The 50 States

The 50 States

Second Edition

Edited by
Charles F. Bahmueller
Center for Civic Education
Calabasas, California

Managing Editor
R. Kent Rasmussen

Contributors

Carl L. Bankston III
Tulane University

Sarah Hilbert
Pasadena, California

Kevin M. Mitchell
Glendale, California

Lauren M. Mitchell
Glendale, California

Rose Secrest
Chattanooga, Tennessee

R. Baird Shuman
University of Illinois

Rowena Wildin
Altadena, California

Michael Witkoski
University of South Carolina

SALEM PRESS, INC.
PASADENA, CALIFORNIA   HACKENSACK, NEW JERSEY

Editor in Chief: Dawn P. Dawson

Managing Editor: R. Kent Rasmussen *Production Editor:* Joyce I. Buchea
Research Supervisor: Jeffry Jensen *Graphics and Design:* James Hutson
Manuscript Editor: Sarah M. Hilbert *Layout:* William Zimmerman
Editorial Assistant: Dana Garey *Photo Editor:* Cynthia Breslin Beres

Cover photos (pictured clockwise, from top left): Rainbow Bridge National Monument, Utah (© Claude Haeusermann/Dreamstime.com); New York City skyscrapers (© Nicholas Koravos/Dreamstime.com); Midwestern farm (© Robert Kyllo/Dreamstime.com); Waikiki Beach, Hawaii (© Tina Lau/Dreamstime.com)

Library of Congress Cataloging-in-Publication Data

The 50 states / edited by Charles F. Bahmueller ; managing editor, R. Kent Rasmussen. — 2nd ed.
   p. cm.
Includes bibliographical references and index.
ISBN 978-1-58765-367-4 (alk. paper)
  1. U.S. states—Miscellanea. 2. United States—Miscellanea. I. Bahmueller, Charles F. II. Rasmussen, R. Kent. III. Title: Fifty states.

E180.A15 2007
973—dc22

2007005350

First Printing

PRINTED IN THE UNITED STATES OF AMERICA

CONTENTS

Contents

Contents

Contents

Contents

Publisher's Note

This volume is the first revision of Salem Press's popular *The 50 States*, which was first published in 2000. Like the first edition, this second edition is designed to serve the needs of students and members of the public seeking basic and up-to-date information on individual American states. To meet users' needs, this revised edition brings the contents of the volume as up to date as possible. It also adds an entirely new chapter on the District of Columbia and vastly expands the appendix resources offered to users.

Like the first edition, *The 50 States, Second Edition* aims to help users find the information they want as quickly and efficiently as possible. To that end, each state and the District of Columbia form the subjects of their own chapters. Moreover, every chapter presents the same kinds of information, in the same formats, and in the same order. The chapters themselves are arranged alphabetically, by the states' names, with the District of Columbia following Wyoming.

Organization of the Chapters

Because of the praise with which librarians and users greeted the first edition, the basic arrangement of *The 50 States, Second Edition* has been only slightly modified. Each chapter in *The 50 States* opens with a profile listing basic data on population, geography, history, and other facts. A brief history of the state follows, emphasizing the events and forces that have worked to make the state what it is today. Additional historical facts are summarized in a Time Line, which is followed by Notes for Further Study, which provide brief descriptions of both published books and resources on the World Wide Web. Information in all these sections has been brought up to date in this new edition.

Note that mileage figures given for each state's "coastline" reflect the broad contours of the states' *marine* seacoasts. "Shoreline" mileage figures encompass the states' seacoasts, offshore islands, and all inland shores touching tidal waters, including rivers and creeks, that are at least one hundred feet wide. It should be understood that many of these figures are approximations.

Every chapter on a state also contains a list of all the counties in the state, giving their populations and areas. The updated lists in this revised edition have been expanded to include each county's rank in both area and population within its state. Every county list is complemented by a map of the state showing the locations of all the counties. Each chapter also has an updated list of all the state's cities and towns of at least ten thousand residents—or six thousand residents for states lacking fifteen towns with ten thousand residents. Every state chapter also has a map of the state's cities and towns and a map showing the state's major physical features. Each chapter also has four or five photographs illustrating places of historical, economic, political, or scenic interest.

Statistical Tables

The bulk of every state chapter is made up of 40 statistical tables, arranged under these subject headings:

- Demographics
- Vital Statistics
- Economy
- Land Use
- Government and Finance
- Politics
- Health and Medical Care
- Housing
- Education
- Transportation and Travel
- Crime and Law Enforcement

Drawing primarily on the latest federal government statistics—most notably, the results of the U.S. Census of 2000—the tables emphasize current data on the subjects likely to be of greatest interest to readers. The tables organize and manipulate their data to make them as easy as possible for students to understand. Although many tables are similar in appearance to their counterparts in the first edition of *The 50 States*, most of their data are entirely new. New table topics added to this edition include abortion rates, numbers of medical professionals, smoking rates, values of owner-occupied houses, and retail gasoline prices—all subjects of great national interest in the early twenty-first century.

The Editors have made every effort to present data in forms that can be readily understood. Many tables contain special features not found in government-published compilations of statistics, such as figures showing how each state ranks nationally in important statistical categories and figures showing each state's share of national totals. For example, the first demographic table gives state and national population totals for selected years between 1970 and 2004, as well as each state's share of the national totals and its rank among all the states. It should be noted that as the District of Columbia is not a state, its figures are not included in the national ranking numbers. However, tables in the District of Columbia chapter give the ranking numbers that the district would have, were it a state.

The tables offer comprehensive population data, including projections of each state's population growth through the year 2030. Other tables summarize such vital statistics as infant mortality rates and marriage, divorce, and death rates. Economic data are provided in tables summarizing statistics on housing, land use, gross state products, personal income, and agricultural data. This volume also offers statistics on state government revenue and expenditures. Political data include lists of all state governors and the political makeups of state and federal legislators, updated through early 2007, and voter participation in presidential elections. Other tables offer data on transportation, health, education, crime, and law enforcement.

Users should be able to find most of the information they seek by simply turning to the chapters for the states that interest them. If they need additional help, they can refer to the subject index at the end of the volume.

Appendixes

One of the biggest changes in *The 50 States, Second Edition* is a ninefold increase in the number of appendixes, from four to thirty-six. Thirty of these appendixes summarize national data for the same subjects covered in statistical tables within the chapters. For example, one appendix summarizes data on total state populations from 1980 through 2004. Readers can use these appendixes to see at a glance how the data of the various states compare. Other appendixes summarize data on the largest cities and counties in the United States and rank the states by their land areas. Finally, the appendix section also includes an annotated General Bibliography, which covers publications on the states collectively, and a Guide to Web Resources, which offers strategies on finding information about the states on the Web, as well as descriptions of some of the most useful sites.

Abbreviations Used in Maps

NB National Battlefield
NBP National Battlefield Park
NBS National Battlefield Site
NHP National Historical Park
NHS National Historic Site
NL National Lakeshore
NM National Monument
NMem National Memorial
NMP National Military Park
NP National Park

NPres National Preserve
NR National River
NRA National Recreation Area
NRes National Reserve
NS National Seashore
NST National Scenic Trail
NVM National Volcanic Monument
Pkwy National Parkway
WSR Wild and Scenic River

The 50 States

United States of America

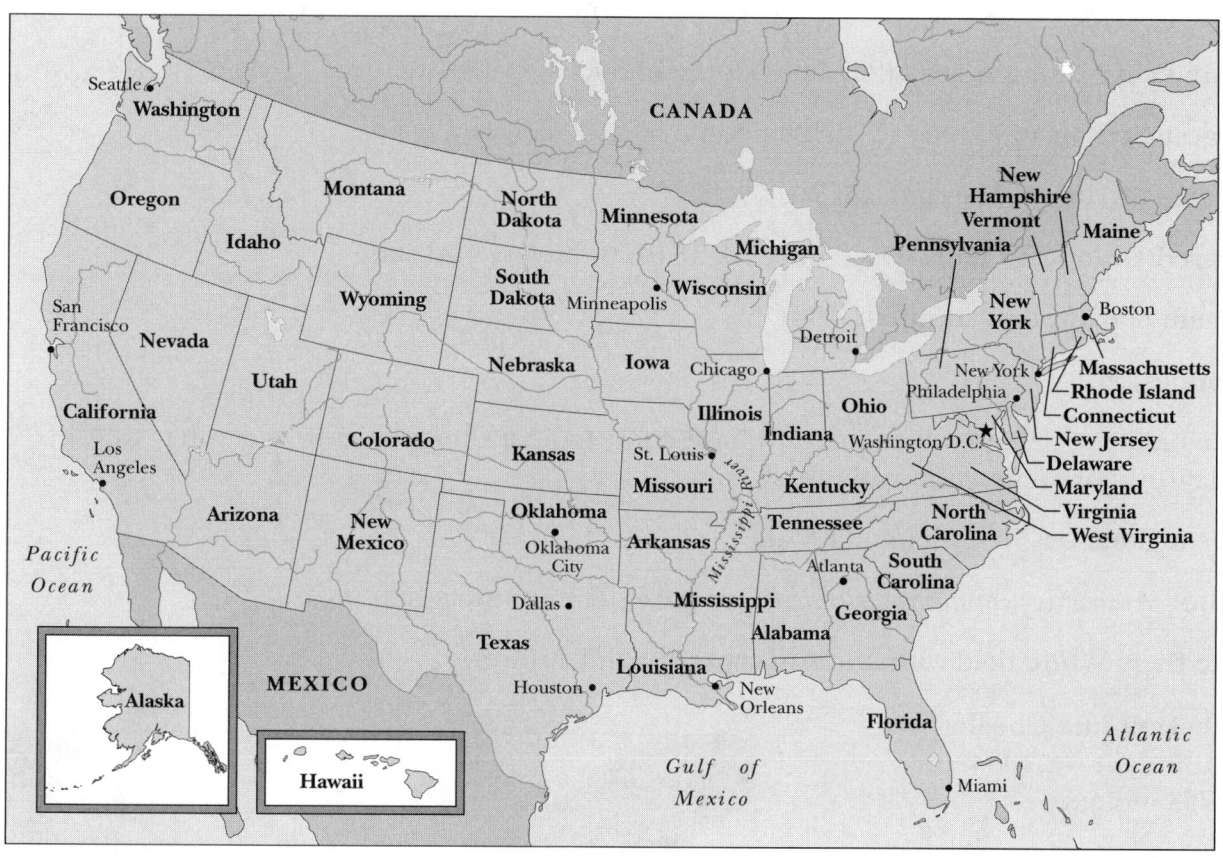

Alabama

Location: Southeast

Area and rank: 50,750 square miles (131,443 square kilometers); 52,423 square miles (135,776 square kilometers) including water; twenty-eighth largest state in area

Coastline: 53 miles (85 kilometers) on the Gulf of Mexico

Shoreline: 607 miles (977 kilometers)

Population and rank: 4,530,000 (2004); twenty-third largest state in population

Capital city: Montgomery (201,568 people in 2000 census)

Largest city: Birmingham (242,820 people in 2000 census)

Became territory: March 3, 1817

Entered Union and rank: December 14, 1819; twenty-second state

Present constitution adopted: 1901

Counties: 67

State name: "Alabama" is thought to have come from a Choctaw word meaning "thicket-clearers" or "vegetation gatherers"

State nickname: Yellowhammer State

Motto: *Audemus jura nostra defendere* (We dare defend our rights)

State flag: White field with crimson cross of Saint Andrew

Highest point: Cheaha Mountain—2,405 feet (733 meters)

Lowest point: Gulf of Mexico—sea level

Highest recorded temperature: 112 degrees Fahrenheit (44 degrees Celsius)—Centerville, 1925

Lowest recorded temperature: –27 degrees Fahrenheit (–33 degrees Celsius)—New Market, 1966

State song: "Alabama" ("Sweet Home Alabama" is unofficial)

State tree: Southern pine (longleaf)

State flower: Camellia

State bird: Yellowhammer

State fish: Tarpon (saltwater); Largemouth bass (freshwater)

State capitol building at Mobile. (©Perry Watson/Dreamstime.com)

Alabama History

Alabama is in the southeastern part of the United States, between Mississippi to the west and Georgia and Florida to the east. Most of Alabama's southern border adjoins Florida, but a small portion of the state extends down to the Gulf of Mexico. The northern part of Alabama, just below Tennessee, is known as the Appalachian region. It is made up of high plateaus, ridges, valleys, and the high Talladega Mountains. The Piedmont Plateau, another rocky region, extends from the Talladega Mountains to the Georgia border. Until well into the twentieth century, many of the people in the high lands of Alabama lived the isolated lives of mountain and hill dwellers. The Interior Low Plateau region is the part of northern Alabama drained by the Tennessee River. Below the northern uplands, the Gulf Coastal Plains extend south to the Gulf of Mexico. The Gulf Coastal Plains include the Black Belt, a dark-soiled prairie.

The Tennessee River area and the Black Belt have rich soil. Together with Alabama's hot, humid climate, this has made these territories ideal for agriculture. As a result, agriculture tended to dominate the state's economic activities until the second half of the twentieth century. Worldwide demand for cotton in the nineteenth century led the state to specialize in cotton production. Since cotton was a crop that required a great deal of unskilled labor, this created a reliance on slavery that profoundly affected the state's history.

Early History. Before the arrival of the Europeans, Alabama was dominated by Native Americans known as the Mound Builders, after their ceremonial earth mounds. The best-known archeological site of the Mound Builders in Alabama is at Moundville on the Black Warrior River in central Alabama. Moundville was a large and complex society, second in size and organization only to the Cahokia site of Mound Builder culture in Illinois. Both a populous town and a political and religious center, the Moundville community itself probably housed about one thousand people at its height and was surrounded by around ten thousand people living in the Black Warrior River Valley. This settlement lasted from about 1000 C.E. to about 1450.

In the eighteenth century, the Creek were one of the largest and predominant Native American groups in Alabama. The Creek, who lived in villages of log houses, sided with the British against the Americans in both the Revolutionary War and the War of 1812. At war with the Americans, they were defeated by General Andrew Jackson, and by 1828 they agreed to give up all of their lands and move to Indian Territory in modern Oklahoma. The Cherokee, who were spread throughout the Southeast, were also well represented in Alabama. In 1838, most of the Cherokee were also forced to relocate to Indian Territory. Similarly, most of the Choctaw and the Chickasaw were removed from Alabama and the adjacent states.

Exploration and Settlement. Spanish explorers reached Alabama around 1540. The Spanish attempted to establish a settlement at Mobile Bay but soon deserted it, leaving cattle, hogs, and horses behind, all of which became part of local Native American ways of life. The French claimed much of Alabama as part of their vast Louisiana territory, and they built forts and trading posts. After France and Great Britain fought the French and Indian Wars (1754-1763), Alabama fell under the control of the British. The coastal area, including Mobile Bay, became part of West Florida. North of West Florida, all of Alabama was reserved by the British for the Native Americans.

During the American Revolution, Spain captured Mobile from the British, shutting the British out of Alabama. After the Revolution, West Florida became Spanish land, and interior Alabama was turned over to the new United States. After several years of border disputes, the United States and Spain finally agreed in 1795 that latitude thirty-one degrees north would be the boundary between U.S. land and West Florida; this would continue to be the boundary between Alabama and the Florida Panhandle. In 1798, the U.S. Congress formed the Mississippi Territory, made up of modern Mississippi and Alabama. The portion of the territory along the Mississippi River became the state of Mississippi in 1817, and in 1819 Alabama was admitted to the Union as the twenty-second state.

Slavery and Civil War. Alabama's rich soil led to an influx of settlers. Worldwide demand for cotton made this crop enormously profitable for a few wealthy landowners. Black slaves worked the cotton plantations, and between 1830 and 1860 the state's slave population grew by 270 percent, while the white population grew by only 170 percent. Although the big plantation owners made up only about 6 to 7 percent of Alabama's population, they were enormously influential and dominated the state's society. The majority of white Alabamians, especially in the hills and mountains, were small subsistence farmers.

Slavery became a contentious issue in the United States in the first half of the nineteenth century. As new territories entered the United States, many northern leaders opposed the spread of slavery. The southern political leadership, dominated by the plantation owners, saw slavery as essential to the southern agricultural way of life and feared falling under the control of the populous north. In 1861, Alabama joined other southern states in seceding from the United States and forming the Confederate States of America. The bitter Civil War ensued. By 1865 Alabama and the other southern states were defeated and occupied by northern troops.

With the end of the Civil War, Alabama's slaves received freedom. However, there were few economic opportunities for them and most had to take jobs working as low-income agricultural laborers for white landowners. The American Missionary Association and the Federal Freedmen's Bureau helped to establish schools that formed a basis for future African American education. Although African Americans received the right to vote during Reconstruction, the period from after the Civil War to 1877, when Union troops withdrew from the South, relatively few Alabamian blacks were able to take positions of political leadership because of the former slaves' lack of education and experience. By 1874, white southern Democrats managed to take control of the state government. Throughout the nineteenth century, the white state government established legal segregation and restriction of the rights of African Americans.

The Civil Rights Era. During the 1950's and 1960's, African Americans in Alabama and other southern states began organizing to oppose segregation and racial discrimination. In 1955, Rosa Parks, a black citizen of Montgomery, Alabama, was arrested when she refused to give up her seat on a bus to a white passenger. In response, the African American residents of Montgomery, under the leadership of the clergyman Dr. Martin Luther King, Jr., organized a boycott of the city's public transportation system. The successful boycott made King a national civil rights leader, and he went on to advocate desegregation campaigns and marches throughout the South.

Alabama Governor George Wallace, first elected in 1962, came to national prominence as a result of his opposition to integration. Wallace had experienced defeat in a first run for governor in 1959, when he refused the support of the Ku Klux Klan and ran a campaign of racial moderation. After that defeat, he became a staunch segregationist and attempted to block the integration of Alabama's schools and universities. On the

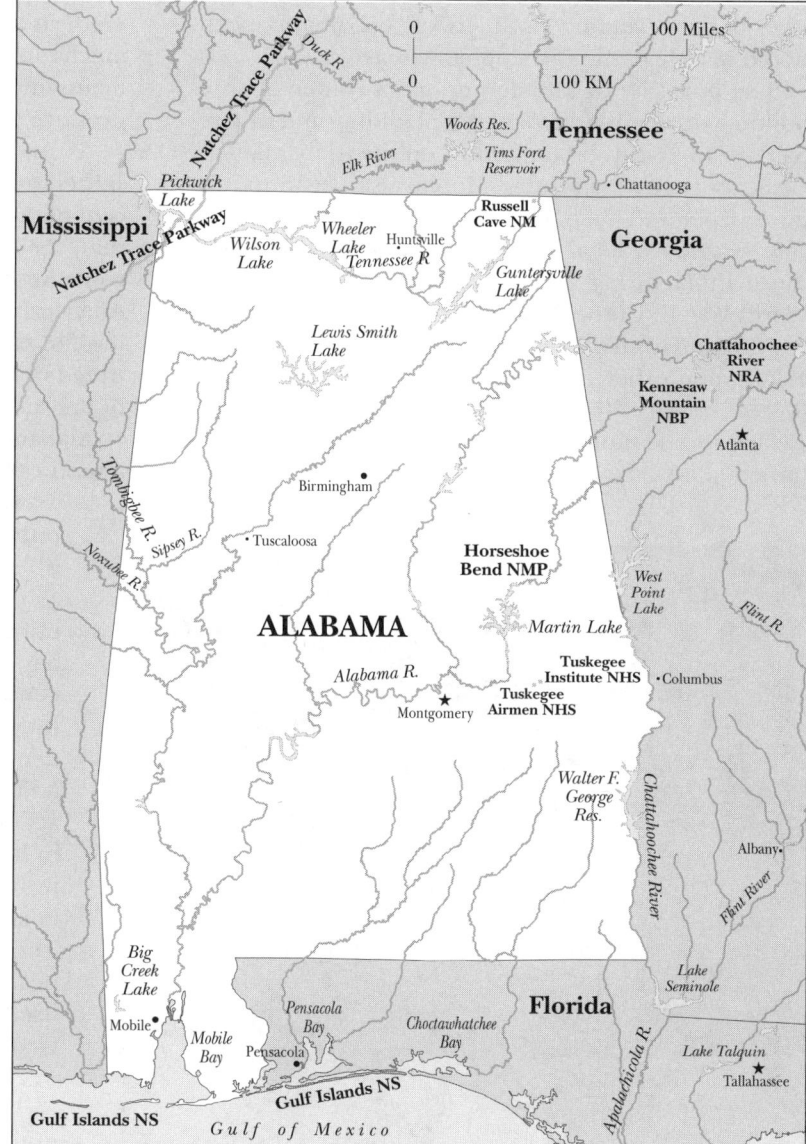

basis of the national recognition brought by his segregationist policies, Wallace ran for president of the United States in 1968 as the candidate of the American Independent Party.

Although racial inequality continued to be a problem in Alabama, segregation became illegal, and black Alabamians achieved substantial social and political influence. From 1969 to 1970, the percentage of African American students attending integrated schools increased from 15 percent to 80 percent. In 1982, when George Wallace was elected to his third term as governor, he actively appealed to black voters and renounced his earlier racial positions.

Alabama's Industrialization. Alabama saw substantial industrialization over the course of the twentieth century. In 1907, United States Steel Corporation established a steel industry in Birmingham. Iron and steel became leading products of Alabama, concentrated mainly in the Birmingham area.

The port city of Mobile became a center of shipbuilding during World War I. Shipbuilding and ship repair continued to be important on the Alabama Gulf Coast, but the area around Mobile also began to produce paper and chemical products. The city of Huntsville became a focal point of U.S. government missile manufacturing and the aerospace industry after World War II. Cutbacks in federal government spending caused Huntsville to diversify its economy after the 1970's, and other high technology industries located there.

Despite the rapid industrialization, agriculture continued to be a major economic activity. However, most modern agricultural activities in Alabama are heavily mechanized and use relatively little labor. Cotton remains important, but many of the old cotton fields now produce peanuts, soybeans, corn, and other crops.

As Alabama has industrialized, its population has shifted from rural areas to urban areas. In 1990, 60 percent of the people in the state lived in places with more than 2,500 inhabitants. Birmingham was the largest concentration, with a population of 266,000. African Americans, who lived almost entirely in rural areas during the early twentieth century, were heavily concentrated in larger cities in the southern and central parts of the state by 1990.

Alabama in the Twenty-first Century. Just before and after the turn of the twenty-first century, Alabama faced a series of issues that gave an uneven texture to its public life. In 1999, the state's politics were roiled when a dispute between the Democratic leadership of the state senate and the lieutenant governor closed the senate down for twelve of the thirty days devoted annually to its meetings. The state's conservative leaning was evident when in 2002 Judge Roy Moore of the Alabama Supreme Court denounced homosexuality as an "inherent evil" and an "abhorrent, immoral, detestable, crime against nature." Two years later, Moore failed in his attempt to place the Ten Commandments in the court's lobby and was removed from the bench for defying the court's rulings against him. The U.S. Supreme Court refused to hear his appeal. Within national politics, the state found itself among the "red states" that supported George W. Bush's election to the presidency both in 2000 and in 2004.

The state's prominent place as a battleground of the Civil Rights movement once again figured prominently in its public life. The turn of the twenty-first century saw the perpetrators of the 1963 Birmingham church bombing that took the lives of four African American girls finally charged with murder and placed on trial; those found guilty were jailed for life. A library named for renowned civil rights activist Rosa Parks was dedicated in 2000. Parks herself received national accolades for moral courage when she died in 2005.

Two hurricanes wreaked havoc on the state's Gulf coast. In September, 2004, the Gulf coast was badly damaged by Hurricane Ivan. In August of the following year, it was devastated by Hurricane Katrina but received scant attention nationally, since attention was focused on the catastrophe that the hurricane had visited upon New Orleans and its vicinity.

Carl L. Bankston III
Updated by the Editor

The somewhat whimsical Boll Weevil Monument in Enterprise recalls the important part cotton has played in Alabama's history. (Alabama Bureau of Tourism & Travel/Dan Brothers)

Dauphin Street in Mobile, Alabama's second-largest city. (Alabama Bureau of Tourism & Travel/Karim Shamsi Basha)

Alabama Time Line

700-1300	Mound Builders of the Mississippian culture build ceremonial mounds in the eastern part of North America, including Moundville in Alabama's Hale County.
1519	Spaniard Alonzo Alvárez de Piñeda sails into Mobile Bay.
July 2, 1540	Spanish explorer Hernando de Soto reaches Mobile, Alabama, while exploring southeastern North America.
1682	French explorer René-Robert Cavalier, sieur de La Salle, travels down the Mississippi to its mouth and claims all lands along the river in the name of France.
1712	French settlement and fort are established at Mobile, on the Gulf of Mexico.
1763	Great Britain takes control of Alabama and other parts of the Mississippi region after winning the French and Indian War.
Mar. 4, 1780	Spanish capture Mobile during the American Revolution.
1799	American surveyor marks the thirty-first latitude as the boundary between Spanish West Florida and the United States.
1802	State of Georgia gives up its claims on most of the lands of modern Alabama.
1805-1806	Choctaw, Chickasaw, and Cherokee lands are opened up to settlement by non-Native Americans.
Apr. 15, 1813	Spanish surrender Mobile to American forces; United States annexes part of Spanish West Florida, including the Alabama coast.
July, 1813	Creek Indian Wars begin between the United States and the Creeks.

(continued)

Dec. 14, 1819	Alabama becomes the twenty-second state of the Union.
1826	Alabama's capital is moved from St. Stephens to Tuscaloosa.
Sept. 27, 1830	Choctaws cede the rest of their lands to Alabama and are removed to Oklahoma.
1846	Alabama's general assembly votes to move the capital to Montgomery.
1856	Large-scale coal mining begins in Alabama when the Alabama Coal Mining Company establishes underground mines.
Jan. 11, 1861	Alabama convention votes to secede from the Union.
May 26, 1865	Last Confederate army unit surrenders, ending the Civil War.
1868	Alabama ratifies a new constitution, recognizing the right of blacks to vote; is then readmitted to the United States.
1871	Birmingham is founded.
1874	Conservative Democrats regain control of the Alabama state government.
Feb. 10, 1881	Booker T. Washington founds Tuskegee Institute (later Tuskegee University), a renowned African American center of higher education.
1901	New state constitution is ratified that effectively disenfranchises black Alabamians and greatly reduces the number of poor white voters.
1907	U.S. Steel Corporation establishes a steel industry in Birmingham.
1948	Democratic president Harry S. Truman's support for civil rights prompts conservative southern Democrats to form Dixiecrat Party, which nominates Strom Thurmond for president.
1955-1956	Montgomery bus boycott follows refusal of seamstress Rosa Parks to give up her bus seat to a white passenger.
1963	George C. Wallace begins the first of his four terms as governor.
1965	Civil rights march from Montgomery to Selma calls national attention to the need for a national voting rights bill.
1982	George Wallace is elected with black support to his third term as governor.
1987	Guy Hunt becomes the first Republican governor since Reconstruction.
1991	Alabama's state universities are ordered by a federal district judge to hire more minority faculty members.
2000-2003	Perpetrators of the 1963 church bombings are criminally charged and those found guilty are jailed.
2000	Library named for civil rights hero Rosa Parks is dedicated.
2003	Judge Roy Moore is removed from the state supreme court over his insistence that the Ten Commandments be posted on state property.
Sept. 16, 2004	Hurricane Ivan causes disastrous damage on state's Gulf of Mexico coast.
Aug. 29, 2005	Hurricane Katrina devastates Alabama's Gulf coast.

Notes for Further Study

Published Sources. *Alabama: The History of a Deep South State* (1994) by William Warren Rogers, Robert David Ward, Willia Rogers, and Leah R. Atkins is an excellent history of Alabama. It is divided into three sections. The first ends with Alabama's Civil War defeat in 1865, the second covers the state from the end of the war to the 1920's, and the third covers Alabama to 1993. Allen Cronenberg's *Forth to the Mighty Conflict: Alabama and World War II* (1995) is an intriguing examination of the impact of World War II on the state and of the role played by Alabamians in this modern struggle. Some of the most interesting parts of the book concern the Tuskegee Army Air Field, where African American pilots learned to fly, and the prisoner-of-war camps for German soldiers in Alabama.

Readers will find an in-depth look at the beginnings of the Civil Rights movement in *Alabama in Daybreak of Freedom: The Montgomery Bus Boycott* (1997), a documentary history assembled by editor Stewart Burns. Historian Glenn T. Eskew pro-

vides a look at another center of the Civil Rights movement in *But for Birmingham: The Local and National Movements in the Civil Rights Struggle* (1997), which describes the movement in Birmingham from the end of World War II onward. Winner of the 2002 Pulitzer Prize for General Nonfiction, Diane McWhorter's *Carry Me Home: Birmingham, Alabama—The Climactic Battle of the Civil Rights Revolution* (2001) details a pivotal year—1963—in the Civil Rights movement.

Marshall Frady's *Wallace* (1996) is a political biography of the controversial Alabama governor and U.S. presidential candidate George Wallace. Frady provides a detailed portrait of this complex individual, and he argues that Wallace's 1968 campaign for president helped to build a conservative working-class voting block that later contributed to the election of President Ronald Reagan. *Alabama Governors: A Political History of the State* (2001), edited by Samuel L. Webb and Margaret E. Armbrester, brings together biographical essays written by thirty-four noted historians and political scientists. Wayne Flint's *Alabama in the Twentieth Century* (2004) is an engaging, academic discussion of the state's achievements and failures. Young adults will appreciate the work of three books in particular: *Alabama Native Americans* (2004) by Carole Marsh, *Alabama* (2005) by Vanessa Brown, and *Alabama: The Heart of Dixie* (2002) by Michael A. Martin.

Web Resources. The Alabama Department of Archives and History has a wide range of Internet links available (www.archives.state.al.us). Use the About Alabama link to access information on nearly any aspect of Alabama history or modern life in Alabama. Those interested in learning about their family connections to Alabama's Civil War history will want to look at the Alabama Civil War Roots Homepage (www.rootsweb.com/~alcwroot). The purpose of this page is to help people find their Alabama Civil War ancestors, on both the Union and Confederate sides. Another good resource on the Civil War in Alabama is the Alabama Civil War Regimental Histories page (www.tarleton.edu/~kjones/alregts .html), which offers brief histories of infantry and cavalry units raised in Alabama. Outdoor enthusiasts planning a trip to Alabama might want to consult Outdoor Alabama (www.outdooralabama.com/) for information on hunting, fishing, state parks, and wildlife watching. The Alabama Bureau of Tourism and Travel also has an informative site for visitors (www.800alabama.com/).

Birmingham's Civil Rights Institute is a memorial to the city's central role in the Civil Rights movement. (Alabama Bureau of Tourism & Travel/Karim Shamsi Basha)

Counties

County	2000 pop.	Rank in pop.	Sq. miles	Rank in area	County	2000 pop.	Rank in pop.	Sq. miles	Rank in area
Autauga	43,671	28	596.0	55	Cullman	77,483	16	738.5	27
Baldwin	140,415	7	1,596.5	1	Dale	49,129	26	561.1	64
Barbour	29,038	39	885.0	16	Dallas	46,365	27	980.8	10
Bibb	20,826	50	622.4	45	DeKalb	64,452	21	778.0	23
Blount	51,024	24	645.7	38	Elmore	65,874	18	621.6	46
Bullock	11,714	66	625.1	44	Escambia	38,440	32	947.5	12
Butler	21,399	48	776.9	24	Etowah	103,459	11	534.8	67
Calhoun	112,249	9	608.5	51	Fayette	18,495	51	627.8	43
Chambers	36,583	34	597.4	54	Franklin	31,223	36	635.7	41
Cherokee	23,988	45	553.2	66	Geneva	25,764	41	576.4	60
Chilton	39,593	31	694.1	31	Greene	9,974	67	646.0	37
Choctaw	15,922	55	913.6	13	Hale	17,185	53	643.8	39
Clarke	27,867	40	1,238.5	3	Henry	16,310	54	562.0	63
Clay	14,254	58	605.1	52	Houston	88,787	12	580.4	59
Cleburne	14,123	59	560.2	65	Jackson	53,926	23	1,078.8	7
Coffee	43,615	29	679.2	33	Jefferson	662,047	1	1,112.7	5
Colbert	54,984	22	594.6	56	Lamar	15,904	56	604.9	53
Conecuh	14,089	60	850.9	18	Lauderdale	87,966	13	669.5	35
Coosa	12,202	64	652.5	36	Lawrence	34,803	35	693.4	32
Covington	37,631	33	1,034.7	8	Lee	115,092	8	608.8	50
Crenshaw	13,665	61	609.6	49	Limestone	65,676	19	568.1	61

(continued)

County	2000 pop.	Rank in pop.	Sq. miles	Rank in area
Lowndes	13,473	62	718.0	30
Macon	24,105	44	610.6	48
Madison	276,700	3	805.0	19
Marengo	22,539	46	977.1	11
Marion	31,214	37	741.5	25
Marshall	82,231	14	567.1	62
Mobile	399,843	2	1,233.4	4
Monroe	24,324	43	1,026.0	9
Montgomery	223,510	4	789.9	22
Morgan	111,064	10	582.2	57
Perry	11,861	65	719.5	28
Pickens	20,949	49	881.5	17
Pike	29,605	38	671.1	34
Randolph	22,380	47	581.1	58

County	2000 pop.	Rank in pop.	Sq. miles	Rank in area
Russell	49,756	25	641.1	40
St. Clair	64,742	20	634.0	42
Shelby	143,293	6	794.9	20
Sumter	14,798	57	905.0	14
Talladega	80,321	15	739.6	26
Tallapoosa	41,475	30	718.0	29
Tuscaloosa	164,875	5	1,325.3	2
Walker	70,713	17	794.5	21
Washington	18,097	52	1,080.7	6
Wilcox	13,183	63	888.8	15
Winston	24,843	42	614.5	47

Source: U.S. Census Bureau; National Association of Counties.

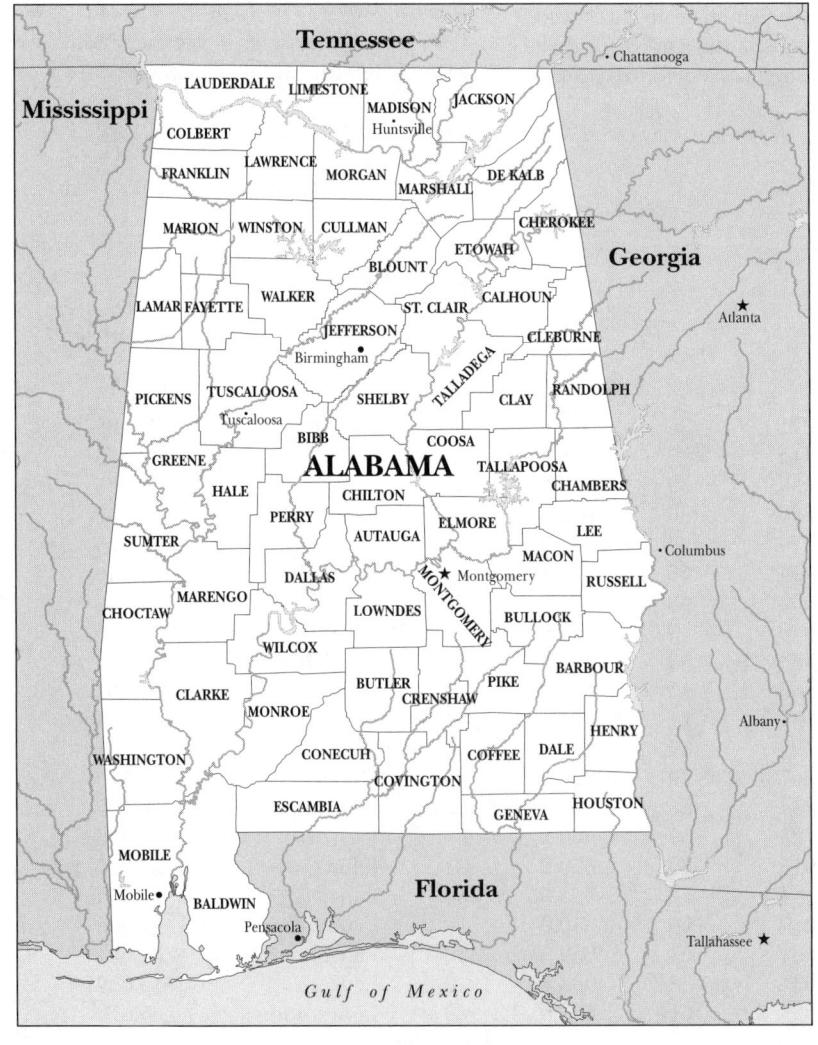

After World War II, Huntsville became an aerospace and space technology hub; it is now home to the U.S. Space and Rocket Center. (Alabama Bureau of Tourism & Travel/Karim Shamsi Basha)

Cities
With 10,000 or more residents

Rank	City	Population	Rank	City	Population
1	Birmingham	242,820	15	Phenix City	28,265
2	Montgomery (capital)	201,568	16	Homewood	25,043
3	Mobile	198,915	17	Vestavia Hills	24,476
4	Huntsville	158,216	18	Prattville	24,303
5	Tuscaloosa	77,906	19	Anniston	24,276
6	Hoover	62,742	20	Opelika	23,498
7	Dothan	57,737	21	Center Point	22,784
8	Decatur	53,929	22	Alabaster	22,619
9	Auburn	42,987	23	Smiths	21,756
10	Gadsden	38,978	24	Enterprise	21,178
11	Florence	36,264	25	Mountain Brook	20,604
12	Bessemer	29,672	26	Selma	20,512
13	Madison	29,329	27	Northport	19,435
14	Prichard	28,633	28	Athens	18,967

(continued)

Rank	City	Population
29	Albertville	17,247
30	Daphne	16,581
31	Tillmans Corner	15,685
32	Hueytown	15,364
33	Talladega	15,143
34	Ozark	15,119
35	Alexander City	15,008
36	Scottsboro	14,762
37	Oxford	14,592
38	Pelham	14,369
39	Jasper	14,052
40	Cullman	13,995
41	Troy	13,935
42	Eufaula	13,908
43	Fort Payne	12,938
44	Trussville	12,924

Rank	City	Population
45	Sylacauga	12,616
46	Fairhope	12,480
47	Fairfield	12,381
48	Saraland	12,288
49	Hartselle	12,019
50	Muscle Shoals	11,924
51	Tuskegee	11,846
52	Gardendale	11,626
53	Saks	10,698
54	Forestdale	10,509
55	Leeds	10,455
56	Millbrook	10,386
57	Helena	10,296

Population figures are from 2000 census.
Source: U.S. Bureau of the Census.

Index to Tables

DEMOGRAPHICS

Resident state and national populations, 1970-2004

Population figures given in thousands

	State pop.	U.S. pop.	Share	Rank
1970	3,444	203,302	1.7%	21
1980	3,894	226,546	1.7%	22
1985	3,973	237,924	1.7%	22
1990	4,040	248,765	1.6%	22
1995	4,297	262,761	1.6%	23
2000	4,447	281,425	1.6%	23
2004	4,530	293,655	1.5%	23

Source: U.S. Census Bureau, Current Population Reports, 2006.

Resident population by age, 2004

Age Group	Total persons
Under 5 years.	296,000
5 to 17 years.	798,000
18 to 24 years	456,000
25 to 34 years	603,000
35 to 44 years	651,000
45 to 54 years	648,000
55 to 64 years	480,000
65 to 74 years	325,000
75 to 84 years	207,000
85 years and older	66,000
All age groups.	4,530,000
Portion of residents 65 and older	13.2%
National rank in portion of oldest residents	17
National average	12.4%

Population figures are rounded to nearest thousand persons;
figures include armed forces personnel stationed in state.
Source: U.S. Bureau of the Census, 2006.

Resident population by race, Hispanic origin, 2004

Category	State pop.	Share	U.S.
All residents	4,530	100.00%	100.00%
Non-Hispanic white	3,148	69.49%	67.37%
Hispanic white	87	1.92%	13.01%
Other Hispanic	11	0.24%	1.06%
African American	1,194	26.36%	12.77%
Native American	23	0.51%	0.96%
Asian, Pacific Islander	39	0.86%	4.37%
Two or more categories	39	0.86%	1.51%

Population figures are in thousands. Persons counted as
"Hispanic" (Latino) may be of any race. Because of overlapping
categories, categories may not add up to 100%. Shares in
column 3 are percentages of each category within the state;
these figures may be compared to the national percentages in
column 4.
Source: U.S. Bureau of the Census, 2006.

Projected state population, 2000-2030

Year	Population
2000	4,447,000
2005	4,527,000
2010	4,596,000
2015	4,663,000
2020	4,729,000
2025	4,800,000
2030	4,874,000
Population increase, 2000-2030	427,000
Percentage increase, 2000-2030	9.6

Projections are based on data from the 2000 census.
Source: U.S. Census Bureau.

VITAL STATISTICS

Infant mortality rates, 1980-2002

	1980	1990	2000	2002
All state residents	15.1	10.8	9.4	9.1
All U.S. residents	12.6	9.2	9.4	9.1
All state white residents	11.6	8.1	6.6	7.1
All U.S. white residents	10.6	7.6	5.7	5.8
All state black residents	21.6	16.0	15.4	13.9
All U.S. black residents	22.2	18.0	14.1	14.4

Figures represent deaths per 1,000 live births of resident infants
under 1 year old, exclusive of fetal deaths. Figures for all
residents include members of other racial categories not listed
separately.
Source: U.S. Census Bureau, *Statistical Abstract of the United States,*
2006.

Abortion rates, 1990 and 2000

	1990	2000
Total abortions	17,000	14,000
Rate per 1,000 women	18.1	14.3
U.S. rate	25.7	21.3
Rank	27	26

Numbers of abortions are rounded to nearest thousand; ranks are
based on rates.
Source: U.S. Census Bureau.

Marriages and divorces, 2004

Total marriages	40,600
Rate per 1,000 population	9.0
National rate per 1,000 population	7.4
Rank among all states	8
Total divorces	21,500
Rate per 1,000 population	4.7
National rate per 1,000 population	3.7
Rank among all states	9

Figures are for all marriages and divorces performed within the
state, including those of nonresidents; totals are rounded to the
nearest hundred. Ranks are for highest to lowest figures; note
that divorce data are not available for five states.
Source: U.S. National Center for Health Statistics, *Vital Statistics of
the United States,* 2006.

Death rates by leading causes, 2002
Deaths per 100,000 resident population

Cause	State	U.S.
Heart disease	294.1	241.7
Cancer	216.2	193.2
Cerebrovascular diseases	71.3	56.4
Accidents other than motor vehicle	49.7	37.0
Motor vehicle accidents	24.9	15.7
Chronic lower respiratory diseases	51.9	43.3
Diabetes mellitus	33.1	25.4
HIV	4.2	4.9
Suicide	11.5	11.0
Homicide	9.3	6.1
All causes	1,026.8	847.3
Rank in overall death rate among states		4

Figures exclude nonresidents who died in the state. Causes of
death follow International Classification of Diseases. Rank is
from highest to lowest death rate in the United States.
Source: U.S. National Center for Health Statistics, *National Vital
Statistics Report,* 2006.

ECONOMY

Gross state product, 1990-2004
In current dollars

Year	State product	Nat'l product	State share
1990	$71.1 billion	$5.67 trillion	1.25%
2000	$114.2 billion	$9.75 trillion	1.17%
2002	$123.8 billion	$10.41 trillion	1.19%
2003	$130.8 billion	$10.92 trillion	1.20%
2004	$138.5 billion	$11.65 trillion	1.19%

Source: U.S. Bureau of Economic Analysis, *Survey of Current Business,* July, 2005.

Gross state product by industry, 2003
In billions of dollars

Construction	$4.9
Manufacturing	21.6
Wholesale trade	7.2
Retail trade	11.3
Finance & insurance	6.6
Information	4.0
Professional services	7.2
Health care & social assistance	8.1
Government	19.0
Total state product	$122.7
Total U.S. product	$10,289.2
State share of U.S. total	1.19%
Rank among all states	25

Total figures include industries not listed separately. Amounts are in chained 2000 dollars.
Source: U.S. Bureau of Economic Analysis, *Survey of Current Business,* July, 2005.

Personal income per capita, 1990-2004
In current dollars

	1990	2000	2004
Per capita income	$15,723	$23,764	$27,795
U.S. average	$19,477	$29,845	$32,937
Rank among states	42	44	40

Source: U.S. Bureau of Economic Analysis, *Survey of Current Business,* April, 2005.

Energy consumption, 2001
In trillions of British thermal units (BTU), except as noted

Total energy consumption

Total state energy consumption	1,943
Total U.S. energy consumption	96,275
State share of U.S. total	2.02%
Rank among states	17

Per capita consumption (In millions of BTU)

Total state per capita consumption	435
Total U.S. per capita consumption	338
Rank among states	9

End-use sectors

Residential	380
Commercial	254
Industrial	863
Transportation	446

Sources of energy

Petroleum	540
Natural gas	342
Coal	846
Hydroelectric power	85
Nuclear electric power	317

Figures for totals include categories not listed separately.
Source: U.S. Energy Information Administration, *State Energy Data Report,* 2001.

Nonfarm employment by sectors, 2004

Total	1,902,000
Construction	104,000
Manufacturing	291,000
Trade, transportation, utilities	376,000
Information	31,000
Finance, insurance, real estate	97,000
Professional & business services	197,000
Education & health services	192,000
Leisure, hospitality, arts, organizations	160,000
Other services, including repair & maintenance	82,000
Government	360,000

Figures are rounded to nearest thousand persons. "Total" includes mining and natural resources, not listed separately.
Source: U.S. Bureau of Labor Statistics, 2006.

Foreign exports, 1990-2004
In millions of dollars

Year	State	U.S.	State share
1990	2,834	394,045	0.72%
1996	5,170	624,767	0.83%
1997	5,932	688,896	0.86%
2000	7,317	712,055	0.94%
2003	8,340	724,006	1.23%
2004	9,037	769,332	1.17%

Rank among all states in 2004 24

U.S. total does not include U.S. dependencies.
Source: U.S. Census Bureau, *U.S. Merchandise Trade,* series FT 900, 2000; U.S. Census Bureau, *U.S. International Trade in Goods and Services,* Series FT 900, 2005.

LAND USE

Federally owned land, 2003
Areas in acres

	State	U.S.	State share
Total area	32,678,000	2,271,343,000	1.44%
Nonfederal land	31,476,000	1,599,584,000	1.97%
Federal land	1,202,000	671,759,000	0.18%
Federal share	3.7%	29.6%	—

Areas are rounded to nearest thousand acres. Figures for federally owned land do not include trust properties.
Source: U.S. General Services Administration, *Federal Real Property Profile,* 2006.

Land use, 1997
In acres, rounded to nearest thousand

Total surface area	33,424,000
Total nonfederal rural land.	28,950,000
Percentage rural land	86.6%
Cropland	2,954,000
Conservation Reserve Program (CRP*) land. . . .	522,000
Pastureland	3,528,000
Rangeland	74,000
Forestland	21,261,000
Other rural land	612,000

*CRP is a federal program begun in 1985 to assist private landowners to convert highly erodible cropland to vegetative cover for ten years. Note that some categories of land overlap.
Source: U.S. Department of Agriculture, Natural Resources and Conservation Service, and Iowa State University, Statistical Laboratory, S*ummary Report, 1997 National Resources Inventory,* revised December, 2000.

Farms and crop acreage, 2004

	State	U.S.	Share	Rank
Farms	44,000	2,113,000	2.08%	21
Acres (millions)	9	937	0.96%	31
Acres per farm	198	443	—	34

Source: U.S. Department of Agriculture, National Agricultural Statistics Service. Numbers of farms are rounded to nearest thousand units; acreage figures are rounded to nearest million. Rankings, including ties, are based on rounded figures.

GOVERNMENT AND FINANCE

Units of local government, 2002

	State	Total U.S.	Rank
All local governments	1,171	87,525	26
Counties	67	3,034	20
Municipalities	451	19,429	19
Townships	0	16,504	—
School districts	128	13,506	30
Special districts	525	35,052	26

Only 48 states have county governments, 20 states have township governments ("towns" in New England, Minnesota, New York, and Wisconsin), and 46 states have school districts. Special districts encompass such functions as natural resources, fire protection, and housing and community development.
Source: U.S. Census Bureau, *Census of Governments.*

State government revenue, 2002

Total revenue	$14,942 mill.
General revenue	$15,986 mill.
Per capita revenue	$3,567
U.S. per capita average	$3,689
Rank among states	35

Intergovernment revenue	
Total	$6,275 mill.
From federal government	$5,795 mill.

Charges and miscellaneous	
Total	$3,201 mill.
Current charges	$2,286 mill.
Misc. general income	$915 mill.
Insurance trust revenue	−$1,204 mill.

Taxes	
Total	$6,510 mill.
Per capita taxes	$1,453
Rank among states	47
Property taxes	$195 mill.
Sales taxes	$3,383 mill.
License taxes	$395 mill.
Individual income taxes	$2,031 mill.
Corporate income taxes	$323 mill.
Other taxes	$183 mill.

Total revenue figures include items not listed separately here.
Source: U.S. Bureau of the Census.

State government expenditures, 2002

General expenditures

Total state expenditures	$17,996 mill.
Intergovernmental	$4,096 mill.

Per capita expenditures

State	$3,608
Average of all states	$3,859
Rank among states	33

Selected direct expenditures

Education	$3,231 mill.
Public welfare	$4,110 mill.
Health, hospital	$1,821 mill.
Highways	$1,064 mill.
Police protection	$100 mill.
Corrections	$325 mill.
Natural resources	$228 mill.
Parks and recreation	$23 mill.
Government administration	$415 mill.
Interest on debt	$242 mill.
Total direct expenditures	$12,065 mill.

Totals include items not listed separately.
Source: U.S. Census Bureau.

POLITICS

Governors since statehood

D = Democrat; R = Republican; O = other;
(r) resigned; (d) died in office; (i) removed from office

William W. Bibb (O)	(d) 1819-1820
Thomas Bibb (O)	1820-1821
Israel Pickens (O)	1821-1825
John Murphy (D)	1825-1829
Gabriel Moore (D)	(r) 1829-1831
Samuel B. Moore (D)	1831
John Gayle (D)	1831-1835
Clement C. Clay (D)	(r) 1835-1837
Hugh McVay (D)	1837
Arthur P. Bagby (D)	1837-1841
Benjamin Fitzpatrick (D)	1841-1845
Joshua L. Martin (O)	1845-1847
Reuben Chapman (D)	1847-1849
Henry W. Collier (D)	1849-1853
John A. Winston (D)	1853-1857
Andrew B. Moore (D)	1857-1861
John G. Shorter (D)	1861-1863
Thomas H. Watts (D)	(i) 1863-1865
Lewis E. Parsons	1865
Robert M. Patton	1865-1868
William H. Smith (R)	1868-1870
Robert B. Lindsay (D)	1870-1872
David P. Lewis (R)	1872-1874
George S. Houston (D)	1874-1878
Rufus W. Cobb (D)	1878-1882
Edward A. O'Neal (D)	1882-1886
Thomas Seay (D)	1886-1890

Thomas G. Jones (D)	1890-1894
William C. Oates (D)	1894-1896
Joseph F. Johnston (D)	1896-1900
William D. Jelks (D)	1900
William J. Samford (D)	(d) 1900-1901
William D. Jelks (D)	1901-1907
Braxton B. Comer (D)	1907-1911
Emmet O'Neal (D)	1911-1915
Charles Henderson (D)	1915-1919
Thomas E. Kilby (D)	1919-1923
William W. Brandon (D)	1923-1927
(David) Bibb Graves (D)	1927-1931
Benjamin M. Miller (D)	1931-1935
(David) Bibb Graves (D)	1935-1939
Frank M. Dixon (D)	1939-1943
Chauncey M. Sparks (D)	1943-1947
James E. Folsom (D)	1947-1951
(Seth) Gordon Persons (D)	1951-1955
James E. Folsom (D)	1955-1959
John M. Patterson (D)	1959-1963
George C. Wallace, Jr. (D)	1963-1967
Lurleen B. Wallace (D)	(d) 1967-1968
Albert P. Brewer (D)	1968-1971
George C. Wallace, Jr. (D)	1971-1979
Forrest ("Fob") H. James (D)	1979-1983
George C. Wallace, Jr. (D)	1983-1987
Guy Hunt (R)	1987-1993
James E. Folsom (D)	1993-1995
Forrest ("Fob") H. James (D)	1995-1999
Don Siegelman (D)	1999-2003
Robert R. Riley (R)	2003-

Composition of congressional delegations, 1989-2007

	Dem	Rep	Total
House of Representatives			
101st Congress, 1989			
State delegates	4	2	6
Total U.S.	259	174	433
102d Congress, 1991			
State delegates	5	2	7
Total U.S.	267	167	434
103d Congress, 1993			
State delegates	4	3	7
Total U.S.	258	176	434
104th Congress, 1995			
State delegates	2	5	7
Total U.S.	197	236	433
105th Congress, 1997			
State delegates	2	5	7
Total U.S.	206	228	434
106th Congress, 1999			
State delegates	2	5	7
Total U.S.	211	222	433

(continued)

	Dem	Rep	Total
107th Congress, 2001			
State delegates	2	5	7
Total U.S.	211	221	432
108th Congress, 2003			
State delegates	2	5	7
Total U.S.	205	229	434
109th Congress, 2005			
State delegates	2	5	7
Total U.S.	202	231	433
110th Congress, 2007			
State delegates	2	5	7
Total U.S.	233	202	435

Senate

	Dem	Rep	Total
101st Congress, 1989			
State delegates	2	0	2
Total U.S.	55	45	100
102d Congress, 1991			
State delegates	2	0	2
Total U.S.	56	44	100
103d Congress, 1993			
State delegates	2	0	2
Total U.S.	57	43	100
104th Congress, 1995			
State delegates	0	2	2
Total U.S.	46	53	99
105th Congress, 1997			
State delegates	0	2	2
Total U.S.	45	55	100
106th Congress, 1999			
State delegates	0	2	2
Total U.S.	45	54	99
107th Congress, 2001			
State delegates	0	2	2
Total U.S.	50	50	100
108th Congress, 2003			
State delegates	0	2	2
Total U.S.	48	51	99
109th Congress, 2005			
State delegates	0	2	2
Total U.S.	44	55	99
110th Congress, 2007			
State delegates	0	2	2
Total U.S.	49	49	98

Figures are for starts of first sessions. Totals are for Democrat (Dem.) and Republican (Rep.) members only. House membership totals under 435 and Senate totals under 100 reflect vacancies and seats held by independent party members. When the 110th Congress opened, the Senate's two independent members caucused with the Democrats, giving the Democrats control of the Senate.
Source: U.S. Congress, *Congressional Directory.*

Composition of state legislature, 1990-2006

	Democrats	Republicans
State House (105 seats)		
1990	82	23
1992	82	23
1994	74	31
1996	72	33
1998	69	36
2000	68	37
2002	67	38
2004	63	42
2006	62	43
State Senate (35 seats)		
1990	28	7
1992	27	8
1994	23	12
1996	22	12
1998	23	12
2000	24	11
2002	24	11
2004	25	10
2006	23	43

Figures for total seats may include independents and minor party members. Numbers reflect results of elections in listed years; elected members usually take their seats in the years that follow.
Source: Council of State Governments; *State Elective Officials and the Legislatures.*

Voter participation in presidential elections, 2000 and 2004

	2000	2004
Voting age population		
State	3,330,000	3,436,000
Total United States	209,831,000	220,377,000
State share of U.S. total	1.59	1.56
Rank among states	22	22
Portion of voting age population casting votes		
State	50.0%	54.8%
United States	50.3%	55.5%
Rank among states	33	34

Population figures are rounded to nearest thousand and include all residents, regardless of eligibility to vote.
Source: U.S. Census Bureau.

HEALTH AND MEDICAL CARE

Medical professionals
Physicians in 2003 and nurses in 2001

	U.S.	State
Physicians in 2003		
Total	774,849	9,547
Share of U.S. total		1.23%
Rate	266	212
Rank		40
Nurses in 2001		
Total	2,262,020	36,400
Share of U.S. total		1.61%
Rate	793	814
Rank		28

Rates are numbers of physicians and nurses per 100,000 resident population; ranks are based on rates.
Source: American Medical Association, *Physician Characteristics and Distribution in the U.S.*; U.S. Department of Health and Human Services, Health Resources and Services Administration.

Health insurance coverage, 2003

	State	U.S.
Total persons covered	3,798,000	243,320,000
Total persons not covered	629,000	44,961,000
Portion not covered	14.2%	15.6%
Rank among states	24	—
Children not covered	95,000	8,373,000
Portion not covered	8.7%	11.4%
Rank among states	28	—

Totals are rounded to nearest thousand. Ranks are from the highest to the lowest percentages of persons *not* insured.
Source: U.S. Census Bureau, Current Population Reports.

AIDS, syphilis, and tuberculosis cases, 2003

Disease	U.S. cases	State cases	Rank
AIDS	44,232	471	23
Syphilis	34,270	566	16
Tuberculosis	14,874	258	16

Source: U.S. Centers for Disease Control and Prevention.

Cigarette smoking, 2003
Residents over age 18 who smoke

	U.S.	State	Rank
All smokers	22.1%	25.3%	13
Male smokers	24.8%	28.5%	9
Female smokers	20.3%	22.4%	13

Cigarette smokers are defined as persons who reported having smoked at least 100 cigarettes during their lifetimes and who currently smoked at least occasionally.
Source: U.S. Centers for Disease Control and Prevention, *Morbidity and Mortality Weekly Report*, 53, no. 44 (November 12, 2004).

HOUSING

Home ownership rates, 1985-2004

	1985	1990	1995	2000	2004
State	70.4%	68.4%	70.1%	73.2%	78.0%
Total U.S.	63.9%	63.9%	64.7%	67.4%	69.0%
Rank among states	10	19	15	14	2

Net change in state home ownership rate, 1985-2004 . . . . +7.6%
Net change in U.S. home ownership rate, 1985-2004 . . . . +5.1%

Percentages represent the proportion of owner households to total occupied households.
Source: U.S. Census Bureau, 2006.

Home sales, 2000-2004
In thousands of units

Existing home sales	2000	2002	2003	2004
State sales	67.0	82.2	93.7	112.0
Total U.S. sales	5,171	5,631	6,183	6,784
State share of U.S. total	1.30%	1.46%	1.52%	1.65%
Sales rank among states	24	23	23	23

Units include single-family homes, condos, and co-ops.
Source: National Association of Realtors, Washington, D.C., *Real Estate Outlook: Market Trends & Insights*.

Values of owner-occupied homes, 2003

	State	U.S.
Total units	947,000	58,809,000
Value of units		
Under $100,000	52.8%	29.6%
$100,000-199,999	35.0%	36.9%
$200,000 or more	12.2%	33.5%
Median value	$96,106	$142,275
Rank among all states 44		

Units are owner-occupied one-family houses whose numbers are rounded to nearest thousand. Data are extrapolated from survey samples.
Source: U.S. Census Bureau, American Community Survey.

EDUCATION

Public school enrollment, 2002

Prekindergarten through grade 8
State enrollment 534,000
Total U.S. enrollment. 34,135,000
State share of U.S. total 1.56%

Grades 9 through 12
State enrollment 206,000
Total U.S. enrollment. 14,067,000
State share of U.S. total 1.46%

Enrollment rates
State public school enrollment rate. 90.8%
Overall U.S. rate 90.4%
Rank among states in 2002. 22
Rank among states in 1995 6

Enrollment figures (which include unclassified students) are rounded to nearest thousand pupils during fall school term. Enrollment rates are based on enumerated resident population estimate for July 1, 2002.
Source: U.S. National Center for Education Statistics.

Public college finances, 2003-2004

FTE enrollment in public institutions of higher education
Students in state institutions. 183,300
Students in all U.S. public institutions 9,916,600
State share of U.S. total 1.85
Rank among states 18

State and local government appropriations for higher education
State appropriation per FTE $4,693
National average $5,716
Rank among states 39
State & local tax revenue going to higher education 12.0%

FTE = full-time equivalent in public postsecondary programs, including summer sessions; student numbers are rounded to nearest hundred. Funding figures for 2003-2004 academic year include financial aid to students in state public institutions and exclude money for research, agriculture experiment stations, teaching hospitals, and medical schools; figures are rounded to nearest thousand dollars.
Source: Higher Education Executive Officers, Denver, Colorado.

TRANSPORTATION AND TRAVEL

Highway mileage, 2003

Interstate highways 905
Other freeways and expressways 21
Arterial roads 8,795
Collector roads. 20,530
Local roads. 64,183
Urban roads 20,958
Rural roads. 73,476
Total state mileage. 94,434
U.S. total 3,974,107
State share 2.38%
Rank among states 19

Note that combined urban and rural road mileage matches the total of the other categories.
Source: U.S. Federal Highway Administration.

Motor vehicle registrations and driver licenses, 2003

Vehicle registrations	State	U.S.	Share	Rank
Autos, trucks, buses	4,329,000	231,390,000	1.87%	20
Autos only	1,771,000	135,670	1.31%	27
Motorcycles	70,000	5,328,000	1.31%	24
Driver licenses	3,598,000	196,166,000	1.83%	20

Figures, which do not include vehicles owned by military services, are rounded to the nearest thousand. Figures for automobiles include taxis.
Source: U.S. Federal Highway Administration.

Domestic travel expenditures, 2003

Spending by U.S. residents on overnight trips and
day trips of at least 50 miles from home

Total expenditures within state . . . . $5.55 bill.
Total expenditures within U.S. . . . . $490.87 bill.
State share of U.S. total 1.1%
Rank among states 29

Source: Travel Industry Association of America.

Retail gasoline prices, 2003-2007

Average price per gallon at the pump

Year	U.S.	State
2003	$1.267	$1.194
2004	$1.316	$1.258
2005	$1.644	$1.621
2007	$2.298	$2.172

Excise tax per gallon in 2004 . . . . 18.0¢
Rank among all states in 2007 prices 39

Prices are averages of all grades of gasoline sold at the pump
during March months in 2003-2005 and during February, 2007.
Averages for 2006, during which prices rose higher, are not
available.
Source: U.S. Energy Information Agency, *Petroleum Marketing
Monthly* (2003-2005 data); American Automobile Association
(2007 data).

CRIME AND LAW ENFORCEMENT

State and local police officers, 2000-2004

	2000	2002	2004
Total officers			
U.S.	654,601	665,555	675,734
State	10,161	9,351	9,472*
*Net change, 2000-2004			−6.78%
Officers per 1,000 residents			
U.S.	2.33	2.31	2.30
State	2.28	2.09	2.09
State rank	19	26	23

Totals include state and local police and sheriffs.
Source: Carsey Institute, University of New Hampshire.

Crime rates, 2003

Incidents per 100,000 residents

Crimes	State	U.S.
Violent crimes		
Total incidents	430	475
Murder	7	6
Forcible rape	37	32
Robbery	134	142
Aggravated assault	252	295
Property crimes		
Total incidents	4,049	3,588
Burglary	961	741
Larceny/theft	2,756	2,415
Motor vehicle theft	332	433
All crimes	4,479	4,063

Source: U.S. Federal Bureau of Investigation, *Crime in the United
States,* annual.

State prison populations, 1980-2003

	State	U.S.	State share
1980	6,543	305,458	2.14%
1990	15,665	708,393	2.21%
1996	21,760	1,025,624	2.12%
2000	26,332	1,391,261	1.89%
2003	29,253	1,470,045	1.99%

State figures exclude prisoners in federal penitentiaries.
Source: U.S. Bureau of Justice Statistics, *Prisoners in 2003.*

Alaska

Location: Northwest of Canada

Area and rank: 570,374 square miles (1,477,267 square kilometers); 656,424 square miles (1,700,138 square kilometers) including water; largest state in area

Coastline: 6,640 miles (10,686 kilometers) on the Pacific and Arctic Oceans

Shoreline: 33,904 miles (54,563 kilometers)

Population and rank: 655,000 (2004); forty-seventh state in population

Capital city: Juneau (30,711 people in 2000 census)

Largest city: Anchorage (260,283 people in 2000 census)

Became territory: 1912

Entered Union and rank: January 3, 1959; forty-ninth state

Present constitution adopted: April 24, 1956

Boroughs: 16

State name: "Alaska" comes from an Aleut word meaning "great land" or "that which the sea breaks against"

State nicknames: The Last Frontier; Land of the Midnight Sun

Motto: North to the Future

State flag: Blue field with eight gold stars forming Ursa Major and the North Star

Highest point: Mount McKinley—20,320 feet (6,194 meters)

Lowest point: Pacific Ocean—sea level

Highest recorded temperature: 100 degrees Fahrenheit (38 degrees Celsius)— Fort Yukon, 1915

Lowest recorded temperature: −80 degrees Fahrenheit (−62 degrees Celsius)—Prospect Creek, 1971

State song: "Alaska's Flag"

State tree: Sitka spruce

State flower: Forget-me-not

State bird: Willow ptarmigan

State fish: King salmon

National parks: Denali, Gates of the Arctic, Glacier Bay, Katmai, Kenai Fjords, Kobuk Valley, Lake Clark, Wrangell-St. Elias

Cruise ship entering the harbor of Ketchikan. With hundreds of miles of scenic coastlines, Alaska has become a popular tourist destination. (©Stanley Rippel/Dreamstime.com)

Alaska History

Alaska must be described in terms of absolutes and superlatives. When it was admitted to the Union in 1959, it became the first state outside the forty-eight contiguous states. It is the northernmost state, and remarkably, it is also the westernmost and easternmost state, extending from 130 degrees west latitude, across the 180 degree meridian, to 172 degrees east latitude. Its longitude runs from Barrow in the Arctic at 72 degrees north to the southernmost point in the Aleutian Islands, where its longitude is 52 degrees north, giving it greater longitude than the entire forty-eight contiguous states and almost as much latitude. Alaska lies geographically in four time zones, although, for practical purposes, two official time zones have been established.

Alaska is the only state that borders the Arctic Ocean and extends into the Arctic Circle. It lies closest to Asia of any of the states, its western extreme on Little Diomede Island being just two miles from the Russian island of Big Diomede. On the east and north, its border with Canada is the longest of any state. The shortest air routes between the United States and Asia are directly over Alaska, which has the largest oil and natural gas reserves in the United States. With a land mass of 570,374 square miles, it is the largest state, more than twice the size of Texas. Alaska has the largest glaciers and the most volcanoes of any U.S. state. With 1.1 per-sons per square mile, it has the lowest population density in the United States. Alaska's Mount McKinley, at 20,320 feet, is the highest point in the North American continent.

Early History. Alaska's earliest inhabitants were the Tlingit-Haidas and members of the Athabascan Tribes. The Aleuts and Eskimos, or Inuits, crossed the Bering Strait from Russia more than four thousand years ago and settled along the coast, surviving largely by fishing and hunting. These migrants were likely Asians who came to the region when what is now Alaska was linked to mainland Asia by a land bridge. By 1750, some seventy thousand native Inuits lived in Alaska (that number has not significantly changed). Aleuts were driven from the Aleutian Islands by the Russians in the eighteenth and nineteenth centuries and by the American military forces during World War II.

The earliest incursions by westerners occurred in 1741, when Vitus Bering, a Dane supported in his ventures by Russia, sailed to Alaska and established the first settlement on Kodiak Island in 1784. The fur business, important and lucrative in early Alaska, thrived with the establishment in 1799 of the Russian-American Company. It controlled the fur trade from its headquarters in Archangel, present-day Sitka.

Russia owned Alaska until 1867, when President Andrew Johnson's secretary of state, William H. Seward,

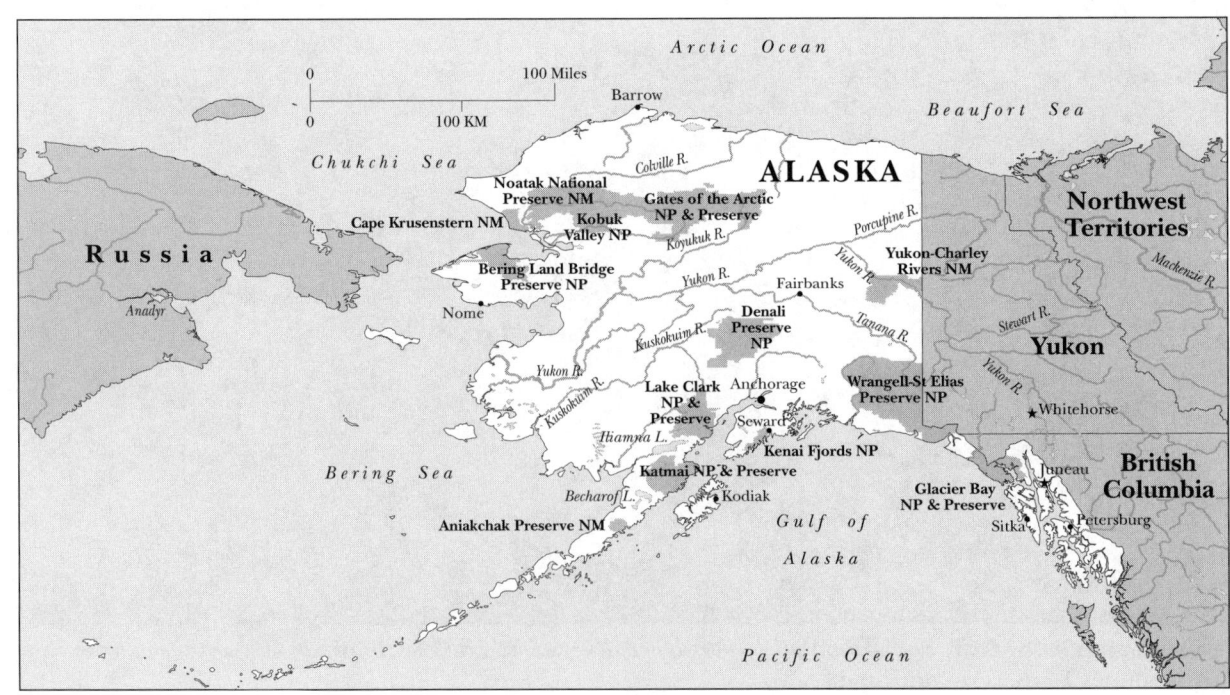

negotiated its purchase by the United States for $7.2 million. Although the U.S. Senate approved this purchase enthusiastically, buying this little-known area, which most people considered a frozen wasteland, was unpopular and known as "Seward's Folly." This "folly" paid off handsomely when a major gold strike was made near Juneau in 1880, unleashing a gold rush to the region and stimulating the exploration of Alaska for its mineral wealth.

In 1896, gold was discovered in Canada's Klondike, and, in 1898, at Fairbanks, causing another gold rush. Fish canneries built in the southeastern part of the area during the 1880's and 1890's imported workers from the United States. American traders moving to Alaska in search of riches established a route along the Yukon, the fourth longest river in the northern hemisphere.

Steps Toward Statehood. As Alaska became more viable economically, Congress viewed it with increased interest. In 1884, Alaska was made a judicial district, with Sitka as its capital. In 1906, it was permitted one elected delegate in the United States House of Representatives. The region was granted territorial status in 1912, and Juneau was declared its capital. Its political powers, however, were limited. Statehood was first proposed in Congress in 1916 but was rejected. In 1946, however, Alaskans, in a state referendum, approved statehood. Ten years later, a state constitution was adopted. On January 3, 1959, Alaska was admitted to the Union as the forty-ninth state.

When statehood was first proposed for Alaska in 1916, the state was extremely isolated from the rest of the country. Many U.S. citizens had gone there to work during the last half of the nineteenth century, but communication and transportation were limited. With the advent of radios and telephones, these problems began to fade, although it was many years before telephone communication with the "lower 48," as the United States mainland was called, was perfected. Almost simultaneously with better telephone communication came the development of air transportation, which had evolved rapidly during World War I and was, by the 1920's, becoming a major factor in transportation worldwide.

Alaska's enormous spaces made it an ideal venue for private aircraft. During the late 1920's and the 1930's, many Alaskans owned private planes, shrinking perceptibly the time they needed to cover the state's huge expanses. Commercial aircraft began to serve Alaska's major cities, and Anchorage became a refueling stop

The discovery of gold in 1898 drew prospectors from all over the world to Alaska and Canada's Klondike in one of the last great gold rushes. (Alaska Division of Tourism)

for planes flying from the United States and Canada to Asia.

These factors eliminated some of the earlier objections to statehood. Also, because the Japanese attacked and eventually occupied some of the Aleutian Islands during World War II, Americans became increasingly aware of Alaska's defensive importance.

Alaska's Economy. From its earliest days, Alaska had a stable economy. While mainland America struggled economically during the Great Depression of the 1930's, Alaska was undergoing an economic rebirth brought on largely by gold mining. Alaska had thriving copper mines as well. As revenues increased, the territorial government built much-needed roads, whose construction employed thousands of workers, many of whom came to Alaska and remained there as permanent residents.

World War II had a profound effect on the Alaskan economy. With Japan's invasion of the Aleutian Islands in 1942, the United States deployed about 200,000 military personnel to Alaska, where major military installations were built at Adak, Anchorage, Fairbanks, Kodiak, and Sitka. The Alcan highway was completed, creating a road link among Alaska's major cities.

Throughout the 1950's, military construction in Alaska continued at a brisk pace. This activity brought both construction workers and military personnel to the area in large numbers. Many, impressed by Alaska's grandeur and economic opportunities, remained there when the work that originally brought them to Alaska was completed.

In 1957, huge oil deposits were discovered in Alaska's Kenai Peninsula, and shortly thereafter other vast fields were found at Prudhoe Bay. Despite the harsh climate and great distances involved, the eight-hundred-mile long trans-Alaska oil pipeline was completed in 1977. Alaska became so oil rich that it was able to finance a giant expansion and still give each of its citizens more than one thousand dollars a year as a cash bonus for several years. It had no need for a state income tax.

The oil boom waned during the 1980's and by the mid-1980's was virtually over. The state by this time had attracted many new residents who viewed Alaska as the land of opportunity. Its population increased by 36.9 percent between 1980 and 1990, reaching just over 550,000 in 1990. The 1997 population registered a more than 10 percent increase, having grown to almost 610,000.

Following the oil boom, Alaska struggled to attract tourist dollars. It also began establishing trade with such Asian countries as South Korea, Taiwan, and Japan, although the slowing of the Asian economy in 1998 and 1999 temporarily stalled some of these efforts. Alaska's abundance of many resources that Asia does not have makes trade enviable. Natural gas devel-

opment also became vigorously pursued within the state, which also did a great deal to increase the amount of metal mining done within its boundaries. Alaska has deposits of every known mineral except bauxite.

The Threat of Oil Spills. Environmentalists were concerned about the building of the Trans-Alaska Pipeline because portions of it were laid in areas with geological faults. However, the pipelines have been fashioned to resist the earthquakes that are common in fault areas. A severe earthquake in 1964, followed by a tsunami, a huge tidal wave, devastated much of coastal Alaska, doing considerable damage in Anchorage, Kodiak, Seward, and Valdez. At this time, there was no pipeline that might rupture. The potential for destruction of the pipeline is slight, but still a cause for concern.

In 1989, a huge supertanker, the *Exxon Valdez*, foundered in Prince William Sound and spilled more than 240,000 barrels of oil into the surrounding water. The result was catastrophic: Commercial fishing was so negatively impacted that many who fished for a living were forced out of business. The wholesale destruction of wildlife would take the area years from which to recover completely. If any good came out of the *Exxon Valdez* disaster, it is that the shipping of oil on supertankers be-

Completion of the Trans-Alaska Pipeline in 1977 raised Alaska to an unprecedented level of prosperity. (© Vera Bogaerts/ iStockphoto)

Alaska's largest city, Anchorage has four times as many residents as the state's next two largest cities, Fairbanks and Juneau, combined. (PhotoDisc)

came more strenuously regulated. Many new tankers have double hulls so that if the hull is punctured, the oil will not leak into the surrounding ocean.

The conflict between those who wish to exploit Alaska's natural resources and those who oppose these policies on environmentalist grounds played a considerable role in the state's public life during the early twenty-first century. These debates were heightened by a 150,000-gallon oil spill from the Trans-Alaska Pipeline in 2001.

The question of oil drilling in the state's Arctic National Wildlife Refuge (ANWR) was as much a national as a state issue, roiling national politics year after year following the era of the Carter administration. Drilling became an intense issue in the new century as oil prices rose and national security became a greater public concern. In 2002, for example, after considerable debate and a negative National Research Council report, Congress rejected ANWR oil drilling. The next year, despite a national security appeal from President George W. Bush, the Senate narrowly rejected drilling. In 2005, however, the Senate accepted it, and the provision was dropped from the House version of the energy bill. Drilling in ANWR continued to be unapproved at mid-decade.

National Security and Politics. Another issue that affected public life in Alaska was the state's security from attack by the missiles of the Democratic People's Republic of Korea (DPRK). Following 1998, the North Koreans maintained a moratorium on missile testing after receiving stern warnings from the United States and its allies. However, in the summer of 2006, the issue again arose when the DPRK tested a number of short-range and long-range missiles. Although the long-range test was a failure, Alaska was put on notice that it was a possible future target. The DPRK claim, backed by Western intelligence, that it had nuclear weapons made Alaska's security a serious public issue.

To counter these security concerns, the Bush administration increased funding for a missile defense system, some of which would be deployed in Alaska. Critics wondered, however, how effective the system really was, especially after test failures, including one in 2004. Nevertheless, in late 2004, six ground-based missiles were placed in silos at Fort Greely.

Politically, Alaska remained split between Republican and Democrat office holders, with Republicans in Congress and a Democrat in the statehouse in Juneau. If anything, however, the state leaned to the political right, voting for the Republican presidential candidate,

Rising to an altitude of 20,320 feet, Alaska's Mount McKinley is the tallest mountain in North America. (PhotoDisc)

Bush, in 2000 and 2004. On social issues, the state also leaned to the right, rejecting same-sex marriage and the partial legalization of marijuana. In August, 2006, former U.S. senator and current governor Frank Murkowski, who had very low approval ratings from the public, lost his bid for reelection in the Republican primary election in what was a landslide victory for former Wasilla mayor Sarah Palin, who took 50 percent of the vote. Murkowski got only 19 percent—identical to his approval rating.

R. Baird Shuman
Updated by the Editor

Alaska Time Line

c. 10,000 B.C.E.	Human habitation of the area toward the end of the last Ice Age is documented.
c. 650 C.E.	Aleuts and Eskimos separate; Eskimos divide into Yupic and Inupiaq.
c. 1000 C.E.	Eskimos migrate from Alaska to Greenland.
1741	Vitus Bering lands off Kayak Island.
1774-1792	Spanish explore Alaska's west coast.
1778	British captain James Cook surveys Alaska coast.
1784	Russian Grigori Sheilikhov establishes Russian settlement near present-day Kodiak.
1791	British captain George Vancouver charts southeastern Alaska.
1799	Czar Paul I charters Russian-American Company.
1802	Tlingit Indians attack Russian-American Company, killing 408.
1823	Father Ivan Veniaminov works among the Aleuts.
1824-1825	Boundaries of Russian settlement in Alaska are fixed.

Mar. 30, 1867	United States purchases Alaska from Russia for $7.2 million.
1876	First Protestant mission in Alaska is established at Wrangell.
1878	First salmon cannery is built at Klawock.
1880	Gold is discovered at Juneau.
1884	Alaska becomes a judicial district with the capital at Sitka; native land rights are preserved and laws of Oregon are enforced.
1891	Sheldon Jackson introduces reindeer into Alaska to compensate for near-extinction of whales and walrus.
1898	Klondike gold rush begins, continuing for twenty years.
1900	United States Congress reforms Alaska's civil government, making Juneau the capital.
1906	Alaska is permitted to elect one delegate to the United States House of Representatives.
1911	Alaska signs international agreement to restrict seal hunting off Pribilof and other islands.
Aug. 24, 1912	Alaska is granted territorial status.
1913	Women receive voting rights.
1916	Alaskan statehood is first proposed in Congress.
1917	University of Alaska is founded.
1923	Alaska Railroad is completed, connecting Anchorage and Seward with Fairbanks.
1923	Alaska Agricultural College and School of Mines opens.
1924	Lieutenant Carl Ben Eielson flies first airmail.
1931	Federal Building is completed in Juneau.
1935	Matanuska agricultural colony is established under New Deal.
1942	Japanese bomb Dutch Harbor.
June 7, 1942	Japan invades and occupies Kiska and Attu in the Aleutian Islands.
Nov. 20, 1942	Alcan Highway, running from Great Falls, Montana, to Fairbanks, is completed.
1943	United States recaptures Aleutians from the Japanese.
1945	Racial discrimination in public accommodations is ruled illegal.
1946	Alaskans approve statehood in statewide referendum.
1952	First pulp and paper mill is built outside Ketchikan.
1955	Eklutna Power Project opens near Palmer.
1955	Military fuel pipeline opens between Haines and Fairbanks.
1956	Alaskans adopt state constitution.
1957	Oil is discovered on Kenai Peninsula.
Jan. 3, 1959	Alaska is granted statehood.
1963	Alaska's first oil refinery opens.
Mar. 27, 1964	Most severe earthquake in North America's history strikes; tsunamis devastate Anchorage, Kodiak, Seward, and Valdez.
Aug. 14-15, 1967	Record floods damage Fairbanks.
1971	Alaska Native Land Claims Settlement bill is enacted.
1977	Trans-Alaska oil pipeline is completed.
1981	Alaska National Interest Lands Conservation bill is enacted.
1988	Forest fires destroy over two million acres.
1988	Border between Alaska and eastern Soviet Union opens.
Mar. 24, 1989	*Exxon Valdez* spills 240,000 barrels of oil into Prince William Sound.
1996	Exxon Corporation pays Alaska $900 million for clean-up following *Exxon Valdez* oil spill.
1997	Congress passes bill to phase out largest factory trawlers for bottom fishing on the Bering Sea.
1997	Alaska ranks among the top three states in per-pupil expenditures for public education.
1998	Federal budget gives Alaska pollock processors $100 million.
1999	Alaska and Canada sign pact to protect endangered salmon species.
2003	Wildfires burn 3.6 million acres across the state.
2003	U.S. Senate rejects ANWR oil drilling.
2005	U.S. Senate approves ANWR drilling, but the House omits it from energy bill.
July 4, 2006	Alaska's security is threatened by the resumption of missile testing by North Korea.
Aug. 22, 2006	Governor Frank Murkowski loses reelection bid in Republican primary, gaining just 19 percent of the vote.

Notes for Further Study

Published Sources. Robert Hedin and Gary Holthaus's *The Great Land: Reflections on Alaska* (1994) offers comprehensive overviews of the state. George W. Rogers, in *Change in Alaska: People, Petroleum, Politics* (1970), considers what the oil discoveries at Kenai Peninsula and Prudhoe mean to the state and is especially useful when read in conjunction with Robert B. Weeden's *Messages from Earth: Nature and Human Prospect in Alaska* (1992) and Craig A. Doherty and Katherine M. Doherty's *The Alaska Pipeline* (1998). Bryan Cooper's *Alaska: The Last Frontier* (1973) also focuses on the effect that the petroleum discoveries of the late 1960's and early 1970's had upon the ecology and economy of Alaska. Jeff Wheelwright's *Degrees of Disaster: Prince William Sound—How Nature Reels and Rebounds* (1994) considers the aftermath of the *Exxon Valdez* oil spill. Taking a step further back into the state's history, Lydia T. Black uses text, detailed maps, and color illustrations to examine the merging of Russian and Alaskan history in *Russians in Alaska, 1732-1867* (2004).

Owen K. Mason, William J. Neal, and Orrin H. Pilkey consider threats to the Alaskan coastline in *Living with the Coast of Alaska* (1997). David S. Case considers how native Alaskans adapt to American laws in *Alaska Natives and American Laws* (1997), while Michael Jenning, in *Alaska Native Political Leadership and Higher Education: One University, Two Universes* (2004), focuses on the ways in which imperial notions of education altered indigenous peoples' relationship to and understanding of their land. Theodore Lane considers the special climatic conditions of Alaska and how to cope with them in *Developing America's Northern Frontier* (1987). The state's harsh elements provide the backbone for two "true story" adventure books: *The Last Frontier: Incredible Tales of Survival, Exploration, and Adventure from "Alaska Magazine"* (2004), which tells stories of events as disparate as earthquakes, tidal waves, bear attacks, and influenza epidemics in its lively focus on Alaska's wilderness; and *Tales from the Edge: True Adventures in Alaska* (2005), edited by Larry Kaniut, which thrills readers with stories of humans struggling against the oftentimes inhospitable environment. In *Looking for Alaska* (2001), Peter Jenkins examines the lives and cultures he encounters during his eighteen-month sojourn across the state. Carole Marsh's *Alaska Timeline: A Chronology of Alaska History, Mystery, Trivia, Legend, Lore, and More* (1992) is aimed at the juvenile market and is a worthwhile study. Kathleen Thompson's *Alaska* (1988) is also written with juveniles in mind.

Web Resources. Alaska's government Web site (www.state.ak.us) is a well-organized portal for a wealth of information about the state. The home page is divided into three main categories, and readers will likely find the most interesting information under the heading Of Interest, including links to Alaska Communities and Alaska Facts and Visitor Info. The state's tourist Web site (www.commerce.state.ak.us/tourism) is directed at the traveler and includes interactive maps and photo galleries, as well as the requisite tourist amenity information for numerous cities and towns. Those planning outdoor activities in the state should consult the Alaska Travel Adventures Web site (www.alaskaadventures.com). Bike tours are advertised on Alaska Bike Tours' Web site (www.alaskabike.com). Fishing enthusiasts will find information on the *Alaska Angler*'s Web site (www.alaskaangler.com) and on the Alaska Fly Fisher's Web site (www.akflyfishers.com). Alaska Whale Tours (www.whale-watching-alaska.com/) covers whale watching thoroughly. Alaska national parklands are described on the National Parklands Web site (www.nps.gov/akso), while an insider's guide to traveling in the state can be found on the Alaska Travel Tips Web site (www.alaskaparks.com).

For scientific information about Alaska's Arctic regions, the Arctic Research Consortium's Web site (www.arcus.org) is helpful. The University of Alaska Anchorage Justice Center (justice.uaa.alaska.edu/rlinks/natives/index.html) operates a Web page index to numerous resources about the state's native peoples, including information on specific tribes, self-governance, environment, and organizations and associations. The Alaska Native Heritage Center (www.alaskanative.net/2.asp), a museum in Anchorage, has an informative Web site that supports museum efforts and provides online information about several Alaskan indigenous communities. The Klondike Gold Rush was a preeminent event in the state's history and several Web sites are dedicated to it, including the Klondike Gold Rush National Park (www.nps.gov/KLGO/home.htm), Explore North's index listing (www.explorenorth.com/library/ya/bl22y.htm) to a wide variety of Klondike resources, and the Klondike Gold Rush site (library.thinkquest.org/5181/).

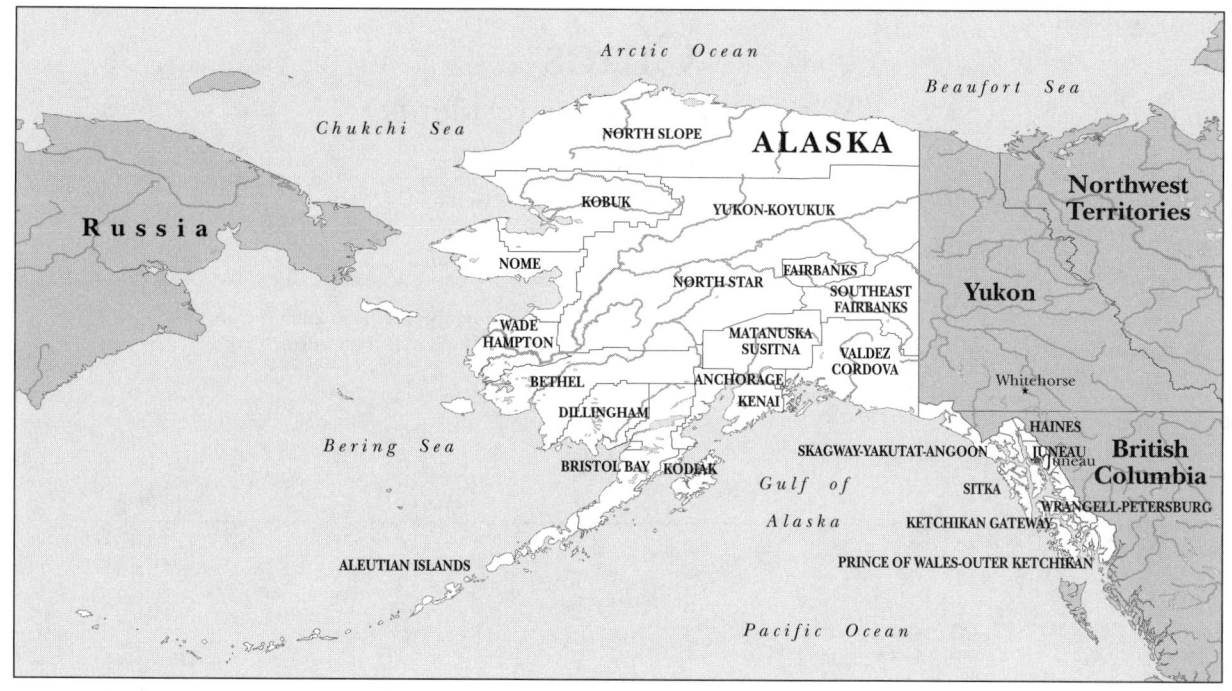

Counties

County	2000 pop.	Rank in pop.	Sq. miles	Area rank
Aleutians East (b)	2,697	22	6,984.8	18
Aleutians West (c)	5,465	19	4,397	21
Anchorage (b)	260,283	1	1,697.6	25
Bethel (c)	16,006	6	40,633	3
Bristol Bay (b)	1,258	26	519.2	27
Denali (b)	1,893	24	12,750	14
Dillingham (c)	4,922	20	18,675	10
Fairbanks North Star (b)	82,840	2	7,362.4	16
Haines (b)	2,392	23	2,357.0	24
Juneau (b)	30,711	5	2,593.6	23
Kenai Peninsula (b)	49,691	4	16,078.9	12
Ketchikan Gateway (b)	14,070	7	1,219.6	26
Kodiak Island (b)	13,913	8	6,462.6	19
Lake and Peninsula (b)	1,823	25	23,632.3	8
Matanuska-Susitna (b)	59,322	3	24,693.6	7
Nome (c)	9,196	10	23,001	9

County	2000 pop.	Rank in pop.	Sq. miles	Area rank
North Slope (b)	7,385	12	87,860.5	2
Northwest Arctic (b)	7,208	13	35,862.5	5
Prince of Wales-Outer Ketchikan (c)	6,145	18	7,324	17
Sitka (b)	8,835	11	2,881.5	22
Skagway-Hoonah-Angoon (c)	3,426	21	12,881	13
Southeast Fairbanks (c)	6,174	17	25,994	6
Valdez-Cordova (c)	10,195	9	36,945	4
Wade Hampton (c)	7,028	14	17,124	11
Wrangell-Petersburg (c)	6,684	15	5,808	20
Yakutat City (b)	808	27	7,650	15
Yukon-Koyukuk (c)	6,551	16	157,121	1

(b) = borough; (c) = census area.

Source: U.S. Census Bureau; National Association of Counties.

Cities
With 6,000 or more residents

Rank	City	Population
1	Anchorage	260,283
2	Juneau (capital)	30,711
3	Fairbanks	30,224
4	College	11,402
5	Sitka	8,835
6	Ketchikan	7,922
7	Knik-Fairview	7,049

Rank	City	Population
8	Kenai	6,942
9	Lakes	6,706
10	Kodiak	6,334

Population figures are from 2000 census.
Source: U.S. Bureau of the Census.

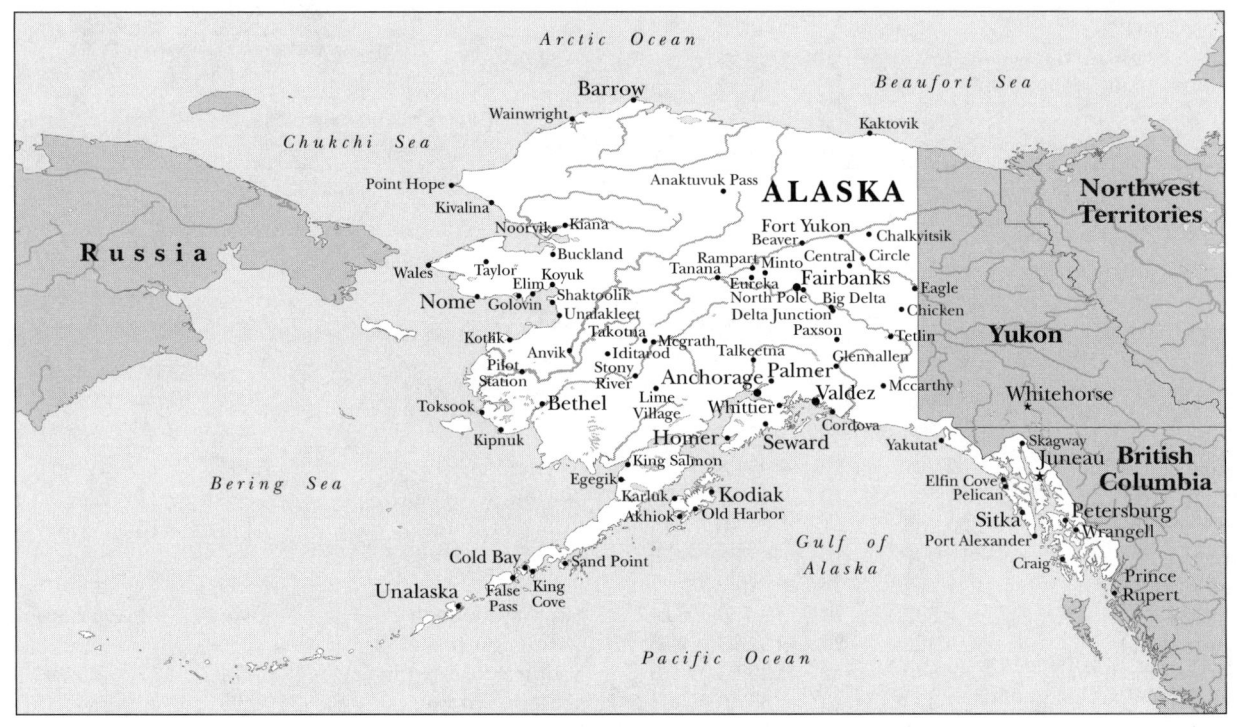

Index to Tables

DEMOGRAPHICS

VITAL STATISTICS

ECONOMY

LAND USE

GOVERNMENT AND FINANCE

POLITICS

HEALTH AND MEDICAL CARE

HOUSING

EDUCATION

TRANSPORTATION AND TRAVEL

CRIME AND LAW ENFORCEMENT

DEMOGRAPHICS

Resident state and national populations, 1970-2004

Population figures given in thousands

	State pop.	U.S. pop.	Share	Rank
1970	303	203,302	0.1%	50
1980	402	226,546	0.2%	50
1985	532	237,924	0.2%	48
1990	550	248,765	0.2%	49
1995	604	262,761	0.2%	48
2000	627	281,425	0.2%	47
2004	655	293,655	0.2%	47

Source: U.S. Census Bureau, Current Population Reports, 2006.

Resident population by age, 2004

Age Group	Total persons
Under 5 years	50,000
5 to 17 years	138,000
18 to 24 years	74,000
25 to 34 years	81,000
35 to 44 years	102,000
45 to 54 years	107,000
55 to 64 years	61,000
65 to 74 years	26,000
75 to 84 years	13,000
85 years and older	4,000
All age groups	655,000
Portion of residents 65 and older	6.4%
National rank in portion of oldest residents	50
National average	12.4%

Population figures are rounded to nearest thousand persons; figures include armed forces personnel stationed in state.
Source: U.S. Bureau of the Census, 2006.

Resident population by race, Hispanic origin, 2004

Category	State pop.	Share	U.S.
All residents	655	100.00%	100.00%
Non-Hispanic white	438	66.87%	67.37%
Hispanic white	26	3.97%	13.01%
Other Hispanic	6	0.92%	1.06%
African American	24	3.66%	12.77%
Native American	104	15.88%	0.96%
Asian, Pacific Islander	34	5.19%	4.37%
Two or more categories	31	4.73%	1.51%

Population figures are in thousands. Persons counted as "Hispanic" (Latino) may be of any race. Because of overlapping categories, categories may not add up to 100%. Shares in column 3 are percentages of each category within the state; these figures may be compared to the national percentages in column 4.
Source: U.S. Bureau of the Census, 2006.

Projected state population, 2000-2030

Year	Population
2000	627,000
2005	661,000
2010	694,000
2015	733,000
2020	774,000
2025	821,000
2030	868,000
Population increase, 2000-2030	241,000
Percentage increase, 2000-2030	38.4

Projections are based on data from the 2000 census.
Source: U.S. Census Bureau.

VITAL STATISTICS

Infant mortality rates, 1980-2002

	1980	1990	2000	2002
All state residents	12.3	10.5	6.8	5.5
All U.S. residents	12.6	9.2	9.4	9.1
All state white residents	9.4	7.6	5.8	4.2
All U.S. white residents	10.6	7.6	5.7	5.8
All state black residents	19.5	—	—	—
All U.S. black residents	22.2	18.0	14.1	14.4

Figures represent deaths per 1,000 live births of resident infants under 1 year old, exclusive of fetal deaths. Figures for all residents include members of other racial categories not listed separately. The Census Bureau considers the post-1980 figures for black residents to be too small to be statistically meaningful.
Source: U.S. Census Bureau, *Statistical Abstract of the United States,* 2006.

Abortion rates, 1990 and 2000

	1990	2000
Total abortions	2,000	2,000
Rate per 1,000 women	16.5	11.7
U.S. rate	25.7	21.3
Rank	29	12

Numbers of abortions are rounded to nearest thousand; ranks are based on rates.
Source: U.S. Census Bureau.

Marriages and divorces, 2004

Total marriages	5,400
Rate per 1,000 population	8.3
National rate per 1,000 population	7.4
Rank among all states	13
Total divorces	3,100
Rate per 1,000 population	4.8
National rate per 1,000 population	3.7
Rank among all states	7

Figures are for all marriages and divorces performed within the state, including those of nonresidents; totals are rounded to the nearest hundred. Ranks are for highest to lowest figures; note that divorce data are not available for five states.
Source: U.S. National Center for Health Statistics, *Vital Statistics of the United States,* 2006.

Death rates by leading causes, 2002
Deaths per 100,000 resident population

Cause	State	U.S.
Heart disease	88.1	241.7
Cancer	111.1	193.2
Cerebrovascular diseases	24.5	56.4
Accidents other than motor vehicle	53.7	37.0
Motor vehicle accidents	17.4	15.7
Chronic lower respiratory diseases	22.1	43.3
Diabetes mellitus	13.4	25.4
HIV	n/a	4.9
Suicide	20.5	11.0
Homicide	6.2	6.1
All causes	470.7	847.3
Rank in overall death rate among states		50

Figures exclude nonresidents who died in the state. Causes of death follow International Classification of Diseases. Rank is from highest to lowest death rate in the United States.
Source: U.S. National Center for Health Statistics, *National Vital Statistics Report,* 2006.

ECONOMY

Gross state product, 1990-2004
In current dollars

Year	State product	Nat'l product	State share
1990	$25.0 billion	$5.67 trillion	0.44%
2000	$27.6 billion	$9.75 trillion	0.28%
2002	$29.7 billion	$10.41 trillion	0.29%
2003	$31.7 billion	$10.92 trillion	0.29%
2004	$33.9 billion	$11.65 trillion	0.29%

Source: U.S. Bureau of Economic Analysis, *Survey of Current Business,* July, 2005.

Gross state product by industry, 2003
In billions of dollars

Construction	$1.4
Manufacturing	0.6
Wholesale trade	0.7
Retail trade	1.8
Finance & insurance	1.0
Information	0.9
Professional services	1.0
Health care & social assistance	1.6
Government	5.5
Total state product	$28.1
Total U.S. product	$10,289.2
State share of U.S. total	0.27%
Rank among all states	45

Total figures include industries not listed separately. Amounts are in chained 2000 dollars.

Source: U.S. Bureau of Economic Analysis, *Survey of Current Business,* July, 2005.

Personal income per capita, 1990-2004
In current dollars

	1990	2000	2004
Per capita income	$22,804	$29,867	$34,454
U.S. average	$19,477	$29,845	$32,937
Rank among states	6	15	13

Source: U.S. Bureau of Economic Analysis, *Survey of Current Business,* April, 2005.

Energy consumption, 2001
In trillions of British thermal units (BTU), except as noted

Total energy consumption

Total state energy consumption	737
Total U.S. energy consumption	96,275
State share of U.S. total	0.77%
Rank among states	35

Per capita consumption (In millions of BTU)

Total state per capita consumption	1,164
Total U.S. per capita consumption	338
Rank among states	1

End-use sectors

Residential	53
Commercial	65
Industrial	413
Transportation	206

Sources of energy

Petroleum	292
Natural gas	413
Coal	16
Hydroelectric power	14
Nuclear electric power	0

Figures for totals include categories not listed separately.
Source: U.S. Energy Information Administration, *State Energy Data Report,* 2001.

Nonfarm employment by sectors, 2004

Total	304,000
Construction	18,000
Manufacturing	12,000
Trade, transportation, utilities	62,000
Information	7,000
Finance, insurance, real estate	15,000
Professional & business services	23,000
Education & health services	35,000
Leisure, hospitality, arts, organizations	30,000
Other services, including repair & maintenance	12,000
Government	81,000

Figures are rounded to nearest thousand persons. "Total" includes mining and natural resources, not listed separately.
Source: U.S. Bureau of Labor Statistics, 2006.

Foreign exports, 1990-2004
In millions of dollars

Year	State	U.S.	State share
1990	2,850	394,045	0.72%
1996	2,879	624,767	0.46%
1997	2,721	688,896	0.39%
2000	2,464	712,055	0.31%
2003	2,739	724,006	0.41%
2004	3,157	769,332	0.41%

Rank among all states in 2004 37

U.S. total does not include U.S. dependencies.
Source: U.S. Census Bureau, *U.S. Merchandise Trade*, series FT 900, 2000; U.S. Census Bureau, *U.S. International Trade in Goods and Services*, Series FT 900, 2005.

LAND USE

Federally owned land, 2003
Areas in acres

	State	U.S.	State share
Total area	365,482,000	2,271,343,000	16.09%
Nonfederal land	121,635,000	1,599,584,000	7.60%
Federal land	243,847,000	671,759,000	36.30%
Federal share	66.7%	29.6%	—

Areas are rounded to nearest thousand acres. Figures for federally owned land do not include trust properties.
Source: U.S. General Services Administration, *Federal Real Property Profile*, 2006.

Farms and crop acreage, 2004

	State	U.S.	Share	Rank
Farms	1,000	2,113,000	0.05%	49
Acres (millions)	1	937	0.11%	41
Acres per farm	1,452	443	—	6

Source: U.S. Department of Agriculture, National Agricultural Statistics Service. Numbers of farms are rounded to nearest thousand units; acreage figures are rounded to nearest million. Rankings, including ties, are based on rounded figures.

GOVERNMENT AND FINANCE

Units of local government, 2002

	State	Total U.S.	Rank
All local governments	175	87,525	48
Counties	12	3,034	44
Municipalities	149	19,429	37
Townships	0	16,504	—
School districts	0	13,506	—
Special districts	14	35,052	50

Only 48 states have county governments, 20 states have township governments ("towns" in New England, Minnesota, New York, and Wisconsin), and 46 states have school districts. Special districts encompass such functions as natural resources, fire protection, and housing and community development.
Source: U.S. Census Bureau, *Census of Governments.*

State government revenue, 2002

Total revenue. $5,019 mill.
General revenue . . . . $5,423 mill.
Per capita revenue $8,462
U.S. per capita average $3,689
Rank among states 1

Intergovernment revenue
Total . . . . $1,556 mill.
From federal government . . . . $1,551 mill.

Charges and miscellaneous
Total . . . . $2,777 mill.
Current charges . . . . $338 mill.
Misc. general income . . . . $2,439 mill.
Insurance trust revenue . . . . −$421 mill.

Taxes
Total . . . . $1,090 mill.
Per capita taxes $1,700
Rank among states 32
Property taxes . . . . $50 mill.
Sales taxes . . . . $142 mill.
License taxes. . . . . $74 mill.
Individual income taxes . . . . (nil)
Corporate income taxes . . . . $269 mill.
Other taxes . . . . $554 mill.

Total revenue figures include items not listed separately here.
Source: U.S. Bureau of the Census.

State government expenditures, 2002

General expenditures

Total state expenditures . . . . $7,402 mill.
Intergovernmental. . . . . $1,056 mill.

Per capita expenditures

State. $10,456
Average of all states $3,859
Rank among states. 1

Selected direct expenditures

Education. . . . . $882 mill.
Public welfare . . . . $1,029 mill.
Health, hospital . . . . $141 mill.
Highways . . . . $667 mill.
Police protection . . . . $63 mill.
Corrections. $174 mill.
Natural resources . . . . $238 mill.
Parks and recreation . . . . $9 mill.
Government administration. . . . . $361 mill.
Interest on debt . . . . $276 mill.
Total direct expenditures . . . . $5,647 mill.

Totals include items not listed separately.
Source: U.S. Census Bureau.

POLITICS

Governors since statehood

D = Democrat; R = Republican; O = other;
(r) resigned; (d) died in office; (i) removed from office

William A. Egan (D) 1959-1966
Walter J. Hickel (R) . . . . (r) 1966-1969
Keith H. Miller (R) 1969-1970
William A. Egan (D) 1970-1974
Jay S. Hammond (R). 1974-1982
William Sheffield (D) 1982-1986
Steve Cowper (D) 1986-1990
Walter J. Hickel (O) 1990-1994
Tony Knowles (D) 1994-2002
Frank Murkowski (R) 2002-2006
Sarah Palin (R). 2006-

Composition of congressional delegations, 1989-2007

	Dem	Rep	Total
House of Representatives			
101st Congress, 1989			
State delegates	0	1	1
Total U.S.	259	174	433
102d Congress, 1991			
State delegates	0	1	1
Total U.S.	267	167	434
103d Congress, 1993			
State delegates	0	1	1
Total U.S.	258	176	434
104th Congress, 1995			
State delegates	0	1	1
Total U.S.	197	236	433
105th Congress, 1997			
State delegates	0	1	1
Total U.S.	206	228	434
106th Congress, 1999			
State delegates	0	1	1
Total U.S.	211	222	433
107th Congress, 2001			
State delegates	0	1	1
Total U.S.	211	221	432
108th Congress, 2003			
State delegates	0	1	1
Total U.S.	205	229	434
109th Congress, 2005			
State delegates	0	1	1
Total U.S.	202	231	433
110th Congress, 2007			
State delegates	0	1	1
Total U.S.	233	202	435
Senate			
101st Congress, 1989			
State delegates	0	2	2
Total U.S.	55	45	100
102d Congress, 1991			
State delegates	0	2	2
Total U.S.	56	44	100
103d Congress, 1993			
State delegates	0	2	2
Total U.S.	57	43	100
104th Congress, 1995			
State delegates	0	2	2
Total U.S.	46	53	99
105th Congress, 1997			
State delegates	0	2	2
Total U.S.	45	55	100

(continued)

	Dem	Rep	Total
106th Congress, 1999			
State delegates	0	2	2
Total U.S.	45	54	99
107th Congress, 2001			
State delegates	0	2	2
Total U.S.	50	50	100
108th Congress, 2003			
State delegates	0	2	2
Total U.S.	48	51	99
109th Congress, 2005			
State delegates	0	2	2
Total U.S.	44	55	99
110th Congress, 2007			
State delegates	0	2	2
Total U.S.	49	49	98

Figures are for starts of first sessions. Totals are for Democrat (Dem.) and Republican (Rep.) members only. House membership totals under 435 and Senate totals under 100 reflect vacancies and seats held by independent party members. When the 110th Congress opened, the Senate's two independent members caucused with the Democrats, giving the Democrats control of the Senate.
Source: U.S. Congress, *Congressional Directory.*

Composition of state legislature, 1990-2006

	Democrats	Republicans
State House (40 seats)		
1990	23	17
1992	20	18
1994	17	22
1996	16	24
1998	14	26
2000	14	26
2002	13	27
2004	14	26
2006	17	23
State Senate (20 seats)		
1990	10	10
1992	10	10
1994	8	12
1996	7	13
1998	5	15
2000	5	15
2002	6	14
2004	8	12
2006	9	11

Figures for total seats may include independents and minor party members. Numbers reflect results of elections in listed years; elected members usually take their seats in the years that follow.
Source: Council of State Governments; *State Elective Officials and the Legislatures.*

Voter participation in presidential elections, 2000 and 2004

	2000	2004
Voting age population		
State	437,000	467,000
Total United States	209,831,000	220,377,000
State share of U.S. total	0.21	0.21
Rank among states	49	49
Portion of voting age population casting votes		
State	65.3%	66.9%
United States	50.3%	55.5%
Rank among states	3	6

Population figures are rounded to nearest thousand and include all residents, regardless of eligibility to vote.
Source: U.S. Census Bureau.

HEALTH AND MEDICAL CARE

Medical professionals
Physicians in 2003 and nurses in 2001

	U.S.	State
Physicians in 2003		
Total	774,849	1,439
Share of U.S. total		0.19%
Rate	266	222
Rank		35
Nurses in 2001		
Total	2,262,020	4,930
Share of U.S. total		0.22%
Rate	793	778
Rank		33

Rates are numbers of physicians and nurses per 100,000 resident population; ranks are based on rates.
Source: American Medical Association, *Physician Characteristics and Distribution in the U.S.*; U.S. Department of Health and Human Services, Health Resources and Services Administration.

Health insurance coverage, 2003

	State	U.S.
Total persons covered	523,000	243,320,000
Total persons not covered	122,000	44,961,000
Portion not covered	18.9%	15.6%
Rank among states	6	—
Children not covered	24,000	8,373,000
Portion not covered	12.3%	11.4%
Rank among states	15	—

Totals are rounded to nearest thousand. Ranks are from the highest to the lowest percentages of persons *not* insured.
Source: U.S. Census Bureau, Current Population Reports.

AIDS, syphilis, and tuberculosis cases, 2003

Disease	U.S. cases	State cases	Rank
AIDS	44,232	17	45
Syphilis	34,270	8	45
Tuberculosis	14,874	57	35

Source: U.S. Centers for Disease Control and Prevention.

Cigarette smoking, 2003
Residents over age 18 who smoke

	U.S.	State	Rank
All smokers	22.1%	26.3%	5
Male smokers	24.8%	30.3%	4
Female smokers	20.3%	21.9%	17

Cigarette smokers are defined as persons who reported having smoked at least 100 cigarettes during their lifetimes and who currently smoked at least occasionally.
Source: U.S. Centers for Disease Control and Prevention, *Morbidity and Mortality Weekly Report*, 53, no. 44 (November 12, 2004).

HOUSING

Home ownership rates, 1985-2004

	1985	1990	1995	2000	2004
State	61.2%	58.4%	60.9%	66.4%	67.2%
Total U.S.	63.9%	63.9%	64.7%	67.4%	69.0%
Rank among states	43	46	44	40	42

Net change in state home ownership rate,
1985-2004 . . . . +6.0%
Net change in U.S. home ownership rate,
1985-2004 . . . . +5.1%

Percentages represent the proportion of owner households to total occupied households.
Source: U.S. Census Bureau, 2006.

Home sales, 2000-2004
In thousands of units

Existing home sales	2000	2002	2003	2004
State sales	14.3	17.2	18.4	23.0
Total U.S. sales	5,171	5,631	6,183	6,784
State share of U.S. total	0.28%	0.31%	0.30%	0.34%
Sales rank among states	45	44	44	44

Units include single-family homes, condos, and co-ops.
Source: National Association of Realtors, Washington, D.C., *Real Estate Outlook: Market Trends & Insights.*

Values of owner-occupied homes, 2003

	State	U.S.
Total units	112,000	58,809,000
Value of units		
Under $100,000	13.2%	29.6%
$100,000-199,999	50.9%	36.9%
$200,000 or more	35.9%	33.5%
Median value	$174,146	$142,275
Rank among all states 12		

Units are owner-occupied one-family houses whose numbers are rounded to nearest thousand. Data are extrapolated from survey samples.
Source: U.S. Census Bureau, American Community Survey.

EDUCATION

Public school enrollment, 2002

Prekindergarten through grade 8
State enrollment 94,000
Total U.S. enrollment. 34,135,000
State share of U.S. total 0.28%

Grades 9 through 12
State enrollment. 40,000
Total U.S. enrollment. 14,067,000
State share of U.S. total 0.28%

Enrollment rates
State public school enrollment rate. 94.9%
Overall U.S. rate 90.4%
Rank among states in 2002 6
Rank among states in 1995. 13

Enrollment figures (which include unclassified students) are rounded to nearest thousand pupils during fall school term. Enrollment rates are based on enumerated resident population estimate for July 1, 2002.
Source: U.S. National Center for Education Statistics.

Public college finances, 2003-2004

FTE enrollment in public institutions of higher education

Students in state institutions 37,600
Students in all U.S. public institutions 9,916,600
State share of U.S. total 0.38
Rank among states 40

State and local government appropriations for higher education

State appropriation per FTE $5,269
National average $5,716
Rank among states 29
State & local tax revenue going to higher
    education 10.2%

FTE = full-time equivalent in public postsecondary programs,
    including summer sessions; student numbers are rounded to
    nearest hundred. Funding figures for 2003-2004 academic year
    include financial aid to students in state public institutions and
    exclude money for research, agriculture experiment stations,
    teaching hospitals, and medical schools; figures are rounded to
    nearest thousand dollars.
Source: Higher Education Executive Officers, Denver, Colorado.

TRANSPORTATION AND TRAVEL

Highway mileage, 2003

Interstate highways 1,082
Arterial roads 1,513
Collector roads 2,753
Local roads 8,882
Urban roads 2,070
Rural roads 12,160
Total state mileage 14,230
U.S. total 3,974,107
State share 0.36%
Rank among states 47

Note that combined urban and rural road mileage matches the
    total of the other categories.
Source: U.S. Federal Highway Administration.

Motor vehicle registrations and driver licenses, 2003

Vehicle registrations	State	U.S.	Share	Rank
Autos, trucks, buses	637,000	231,390,000	0.28%	48
Autos only	261,000	135,670	0.19%	49
Motorcycles	20,000	5,328,000	0.38%	46
Driver licenses	481,000	196,166,000	0.25%	48

Figures, which do not include vehicles owned by military services,
    are rounded to the nearest thousand. Figures for automobiles
    include taxis.
Source: U.S. Federal Highway Administration.

Domestic travel expenditures, 2003

Spending by U.S. residents on overnight trips and
day trips of at least 50 miles from home

Total expenditures within state . . . . $1.38 bill.
Total expenditures within U.S. . . . . $490.87 bill.
State share of U.S. total 0.3%
Rank among states 47

Source: Travel Industry Association of America.

Retail gasoline prices, 2003-2007

Average price per gallon at the pump

Year	U.S.	State
2003	$1.267	n/a
2004	$1.316	$1.475
2005	$1.644	$1.872
2007	$2.298	$2.441

Excise tax per gallon in 2004 . . . . 8.0¢
Rank among all states in 2007 prices 8

Prices are averages of all grades of gasoline sold at the pump
    during March months in 2003-2005 and during February, 2007.
    Averages for 2006, during which prices rose higher, are not
    available.
Source: U.S. Energy Information Agency, *Petroleum Marketing
    Monthly* (2003-2005 data); American Automobile Association
    (2007 data).

CRIME AND LAW ENFORCEMENT

State and local police officers, 2000-2004

	2000	2002	2004
Total officers			
U.S.	654,601	665,555	675,734
State	1,116	1,161	1,213*
*Net change, 2000-2004			+8.69%
Officers per 1,000 residents			
U.S.	2.33	2.31	2.30
State	1.78	1.81	1.85
State rank	37	37	35

Totals include state and local police and sheriffs.
Source: Carsey Institute, University of New Hampshire.

Crime rates, 2003
Incidents per 100,000 residents

Crimes	State	U.S.
Violent crimes		
Total incidents	593	475
Murder	6	6
Forcible rape	93	32
Robbery	68	142
Aggravated assault	427	295
Property crimes		
Total incidents	3,742	3,588
Burglary	594	741
Larceny/theft	2,771	2,415
Motor vehicle theft	377	433
All crimes	4,335	4,063

Source: U.S. Federal Bureau of Investigation, *Crime in the United States*, annual.

State prison populations, 1980-2003

	State	U.S.	State share
1980	822	305,458	0.27%
1990	2,622	708,393	0.37%
1996	3,716	1,025,624	0.36%
2000	4,173	1,391,261	0.30%
2003	4,527	1,470,045	0.31%

State figures include jail inmates but exclude prisoners in federal penitentiaries.
Source: U.S. Bureau of Justice Statistics, *Prisoners in 2003.*

Arizona

Location: Southwest

Area and rank: 114,000 square miles (295,249 square kilometers); 114,006 square miles (295,276 square kilometers) including water; sixth largest state in area

Coastline: none (c. 40 miles from Gulf of California)

Population and rank: 5,744,000 (2004); eighteenth largest state in population

Capital and largest city: Phoenix (1,321,045 people in 2000 census)

Became territory: February 24, 1863

Entered Union and rank: February 14, 1912; forty-eighth state

Present constitution adopted: 1911

Counties: 15

State name: "Arizona" derives from the American Indian "Arizonac," which means "little spring" or "young spring"

State nickname: Grand Canyon State

Motto: *Ditat Deus* (God enriches)

State flag: Blue field on bottom half; thirteen red and yellow rays and a copper star on top half

Highest point: Humphreys Peak—12,633 feet (3,851 meters)

Lowest point: Colorado River—70 feet (21 meters)

Highest recorded temperature: 127 degrees Fahrenheit (53 degrees Celsius)—Parker, 1905

Lowest recorded temperature: −40 degrees Fahrenheit (−40 degrees Celsius)—Hawley Lake, 1971

State song: "Arizona March Song"

State tree: Palo Verde

State flower: Saguaro cactus blossom

State bird: Cactus wren

State fish: Apache trout

National parks: Grand Canyon, Petrified Forest, Saguaro

Central business district of Arizona's capital and largest city, Phoenix, with the Phoenix Mountains to the north in the background.

Arizona History

Arizona's arid climate and southwest location combined to play influential roles in its history. Lack of rain has placed water at the center of Arizona's concerns, because without water, economic development is impossible. During the 1850's, the federal government even imported camels for a route through Arizona. The state was later than others in developing, with a population of barely forty thousand in 1880. On the other hand, the completion of a number of significant dams before and after World War II provided copious water and electric power, and the state's warm winters attract millions of new arrivals.

Early History. American Indians are believed to have inhabited Arizona for thousands of years, probably as early as 25,000 B.C.E. First to have settled were the Anasazi, ancestors of today's Pueblo, Hohokam, and Mogollon peoples. Not long before the entrance of Europeans to the region, the Navajos and Apaches arrived. In the sixteenth century, Spanish and Native Americans came in contact with each other. A succession of Spanish expeditions arrived, headed by priests such as Franciscan friar Marcos de Niza, who came in 1539 searching for the fabled Seven Cities of Cibola. Other adventurers arrived, such as Francisco Vásquez de Coronado, who explored the region from 1540 to 1542. More explorers entered the region later in the century searching for precious metals.

In the next century a number of priests came in search of American Indian souls to save and began erecting missions. Perhaps the most illustrious was Father Eusebio Francisco Kino, a Jesuit mathematics professor of German origin, who went to Mexico in 1680. Kino thoroughly explored the region, covering twenty thousand miles and finding an overland route to California. Kino also founded several missions, including San Xavier del Bac Mission, located near Tucson, established in 1692. It is the only surviving Mexican Baroque church in the United States.

In the eighteenth century Spanish activity continued. In 1776, when the American colonies declared

Apache leaders Geronimo (center left with arms on knees) and Nana (to Geronimo's right) negotiating with General George Crook (second from right with white hat) around 1886, during one of several attempts to end the region's Apache wars. (Library of Congress)

independence from Britain, Spanish cleric Father Francisco Silvestre Vélez de Escalante undertook important explorations of the Colorado River region. The previous year, Tucson had been founded when a fortress, Old Pueblo, was constructed there. In succeeding years, Spanish troops were busy dealing with hostile American Indians. During the 1780's they conquered the Yumas, and in 1790 negotiations with the Apaches resulted in a peace lasting until 1822. Peace with the Navahos after their military defeat in 1806 lasted thirteen years.

American involvement in the region began during the 1820's, when traders and trappers entered the territory. From 1828, trapper, scout, and soldier Kit Carson used Taos, New Mexico, as a base for expeditions, which in some cases traveled through Arizona. Another famous trapper and scout, Pauline Weaver, arrived in 1830 and was active more than thirty years later when he led gold-hunting parties. In these years modern Arizona was part of Mexico, which gained independence from Spain after its War of Independence, begun in 1810.

From Spanish to American Rule. Arizona passed from Mexican to American hands as a consequence of the Mexican-American War (1846-1848). The terms of the Treaty of Guadalupe Hidalgo called for Mexico to cede all lands north of the Gila River, which runs through southern Arizona. Thus Arizona became part of New Mexico, which became a territory after its annexation to the United States.

The Gila River border proved problematic, however, when plans for a transcontinental railroad were being drawn up, since the best route ran south of the river. Accordingly, an American diplomat, James Gadsden, American Minister to Mexico, negotiated transfer of the required land. In 1853, by the terms of the Gadsden Purchase, Mexico agreed to sell a strip of territory along its northern border between Texas and California for $10 million.

Arizona was still part of New Mexico when the Civil War broke out. In 1861, when southern President Jefferson Davis declared New Mexico part of the Confederacy, Kit Carson was asked to raise a force to defend the territory against invasion. When the Confederacy sent troops to the region in 1862, the only Civil War battle on Arizona soil occurred, resulting in Union victory. Thereafter, claims of the Confederacy to the region

rang hollow. To ensure its status, however, Congress made Arizona a separate territory in 1863. Prescott was the new territory's first capital, though the site changed from one place to another until Phoenix became the permanent capital in 1889.

Native American Relations. During the Civil War, the area was nearly emptied of European settlers. Yet after the war, when miners and ranchers returned, American Indian attacks became a serious matter. In 1864, Kit Carson led a successful campaign against the Navahos. The defeated Navahos were then required to trek, many of them on foot, to Bosque Redondo, New Mexico, some three hundred miles away. The event became known as the Long Walk. They remained there until 1868, when they made the Long Walk Home. The Apaches, however, remained hostile and active in Arizona. With such leaders as Cochise, Mangas Coloradas, and Geronimo, the Apaches were a formidable threat, attacking not only ranches but also towns and even forts. Not until 1886 did the last raiding party led by Geronimo surrender to federal forces.

Despite problems with Native Americans, much economic progress was made. Mining made great strides during the 1870's, and after 1886 grazing prospered despite frequent range wars between cattle and sheep ranchers. During the 1880's copper was discovered near Bisbee, in the southeast. Eventually copper became an important state resource. Settlement of the territory was assisted by several congressional acts, such as the Homestead Act (1862), which gave land to settlers but required them to develop it to make good their claims. A tremendous boost to the state's development occurred when the first transcontinental railroad appeared in 1877. Six years later, track for a second railroad was laid in northern Arizona. Population, which was a dismal 9,658 in 1870, jumped to more than 40,000 ten years later and reached 88,000 in 1890. At the close of the century, it was 123,000, and in 1910, just prior to statehood, it passed 200,000.

From Territory to Statehood. With the American Indian menace behind them, Arizonans of the 1890's agitated for statehood. Not until 1910, however, could Congress be persuaded to pass enabling legislation. Accordingly, a constitution was adopted. Like those of other western states, it provided for the initiative and referendum and allowed recall of public officials. This provision included recall of judges by voters, but President William Howard Taft strongly objected and refused to agree to Arizona statehood unless it was removed. He believed that judicial independence, essential for constitutional government, would be fatally compromised by such a provision. The offending provision was therefore deleted. Upon attaining statehood, however, voters restored the provision.

The constitution provides for a governor elected for no more than two four-year terms. Four other executive branch officials are elected—a secretary of state, attorney general, treasurer, and superintendent of public instruction. These officials form a line of succession if a governor dies, resigns, or is removed from office; they, too, are limited to two four-year terms. Members of the bicameral legislature can be elected to a maximum of four two-year terms. The state's supreme court justices are appointed by the governor to six-year terms, at the end of which voters decide whether to retain them. The recall provision was most notably used in 1988 to remove a sitting governor.

Social and Economic Progress. By the time Arizona achieved statehood, it had begun the process of advancing from an extraction to a manufacturing economy. With the emergence of labor unions in mines, labor strife became familiar. Among militant labor organizers were the Marxist International Workers

of the World (IWW). A notorious event in the state's labor history involving the IWW was the "Bisbee deportation" of July 12, 1917, during World War I. In this incident, some two thousand persons, most of them copper miners called out on strike by the IWW, were arrested by armed civilians, headed by the sheriff. Those who refused to abandon the strike, nearly 1,200 men, were loaded onto cattle cars and taken across the New Mexico border. There, they were unloaded in the desert, where they spent two unsheltered days before U.S. troops arrived. Hundreds of civil suits were filed afterward and settled out of court.

Along with neighboring states, the American entrance into World War I gave a significant, though temporary, boost to Arizona's economy, when the price of minerals skyrocketed. During the two decades following the war, the federal government continued planning and constructing a series of dams and reservoirs that eventually would be of tremendous value to the state's economy by allowing irrigation, cheap power, and flood control. The Roosevelt Dam had been constructed prior to statehood. After the war, further projects included the Coolidge Dam on the Upper Gila

Hoover Dam as it neared completion during the mid-1930's. (Bureau of Reclamation)

River in south central Arizona, other dams on the Verde and Salt Rivers, and the great Hoover Dam, one of the century's great engineering projects, on the Arizona-Nevada border. In 1922, the Colorado River Compact devised a scheme for water sharing among seven states, including Arizona. As further irrigation became possible, agriculture prospered. The 1930's Depression years, however, were as difficult for Arizona as for the rest of the nation.

World War II and Postwar Developments. The state's economy rebounded through federal spending during World War II, when numerous air bases were opened due to the state's ideal flying weather. After the war the boom continued. Between 1940 and 1960, population nearly tripled, reaching 1.3 million. Adequate water supplies allowed manufacturing to expand, especially after 1963, when the U.S. Supreme Court awarded the state rights to 2.8 million acre feet of water a year from the Colorado River. By then, Arizona's extraction economy had been transformed by industrialization.

By the 1990's the state had undergone a second transformation. Manufacturing accounted for only 12 percent of its income, though high-tech industries were making their mark. Agriculture was just 2 percent and mining a scant 1 percent of state income. The lion's share was now taken up by services, including a thriving tourist industry. Society had also been transformed by a postwar flight from the eastern and midwestern "rust belt" to the warmer climate and economic opportunities of the Southwest. From a raw frontier territory at the start of the century, Arizona had become a prosperous modern, postindustrial society, with a rich and colorful past and a confident future.

Twenty-first Century Prosperity. As the new millennium approached, Arizona could find much satisfaction in its growing prosperity. People flocked to the state, where a bountiful economy beckoned, especially in the Phoenix-Tucson area. In 1999, the U.S. poverty rate reached a twenty-year low; Arizona was one of seven states with a statistically significant drop in poverty. Following the 2000 census, which reflected the state's population increase, Arizona gained two new members in the U.S. House of Representatives.

Politically, the state remained somewhat right of center, voting for the Republican presidential candidate, George W. Bush, in both 2000 and 2004. Both of its U.S. senators and four of its five members of the House were Republican, and the two seats created in

In 2006, after playing before sweltering crowds in Arizona's desert heat, the National Football League's Cardinals began playing in a new air-conditioned stadium with a unique innovation: a real-grass field that rolls out of the covered stadium into the sunlight.

2002 went to Republicans. The state governor elected in 2002, Janet Napolitano, however, was a Democrat.

Wildfires. Many of the Western states struggled with historic droughts during the 1990's and into the early twenty-first century, and Arizona was no exception. One serious consequence of the droughts was the recurrence of wildfires, some of which consumed hundreds of thousands of acres. The wildfires in 1999 were so prevalent and destructive that they were said to be "the worst wildfire season in a generation." Other fires, not all of them of natural origin, followed annually. The devastating Rodeo-Chediski fire of 2002, in east-central Arizona, burned more than 400,000 acres.

Illegal Immigration. By the late 1990's, a simmering controversy plagued the state regarding illegal immigrants flowing north from the Mexican border. In 2000, Arizonans sought to shore up social cohesion by passing an initiative, Proposition 203, abolishing bilingual education and replacing it with English immersion education for immigrant students. Four years later, in 2004, the state's voters, fearful of noncitizen influence at the polls, passed an initiative requiring proof of U.S. citizenship for voting.

Tragic circumstances surrounded other aspects of illegal immigration. In 2001, fourteen illegal immigrants who had been abandoned by smugglers in the Arizona desert were found dead some thirty miles north of the Mexican border. Others, more fortunate, were found alive but dehydrated and exhausted. Several years later, on August 15, 2005, Governor Napolitano declared a state of emergency in four counties bordering Mexico because of problems caused by a heavy influx of illegal immigrants.

During the same year, about thirteen hundred citizen volunteers—declaring themselves part of the Minuteman Project after the Revolutionary-era defenders of the American colonies—spent a month patrolling border areas for illegal immigrants and informing Border Patrol agents of immigrant activity they witnessed.

Despite its problems, Arizona entered the third millennium in a dynamically prosperous position, with the continued arrival of Americans from other parts to the country eager to take advantage of the state's warm climate and its growing economic opportunities.

Charles F. Bahmueller
Updated by the Editor

Arizona Time Line

500 c.e.-1450	Hohokam tribes flourish; build more than two hundred miles of canals for water for irrigation and domestic use.
c. 1000	Cochise tribe settles near present-day Bisbee.
1526	Don José de Basconales crosses part of Arizona.
1536	Explorer Alvar Núñez Cabeza de Vaca crosses part of southwest Arizona.
1539	Franciscan friar Marcos de Niza explores in Arizona, searching for rich Seven Cities of Cibola.
1540	Francisco Vásquez de Coronado explores Arizona region.
1581-1583	Spanish expeditions through Arizona find precious metals.
1620	Franciscan missionaries appeal to Hopi tribe.
1680	Father Eusebio Francisco Kino begins missionary work.
1700	Father Kino founds San Xavier del Bac Mission.
1752	First white settlement is founded by Spanish at Tubac.
1776	Tucson is founded as Spanish fort.
1776	Father Francisco Silvestre Vélez de Escalante explores Colorado River region.
1782	Spanish military forces conquer Yuma tribe.
1804-1806	Navaho Indians are defeated by Spanish military; peace endures for thirteen years.
1821	Arizona becomes province of Mexico; Santa Fe Trail opens.
1824	American traders begin exploring Apache territory.
1827	Mexican Republic expels Franciscans, ending missionary era.
1830	American trapper and scout Pauline Weaver begins Arizona travels.
Dec. 17, 1846	Mormon battalion occupies Tucson; raises U.S. flag on road from Santa Fe to the Pacific.
1848	Mexico cedes all land north of Gila River to United States in Treaty of Guadalupe Hidalgo.
Sept. 9, 1850	Territory of New Mexico, which includes Arizona, is established.
1853	Gadsden Purchase makes southern Arizona U.S. land.
1860	First newspaper, the *Weekly Arizonan*, begins publication.
1860	Apache chief Cochise leads raids on settlers.
1861	Southern president Jefferson Davis declares Arizona a Confederate territory.
1862	Sole Civil War battle in Arizona fought at Picacho Peak, near Tucson; results in Union victory.
Feb. 24, 1863	Union president Abraham Lincoln creates Arizona Territory; Prescott is made capital.
1864	Navahos are forced to walk three hundred miles from Arizona to Fort Sumner, New Mexico, after military defeat in an event remembered as The Long Walk.
1866	First public schools open, in Prescott and Tucson.
1867	Treaty establishing Navaho Reservation is signed.
Apr. 30, 1871	Grant Camp Massacre occurs, in which 108 Apaches are killed by whites.
1875	First copper is mined at Clifton.
1879	Tombstone is founded after gold is discovered.
1880	First railroad crosses state.

Oct. 26, 1881	Gunfight at the O.K. Corral, among Wyatt Earp, Doc Holliday, and others, takes place in Tombstone.
1883	Santa Fe Railroad crosses northern region of Arizona.
1907	Arizona is nation's leading copper producer.
1911	Roosevelt Dam is dedicated.
Feb. 14, 1912	Arizona becomes forty-eighth state.
1919	Grand Canyon National Park is established.
1928	Coolidge Dam is dedicated.
1936	Boulder (now Hoover) Dam, on Arizona-Nevada border, is completed.
1942	Almost eighteen thousand Japanese Americans are interned in Poston.
1948	Arizona's Native Americans win right to vote.
1962	U.S. Supreme Court gives Arizona Colorado River water rights.
1963	Judge Lorna Lockwood becomes first female state supreme court chief justice.
1969	Navajo Community College, the first college on an Indian reservation, opens in Tsaile.
1974	Construction begins on Central Arizona Project, designed to assure Arizona sufficient water.
1991	Central Arizona Project is completed.
1997	Arizona's population is estimated at 4,554,966.
May 23-24, 2001	Fourteen illegal immigrants, abandoned by smugglers, are found dead in the Arizona desert.
Oct. 16, 2003	Colorado River Water Pact is signed guaranteeing stable access to water from the Colorado River to Arizona and to seven other Colorado River Basin states.
Nov. 4, 2003	Mexico's president Vicente Fox visits the state in search of agreement on the regularization of the status of illegal Mexican immigrants; he meets with Arizona governor and governors of three other border states.
Aug. 15, 2005	Governor declares a state of emergency in border counties because of a heavy influx of illegal immigrants.
Aug. 12, 2006	State-of-the-art, retractable roof, air-conditioned Cardinals Stadium, which cost $455 million to build, opens in Glendale, Arizona.

Notes for Further Study

Published Sources. Among books useful for an understanding of government in Arizona are David R. Berman's *Arizona Politics and Government: The Quest for Autonomy, Democracy, and Development* (1998), Gerald E. Hansen and Douglas A. Brown's *Arizona: Its Constitution and Government* (1993), and *The Arizona Constitution Study Guide* (8th ed., 2005). There is also an annually updated yearbook series, *Arizona Yearbook: A Guide to Government in the Grand Canyon State.* On Arizona's geography, see Malcolm L. Comeaux's *Arizona: A Geography* (1982); for place names, there is Will Croft Barnes's *Arizona Place Names* (1988); and for a historical atlas, one should consult Henry Pickering Walker's *Historical Atlas of Arizona* (1987).

For natural history, an excellent source is *The Smithsonian Guide to Natural America: The Southwest—New Mexico and Arizona* (1995). For an overview of Arizona history, see Robert Wozinicki's *History of Arizona* (1987); Donald Gawronski's *An Introduction to Arizona and Government* (1988); and Thomas G. Aylesworth, et al. *The West: Arizona, Nevada, Utah* (1995). Eminent folk historian Marshall Trimble has also written *Arizona: A Cavalcade of History* (Rev. ed., 2003), a solid overview of the state's past. Travelers should also consult Trimble's *Roadside History of Arizona* (2d ed., 2004) and Anne O'Brien's *Traveling Indian Arizona* (2006), which introduces readers to the modern-day culture, traditions, cuisine, and arts of the state's

twenty-one tribal communities. Studies on Native Americans include W. E. Coffer's *Sipapu: The Story of the Indians of Arizona and New Mexico* (1986). Regarding individual tribes, Ruth Underhill studies *The Papago and Pima Indians of Arizona* (1990), and Franck C. Lockwood examines *The Apache Indians* (1987). Ancient Indian culture is explored in James J. Reid and Stephanie Whittlesey's *The Archeology of Ancient Arizona* (1997). Few Americans know that the Civil War was fought as far west as the territory that was to become Arizona. In *The Civil War in Arizona: The Story of the California Volunteers, 1861-1865* (2006), Andrew E. Masich chronicles the struggles of the California Column, a group of volunteer soldiers who served in the U.S. Army from 1861 to 1866 and played a key role in creating and shaping Arizona Territory. Young audiences will appreciate the survey of the state found in *Arizona* (2005) by Vanessa Brown.

Web Resources. The official state of Arizona Web site (www.state.az.us) is a good starting place for information on the state, especially by using the Find by Category heading on the home page. Arizona Travel (www.arizonaguide.com/) is a comprehensive site with a wealth of information for those planning a trip to the state. The governor's site (governor .state.az.us/) and the State of Arizona Legislative Information System (www.azleg.state.az.us/) offer resources on the political workings in the state. The Census Bureau provides

Straddling the northwestern corner of Arizona, the Grand Canyon is a deep gorge, cut by the Colorado River, that stretches about 280 miles. (PhotoDisc)

pages on individual states, which are good resources for statistical information on state demographics (quickfacts.census.gov/qfd/states/04000.html).

Useful links to Arizona history sites include the Prescott site (prescott.org/history.htm) and the Arizona Heritage Traveler (www.azhistorytraveler.org/templates/index.php); click on Attractions A-Z in the top navigation bar.

For a taste of the state's varied ethnic history, see the Promise of Gold Mountain: Tucson's Chinese Heritage (parentseyes.arizona.edu/promise/). The Arizona state historical society maintains information on library archives on Arizona history (www.arizonahistoricalsociety.org/). Access Genealogy (www.accessgenealogy.com/native/arizona/) maintains a very useful page on the history of many of the state's tribal communities, as does AzCentral (www.azcentral.com/culturesaz/amindian/timelineamind.html).

Information on individual tribes may also be researched; consult pages on the Hohokum Indians in Arizona (www.nativeamericans.com/Hohokam.htm) or the Hopi (www.crystalinks.com/hopi1.html).

Counties

County	2000 pop.	Rank in pop.	Sq. miles	Rank in area
Apache	69,423	10	11,205.7	3
Cochise	117,755	7	6,170.0	8
Coconino	116,320	8	18,619.1	1
Gila	51,335	11	4,768.1	11
Graham	33,489	13	4,629.6	12
Greenlee	8,547	15	1,847.1	14
La Paz	19,715	14	4,499.6	13
Maricopa	3,072,149	1	9,204.0	5
Mohave	155,032	6	13,312.4	2

County	2000 pop.	Rank in pop.	Sq. miles	Rank in area
Navajo	97,470	9	9,953.8	4
Pima	843,746	2	9,187.0	6
Pinal	179,727	3	5,370.0	10
Santa Cruz	38,381	12	1,237.7	15
Yavapai	167,517	4	8,123.5	7
Yuma	160,026	5	5,514.4	9

Source: U.S. Census Bureau; National Association of Counties.

Cities
With 10,000 or more residents

Rank	City	Population	Rank	City	Population
1	Phoenix (capital)	1,321,045	27	Nogales	20,878
2	Tucson	486,699	28	Fortuna Foothills	20,478
3	Mesa	396,375	29	Fountain Hills	20,235
4	Glendale	218,812	30	Kingman	20,069
5	Scottsdale	202,705	31	Goodyear	18,911
6	Chandler	176,581	32	Green Valley	17,283
7	Tempe	158,625	33	Florence	17,054
8	Gilbert	109,697	34	Tanque Verde	16,195
9	Peoria	108,364	35	San Luis	15,322
10	Yuma	77,515	36	Flowing Wells	15,050
11	Casas Adobes	54,011	37	New Kingman-Butler	14,810
12	Catalina Foothills	53,794	38	Sierra Vista Southeast	14,348
13	Flagstaff	52,894	39	Douglas	14,312
14	Lake Havasu City	41,938	40	Mohave Valley	13,694
15	Sun City	38,309	41	Paradise Valley	13,664
16	Sierra Vista	37,775	42	Payson	13,620
17	Avondale	35,883	43	Marana	13,556
18	Prescott	33,938	44	Sun Lakes	11,936
19	Bullhead City	33,769	45	New River	10,740
20	Apache Junction	31,814	46	Cottonwood-Verde Village	10,610
21	Surprise	30,848	47	Eloy	10,375
22	Oro Valley	29,700	48	Sedona	10,192
23	Sun City West	26,344			
24	Casa Grande	25,224			
25	Drexel Heights	23,849			
26	Prescott Valley	23,535			

Population figures are from 2000 census.
Source: U.S. Bureau of the Census.

Index to Tables

DEMOGRAPHICS

Resident state and national populations, 1970-2004

Population figures given in thousands

	State pop.	U.S. pop.	Share	Rank
1970	1,775	203,302	0.9%	33
1980	2,718	226,546	1.2%	29
1985	3,184	237,924	1.3%	28
1990	3,665	248,765	1.5%	24
1995	4,432	262,761	1.6%	22
2000	5,131	281,425	1.8%	20
2004	5,744	293,655	2.0%	18

Source: U.S. Census Bureau, Current Population Reports, 2006.

Resident population by age, 2004

Age Group	Total persons
Under 5 years	450,000
5 to 17 years	1,097,000
18 to 24 years	571,000
25 to 34 years	830,000
35 to 44 years	800,000
45 to 54 years	719,000
55 to 64 years	545,000
65 to 74 years	396,000
75 to 84 years	250,000
85 years and older	86,000
All age groups	5,744,000
Portion of residents 65 and older	12.7%
National rank in portion of oldest residents	26
National average	12.4%

Population figures are rounded to nearest thousand persons;
figures include armed forces personnel stationed in the state.
Source: U.S. Bureau of the Census, 2006.

Resident population by race, Hispanic origin, 2004

Category	State pop.	Share	U.S.
All residents	5,744	100.00%	100.00%
Non-Hispanic white	3,510	61.11%	67.37%
Hispanic white	1,523	26.51%	13.01%
Other Hispanic	86	1.50%	1.06%
African American	203	3.53%	12.77%
Native American	289	5.03%	0.96%
Asian, Pacific Islander	133	2.32%	4.37%
Two or more categories	86	1.50%	1.51%

Population figures are in thousands. Persons counted as "Hispanic" (Latino) may be of any race. Because of overlapping categories, categories may not add up to 100%. Shares in column 3 are percentages of each category within the state; these figures may be compared to the national percentages in column 4.
Source: U.S. Bureau of the Census, 2006.

Projected state population, 2000-2030

Year	Population
2000	5,131,000
2005	5,868,000
2010	6,637,000
2015	7,495,000
2020	8,456,000
2025	9,532,000
2030	10,712,000
Population increase, 2000-2030	5,581,000
Percentage increase, 2000-2030	108.8

Projections are based on data from the 2000 census.
Source: U.S. Census Bureau.

VITAL STATISTICS

Infant mortality rates, 1980-2002

	1980	1990	2000	2002
All state residents	12.4	8.8	6.7	6.4
All U.S. residents	12.6	9.2	9.4	9.1
All state white residents	11.8	7.8	6.2	6.2
All U.S. white residents	10.6	7.6	5.7	5.8
All state black residents	18.4	20.6	17.6	13.0
All U.S. black residents	22.2	18.0	14.1	14.4

Figures represent deaths per 1,000 live births of resident infants under 1 year old, exclusive of fetal deaths. Figures for all residents include members of other racial categories not listed separately.
Source: U.S. Census Bureau, *Statistical Abstract of the United States,* 2006.

Abortion rates, 1990 and 2000

	1990	2000
Total abortions	21,000	18,000
Rate per 1,000 women	23.5	16.5
U.S. rate	25.7	21.3
Rank	18	21

Numbers of abortions are rounded to nearest thousand; ranks are based on rates.
Source: U.S. Census Bureau.

Marriages and divorces, 2004

Total marriages	37,900
Rate per 1,000 population	6.6
National rate per 1,000 population	7.4
Rank among all states	32
Total divorces	24,400
Rate per 1,000 population	4.2
National rate per 1,000 population	3.7
Rank among all states	15

Figures are for all marriages and divorces performed within the state, including those of nonresidents; totals are rounded to the nearest hundred. Ranks are for highest to lowest figures; note that divorce data are not available for five states.
Source: U.S. National Center for Health Statistics, *Vital Statistics of the United States,* 2006.

Death rates by leading causes, 2002
Deaths per 100,000 resident population

Cause	State	U.S.
Heart disease	198.9	241.7
Cancer	171.5	193.2
Cerebrovascular diseases	46.5	56.4
Accidents other than motor vehicle	47.2	37.0
Motor vehicle accidents	20.3	15.7
Chronic lower respiratory diseases	47.2	43.3
Diabetes mellitus	22.6	25.4
HIV	3.0	4.9
Suicide	16.2	11.0
Homicide	9.2	6.1
All causes	784.7	847.3
Rank in overall death rate among states		36

Figures exclude nonresidents who died in the state. Causes of death follow International Classification of Diseases. Rank is from highest to lowest death rate in the United States.
Source: U.S. National Center for Health Statistics, *National Vital Statistics Report,* 2006.

ECONOMY

Gross state product, 1990-2004
In current dollars

Year	State product	Nat'l product	State share
1990	$69.3 billion	$5.67 trillion	1.22%
2000	$157.6 billion	$9.75 trillion	1.62%
2002	$173.1 billion	$10.41 trillion	1.66%
2003	$183.3 billion	$10.92 trillion	1.68%
2004	$199.7 billion	$11.65 trillion	1.71%

Source: U.S. Bureau of Economic Analysis, *Survey of Current Business,* July, 2005.

Gross state product by industry, 2003
In billions of dollars

Construction	$9.2
Manufacturing	26.0
Wholesale trade	10.0
Retail trade	16.0
Finance & insurance	14.5
Information	5.9
Professional services	9.6
Health care & social assistance	10.9
Government	20.3
Total state product	$175.5
Total U.S. product	$10,289.2
State share of U.S. total	1.71%
Rank among all states	22

Total figures include industries not listed separately. Amounts are in chained 2000 dollars.
Source: U.S. Bureau of Economic Analysis, *Survey of Current Business,* July, 2005.

Personal income per capita, 1990-2004
In current dollars

	1990	2000	2004
Per capita income	$17,005	$25,660	$28,442
U.S. average	$19,477	$29,845	$32,937
Rank among states	35	37	38

Source: U.S. Bureau of Economic Analysis, *Survey of Current Business,* April, 2005.

Energy consumption, 2001
In trillions of British thermal units (BTU), except as noted

Total energy consumption

Total state energy consumption	1,353
Total U.S. energy consumption	96,275
State share of U.S. total	1.41%
Rank among states	26

Per capita consumption (In millions of BTU)

Total state per capita consumption	255
Total U.S. per capita consumption	338
Rank among states	43

End-use sectors

Residential	344
Commercial	312
Industrial	221
Transportation	476

Sources of energy

Petroleum	524
Natural gas	245
Coal	424
Hydroelectric power	80
Nuclear electric power	300

Figures for totals include categories not listed separately.
Source: U.S. Energy Information Administration, *State Energy Data Report,* 2001.

Nonfarm employment by sectors, 2004

Total	2,374,000
Construction	190,000
Manufacturing	176,000
Trade, transportation, utilities	462,000
Information	48,000
Finance, insurance, real estate	164,000
Professional & business services	334,000
Education & health services	260,000
Leisure, hospitality, arts, organizations	241,000
Other services, including repair & maintenance	89,000
Government	401,000

Figures are rounded to nearest thousand persons. "Total" includes mining and natural resources, not listed separately.
Source: U.S. Bureau of Labor Statistics, 2006.

Foreign exports, 1990-2004
In millions of dollars

Year	State	U.S.	State share
1990	3,729	394,045	0.95%
1996	10,503	624,767	1.68%
1997	13,820	688,896	2.01%
2000	14,334	712,055	1.83%
2003	13,323	724,006	1.97%
2004	13,423	769,332	1.74%

Rank among all states in 2004 17

U.S. total does not include U.S. dependencies.
Source: U.S. Census Bureau, *U.S. Merchandise Trade*, series FT 900, 2000; U.S. Census Bureau, *U.S. International Trade in Goods and Services*, Series FT 900, 2005.

LAND USE

Federally owned land, 2003
Areas in acres

	State	U.S.	State share
Total area	72,688,000	2,271,343,000	3.20%
Nonfederal land	36,193,000	1,599,584,000	2.26%
Federal land	36,495,000	671,759,000	5.43%
Federal share	50.2%	29.6%	—

Areas are rounded to nearest thousand acres. Figures for federally owned land do not include trust properties.
Source: U.S. General Services Administration, *Federal Real Property Profile,* 2006.

Land use, 1997
In acres, rounded to nearest thousand

Total surface area	72,964,000
Total nonfederal rural land.	40,858,000
Percentage rural land	56.0%
Cropland	1,212,000
Conservation Reserve Program (CRP*) land	(nil)
Pastureland.	73,000
Rangeland	32,323,000
Forestland.	4,216,000
Other rural land	3,035,000

*CRP is a federal program begun in 1985 to assist private landowners to convert highly erodible cropland to vegetative cover for ten years. Note that some categories of land overlap.
Source: U.S. Department of Agriculture, Natural Resources and Conservation Service, and Iowa State University, Statistical Laboratory, S*ummary Report, 1997 National Resources Inventory,* revised December, 2000.

Farms and crop acreage, 2004

	State	U.S.	Share	Rank
Farms	10,000	2,113,000	0.47%	38
Acres (millions)	26	937	2.77%	16
Acres per farm	2,588	443	—	2

Source: U.S. Department of Agriculture, National Agricultural Statistics Service. Numbers of farms are rounded to nearest thousand units; acreage figures are rounded to nearest million. Rankings, including ties, are based on rounded figures.

GOVERNMENT AND FINANCE

Units of local government, 2002

	State	Total U.S.	Rank
All local governments	638	87,525	39
Counties	15	3,034	42
Municipalities	87	19,429	41
Townships	0	16,504	—
School districts	231	13,506	22
Special districts	305	35,052	36

Only 48 states have county governments, 20 states have township governments ("towns" in New England, Minnesota, New York, and Wisconsin), and 46 states have school districts. Special districts encompass such functions as natural resources, fire protection, and housing and community development.
Source: U.S. Census Bureau, *Census of Governments.*

State government revenue, 2002

Total revenue	$17,298 mill.
General revenue	$15,860 mill.
Per capita revenue	$2,916
U.S. per capita average	$3,689
Rank among states	46
Intergovernment revenue	
Total	$5,260 mill.
From federal government	$4,875 mill.
Charges and miscellaneous	
Total	$2,123 mill.
Current charges	$925 mill.
Misc. general income	$1,198 mill.
Insurance trust revenue	$1,414 mill.
Taxes	
Total	$8,477 mill.
Per capita taxes	$1,558
Rank among states	40
Property taxes	$329 mill.
Sales taxes	$5,352 mill.
License taxes	$271 mill.
Individual income taxes	$2,091 mill.
Corporate income taxes	$346 mill.
Other taxes	$88 mill.

Total revenue figures include items not listed separately here.
Source: U.S. Bureau of the Census.

State government expenditures, 2002

General expenditures

Total state expenditures . . . . $18,119 mill.
Intergovernmental . . . . $6,969 mill.

Per capita expenditures

State $2,986
Average of all states $3,859
Rank among states 47

Selected direct expenditures

Education. . . . . $2,212 mill.
Public welfare . . . . $2,780 mill.
Health, hospital . . . . $610 mill.
Highways . . . . $1,127 mill.
Police protection . . . . $151 mill.
Corrections . . . . $642 mill.
Natural resources . . . . $199 mill.
Parks and recreation . . . . $42 mill.
Government administration . . . . $459 mill.
Interest on debt . . . . $186 mill.
Total direct expenditures . . . . $9,278 mill.

Totals include items not listed separately.
Source: U.S. Census Bureau.

POLITICS

Governors since statehood

D = Democrat; R = Republican; O = other;
(r) resigned; (d) died in office; (i) removed from office

George W. P. Hunt (D) 1912-1917
Thomas E. Campbell (R) . . . . (i) 1917
George W. P. Hunt (D) 1917-1919
Thomas E. Campbell (R) 1919-1923
George W. P. Hunt (D) 1923-1929
John C. Phillips (R) 1929-1931
George W. P. Hunt (D) 1931-1933
Benjamin B. Moeur (D) 1933-1937
Rawghlie C. Stanford (D) 1937-1939
Robert T. Jones (D) 1939-1941
Sidney P. Osborn (D) . . . . (d) 1941-1948
Daniel E. Garvey (D) 1948-1951
(John) Howard Pyle (R) 1951-1955
Ernest W. McFarland (D) 1955-1959
Paul J. Fannin (R) 1959-1965
Samuel P. Goddard, Jr. (D) 1965-1967
John R. (Jack) Williams (R) 1967-1975
Raul H. Castro (D) . . . . (r) 1975-1977
Wesley Bolin (D) . . . . (d) 1977-1978
Bruce Babbitt (D) 1978-1987
Evan Mecham (R) 1987-1988
Rose Mofford (R) 1988-1991
Fife Symington (R) . . . . (r) 1991-1997
Jane Dee Hull (R) 1997-2003
Janet Napolitano (D) 2003-

Composition of congressional delegations, 1989-2007

	Dem	Rep	Total
House of Representatives			
101st Congress, 1989			
State delegates	1	4	5
Total U.S.	259	174	433
102d Congress, 1991			
State delegates	1	4	5
Total U.S.	267	167	434
103d Congress, 1993			
State delegates	3	3	6
Total U.S.	258	176	434
104th Congress, 1995			
State delegates	1	5	6
Total U.S.	197	236	433
105th Congress, 1997			
State delegates	1	5	6
Total U.S.	206	228	434
106th Congress, 1999			
State delegates	1	5	6
Total U.S.	211	222	433
107th Congress, 2001			
State delegates	1	5	6
Total U.S.	211	221	432
108th Congress, 2003			
State delegates	2	6	8
Total U.S.	205	229	434
109th Congress, 2005			
State delegates	2	6	8
Total U.S.	202	231	433
110th Congress, 2007			
State delegates	4	4	8
Total U.S.	233	202	435
Senate			
101st Congress, 1989			
State delegates	1	1	2
Total U.S.	55	45	100
102d Congress, 1991			
State delegates	1	1	2
Total U.S.	56	44	100
103d Congress, 1993			
State delegates	1	1	2
Total U.S.	57	43	100
104th Congress, 1995			
State delegates	0	2	2
Total U.S.	46	53	99
105th Congress, 1997			
State delegates	0	2	2
Total U.S.	45	55	100

(continued)

	Dem	Rep	Total
106th Congress, 1999			
State delegates	0	2	2
Total U.S.	45	54	99
107th Congress, 2001			
State delegates	0	2	2
Total U.S.	50	50	100
108th Congress, 2003			
State delegates	0	2	2
Total U.S.	48	51	99
109th Congress, 2005			
State delegates	0	2	2
Total U.S.	44	55	99
110th Congress, 2007			
State delegates	0	2	2
Total U.S.	49	49	98

Figures are for starts of first sessions. Totals are for Democrat (Dem.) and Republican (Rep.) members only. House membership totals under 435 and Senate totals under 100 reflect vacancies and seats held by independent party members. When the 110th Congress opened, the Senate's two independent members caucused with the Democrats, giving the Democrats control of the Senate.
Source: U.S. Congress, *Congressional Directory.*

Composition of state legislature, 1990-2006

	Democrats	Republicans
State House (60 seats)		
1990	27	33
1992	25	35
1994	22	38
1996	22	38
1998	20	40
2000	20	40
2002	21	39
2004	22	38
2006	27	33
State Senate (30 seats)		
1990	17	13
1992	12	18
1994	11	19
1996	12	18
1998	14	16
2000	14	16
2002	15	15
2004	13	17
2006	13	17

Figures for total seats may include independents and minor party members. Numbers reflect results of elections in listed years; elected members usually take their seats in the years that follow.
Source: Council of State Governments; *State Elective Officials and the Legislatures.*

Voter participation in presidential elections, 2000 and 2004

	2000	2004
Voting age population		
State	3,788,000	4,197,000
Total United States	209,831,000	220,377,000
State share of U.S. total	1.81	1.90
Rank among states	20	19
Portion of voting age population casting votes		
State	40.4%	48.0%
United States	50.3%	55.5%
Rank among states	49	46

Population figures are rounded to nearest thousand and include all residents, regardless of eligibility to vote.
Source: U.S. Census Bureau.

HEALTH AND MEDICAL CARE

Medical professionals
Physicians in 2003 and nurses in 2001

	U.S.	State
Physicians in 2003		
Total	774,849	11,679
Share of U.S. total		1.50%
Rate	266	209
Rank		43
Nurses in 2001		
Total	2,262,020	34,880
Share of U.S. total		1.54%
Rate	793	657
Rank		44

Rates are numbers of physicians and nurses per 100,000 resident population; ranks are based on rates.
Source: American Medical Association, *Physician Characteristics and Distribution in the U.S.*; U.S. Department of Health and Human Services, Health Resources and Services Administration.

Health insurance coverage, 2003

	State	U.S.
Total persons covered	4,626,000	243,320,000
Total persons not covered	951,000	44,961,000
Portion not covered	17.0%	15.6%
Rank among states	16	—
Children not covered	223,000	8,373,000
Portion not covered	14.6%	11.4%
Rank among states	7	—

Totals are rounded to nearest thousand. Ranks are from the highest to the lowest percentages of persons *not* insured.
Source: U.S. Census Bureau, Current Population Reports.

AIDS, syphilis, and tuberculosis cases, 2003

Disease	U.S. cases	State cases	Rank
AIDS	44,232	628	19
Syphilis	34,270	1,106	8
Tuberculosis	14,874	295	11

Source: U.S. Centers for Disease Control and Prevention.

Cigarette smoking, 2003
Residents over age 18 who smoke

	U.S.	State	Rank
All smokers	22.1%	21.0%	35
Male smokers	24.8%	23.8%	28
Female smokers	20.3%	18.2%	39

Cigarette smokers are defined as persons who reported having smoked at least 100 cigarettes during their lifetimes and who currently smoked at least occasionally.

Source: U.S. Centers for Disease Control and Prevention, *Morbidity and Mortality Weekly Report,* 53, no. 44 (November 12, 2004).

HOUSING

Home ownership rates, 1985-2004

	1985	1990	1995	2000	2004
State	64.7%	64.5%	62.9%	68.0%	68.7%
Total U.S.	63.9%	63.9%	64.7%	67.4%	69.0%
Rank among states	36	36	41	38	40

Net change in state home ownership rate, 1985-2004	+4.0%
Net change in U.S. home ownership rate, 1985-2004	+5.1%

Percentages represent the proportion of owner households to total occupied households.
Source: U.S. Census Bureau, 2006.

Home sales, 2000-2004
In thousands of units

Existing home sales	2000	2002	2003	2004
State sales	104.8	128.2	149.6	186.8
Total U.S. sales	5,171	5,631	6,183	6,784
State share of U.S. total	2.03%	2.28%	2.42%	2.75%
Sales rank among states	18	13	13	12

Units include single-family homes, condos, and co-ops.
Source: National Association of Realtors, Washington, D.C., *Real Estate Outlook: Market Trends & Insights.*

Values of owner-occupied homes, 2003

	State	U.S.
Total units	1,165,000	58,809,000
Value of units		
Under $100,000	20.5%	29.6%
$100,000-199,999	52.2%	36.9%
$200,000 or more	27.4%	33.5%
Median value	$146,124	$142,275
Rank among all states 20		

Units are owner-occupied one-family houses whose numbers are rounded to nearest thousand. Data are extrapolated from survey samples.
Source: U.S. Census Bureau, American Community Survey.

EDUCATION

Public school enrollment, 2002

Prekindergarten through grade 8
State enrollment 660,000
Total U.S. enrollment 34,135,000
State share of U.S. total 1.93%

Grades 9 through 12
State enrollment 277,000
Total U.S. enrollment 14,067,000
State share of U.S. total 1.97%

Enrollment rates
State public school enrollment rate 88.6%
Overall U.S. rate 90.4%
Rank among states in 2002 34
Rank among states in 1995 17

Enrollment figures (which include unclassified students) are rounded to nearest thousand pupils during fall school term. Enrollment rates are based on enumerated resident population estimate for July 1, 2002.
Source: U.S. National Center for Education Statistics.

Public college finances, 2003-2004

FTE enrollment in public institutions of higher education

Students in state institutions 211,200
Students in all U.S. public institutions 9,916,600
State share of U.S. total 2.13
Rank among states 14

State and local government appropriations for higher education

State appropriation per FTE $5,699
National average $5,716
Rank among states 21
State & local tax revenue going to higher
education 8.5%

FTE = full-time equivalent in public postsecondary programs,
including summer sessions; student numbers are rounded to
nearest hundred. Funding figures for 2003-2004 academic year
include financial aid to students in state public institutions and
exclude money for research, agriculture experiment stations,
teaching hospitals, and medical schools; figures are rounded to
nearest thousand dollars.
Source: Higher Education Executive Officers, Denver, Colorado.

TRANSPORTATION AND TRAVEL

Highway mileage, 2003

Interstate highways 1,167
Other freeways and expressways 150
Arterial roads 4,664
Collector roads 8,549
Local roads 42,999

Urban roads 21,900
Rural roads 35,629

Total state mileage 57,529
U.S. total 3,974,107
State share 1.45%
Rank among states 34

Note that combined urban and rural road mileage matches the
total of the other categories.
Source: U.S. Federal Highway Administration.

Motor vehicle registrations and driver licenses, 2003

Vehicle registrations	State	U.S.	Share	Rank
Autos, trucks, buses	3,574,000	231,390,000	1.54%	23
Autos only	1,992,000	135,670	1.47%	23
Motorcycles	208,000	5,328,000	3.90%	9
Driver licenses	3,819,000	196,166,000	1.95%	18

Figures, which do not include vehicles owned by military services,
are rounded to the nearest thousand. Figures for automobiles
include taxis.
Source: U.S. Federal Highway Administration.

Domestic travel expenditures, 2003

Spending by U.S. residents on overnight trips and
day trips of at least 50 miles from home

Total expenditures within state . . . . $9.15 bill.
Total expenditures within U.S. . . . . $490.87 bill.
State share of U.S. total 1.9%
Rank among states 18

Source: Travel Industry Association of America.

Retail gasoline prices, 2003-2007

Average price per gallon at the pump

Year	U.S.	State
2003	$1.267	$1.518
2004	$1.316	$1.585
2005	$1.644	$1.724
2007	$2.298	$2.341

Excise tax per gallon in 2004 . . . . 18.0¢
Rank among all states in 2007 prices 14

Prices are averages of all grades of gasoline sold at the pump
during March months in 2003-2005 and during February, 2007.
Averages for 2006, during which prices rose higher, are not
available.
Source: U.S. Energy Information Agency, *Petroleum Marketing
Monthly* (2003-2005 data); American Automobile Association
(2007 data).

CRIME AND LAW ENFORCEMENT

State and local police officers, 2000-2004

	2000	2002	2004
Total officers			
U.S.	654,601	665,555	675,734
State	10,434	10,964	11,317*
*Net change, 2000-2004			+8.46%
Officers per 1,000 residents			
U.S.	2.33	2.31	2.30
State	2.03	2.02	1.97
State rank	28	30	29

Totals include state and local police and sheriffs.
Source: Carsey Institute, University of New Hampshire.

Crime rates, 2003
Incidents per 100,000 residents

Crimes	State	U.S.
Violent crimes		
Total incidents	513	475
Murder	8	6
Forcible rape	33	32
Robbery	137	142
Aggravated assault	336	295
Property crimes		
Total incidents	5,632	3,588
Burglary	1,050	741
Larceny/theft	3,561	2,415
Motor vehicle theft	1,021	433
All crimes	6,145	4,063

Source: U.S. Federal Bureau of Investigation, *Crime in the United States*, annual.

State prison populations, 1980-2003

	State	U.S.	State share
1980	4,372	305,458	1.43%
1990	14,261	708,393	2.01%
1996	22,493	1,025,624	2.19%
2000	26,510	1,391,261	1.91%
2003	31,170	1,470,045	2.12%

State figures exclude prisoners in federal penitentiaries.
Source: U.S. Bureau of Justice Statistics, *Prisoners in 2003.*

Arkansas

Location: South

Area and rank: 52,075 square miles (134,875 square kilometers); 53,182 square miles (137,741 square kilometers) including water; twenty-seventh largest state in area

Coastline: none

Population and rank: 2,753,000 (2004); thirty-second largest state in population

Capital and largest city: Little Rock (183,133 people in 2000 census)

Became territory: March 2, 1819

Entered Union and rank: June 15, 1836; twenty-fifth state

State capitol building in Little Rock. (A. C. Haralson/Arkansas Department of Parks & Tourism)

Present constitution adopted: 1874

Counties: 75

State name: "Arkansas" comes from a Quapaw Indian word

State nickname: The Natural State

Motto: *Regnat populus* (The people rule)

State flag: Red field with four stars and white diamond with name "Arkansas"

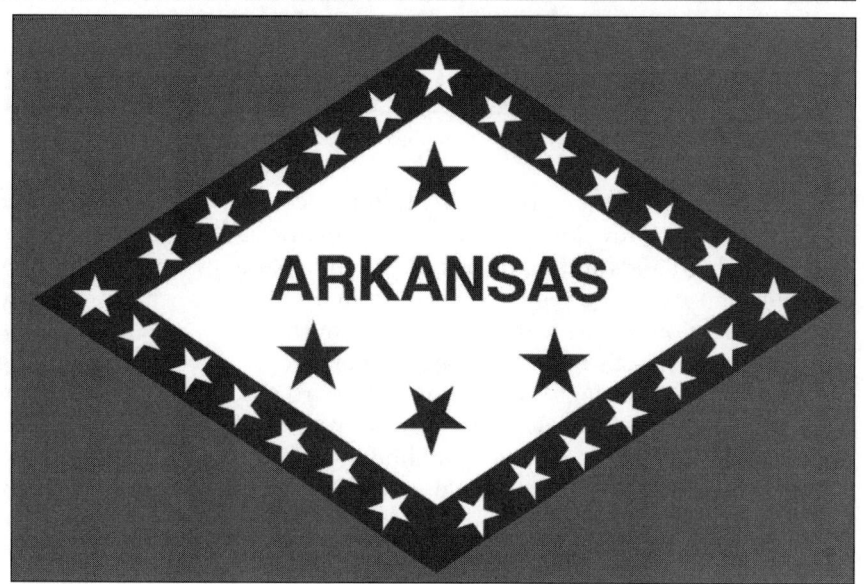

Highest point: Magazine Mountain—2,753 feet (839 meters)

Lowest point: Ouachita River—55 feet (17 meters)

Highest recorded temperature: 120 degrees Fahrenheit (49 degrees Celsius)—Ozark, 1936

Lowest recorded temperature: –29 degrees Fahrenheit (–34 degrees Celsius)—Pond, 1905

State songs: "Arkansas"; "Oh, Arkansas"

State tree: Pine

State flower: Apple blossom

State bird: Mockingbird

National parks: Hot Springs

Arkansas History

The history of Arkansas was greatly influenced by the natural division of the area into northwestern highlands and southeastern lowlands. Running through these two regions as it flows in a southeasterly direction to meet the Mississippi River, the Arkansas River has also been of major importance in the area's history. As long as ten thousand years ago, hunters and gatherers wandered the land surrounding the Arkansas River, attracted by the abundant wildlife. About one thousand years ago, bluff dwellers and mound builders grew crops in the area's fertile soil. By the time Europeans arrived in the New World, the primary groups of Native Americans inhabiting the area were the Osage, in Missouri and northwestern Arkansas; the Caddo, in Louisiana and southwestern Arkansas; and the Quapaw, along the Arkansas River. All three groups were forced into Oklahoma by the middle of the nineteenth century.

Exploration and Settlement. The first Europeans to reach the area were led northwest from Florida by Spanish explorer Hernando de Soto in 1541. A French expedition led by Jacques Marquette and Louis Jolliet reached the area in 1673 by traveling south from Michigan. In 1682, a similar expedition was led by René-Robert Cavelier, sieur de La Salle. La Salle claimed the entire valley of the Mississippi River, including all of Arkansas, for France. This enormous area was named Louisiana in honor of King Louis XIV of France.

Despite La Salle's claim to the area, European settlement of the area began modestly. In 1686, French explorer Henri de Tonti established Arkansas Post, the first permanent European settlement in the area, near the point where the Arkansas River meets the Mississippi River. Starting with a population of six residents, Arkansas Post grew to become the largest city in Arkansas until the nineteenth century. In 1722, French explorer Bernard de la Harpe led an expedition along the Arkansas River and named a natural rock formation Little Rock. Nearly a century later, a city of the same name was founded there.

Road to Statehood. Settlement of the area continued slowly throughout the eighteenth century. In 1762, France ceded Louisiana to Spain. In order to encourage settlers, Spain offered free land and freedom from taxes to all who chose to live there. In 1783, British forces attacked Arkansas Post but were defeated by the Spanish and Quapaw. By 1799 Arkansas had nearly four hundred European settlers.

In 1800, Louisiana was returned to France. Three years later, the United States purchased this vast area, doubling the size of the young nation, for a payment of more than twenty-seven million dollars. At first a part of the huge Louisiana Territory, in 1812 Arkansas became part of the newly created Missouri Territory, then became a separate territory in 1819. In 1824, the western section of the area became part of the Indian Territory (Oklahoma), giving Arkansas its modern boundaries. By 1836 Arkansas had the sixty thousand residents necessary for statehood, primarily settlers from eastern states, and it was admitted as the twenty-fifth state.

The Civil War. Along with those who arrived from the eastern United States, the 1840's and 1850's brought large numbers of Irish and German immigrants to the area. The mountains and plateaus of the northwest supported small farms, while the lowlands of the southeast developed large cotton plantations dependent on slaves. By 1860 the population of Arkansas reached 435,000. About one-quarter of the inhabitants were slaves.

Arkansas seceded from the Union on May 6, 1861, nearly a month after the Civil War broke out. The delay in joining the Confederacy may have been due to strong Union sympathies in the northwest part of the state. About six thousand residents of the state fought for the Union, while about fifty-eight thousand fought for the Confederacy. Several important Civil War battles were fought in northern Arkansas, near the border with Missouri. The Battle of Pea Ridge (March 7-8, 1862) led to heavy losses on both sides, as Union forces drove back an attack by the Confederates, ending the threat of a Confederate invasion of Missouri. In September of 1863, Union forces took control of Little Rock.

From the end of the war until the middle of the 1870's, a period known as Reconstruction, Arkansas and the other former Confederate states were occupied by federal troops and ruled by state governments dominated by the Republican Party. Arkansas was readmitted to the Union under Republican control in 1868. The Republican government, which attempted to win civil rights for freed slaves, was seen as an artificial structure imposed by the northern states. It was opposed, often violently, by many white Arkansans, leading to increased repression of African Americans after Reconstruction. After federal troops were withdrawn, the Democratic Party returned to power in 1874, completely dominating state politics for nearly a century.

After the War. Economic recovery after the devastation of the Civil War was difficult for Arkansans. The plantation system of the southeastern region of the state, which relied on slavery, was replaced with sharecropping. Under this system, tenants lived on and farmed a landowner's property, paying rent in the form of crops, usually cotton. The social and economic gap between the farmer and the landlord was often a large one.

An economic depression in the southern states during the late nineteenth century led to widespread poverty. The situation became even worse in 1885, when the state government defaulted on huge debts, including fourteen million dollars of interest payments. Race relations were also a severe problem, with the state government completely controlled by the Democratic Party, which excluded African Americans.

The Twentieth Century. Along with the rest of the country, Arkansas experienced a large increase in the number of European immigrants at the end of the nineteenth century. Although the pace of economic

growth remained slow, the state began to develop new resources during the early years of the twentieth century. Rice, which would later become a major crop, was first planted in 1904. With the rise of the automobile and the increasing industrialization of the United States, the discovery of oil and natural gas deposits in 1921 was an important boost to the economy. The many rivers in Arkansas became an important resource, and modern dams were built beginning during the 1920's.

Arkansas, along with the rest of the United States, suffered a severe economic setback with the Great Depression of the 1930's. Adding to the problem, years of drought forced many farmers to abandon their lands. The Southern Farm Tenants Union, created by Arkansas sharecroppers at this time, had an important influ-

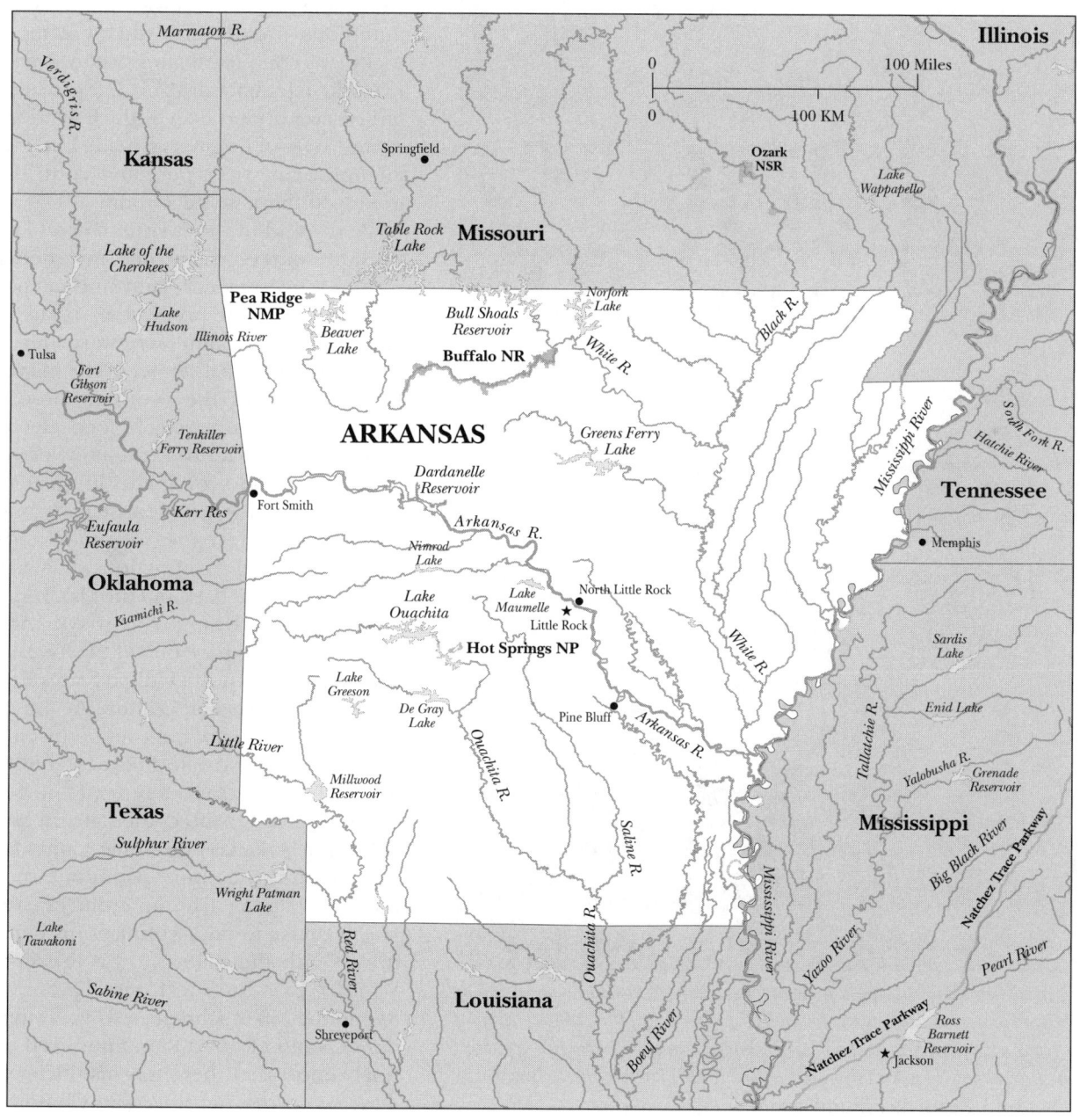

ence on national farm policies. It was not until the United States entered World War II in 1941 that the economy began to recover. The enormous defense industry created by the war effort, as well as the technological and economic growth that followed the war, led to major changes in Arkansas society.

The number of Arkansans living in rural areas decreased, and many small family farms were replaced by large agricultural enterprises. Little Rock and other major cities experienced a rapid increase in population. Women entered the workplace in greater numbers. The most important social change during the middle of the twentieth century was the struggle to win civil rights for African Americans.

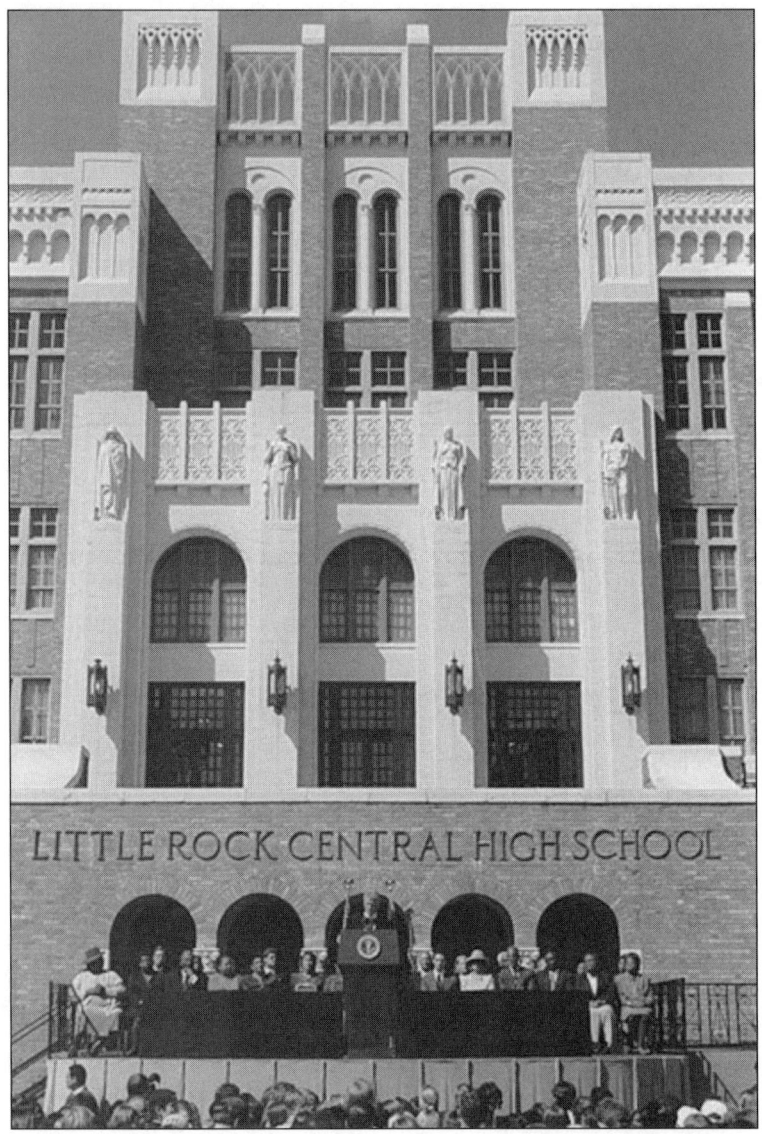

U.S. president Bill Clinton—a former governor of Arkansas—speaking at a 1997 ceremony celebrating the fortieth anniversary of the desegregation of Little Rock's Central High School. The scene of a major civil rights confrontation, the school is now designated a National Historic Site. (National Archives and Records Administration)

The attention of the world was focused on race relations in Arkansas in September of 1957. Three years earlier, the Supreme Court had declared public school segregation unconstitutional. To comply with the Court's decision, the school board of Little Rock created a plan to desegregate the city's schools. When nine African American students attempted to attend the city's Central High School, Governor Orval E. Faubus ordered the state militia to prevent them from entering. In response, President Dwight David Eisenhower sent federal troops to enforce the desegregation process.

Economic Growth. Economic development continued steadily throughout the second half of the twentieth century. During the 1960's, rice, soybeans, and poultry replaced cotton as the most important agricultural products. The McClellan-Kerr Arkansas River Navigation System, an ambitious project of building dams and locks, was completed after twenty-five years of work, in January of 1971. The project, the largest ever undertaken by the United States Army Corps of Engineers, made Little Rock an important river port and contributed greatly to the state's economy.

By the end of the twentieth century, important sources of income included fish farming, hydroelectric and nuclear power production, food processing, retail merchandising, computer software development, and financial services. The manufacturing sector of the economy produced clothing, furniture, machinery, electrical equipment, metal products, and electronic devices. With improvements in transportation, tourism became a particularly important source of revenue, with thousands of visitors traveling to attractions such as Hot Springs National Park and the Ozark Mountains each year. Despite this growth, Arkansas continued to have one of the lowest per-capita incomes in the United States.

Former Governor Clinton. At the close of the last decade of the twentieth century, Arkansas's close ties to President Bill Clinton, its former attorney general and governor, continued to affect the state. In May of 2000, the Arkansas Supreme Court Committee of Professional Conduct recommended barring Clinton from practicing law in the state on account of his denying under oath the nature of his liaison with White House intern Monica Lewinsky. In September, in Washington, D.C., Independent Counsel Robert Ray announced in his final report that there was insufficient evidence to prosecute President Clinton and

First Lady Hillary Rodham Clinton for criminal wrongdoing in the scandal involving the Whitewater real estate partnership in northern Arkansas. This report concluded the investigation of the Clintons, which began in 1994 and eventually cost taxpayers $65 million.

At the end of the year, the outgoing president again figured in Arkansas news when he pardoned a vice president of Arkansas-based giant Tyson Foods, Archibald Schaffer III. Schaffer was convicted of a felony in making illegal gifts in 1993 to Secretary of Agriculture Mike Espy and subsequently lying about them to investigators. In January, 2001, former president Clinton reached an agreement with the independent counsel that suspended his license to practice law in Arkansas for five years, imposed a twenty-five-thousand-dollar fine, and required Clinton to agree not to seek repayment of legal fees. The agreement shielded him from being tried for perjury and obstruction of justice.

Politics and Elections. Notwithstanding Arkansas's strong previous support of the Democratic Party, in the 2000 election, the state sent its six electoral votes to presidential candidate George W. Bush, who defeated Democrat Al Gore by 51-46 percent. Independent Ralph Nader, with just 1.5 percent of the vote, did not figure in the outcome. One Republican congressional incumbent was unseated by a Democratic challenger, giving the Democrats a 3-1 edge in the state's congressional delegation. Two years later, Arkansas reelected its colorful and sometimes controversial governor Mike Huckabee, who won by a 53-47 percent margin. In 2004, Bush again claimed the state's electoral votes, defeating John Kerry 56 to 44 percent. U.S. senator Blanche Lincoln, a Democrat, was also reelected.

Huckabee, frequently mentioned as a possible presidential candidate in 2008, became governor in 1996 when the sitting governor resigned after a felony conviction in the Whitewater scandal. He subsequently showed a marked interest in health care matters and created a health insurance program for the needy shortly after assuming office. Huckabee also made an example of himself in shedding more than one hundred pounds after being diagnosed a diabetic. He successfully advocated using all funds from the state's tobacco settlement revenues for health care.

After about 70,000 refugees from Hurricane Katrina entered the state in the fall of 2006, Huckabee orga-

After President Bill Clinton left office, the Clinton Presidential Center and Park opened in Little Rock. The center includes a replica of the White House's Oval Office, a presidential library and archive, and the interactive museum pictured here. (Arkansas Parks & Tourism)

nized a program to shelter them throughout the state and expedited prescription drug and other health care needs. Huckabee's critics, however, contend that the governor, a devoutly religious graduate of Baptist educational institutions, failed to abide by separation of church and state practices, especially in his dealings with Reclaim America for Christ conferences. He has also been criticized both for his refusal to open his financial affairs to public scrutiny and for his purchase of a jet plane and his use of it for personal travel. His most controversial action as governor was his pardon of a convicted rapist. Upon release, the pardoned man, Wayne DuMond, raped and murdered a woman in Missouri.

Rose Secrest
Updated by the Editor

Arkansas Time Line

June 18, 1541	Hernando de Soto crosses the Mississippi River and leads the first Europeans to the area.
July, 1673	Jacques Marquette and Louis Jolliet lead the first French expedition to the area.
Mar. 13, 1682	René-Robert Cavelier, sieur de La Salle, explores the area and claims the entire Mississippi valley for France, naming it Louisiana.
1686	Henri de Tonti establishes the first permanent European settlement at Arkansas Post.
1722	Bernard de la Harpe explores the Arkansas River and names Little Rock.
1762	Louisiana is ceded to Spain.
1783	British forces attack Arkansas Post.
1800	Louisiana is returned to France.
1803	United States purchases Louisiana.
1811-1812	Series of large earthquakes centered in New Madrid, Missouri, damage the area.
1812	Arkansas becomes part of the Missouri Territory.
1817	First post office is established.
Mar. 2, 1819	Arkansas Territory is created.
Nov. 20, 1819	First Arkansas newspaper, the *Arkansas Gazette*, is established.
1820	Border between Missouri and Arkansas is established as the line dividing future slave states and free states.
Oct. 25, 1821	Capital is moved from Arkansas Post to Little Rock.
1824	Western part of Arkansas becomes part of the Indian Territory.
1830	Congress marks boundary between Arkansas and Indian Territory.
June 15, 1836	Arkansas becomes the twenty-fifth state.
1858	First railroad is established.
1859	All free blacks are ordered out of the state by the end of the year.
1860	Population reaches 435,450, including 111,115 slaves.
May 6, 1861	Arkansas secedes from the Union.
Sept. 10, 1863	Union forces occupy Little Rock.
1864	State government dominated by the Republican Party is established.
1864	Unionists abolish slavery in Arkansas and adopt a new state constitution.
Aug., 1866	Laws passed prohibiting blacks from jury duty, militia service, and attendance at white schools.
Mar. 2, 1867	Reconstruction Act is passed in Congress, voiding the government of Arkansas and nine other southern states.
Mar. 13, 1868	New constitution is adopted, freeing blacks and disenfranchising ex-Confederate soldiers.
June 22, 1868	Arkansas is readmitted to the Union.
Nov., 1868	Martial law is declared in much of the state, as battles with the Ku Klux Klan become more frequent.
1872	University of Arkansas is established.
Oct. 13, 1874	New constitution restores franchise to all whites and gives full civil rights to blacks.
1885	State government defaults on millions of dollars of debt.
1891	Jim Crow laws go into effect, segregating trains and waiting stations.
1898	Whites-only primary elections are established.
1900	Population reaches 1.3 million.
1904	First rice crop is planted.
1906	Diamonds are discovered near Murfreesboro, leading to the only diamond-mining site in the United States.
1908	Ozark National Forest is established.
1921	Hot Springs National Park is established.
1921	Oil and natural gas are discovered.
1921	Commercial radio broadcasts begin.
1928	Law is passed prohibiting teaching of evolution theory in public schools, which would not be overturned until 1968, by the U.S. Supreme Court.
1930's	Drought and economic depression lead to widespread poverty.
1930's	Southern Farm Tenants Union is created.
1931	Hattie W. Caraway is first woman elected to U.S. Senate.
1940's	World War II defense industry leads to economic recovery.

1953	Commercial television broadcasts begin.
1957	Federal troops enter Little Rock after the state militia is called out to prevent school integration.
1960's	Rice, soybeans, and poultry replace cotton as the leading agricultural products.
1966	Winthrop Rockefeller is elected the first Republican governor since 1874.
1971	McClellan-Kerr Arkansas River Navigation System is completed.
1983	Arkansas requires teachers to pass basic skills tests, becoming the first state to do so.
1990	Population reaches 2.35 million.
Nov. 3, 1992	Bill Clinton becomes the first Arkansan elected president of the United States.
1993	M. Jocelyn Elders, former director of the state Department of Health, becomes the first African American Surgeon General of the United States.
1996	Severe tornadoes kill at least twelve people and do more than $300 million worth of property damage.
1998	Eleven-year-old and thirteen-year-old boys kill four fellow students and a teacher, wounding ten others, in a schoolyard shooting in Jonesboro, leading to a national debate on the issue of school violence.
May 2000	Committee of the Arkansas State Bar Association recommends disbarring President Bill Clinton for lying under oath.
Sept. 19, 2000	Independent Counsel Robert Ray closes books on Whitewater real estate partnership of northern Arkansas.
Jan. 2001	Bill Clinton agrees to five-year suspension of his Arkansas law license on account of false statements made under oath.
Nov. 5, 2002	Mike Huckabee is reelected governor.
Nov. 2, 2004	George W. Bush wins Arkansas presidential election by 54 to 46 percent; Democratic U.S. senator Blanche Lincoln is reelected 56 to 44 percent.

Notes for Further Study

Published Sources. For an overall view of Arkansas's physical geography, the *Arkansas Atlas and Gazetteer* (1997) from the DeLorme Mapping Company is an excellent resource. The state government can be understood by reading *The Arkansas Constitution: A Reference Guide* (1993) by Kay Collett Goss. The botany of the state is discussed in *Keys to the Flora of Arkansas* (1994) by Edwin B. Smith.

Among the many outstanding books devoted to the state's past are *Cultural Encounters in the Early South: Indians and Europeans in Arkansas* (1995) by Jeannie M. Whayne; *Colonial Arkansas, 1686-1804: A Social and Cultural History* (1991) by Morris S. Arnold; *Territorial Ambition: Land and Society in Arkansas, 1800-1840* (1993) by Charles S. Bolton; *Rebellion and Realignment: Arkansas's Road to Secession* (1987) by James M. Woods; *Rugged and Sublime: The Civil War in Arkansas* (1994), edited by Mark K. Christ; *War and Wartime Changes: The Transformation of Arkansas, 1940-1945* (1986) by Calvin C. Smith; and *Warriors Don't Cry: A Searing Memoir of the Battle to Integrate Little Rock's Central High* (1994) by Melba Pattillo Beals. Younger audiences will appreciate the scholarly but still accessible account of the state's history published by the University of Arkansas Press, *Arkansas History for Young People* (3d ed., 2003) by T. Harri Baker and Jane Browning. Carole Marsh's *Arkansas Native Americans* (2004) is also designed for younger readers.

During the 1930's, the Federal Writers' Project, sponsored by the Works Progress Administration (WPA), worked to interview as many former slaves as possible. Employed authors interviewed more than two thousand former slaves, over one third of them in Arkansas. Editor George E. Lankford brings together all 176 of the testimonies describing slavery in Arkansas in *Bearing Witness: Memories of Arkansas Slavery—Narratives from the 1930's WPA Collections* (2003). Immense changes occurred within the state as it changed from a primarily rural society in the early 1900's to an expanded manufacturing economy in subsequent decades. Ben F. Johnson details this evolution in *Arkansas in Modern America: 1930-1999* (2000). For travelers planning a visit to the state, Patti DeLano's *Arkansas: Off the Beaten Path* (2006) is a solid resource.

Web Resources. A number of excellent Web sites devoted to Arkansas have been developed by government agencies, universities, and private organizations and individuals. A good place to start is the official state government site (www.state.ar.us/), which provides links to agencies dealing with government, tourism, and business, as well as links to local communities and information about state laws. More specific sites include Arkansas—The Natural State (www.arkansas.com) from the Arkansas Department of Parks and Tourism; the Arkansas Department of Economic Development (www.1800arkansas.com) for information on business; and Arkansas Quickfacts (quickfacts.census.gov/qfd/states/05000.html) from the United States Census Bureau, providing numerous demographic statistics for every major town and city in the state.

Barge loaded with agricultural produce on the Arkansas River, a major tributary of the Mississippi. (A. C. Haralson/Arkansas Department of Parks & Tourism)

Arkansas history is presented in numerous Web sites. A good place to start is the Arkansas History Commission (www .ark-ives.com/). More specific information can be found in Web sites such as the Civil War in Arkansas (www.civilwarbuff .org), the Official Quapaw Website (www.geocities.com/Ath ens/Aegean/1388), Persistence of the Spirit (www.aristotle .net/persistence), which concerns African Americans, and Little Rock Central High (www.centralhigh57.org/), which details the famous attempts at school desegregation in the fall of 1957.

Counties

County	2000 pop.	Rank in pop.	Sq. miles	Rank in area	County	2000 pop.	Rank in pop.	Sq. miles	Rank in area
Arkansas	20,749	36	988.5	3	Craighead	82,148	9	710.8	28
Ashley	24,209	29	921.4	6	Crawford	53,247	12	595.5	60
Baxter	38,386	18	554.4	70	Crittenden	50,866	15	610.5	51
Benton	153,406	3	843.3	12	Cross	19,526	39	615.9	49
Boone	33,948	21	591.2	61	Dallas	9,210	69	667.5	32
Bradley	12,600	58	650.7	36	Desha	15,341	51	765.0	21
Calhoun	5,744	75	628.3	45	Drew	18,723	40	828.2	14
Carroll	25,357	28	633.8	42	Faulkner	86,014	6	647.4	37
Chicot	14,117	55	644.1	39	Franklin	17,771	44	609.6	52
Clark	23,546	32	865.5	10	Fulton	11,642	60	618.2	48
Clay	17,609	45	639.3	40	Garland	88,068	5	678.1	31
Cleburne	24,046	30	553.1	71	Grant	16,464	47	631.8	44
Cleveland	8,571	72	597.8	58	Greene	37,331	19	577.6	66
Columbia	25,603	27	766.2	19	Hempstead	23,587	31	728.8	25
Conway	20,336	37	556.2	69	Hot Spring	30,353	22	615.0	50

County	2000 pop.	Rank in pop.	Sq. miles	Rank in area	County	2000 pop.	Rank in pop.	Sq. miles	Rank in area
Howard	14,300	53	587.5	62	Pike	11,303	62	603.1	56
Independence	34,233	20	763.8	22	Poinsett	25,614	26	757.8	23
Izard	13,249	57	580.7	65	Polk	20,229	38	859.5	11
Jackson	18,418	41	633.6	43	Pope	54,469	11	812.0	16
Jefferson	84,278	7	884.8	9	Prairie	9,539	67	646.0	38
Johnson	22,781	33	662.2	34	Pulaski	361,474	1	771.0	18
Lafayette	8,559	73	526.5	75	Randolph	18,195	42	651.9	35
Lawrence	17,774	43	586.6	64	St. Francis	29,329	23	633.9	41
Lee	12,580	59	601.7	57	Saline	83,529	8	724.8	26
Lincoln	14,492	52	561.2	68	Scott	10,996	63	893.9	8
Little River	13,628	56	531.8	74	Searcy	8,261	74	667.2	33
Logan	22,486	34	709.9	29	Sebastian	115,071	4	536.4	73
Lonoke	52,828	13	765.5	20	Sevier	15,757	50	564.0	67
Madison	14,243	54	837.0	13	Sharp	17,119	46	604.4	55
Marion	16,140	49	597.7	59	Stone	11,499	61	606.6	54
Miller	40,443	17	624.1	46	Union	45,629	16	1,039.0	1
Mississippi	51,979	14	898.3	7	Van Buren	16,192	48	711.6	27
Monroe	10,254	64	606.7	53	Washington	157,715	2	950.2	4
Montgomery	9,245	68	781.0	17	White	67,165	10	1,034.1	2
Nevada	9,955	66	620.0	47	Woodruff	8,741	70	586.6	63
Newton	8,608	71	823.0	15	Yell	21,139	35	927.9	5
Ouachita	28,790	24	732.5	24					
Perry	10,209	65	551.0	72					
Phillips	26,445	25	692.7	30					

Source: U.S. Census Bureau; National Association of Counties.

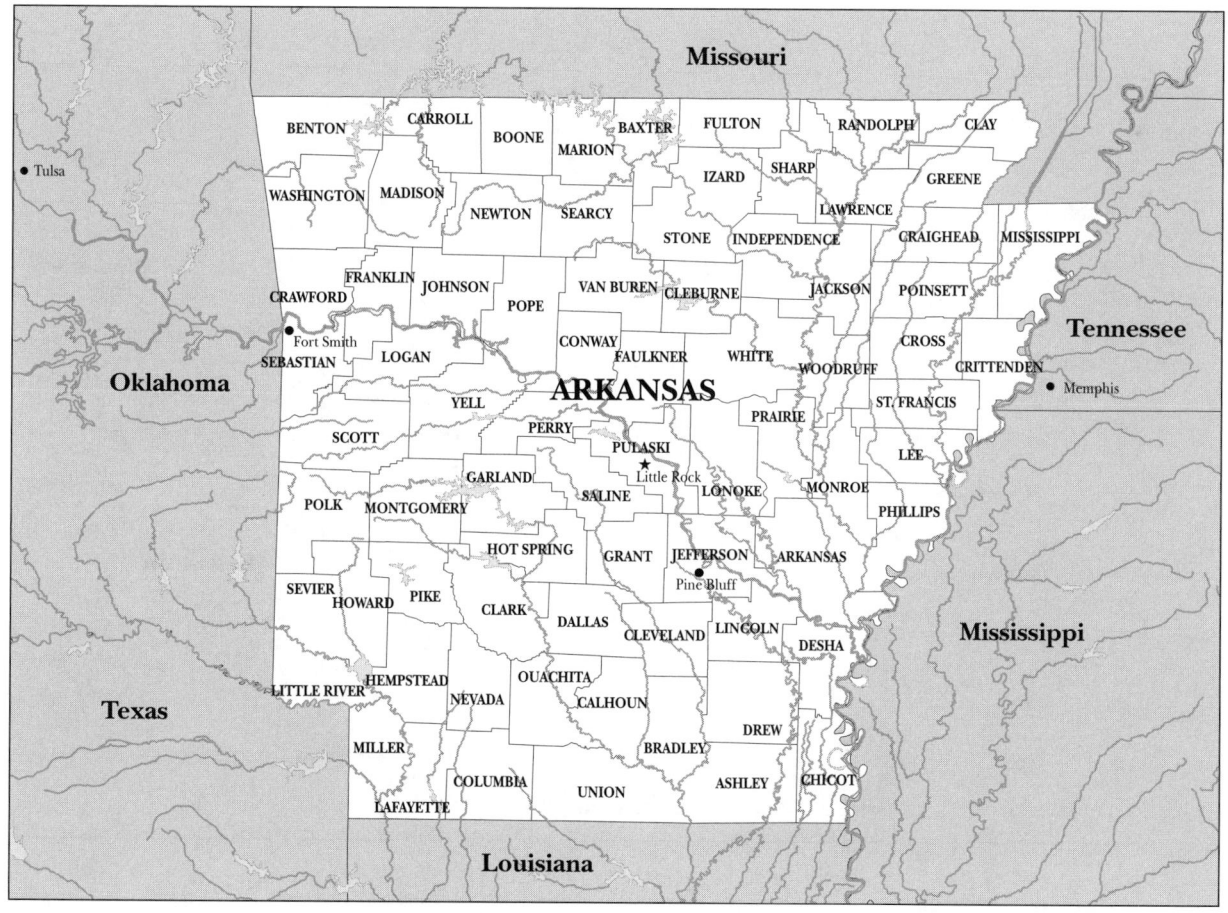

Cities
With 10,000 or more residents

Rank	City	Population	Rank	City	Population
1	Little Rock (capital)	183,133	19	Bentonville	19,730
2	Fort Smith	80,268	20	Van Buren	18,986
3	North Little Rock	60,433	21	Searcy	18,928
4	Fayetteville	58,047	22	Blytheville	18,272
5	Jonesboro	55,515	23	Bella Vista	16,582
6	Pine Bluff	55,085	24	Cabot	15,261
7	Springdale	45,798	25	Forrest City	14,774
8	Conway	43,167	26	Camden	13,154
9	Rogers	38,829	27	Harrison	12,152
10	Hot Springs	35,750	28	Mountain Home	11,012
11	Jacksonville	29,916	29	Arkadelphia	10,912
12	West Memphis	27,666	30	Magnolia	10,858
13	Texarkana	26,448	31	Siloam Springs	10,843
14	Russellville	23,682	32	Hope	10,616
15	Paragould	22,017	33	Maumelle	10,557
16	Benton	21,906			
17	El Dorado	21,530			
18	Sherwood	21,511			

Population figures are from 2000 census.

Source: U.S. Bureau of the Census.

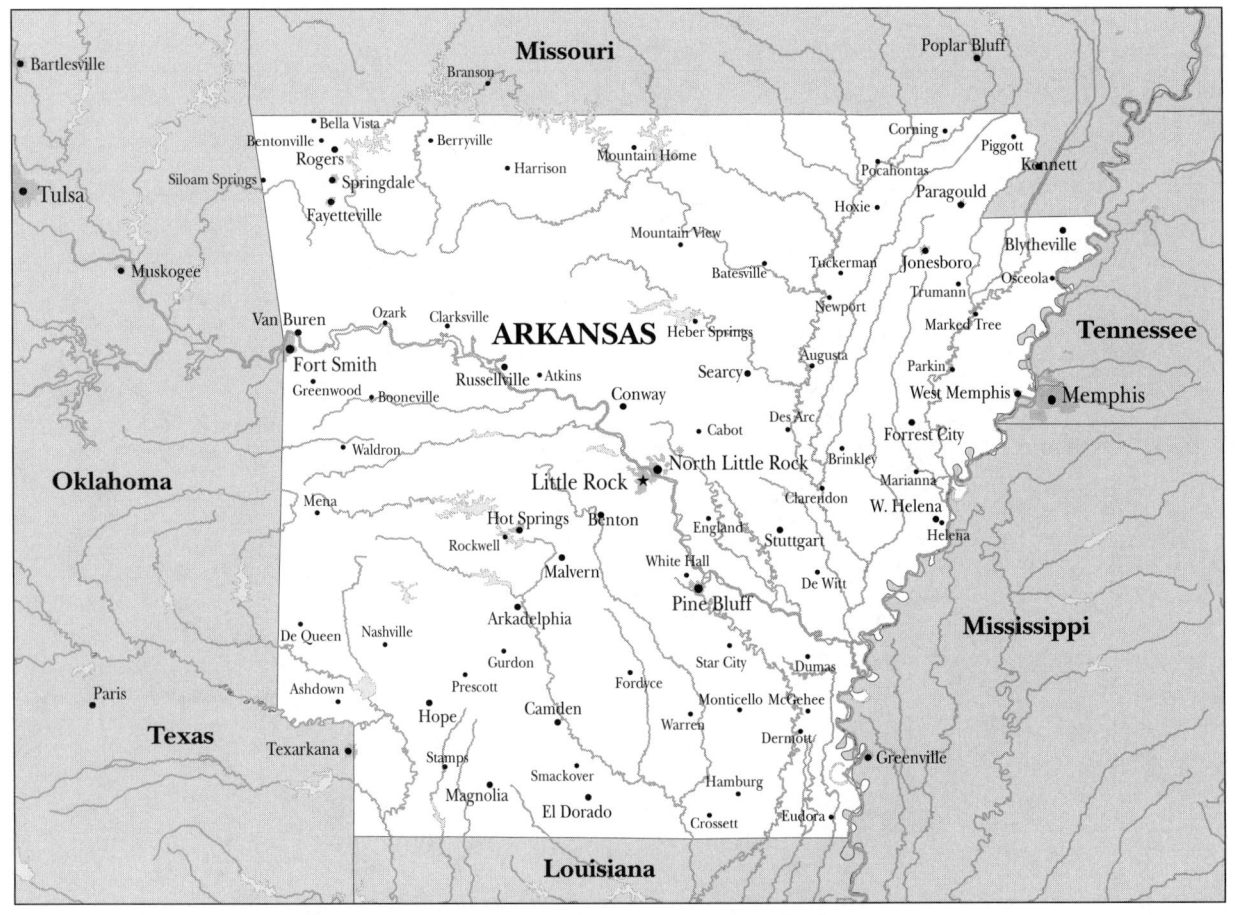

Index to Tables

DEMOGRAPHICS

Resident state and national populations, 1970-2004

Population figures given in thousands

	State pop.	U.S. pop.	Share	Rank
1970	1,923	203,302	0.9%	32
1980	2,286	226,546	1.0%	33
1985	2,327	237,924	1.0%	33
1990	2,351	248,765	0.9%	33
1995	2,535	262,761	0.9%	33
2000	2,673	281,425	1.0%	33
2004	2,753	293,655	0.9%	32

Source: U.S. Census Bureau, Current Population Reports, 2006.

Resident population by age, 2004

Age Group	Total persons
Under 5 years	186,000
5 to 17 years	491,000
18 to 24 years	280,000
25 to 34 years	360,000
35 to 44 years	385,000
45 to 54 years	376,000
55 to 64 years	294,000
65 to 74 years	205,000
75 to 84 years	128,000
85 years and older	48,000
All age groups	2,753,000

Portion of residents 65 and older	13.8%
National rank in portion of oldest residents	9
National average	12.4%

Population figures are rounded to nearest thousand persons;
figures include armed forces personnel stationed in the state.
Source: U.S. Bureau of the Census, 2006.

Resident population by race, Hispanic origin, 2004

Category	State pop.	Share	U.S.
All residents	2,753	100.00%	100.00%
Non-Hispanic white	2,126	77.22%	67.37%
Hispanic white	112	4.07%	13.01%
Other Hispanic	9	0.33%	1.06%
African American	434	15.76%	12.77%
Native American	20	0.73%	0.96%
Asian, Pacific Islander	28	1.02%	4.37%
Two or more categories	32	1.16%	1.51%

Population figures are in thousands. Persons counted as "Hispanic" (Latino) may be of any race. Because of overlapping categories, categories may not add up to 100%. Shares in column 3 are percentages of each category within the state; these figures may be compared to the national percentages in column 4.
Source: U.S. Bureau of the Census, 2006.

Projected state population, 2000-2030

Year	Population
2000	2,673,000
2005	2,777,000
2010	2,875,000
2015	2,969,000
2020	3,060,000
2025	3,151,000
2030	3,240,000
Population increase, 2000-2030	567,000
Percentage increase, 2000-2030	21.2

Projections are based on data from the 2000 census.
Source: U.S. Census Bureau.

VITAL STATISTICS

Infant mortality rates, 1980-2002

	1980	1990	2000	2002
All state residents	12.7	9.2	8.4	8.3
All U.S. residents	12.6	9.2	9.4	9.1
All state white residents	10.3	8.4	7.0	6.9
All U.S. white residents	10.6	7.6	5.7	5.8
All state black residents	20.0	13.9	13.7	13.9
All U.S. black residents	22.2	18.0	14.1	14.4

Figures represent deaths per 1,000 live births of resident infants under 1 year old, exclusive of fetal deaths. Figures for all residents include members of other racial categories not listed separately.
Source: U.S. Census Bureau, S*tatistical Abstract of the United States*, 2006.

Abortion rates, 1990 and 2000

	1990	2000
Total abortions	7,000	6,000
Rate per 1,000 women	13.5	9.8
U.S. rate	25.7	21.3
Rank	36	38

Numbers of abortions are rounded to nearest thousand; ranks are based on rates.
Source: U.S. Census Bureau.

Marriages and divorces, 2004

Total marriages	35,700
Rate per 1,000 population	13.0
National rate per 1,000 population	7.4
Rank among all states	3
Total divorces	17,400
Rate per 1,000 population	6.3
National rate per 1,000 population	3.7
Rank among all states	2

Figures are for all marriages and divorces performed within the state, including those of nonresidents; totals are rounded to the nearest hundred. Ranks are for highest to lowest figures; note that divorce data are not available for five states.
Source: U.S. National Center for Health Statistics, *Vital Statistics of the United States*, 2006.

Death rates by leading causes, 2002
Deaths per 100,000 resident population

Cause	State	U.S.
Heart disease	307.4	241.7
Cancer	231.8	193.2
Cerebrovascular diseases	82.4	56.4
Accidents other than motor vehicle	48.4	37.0
Motor vehicle accidents	25.6	15.7
Chronic lower respiratory diseases	53.2	43.3
Diabetes mellitus	29.3	25.4
HIV	3.0	4.9
Suicide	13.9	11.0
Homicide	7.2	6.1
All causes	1,052.1	847.3
Rank in overall death rate among states		3

Figures exclude nonresidents who died in the state. Causes of death follow International Classification of Diseases. Rank is from highest to lowest death rate in the United States.
Source: U.S. National Center for Health Statistics, *National Vital Statistics Report*, 2006.

ECONOMY

Gross state product, 1990-2004
In current dollars

Year	State product	Nat'l product	State share
1990	$38.1 billion	$5.67 trillion	0.67%
2000	$66.2 billion	$9.75 trillion	0.68%
2002	$71.2 billion	$10.41 trillion	0.68%
2003	$74.5 billion	$10.92 trillion	0.68%
2004	$80.1 billion	$11.65 trillion	0.69%

Source: U.S. Bureau of Economic Analysis, *Survey of Current Business,* July, 2005.

Gross state product by industry, 2003
In billions of dollars

Construction $2.9
Manufacturing 13.4
Wholesale trade 4.7
Retail trade 5.9
Finance & insurance 3.2
Information 3.1
Professional services 2.4
Health care & social assistance 5.1
Government 8.6

Total state product $69.7
Total U.S. product $10,289.2
State share of U.S. total 0.68%
Rank among all states 34

Total figures include industries not listed separately. Amounts are in chained 2000 dollars.
Source: U.S. Bureau of Economic Analysis, *Survey of Current Business,* July, 2005.

Personal income per capita, 1990-2004
In current dollars

	1990	2000	2004
Per capita income	$14,460	$21,925	$25,725
U.S. average	$19,477	$29,845	$32,937
Rank among states	49	48	49

Source: U.S. Bureau of Economic Analysis, *Survey of Current Business,* April, 2005.

Energy consumption, 2001
In trillions of British thermal units (BTU), except as noted

Total energy consumption
Total state energy consumption 1,106
Total U.S. energy consumption 96,275
State share of U.S. total 1.15%
Rank among states 30

Per capita consumption (In millions of BTU)
Total state per capita consumption 411
Total U.S. per capita consumption 338
Rank among states 11

End-use sectors
Residential 219
Commercial 148
Industrial 462
Transportation 278

Sources of energy
Petroleum 379
Natural gas 232
Coal 274
Hydroelectric power 26
Nuclear electric power 154

Figures for totals include categories not listed separately.
Source: U.S. Energy Information Administration, *State Energy Data Report,* 2001.

Nonfarm employment by sectors, 2004

Total 1,159,000
Construction 52,000
Manufacturing 204,000
Trade, transportation, utilities 242,000
Information 20,000
Finance, insurance, real estate 51,000
Professional & business services 108,000
Education & health services 143,000
Leisure, hospitality, arts, organizations 91,000
Other services, including repair & maintenance . . . 41,000
Government 201,000

Figures are rounded to nearest thousand persons. "Total" includes mining and natural resources, not listed separately.
Source: U.S. Bureau of Labor Statistics, 2006.

Foreign exports, 1990-2004
In millions of dollars

Year	State	U.S.	State share
1990	920	394,045	0.23%
1996	2,003	624,767	0.32%
1997	2,305	688,896	0.33%
2000	2,599	712,055	0.33%
2003	2,962	724,006	0.44%
2004	3,493	769,332	0.45%

Rank among all states in 2004 32

U.S. total does not include U.S. dependencies.
Source: U.S. Census Bureau, *U.S. Merchandise Trade,* series FT 900, 2000; U.S. Census Bureau, *U.S. International Trade in Goods and Services,* Series FT 900, 2005.

LAND USE

Federally owned land, 2003
Areas in acres

	State	U.S.	State share
Total area	33,599,000	2,271,343,000	1.48%
Nonfederal land	29,643,000	1,599,584,000	1.85%
Federal land	3,956,000	671,759,000	0.59%
Federal share	11.8%	29.6%	—

Areas are rounded to nearest thousand acres. Figures for federally owned land do not include trust properties.
Source: U.S. General Services Administration, *Federal Real Property Profile,* 2006.

Land use, 1997
In acres, rounded to nearest thousand

Total surface area 34,037,000
Total nonfederal rural land. 28,638,000
Percentage rural land 84.1%
Cropland 7,625,000
Conservation Reserve Program (CRP*) land 230,000
Pastureland 5,351,000
Rangeland 38,000
Forestland 15,011,000
Other rural land 384,000

*CRP is a federal program begun in 1985 to assist private landowners to convert highly erodible cropland to vegetative cover for ten years. Note that some categories of land overlap.
Source: U.S. Department of Agriculture, Natural Resources and Conservation Service, and Iowa State University, Statistical Laboratory, *Summary Report, 1997 National Resources Inventory,* revised December, 2000.

Farms and crop acreage, 2004

	State	U.S.	Share	Rank
Farms	48,000	2,113,000	2.27%	18
Acres (millions)	14	937	1.49%	22
Acres per farm	303	443	—	22

Source: U.S. Department of Agriculture, National Agricultural Statistics Service. Numbers of farms are rounded to nearest thousand units; acreage figures are rounded to nearest million. Rankings, including ties, are based on rounded figures.

GOVERNMENT AND FINANCE

Units of local government, 2002

	State	Total U.S.	Rank
All local governments	1,588	87,525	20
Counties	75	3,034	18
Municipalities	499	19,429	17
Townships	0	16,504	—
School districts	310	13,506	17
Special districts	704	35,052	16

Only 48 states have county governments, 20 states have township governments ("towns" in New England, Minnesota, New York, and Wisconsin), and 46 states have school districts. Special districts encompass such functions as natural resources, fire protection, and housing and community development.
Source: U.S. Census Bureau, *Census of Governments.*

State government revenue, 2002

Total revenue . . . . $10,297 mill.
General revenue . . . . $10,533 mill.
Per capita revenue $3,890
U.S. per capita average $3,689
Rank among states 24

Intergovernment revenue
Total . . . . $3,429 mill.
From federal government . . . . $3,410 mill.

Charges and miscellaneous
Total . . . . $1,878 mill.
Current charges . . . . $1,177 mill.
Misc. general income . . . . $701 mill.
Insurance trust revenue . . . . −$236 mill.

Taxes
Total . . . . $5,226 mill.
Per capita taxes $1,931
Rank among states 20
Property taxes . . . . $487 mill.
Sales taxes . . . . $2,649 mill.
License taxes . . . . $273 mill.
Individual income taxes . . . . $1,563 mill.
Corporate income taxes . . . . $177 mill.
Other taxes . . . . $78 mill.

Total revenue figures include items not listed separately here.
Source: U.S. Bureau of the Census.

State government expenditures, 2002

General expenditures
Total state expenditures . . . . $11,521 mill.
Intergovernmental . . . . $3,071 mill.

Per capita expenditures
State $3,930
Average of all states $3,859
Rank among states 25

Selected direct expenditures
Education. . . . . $1,832 mill.
Public welfare . . . . $2,578 mill.
Health, hospital . . . . $722 mill.
Highways . . . . $942 mill.
Police protection . . . . $72 mill.
Corrections. . . . . $284 mill.
Natural resources . . . . $206 mill.
Parks and recreation . . . . $75 mill.
Government administration. . . . . $405 mill.
Interest on debt . . . . $138 mill.
Total direct expenditures . . . . $7,563 mill.

Totals include items not listed separately.
Source: U.S. Census Bureau.

POLITICS

Governors since statehood
D = Democrat; R = Republican; O = other;
(r) resigned; (d) died in office; (i) removed from office

James S. Conway (D) 1836-1840
Archibald Yell (D) . . . . (r) 1840-1844
Samuel Adams (D) 1844
Thomas S. Drew (D) 1844-1849
Richard C. Byrd (D) 1849
John S. Roane (D) 1849-1852
Elias N. Conway (D) 1852-1860
Henry M. Rector (D) . . . . (r) 1860-1862
Thomas Fletcher (D) 1862
Harris Flanagin (D) . . . . (i) 1862-1864
Isaac Murphy (O). 1864-1868
Powell Clayton (R) . . . . (r) 1868-1871
Ozra A. Hadley (R) 1871-1873
Elisha Baxter (R) 1873-1874
Augustus H. Garland (D). 1874-1877
William R. Miller (D) 1877-1881
Thomas J. Churchill (D) 1881-1883
James H. Berry (D) 1883-1885
Simon P. Hughes (D) 1885-1889
James P. Eagle (D) 1889-1893
William M. Fishback (D) 1893-1895
James P. Clarke (D). 1895-1897
Daniel W. Jones (D) 1897-1901
Jefferson Davis (D) 1901-1907
John S. Little (D) 1907-1909
George W. Donaghey (D) 1909-1913

James T. Robinson (D) . . . . (r) 1913
William K. Oldham (D) 1913
J. Marion Futrell (D) 1913
George W. Hays (D) 1913-1917
Charles H. Brough (D) 1917-1921
Thomas C. McRae (D) 1921-1925
Thomas J. Terral (D) 1925-1927
John E. Martineau (D) . . . . (r) 1927-1928
Harvey Parnell (D) 1928-1933
J. Marion Futrell (D) 1933-1937
Carl E. Bailey (D) 1937-1941
Homer M. Adkins (D) 1941-1945
Benjamin T. Laney (D) 1945-1949
Sidney S. McMath (D) 1949-1953
Francis A. Cherry (D) 1953-1955
Orval E. Faubus (D) 1955-1967
Winthrop Rockefeller (R) 1967-1971
Dale L. Bumpers (D) . . . . (r) 1971-1975
Robert C. Riley (D) 1975
David H. Pryor (D) 1975-1979
William J. Clinton (D) 1979-1992
Jim Guy Tucker (D). . . . . (r) 1992-1996
Mike Huckabee (R). 1996-

Composition of congressional delegations, 1989-2007

	Dem	Rep	Total
House of Representatives			
101st Congress, 1989			
State delegates	3	1	4
Total U.S.	259	174	433
102d Congress, 1991			
State delegates	3	1	4
Total U.S.	267	167	434
103d Congress, 1993			
State delegates	2	2	4
Total U.S.	258	176	434
104th Congress, 1995			
State delegates	2	2	4
Total U.S.	197	236	433
105th Congress, 1997			
State delegates	2	2	4
Total U.S.	206	228	434
106th Congress, 1999			
State delegates	2	2	4
Total U.S.	211	222	433
107th Congress, 2001			
State delegates	3	1	4
Total U.S.	211	221	432
108th Congress, 2003			
State delegates	3	1	4
Total U.S.	205	229	434

(continued)

	Dem	Rep	Total
109th Congress, 2005			
State delegates	3	1	4
Total U.S.	202	231	433
110th Congress, 2007			
State delegates	3	1	4
Total U.S.	233	202	435
Senate			
101st Congress, 1989			
State delegates	2	0	2
Total U.S.	55	45	100
102d Congress, 1991			
State delegates	2	0	2
Total U.S.	56	44	100
103d Congress, 1993			
State delegates	2	0	2
Total U.S.	57	43	100
104th Congress, 1995			
State delegates	1	1	2
Total U.S.	46	53	99
105th Congress, 1997			
State delegates	1	1	2
Total U.S.	45	55	100
106th Congress, 1999			
State delegates	1	1	2
Total U.S.	45	54	99
107th Congress, 2001			
State delegates	1	1	2
Total U.S.	50	50	100
108th Congress, 2003			
State delegates	2	0	2
Total U.S.	48	51	99
109th Congress, 2005			
State delegates	2	0	2
Total U.S.	44	55	99
110th Congress, 2007			
State delegates	2	0	2
Total U.S.	49	49	98

Figures are for starts of first sessions. Totals are for Democrat (Dem.) and Republican (Rep.) members only. House membership totals under 435 and Senate totals under 100 reflect vacancies and seats held by independent party members. When the 110th Congress opened, the Senate's two independent members caucused with the Democrats, giving the Democrats control of the Senate.

Source: U.S. Congress, *Congressional Directory.*

Composition of state legislature, 1990-2006

	Democrats	Republicans
State House (100 seats)		
1990	90	9
1992	88	11
1994	88	12
1996	86	13
1998	75	25
2000	75	25
2002	70	30
2004	72	28
2006	75	25
State Senate (35 seats)		
1990	31	4
1992	30	5
1994	28	7
1996	28	6
1998	29	6
2000	29	6
2002	27	8
2004	27	8
2006	27	8

Figures for total seats may include independents and minor party members. Numbers reflect results of elections in listed years; elected members usually take their seats in the years that follow.

Source: Council of State Governments; *State Elective Officials and the Legislatures.*

Voter participation in presidential elections, 2000 and 2004

	2000	2004
Voting age population		
State	1,998,000	2,076,000
Total United States	209,831,000	220,377,000
State share of U.S. total	0.95	0.94
Rank among states	32	32
Portion of voting age population casting votes		
State	46.1%	50.8%
United States	50.3%	55.5%
Rank among states	41	43

Population figures are rounded to nearest thousand and include all residents, regardless of eligibility to vote.

Source: U.S. Census Bureau.

HEALTH AND MEDICAL CARE

Medical professionals
Physicians in 2003 and nurses in 2001

	U.S.	State
Physicians in 2003		
Total	774,849	5,516
Share of U.S. total		0.71%
Rate	266	202
Rank		44
Nurses in 2001		
Total	2,262,020	19,860
Share of U.S. total		0.88%
Rate	793	737
Rank		39

Rates are numbers of physicians and nurses per 100,000 resident population; ranks are based on rates.
Source: American Medical Association, *Physician Characteristics and Distribution in the U.S.*; U.S. Department of Health and Human Services, Health Resources and Services Administration.

Health insurance coverage, 2003

	State	U.S.
Total persons covered	2,206,000	243,320,000
Total persons not covered	465,000	44,961,000
Portion not covered	17.4%	15.6%
Rank among states	12	—
Children not covered	71,000	8,373,000
Portion not covered	10.5%	11.4%
Rank among states	20	—

Totals are rounded to nearest thousand. Ranks are from the highest to the lowest percentages of persons *not* insured.
Source: U.S. Census Bureau, Current Population Reports.

AIDS, syphilis, and tuberculosis cases, 2003

Disease	U.S. cases	State cases	Rank
AIDS	44,232	189	31
Syphilis	34,270	296	23
Tuberculosis	14,874	127	27

Source: U.S. Centers for Disease Control and Prevention.

Cigarette smoking, 2003
Residents over age 18 who smoke

	U.S.	State	Rank
All smokers	22.1%	24.8%	16
Male smokers	24.8%	27.6%	14
Female smokers	20.3%	22.3%	14

Cigarette smokers are defined as persons who reported having smoked at least 100 cigarettes during their lifetimes and who currently smoked at least occasionally.
Source: U.S. Centers for Disease Control and Prevention, *Morbidity and Mortality Weekly Report*, 53, no. 44 (November 12, 2004).

HOUSING

Home ownership rates, 1985-2004

	1985	1990	1995	2000	2004
State	66.6%	67.8%	67.2%	68.9%	69.1%
Total U.S.	63.9%	63.9%	64.7%	67.4%	69.0%
Rank among states	32	24	28	33	37

Net change in state home ownership rate, 1985-2004 . . . . +2.5%
Net change in U.S. home ownership rate, 1985-2004 . . . . +5.1%

Percentages represent the proportion of owner households to total occupied households.
Source: U.S. Census Bureau, 2006.

Home sales, 2000-2004
In thousands of units

Existing home sales	2000	2002	2003	2004
State sales	45.0	52.2	53.8	60.9
Total U.S. sales	5,171	5,631	6,183	6,784
State share of U.S. total	0.87%	0.93%	0.87%	0.90%
Sales rank among states	32	33	33	33

Units include single-family homes, condos, and co-ops.
Source: National Association of Realtors, Washington, D.C., *Real Estate Outlook: Market Trends & Insights.*

Values of owner-occupied homes, 2003

	State	U.S.
Total units	556,000	58,809,000
Value of units		
Under $100,000	63.0%	29.6%
$100,000-199,999	28.5%	36.9%
$200,000 or more	8.5%	33.5%
Median value	$83,699	$142,275
Rank among all states 49		

Units are owner-occupied one-family houses whose numbers are
rounded to nearest thousand. Data are extrapolated from
survey samples.
Source: U.S. Census Bureau, American Community Survey.

EDUCATION

Public school enrollment, 2002

Prekindergarten through grade 8
State enrollment 319,000
Total U.S. enrollment. 34,135,000
State share of U.S. total 0.93%

Grades 9 through 12
State enrollment 132,000
Total U.S. enrollment. 14,067,000
State share of U.S. total 0.94%

Enrollment rates
State public school enrollment rate. 90.6%
Overall U.S. rate 90.4%
Rank among states in 2002. 24
Rank among states in 1995. 11

Enrollment figures (which include unclassified students) are
rounded to nearest thousand pupils during fall school term.
Enrollment rates are based on enumerated resident population
estimate for July 1, 2002.
Source: U.S. National Center for Education Statistics.

Public college finances, 2003-2004

FTE enrollment in public institutions of higher education
Students in state institutions 97,700
Students in all U.S. public institutions 9,916,600
State share of U.S. total 0.99
Rank among states 33

**State and local government appropriations for higher
education**
State appropriation per FTE $5,233
National average $5,716
Rank among states 31
State & local tax revenue going to higher
education 9.6%

FTE = full-time equivalent in public postsecondary programs,
including summer sessions; student numbers are rounded to
nearest hundred. Funding figures for 2003-2004 academic year
include financial aid to students in state public institutions and
exclude money for research, agriculture experiment stations,
teaching hospitals, and medical schools; figures are rounded to
nearest thousand dollars.
Source: Higher Education Executive Officers, Denver, Colorado.

TRANSPORTATION AND TRAVEL

Highway mileage, 2003

Interstate highways	656
Other freeways and expressways	90
Arterial roads	6,839
Collector roads.	20,077
Local roads	70,879
Urban roads	10,808
Rural roads	87,733
Total state mileage	98,541
U.S. total	3,974,107
State share	2.48%
Rank among states	17

Note that combined urban and rural road mileage matches the
total of the other categories.
Source: U.S. Federal Highway Administration.

Motor vehicle registrations and driver licenses, 2003

Vehicle registrations	State	U.S.	Share	Rank
Autos, trucks, buses	1,889,000	231,390,000	0.82%	34
Autos only	955,000	135,670	0.70%	32
Motorcycles	38,000	5,328,000	0.71%	36
Driver licenses	1,998,000	196,166,000	1.02%	30

Figures, which do not include vehicles owned by military services,
are rounded to the nearest thousand. Figures for automobiles
include taxis.
Source: U.S. Federal Highway Administration.

Domestic travel expenditures, 2003
Spending by U.S. residents on overnight trips and
day trips of at least 50 miles from home

Total expenditures within state . . . . $3.97 bill.
Total expenditures within U.S. . . . . $490.87 bill.
State share of U.S. total 0.8%
Rank among states 35

Source: Travel Industry Association of America.

Retail gasoline prices, 2003-2007
Average price per gallon at the pump

Year	U.S.	State
2003	$1.267	$1.203
2004	$1.316	$1.242
2005	$1.644	$1.590
2007	$2.298	$2.164

Excise tax per gallon in 2004 . . . . 21.5¢
Rank among all states in 2007 prices 40

Prices are averages of all grades of gasoline sold at the pump
during March months in 2003-2005 and during February, 2007.
Averages for 2006, during which prices rose higher, are not
available.
Source: U.S. Energy Information Agency, *Petroleum Marketing
Monthly* (2003-2005 data); American Automobile Association
(2007 data).

CRIME AND LAW ENFORCEMENT

State and local police officers, 2000-2004

	2000	2002	2004
Total officers			
U.S.	654,601	665,555	675,734
State	4,903	5,064	5,234*
*Net change, 2000-2004			+6.75%
Officers per 1,000 residents			
U.S.	2.33	2.31	2.30
State	1.83	1.87	1.90
State rank	35	35	31

Totals include state and local police and sheriffs.
Source: Carsey Institute, University of New Hampshire.

Crime rates, 2003
Incidents per 100,000 residents

Crimes	State	U.S.
Violent crimes		
Total incidents	456	475
Murder	6	6
Forcible rape	33	32
Robbery	82	142
Aggravated assault	335	295
Property crimes		
Total incidents	3,621	3,588
Burglary	914	741
Larceny/theft	2,487	2,415
Motor vehicle theft	221	433
All crimes	4,077	4,063

Source: U.S. Federal Bureau of Investigation, *Crime in the United
States*, annual.

State prison populations, 1980-2003

	State	U.S.	State share
1980	2,911	305,458	0.95%
1990	7,322	708,393	1.03%
1996	9,407	1,025,624	0.92%
2000	11,915	1,391,261	0.86%
2003	13,084	1,470,045	0.89%

State figures exclude prisoners in federal penitentiaries.
Source: U.S. Bureau of Justice Statistics, *Prisoners in 2003.*

California

Location: Pacific coast

Area and rank: 155,973 square miles (403,970 square kilometers); 163,707 square miles (424,000 square kilometers) including water; third largest state in area

Coastline: 840 miles (1,394 kilometers) on the Pacific Ocean

Shoreline: 3,427 miles (5,512 kilometers)

Population and rank: 35,894,000 (2004); largest state in population

Capital city: Sacramento (407,018 people in 2000 census)

Largest city: Los Angeles (3,694,820 people in 2000 census)

Entered Union and rank: September 9, 1850; thirty-first state

Present constitution adopted: 1879

Counties: 58

State name: "California" is believed to have derived from a name in a Spanish romance written around 1500

State nickname: Golden State

Motto: *Eureka!* (Greek for "I have found it!")

State flag: Star above grizzly bear on white background above red stripe

Highest point: Mount Whitney—14,494 feet (4,418 meters); highest point in continental United States

Lowest point: Death Valley—282 feet (87 meters) below sea level; lowest point in United States

Highest recorded temperature: 134 degrees Fahrenheit (57 degrees Celsius)— Death Valley, 1913

Lowest recorded temperature: −45 degrees Fahrenheit (−43 degrees Celsius)—Boca, 1937

State song: "I Love You, California" ("California, Here I Come" is unofficial)

State tree: California redwoods

State flower: Golden poppy

State bird: California valley quail

State fish: Golden trout

State animal: California grizzly bear

National parks: Channel Islands, Death Valley, Joshua Tree, Kings Canyon, Lassen Volcanic, Redwood, Sequoia, Yosemite

Governor Gray Davis (right) showing actor Arnold Schwarzenegger his private office shortly after Davis lost his job in a special recall election and Schwarzenegger was elected at the same time to succeed him. Schwarzenegger followed Ronald Reagan in being the second actor with no political experience to be elected California's governor. (AP/Wide World Photos)

California History

To an extent much greater than in other states, California is a naturally defined region with a distinct history of its own. Its differences begin with its natural geography. Bounded by the Pacific Ocean on the west and the Sierra Madre range along the east, California had limited contacts with the outside world until the mid-nineteenth century. Until then, little was known about its abundant natural resources beyond the fact it had an equable climate and fertile land.

An estimated 300,000 Native Americans inhabited the region before Europeans arrived. Though they were among the most numerous and prosperous native societies in North America, most of them lived outside the main currents of Native American history. Compared to many cultures outside California, their culture was simple. Metallurgy, pottery, intensive cultivation, horses and draft animals were all unknown to them. With economies based mostly on fishing, hunting, and gathering, they nevertheless achieved comparatively high levels of prosperity and lived largely peaceful lives.

Early Exploration. European contact with California began in 1542, when the Spanish navigator Juan Rodríguez Cabrillo found San Diego Bay. English navigator Francis Drake followed thirty-seven years later, when he reached Northern California. Little came out of these early explorations. Busy colonizing Mexico, Spain paid little attention to the California region over the next two centuries. Permanent European interest in the region finally began during the late eighteenth century, when Spain authorized members of the Franciscan order to build a chain of mission stations up the California coast. Father Junipero Serra founded California's first mission at San Diego in 1769; twenty other mission stations followed over the next fifty-four years.

During those years California was nominally a Spanish colony, but the government exercised only light control, and the burden of imposing European culture on California's peoples was left to the Franciscans. The missionaries began systematic agricultural development and gathered American Indian communities around their mission stations. Meanwhile, Russian traders established posts north of the mission chain without interference. After a half century of formal Spanish colonization, the non-native residents of California numbered only about 3,300—a fraction of the number of Native Americans.

Mexican Rule. By this time, Spain was losing its hold on its New World empire and Mexico was in open revolt. When Mexico won its independence from Spain in 1821, California's Spanish governor peacefully recognized Mexican rule, and California became a Mexican province. Mexico then followed Spain's example by taking little active interest in the region until the early 1830's, when it began secularizing California's mission stations and distributing titles to large blocs of land among favored families. In 1837, the Mexican government granted California's administration a large measure of autonomy, continuing California's tradition of comparative isolation.

Secularization was a disaster to the American Indian communities attached to the former mission stations. The departure of the Franciscans left the indigenous peoples at the mercy of private landlords, who had little interest in their welfare. Most Native Americans left the missions for their original homes, where harsh economic conditions and European diseases reduced their numbers greatly. By the turn of the twentieth century their numbers fell to their lowest level ever—about 15,000 people, about one-twentieth their precolonial number.

By the early 1840's, Americans hungry for land and new opportunities were moving west and settling in California. Conflicts soon arose between these new, non-Spanish-speaking residents and the established Spanish and Mexican settlers, known as *Californios.* Soon, the U.S. government was taking an interest in the region, which it feared might be occupied by Great Britain or Russia. In 1845, it instructed its consul in Monterey to promote local interest in annexation to the United States. The following year, disgruntled American settlers in northern California found an excuse for rebelling against the Mexican regime and proclaimed an independent republic in Sonoma—a short-lived rebellion known as the "Bear Flag Revolt," after the flag the rebels used.

For reasons largely unrelated to California, the United States declared war against Mexico in 1846. Placed under military rule by Mexico, California played a small role in the Mexican-American War. The Mexican government surrendered California to the United States when John C. Frémont arrived with an occupation force in 1847. In the peace accord that followed, Mexico formally ceded California, along with most of what became the American Southwest, to the United States. California's territorial status was short-lived. Two years later, before its territorial government was fully organized, California entered the Union as a state. Its rapid transition to statehood owed much to an unexpected and spectacular event that fundamentally changed the region's future: the discovery of gold near Sacramento.

The Gold Rush and Statehood. Scarcely a week before the treaty ending the Mexican-American War was signed, news of the discovery of gold in northern California became public, and the seeds of one of the world's great gold rushes began. The effect the gold rush had on California would be difficult to overstate. Within a matter of only a few years, California was transformed from a sleepy backwater to perhaps the fastest-growing economy in the world. Hundreds of thousands of people poured into the state from the East and other parts of the world. Within ten years California's non-Indian population rose from less than 10,000 to several hundred thousands. Meanwhile, San Francisco grew from little more than a village to a booming metropolitan center offering virtually every service and amenity

available in big eastern cities and controlling the commerce of the West Coast.

The multitudes who rushed to California dreamt of striking it rich from mineral wealth; however, the real fortunes made there grew mostly out of the many enterprises that arose to support the gold industry. Great profits were made in agriculture, retail trade, transportation, and countless other industries and services. For the first time, agriculture was undertaken on a large scale. As the gold rush made food production a critical priority, the agricultural potential of California's great Central Valley was finally recognized. Eventually, California's agricultural production would not only lead

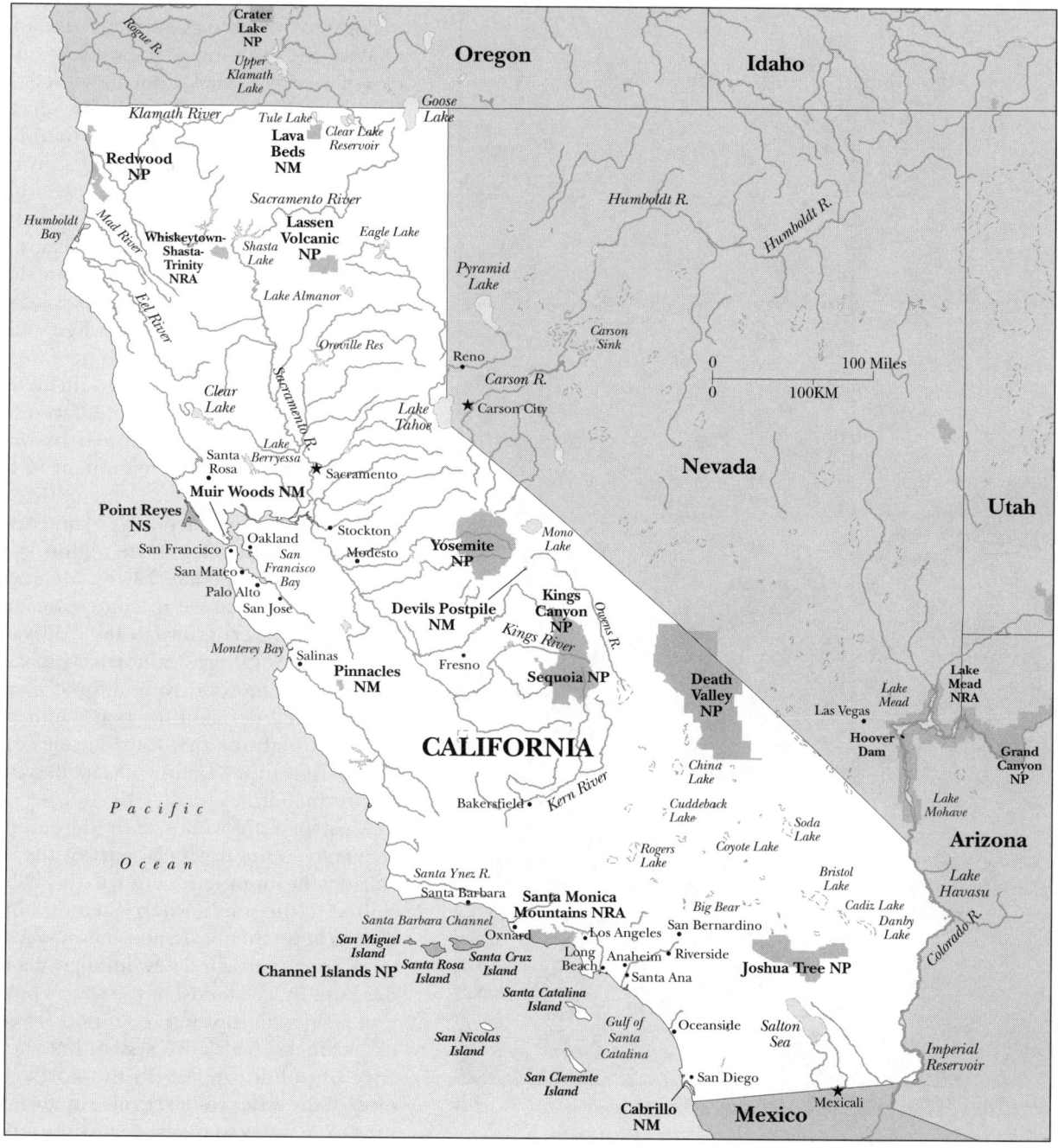

the nation, but reach a level exceeded by only a handful of nations in the world.

The gold rush peaked during the early 1850's. By 1861, when the Civil War began, it was essentially over. Nevertheless, California's economy continued to expand. The war interrupted commerce with the eastern United States but actually helped the local economy. Once again isolated from the East, California had to diversify its production to make up for what it could not import. Pro-Unionists outnumbered Confederate sympathizers within California, but the state played no direct role in the war.

Completed in 1937, the Golden Gate Bridge spans the mile-wide gap separating San Francisco Bay from the Pacific Ocean. (PhotoDisc)

Communications. When California attained statehood in 1850, it was separated from the rest of the states by the Central Plains, Rocky Mountains, and arid Southwest. With people and goods arriving at increasing rates, cheaper and more rapid transportation became a paramount need. With overland slow and expensive, much goods and people reaching the state came by ship—by way of Central America. In 1860, the Pony Express was begun to speed mail service between California and the East. It lasted little more than a year—but only because it was displaced by transcontinental telegraph service. Completion of the first transcontinental railroad in 1869 linked California's capital, Sacramento, with St. Joseph, Missouri. These new links with the East were major steps in ending California's isolation.

With the building of the railway and the end of the Civil War, California settled down to a period of steady growth and development. Settlers continued to pour in from the East, doubling the state's population every decade—a rate of growth that continued through most of the twentieth century. As the proportion of European Americans rose, their tolerance for other immigrants diminished and racially discriminatory laws were passed. Particular targets of white intolerance were the thousands of Chinese workers who had come to California to help build the railroads. Most of these people stayed working at low-paying jobs shunned by whites, who pressed the state government to legislate against Asians.

Agricultural production grew and diversified until California led the nation in production during the late 1940's. Meanwhile, other industries arose to contribute to the state's growing economy. In 1895, oil was discovered in Southern California, just as the invention of motor-driven automobiles was creating new demand for petroleum products. Through the first four decades of the twentieth century, California led all states in oil production.

Most of California's early development occurred in the northern part of the state. During the twentieth century, the balance shifted to the south, where such new industries as petrochemicals, aeronautics, and entertainment attracted new immigrants from the East. By 1920 most of the state's population resided in southern counties. However, its bicameral legislative system left the balance of political power in the north. With most of the water resources also in the north, supplying water to the largely arid south be-

Sacramento's state capitol building after its major renovation was completed in 1982. (California State Capitol Museum)

came a critical issue in state politics. Correction of the political imbalance finally came during the early 1960's, after a U.S. Supreme Court decision forced reapportionment of the state legislature. By this time, California ranked as the most populous state in the nation.

Over the next four decades, a central issue in state politics was the changing composition of the population. Opposition to immigrants of all kinds is an issue with roots going back to the late nineteenth century. During the Great Depression of the 1930's, for example, the state tried, unsuccessfully, to keep out swarms of poor farmers fleeing the drought-stricken Midwest. After World War II, Californians became alarmed by the rising influx of Mexicans seeking higher-paying jobs—particularly in agriculture. Immigration from Asia, Mexico, and Central America grew through the rest of the twentieth century, making California the most multicultural state in the Union.

Twenty-first Century Developments. As California moved toward the new millennium, it faced new challenges arising from its burgeoning population and the consequent pressure on its resources. During the late 1990's, the energy supply became a critical issue. The year 2000 saw a sharp rise in energy prices that was soon followed by unprecedented power blackouts due to a shortage of electricity. In January, 2001, Governor Grey Davis declared a state of emergency, and North California's largest power utility, Pacific Gas and Electric, filed for bankruptcy. Over the next several years, the power shortage was alleviated, but dissatisfaction over the governor's handling of the crisis led to calls for an unprecedented recall election.

In October, 2003, after more than 1.3 million signatures on recall petitions were validated, a special recall election was held. Voters were asked to decide on two issues: first, whether Governor Davis should be recalled; second, who should replace him if a majority of voters endorsed his recall. Requirements for candidacy were so low that 135 people qualified for listing on the ballot. Davis, a Democrat, was voted out of office by a decisive margin and became only the second U.S. governor in history to be recalled (the first was North Dakota's governor in 1921). Actor Arnold Schwarzenegger was elected to replace him. Candidates in the special election did not run on party affiliations, but Schwarzenegger was known to be a registered Republican. In 2006, he won his party's nomination for reelection and defeated Democratic candidate Phil Angelides, the state treasurer.

R. Kent Rasmussen

California Time Line

1521	Spain conquers Mexico.
Sept. 28, 1542	Juan Rodríguez Cabrillo is the first European to sight California's coast.
1579	Sir Francis Drake lands in Northern California.
1602	Sebastían Vizcaíno sails along California coast.
1700's	Estimated American Indian population is nearly 300,000 people.
1769-1823	Franciscans build twenty-one mission stations between San Diego and Sonoma.
1773	Spanish colonization begins.
1812	Russians establish trading posts in Northern California.
1820	Estimated *non*-Native American population is 3,270.
1821	Newly independent, Mexico makes California a province.
1833-1840	Mexico secularizes California missions and distributes lands among favored families.
1837	Mexico grants California government considerable autonomy.
1841	American settlers begin migrating to California from Missouri.
June 14, 1846	Americans raise "Bear Flag" republic revolt in Sonoma.
May, 1846	United States declares war on Mexico, which places California under military rule.
1847	California becomes U.S. territory when Mexico surrenders it to John C. Frémont's force.
1848	Signing of Treaty of Guadalupe Hidalgo ends Mexican-American War.
Jan. 24, 1848	Discovery of gold near Sacramento launches gold rush, promoting rapid, long-term development.
1849	Convention votes against forming a territorial government, instead drafts bilingual state constitution, which voters ratify.
Sept. 9, 1850	California is admitted to the Union.
1854	Sacramento becomes permanent state capital.
1860-1861	Pony Express improves mail service with the East.
Oct. 1861	Transcontinental telegraph reaches California.
1868	University of California is founded in Berkeley.
1869	Completion of transcontinental railroad ends California's isolation.
1872	State laws are codified for the first time.
May 7, 1879	Voters ratify new constitution.
1890	Yosemite becomes state's first national park.
1895	Oil is discovered in Southern California.
1900	Native American population drops to about 15,500 people.
Oct., 1906	Earthquake and fire level San Francisco.

The interior of San Francisco's Majestic Theater offers a dramatic view of the damage wrought by the 1906 earthquake. (California State Capitol Museum)

1908	Film industry begins in Los Angeles.
1914	Opening of Panama Canal improves communications with the East Coast, lowering shipping and transportation costs.
1920	Southern California overtakes the north in population, but legislature refuses to reapportion.
Feb. 3, 1923	Mount Lassen erupts.
1930's	Great Depression sends many farmers from the Great Plains to California, which tries to keep them out.
1931	Master plan for distributing water throughout the state is created.
Nov., 1934	Voters endorse calling of new constitutional convention, but legislature never acts to organize it.
1937	Golden Gate Bridge opens in San Francisco Bay.
Nov., 1938	Culbert Olson is first Democrat elected governor.
1940	First freeway in United States opens in Pasadena.
Feb., 1942	Federal government orders internment of state's Japanese American population after World War II begins.
1942-1945	World War II spurs industrial and economic growth.
1945	State Water Resources Board is created to distribute state's limited water supplies.
1947	State's agriculture ranks first among U.S. states.
1953	Governor Earl Warren becomes chief justice of the United States.
1959	California is first state to adopt master highway plan.
1960	State prepares master plan for higher education.
1964	California surpasses New York as most populous state.
Nov., 1964	Ronald Reagan is elected governor.
Aug., 1965	Nation's first modern racially motivated rioting erupts in Los Angeles's Watts district.
Nov., 1966	First elections after reapportionment are held.
Feb. 9, 1971	Massive earthquake devastates Los Angeles area.
June 6, 1978	Voters approve referendum Prop 13, mandating statewide reduction in property tax of 57 percent.
Nov., 1980	Ronald Reagan is elected president of the United States.
Oct. 17, 1989	Earthquake devastates San Francisco Bay Area.
Oct. 20, 1991	Most destructive urban wildfire in U.S. history burns parts of Berkeley and Oakland.
Apr. 29, 1992	Acquittal of policemen charged with beating Rodney King touches off rioting in Los Angeles.
Jan. 17, 1994	Massive earthquake devastates Southern California.
Nov., 1998	Grey Davis is first Democrat elected governor since 1978.
2000	Significant rise in energy prices signals beginning of energy crisis that worsens as power blackouts occur.
Jan. 17, 2000	Governor Davis responds to energy crisis by declaring a state of emergency.
Nov., 2002	Despite energy crisis, Davis is reelected governor by a wide margin.
Feb. 5, 2003	Movement to recall Davis is launched.
Oct. 7, 2003	In special recall election, Davis is voted out of office, and actor Arnold Schwarzenegger is elected from among 135 candidates to complete his term.
Nov. 13, 2003	Davis ends the state of emergency four days before leaving office.
Nov. 8, 2005	In another special selection, voters reject all four ballot initiatives proposed by Schwarzenegger to reform the state government.
Nov., 2006	Schwarzenegger defeats Democrat Phil Angelides in his first bid for reelection.
Jan., 2007	San Francisco congresswoman Nancy Pelosi becomes the Speaker of the House of Representatives.

Notes for Further Study

Published Sources. As the largest state in the nation, California offers the most abundant resources for further study. Thousands of published books cover every imaginable aspect of the state's history, peoples, politics, economy, and natural resources. Especially abundant are travel guides. These not only provide practical guides to the state as a whole, its major cities, and regions, but also are filled with statistics, historical facts, and other useful information. Vast amounts of diverse information can also be obtained from government agencies at all levels. A good starting point for general information on the state is *California Almanac* (7th ed., 1996), edited by James S. Fay. Warren A. Beck and Ynez D. Haase's *Historical Atlas of*

California (1975) remains a standard source on historical geography. For an updated version of a classic history text emphasizing forces that have made California unique, see Carey McWilliams and Lewis H. Lapham's *California: The Great Exception* (1999). Another overview can be found in *California: An Interpretive History* (8th ed., 2003) by James J. Rawls and Walton Bean. California historian Kevin Starr brings together a discussion of the state's history and the myths surrounding it in *California: A History* (2005).

Agriculture forms a substantial portion of California's economy, and Richard A. Walker examines the modern agro-industrial system of production in the state in *The Conquest of Bread: One Hundred Fifty Years of Agribusiness in California*. Editors Charles F. Hohm and James A. Glynn focus the chapters in *California's Social Problems* (2d ed., 2002) on the important challenges facing the state's communities, including those involving health, institutional change, population growth, and environmental decline. C. L. Keyworth's *California Indians* (1999) is a comprehensive guide to the history, cultures, and modern condition of the state's diverse Native American peoples. An authoritative analysis of how government works in the state can be found both in Mona Field and Charles P. Sohner's *California Government and Politics Today* (8th ed., 1999) and in *California Politics and Government: A Practical Approach* (8th ed., 2006) by Larry N. Gerston and Terry Christensen.

Web Resources. The range of Web sites offering useful information on California is too broad even to summarize. However, many of the sites are so well connected by links and are so easy to find with Web search engines that the addresses of only a few will suffice to direct users to most of the rest.

An excellent starting point is the official California Tourist Bureau site (gocalif.ca.gov/state/tourism/tour_homepage .jsp?PrimaryCat=Tourism+Home), providing links to maps and travel information. Welcome to California (www.ca.gov/ state/portal/myca_homepage.jsp) is a thorough site, providing residents and visitors with information on the state's history and culture, travel and transportation, environmental and natural resources, and health and safety, among many other topics. Among specialized sites, readers will find interest in California State Library (www.library.ca.gov/history/ cahinsig.cfm), which hosts a page detailing all the state's insignia, such as the state flower, state gemstone, and state seal; California Coastal Geography (ceres.ca.gov/ceres/calweb/ coastal/geography.html); Gold Rush! (www .museumca.org/ goldrush/), detailing the influx of settlers and miners following the 1848 discovery of gold; and A History of Mexican Americans in California (www.lasculturas.com/lib/sd/ blsd092200a.php).

Another good starting point on the Web is the Law Library of Congress (www.loc.gov/law/guide/us-ca.html), which provides links to the office of the governor, state agencies, and the California Legislative Assembly, among many others. The California State Association of Counties Web site (www.csac.counties.org/) offers profiles of every county, as well as links to individual Web sites for most of them. The county sites, in turn, provide additional information on local matters and government agencies. The Official California Legislative Information site (www.leginfo.ca.gov) provides full information on current legislative activity and pending legislation.

Counties

County	2000 pop.	Rank in pop.	Sq. miles	Rank in area	County	2000 pop.	Rank in pop.	Sq. miles	Rank in area
Alameda	1,443,741	7	737.5	50	Mariposa	17,130	53	1,451.2	31
Alpine	1,208	58	738.7	49	Mendocino	86,265	37	3,509.3	15
Amador	35,100	46	592.6	54	Merced	210,554	26	1,928.9	25
Butte	203,171	27	1,639.6	28	Modoc	9,449	56	3,944.4	12
Calaveras	40,554	45	1,020.2	40	Mono	12,853	55	3,044.5	19
Colusa	18,804	51	1,150.8	39	Monterey	401,762	18	3,321.9	16
Contra Costa	948,816	9	720.3	51	Napa	124,279	34	753.9	48
Del Norte	27,507	48	1,007.9	42	Nevada	92,033	36	957.7	44
El Dorado	156,299	30	1,711.5	27	Orange	2,846,289	2	789.7	47
Fresno	799,407	10	5,963.2	6	Placer	248,399	23	1,404.4	32
Glenn	26,453	49	1,314.9	36	Plumas	20,824	50	2,554.0	22
Humboldt	126,518	33	3,572.8	14	Riverside	1,545,387	6	7,208.2	4
Imperial	142,361	31	4,175.1	10	Sacramento	1,223,499	8	965.7	43
Inyo	17,945	52	10,192.1	2	San Benito	53,234	43	1,389.1	35
Kern	661,645	14	8,141.6	3	San Bernardino	1,709,434	4	20,062.2	1
Kings	129,461	32	1,389.5	34	San Diego	2,813,833	3	4,204.5	9
Lake	58,309	40	1,258.5	38	San Francisco	776,733	11	46.7	58
Lassen	33,828	47	4,557.5	8	San Joaquin	563,598	15	1,399.3	33
Los Angeles	9,519,338	1	4,060.0	11	San Luis				
Madera	123,109	35	2,138.4	24	Obispo	246,681	25	3,304.5	17
Marin	247,289	24	519.8	55	San Mateo	707,161	13	449.1	56

County	2000 pop.	Rank in pop.	Sq. miles	Rank in area
Santa Barbara	399,347	19	2,738.5	21
Santa Clara	1,682,585	5	1,291.2	37
Santa Cruz	255,602	22	445.7	57
Shasta	163,256	29	3,785.7	13
Sierra	3,555	57	953.4	45
Siskiyou	44,301	44	6,287.3	5
Solano	394,542	20	828.2	46
Sonoma	458,614	16	1,576.2	29
Stanislaus	446,997	17	1,494.6	30
Sutter	78,930	38	602.7	53

County	2000 pop.	Rank in pop.	Sq. miles	Rank in area
Tehama	56,039	41	2,951.0	20
Trinity	13,022	54	3,178.9	18
Tulare	368,021	21	4,824.3	7
Tuolumne	54,501	42	2,235.6	23
Ventura	753,197	12	1,845.9	26
Yolo	168,660	28	1,012.4	41
Yuba	60,219	39	630.5	52

Source: U.S. Census Bureau; National Association of Counties.

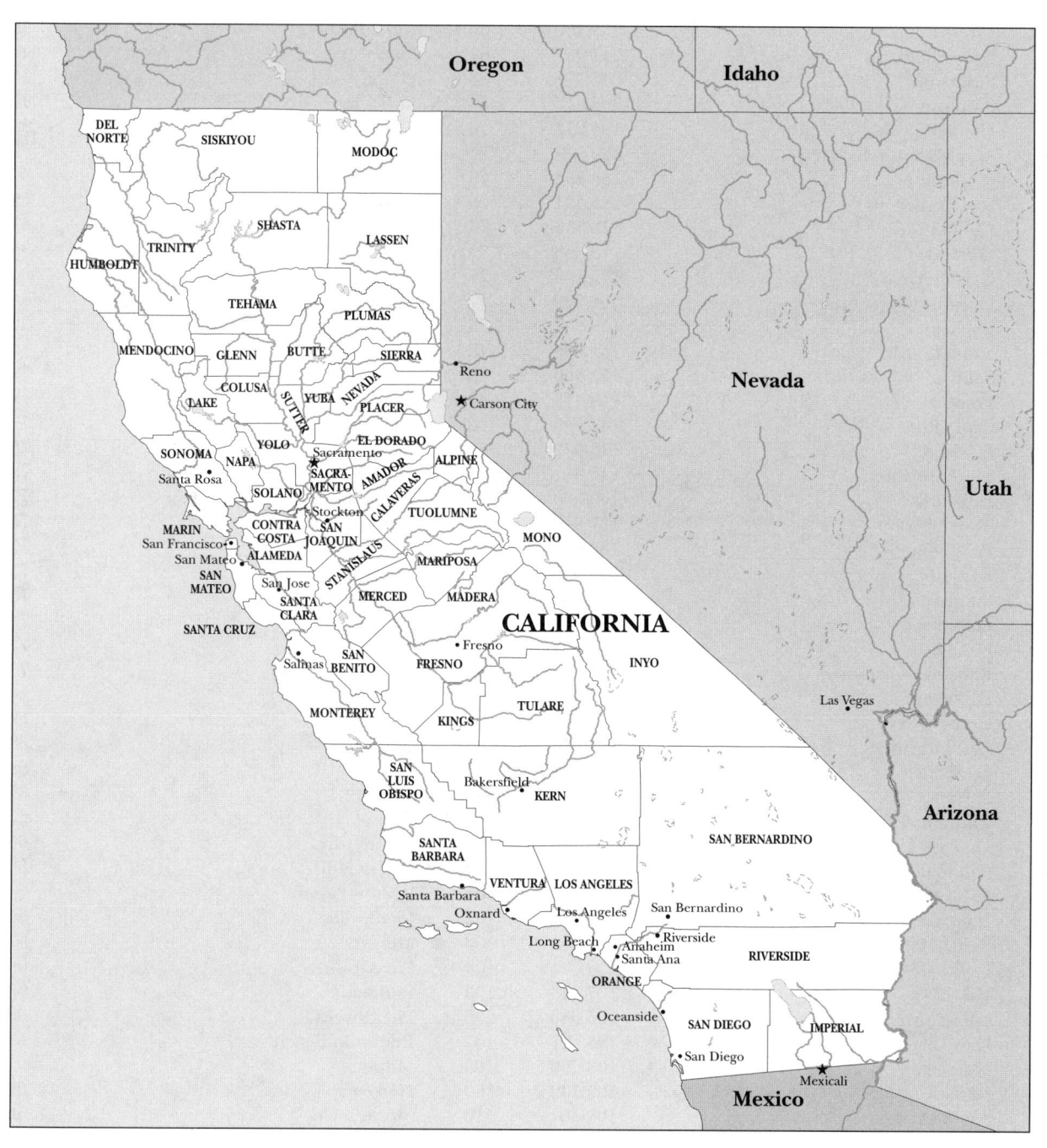

Cities
With 10,000 or more residents

Rank	City	Population	Rank	City	Population
1	Los Angeles	3,694,820	56	San Buenaventura (Ventura)	100,916
2	San Diego	1,223,400	57	Burbank	100,316
3	San Jose	894,943	58	Richmond	99,216
4	San Francisco	776,733	59	South Gate	96,375
5	Long Beach	461,522	60	Fairfield	96,178
6	Fresno	427,652	61	Arden-Arcade	96,025
7	Sacramento (capital)	407,018	62	El Cajon	94,869
8	Oakland	399,484	63	Compton	93,493
9	Santa Ana	337,977	64	Mission Viejo	93,102
10	Anaheim	328,014	65	San Mateo	92,482
11	Riverside	255,166	66	Santa Barbara	92,325
12	Bakersfield	247,057	67	Rialto	91,873
13	Stockton	243,771	68	Visalia	91,565
14	Fremont	203,413	69	Antioch	90,532
15	Glendale	194,973	70	Vista	89,857
16	Huntington Beach	189,594	71	Carson	89,730
17	Modesto	188,856	72	Vacaville	88,625
18	San Bernardino	185,401	73	Westminster	88,207
19	Chula Vista	173,556	74	Alhambra	85,804
20	Oxnard	170,358	75	Citrus Heights	85,071
21	Garden Grove	165,196	76	Hawthorne	84,112
22	Oceanside	161,029	77	Santa Monica	84,084
23	Ontario	158,007	78	Whittier	83,680
24	Santa Clarita	151,088	79	Redding	80,865
25	Salinas	151,060	80	Roseville	79,921
26	Pomona	149,473	81	San Leandro	79,452
27	Santa Rosa	147,595	82	Lakewood	79,345
28	Irvine	143,072	83	Buena Park	78,282
29	Moreno Valley	142,381	84	Carlsbad	78,247
30	Hayward	140,030	85	Santa Maria	77,423
31	Torrance	137,946	86	Baldwin Park	75,837
32	Pasadena	133,936	87	Redwood City	75,402
33	Escondido	133,559	88	Livermore	73,345
34	Sunnyvale	131,760	89	Bellflower	72,878
35	Fontana	128,929	90	Napa	72,585
36	Orange	128,821	91	Alameda	72,259
37	Rancho Cucamonga	127,743	92	Mountain View	70,708
38	Fullerton	126,003	93	Newport Beach	70,032
39	Corona	124,966	94	Lynwood	69,845
40	East Los Angeles	124,283	95	Clovis	68,468
41	Concord	121,780	96	Upland	68,393
42	Lancaster	118,718	97	Tustin	67,504
43	Thousand Oaks	117,005	98	Chino	67,168
44	Vallejo	116,760	99	Union City	66,869
45	Palmdale	116,670	100	Chino Hills	66,787
46	El Monte	115,965	101	Walnut Creek	64,296
47	Inglewood	112,580	102	Victorville	64,029
48	Simi Valley	111,351	103	Merced	63,893
49	Costa Mesa	108,724	104	Pleasanton	63,654
50	Downey	107,323	105	Redlands	63,591
51	West Covina	105,080	106	Pico Rivera	63,428
52	Daly City	103,621	107	Redondo Beach	63,261
53	Norwalk	103,298	108	Milpitas	62,698
54	Berkeley	102,743	109	Hesperia	62,582
55	Santa Clara	102,361	110	Montebello	62,150

Rank	City	Population	Rank	City	Population
111	Laguna Niguel	61,891	170	Highland	44,605
112	Huntington Park	61,348	171	Murrieta	44,282
113	South San Francisco	60,552	172	Watsonville	44,265
114	Davis	60,308	173	North Highlands	44,187
115	Florence-Graham	60,197	174	San Luis Obispo	44,174
116	Monterey Park	60,051	175	Bell Gardens	44,054
117	Elk Grove	59,984	176	Tulare	43,994
118	Chico	59,954	177	Madera	43,207
119	La Habra	58,974	178	Palm Springs	42,807
120	Yorba Linda	58,918	179	Cathedral City	42,647
121	Hemet	58,812	180	Altadena	42,610
122	Lake Forest	58,707	181	Newark	42,471
123	Palo Alto	58,598	182	Rohnert Park	42,236
124	Encinitas	58,014	183	Danville	41,715
125	Gardena	57,746	184	Hanford	41,686
126	Temecula	57,716	185	Gilroy	41,464
127	Castro Valley	57,292	186	Yucaipa	41,207
128	Camarillo	57,077	187	Palm Desert	41,155
129	Lodi	56,999	188	Rancho Palos Verdes	41,145
130	Tracy	56,929	189	Lompoc	41,103
131	Pittsburg	56,769	190	La Puente	41,063
132	Diamond Bar	56,287	191	Aliso Viejo	40,166
133	San Rafael	56,063	192	San Bruno	40,165
134	Turlock	55,810	193	San Gabriel	39,804
135	Paramount	55,266	194	Porterville	39,615
136	Goleta	55,204	195	Delano	38,824
137	South Whittier	55,193	196	Culver City	38,816
138	Rancho Cordova	55,060	197	Pacifica	38,390
139	Fountain Valley	54,978	198	Campbell	38,138
140	San Marcos	54,977	199	El Centro	37,835
141	La Mesa	54,749	200	Stanton	37,403
142	Santa Cruz	54,593	201	Monrovia	36,929
143	Petaluma	54,548	202	Yuba City	36,758
144	National City	54,260	203	Bell	36,664
145	Apple Valley	54,239	204	Parkway-South Sacramento	36,468
146	Rosemead	53,505	205	Rocklin	36,330
147	Hacienda Heights	53,122	206	Perris	36,189
148	Arcadia	53,054	207	Martinez	35,866
149	Santee	52,975	208	West Hollywood	35,716
150	Folsom	51,884	209	Brea	35,410
151	Cerritos	51,488	210	Dana Point	35,110
152	Cupertino	50,546	211	San Dimas	34,980
153	San Clemente	49,936	212	Ceres	34,609
154	Carmichael	49,742	213	Hollister	34,413
155	Glendora	49,415	214	Laguna	34,309
156	Manteca	49,258	215	Willowbrook	34,138
157	Woodland	49,151	216	Claremont	33,998
158	Indio	49,116	217	Manhattan Beach	33,852
159	Rowland Heights	48,553	218	San Juan Capistrano	33,826
160	Poway	48,044	219	Beverly Hills	33,784
161	Colton	47,662	220	Morgan Hill	33,556
162	Novato	47,630	221	Temple City	33,377
163	Rancho Santa Margarita	47,214	222	Montclair	33,049
164	Covina	46,837	223	Pleasant Hill	32,837
165	La Mirada	46,783	224	La Presa	32,721
166	Placentia	46,488	225	Lawndale	31,711
167	Cypress	46,229	226	Seaside	31,696
168	San Ramon	44,722	227	La Verne	31,638
169	Azusa	44,712	228	Westmont	31,623

(continued)

Rank	City	Population	Rank	City	Population
229	West Sacramento	31,615	241	Lake Elsinore	28,928
230	Moorpark	31,415	242	Orcutt	28,830
231	Laguna Hills	31,178	243	Foster City	28,803
232	Menlo Park	30,785	244	Santa Paula	28,598
233	San Pablo	30,215	245	Los Gatos	28,592
234	Walnut	30,004	246	Burlingame	28,158
235	Dublin	29,973	247	Maywood	28,083
236	Saratoga	29,843	248	Fair Oaks	28,008
237	Monterey	29,674	249	Oildale	27,885
238	East Palo Alto	29,506	250	San Carlos	27,718
239	Rubidoux	29,180	251	Los Altos	27,693
240	Fallbrook	29,100	252	Florin	27,653

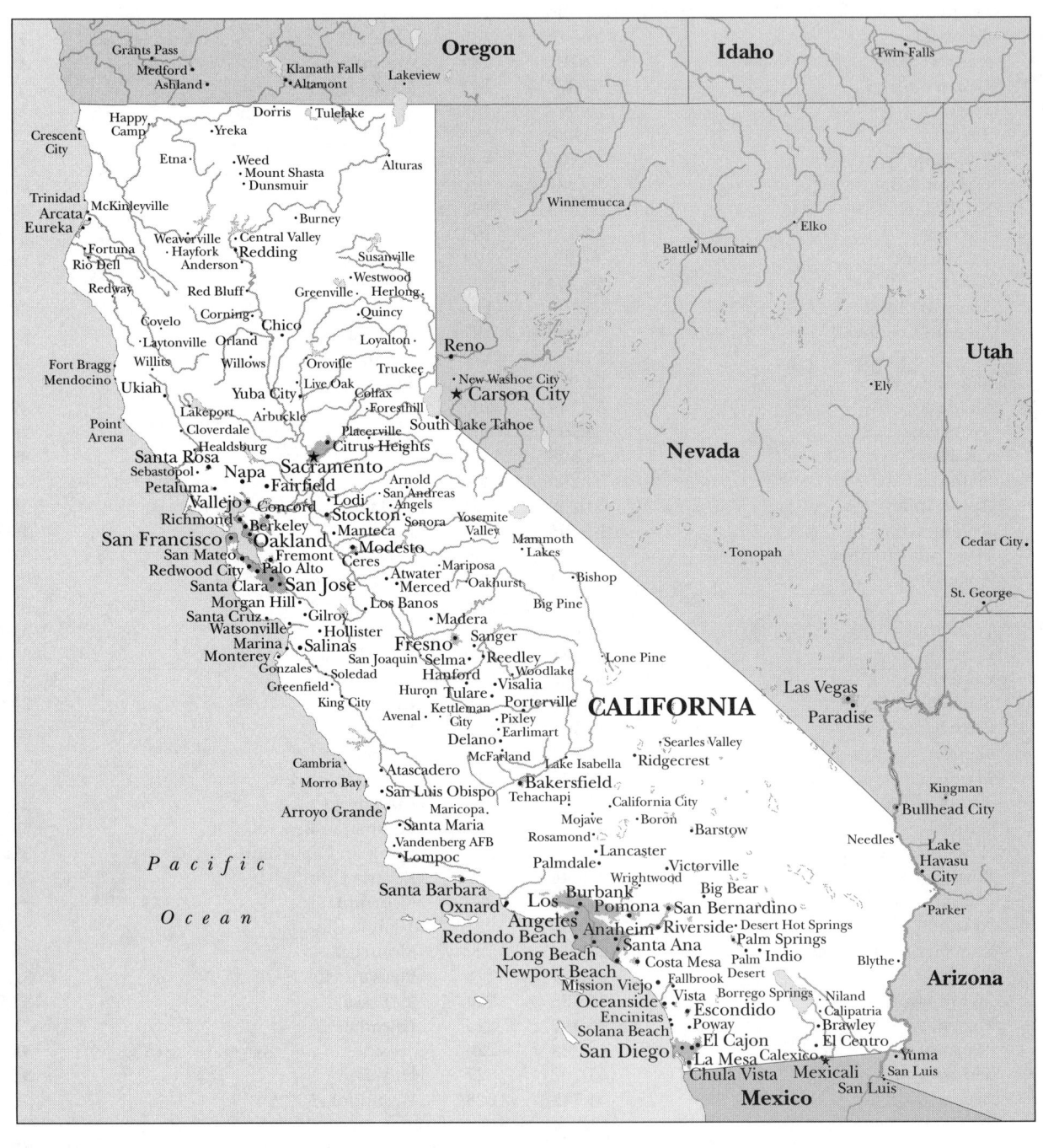

Rank	City	Population	Rank	City	Population
253	Calexico	27,109	312	Lakeside	19,560
254	Imperial Beach	26,992	313	Hercules	19,488
255	Benicia	26,865	314	Galt	19,472
256	Orangevale	26,705	315	Selma	19,444
257	Spring Valley	26,663	316	Granite Bay	19,388
258	Atascadero	26,411	317	Bloomington	19,318
259	Paradise	26,408	318	Pinole	19,039
260	Eureka	26,128	319	Sanger	18,931
261	Suisun City	26,118	320	Casa de Oro-Mount Helix	18,874
262	Los Banos	25,869	321	Loma Linda	18,681
263	Oakley	25,619	322	Hermosa Beach	18,566
264	West Whittier-Los Nietos	25,129	323	La Crescenta-Montrose	18,532
265	Belmont	25,123	324	Isla Vista	18,344
266	Marina	25,101	325	Adelanto	18,130
267	Ridgecrest	24,927	326	El Dorado Hills	18,016
268	Lemon Grove	24,918	327	Sun City	17,773
269	El Paso de Robles (Paso Robles)	24,297	328	Mira Loma	17,617
270	South Pasadena	24,292	329	Orinda	17,599
271	Cudahy	24,208	330	Santa Fe Springs	17,438
272	Norco	24,157	331	Foothill Farms	17,426
273	Seal Beach	24,157	332	Yucca Valley	16,865
274	Coronado	24,100	333	Dinuba	16,844
275	Tustin Foothills	24,044	334	Arcata	16,651
276	Lafayette	23,908	335	Live Oak	16,628
277	San Jacinto	23,779	336	Desert Hot Springs	16,582
278	Laguna Beach	23,727	337	Laguna Woods	16,507
279	La Quinta	23,694	338	Albany	16,444
280	South Lake Tahoe	23,609	339	Prunedale	16,432
281	San Fernando	23,564	340	Artesia	16,380
282	Banning	23,562	341	Moraga	16,290
283	Brentwood	23,302	342	Walnut Park	16,180
284	El Cerrito	23,171	343	Dixon	16,103
285	Atwater	23,113	344	El Segundo	16,033
286	Lennox	22,950	345	Arroyo Grande	15,851
287	Rosemont	22,904	346	Riverbank	15,826
288	Windsor	22,744	347	Ramona	15,691
289	Coachella	22,724	348	Alamo	15,626
290	West Puente Valley	22,589	349	Pacific Grove	15,522
291	Brawley	22,052	350	Oakdale	15,503
292	San Lorenzo	21,898	351	Ukiah	15,497
293	Port Hueneme	21,845	352	North Fair Oaks	15,440
294	Valinda	21,776	353	La Palma	15,408
295	Bay Point	21,534	354	Bostonia	15,169
296	Duarte	21,486	355	Avocado Heights	15,148
297	Wasco	21,263	356	Vincent	15,097
298	South El Monte	21,144	357	Glen Avon	14,853
299	West Carson	21,138	358	East Hemet	14,823
300	Barstow	21,119	359	Hawaiian Gardens	14,779
301	Ashland	20,793	360	Twentynine Palms	14,764
302	Reedley	20,756	361	Avenal	14,674
303	Millbrae	20,718	362	Cameron Park	14,549
304	Agoura Hills	20,537	363	East San Gabriel	14,512
305	La Canada Flintridge	20,318	364	Corcoran	14,458
306	South San Jose Hills	20,218	365	Baywood-Los Osos	14,351
307	Rancho San Diego	20,155	366	Rosamond	14,349
308	Lomita	20,046	367	Carpinteria	14,194
309	Calabasas	20,033	368	Wildomar	14,064
310	Winter Gardens	19,771	369	Truckee	13,864
311	Lemoore	19,712	370	Cherryland	13,837

(continued)

Rank	City	Population
371	Fillmore	13,643
372	Mill Valley	13,600
373	McKinleyville	13,599
374	Susanville	13,541
375	Alum Rock	13,479
376	Linda	13,474
377	Palos Verdes Estates	13,340
378	Stanford	13,315
379	Lamont	13,296
380	Rancho Mirage	13,249
381	Red Bluff	13,147
382	Alpine	13,143
383	Clearlake	13,142
384	Grover Beach	13,067
385	Coto de Caza	13,057
386	Oroville	13,004
387	Solana Beach	12,979
388	Arvin	12,956
389	San Marino	12,945
390	Shafter	12,736
391	South Yuba City	12,651
392	Nipomo	12,626
393	Greenfield	12,583
394	Malibu	12,575
395	Commerce	12,568
396	Salida	12,560
397	Auburn	12,462
398	Bonita	12,401
399	San Anselmo	12,378
400	Marysville	12,268
401	El Sobrante	12,260
402	Blythe	12,155
403	Larkspur	12,014
404	North Auburn	11,847
405	Half Moon Bay	11,842
406	Coalinga	11,668
407	Grand Terrace	11,626
408	Patterson	11,606
409	Los Alamitos	11,536
410	Lake Los Angeles	11,523
411	Scotts Valley	11,385
412	Beaumont	11,384
413	Soledad	11,263
414	Pedley	11,207
415	Lincoln	11,205
416	Parlier	11,145
417	Chowchilla	11,127
418	King City	11,094
419	Olivehurst	11,061
420	View Park-Windsor Hills	10,958
421	Tehachapi	10,957
422	Piedmont	10,952
423	Grass Valley	10,922
424	Foothill Ranch	10,899
425	Hillsborough	10,825
426	Clayton	10,762
427	Healdsburg	10,722
428	Tamalpais-Homestead Valley	10,691

Rank	City	Population
429	Citrus	10,581
430	Sierra Madre	10,578
431	Magalia	10,569
432	Fortuna	10,497
433	Valle Vista	10,488
434	Livingston	10,473
435	Rio Linda	10,466
436	Lathrop	10,445
437	Morro Bay	10,350
438	Rossmoor	10,298
439	Lindsay	10,297
440	La Riviera	10,273
441	Crestline	10,218
442	Ripon	10,146
443	Vineyard	10,109
444	Blackhawk-Camino Tassajara	10,048
445	Capitola	10,033
446	Montecito	10,000

Population figures are from 2000 census.
Source: U.S. Bureau of the Census.

Aerial view of Hollywood's Capitol Records building, which was designed to resemble a record turntable. (PhotoDisc)

Index to Tables

DEMOGRAPHICS

Resident state and national populations, 1970-2004

Population figures given in thousands

	State pop.	U.S. pop.	Share	Rank
1970	19,971	203,302	9.8%	1
1980	23,668	226,546	10.4%	1
1985	26,441	237,924	11.1%	1
1990	29,811	248,765	12.0%	1
1995	31,697	262,761	12.0%	1
2000	33,872	281,425	12.0%	1
2004	35,894	293,655	12.2%	1

Source: U.S. Census Bureau, Current Population Reports, 2006.

Resident population by age, 2004

Age Group	Total persons
Under 5 years	2,634,000
5 to 17 years	6,962,000
18 to 24 years	3,596,000
25 to 34 years	5,253,000
35 to 44 years	5,541,000
45 to 54 years	4,860,000
55 to 64 years	3,225,000
65 to 74 years	1,950,000
75 to 84 years	1,359,000
85 years and older	514,000
All age groups	35,894,000

Portion of residents 65 and older	10.7%
National rank in portion of oldest residents	45
National average	12.4%

Population figures are rounded to nearest thousand persons;
figures include armed forces personnel stationed in the state.
Source: U.S. Bureau of the Census, 2006.

Resident population by race, Hispanic origin, 2004

Category	State pop.	Share	U.S.
All residents	35,894	100.00%	100.00%
Non-Hispanic white	15,982	44.53%	67.37%
Hispanic white	11,728	32.67%	13.01%
Other Hispanic	715	1.99%	1.06%
African American	2,437	6.79%	12.77%
Native American	417	1.16%	0.96%
Asian, Pacific Islander	4,475	12.47%	4.37%
Two or more categories	855	2.38%	1.51%

Population figures are in thousands. Persons counted as "Hispanic" (Latino) may be of any race. Because of overlapping categories, categories may not add up to 100%. Shares in column 3 are percentages of each category within the state; these figures may be compared to the national percentages in column 4.
Source: U.S. Bureau of the Census, 2006.

Projected state population, 2000-2030

Year	Population
2000	33,872,000
2005	36,039,000
2010	38,067,000
2015	40,123,000
2020	42,207,000
2025	44,305,000
2030	46,445,000
Population increase, 2000-2030	12,573,000
Percentage increase, 2000-2030	37.1

Projections are based on data from the 2000 census.
Source: U.S. Census Bureau.

VITAL STATISTICS

Infant mortality rates, 1980-2002

	1980	1990	2000	2002
All state residents	11.1	7.9	5.4	5.5
All U.S. residents	12.6	9.2	9.4	9.1
All state white residents	10.6	7.0	5.1	5.2
All U.S. white residents	10.6	7.6	5.7	5.8
All state black residents	18.0	16.8	12.9	12.9
All U.S. black residents	22.2	18.0	14.1	14.4

Figures represent deaths per 1,000 live births of resident infants under 1 year old, exclusive of fetal deaths. Figures for all residents include members of other racial categories not listed separately.
Source: U.S. Census Bureau, *Statistical Abstract of the United States,* 2006.

Abortion rates, 1990 and 2000

	1990	2000
Total abortions	304,000	236,000
Rate per 1,000 women	41.8	31.2
U.S. rate	25.7	21.3
Rank	4	6

Numbers of abortions are rounded to nearest thousand; ranks are based on rates.
Source: U.S. Census Bureau.

Marriages and divorces

Total marriages in 2004	172,300
Rate per 1,000 population.	4.8
National rate per 1,000 population	7.4
Rank among all states in 2004	49
Total divorces in 1990	128,000
Rate per 1,000 population in 1990	4.3
National rate per 1,000 population in 2004	3.7
Rank among all states in 2004	n/a

Figures are for all marriages and divorces performed within the state, including those of nonresidents; totals are rounded to the nearest hundred. Ranks are for highest to lowest figures; note that 2004 divorce data are not available for California and four other states.
Source: U.S. National Center for Health Statistics, *Vital Statistics of the United States,* 2006.

Death rates by leading causes, 2002
Deaths per 100,000 resident population

Cause	State	U.S.
Heart disease	195.9	241.7
Cancer	154.2	193.2
Cerebrovascular diseases	50.2	56.4
Accidents other than motor vehicle	28.8	37.0
Motor vehicle accidents	12.1	15.7
Chronic lower respiratory diseases	36.1	43.3
Diabetes mellitus	19.4	25.4
HIV	4.1	4.9
Suicide	9.2	11.0
Homicide	7.1	6.1
All causes	668.0	847.3
Rank in overall death rate among states		47

Figures exclude nonresidents who died in the state. Causes of death follow International Classification of Diseases. Rank is from highest to lowest death rate in the United States.
Source: U.S. National Center for Health Statistics, *National Vital Statistics Report,* 2006.

ECONOMY

Gross state product, 1990-2004
In current dollars

Year	State product	Nat'l product	State share
1990	$788.3 billion	$5.67 trillion	13.89%
2000	$1,291.1 billion	$9.75 trillion	13.24%
2002	$1,363.6 billion	$10.41 trillion	13.10%
2003	$1,438.1 billion	$10.92 trillion	13.16%
2004	$1,543.8 billion	$11.65 trillion	13.25%

Source: U.S. Bureau of Economic Analysis, *Survey of Current Business,* July, 2005.

Gross state product by industry, 2003
In billions of dollars

Construction	$53.8
Manufacturing	181.5
Wholesale trade	80.1
Retail trade	106.9
Finance & insurance	96.3
Information	85.4
Professional services	109.0
Health care & social assistance	75.3
Government	142.9
Total state product	$1,369.2
Total U.S. product	$10,289.2
State share of U.S. total	13.31%
Rank among all states	1

Total figures include industries not listed separately. Amounts are in chained 2000 dollars.
Source: U.S. Bureau of Economic Analysis, *Survey of Current Business,* July, 2005.

Personal income per capita, 1990-2004
In current dollars

	1990	2000	2004
Per capita income	$21,638	$32,464	$35,019
U.S. average	$19,477	$29,845	$32,937
Rank among states	8	8	12

Source: U.S. Bureau of Economic Analysis, *Survey of Current Business,* April, 2005.

Energy consumption, 2001
In trillions of British thermal units (BTU), except as noted

Total energy consumption

Total state energy consumption	7,853
Total U.S. energy consumption	96,275
State share of U.S. total	8.16%
Rank among states	2

Per capita consumption (In millions of BTU)

Total state per capita consumption	227
Total U.S. per capita consumption	338
Rank among states	48

End-use sectors

Residential	1,446
Commercial	1,509
Industrial	1,928
Transportation	2,971

Sources of energy

Petroleum	3,604
Natural gas	2,514
Coal	68
Hydroelectric power	256
Nuclear electric power	347

Figures for totals include categories not listed separately.
Source: U.S. Energy Information Administration, *State Energy Data Report,* 2001.

Nonfarm employment by sectors, 2004

Total	14,539,000
Construction	847,000
Manufacturing	1,533,000
Trade, transportation, utilities	2,753,000
Information	483,000
Finance, insurance, real estate	903,000
Professional & business services	2,099,000
Education & health services	1,562,000
Leisure, hospitality, arts, organizations	1,442,000
Other services, including repair & maintenance	505,000
Government	2,390,000

Figures are rounded to nearest thousand persons. "Total" includes mining and natural resources, not listed separately.
Source: U.S. Bureau of Labor Statistics, 2006.

Foreign exports, 1990-2004
In millions of dollars

Year	State	U.S.	State share
1990	44,520	394,045	11.30%
1996	93,418	624,767	14.95%
1997	99,161	688,896	14.39%
2000	119,640	712,055	15.29%
2003	93,995	724,006	13.91%
2004	109,968	769,332	14.29%

Rank among all states in 2004. 2

U.S. total does not include U.S. dependencies.
Source: U.S. Census Bureau, *U.S. Merchandise Trade,* series FT 900, 2000; U.S. Census Bureau, *U.S. International Trade in Goods and Services,* Series FT 900, 2005.

LAND USE

Federally owned land, 2003
Areas in acres

	State	U.S.	State share
Total area	100,207,000	2,271,343,000	4.41%
Nonfederal land	53,227,000	1,599,584,000	3.33%
Federal land	46,980,000	671,759,000	6.99%
Federal share	46.9%	29.6%	—

Areas are rounded to nearest thousand acres. Figures for federally owned land do not include trust properties.
Source: U.S. General Services Administration, *Federal Real Property Profile,* 2006.

Land use, 1997
In acres, rounded to nearest thousand

Total surface area 101,510,000
Total nonfederal rural land. 47,555,000
Percentage rural land 46.8%
Cropland 9,635,000
Conservation Reserve Program (CRP*) land. . . . 173,000
Pastureland 1,049,000
Rangeland 18,269,000
Forestland 13,936,000
Other rural land 4,494,000

*CRP is a federal program begun in 1985 to assist private landowners to convert highly erodible cropland to vegetative cover for ten years. Note that some categories of land overlap.
Source: U.S. Department of Agriculture, Natural Resources and Conservation Service, and Iowa State University, Statistical Laboratory, S*ummary Report, 1997 National Resources Inventory,* revised December, 2000.

Farms and crop acreage, 2004

	State	U.S.	Share	Rank
Farms	77,000	2,113,000	3.64%	8
Acres (millions)	27	937	2.88%	15
Acres per farm	347	443	—	20

Source: U.S. Department of Agriculture, National Agricultural Statistics Service. Numbers of farms are rounded to nearest thousand units; acreage figures are rounded to nearest million. Rankings, including ties, are based on rounded figures.

GOVERNMENT AND FINANCE

Units of local government, 2002

	State	Total U.S.	Rank
All local governments	4,409	87,525	4
Counties	57	3,034	26
Municipalities	475	19,429	18
Townships	0	16,504	—
School districts	1,047	13,506	2
Special districts	2,830	35,052	2

Only 48 states have county governments, 20 states have township governments ("towns" in New England, Minnesota, New York, and Wisconsin), and 46 states have school districts. Special districts encompass such functions as natural resources, fire protection, and housing and community development.
Source: U.S. Census Bureau, *Census of Governments.*

State government revenue, 2002

Total revenue . . . . $151,245 mill.
General revenue. . . . . $141,481 mill.
Per capita revenue $4,044
U.S. per capita average $3,689
Rank among states 18

Intergovernment revenue
Total . . . . $43,861 mill.
From federal government . . . . $40,843 mill.

Charges and miscellaneous
Total . . . . $19,865 mill.
Current charges. . . . . $11,456 mill.
Misc. general income . . . . $8,408 mill.
Insurance trust revenue . . . . $5,520 mill.

Taxes
Total . . . . $77,755 mill.
Per capita taxes $2,221
Rank among states. 8
Property taxes . . . . $1,952 mill.
Sales taxes . . . . $30,702 mill.
License taxes . . . . $5,693 mill.
Individual income taxes . . . . $33,047 mill.
Corporate income taxes . . . . $5,333 mill.
Other taxes . . . . $1,029 mill.

Total revenue figures include items not listed separately here.
Source: U.S. Bureau of the Census.

State government expenditures, 2002

General expenditures
Total state expenditures. . . . . $184,928 mill.
Intergovernmental . . . . $74,687 mill.

Per capita expenditures
State $4,521
Average of all states $3,859
Rank among states 11

Selected direct expenditures
Education . . . . $17,289 mill.
Public welfare . . . . $23,014 mill.
Health, hospital . . . . $6,835 mill.
Highways . . . . $5,696 mill.
Police protection . . . . $1,132 mill.
Corrections . . . . $5,334 mill.
Natural resources . . . . $2,977 mill.
Parks and recreation . . . . $537 mill.
Government administration . . . . $6,816 mill.
Interest on debt . . . . $3,405 mill.
Total direct expenditures. . . . . $83,548 mill.

Totals include items not listed separately.
Source: U.S. Census Bureau.

POLITICS

Governors since statehood
D = Democrat; R = Republican; O = other;
(r) resigned; (d) died in office; (i) removed from office

Peter H. Burnett (D) . . . . (r) 1849-1851
John McDougal (D) 1851-1852
John Bigler (D) 1852-1856
John Neely Johnson (O) 1856-1858
John B. Weller (D) 1858-1860
Milton S. Latham (D) . . . . (r) 1860-1860
John G. Downey (D) 1860-1862
Leland Stanford (R) 1862-1863
Frederick F. Low (O) 1863-1867
Henry H. Haight (D) 1867-1871
Newton Booth (R) . . . . (r) 1871-1875
Romualdo Pacheco (R) 1875-1875
William Irwin (D) 1875-1880
George C. Perkins (R) 1880-1883
George Stoneman (D) 1883-1887
Washington Bartlett (D) . . . . (d) 1887-1887
Robert W. Waterman (R) 1887-1891
Henry H. Markham (R) 1891-1895
James H. Budd (D) 1895-1899
Henry T. Gage (R) 1899-1903
George C. Pardee (R) 1903-1907
James N. Gillette (R) 1907-1911
Hiram W. Johnson (R) . . . . (r) 1911-1917
William D. Stephens (R) 1917-1923
Friend W. Richardson (R) 1923-1927
Clement C. Young (R) 1927-1931
James Rolph, Jr. (R) . . . . (d) 1931-1934

Frank F. Merriam (R) 1934-1939
Culbert L. Olson (D) 1939-1943
Earl Warren (R) . . . . (r) 1943-1953
Goodwin J. Knight (R) 1953-1959
Edmund G. ("Pat") Brown (D) 1959-1967
Ronald W. Reagan (R) 1967-1975
Edmund G. ("Jerry") Brown, Jr. (D) 1975-1983
George Deukmejian (R) 1983-1991
Pete Wilson (R) 1991-1999
Gray Davis (D) . . . . (i) 1999-2003
Arnold Schwarzenegger (R) 2003-

Composition of congressional delegations, 1989-2007

	Dem	Rep	Total
House of Representatives			
101st Congress, 1989			
State delegates	27	18	45
Total U.S.	259	174	433
102d Congress, 1991			
State delegates	26	19	45
Total U.S.	267	167	434
103d Congress, 1993			
State delegates	30	22	52
Total U.S.	258	176	434
104th Congress, 1995			
State delegates	29	23	52
Total U.S.	197	236	433
105th Congress, 1997			
State delegates	28	24	52
Total U.S.	206	228	434
106th Congress, 1999			
State delegates	28	24	52
Total U.S.	211	222	433
107th Congress, 2001			
State delegates	31	20	51
Total U.S.	211	221	432
108th Congress, 2003			
State delegates	33	20	53
Total U.S.	205	229	434
109th Congress, 2005			
State delegates	33	20	53
Total U.S.	202	231	433
110th Congress, 2007			
State delegates	34	19	53
Total U.S.	233	202	435
Senate			
101st Congress, 1989			
State delegates	1	1	2
Total U.S.	55	45	100

(continued)

	Dem	Rep	Total
102d Congress, 1991			
State delegates	1	1	2
Total U.S.	56	44	100
103d Congress, 1993			
State delegates	2	0	2
Total U.S.	57	43	100
104th Congress, 1995			
State delegates	2	0	2
Total U.S.	46	53	99
105th Congress, 1997			
State delegates	2	0	2
Total U.S.	45	55	100
106th Congress, 1999			
State delegates	2	0	2
Total U.S.	45	54	99
107th Congress, 2001			
State delegates	2	0	2
Total U.S.	50	50	100
108th Congress, 2003			
State delegates	2	0	2
Total U.S.	48	51	99
109th Congress, 2005			
State delegates	2	0	2
Total U.S.	44	55	99
110th Congress, 2007			
State delegates	2	0	2
Total U.S.	49	49	98

Figures are for starts of first sessions. Totals are for Democrat (Dem.) and Republican (Rep.) members only. House membership totals under 435 and Senate totals under 100 reflect vacancies and seats held by independent party members. When the 110th Congress opened, the Senate's two independent members caucused with the Democrats, giving the Democrats control of the Senate.

Source: U.S. Congress, *Congressional Directory.*

Composition of state legislature, 1990-2006

	Democrats	Republicans
State Assembly (80 seats)		
1990	47	33
1992	47	33
1994	39	40
1996	43	37
1998	47	32
2000	46	32
2002	48	32
2004	48	32
2006	48	32
State Senate (40 seats)		
1990	25	13
1992	21	16
1994	21	17
1996	25	15
1998	25	15
2000	25	15
2002	25	15
2004	25	15
2006	25	15

Figures for total seats may include independents and minor party members. Numbers reflect results of elections in listed years; elected members usually take their seats in the years that follow.

Source: Council of State Governments; *State Elective Officials and the Legislatures.*

Voter participation in presidential elections, 2000 and 2004

	2000	2004
Voting age population		
State	24,728,000	26,297,000
Total United States	209,831,000	220,377,000
State share of U.S. total	11.78	11.93
Rank among states	1	1
Portion of voting age population casting votes		
State	44.3%	47.2%
United States	50.3%	55.5%
Rank among states	45	48

Population figures are rounded to nearest thousand and include all residents, regardless of eligibility to vote.

Source: U.S. Census Bureau.

HEALTH AND MEDICAL CARE

Medical professionals
Physicians in 2003 and nurses in 2001

	U.S.	State
Physicians in 2003		
Total	774,849	92,470
Share of U.S. total		11.88%
Rate	266	261
Rank		18
Nurses in 2001		
Total	2,262,020	185,550
Share of U.S. total		8.20%
Rate	793	536
Rank		49

Rates are numbers of physicians and nurses per 100,000 resident population; ranks are based on rates.
Source: American Medical Association, *Physician Characteristics and Distribution in the U.S.;* U.S. Department of Health and Human Services, Health Resources and Services Administration.

Health insurance coverage, 2003

	State	U.S.
Total persons covered	28,895,000	243,320,000
Total persons not covered	6,499,000	44,961,000
Portion not covered	18.4%	15.6%
Rank among states	9	—
Children not covered	1,196,000	8,373,000
Portion not covered	12.5%	11.4%
Rank among states	13	—

Totals are rounded to nearest thousand. Ranks are from the highest to the lowest percentages of persons *not* insured.
Source: U.S. Census Bureau, Current Population Reports.

AIDS, syphilis, and tuberculosis cases, 2003

Disease	U.S. cases	State cases	Rank
AIDS	44,232	5,967	1
Syphilis	34,270	4,202	1
Tuberculosis	14,874	3,227	1

Source: U.S. Centers for Disease Control and Prevention.

Cigarette smoking, 2003
Residents over age 18 who smoke

	U.S.	State	Rank
All smokers	22.1%	16.8%	49
Male smokers	24.8%	20.5%	42
Female smokers	20.3%	13.2%	49

Cigarette smokers are defined as persons who reported having smoked at least 100 cigarettes during their lifetimes and who currently smoked at least occasionally.
Source: U.S. Centers for Disease Control and Prevention, *Morbidity and Mortality Weekly Report,* 53, no. 44 (November 12, 2004).

HOUSING

Home ownership rates, 1985-2004

	1985	1990	1995	2000	2004
State	54.2%	53.8%	55.4%	57.1%	59.7%
Total U.S.	63.9%	63.9%	64.7%	67.4%	69.0%
Rank among states	48	49	48	48	49

Net change in state home ownership rate,
1985-2004 . . . . +5.5%
Net change in U.S. home ownership rate,
1985-2004 . . . . +5.1%

Percentages represent the proportion of owner households to total occupied households.
Source: U.S. Census Bureau, 2006.

Home sales, 2000-2004
In thousands of units

Existing home sales	2000	2002	2003	2004
State sales	573.5	565.1	577.6	610.1
Total U.S. sales	5,171	5,631	6,183	6,784
State share of U.S. total	11.09%	10.04%	9.34%	8.99%
Sales rank among states	1	1	1	1

Units include single-family homes, condos, and co-ops.
Source: National Association of Realtors, Washington, D.C., *Real Estate Outlook: Market Trends & Insights.*

Values of owner-occupied homes, 2003

	State	U.S.
Total units	5,921,000	58,809,000
Value of units		
Under $100,000	5.1%	29.6%
$100,000-199,999	17.8%	36.9%
$200,000 or more	77.1%	33.5%
Median value	$334,426	$142,275
Rank among all states 1		

Units are owner-occupied one-family houses whose numbers are
  rounded to nearest thousand. Data are extrapolated from
  survey samples.
Source: U.S. Census Bureau, American Community Survey.

EDUCATION

Public school enrollment, 2002

Prekindergarten through grade 8
State enrollment 4,529,000
Total U.S. enrollment. 34,135,000
State share of U.S. total. 13.27%

Grades 9 through 12
State enrollment 1,828,000
Total U.S. enrollment. 14,067,000
State share of U.S. total. 12.99%

Enrollment rates
State public school enrollment rate. 92.6%
Overall U.S. rate 90.4%
Rank among states in 2002. 10
Rank among states in 1995. 24

Enrollment figures (which include unclassified students) are
  rounded to nearest thousand pupils during fall school term.
  Enrollment rates are based on enumerated resident population
  estimate for July 1, 2002.
Source: U.S. National Center for Education Statistics.

Public college finances, 2003-2004

FTE enrollment in public institutions of higher education
Students in state institutions 1,623,500
Students in all U.S. public institutions 9,916,600
State share of U.S. total 16.37
Rank among states 1

**State and local government appropriations for higher
  education**
State appropriation per FTE $6,103
National average $5,716
Rank among states 15
State & local tax revenue going to higher
  education 9.7%

FTE = full-time equivalent in public postsecondary programs,
  including summer sessions; student numbers are rounded to
  nearest hundred. Funding figures for 2003-2004 academic year
  include financial aid to students in state public institutions and
  exclude money for research, agriculture experiment stations,
  teaching hospitals, and medical schools; figures are rounded to
  nearest thousand dollars.
Source: Higher Education Executive Officers, Denver, Colorado.

TRANSPORTATION AND TRAVEL

Highway mileage, 2003

Interstate highways	2,458
Other freeways and expressways	1,434
Arterial roads.	27,133
Collector roads.	32,074
Local roads	106,450
Urban roads	85,622
Rural roads.	83,927
Total state mileage	169,549
U.S. total	3,974,107
State share	4.27%
Rank among states	2

Note that combined urban and rural road mileage matches the
  total of the other categories.
Source: U.S. Federal Highway Administration.

Motor vehicle registrations and driver licenses, 2003

Vehicle registrations	State	U.S.	Share	Rank
Autos, trucks, buses	30,248,000	231,390,000	13.07%	1
Autos only	18,699,000	135,670	13.78%	1
Motorcycles	547,000	5,328,000	10.27%	1
Driver licenses	22,657,000	196,166,000	11.55%	1

Figures, which do not include vehicles owned by military services,
  are rounded to the nearest thousand. Figures for automobiles
  include taxis.
Source: U.S. Federal Highway Administration.

Domestic travel expenditures, 2003

Spending by U.S. residents on overnight trips and
day trips of at least 50 miles from home

Total expenditures within state . . . . $61.08 bill.
Total expenditures within U.S. . . . . $490.87 bill.
State share of U.S. total 12.4%
Rank among states 1

Source: Travel Industry Association of America.

Retail gasoline prices, 2003-2007

Average price per gallon at the pump

Year	U.S.	State
2003	$1.267	$1.598
2004	$1.316	$1.641
2005	$1.644	$1.818
2007	$2.298	$2.693

Excise tax per gallon in 2004 . . . . 18.0¢
Rank among all states in 2007 prices 2

Prices are averages of all grades of gasoline sold at the pump
during March months in 2003-2005 and during February, 2007.
Averages for 2006, during which prices rose higher, are not
available.
Source: U.S. Energy Information Agency, *Petroleum Marketing
Monthly* (2003-2005 data); American Automobile Association
(2007 data).

CRIME AND LAW ENFORCEMENT

State and local police officers, 2000-2004

	2000	2002	2004
Total officers			
U.S.	654,601	665,555	675,734
State	69,113	74,174	73,864*
*Net change, 2000-2004			+6.87%
Officers per 1,000 residents			
U.S.	2.33	2.31	2.30
State	2.04	2.12	2.06
State rank	27	24	25

Totals include state and local police and sheriffs.
Source: Carsey Institute, University of New Hampshire.

Crime rates, 2003

Incidents per 100,000 residents

Crimes	State	U.S.
Violent crimes		
Total incidents	579	475
Murder	7	6
Forcible rape	28	32
Robbery	180	142
Aggravated assault	365	295
Property crimes		
Total incidents	3,424	3,588
Burglary	683	741
Larceny/theft	2,061	2,415
Motor vehicle theft	680	433
All crimes	4,003	4,063

Source: U.S. Federal Bureau of Investigation, *Crime in the United
States,* annual.

State prison populations, 1980-2003

	State	U.S.	State share
1980	24,569	305,458	8.04%
1990	97,309	708,393	13.74%
1996	146,049	1,025,624	14.24%
2000	163,001	1,391,261	11.72%
2003	164,487	1,470,045	11.19%

State figures exclude prisoners in federal penitentiaries.
Source: U.S. Bureau of Justice Statistics, *Prisoners in 2003.*

Colorado

Location: Rocky Mountains

Area and rank: 103,730 square miles (268,660 square kilometers); 104,100 square miles (269,619 square kilometers) including water; eighth largest state in area

Coastline: none

Population and rank: 4,601,000 (2004); twenty-second largest state in population

Capital and largest city: Denver (554,636 people in 2000 census)

Became territory: February 28, 1861

Entered Union and rank: August 1, 1876; thirty-eighth state

Present constitution adopted: 1876

Counties: 63

State name: "Colorado" is derived from the Spanish for "ruddy" or "red"

State nickname: Centennial State

Motto: *Nil sine numine* (Nothing without providence)

State flag: Blue and white stripes with red letter C and yellow disk in center

Highest point: Mount Elbert—14,433 feet (4,399 meters)

Lowest point: Arkansas River—3,350 feet (1,021 meters)

Highest recorded temperature: 118 degrees Fahrenheit (48 degrees Celsius)— Bennett, 1888

Lowest recorded temperature: −61 degrees Fahrenheit (−52 degrees Celsius)— Maybell, 1985

State song: "Where the Columbines Grow"

State tree: Colorado blue spruce

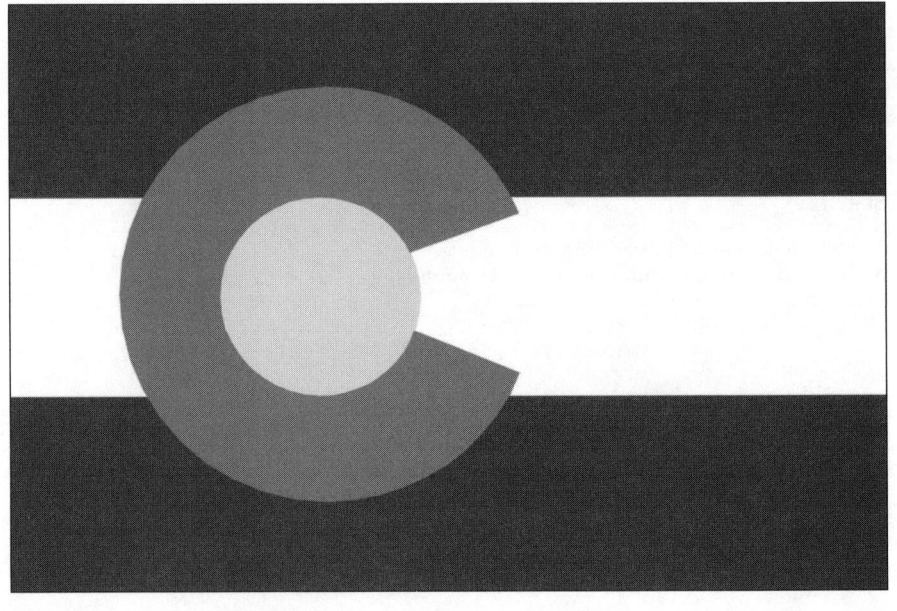

State flower: Rocky Mountain columbine

State bird: Lark bunting

State fish: Greenback cutthroat trout

State animal: Rocky Mountain bighorn sheep

National parks: Black Canyon of the Gunnison, Mesa Verde, Rocky Mountain

State capitol building in Denver. (Denver Metro Convention & Visitors Bureau)

Colorado History

The history of Colorado is marked by its geographical features, divided as it is by the Rocky Mountains, with rugged territory lying to the west and agriculturally productive plains to the east. Mining in the central and western parts of the state was influential in its early history; while agriculture, and its thirst for water in the parched eastern plains, was influential in later decades. Colorado's mountainous terrain has attracted generations of tourists, who flock to winter and summer recreational attractions.

Early History. The earliest inhabitants of the area were nomadic hunters, around 10,000 B.C.E. About the first century C.E., the southwestern area of the state was populated by a people known as the Basket Makers. By 800, the Cliff Dwellers had established their civilization in the state's mesa country. From 1000 the civilization of the Cliff Dwellers flourished, but around 1300, for unknown reasons, it died out.

Though their origins are unknown, many other Native American peoples populated today's Colorado when whites arrived. A number of Apache bands raided Colorado territory, but only one such band, the Jicarilla, lived permanently in Colorado and its environs, mainly in the southeastern portion. Bannock and Shoshone tribes roamed over the northwest corner of the state. The Cheyenne, Arapaho, and Comanche tribes hunted and made war in eastern areas, as did the Kiowa and the Kiowa Apaches, who always accompanied them. The Navahos occasionally entered the state from New Mexico, but the Ute occupied the state's entire central and western portions. Most of the Pueblos inhabited the state's southwest, in Colorado's famous cliff ruins, sometimes intermarrying with the Utes.

Spanish Exploration. In the sixteenth century the Spanish became the area's first European explorers. Searching for rich cities of gold, Francisco Vásquez de Coronado arrived in 1541. During the next two-and-a-half centuries, a number of Spanish explorers traversed

Last occupied during the thirteenth century, the Cliff Palace ruins in Mesa Verde National Park contain some of the oldest and best-preserved pre-Columbian dwellings in North America. (PhotoDisc)

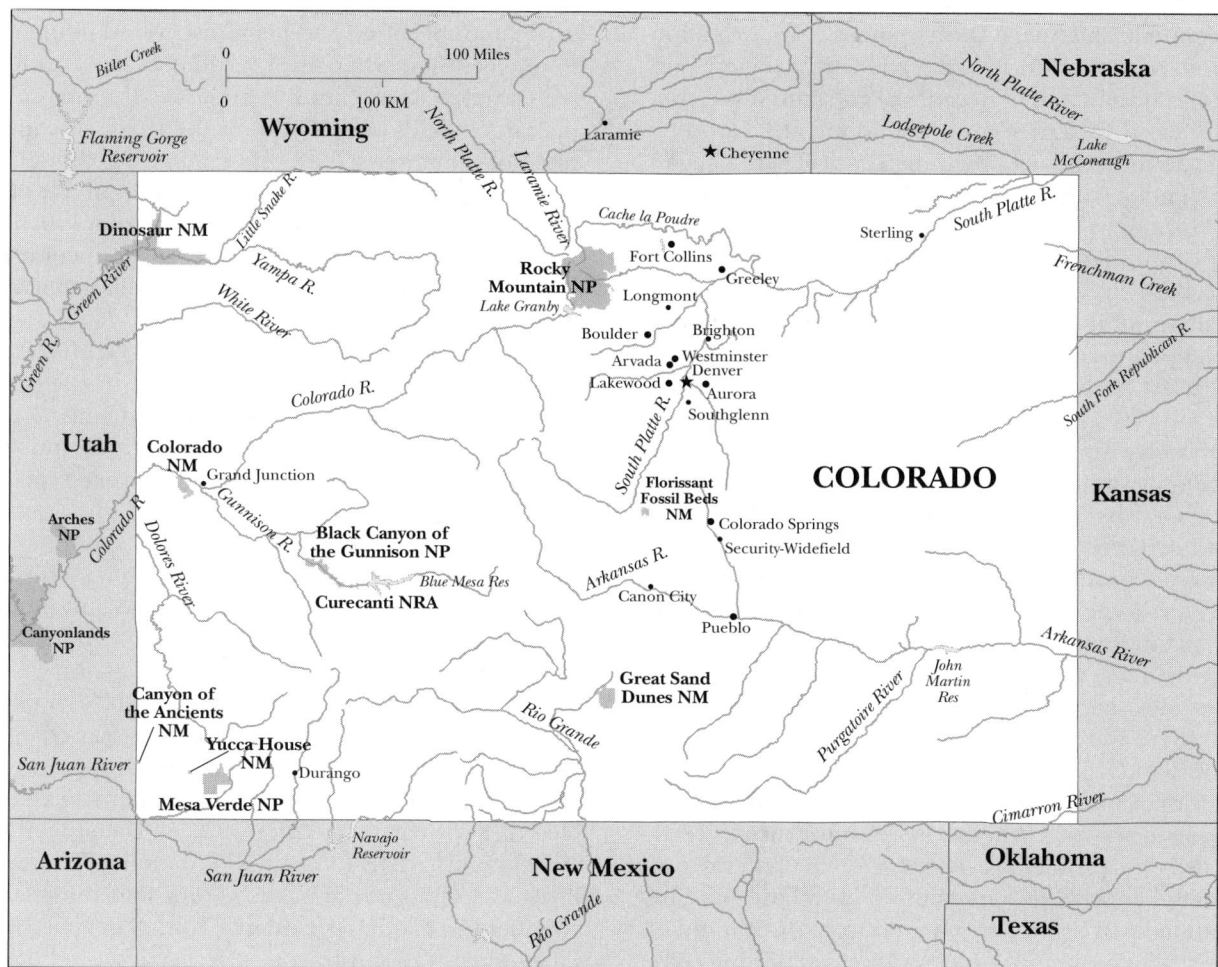

parts of what became Colorado, among them Juan de Ulibarri, who claimed the territory for the Spanish crown.

American Exploration and Settlement. In 1803, parts of Colorado were sold to the United States when the administration of Thomas Jefferson concluded the Louisiana Purchase with France. Thereafter, the territory was explored by a series of American expeditions: in 1806 by Zebulon Pike, for whom Pikes Peak is named; in 1820 by Stephen Long; from 1842 to 1853 by John C. Frémont; and in 1853 by the Gunnison-Beckwith expedition. In 1833, Bent's Fort, the first permanent American settlement in Colorado, was completed. The area was also inhabited by various nomadic Indian tribes, as well as by American "mountain men," who lived by trapping and fur trading. Among them were those who became the subjects of American folklore, such as Kit Carson and Jim Bridger.

From Territory to Statehood. In 1848, Mexico ceded part of Colorado to the United States with the Treaty of Guadelupe Hidalgo, which ended the Mexican War. Two years later, a portion of the western area of modern Colorado became part of Utah Territory. In 1854, some eastern areas were incorporated into Kansas and Nebraska Territories. In 1858, gold was found in Colorado, first at Cherry Creek, near Denver. The next year, a rich vein was discovered in Central City. These finds brought thousands of adventurers in search of a new life, who adopted the slogan "Pikes Peak or Bust." The miners ignored the claims of American Indians to the land that had been deeded to them in past treaties. In place of Indian lands, newcomers attempted to set up a new, so-called Jefferson Territory, which Congress did not approve. After Kansas became a state in 1861, Colorado Territory was organized, with much the same boundaries as the subsequent state.

Colorado entered the Civil War on the Union side in 1861 and was the scene of significant fighting in the western phases of the war. Other notable events of these early years were wars between whites and American Indians, and a number of gold and silver strikes. By the late 1860's new mining methods brought both further prosperity and more immigration from the East. The increased population was a key factor in the territory's seeking statehood. After several failures, statehood was finally attained in 1876.

Economic and Social Development. The formation of modern Colorado was preceded by a society and economy dominated by decades of gold and silver mining followed by agricultural development. The same year statehood was achieved, the Leadville area began to surrender its millions of dollars of gold and silver ore. More than a decade later, Cripple Creek was the scene of another notable gold strike. This discovery was especially welcome, because the free coinage of silver sent silver mining into a tailspin that the Cripple Creek find helped to offset.

The last of the battles with American Indian tribes came in 1879, when the Utes rebelled. In the last uprising by Native Americans in the American West, the Utes massacred Nathan Meeker, an Indian agent, and his workers in what would become the town of Meeker, in the White River Valley in northwestern Colorado. This massacre resulted in the Utes' forcible removal to eastern Utah. Some Native Americans, however, appear to have maintained their presence, though in modest numbers. For example, in 1845, the Jicarilla Apaches were said to number 800. According to the census of 1910, there were 694, and in 1937, the Report of the U.S. Indian Office said there were 714.

If Indian wars were at an end, other conflicts were not long in arriving. When a depression struck in 1893, serious labor problems erupted after the federal government canceled its agreement to purchase substantial amounts of silver. Silver miners were thrown out of work; strikes by miners, now employees of mining companies, not independent adventurers, occurred in silver mines in 1893-1894 and 1903-1904 and in coal mines in 1913-1914. These strikes were settled with military force, a graphic reminder that the days of the romantic West were over.

The Twentieth Century. The opening of the twentieth century saw the beginning of the natural conservation movement that attracted tourists. In 1906, Congress created Mesa Verde National Park to preserve the remains of ancient Indian culture, and nine years later Rocky Mountain National Park was established. During these years, the economy depended on agriculture, as Colorado became the most irrigated state in the Union. Canning and other industries grew along with agriculture. In 1899, Colorado's first sugar beet factory began operations at Grand Junction; seven years later the U.S. Mint opened in Denver.

The advent of another industry, however, augured well for the future, when oil production and refining became prominent sources of income. With the plentiful availability of oil throughout the nation came the advent of the automobile. America's love affair with the automobile, coupled with the unsurpassed beauty of western Colorado, gave rise to the state's considerable tourist industry, which developed rapidly after World War I. Colorado, moreover, has its own oil sources.

Small amounts of oil had been discovered in the nineteenth century, when in 1862 the first oil well was drilled near Canon City. But in the next century more, and larger, fields were found. By the 1920's, the importance of oil surpassed all other minerals, though not until after World War II and the development of the Rangley oil field in 1946 in northwest Colorado did oil production approach its zenith. Oil production rose from 1.7 million barrels in 1940 to 23 million barrels in 1950.

Like the rest of the nation, Colorado suffered considerably during the Great Depression of the 1930's. World War II lifted the state from its doldrums, as its oil and minerals were in great demand. Military and other federal installations opened in several areas, especially around Denver, the state's capital.

Postwar Developments. Colorado's population, which had grown to 800,000 in 1910, grew swiftly after World War II. With population increase and demand for expansion of agriculture came the need for water. Irrigation had begun in the nineteenth century. Large irrigation projects existed from the 1860's, but after the war a series of irrigation projects was carried out. In 1947, the Alva B. Adams Tunnel, which carries water eastward through the Rocky Mountains, was completed. Two years later Cherry Creek Dam, near Denver, was finished. In 1959, the Colorado-Big Thompson Project, a series of dams, reservoirs, and tunnels, was completed, of which the Adams Tunnel is a part. More water-conservation projects were carried out between the 1950's and the 1980's, such as the Colorado River Storage Project, begun in 1956, and the Frying Pan-Arkansas project, begun during the early 1960's and completed in 1985.

Other significant postwar changes in the state's economy changed the complexion of its society. Manufacturing replaced agriculture in importance by the mid-1950's. Federal agencies sank important new roots in the state, opening the laboratory of the National Bureau of Standards in Boulder in 1954, the United States Air Force Academy in 1958, and the North American Air Defense Command in 1966, sunk some twelve hundred feet deep in Cheyenne Mountain.

By the 1990's Colorado had emerged as both a significant area of urban development below the eastern slopes of the Rocky Mountains and one of the nation's most popular recreation areas. The upscale mountain community of Vail, for example, serves as an icon of winter sports, and the state's national parks and other scenic wonders draw millions of vacationers each year. At the same time, the nation's academic life benefited from its universities, and several of its political figures reached national stature. If in its early decades, Colorado, seemingly connected more to the West, felt marginal to powerful eastern states, a century after its admittance to the Union the state became fully integrated into the nation's life. Signs of this integration include its thriving urban life, especially in its capital and environs; its significant defense installations; and its sports teams, such as those in professional baseball, basketball, and football.

At the end of the twentieth century, Colorado's prosperity continued. Population increase gained the state a further representative in Congress after the census in 2000. Greater Denver experienced more than 30 percent growth over the previous decade; more than one third of the state was now Hispanic. In 2000, the state's reputation as a tourist destination was enhanced when President Bill Clinton created a new national monument, Canyon of the Ancients, in Colorado's southwest. Natural forces, however, did not always cooperate with the state's upbeat economic life. Wildfires bedeviled the state throughout the first half of the new decade; those of 2000 were called the "worst in a generation."

Headline Cases. Tragedy also touched the state. On April 20, 1999, the nation was shocked when two disturbed high school students, Eric Harris and Dylan Klebold, opened fire on classmates and faculty at Columbine High School in Littleton. The students, who timed the attack to coincide with Adolf Hitler's birthday, killed twelve students and one teacher in the span of sixteen minutes, an act caught on the school's video cameras. Much soul-searching ensued, but the affair was not concluded before two more Columbine students were slain at a restaurant near the school on Valentine's Day, 2000, and another Columbine student took his life in May. The school library, where most of the shooting took place, was demolished and another opened later in its place in June, 2001.

The state also made national headlines for several months when, in July, 2003, a hotel employee in Eagle, a small town near Vail, accused a famous basketball player of rape. A complex set of legal actions began, including an indictment of Kobe Bryant of the Los Angeles Lakers on a sexual assault charge. The case reached a climax just before a trial was to start, when the accuser decided not to testify, and Bryant issued a quasi-apologetic statement. A civil lawsuit by the accuser eventuated in an out-of-court settlement of unspecified terms.

Finally, the state's best-known institution of higher learning, the University of Colorado at Boulder, became the focus of national attention in January, 2005, when the public became aware of controversial statements made by professor Ward Churchill about the victims of the September 11, 2001, terrorist attacks on the World Trade Center in New York. Churchill said that they were no more than "little Eichmanns," a reference to a Nazi bureaucrat who was a principal organizer of the Holocaust of the Jews during World War II. A uni-

With more than one-half million residents, Denver is both Colorado's capital and its largest city. (PhotoDisc)

versity investigation accused the professor, who refused to retract his remarks, of plagiarism and other academic misdeeds but stopped short of recommending that he be fired. His removal, however, which had been called for by Colorado's governor, remained a possibility.

Political Developments. Politically, Colorado moved from being a more Republican state to a centrist position during the early twenty-first century. In 2003, its congressional representation included two Republican U.S. senators and five of seven Republican members of the House of Representatives. By 2006, however, it had one senator of each party and four Republicans and three Democrats in the House. Governor William F. "Bill" Owens, a Republican, was reelected in 2002.

Charles F. Bahmueller
Updated by the Editor

Colorado Time Line

c. 1000 c.e.	Indian cliff dwellers live in southwestern part of state.
1500's	Spanish explorers searching for legendary golden cities travel through parts of the state.
1541	Spaniard Francisco Vásquez de Coronado probably crosses southeastern corner of the state.
1700	French explorers reach the Rocky Mountains.
1706	Juan de Uribarri, leader of a Spanish expedition to capture runaway Indian slaves, claims the area for Philip V of Spain.
c. 1776	Two Franciscan monks explore much of western and southwestern areas seeking a route to the California missions.
1779	Juan Bautista de Anza explores territory for Spain.
1803	Portions of Colorado become part of the United States through the Louisiana Purchase.
1806	Zebulon Pike explores Pikes Peak.
1820	Stephen Long explores western boundary of Colorado.

Nineteenth century painter Frederic Remington's fanciful depiction of Coronado's march through Colorado in 1541. (Library of Congress)

In 2001, INVESCO Field at Mile High replaced Mile-High Stadium as the home of the Denver Broncos and other professional sports franchises. Since the Broncos began in 1960, Denver has demonstrated exceptional levels of fan support for its teams. (©Matthew Trump)

1835	Bent's Old Fort is founded; first permanent American settlement of future state.
1842-1853	Sponsored by the federal government, John C. Frémont explores Colorado on five occasions.
1845	Portion of future state is acquired in connection with annexation of Texas.
1848	Entirety of Colorado is acquired in the Treaty of Guadalupe Hidalgo, which ended the Mexican War.
1854	Parts of Colorado are incorporated in the Kansas and Nebraska Territories.
1858	Gold is discovered at Cherry Creek, near Denver.
1858-1859	Agricultural irrigation begins.
1859	Rich gold vein is discovered in Central City; Colorado Gold Rush attracts thousands of fortune hunters.
1859	Production of gold begins; reaches peak in 1900.
1860's	Wars with American Indians take place.
Feb. 28, 1861	Colorado Territory is organized; Cheyenne tribes give up most of their lands.
1861-1865	Entering on Union side, Colorado Territory is scene of Civil War fighting.
1867	Denver becomes permanent capital.
1867	Treaty of Medicine Lodge is signed; Cheyenne and Arapaho move to Indian Territory (Oklahoma).
1870	Denver Pacific Railroad is completed to Denver.
1876	Convention meeting in Denver adopts state constitution (March), which is ratified by voters (July).
1876	Gold mining in Leadville area is especially productive.
Aug. 1, 1876	Colorado enters the Union as the thirty-eighth state.
1877	University of Colorado at Boulder is founded.
1878	Adoption of Bland-Allison Act stimulates production of silver, causing silver boom.
1879	Ute tribes, originally given most of western Colorado, are relocated after massacre of Indian agent Nathan Meeker and his colleagues.
1890's	Following rapid growth, state experiences economic depression and severe labor strife.
1891	Gold production begins at Cripple Creek mine.
Nov. 2, 1893	Women receive voting rights.
1906	U.S. Mint opens in Denver.
1906	Congress establishes Mesa Verde National Park.
Apr. 20, 1914	National Guardsmen burn a tent colony of striking Colorado Fuel and Iron Corporation miners, killing twenty; ten-day uprising follows, resulting in dispatch of federal troops.
1915	Rocky Mountain National Park is established.

(continued)

1924	Ku Klux Klan members are elected to major state offices; Klan-endorsed politicians become governor and senator.
1927	Moffat Tunnel through the Rocky Mountains is completed.
1942	Relocation center for West Coast Japanese Americans is established near Granada.
1954	Air Force Academy is authorized by Congress, with temporary quarters at Lowry Air Force Base; permanent quarters at Colorado Springs opens four years later.
1957	North American Air Defense Command (NORAD) is established in Colorado Springs.
1959	Series of dams for irrigation, known as the Colorado-Big Thompson Project, is completed.
1961	National Center for Atmospheric Research is created at Boulder.
Apr. 25, 1967	Colorado is first to pass liberal abortion laws.
1990's	Economic boom turns state's electorate toward political right.
1998	Marked Republican plurality of 120,000 voters replaces previous slight Democratic Party advantage.
Apr. 20, 1999	Two disturbed students at Columbine High School in Littleton murder twelve students and one teacher and injure twenty-four in a planned shooting attack.
June, 2002	Hayman wildfire near Denver is the largest wildfire recorded in state's history.
July 18, 2003	Basketball star Kobe Bryant is accused of raping a hotel employee in Eagle; charges are later dropped after he issues apology.
Jan., 2005	University of Colorado professor Ward Churchill becomes center of national controversy after he calls World Trade Center 9/11 victims "little Eichmanns."

Notes for Further Study

Published Sources. A standard history of Colorado is *Colorado: A History of the Centennial State* (4th ed., 2005) by Carl Abbott et al. and *Colorado History* (9th ed., 2006) by Carl Ubbelohde, Duane A. Smith, and Maxine Benson. Informal volumes of colorful incidents and facets of the state's past constitute Abott Fay's *I Never Knew That About Colorado: A Quaint Volume of Forgotten Lore* (1997) and Muriel Marshall's *Where Rivers Meet: Lore from the Colorado Frontier* (1996). Maxine Benson's *1001 Colorado Place Names* (1995) discusses place names chosen for their historical, geographical, or geological significance. A good guide to the state is *Colorado* (4th ed., 1998) by Jon Klusmire and Paul Chesley. For the state's politics and government, readers should consult Roger A. Walton's *Colorado: A Practical Guide to Its Government and Politics* (6th rev. ed., 1991) or *Cornerstones and Communities: A Historical Overview of Colorado's County Seats and Court Houses* (2001), edited by William Virden and Barbara Teel. A useful guide to the state's geography is *Colorado: A Geography* (1983) by Mel Griffiths and Lynell Rubright. Sally Crum's *People of the Red Earth: Native Americans of Colorado* (1998) uses archaeological evidence in discussing Colorado's original inhabitants.

Tourism is a large portion of the state economy, and guidebooks are often a good place to turn to get accessible history of the state. Two notable titles are *John Fielder's Best of Colorado: Photography and Text* (2002) and *Colorado Guide* (5th rev. ed., 2005) by Bruce Caughey and Dean Winstanley.

Web Resources. Those visiting the state or wishing to know more about it might begin with the state of Colorado home page (www.state.co.us). The site includes pages on points of interest; road, ski, weather, and air pollution conditions; doing business in Colorado; and information on the state's elected officials, among other topics. Colorado.com (www.colorado.com/) is another good site for travelers.

For public affairs, one can turn to Citizen's Guide to Colorado (www.state.co.us/citizens.html), published by the Colorado governor's office, which includes links both to state agencies and to nonstate resources, as well as to organizational phone listings. The U.S. Census Bureau Quickfacts (quickfacts.census.gov/qfd/states/08000.html) allows one to select any county or city in the state and view a range of related demographic statistics.

Counties

County	2000 pop.	Rank in pop.	Sq. miles	Rank in area	County	2000 pop.	Rank in pop.	Sq. miles	Rank in area
Adams	363,857	5	1,192.0	39	Bent	5,998	45	1,514.0	32
Alamosa	14,966	28	722.8	53	Boulder	291,288	6	742.5	51
Arapahoe	487,967	4	803.2	48	Chaffee	16,242	26	1,013.5	43
Archuleta	9,898	36	1,349.4	33	Cheyenne	2,231	57	1,781.5	24
Baca	4,517	51	2,555.9	11	Clear Creek	9,322	38	395.5	59

County	2000 pop.	Rank in pop.	Sq. miles	Rank in area
Conejos	8,400	39	1,287.3	34
Costilla	3,663	54	1,227.0	38
Crowley	5,518	48	789.0	49
Custer	3,503	55	738.9	52
Delta	27,834	17	1,142.2	40
Denver	554,636	1	153.3	62
Dolores	1,844	58	1,067.0	42
Douglas	175,766	9	840.2	47
Eagle	41,659	15	1,688.0	27
El Paso	19,872	24	2,126.7	19
Elbert	516,929	3	1,850.9	21
Fremont	46,145	12	1,533.0	31
Garfield	43,791	14	2,947.5	8
Gilpin	4,757	50	149.9	63
Grand	12,442	34	1,849.8	22
Gunnison	13,956	32	3,239.2	5
Hinsdale	790	62	1,117.8	41
Huerfano	7,862	41	1,590.9	30
Jackson	1,577	60	1,613.3	29
Jefferson	527,056	2	772.2	50
Kiowa	1,622	59	1,771.1	25
Kit Carson	8,011	40	2,161.0	18
La Plata	43,941	13	1,692.1	26
Lake	7,812	42	376.9	61
Larimer	251,494	7	2,601.4	9
Las Animas	15,207	27	4,773.0	1
Lincoln	6,087	44	2,586.3	10
Logan	20,504	22	1,838.6	23

County	2000 pop.	Rank in pop.	Sq. miles	Rank in area
Mesa	116,255	11	3,327.9	4
Mineral	831	61	875.8	46
Moffat	13,184	33	4,742.5	2
Montezuma	23,830	19	2,036.9	20
Montrose	33,432	16	2,240.7	16
Morgan	27,171	18	1,285.5	36
Otero	20,311	23	1,262.9	37
Ouray	3,742	53	542.1	58
Park	14,523	30	2,200.8	17
Phillips	4,480	52	687.7	54
Pitkin	14,872	29	970.2	44
Prowers	14,483	31	1,640.5	28
Pueblo	141,472	10	2,388.8	13
Rio Blanco	5,986	46	3,221.2	6
Rio Grande	12,413	35	912.6	45
Routt	19,690	25	2,361.8	15
Saguache	5,917	47	3,168.7	7
San Juan	558	63	387.5	60
San Miguel	6,594	43	1,286.5	35
Sedgwick	2,747	56	548.3	57
Summit	23,548	20	608.2	55
Teller	20,555	21	557.1	56
Washington	4,926	49	2,521.2	12
Weld	180,936	8	3,992.8	3
Yuma	9,841	37	2,366.1	14

Source: U.S. Census Bureau; National Association of Counties.

Cities

With 10,000 or more residents

Rank	City	Population	Rank	City	Population
1	Denver (capital)	554,636	27	Lafayette	23,197
2	Colorado Springs	360,890	28	Commerce City	20,991
3	Aurora	276,393	29	Brighton	20,905
4	Lakewood	144,126	30	Castle Rock	20,224
5	Fort Collins	118,652	31	Louisville	18,937
6	Arvada	102,153	32	Sherrelwood	17,657
7	Pueblo	102,121	33	Clifton	17,345
8	Westminster	100,940	34	Golden	17,159
9	Boulder	94,673	35	Pueblo West	16,899
10	Thornton	82,384	36	Canon City	15,431
11	Greeley	76,930	37	Fountain	15,197
12	Longmont	71,093	38	Cimarron Hills	15,194
13	Highlands Ranch	70,931	39	Durango	13,922
14	Loveland	50,608	40	Black Forest	13,247
15	Southglenn	43,520	41	Welby	12,973
16	Grand Junction	41,986	42	Montrose	12,344
17	Littleton	40,340	43	Federal Heights	12,065
18	Broomfield	38,272	44	Sterling	11,360
19	Wheat Ridge	32,913	45	Greenwood Village	11,035
20	Englewood	31,727	46	Fort Morgan	11,034
21	Northglenn	31,575	47	Berkley	10,743
22	Ken Caryl	30,887	48	Fort Carson	10,566
23	Security-Widefield	29,845			
24	Castlewood	25,567			
25	Columbine	24,095			
26	Parker	23,558			

Population figures are from 2000 census.

Source: U.S. Bureau of the Census.

Index to Tables

DEMOGRAPHICS

Resident state and national populations, 1970-2004

Population figures given in thousands

	State pop.	U.S. pop.	Share	Rank
1970	2,210	203,302	1.1%	30
1980	2,890	226,546	1.3%	28
1985	3,209	237,924	1.4%	26
1990	3,294	248,765	1.3%	26
1995	3,827	262,761	1.4%	25
2000	4,302	281,425	1.5%	24
2004	4,601	293,655	1.6%	22

Source: U.S. Census Bureau, Current Population Reports, 2006.

Resident population by age, 2004

Age Group	Total persons
Under 5 years	339,000
5 to 17 years	840,000
18 to 24 years	457,000
25 to 34 years	717,000
35 to 44 years	709,000
45 to 54 years	668,000
55 to 64 years	421,000
65 to 74 years	241,000
75 to 84 years	154,000
85 years and older	56,000
All age groups	4,601,000

Portion of residents 65 and older	9.8%
National rank in portion of oldest residents	47
National average	12.4%

Population figures are rounded to nearest thousand persons;
figures include armed forces personnel stationed in the state.
Source: U.S. Bureau of the Census, 2006.

Resident population by race, Hispanic origin, 2004

Category	State pop.	Share	U.S.
All residents	4,601	100.00%	100.00%
Non-Hispanic white	3,334	72.46%	67.37%
Hispanic white	820	17.82%	13.01%
Other Hispanic	59	1.28%	1.06%
African American	189	4.11%	12.77%
Native American	52	1.13%	0.96%
Asian, Pacific Islander	122	2.65%	4.37%
Two or more categories	82	1.78%	1.51%

Population figures are in thousands. Persons counted as "Hispanic" (Latino) may be of any race. Because of overlapping categories, categories may not add up to 100%. Shares in column 3 are percentages of each category within the state; these figures may be compared to the national percentages in column 4.
Source: U.S. Bureau of the Census, 2006.

Projected state population, 2000-2030

Year	Population
2000	4,302,000
2005	4,618,000
2010	4,832,000
2015	5,049,000
2020	5,279,000
2025	5,523,000
2030	5,792,000
Population increase, 2000-2030	1,490,000
Percentage increase, 2000-2030	34.7

Projections are based on data from the 2000 census.
Source: U.S. Census Bureau.

VITAL STATISTICS

Infant mortality rates, 1980-2002

	1980	1990	2000	2002
All state residents	10.1	8.8	6.2	6.1
All U.S. residents	12.6	9.2	9.4	9.1
All state white residents	9.8	7.8	5.6	5.5
All U.S. white residents	10.6	7.6	5.7	5.8
All state black residents	19.1	19.4	19.5	21.1
All U.S. black residents	22.2	18.0	14.1	14.4

Figures represent deaths per 1,000 live births of resident infants under 1 year old, exclusive of fetal deaths. Figures for all residents include members of other racial categories not listed separately.
Source: U.S. Census Bureau, *Statistical Abstract of the United States,* 2006.

Abortion rates, 1990 and 2000

	1990	2000
Total abortions	20,000	16,000
Rate per 1,000 women	23.6	15.9
U.S. rate	25.7	21.3
Rank	17	23

Numbers of abortions are rounded to nearest thousand; ranks are based on rates.
Source: U.S. Census Bureau.

Marriages and divorces, 2004

Total marriages	34,500
Rate per 1,000 population	7.5
National rate per 1,000 population	7.4
Rank among all states	22
Total divorces	20,200
Rate per 1,000 population	4.4
National rate per 1,000 population	3.7
Rank among all states	13

Figures are for all marriages and divorces performed within the state, including those of nonresidents; totals are rounded to the nearest hundred. Ranks are for highest to lowest figures; note that divorce data are not available for five states.
Source: U.S. National Center for Health Statistics, *Vital Statistics of the United States,* 2006.

Death rates by leading causes, 2002
Deaths per 100,000 resident population

Cause	State	U.S.
Heart disease	142.6	241.7
Cancer	141.7	193.2
Cerebrovascular diseases	42.5	56.4
Accidents other than motor vehicle	40.2	37.0
Motor vehicle accidents	17.3	15.7
Chronic lower respiratory diseases	41.0	43.3
Diabetes mellitus	14.6	25.4
HIV	2.3	4.9
Suicide	16.1	11.0
Homicide	4.1	6.1
All causes	648.2	847.3
Rank in overall death rate among states		48

Figures exclude nonresidents who died in the state. Causes of death follow International Classification of Diseases. Rank is from highest to lowest death rate in the United States.
Source: U.S. National Center for Health Statistics, *National Vital Statistics Report,* 2006.

ECONOMY

Gross state product, 1990-2004
In current dollars

Year	State product	Nat'l product	State share
1990	$74.2 billion	$5.67 trillion	1.31%
2000	$171.4 billion	$9.75 trillion	1.76%
2002	$181.2 billion	$10.41 trillion	1.74%
2003	$188.4 billion	$10.92 trillion	1.72%
2004	$200.0 billion	$11.65 trillion	1.72%

Source: U.S. Bureau of Economic Analysis, *Survey of Current Business,* July, 2005.

Gross state product by industry, 2003
In billions of dollars

Construction	$9.7
Manufacturing	14.8
Wholesale trade	9.9
Retail trade	13.2
Finance & insurance	12.4
Information	17.2
Professional services	15.1
Health care & social assistance	9.8
Government	20.4
Total state product	$178.3
Total U.S. product	$10,289.2
State share of U.S. total	1.73%
Rank among all states	21

Total figures include industries not listed separately. Amounts are in chained 2000 dollars.

Source: U.S. Bureau of Economic Analysis, *Survey of Current Business,* July, 2005.

Personal income per capita, 1990-2004
In current dollars

	1990	2000	2004
Per capita income	$19,575	$33,370	$36,063
U.S. average	$19,477	$29,845	$32,937
Rank among states	18	7	7

Source: U.S. Bureau of Economic Analysis, *Survey of Current Business,* April, 2005.

Energy consumption, 2001
In trillions of British thermal units (BTU), except as noted

Total energy consumption

Total state energy consumption	1,270
Total U.S. energy consumption	96,275
State share of U.S. total	1.32%
Rank among states	27

Per capita consumption (In millions of BTU)

Total state per capita consumption	287
Total U.S. per capita consumption	338
Rank among states	39

End-use sectors

Residential	303
Commercial	287
Industrial	294
Transportation	386

Sources of energy

Petroleum	462
Natural gas	385
Coal	400
Hydroelectric power	13
Nuclear electric power	0

Figures for totals include categories not listed separately.
Source: U.S. Energy Information Administration, *State Energy Data Report,* 2001.

Nonfarm employment by sectors, 2004

Total	2,179,000
Construction	151,000
Manufacturing	155,000
Trade, transportation, utilities	407,000
Information	81,000
Finance, insurance, real estate	155,000
Professional & business services	299,000
Education & health services	219,000
Leisure, hospitality, arts, organizations	252,000
Other services, including repair & maintenance	87,000
Government	359,000

Figures are rounded to nearest thousand persons. "Total" includes mining and natural resources, not listed separately.
Source: U.S. Bureau of Labor Statistics, 2006.

Foreign exports, 1990-2004
In millions of dollars

Year	State	U.S.	State share
1990	2,274	394,045	0.58%
1996	4,883	624,767	0.78%
1997	5,120	688,896	0.74%
2000	6,593	712,055	0.84%
2003	6,109	724,006	0.90%
2004	6,651	769,332	0.86%

Rank among all states in 2004 27

U.S. total does not include U.S. dependencies.
Source: U.S. Census Bureau, *U.S. Merchandise Trade,* series FT 900, 2000; U.S. Census Bureau, *U.S. International Trade in Goods and Services,* Series FT 900, 2005.

LAND USE

Federally owned land, 2003
Areas in acres

	State	U.S.	State share
Total area	66,486,000	2,271,343,000	2.93%
Nonfederal land	43,311,000	1,599,584,000	2.71%
Federal land	23,175,000	671,759,000	3.45%
Federal share	34.9%	29.6%	—

Areas are rounded to nearest thousand acres. Figures for federally owned land do not include trust properties.
Source: U.S. General Services Administration, *Federal Real Property Profile,* 2006.

Land use, 1997
In acres, rounded to nearest thousand

Total surface area	66,625,000
Total nonfederal rural land.	40,850,000
Percentage rural land	61.3%
Cropland	8,770,000
Conservation Reserve Program (CRP*) land. . .	1,890,000
Pastureland	1,211,000
Rangeland	24,574,000
Forestland.	3,442,000
Other rural land	964,000

*CRP is a federal program begun in 1985 to assist private landowners to convert highly erodible cropland to vegetative cover for ten years. Note that some categories of land overlap.
Source: U.S. Department of Agriculture, Natural Resources and Conservation Service, and Iowa State University, Statistical Laboratory, *Summary Report, 1997 National Resources Inventory,* revised December, 2000.

Farms and crop acreage, 2004

	State	U.S.	Share	Rank
Farms	31,000	2,113,000	1.47%	28
Acres (millions)	31	937	3.31%	11
Acres per farm	1,000	443	—	9

Source: U.S. Department of Agriculture, National Agricultural Statistics Service. Numbers of farms are rounded to nearest thousand units; acreage figures are rounded to nearest million. Rankings, including ties, are based on rounded figures.

GOVERNMENT AND FINANCE

Units of local government, 2002

	State	Total U.S.	Rank
All local governments	1,928	87,525	16
Counties	62	3,034	24
Municipalities	270	19,429	29
Townships	0	16,504	—
School districts	182	13,506	24
Special districts	1,414	35,052	7

Only 48 states have county governments, 20 states have township governments ("towns" in New England, Minnesota, New York, and Wisconsin), and 46 states have school districts. Special districts encompass such functions as natural resources, fire protection, and housing and community development.
Source: U.S. Census Bureau, *Census of Governments.*

State government revenue, 2002

Total revenue	$11,809 mill.
General revenue	$13,875 mill.
Per capita revenue	$3,085
U.S. per capita average	$3,689
Rank among states	40
Intergovernment revenue	
Total	$3,866 mill.
From federal government	$3,806 mill.
Charges and miscellaneous	
Total	$3,086 mill.
Current charges	$1,471 mill.
Misc. general income	$1,615 mill.
Insurance trust revenue	−$2,065 mill.
Taxes	
Total	$6,923 mill.
Per capita taxes	$1,538
Rank among states	42
Property taxes	(nil)
Sales taxes	$2,835 mill.
License taxes	$278 mill.
Individual income taxes	$3,476 mill.
Corporate income taxes	$205 mill.
Other taxes	$130 mill.

Total revenue figures include items not listed separately here.
Source: U.S. Bureau of the Census.

State government expenditures, 2002

General expenditures
Total state expenditures . . . . $16,823 mill.
Intergovernmental . . . . $4,295 mill.

Per capita expenditures
State $3,257
Average of all states $3,859
Rank among states 44

Selected direct expenditures
Education. . . . . $3,009 mill.
Public welfare . . . . $2,283 mill.
Health, hospital . . . . $894 mill.
Highways . . . . $1,134 mill.
Police protection. . . . . $100 mill.
Corrections. $639 mill.
Natural resources . . . . $177 mill.
Parks and recreation . . . . $61 mill.
Government administration. . . . . $422 mill.
Interest on debt . . . . $326 mill.
Total direct expenditures. . . . . $10,366 mill.

Totals include items not listed separately.
Source: U.S. Census Bureau.

POLITICS

Governors since statehood
D = Democrat; R = Republican; O = other;
(r) resigned; (d) died in office; (i) removed from office

John L. Routt (R) 1876-1879
Frederick W. Pitkin (R) 1879-1883
James B. Grant (D) 1883-1885
Benjamin H. Eaton (R) 1885-1887
Alva Adams (D) 1887-1889
Job A. Cooper (R) 1889-1891
John L. Routt (R) 1891-1893
Davis H. Waite (D) 1893-1895
Albert W. McIntire (R) 1895-1897
Alva Adams (D) 1897-1899
Charles S. Thomas (O) 1899-1901
James B. Orman (O). 1901-1903
James H. Peabody (R) 1903-1905
Alva Adams (D) . . . . (r) 1905
James H. Peabody (R) 1905
Jesse F. McDonald (R) 1905-1907
Henry A. Buchtel (R) 1907-1909
John F. Shafroth (D). 1909-1913
Elias M. Ammons (D) 1913-1915
George A. Carlson (R) 1915-1917
Julius C. Gunter (D) 1917-1919
Oliver H. Shoup (R) 1919-1923
William E. Sweet (D) 1923-1925
Clarence J. Morley (R) 1925-1927
William H. Adams (D). 1927-1933

Edwin C. Johnson (D) . . . . (r) 1933-1937
Ray H. Talbot (D) 1937
Teller Ammons (D) 1937-1939
Ralph L. Carr (R) 1939-1943
John C. Vivian (R) 1943-1947
William L. Knous (D) . . . . (r) 1947-1950
Walter W. Johnson (D) 1950-1951
Daniel I. J. Thornton (R) 1951-1955
Edwin C. Johnson (D) 1955-1957
Stephen L. R. McNichols (D) 1957-1963
John A. Love (R) . . . . (r) 1963-1973
John D. Vanderhoof (R) 1973-1975
Richard D. Lamm (D) 1975-1987
Roy Romer (D). 1987-1999
Bill Owens (R) 1999-2007
Bill Ritter (D) 2007-

Composition of congressional delegations, 1989-2007

	Dem	Rep	Total
House of Representatives			
101st Congress, 1989			
State delegates	3	3	6
Total U.S.	259	174	433
102d Congress, 1991			
State delegates	3	3	6
Total U.S.	267	167	434
103d Congress, 1993			
State delegates	2	4	6
Total U.S.	258	176	434
104th Congress, 1995			
State delegates	2	4	6
Total U.S.	197	236	433
105th Congress, 1997			
State delegates	2	4	6
Total U.S.	206	228	434
106th Congress, 1999			
State delegates	2	4	6
Total U.S.	211	222	433
107th Congress, 2001			
State delegates	2	4	6
Total U.S.	211	221	432
108th Congress, 2003			
State delegates	2	5	7
Total U.S.	205	229	434
109th Congress, 2005			
State delegates	3	4	7
Total U.S.	202	231	433
110th Congress, 2007			
State delegates	4	3	7
Total U.S.	233	202	435

(continued)

	Dem	Rep	Total
Senate			
101st Congress, 1989			
State delegates	1	1	2
Total U.S.	55	45	100
102d Congress, 1991			
State delegates	1	1	2
Total U.S.	56	44	100
103d Congress, 1993			
State delegates	1	1	2
Total U.S.	57	43	100
104th Congress, 1995			
State delegates	0	2	2
Total U.S.	46	53	99
105th Congress, 1997			
State delegates	0	2	2
Total U.S.	45	55	100
106th Congress, 1999			
State delegates	0	2	2
Total U.S.	45	54	99
107th Congress, 2001			
State delegates	0	2	2
Total U.S.	50	50	100
108th Congress, 2003			
State delegates	0	2	2
Total U.S.	48	51	99
109th Congress, 2005			
State delegates	1	1	2
Total U.S.	44	55	99
110th Congress, 2007			
State delegates	1	1	2
Total U.S.	49	49	98

Figures are for starts of first sessions. Totals are for Democrat (Dem.) and Republican (Rep.) members only. House membership totals under 435 and Senate totals under 100 reflect vacancies and seats held by independent party members. When the 110th Congress opened, the Senate's two independent members caucused with the Democrats, giving the Democrats control of the Senate.

Source: U.S. Congress, *Congressional Directory.*

Composition of state legislature, 1990-2006

	Democrats	Republicans
State House (65 seats)		
1990	27	38
1992	31	34
1994	24	41
1996	24	41
1998	25	40
2000	25	40
2002	28	37
2004	35	30
2006	39	26
State Senate (35 seats)		
1990	12	23
1992	16	19
1994	16	19
1996	15	20
1998	15	20
2000	15	20
2002	17	18
2004	18	17
2006	20	15

Figures for total seats may include independents and minor party members. Numbers reflect results of elections in listed years; elected members usually take their seats in the years that follow.

Source: Council of State Governments; *State Elective Officials and the Legislatures.*

Voter participation in presidential elections, 2000 and 2004

	2000	2004
Voting age population		
State	3,219,000	3,423,000
Total United States	209,831,000	220,377,000
State share of U.S. total	1.53	1.55
Rank among states	24	23
Portion of voting age population casting votes		
State	54.1%	62.2%
United States	50.3%	55.5%
Rank among states	23	16

Population figures are rounded to nearest thousand and include all residents, regardless of eligibility to vote.

Source: U.S. Census Bureau.

HEALTH AND MEDICAL CARE

Medical professionals
Physicians in 2003 and nurses in 2001

	U.S.	State
Physicians in 2003		
Total	774,849	11,600
Share of U.S. total		1.49%
Rate	266	255
Rank		20
Nurses in 2001		
Total	2,262,020	33,510
Share of U.S. total		1.48%
Rate	793	756
Rank		36

Rates are numbers of physicians and nurses per 100,000 resident population; ranks are based on rates.
Source: American Medical Association, *Physician Characteristics and Distribution in the U.S.*; U.S. Department of Health and Human Services, Health Resources and Services Administration.

Health insurance coverage, 2003

	State	U.S.
Total persons covered	3,708,000	243,320,000
Total persons not covered	772,000	44,961,000
Portion not covered	17.2%	15.6%
Rank among states	14	—
Children not covered	159,000	8,373,000
Portion not covered	13.7%	11.4%
Rank among states	8	—

Totals are rounded to nearest thousand. Ranks are from the highest to the lowest percentages of persons *not* insured.
Source: U.S. Census Bureau, Current Population Reports.

AIDS, syphilis, and tuberculosis cases, 2003

Disease	U.S. cases	State cases	Rank
AIDS	44,232	368	25
Syphilis	34,270	144	31
Tuberculosis	14,874	111	29

Source: U.S. Centers for Disease Control and Prevention.

Cigarette smoking, 2003
Residents over age 18 who smoke

	U.S.	State	Rank
All smokers	22.1%	18.5%	47
Male smokers	24.8%	19.6%	47
Female smokers	20.3%	17.5%	47

Cigarette smokers are defined as persons who reported having smoked at least 100 cigarettes during their lifetimes and who currently smoked at least occasionally.
Source: U.S. Centers for Disease Control and Prevention, *Morbidity and Mortality Weekly Report*, 53, no. 44 (November 12, 2004).

HOUSING

Home ownership rates, 1985-2004

	1985	1990	1995	2000	2004
State	63.6%	59.0%	64.6%	68.3%	71.1%
Total U.S.	63.9%	63.9%	64.7%	67.4%	69.0%
Rank among states	38	43	39	36	30

Net change in state home ownership rate, 1985-2004	+7.5%
Net change in U.S. home ownership rate, 1985-2004	+5.1%

Percentages represent the proportion of owner households to total occupied households.
Source: U.S. Census Bureau, 2006.

Home sales, 2000-2004
In thousands of units

Existing home sales	2000	2002	2003	2004
State sales	111.5	109.4	112.4	126.0
Total U.S. sales	5,171	5,631	6,183	6,784
State share of U.S. total	2.16%	1.94%	1.82%	1.86%
Sales rank among states	15	21	21	21

Units include single-family homes, condos, and co-ops.
Source: National Association of Realtors, Washington, D.C., *Real Estate Outlook: Market Trends & Insights*.

Values of owner-occupied homes, 2003

	State	U.S.
Total units	1,062,000	58,809,000
Value of units		
Under $100,000	4.3%	29.6%
$100,000-199,999	41.1%	36.9%
$200,000 or more	54.5%	33.5%
Median value	$210,398	$142,275
Rank among all states 6		

Units are owner-occupied one-family houses whose numbers are
rounded to nearest thousand. Data are extrapolated from
survey samples.
Source: U.S. Census Bureau, American Community Survey.

EDUCATION

Public school enrollment, 2002

Prekindergarten through grade 8
State enrollment 534,000
Total U.S. enrollment. 34,135,000
State share of U.S. total 1.56%

Grades 9 through 12
State enrollment 217,000
Total U.S. enrollment. 14,067,000
State share of U.S. total 1.54%

Enrollment rates
State public school enrollment rate. 91.0%
Overall U.S. rate 90.4%
Rank among states in 2002. 21
Rank among states in 1995. 25

Enrollment figures (which include unclassified students) are
rounded to nearest thousand pupils during fall school term.
Enrollment rates are based on enumerated resident population
estimate for July 1, 2002.
Source: U.S. National Center for Education Statistics.

Public college finances, 2003-2004

FTE enrollment in public institutions of higher education
Students in state institutions 161,200
Students in all U.S. public institutions 9,916,600
State share of U.S. total 1.63
Rank among states 22

**State and local government appropriations for higher
education**
State appropriation per FTE $3,202
National average $5,716
Rank among states 49
State & local tax revenue going to higher
education 4.6%

FTE = full-time equivalent in public postsecondary programs,
including summer sessions; student numbers are rounded to
nearest hundred. Funding figures for 2003-2004 academic year
include financial aid to students in state public institutions and
exclude money for research, agriculture experiment stations,
teaching hospitals, and medical schools; figures are rounded to
nearest thousand dollars.
Source: Higher Education Executive Officers, Denver, Colorado.

TRANSPORTATION AND TRAVEL

Highway mileage, 2003

Interstate highways 956
Other freeways and expressways 279
Arterial roads 8,191
Collector roads. 16,586
Local roads. 60,809
Urban roads 18,128
Rural roads. 68,693
Total state mileage. 86,821
U.S. total 3,974,107
State share 2.18%
Rank among states 22

Note that combined urban and rural road mileage matches the
total of the other categories.
Source: U.S. Federal Highway Administration.

Motor vehicle registrations and driver licenses, 2003

Vehicle registrations	State	U.S.	Share	Rank
Autos, trucks, buses	2,027,000	231,390,000	0.88%	31
Autos only	888,000	135,670	0.65%	33
Motorcycles	8,000	5,328,000	0.15%	50
Driver licenses	2,975,000	196,166,000	1.52%	24

Figures, which do not include vehicles owned by military services,
are rounded to the nearest thousand. Figures for automobiles
include taxis.
Source: U.S. Federal Highway Administration.

Domestic travel expenditures, 2003

Spending by U.S. residents on overnight trips and day trips of at least 50 miles from home

Total expenditures within state . . . . $9.19 bill.
Total expenditures within U.S. . . . . $490.87 bill.
State share of U.S. total 1.9%
Rank among states 16

Source: Travel Industry Association of America.

Retail gasoline prices, 2003-2007

Average price per gallon at the pump

Year	U.S.	State
2003	$1.267	$1.296
2004	$1.316	$1.328
2005	$1.644	$1.670
2007	$2.298	$2.246

Excise tax per gallon in 2004 . . . . 22.0¢
Rank among all states in 2007 prices 28

Prices are averages of all grades of gasoline sold at the pump during March months in 2003-2005 and during February, 2007. Averages for 2006, during which prices rose higher, are not available.
Source: U.S. Energy Information Agency, *Petroleum Marketing Monthly* (2003-2005 data); American Automobile Association (2007 data).

CRIME AND LAW ENFORCEMENT

State and local police officers, 2000-2004

	2000	2002	2004
Total officers			
U.S.	654,601	665,555	675,734
State	9,381	10,704	10,528*
*Net change, 2000-2004			+12.23%
Officers per 1,000 residents			
U.S.	2.33	2.31	2.30
State	2.18	2.38	2.29
State rank	23	12	17

Totals include state and local police and sheriffs.
Source: Carsey Institute, University of New Hampshire.

Crime rates, 2003

Incidents per 100,000 residents

Crimes	State	U.S.
Violent crimes		
Total incidents	345	475
Murder	4	6
Forcible rape	42	32
Robbery	82	142
Aggravated assault	218	295
Property crimes		
Total incidents	3,941	3,588
Burglary	711	741
Larceny/theft	2,731	2,415
Motor vehicle theft	499	433
All crimes	4,286	4,063

Source: U.S. Federal Bureau of Investigation, *Crime in the United States,* annual.

State prison populations, 1980-2003

	State	U.S.	State share
1980	2,629	305,458	0.86%
1990	7,671	708,393	1.08%
1996	12,438	1,025,624	1.21%
2000	16,833	1,391,261	1.21%
2003	19,671	1,470,045	1.34%

State figures exclude prisoners in federal penitentiaries.
Source: U.S. Bureau of Justice Statistics, *Prisoners in 2003.*

Connecticut

Location: New England

Area and rank: 4,845 square miles (12,550 square kilometers); 5,544 square miles (14,359 square kilometers) including water; forty-eighth largest state in area

Shoreline: 618 miles (995 kilometers) on Long Island Sound

Population and rank: 3,504,000 (2004); twenty-ninth largest state in population

Capital city: Hartford (121,578 people in 2000 census)

Largest city: Bridgeport (139,529 people in 2000 census)

Entered Union and rank: January 9, 1788; fifth state

Present constitution adopted: December 30, 1965

A mixture of Gothic and Renaissance architectural styles, the state capitol building in Hartford was completed in 1878. Almost a century later, it was designated a National Historic Landmark. (Courtesy, State of Connecticut/Dan Duggan)

Counties: 8

State name: "Connecticut" is derived from the Indian word "Quinnehtukqut," meaning "beside the long tidal river"

State nickname: Nutmeg State

Motto: *Qui transtulit sustinet* (He who transplanted still sustains)

State flag: Azure field with state coat of arms above banner with state motto

Highest point: Mount Frissell—2,380 feet (725 meters)

Lowest point: Long Island Sound—sea level

Highest recorded temperature: 105 degrees Fahrenheit (41 degrees Celsius)—Waterbury, 1926

Lowest recorded temperature: –32 degrees Fahrenheit (–36 degrees Celsius)—Falls Village, 1943

State song: "Yankee Doodle"

State tree: White Oak

State flower: Mountain Laurel

State bird: American robin

State fish: (none)

State animal: Sperm whale

Connecticut History

Connecticut is the third smallest state in area in the Union, after Rhode Island and Delaware. It is also the fourth most densely populated state. Positioned at the southernmost part of New England, Connecticut is bordered by New York on the west, Rhode Island on the east, Massachusetts on the north, and Long Island Sound—an arm of the Atlantic Ocean—on the south. Like most New England states, Connecticut is shaped by its abundance of water. It has more than 1,000 lakes and 8,400 miles of rivers and streams. The three major rivers flowing through the state, the Connecticut, the Housatonic, and the Thames, provide ports, fishing, and power for industry.

The Connecticut River Valley has very fertile land; potatoes, corn, onions, lettuce, tobacco, and other crops are grown there. Forests cover 60 percent of the state, making Connecticut one of the most wooded states in the Union. Maple trees are used to supply sugar and syrup. Until the nineteenth century, salmon fishing was a highly profitable industry. After a dam was built on the Connecticut River, preventing salmon from reaching their spawning grounds, the salmon supply was depleted.

Early History. Connecticut was inhabited by American Indian tribes for thousands of years before the first Europeans came to North America. By the seventeenth century, approximately twenty thousand Algonquian Indians lived in the region. The dominant tribe was the Pequot, a warrior group who conquered most of the Connecticut River Valley during the sixteenth century. Other tribes included the Narragansetts, Quinnipiacs, Mohegans, and Saukiogs, who hunted moose, deer, and bear and grew corn, beans, and squash.

Dutch explorer Adriaen Block sailed the Connecticut River in 1614, meeting friendly Podunk Indians. In 1633, Dutch settlers built the House of Good Hope trading post near modern Hartford, where they traded with the Native Americans. In the same year, English settlers founded Windsor. Violence erupted between the settlers and the Pequots in 1637 over land disputes. The Native Americans were defeated during the Pequot War, with losses of six hundred people. Many remaining Native Americans left the state, and by 1990, Indians made up only 0.2 percent of the population.

Colonization. In 1638, 250 Puritans from the Massachusetts Bay Colony established the New Haven Colony. The government was based on the Fundamental Agreement, which stated that the Bible was the supreme law. The colony was not inclusive; only Puritans were allowed to vote or hold office.

The residents of Wethersfield, Windsor, and Hartford joined to form the Colony of Connecticut in 1639. This colony's government was based on the teachings of Reverend Thomas Hooker, which were known as the Fundamental Orders. A Puritan preacher, Hooker believed that the right to vote should belong to all, regardless of their religion. The Fundamental Orders, which served as Connecticut's constitution for many years, were the first document in the New World to give the government its power from the "free consent of the people."

In 1643, Connecticut, New Haven, Massachussetts, and Plymouth colonies banded together, forming the Confederation of New England. The colonies stayed independent of each other but made a pact to act together in times of war. In 1662, the Connecticut colony received a royal charter, allowing it self-rule. The charter was revoked, however, twenty-three years later by King James. Edmund Andros, acting for the duke of York, tried to claim the area west of the Connecticut River for the New York colony. The residents of Connecticut refused to turn over their charter, supposedly hiding it in an oak tree, and they were able to resume self-rule in 1689. Connecticut became a state, the fifth in the Union, in 1788.

The American Revolution. Connecticut played a major role in the American Revolution. It sent thirty thousand soldiers into action—more, in relation to its population, than any other colony. These men included more than three hundred black soldiers. General George Washington called Connecticut the "Provisions State" because it sent so many supplies and munitions to the soldiers. The colony's navy captured more than forty British ships.

Connecticut produced both villains and heroes. One of its residents, Benedict Arnold, became a spy for the British, led English troops in an attack at Fort Griswold, and burned down the city of New London. Connecticut's Nathan Hale was a spy for the Union and became famous for the last words he uttered before the British hanged him.

Slavery in Connecticut. During the mid-eighteenth century, about three to five thousand black people lived in the colony, most of them slaves. A law was passed in 1774 prohibiting residents from bringing in new slaves, and the 1784 Connecticut Emancipation Law allowed children born to slaves to be freed at the age of twenty-five. After the Revolution, all slaves who fought were freed.

A well-publicized Connecticut court case in 1839 brought the issue of slavery to national attention. Africans carried in the Spanish slave ship *Amistad* mutinied and tried to force the crew to to turn the ship back to Africa. The crew instead secretly headed for Long Island, and the rebels, led by Joseph Cinqué, stood trial in Hartford for murder and piracy. In 1840, the U.S. Supreme Court ruled that the Africans were born free and taken as slaves against their will, so they were returned home. Slavery was banished in Connecticut in 1848. Later, the antislavery state sent more than fifty-seven thousand men to fight in the Civil War on the Union side.

Industry. In its early days, Connecticut's economy depended on agriculture and fishing. Its economy grew during the early nineteenth century with the construction of cotton, wool, and paper mills. Samuel Colt invented the six-shooter, the first repeating pistol, and its factories boomed. A machine to remove seeds from cotton, the cotton gin, invented in 1793 by Eli Whitney, added to the growth of industry.

Connecticut was hit hard by the Great Depression of the 1930's, with 22 percent of the state's workers unemployed. However, its economy bounced back during World War II. Connecticut produced more war supplies per person than any other state. During the late 1940's, more than half of its adult population worked in factories. Most of the industry was centered in ten towns, especially New Haven, Bridgeport, and Danbury, and half of Connecticut residents lived in these factory towns.

After the 1950's, textile production and other factory work subsided, and service jobs grew. Most middle-class families left the cities, and poverty increased in urban areas. Urban renewal programs initiated during the 1950's-1970's could not counter the riots that took place in poor areas in 1967.

Economy. By the end of the twentieth century, Hartford was the insurance capital of the world, a position it had held since the late eighteenth century. Groton was the submarine capital of the world during the early part of the century, but massive layoffs in the defense industry during the 1990's forced the closure of many shipyards and factories. Connecticut's population fell by several thousand during this period.

The state's economy was revitalized by the Mashantucket Pequot Indian Foxwoods Casino, which opened in 1993 as the largest casino in the Western Hemisphere. Paying the state one-quarter of its earnings, the casino pumps about $1 billion per year into Connecticut's economy. Nevertheless, the state imposed its first income tax in 1993, to the dismay of many.

Politics. Connecticut traditionally has been a Republican state. In 1974, however, Ella T. Grasso, a Democrat and the first Connecticut governor of Italian descent, became the first woman governor of a state elected in her own right. In 1981, Thirman Milner of Hartford became the first African American mayor of a New England city.

In 2000 Connecticut was honored when one of its U.S. senators, Joe Lieberman, was chosen running mate of Vice President Al Gore in his bid for the presidency. The state voted for the Democratic ticket, which lost in a narrow defeat. Lieberman, however, was reelected senator.

Social Issues and Headline Cases. Crime rates fell during the 1990's, and efforts were made to clean up Connecticut's deteriorating inner cities. The state government instituted a drug-policy reform in which drug addicts received methadone (a heroin substitute) treatments and thereby possibly avoided long-term imprisonment. Connecticut was the first state to place drug courts in every jurisdiction. About 75 percent of the defendants stay in the program, compared to about 25 percent in regular drug-treatment programs.

In July, 2000, West Nile virus was found in a dead bird, and authorities announced that the disease had circulated undetected in the state in 1999. In addition, the new national census did not benefit the state; it lost a representative in Congress as a result of declining population.

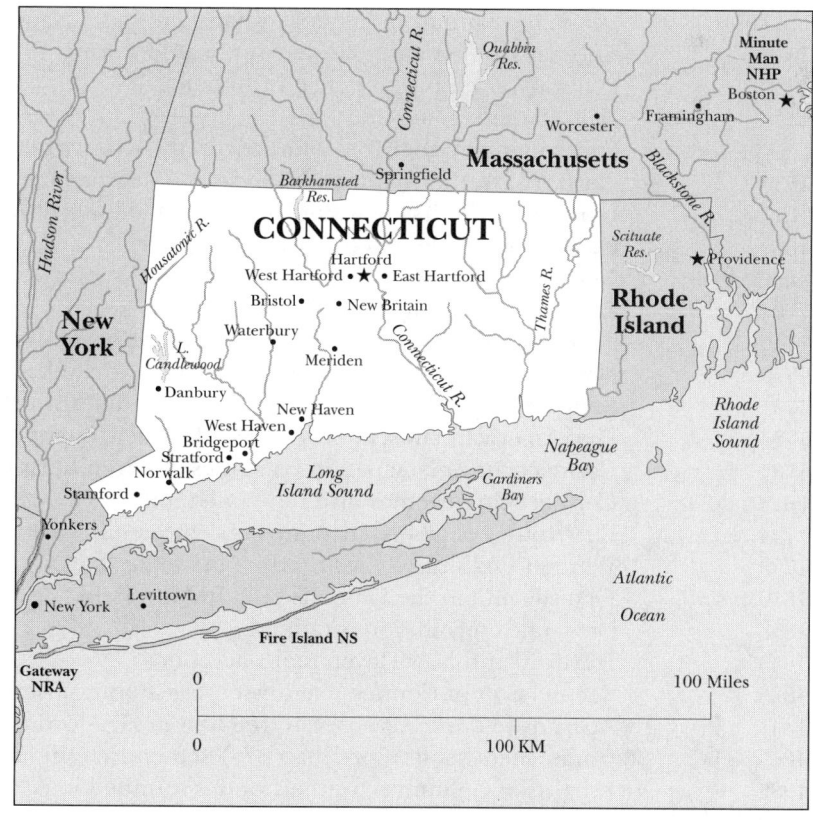

In 2001, the state took a leading role in the national debate over the death penalty when Governor John Rowland signed a measure into law that mandated a study of the state's death penalty system. The study was to determine if racial or economic factors are used in decisions for execution. In 2002, Connecticut was the site of a sensational murder trial involving Michael Skakel, a nephew of Ethel and Robert Kennedy. The case involved the 1975 murder of a young woman. The defendant was convicted and sentenced to twenty years to life.

Two important public controversies erupted in the first years of the new century. One of them concerned pedophilia in the Roman Catholic Church. In 2002, Cardinal Edward Egan was accused of mishandling child molestation cases. Written evidence from previous years indicated both that he allowed priests accused of such crimes to continue working and that he failed to inform the authorities, contrary to legal requirements. In 2003, the matter was concluded when a suit involving forty people molested by sixteen priests was settled for $21 million. Finally, Governor Rowland be-

came implicated in a bribery scandal when he was found to have accepted cash and gifts from state contractors. His resignation was effective on July 1, 2004.

2006 Democratic Primary. On August 8, 2006, Ned Lamont, scion of a wealthy Connecticut family, defeated Senator Lieberman in the Democratic primary election to gain the party's formal endorsement in the election for the senator's seat in November. The outcome caused a sensation both in the state and in the nation, since Lieberman had been Al Gore's running mate in 2000 and a strong fixture in the Democratic Party in Connecticut for many years. However, Lieberman's strong support for the Iraq War—which, for many Connecticut Democrats, tied him too closely to President George W. Bush—hurt his support. Many Democratic voters had soured on the war, and Lamont took full advantage of these sentiments. On August 9, however, Lieberman announced that he would run in the November election as an "independent Democrat." He won the ensuing contest.

Lauren M. Mitchell
Updated by the Editor

Connecticut Time Line

1600's	Connecticut area is inhabited by Native American Algonquians dominated by Pequots.
1614	Dutch explorer Adriaen Block sails up Connecticut River and claims region for Holland.
1633	English settle Windsor.
June 6, 1633	Dutch buy land from Pequot Indians and build trading post at modern Hartford.
1636	Thomas Hooker and followers settle at Hartford.
1637	Pequot War ends with defeat of Indians.
1638	New Haven is founded.
Jan. 14, 1639	Fundamental Orders of Connecticut, the first written constitution, is adopted.
1639	Hartford, Wethersfield, and Windsor unite, forming Connecticut Colony.
1647	Connecticut is first New England colony to hang a woman convicted of witchcraft.
1662	Connecticut Colony is officially chartered.
Jan. 5, 1665	New Haven becomes part of Connecticut Colony.
1701	Yale University is founded in New Haven.
1740	First tinware in New World is made in central Connecticut by Edward and William Pattison.
1779	New Haven is attacked, and Fairfield and Norwalk are burned during Revolutionary War.
1781	Benedict Arnold, a Connecticut traitor leading British troops, burns New London.
1784	First American law school is founded in New Litchfield.
1784	Connecticut Emancipation Law rules children born to slaves become free at age twenty-five.
Jan. 9, 1788	Connecticut becomes fifth state in Union.
1794	Eli Whitney of Connecticut invents cotton gin.
1798	Whitney establishes mass production at gun-making plant in Whitneyville.
1810	First silk mill in the Union is built in Mansfield.
1818	New state constitution is ratified.
1833	Hartford and New Haven Railroad opens.
1835	Samuel Colt of Connecticut invents six-shooter pistol.
1841	Africans sold into slavery win freedom in Hartford trials after mutiny of *Amistad*.
1861-1865	Connecticut sends more than 57,000 men to fight in the Civil War for the Union.
1882	Knights of Columbus brotherhood is founded in New Haven.

Replica of the Amistad *slave ship at Mystic Harbor.* (PhotoDisc)

1888	Great Blizzard of 1888 leaves hundreds dead.
1910	U.S. Coast Guard Academy moves to New London.
1917	U.S. naval submarine base opens at Groton.
1917-1918	During World War I, Connecticut is supply center; sends more than 60,000 men to fight.
1930's	Great Depression hits the industrial state hard; 150,000 are unemployed.
1941-1945	During World War II, Connecticut is supply center.
1943	Connecticut is first state to establish a civil rights commission.
Jan., 1954	First atomic-powered submarine, *Nautilus*, is launched at Groton.
1965	New state constitution is ratified.
1969	Race riots occur in black and Puerto Rican parts of Hartford.
1973	Waste agency opens, to combat widespread pollution.
1974	Connecticut's Ella Grasso is first woman to be elected a state governor without succeeding her husband.
1979	State bans construction of new nuclear plants.
1981	Thirman Milner of Hartford becomes first black mayor of a New England city.
1984	Ellen Ash Peters is first woman named to Connecticut supreme court.
1991	City of Bridgeport files for bankruptcy.
1991	First Connecticut state income tax is established.
1996	*Sheff v. O'Neill* case, claiming racial segregation in schools, reaches state supreme court.
July 5, 2000	Potentially deadly West Nile virus reported found in Fairfield County, as well as in adjoining states; the disease is also found to have circulated undetected in 1999.
Nov. 21, 2001	Elderly Connecticut resident Ottilie Lundgren dies mysteriously of inhalation anthrax.
Oct., 2003	Lawsuit settling child molestation in the Roman Catholic Church involving forty Connecticut victims is settled for $21 million.
June 20, 2004	Governor John G. Rowland announces his resignation as governor, effective July 1.
Aug. 8, 2006	Ned Lamont defeats Senator Joe Lieberman in Democratic Party primary election for U.S. Senate.

Notes for Further Study

Published Sources. Among the many books on Connecticut state history, a good place to start is *Connecticut* (1989) by William Hubbell and Roger Eddy. *Connecticut: An Explorer's Guide* (1999) by Barnett D. Laschever and Andi Marie Fusco and *Connecticut: Driving Through History* (1998) by Suzanne Staubach are excellent travel books that give tourist information and history lessons. Two accessible books for young adults on the state's history are *Connecticut* (2004) by Emily Lauren and Dina McClellan and *Primary Source History of the Colony of Connecticut* (2005) by Ann Malaspina. Richard Radune explores a particular aspect the colonial history of Connecticut in *Pequot Plantation: The Story of an Early Colonial Settlement* (2005).

Useful books on Native Americans in Connecticut include *Algonquians of the East Coast* (1996), published by Time-Life Books. It reveals the history, customs, and mythology of this important Connecticut tribe, with many photographs. Alfred A. Cave's excellent *The Pequot War* (1997) explains the Puritan belief that Native Americans were "agents of Satan" and were to be destroyed. *The Puritan Family: Religion and Domestic Relations in Seventeenth Century New England* (1990), by Edmund Sears Morgan, discusses the Puritan ideal of social virtue and the communities established by Puritans in New England.

Howard Jones's *Mutiny on the "Amistad": The Saga of a Slave Revolt and Its Impact on American Abolition, Law, and Diplomacy* (1988) is a full-scale treatment of the infamous case in which African slaves won their freedom. Another excellent study is *Black Mutiny: The Revolt on the Schooner "Amistad"* (1953) by William A. Owens and Michael E. Dyson, which provides one of the most detailed accounts of the *Amistad* mutiny. *Colt: The Making of an American Legend* (1996) by William Hosley, Constance McLaughlin Green's *Eli Whitney and the Birth of American Technology* (1998), and *Eli Whitney, Great Inventor: Discovery Biography* (1991) by Jean Lee Latham and Louis F. Cary are good biographies of these important Connecticut industrial leaders.

Web Resources. The best starting place on the Internet is the official state of Connecticut site (www.state.ct.us), which covers government information, news, history, and tourist attractions. Other good tourist sites are the Connecticut Tourism Home Page (www.tourism.state.ct.us/), Visit Connecticut (www.visitconnecticut.com), and Connecticut.com (www.connecticut.com), which provides a state photograph gallery and a section for children, among other features.

For state and county data from the U.S. Census Bureau, see Connecticut QuickFacts (quickfacts.census.gov/qfd/states/

Hartford, Connecticut's capital and third-largest city, after Bridgeport and New Haven, is the center of the nation's insurance industry. (Michael Czaczkes)

09000.html). Two good resources for state news, which are updated daily, are Connecticut Central (www.ctcentral.com), with news from the *New Haven Register* and *The Middletown Press*, and *The Hartford Courant* (www.courant.com), which also provides the history of the newspaper. For specific history, the Pequot Web site (www.pequotwar.com/) has much data on the Pequot War in Connecticut. More information on Native Americans can be found at Nipmuc Indian Association of Connecticut (www.nativetech.org/Nipmuc/), with news of Nipmucs and links to other American Indian Web sites. The Fundamental Orders of 1639 site (www.constitution.org/bcp/fo_1639.htm) gives the history of the constitution and reprints it. The *Amistad* mutiny is discussed at the Amistad Case (www.archives.gov/education/lessons/amistad/), which provides legal documents. The Connecticut Society of the Sons of the American Revolution (www.connecticutsar.org/) provides links to biographies of state patriots, a list of articles detailing the state's involvement in the war, and a time line of events.

Counties

County	2000 pop.	Rank in pop.	Sq. miles	Rank in area
Fairfield	882,567	1	837	3
Hartford	857,183	2	751	5
Litchfield	182,193	5	945	1
Middlesex	155,071	6	439	7
New Haven	824,008	3	862	2
New London	259,088	4	772	4
Tolland	136,364	7	417	8
Windham	109,091	8	521	6

Source: U.S. Census Bureau; National Association of Counties.

Cities
With 10,000 or more residents

Rank	City	Population	Rank	City	Population
1	Bridgeport	139,529	17	Milford	50,594
2	New Haven	123,626	18	Stratford	49,976
3	Hartford (capital)	121,578	19	East Hartford	49,575
4	Stamford	117,083	20	Enfield	45,212
5	Waterbury	107,271	21	Middletown	43,167
6	Norwalk	82,951	22	Wallingford	43,026
7	Danbury	74,848	23	Groton	39,907
8	New Britain	71,538	24	Southington	39,728
9	West Hartford	63,589	25	Shelton	38,101
10	Greenwich	61,101	26	Norwich	36,117
11	Bristol	60,062	27	Torrington	35,202
12	Meriden	58,244	28	Trumbull	34,243
13	Fairfield	57,340	29	Glastonbury	31,876
14	Hamden	56,913	30	Naugatuck	30,989
15	Manchester	54,740	31	Central Manchester	30,595
16	West Haven	52,360	32	Newington	29,306

(continued)

Rank	City	Population	Rank	City	Population
33	Branford	28,683	68	Plainville	17,328
34	Cheshire	28,543	69	Killingly	16,472
35	Windsor	28,237	70	Avon	15,832
36	East Haven	28,189	71	Willimantic	15,823
37	Vernon	28,063	72	Brookfield	15,664
38	New Milford	27,121	73	Seymour	15,454
39	Wethersfield	26,271	74	Wolcott	15,215
40	Westport	25,749	75	Ledyard	14,687
41	New London	25,671	76	Plainfield	14,619
42	Newtown	25,031	77	Colchester	14,551
43	South Windsor	24,412	78	New Fairfield	13,953
44	Ridgefield	23,643	79	North Branford	13,906
45	Farmington	23,641	80	Suffield	13,552
46	Simsbury	23,234	81	East Hampton	13,352
47	North Haven	23,035	82	Orange	13,233
48	Windham	22,857	83	Tolland	13,146
49	Watertown	21,661	84	Clinton	13,094
50	Guilford	21,398	85	Ellington	12,921
51	Mansfield	20,720	86	Cromwell	12,871
52	Darien	19,607	87	Derby	12,391
53	Bloomfield	19,587	88	Windsor Locks	12,043
54	New Canaan	19,395	89	Plymouth	11,634
55	Monroe	19,247	90	Coventry	11,504
56	Waterford	19,152	91	Stafford	11,307
57	Southbury	18,567	92	Storrs	10,996
58	Ansonia	18,554	93	Griswold	10,807
59	Montville	18,546	94	Winchester	10,664
60	Berlin	18,215	95	Somers	10,417
61	East Lyme	18,118	96	Old Saybrook	10,367
62	Bethel	18,067	97	Granby	10,347
63	Rocky Hill	17,966	98	Conning Towers-Nautilus Park	10,241
64	Stonington	17,906	99	Weston	10,037
65	Madison	17,858			
66	Wilton	17,633			
67	Wallingford Center	17,509			

Population figures are from 2000 census.
Source: U.S. Bureau of the Census.

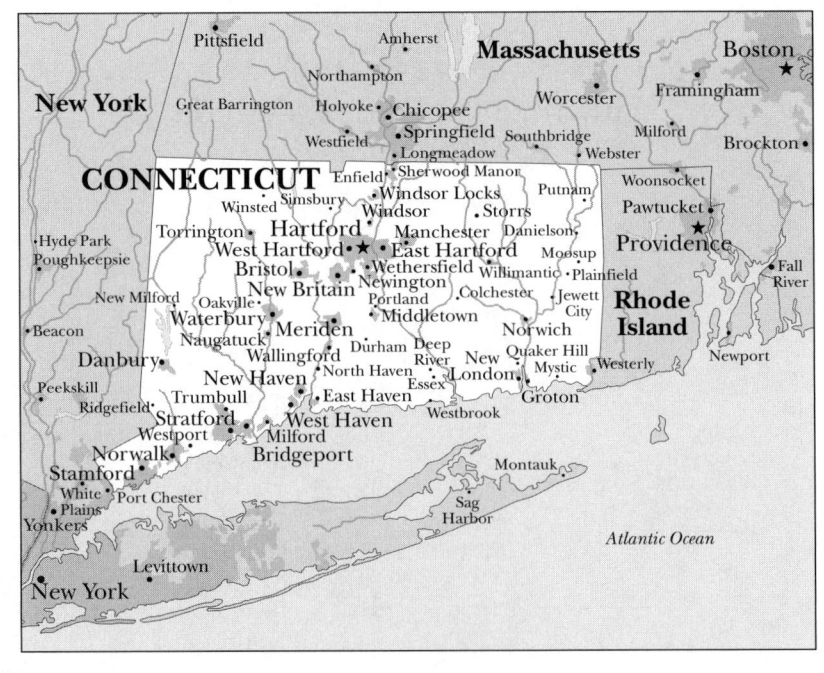

Index to Tables

DEMOGRAPHICS

Resident state and national populations, 1970-2004

Population figures given in thousands

	State pop.	U.S. pop.	Share	Rank
1970	3,032	203,302	1.5%	24
1980	3,108	226,546	1.4%	25
1985	3,201	237,924	1.3%	27
1990	3,287	248,765	1.3%	27
1995	3,324	262,761	1.2%	28
2000	3,406	281,425	1.2%	29
2004	3,504	293,655	1.2%	29

Source: U.S. Census Bureau, Current Population Reports, 2006.

Resident population by age, 2004

Age Group	Total persons
Under 5 years	213,000
5 to 17 years	626,000
18 to 24 years	311,000
25 to 34 years	409,000
35 to 44 years	565,000
45 to 54 years	532,000
55 to 64 years	374,000
65 to 74 years	217,000
75 to 84 years	175,000
85 years and older	82,000
All age groups	3,504,000

Portion of residents 65 and older	13.5%
National rank in portion of oldest residents	12
National average	12.4%

Population figures are rounded to nearest thousand persons;
figures include armed forces personnel stationed in the state.
Source: U.S. Bureau of the Census, 2006.

Resident population by race, Hispanic origin, 2004

Category	State pop.	Share	U.S.
All residents	3,504	100.00%	100.00%
Non-Hispanic white	2,658	75.86%	67.37%
Hispanic white	325	9.28%	13.01%
Other Hispanic	47	1.34%	1.06%
African American	352	10.05%	12.77%
Native American	12	0.34%	0.96%
Asian, Pacific Islander	111	3.17%	4.37%
Two or more categories	46	1.31%	1.51%

Population figures are in thousands. Persons counted as "Hispanic" (Latino) may be of any race. Because of overlapping categories, categories may not add up to 100%. Shares in column 3 are percentages of each category within the state; these figures may be compared to the national percentages in column 4.
Source: U.S. Bureau of the Census, 2006.

Projected state population, 2000-2030

Year	Population
2000	3,406,000
2005	3,503,000
2010	3,577,000
2015	3,635,000
2020	3,676,000
2025	3,691,000
2030	3,689,000
Population increase, 2000-2030	283,000
Percentage increase, 2000-2030	8.3

Projections are based on data from the 2000 census.
Source: U.S. Census Bureau.

VITAL STATISTICS

Infant mortality rates, 1980-2002

	1980	1990	2000	2002
All state residents	11.2	7.9	6.6	6.5
All U.S. residents	12.6	9.2	9.4	9.1
All state white residents	10.2	6.3	5.6	5.5
All U.S. white residents	10.6	7.6	5.7	5.8
All state black residents	19.1	17.6	14.4	14.2
All U.S. black residents	22.2	18.0	14.1	14.4

Figures represent deaths per 1,000 live births of resident infants under 1 year old, exclusive of fetal deaths. Figures for all residents include members of other racial categories not listed separately.
Source: U.S. Census Bureau, *Statistical Abstract of the United States,* 2006.

Abortion rates, 1990 and 2000

	1990	2000
Total abortions	20,000	15,000
Rate per 1,000 women	26.0	21.1
U.S. rate	25.7	21.3
Rank	12	15

Numbers of abortions are rounded to nearest thousand; ranks are based on rates.
Source: U.S. Census Bureau.

Marriages and divorces, 2004

Total marriages	16,500
Rate per 1,000 population	4.7
National rate per 1,000 population	7.4
Rank among all states	50
Total divorces	10,300
Rate per 1,000 population	2.9
National rate per 1,000 population	3.7
Rank among all states	38

Figures are for all marriages and divorces performed within the state, including those of nonresidents; totals are rounded to the nearest hundred. Ranks are for highest to lowest figures; note that divorce data are not available for five states.
Source: U.S. National Center for Health Statistics, *Vital Statistics of the United States,* 2006.

Death rates by leading causes, 2002
Deaths per 100,000 resident population

Cause	State	U.S.
Heart disease	254.7	241.7
Cancer	207.0	193.2
Cerebrovascular diseases	53.8	56.4
Accidents other than motor vehicle	34.2	37.0
Motor vehicle accidents	10.1	15.7
Chronic lower respiratory diseases	42.0	43.3
Diabetes mellitus	19.5	25.4
HIV	5.4	4.9
Suicide	7.5	11.0
Homicide	2.8	6.1
All causes	870.5	847.3
Rank in overall death rate among states		26

Figures exclude nonresidents who died in the state. Causes of death follow International Classification of Diseases. Rank is from highest to lowest death rate in the United States.
Source: U.S. National Center for Health Statistics, *National Vital Statistics Report,* 2006.

ECONOMY

Gross state product, 1990-2004
In current dollars

Year	State product	Nat'l product	State share
1990	$99.0 billion	$5.67 trillion	1.74%
2000	$160.7 billion	$9.75 trillion	1.65%
2002	$167.2 billion	$10.41 trillion	1.61%
2003	$174.1 billion	$10.92 trillion	1.59%
2004	$187.1 billion	$11.65 trillion	1.61%

Source: U.S. Bureau of Economic Analysis, *Survey of Current Business,* July, 2005.

Gross state product by industry, 2003
In billions of dollars

Construction	$4.9
Manufacturing	21.1
Wholesale trade	9.2
Retail trade	11.4
Finance & insurance	27.1
Information	6.8
Professional services	12.7
Health care & social assistance	11.6
Government	13.8
Total state product	$164.1
Total U.S. product	$10,289.2
State share of U.S. total	1.59%
Rank among all states	23

Total figures include industries not listed separately. Amounts are in chained 2000 dollars.
Source: U.S. Bureau of Economic Analysis, *Survey of Current Business,* July, 2005.

Personal income per capita, 1990-2004
In current dollars

	1990	2000	2004
Per capita income	$26,504	$41,489	$45,398
U.S. average	$19,477	$29,845	$32,937
Rank among states	1	1	1

Source: U.S. Bureau of Economic Analysis, *Survey of Current Business,* April, 2005.

Energy consumption, 2001
In trillions of British thermal units (BTU), except as noted

Total energy consumption

Total state energy consumption	853
Total U.S. energy consumption	96,275
State share of U.S. total	0.89%
Rank among states	33

Per capita consumption (In millions of BTU)

Total state per capita consumption	249
Total U.S. per capita consumption	338
Rank among states	45

End-use sectors

Residential	267
Commercial	215
Industrial	134
Transportation	238

Sources of energy

Petroleum	439
Natural gas	149
Coal	40
Hydroelectric power	3
Nuclear electric power	161

Figures for totals include categories not listed separately.
Source: U.S. Energy Information Administration, *State Energy Data Report,* 2001.

Nonfarm employment by sectors, 2004

Total	1,651,000
Construction	66,000
Manufacturing	198,000
Trade, transportation, utilities	308,000
Information	39,000
Finance, insurance, real estate	141,000
Professional & business services	198,000
Education & health services	268,000
Leisure, hospitality, arts, organizations	128,000
Other services, including repair & maintenance	63,000
Government	242,000

Figures are rounded to nearest thousand persons. "Total" includes mining and natural resources, not listed separately.
Source: U.S. Bureau of Labor Statistics, 2006.

Foreign exports, 1990-2004
In millions of dollars

Year	State	U.S.	State share
1990	4,356	394,045	1.11%
1996	6,100	624,767	0.98%
1997	7,058	688,896	1.02%
2000	8,047	712,055	1.03%
2003	8,136	724,006	1.20%
2004	8,559	769,332	1.11%

Rank among all states in 2004 26

U.S. total does not include U.S. dependencies.
Source: U.S. Census Bureau, *U.S. Merchandise Trade*, series FT 900, 2000; U.S. Census Bureau, *U.S. International Trade in Goods and Services*, Series FT 900, 2005.

LAND USE

Federally owned land, 2003
Areas in acres

	State	U.S.	State share
Total area	3,135,000	2,271,343,000	0.14%
Nonfederal land	3,120,000	1,599,584,000	0.20%
Federal land	15,000	671,759,000	0.00%
Federal share	0.5%	29.6%	—

Areas are rounded to nearest thousand acres. Figures for federally owned land do not include trust properties.
Source: U.S. General Services Administration, *Federal Real Property Profile*, 2006.

Land use, 1997
In acres, rounded to nearest thousand

Total surface area.	3,195,000
Total nonfederal rural land	2,178,000
Percentage rural land	68.2%
Cropland	204,000
Conservation Reserve Program (CRP*) land	(nil)
Pastureland.	112,000
Rangeland	(nil)
Forestland.	1,759,000
Other rural land	103,000

*CRP is a federal program begun in 1985 to assist private landowners to convert highly erodible cropland to vegetative cover for ten years. Note that some categories of land overlap.
Source: U.S. Department of Agriculture, Natural Resources and Conservation Service, and Iowa State University, Statistical Laboratory, *Summary Report, 1997 National Resources Inventory*, revised December, 2000.

Farms and crop acreage, 2004

	State	U.S.	Share	Rank
Farms	4,000	2,113,000	0.19%	45
Acres (millions)	0.35*	937	—	48
Acres per farm	86	443	—	47

Source: U.S. Department of Agriculture, National Agricultural Statistics Service. Numbers of farms are rounded to nearest thousand units; acreage figures are rounded to nearest million; *Connecticut has fewer than 500,000 acres of farmland. Rankings, including ties, are based on rounded figures.

GOVERNMENT AND FINANCE

Units of local government, 2002

	State	Total U.S.	Rank
All local governments	580	87,525	41
Counties	0	3,034	—
Municipalities	30	19,429	45
Towns (townships)	149	16,504	19
School districts	17	13,506	42
Special districts	384	35,052	31

Only 48 states have county governments, 20 states have township governments ("towns" in New England, Minnesota, New York, and Wisconsin), and 46 states have school districts. Special districts encompass such functions as natural resources, fire protection, and housing and community development.
Source: U.S. Census Bureau, *Census of Governments.*

State government revenue, 2002

Total revenue	$16,993 mill.
General revenue	$15,382 mill.
Per capita revenue	$4,447
U.S. per capita average	$3,689
Rank among states	6
Intergovernment revenue	
Total	$3,769 mill.
From federal government	$3,686 mill.
Charges and miscellaneous	
Total	$2,580 mill.
Current charges	$1,076 mill.
Misc. general income	$1,504 mill.
Insurance trust revenue	$1,589 mill.
Taxes	
Total	$9,033 mill.
Per capita taxes	$2,611
Rank among states	4
Property taxes	(nil)
Sales taxes	$4,516 mill.
License taxes	$405 mill.
Individual income taxes	$3,685 mill.
Corporate income taxes	$149 mill.
Other taxes	$277 mill.

Total revenue figures include items not listed separately here.
Source: U.S. Bureau of the Census.

State government expenditures, 2002

General expenditures

Total state expenditures	$20,117 mill.
Intergovernmental	$3,735 mill.

Per capita expenditures

State	$5,070
Average of all states	$3,859
Rank among states	6

Selected direct expenditures

Education	$2,218 mill.
Public welfare	$3,362 mill.
Health, hospital	$1,749 mill.
Highways	$817 mill.
Police protection	$164 mill.
Corrections	$638 mill.
Natural resources	$194 mill.
Parks and recreation	$104 mill.
Government administration	$913 mill.
Interest on debt	$1,138 mill.
Total direct expenditures	$13,802 mill.

Totals include items not listed separately.
Source: U.S. Census Bureau.

POLITICS

Governors since statehood

D = Democrat; R = Republican; O = other;
(r) resigned; (d) died in office; (i) removed from office

Jonathan Trumbull	1776-1784
Matthew Griswold	1784-1786
Samuel Huntington (O)	(d) 1786-1796
Oliver Wolcott (O)	(d) 1796-1797
Jonathan Trumbull, Jr. (O)	(d) 1797-1809
John Treadwell (O)	1809-1811
Robert Griswold (O)	(d) 1811-1812
John Cotton Smith (O)	1812-1817
Oliver Wolcott II (O)	1817-1827
Gideon Tomlinson (O)	1827-1831
John S. Peters (O)	1831-1833
Henry W. Edwards (D)	1833-1834
Samuel A. Foot (O)	1834-1835
Henry W. Edwards (D)	1835-1838
William W. Ellsworth (O)	1838-1842
Chauncey F. Cleveland (D)	1842-1844
Roger S. Baldwin (O)	1844-1846
Isaac Toucey (D)	1846-1847
Clark Bissell (O)	1847-1849
Joseph Trumbull (O)	1849-1850
Thomas H. Seymour (D)	(r) 1850-1853
Charles H. Pond (D)	1853-1854
Henry Dutton (O)	1854-1855
William T. Minor (O)	1855-1857
Alexander H. Holley (R)	1857-1858
William A. Buckingham (R)	1858-1866
Joseph R. Hawley (R)	1866-1867
James E. English (D)	1867-1869
Marshall Jewell (R)	1869-1870
James E. English (D)	1870-1871
Marshall Jewell (R)	1871-1873
Charles R. Ingersoll (R)	1873-1877
Richard D. Hubbard (D)	1877-1879
Charles B. Andrews (R)	1879-1881
Hobart B. Bigelow (R)	1881-1883
Thomas M. Waller (D)	1883-1885
Henry B. Harrison (R)	1885-1887
Phineas C. Lounsbury (R)	1887-1889
Morgan G. Bulkeley (R)	1889-1893
Luzon B. Morris (D)	1893-1895
Owen Vincent Coffin (R)	1895-1897
Lorrin A. Cooke (R)	1897-1899
George S. Lounsbury (R)	1899-1901
George P. McLean (R)	1901-1903
Abiram Chamberlain (R)	1903-1905
Harry Roberts (R)	1905-1907
Rollin S. Woodruff (R)	1907-1909
George L. Lilley (R)	(d) 1909
Frank B. Weeks (R)	1909-1911
Simeon E. Baldwin (D)	1911-1915
Marcus H. Holcomb (R)	1915-1921
Everett J. Lake (R)	1921-1923
Charles A. Templeton (R)	1923-1925
Hiram Bingham (R)	(r) 1925
John H. Trumbull (R)	1925-1931
Wilbur L. Cross (D)	1931-1939
Raymond E. Baldwin (R)	1939-1941
Robert A. Hurley (D)	1941-1943
Raymond E. Baldwin (R)	(r) 1943-1946
Wilbert Snow (D)	1946-1947
James L. McConaughty (R)	(d) 1947-1948
James C. Shannon (R)	1948-1949
Charles B. Bowles (D)	1949-1951
John D. Lodge (R)	1951-1955
Abraham Ribicoff (D)	(r) 1955-1961
John N. Dempsey (D)	1961-1971
Thomas J. Meskill (R)	1971-1975
Ella T. Grasso (D)	1975-1980
William A. O'Neill (D)	1981-1991
Lowell P. Weicker, Jr. (O)	1991-1995
John G. Rowland (R)	1995-2004
M. Jodi Rell (R)	2004-

Composition of congressional delegations, 1989-2007

	Dem	Rep	Total
House of Representatives			
101st Congress, 1989			
State delegates	3	3	6
Total U.S.	259	174	433
102d Congress, 1991			
State delegates	3	3	6
Total U.S.	267	167	434
103d Congress, 1993			
State delegates	3	3	6
Total U.S.	258	176	434
104th Congress, 1995			
State delegates	4	2	6
Total U.S.	197	236	433
105th Congress, 1997			
State delegates	4	2	6
Total U.S.	206	228	434
106th Congress, 1999			
State delegates	4	2	6
Total U.S.	211	222	433
107th Congress, 2001			
State delegates	3	3	6
Total U.S.	211	221	432
108th Congress, 2003			
State delegates	2	3	5
Total U.S.	205	229	434
109th Congress, 2005			
State delegates	2	3	5
Total U.S.	202	231	433
110th Congress, 2007			
State delegates	4	1	5
Total U.S.	233	202	435
Senate			
101st Congress, 1989			
State delegates	2	0	2
Total U.S.	55	45	100
102d Congress, 1991			
State delegates	2	0	2
Total U.S.	56	44	100
103d Congress, 1993			
State delegates	2	0	2
Total U.S.	57	43	100
104th Congress, 1995			
State delegates	2	0	2
Total U.S.	46	53	99
105th Congress, 1997			
State delegates	2	0	2
Total U.S.	45	55	100

	Dem	Rep	Total
106th Congress, 1999			
State delegates	2	0	2
Total U.S.	45	54	99
107th Congress, 2001			
State delegates	2	0	2
Total U.S.	50	50	100
108th Congress, 2003			
State delegates	2	0	2
Total U.S.	48	51	99
109th Congress, 2005			
State delegates	2	0	2
Total U.S.	44	55	99
110th Congress, 2007			
State delegates	2*	0	2
Total U.S.	49	49	98

Figures are for starts of first sessions. Totals are for Democrat (Dem.) and Republican (Rep.) members only. House membership totals under 435 and Senate totals under 100 reflect vacancies and seats held by independent party members. When the 110th Congress opened, the Senate's two independent members caucused with the Democrats, giving the Democrats control of the Senate. *Democratic incumbent Joseph Lieberman returned to the Senate in 2007 as an independent but continued to caucus with Democrats.
Source: U.S. Congress, *Congressional Directory.*

Composition of state legislature, 1990-2006

	Democrats	Republicans
State House (151 seats)		
1990	87	64
1992	85	64
1994	90	61
1996	97	54
1998	96	54
2000	96	56
2002	95	56
2004	99	52
2006	107	44
State Senate (36 seats)		
1990	20	16
1992	19	17
1994	17	19
1996	19	17
1998	19	17
2000	19	17
2002	21	15
2004	24	12
2006	24	12

Figures for total seats may include independents and minor party members. Numbers reflect results of elections in listed years; elected members usually take their seats in the years that follow.
Source: Council of State Governments; *State Elective Officials and the Legislatures.*

Voter participation in presidential elections, 2000 and 2004

	2000	2004
Voting age population		
State	2,570,000	2,665,000
Total United States	209,831,000	220,377,000
State share of U.S. total	1.22	1.21
Rank among states	28	28
Portion of voting age population casting votes		
State	56.8%	59.2%
United States	50.3%	55.5%
Rank among states	14	20

Population figures are rounded to nearest thousand and include all residents, regardless of eligibility to vote.
Source: U.S. Census Bureau.

HEALTH AND MEDICAL CARE

Medical professionals
Physicians in 2003 and nurses in 2001

	U.S.	State
Physicians in 2003		
Total	774,849	12,603
Share of U.S. total		1.62%
Rate	266	362
Rank		5
Nurses in 2001		
Total	2,262,020	32,740
Share of U.S. total		1.45%
Rate	793	953
Rank		8

Rates are numbers of physicians and nurses per 100,000 resident population; ranks are based on rates.
Source: American Medical Association, *Physician Characteristics and Distribution in the U.S.*; U.S. Department of Health and Human Services, Health Resources and Services Administration.

Health insurance coverage, 2003

	State	U.S.
Total persons covered	3,065,000	243,320,000
Total persons not covered	357,000	44,961,000
Portion not covered	10.4%	15.6%
Rank among states	44	—
Children not covered	71,000	8,373,000
Portion not covered	8.3%	11.4%
Rank among states	35	—

Totals are rounded to nearest thousand. Ranks are from the highest to the lowest percentages of persons *not* insured.
Source: U.S. Census Bureau, Current Population Reports.

AIDS, syphilis, and tuberculosis cases, 2003

Disease	U.S. cases	State cases	Rank
AIDS	44,232	733	17
Syphilis	34,270	207	25
Tuberculosis	14,874	111	29

Source: U.S. Centers for Disease Control and Prevention.

Cigarette smoking, 2003
Residents over age 18 who smoke

	U.S.	State	Rank
All smokers	22.1%	18.7%	46
Male smokers	24.8%	19.7%	46
Female smokers	20.3%	17.9%	43

Cigarette smokers are defined as persons who reported having smoked at least 100 cigarettes during their lifetimes and who currently smoked at least occasionally.
Source: U.S. Centers for Disease Control and Prevention, *Morbidity and Mortality Weekly Report*, 53, no. 44 (November 12, 2004).

HOUSING

Home ownership rates, 1985-2004

	1985	1990	1995	2000	2004
State	69.0%	67.9%	68.2%	70.0%	71.7%
Total U.S.	63.9%	63.9%	64.7%	67.4%	69.0%
Rank among states	19	23	21	28	26

Net change in state home ownership rate, 1985-2004 . . . . +2.7%
Net change in U.S. home ownership rate, 1985-2004 . . . . +5.1%

Percentages represent the proportion of owner households to total occupied households.
Source: U.S. Census Bureau, 2006.

Home sales, 2000-2004
In thousands of units

Existing home sales	2000	2002	2003	2004
State sales	61.5	64.2	63.5	72.5
Total U.S. sales	5,171	5,631	6,183	6,784
State share of U.S. total	1.19%	1.14%	1.03%	1.07%
Sales rank among states	29	29	31	31

Units include single-family homes, condos, and co-ops.
Source: National Association of Realtors, Washington, D.C., *Real Estate Outlook: Market Trends & Insights*.

Values of owner-occupied homes, 2003

	State	U.S.
Total units	765,000	58,809,000
Value of units		
Under $100,000	4.7%	29.6%
$100,000-199,999	37.4%	36.9%
$200,000 or more	58.0%	33.5%
Median value	$226,202	$142,275
Rank among all states 5		

Units are owner-occupied one-family houses whose numbers are
rounded to nearest thousand. Data are extrapolated from
survey samples.
Source: U.S. Census Bureau, American Community Survey.

EDUCATION

Public school enrollment, 2002

Prekindergarten through grade 8
State enrollment 406,000
Total U.S. enrollment. 34,135,000
State share of U.S. total 1.19%

Grades 9 through 12
State enrollment 164,000
Total U.S. enrollment. 14,067,000
State share of U.S. total 1.17%

Enrollment rates
State public school enrollment rate. 91.3%
Overall U.S. rate 90.4%
Rank among states in 2002. 19
Rank among states in 1995. 28

Enrollment figures (which include unclassified students) are
rounded to nearest thousand pupils during fall school term.
Enrollment rates are based on enumerated resident population
estimate for July 1, 2002.
Source: U.S. National Center for Education Statistics.

Public college finances, 2003-2004

FTE enrollment in public institutions of higher education
Students in state institutions 70,000
Students in all U.S. public institutions 9,916,600
State share of U.S. total 0.71
Rank among states 36

**State and local government appropriations for higher
    education**
State appropriation per FTE $8,916
National average $5,716
Rank among states 4
State & local tax revenue going to higher
    education 5.0%

FTE = full-time equivalent in public postsecondary programs,
including summer sessions; student numbers are rounded to
nearest hundred. Funding figures for 2003-2004 academic year
include financial aid to students in state public institutions and
exclude money for research, agriculture experiment stations,
teaching hospitals, and medical schools; figures are rounded to
nearest thousand dollars.
Source: Higher Education Executive Officers, Denver, Colorado.

TRANSPORTATION AND TRAVEL

Highway mileage, 2003

Interstate highways	346
Other freeways and expressways	236
Arterial roads	2,785
Collector roads	3,037
Local roads.	14,685
Urban roads	14,969
Rural roads	6,120
Total state mileage.	21,089
U.S. total	3,974,107
State share	0.53%
Rank among states	44

Note that combined urban and rural road mileage matches the
total of the other categories.
Source: U.S. Federal Highway Administration.

Motor vehicle registrations and driver licenses, 2003

Vehicle registrations	State	U.S.	Share	Rank
Autos, trucks, buses	2,964,000	231,390,000	1.28%	29
Autos only	2,041,000	135,670	1.50%	21
Motorcycles	63,000	5,328,000	1.18%	27
Driver licenses	2,660,000	196,166,000	1.36%	27

Figures, which do not include vehicles owned by military services,
are rounded to the nearest thousand. Figures for automobiles
include taxis.
Source: U.S. Federal Highway Administration.

Domestic travel expenditures, 2003

Spending by U.S. residents on overnight trips and
day trips of at least 50 miles from home

Total expenditures within state	$6.709 bill.
Total expenditures within U.S.	$490.87 bill.
State share of U.S. total	1.4%
Rank among states	26

Source: Travel Industry Association of America.

Retail gasoline prices, 2003-2007

Average price per gallon at the pump

Year	U.S.	State
2003	$1.267	$1.256
2004	$1.316	$1.333
2005	$1.644	$1.615
2007	$2.298	$2.464

Excise tax per gallon in 2004	25.0¢
Rank among all states in 2007 prices	7

Prices are averages of all grades of gasoline sold at the pump
during March months in 2003-2005 and during February, 2007.
Averages for 2006, during which prices rose higher, are not
available.

Source: U.S. Energy Information Agency, *Petroleum Marketing
Monthly* (2003-2005 data); American Automobile Association
(2007 data).

CRIME AND LAW ENFORCEMENT

State and local police officers, 2000-2004

	2000	2002	2004
Total officers			
U.S.	654,601	665,555	675,734
State	7,761	7,788	7,898*
*Net change, 2000-2004			+1.77%
Officers per 1,000 residents			
U.S.	2.33	2.31	2.30
State	2.28	2.25	2.25
State rank	19	19	20

Totals include state and local police and sheriffs.
Source: Carsey Institute, University of New Hampshire.

Crime rates, 2003

Incidents per 100,000 residents

Crimes	State	U.S.
Violent crimes		
Total incidents	308	475
Murder	3	6
Forcible rape	19	32
Robbery	119	142
Aggravated assault	168	295
Property crimes		
Total incidents	2,607	3,588
Burglary	448	741
Larceny/theft	1,842	2,415
Motor vehicle theft	317	433
All crimes	2,915	4,063

Source: U.S. Federal Bureau of Investigation, *Crime in the United
States,* annual.

State prison populations, 1980-2003

	State	U.S.	State share
1980	4,308	305,458	1.41%
1990	10,500	708,393	1.48%
1996	15,007	1,025,624	1.46%
2000	18,355	1,391,261	1.32%
2003	19,846	1,470,045	1.35%

State figures include jail inmates but exclude prisoners in federal
penitentiaries.
Source: U.S. Bureau of Justice Statistics, *Prisoners in 2003.*

Delaware

Location: Atlantic coast

Area and rank: 1,982 square miles (5,153 square kilometers); 2,489 square miles (6,447 square kilometers) including water; forty-ninth largest state in area

Coastline: 28 miles (45 kilometers) on the Atlantic Ocean

Shoreline: 381 miles (613 kilometers)

Population and rank: 830,000 (2004); forty-fifth largest state in population

Capital city: Dover (32,135 people in 2000 census)

Largest city: Wilmington (72,664 people in 2000 census)

Entered Union and rank: December 7, 1787; first state

The architecture of the center of the University of Delaware campus, in Newark, recalls that of the University of Virginia, whose main buildings were designed by Thomas Jefferson.

Present constitution adopted: 1897

Counties: 3

State name: "Delaware" was named after the Delaware River and Bay, which was named for Sir Thomas West, Baron De La Warr

State nickname: Diamond State; First State; Small Wonder

Motto: Liberty and independence

State flag: Blue field with yellow diamond with state coat of arms and date of entrance to Union

DECEMBER 7, 1787

Highest point: Ebright Road—442 feet (135 meters)

Lowest point: Atlantic Ocean—sea level

Highest recorded temperature: 110 degrees Fahrenheit (43 degrees Celsius)—Millsboro, 1930

Lowest recorded temperature: –17 degrees Fahrenheit (–27 degrees Celsius)—Millsboro, 1893

State song: "Our Delaware"

State tree: American holly

State flower: Peach blossom

State bird: Blue Hen chicken

State fish: Weakfish

Delaware History

Of the fifty states, only Rhode Island is smaller in land mass than Delaware, which stretches one hundred miles from north to south and varies in width from ten to thirty-five miles. Bounded on the north by Pennsylvania, on the south and west by Maryland, and on the east by the Atlantic Ocean and the Delaware River, whose east bank is in New Jersey, this small state, with a land mass of 1,982 square miles, has just three counties, New Castle in the north, Kent in the middle, and Sussex in the south. The state's mean elevation is about sixty feet.

Early History. As early as 1609, English explorer Henry Hudson sailed on what became known as the Delaware River and the Delaware Bay. By 1631, the Dutch had established the first European settlement in the area around present-day Lewes, in the southeastern part of the state. Long before European settlement began in the region, prehistoric Indians occupied the area. Archaeological excavations at Island Field, twenty miles south of Dover, Delaware's capital, unearthed Indian graves that were close to one thousand years old. The Native Americans in this area are thought to have been the Owascos, a tribe related to the Iroquois, who inhabited the Finger Lakes region in New York.

Later American Indian inhabitants in northern Delaware included the Lenni-Lenape, also called the Delaware. Near the ocean and on the Delaware Bay lived the Nanticoke and Assateague tribes. These Indians massacred the first Dutch settlers in the area near Lewes. When more permanent settlement occurred with the arrival of the Swedes, these tribes disappeared from the area.

Permanent Settlements in Delaware. By 1638 a permanent Swedish settlement was established at Fort Christina, which is close to Wilmington on the Delaware River in the state's north. Peter Minuit, who had

Governor Ross mansion in Dover. (Courtesy, Delaware Tourism Office)

been colonial governor of New Amsterdam (present-day New York), helped create this settlement for the New Sweden Company, partly sponsored by the Dutch. They soon withdrew their support, leaving a hearty band of Swedes to manage as well as they could on their own. Their governor, Johan Printz, was an able leader who almost single-handedly sustained the beleaguered community.

This settlement, which eventually extended from below Wilmington to Philadelphia, had about one thousand inhabitants. It was eventually overcome in 1655 by Dutch forces sent from New Amsterdam. In 1664, however, the British, rankling at the inroads the Dutch were making on English trade, assaulted New Amsterdam and captured it, then, after a considerable battle, took the Dutch fort at New Castle. The whole of New York and Delaware became part of the province of New York. Delaware remained so until 1682, when the duke of York gave Delaware to William Penn, who owned Pennsylvania.

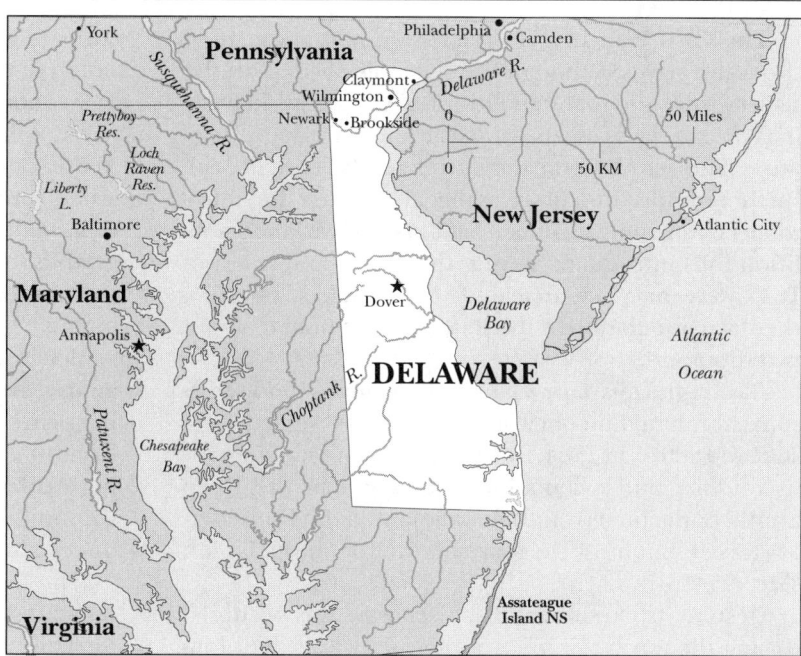

At first, Penn, whose colony needed more direct access to the ocean, tried to merge his two holdings, but the people in southern Delaware feared that their colony might in time be overwhelmed by Pennsylvania, many times its size. In 1704, Penn finally permitted the people of Delaware to form their own assembly and, although the area had the same governor as Pennsylvania, to make their own laws.

The Revolt Against England. Although sentiment about gaining independence from England was spreading, Delaware had many loyalists among its inhabitants. George Read, one of Delaware's three delegates to the Continental Congress in 1774, voted against the colonies' declaring independence from England. Had another delegate, Caesar Rodney, not ridden on horseback all night from Dover, Delaware, to Philadelphia to cast the deciding vote, Delaware might not have joined the twelve other colonies in supporting the Declaration of Independence.

In 1777, British forces making their way from the Chesapeake Bay to Philadelphia invaded Delaware. George Washington's army had dug in close to Wilmington, but the British troops cut into Pennsylvania south of Wilmington and finally met Washington's men at Brandywine. After the Battle of Brandywine, the British took Wilmington and controlled it until they gained complete control of the Delaware River in June, 1778.

After the Revolutionary War, Delaware, in 1787, became the first of the newly formed states to ratify the United States Constitution, thereby earning one of its nicknames, the First State. Because of its size, Delaware feared it would be viewed as politically inferior to larger states. During the Constitutional Convention in 1787, Delaware called for equal representation for all states. Finally, the Delaware delegation accepted a compromise whereby every state would have two senators but would have representation in the House of Representatives based on each state's population.

The War of 1812. Delaware, which was a Federalist state, opposed the War of 1812. Once the United States entered that war, however, Delaware gave its reluctant support. Residents of the state feared an invasion when the British took Washington and, after burning the executive mansion, attacked Baltimore. Delaware was spared by the British, whose only assault on it was an abortive bombardment of Lewes in 1813.

The du Pont Company. In 1802, E. I. du Pont built a munitions factory on the Brandywine River. This marked the beginning of the highly influential enterprise E. I. du Pont de Nemours and Company, which grew into one of the most important chemical companies in the world. The presence of this company in Delaware eventually attracted other corporations to the region.

In time changing its name to the du Pont Company, having long since expanded from its original munitions manufacturing, it boasts a large nylon plant in Seaford, in the southwestern part of Delaware, and two major pigment factories in other parts of the state. Its home offices and laboratories are located in both Wilmington and Newark, Delaware. A large refinery in Delaware City drew many petrochemical companies to the state.

The Civil War. In 1790, Delaware had about nine thousand slaves, although the state was divided on the slavery issue and many abolitionists were active in helping African slaves escape from the South through Delaware. The state's first constitution, in 1776, made the further importation of slaves illegal. Because the state's tobacco industry was dependent upon slave labor, abolition bills introduced during the 1790's and again in 1847 were narrowly defeated. Nevertheless, by 1860, the slave population in the state had declined to about two thousand.

Although Delaware was staunchly opposed to secession, Abraham Lincoln won no electoral votes from the state in 1860 or in 1864. Delaware was more northern in its outlook and orientation than states in the Deep South. Some men from Delaware joined the Confederate forces, but most Delawareans fought on the Union side.

Despite its Union leanings, Delaware was occupied during the war by Union troops sent by President Lincoln to disarm some of the militia whose loyalty was suspect and to guard the polling places during elections. At war's end, many of the people in Delaware were so incensed by the federal government's punitive mea-

sures that the state became solidly Democrat, as did much of the Deep South.

Economy. Strategically situated on the Delaware River, Wilmington became a center of industrial activity in the state. In the city and its environs are textile mills, a steel foundry, automobile assembly operations, paper mills, and tanneries. Many large national corporations established their headquarters in Delaware, primarily in Wilmington, because of state's favorable business climate.

Because of its location near the point where the Delaware River flows into the Atlantic Ocean, Wilmington has proved an ideal location for shipbuilders, who built iron-hulled ships during the nineteenth century. During World War II, the largest employer in the state was a shipbuilding company based in Wilmington that produced ships for the U.S. Navy and Merchant Marine.

The Dover Air Force Base helped Delaware's economy substantially. The national headquarters of the International Reading Association in Newark, whose outreach is enormous, serves ninety thousand members in ninety-nine countries and employs more than eighty people in its headquarters. In 1998, nearly one-third of the people who worked in Delaware worked in the ser-

Kent County farm country. (Courtesy, Delaware Tourism Office)

vice sector, whereas slightly more than 20 percent were engaged in construction and about 15 percent in some aspect of manufacturing. The unemployment rate in that year was about 4 percent. The 1997 per-capita income was $29,022, up from $10,339 in 1980. The state had 2,667 federal employees in 1997 with average annual salaries of $40,159.

Despite its size, Delaware has a thriving agricultural industry that produces soybeans, lima beans, corn, potatoes, mushrooms, and various grains. It also produces considerable livestock, mainly chickens, hogs, and cattle. Its timber industry produced fifteen million board feet in 1998. Although it is not rich in minerals, Delaware produces magnesium, as well as sand, gravel, and gemstones.

Delaware's Population. A few of Delaware's Native American population, especially descendants of the Nanticoke and Moor tribes, remain in Kent and Sussex counties, although most of the native population was driven out or killed in combat with the Europeans who settled the state. In 1770, more than 20 percent of Delaware's population was African American; in 1998, 16.9 percent was black and less than 3 percent Hispanic.

During the mid-nineteenth century, many Germans and Irish came to Delaware. By the end of the century, southern and eastern Europeans began to arrive in large numbers, seeking work in the state's thriving industries. The first decades of the twentieth century saw the arrival of many Ukrainians and Greeks. As industry grew, many people arrived from other states to take advantage of Delaware's economic opportunities. In 1998, about 3 percent of the state's population was foreign born.

Delaware, lying in the highly urbanized corridor that runs from Boston to Richmond, Virginia, experienced rapid population growth in the last third of the twentieth century. Its population density of 340.8 people per square mile is among the greatest in the United States, and its population of three-quarters of a million should exceed the million mark well before 2010.

Politics. As Delaware approached the twenty-first century, it was clear that change in its political landscape was imminent. This small state had just four major offices—governor, one member of the House of Representatives, and two U.S. senators. These offices had been held by a few individuals for a considerable period. The incumbent member of the House, Michael Castle, had been a popular governor before term limits directed him to Washington, D.C. William Roth had been senator since 1970—a duration of thirty years by the end of his term—and was nearly eighty years old. The popular governor, Thomas R. Carper, was also barred from reelection by term limits. The other U.S. senator, Democrat Joe Biden, was a well-regarded and stable fixture in the state; he was not up for reelection in 2000.

Although Castle aspired to the U.S. Senate, he was unwilling to challenge fellow Republican Roth in election primaries. However, Democrat Carper had no such inhibitions. When the election took place, Carper ousted Roth, mostly, it was said, because of Roth's advanced age. Veteran state politician Ruth Ann Minner was elected governor. Castle fended off his Democrat opponent without difficulty and remained the state's congress member in 2000 and in succeeding elections. In 2002, Biden easily overwhelmed his Republican opposition, winning by 58 to 41 percent of the vote. In 2004, Minner was reelected by a 51-46 percent margin.

Court Cases. Delaware found itself at the center of national attention in the autumn of 2004. In a bitter dispute, top Walt Disney Company management, in particular Chief Executive Michael Eisner, fought a courtroom battle in Delaware with Disney shareholders, led by Walt Disney's nephew Roy E. Disney, over business decisions costing the company hundreds of millions of dollars. At issue was a severance payment to former Eisner friend and Disney president Michael Ovitz. In the end, after dramatic and emotional testimony, Disney management prevailed. Critics said that pertinent Delaware law affecting the central issue of the trial, the "business judgment rule," reflected a race to the bottom of bad law. In June, 2006, the Delaware Supreme Court affirmed the decision. In 2003, in a quite different case, the Delaware-based DuPont Company, the chemical giant, agreed to a $348 million settlement of a site over its perfluorooctanoic chemical, which was found in a West Virginia water supply.

Hurricanes. Situated partially on the Atlantic Ocean in the direct path of storms moving up the Atlantic Coast from the south, Delaware has long been prey to hurricanes. Even though many are downgraded to lesser storms when they reach Delaware's shores, some still pack a sufficient punch to cause damage. Thus, when the remnants of Hurricane Gordon in September, 2000, and Tropical Storm Allison in June, 2001, passed through the state, they dumped considerable rain, though they did little damage. However, in July, 2003, torrential rains from the remains of Tropical Storm Bill flooded hundreds of homes, trapped motorists, and damaged infrastructure. A few months later, in September, Hurricane Isabel did enough damage, including prolonged power outages, that President George W. Bush declared the state a disaster area. Storms in later years did similar damage and in some cases caused tornadoes.

R. Baird Shuman
Updated by the Editor

Delaware Time Line

1609	Henry Hudson explores the Delaware River and Delaware Bay for the Dutch East Indies.
1610	Samuel Argall of Virginia blown off course into a bay that he names for his governor, Lord De La Warr.
1631	Dutch found a settlement near present-day Lewes.
1632	Native Americans destroy the Dutch settlement.
1638	Swedish settlement is established at Fort Christina.
1655	Dutch conquer the Swedish settlement and add it to the New Netherland settlement.
1664	New Netherland is taken by the British and renamed New York.
1682	Duke of York gives Delaware to William Penn.
1704	Delaware's General Assembly meets apart from Pennsylvania's legislature and makes its own laws.
1739	Wilmington receives its royal charter.
1743	University of Delaware opens in Newark.
1776	Delaware breaks from England, writes constitution for Delaware State.
1777	British capture Wilmington; Delaware General Assembly moves to Dover from New Castle.
Dec. 7, 1787	Delaware becomes the first state to ratify the United States Constitution.
1792	Delaware adopts second state constitution.
1802	E. I. du Pont opens powder mill on the Brandywine.
1813	British bombard Lewes in War of 1812.
1829	Chesapeake and Delaware Canal opens.
1829	Free public schools are mandated.
1831	Third state constitution is adopted.
1838	Philadelphia, Wilmington, and Baltimore Railroad is completed.
1861	Delaware refuses to join secession movement.
1897	New state constitution is adopted.
1912	Wilmington Society of the Fine Arts opens its museum, which grows into the Delaware Art Museum.
1917	Passage of state income and inheritance taxes.
1924	Completion of first highway running the length of Delaware.
1951	Delaware Memorial Bridge opens, linking Delaware and New Jersey.
1956	International Reading Association is established in Newark.
1966	Reorganized state government is established in New Castle County.
1968	Legislative reapportionment is completed.
1969	Henry Francis du Pont dies, leaving Winterthur, his 125-room residence, and most of its contents as a public museum in Wilmington.
1976	Rockwood Museum opens in New Castle; Willington Square with its six restored colonial homes relocated in a Wilmington park.
1981	Financial Center Development Act is enacted.
1987	Senator Joseph Biden withdraws presidential bid after being charged with plagiarism.

Chesapeake and Delaware Canal Bridge. (Courtesy, Delaware Tourism Office)

1988	Legislature passes law restricting hostile takeovers of businesses incorporated in-state.
1990	Laws passed enabling banks to sell and underwrite insurance.
1997	Seventeen hazardous waste sites placed on National Priority List.
Nov. 7, 2000	Al Gore wins Delaware's presidential electoral votes; Governor Thomas R. Carper defeats Senator William Roth for U.S. Senate seat. Ruth Ann Minner is elected governor.
Sept., 2003	Hurricane Isabel causes severe power outages and millions of dollars in damage.
Dec. 13, 2003	Former senator Roth, responsible for the tax-free Individual Retirement Accounts (IRAs) that bear his name, dies in Washington, D.C.
Nov. 2, 2004	John Kerry defeats George W. Bush in presidential balloting, despite his national loss; Minner is re-elected governor.

Notes for Further Study

Published Sources. One of the best comprehensive histories of Delaware is John A. Munroe's *History of Delaware* (5th ed., 2006). It relates how the state came into being and is especially effective in outlining clearly the chaotic situation that resulted in Delaware once being a part of New York. Historical maps, archival illustrations, and first-person accounts help tell the story of the state's history in National Geographic's *Delaware 1638-1776* (2006). Slavery existed but never really flourished in Delaware; Alice Dunbar-Nelson's essay, "Delaware: A Jewel of Inconsistencies," written in the 1920's and reproduced in *These "Colored" United States: African American Essays from the 1920's* (1996), edited by Tom Lutz and Susanne Ashton, offers an interesting retrospective view of the situation by an African American who was affected by the ambivalent situation regarding people of color in the state. William H. Williams's *Slavery and Freedom in Delaware, 1639-1865* (1996) examines how slavery existed in a state that had few slave owners and many active abolitionists. William W. Boyer examines politics and public policy in *Governing Delaware: Policy Problems of the First State* (2000). For young adults, Roberta Wiener and James R. Arnold provide a concise history of the state with *Delaware* (2004), while

Aaron Raymond discusses the colonial era for this audience in *Primary Source History of the Colony of Delaware* (2006).

Jay F. Custer's *Delaware Prehistoric Archaeology: An Ecological Approach* (1984) reaches useful conclusions about the earliest

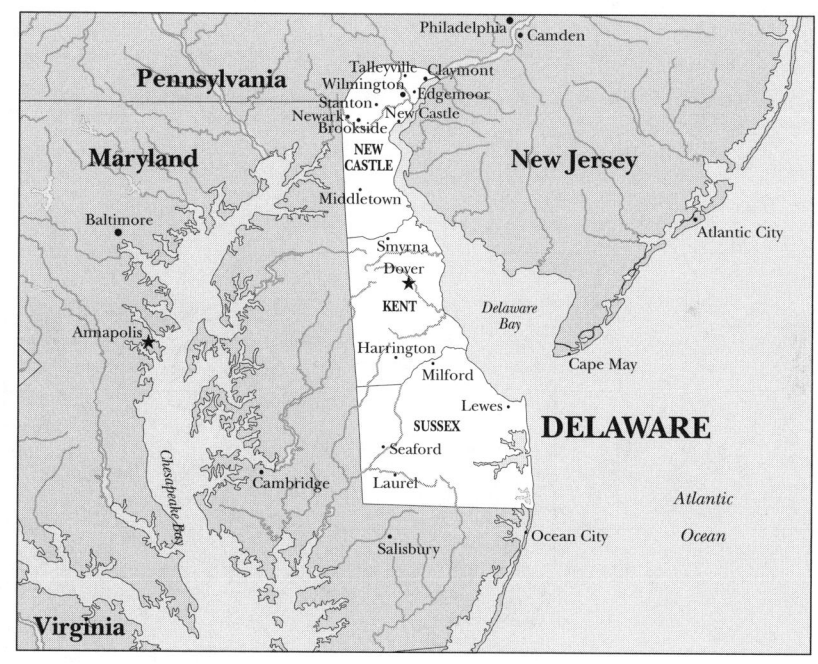

Counties

history of the Delaware area based on archaelogical findings. His *Prehistoric Culture in the Delmarva Peninsula: An Archeological Study* (1989) also delves into some of the state's ancient history as revealed in artifacts and ancient burial grounds. David McCutchen offers cogent insights into early Indian cultures in *The Red Record: The Wallam Plum—The Oldest Native North American History* (1993). A reliable study of later Native Americans in Delaware is found in C. A. Weslager's *The Delaware Indians: A History* (1972) and in John Bierhorst's *Myth of the Lenape: Guide and Texts* (1995). The latter presents the folk traditions of these Delaware Indians. In *New Sweden in America*

County	2000 pop.	Rank in pop.	Sq. miles	Rank in area
Kent	126,697	3	590.7	2
New Castle	500,265	1	426.3	3
Sussex	156,638	2	937.7	1

Source: U.S. Census Bureau; National Association of Counties.

(1995), edited by Carol E. Hoffecker and others, one will find six informative essays that touch on the early Swedish settlement of Delaware in the seventeenth century.

Web Resources. A reasonable starting point for finding out more about Delaware and for locating other Web sites and their addresses is the state's Web site (www.delaware .gov/). This Web site offers material about many aspects of state government, tourism, history, commerce, economy, and population. A Web site run by the state's department of tourism (www.visitdelaware.com/) also provides comprehensive information about many of the state's attractions and facilities.

Research resources can be found on the University of Dela-

ware Library's Web site (www.lib.udel.edu). A good source for information about business and commerce is found on the Delaware State Chamber of Commerce (www.dscc.com/). For those interested in visiting any of the state's history museums, detailed information about their collections and visitor information can be found by using the links on Census Finder Historical Museums of Delaware (www.censusfinder .com/delaware-historical-museums.htm). For those interested in researching state history or one's ancestry in the state, the Historical Society of Delaware (www.hsd.org/) and Moors and Naticokes: History and Genealogy of Delaware (members.aol.com/jacklyn001/main.htm?f=fs) are good destinations.

Cities
With 6,000 or more residents

Rank	City	Population
1	Wilmington	72,664
2	Dover (capital)	32,135
3	Newark	28,547
4	Pike Creek	19,751
5	Bear	17,593
6	Brookside	14,806
7	Hockessin	12,902
8	Glasgow	12,840
9	Claymont	9,220

Rank	City	Population
10	North Star	8,277
11	Wilmington Manor	8,262
12	Milford	6,732
13	Seaford	6,699
14	Middletown	6,161

Population figures are from 2000 census.
Source: U.S. Bureau of the Census.

Index to Tables

DEMOGRAPHICS

Resident state and national populations, 1970-2004

Population figures given in thousands

	State pop.	U.S. pop.	Share	Rank
1970	548	203,302	0.3%	46
1980	594	226,546	0.3%	47
1985	618	237,924	0.3%	47
1990	666	248,765	0.3%	46
1995	730	262,761	0.3%	46
2000	784	281,425	0.3%	45
2004	830	293,655	0.3%	45

Source: U.S. Census Bureau, Current Population Reports, 2006.

Resident population by age, 2004

Age Group	Total persons
Under 5 years	54,000
5 to 17 years.	140,000
18 to 24 years.	84,000
25 to 34 years	110,000
35 to 44 years	128,000
45 to 54 years	119,000
55 to 64 years.	87,000
65 to 74 years.	58,000
75 to 84 years.	38,000
85 years and older	13,000
All age groups.	830,000

Portion of residents 65 and older	13.1%
National rank in portion of oldest residents	19
National average	12.4%

Population figures are rounded to nearest thousand persons;
figures include armed forces personnel stationed in the state.
Source: U.S. Bureau of the Census, 2006.

Resident population by race, Hispanic origin, 2004

Category	State pop.	Share	U.S.
All residents	830	100.00%	100.00%
Non-Hispanic white	583	70.24%	67.37%
Hispanic white	42	5.06%	13.01%
Other Hispanic	6	0.72%	1.06%
African American	169	20.36%	12.77%
Native American	3	0.36%	0.96%
Asian, Pacific Islander	21	2.53%	4.37%
Two or more categories	11	1.33%	1.51%

Population figures are in thousands. Persons counted as "Hispanic" (Latino) may be of any race. Because of overlapping categories, categories may not add up to 100%. Shares in column 3 are percentages of each category within the state; these figures may be compared to the national percentages in column 4.
Source: U.S. Bureau of the Census, 2006.

Projected state population, 2000-2030

Year	Population
2000	784,000
2005	837,000
2010	884,000
2015	927,000
2020	963,000
2025	991,000
2030	1,013,000
Population increase, 2000-2030	229,000
Percentage increase, 2000-2030	29.2

Projections are based on data from the 2000 census.
Source: U.S. Census Bureau.

VITAL STATISTICS

Infant mortality rates, 1980-2002

	1980	1990	2000	2002
All state residents	13.9	10.1	9.2	8.7
All U.S. residents	12.6	9.2	9.4	9.1
All state white residents	9.8	9.7	7.9	7.3
All U.S. white residents	10.6	7.6	5.7	5.8
All state black residents	27.9	20.1	14.8	12.9
All U.S. black residents	22.2	18.0	14.1	14.4

Figures represent deaths per 1,000 live births of resident infants under 1 year old, exclusive of fetal deaths. Figures for all residents include members of other racial categories not listed separately.
Source: U.S. Census Bureau, *Statistical Abstract of the United States,* 2006.

Abortion rates, 1990 and 2000

	1990	2000
Total abortions	6,000	5,000
Rate per 1,000 women	34.9	31.3
U.S. rate	25.7	21.3
Rank	5	5

Numbers of abortions are rounded to nearest thousand; ranks are based on rates.
Source: U.S. Census Bureau.

Marriages and divorces, 2004

Total marriages	5,100
Rate per 1,000 population	6.1
National rate per 1,000 population	7.4
Rank among all states	42
Total divorces	3,100
Rate per 1,000 population	3.7
National rate per 1,000 population	3.7
Rank among all states	24

Figures are for all marriages and divorces performed within the state, including those of nonresidents; totals are rounded to the nearest hundred. Ranks are for highest to lowest figures; note that divorce data are not available for five states.
Source: U.S. National Center for Health Statistics, *Vital Statistics of the United States,* 2006.

Death rates by leading causes, 2002
Deaths per 100,000 resident population

Cause	State	U.S.
Heart disease	237.6	241.7
Cancer	200.8	193.2
Cerebrovascular diseases	50.2	56.4
Accidents other than motor vehicle	36.2	37.0
Motor vehicle accidents	15.0	15.7
Chronic lower respiratory diseases	43.3	43.3
Diabetes mellitus	26.6	25.4
HIV	8.7	4.9
Suicide	9.2	11.0
Homicide	4.7	6.1
All causes	849.8	847.3
Rank in overall death rate among states		30

Figures exclude nonresidents who died in the state. Causes of death follow International Classification of Diseases. Rank is from highest to lowest death rate in the United States.
Source: U.S. National Center for Health Statistics, *National Vital Statistics Report,* 2006.

ECONOMY

Gross state product, 1990-2004
In current dollars

Year	State product	Nat'l product	State share
1990	$20.1 billion	$5.67 trillion	0.35%
2000	$42.4 billion	$9.75 trillion	0.43%
2002	$47.0 billion	$10.41 trillion	0.45%
2003	$50.5 billion	$10.92 trillion	0.46%
2004	$54.5 billion	$11.65 trillion	0.47%

Source: U.S. Bureau of Economic Analysis, *Survey of Current Business,* July, 2005.

Gross state product by industry, 2003
In billions of dollars

Construction	$1.4
Manufacturing	4.8
Wholesale trade	1.8
Retail trade	2.4
Finance & insurance	15.2
Information	0.9
Professional services	2.8
Health care & social assistance	2.2
Government	3.8
Total state product	$47.0
Total U.S. product	$10,289.2
State share of U.S. total	0.46%
Rank among all states	38

Total figures include industries not listed separately. Amounts are in chained 2000 dollars.
Source: U.S. Bureau of Economic Analysis, *Survey of Current Business,* July, 2005.

Personal income per capita, 1990-2004
In current dollars

	1990	2000	2004
Per capita income	$21,422	$30,869	$35,861
U.S. average	$19,477	$29,845	$32,937
Rank among states	9	13	8

Source: U.S. Bureau of Economic Analysis, *Survey of Current Business,* April, 2005.

Energy consumption, 2001
In trillions of British thermal units (BTU), except as noted

Total energy consumption
Total state energy consumption	293
Total U.S. energy consumption	96,275
State share of U.S. total	0.30%
Rank among states	46

Per capita consumption (In millions of BTU)
Total state per capita consumption	368
Total U.S. per capita consumption	338
Rank among states	21

End-use sectors
Residential	62
Commercial	52
Industrial	113
Transportation	66

Sources of energy
Petroleum	147
Natural gas	52
Coal	38
Hydroelectric power	0
Nuclear electric power	0

Figures for totals include categories not listed separately.
Source: U.S. Energy Information Administration, *State Energy Data Report,* 2001.

Nonfarm employment by sectors, 2004

Total	424,000
Construction	26,000
Manufacturing	35,000
Trade, transportation, utilities	81,000
Information	7,000
Finance, insurance, real estate	45,000
Professional & business services	62,000
Education & health services	52,000
Leisure, hospitality, arts, organizations	40,000
Other services, including repair & maintenance	19,000
Government	58,000

Figures are rounded to nearest thousand persons. "Total" includes mining and natural resources, not listed separately.
Source: U.S. Bureau of Labor Statistics, 2006.

Foreign exports, 1990-2004
In millions of dollars

Year	State	U.S.	State share
1990	1,344	394,045	0.34%
1996	1,594	624,767	0.26%
1997	2,067	688,896	0.30%
2000	2,197	712,055	0.28%
2003	1,886	724,006	0.28%
2004	2,053	769,332	0.27%

Rank among all states in 2004 43

U.S. total does not include U.S. dependencies.
Source: U.S. Census Bureau, *U.S. Merchandise Trade,* series FT 900, 2000; U.S. Census Bureau, *U.S. International Trade in Goods and Services,* Series FT 900, 2005.

LAND USE

Federally owned land, 2003
Areas in acres

	State	U.S.	State share
Total area	1,266,000	2,271,343,000	0.06%
Nonfederal land	1,236,000	1,599,584,000	0.08%
Federal land	30,000	671,759,000	0.00%
Federal share	2.3%	29.6%	—

Areas are rounded to nearest thousand acres. Figures for federally owned land do not include trust properties.
Source: U.S. General Services Administration, *Federal Real Property Profile,* 2006.

Land use, 1997
In acres, rounded to nearest thousand

Total surface area.	1,534,000
Total nonfederal rural land	988,000
Percentage rural land	64.4%
Cropland	485,000
Conservation Reserve Program (CRP*) land	1,000
Pastureland.	24,000
Rangeland	(nil)
Forestland.	352,000
Other rural land	128,000

*CRP is a federal program begun in 1985 to assist private landowners to convert highly erodible cropland to vegetative cover for ten years. Note that some categories of land overlap.
Source: U.S. Department of Agriculture, Natural Resources and Conservation Service, and Iowa State University, Statistical Laboratory, *Summary Report, 1997 National Resources Inventory,* revised December, 2000.

Farms and crop acreage, 2004

	State	U.S.	Share	Rank
Farms	2,000	2,113,000	0.09%	48
Acres (millions)	1	937	0.11%	41
Acres per farm	230	443	—	29

Source: U.S. Department of Agriculture, National Agricultural Statistics Service. Numbers of farms are rounded to nearest thousand units; acreage figures are rounded to nearest million. Rankings, including ties, are based on rounded figures.

GOVERNMENT AND FINANCE

Units of local government, 2002

	State	Total U.S.	Rank
All local governments	339	87,525	45
Counties	3	3,034	47
Municipalities	57	19,429	42
Townships	0	16,504	—
School districts	19	13,506	41
Special districts	260	35,052	40

Only 48 states have county governments, 20 states have township governments ("towns" in New England, Minnesota, New York, and Wisconsin), and 46 states have school districts. Special districts encompass such functions as natural resources, fire protection, and housing and community development.
Source: U.S. Census Bureau, *Census of Governments.*

State government revenue, 2002

Total revenue.	$4,842 mill.
General revenue	$4,633 mill.
Per capita revenue	$5,748
U.S. per capita average	$3,689
Rank among states.	2
Intergovernment revenue	
Total	$922 mill.
From federal government	$891 mill.
Charges and miscellaneous	
Total	$1,538 mill.
Current charges	$623 mill.
Misc. general income	$914 mill.
Insurance trust revenue	$199 mill.
Taxes	
Total	$2,174 mill.
Per capita taxes	$2,697
Rank among states.	2
Property taxes	(nil)
Sales taxes	$323 mill.
License taxes	$780 mill.
Individual income taxes	$717 mill.
Corporate income taxes	$252 mill.
Other taxes	$102 mill.

Total revenue figures include items not listed separately here.
Source: U.S. Bureau of the Census.

State government expenditures, 2002

General expenditures
Total state expenditures . . . . $4,646 mill.
Intergovernmental . . . . $823 mill.

Per capita expenditures
State $5,252
Average of all states $3,859
Rank among states 4

Selected direct expenditures
Education. . . . . $733 mill.
Public welfare . . . . $659 mill.
Health, hospital . . . . $311 mill.
Highways . . . . $332 mill.
Police protection . . . . $68 mill.
Corrections. $245 mill.
Natural resources . . . . $68 mill.
Parks and recreation . . . . $50 mill.
Government administration. . . . . $331 mill.
Interest on debt . . . . $255 mill.
Total direct expenditures . . . . $3,410 mill.

Totals include items not listed separately.
Source: U.S. Census Bureau.

POLITICS

Governors since statehood
D = Democrat; R = Republican; O = other;
(r) resigned; (d) died in office; (i) removed from office

John McKinly. 1777
Thomas McKean 1777
George Read 1777-1778
Caesar Rodney 1778-1781
John Dickinson. . . . . (r) 1781-1782
John Cook 1782-1783
Nicholas Van Dyke 1783-1786
Thomas Collins . . . . (d) 1786-1789
Jehu Davis 1789
Joshua Clayton (O) 1789-1796
Gunning Bedford (O). . . . . (d) 1796-1797
Daniel Rogers (O) 1797-1799
Richard Bassett (O) . . . . (r) 1799-1801
James Sykes (O) 1801-1802
David Hall (O) 1802-1805
Nathaniel Mitchell (O) 1805-1808
George Truitt (O) 1808-1811
Joseph Haslet (O) 1811-1814
Daniel Rodney (O) 1814-1817
John Clark (O). 1817-1820
Jacob Stout (O) 1820-1821
John Collins (O). . . . . (d) 1821-1822
Caleb Rodney (O) 1822-1823
Joseph Haslet (O) . . . . (d) 1823
Charles Thomas (O). 1823-1824
Samuel Paynter (O) 1824-1827
Charles Polk (O). 1827-1830

David Hazzard (D) 1830-1833
Caleb P. Bennett (D) . . . . (d) 1833-1836
Charles Polk (O) 1836-1837
Cornelius P. Comegys (O) 1837-1841
William B. Cooper (O) 1841-1845
Thomas Stockton (O) . . . . (d) 1845-1846
Joseph Maull (O) . . . . (d) 1846
William Temple (O) 1846-1847
William Tharp (D) 1847-1851
William H. H. Ross (D) 1851-1855
Peter F. Causey (O) 1855-1859
William Burton (D) 1859-1863
William Cannon (O) . . . . (d) 1863-1865
Gove Saulsbury (D) 1865-1871
James Ponder (D) 1871-1875
John P. Cochran (D) 1875-1879
John W. Hall (D). 1879-1883
Charles C. Stockley (D) 1883-1887
Benjamin T. Biggs (D) 1887-1891
Robert J. Reynolds (D) 1891-1895
Joshua H. Marvel (R) . . . . (d) 1895
William T. Watson (D) 1895-1897
Ebe W. Tunnell (D) 1897-1901
John Hunn (R). 1901-1905
Preston Lea (R) 1905-1909
Simeon S. Pennewell (R) 1909-1913
Charles R. Miller (R) 1913-1917
John G. Townsend, Jr. (R) 1917-1921
William D. Denney (R) 1921-1925
Robert P. Robinson (R) 1925-1929
Clayton Douglass Buck (R) 1929-1937
Richard C. McMullen (D) 1937-1941
Walter W. Bacon (R). 1941-1949
Elbert N. Carvel (D) 1949-1953
James Caleb Boggs (R) . . . . (r) 1953-1960
David P. Buckson (R) 1960-1961
Elbert N. Carvel (D) 1961-1965
Charles L. Terry, Jr. (D) 1965-1969
Russell W. Peterson (R) 1969-1973
Sherman W. Tribbitt (D) 1973-1977
Pierre Samuel du Pont IV (R) 1977-1985
Michael N. Castle (R) 1985-1993
Thomas R. Carper (D). . . . . (r) 1993-2001
Ruth Ann Minner (D) 2001-

Governors were called state presidents before 1792.

Composition of congressional delegations, 1989-2007

	Dem	Rep	Total
House of Representatives			
101st Congress, 1989			
State delegates	1	0	1
Total U.S.	259	174	433
102d Congress, 1991			
State delegates	1	0	1
Total U.S.	267	167	434
103d Congress, 1993			
State delegates	0	1	1
Total U.S.	258	176	434
104th Congress, 1995			
State delegates	0	1	1
Total U.S.	197	236	433
105th Congress, 1997			
State delegates	0	1	1
Total U.S.	206	228	434
106th Congress, 1999			
State delegates	0	1	1
Total U.S.	211	222	433
107th Congress, 2001			
State delegates	0	1	1
Total U.S.	211	221	432
108th Congress, 2003			
State delegates	0	1	1
Total U.S.	205	229	434
109th Congress, 2005			
State delegates	0	1	1
Total U.S.	202	231	433
110th Congress, 2007			
State delegates	0	1	1
Total U.S.	233	202	435
Senate			
101st Congress, 1989			
State delegates	1	1	2
Total U.S.	55	45	100
102d Congress, 1991			
State delegates	1	1	2
Total U.S.	56	44	100
103d Congress, 1993			
State delegates	1	1	2
Total U.S.	57	43	100
104th Congress, 1995			
State delegates	1	1	2
Total U.S.	46	53	99
105th Congress, 1997			
State delegates	1	1	2
Total U.S.	45	55	100

	Dem	Rep	Total
106th Congress, 1999			
State delegates	1	1	2
Total U.S.	45	54	99
107th Congress, 2001			
State delegates	2	0	2
Total U.S.	50	50	100
108th Congress, 2003			
State delegates	2	0	2
Total U.S.	48	51	99
109th Congress, 2005			
State delegates	2	0	2
Total U.S.	44	55	99
110th Congress, 2007			
State delegates	2	0	2
Total U.S.	49	49	98

Figures are for starts of first sessions. Totals are for Democrat (Dem.) and Republican (Rep.) members only. House membership totals under 435 and Senate totals under 100 reflect vacancies and seats held by independent party members. When the 110th Congress opened, the Senate's two independent members caucused with the Democrats, giving the Democrats control of the Senate.

Source: U.S. Congress, *Congressional Directory*.

Composition of state legislature, 1990-2006

	Democrats	Republicans
State House (41 seats)		
1990	17	24
1992	18	23
1994	14	27
1996	14	27
1998	15	26
2000	15	26
2002	12	29
2004	15	25
2006	18	23
State Senate (21 seats)		
1990	15	6
1992	15	6
1994	12	9
1996	13	8
1998	13	8
2000	13	8
2002	13	8
2004	13	8
2006	13	8

Figures for total seats may include independents and minor party members. Numbers reflect results of elections in listed years; elected members usually take their seats in the years that follow.

Source: Council of State Governments; *State Elective Officials and the Legislatures*.

Voter participation in presidential elections, 2000 and 2004

	2000	2004
Voting age population		
State	592,000	637,000
Total United States	209,831,000	220,377,000
State share of U.S. total	0.28	0.29
Rank among states	45	45
Portion of voting age population casting votes		
State	55.3%	58.9%
United States	50.3%	55.5%
Rank among states	19	22

Population figures are rounded to nearest thousand and include all residents, regardless of eligibility to vote.
Source: U.S. Census Bureau.

HEALTH AND MEDICAL CARE

Medical professionals
Physicians in 2003 and nurses in 2001

	U.S.	State
Physicians in 2003		
Total	774,849	2,069
Share of U.S. total		0.27%
Rate	266	253
Rank		22
Nurses in 2001		
Total	2,262,020	7,280
Share of U.S. total		0.32%
Rate	793	913
Rank		14

Rates are numbers of physicians and nurses per 100,000 resident population; ranks are based on rates.
Source: American Medical Association, *Physician Characteristics and Distribution in the U.S.*; U.S. Department of Health and Human Services, Health Resources and Services Administration.

Health insurance coverage, 2003

	State	U.S.
Total persons covered	729,000	243,320,000
Total persons not covered	91,000	44,961,000
Portion not covered	11.1%	15.6%
Rank among states	37	—
Children not covered	17,000	8,373,000
Portion not covered	8.5%	11.4%
Rank among states	30	—

Totals are rounded to nearest thousand. Ranks are from the highest to the lowest percentages of persons *not* insured.
Source: U.S. Census Bureau, Current Population Reports.

AIDS, syphilis, and tuberculosis cases, 2003

Disease	U.S. cases	State cases	Rank
AIDS	44,232	216	29
Syphilis	34,270	47	38
Tuberculosis	14,874	33	40

Source: U.S. Centers for Disease Control and Prevention.

Cigarette smoking, 2003
Residents over age 18 who smoke

	U.S.	State	Rank
All smokers	22.1%	21.9%	29
Male smokers	24.8%	26.0%	21
Female smokers	20.3%	18.2%	41

Cigarette smokers are defined as persons who reported having smoked at least 100 cigarettes during their lifetimes and who currently smoked at least occasionally.
Source: U.S. Centers for Disease Control and Prevention, *Morbidity and Mortality Weekly Report*, 53, no. 44 (November 12, 2004).

HOUSING

Home ownership rates, 1985-2004

	1985	1990	1995	2000	2004
State	70.3%	67.7%	71.7%	72.0%	77.3%
Total U.S.	63.9%	63.9%	64.7%	67.4%	69.0%
Rank among states	11	26	6	17	3

Net change in state home ownership rate,
1985-2004 . . . . +7.0%
Net change in U.S. home ownership rate,
1985-2004 . . . . +5.1%

Percentages represent the proportion of owner households to total occupied households.
Source: U.S. Census Bureau, 2006.

Home sales, 2000-2004
In thousands of units

Existing home sales	2000	2002	2003	2004
State sales	12.9	14.5	15.8	18.9
Total U.S. sales	5,171	5,631	6,183	6,784
State share of U.S. total	0.25%	0.26%	0.26%	0.28%
Sales rank among states	46	47	46	46

Units include single-family homes, condos, and co-ops.
Source: National Association of Realtors, Washington, D.C., *Real Estate Outlook: Market Trends & Insights.*

Values of owner-occupied homes, 2003

	State	U.S.
Total units	185,000	58,809,000
Value of units		
Under $100,000	14.5%	29.6%
$100,000-199,999	49.6%	36.9%
$200,000 or more	35.8%	33.5%
Median value	$165,739	$142,275
Rank among all states 16		

Units are owner-occupied one-family houses whose numbers are
rounded to nearest thousand. Data are extrapolated from
survey samples.
Source: U.S. Census Bureau, American Community Survey.

EDUCATION

Public school enrollment, 2002

Prekindergarten through grade 8
State enrollment 82,000
Total U.S. enrollment 34,135,000
State share of U.S. total 0.24%

Grades 9 through 12
State enrollment 34,000
Total U.S. enrollment 14,067,000
State share of U.S. total 0.24%

Enrollment rates
State public school enrollment rate 81.6%
Overall U.S. rate 90.4%
Rank among states in 2002 50
Rank among states in 1995 48

Enrollment figures (which include unclassified students) are
rounded to nearest thousand pupils during fall school term.
Enrollment rates are based on enumerated resident population
estimate for July 1, 2002.
Source: U.S. National Center for Education Statistics.

Public college finances, 2003-2004

FTE enrollment in public institutions of higher education
Students in state institutions 31,000
Students in all U.S. public institutions 9,916,600
State share of U.S. total 0.31
Rank among states 45

**State and local government appropriations for higher
education**
State appropriation per FTE $10,907
National average $5,716
Rank among states 2
State & local tax revenue going to higher
education 6.8%

FTE = full-time equivalent in public postsecondary programs,
including summer sessions; student numbers are rounded to
nearest hundred. Funding figures for 2003-2004 academic year
include financial aid to students in state public institutions and
exclude money for research, agriculture experiment stations,
teaching hospitals, and medical schools; figures are rounded to
nearest thousand dollars.
Source: Higher Education Executive Officers, Denver, Colorado.

TRANSPORTATION AND TRAVEL

Highway mileage, 2003

Interstate highways	41
Other freeways and expressways	14
Arterial roads	630
Collector roads	939
Local roads	4,270
Urban roads	2,029
Rural roads	3,865
Total state mileage	5,894
U.S. total	3,974,107
State share	0.15%
Rank among states	49

Note that combined urban and rural road mileage matches the
total of the other categories.
Source: U.S. Federal Highway Administration.

Motor vehicle registrations and driver licenses, 2003

Vehicle registrations	State	U.S.	Share	Rank
Autos, trucks, buses	687,000	231,390,000	0.30%	47
Autos only	419,000	135,670	0.31%	45
Motorcycles	15,000	5,328,000	0.28%	49
Driver licenses	585,000	196,166,000	0.30%	45

Figures, which do not include vehicles owned by military services,
are rounded to the nearest thousand. Figures for automobiles
include taxis.
Source: U.S. Federal Highway Administration.

Domestic travel expenditures, 2003
Spending by U.S. residents on overnight trips and day trips of at least 50 miles from home

Total expenditures within state . . . . $1.14 bill.
Total expenditures within U.S. . . . . $490.87 bill.
State share of U.S. total 0.2%
Rank among states 50

Source: Travel Industry Association of America.

Retail gasoline prices, 2003-2007
Average price per gallon at the pump

Year	U.S.	State
2003	$1.267	$1.212
2004	$1.316	$1.272
2005	$1.644	$1.542
2007	$2.298	$2.226

Excise tax per gallon in 2004 . . . . 23.0¢
Rank among all states in 2007 prices 32

Prices are averages of all grades of gasoline sold at the pump during March months in 2003-2005 and during February, 2007. Averages for 2006, during which prices rose higher, are not available.
Source: U.S. Energy Information Agency, *Petroleum Marketing Monthly* (2003-2005 data); American Automobile Association (2007 data).

CRIME AND LAW ENFORCEMENT

State and local police officers, 2000-2004

	2000	2002	2004
Total officers			
U.S.	654,601	665,555	675,734
State	2,139	2,206	2,263*
*Net change, 2000-2004			+5.80%
Officers per 1,000 residents			
U.S.	2.33	2.31	2.30
State	2.73	2.74	2.73
State rank	5	5	5

Totals include state and local police and sheriffs.
Source: Carsey Institute, University of New Hampshire.

Crime rates, 2003
Incidents per 100,000 residents

Crimes	State	U.S.
Violent crimes		
Total incidents	658	475
Murder	3	6
Forcible rape	43	32
Robbery	170	142
Aggravated assault	442	295
Property crimes		
Total incidents	3,384	3,588
Burglary	730	741
Larceny/theft	2,302	2,415
Motor vehicle theft	352	433
All crimes	4,042	4,063

Source: U.S. Federal Bureau of Investigation, *Crime in the United States*, annual.

State prison populations, 1980-2003

	State	U.S.	State share
1980	1,474	305,458	0.48%
1990	3,471	708,393	0.49%
1996	5,110	1,025,624	0.50%
2000	6,921	1,391,261	0.50%
2003	6,794	1,470,045	0.46%

State figures include jail inmates but exclude prisoners in federal penitentiaries.
Source: U.S. Bureau of Justice Statistics, *Prisoners in 2003*.

Florida

Location: Southeast coast

Area and rank: 53,997 square miles (139,852 square kilometers); 65,758 square miles (170,313 square kilometers) including water; twenty-sixth largest state in area

Coastline: 1,350 miles (2,173 kilometers) on the Atlantic Ocean and Gulf of Mexico

Shoreline: 8,426 miles (13,560 kilometers)

Population and rank: 17,397,000 (2004); fourth largest state in population

Capital city: Tallahassee (150,624 people in 2000 census)

State capitol building in Tallahassee. (Visit Florida)

Largest city: Jacksonville (consolidated city, coextensive with Duval County; 735,617 people in 2000 census)

Became territory: March 30, 1822

Entered Union and rank: March 3, 1845; twenty-seventh state

Present constitution adopted: 1968

Counties: 67

State name: "Florida" comes from the Spanish for "feast of flowers," which relates to Easter celebrations

State nickname: Sunshine State

Motto: In God we trust

State flag: White field with red cross of Saint Andrew and state seal in center

Highest point: Geological survey section 30, T6 north, R20 west—345 feet (105 meters)

Lowest point: Atlantic Ocean—sea level

Highest recorded temperature: 109 degrees Fahrenheit (43 degrees Celsius)—Monticello, 1931

Lowest recorded temperature: –2 degrees Fahrenheit (–19 degrees Celsius)—Tallahassee, 1899

State songs: "Swannee River"; "Florida, My Florida"

State flower: Orange blossom

State bird: Mockingbird

National parks: Biscayne, Dry Tortugas, Everglades

Florida History

Although Florida has a long and varied history, many of the most important developments in the state, especially in terms of economic, political, and demographic changes, took place after the 1950's. Because of its geographic location, which promotes the influence of West Indian and Caribbean cultures, and its pleasant, tropical climate, which has attracted large numbers of residents from both the Northern and Southern Hemispheres, Florida developed a unique and distinctive character.

Early History. Native Americans arrived in Florida sometime around 10,000 B.C.E. and slowly made their way south, not reaching the southern tip of the peninsula until about 1400 B.C.E. Archaeological evidence from northeastern Florida and southeastern Georgia indicates that inhabitants of these areas invented pottery in the period around 2000 B.C.E. This would place their development of pottery approximately eight hundred years before other North American cultures.

Because of the abundance of game and marine life, early Native Americans in the Florida area were primarily hunters and fishers, rather than farmers. Great respect was paid to the dead, who were interred in large burial mounds. By 1,500 C.E., a sun worship cult, also centered around large earthen mounds, spread through the region. The tribes discovered agriculture and grew corn, beans, and squash, among other crops.

Along the northern Gulf coast lived the Panzacola, Chatot, and Apalachicola; farther west were the Apalachee. The lower part of the peninsula, from Tampa Bay extending south, was inhabited by the warrior Calusa, for whom warfare seemed to be part of religious practice. In the north, the dominant group was the Timucua, who were the first Native Americans to encounter Europeans. By far the most famous of Florida tribes, however, were the Seminoles, who entered the state in 1750. The word *seminole* means "runaway" in the Creek language, and the people themselves were Creek Indians who came from Alabama and Georgia. At first scattered in small groups, the Seminoles united against those who wanted to remove them from Florida, first the Spanish and English and later the Americans.

Exploration and Settlement. The first European contact with Florida began in 1513, when Juan Ponce de León landed on the coast, claimed the land for

Hernando de Soto landing at Tampa Bay in 1539. (Library of Congress)

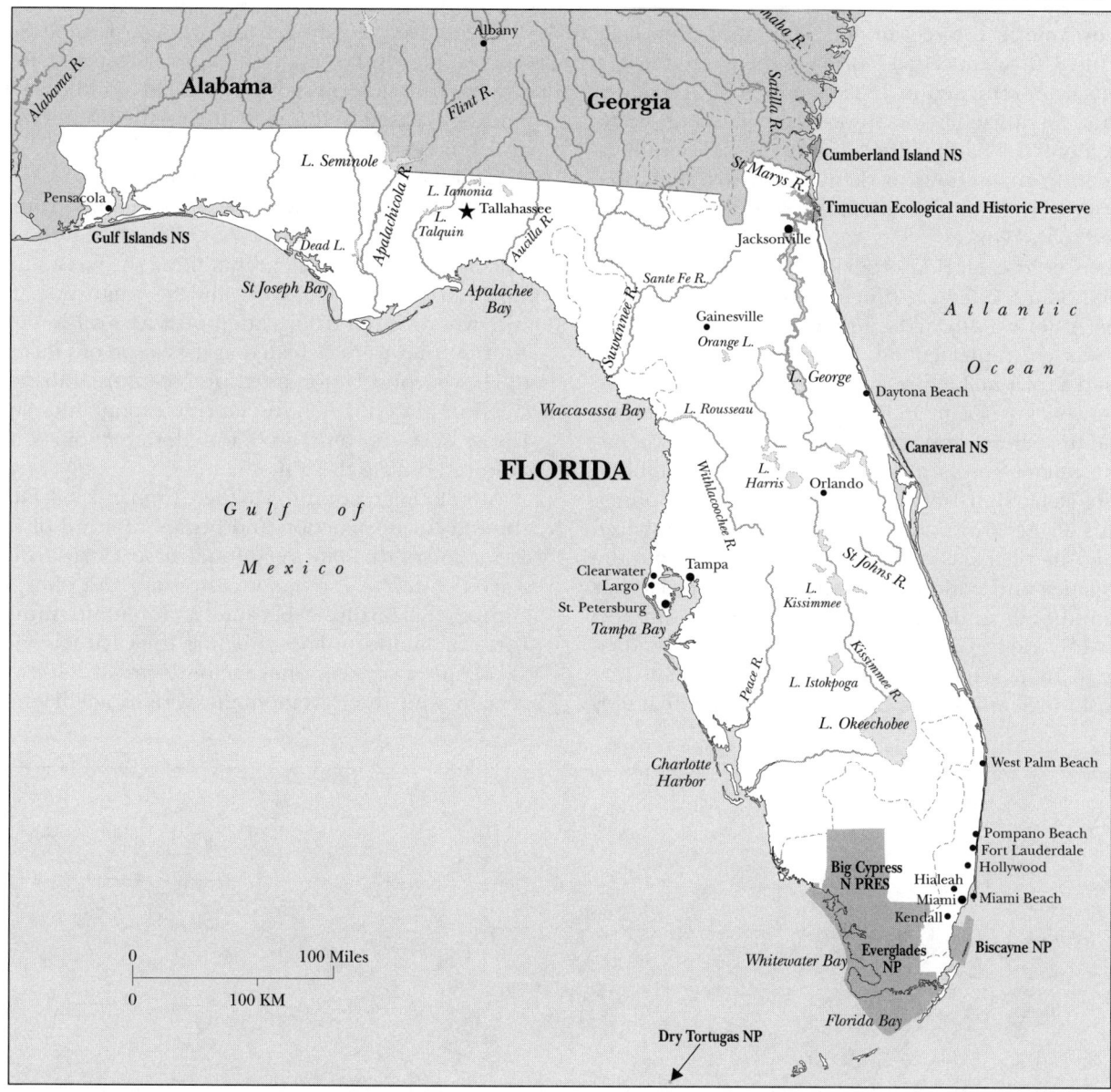

Spain, and bestowed its current name, either because it was Easter (*Pascua Florida*, in Spanish) or because of the many flowering plants he discovered (*florida* also means "flowery" in Spanish). After Ponce de León's death during a battle with Native Americans in 1521, several other Spanish explorers, including Hernando de Soto, sought to establish a permanent presence in Florida. It was not until 1565, however, that a Spanish colony was founded at St. Augustine, becoming the first permanent European settlement in what is now the United States.

As they did elsewhere with their New World colonies, the Spanish implemented both imperial rule and the Catholic religion. Settlements and missions were established throughout Florida, but these were destroyed during the early eighteenth century in raids by Native Americans and British settlers from South Carolina. In 1763, as part of the treaties which ended the French and Indian War, Spain ceded Florida to the British in exchange for Cuba. The British divided the colony into East and West Florida.

Immigration increased the English population of Florida, and during the American Revolution the residents remained loyal to that crown. However, in 1778, Spain, which had become an American ally, seized West Florida. In 1783, at the end of the Revolution, Spain regained all of Florida. While many English settlers left for British possessions in the West Indies, others remained behind, stubbornly defiant to the Spanish and fearful of possible takeover by French forces.

Steps to Statehood. During the War of 1812 the British used Pensacola as a naval base, prompting its capture by American forces under General Andrew Jackson. In 1819, Spain ceded Florida to the United States, and Jackson returned in 1822 as military governor of the new territory. The northwestern portion of the region, along the panhandle, became the site of numerous cotton plantations worked by slaves. Tallahassee was named the capital in 1823. In 1845, Florida was admitted to the Union.

Even before Florida officially became part of the United States, efforts had been under way to remove Native Americans from the territory. This ongoing conflict was concentrated on the Seminoles, who had formed a formidable presence against the threat from the Americans. From 1835 to 1842 the United States waged the Seminole War against the tribe. The war was begun when Osceola, a young Seminole chief, publicly rejected a harsh treaty with the United States by plunging his dagger through the document. Outnumbered by the Americans, Osceola led the Seminoles into the Everglades and conducted guerrilla warfare. He was captured while under a flag of truce and imprisoned in Fort Moultrie at Charleston, South Carolina; he died there in 1838. Without his leadership, the tide turned against the Seminoles, and after their final defeat they were removed to lands in the western United States. Only a handful remained behind, hidden in the swamps and wilderness of Florida. The number of Seminoles increased in the state during the twentieth century, however.

Civil War and Reconstruction. In 1861, Florida joined other southern states in seceding from the Union. During the Civil War, Union naval forces quickly captured strong points along the coast, including Fernandina, Pensacola, and St. Augustine. However, when Union troops attempted an invasion of the interior, they were defeated at the battle of Olustee in 1864. A second Union attempt to capture Tallahassee failed in March, 1865; the Florida capital and Austin, Texas, were the only two Confederate capitals never captured during the war.

After being readmitted to the Union in 1868, Florida entered Reconstruction and began a period of transformation of the state's economic base. Citrus fruits replaced cotton as the major cash crop, and phosphate mining for fertilizer became a dominant industry. Tourism, almost unknown before the Civil War, began to become a key economic factor during the 1880's, especially with the development of railroads. Henry B.

Highway connecting the islands of the Florida Keys at the southern tip of the state's mainland. (PhotoDisc)

Plant completed the Kissimmee-Tampa cross-state railroad in 1884, and Henry M. Flagler inaugurated the Jacksonville-Miami Line in 1896. The two systems linked Florida and its produce to the rich markets of the Northeast and encouraged the growth of the tourism and retirement industries. Starting during the early twentieth century, the state's population began to double approximately every twenty years.

The Florida real estate boom of the 1920's saw a dramatic increase in settlers, but by the middle of the decade the boom had ended. In addition, massive hurricanes in 1926 and 1928 further damaged the state's economy, which was severely affected by the Great Depression of 1929. President Franklin Roosevelt's New Deal brought relief and massive defense spending before and during World War II, helping bring the state into the modern age.

A Mixed Economy. Cape Canaveral on the east coast of Florida was one of the oldest sites to be named by Europeans on the North American continent. During the 1950's and 1960's it became the site of the nation's newest explorers, as the National Aeronautics and Space Administration (NASA) chose it for the site of the American space program. In 1958, it saw the launch of the first U.S. satellite, in 1961 and 1962 the first American manned space flight and orbital mission, and in 1969 the first lunar mission.

Modern Florida developed a mixed economy that depends upon traditional areas such as manufacturing and agriculture and also relies heavily on tourism. Companies that produce computer equipment and accessories have taken the lead in manufacturing. Citrus fruits, first introduced to Florida during the 1570's, are a strong staple, with Florida producing more than three-quarters of the total U.S. harvest of grapefruit and oranges. In addition, the state's pine forests are valuable sources of materials for pulp and paper, as well as turpentine and other products. The almost year-round growing season has made Florida a leader in truck-farm agriculture; Florida ships tomatoes, vegetables, and other produce throughout the nation.

A Multicultural State. The Cuban Revolution of 1959, which brought Fidel Castro and the Communist Party to power, saw a massive emigration from that island, largely among the professional, upper, and middle classes. Conservative in politics and religion, Cubans brought with them a tradition of respect for

Launch of the space shuttle Endeavour from Cape Canaveral in June, 2006. (National Aeronautics and Space Administration)

learning and for the free enterprise system. Although their initial plans had been for an early return to their home, these immigrants established themselves in southern Florida, especially in the Miami area, where they developed a strong economy and thriving culture. By the late 1970's, southern Florida had become a multicultural, bilingual area.

These developments were not without difficulty. In 1986, Bob Martinez became the first Hispanic to be elected governor of Florida. Significantly, he won election as a Republican. However, many conservatives, disturbed at the increasing power of Hispanic voters, pushed hard to win approval in 1988 of an amendment to the state constitution that made English the official language of state government. Adding to the situation were sometimes tense relations between the white, Hispanic, and African American populations; during the early 1980's these tensions caused riots to flare in the Miami area.

Tourism and Nature. Tourism, long a staple of the modern Florida economy, received a major boost in 1971 with the opening of Walt Disney World near Orlando. Disney's Epcot Center followed in 1982. Soon, Disney World became the single most popular tourist destination in the United States. Other attractions, including Sea World, Universal Studios theme park, and Busch Gardens, increased Florida's appeal as a tourist destination. Added to these are the state's natural attractions, such as the Everglades, the Florida Keys, and the unique John Pennekamp Coral Reef State Park near Key Largo, which is entirely underwater and features living coral formations. In 1990, a record-breaking 41 million visitors from around the world visited Florida.

Although much of Florida's appeal rested upon its environment, much of that environment had been devastated by natural forces or harmed by human intervention. In 1992, the state was struck by Hurricane Andrew, at that time the costliest natural disaster in U.S. history. The storm raged through southern Florida, ruining entire communities and causing more than $20 billion in damages.

As the state entered the twenty-first century, it began to address a potentially fatal threat to its environment. Decades of systematic draining of wetlands, including the vast expanse of the Everglades, to accommodate expanding human population and development seriously endangered the environment and wildlife. Finally realizing the seriousness of the situation, the U.S. Army Corps of Engineers and other organizations abandoned long-standing projects such as the Cross Florida Barge Canal and began efforts to reverse years of neglect and active damage. These efforts became critical for a state more dependent than most on its natural environment for its prosperity and continued growth.

Headlines and Controversy. Florida gained national attention at the end of the twentieth century as the center of a series of controversies. One regarded the fate of a six-year-old Cuban boy, Elián González. In late November, 1999, the boy's mother drowned while escaping from Cuba. Rescued by American fishermen, the boy was taken in by relatives in Miami, where his plight captured the nation's imagination. Miami's large Cuban émigré community was adamant that he stay in the United States, while many felt that he should be returned to his father in Cuba. In the end, he was forcibly seized by federal agents and sent back to Cuba to be with his father.

A second controversy occurred in November, 2000, when the state nearly deadlocked in the presidential election between George W. Bush and Al Gore. Questions surrounding what recounting of votes should be done and who had authority to order such recounts were at the center of the intense weeks-long political controversy. After a flurry of legal maneuvers, including decisions by the Florida Supreme Court, the issue landed at the U.S. Supreme Court. On December 12, 2000, the Court ruled in favor of the Bush campaign, ordering a halt to a vote recount. The following day, Gore conceded. His supporters remained embittered. It was later determined, however, that the recount method most favored by the Gore campaign was the one that would have most increased Bush's lead.

A third cause célèbre centered upon a forty-two-year-old woman, Terri Schiavo, who, by 2005, had been comatose for fifteen years. Doctors pronounced her in a persistent vegetative state and said she would never regain consciousness. A long conflict had taken place between her parents and her husband over whether, in these circumstances, life support should be withdrawn and she be allowed to die. Americans followed the debate, with some arguing that Schiavo was a human being and that it was not right, as her husband wished, to allow her to die. In the end, after attempts in Congress and the Florida State legislature, as well as extensive legal maneuvering, failed, a judge's order on March 18, 2005, that her feeding tube be withdrawn was carried out. On March 31, Schiavo died.

Hurricane Alley. A series of hurricanes battered the state in the twenty-first century, following Hurricane Gordon, a storm in 2000 that was relatively weak but nonetheless killed one person and displaced twenty thousand. However, in August, 2004, Hurricane Charley, the second most costly hurricane in Florida's history, made landfall, causing some $20 billion in damage. One million people were without electricity, and the infrastructure of southwestern Florida was devastated. Charley was followed on September 13 by Hurricane Francis, on September 16 by Hurricane Ivan, and on September 25 by Hurricane Jeanne. Each was a considerable, damaging storm. Altogether, Florida's four hurricanes in August and September of 2004 did $42 billion in damage and destroyed twenty-five thousand homes, with another forty thousand sustaining major damage.

In 2005, Hurricane Katrina swept across the state, en route to catastrophic destruction on the Gulf Coast, especially in Louisiana. In Florida, Katrina killed fourteen people and left one million people in the dark, but its winds were relatively modest. The storm developed its most destructive force after leaving the state and traveling across the Gulf of Mexico.

Despite its hurricane destruction, Florida remained prosperous. Its population gains were enough to gain it another member of Congress to its delegation following the 2000 census. Retirees continued to flock to the state, which has no state income tax.

Michael Witkoski
Updated by the Editor

Florida Time Line

Apr. 3, 1513	Juan Ponce de León discovers territory he calls Florida and claims for Spain.
May, 1539	Hernando de Soto lands near what is now Tampa Bay and begins exploration.
1564	French Huguenots establish settlement on St. Johns River.
1565	Spanish mariner Pedro Menéndez de Avilés founds St. Augustine, the oldest city in the Union, and kills French Huguenot colonists, establishing Spanish power.
1570's	Citrus trees are introduced into Florida.
1698	Spanish establish settlement at Pensacola.
1750	Seminoles migrate to Florida from Georgia.
1763	Spain trades Florida to Britain.
1783	Britain cedes Florida back to Spain.
1814	General Andrew Jackson seizes Pensacola in War of 1812.
1819	Spain cedes East Florida to United States.
Mar. 30, 1822	Territory of Florida is established.
1835-1842	Seminole War rages as settlers try to push Native Americans from area.
Mar. 3, 1845	Florida enters the Union as the twenty-seventh state.
1853	University of Florida is founded at Gainesville.
Jan. 10, 1861	Florida is the third state to secede from the Union.
July 4, 1868	Florida is readmitted to the Union.
1884	Phosphate deposits are found on Peace River.
1884	Henry B. Plant completes cross-state railroad.
1886	Henry M. Flagler opens Jacksonville-Miami railroad.
1906	Draining operations begin in the Everglades.
1947	Everglades National Park is created.
1954	Sunshine Skyway across Tampa Bay opens.
1958	NASA begins administration of Cape Canaveral aerospace center.
1963	Cape Canaveral is renamed Cape Kennedy.
1968	New state constitution is adopted.
1969	All public schools, including colleges and universities, come under a unified system.
1971	Construction on Cross Florida Barge Canal halted for environmental reasons.
1971	Walt Disney World opens.
1973	Cape Kennedy is renamed Cape Canaveral.
1982	Epcot Center opens at Walt Disney World.
1985	Xavier Suarez becomes first Cuban American elected mayor of Miami.
1986	Republican Bob Martinez becomes first Hispanic elected governor.
1988	English is made the official language of state government through a constitutional amendment.
1990	41 million people visit Florida, a state record.
Aug. 24, 1992	Hurricane Andrew devastates southern Florida.
June 28, 2000	Six-year-old Elián González is returned to his father in Cuba.
Nov. 7-Dec. 13, 2000	Florida is center of national political controversy when presidential voting is nearly equal between the major party candidates.
Aug.-Sept 2004	Series of hurricanes hits the state, causing the deaths of eighty-six people and more than $42 billion in damage.
Mar. 31, 2005	National controversy over continuance of life support for Terri Schiavo ends with her death.
Aug. 25, 2005	Hurricane Katrina cuts a swath through the state, killing fourteen persons.

Notes for Further Study

Published Sources. Charlton Tebeau's *A History of Florida* (3d rev. ed., 1999) provides a good start to understanding the growth and development of the state, especially from statehood to Civil War and Reconstruction. *Florida: A Short History* (1993) by Michael Gannon is another excellent introductory survey of the state and its development. David Nolan's *Fifty Feet in Paradise: The Booming of Florida* (1984) discusses Florida's checkered history in the modern era, as the state went through several periods of growth and recession. *Land of Sunshine, State of Dreams: A Social History of Modern Florida*

(2005) by Gary R. Mormino examines the state's explosive growth following 1950 as a result of immigration and the combined pull of tourism, retirement communities, and new technology sectors. Michael Grunwald, in *The Swamp: The Everglades, Florida, and the Politics of Paradise* (2006), examines the region's population growth from another angle: the environmental destruction of the Everglades and efforts to restore them. Tourism is a critical sector in Florida, and two books explore the early efforts of railroad tycoon Henry Flagler to establish the state as a vacationer's destination: *Last Train to Paradise: Henry Flagler and the Spectacular Rise and Fall of the Railroad That Crossed an Ocean* (2002) by Les Standiford and *The Architecture of Leisure: The Florida Resort Hotels of Henry Flagler and Henry Plant* (2002) by Susan R. Braden. David R. Colburn and Lance de Haven-Smith's work, *Government in the Sunshine State: Florida Since Statehood* (1999), examines several aspects of state politics.

Hernando de Soto and the Indians of Florida (1993) by Jerald T. Milanich and Charles Hudson looks at the beginning of an often troubled relationship between Native Americans and later-arriving European settlers. David Colburn's *The African American Heritage of Florida* (1995) is an important and interesting survey of African American contributions to the state during its history.

Web Resources. Practically every aspect of Florida history, culture, politics, economics, and leisure can be accessed through a Web site, and most of the general sites provide easy reference to specific areas. Perhaps the best portal site is My Florida (www.myflorida.com/). Using the navigation on the left-hand side, site visitors will need to choose the category that pertains to them—Visitor, Floridian, Business, or Government—wherein one can find numerous links to specific information on that category. For official information about the state, including statistics and links to agencies and departments, choose the Government category on My Florida (www.myflorida.com/taxonomy/government/). My Florida also has a comprehensive section for children (dhr.dos.state.fl.us/kids/), which explains the state's history, culture, and Native American history, among other topics.

For those who are interested in Florida history, a variety of sites offer valuable information and links to other pages. Florida Smart (www.floridasmart.com/commculture/history.htm) offers countless links to historical information and associations and to facts about the state (www.floridasmart.com/information/facts/factshome.htm). For those who wish information about Florida's Native Americans, the Seminole Tribe of Florida has its own site (www.seminoletribe.com). One of the many legacies of Henry Flagler, the railroad tycoon and resort developer, is the Flagler Museum in Palm Beach (www.flagler.org/). Its Web site offers a thorough biography of Flagler and a description of the collections one will find when visiting the museum.

Counties

County	2000 pop.	Rank in pop.	Sq. miles	Rank in area	County	2000 pop.	Rank in pop.	Sq. miles	Rank in area
Alachua	217,955	20	874.3	22	Highlands	87,366	34	1,028.5	14
Baker	22,259	52	585.2	46	Hillsborough	998,948	4	1,051.0	12
Bay	148,217	25	763.7	29	Holmes	18,564	56	482.5	61
Bradford	26,088	50	293.2	65	Indian River	112,947	33	503.2	59
Brevard	476,230	9	1,018.5	15	Jackson	46,755	41	915.8	20
Broward	1,623,018	2	1,208.9	7	Jefferson	12,902	63	597.8	45
Calhoun	13,017	62	567.4	51	Lafayette	7,022	66	542.8	55
Charlotte	141,627	26	693.7	34	Lake	210,528	21	953.1	18
Citrus	118,085	31	583.6	47	Lee	440,888	11	803.6	24
Clay	140,814	27	601.1	44	Leon	239,452	19	666.8	37
Collier	251,377	18	2,025.5	2	Levy	34,450	47	1,118.4	9
Columbia	56,513	38	797.2	25	Liberty	7,021	67	835.9	23
Dade	2,253,362	1	1,944.7	3	Madison	18,733	55	692.0	35
DeSoto	32,209	48	637.3	41	Manatee	264,002	16	741.2	31
Dixie	13,827	58	704.1	33	Marion	258,916	17	1,579.0	5
Duval	778,879	7	773.9	27	Martin	126,731	29	555.7	53
Escambia	294,410	15	663.6	38	Monroe	79,589	35	997.3	17
Flagler	49,832	40	485.0	60	Nassau	57,663	37	651.6	39
Franklin	11,057	64	534.0	56	Okaloosa	170,498	24	935.8	19
Gadsden	45,087	42	516.2	57	Okeechobee	35,910	45	774.3	26
Gilchrist	14,437	57	348.9	63	Orange	896,344	6	907.6	21
Glades	10,576	65	773.5	28	Osceola	172,493	23	1,322.0	6
Gulf	13,332	60	565.1	52	Palm Beach	1,131,184	3	2,034.3	1
Hamilton	13,327	61	514.9	58	Pasco	344,765	13	745.0	30
Hardee	26,938	49	637.4	40	Pinellas	921,482	5	280.2	66
Hendry	36,210	44	1,152.7	8	Polk	483,924	8	1,874.9	4
Hernando	130,802	28	478.3	62	Putnam	70,423	36	722.2	32

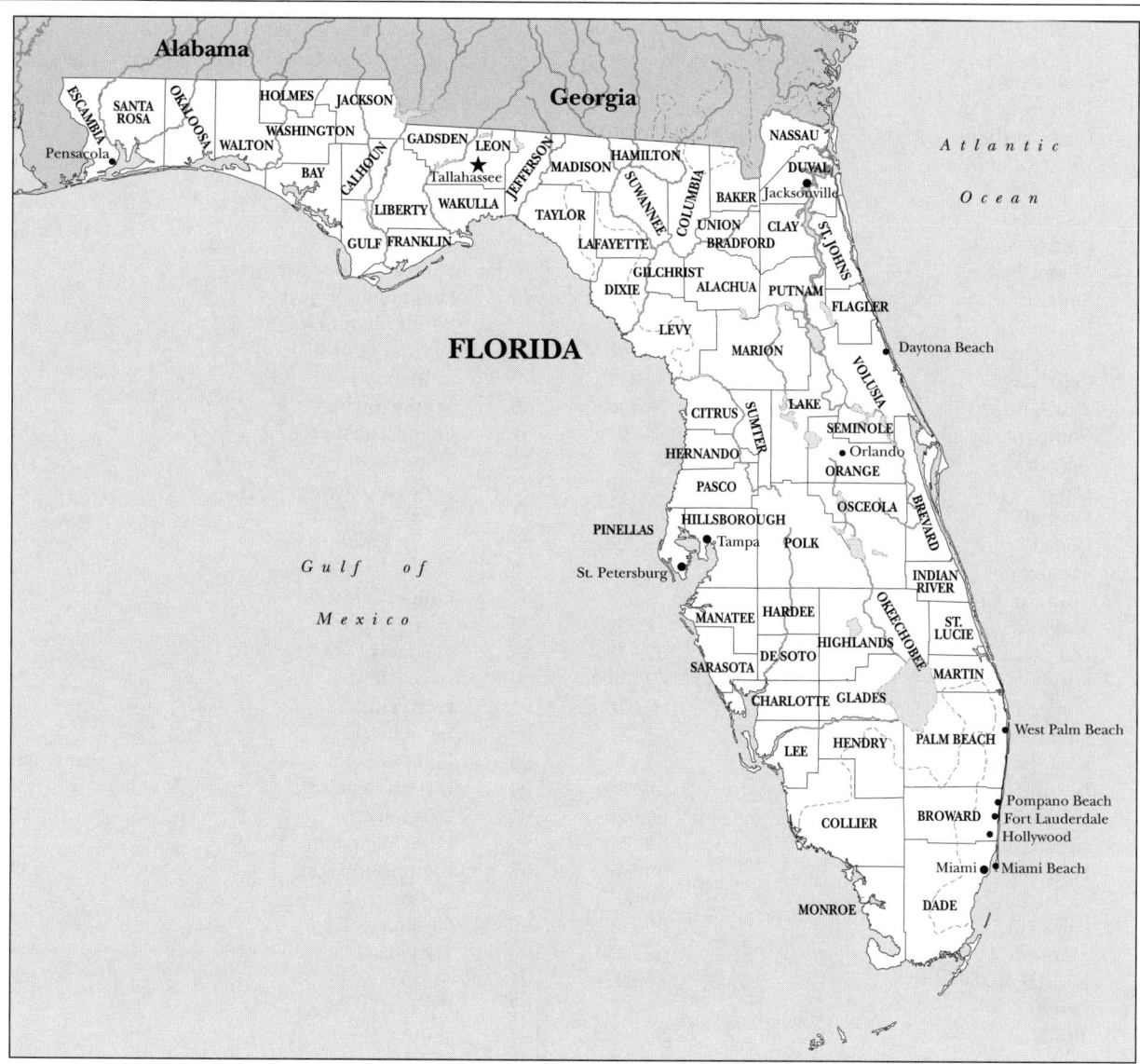

County	2000 pop.	Rank in pop.	Sq. miles	Rank in area
St. Johns	123,135	30	609.0	42
St. Lucie	192,695	22	572.5	49
Santa Rosa	117,743	32	1,015.8	16
Sarasota	325,957	14	571.8	50
Seminole	365,196	12	308.2	64
Sumter	53,345	39	545.7	54
Suwannee	34,844	46	687.7	36
Taylor	19,256	54	1,041.9	13

County	2000 pop.	Rank in pop.	Sq. miles	Rank in area
Union	13,442	59	240.3	67
Volusia	443,343	10	1,105.9	10
Wakulla	22,863	51	606.7	43
Walton	40,601	43	1,057.7	11
Washington	20,973	53	579.9	48

Source: U.S. Census Bureau; National Association of Counties.

Cities

With 10,000 or more residents

Rank	City	Population	Rank	City	Population
1	Jacksonville	735,617	5	Hialeah	226,419
2	Miami	362,470	6	Orlando	185,951
3	Tampa	303,447	7	Fort Lauderdale	152,397
4	St. Petersburg	248,232	8	Tallahassee (capital)	150,624

(continued)

Rank	City	Population	Rank	City	Population
9	Hollywood	139,357	68	Fort Pierce	37,516
10	Pembroke Pines	137,427	69	Panama City	36,417
11	Coral Springs	117,549	70	Country Club	36,310
12	Clearwater	108,787	71	Ormond Beach	36,301
13	Cape Coral	102,286	72	Merritt Island	36,090
14	Gainesville	95,447	73	Dunedin	35,691
15	Port St. Lucie	88,769	74	Lake Worth	35,133
16	Miami Beach	87,933	75	Palm Beach Gardens	35,058
17	Sunrise	85,779	76	Hallandale	34,282
18	Plantation	82,934	77	South Miami Heights	33,522
19	West Palm Beach	82,103	78	Greater Carrollwood	33,519
20	Palm Bay	79,413	79	Lehigh Acres	33,430
21	Lakeland	78,452	80	Bonita Springs	32,797
22	Pompano Beach	78,191	81	Egypt Lake-Leto	32,782
23	Brandon	77,895	82	Palm Coast	32,732
24	Davie	75,720	83	Golden Glades	32,623
25	Kendall	75,226	84	West Little River	32,498
26	Boca Raton	74,764	85	North Lauderdale	32,264
27	Miramar	72,739	86	Homestead	31,909
28	Town 'n' Country	72,523	87	Lauderdale Lakes	31,705
29	Melbourne	71,382	88	Winter Springs	31,666
30	Deltona	69,543	89	Oakland Park	30,966
31	Largo	69,371	90	Lakeside	30,927
32	Spring Hill	69,078	91	University	30,736
33	Deerfield Beach	64,583	92	Westchester	30,271
34	Daytona Beach	64,112	93	Plant City	29,915
35	Boynton Beach	60,389	94	Riviera Beach	29,884
36	Delray Beach	60,020	95	East Lake	29,394
37	North Miami	59,880	96	Lake Magdalene	28,755
38	Fountainbleau	59,549	97	Richmond West	28,082
39	Carol City	59,443	98	Cooper City	27,939
40	Palm Harbor	59,248	99	Greenacres	27,569
41	Lauderhill	57,585	100	Ferry Pass	27,176
42	Kendale Lakes	56,901	101	Apopka	26,642
43	Pensacola	56,255	102	University Park	26,538
44	Tamarac	55,588	103	Winter Haven	26,487
45	Tamiami	54,788	104	Oviedo	26,316
46	Margate	53,909	105	Key West	25,478
47	Sarasota	52,715	106	Aventura	25,267
48	Bradenton	49,504	107	Cutler Ridge	24,781
49	Weston	49,286	108	Ocoee	24,391
50	Fort Myers	48,208	109	Coral Terrace	24,380
51	Kissimmee	47,814	110	Winter Park	24,090
52	The Hammocks	47,379	111	Bayonet Point	23,577
53	Port Charlotte	46,451	112	The Crossings	23,557
54	Ocala	45,943	113	Wekiwa Springs	23,169
55	Port Orange	45,823	114	Norland	22,995
56	Pinellas Park	45,658	115	North Port	22,797
57	Coconut Creek	43,566	116	Miami Lakes	22,676
58	Coral Gables	42,249	117	Casselberry	22,629
59	Pine Hills	41,764	118	Oak Ridge	22,349
60	Altamonte Springs	41,200	119	Brent	22,257
61	North Miami Beach	40,786	120	Leisure City	22,152
62	Titusville	40,670	121	West Pensacola	21,939
63	North Fort Myers	40,214	122	Holiday	21,904
64	Jupiter	39,328	123	Boca Del Mar	21,832
65	Sanford	38,291	124	Yeehaw Junction	21,778
66	Wellington	38,216	125	West and East Lealman	21,753
67	Kendall West	38,034	126	Wright	21,697

Rank	City	Population	Rank	City	Population
127	South Bradenton	21,587	186	Opa-locka	14,951
128	Royal Palm Beach	21,523	187	Belle Glade	14,906
129	Bellview	21,201	188	Marco Island	14,879
130	Tarpon Springs	21,003	189	Crestview	14,766
131	Jacksonville Beach	20,990	190	Stuart	14,633
132	Naples	20,976	191	Keystone	14,627
133	Land O' Lakes	20,971	192	Gladeview	14,468
134	Golden Gate	20,951	193	Scott Lake	14,401
135	Temple Terrace	20,918	194	Conway	14,394
136	De Land	20,904	195	Brownsville	14,393
137	Greater Northdale	20,461	196	Winter Garden	14,351
138	Doral	20,438	197	Punta Gorda	14,344
139	Vero Beach South	20,362	198	Callaway	14,233
140	Citrus Park	20,226	199	Sweetwater	14,226
141	Rockledge	20,170	200	Fairview Shores	13,898
142	Palm City	20,097	201	Parkland	13,835
143	St. Cloud	20,074	202	Longwood	13,745
144	Dania Beach	20,061	203	Miami Springs	13,712
145	New Smyrna Beach	20,048	204	Palmetto Estates	13,675
146	Fort Walton Beach	19,973	205	Poinciana	13,647
147	Palm Valley	19,860	206	South Venice	13,539
148	Bloomingdale	19,839	207	Olympia Heights	13,452
149	Immokalee	19,763	208	Atlantic Beach	13,368
150	Hialeah Gardens	19,297	209	South Daytona	13,177
151	Pinecrest	19,055	210	Haines City	13,174
152	Ensley	18,752	211	Elfers	13,161
153	Edgewater	18,668	212	Lockhart	12,944
154	Lake Worth Corridor	18,663	213	Goldenrod	12,871
155	Jasmine Estates	18,213	214	Hudson	12,765
156	Venice	17,764	215	Fruitville	12,741
157	Vero Beach	17,705	216	Wilton Manors	12,697
158	Palm River-Clair Mel	17,589	217	Forest City	12,612
159	Ives Estates	17,586	218	Palmetto	12,571
160	Cutler	17,390	219	Lakeland Highlands	12,557
161	Bayshore Gardens	17,350	220	Gulfport	12,527
162	Myrtle Grove	17,211	221	Cocoa Beach	12,482
163	Safety Harbor	17,203	222	Homosassa Springs	12,458
164	Sunset	17,150	223	Lynn Haven	12,451
165	Lutz	17,081	224	Kings Point	12,207
166	Ojus	16,642	225	Holly Hill	12,119
167	Sandalfoot Cove	16,582	226	Port St. John	12,112
168	Bellair-Meadowbrook Terrace	16,539	227	Cypress Lake	12,072
169	Pinewood	16,523	228	North Palm Beach	12,064
170	Cocoa	16,412	229	Riverview	12,035
171	Greater Sun Center	16,321	230	Maitland	12,019
172	San Carlos Park	16,317	231	Citrus Ridge	12,015
173	Glenvar Heights	16,243	232	Westwood Lakes	12,005
174	Englewood	16,196	233	Oldsmar	11,910
175	Sebastian	16,181	234	Key Largo	11,886
176	New Port Richey	16,117	235	Lady Lake	11,828
177	Fruit Cove	16,077	236	Iona	11,756
178	Leesburg	15,956	237	Palm Springs	11,699
179	Sarasota Springs	15,875	238	Niceville	11,684
180	De Bary	15,559	239	Gulf Gate Estates	11,647
181	Bartow	15,340	240	St. Augustine	11,592
182	Sunny Isles Beach	15,315	241	Lake Mary	11,458
183	Florida Ridge	15,217	242	Hobe Sound	11,376
184	Warrington	15,207	243	Gonzalez	11,365
185	Eustis	15,106	244	Villas	11,346

(continued)

Rank	City	Population
245	Hamptons at Boca Raton	11,306
246	Meadow Woods	11,286
247	Destin	11,119
248	Westchase	11,116
249	Jensen Beach	11,100
250	Azalea Park	11,073
251	Auburndale	11,032
252	Seminole	10,890
253	Upper Grand Lagoon	10,889
254	Zephyrhills	10,833
255	Lighthouse Point	10,767
256	South Miami	10,741
257	Country Walk	10,653
258	Fernandina Beach	10,549

Rank	City	Population
259	Key Biscayne	10,507
260	Palm Beach	10,468
261	Lakewood Park	10,458
262	Miami Shores	10,380
263	Middleburg	10,338
264	Marathon	10,255
265	Lake Wales	10,194
266	Union Park	10,191
267	Port Salerno	10,141
268	Princeton	10,090
269	Palatka	10,033

Population figures are from 2000 census.

Source: U.S. Bureau of the Census.

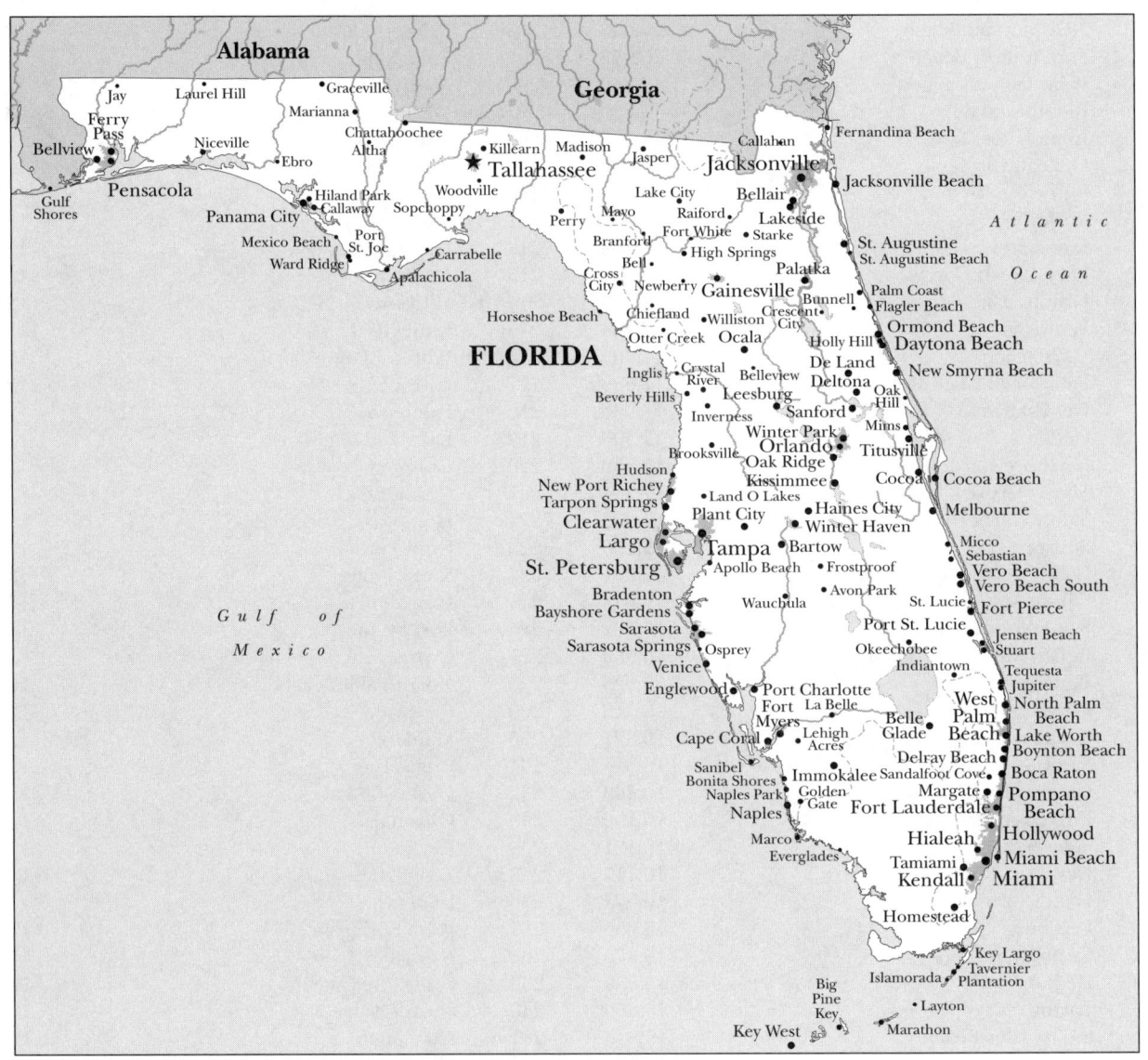

Index to Tables

DEMOGRAPHICS

Resident state and national populations, 1970-2004

Population figures given in thousands

	State pop.	U.S. pop.	Share	Rank
1970	6,791	203,302	3.3%	9
1980	9,746	226,546	4.3%	7
1985	11,351	237,924	4.8%	6
1990	12,938	248,765	5.2%	4
1995	14,538	262,761	5.4%	4
2000	15,983	281,425	5.7%	4
2004	17,397	293,655	5.9%	4

Source: U.S. Census Bureau, Current Population Reports, 2006.

Resident population by age, 2004

Age Group	Total persons
Under 5 years	1,091,000
5 to 17 years	2,912,000
18 to 24 years	1,549,000
25 to 34 years	2,142,000
35 to 44 years	2,530,000
45 to 54 years	2,380,000
55 to 64 years	1,865,000
65 to 74 years	1,475,000
75 to 84 years	1,073,000
85 years and older	380,000
All age groups	17,397,000

Portion of residents 65 and older	16.8%
National rank in portion of oldest residents	1
National average	12.4%

Population figures are rounded to nearest thousand persons;
figures include armed forces personnel stationed in the state.
Source: U.S. Bureau of the Census, 2006.

Resident population by race, Hispanic origin, 2004

Category	State pop.	Share	U.S.
All residents	17,397	100.00%	100.00%
Non-Hispanic white	10,920	62.77%	67.37%
Hispanic white	3,102	17.83%	13.01%
Other Hispanic	203	1.17%	1.06%
African American	2,726	15.67%	12.77%
Native American	74	0.43%	0.96%
Asian, Pacific Islander	366	2.10%	4.37%
Two or more categories	209	1.20%	1.51%

Population figures are in thousands. Persons counted as "Hispanic" (Latino) may be of any race. Because of overlapping categories, categories may not add up to 100%. Shares in column 3 are percentages of each category within the state; these figures may be compared to the national percentages in column 4.
Source: U.S. Bureau of the Census, 2006.

Projected state population, 2000-2030

Year	Population
2000	15,983,000
2005	17,510,000
2010	19,252,000
2015	21,204,000
2020	23,407,000
2025	25,912,000
2030	28,686,000
Population increase, 2000-2030	12,703,000
Percentage increase, 2000-2030	79.5

Projections are based on data from the 2000 census.
Source: U.S. Census Bureau.

VITAL STATISTICS

Infant mortality rates, 1980-2002

	1980	1990	2000	2002
All state residents	14.6	9.6	7.0	7.5
All U.S. residents	12.6	9.2	9.4	9.1
All state white residents	11.8	6.7	5.4	5.8
All U.S. white residents	10.6	7.6	5.7	5.8
All state black residents	22.8	16.8	12.6	13.6
All U.S. black residents	22.2	18.0	14.1	14.4

Figures represent deaths per 1,000 live births of resident infants under 1 year old, exclusive of fetal deaths. Figures for all residents include members of other racial categories not listed separately.
Source: U.S. Census Bureau, *Statistical Abstract of the United States,* 2006.

Abortion rates, 1990 and 2000

	1990	2000
Total abortions	85,000	103,000
Rate per 1,000 women	29.3	31.9
U.S. rate	25.7	21.3
Rank	8	4

Numbers of abortions are rounded to nearest thousand; ranks are based on rates.
Source: U.S. Census Bureau.

Marriages and divorces, 2004

Total marriages	156,400
Rate per 1,000 population	9.0
National rate per 1,000 population	7.4
Rank among all states	8
Total divorces	82,700
Rate per 1,000 population	4.8
National rate per 1,000 population	3.7
Rank among all states	7

Figures are for all marriages and divorces performed within the state, including those of nonresidents; totals are rounded to the nearest hundred. Ranks are for highest to lowest figures; note that divorce data are not available for five states.
Source: U.S. National Center for Health Statistics, *Vital Statistics of the United States,* 2006.

Death rates by leading causes, 2002
Deaths per 100,000 resident population

Cause	State	U.S.
Heart disease	294.6	241.7
Cancer	234.2	193.2
Cerebrovascular diseases	61.4	56.4
Accidents other than motor vehicle	44.3	37.0
Motor vehicle accidents	19.1	15.7
Chronic lower respiratory diseases	54.2	43.3
Diabetes mellitus	27.4	25.4
HIV	10.3	4.9
Suicide	14.0	11.0
Homicide	6.0	6.1
All causes	1,004.1	847.3
Rank in overall death rate among states		7

Figures exclude nonresidents who died in the state. Causes of death follow International Classification of Diseases. Rank is from highest to lowest death rate in the United States.
Source: U.S. National Center for Health Statistics, *National Vital Statistics Report,* 2006.

ECONOMY

Gross state product, 1990-2004
In current dollars

Year	State product	Nat'l product	State share
1990	$257.2 billion	$5.67 trillion	4.53%
2000	$470.1 billion	$9.75 trillion	4.82%
2002	$522.3 billion	$10.41 trillion	5.02%
2003	$553.7 billion	$10.92 trillion	5.07%
2004	$594.5 billion	$11.65 trillion	5.10%

Source: U.S. Bureau of Economic Analysis, *Survey of Current Business,* July, 2005.

Gross state product by industry, 2003
In billions of dollars

Construction	$26.7
Manufacturing	31.0
Wholesale trade	35.3
Retail trade	47.4
Finance & insurance	37.3
Information	24.6
Professional services	31.4
Health care & social assistance	37.0
Government	59.0
Total state product	$517.9
Total U.S. product	$10,289.2
State share of U.S. total	5.03%
Rank among all states	4

Total figures include industries not listed separately. Amounts are in chained 2000 dollars.
Source: U.S. Bureau of Economic Analysis, *Survey of Current Business,* July, 2005.

Personal income per capita, 1990-2004
In current dollars

	1990	2000	2004
Per capita income	$19,564	$28,509	$31,455
U.S. average	$19,477	$29,845	$32,937
Rank among states	19	20	23

Source: U.S. Bureau of Economic Analysis, *Survey of Current Business,* April, 2005.

Energy consumption, 2001
In trillions of British thermal units (BTU), except as noted

Total energy consumption

Total state energy consumption	4,135
Total U.S. energy consumption	96,275
State share of U.S. total	4.29%
Rank among states	3

Per capita consumption (In millions of BTU)

Total state per capita consumption	253
Total U.S. per capita consumption	338
Rank among states	44

End-use sectors

Residential	1,193
Commercial	958
Industrial	598
Transportation	1,386

Sources of energy

Petroleum	1,990
Natural gas	570
Coal	726
Hydroelectric power	2
Nuclear electric power	330

Figures for totals include categories not listed separately.
Source: U.S. Energy Information Administration, *State Energy Data Report,* 2001.

Nonfarm employment by sectors, 2004

Total	7,504,000
Construction	491,000
Manufacturing	388,000
Trade, transportation, utilities	1,498,000
Information	168,000
Finance, insurance, real estate	501,000
Professional & business services	1,290,000
Education & health services	919,000
Leisure, hospitality, arts, organizations	854,000
Other services, including repair & maintenance	320,000
Government	1,069,000

Figures are rounded to nearest thousand persons. "Total" includes mining and natural resources, not listed separately.
Source: U.S. Bureau of Labor Statistics, 2006.

Foreign exports, 1990-2004
In millions of dollars

Year	State	U.S.	State share
1990	11,634	394,045	2.95%
1996	20,744	624,767	3.32%
1997	23,234	688,896	3.37%
2000	26,543	712,055	3.39%
2003	24,953	724,006	3.69%
2004	28,982	769,332	3.77%

Rank among all states in 2004. 8

U.S. total does not include U.S. dependencies.
Source: U.S. Census Bureau, *U.S. Merchandise Trade,* series FT 900, 2000; U.S. Census Bureau, *U.S. International Trade in Goods and Services,* Series FT 900, 2005.

LAND USE

Federally owned land, 2003
Areas in acres

	State	U.S.	State share
Total area	34,721,000	2,271,343,000	1.53%
Nonfederal land	30,116,000	1,599,584,000	1.88%
Federal land	4,606,000	671,759,000	0.69%
Federal share	13.3%	29.6%	—

Areas are rounded to nearest thousand acres. Figures for federally owned land do not include trust properties.
Source: U.S. General Services Administration, *Federal Real Property Profile,* 2006.

Land use, 1997
In acres, rounded to nearest thousand

Total surface area	37,534,000
Total nonfederal rural land.	25,498,000
Percentage rural land	67.9%
Cropland	2,752,000
Conservation Reserve Program (CRP*) land	120,000
Pastureland	4,231,000
Rangeland	3,229,000
Forestland	12,536,000
Other rural land	2,630,000

*CRP is a federal program begun in 1985 to assist private landowners to convert highly erodible cropland to vegetative cover for ten years. Note that some categories of land overlap.
Source: U.S. Department of Agriculture, Natural Resources and Conservation Service, and Iowa State University, Statistical Laboratory, *Summary Report, 1997 National Resources Inventory,* revised December, 2000.

Farms and crop acreage, 2004

	State	U.S.	Share	Rank
Farms	43,000	2,113,000	2.04%	22
Acres (millions)	10	937	1.07%	29
Acres per farm	235	443	—	28

Source: U.S. Department of Agriculture, National Agricultural Statistics Service. Numbers of farms are rounded to nearest thousand units; acreage figures are rounded to nearest million. Rankings, including ties, are based on rounded figures.

GOVERNMENT AND FINANCE

Units of local government, 2002

	State	Total U.S.	Rank
All local governments	1,191	87,525	25
Counties	66	3,034	21
Municipalities	404	19,429	21
Townships	0	16,504	—
School districts	95	13,506	34
Special districts	626	35,052	20

Only 48 states have county governments, 20 states have township governments ("towns" in New England, Minnesota, New York, and Wisconsin), and 46 states have school districts. Special districts encompass such functions as natural resources, fire protection, and housing and community development.
Source: U.S. Census Bureau, *Census of Governments.*

State government revenue, 2002

Total revenue . . . . $47,890 mill.
General revenue . . . . $46,995 mill.
Per capita revenue $2,817
U.S. per capita average $3,689
Rank among states 49

Intergovernment revenue
Total . . . . $13,141 mill.
From federal government . . . . $12,786 mill.

Charges and miscellaneous
Total . . . . $8,502 mill.
Current charges . . . . $2,927 mill.
Misc. general income . . . . $5,575 mill.
Insurance trust revenue . . . . $881 mill.

Taxes
Total . . . . $25,352 mill.
Per capita taxes $1,519
Rank among states 43
Property taxes . . . . $428 mill.
Sales taxes . . . . $19,456 mill.
License taxes . . . . $1,557 mill.
Individual income taxes . . . . (nil)
Corporate income taxes . . . . $1,219 mill.
Other taxes . . . . $2,692 mill.

Total revenue figures include items not listed separately here.
Source: U.S. Bureau of the Census.

State government expenditures, 2002

General expenditures
Total state expenditures . . . . $51,834 mill.
Intergovernmental . . . . $14,054 mill.

Per capita expenditures
State $2,833
Average of all states $3,859
Rank among states 50

Selected direct expenditures
Education. . . . . $5,105 mill.
Public welfare . . . . $11,874 mill.
Health, hospital . . . . $2,839 mill.
Highways . . . . $4,707 mill.
Police protection . . . . $425 mill.
Corrections . . . . $2,200 mill.
Natural resources . . . . $1,395 mill.
Parks and recreation . . . . $178 mill.
Government administration . . . . $1,914 mill.
Interest on debt . . . . $1,052 mill.
Total direct expenditures. . . . . $33,233 mill.

Totals include items not listed separately.
Source: U.S. Census Bureau.

POLITICS

Governors since statehood

D = Democrat; R = Republican; O = other;
(r) resigned; (d) died in office; (i) removed from office

William D. Moseley (D) 1845-1849
Thomas Brown (O) 1849-1853
James E. Broome (D) 1853-1857
Madison S. Perry (D) 1857-1861
John Milton (D) . . . . (d) 1861-1865
Abram K. Allison (D) . . . . (i) 1865
William Marvin 1865
David S. Walker 1865-1868
Harrison Reed (R) 1868-1873
Ossian B. Hart (R) . . . . (d) 1873-1874
Marcellus L. Stearns (R) 1874-1877
George F. Drew (D) 1877-1881
William D. Bloxham (D) 1881-1885
Edward A. Perry (D) 1885-1889
Francis P. Fleming (D) 1889-1893
Henry L. Mitchell (D) 1893-1897
William D. Bloxham (D) 1897-1901
William S. Jennings (D) 1901-1905
Napoleon B. Broward (D) 1905-1909
Albert W. Gilchrist (D) 1909-1913
Park Trammell (D) 1913-1917
Sidney J. Catts (O) 1917-1921
Gary A. Hardee (D) 1921-1925
John W. Martin (D) 1925-1929
Doyle E. Carlton (D) 1929-1933
David Sholtz (D) 1933-1937

Frederick P. Cone (D) 1937-1941
Spessard L. Holland (D) 1941-1945
Millard F. Caldwell, Jr. (D) 1945-1949
Fuller Warren (D) 1949-1953
Daniel T. McCarty (D) . . . . (d) 1953
Charles E. Johns (D) 1953-1955
Thomas Leroy Collins (D) 1955-1961
Cecil Farris Bryant (D) 1961-1965
William Hayden Burns (D) 1965-1967
Claude R. Kirk, Jr. (R) 1967-1971
Reubin O. Askew (D) 1971-1979
Robert Graham (D) 1979-1987
Bob Martinez (R) 1987-1991
Lawton Chiles (D) 1991-1999
Jeb Bush (R) 1999-2007
Charlie Crist (R) 2007-

Composition of congressional delegations, 1989-2007

	Dem	Rep	Total
House of Representatives			
101st Congress, 1989			
State delegates	10	9	19
Total U.S.	259	174	433
102d Congress, 1991			
State delegates	9	10	19
Total U.S.	267	167	434
103d Congress, 1993			
State delegates	10	13	23
Total U.S.	258	176	434
104th Congress, 1995			
State delegates	8	15	23
Total U.S.	197	236	433
105th Congress, 1997			
State delegates	8	15	23
Total U.S.	206	228	434
106th Congress, 1999			
State delegates	8	15	23
Total U.S.	211	222	433
107th Congress, 2001			
State delegates	8	15	23
Total U.S.	211	221	432
108th Congress, 2003			
State delegates	7	18	25
Total U.S.	205	229	434
109th Congress, 2005			
State delegates	7	18	25
Total U.S.	202	231	433
110th Congress, 2007			
State delegates	9	16	25
Total U.S.	233	202	435

(continued)

	Dem	Rep	Total
Senate			
101st Congress, 1989			
State delegates	1	1	2
Total U.S.	55	45	100
102d Congress, 1991			
State delegates	1	1	2
Total U.S.	56	44	100
103d Congress, 1993			
State delegates	1	1	2
Total U.S.	57	43	100
104th Congress, 1995			
State delegates	1	1	2
Total U.S.	46	53	99
105th Congress, 1997			
State delegates	1	1	2
Total U.S.	45	55	100
106th Congress, 1999			
State delegates	1	1	2
Total U.S.	45	54	99
107th Congress, 2001			
State delegates	2	0	2
Total U.S.	50	50	100
108th Congress, 2003			
State delegates	2	0	2
Total U.S.	48	51	99
109th Congress, 2005			
State delegates	1	1	2
Total U.S.	44	55	99
110th Congress, 2007			
State delegates	1	1	2
Total U.S.	49	49	98

Figures are for starts of first sessions. Totals are for Democrat (Dem.) and Republican (Rep.) members only. House membership totals under 435 and Senate totals under 100 reflect vacancies and seats held by independent party members. When the 110th Congress opened, the Senate's two independent members caucused with the Democrats, giving the Democrats control of the Senate.

Source: U.S. Congress, *Congressional Directory.*

Composition of state legislature, 1990-2006

	Democrats	Republicans
State House (120 seats)		
1990	74	46
1992	71	49
1994	63	57
1996	59	61
1998	46	73
2000	45	75
2002	39	81
2004	36	84
2006	41	79
State Senate (40 seats)		
1990	22	18
1992	20	20
1994	19	21
1996	17	23
1998	15	25
2000	15	25
2002	14	26
2004	14	26
2006	14	26

Figures for total seats may include independents and minor party members. Numbers reflect results of elections in listed years; elected members usually take their seats in the years that follow.

Source: Council of State Governments; *State Elective Officials and the Legislatures.*

Voter participation in presidential elections, 2000 and 2004

	2000	2004
Voting age population		
State	12,383,000	13,394,000
Total United States	209,831,000	220,377,000
State share of U.S. total	5.90	6.08
Rank among states	4	4
Portion of voting age population casting votes		
State	48.2%	56.8%
United States	50.3%	55.5%
Rank among states	36	27

Population figures are rounded to nearest thousand and include all residents, regardless of eligibility to vote.

Source: U.S. Census Bureau.

HEALTH AND MEDICAL CARE

Medical professionals
Physicians in 2003 and nurses in 2001

	U.S.	State
Physicians in 2003		
Total	774,849	42,213
Share of U.S. total		5.42%
Rate	266	248
Rank		25
Nurses in 2001		
Total	2,262,020	129,610
Share of U.S. total		5.73%
Rate	793	792
Rank		31

Rates are numbers of physicians and nurses per 100,000 resident population; ranks are based on rates.
Source: American Medical Association, *Physician Characteristics and Distribution in the U.S.*; U.S. Department of Health and Human Services, Health Resources and Services Administration.

Health insurance coverage, 2003

	State	U.S.
Total persons covered	13,849,000	243,320,000
Total persons not covered	3,071,000	44,961,000
Portion not covered	18.2%	15.6%
Rank among states	10	—
Children not covered	616,000	8,373,000
Portion not covered	15.5%	11.4%
Rank among states	5	—

Totals are rounded to nearest thousand. Ranks are from the highest to the lowest percentages of persons *not* insured.
Source: U.S. Census Bureau, Current Population Reports.

AIDS, syphilis, and tuberculosis cases, 2003

Disease	U.S. cases	State cases	Rank
AIDS	44,232	4,774	3
Syphilis	34,270	3,282	4
Tuberculosis	14,874	1,046	4

Source: U.S. Centers for Disease Control and Prevention.

Cigarette smoking, 2003
Residents over age 18 who smoke

	U.S.	State	Rank
All smokers	22.1%	23.9%	20
Male smokers	24.8%	26.0%	21
Female smokers	20.3%	22.1%	16

Cigarette smokers are defined as persons who reported having smoked at least 100 cigarettes during their lifetimes and who currently smoked at least occasionally.
Source: U.S. Centers for Disease Control and Prevention, *Morbidity and Mortality Weekly Report*, 53, no. 44 (November 12, 2004).

HOUSING

Home ownership rates, 1985-2004

	1985	1990	1995	2000	2004
State	67.2%	65.1%	66.6%	68.4%	72.2%
Total U.S.	63.9%	63.9%	64.7%	67.4%	69.0%
Rank among states	30	32	32	35	23

Net change in state home ownership rate,
1985-2004 . . . . +5.0%
Net change in U.S. home ownership rate,
1985-2004 . . . . +5.1%

Percentages represent the proportion of owner households to total occupied households.
Source: U.S. Census Bureau, 2006.

Home sales, 2000-2004
In thousands of units

Existing home sales	2000	2002	2003	2004
State sales	393.6	429.3	476.1	526.5
Total U.S. sales	5,171	5,631	6,183	6,784
State share of U.S. total	7.61%	7.62%	7.70%	7.76%
Sales rank among states	2	2	2	2

Units include single-family homes, condos, and co-ops.
Source: National Association of Realtors, Washington, D.C., *Real Estate Outlook: Market Trends & Insights*.

Values of owner-occupied homes, 2003

	State	*U.S.*
Total units	3,508,000	58,809,000
Value of units		
Under $100,000	26.4%	29.6%
$100,000-199,999	44.4%	36.9%
$200,000 or more	29.1%	33.5%
Median value	$144,507	$142,275
Rank among all states 21		

Units are owner-occupied one-family houses whose numbers are
rounded to nearest thousand. Data are extrapolated from
survey samples.
Source: U.S. Census Bureau, American Community Survey.

EDUCATION

Public school enrollment, 2002

Prekindergarten through grade 8
State enrollment 1,809,000
Total U.S. enrollment 34,135,000
State share of U.S. total 5.30%

Grades 9 through 12
State enrollment 731,000
Total U.S. enrollment 14,067,000
State share of U.S. total 5.20%

Enrollment rates
State public school enrollment rate 89.7%
Overall U.S. rate 90.4%
Rank among states in 2002 30
Rank among states in 1995 31

Enrollment figures (which include unclassified students) are
rounded to nearest thousand pupils during fall school term.
Enrollment rates are based on enumerated resident population
estimate for July 1, 2002.
Source: U.S. National Center for Education Statistics.

Public college finances, 2003-2004

FTE enrollment in public institutions of higher education
Students in state institutions 526,700
Students in all U.S. public institutions 9,916,600
State share of U.S. total 5.31
Rank among states 3

**State and local government appropriations for higher
education**
State appropriation per FTE $4,293
National average $5,716
Rank among states 44
State & local tax revenue going to higher
education 5.8%

FTE = full-time equivalent in public postsecondary programs,
including summer sessions; student numbers are rounded to
nearest hundred. Funding figures for 2003-2004 academic year
include financial aid to students in state public institutions and
exclude money for research, agriculture experiment stations,
teaching hospitals, and medical schools; figures are rounded to
nearest thousand dollars.
Source: Higher Education Executive Officers, Denver, Colorado.

TRANSPORTATION AND TRAVEL

Highway mileage, 2003

Interstate highways 1,471
Other freeways and expressways 470
Arterial roads 12,162
Collector roads 14,194
Local roads 92,078
Urban roads 68,479
Rural roads 51,896
Total state mileage 120,375
U.S. total 3,974,107
State share 3.03%
Rank among states 10

Note that combined urban and rural road mileage matches the
total of the other categories.
Source: U.S. Federal Highway Administration.

Motor vehicle registrations and driver licenses, 2003

Vehicle registrations	*State*	*U.S.*	*Share*	*Rank*
Autos, trucks, buses	14,526,000	231,390,000	6.28%	3
Autos only	8,564,000	135,670	6.31%	2
Motorcycles	386,000	5,328,000	7.24%	2
Driver licenses	12,906,000	196,166,000	6.58%	3

Figures, which do not include vehicles owned by military services,
are rounded to the nearest thousand. Figures for automobiles
include taxis.
Source: U.S. Federal Highway Administration.

Domestic travel expenditures, 2003

Spending by U.S. residents on overnight trips and
day trips of at least 50 miles from home

Total expenditures within state	$42.89 bill.
Total expenditures within U.S.	$490.87 bill.
State share of U.S. total	8.7%
Rank among states	2

Source: Travel Industry Association of America.

Retail gasoline prices, 2003-2007

Average price per gallon at the pump

Year	U.S.	State
2003	$1.267	$1.252
2004	$1.316	$1.301
2005	$1.644	$1.621
2007	$2.298	$2.333

Excise tax per gallon in 2004	14.5¢
Rank among all states in 2007 prices	16

Prices are averages of all grades of gasoline sold at the pump
during March months in 2003-2005 and during February, 2007.
Averages for 2006, during which prices rose higher, are not
available.
Source: U.S. Energy Information Agency, *Petroleum Marketing
Monthly* (2003-2005 data); American Automobile Association
(2007 data).

CRIME AND LAW ENFORCEMENT

State and local police officers, 2000-2004

	2000	2002	2004
Total officers			
U.S.	654,601	665,555	675,734
State	39,033	41,511	44,037*
*Net change, 2000-2004			+12.82%
Officers per 1,000 residents			
U.S.	2.33	2.31	2.30
State	2.44	2.49	2.53
State rank	9	10	9

Totals include state and local police and sheriffs.
Source: Carsey Institute, University of New Hampshire.

Crime rates, 2003

Incidents per 100,000 residents

Crimes	State	U.S.
Violent crimes		
Total incidents	730	475
Murder	5	6
Forcible rape	40	32
Robbery	185	142
Aggravated assault	500	295
Property crimes		
Total incidents	4,452	3,588
Burglary	1,003	741
Larceny/theft	2,970	2,415
Motor vehicle theft	479	433
All crimes	5,182	4,063

Source: U.S. Federal Bureau of Investigation, *Crime in the United
States,* annual.

State prison populations, 1980-2003

	State	U.S.	State share
1980	20,735	305,458	6.79%
1990	44,387	708,393	6.27%
1996	63,763	1,025,624	6.22%
2000	71,319	1,391,261	5.13%
2003	79,594	1,470,045	5.41%

State figures exclude prisoners in federal penitentiaries.
Source: U.S. Bureau of Justice Statistics, *Prisoners in 2003.*

Georgia

Location: Southeast coast

Area and rank: 57,919 square miles (150,010 square kilometers); 59,441 square miles (153,952 square kilometers) including water; twenty-second largest state in area

Coastline: 100 miles (161 kilometers) on the Atlantic Ocean

Shoreline: 2,344 miles (3,772 kilometers)

Population and rank: 8,829,000 (2004); ninth largest state in population

Capital and largest city: Atlanta (416,474 people in 2000 census)

Entered Union and rank: January 2, 1788; fourth state

Present constitution adopted: 1983

Counties: 159

State name: Georgia takes its name from King George II of England

Skyline of Atlanta, Georgia's capital and largest city. (Georgia Department of Industry, Trade & Tourism)

State nickname: Peach State; Empire State of the South

Motto: Wisdom, justice, and moderation

State flag: One-third is blue field with state coat of arms; two-thirds are the Confederate flag— red field with blue and white cross of Saint Andrew and thirteen white stars

Highest point: Brasstown Bald—4,784 feet (1,458 meters)

Lowest point: Atlantic Ocean—sea level

Highest recorded temperature: 113 degrees Fahrenheit (45 degrees Celsius)—Greenville, 1978

Lowest recorded temperature: –17 degrees Fahrenheit (–27 degrees Celsius)—CCC Camp F-16, 1940

State song: "Georgia on My Mind"

State tree: Live oak

State flower: Cherokee rose

State bird: Brown thrasher

Georgia History

The last of the original thirteen English colonies to be founded, and the largest state east of the Mississippi River, Georgia has twice led its region in being the forerunner of the "New South," first following the Civil War and then during the second half of the twentieth century. A state of immense geographical variation, changing in elevation from nearly a mile to sea level, it transformed itself from a primarily agricultural state to one that embraced modern manufacturing and technology. Its capital, Atlanta, is one of the largest and fastest-growing cities in the South and a metropolis of truly international distinction.

Early History. In approximately 12,000 B.C.E. the first inhabitants lived along the rivers and coasts of what would become Georgia with a diet of fish and shellfish. They were followed first by nomadic hunters and then by more settled residents who developed agriculture. When Europeans arrived during the mid-sixteenth century, the Native American Cherokee and Creek tribes were dominant in the eastern and coastal areas. Along the coast the Yamacraw, a group of the Creek, were well established. The Chickasaw and Choctaw inhabited the western portion of the territory.

A Native American chief named Guale was the first to make lasting contact with the Europeans, meeting the Spanish soldier Pedro Menéndez de Avilés in 1566. As a result, for a time the entire coastal region was called Guale. The British, French, and Spanish competed to make the Native American tribes their allies, with hopes of using them to defend their own colonies and eliminate those of their competitors. After the Yamasee War (1715-1728) nearly destroyed the British colony of Carolina, the British were determined to settle a buffer colony between themselves and the Spanish in Florida. That colony would become Georgia.

Exploration and Settlement. Spain, with strongholds established throughout the Caribbean and in Florida, sent the first European explorers into the area of Georgia. In 1540, Hernando de Soto passed through Georgia on his lengthy and difficult expedition in search of the fabled Seven Cities of Gold, which were rumored to possess wealth in excess of anything yet found in the New World. French Huguenots under Jean Ribaut landed along the coast in 1562, the same year Ribaut sought to colonize the Port Royal region to the north, in what is now South Carolina. Both attempts were failures. In order to strengthen its position and defend its Florida possessions, Spain established a string of missions and forts running along the coast from northern Florida to the sea islands.

The English responded by thrusting south, forcing the Spanish back to St. Augustine. To create a barrier between the Spanish and the rapidly growing colonies to the north, King George II granted a charter for a colony in 1732. General James Edward Oglethorpe, who wished to open the colony for debtors to give them a fresh start on life, was placed in command of the venture. In 1733, with just over one hundred colonists, Oglethorpe arrived at the bluffs of the Savannah River and struck a deal with Yamacraw chief Tomochichi for land along the river. Oglethorpe laid out the city of Savannah with a gridlike pattern of squares, which would remain.

The Spanish threat was effectively ended in 1742 with Oglethorpe's victory at the battle of Bloody Marsh on Saint Simons Island. Georgia grew rapidly with an economy based on rice, indigo, and cotton. Slave imports were banned in the colony in 1735, but crops were grown best under the plantation system, and in 1749 the slave trade was legalized. The territory up the Savannah River was explored and settled; in 1753 the city of Augusta was founded. In 1754, Georgia became a royal colony.

Revolution and the New Nation. As the colonies moved toward independence, Georgia convened a Provincial Congress in 1775, and its Council of Safety sent delegates to the Continental Congress in Philadelphia. The year following the declaration of American independence, Georgia ratified its first state constitution. In 1778, as the British pursued a southern strategy to pacify the rebellion, their troops seized Savannah. American and French troops were repulsed in a bloody attempt to retake the city, which the British continued to hold until the end of the Revolution.

Georgia became the fourth state to ratify the Constitution, and it joined the Union in 1788, with Augusta, on the Savannah River, as its capital. Its western lands were rapidly developed, and this growth led to the Yazoo Fraud, during which members of the state legislature sold 50 million acres to phantom land companies (most of which were owned by the legislators themselves), which resold them to the public. In the end, the federal government had to pay more than $4 million to settle claims from the incident.

The western movement also prompted the removal of the Cherokee and Creek Indians from Georgia. The Creek began selling their lands in 1827 and moved to Arkansas. Although the Cherokee had tried to fashion a compromise with the European settlers, the discovery of gold on their territory doomed those efforts. Georgia ordered the removal of the Native Americans in 1832, and six years later the tribe began its Trail of Tears to Indian Territory, now the state of Oklahoma.

One of the most important developments in American history occurred near Savannah in 1793, when Eli Whitney invented the cotton gin. This device automatically separated cotton seed from cotton fiber, a time-consuming task which before had been done only by hand. The cotton gin made possible the booming growth of cotton farming in the South, including Georgia, where the rich soil in the central part of the state made the crop highly profitable.

Civil War and Reconstruction. In 1861, Georgia joined with seven other southern states and seceded from the Union. Later that year, in the temporary capital of Montgomery, Alabama, Alexander H. Stephens

of Georgia was elected vice president of the Confederacy. While Georgia soldiers were fighting along the front lines in Tennessee and Virginia, Union forces bombarded and captured Fort Pulaski at the mouth of the Savannah River and clamped a tight blockade on the Georgia coastline. In 1863, after capturing Chattanooga, Tennessee, a Union army advancing into Georgia was surprised and overcome at the Battle of Chickamauga. The following year, the Federals returned under General William Tecumseh Sherman to strike at the strategic railroad center of Atlanta. After months of siege, Atlanta fell and was burned. Sherman then embarked on his March to the Sea, leaving a swath of destruction through Georgia sixty miles wide and capturing Savannah in December.

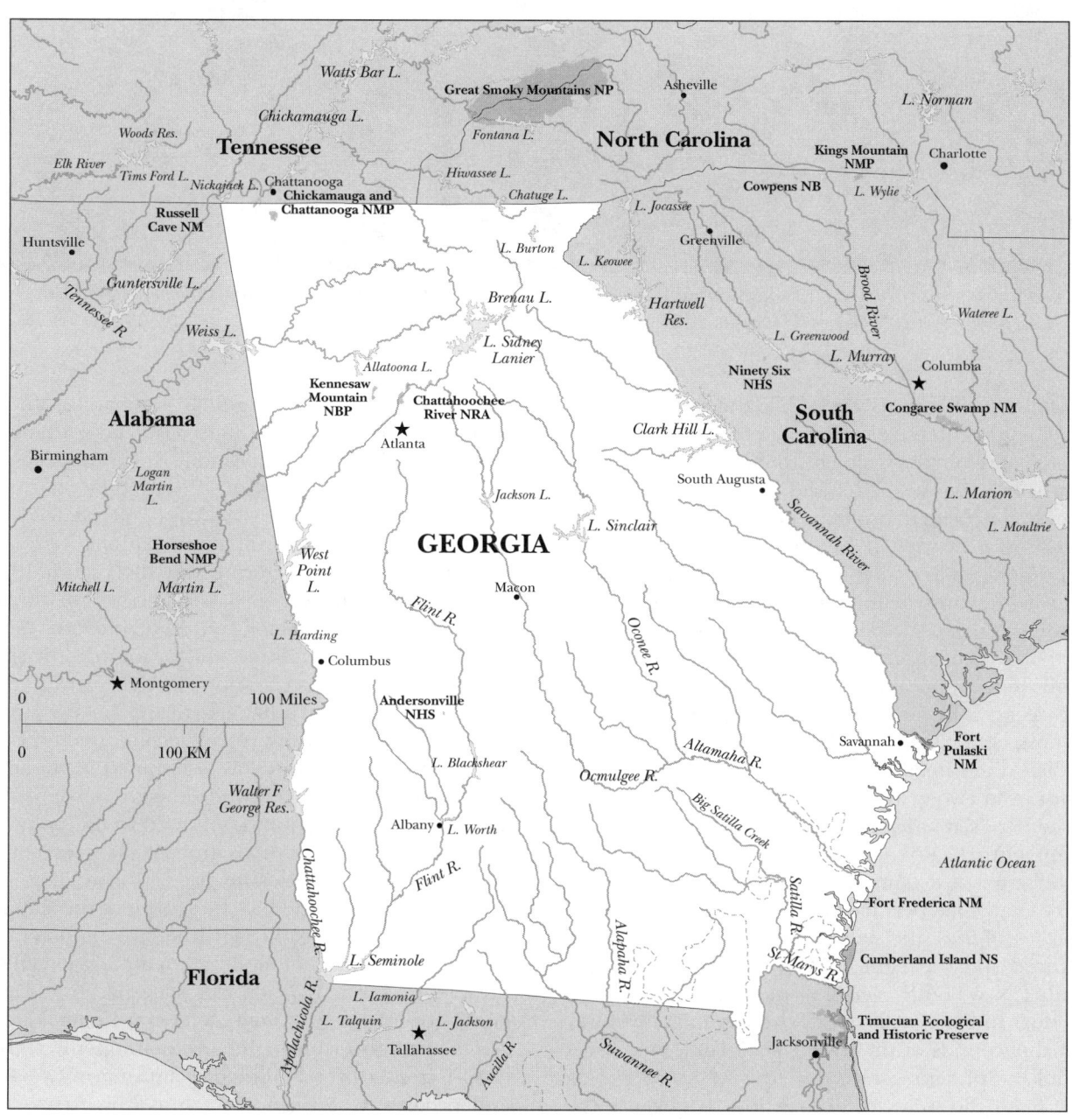

This monumental relief carved on Stone Mountain, near Atlanta, honors (left to right), Confederate leaders Jefferson Davis, Robert E. Lee, and Thomas "Stonewall" Jackson. (PhotoDisc)

Following the war, Georgia, like the rest of the defeated South, entered a period of Reconstruction. It attempted to rejoin the Union in 1868 but was refused re-entry in 1869 because it refused to ratify the Fifteenth Amendment, which prohibits denying voting rights because of race. When Georgia complied with this amendment it was readmitted to the Union, in 1870.

During Reconstruction, Georgia began to rebuild its economy, repairing and expanding its railroad system, which had been largely destroyed during the Civil War, and diversifying its agricultural base to include corn, fruit—especially peaches—tobacco, and livestock. However, cotton, which had been a major crop before the Civil War, remained an essential part of the state's economy, and when a boll weevil infestation struck during the 1920's, it was a severe blow to Georgia's farmers and the entire state.

The state was making strides in other areas. In 1879, Henry Grady had become one of the owners of the Atlanta *Constitution*, the state's largest newspaper. As an unofficial spokesperson for Georgia, Grady prophesied the "New South," which would embrace progress, introduce industry and manufacturing, and move away from the wounds of the Civil War. Atlanta took as its symbol the phoenix, since the city had literally risen anew from the ashes of destruction. It became the headquarters of large regional companies, an economic powerhouse in the Southeast, and a literal symbol of Grady's New South. Among the local success stories was the rise of Coca-Cola, invented by pharmacist John Styth Pemberton in 1886 and, after a few years, the most popular soft drink in the nation.

The Modern Age. During the 1940's and 1950's, manufacturing in Georgia passed agriculture, forestry, and fishing as the major source of income. Textile mills, in particular, became a major force in the state's economy. Georgia became one of the world's largest sources of kaolin and fuller's earth, the first used in producing paper and dishware, the second used for cat litter. High-quality granite was also mined in the upper portion of the state. Meanwhile, the growth of banking and financial institutions continued to the point that Atlanta became known as the "Wall Street of the South," while businesses involved with modern technology also contributed to the growth of the state.

Georgia's passage through the civil rights era was aided by a tradition of moderation among its political leadership. From 1877 on, the state had only Democratic governors. Although Democrat Lester Maddox was elected governor in 1966 with an openly segregationist agenda, broad-minded Atlanta mayor Ivan Allen and progressive governors such as Ellis Arnall, Carl

Sanders, and Jimmy Carter were more representative and helped bring the state through a potentially difficult period. Carter in 1976 was elected president of the United States. In 1972, Maynard Jackson was elected mayor of Atlanta, the first African American chosen to lead a large southern city. Also that year, Andrew Young became the first African American elected to Congress from Georgia since the end of Reconstruction. This period of Georgia's history is regarded as marking the birth of the second "New South," which combined economic development with racial progress.

Georgia's economy is strong, with its deep-water port of Savannah one of the most active on the East Coast. Atlanta's Hartsville International Airport is one of the largest and best equipped in the world. Natural resources contribute to the state's revenues.

The New South. As the new millennium approached, Georgia remained at the head of the economy and society of the New South. With Atlanta at its economic heart, Georgia was modern, forward looking, and prosperous. The city's gleaming international airport was one of the busiest in the United States. Emblematic of the state's growing economic status was the announcement in 2000 that Atlanta-based United Parcel Service (UPS) received permission for six flights a week to be initiated to China. Population growth in greater Atlanta pointed in the same upward trajectory, with a 39 percent increase over the previous decade. The state had outgrown most other states and earned an additional two seats in the U.S. House of Representatives in Washington, D.C.

Political Change and Legal Controversy. Also symbolic of the dynamics of the New South's politics was the aftermath of the election of Zell Miller, a Democrat, to the U.S. Senate over Republican senator Mack Mattingly. Miller had been appointed to the seat upon the death of Senator Paul Coverdell. Miller, however, turned against Democrats and critics of the administration of George W. Bush to back the president's reelection in 2004. He delivered a fiery keynote speech at the Republican National Convention in New York, all the while remaining a Democrat.

On July 24, 2000, the University of Georgia at Athens lost a closely watched affirmative action suit before the U.S. Eleventh Circuit Court of Appeals. Three women sued the university when minority candidates gained admission to the university, notwithstanding the plaintiffs' high scores on the Scholastic Aptitude Test. The awarding of bonus points for race by the university was found unconstitutional. The Court demanded that admissions officials "fully and fairly" analyze applicants "as individuals and not merely as members of groups."

One of the great plantation houses of nineteenth century Savannah. (Georgia Department of Industry, Trade & Tourism)

In the 2002 midterm elections, Republican Saxby Chambliss, by 53 to 46 percent, took the seat of U.S. senator Max Cleland, a decorated Vietnam War veteran and a member of the Senate's liberal wing. Once again, the politics of the New South rejected the domination of the "Solid South" of yore, when the real race for public office took place in the Democratic Party primaries and not in the general election, where the outcome was typically a foregone conclusion. Further evidence of these changes lay in the fact that a black Republican candidate for Congress beat a white Democrat in a heavily Democratic redrawn congressional district.

Michael Witkoski
Updated by the Editor

Georgia Time Line

1540	Spanish explorer Hernando de Soto marches through part of Georgia in his quest for gold.
1566	Spanish mariner Pedro Menéndez de Avilés builds a fort on Saint Catherine's Island.
June 9, 1732	George II grants charter giving imprisoned English debtors the right to settle in Georgia.
Feb. 12, 1733	General James Oglethorpe founds Savannah.
1735	Georgia bans importation of slaves.
1736	Methodist preachers John and Charles Wesley arrive at Savannah.
1742	Oglethorpe's troops defeat Spaniards at battle of Bloody Marsh on Saint Simons Island.
1749	Slave trade is legalized.
1754	Georgia becomes a royal colony.
1775	Provincial Congress meets in Savannah.
Feb. 5, 1777	First state constitution is ratified in Savannah.
1778	British troops capture Savannah during the Revolution.
July 12, 1782	British abandon Savannah.
1785	University of Georgia is founded at Athens.
1786	Augusta is named state capital.
Jan. 2, 1788	Georgia enters the Union as the fourth state.
June 20, 1793	Eli Whitney invents the cotton gin near Savannah.
1795	Louisville is named state capital.
1804	Milledgeville is named state capital.
1827	Creek Indians begin selling their lands east of Flint River to Georgia.
1828-1838	Conflicts with Cherokee over land claims lead to their removal from Georgia.
1836	Georgia Female College, now Wesleyan College, the first college chartered to grant degrees to women, opens in Macon.
1837	City of Terminus, later Atlanta, is founded.
Jan. 19, 1861	Georgia secedes from Union.
Feb. 18, 1861	Georgian Alexander H. Stephens becomes vice president of the Confederacy.
Sept. 20, 1863	Union army is defeated at Battle of Chickamauga.
1864	Union general William Tecumseh Sherman captures and burns Atlanta; Union army marches to the sea and captures Savannah.
1868	Federal troops leave state.
1868	Atlanta is named state capital.
July 15, 1870	Georgia is readmitted to Union.
1875	First commercial peach orchard in Georgia is established.
1886	Pharmacist John Styth Pemberton of Atlanta invents Coca-Cola.
1888	Georgia Institute of Technology opens in Atlanta.
1912	Girl Scouts of America are formed by Juliette Gordon Low of Savannah.
1921	Boll weevil infestation damages Georgia's cotton crop.
1960	Future governor Lester Maddox organizes Georgians Unwilling to Surrender (GUTS), which boycotts businesses that change their segregation policies.
1966	Race riots take place in Atlanta.
1972	Maynard Jackson becomes the first African American elected mayor of Atlanta.

The Atlanta home in which civil rights leader Martin Luther King, Jr., was born is now a National Historic Site. (Georgia Department of Industry, Trade & Tourism)

1972	Andrew Young is elected the first African American congressman from Georgia since Reconstruction.
1976	Former governor Jimmy Carter is elected president of the United States.
1980	World's largest airport terminal opens in Atlanta.
1983	New state constitution is adopted.
1987	Gwinnet County in Atlanta is the fastest-growing county in the United States for the second year.
1991	Georgia carries out the most executions in the country.
1992	Governor Zell Miller announces legislation to remove the Confederate battle symbol from the state flag.
2000	Georgia gains two seats in the U.S. House of Representatives after the 2000 census shows substantial population growth in the state compared with other states.
July 24, 2000	Three women candidates for admission at the University of Georgia at Athens who were denied admission in favor of less-qualified minority candidates win their case in U.S. federal court.
Nov. 5, 2002	Republican Saxby Chambliss, a conservative, defeats Democratic senator Max Cleland, a veteran of the Vietnam War and one-term senator.
Dec. 10, 2004	Former president and former Georgia governor Jimmy Carter receives the Nobel Peace Prize in Oslo, Norway.

Notes for Further Study

Published Sources. A good starting place for information on the state is *A History of Georgia* (2d ed., 1991), edited by Kenneth Coleman. This is a solid traditional history of the state, well researched and documented, which explores a wide range of topics. Robin S. Doak takes an accessible approach to the history of the state with *Georgia* (2005), a book for young adults. Another book for the younger audience is *Primary Source History of the Colony of Georgia* (2005) by Liz Sonneborn. Two good sources on Georgia residents are James C. Cobb's *Georgia Odyssey* (1997) and Lane Mills's *The People of Georgia: An Illustrated History* (2d ed., 1992), a popular history on individuals and groups, from the earliest times to the modern era, who shaped developments in the Peach State. *Civil War Savannah* (1997) by Derek Smith explores one of the South's most important cities during the Civil War. *The Archaeology and History of the Native Georgia Tribes* (2002) by Max E. White uses evidence from select archaeological sites, maps, photographs, and vivid fictional vignettes to highlight the history of the state's indigenous communities. During the Great Depression, unemployed writers and researchers were recruited by the Federal Writers' Project of the Works Progress Administration (WPA) to interview former slaves and collect the memories of their enslaved years. *On Jordan's Stormy Banks: Personal Accounts of Slavery in Georgia* (2000) is one result of this project, a collection of dramatic reminiscences brought together by Andrew White. Rebecca S. Montgomery's *Politics of Education in the New South: Women and Reform in Georgia, 1890-1930* (2006) is a fascinating study of the way in which post-Civil War women activists advocated a fair and just system of education as a way of providing economic opportunity for women and the rural and urban poor.

Web Resources. The state of Georgia has a Web site that provides a wealth of information and directs visitors to other locations (www.state.ga.us). A valuable source of information for tourists, businesspeople, and residents can be found at the site hosted by the Georgia Department of Industry, Trade and Tourism (www .georgia.org). Roadside America Attractions also has a good site for visitors to the state (www.roadsideamerica.com/map/ga .html). For information specifically about Georgia's rich historical heritage, the Georgia History site (www.cviog .uga.edu/Projects/gainfo/ gahist.htm) is an excellent starting place. It is well supplemented and amplified by a visit to the site of the Georgia Department of Archives and History (www.georgiaarchives.org/ who_are_we/default .htm). For those interested in Georgia's natural resources, an excellent site is Links to Georgia Geoscience Sites (gpc.edu/~pgore/georgia.htm).

State capitol building in Atlanta. The statue in the foreground is of former governor Richard B. Russell. (©Gabriel Eckert/Dreamstime.com)

Counties

County	2000 pop.	Rank in pop.	Sq. miles	Rank in area	County	2000 pop.	Rank in pop.	Sq. miles	Rank in area
Appling	17,419	90	508.8	23	Fayette	91,263	19	197.4	140
Atkinson	7,609	141	338.1	84	Floyd	90,565	20	513.3	20
Bacon	10,103	126	285.0	104	Forsyth	98,407	15	225.8	130
Baker	4,074	152	343.2	80	Franklin	20,285	83	263.3	115
Baldwin	44,700	39	258.5	117	Fulton	816,006	1	528.7	17
Banks	14,422	105	233.7	126	Gilmer	23,456	68	426.7	50
Barrow	46,144	37	162.2	153	Glascock	2,556	157	144.2	156
Bartow	76,019	26	459.9	35	Glynn	67,568	28	422.4	52
Ben Hill	17,484	89	251.8	118	Gordon	44,104	40	355.2	75
Berrien	16,235	94	452.5	38	Grady	23,659	66	458.2	37
Bibb	153,887	9	250.0	119	Greene	14,406	106	388.4	62
Bleckley	11,666	114	217.4	132	Gwinnett	588,448	4	432.9	48
Brantley	14,629	104	444.4	41	Habersham	35,902	50	278.2	110
Brooks	16,450	93	493.7	28	Hall	139,277	11	393.7	59
Bryan	23,417	69	441.8	43	Hancock	10,076	127	473.3	32
Bulloch	55,983	35	682.6	7	Haralson	25,690	59	282.2	108
Burke	22,243	74	830.6	2	Harris	23,695	64	463.8	34
Butts	19,522	86	186.6	144	Hart	22,997	70	232.2	127
Calhoun	6,320	149	280.2	109	Heard	11,012	117	296.1	99
Camden	43,664	41	629.9	11	Henry	119,341	12	322.7	93
Candler	9,577	130	247.0	122	Houston	110,765	13	376.8	66
Carroll	87,268	23	499.3	27	Irwin	9,931	128	356.8	73
Catoosa	53,282	36	162.2	152	Jackson	41,589	44	342.4	82
Charlton	10,282	124	780.8	5	Jasper	11,426	116	370.5	68
Chatham	232,048	6	440.4	46	Jeff Davis	12,684	109	333.4	86
Chattahoochee	14,882	103	248.8	120	Jefferson	17,266	92	527.7	18
Chattooga	25,470	60	313.8	94	Jenkins	8,575	136	349.8	76
Cherokee	141,903	10	423.7	51	Johnson	8,560	137	304.4	97
Clarke	101,489	14	120.8	159	Jones	23,639	67	393.8	58
Clay	3,357	155	195.2	142	Lamar	15,912	96	184.8	147
Clayton	236,517	5	142.6	157	Lanier	7,241	142	186.8	143
Clinch	6,878	144	809.4	4	Laurens	44,874	38	812.6	3
Cobb	607,751	3	340.2	83	Lee	24,757	62	355.8	74
Coffee	37,413	48	599.1	12	Liberty	61,610	30	519.1	19
Colquitt	42,053	43	552.3	15	Lincoln	8,348	138	211.1	134
Columbia	89,288	21	290.0	101	Long	10,304	123	401.0	56
Cook	15,771	97	229.1	129	Lowndes	92,115	18	504.3	24
Coweta	89,215	22	443.1	42	Lumpkin	21,016	81	284.5	105
Crawford	12,495	111	325.1	90	McDuffie	21,231	79	259.8	116
Crisp	21,996	75	273.8	112	McIntosh	10,847	119	433.5	47
Dade	15,154	101	173.9	149	Macon	14,074	107	403.3	55
Dawson	15,999	95	211.0	135	Madison	25,730	58	284.4	106
Decatur	28,240	53	596.8	13	Marion	7,144	143	367.1	70
De Kalb	665,865	2	268.3	113	Meriwether	22,534	72	503.4	25
Dodge	19,171	87	500.6	26	Miller	6,383	147	283.1	107
Dooly	11,525	115	393.0	61	Mitchell	23,932	63	512.0	21
Dougherty	96,065	16	329.7	87	Monroe	21,757	78	395.7	57
Douglas	92,174	17	199.3	138	Montgomery	8,270	139	245.3	123
Early	12,354	112	511.3	22	Morgan	15,457	99	349.7	77
Echols	3,754	154	404.2	54	Murray	36,506	49	344.4	79
Effingham	37,535	47	479.5	31	Muscogee	186,291	8	216.3	133
Elbert	20,511	82	368.8	69	Newton	62,001	29	276.4	111
Emanuel	21,837	77	686.0	6	Oconee	26,225	56	185.8	145
Evans	10,495	122	185.0	146	Oglethorpe	12,635	110	441.1	45
Fannin	19,798	85	385.8	63	Paulding	81,678	25	313.6	95

(continued)

County	2000 pop.	Rank in pop.	Sq. miles	Rank in area	County	2000 pop.	Rank in pop.	Sq. miles	Rank in area
Peach	23,668	65	151.1	155	Talbot	6,498	146	393.2	60
Pickens	22,983	71	232.1	128	Taliaferro	2,077	159	195.4	141
Pierce	15,636	98	343.0	81	Tattnall	22,305	73	483.7	30
Pike	13,688	108	218.4	131	Taylor	8,815	134	377.5	65
Polk	38,127	46	311.2	96	Telfair	11,794	113	441.2	44
Pulaski	9,588	129	247.4	121	Terrell	10,970	118	335.5	85
Putnam	18,812	88	344.5	78	Thomas	42,737	42	548.4	16
Quitman	2,598	156	151.6	154	Tift	38,407	45	265.1	114
Rabun	15,050	102	371.1	67	Toombs	26,067	57	366.7	71
Randolph	7,791	140	429.3	49	Towns	9,319	133	166.5	151
Richmond	199,775	7	324.1	91	Treutlen	6,854	145	200.7	137
Rockdale	70,111	27	130.7	158	Troup	58,779	33	413.9	53
Schley	3,766	153	167.6	150	Turner	9,504	131	286.1	102
Screven	15,374	100	648.5	9	Twiggs	10,590	121	360.4	72
Seminole	9,369	132	238.1	125	Union	17,289	91	322.7	92
Spalding	58,417	34	198.0	139	Upson	27,597	54	325.5	89
Stephens	25,435	61	179.3	148	Walker	61,053	31	446.3	40
Stewart	5,252	151	458.7	36	Walton	60,687	32	329.3	88
Sumter	33,200	52	485.3	29	Ware	35,483	51	902.6	1

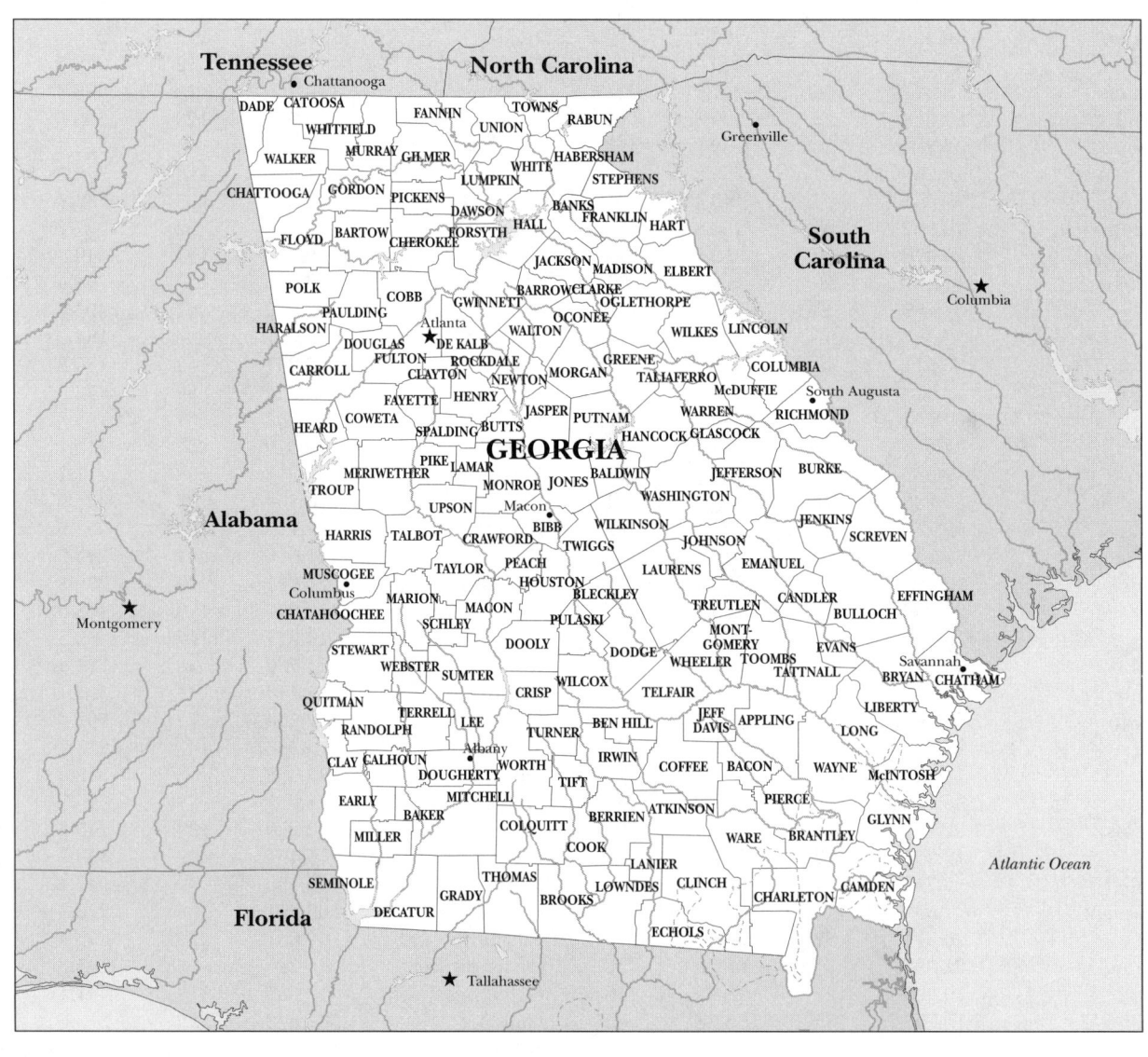

County	2000 pop.	Rank in pop.	Sq. miles	Rank in area
Warren	6,336	148	285.5	103
Washington	21,176	80	680.5	8
Wayne	26,565	55	644.7	10
Webster	2,390	158	209.6	136
Wheeler	6,179	150	297.7	98
White	19,944	84	241.6	124
Whitfield	83,525	24	290.0	100

County	2000 pop.	Rank in pop.	Sq. miles	Rank in area
Wilcox	8,577	135	380.4	64
Wilkes	10,687	120	471.4	33
Wilkinson	10,220	125	446.6	39
Worth	21,967	76	569.8	14

Source: U.S. Census Bureau; National Association of Counties.

Cities
With 10,000 or more residents

Rank	City	Population
1	Atlanta (capital)	416,474
2	Augusta-Richmond County	195,182
3	Columbus	185,781
4	Savannah	131,510
5	Athens-Clarke County	100,266
6	Macon	97,255
7	Sandy Springs	85,781
8	Roswell	79,334
9	Albany	76,939
10	Marietta	58,748
11	Warner Robins	48,804
12	Valdosta	43,724
13	Smyrna	40,999
14	East Point	39,595
15	North Atlanta	38,579
16	Rome	34,980
17	Alpharetta	34,854
18	Redan	33,841
19	Dunwoody	32,808
20	Peachtree City	31,580
21	Hinesville	30,392
22	Mableton	29,733
23	Candler-McAfee	28,294
24	Dalton	27,912
25	Martinez	27,749
26	Tucker	26,532
27	LaGrange	25,998
28	Gainesville	25,578
29	Griffin	23,451
30	Statesboro	22,698
31	Lawrenceville	22,397
32	Duluth	22,122
33	Kennesaw	21,675
34	Forest Park	21,447
35	College Park	20,382
36	Douglasville	20,065
37	Carrollton	19,843
38	Belvedere Park	18,945
39	North Druid Hills	18,852
40	Milledgeville	18,757
41	Thomasville	18,162
42	Decatur	18,147
43	Evans	17,727
44	Americus	17,013
45	Newnan	16,242
46	Cartersville	15,925
47	Dublin	15,857
48	Brunswick	15,600
49	Snellville	15,351
50	Waycross	15,333
51	North Decatur	15,270
52	Tifton	15,060
53	Moultrie	14,387
54	Wilmington Island	14,213
55	St. Marys	13,761
56	Acworth	13,422
57	St. Simons	13,381
58	Druid Hills	12,741
59	Powder Springs	12,481
60	Riverdale	12,478
61	Panthersville	11,791
62	Mountain Park	11,753
63	Fort Benning South	11,737
64	Bainbridge	11,722
65	Union City	11,621
66	Cordele	11,608
67	Covington	11,547
68	Monroe	11,407
69	Sugar Hill	11,399
70	Lilburn	11,307
71	Garden City	11,289
72	Fort Stewart	11,205
73	Fayetteville	11,148
74	Conyers	10,689
75	Buford	10,668
76	Calhoun	10,667
77	Douglas	10,639
78	Georgetown	10,599
79	Kingsland	10,506
80	Vidalia	10,491
81	Winder	10,201
82	Woodstock	10,050

Population figures are from 2000 census.
Source: U.S. Bureau of the Census.

Index to Tables

DEMOGRAPHICS

Resident state and national populations, 1970-2004

Population figures given in thousands

	State pop.	U.S. pop.	Share	Rank
1970	4,588	203,302	2.3%	15
1980	5,463	226,546	2.4%	13
1985	5,963	237,924	2.5%	11
1990	6,478	248,765	2.6%	11
1995	7,328	262,761	2.7%	10
2000	8,187	281,425	2.9%	10
2004	8,829	293,655	3.0%	9

Source: U.S. Census Bureau, Current Population Reports, 2006.

Resident population by age, 2004

Age Group	Total persons
Under 5 years	679,000
5 to 17 years	1,654,000
18 to 24 years	902,000
25 to 34 years	1,364,000
35 to 44 years	1,392,000
45 to 54 years	1,189,000
55 to 64 years	803,000
65 to 74 years	477,000
75 to 84 years	275,000
85 years and older	95,000
All age groups	8,829,000

Portion of residents 65 and older	9.6%
National rank in portion of oldest residents	48
National average	12.4%

Population figures are rounded to nearest thousand persons;
figures include armed forces personnel stationed in the state.
Source: U.S. Bureau of the Census, 2006.

Resident population by race, Hispanic origin, 2004

Category	State pop.	Share	U.S.
All residents	8,829	100.00%	100.00%
Non-Hispanic white	5,319	60.24%	67.37%
Hispanic white	544	6.16%	13.01%
Other Hispanic	54	0.61%	1.06%
African American	2,613	29.60%	12.77%
Native American	27	0.31%	0.96%
Asian, Pacific Islander	237	2.68%	4.37%
Two or more categories	90	1.02%	1.51%

Population figures are in thousands. Persons counted as "Hispanic" (Latino) may be of any race. Because of overlapping categories, categories may not add up to 100%. Shares in column 3 are percentages of each category within the state; these figures may be compared to the national percentages in column 4.
Source: U.S. Bureau of the Census, 2006.

Projected state population, 2000-2030

Year	Population
2000	8,187,000
2005	8,926,000
2010	9,589,000
2015	10,231,000
2020	10,844,000
2025	11,439,000
2030	12,018,000
Population increase, 2000-2030	3,831,000
Percentage increase, 2000-2030	46.8

Projections are based on data from the 2000 census.
Source: U.S. Census Bureau.

VITAL STATISTICS

Infant mortality rates, 1980-2002

	1980	1990	2000	2002
All state residents	14.5	12.4	8.5	8.9
All U.S. residents	12.6	9.2	9.4	9.1
All state white residents	10.8	7.4	5.9	6.6
All U.S. white residents	10.6	7.6	5.7	5.8
All state black residents	21.0	18.3	13.9	13.7
All U.S. black residents	22.2	18.0	14.1	14.4

Figures represent deaths per 1,000 live births of resident infants under 1 year old, exclusive of fetal deaths. Figures for all residents include members of other racial categories not listed separately.
Source: U.S. Census Bureau, *Statistical Abstract of the United States,* 2006.

Abortion rates, 1990 and 2000

	1990	2000
Total abortions	40,000	32,000
Rate per 1,000 women	23.7	16.9
U.S. rate	25.7	21.3
Rank	16	20

Numbers of abortions are rounded to nearest thousand; ranks are based on rates.
Source: U.S. Census Bureau.

Marriages and divorces

Total marriages in 2004	64,500
Rate per 1,000 population.	7.3
National rate per 1,000 population	7.4
Rank among all states	26
Total divorces in 2000	30,700
Rate per 1,000 population.	3.9
National rate per 1,000 population in 2004	3.7
Rank among all states in 2004	n/a

Figures are for all marriages and divorces performed within the state, including those of nonresidents; totals are rounded to the nearest hundred. Ranks are for highest to lowest figures; note that 2004 divorce data are not available for Georgia and four other states.
Source: U.S. National Center for Health Statistics, *Vital Statistics of the United States,* 2006.

Death rates by leading causes, 2002
Deaths per 100,000 resident population

Cause	State	U.S.
Heart disease	204.8	241.7
Cancer	163.3	193.2
Cerebrovascular diseases	49.8	56.4
Accidents other than motor vehicle	38.9	37.0
Motor vehicle accidents	17.8	15.7
Chronic lower respiratory diseases	36.9	43.3
Diabetes mellitus	18.4	25.4
HIV	8.3	4.9
Suicide	10.6	11.0
Homicide	7.9	6.1
All causes	764.6	847.3
Rank in overall death rate among states		42

Figures exclude nonresidents who died in the state. Causes of death follow International Classification of Diseases. Rank is from highest to lowest death rate in the United States.
Source: U.S. National Center for Health Statistics, *National Vital Statistics Report,* 2006.

ECONOMY

Gross state product, 1990-2004
In current dollars

Year	State product	Nat'l product	State share
1990	$139.5 billion	$5.67 trillion	2.46%
2000	$291.0 billion	$9.75 trillion	2.98%
2002	$307.4 billion	$10.41 trillion	2.95%
2003	$321.2 billion	$10.92 trillion	2.94%
2004	$340.7 billion	$11.65 trillion	2.92%

Source: U.S. Bureau of Economic Analysis, *Survey of Current Business,* July, 2005.

Gross state product by industry, 2003
In billions of dollars

Construction	$13.4
Manufacturing	43.0
Wholesale trade	23.7
Retail trade	22.8
Finance & insurance	18.8
Information	21.3
Professional services	18.8
Health care & social assistance	16.2
Government	37.2
Total state product	$303.0
Total U.S. product	$10,289.2
State share of U.S. total	2.94%
Rank among all states	10

Total figures include industries not listed separately. Amounts are in chained 2000 dollars.
Source: U.S. Bureau of Economic Analysis, *Survey of Current Business,* July, 2005.

Personal income per capita, 1990-2004
In current dollars

	1990	2000	2004
Per capita income	$17,603	$27,989	$30,051
U.S. average	$19,477	$29,845	$32,937
Rank among states	29	26	34

Source: U.S. Bureau of Economic Analysis, *Survey of Current Business,* April, 2005.

Energy consumption, 2001
In trillions of British thermal units (BTU), except as noted

Total energy consumption
Total state energy consumption	2,881
Total U.S. energy consumption	96,275
State share of U.S. total	2.99%
Rank among states	10

Per capita consumption (In millions of BTU)
Total state per capita consumption	343
Total U.S. per capita consumption	338
Rank among states	26

End-use sectors
Residential	642
Commercial	503
Industrial	876
Transportation	860

Sources of energy
Petroleum	1,034
Natural gas	363
Coal	772
Hydroelectric power	21
Nuclear electric power	352

Figures for totals include categories not listed separately.
Source: U.S. Energy Information Administration, *State Energy Data Report,* 2001.

Nonfarm employment by sectors, 2004

Total	3,890,000
Construction	198,000
Manufacturing	445,000
Trade, transportation, utilities	828,000
Information	119,000
Finance, insurance, real estate	218,000
Professional & business services	511,000
Education & health services	407,000
Leisure, hospitality, arts, organizations	358,000
Other services, including repair & maintenance	156,000
Government	638,000

Figures are rounded to nearest thousand persons. "Total" includes mining and natural resources, not listed separately.
Source: U.S. Bureau of Labor Statistics, 2006.

Foreign exports, 1990-2004
In millions of dollars

Year	State	U.S.	State share
1990	5,763	394,045	1.46%
1996	10,982	624,767	1.76%
1997	12,949	688,896	1.88%
2000	14,925	712,055	1.91%
2003	16,286	724,006	2.41%
2004	19,633	769,332	2.55%

Rank among all states in 2004 11

U.S. total does not include U.S. dependencies.
Source: U.S. Census Bureau, *U.S. Merchandise Trade,* series FT 900, 2000; U.S. Census Bureau, *U.S. International Trade in Goods and Services,* Series FT 900, 2005.

LAND USE

Federally owned land, 2003
Areas in acres

	State	U.S.	State share
Total area	37,295,000	2,271,343,000	1.64%
Nonfederal land	34,981,000	1,599,584,000	2.19%
Federal land	2,314,000	671,759,000	0.34%
Federal share	6.2%	29.6%	—

Areas are rounded to nearest thousand acres. Figures for federally owned land do not include trust properties.
Source: U.S. General Services Administration, *Federal Real Property Profile,* 2006.

Land use, 1997
In acres, rounded to nearest thousand

Total surface area	37,741,000
Total nonfederal rural land.	30,648,000
Percentage rural land	81.2%
Cropland	4,757,000
Conservation Reserve Program (CRP*) land. . . .	595,000
Pastureland	2,865,000
Rangeland	(nil)
Forestland	21,560,000
Other rural land	872,000

*CRP is a federal program begun in 1985 to assist private landowners to convert highly erodible cropland to vegetative cover for ten years. Note that some categories of land overlap.
Source: U.S. Department of Agriculture, Natural Resources and Conservation Service, and Iowa State University, Statistical Laboratory, S*ummary Report, 1997 National Resources Inventory,* revised December, 2000.

Farms and crop acreage, 2004

	State	U.S.	Share	Rank
Farms	49,000	2,113,000	2.32%	17
Acres (millions)	11	937	1.17%	27
Acres per farm	218	443	—	30

Source: U.S. Department of Agriculture, National Agricultural Statistics Service. Numbers of farms are rounded to nearest thousand units; acreage figures are rounded to nearest million. Rankings, including ties, are based on rounded figures.

GOVERNMENT AND FINANCE

Units of local government, 2002

	State	Total U.S.	Rank
All local governments	1,448	87,525	21
Counties	156	3,034	2
Municipalities	531	19,429	16
Townships	0	16,504	—
School districts	180	13,506	25
Special districts	581	35,052	22

Only 48 states have county governments, 20 states have township governments ("towns" in New England, Minnesota, New York, and Wisconsin), and 46 states have school districts. Special districts encompass such functions as natural resources, fire protection, and housing and community development.
Source: U.S. Census Bureau, *Census of Governments.*

State government revenue, 2002

Total revenue	$24,847 mill.
General revenue	$26,114 mill.
Per capita revenue	$3,058
U.S. per capita average	$3,689
Rank among states	45

Intergovernment revenue	
Total	$8,611 mill.
From federal government	$8,541 mill.

Charges and miscellaneous	
Total	$3,731 mill.
Current charges	$1,895 mill.
Misc. general income	$1,836 mill.
Insurance trust revenue	−$1,268 mill.

Taxes	
Total	$13,772 mill.
Per capita taxes	$1,612
Rank among states	38
Property taxes	$54 mill.
Sales taxes	$6,018 mill.
License taxes	$494 mill.
Individual income taxes	$6,488 mill.
Corporate income taxes	$568 mill.
Other taxes	$151 mill.

Total revenue figures include items not listed separately here.
Source: U.S. Bureau of the Census.

State government expenditures, 2002

General expenditures
Total state expenditures . . . . $30,053 mill.
Intergovernmental . . . . $8,645 mill.

Per capita expenditures
State $3,180
Average of all states $3,859
Rank among states 46

Selected direct expenditures
Education. . . . . $5,011 mill.
Public welfare . . . . $6,013 mill.
Health, hospital . . . . $1,094 mill.
Highways . . . . $1,990 mill.
Police protection. . . . . $255 mill.
Corrections. $1,233 mill.
Natural resources . . . . $494 mill.
Parks and recreation . . . . $162 mill.
Government administration. . . . . $660 mill.
Interest on debt . . . . $433 mill.
Total direct expenditures. . . . . $18,521 mill.

Totals include items not listed separately.
Source: U.S. Census Bureau.

POLITICS

Governors since statehood
D = Democrat; R = Republican; O = other;
(r) resigned; (d) died in office; (i) removed from office

John A. Treutlen 1777-1778
John Houstoun. 1778-1779
George Walton 1779-1780
Richard Howley 1780-1781
Nathan Brownson 1781-1782
John Martin 1782-1783
Lyman Hall. 1783-1784
John Houstoun. 1784-1785
Samuel Elbert 1785-1786
Edward Telfair 1786-1787
George Mathews 1787-1788
George Handley 1788-1789
George Walton (O) 1789
Edward Telfair (O) 1789-1793
George Mathews (O) 1793-1796
Jared Irwin (O) 1796-1798
James Jackson (O) . . . . (r) 1798-1801
David Emanuel (O) 1801
Josiah Tattnall (O) . . . . (r) 1801-1802
John Milledge (O) . . . . (r) 1802-1806
Jared Irwin (O) 1806-1809
David B. Mitchell (O) 1809-1813
William Rabun (O) . . . . (d) 1813-1819
Matthew Talbot (O) 1819
John Clark (O). 1819-1823
George M. Troup (O) 1823-1827
John Forsyth (O). 1827-1829

George R. Gilmer (D) 1829-1831
Wilson Lumpkin (D) 1831-1835
William Schley (D). 1835-1837
George R. Gilmer (O) 1837-1839
Charles J. McDonald (D) 1839-1843
George W. Crawford (O) 1843-1847
George W. B. Towns (D). 1847-1851
Howell Cobb (D) 1851-1853
Herschel V. Johnson (D) 1853-1857
Joseph E. Brown (D) . . . . (i) 1857-1865
James Johnson (D). 1865
Charles J. Jenkins (D) . . . . (i) 1865-1868
Thomas H. Ruger . . . . (i) 1868
Rufus B. Bullock (R) . . . . (r) 1868-1871
Benjamin Conley (R) 1871-1872
James M. Smith (R) 1872-1877
Alfred M. Colquitt (D). 1877-1882
Alexander H. Stephens (D). . . . . . . (d) 1882-1883
James S. Boynton (D) 1883
Henry D. McDaniel (D) 1883-1886
John B. Gordon (D) 1886-1890
William J. Northern (D) 1890-1894
William Y. Atkinson (D) 1894-1898
Allen D. Candler (D) 1898-1902
Joseph M. Terrell (D) 1902-1907
Michael Hoke Smith (D) 1907-1909
Joseph M. Brown (D) 1909-1911
Michael Hoke Smith (D) . . . . (r) 1911
John M. Slaton (D) 1911-1912
Joseph M. Brown (D) 1912-1913
John M. Slaton (D) 1913-1915
Nathaniel E. Harris (D) 1915-1917
Hugh M. Dorsey (D). 1917-1921
Thomas W. Hardwick (D) 1921-1923
Clifford M. Walker (D) 1923-1927
Lamartine G. Hardman (D). 1927-1931
Richard B. Russell, Jr. (D) 1931-1933
Eugene Talmadge (D). 1933-1937
Eurith D. Rivers (D) 1937-1941
Eugene Talmadge (D). 1941-1943
Ellis G. Arnall (D) 1943-1947
Herman Talmadge (D) . . . . (i) 1947
Ellis G. Arnall (D) . . . . (r) 1947
Melvin E. Thompson (D) 1947-1948
Herman Talmadge (D) 1948-1955
Samuel Marvin Griffin (D) 1955-1959
Samuel Ernest Vandiver, Jr. (D) 1959-1963
Carl E. Sanders (D) 1963-1967
Lester G. Maddox (D) 1967-1971
Jimmy (James E.) Carter (D) 1971-1975
George D. Busbee (D). 1975-1983
Joe Frank Harris (D). 1983-1991
Zell Miller (D) 1991-1999
Roy Barnes (D) 1999-2003
George E. "Sonny" Perdue III (R) 2003-

Composition of congressional delegations, 1989-2007

	Dem	Rep	Total
House of Representatives			
101st Congress, 1989			
State delegates	9	1	10
Total U.S.	259	174	433
102d Congress, 1991			
State delegates	9	1	10
Total U.S.	267	167	434
103d Congress, 1993			
State delegates	7	4	11
Total U.S.	258	176	434
104th Congress, 1995			
State delegates	3	8	11
Total U.S.	197	236	433
105th Congress, 1997			
State delegates	3	8	11
Total U.S.	206	228	434
106th Congress, 1999			
State delegates	3	8	11
Total U.S.	211	222	433
107th Congress, 2001			
State delegates	3	8	11
Total U.S.	211	221	432
108th Congress, 2003			
State delegates	5	8	13
Total U.S.	205	229	434
109th Congress, 2005			
State delegates	6	7	13
Total U.S.	202	231	433
110th Congress, 2007			
State delegates	6	7	13
Total U.S.	233	202	435
Senate			
101st Congress, 1989			
State delegates	2	0	2
Total U.S.	55	45	100
102d Congress, 1991			
State delegates	2	0	2
Total U.S.	56	44	100
103d Congress, 1993			
State delegates	1	1	2
Total U.S.	57	43	100
104th Congress, 1995			
State delegates	1	1	2
Total U.S.	46	53	99
105th Congress, 1997			
State delegates	1	1	2
Total U.S.	45	55	100

	Dem	Rep	Total
106th Congress, 1999			
State delegates	1	1	2
Total U.S.	45	54	99
107th Congress, 2001			
State delegates	2	0	2
Total U.S.	50	50	100
108th Congress, 2003			
State delegates	1	1	2
Total U.S.	48	51	99
109th Congress, 2005			
State delegates	0	2	2
Total U.S.	44	55	99
110th Congress, 2007			
State delegates	0	2	2
Total U.S.	49	49	98

Figures are for starts of first sessions. Totals are for Democrat (Dem.) and Republican (Rep.) members only. House membership totals under 435 and Senate totals under 100 reflect vacancies and seats held by independent party members. When the 110th Congress opened, the Senate's two independent members caucused with the Democrats, giving the Democrats control of the Senate.

Source: U.S. Congress, *Congressional Directory*.

Composition of state legislature, 1990-2006

	Democrats	Republicans
State House (180 seats)		
1990	145	35
1992	128	51
1994	114	65
1996	106	74
1998	102	78
2000	101	78
2002	107	72
2004	80	99
2006	74	106
State Senate (56 seats)		
1990	45	11
1992	41	15
1994	35	20
1996	34	22
1998	33	22
2000	34	22
2002	26	30
2004	22	34
2006	22	34

Figures for total seats may include independents and minor party members. Numbers reflect results of elections in listed years; elected members usually take their seats in the years that follow.

Source: Council of State Governments; *State Elective Officials and the Legislatures*.

Voter participation in presidential elections, 2000 and 2004

	2000	2004
Voting age population		
State	6,050,000	6,497,000
Total United States	209,831,000	220,377,000
State share of U.S. total	2.88	2.95
Rank among states	11	10
Portion of voting age population casting votes		
State	42.7%	50.8%
United States	50.3%	55.5%
Rank among states	46	43

Population figures are rounded to nearest thousand and include all residents, regardless of eligibility to vote.
Source: U.S. Census Bureau.

HEALTH AND MEDICAL CARE

Medical professionals
Physicians in 2003 and nurses in 2001

	U.S.	State
Physicians in 2003		
Total	774,849	19,222
Share of U.S. total		2.47%
Rate	266	221
Rank		36
Nurses in 2001		
Total	2,262,020	58,600
Share of U.S. total		2.59%
Rate	793	697
Rank		41

Rates are numbers of physicians and nurses per 100,000 resident population; ranks are based on rates.
Source: American Medical Association, *Physician Characteristics and Distribution in the U.S.*; U.S. Department of Health and Human Services, Health Resources and Services Administration.

Health insurance coverage, 2003

	State	U.S.
Total persons covered	7,162,000	243,320,000
Total persons not covered	1,409,000	44,961,000
Portion not covered	16.4%	15.6%
Rank among states	18	—
Children not covered	314,000	8,373,000
Portion not covered	13.7%	11.4%
Rank among states	8	—

Totals are rounded to nearest thousand. Ranks are from the highest to the lowest percentages of persons *not* insured.
Source: U.S. Census Bureau, Current Population Reports.

AIDS, syphilis, and tuberculosis cases, 2003

Disease	U.S. cases	State cases	Rank
AIDS	44,232	1,907	5
Syphilis	34,270	2,152	5
Tuberculosis	14,874	526	6

Source: U.S. Centers for Disease Control and Prevention.

Cigarette smoking, 2003
Residents over age 18 who smoke

	U.S.	State	Rank
All smokers	22.1%	22.8%	22
Male smokers	24.8%	25.8%	23
Female smokers	20.3%	20.0%	29

Cigarette smokers are defined as persons who reported having smoked at least 100 cigarettes during their lifetimes and who currently smoked at least occasionally.
Source: U.S. Centers for Disease Control and Prevention, *Morbidity and Mortality Weekly Report*, 53, no. 44 (November 12, 2004).

HOUSING

Home ownership rates, 1985-2004

	1985	1990	1995	2000	2004
State	62.7%	64.3%	66.6%	69.8%	70.9%
Total U.S.	63.9%	63.9%	64.7%	67.4%	69.0%
Rank among states	39	38	32	30	32

Net change in state home ownership rate, 1985-2004 . . . . +8.2%
Net change in U.S. home ownership rate, 1985-2004 . . . . +5.1%

Percentages represent the proportion of owner households to total occupied households.
Source: U.S. Census Bureau, 2006.

Home sales, 2000-2004
In thousands of units

Existing home sales	2000	2002	2003	2004
State sales	143.6	173.9	174.0	215.8
Total U.S. sales	5,171	5,631	6,183	6,784
State share of U.S. total	2.78%	3.09%	2.81%	3.18%
Sales rank among states	10	9	10	8

Units include single-family homes, condos, and co-ops.
Source: National Association of Realtors, Washington, D.C., *Real Estate Outlook: Market Trends & Insights*.

Values of owner-occupied homes, 2003

	State	U.S.
Total units	1,745,000	58,809,000
Value of units		
Under $100,000	28.0%	29.6%
$100,000-199,999	45.9%	36.9%
$200,000 or more	26.1%	33.5%
Median value	$140,734	$142,275
Rank among all states 23		

Units are owner-occupied one-family houses whose numbers are rounded to nearest thousand. Data are extrapolated from survey samples.

Source: U.S. Census Bureau, American Community Survey.

EDUCATION

Public school enrollment, 2002

Prekindergarten through grade 8
State enrollment 1,089,000
Total U.S. enrollment. 34,135,000
State share of U.S. total 3.19%

Grades 9 through 12
State enrollment 407,000
Total U.S. enrollment. 14,067,000
State share of U.S. total 2.89%

Enrollment rates
State public school enrollment rate. 92.1%
Overall U.S. rate 90.4%
Rank among states in 2002. 14
Rank among states in 1995 7

Enrollment figures (which include unclassified students) are rounded to nearest thousand pupils during fall school term. Enrollment rates are based on enumerated resident population estimate for July 1, 2002.

Source: U.S. National Center for Education Statistics.

Public college finances, 2003-2004

FTE enrollment in public institutions of higher education
Students in state institutions 210,000
Students in all U.S. public institutions 9,916,600
State share of U.S. total 2.12
Rank among states 15

State and local government appropriations for higher education
State appropriation per FTE $8,231
National average. $5,716
Rank among states 6
State & local tax revenue going to higher education 8.6%

FTE = full-time equivalent in public postsecondary programs, including summer sessions; student numbers are rounded to nearest hundred. Funding figures for 2003-2004 academic year include financial aid to students in state public institutions and exclude money for research, agriculture experiment stations, teaching hospitals, and medical schools; figures are rounded to nearest thousand dollars.

Source: Higher Education Executive Officers, Denver, Colorado.

TRANSPORTATION AND TRAVEL

Highway mileage, 2003

Interstate highways	1,245
Other freeways and expressways	123
Arterial roads.	13,126
Collector roads.	23,342
Local roads.	78,698
Urban roads	28,557
Rural roads.	87,977
Total state mileage	116,534
U.S. total	3,974,107
State share	2.93%
Rank among states	11

Note that combined urban and rural road mileage matches the total of the other categories.

Source: U.S. Federal Highway Administration.

Motor vehicle registrations and driver licenses, 2003

Vehicle registrations	State	U.S.	Share	Rank
Autos, trucks, buses	7,730,000	231,390,000	3.34%	9
Autos only	4,192,000	135,670	3.09%	10
Motorcycles	118,000	5,328,000	2.21%	17
Driver licenses	5,758,000	196,166,000	2.94%	10

Figures, which do not include vehicles owned by military services, are rounded to the nearest thousand. Figures for automobiles include taxis.

Source: U.S. Federal Highway Administration.

Domestic travel expenditures, 2003

Spending by U.S. residents on overnight trips and
day trips of at least 50 miles from home

Total expenditures within state	$14.52 bill.
Total expenditures within U.S.	$490.87 bill.
State share of U.S. total	3.0%
Rank among states	9

Source: Travel Industry Association of America.

Retail gasoline prices, 2003-2007

Average price per gallon at the pump

Year	U.S.	State
2003	$1.267	$1.207
2004	$1.316	$1.279
2005	$1.644	$1.649
2007	$2.298	$2.174

Excise tax per gallon in 2004	7.5¢
Rank among all states in 2007 prices	37

Prices are averages of all grades of gasoline sold at the pump
during March months in 2003-2005 and during February, 2007.
Averages for 2006, during which prices rose higher, are not
available.
Source: U.S. Energy Information Agency, *Petroleum Marketing
Monthly* (2003-2005 data); American Automobile Association
(2007 data).

CRIME AND LAW ENFORCEMENT

State and local police officers, 2000-2004

	2000	2002	2004
Total officers			
U.S.	654,601	665,555	675,734
State	20,466	18,753	21,270*
*Net change, 2000-2004			+3.93%
Officers per 1,000 residents			
U.S.	2.33	2.31	2.30
State	2.50	2.19	2.41
State rank	8	21	14

Totals include state and local police and sheriffs.
Source: Carsey Institute, University of New Hampshire.

Crime rates, 2003

Incidents per 100,000 residents

Crimes	State	U.S.
Violent crimes		
Total incidents	454	475
Murder	8	6
Forcible rape	26	32
Robbery	162	142
Aggravated assault	259	295
Property crimes		
Total incidents	4,255	3,588
Burglary	909	741
Larceny/theft	2,846	2,415
Motor vehicle theft	499	433
All crimes	4,709	4,063

Source: U.S. Federal Bureau of Investigation, *Crime in the United
States*, annual.

State prison populations, 1980-2003

	State	U.S.	State share
1980	12,178	305,458	3.99%
1990	22,411	708,393	3.16%
1996	35,139	1,025,624	3.43%
2000	44,232	1,391,261	3.18%
2003	47,208	1,470,045	3.21%

State figures exclude prisoners in federal penitentiaries.
Source: U.S. Bureau of Justice Statistics, *Prisoners in 2003.*

Hawaii

Location: South Pacific Ocean

Area and rank: 6,423 square miles (16,637 square kilometers); 10,932 square miles (28,314 square kilometers) including water; forty-seventh largest state in area

Coastline: 750 miles (1,207 kilometers) on the Pacific Ocean

Shoreline: 1,052 miles (1,693 kilometers)

Population and rank: 1,263,000 (2004); forty-second largest state in population

Capital and largest city: Honolulu (371,657 people in 2000 census)

Became territory: 1900

Entered Union and rank: August 21, 1959; fiftieth state

Honolulu, Hawaii's capital city, is home to a third of the state's residents, as well as a large, changing tourist population. (PhotoDisc)

Present constitution adopted: 1950

Counties: 4 and Kalawao, a nonfunctioning county

State name: Hawaii appears to have taken its name from either Hawaii Loa, the islands' traditional discoverer, or the traditional home of the Polynesians, known as Hawaii or Hawaiki.

State nickname: Aloha State

Motto: *Ua mau ke ea o ka aina i ka pono* (The life of the land is perpetuated in righteousness)

State flag: Eight stripes of red, white, and blue, with the Union Jack in the upper left corner

Highest point: Puu Wekiu—13,796 feet (4,205 meters)

Lowest point: Pacific Ocean—sea level

Highest recorded temperature: 100 degrees Fahrenheit (38 degrees Celsius)—Pahala, 1931

Lowest recorded temperature: 14 degrees Fahrenheit (–10 degrees Celsius)—Haleukala, 1961

State song: "Hawai'i Pono'i"

State tree: Kukui (Candlenut)

State flower: Pua Aloalo (Hibiscus)

State bird: Nene (Hawaiian goose)

National parks: Haleakala; Hawaii Volcanoes

Hawaii History

Hawaii is unique in many ways. It is the only one of the fifty United States that lies outside the northern hemisphere and is, with Alaska, one of two states that is not part of the contiguous forty-eight states that, until 1959, constituted the United States of America. It is the only state that is composed of a group of islands, running from the big island of Hawaii to the islet of Kure at Hawaii's northwest extreme. Ka Lae, or South Cape, on the big island, is the southernmost point in the United States.

Hawaii is also the most multiethnic state in the Union. Some 40 percent of Hawaiian marriages are interracial. In this state of idyllic islands with inviting beaches, one can ascend the big island's Mauna Loa volcano in winter and, at an altitude of almost fourteen thousand feet, go skiing. Although 80 percent of the state's population lives in bustling, crowded cities, mainly Honolulu, Hawaiians are probably the most relaxed of all Americans.

Early History. As early as the middle of the eighth century, people sailed from the South Seas to Hawaii, presumably intent on colonizing some of its islands. Most of these people were Southeast Asians who had made their arduous way to Tahiti and the Marquesa Islands. In time, sailing in large double-hulled canoes, they continued to Hawaii, carrying with them roots and seeds to plant, as well as animals, mostly pigs and chickens, to raise.

These seamen knew enough about sailing and about the currents of the Pacific Ocean, presumably, to make trips from Tahiti to Hawaii and safely back to Tahiti. Seemingly they did this regularly between 1100 and 1400. An influx of foreigners resumed, however, in the eighteenth century, this time from Europe as well as Asia. The native Hawaiian population, which exceeded 225,000 toward the end of that century, plummeted to about 50,000 one hundred years later, as many natives fell victim to diseases that visitors brought to the islands.

Although Spanish seamen sailed from Manila in the Philippines to the west coast of Mexico in the seventeenth century, they seem to have passed north of the Hawaiian archipelago and were unaware of this chain of volcanic islands. Captain James Cook, in January, 1778, was probably the first European to find the Hawaiian islands, calling them the Sandwich Islands after the earl of Sandwich, from whom he had financial support for his explorations. In February, 1779, Captain Cook was killed by natives on the big island of Hawaii in an argument over some thefts from his ship. In time, trade with white merchants began to flourish, Hawaii's chief export being sandalwood. As foreign merchants

Waterfalls on the island of Kauai. Containing some of the world's most spectacular tropical scenery, the Hawaiian islands are frequently used for feature film locations. (©David Pruter/Dreamstime.com)

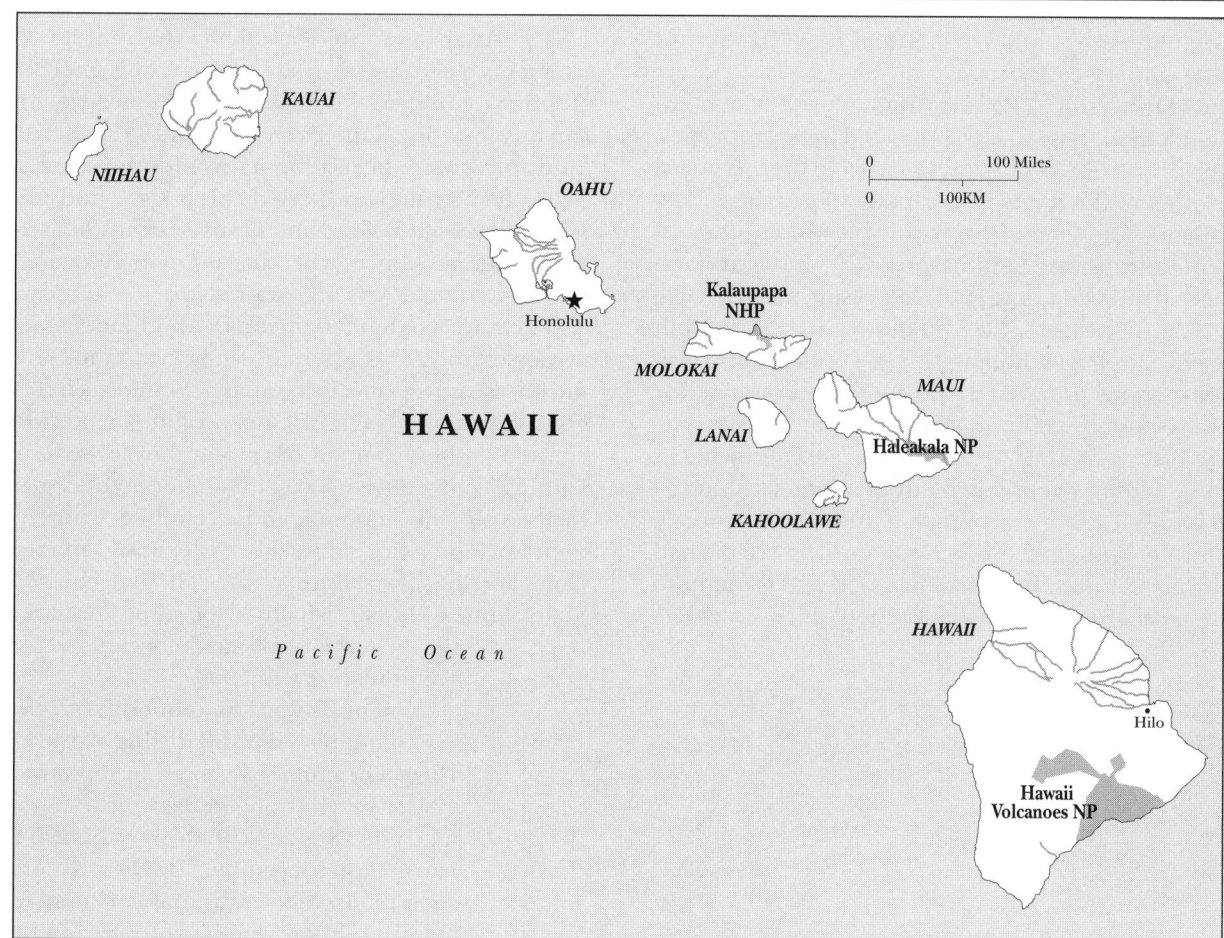

came to Hawaii to trade, the social structure of the islands began to change.

The Kingdom of Hawaii. In 1810, Kamehameha I, a warrior chief, founded the Kingdom of Hawaii after gaining the loyal support of Kauai's chieftain. Although a native Hawaiian gained political control, the islands had already been altered appreciably by the influx of people from the West who came there to do business. Upon the king's death in 1819, Kamehameha II, who welcomed traders from the West, was given the reins of power. Under his jurisdiction, the kapu system, based on the ancient laws and taboos that had long prevailed in the islands, began to give way to Western customs.

The following year, the first Christian missionaries arrived from New England. These Congregationalists were soon followed by Methodists from the United States, Roman Catholics from France, Anglicans from Britain, and Lutherans from Germany. Mormon missionaries arrived considerably later and had such great success in winning Hawaiians to Mormonism that they ultimately established a branch of Brigham Young University and a Mormon temple and information center on Oahu's northeast coast.

The pusillanimous Hawaiians, who were traditionally polytheistic, were easy to convert to Christianity, although they still preserved the myths of many of their deities, such as Pele and Maui. The arrival of the missionaries marked a wave of immigration to the islands and also heralded an era of interracial interchanges and interracial marriage, thereby minimizing many of the ethnic divisions that characterize some societies.

The next wave of immigration came during the 1850's, when large numbers of Chinese immigrants arrived, drawn to Hawaii by its climate, its strategic location, and its commercial possibilities. The Chinese, many of whom initially worked on the sugar and pineapple plantations, soon gravitated to urban centers, mostly to Honolulu, to establish businesses. Soon they had the highest family income of all the ethnic groups in the islands.

During the nineteenth century, significant numbers of immigrants arrived, first from Japan around 1860, then from Scandinavia, Spain, Madeira, the Azores, Puerto Rico, and Germany. The overwhelming influx was from Asia. About half of Hawaii's population is of Asian ancestry. Intermarriage reduced the number of full-blooded Hawaiians from about 225,000 at the end of the eighteenth century to less than 10,000 at the end of the twentieth century.

Land Ownership. The king originally owned most of the state's land, held as crown lands. These properties, broken up in 1848, eventually reverted to the territorial government, which now owns about 40 percent of Hawaii's land. The federal government owns another 10 percent, and private land barons own all but about 3 percent of the remaining land. As a result, many people who own houses or other buildings in Hawaii built them on leased land. Long-term leases offer homeowners some protection, but when the leases come up for renewal, substantial increases are usually imposed.

The Bishop Estate is the largest private landowner in Hawaii, holding about 9 percent of all the land in the state. It uses the large income that these lands produce to fund the Kamehameha School, initially established to educate children of Hawaiian blood and thought to be the most affluent secondary school in the world.

A statue of Hawaii's King Kamehameha I stands in front of Hawaii's judiciary building in Honolulu. (Hawaii Visitors & Convention Bureau/ Robert Coello)

The Annexation of Hawaii. By the middle of the nineteenth century, during the reign of Kamehameha III, the kingdom was increasingly influenced by American missionaries. Kamehameha III in 1843 ceded the islands to Britain, but within a few months, the United States had strongly protested this action, and, shortly thereafter, both Britain and France acknowledged Hawaii's independence. The kingdom was reformed under the Organic Acts of 1845-1847.

The reigns of Kamehameha IV and Kamehameha V witnessed the growth of huge sugar plantations owned mostly by Americans. U.S. financial interests in Hawaii grew before the reign of Queen Liliuokalani, who ascended to the throne in 1891. She showed signs of becoming a more absolute ruler than her predecessors, so in 1893 she was deposed, and a republic, whose president was American Sanford B. Dole, was soon created. Dole and his legislature requested that the United States annex Hawaii, which, after some hesitation, it did in 1898. It officially became a United States territory in 1900.

Moving Toward Statehood. With the advent of military aircraft during World War I, Hawaii began to be viewed by military leaders as a first line of defense for the continental United States. With the bombing of Pearl Harbor on December 7, 1941, Americans soon realized how vulnerable Hawaii was to attack and how vital it was both as a line of defense and as a staging area for a Pacific war.

During the early days of the war, Nisei (second-generation) Japanese in Hawaii were viewed with a combination of distrust and contempt. They were barred from service in the U.S. armed forces, although they were not incarcerated in camps, as their counterparts on the mainland West Coast had been. Eventually they were admitted to the armed forces and, as members of the 100th Infantry Battalion and the 442d Regimental Combat Team, performed heroically in some of the most desperate battles of the conflict, proving their loyalty.

Shortly after the war, mainland labor unions called plantation strikes in Hawaii that paralyzed shipping. The five business cartels that controlled a great deal of the islands' economy were forced to make substantial concessions to plantation workers. Many Japanese Americans rose to political power and did a great deal to reform state government. As the territory attracted large numbers of new inhabitants and gained considerable affluence, agitation for statehood grew. In 1959, statehood was conferred.

Japan's surprise attack on the U.S. Naval Base at Pearl Harbor on December 7, 1941, brought the United States into World War II. (National Archives)

The Growth of Tourism. Hawaii's economy during the nineteenth century and the first half of the twentieth came largely from the sale of sandalwood, sugar, and pineapples, although the federal and territorial governments increasingly provided jobs that bolstered the economy. In 1970, seventy thousand of the islands' population of less than one million were employed in state and federal jobs. By 1997 the federal government employed only 20,221 people in Hawaii at an average salary of $39,984.

Although the federal government spends a billion dollars a year in Hawaii, its expenditures are far exceeded by the revenues generated for the state through tourism, which in 1996 amounted to more than fourteen billion dollars. The Hawaiian Chamber of Commerce is among the most efficient and accommodating in the United States. The five islands that are most often visited, Oahu, Maui, Hawaii, Molokai, and Kauai, have excellent tourist facilities and offer breathtaking beaches and waves that attract surfers from around the world. Of the inhabited islands, only Lanai, owned by the Dole Corporation, discourages tourism.

Honolulu is Hawaii's most-visited city. Waikiki Beach, close to the main section of Honolulu, is lined with elegant hotels. Its beaches are filled with tourists and surfers throughout the year. Such natural attractions as the Haleakala Volcano on Maui, the Mauna Loa and Mauna Kea volcanoes on Hawaii, Diamond Head on Oahu, and the Waimea Canyon on Kauai are popular among tourists.

Political Developments and Controversies. At the end of last decade of the twentieth century, Hawaii continued to lean to the political left in its congressional representation and in its legislature, with one significant exception. In 2000, with the election of Linda Lingle, the state elected its first Republican governor. In doing so, the state also elected its first woman governor and its first Jewish governor. However, the state continued it practice of electing a Democrat to the U.S. House of Representatives. In 2002, Representative Patsy Takemoto Mink, a twelve-term Democratic congresswoman, died prior to the general election but was elected nonetheless by a margin of 56-40 percent.

During the same period, the state was involved in two political controversies that drew national attention. During 1999, the state's Office of Hawaiian Affairs decided that it would allow only Hawaiians of indigenous descent to vote for Trustees of the Office. This policy was challenged in the courts as unconstitutional discriminatory. Early in 2000, the U.S. Supreme Court, in *Rice v. Cayetano*, denied the legitimacy of allowing only native Hawaiians to vote for trustees of the Office of Hawaiian Affairs as unconstitutional racial discrimination.

A second controversy regarded a law proposed by Hawaiian senator Daniel Akaka known as the Native Hawaiian Governmental Reorganization Act of 2005. The proposed law would allow Hawaiians of indigenous descent to group themselves as a sovereign, autonomous nation, just as American Indian tribes are constituted. Opponents dissented from this proposal, which nonetheless passed the U.S. House of Representatives. In June, 2006, however, the bill was effectively killed before being voted upon in the Senate because a procedural vote denied the bill the sixty votes required to cut off debate (called "cloture" in the Senate). The matter was not necessarily settled, however, because the bill could be reintroduced at a later time.

Tragedy and Natural Disaster. Another noteworthy event was the tragic accident that took place in the waters off Hawaii early in 2001. On February 9, during a training exercise, the submarine USS *Greeneville* collided with a Japanese fishing and high school training ship, the *Ehime Maru*. The Japanese vessel sank, drowning nine persons, including four high school students. Relations between the United States and Japan were strained for some time afterward.

In spring, 2006, nature played a role in the islands' history, as rains of biblical proportions descended upon the islands, especially Oahu and Kauai. The rains, which began on February 19, lasted for forty days and nights, killing seven persons on Kauai and leaving untold damage.

R. Baird Shuman
Updated by the Editor

Hawaii Time Line

750-800	First Polynesians begin to colonize the islands.
Jan. 18, 1778	James Cook discovers the Hawaiian archipelago and calls it the Sandwich Islands.
1810	Kamehameha I conquers the islands and establishes the Kingdom of Hawaii.
1819	Kamehameha I dies; Kamehameha II abolishes the kapu system.
1820	First Christian missionaries arrive from the United States.
1835	Ladd and Company establishes first sugar plantation on Kauai.
1840	Kamehameha III drafts first Hawaiian constitution.
1843	Kamehameha III cedes islands to Great Britain.
1845	Britain and France recognize Hawaii's independence.
1846	Redistribution of Hawaiian land begins, most going to the state.
1851	First Chinese laborers arrive to work on sugar plantations.
1868	First Japanese laborers arrive to work on Hawaiian plantations.
1886	Exportable pineapple strain, "Smooth Cayenne," introduced.
Jan. 17, 1893	Queen Liliuokalani deposed; republic is established by American business leaders.
July 4, 1894	New constitution introduced, establishing Republic of Hawaii; Sanford B. Dole is president.
Aug. 12, 1898	United States annexes Hawaii.
1900	Hawaii given territorial status by Organic Act; Sanford Dole named first territorial governor.
1901	First successful pineapple cannery is established.
1903	Territorial legislature asks Congress for statehood.
1907	University of Hawaii is established.
1916	Hawaii Volcanoes National Park and Haleakala National Park are established.
1927	First nonstop flight is made from American mainland.
1929	Regular air service is established among Hawaii's islands.
1935	Pan American Airlines launches first commercial flight across the Pacific with the China Clipper.
Dec. 7, 1941	Japanese attack Pearl Harbor.
1943	100th Infantry Battalion and 442d Regimental Combat Team admit Nisei Japanese.
1946	Plantation strikes launched by International Longshoremen's and Warehousemen's Union (ILWU).
1947	First statehood bill fails in U.S. Congress.
1949	Hawaiian waterfront is paralyzed for 178 days by ILWU strike.

1950	Constitutional Convention drafts constitution for state of Hawaii.
1955	Democrats take control of both legislative houses for the first time in Hawaii's history.
Aug. 21, 1959	Hawaii becomes fiftieth state.
May 23, 1960	Thirty-five-foot tidal wave kills fifty-seven, causes $50 million in damage.
1967	Mauna Kea Observatory opens.
1968	President Lyndon B. Johnson confers with South Vietnam's President Nguyen Van Thieu in Honolulu.
1972	First full Hawaiian medical school is approved.
1973	First Hawaiian school of law is established.
1985	Marijuana crop is estimated at $4 billion, ten times the worth of the sugar crop.
1986	Kilauea volcano erupts, destroying everything in its path.
1994	United States Navy negates 1941 agreement that gave it Kahoolawe Island as a gunnery site.
Feb. 23, 2000	U.S. Supreme Court's *Rice v. Cayetano* ruling denies the legitimacy of allowing only Native Hawaiians to vote for trustees of the Office of Hawaiian Affairs.
Nov. 7, 2000	Linda Lingle elected Hawaii's first Republican, first female, and first Jewish governor.
Feb. 9, 2001	Submarine USS *Greeneville* collides with a Japanese training ship off Hawaii, drowning nine persons, including four high school students.
Nov. 5, 2002	Hawaii reelects a recently deceased congresswoman, Patsy Takemoto Mink, a twelve-term member of Congress.
Aug. 19, 2004	Hiram Fong, one of Hawaii's first senators and the state's first Chinese American senator, dies at the age of ninety-six.
June 6, 2006	Vote of the U.S. Senate fails to allow a vote on the Native Hawaiian Governmental Act of 2005.
Oct. 15, 2006	Earthquake with magnitude of 6.6 hits island of Hawaii.

Mount Kilauea, on the island of Hawaii, has the largest crater of any active volcano in the world. Mark Twain visited Italy's Mount Vesuvius after seeing Kilauea and called it a "soup-kettle" by comparison to the Hawaiian volcano. (Hawaii Visitors & Convention Bureau/Warren Bolster)

Notes for Further Study

Published Sources. One of the best brief accounts of Hawaii's ethnic situation is found in William Petersen's *Ethnicity Counts* (1997), which devotes ten pages to the multiethnicity of the islands. The book is excellent for its comparisons and contrasts with other places. Wayne S. Wooden's *Return to Paradise: Continuity and Change in Hawaii* (1995) also touches on the islands' ethnicity, as does Mary Ann Lynch's *Hawaii: The Land, the People, the Cities* (1991), which is richly illustrated. Eleanor C. Nordyke's second edition of *The Peopling of Hawai'i* (1989) offers specifics about the origins of the Hawaiian people and about the state's ethnicity. Nancy J. Morris and Love Dean compiled *Hawai'i* (1992), a fine source about the prehistory and languages of the islands. Bonnie Friedman, Paul Wood, and others offer eyewitness views of the islands in *Hawaii* (1998) and provide useful maps of the areas about which the many contributors write.

Two books cover interesting historical aspects of the islands' local communities: *The Colony: The Harrowing True Story of the Exiles of Molokai* by John Tayman (2006) explores the history and survival of nine thousand exiled leprosy sufferers on the island of Molokai between 1866 and 1969. In another fascinating historical account, Noenoe K. Silva, while doing preliminary research into her book, discovered numerous primary documents that detailed native Hawaiians' organization of a substantial petition drive to protest the late nineteenth century plans to allow the United States to annex Hawaii. Her work, *Aloha Betrayed: Native Hawaiian Resistance to American Colonialism* (2004), fills a gap in Hawaiian history and gives voice to a group that was once considered acquiescent to white imperialism.

For young readers interested in knowing more about Hawaii, the second revised edition of Joyce Johnson's *Hawaii* (2001), part of the Hello USA! series, is a short, attractive book filled with entertaining facts about daily life, history, and environmental issues. Also of interest is Penelope J. Neri's *Hawaii* (2003), which covers the state's topography, climate, history, government, and culture for a young-adult audience. For a reader-friendly guide to the state, John H. Chambers's *Hawaii* (2006), part of the On the Road Histories series, begins with the volcanic origins of the islands, covers the exploration of Captain Cook, and continues up through the modern era and the process of statehood.

Web Resources. The most comprehensive Web site on Hawaii is that run by the state government (www.hawaii.gov). The Visitors' Department Web site (www.gohawaii.com) offers extensive, up-to-date information about every aspect of

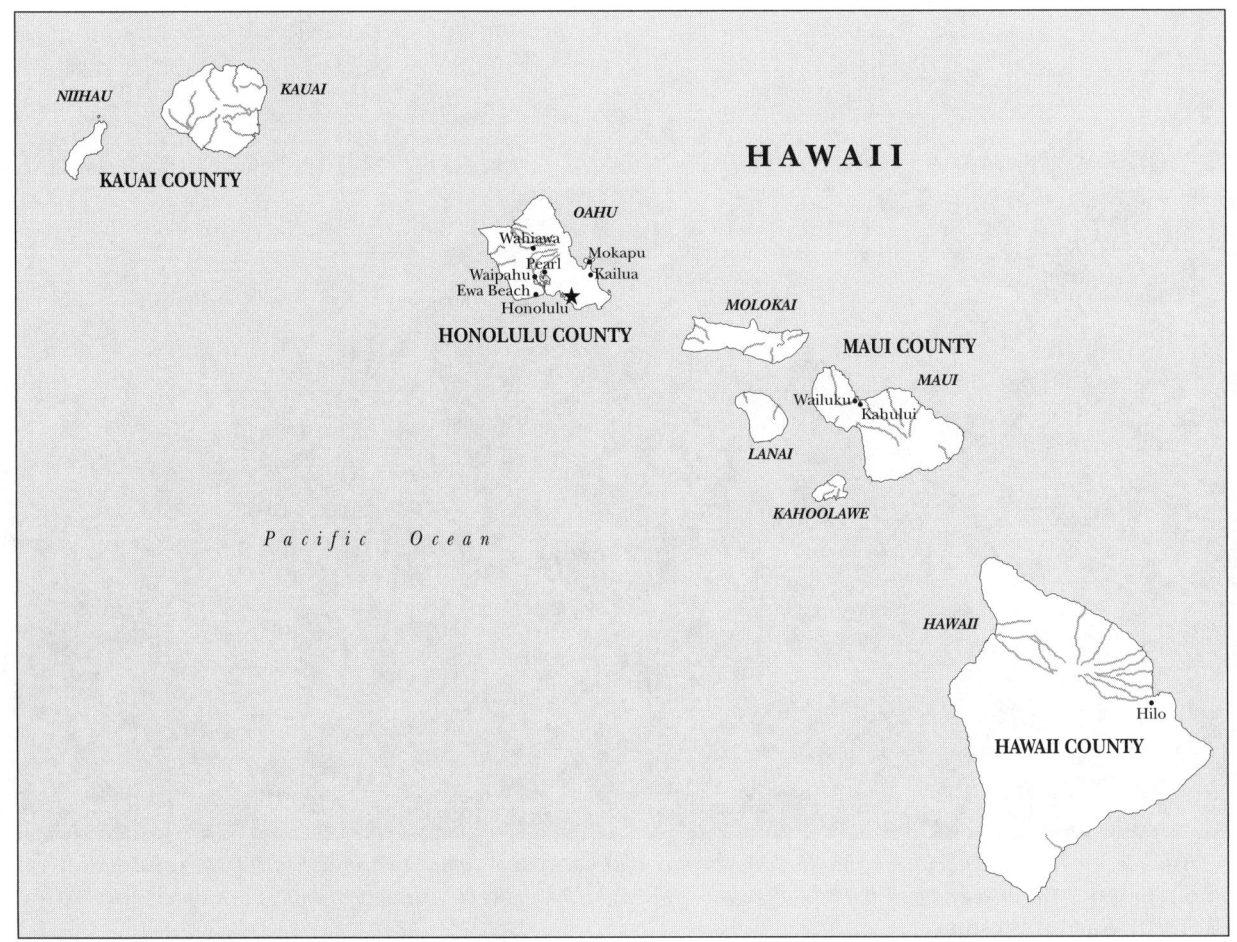

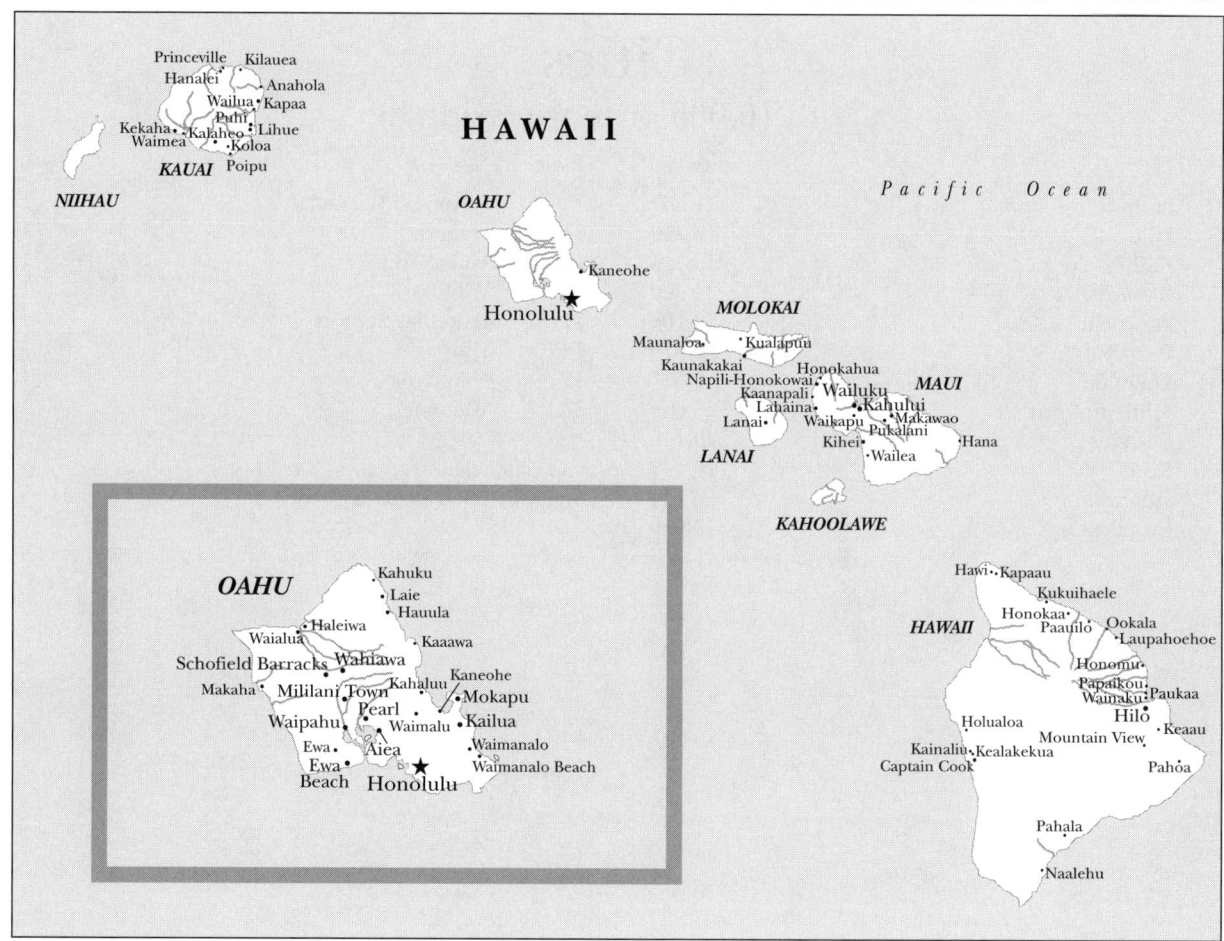

tourism in the state. The Web site of Honolulu's newspaper, *The Star-Bulletin* (www.starbulletin.com), is excellent for covering developments in the state generally and in Honolulu specifically. It includes classified advertisements that can be useful. The *Islander Magazine* (www.islander-magazine.com) offers specific information about tourist attractions and coming events that might interest visitors.

Counties

County	2000 pop.	Rank in pop.	Sq. miles	Rank in area
Hawaii	148,677	2	4,028.2	1
Honolulu	876,156	1	600.2	4
Kauai	58,463	4	622.5	3
Maui	128,094	3	1,159.3	2

Molokai's Kalawao County is administratively part of Maui County.
Source: U.S. Census Bureau; National Association of Counties.

The individual islands most visited by tourists have their own Web sites: Maui (www.visitmaui.com), Molokai (visitmolokai.com/), Hawaii (www.bigisland.com/ and www.hawaiibigisland.com), Kauai (www.kauaivisitorsbureau.org and www.kauai-hawaii.com), and Oahu (www.oahuvacations.com). The Hawaii Visitors Bureau maintains its own Web site (www.visit.hawaii.org). Those interested in Hawaii's volcanoes or in volcanology should consult the sites for Hawaii Volcanoes National Park (www.nps.gov.havo and www.hawaii.volcanoes.national-park.com/) or the Hawaii Center for Volcanology Web site (www.soest.hawaii.edu/GG/hcv.html). Users interested in the cultural aspects of the islands will find valuable information on the Web site of the Honolulu Academy of Arts (www.honoluluacademy.org) or the Hawaii Art Web site (www.hawaiiart.com). Those wishing to learn more about business in Hawaii should consult Hawaii Business (www.hawaiibusiness.com). For information on the islands' history or genealogy research, consult Hawaiian Roots (www.hawaiian-roots.com/index.htm). The Hawaiian Historical Society also has a good Internet site (www.hawaiianhistory.org/).

Cities
With 10,000 or more residents

Rank	City	Population	Rank	City	Population
1	Honolulu (capital)	371,657	13	Schofield Barracks	14,428
2	Hilo	40,759	14	Halawa	13,891
3	Kailua	36,513	15	Makakilo City	13,156
4	Kaneohe	34,970	16	Wailuku	12,296
5	Waipahu	33,108	17	Kaneohe Station	11,827
6	Pearl City	30,976	18	Waipio	11,672
7	Waimalu	29,371	19	Nanakuli	10,814
8	Mililani Town	28,608	20	Waianae	10,506
9	Kahului	20,146			
10	Kihei	16,749			
11	Wahiawa	16,151			
12	Ewa Beach	14,650			

Population figures are from 2000 census.
Source: U.S. Bureau of the Census.

Index to Tables

DEMOGRAPHICS

Resident state and national populations, 1970-2004

Population figures given in thousands

	State pop.	U.S. pop.	Share	Rank
1970	770	203,302	0.4%	40
1980	965	226,546	0.4%	39
1985	1,040	237,924	0.4%	39
1990	1,108	248,765	0.4%	41
1995	1,197	262,761	0.4%	40
2000	1,212	281,425	0.4%	42
2004	1,263	293,655	0.4%	42

Source: U.S. Census Bureau, Current Population Reports, 2006.

Resident population by age, 2004

Age Group	Total persons
Under 5 years	89,000
5 to 17 years	210,000
18 to 24 years	126,000
25 to 34 years	161,000
35 to 44 years	180,000
45 to 54 years	186,000
55 to 64 years	138,000
65 to 74 years	79,000
75 to 84 years	68,000
85 years and older	25,000
All age groups	1,263,000

Portion of residents 65 and older	13.6%
National rank in portion of oldest residents	11
National average	12.4%

Population figures are rounded to nearest thousand persons;
  figures include armed forces personnel stationed in the state.
Source: U.S. Bureau of the Census, 2006.

Resident population by race, Hispanic origin, 2004

Category	State pop.	Share	U.S.
All residents	1,263	100.00%	100.00%
Non-Hispanic white	295	23.36%	67.37%
Hispanic white	40	3.17%	13.01%
Other Hispanic	60	4.75%	1.06%
African American	28	2.22%	12.77%
Native American	4	0.32%	0.96%
Asian, Pacific Islander	642	50.83%	4.37%
Two or more categories	254	20.11%	1.51%

Population figures are in thousands. Persons counted as "Hispanic" (Latino) may be of any race. Because of overlapping categories, categories may not add up to 100%. Shares in column 3 are percentages of each category within the state; these figures may be compared to the national percentages in column 4.
Source: U.S. Bureau of the Census, 2006.

Projected state population, 2000-2030

Year	Population
2000	1,212,000
2005	1,277,000
2010	1,341,000
2015	1,386,000
2020	1,412,000
2025	1,439,000
2030	1,466,000
Population increase, 2000-2030	254,000
Percentage increase, 2000-2030	21.0

Projections are based on data from the 2000 census.
Source: U.S. Census Bureau.

VITAL STATISTICS

Infant mortality rates, 1980-2002

	1980	1990	2000	2002
All state residents	10.3	6.7	8.1	7.3
All U.S. residents	12.6	9.2	9.4	9.1
All state white residents	11.6	6.1	6.5	—
All U.S. white residents	10.6	7.6	5.7	5.8

Figures represent deaths per 1,000 live births of resident infants under 1 year old, exclusive of fetal deaths. Figures for all residents include members of other racial categories not listed separately. The Census Bureau considers the figures for black residents and for white residents in 2002 to be too small to be statistically meaningful.
Source: U.S. Census Bureau, *Statistical Abstract of the United States,* 2006.

Abortion rates, 1990 and 2000

	1990	2000
Total abortions	12,000	6,000
Rate per 1,000 women	46.0	22.1
U.S. rate	25.7	21.3
Rank	1	11

Numbers of abortions are rounded to nearest thousand; ranks are based on rates.
Source: U.S. Census Bureau.

Marriages and divorces

Total marriages in 2004	28,400
Rate per 1,000 population	22.5
National rate per 1,000 population	7.4
Rank among all states	2
Total divorces in 2000	4,600
Rate per 1,000 population in 2000	3.9
National rate per 1,000 population in 2004	3.7
Rank among all states in 2004	n/a

Figures are for all marriages and divorces performed within the state, including those of nonresidents; totals are rounded to the nearest hundred. Ranks are for highest to lowest figures; note that 2004 divorce data are not available for Hawaii and four other states.
Source: U.S. National Center for Health Statistics, *Vital Statistics of the United States,* 2006.

Death rates by leading causes, 2002
Deaths per 100,000 resident population

Cause	State	U.S.
Heart disease	201.8	241.7
Cancer	156.2	193.2
Cerebrovascular diseases	65.2	56.4
Accidents other than motor vehicle	31.6	37.0
Motor vehicle accidents	9.7	15.7
Chronic lower respiratory diseases	21.3	43.3
Diabetes mellitus	16.4	25.4
HIV	2.1	4.9
Suicide	9.6	11.0
Homicide	3.1	6.1
All causes	707.0	847.3
Rank in overall death rate among states		46

Figures exclude nonresidents who died in the state. Causes of death follow International Classification of Diseases. Rank is from highest to lowest death rate in the United States.
Source: U.S. National Center for Health Statistics, *National Vital Statistics Report,* 2006.

ECONOMY

Gross state product, 1990-2004
In current dollars

Year	State product	Nat'l product	State share
1990	$31.9 billion	$5.67 trillion	0.56%
2000	$40.2 billion	$9.75 trillion	0.41%
2002	$43.8 billion	$10.41 trillion	0.42%
2003	$46.7 billion	$10.92 trillion	0.43%
2004	$50.1 billion	$11.65 trillion	0.43%

Source: U.S. Bureau of Economic Analysis, *Survey of Current Business,* July, 2005.

Gross state product by industry, 2003
In billions of dollars

Construction	$2.0
Manufacturing	0.8
Wholesale trade	1.6
Retail trade	3.6
Finance & insurance	2.0
Information	1.3
Professional services	2.0
Health care & social assistance	2.9
Government	9.2
Total state product	$43.0
Total U.S. product	$10,289.2
State share of U.S. total	0.42%
Rank among all states	41

Total figures include industries not listed separately. Amounts are in chained 2000 dollars.
Source: U.S. Bureau of Economic Analysis, *Survey of Current Business,* July, 2005.

Personal income per capita, 1990-2004
In current dollars

	1990	2000	2004
Per capita income	$22,186	$28,422	$32,160
U.S. average	$19,477	$29,845	$32,937
Rank among states	7	22	20

Source: U.S. Bureau of Economic Analysis, *Survey of Current Business,* April, 2005.

Energy consumption, 2001
In trillions of British thermal units (BTU), except as noted

Total energy consumption
Total state energy consumption	282
Total U.S. energy consumption	96,275
State share of U.S. total	0.29%
Rank among states	47

Per capita consumption (In millions of BTU)
Total state per capita consumption	230
Total U.S. per capita consumption	338
Rank among states	47

End-use sectors
Residential	35
Commercial	39
Industrial	77
Transportation	132

Sources of energy
Petroleum	240
Natural gas	3
Coal	18
Hydroelectric power	1
Nuclear electric power	0

Figures for totals include categories not listed separately.
Source: U.S. Energy Information Administration, *State Energy Data Report,* 2001.

Nonfarm employment by sectors, 2004

Total	582,000
Construction	29,000
Manufacturing	15,000
Trade, transportation, utilities	112,000
Information	11,000
Finance, insurance, real estate	29,000
Professional & business services	71,000
Education & health services	67,000
Leisure, hospitality, arts, organizations	104,000
Other services, including repair & maintenance	24,000
Government	120,000

Figures are rounded to nearest thousand persons. "Total" includes mining and natural resources, not listed separately.
Source: U.S. Bureau of Labor Statistics, 2006.

Foreign exports, 1990-2004
In millions of dollars

Year	State	U.S.	State share
1990	179	394,045	0.05%
1996	284	624,767	0.05%
1997	334	688,896	0.05%
2000	387	712,055	0.05%
2003	368	724,006	0.05%
2004	405	769,332	0.05%

Rank among all states in 2004 50

U.S. total does not include U.S. dependencies.
Source: U.S. Census Bureau, *U.S. Merchandise Trade,* series FT 900, 2000; U.S. Census Bureau, *U.S. International Trade in Goods and Services,* Series FT 900, 2005.

LAND USE

Federally owned land, 2003
Areas in acres

	State	U.S.	State share
Total area	4,106,000	2,271,343,000	0.18%
Nonfederal land	3,434,000	1,599,584,000	0.21%
Federal land	672,000	671,759,000	0.10%
Federal share	16.4%	29.6%	—

Areas are rounded to nearest thousand acres. Figures for federally owned land do not include trust properties.
Source: U.S. General Services Administration, *Federal Real Property Profile,* 2006.

Land use, 1997
In acres, rounded to nearest thousand

Total surface area. 4,158,000
Total nonfederal rural land 3,565,000
Percentage rural land 85.7%
Cropland 246,000
Conservation Reserve Program (CRP*) land . . . . . (nil)
Pastureland. 36,000
Rangeland 1,009,000
Forestland. 1,635,000
Other rural land 639,000

*CRP is a federal program begun in 1985 to assist private landowners to convert highly erodible cropland to vegetative cover for ten years. Note that some categories of land overlap.
Source: U.S. Department of Agriculture, Natural Resources and Conservation Service, and Iowa State University, Statistical Laboratory, S*ummary Report, 1997 National Resources Inventory,* revised December, 2000.

Farms and crop acreage, 2004

	State	U.S.	Share	Rank
Farms	6,000	2,113,000	0.28%	42
Acres (millions)	1	937	0.11%	41
Acres per farm	236	443	—	27

Source: U.S. Department of Agriculture, National Agricultural Statistics Service. Numbers of farms are rounded to nearest thousand units; acreage figures are rounded to nearest million. Rankings, including ties, are based on rounded figures.

GOVERNMENT AND FINANCE

Units of local government, 2002

	State	Total U.S.	Rank
All local governments	19	87,525	50
Counties	3	3,034	47
Municipalities	1	19,429	50
Townships	0	16,504	—
School districts	0	13,506	—
Special districts	15	35,052	49

Only 48 states have county governments, 20 states have township governments ("towns" in New England, Minnesota, New York, and Wisconsin), and 46 states have school districts. Special districts encompass such functions as natural resources, fire protection, and housing and community development.
Source: U.S. Census Bureau, *Census of Governments.*

State government revenue, 2002

Total revenue. . . . . $5,869 mill.
General revenue . . . . $6,042 mill.
Per capita revenue $4,894
U.S. per capita average $3,689
Rank among states. 3

Intergovernment revenue
Total . . . . $1,367 mill.
From federal government . . . . $1,365 mill.

Charges and miscellaneous
Total . . . . $1,255 mill.
Current charges . . . . $766 mill.
Misc. general income . . . . $489 mill.
Insurance trust revenue . . . . −$174 mill.

Taxes
Total . . . . $3,421 mill.
Per capita taxes $2,756
Rank among states. 1
Property taxes . . . . (nil)
Sales taxes . . . . $2,118 mill.
License taxes . . . . $112 mill.
Individual income taxes . . . . $1,112 mill.
Corporate income taxes. . . . . $53 mill.
Other taxes . . . . $27 mill.

Total revenue figures include items not listed separately here.
Source: U.S. Bureau of the Census.

State government expenditures, 2002

General expenditures

Total state expenditures	$7,446 mill.
Intergovernmental.	$130 mill.

Per capita expenditures

State	$5,386
Average of all states	$3,859
Rank among states.	2

Selected direct expenditures

Education.	$2,257 mill.
Public welfare	$1,112 mill.
Health, hospital	$620 mill.
Highways	$236 mill.
Police protection	$6 mill.
Corrections.	$157 mill.
Natural resources	$98 mill.
Parks and recreation	$50 mill.
Government administration.	$372 mill.
Interest on debt	$462 mill.
Total direct expenditures	$6,553 mill.

Totals include items not listed separately.
Source: U.S. Census Bureau.

POLITICS

Governors since statehood

D = Democrat; R = Republican; O = other;
(r) resigned; (d) died in office; (i) removed from office

William F. Quinn (R)	1959-1962
John A. Burns (D)	1962-1974
George R. Ariyoshi (D).	1974-1986
John Waihee (D)	1986-1998
Benjamin J. Cayetano (D)	1998-2002
Linda Lingle (R)	2002-

Composition of congressional delegations, 1989-2007

	Dem	Rep	Total
House of Representatives			
101st Congress, 1989			
State delegates	1	1	2
Total U.S.	259	174	433
102d Congress, 1991			
State delegates	2	0	2
Total U.S.	267	167	434
103d Congress, 1993			
State delegates	2	0	2
Total U.S.	258	176	434
104th Congress, 1995			
State delegates	2	0	2
Total U.S.	197	236	433
105th Congress, 1997			
State delegates	2	0	2
Total U.S.	206	228	434
106th Congress, 1999			
State delegates	2	0	2
Total U.S.	211	222	433
107th Congress, 2001			
State delegates	2	0	2
Total U.S.	211	221	432
108th Congress, 2003			
State delegates	2	0	2
Total U.S.	205	229	434
109th Congress, 2005			
State delegates	2	0	2
Total U.S.	202	231	433
110th Congress, 2007			
State delegates	2	0	2
Total U.S.	233	202	435
Senate			
101st Congress, 1989			
State delegates	2	0	2
Total U.S.	55	45	100
102d Congress, 1991			
State delegates	2	0	2
Total U.S.	56	44	100
103d Congress, 1993			
State delegates	2	0	2
Total U.S.	57	43	100
104th Congress, 1995			
State delegates	2	0	2
Total U.S.	46	53	99
105th Congress, 1997			
State delegates	2	0	2
Total U.S.	45	55	100

(continued)

	Dem	Rep	Total
106th Congress, 1999			
State delegates	2	0	2
Total U.S.	45	54	99
107th Congress, 2001			
State delegates	2	0	2
Total U.S.	50	50	100
108th Congress, 2003			
State delegates	2	0	2
Total U.S.	48	51	99
109th Congress, 2005			
State delegates	2	0	2
Total U.S.	44	55	99
110th Congress, 2007			
State delegates	2	0	2
Total U.S.	49	49	98

Figures are for starts of first sessions. Totals are for Democrat (Dem.) and Republican (Rep.) members only. House membership totals under 435 and Senate totals under 100 reflect vacancies and seats held by independent party members. When the 110th Congress opened, the Senate's two independent members caucused with the Democrats, giving the Democrats control of the Senate.

Source: U.S. Congress, *Congressional Directory.*

Composition of state legislature, 1990-2006

	Democrats	Republicans
State House (51 seats)		
1990	45	6
1992	47	4
1994	44	7
1996	39	12
1998	39	12
2000	39	12
2002	36	15
2004	41	10
2006	43	8
State Senate (25 seats)		
1990	22	3
1992	22	3
1994	23	2
1996	23	2
1998	23	2
2000	23	2
2002	20	5
2004	20	5
2006	20	5

Figures for total seats may include independents and minor party members. Numbers reflect results of elections in listed years; elected members usually take their seats in the years that follow.

Source: Council of State Governments; *State Elective Officials and the Legislatures.*

Voter participation in presidential elections, 2000 and 2004

	2000	2004
Voting age population		
State	917,000	964,000
Total United States	209,831,000	220,377,000
State share of U.S. total	0.44	0.44
Rank among states	40	42
Portion of voting age population casting votes		
State	40.1%	44.5%
United States	50.3%	55.5%
Rank among states	50	50

Population figures are rounded to nearest thousand and include all residents, regardless of eligibility to vote.

Source: U.S. Census Bureau.

HEALTH AND MEDICAL CARE

Medical professionals
Physicians in 2003 and nurses in 2001

	U.S.	State
Physicians in 2003		
Total	774,849	3,901
Share of U.S. total		0.50%
Rate	266	310
Rank		7
Nurses in 2001		
Total	2,262,020	8,680
Share of U.S. total		0.38%
Rate	793	707
Rank		40

Rates are numbers of physicians and nurses per 100,000 resident population; ranks are based on rates.

Source: American Medical Association, *Physician Characteristics and Distribution in the U.S.;* U.S. Department of Health and Human Services, Health Resources and Services Administration.

Health insurance coverage, 2003

	State	U.S.
Total persons covered	1,126,000	243,320,000
Total persons not covered	127,000	44,961,000
Portion not covered	10.1%	15.6%
Rank among states	48	—
Children not covered	23,000	8,373,000
Portion not covered	7.4%	11.4%
Rank among states	41	—

Totals are rounded to nearest thousand. Ranks are from the highest to the lowest percentages of persons *not* insured.

Source: U.S. Census Bureau, Current Population Reports.

AIDS, syphilis, and tuberculosis cases, 2003

Disease	U.S. cases	State cases	Rank
AIDS	44,232	110	36
Syphilis	34,270	59	37
Tuberculosis	14,874	117	28

Source: U.S. Centers for Disease Control and Prevention.

Cigarette smoking, 2003
Residents over age 18 who smoke

	U.S.	State	Rank
All smokers	22.1%	17.3%	48
Male smokers	24.8%	20.1%	43
Female smokers	20.3%	14.4%	48

Cigarette smokers are defined as persons who reported having smoked at least 100 cigarettes during their lifetimes and who currently smoked at least occasionally.
Source: U.S. Centers for Disease Control and Prevention, *Morbidity and Mortality Weekly Report*, 53, no. 44 (November 12, 2004).

HOUSING

Home ownership rates, 1985-2004

	1985	1990	1995	2000	2004
State	51.0%	55.5%	50.2%	55.2%	60.9%
Total U.S.	63.9%	63.9%	64.7%	67.4%	69.0%
Rank among states	49	48	50	49	48

Net change in state home ownership rate,
1985-2004 . . . . +9.9%
Net change in U.S. home ownership rate,
1985-2004 . . . . +5.1%

Percentages represent the proportion of owner households to total occupied households.
Source: U.S. Census Bureau, 2006.

Home sales, 2000-2004
In thousands of units

Existing home sales	2000	2002	2003	2004
State sales	22.1	28.1	34.4	35.5
Total U.S. sales	5,171	5,631	6,183	6,784
State share of U.S. total	0.43%	0.50%	0.56%	0.52%
Sales rank among states	42	39	38	39

Units include single-family homes, condos, and co-ops.
Source: National Association of Realtors, Washington, D.C., *Real Estate Outlook: Market Trends & Insights.*

Values of owner-occupied homes, 2003

	State	U.S.
Total units	185,000	58,809,000
Value of units		
Under $100,000	6.2%	29.6%
$100,000-199,999	16.0%	36.9%
$200,000 or more	77.8%	33.5%
Median value	$324,661	$142,275
Rank among all states 2		

Units are owner-occupied one-family houses whose numbers are rounded to nearest thousand. Data are extrapolated from survey samples.
Source: U.S. Census Bureau, American Community Survey.

EDUCATION

Public school enrollment, 2002

Prekindergarten through grade 8
State enrollment 131,000
Total U.S. enrollment. 34,135,000
State share of U.S. total 0.38%

Grades 9 through 12
State enrollment. 53,000
Total U.S. enrollment. 14,067,000
State share of U.S. total 0.38%

Enrollment rates
State public school enrollment rate. 86.3%
Overall U.S. rate 90.4%
Rank among states in 2002. 44
Rank among states in 1995. 50

Enrollment figures (which include unclassified students) are rounded to nearest thousand pupils during fall school term. Enrollment rates are based on enumerated resident population estimate for July 1, 2002.
Source: U.S. National Center for Education Statistics.

Public college finances, 2003-2004

FTE enrollment in public institutions of higher education

Students in state institutions 35,400
Students in all U.S. public institutions 9,916,600
State share of U.S. total 0.36
Rank among states 43

State and local government appropriations for higher education

State appropriation per FTE $9,566
National average $5,716
Rank among states 3
State & local tax revenue going to higher
education 8.7%

FTE = full-time equivalent in public postsecondary programs,
including summer sessions; student numbers are rounded to
nearest hundred. Funding figures for 2003-2004 academic year
include financial aid to students in state public institutions and
exclude money for research, agriculture experiment stations,
teaching hospitals, and medical schools; figures are rounded to
nearest thousand dollars.
Source: Higher Education Executive Officers, Denver, Colorado.

TRANSPORTATION AND TRAVEL

Highway mileage, 2003

Interstate highways 55
Other freeways and expressways 34
Arterial roads 752
Collector roads 831
Local roads 2,637
Urban roads 2,128
Rural roads 2,181
Total state mileage 4,309
U.S. total 3,974,107
State share 0.11%
Rank among states 50

Note that combined urban and rural road mileage matches the
total of the other categories.
Source: U.S. Federal Highway Administration.

Motor vehicle registrations and driver licenses, 2003

Vehicle registrations	State	U.S.	Share	Rank
Autos, trucks, buses	903,000	231,390,000	0.39%	43
Autos only	525,000	135,670	0.39%	43
Motorcycles	22,000	5,328,000	0.41%	45
Driver licenses	834,000	196,166,000	0.43%	42

Figures, which do not include vehicles owned by military services,
are rounded to the nearest thousand. Figures for automobiles
include taxis.
Source: U.S. Federal Highway Administration.

Domestic travel expenditures, 2003
Spending by U.S. residents on overnight trips and
day trips of at least 50 miles from home

Total expenditures within state . . . . $7.49 bill.
Total expenditures within U.S. . . . . $490.87 bill.
State share of U.S. total 1.5%
Rank among states 23

Source: Travel Industry Association of America.

Retail gasoline prices, 2003-2007
Average price per gallon at the pump

Year	U.S.	State
2003	$1.267	$1.560
2004	$1.316	$1.616
2005	$1.644	$1.980
2007	$2.298	$3.003

Excise tax per gallon in 2004 . . . . 16.0¢
Rank among all states in 2007 prices 1

Prices are averages of all grades of gasoline sold at the pump
during March months in 2003-2005 and during February, 2007.
Averages for 2006, during which prices rose higher, are not
available.
Source: U.S. Energy Information Agency, *Petroleum Marketing
Monthly* (2003-2005 data); American Automobile Association
(2007 data).

CRIME AND LAW ENFORCEMENT

State and local police officers, 2000-2004

	2000	2002	2004
Total officers			
U.S.	654,601	665,555	675,734
State	2,864	2,799	2,712*
*Net change, 2000-2004			−5.31%
Officers per 1,000 residents			
U.S.	2.33	2.31	2.30
State	2.36	2.26	2.15
State rank	15	17	22

Totals include state and local police and sheriffs.
Source: Carsey Institute, University of New Hampshire.

Crime rates, 2003
Incidents per 100,000 residents

Crimes	State	U.S.
Violent crimes		
Total incidents	270	475
Murder	2	6
Forcible rape	29	32
Robbery	93	142
Aggravated assault	147	295
Property crimes		
Total incidents	5,238	3,588
Burglary	907	741
Larceny/theft	3,563	2,415
Motor vehicle theft	767	433
All crimes	5,508	4,063

Source: U.S. Federal Bureau of Investigation, *Crime in the United States,* annual.

State prison populations, 1980-2003

	State	U.S.	State share
1980	985	305,458	0.32%
1990	2,533	708,393	0.36%
1996	4,011	1,025,624	0.39%
2000	5,053	1,391,261	0.36%
2003	5,828	1,470,045	0.40%

State figures include jail inmates but exclude prisoners in federal penitentiaries.
Source: U.S. Bureau of Justice Statistics, *Prisoners in 2003.*

Idaho

Location: Northwest

Area and rank: 82,751 square miles (214,325 square kilometers); 83,574 square miles (216,457 square kilometers) including water; eleventh largest state in area

Coastline: none

Population and rank: 1,393,000 (2004); fortieth largest state in population

Capital and largest city: Boise (185,787 people in 2000 census)

Became territory: March 4, 1863

Entered Union and rank: July 3, 1890; forty-third state

Present constitution adopted: 1890

Counties: 44, as well as a small part of Yellowstone National Park

Boise skyline, showing the capitol building. (Idaho Department of Commerce)

State name: "Idaho" is an invented name whose meaning is unknown

State nicknames: Gem State; Spud State; Panhandle State

Motto: *Esto perpetua* (It is forever)

State flag: Blue field with state seal and red band with words "State of Idaho"

Highest point: Borah Peak—12,662 feet (3,859 meters)

Lowest point: Snake River—5,000 feet (1,524 meters)

Highest recorded temperature: 118 degrees Fahrenheit (48 degrees Celsius)—Orotino, 1934

Lowest recorded temperature: –60 degrees Fahrenheit (–51 degrees Celsius)—Island Park Dam, 1943

State song: "Here We Have Idaho"

State tree: White pine

State flower: Syringa

State bird: Mountain bluebird

State fish: Cutthroat trout

National parks: Yellowstone

Idaho History

Idaho's history is marked by its frontier origins. The state was settled later than neighboring Washington and Oregon, as pioneers passed through during the 1840's without stopping to settle until valuable gold strikes brought miners in significant numbers. The rough character of Idaho's early days was reflected in the violence of its first decades as a state, which came to a close only around the time of the U.S. entrance into World War I. This background is sometimes still apparent in extremist political groups, some of which are racist or anarchist.

Early History. Idaho was first inhabited by various American Indian tribes, such as the Nez Perce, Coeur d'Alene, Pend d'Oreille, Kutenai, Paiute Shoshone, and Bannock. The origins of the indigenous inhabitants extend back around fourteen thousand years.

Other ancient cultures flourished from eight thousand years ago until about the seventeenth century. By the eighteenth century, Shoshone bands (fragments of tribes) had obtained horses from European contacts, but these contacts decimated the native population by spreading smallpox.

No whites are known to have explored Idaho before Meriwether Lewis and William Clark led their famous expedition through Lemhi Pass in Idaho in 1805. Traveling through the Bitterroot Mountains, the explorers built canoes with the assistance of the Shoshone and Nez Perce and floated down the Clearwater and Snake Rivers to the Columbia. Four years later, Canadian explorer David Thompson built Kullyspell House, known as the first non-native house in the Pacific Northwest, near Pend Oreille Lake. Decades later, during the 1830's, Forts Hall and Boise, site of the future state's capital, were founded.

Presettlement Decades. Missionaries, a constant feature of the early days of the Pacific Northwest, soon made their appearance in Idaho, bringing Christianity and—in their eyes—civilization to the native tribes. Henry Spalding arrived in 1836 and established the state's first school. He also created its first irrigation system and planted its first potatoes, both of which were to play significant roles in Idaho's later economic development. The 1840's saw the arrival of the wagon trains headed west on the Oregon Trail. The steady stream of humanity became a flood in 1849, as twenty thousand forty-niners came through on their way to California's goldfields. Continuing heavy traffic led to the establishment of the U.S. military post Cantonment Loring near Fort Hall. There were still no settlers, however, even after French Canadians discovered gold on the Pend Oreille River in 1852, the year before a large piece of Oregon Territory broke off to form Washington Territory, of which Idaho was a part. The first permanent community had not even been founded when Oregon was admitted to the Union at the end of the decade. Mormon missionaries had established the Salmon River Mission (Fort Lemhi) in mid-decade, but it was not a success and was abandoned in 1858.

From Territory to Statehood. Only in 1860, when much of the rest of the nation was gearing up for a bloody civil war, were roots for the first town put down, when Franklin, just over the Utah border, was founded by Mormons. The next several years, however, were to change Idaho's sparsely populated character, as major mining strikes were made in Pierce, Florence, Idaho City, and Silver City. Just two years after the first town was settled, the new community of Lewiston saw the region's first newspaper, the *Golden Age.* By 1863, the region east of Washington and Oregon was ready to take a giant step to statehood when it became a territory, with Lewiston as its capital.

This rapid invasion by European settlers was viewed with great alarm by the Native Americans. American Indian wars followed until the end of the 1870's, as Nez Perce, Bannock, and Sheepeater Indian wars followed in successive years. Thus, in 1877, after years of abuse by settlers, the Nez Perce resisted efforts to send them from Oregon to Lapwai Reservation in Idaho. In June, they crushed U.S. Army troops and settler volunteers at White Bird Canyon, in north-central Idaho. Forced to retreat after federal reinforcements arrived, the Nez Perce surrendered in Montana in October.

Other American Indians, in accordance with federal policy, were also settled on reservations provided by treaties. Conditions on reservations were in some cases so poor that rebellions took place. Thus, the Bannock Indians rebelled in 1878, when food on their reservation became inadequate and settlers objected to their foraging on cattle grazing land. However, they too were defeated by federal troops.

Economic Development and Statehood. In the meantime, other events were unfolding that foretold the new territory's social and economic future. The first wave of modern technology made its appearance in 1866, as the first telegraph service reached the territory. A harbinger of modern social conflict arrived the next year, when the Owyhee Miners' League, Idaho's first labor union, made its appearance. Early in the following decade the first U.S. assay office and Idaho's first prison were built. Soon after, railroad service came to Franklin, and the way was open for even greater emigration from the restless east. By the next century these immigrants included English, Chinese, Czech, Dutch, French, French Canadian, German, Mexican, and Scandinavian settlers.

From the 1880's on, technological developments and their economic consequences followed with stunning speed for a region that was so recently an untamed wilderness. During the early 1880's electric light was introduced, and telephone service followed in 1883. The following year, an enormous silver strike, eventually recognized as the nation's largest, was registered in the

Frederic Remington's depiction of Chief Joseph surrendering the Nez Perce to U.S. cavalry troops in northern Montana in 1877, after leading five thousand troops on a five-month chase. (Library of Congress)

Coeur d'Alene mining district, and more settlers arrived. By the close of the decade, Idaho was ready to trade its position as territory for the status of state. In 1889, a constitutional convention convened on Independence Day to institute a new frame of government. The next year Idaho was admitted to the Union.

Government and Social Conflict. Government under the new state constitution, as in neighboring Washington, reflected the frontier distrust of power in the form of a powerful state governor. Accordingly, executive control was divided into a number of elective offices in which the secretary of state, state controller, state treasurer, attorney general, and superintendent of public instruction are separately elected rather than appointed by the governor. The governor is also denied the power of pardoning criminals. The state constitution underlines a commitment to liberal democracy. It opens with a declaration of the "inalienable rights of man" and a detailed enumeration of individual rights, the central idea of classical liberalism. Immediately following is the forthright statement that "All political power is inherent in the people," the key democratic idea of popular sovereignty. In keeping with a strong tradition of frontier democracy, voters have the right to the initiative, referendum, and recall.

While a framework for orderly government was in place, Idaho's rough-and-ready frontier origins could hardly disappear overnight. This became evident during the 1890's as serious violence broke out between union miners and mine owners. In 1892, the Coeur d'Alene mining area was the scene of dynamiting and shootings. More violence broke out when a new strike occurred in 1899. The strike was broken when the governor, Frank Steunenberg, called out federal troops.

Much bitterness remained, however. In 1905, former governor Steunenberg was murdered by a bomb. The perpetrator, a member of the Western Federation of Miners, an organization of the militant Marxist International Workers of the World (IWW), confessed but implicated three union officials. When a sensational trial was held in 1907, renowned defense attorney Clarence Darrow gained acquittals of two officials, and charges against the third were dropped. The prosecutor, William E. Borah, nevertheless won national fame and was elected six times to the U.S. Senate, where he became a stalwart foreign policy isolationist.

Two World Wars and Depression. Before World War I, the state's economy benefited from irrigation projects. A dam on the Snake River completed in 1906, for example, opened more than 100,000 acres of land for agriculture. The war created an agricultural boom when wartime food shortages brought demand for farm products. The end of the war, however, brought an economic downturn, whose effects were felt into the 1920's. Matters were worse in the Great Depression of the 1930's, when many banks collapsed. Federal spending

helped to a degree through a highway construction program and employment in the Civilian Conservation Corps (CCC).

World War II brought renewed prosperity, as in the rest of the nation, with massive federal spending for war needs. People of Japanese descent who were relocated from western portions of Oregon and Washington went to work in agriculture, where conscription had made labor scarce. Wartime industry made a lasting change in the economy, since in the postwar period manufacturing begun by defense needs continued, resulting in increased urbanization. By 1960, half of the population lived in cities or towns.

Postwar Economy and Society. As in neighboring states, postwar economic growth was also stimulated by development of cheap hydroelectric power. A series of dams was built during the 1950's, and projects continued during the 1960's. In 1976, one of the dams collapsed, and several rural communities were inundated, causing loss of life and considerable damage. During the 1970's, the state's prosperity brought a rapid increase in population, which rose nearly one-third between 1970 and 1980.

By the 1990's, Idaho's economy was balanced between agriculture, mining, and nonagricultural industries. Various high-tech industries moved to the Boise area; food processing and wood products remained important. A tourist industry that, led by development of winter sports in Sun Valley, had grown up beginning during the 1950's was also important. Politically, the state was divided between conservationists and their opponents, and outsiders frequently noted the activity of unsavory fringe political groups, such as anarchists and neo-Nazis. Observers noted that the wise and efficient use of the state's natural resources would principally determine its future prosperity.

At the end of the twentieth century, Idaho's politics remained predominantly Republican. The state voted for Texas governor George W. Bush and Richard Cheney, a former congressman from neighboring Wyoming, in the presidential election on November 7, by a 68-28 percent margin, and again in 2004 by a similar margin (68-30 percent). Indicative of the political leanings of the state was the wide margin by which Idaho's new congressman in Washington, D.C., C. L. (Butch) Otter, defeated his opponent by a 65-32 percent margin in 2000.

Wildfires and Wildlife. Idaho, as common in other Western states, was the victim of annual wildfires, exacerbated by lingering drought. The state had experienced wildfires in the past, but they seemed to intensify around the turn of the new century. Fires during the 2000 season were said to be the worst on record, destroying some 6.7 million acres in the seven most stricken states, including Idaho. The federal government became involved in helping to organize a plan among the states to limit the damage that the fires were causing. Acting in a nonpartisan spirit, the seven states unanimously endorsed the plan proposed by the U.S. secretary of the interior and the secretary of agriculture. The plan avoided discussion of contentious issues such as harvesting timber but instead emphasized fire prevention and local decision making. The federal government paid the states $800 million to replenish emergency funds that were depleted during the fire season.

Aside from the fire problem, the state was involved in other environmental controversies involving natural resources. One of these involved a plan to reintroduce grizzly bears in the Selway-Bitterroot Wilderness area in Idaho and Montana. The return of the bears did not take place because a federal judge in Boise, Idaho's state capital, ruled that introducing the animals would cause irreplaceable harm to the Idaho economy and its timber and mining industries.

Aryan Nations Lawsuit. Also during 2000, the victims of a 1998 neo-Nazi assault outside the compound of the so-called Aryan Nations founded by Richard Butler won a $6.3 million settlement in their lawsuit over

Idaho's lowest altitudes occur in the basin of the Snake River. (PhotoDisc)

the incident, effectively putting Butler and his group out of business. As a result, Butler agreed to give up the name Aryan Nations. The following year, the victims bought Butler's compound, where the group had been headquartered, and converted it into a human rights center.

Charles F. Bahmueller

Idaho Time Line

6000 B.C.E.-1700's American Indian cultures flourish.

1810	Fort Henry, first American fur post west of Rocky Mountains, is established near St. Anthony.
1811	Party based at Astoria on the Pacific Coast explores portions of the future Oregon Trail in Idaho.
1819	Canadian Donald Mackenzie holds rendezvous with American Indians on the Boise River; attempts to establish post.
1820	Mackenzie negotiates peace treaty with the Shoshone on Little Lost River.
1821	Hudson's Bay Company and North West Company merge.
1822	Founding of Rocky Mountain Fur Company.
1830	Captain B. L. E. Bonneville leads wagon train across South Pass to Green River.
1834	Forts Laramie, Boise, and Hall are established.
1843	First Oregon Trail wagons cross Idaho.
June 15, 1846	Treaty with Great Britain settles the Oregon boundary dispute; all land below the forty-ninth parallel is American.
Aug. 14, 1848	Oregon Territory is created, which includes Idaho.
1852	French Canadians discover gold on the Pend Oreille River.
1853	Idaho becomes part of Washington Territory.
1863	Major mining strikes take place near Pierce, Florence, Idaho City, and Silver City.
Mar. 4, 1863	Idaho Territory is established.
1864	Territorial legislature approves moving capital to Boise.
1867	Owyhee Miners' League, state's first labor union, is organized.

(continued)

1874	First railroad service in Idaho begins at Franklin.
1877-1879	Nez Perce, Bannock, and Sheepeater Indians war with settlers.
1884	Silver is discovered in the Coeur d'Alene mining district.
Nov. 5, 1889	State constitution is ratified.
1889	Territorial legislature establishes University of Idaho.
July 3, 1890	Idaho becomes the forty-third state.
1904	Completion of Milner Dam brings irrigation to the south side of the Snake River.
1910	Forest fires consume one-sixth of north Idaho's forests.
1912	State Board of Education is established.
1914	Moses Alexander is elected the first Jewish governor in the United States.
1924	Craters of the Moon National Monument is established.
1926	First commercial airmail service in the United States begins in Boise.
1934	Idaho is nation's leading silver producer.
1936	Sun Valley winter sports resort is established by Union Pacific Railroad; world's first ski chair lift opens there.
1942	Almost ten thousand Japanese Americans are placed in an internment camp near Eden.
1949	National Reactor Testing Station (NRTS) is established.
1951	NRTS becomes site of the world's first use of nuclear fission to produce electricity.
1958	Idaho leads the nation in mining of silver, lead, and cobalt.
1966	Voters uphold 3 percent state sales tax.
1975	Port of Lewiston opens Idaho to oceangoing shipping.
June 5, 1976	Teton Dam collapses, killing eleven and forcing thousands to flee.
1978	Voters approve tax limitation placing severe restrictions on use of the property tax.
1985	Idaho produces one-fourth of U.S. potatoes.
1986	Voters adopt constitutional amendment prohibiting the payment of union dues as a necessity for employment.
1992	First woman appointed to Idaho Supreme Court.
June-Sept., 2000	Idaho experiences extensive, destructive wildfires that also severely affect six other western states.
Nov. 7, 2000	Idaho votes for George W. Bush and Richard Cheney for president and vice president, respectively. The state's other representatives in Washington remain Republican.

Notes for Further Study

Published Sources. For an introduction to the state, see Rick Ardinger and M. L. Peterson's *Celebrating Idaho: The Centennial in Words and Pictures* (1991). Books on Idaho's history include Leonard J. Arrington's *History of Idaho* (2 vols., 1994) and Dorothy Dutton's *A Rendezvous with Idaho History* (1994). One facet of ethnic history is described in *History of the Jews in Utah and Idaho, 1853-1950* (1973) by Juanita Brooks.

Good books on Idaho geography include Lalia Phipps Boone's *Idaho Place Names: A Geographical Dictionary* (1988) and Delorme Mapping's *Idaho Atlas and Gazetteer* (5th ed., 2002). American Indian history is surveyed in *Indians of Idaho* (1978) by Deward Walker. For information on the great Nez Perce leader Chief Joseph, readers should consult Clifford E. Trafzer's *Chief Joseph's Allies: The Palouse Indians and the Nez Perce* (1992) or *Chief Joseph: Guardian of the People* (2005) by Candy Moulton. The Bannock Indians are studied both in Brigham D. Mardsen's *The Bannock of Idaho* (1996) and, along with the Shoshone, in John W. Heaton's *The Shoshone-Bannocks: Culture and Commerce at Fort Hall, 1870-1940* (2005). Laura Woodworth-Ney uses a number of historical documents to examine the development of one of Idaho's reservations in *Mapping Identity: The Creation of the Coeur d'Alene Indian*

Reservation, 1805-1902 (2004). The life and work of an important Idaho photographer is detailed in Joanna Cohan Scherer's *A Danish Photographer of Idaho Indians: Benedicte Wrensted* (2005).

The state's government is discussed in *Governing Idaho: Politics, People, and Power* (2005) by James Weatherby and Randy Strapilus. Idaho's constitution is examined in Dennis C. Colson's *Idaho's Constitution: The Tie That Binds* (rev. ed., 2003). Jennifer Eastman Attebery's *Building Idaho: An Architectural History* (1991) treats the state's architecture. Those interested in archaeology of the state should see Mark Plew's *Introduction to the Archaeology of Southern Idaho* (1986). For those interested in general travel in Idaho, Cort Conley's *Idaho for the Curious: A Guide* (2003) and *Idaho Off the Beaten Path* (5th ed., 2004) by Julie Fanselow are excellent guides.

Web Resources. For information on politics and government in Idaho, a good place to start is the state of Idaho home page (www.accessidaho.org/), which contains information on and links to state agencies and major offices, as well as commerce, education, the environment, and many related topics. A federal government agency particularly significant in Idaho is the Bureau of Land Management (BLM), whose

work is outlined on its home page (www.id .blm.gov/). The Idaho section of the American Local History Network (www .usgennet .org/usa/id/state1/alhn/index.htm) has a variety of information and links, including local, ethnic, and cultural history; schools and education; genealogy; geography; government (including the Idaho Constitution); military records; museums; and other topics. Other information on the state is found on the Libraries Linking Idaho home page (www.lili.org/lili/). The state historical society home page (www.idahohistory.net/) is useful for learning about the early days of Idaho. State geography information especially suitable to young people can be accessed at Kidport (kidport.com/RefLib/ UsaGeography/Facts/Idaho.htm). Travelers may wish to consult Virtual Tourist: Travel in Idaho (www.virtualtourist.com/ travel/North_America/United_States _of_ America/Idaho/TravelGuide-Idaho.html).

For information on Native Americans, readers should view the home pages maintained by various tribes—for example, the Nez Perce home page (www.nezperce.org/). The sites for Bannock, Cayuse, and other Idaho Native Americans (www.rootsweb .com/~idreserv/fhhist.html and www .bannockindians.com/), along with that for Coeur d'Alene tribal history (www.rootsweb .com/~idreserv/cdhist.html), are also informative.

Counties

County	2000 pop.	Rank in pop.	Sq. miles	Rank in area	County	2000 pop.	Rank in pop.	Sq. miles	Rank in area
Ada	300,904	1	1,055.0	31	Custer	4,342	37	4,925.6	3
Adams	3,476	41	1,364.7	22	Elmore	29,130	11	3,077.8	6
Bannock	75,565	5	1,113.2	27	Franklin	11,329	24	665.5	37
Bear Lake	6,411	35	971.4	32	Fremont	11,819	23	1,866.8	16
Benewah	9,171	28	776.0	34	Gem	15,181	20	562.6	40
Bingham	41,735	7	2,094.8	12	Gooding	14,155	21	730.8	36
Blaine	18,991	17	2,644.9	7	Idaho	15,511	19	8,485.2	1
Boise	6,670	34	1,902.5	14	Jefferson	19,155	16	1,095.1	28
Bonner	36,835	9	1,737.6	19	Jerome	18,342	18	599.9	38
Bonneville	82,522	4	1,868.6	15	Kootenai	108,685	3	1,245.2	24
Boundary	9,871	27	1,268.8	23	Latah	34,935	10	1,076.7	29
Butte	2,899	42	2,232.9	11	Lemhi	7,806	30	4,564.3	4
Camas	991	44	1,075.0	30	Lewis	3,747	40	479.1	41
Canyon	131,441	2	589.8	39	Lincoln	4,044	39	1,205.6	25
Caribou	7,304	33	1,766.1	17	Madison	27,467	12	471.6	42
Cassia	21,416	13	2,566.6	9	Minidoka	20,174	15	759.7	35
Clark	1,022	43	1,764.7	18	Nez Perce	37,410	8	849.1	33
Clearwater	8,930	29	2,461.6	10	Oneida	4,125	38	1,200.4	26

(continued)

County	2000 pop.	Rank in pop.	Sq. miles	Rank in area
Owyhee	10,644	25	7,678.4	2
Payette	20,578	14	407.5	44
Power	7,538	32	1,405.7	21
Shoshone	13,771	22	2,634.0	8
Teton	5,999	36	450.4	43

County	2000 pop.	Rank in pop.	Sq. miles	Rank in area
Twin Falls	64,284	6	1,925.1	13
Valley	7,651	31	3,678.2	5
Washington	9,977	26	1,456.4	20

Source: U.S. Census Bureau; National Association of Counties.

Cities
With 10,000 or more residents

Rank	City	Population
1	Boise (capital)	185,787
2	Nampa	51,867
3	Pocatello	51,466
4	Idaho Falls	50,730
5	Meridian	34,919
6	Coeur d'Alene	34,514
7	Twin Falls	34,469
8	Lewiston	30,904
9	Caldwell	25,967
10	Moscow	21,291

Rank	City	Population
11	Rexburg	17,257
12	Post Falls	17,247
13	Mountain Home	11,143
14	Eagle	11,085
15	Garden City	10,624
16	Blackfoot	10,419

Population figures are from 2000 census.
Source: U.S. Bureau of the Census.

Index to Tables

DEMOGRAPHICS

Resident state and national populations, 1970-2004

Population figures given in thousands

	State pop.	U.S. pop.	Share	Rank
1970	713	203,302	0.4%	42
1980	944	226,546	0.4%	41
1985	994	237,924	0.4%	41
1990	1,007	248,765	0.4%	42
1995	1,177	262,761	0.4%	41
2000	1,294	281,425	0.5%	39
2004	1,393	293,655	0.5%	39

Source: U.S. Census Bureau, Current Population Reports, 2006.

Resident population by age, 2004

Age Group	Total persons
Under 5 years	103,000
5 to 17 years	269,000
18 to 24 years	157,000
25 to 34 years	185,000
35 to 44 years	192,000
45 to 54 years	194,000
55 to 64 years	135,000
65 to 74 years	83,000
75 to 84 years	53,000
85 years and older	22,000
All age groups	1,393,000

Portion of residents 65 and older	11.4%
National rank in portion of oldest residents	40
National average	12.4%

Population figures are rounded to nearest thousand persons;
figures include armed forces personnel stationed in the state.
Source: U.S. Bureau of the Census, 2006.

Resident population by race, Hispanic origin, 2004

Category	State pop.	Share	U.S.
All residents	1,393	100.00%	100.00%
Non-Hispanic white	1,215	87.22%	67.37%
Hispanic white	116	8.33%	13.01%
Other Hispanic	8	0.57%	1.06%
African American	8	0.57%	12.77%
Native American	20	1.44%	0.96%
Asian, Pacific Islander	16	1.15%	4.37%
Two or more categories	19	1.36%	1.51%

Population figures are in thousands. Persons counted as "Hispanic" (Latino) may be of any race. Because of overlapping categories, categories may not add up to 100%. Shares in column 3 are percentages of each category within the state; these figures may be compared to the national percentages in column 4.
Source: U.S. Bureau of the Census, 2006.

Projected state population, 2000-2030

Year	Population
2000	1,294,000
2005	1,407,000
2010	1,517,000
2015	1,630,000
2020	1,741,000
2025	1,853,000
2030	1,970,000
Population increase, 2000-2030	676,000
Percentage increase, 2000-2030	52.2

Projections are based on data from the 2000 census.
Source: U.S. Census Bureau.

VITAL STATISTICS

Infant mortality rates, 1980-2002

	1980	1990	2000	2002
All state residents	10.7	8.7	7.5	6.1
All U.S. residents	12.6	9.2	9.4	9.1
All state white residents	10.7	8.6	7.5	6.1
All U.S. white residents	10.6	7.6	5.7	5.8

Figures represent deaths per 1,000 live births of resident infants under 1 year old, exclusive of fetal deaths. Figures for all residents include members of other racial categories not listed separately. The Census Bureau considers the figures for black residents to be too small to be statistically meaningful.
Source: U.S. Census Bureau, *Statistical Abstract of the United States,* 2006.

Abortion rates, 1990 and 2000

	1990	2000
Total abortions	2,000	2,000
Rate per 1,000 women	7.2	7.0
U.S. rate	25.7	21.3
Rank	48	43

Numbers of abortions are rounded to nearest thousand; ranks are based on rates.
Source: U.S. Census Bureau.

Marriages and divorces, 2004

Total marriages	15,200
Rate per 1,000 population	10.9
National rate per 1,000 population	7.4
Rank among all states	5
Total divorces	7,100
Rate per 1,000 population	5.1
National rate per 1,000 population	3.7
Rank among all states	4

Figures are for all marriages and divorces performed within the state, including those of nonresidents; totals are rounded to the nearest hundred. Ranks are for highest to lowest figures; note that divorce data are not available for five states.
Source: U.S. National Center for Health Statistics, *Vital Statistics of the United States,* 2006.

Death rates by leading causes, 2002
Deaths per 100,000 resident population

Cause	State	U.S.
Heart disease	188.8	241.7
Cancer	159.4	193.2
Cerebrovascular diseases	54.9	56.4
Accidents other than motor vehicle	45.6	37.0
Motor vehicle accidents	22.1	15.7
Chronic lower respiratory diseases	44.4	43.3
Diabetes mellitus	24.0	25.4
HIV	n/a	4.9
Suicide	15.1	11.0
Homicide	2.4	6.1
All causes	739.9	847.3
Rank in overall death rate among states		44

Figures exclude nonresidents who died in the state. Causes of death follow International Classification of Diseases. Rank is from highest to lowest death rate in the United States.
Source: U.S. National Center for Health Statistics, *National Vital Statistics Report,* 2006.

ECONOMY

Gross state product, 1990-2004
In current dollars

Year	State product	Nat'l product	State share
1990	$17.8 billion	$5.67 trillion	0.31%
2000	$35.2 billion	$9.75 trillion	0.36%
2002	$38.3 billion	$10.41 trillion	0.37%
2003	$40.4 billion	$10.92 trillion	0.37%
2004	$43.4 billion	$11.65 trillion	0.37%

Source: U.S. Bureau of Economic Analysis, *Survey of Current Business,* July, 2005.

Gross state product by industry, 2003
In billions of dollars

Construction $2.2
Manufacturing 7.1
Wholesale trade 2.1
Retail trade 3.5
Finance & insurance 1.6
Information 0.8
Professional services 2.5
Health care & social assistance 2.4
Government 5.0

Total state product $38.8
Total U.S. product $10,289.2
State share of U.S. total 0.38%
Rank among all states 42

Total figures include industries not listed separately. Amounts are in chained 2000 dollars.
Source: U.S. Bureau of Economic Analysis, *Survey of Current Business,* July, 2005.

Personal income per capita, 1990-2004
In current dollars

	1990	2000	2004
Per capita income	$15,724	$24,075	$27,098
U.S. average	$19,477	$29,845	$32,937
Rank among states	41	42	44

Source: U.S. Bureau of Economic Analysis, *Survey of Current Business,* April, 2005.

Energy consumption, 2001
In trillions of British thermal units (BTU), except as noted

Total energy consumption
Total state energy consumption 501
Total U.S. energy consumption 96,275
State share of U.S. total 0.52%
Rank among states 40

Per capita consumption (In millions of BTU)
Total state per capita consumption 379
Total U.S. per capita consumption 338
Rank among states 19

End-use sectors
Residential 105
Commercial 95
Industrial 180
Transportation 122

Sources of energy
Petroleum 155
Natural gas 82
Coal 11
Hydroelectric power 74
Nuclear electric power 0

Figures for totals include categories not listed separately.
Source: U.S. Energy Information Administration, *State Energy Data Report,* 2001.

Nonfarm employment by sectors, 2004

Total 587,000
Construction 40,000
Manufacturing 62,000
Trade, transportation, utilities 118,000
Information 10,000
Finance, insurance, real estate 28,000
Professional & business services 73,000
Education & health services 65,000
Leisure, hospitality, arts, organizations 56,000
Other services, including repair & maintenance . . . 18,000
Government 114,000

Figures are rounded to nearest thousand persons. "Total" includes mining and natural resources, not listed separately.
Source: U.S. Bureau of Labor Statistics, 2006.

Foreign exports, 1990-2004
In millions of dollars

Year	State	U.S.	State share
1990	898	394,045	0.23%
1996	1,571	624,767	0.25%
1997	1,664	688,896	0.24%
2000	3,559	712,055	0.45%
2003	2,096	724,006	0.31%
2004	2,915	769,332	0.38%

Rank among all states in 2004 38

U.S. total does not include U.S. dependencies.
Source: U.S. Census Bureau, *U.S. Merchandise Trade,* series FT 900, 2000; U.S. Census Bureau, *U.S. International Trade in Goods and Services,* Series FT 900, 2005.

LAND USE

Federally owned land, 2003
Areas in acres

	State	U.S.	State share
Total area	52,933,000	2,271,343,000	2.33%
Nonfederal land	17,797,000	1,599,584,000	1.11%
Federal land	35,136,000	671,759,000	5.23%
Federal share	66.4%	29.6%	—

Areas are rounded to nearest thousand acres. Figures for federally owned land do not include trust properties.
Source: U.S. General Services Administration, *Federal Real Property Profile,* 2006.

Land use, 1997
In acres, rounded to nearest thousand

Total surface area	53,488,000
Total nonfederal rural land.	18,618,000
Percentage rural land	34.8%
Cropland	5,517,000
Conservation Reserve Program (CRP*) land	785,000
Pastureland	1,315,000
Rangeland	6,501,000
Forestland.	3,948,000
Other rural land	553,000

*CRP is a federal program begun in 1985 to assist private landowners to convert highly erodible cropland to vegetative cover for ten years. Note that some categories of land overlap.
Source: U.S. Department of Agriculture, Natural Resources and Conservation Service, and Iowa State University, Statistical Laboratory, S*ummary Report, 1997 National Resources Inventory,* revised December, 2000.

Farms and crop acreage, 2004

	State	U.S.	Share	Rank
Farms	25,000	2,113,000	1.18%	32
Acres (millions)	12	937	1.28%	24
Acres per farm	472	443	—	14

Source: U.S. Department of Agriculture, National Agricultural Statistics Service. Numbers of farms are rounded to nearest thousand units; acreage figures are rounded to nearest million. Rankings, including ties, are based on rounded figures.

GOVERNMENT AND FINANCE

Units of local government, 2002

	State	Total U.S.	Rank
All local governments	1,158	87,525	27
Counties	44	3,034	32
Municipalities	200	19,429	35
Townships	0	16,504	—
School districts	116	13,506	31
Special districts	798	35,052	13

Only 48 states have county governments, 20 states have township governments ("towns" in New England, Minnesota, New York, and Wisconsin), and 46 states have school districts. Special districts encompass such functions as natural resources, fire protection, and housing and community development.
Source: U.S. Census Bureau, *Census of Governments.*

State government revenue, 2002

Total revenue.	$4,488 mill.
General revenue	$4,375 mill.
Per capita revenue	$3,257
U.S. per capita average	$3,689
Rank among states	32
Intergovernment revenue	
Total	$1,330 mill.
From federal government	$1,324 mill.
Charges and miscellaneous	
Total	$774 mill.
Current charges	$383 mill.
Misc. general income	$391 mill.
Insurance trust revenue	$48 mill.
Taxes	
Total	$2,271 mill.
Per capita taxes	$1,691
Rank among states	34
Property taxes	(nil)
Sales taxes	$1,116 mill.
License taxes	$222 mill.
Individual income taxes	$842 mill.
Corporate income taxes.	$77 mill.
Other taxes	$13 mill.

Total revenue figures include items not listed separately here.
Source: U.S. Bureau of the Census.

State government expenditures, 2002

General expenditures

Total state expenditures	$5,234 mill.
Intergovernmental	$1,407 mill.

Per capita expenditures

State	$3,444
Average of all states	$3,859
Rank among states	38

Selected direct expenditures

Education	$704 mill.
Public welfare	$1,003 mill.
Health, hospital	$143 mill.
Highways	$383 mill.
Police protection	$44 mill.
Corrections	$170 mill.
Natural resources	$164 mill.
Parks and recreation	$37 mill.
Government administration	$222 mill.
Interest on debt	$142 mill.
Total direct expenditures	$3,218 mill.

Totals include items not listed separately.
Source: U.S. Census Bureau.

POLITICS

Governors since statehood

D = Democrat; R = Republican; O = other;
(r) resigned; (d) died in office; (i) removed from office

George L. Shoup (R)	(r) 1890
Norman B. Willey (R)	1890-1893
William J. McConnell (R)	1893-1897
Frank Steunenberg (D)	1897-1901
Frank W. Hunt (D)	1901-1903
John T. Morrison (R)	1903-1905
Frank R. Gooding (R)	1905-1909
James H. Brady (R)	1909-1911
James W. Hawley (D)	1911-1913
John M. Haines (R)	1913-1915
Moses Alexander (D)	1915-1919
David W. Davis (R)	1919-1923
Charles C. Moore (R)	1923-1927
H. Clarence Baldridge (R)	1927-1931
Charles Ben Ross (D)	1931-1937
Barzilla W. Clark (D)	1937-1939
Clarence A. Bottolfsen (R)	1939-1941
Chase A. Clark (D)	1941-1943
Clarence A. Bottolfsen (R)	1943-1945
Charles C. Gossett (D)	(r) 1945
Arnold Williams (D)	1945-1947
Charles A. Robins (R)	1947-1951
Leonard B. Jordan (R)	1951-1955
Robert E. Smylie (R)	1955-1967
Donald W. Samuelson (R)	1967-1971
Cecil D. Andrus (D)	(r) 1971-1977
John V. Evans (D)	1977-1987
Cecil D. Andrus (D)	1987-1995
Phillip E. Batt (R)	1995-1999
Dirk Kempthorne (R)	(r) 1999-2006
Jim Risch (R)	2006-2007
C. L. "Butch" Otter (R)	2007-

Composition of congressional delegations, 1989-2007

	Dem	Rep	Total
House of Representatives			
101st Congress, 1989			
State delegates	1	1	2
Total U.S.	259	174	433
102d Congress, 1991			
State delegates	2	0	2
Total U.S.	267	167	434
103d Congress, 1993			
State delegates	1	1	2
Total U.S.	258	176	434
104th Congress, 1995			
State delegates	0	2	2
Total U.S.	197	236	433
105th Congress, 1997			
State delegates	0	2	2
Total U.S.	206	228	434
106th Congress, 1999			
State delegates	0	2	2
Total U.S.	211	222	433
107th Congress, 2001			
State delegates	0	2	2
Total U.S.	211	221	432
108th Congress, 2003			
State delegates	0	2	2
Total U.S.	205	229	434
109th Congress, 2005			
State delegates	0	2	2
Total U.S.	202	231	433
110th Congress, 2007			
State delegates	0	2	2
Total U.S.	233	202	435
Senate			
101st Congress, 1989			
State delegates	0	2	2
Total U.S.	55	45	100
102d Congress, 1991			
State delegates	0	2	2
Total U.S.	56	44	100

(continued)

	Dem	Rep	Total
103d Congress, 1993			
State delegates	0	2	2
Total U.S.	57	43	100
104th Congress, 1995			
State delegates	0	2	2
Total U.S.	46	53	99
105th Congress, 1997			
State delegates	0	2	2
Total U.S.	45	55	100
106th Congress, 1999			
State delegates	0	2	2
Total U.S.	45	54	99
107th Congress, 2001			
State delegates	0	2	2
Total U.S.	50	50	100
108th Congress, 2003			
State delegates	0	2	2
Total U.S.	48	51	99
109th Congress, 2005			
State delegates	0	2	2
Total U.S.	44	55	99
110th Congress, 2007			
State delegates	0	2	2
Total U.S.	49	49	98

Figures are for starts of first sessions. Totals are for Democrat (Dem.) and Republican (Rep.) members only. House membership totals under 435 and Senate totals under 100 reflect vacancies and seats held by independent party members. When the 110th Congress opened, the Senate's two independent members caucused with the Democrats, giving the Democrats control of the Senate.

Source: U.S. Congress, *Congressional Directory.*

Composition of state legislature, 1990-2006

	Democrats	Republicans
State House (84 seats in 1990; 70 seats thereafter)		
1990	28	56
1992	20	50
1994	13	57
1996	11	59
1998	12	58
2000	12	58
2002	16	54
2004	13	57
2006	19	51
State Senate (35 seats)		
1990	21	21
1992	12	23
1994	8	27
1996	5	30
1998	4	31
2000	4	31
2002	7	28
2004	7	28
2006	7	28

Figures for total seats may include independents and minor party members. Numbers reflect results of elections in listed years; elected members usually take their seats in the years that follow.

Source: Council of State Governments; *State Elective Officials and the Legislatures.*

Voter participation in presidential elections, 2000 and 2004

	2000	2004
Voting age population		
State	930,000	1,021,000
Total United States	209,831,000	220,377,000
State share of U.S. total	0.44	0.46
Rank among states	40	40
Portion of voting age population casting votes		
State	53.9%	58.6%
United States	50.3%	55.5%
Rank among states	24	23

Population figures are rounded to nearest thousand and include all residents, regardless of eligibility to vote.

Source: U.S. Census Bureau.

HEALTH AND MEDICAL CARE

Medical professionals
Physicians in 2003 and nurses in 2001

	U.S.	State
Physicians in 2003		
Total	774,849	2,324
Share of U.S. total		0.30%
Rate	266	170
Rank		50
Nurses in 2001		
Total	2,262,020	8,400
Share of U.S. total		0.37%
Rate	793	636
Rank		45

Rates are numbers of physicians and nurses per 100,000 resident population; ranks are based on rates.
Source: American Medical Association, *Physician Characteristics and Distribution in the U.S.*; U.S. Department of Health and Human Services, Health Resources and Services Administration.

Health insurance coverage, 2003

	State	U.S.
Total persons covered	1,107,000	243,320,000
Total persons not covered	253,000	44,961,000
Portion not covered	18.6%	15.6%
Rank among states	8	—
Children not covered	51,000	8,373,000
Portion not covered	13.7%	11.4%
Rank among states	8	—

Totals are rounded to nearest thousand. Ranks are from the highest to the lowest percentages of persons *not* insured.
Source: U.S. Census Bureau, Current Population Reports.

AIDS, syphilis, and tuberculosis cases, 2003

Disease	U.S. cases	State cases	Rank
AIDS	44,232	25	44
Syphilis	34,270	45	40
Tuberculosis	14,874	13	46

Source: U.S. Centers for Disease Control and Prevention.

Cigarette smoking, 2003
Residents over age 18 who smoke

	U.S.	State	Rank
All smokers	22.1%	19.0%	45
Male smokers	24.8%	19.5%	48
Female smokers	20.3%	18.5%	37

Cigarette smokers are defined as persons who reported having smoked at least 100 cigarettes during their lifetimes and who currently smoked at least occasionally.
Source: U.S. Centers for Disease Control and Prevention, *Morbidity and Mortality Weekly Report*, 53, no. 44 (November 12, 2004).

HOUSING

Home ownership rates, 1985-2004

	1985	1990	1995	2000	2004
State	71.0%	69.4%	72.0%	70.5%	73.7%
Total U.S.	63.9%	63.9%	64.7%	67.4%	69.0%
Rank among states	7	11	5	25	13

Net change in state home ownership rate, 1985-2004 . . . . +2.7%
Net change in U.S. home ownership rate, 1985-2004 . . . . +5.1%

Percentages represent the proportion of owner households to total occupied households.
Source: U.S. Census Bureau, 2006.

Home sales, 2000-2004
In thousands of units

Existing home sales	2000	2002	2003	2004
State sales	24.1	25.7	27.6	32.0
Total U.S. sales	5,171	5,631	6,183	6,784
State share of U.S. total	0.47%	0.46%	0.45%	0.47%
Sales rank among states	40	41	41	41

Units include single-family homes, condos, and co-ops.
Source: National Association of Realtors, Washington, D.C., *Real Estate Outlook: Market Trends & Insights*.

Values of owner-occupied homes, 2003

	State	U.S.
Total units	284,000	58,809,000
Value of units		
Under $100,000	35.4%	29.6%
$100,000-199,999	49.0%	36.9%
$200,000 or more	15.6%	33.5%
Median value	$118,174	$142,275
Rank among all states 32		

Units are owner-occupied one-family houses whose numbers are
rounded to nearest thousand. Data are extrapolated from
survey samples.
Source: U.S. Census Bureau, American Community Survey.

EDUCATION

Public school enrollment, 2002

Prekindergarten through grade 8
State enrollment 173,000
Total U.S. enrollment. 34,135,000
State share of U.S. total 0.51%

Grades 9 through 12
State enrollment. 75,000
Total U.S. enrollment. 14,067,000
State share of U.S. total 0.53%

Enrollment rates
State public school enrollment rate. 91.5%
Overall U.S. rate 90.4%
Rank among states in 2002. 16
Rank among states in 1995. 10

Enrollment figures (which include unclassified students) are
rounded to nearest thousand pupils during fall school term.
Enrollment rates are based on enumerated resident population
estimate for July 1, 2002.
Source: U.S. National Center for Education Statistics.

Public college finances, 2003-2004

FTE enrollment in public institutions of higher education
Students in state institutions 49,800
Students in all U.S. public institutions 9,916,600
State share of U.S. total 0.50
Rank among states 39

**State and local government appropriations for higher
  education**
State appropriation per FTE $6,050
National average. $5,716
Rank among states 16
State & local tax revenue going to higher
  education 10.1%

FTE = full-time equivalent in public postsecondary programs,
including summer sessions; student numbers are rounded to
nearest hundred. Funding figures for 2003-2004 academic year
include financial aid to students in state public institutions and
exclude money for research, agriculture experiment stations,
teaching hospitals, and medical schools; figures are rounded to
nearest thousand dollars.
Source: Higher Education Executive Officers, Denver, Colorado.

TRANSPORTATION AND TRAVEL

Highway mileage, 2003

Interstate highways	611
Arterial roads	3,841
Collector roads.	10,075
Local roads.	32,400
Urban roads	4,410
Rural roads	42,517
Total state mileage.	46,927
U.S. total	3,974,107
State share	1.18%
Rank among states	35

Note that combined urban and rural road mileage matches the
total of the other categories.
Source: U.S. Federal Highway Administration.

Motor vehicle registrations and driver licenses, 2003

Vehicle registrations	*State*	*U.S.*	*Share*	*Rank*
Autos, trucks, buses	1,301,000	231,390,000	0.56%	38
Autos only	554,000	135,670	0.41%	41
Motorcycles	44,000	5,328,000	0.83%	33
Driver licenses	921,000	196,166,000	0.47%	41

Figures, which do not include vehicles owned by military services,
are rounded to the nearest thousand. Figures for automobiles
include taxis.
Source: U.S. Federal Highway Administration.

Domestic travel expenditures, 2003

Spending by U.S. residents on overnight trips and
day trips of at least 50 miles from home

Total expenditures within state . . . . $2.21 bill.
Total expenditures within U.S. . . . . $490.87 bill.
State share of U.S. total 0.4%
Rank among states 40

Source: Travel Industry Association of America.

Retail gasoline prices, 2003-2007

Average price per gallon at the pump

Year	U.S.	State
2003	$1.267	$1.279
2004	$1.316	$1.368
2005	$1.644	$1.572
2007	$2.298	$2.320

Excise tax per gallon in 2004 . . . . 25.0¢
Rank among all states in 2007 prices 19

Prices are averages of all grades of gasoline sold at the pump
during March months in 2003-2005 and during February, 2007.
Averages for 2006, during which prices rose higher, are not
available.
Source: U.S. Energy Information Agency, *Petroleum Marketing
Monthly* (2003-2005 data); American Automobile Association
(2007 data).

CRIME AND LAW ENFORCEMENT

State and local police officers, 2000-2004

	2000	2002	2004
Total officers			
U.S.	654,601	665,555	675,734
State	2,326	2,358	2,444*
*Net change, 2000-2004			+5.07%
Officers per 1,000 residents			
U.S.	2.33	2.31	2.30
State	1.80	1.76	1.75
State rank	36	38	39

Totals include state and local police and sheriffs.
Source: Carsey Institute, University of New Hampshire.

Crime rates, 2003

Incidents per 100,000 residents

Crimes	State	U.S.
Violent crimes		
Total incidents	243	475
Murder	2	6
Forcible rape	37	32
Robbery	18	142
Aggravated assault	186	295
Property crimes		
Total incidents	2,909	3,588
Burglary	570	741
Larceny/theft	2,148	2,415
Motor vehicle theft	191	433
All crimes	3,152	4,063

Source: U.S. Federal Bureau of Investigation, *Crime in the United
States,* annual.

State prison populations, 1980-2003

	State	U.S.	State share
1980	817	305,458	0.27%
1990	1,961	708,393	0.28%
1996	3,832	1,025,624	0.37%
2000	5,535	1,391,261	0.40%
2003	5,887	1,470,045	0.40%

State figures exclude prisoners in federal penitentiaries.
Source: U.S. Bureau of Justice Statistics, *Prisoners in 2003.*

Illinois

Location: Midwest

Area and rank: 55,593 square miles (143,987 square kilometers); 57,918 square miles (150,008 square kilometers) including water; twenty-fourth largest state in area

Coastline: none

Population and rank: 12,714,000 (2004); fifth largest state in population

Capital city: Springfield (111,454 people in 2000 census)

Largest city: Chicago (2,896,016 people in 2000 census)

Illinois's chief city, Chicago is the third largest city in the United States. (PhotoDisc)

Became territory: February 3, 1809

Entered Union and rank: December 3, 1818; twenty-first state

Present constitution adopted: 1970

Counties: 102

State name: "Illinois" is an Algonquin word for "tribe of superior men"

ILLINOIS

State nickname: Prairie State

Motto: State sovereignty, national union

State flag: White field with state seal and name "Illinois" in blue

Highest point: Charles Mound—1,235 feet (376 meters)

Lowest point: Mississippi River—279 feet (85 meters)

Highest recorded temperature: 117 degrees Fahrenheit (47 degrees Celsius)—East St. Louis, 1954

Lowest recorded temperature: –35 degrees Fahrenheit (–37 degrees Celsius)—Mount Carroll, 1930

State song: "Illinois"

State tree: White oak

State flower: Purple violet

State bird: Cardinal

State fish: Bluegill

State animal: White-tailed deer

Illinois History

Situated between the major waterways of the Mississippi River and Lake Michigan, and possessing unusually rich soil for agricultural purposes, Illinois has been an important area of human activity since the earliest days of habitation. The historical development of the region has been sharply divided among the urban northeast area, dominated by Chicago; the central area, a mixture of urban and rural cultures; and the rural southern area, which resembles its southern neighbors, Missouri and Kentucky, more than it does the rest of the state.

Early History. The earliest humans to inhabit the area were hunters and gatherers who roamed the southern part of the region ten thousand years ago. Over the next several thousand years, cultures developed that built permanent villages and depended primarily on the growing of corn. By the year 1300, the Mississippian culture, a highly developed society based on the raising of corn, squash, and beans, dominated central North America. This society, the largest Native American culture north of Mexico, built large, fortified cities and extensive earth-mound monuments. The largest of these monuments were found at Cahokia, the culture's religious center, located in southwestern Illinois.

By the time Europeans arrived in the New World, a large number of Native American peoples, belonging to the Algonquin language group, inhabited the region. Among these were the Kickapoo, Sauk, and Fox in the north; the Potawatomi, Ottawa, and Ojibwa near Lake Michigan; the Illinois, a confederation of five peoples, in the central prairies; and the Cahokia and Tamaroa in the south. These societies relied on agriculture and buffalo hunting for survival. By the end of the first third of the nineteenth century, all these peoples had sold, ceded, or been forced off their native lands and had settled in other areas.

Exploration and Settlement. The first Europeans to visit the Illinois area were led by the French explorers Louis Jolliet and Jacques Marquette in 1673 as they traveled south from Wisconsin along the Mississippi River as far as Arkansas. This expedition also explored the Illinois River on its return journey north. In 1680, the French explorers René-Robert Cavelier, sieur de La Salle, and Henri de Tonti founded Fort Crevecoeur near the modern city of Peoria, followed two years later by Fort Saint Louis near the modern city of Ottawa. After a century of French settlement, the area became British territory at the end of the French and Indian War.

British policy was unfavorable to the economic de-

Springfield, Illinois, house in which Abraham Lincoln lived for seventeen years before becoming president of the United States. (Courtesy, State of Illinois Gallery)

velopment of the area, and settlements often lacked any form of government. Combined with violent encounters with Native Americans living in the area, these factors tended to discourage settlers. By 1773, the number of Europeans in Illinois had declined to about one thousand. The population also included a few hundred slaves.

During the American Revolution, American forces under George Rogers Clark captured British settlements at Kaskaskia and Cahokia in May of 1778, winning the region for the newly created United States. American control of the area was confirmed by the Treaty of Paris, which ended the war in 1783. At first a part of the state of Virginia, the region became part of the new Northwest Territory in 1787; part of the new Indiana Territory in 1800; a separate territory, including parts of modern Wisconsin and Minnesota, in 1809; and a state, with its modern borders, in 1818.

Conflict with Native Americans. Battles between European settlers and Native Americans began long before statehood. In 1730, French forces defeated Fox forces in east central Illinois. In 1803, the Kaskaskia ceded their lands to the United States. In 1812,

Potawatomi forces killed fifty-two Americans and destroyed Fort Dearborn, a military establishment on the site of modern Chicago. The Kickapoo left their native lands in 1819, followed by the Ojibwa, Ottawa, and Potawatomi in 1829. The Illinois sold their land in 1832.

One of the most violent encounters between settlers and American Indians was the Black Hawk War of 1832. Although some leaders of the Sauk and Fox had ceded their lands to the United States in 1804, others refused to leave. Black Hawk, a leader of these people, was driven into Iowa in 1831 but crossed back over the Mississippi River into Illinois the next year with about one thousand followers. Although at first Black Hawk was able to defeat the Illinois militia, lack of supplies forced him to retreat northward into Wisconsin, where most of his followers were killed. The destruction of Black Hawk's people, including women, children, and the elderly, was an important factor in the decision of nearly all Native Americans to leave the area by 1837.

Slavery and the Civil War. At the time of statehood, slaves in Illinois were given the status of indentured servants, due to the fear that permitting slavery would block admission to the Union. In 1824, voters rejected a proposal to hold a constitutional convention for the purpose of making slavery legal. Increasing numbers of settlers from free states during the 1830's and 1840's led to a new state constitution in 1848, which abolished slavery and made it illegal to bring slaves into Illinois.

During the Civil War, most residents of the state were loyal to the Union and to President Abraham Lincoln, who was himself from Illinois. An attempt was made to unite southern Illinois, which was less sympathetic to the Union cause, to the Confederacy, but it ended in failure. About 250,000 residents of Illinois fought for the Union, including Ulysses S. Grant, one of its most capable generals.

The Rise of Chicago. During the early nineteenth century, about two-thirds of the population of Illinois lived in the southern part of the state. Although Jean Baptist Point du Sable, known as the father of Chicago, founded a trading post at the site in 1779, it remained a small settlement for nearly half a century. The opening of the Erie Canal in 1825, linking the Hudson River to Lake Erie, made transportation from eastern states to northern Illinois much easier. In 1837, Chicago had a population of 4,200 and was incorporated as a city.

The opening of the Illinois and Michigan canal in 1848 linked Lake Michigan and the Illinois River, pro-viding Chicago with a waterway to the Mississippi River. By 1852 two railroad lines linked Chicago to eastern states. By 1856 it was the nation's most important railroad center.

The second half of the nineteenth century saw rapid economic growth in Chicago, with the city becoming dominant in iron and steel production, lumber distribution, slaughtering and meat packing, and marketing of produce. The Great Chicago Fire, lasting for two days in October, 1871, killed more than two hundred people, left ninety thousand homeless, and destroyed $200 million worth of property. Despite this disaster, Chicago continued to experience rapid growth. From 1850 to 1880 the population of the city grew from about thirty thousand to more than half a million.

The Twentieth Century. Although Illinois harbored a number of German and Irish immigrants during the 1840's, it was not until the turn of the century that large numbers of immigrants from other nations, including Poland, Hungary, Italy, Norway, Sweden, Austria, and Russia, arrived in the state. Chicago was the center of immigration, with more than three-fourths of its population in 1900 consisting of those born in other countries and their children.

The same period also saw a large increase in the number of African Americans in Illinois. From 1870 to

Contemporary magazine illustration of the Haymarket Riot. (Library of Congress)

One of the first truly major world fairs, Chicago's 1893 Columbian Exposition celebrated the quadrennial of Christopher Columbus's opening of the New World and attracted more than twenty million visitors. (Courtesy, Paul V. Galvan Library/Illinois Institute of Technology)

1910, the population of African Americans increased from 29,000 to more than 100,000. Prior to World War II, large numbers of European Jews immigrated to Illinois. In later years, increasing numbers of Asians and Latin Americans immigrated to the state.

The late nineteenth century and the early twentieth century brought Illinois a reputation for violence, particularly in Chicago, where the Haymarket Riot of 1886 resulted in numerous deaths in a confrontation between police and labor activists. Railroad worker strikes in Chicago in 1894 also led to violence. Elsewhere in the state, strikes by mine workers led to violence in 1898 and 1922. Race riots broke out in Springfield in 1908, in East St. Louis in 1917, and in Chicago in 1919. The 1920's saw an increase in violence against African Americans by the Ku Klux Klan. During the 1920's and 1930's, Chicago was a center of organized crime. Perhaps the most infamous event in the history of crime in Chicago occurred in 1929, when crime leader Al Capone had seven rivals killed in the Saint Valentine's Day Massacre.

Throughout the twentieth century, the Democratic and Republican parties struggled for control of Illinois.

This fact, combined with the state's large number of electoral votes, made Illinois a key target of presidential election campaigns. In general, the city of Chicago has been strongly Democratic, the suburbs and farmlands of the north and central regions strongly Republican, and the southern region mixed.

After the economic recession of the 1970's, the electronic and computer technology industries in Illinois became an important part of the state's economy during the 1980's. Illinois also became a leader in nuclear-power production during the 1990's, when it had thirteen operating nuclear-power plants, more than any other state. These plants supplied more than half of the state's electricity.

Politics. Illinois underwent several political changes at the end of the twentieth century. In the 2000 presidential elections, the state voted for Vice President Al Gore. The state also replaced congressional Democrats with two Republicans, one by a margin of 51 to 49 percent, the other by 53-47 percent. The U.S. Senate remained the same. Following the 2000 census, Illinois lost one seat in the U.S. House of Representatives.

Another notable political event in 2000 was President Bill Clinton's pardoning of former Representative Dan Rostenkowski, the once-powerful chairman of the House Ways and Means Committee. In 1996, Rostenkowski had been convicted of embezzlement and sent to prison for fifteen months.

In 2000, Governor George Ryan declared a moratorium on the application of the death penalty after he learned that following 1987 the state had removed more prison inmates than it had executed from death row as a result of wrongful conviction. A national study had shown that more than two-thirds of all death sentences were overturned on appeal because of procedural or other flaws.

By 2002, the political climate turned decidedly frosty for Governor Ryan, whose campaign committee and two of his former top aides were indicted with a variety of crimes, including racketeering. The indictment forced the governor to abandon a reelection bid. Instead, Democrat Rod Blagojevich resigned his seat in Congress, ran for governor, and won.

Two years later, in 2004, a newly vacated seat in the U.S. Senate was won by Democrat Barack Obama, a lecturer at the University of Chicago Law School. Obama, whose father was an immigrant from Kenya, handily beat Republican candidate Alan Keyes. At the same time, the state remained in the Democrats' column in presidential elections, as John Kerry, aided by a large margin in Cook County where Chicago is located, defeated President George W. Bush, 55-44 percent.

Rose Secrest
Updated by the Editor

Illinois Time Line

1673	Louis Jolliet and Jacques Marquette lead the first European expedition to the area.
1680	René-Robert Cavelier, sieur de La Salle, and Henri de Tonti found Fort Crevecoeur.
1682	La Salle and Tonti found Fort Saint Louis.
1730	Fox forces are defeated in a battle with French settlers.
1763	End of the French and Indian War brings the area under British control.
1778	George Rogers Clark leads American forces to victory over British forces in Kaskaskia and Cahokia.
1779	Jean Baptist Point du Sable founds a trading post at Chicago.
1783	End of the American Revolution brings the area under American control.
1787	Illinois becomes part of the Northwest Territory.
1803	Kaskaskia cede their land to the United States.
1803	Fort Dearborn is established at Chicago.
1809	Illinois Territory is established.
1811-1812	Earthquakes centered near New Madrid, Missouri, cause extensive damage in southern Illinois.
1812	Potawatomi forces destroy Fort Dearborn.
1814	First newspaper, the *Illinois Herald*, is established.
1816	Fort Dearborn is rebuilt.
1816	First bank in Illinois is established.
1818	Population is nearly thirty-five thousand.
Dec. 3, 1818	Illinois becomes the twenty-first state.
1819	Kickapoo leave their native lands.
1820	Capital is moved from Kaskaskia to Vandalia.
1824	Voters defeat a plan for a constitutional convention which would legalize slavery in the state.
1825	Opening of the Erie Canal brings more settlers to Chicago.
1827	Rock Spring Seminary, the first college, is established.
1829	Ojibwa, Ottawa, and Potawatomi cede their lands to the United States.
1832	Black Hawk War leads to the defeat of the Sauk and Fox.
1837	Chicago is incorporated as a city.
1839	Capital is moved to Springfield.
1848	New state constitution abolishes slavery.
1850	Population reaches 850,000; Chicago is home to 30,000.
1852	Railroads connect Chicago with eastern cities.
1867	University of Illinois is established.
1871	Great Chicago Fire devastates the city.

1880	Population of Chicago reaches 500,000.
1883	Ten-story Home Insurance Building, the world's first skyscraper, is built in Chicago.
1886	Haymarket Riot, a confrontation between police and labor activists, breaks out in Chicago.
1894	Strike by railroad workers leads to violence in Chicago.
1898	Strike by mine workers leads to violence in Pana and Virden.
1900	Population reaches nearly five million.
1908	Race riot breaks out in Springfield.
1917	Race riot breaks out in East St. Louis.
1919	Race riot breaks out in Chicago.
1922	Strike by mine workers leads to violence in Williamson County.
1929	Seven Chicago crime leaders are murdered in the Saint Valentine's Day Massacre.
1942	First controlled nuclear chain reaction is achieved at the University of Chicago.
1950	Population reaches nearly nine million.
1957	First nuclear power plant in the United States is established.
1968	Violence breaks out between police and protesters during the Democratic National Convention in Chicago.
1990	Population reaches 11.5 million.
1992	Carol Moseley-Braun of Chicago becomes the first African American woman elected to the United States Senate.
1993	Worst floods in the state's history do $1.5 billion worth of damage in western and southern Illinois.
1994	Members of the Republican Party hold all statewide offices and control both chambers of the state assembly.
1997	Population reaches nearly 12 million, with 85 percent living in urban areas, including 65 percent in the Chicago metropolitan area.
Jan. 31, 2000	Governor George Ryan declares a moratorium on the death penalty.
Nov. 7, 2000	Illinois votes its twenty-two electoral votes for Vice President Al Gore.
Dec., 2000	President Bill Clinton pardons former Illinois congressman Dan Rostenkowski, who had served prison time for embezzling funds.
2002	Indictment of Governor Ryan's campaign committee and two of his former top aides leads to his withdrawal from a reelection bid.
Nov. 2, 2004	Democrat Barack Obama defeats Alan Keyes for the vacant U.S. Senate seat.

Notes for Further Study

Published Sources. Two good places for the beginning student to start are Andrew Santella's *Illinois* (1998)—a simple but clear account of the state's history, geography, ecology, people, economy, cities, and attractions—and his *All Around Illinois: Regions and Resources* (2002). An extremely detailed discussion of the state's physical structure can be found in A. Doyne Horsley's *Illinois: A Geography* (1986), which includes extensive maps. The land and its inhabitants are described in *The Natural Resources of Illinois* (1987), compiled by R. Dan Neely and Carla G. Heister. Two of the best books dealing with the early history of the state are *Frontier Illinois* (1998) by James E. Davis and *French Roots in the Illinois Country: The Mississippi Frontier in Colonial Times* (1998) by Carl J. Ekberg. Two worthwhile books detail specific aspects of the slavery period in Illinois: *Democracy and Slavery in Frontier Illinois: The Bottomland Republic* (2000) by James Simeone and *Escape Betwixt Two Suns: A True Tale of the Underground Railroad in Illinois* (2000) by Carol Pirtle. For more detailed information on the state's history, the University of Illinois publishes numerous volumes dealing with all aspects of the state's past.

Of the many books dealing with Chicago, one of the best for the general reader is *Chicago Sketches: Urban Tales, Stories, and Legends from Chicago History* (1995) by June Skinner Sawyers, a collection of seventy-two colorful essays. A more serious book about the city is David Farber's *Chicago '68* (1988), a dramatic account of the riots that occurred during the Democratic National Convention in 1968. John C. Hudson's *Chicago: A Geography of the City and its Region* (2006) is a thorough book that brings forth a topical and chronological focus to the city's history. In *Chicago Dreaming: Midwesterners and the City, 1871-1919* (2005), Timothy B. Spears examines the influx of rural midwesterners into Chicago during a period of fifty years and how it shaped the young city's identity.

Web Resources. An excellent place to start one's research on the state of Illinois is its official government site (www.state .il.us). It provides information on governmental agencies, tourism, cities and counties, and state facts. For local information, Illinois Counties (www.outfitters.com/illinois/index2 .html) provides brief data on all the state's counties, while Living in Ilinois (illinoisgis.ito.state.il.us/communities/) offers users in-depth information about counties when one uses the drop-down menu, or about cities when one types in a city name. Tourist attractions in the state are discussed in the Illinois @ Travel Notes site (www.travelnotes.org/NorthAmerica/illinois.htm). The physical structure of the region is described in Geologic Information About Illinois (geology.er.usgs.gov/states/midwest.html) from the United States Geologic Survey.

One of the many Web sites devoted to Illinois history, with discussions of Chicago, Abraham Lincoln, Native Americans, early settlers, and the history of transportation, is the Illinois History Resource Page (www.historyillinois.org/hist.html).

An excellent time line can be found at Illinois Historic Preservation Agency (www.state.il.us/hpa/lib/ILChronology.htm). Illinois Alive (history.alliancelibrarysystem.com/illinoisalive/index.cfm) is a unique online history project which covers Illinois in its first century of statehood, 1818-1918. A detailed history of Chicago is found at Chicago Timeline from 1673 (www.chipublib.org/004chicago/chihist.html). The Encyclopedia of Chicago (www.encyclopedia.chicagohistory.org/) offers comprehensive information on the city, while the Chicago's History from the Kids' View (http://library.thinkquest.org/CR0215480/) is an entertaining site for young learners.

Counties

County	2000 pop.	Rank in pop.	Sq. miles	Rank in area	County	2000 pop.	Rank in pop.	Sq. miles	Rank in area
Adams	68,277	21	856.7	12	Jasper	10,117	88	494.4	55
Alexander	9,590	89	236.4	97	Jefferson	40,045	34	571.1	41
Bond	17,633	64	380.2	77	Jersey	21,668	57	369.2	82
Boone	41,786	32	281.4	93	Jo Daviess	22,289	55	601.2	35
Brown	6,950	95	305.7	91	Johnson	12,878	85	346.0	84
Bureau	35,503	42	868.6	8	Kane	404,119	5	520.7	50
Calhoun	5,084	100	253.8	94	Kankakee	103,833	18	677.5	27
Carroll	16,674	70	444.2	61	Kendall	54,544	26	320.7	89
Cass	13,695	82	376.0	79	Knox	55,836	25	716.3	22
Champaign	179,669	12	997.2	5	Lake	644,356	3	447.8	60
Christian	35,372	44	709.1	24	LaSalle	111,509	17	1,135.0	2
Clark	17,008	67	501.5	53	Lawrence	15,452	74	372.0	80
Clay	14,560	79	469.3	59	Lee	36,062	40	725.4	19
Clinton	35,535	41	474.3	58	Livingston	39,678	35	1,043.8	4
Coles	53,196	27	508.3	52	Logan	31,183	49	618.2	33
Cook	5,376,741	1	945.7	6	McDonough	32,913	47	589.3	36
Crawford	20,452	58	443.6	62	McHenry	260,077	7	604.1	34
Cumberland	11,253	87	346.0	85	McLean	150,433	13	1,183.6	1
DeKalb	88,969	19	634.2	30	Macon	114,706	16	580.6	38
DeWitt	16,798	69	397.6	73	Macoupin	49,019	30	863.7	11
Douglas	19,922	60	416.9	70	Madison	258,941	8	725.1	20
DuPage	904,161	2	334.4	87	Marion	41,691	33	572.3	40
Edgar	19,704	61	623.6	31	Marshall	13,180	83	386.1	75
Edwards	6,971	94	222.4	99	Mason	16,038	73	539.0	48
Effingham	34,264	45	478.7	57	Massac	15,161	76	239.1	96
Fayette	21,802	56	716.5	21	Menard	12,486	86	314.3	90
Ford	14,241	81	485.9	56	Mercer	16,957	68	561.1	45
Franklin	39,018	36	412.1	72	Monroe	27,619	51	388.3	74
Fulton	38,250	37	865.7	10	Montgomery	30,652	50	703.8	25
Gallatin	6,445	96	323.7	88	Morgan	36,616	39	568.8	42
Greene	14,761	78	543.1	46	Moultrie	14,287	80	335.6	86
Grundy	37,535	38	420.1	69	Ogle	51,032	28	758.9	17
Hamilton	8,621	90	435.2	66	Peoria	183,433	11	619.6	32
Hancock	20,121	59	794.7	16	Perry	23,094	53	441.0	63
Hardin	4,800	101	178.3	101	Piatt	16,365	71	440.0	64
Henderson	8,213	91	378.8	78	Pike	17,384	65	830.3	14
Henry	51,020	29	823.3	15	Pope	4,413	102	370.9	81
Iroquois	31,334	48	1,116.5	3	Pulaski	7,348	92	200.8	100
Jackson	59,612	24	588.1	37	Putnam	6,086	98	159.8	102

County	2000 pop.	Rank in pop.	Sq. miles	Rank in area	County	2000 pop.	Rank in pop.	Sq. miles	Rank in area
Randolph	33,893	46	578.4	39	Vermilion	83,919	20	899.1	7
Richland	16,149	72	360.2	83	Wabash	12,937	84	223.5	98
Rock Island	149,374	14	426.8	67	Warren	18,735	62	542.6	47
St. Clair	256,082	9	663.9	28	Washington	15,148	77	562.7	44
Saline	26,733	52	383.3	76	Wayne	17,151	66	713.9	23
Sangamon	188,951	10	868.3	9	White	15,371	75	494.9	54
Schuyler	7,189	93	437.4	65	Whiteside	60,653	23	684.8	26
Scott	5,537	99	251.0	95	Will	502,266	4	837.3	13
Shelby	22,893	54	758.6	18	Williamson	61,296	22	424.2	68
Stark	6,332	97	287.9	92	Winnebago	278,418	6	513.8	51
Stephenson	48,979	31	564.3	43	Woodford	35,469	43	528.0	49
Tazewell	128,485	15	648.9	29					
Union	18,293	63	416.2	71					

Source: U.S. Census Bureau; National Association of Counties.

Cities
With 10,000 or more residents

Rank	City	Population	Rank	City	Population
1	Chicago	2,896,016	56	Chicago Heights	32,776
2	Rockford	150,115	57	Glendale Heights	31,765
3	Aurora	142,990	58	East St. Louis	31,542
4	Naperville	128,358	59	Highland Park	31,365
5	Peoria	112,936	60	Granite City	31,301
6	Springfield (capital)	111,454	61	Mundelein	30,935
7	Joliet	106,221	62	Woodridge	30,934
8	Elgin	94,487	63	Carpentersville	30,586
9	Waukegan	87,901	64	Alton	30,496
10	Cicero	85,616	65	Niles	30,068
11	Decatur	81,860	66	Harvey	30,000
12	Arlington Heights	76,031	67	Gurnee	28,834
13	Schaumburg	75,386	68	Lansing	28,332
14	Evanston	74,239	69	Oak Forest	28,051
15	Champaign	67,518	70	Burbank	27,902
16	Palatine	65,479	71	St. Charles	27,896
17	Bloomington	64,808	72	Wilmette	27,651
18	Skokie	63,348	73	Kankakee	27,491
19	Des Plaines	58,720	74	Glen Ellyn	26,999
20	Bolingbrook	56,321	75	Maywood	26,987
21	Mount Prospect	56,265	76	Freeport	26,443
22	Wheaton	55,416	77	Round Lake Beach	25,859
23	Oak Lawn	55,245	78	Dolton	25,614
24	Berwyn	54,016	79	Elmwood Park	25,405
25	Oak Park	52,524	80	Collinsville	24,707
26	Orland Park	51,077	81	Rolling Meadows	24,604
27	Hoffman Estates	49,495	82	Westmont	24,554
28	Downers Grove	48,724	83	Batavia	23,866
29	Tinley Park	48,401	84	West Chicago	23,469
30	Normal	45,386	85	Blue Island	23,463
31	Moline	43,768	86	Park Forest	23,462
32	Buffalo Grove	42,909	87	Algonquin	23,276
33	Elmhurst	42,762	88	Melrose Park	23,171
34	Lombard	42,322	89	Lake in the Hills	23,152
35	Glenview	41,847	90	Roselle	23,115
36	Belleville	41,410	91	Zion	22,866
37	Carol Stream	40,438	92	Darien	22,860
38	Quincy	40,366	93	East Peoria	22,638
39	Rock Island	39,684	94	Morton Grove	22,451
40	Calumet City	39,071	95	South Holland	22,147
41	DeKalb	39,018	96	Villa Park	22,075
42	Hanover Park	38,278	97	O'Fallon	21,910
43	Crystal Lake	38,000	98	Bloomingdale	21,675
44	Park Ridge	37,775	99	McHenry	21,501
45	Bartlett	36,706	100	Edwardsville	21,491
46	Streamwood	36,407	101	Lisle	21,182
47	Urbana	36,395	102	Romeoville	21,153
48	North Chicago	35,918	103	Charleston	21,039
49	Addison	35,914	104	Evergreen Park	20,821
50	Elk Grove Village	34,727	105	Belvidere	20,820
51	Wheeling	34,496	106	Machesney Park	20,759
52	Danville	33,904	107	Libertyville	20,742
53	Pekin	33,857	108	Bensenville	20,703
54	Galesburg	33,706	109	Carbondale	20,681
55	Northbrook	33,435	110	Bellwood	20,535

Rank	City	Population	Rank	City	Population
111	East Moline	20,333	122	Macomb	18,558
112	Woodstock	20,151	123	Grayslake	18,506
113	Vernon Hills	20,120	124	Deerfield	18,420
114	Lake Forest	20,059	125	Ottawa	18,307
115	Loves Park	20,044	126	Mattoon	18,291
116	Alsip	19,725	127	Lake Zurich	18,104
117	Homewood	19,543	128	New Lenox	17,771
118	Geneva	19,515	129	Palos Hills	17,665
119	Franklin Park	19,434	130	Hinsdale	17,349
120	Brookfield	19,085	131	Goodings Grove	17,084
121	Jacksonville	18,940	132	Prospect Heights	17,081

(continued)

Rank	City	Population	Rank	City	Population
133	Westchester	16,824	171	Rantoul	12,857
134	Cahokia	16,391	172	Bradley	12,784
135	Godfrey	16,286	173	Markham	12,620
136	Mount Vernon	16,269	174	Lindenhurst	12,539
137	Country Club Hills	16,169	175	Richton Park	12,533
138	South Elgin	16,100	176	Western Springs	12,493
139	Marion	16,035	177	Winnetka	12,419
140	Dixon	15,941	178	Effingham	12,384
141	Forest Park	15,688	179	Lincolnwood	12,359
142	La Grange	15,608	180	Justice	12,193
143	Cary	15,531	181	Sycamore	12,020
144	Sterling	15,451	182	Morris	11,928
145	Lincoln	15,369	183	Northlake	11,878
146	Bridgeview	15,335	184	Pontiac	11,864
147	Canton	15,288	185	Schiller Park	11,850
148	Bourbonnais	15,256	186	River Forest	11,635
149	Morton	15,198	187	Taylorville	11,427
150	Lockport	15,191	188	Herrin	11,298
151	Riverdale	15,055	189	Wood River	11,296
152	Fairview Heights	15,034	190	Palos Heights	11,260
153	Hazel Crest	14,816	191	Crestwood	11,251
154	Mokena	14,583	192	Worth	11,047
155	Norridge	14,582	193	Washington	10,841
156	Midlothian	14,315	194	River Grove	10,668
157	Streator	14,190	195	Summit	10,637
158	Centralia	14,136	196	North Aurora	10,585
159	Chicago Ridge	14,127	197	Swansea	10,579
160	Hickory Hills	13,926	198	Glen Carbon	10,425
161	Wood Dale	13,535	199	Gages Lake	10,415
162	Warrenville	13,363	200	Sauk Village	10,411
163	Crest Hill	13,329	201	Burr Ridge	10,408
164	Oswego	13,326	202	Frankfort	10,391
165	La Grange Park	13,295	203	Lyons	10,255
166	Murphysboro	13,295	204	Barrington	10,168
167	Lemont	13,098	205	Beach Park	10,072
168	Plainfield	13,038			
169	Kewanee	12,944			
170	Matteson	12,928			

Population figures are from 2000 census.
Source: U.S. Bureau of the Census.

Index to Tables

DEMOGRAPHICS

Resident state and national populations, 1970-2004

Population figures given in thousands

	State pop.	U.S. pop.	Share	Rank
1970	11,110	203,302	5.5%	5
1980	11,427	226,546	5.0%	5
1985	11,400	237,924	4.8%	5
1990	11,431	248,765	4.6%	6
1995	12,008	262,761	4.5%	6
2000	12,420	281,425	4.4%	5
2004	12,714	293,655	4.3%	5

Source: U.S. Census Bureau, Current Population Reports, 2006.

Resident population by age, 2004

Age Group	Total persons
Under 5 years	891,000
5 to 17 years	2,348,000
18 to 24 years	1,260,000
25 to 34 years	1,798,000
35 to 44 years	1,905,000
45 to 54 years	1,782,000
55 to 64 years	1,210,000
65 to 74 years	761,000
75 to 84 years	540,000
85 years and older	219,000
All age groups	12,714,000

Portion of residents 65 and older	12.0%
National rank in portion of oldest residents	38
National average	12.4%

Population figures are rounded to nearest thousand persons;
figures include armed forces personnel stationed in the state.
Source: U.S. Bureau of the Census, 2006.

Resident population by race, Hispanic origin, 2004

Category	State pop.	Share	U.S.
All residents	12,714	100.00%	100.00%
Non-Hispanic white	8,414	66.18%	67.37%
Hispanic white	1,687	13.27%	13.01%
Other Hispanic	88	0.69%	1.06%
African American	1,926	15.15%	12.77%
Native American	39	0.31%	0.96%
Asian, Pacific Islander	513	4.03%	4.37%
Two or more categories	135	1.06%	1.51%

Population figures are in thousands. Persons counted as "Hispanic" (Latino) may be of any race. Because of overlapping categories, categories may not add up to 100%. Shares in column 3 are percentages of each category within the state; these figures may be compared to the national percentages in column 4.
Source: U.S. Bureau of the Census, 2006.

Projected state population, 2000-2030

Year	Population
2000	12,420,000
2005	12,699,000
2010	12,917,000
2015	13,097,000
2020	13,237,000
2025	13,341,000
2030	13,433,000
Population increase, 2000-2030	1,013,000
Percentage increase, 2000-2030	8.2

Projections are based on data from the 2000 census.
Source: U.S. Census Bureau.

VITAL STATISTICS

Infant mortality rates, 1980-2002

	1980	1990	2000	2002
All state residents	14.8	10.7	8.5	7.4
All U.S. residents	12.6	9.2	9.4	9.1
All state white residents	11.7	7.9	6.6	5.6
All U.S. white residents	10.6	7.6	5.7	5.8
All state black residents	26.3	22.4	17.1	16.3
All U.S. black residents	22.2	18.0	14.1	14.4

Figures represent deaths per 1,000 live births of resident infants under 1 year old, exclusive of fetal deaths. Figures for all residents include members of other racial categories not listed separately.
Source: U.S. Census Bureau, *Statistical Abstract of the United States,* 2006.

Abortion rates, 1990 and 2000

	1990	2000
Total abortions	68,000	64,000
Rate per 1,000 women	25.2	23.2
U.S. rate	25.7	21.3
Rank	13	10

Numbers of abortions are rounded to nearest thousand; ranks are based on rates.
Source: U.S. Census Bureau.

Marriages and divorces, 2004

Total marriages	77,800
Rate per 1,000 population	6.1
National rate per 1,000 population	7.4
Rank among all states	42
Total divorces	33,100
Rate per 1,000 population	2.6
National rate per 1,000 population	3.7
Rank among all states	42

Figures are for all marriages and divorces performed within the state, including those of nonresidents; totals are rounded to the nearest hundred. Ranks are for highest to lowest figures; note that divorce data are not available for five states.
Source: U.S. National Center for Health Statistics, *Vital Statistics of the United States,* 2006.

Death rates by leading causes, 2002
Deaths per 100,000 resident population

Cause	State	U.S.
Heart disease	244.6	241.7
Cancer	196.3	193.2
Cerebrovascular diseases	57.0	56.4
Accidents other than motor vehicle	33.5	37.0
Motor vehicle accidents	12.5	15.7
Chronic lower respiratory diseases	38.3	43.3
Diabetes mellitus	23.9	25.4
HIV	3.9	4.9
Suicide	9.1	11.0
Homicide	8.1	6.1
All causes	846.5	847.3
Rank in overall death rate among states		31

Figures exclude nonresidents who died in the state. Causes of death follow International Classification of Diseases. Rank is from highest to lowest death rate in the United States.
Source: U.S. National Center for Health Statistics, *National Vital Statistics Report,* 2006.

ECONOMY

Gross state product, 1990-2004
In current dollars

Year	State product	Nat'l product	State share
1990	$277.2 billion	$5.67 trillion	4.89%
2000	$464.3 billion	$9.75 trillion	4.76%
2002	$486.2 billion	$10.41 trillion	4.67%
2003	$499.7 billion	$10.92 trillion	4.57%
2004	$528.9 billion	$11.65 trillion	4.54%

Source: U.S. Bureau of Economic Analysis, *Survey of Current Business,* July, 2005.

Gross state product by industry, 2003
In billions of dollars

Construction	$20.3
Manufacturing	66.2
Wholesale trade	34.0
Retail trade	31.4
Finance & insurance	46.8
Information	20.5
Professional services	38.1
Health care & social assistance	28.6
Government	43.9
Total state product	$470.1
Total U.S. product	$10,289.2
State share of U.S. total	4.57%
Rank among all states	5

Total figures include industries not listed separately. Amounts are in chained 2000 dollars.
Source: U.S. Bureau of Economic Analysis, *Survey of Current Business,* July, 2005.

Personal income per capita, 1990-2004
In current dollars

	1990	2000	2004
Per capita income	$20,824	$32,185	$34,351
U.S. average	$19,477	$29,845	$32,937
Rank among states	10	9	14

Source: U.S. Bureau of Economic Analysis, *Survey of Current Business,* April, 2005.

Energy consumption, 2001
In trillions of British thermal units (BTU), except as noted

Total energy consumption

Total state energy consumption	3,870
Total U.S. energy consumption	96,275
State share of U.S. total	4.02%
Rank among states	7

Per capita consumption (In millions of BTU)

Total state per capita consumption	309
Total U.S. per capita consumption	338
Rank among states	35

End-use sectors

Residential	928
Commercial	829
Industrial	1,173
Transportation	939

Sources of energy

Petroleum	1,304
Natural gas	971
Coal	994
Hydroelectric power	2
Nuclear electric power	965

Figures for totals include categories not listed separately.
Source: U.S. Energy Information Administration, *State Energy Data Report,* 2001.

Nonfarm employment by sectors, 2004

Total	5,807,000
Construction	267,000
Manufacturing	697,000
Trade, transportation, utilities	1,179,000
Information	121,000
Finance, insurance, real estate	400,000
Professional & business services	796,000
Education & health services	728,000
Leisure, hospitality, arts, organizations	507,000
Other services, including repair & maintenance	259,000
Government	844,000

Figures are rounded to nearest thousand persons. "Total" includes mining and natural resources, not listed separately.
Source: U.S. Bureau of Labor Statistics, 2006.

Foreign exports, 1990-2004
In millions of dollars

Year	State	U.S.	State share
1990	12,965	394,045	3.29%
1996	24,176	624,767	3.87%
1997	26,455	688,896	3.84%
2000	31,438	712,055	4.02%
2003	26,473	724,006	3.92%
2004	30,214	769,332	3.93%

Rank among all states in 2004. 7

U.S. total does not include U.S. dependencies.
Source: U.S. Census Bureau, *U.S. Merchandise Trade,* series FT 900, 2000; U.S. Census Bureau, *U.S. International Trade in Goods and Services,* Series FT 900, 2005.

LAND USE

Federally owned land, 2003
Areas in acres

	State	U.S.	State share
Total area	35,795,000	2,271,343,000	1.58%
Nonfederal land	35,144,000	1,599,584,000	2.20%
Federal land	651,000	671,759,000	0.10%
Federal share	1.8%	29.6%	—

Areas are rounded to nearest thousand acres. Figures for federally owned land do not include trust properties.
Source: U.S. General Services Administration, *Federal Real Property Profile,* 2006.

Land use, 1997
In acres, rounded to nearest thousand

Total surface area	36,059,000
Total nonfederal rural land.	31,675,000
Percentage rural land	87.8%
Cropland.	24,011,000
Conservation Reserve Program (CRP*) land. . . .	726,000
Pastureland	2,502,000
Rangeland	(nil)
Forestland.	3,784,000
Other rural land	652,000

*CRP is a federal program begun in 1985 to assist private landowners to convert highly erodible cropland to vegetative cover for ten years. Note that some categories of land overlap.
Source: U.S. Department of Agriculture, Natural Resources and Conservation Service, and Iowa State University, Statistical Laboratory, *Summary Report, 1997 National Resources Inventory,* revised December, 2000.

Farms and crop acreage, 2004

	State	U.S.	Share	Rank
Farms	73,000	2,113,000	3.45%	11
Acres (millions)	28	937	2.99%	13
Acres per farm	377	443	—	18

Source: U.S. Department of Agriculture, National Agricultural Statistics Service. Numbers of farms are rounded to nearest thousand units; acreage figures are rounded to nearest million. Rankings, including ties, are based on rounded figures.

GOVERNMENT AND FINANCE

Units of local government, 2002

	State	Total U.S.	Rank
All local governments	6,903	87,525	1
Counties	102	3,034	6
Municipalities	1,291	19,429	1
Townships	1,431	16,504	3
School districts	934	13,506	3
Special districts	3,145	35,052	1

Only 48 states have county governments, 20 states have township governments ("towns" in New England, Minnesota, New York, and Wisconsin), and 46 states have school districts. Special districts encompass such functions as natural resources, fire protection, and housing and community development.
Source: U.S. Census Bureau, *Census of Governments.*

State government revenue, 2002

Total revenue . . . . $41,095 mill.
General revenue . . . . $40,340 mill.
Per capita revenue $3,205
U.S. per capita average $3,689
Rank among states 39

Intergovernment revenue
Total . . . . $11,435 mill.
From federal government . . . . $10,449 mill.

Charges and miscellaneous
Total . . . . $6,430 mill.
Current charges . . . . $2,669 mill.
Misc. general income . . . . $3,761 mill.
Insurance trust revenue . . . . $755 mill.

Taxes
Total . . . . $22,475 mill.
Per capita taxes $1,786
Rank among states 24
Property taxes . . . . $57 mill.
Sales taxes . . . . $11,256 mill.
License taxes . . . . $1,914 mill.
Individual income taxes . . . . $7,471 mill.
Corporate income taxes . . . . $1,384 mill.
Other taxes . . . . $393 mill.

Total revenue figures include items not listed separately here.
Source: U.S. Bureau of the Census.

State government expenditures, 2002

General expenditures

Total state expenditures	$49,131 mill.
Intergovernmental	$13,091 mill.

Per capita expenditures

State	$3,391
Average of all states	$3,859
Rank among states	39

Selected direct expenditures

Education	$6,128 mill.
Public welfare	$9,429 mill.
Health, hospital	$3,348 mill.
Highways	$2,983 mill.
Police protection	$359 mill.
Corrections	$1,300 mill.
Natural resources	$426 mill.
Parks and recreation	$288 mill.
Government administration	$1,284 mill.
Interest on debt	$1,847 mill.
Total direct expenditures	$29,587 mill.

Totals include items not listed separately.
Source: U.S. Census Bureau.

POLITICS

Governors since statehood

D = Democrat; R = Republican; O = other;
(r) resigned; (d) died in office; (i) removed from office

Shadrach Bond (O)	1818-1822
Edward Coles (O)	1822-1826
Ninian Edwards (O)	1826-1830
John Reynolds (O)	(r) 1830-1834
William L. D. Ewing (O)	1834
Joseph Duncan (O)	1834-1838
Thomas Carlin (D)	1838-1842
Thomas Ford (D)	1842-1846
Augustus C. French (D)	1846-1853
Joel A. Matteson (D)	1853-1857
William H. Bissell (R)	(d) 1857-1860
John Wood (R)	1860-1861
Richard Yates (R)	1861-1865
Richard J. Oglesby (R)	1865-1869
John M. Palmer (R)	1869-1873
Richard J. Oglesby (R)	(r) 1873
John L. Beveridge (R)	1873-1877
Shelby L. Cullom (R)	(r) 1877-1883
John M. Hamilton (R)	1883-1885
Richard J. Oglesby (R)	1885-1889
Joseph W. Fifer (R)	1889-1893
John P. Altgeld (D)	1893-1897
John R. Tanner (R)	1897-1901
Richard Yates, Jr. (R)	1901-1905
Charles S. Deneen (R)	1905-1913
Edward F. Dunne (D)	1913-1917

Frank O. Lowden (R)	1917-1921
Lennington Small (R)	1921-1929
Louis L. Emmerson (R)	1929-1933
Henry Horner (D)	(d) 1933-1940
John H. Stelle (D)	1940-1941
Dwight H. Green (R)	1941-1949
Adlai E. Stevenson II (D)	1949-1953
William G. Stratton (R)	1953-1961
Otto Kerner, Jr. (D)	(r) 1961-1968
Samuel H. Shapiro (D)	1968-1969
Richard B. Ogilvie (R)	1969-1973
Daniel Walker (D)	1973-1977
James R. Thompson (R)	1977-1991
Jim Edgar (R)	1991-1999
George H. Ryan (R)	1999-2003
Rod R. Blagojevich (D)	2003-

Composition of congressional delegations, 1989-2007

	Dem	Rep	Total
House of Representatives			
101st Congress, 1989			
State delegates	14	8	22
Total U.S.	259	174	433
102d Congress, 1991			
State delegates	15	7	22
Total U.S.	267	167	434
103d Congress, 1993			
State delegates	12	8	20
Total U.S.	258	176	434
104th Congress, 1995			
State delegates	10	10	20
Total U.S.	197	236	433
105th Congress, 1997			
State delegates	10	10	20
Total U.S.	206	228	434
106th Congress, 1999			
State delegates	10	10	20
Total U.S.	211	222	433
107th Congress, 2001			
State delegates	10	10	20
Total U.S.	211	221	432
108th Congress, 2003			
State delegates	9	10	19
Total U.S.	205	229	434
109th Congress, 2005			
State delegates	10	9	19
Total U.S.	202	231	433
110th Congress, 2007			
State delegates	10	9	19
Total U.S.	233	202	435

	Dem	Rep	Total
Senate			
101st Congress, 1989			
State delegates	2	0	2
Total U.S.	55	45	100
102d Congress, 1991			
State delegates	2	0	2
Total U.S.	56	44	100
103d Congress, 1993			
State delegates	2	0	2
Total U.S.	57	43	100
104th Congress, 1995			
State delegates	2	0	2
Total U.S.	46	53	99
105th Congress, 1997			
State delegates	2	0	2
Total U.S.	45	55	100
106th Congress, 1999			
State delegates	1	1	2
Total U.S.	45	54	99
107th Congress, 2001			
State delegates	1	1	2
Total U.S.	50	50	100
108th Congress, 2003			
State delegates	1	1	2
Total U.S.	48	51	99
109th Congress, 2005			
State delegates	2	0	2
Total U.S.	44	55	99
110th Congress, 2007			
State delegates	2	0	2
Total U.S.	49	49	98

Figures are for starts of first sessions. Totals are for Democrat (Dem.) and Republican (Rep.) members only. House membership totals under 435 and Senate totals under 100 reflect vacancies and seats held by independent party members. When the 110th Congress opened, the Senate's two independent members caucused with the Democrats, giving the Democrats control of the Senate.

Source: U.S. Congress, *Congressional Directory.*

Composition of state legislature, 1990-2006

	Democrats	Republicans
State House (118 seats)		
1990	72	46
1992	67	51
1994	54	64
1996	60	58
1998	62	56
2000	62	56
2002	66	52
2004	65	53
2006	66	52
State Senate (59 seats)		
1990	31	28
1992	27	32
1994	26	33
1996	28	31
1998	27	32
2000	27	32
2002	26	32
2004	31	27
2006	37	22

Figures for total seats may include independents and minor party members. Numbers reflect results of elections in listed years; elected members usually take their seats in the years that follow.

Source: Council of State Governments; *State Elective Officials and the Legislatures.*

Voter participation in presidential elections, 2000 and 2004

	2000	2004
Voting age population		
State	9,192,000	9,475,000
Total United States	209,831,000	220,377,000
State share of U.S. total	4.38	4.30
Rank among states	6	6
Portion of voting age population casting votes		
State	51.6%	55.7%
United States	50.3%	55.5%
Rank among states	26	31

Population figures are rounded to nearest thousand and include all residents, regardless of eligibility to vote.

Source: U.S. Census Bureau.

HEALTH AND MEDICAL CARE

Medical professionals
Physicians in 2003 and nurses in 2001

	U.S.	State
Physicians in 2003		
Total	774,849	34,461
Share of U.S. total		4.43%
Rate	266	272
Rank		12
Nurses in 2001		
Total	2,262,020	104,830
Share of U.S. total		4.63%
Rate	793	837
Rank		26

Rates are numbers of physicians and nurses per 100,000 resident population; ranks are based on rates.

Source: American Medical Association, *Physician Characteristics and Distribution in the U.S.*; U.S. Department of Health and Human Services, Health Resources and Services Administration.

Health insurance coverage, 2003

	State	U.S.
Total persons covered	10,810,000	243,320,000
Total persons not covered	1,818,000	44,961,000
Portion not covered	14.4%	15.6%
Rank among states	22	—
Children not covered	320,000	8,373,000
Portion not covered	10.0%	11.4%
Rank among states	22	—

Totals are rounded to nearest thousand. Ranks are from the highest to the lowest percentages of persons *not* insured.

Source: U.S. Census Bureau, Current Population Reports.

AIDS, syphilis, and tuberculosis cases, 2003

Disease	U.S. cases	State cases	Rank
AIDS	44,232	1,734	7
Syphilis	34,270	1,376	7
Tuberculosis	14,874	633	5

Source: U.S. Centers for Disease Control and Prevention.

Cigarette smoking, 2003
Residents over age 18 who smoke

	U.S.	State	Rank
All smokers	22.1%	24.3%	19
Male smokers	24.8%	28.3%	11
Female smokers	20.3%	20.5%	24

Cigarette smokers are defined as persons who reported having smoked at least 100 cigarettes during their lifetimes and who currently smoked at least occasionally.

Source: U.S. Centers for Disease Control and Prevention, *Morbidity and Mortality Weekly Report*, 53, no. 44 (November 12, 2004).

HOUSING

Home ownership rates, 1985-2004

	1985	1990	1995	2000	2004
State	60.6%	63.0%	66.4%	67.9%	72.7%
Total U.S.	63.9%	63.9%	64.7%	67.4%	69.0%
Rank among states	44	40	34	39	20

Net change in state home ownership rate,
1985-2004 . . . . +12.1
Net change in U.S. home ownership rate,
1985-2004 . . . . +5.1%

Percentages represent the proportion of owner households to total occupied households.

Source: U.S. Census Bureau, 2006.

Home sales, 2000-2004
In thousands of units

Existing home sales	2000	2002	2003	2004
State sales	246.8	269.0	275.1	307.5
Total U.S. sales	5,171	5,631	6,183	6,784
State share of U.S. total	4.77%	4.78%	4.45%	4.53%
Sales rank among states	5	5	5	4

Units include single-family homes, condos, and co-ops.

Source: National Association of Realtors, Washington, D.C., *Real Estate Outlook: Market Trends & Insights*.

Values of owner-occupied homes, 2003

	State	U.S.
Total units	2,563,000	58,809,000
Value of units		
Under $100,000	27.8%	29.6%
$100,000-199,999	35.5%	36.9%
$200,000 or more	36.8%	33.5%
Median value	$160,551	$142,275
Rank among all states		18

Units are owner-occupied one-family houses whose numbers are rounded to nearest thousand. Data are extrapolated from survey samples.
Source: U.S. Census Bureau, American Community Survey.

EDUCATION

Public school enrollment, 2002

Prekindergarten through grade 8
State enrollment 1,488,000
Total U.S. enrollment. 34,135,000
State share of U.S. total 4.36%

Grades 9 through 12
State enrollment 597,000
Total U.S. enrollment. 14,067,000
State share of U.S. total 4.24%

Enrollment rates
State public school enrollment rate. 88.5%
Overall U.S. rate 90.4%
Rank among states in 2002. 35
Rank among states in 1995. 44

Enrollment figures (which include unclassified students) are rounded to nearest thousand pupils during fall school term. Enrollment rates are based on enumerated resident population estimate for July 1, 2002.
Source: U.S. National Center for Education Statistics.

Public college finances, 2003-2004

FTE enrollment in public institutions of higher education
Students in state institutions. 378,100
Students in all U.S. public institutions 9,916,600
State share of U.S. total 3.81
Rank among states. 6

State and local government appropriations for higher education
State appropriation per FTE $6,777
National average. $5,716
Rank among states 10
State & local tax revenue going to higher education 8.1%

FTE = full-time equivalent in public postsecondary programs, including summer sessions; student numbers are rounded to nearest hundred. Funding figures for 2003-2004 academic year include financial aid to students in state public institutions and exclude money for research, agriculture experiment stations, teaching hospitals, and medical schools; figures are rounded to nearest thousand dollars.
Source: Higher Education Executive Officers, Denver, Colorado.

TRANSPORTATION AND TRAVEL

Highway mileage, 2003

Interstate highways	2,170
Other freeways and expressways	88
Arterial roads.	14,030
Collector roads.	21,701
Local roads	100,537
Urban roads	37,007
Rural roads	101,519
Total state mileage	138,526
U.S. total	3,974,107
State share	3.49%
Rank among states.	3

Note that combined urban and rural road mileage matches the total of the other categories.
Source: U.S. Federal Highway Administration.

Motor vehicle registrations and driver licenses, 2003

Vehicle registrations	State	U.S.	Share	Rank
Autos, trucks, buses	9,250,000	231,390,000	4.00%	7
Autos only	5,769,000	135,670	4.25%	7
Motorcycles	261,000	5,328,000	4.90%	5
Driver licenses	8,054,000	196,166,000	4.11%	6

Figures, which do not include vehicles owned by military services, are rounded to the nearest thousand. Figures for automobiles include taxis.
Source: U.S. Federal Highway Administration.

Domestic travel expenditures, 2003

Spending by U.S. residents on overnight trips and day trips of at least 50 miles from home

Total expenditures within state . . . . $21.60 bill.
Total expenditures within U.S. . . . . $490.87 bill.
State share of U.S. total 4.4%
Rank among states 5

Source: Travel Industry Association of America.

Retail gasoline prices, 2003-2007

Average price per gallon at the pump

Year	U.S.	State
2003	$1.267	$1.265
2004	$1.316	$1.313
2005	$1.644	$1.647
2007	$2.298	$2.357

Excise tax per gallon in 2004 . . . . 19.0¢
Rank among all states in 2007 prices 11

Prices are averages of all grades of gasoline sold at the pump during March months in 2003-2005 and during February, 2007. Averages for 2006, during which prices rose higher, are not available.
Source: U.S. Energy Information Agency, *Petroleum Marketing Monthly* (2003-2005 data); American Automobile Association (2007 data).

CRIME AND LAW ENFORCEMENT

State and local police officers, 2000-2004

	2000	2002	2004
Total officers			
U.S.	654,601	665,555	675,734
State	36,644	36,389	36,432*
*Net change, 2000-2004			−0.58%
Officers per 1,000 residents			
U.S.	2.33	2.31	2.30
State	2.95	2.89	2.87
State rank	4	4	4

Totals include state and local police and sheriffs.
Source: Carsey Institute, University of New Hampshire.

Crime rates, 2003

Incidents per 100,000 residents

Crimes	State	U.S.
Violent crimes		
Total incidents	557	475
Murder	7	6
Forcible rape	33	32
Robbery	188	142
Aggravated assault	329	295
Property crimes		
Total incidents	3,284	3,588
Burglary	619	741
Larceny/theft	2,336	2,415
Motor vehicle theft	330	433
All crimes	3,841	4,063

Source: U.S. Federal Bureau of Investigation, *Crime in the United States*, annual.

State prison populations, 1980-2003

	State	U.S.	State share
1980	11,899	305,458	3.90%
1990	27,516	708,393	3.88%
1996	38,852	1,025,624	3.79%
2000	45,281	1,391,261	3.25%
2003	43,418	1,470,045	2.95%

State figures exclude prisoners in federal penitentiaries.
Source: U.S. Bureau of Justice Statistics, *Prisoners in 2003*.

Indiana

Location: Midwest

Area and rank: 35,870 square miles (92,904 square kilometers); 36,420 square miles (94,328 square kilometers) including water; thirty-eighth largest state in area

Coastline: none

Population and rank: 6,238,000 (2004); fourteenth largest state in population

Capital and largest city: Indianapolis (781,870 people in 2000 census)

Became territory: May 7, 1800

Entered Union and rank: December 11, 1816; nineteenth state

Present constitution adopted: 1851

Counties: 92

State name: "Indiana" means "land of Indians"

Opening lap of the 2006 Indianapolis 500. An open-wheel automobile race, the "Indy 500" is one of the world's premier single-day sporting events and the biggest annual sporting event in Indiana. (AP/Wide World Photos)

State nickname: Hoosier State

Motto: The Crossroads of America

State flag: Blue field with gold torch surrounded by an outer circle of thirteen stars and an inner half circle of five stars

Highest point: Franklin Township—1,257 feet (383 meters)

Lowest point: Ohio River—320 feet (98 meters)

Highest recorded temperature: 116 degrees Fahrenheit (47 degrees Celsius)—Collegeville, 1936

Lowest recorded temperature: –35 degrees Fahrenheit (–37 degrees Celsius)—Greensburg, 1951

State song: "On the Banks of the Wabash"

State tree: Tulip tree

State flower: Peony

State bird: Cardinal

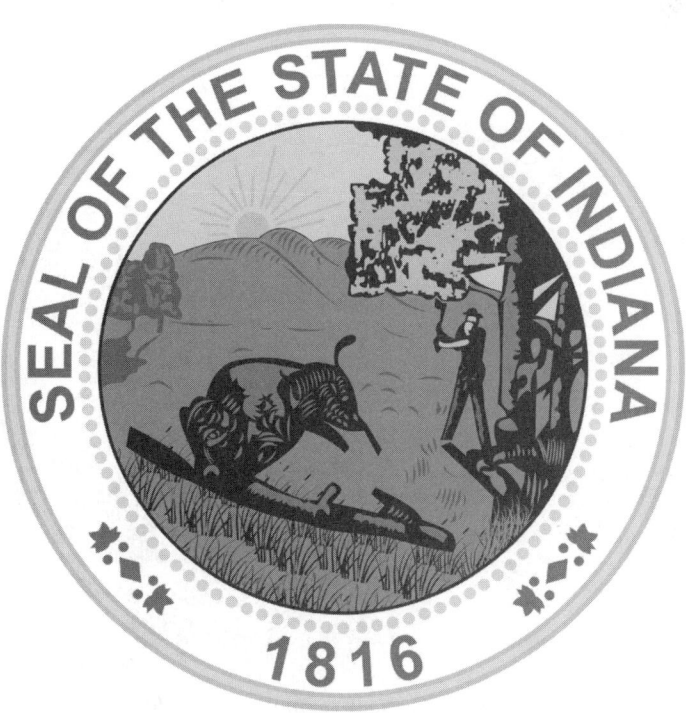

Indiana History

Indiana's central position between earlier settled regions to the east and south and more recently settled regions to the north and west has made it an important area of commerce and transportation since the early years of the United States. Urban areas of the state, particularly in the northwest corner, which is located near the giant city of Chicago, have developed a multiethnic culture in sharp contrast to the white, western European, Protestant culture which dominates the rest of the state.

Early History. Several thousand years ago, early hunting, gathering, and crop-growing societies inhabited areas near the Ohio River. The oldest artifacts from this period have been discovered at Angel Mounds, a large archaeological site near Evansville. By the time Europeans arrived in the New World, the northern and central regions of the area were inhabited by the Miami Confederation, a group of Native Americans belonging to the Algonquin language group. The Miami, who depended largely on the growing of corn and the hunting of buffalo for survival, were organized into a confederation in order to protect their lands from the Iroquois, a large group of various Native American peoples living to the east. During the nineteenth century, the Miami ceded most of their land to the United States. Most of the Miami moved to Oklahoma, but some remained in Indiana.

French and British Settlement. During the seventeenth century, the Iroquois, who were generally hostile to the French, agreed to treaties which allowed the French to trade with the Miami. In 1679, the French explorer René-Robert Cavelier, sieur de La Salle, led an expedition into the northern part of the region by traveling south from Michigan down the Saint Joseph River. At about the same time, traders from the British colonies along the Atlantic coast began to settle in the region along the Wabash River and the Ohio River.

In order to protect their access to the Wabash River, which led to the vital waterway of the Mississippi River, the French built a series of forts in the area. The first was Fort Miami, built in 1704, followed by Fort Ouiatanon, built in 1719, and Fort Vincennes, built in 1732. The effort to win the region for France ended in failure in 1763, when the Treaty of Paris, which ended the French and Indian War, brought the area under British control. Although the British officially banned any further European settlement of the area, this prohibition was largely ignored. The area became part of the British province of Quebec in 1774.

American Settlement. During the American Revolution, American forces led by George Rogers Clark brought the region under the control of the newly created United States in 1779 in a surprise attack on British forces in Vincennes. The Peace of Paris, which ended the war in 1783, officially made the area part of the new nation. The first American settlement in the region was established in 1784 in Clarkville, across the Ohio River from Louisville, Kentucky.

New Harmony community founded by the Wabash River in 1815. (Library of Congress)

The area was part of the Northwest Territory from 1787 to 1800, when the Indiana Territory, which included Michigan, Illinois, Wisconsin, and part of Minnesota, was created. The Michigan Territory was created in 1805, giving the region its modern northern border. In 1809, the Illinois Territory was created, giving the area its modern western border. Indiana became a state in 1816, with its first capital at Corydon.

Wars with Native Americans. Violent conflict with the Native Americans inhabiting the region began as soon as European settlers entered the area. The first phase of American Indian resistance ended in 1794 with the Battle of Fallen Timbers, near the border between Ohio and Indiana. About one thousand Americans led by Anthony Wayne defeated about two thousand Native Americans of the Northwest Indian Confederation, including members of the Miami, Potawatomi, Shawnee, Delaware, Ottawa, Ojibwa, and Iroquois, led by Shawnee chief Bluejacket. As a result of the battle, in 1795 Miami chief Little Turtle ceded much of his people's land to the United States in the Treaty of Fort Greenville.

The opening of this land to non-Indians led to a large increase in the number of settlers from southern states. As a result, Indiana became culturally more southern than other states in the area and was inhabited primarily by Protestants of English, Scottish, Irish, and German ancestry. This rapid increase in the rate of European settlement led to an increase in the number of violent encounters with Native Americans.

The second phase of Native American resistance ended on November 7, 1811, at the Battle of Tippecanoe, near the modern city of Lafayette. During the battle, American forces led by William Henry Harrison defeated Shawnee forces led by Tenskwatawa. Although the two sides suffered equal losses, the battle was generally considered a decisive American victory, and it helped Harrison, a war hero, become president in 1840. Between 1820 and 1840 most Native Americans left the state.

Indianapolis. Settlement in Indiana in the first half of the nineteenth century was centered in the southern part of the state. The economy was based primarily on agriculture and transportation of goods along the Ohio River and the Wabash River. Indianapolis, a planned city designed to resemble Washington, D.C., was founded in 1821 in the center of the state and became

the state capital in 1825. With the rise of railroads during the middle of the nineteenth century and the increase in motor-vehicle traffic in the twentieth century, Indianapolis became one of the largest cities in the world not located on a major waterway. It also went on to be served by more major highways than any other city in the United States.

Education and Industry. The first college in Indiana was founded in Vincennes in 1801. The first major institute of higher education, Indiana University, was founded in Bloomington in 1820. This university went on to become one of the most respected in the United States, with a particularly well-regarded university press. Indiana later became the home of other outstanding universities, with the founding of the University of Notre Dame, near South Bend, in 1842, and Purdue University, in West Lafayette, in 1869.

The Civil War, in which many Indianans fought for the Union, brought a rapid increase in the growth of industry in the state, particularly in the northern region. Natural resources that contributed to this growth included limestone, found in the southern part of the state, and coal, found in the southwest area. The southern half of the state was also the site of the world's largest natural gas field in 1880's, but this resource was depleted by 1898.

Steel production became one of the state's most important industries, particularly with the founding of Gary, located near Chicago, in 1906. At about the same time, automobile manufacturing began in South Bend and Indianapolis. Certain cities specialized in the manufacturing of particular products. Elkhart became known for producing musical instruments in 1875, while Fort Wayne produces a large part of the world's diamond tools. Overall, Indiana is one of the top ten manufacturing states in the nation. Manufacturing accounts for about 40 percent of the state's income. Environmental destruction to the state's unique sand dunes along Lake Michigan, an indirect result of industrial growth, was slowed by the creation of Indiana Dunes National Lakeshore in 1972.

The Twentieth Century. Although much of Indiana retains its character as an enclave of white, Anglo-Saxon, Protestant culture, the growth of the state's cities and the powerful influence of Chicago on the northwest region brought a mixture of ethnic groups to the area. World War I brought a steady flow of African Americans to the industrial centers of the state. By the late twentieth century, African Americans made up about 20 percent of the population of Indianapolis and about 70 percent of the population of Gary. Indianans of Polish ancestry constitute an important ethnic group in South Bend. Other ethnic groups in the state, particularly in northern cities, include Indianans whose ancestors arrived from Hungary, Belgium, and Italy. These groups give northern Indiana a higher percentage of Roman Catholics than the rest of the state, which is about two-thirds Protestant.

Politically, Indiana is generally conservative. The state spends less per capita on education, welfare, and health care than most other states. The amount of federal aid which the state receives per capita is one of the lowest in the nation. Change is slow to come to the state's political system, which still uses the state constitution of 1851. Although this constitution requires changes to be made in legislative districts based on population changes, this rule was disregarded from 1923 to 1963, giving the rural areas more political power than their dwindling population should have allowed. It was

Notre Dame University in South Bend, Indiana, is famous for its legendary football teams but is also one of the nation's top-ranked universities. (Derek Jensen)

not until 1970 that voters approved a proposal to have the state legislature meet annually rather than every two years.

Despite this conservatism, the Republican Party held only a slight advantage in the state after the Civil War. Indiana counties are about one-third Republican, one-third Democratic, and one-third variable. Almost as many liberals and Democrats have been elected from the state as conservatives and Republicans. Indiana state politics are sometimes surprisingly innovative, as when Indianapolis merged with Marion County in 1969 to form a unique type of city/county government.

Church and State. Indiana ended the twentieth century with a political controversy. On March 14, 2000, Governor Frank O'Bannon, a Democrat, signed a bill allowing schools and other government entities to display the Ten Commandments on state property, challenging the constitutional prohibition of an "establishment" of religion. The law made Indiana the first state to allow such an action. Two weeks later, however, after suit was filed by the Indiana American Civil Liberties Union, a federal judge barred placing a Ten Commandments monument on the State House lawn. The judge argued that the monument lacked a secular purpose and implied endorsement of religious belief, contradicting the U.S. Constitution. The following year a similar decision was made by the U.S. Supreme Court. The City of Elkhart placed a stone pillar on its lawn displaying the Ten Commandments. A lower court ruled that the display violated the U.S. Constitution's separation of church and state provision found in the First Amendment. While the city maintained that the pillar stated no religious preference, Justice John Paul Stevens, speaking for the Court, disagreed.

Republican Gains. Politically, Indiana leaned Republican in national politics, though not necessarily in state politics. In the 2000 presidential election, George W. Bush and his running mate Richard Cheney collected the state's twelve electoral votes by a 57-41 percent margin. Both of Indiana's newly elected members of Congress were Republicans. One exception to the Republican preponderance was Governor O'Bannon, a Democrat, who was reelected by the comfortable margin of 56 to 42 percent.

State capitol building in Indianapolis. (Jim West)

Following the 2000 census, Indiana lost a member of Congress to states with larger population increases. Also in 2000, Indiana's highly respected senior senator, Richard Lugar, was elected by landslide proportions (67 to 32 percent). The luster of Senator Lugar's public image was burnished by his nomination for a Nobel Peace Prize for his efforts to reduce Russia's dangerously exposed stockpile of nuclear weapons and materials.

In the 2002 and 2004 elections, Republican strength asserted itself. In 2002, a vacated seat in Congress was won by the Republican candidate, though not by a large margin (50-46 percent). In 2004, President Bush took the state by 55-45 percent; a Republican won over a Democrat in a newly created district; and the governorship went to a Republican, Mitch Daniels, by 53-45 percent over Democratic incumbent Joe Kernan, who had been the successor to Governor O'Bannon, who had died in office. The state legislature, previously Democratically controlled, became tied in party affiliation.

Weak Economy. During the early twenty-first century, Indiana's economy turned in a less than stellar performance, as the national economy declined especially after the September 11, 2001, terrorist attacks. A study found that welfare caseloads in 2001 rose in thirty-three states across the nation before and after the attacks; the largest increases came in Indiana and two other states. The economic recovery regarding unemployment in later years was weak in Indiana, partly because gross national product was lifted by increases in productivity, and new hiring was accordingly less prevalent.

Rose Secrest
Updated by the Editor

Indiana Time Line

Dec. 5, 1679	René-Robert Cavelier, sieur de La Salle, leads a French expedition down the Saint Joseph River from Michigan into Indiana.
1686	Trading post is established at the future site of Fort Wayne.
1704	Fort Miami is founded.
1719	Fort Ouiatanon is founded.
1732	Fort Vincennes is founded.
1763	Defeat of the French in the French and Indian War brings the region under British control.
1774	Indiana becomes part of the British province of Quebec.
Feb. 25, 1779	American forces led by George Rogers Clark defeat British forces at Vincennes.
1783	Defeat of the British in the American Revolution brings the region under American control.
1784	First American settlement in Indiana is founded at Clarkville.
1787	Indiana becomes part of the Northwest Territory.
1794	Battle of Fallen Timbers results in the defeat of a confederation of Native Americans.
1795	Miami people cede much of their land to the United States.
May 7, 1800	Indiana Territory is created.
1801	First college is founded at Vincennes.
1805	Michigan Territory is created from the northern part of the Indiana Territory.
1809	Illinois Territory is created from the western part of the Indiana Territory.
Nov. 7, 1811	Battle of Tippecanoe results in the defeat of the Shawnee.
1815	New Harmony, a utopian community, is founded on the Wabash River.
Dec. 11, 1816	Indiana becomes the nineteenth state.
1818	Bloomington is founded.
1820	Trading post is founded at the future site of South Bend.
1820	Indiana University is founded.
1821	Indianapolis is founded.
1825	Indianapolis becomes the state capital.
1832	Elkhart is founded.
1835	First railroad in the state, a horse-drawn single car, arrives in Shelbyville.
1840	William Henry Harrison, hero of the Battle of Tippecanoe, is elected president of the United States.
1842	University of Notre Dame is founded.
1851	State constitution is adopted.
1869	Purdue University is founded.
1880's	Indiana's "Gas Belt" contains the world's largest producing natural gas field.
1888	Indianapolis resident Benjamin Harrison, grandson of William Henry Harrison, is elected president.
1893	American Railway Union, the first industrial union in the United States, is founded in Terre Haute.
1894	Strike by the American Railway Union leads to violence and intervention by federal troops.
1898	Indiana's natural gas supplies are depleted.
1906	Gary is founded.
May 30, 1911	First Indianapolis 500 automobile race is held.
1912	Indiana native Thomas R. Marshall is elected vice president.

1923-1963	State legislature disregards the state constitution requirement that legislative districts be changed to reflect changes in population.
1969	Indianapolis merges with Marion County to form a single government.
1970	Voters approve a proposal to increase meetings of the state legislature from every two years to every year.
1970	Port of Indiana, an artificial harbor, is opened on Lake Michigan, linking the state to worldwide water traffic.
1972	University of Notre Dame begins accepting female students.
1972	Indiana Dunes National Lakeshore is created.
1975	Indiana and Michigan Electric Company begins generating nuclear power.
1988	Indiana native Dan Quayle is elected vice president.
Oct. 7, 1991	Rose-Hulman Institute of Terre Haute, an all-male school for 117 years, admits women.
Mar. 14, 2000	Governor Frank O'Bannon signs bill allowing schools and other government entities to display the Ten Commandments on state property.
Mar. 28, 2000	Federal court finds that placing a monument with the Ten Commandments on the lawn of the Indiana State House violates the Bill of Rights guarantee of a separation of church and state.
Nov. 7, 2000	Governor Frank O'Bannon reelected by a 56-42 percent margin.
May 29, 2001	U.S. Supreme Court lets stand a ruling that City of Elkhart's Ten Commandments display is unconstitutional.
Nov. 2, 2004	President George Bush wins the state by 55-45 percent and Mitch Daniels wins the governorship by a 53-45 percent margin.

Notes for Further Study

Published Sources. For those unfamiliar with basic facts about the history of Indiana, an excellent starting point is Howard Henry Peckham's *Indiana: A Bicentennial History* (1978), a clear, concise, colorful account of the state's past. For more advanced students, the Indiana Historical Bureau and the Indiana Historical Society, based in Indianapolis, have published several volumes in a series, which includes *Indiana to 1816: The Colonial Period* (1971) by John D. Barnhart and Dorothy L. Riker; *Indiana, 1816-1850: The Pioneer Era* (1998) by Donald F. Carmony; *Indiana in the Civil War Era, 1850-1880* (1965) by Emma Lou Thornburgh; *Indiana in Transition: The Emergence of an Industrial Commonwealth, 1880-1920* (1968) by Clifton J. Phillips; and *Indiana Through Transition and Change: A History of the Hoosier State and its People, 1920-1945* (1968) by James H. Madison.

A detailed and scholarly account of the early years of the state can be found in *Frontier Indiana* by Andrew R. L. Cayton (1996), one of many outstanding historical works published by Indiana University Press, located in Bloomington. *Destination Indiana: Travels Through Hoosier History* (2000) written by Ray E. Boomhower (photography by Darryl Jones) brings together carefully researched text with beautiful photographs of public historic sites throughout Indiana. Two books that focus more on niche history are *At Home in the Hoosier Hills: Agriculture, Politics, and Religion in Southern Indiana, 1810-1870* (2005) by Richard F. Nation and *Centennial Farms of Indiana* (2003), edited by M. Teresa Baer et al., which traces the history of Hoosier farmers, including Native Americans to modern-day agribusiness. *An Amish Patchwork: Indiana's Old Orders in the Modern World* (2005) by Thomas J. Meyers and Steven M. Nolt provides an overview of the beliefs and values of the Amish, their migration history, and the differences between the state's two major Amish ethnic groups (Pennsylvania Dutch and Swiss). The often overlooked story of African Americans in the state is found in a series of articles collected in *Indiana's African-American Heritage: Essays from Black History News and Notes* (1993), edited by Wilma L. Gibbs.

Web Resources. Several excellent Web sites, supplied by government agencies, private organizations, and individuals, are dedicated to the history of Indiana. A good place to start is the official Web site of the state government of Indiana (www.in.gov/). It offers basic information on the state, a list of famous Indianans and the accomplishments for which they are noted, a discussion of the structure of the state government, and links to historical Web sites, among many other features. Visit Indiana (www.visitindiana.net/) provides several links and articles for the visitor to the state.

A unique, detailed, and interactive time line is found at Indiana Local History Genealogy (home.att.net/~Local_History/IN_Timeline.htm). This site is particularly helpful for information on the prehistory of the state, pre-Columbian Native American archaeology, French settlement, and early statehood. Two historical organizations in the state maintain Web sites which are frequently updated. The Indiana Historical Bureau (www.statelib.lib.in.us/www/ihb/ihb.html) includes numerous historical documents and links to historical periodicals, while the Indiana Historical Society (www.indianahistory.org/) includes links to publications and a collection of essays on subjects ranging from biographies of noted Indianans to a history of the state's constitution.

Counties

County	2000 pop.	Rank in pop.	Sq. miles	Rank in area	County	2000 pop.	Rank in pop.	Sq. miles	Rank in area
Adams	33,625	47	339.4	71	Madison	133,358	10	452.2	19
Allen	331,849	3	657.3	1	Marion	860,454	1	396.4	48
Bartholomew	71,435	21	406.9	38	Marshall	45,128	32	444.3	24
Benton	9,421	88	406.3	40	Martin	10,369	87	336.2	73
Blackford	14,048	83	165.1	89	Miami	36,082	41	375.8	61
Boone	46,107	30	422.7	28	Monroe	120,563	11	394.4	50
Brown	14,957	81	312.3	76	Montgomery	37,629	40	504.6	10
Carroll	20,165	73	372.3	64	Morgan	66,689	24	406.5	39
Cass	40,930	35	412.9	32	Newton	14,566	82	401.9	44
Clark	96,472	17	375.2	62	Noble	46,275	28	411.1	34
Clay	26,556	60	357.6	70	Ohio	5,623	92	86.7	92
Clinton	33,866	46	405.1	41	Orange	19,306	74	399.6	45
Crawford	10,743	86	305.7	80	Owen	21,786	69	385.2	54
Daviess	29,820	54	430.7	26	Parke	17,241	78	444.8	23
Dearborn	46,109	29	305.2	81	Perry	18,899	75	381.4	58
Decatur	24,555	64	372.6	63	Pike	12,837	85	336.2	72
DeKalb	40,285	36	362.9	68	Porter	146,798	9	418.2	29
Delaware	118,769	12	393.3	51	Posey	27,061	59	408.5	35
Dubois	39,674	37	430.1	27	Pulaski	13,755	84	433.7	25
Elkhart	182,791	5	463.8	16	Putnam	36,019	42	480.3	15
Fayette	25,588	62	215.0	87	Randolph	27,401	57	452.9	18
Floyd	70,823	23	148.0	91	Ripley	26,523	61	446.4	22
Fountain	17,954	77	395.7	49	Rush	18,261	76	408.3	37
Franklin	22,151	67	386.0	53	St. Joseph	265,559	4	457.3	17
Fulton	20,511	71	368.5	66	Scott	22,960	66	190.4	88
Gibson	32,500	50	488.9	13	Shelby	43,445	33	412.7	33
Grant	73,403	20	414.0	30	Spencer	20,391	72	398.7	46
Greene	33,157	49	542.1	4	Starke	23,556	65	309.3	77
Hamilton	182,740	6	398.0	47	Steuben	33,214	48	308.7	78
Hancock	55,391	25	306.2	79	Sullivan	21,751	70	447.2	21
Harrison	34,325	45	485.3	14	Switzerland	9,065	89	221.2	86
Hendricks	104,093	16	408.4	36	Tippecanoe	148,955	8	499.8	11
Henry	48,508	27	393.0	52	Tipton	16,577	80	260.4	83
Howard	84,964	18	293.1	82	Union	7,349	91	161.6	90
Huntington	38,075	39	382.6	57	Vanderburgh	171,922	7	234.6	85
Jackson	41,335	34	509.3	8	Vermillion	16,788	79	256.9	84
Jasper	30,043	53	559.9	3	Vigo	105,848	15	403.3	43
Jay	21,806	68	383.7	56	Wabash	34,960	43	413.2	31
Jefferson	31,705	51	361.4	69	Warren	8,419	90	364.9	67
Jennings	27,554	56	377.3	60	Warrick	52,383	26	384.1	55
Johnson	115,209	13	320.2	75	Washington	27,223	58	514.5	7
Knox	39,256	38	515.9	6	Wayne	71,097	22	403.6	42
Kosciusko	74,057	19	537.5	5	Wells	27,600	55	370.0	65
La Porte	34,909	44	598.3	2	White	25,267	63	505.3	9
Lagrange	484,564	2	379.6	59	Whitley	30,707	52	335.5	74
Lake	110,106	14	497.0	12					
Lawrence	45,922	31	448.9	20					

Source: U.S. Census Bureau; National Association of Counties.

Cities
With 10,000 or more residents

Rank	City	Population	Rank	City	Population
1	Indianapolis (capital)	781,870	22	Portage	33,496
2	Fort Wayne	205,727	23	Michigan City	32,900
3	Evansville	121,582	24	East Chicago	32,414
4	South Bend	107,789	25	Marion	31,320
5	Gary	102,746	26	Merrillville	30,560
6	Hammond	83,048	27	Goshen	29,383
7	Bloomington	69,291	28	West Lafayette	28,778
8	Muncie	67,430	29	Noblesville	28,590
9	Anderson	59,734	30	Granger	28,284
10	Terre Haute	59,614	31	Valparaiso	27,428
11	Lafayette	56,397	32	Jeffersonville	27,362
12	Elkhart	51,874	33	Hobart	25,363
13	Mishawaka	46,557	34	Schererville	24,851
14	Kokomo	46,113	35	Highland	23,546
15	Richmond	39,124	36	La Porte	21,621
16	Columbus	39,059	37	Munster	21,511
17	Lawrence	38,915	38	Clarksville	21,400
18	Fishers	37,835	39	Crown Point	19,806
19	Carmel	37,733	40	Logansport	19,684
20	New Albany	37,603	41	Franklin	19,463
21	Greenwood	36,037	42	Vincennes	18,701

(continued)

Rank	City	Population
43	Plainfield	18,396
44	Seymour	18,101
45	Shelbyville	17,951
46	New Castle	17,780
47	Huntington	17,450
48	Griffith	17,334
49	Frankfort	16,662
50	Connersville	15,411
51	Crawfordsville	15,243
52	Beech Grove	14,880
53	Greenfield	14,600
54	Brownsburg	14,520
55	Lebanon	14,222
56	Lake Station	13,948
57	Dyer	13,895
58	Bedford	13,768

Rank	City	Population
59	Peru	12,994
60	Speedway	12,881
61	Warsaw	12,415
62	New Haven	12,406
63	Jasper	12,100
64	Auburn	12,074
65	Madison	12,004
66	Wabash	11,743
67	Martinsville	11,698
68	Washington	11,380
69	Chesterton	10,488
70	Greensburg	10,260

Population figures are from 2000 census.

Source: U.S. Bureau of the Census.

Index to Tables

DEMOGRAPHICS

Resident state and national populations, 1970-2004

Population figures given in thousands

	State pop.	U.S. pop.	Share	Rank
1970	5,195	203,302	2.6%	11
1980	5,490	226,546	2.4%	12
1985	5,459	237,924	2.3%	14
1990	5,544	248,765	2.2%	14
1995	5,851	262,761	2.2%	14
2000	6,081	281,425	2.2%	14
2004	6,238	293,655	2.1%	14

Source: U.S. Census Bureau, Current Population Reports, 2006.

Resident population by age, 2004

Age Group	Total persons
Under 5 years	431,000
5 to 17 years	1,170,000
18 to 24 years	632,000
25 to 34 years	826,000
35 to 44 years	907,000
45 to 54 years	886,000
55 to 64 years	614,000
65 to 74 years	388,000
75 to 84 years	279,000
85 years and older	105,000
All age groups	6,238,000

Portion of residents 65 and older	12.4%
National rank in portion of oldest residents	29
National average	12.4%

Population figures are rounded to nearest thousand persons;
  figures include armed forces personnel stationed in the state.
Source: U.S. Bureau of the Census, 2006.

Resident population by race, Hispanic origin, 2004

Category	State pop.	Share	U.S.
All residents	6,238	100.00%	100.00%
Non-Hispanic white	5,280	84.64%	67.37%
Hispanic white	250	4.01%	13.01%
Other Hispanic	19	0.30%	1.06%
African American	548	8.78%	12.77%
Native American	18	0.29%	0.96%
Asian, Pacific Islander	76	1.22%	4.37%
Two or more categories	66	1.06%	1.51%

Population figures are in thousands. Persons counted as "Hispanic" (Latino) may be of any race. Because of overlapping categories, categories may not add up to 100%. Shares in column 3 are percentages of each category within the state; these figures may be compared to the national percentages in column 4.
Source: U.S. Bureau of the Census, 2006.

Projected state population, 2000-2030

Year	Population
2000	6,081,000
2005	6,250,000
2010	6,392,000
2015	6,518,000
2020	6,627,000
2025	6,721,000
2030	6,810,000
Population increase, 2000-2030	729,000
Percentage increase, 2000-2030	12.0

Projections are based on data from the 2000 census.
Source: U.S. Census Bureau.

VITAL STATISTICS

Infant mortality rates, 1980-2002

	1980	1990	2000	2002
All state residents	11.9	9.6	7.8	7.7
All U.S. residents	12.6	9.2	9.4	9.1
All state white residents	10.5	7.9	6.9	6.8
All U.S. white residents	10.6	7.6	5.7	5.8
All state black residents	23.4	17.4	15.8	15.3
All U.S. black residents	22.2	18.0	14.1	14.4

Figures represent deaths per 1,000 live births of resident infants under 1 year old, exclusive of fetal deaths. Figures for all residents include members of other racial categories not listed separately.
Source: U.S. Census Bureau, *Statistical Abstract of the United States,* 2006.

Abortion rates, 1990 and 2000

	1990	2000
Total abortions	16,000	12,000
Rate per 1,000 women	12.0	9.4
U.S. rate	25.7	21.3
Rank	41	41

Numbers of abortions are rounded to nearest thousand; ranks are based on rates.
Source: U.S. Census Bureau.

Marriages and divorces, 2004

Total marriages	48,400
Rate per 1,000 population	7.8
National rate per 1,000 population	7.4
Rank among all states	17
Total divorces	n/a
National rate per 1,000 population	3.7
Rank among all states	n/a

Figures are for all marriages and divorces performed within the state, including those of nonresidents; totals are rounded to the nearest hundred. Ranks are for highest to lowest figures; note that no recent divorce data are available for Indiana.
Source: U.S. National Center for Health Statistics, *Vital Statistics of the United States,* 2006.

Death rates by leading causes, 2002
Deaths per 100,000 resident population

Cause	State	U.S.
Heart disease	248.8	241.7
Cancer	208.9	193.2
Cerebrovascular diseases	60.4	56.4
Accidents other than motor vehicle	34.9	37.0
Motor vehicle accidents	15.6	15.7
Chronic lower respiratory diseases	50.9	43.3
Diabetes mellitus	27.4	25.4
HIV	1.9	4.9
Suicide	12.1	11.0
Homicide	6.3	6.1
All causes	899.4	847.3
Rank in overall death rate among states		22

Figures exclude nonresidents who died in the state. Causes of death follow International Classification of Diseases. Rank is from highest to lowest death rate in the United States.
Source: U.S. National Center for Health Statistics, *National Vital Statistics Report,* 2006.

ECONOMY

Gross state product, 1990-2004
In current dollars

Year	State product	Nat'l product	State share
1990	$110.1 billion	$5.67 trillion	1.94%
2000	$194.7 billion	$9.75 trillion	2.00%
2002	$203.3 billion	$10.41 trillion	1.95%
2003	$213.3 billion	$10.92 trillion	1.95%
2004	$227.3 billion	$11.65 trillion	1.95%

Source: U.S. Bureau of Economic Analysis, *Survey of Current Business,* July, 2005.

Gross state product by industry, 2003
In billions of dollars

Construction	$8.5
Manufacturing	58.4
Wholesale trade	11.0
Retail trade	15.0
Finance & insurance	12.0
Information	4.9
Professional services	7.4
Health care & social assistance	13.4
Government	18.6
Total state product	$201.3
Total U.S. product	$10,289.2
State share of U.S. total	1.96%
Rank among all states	15

Total figures include industries not listed separately. Amounts are in chained 2000 dollars.
Source: U.S. Bureau of Economic Analysis, *Survey of Current Business,* July, 2005.

Personal income per capita, 1990-2004
In current dollars

	1990	2000	2004
Per capita income	$17,491	$27,132	$30,094
U.S. average	$19,477	$29,845	$32,937
Rank among states	30	31	33

Source: U.S. Bureau of Economic Analysis, *Survey of Current Business,* April, 2005.

Energy consumption, 2001
In trillions of British thermal units (BTU), except as noted

Total energy consumption

Total state energy consumption	2,802
Total U.S. energy consumption	96,275
State share of U.S. total	2.91%
Rank among states	11

Per capita consumption (In millions of BTU)

Total state per capita consumption	457
Total U.S. per capita consumption	338
Rank among states	7

End-use sectors

Residential	504
Commercial	397
Industrial	1,296
Transportation	604

Sources of energy

Petroleum	837
Natural gas	514
Coal	1,567
Hydroelectric power	6
Nuclear electric power	0

Figures for totals include categories not listed separately.
Source: U.S. Energy Information Administration, *State Energy Data Report,* 2001.

Nonfarm employment by sectors, 2004

Total	2,930,000
Construction	148,000
Manufacturing	572,000
Trade, transportation, utilities	576,000
Information	41,000
Finance, insurance, real estate	140,000
Professional & business services	266,000
Education & health services	369,000
Leisure, hospitality, arts, organizations	275,000
Other services, including repair & maintenance	109,000
Government	426,000

Figures are rounded to nearest thousand persons. "Total" includes mining and natural resources, not listed separately.
Source: U.S. Bureau of Labor Statistics, 2006.

Foreign exports, 1990-2004
In millions of dollars

Year	State	U.S.	State share
1990	5,273	394,045	1.34%
1996	10,984	624,767	1.76%
1997	12,029	688,896	1.75%
2000	15,386	712,055	1.97%
2003	16,402	724,006	2.43%
2004	19,109	769,332	2.48%

Rank among all states in 2004 13

U.S. total does not include U.S. dependencies.
Source: U.S. Census Bureau, *U.S. Merchandise Trade*, series FT 900, 2000; U.S. Census Bureau, *U.S. International Trade in Goods and Services*, Series FT 900, 2005.

LAND USE

Federally owned land, 2003
Areas in acres

	State	U.S.	State share
Total area	23,158,000	2,271,343,000	1.02%
Nonfederal land	22,624,000	1,599,584,000	1.41%
Federal land	534,000	671,759,000	0.08%
Federal share	2.3%	29.6%	—

Areas are rounded to nearest thousand acres. Figures for federally owned land do not include trust properties.
Source: U.S. General Services Administration, *Federal Real Property Profile*, 2006.

Land use, 1997
In acres, rounded to nearest thousand

Total surface area 23,158,000
Total nonfederal rural land. 20,069,000
Percentage rural land 86.7%
Cropland. 13,407,000
Conservation Reserve Program (CRP*) land 378,000
Pastureland 1,830,000
Rangeland . . . . (nil)
Forestland. 3,781,000
Other rural land 674,000

*CRP is a federal program begun in 1985 to assist private landowners to convert highly erodible cropland to vegetative cover for ten years. Note that some categories of land overlap.
Source: U.S. Department of Agriculture, Natural Resources and Conservation Service, and Iowa State University, Statistical Laboratory, *Summary Report, 1997 National Resources Inventory*, revised December, 2000.

Farms and crop acreage, 2004

	State	U.S.	Share	Rank
Farms	59,000	2,113,000	2.79%	13
Acres (millions)	15	937	1.60%	19
Acres per farm	253	443	—	26

Source: U.S. Department of Agriculture, National Agricultural Statistics Service. Numbers of farms are rounded to nearest thousand units; acreage figures are rounded to nearest million. Rankings, including ties, are based on rounded figures.

GOVERNMENT AND FINANCE

Units of local government, 2002

	State	Total U.S.	Rank
All local governments	3,085	87,525	10
Counties	91	3,034	12
Municipalities	567	19,429	12
Townships	1,008	16,504	9
School districts	294	13,506	19
Special districts	1,125	35,052	11

Only 48 states have county governments, 20 states have township governments ("towns" in New England, Minnesota, New York, and Wisconsin), and 46 states have school districts. Special districts encompass such functions as natural resources, fire protection, and housing and community development.
Source: U.S. Census Bureau, *Census of Governments.*

State government revenue, 2002

Total revenue . . . . $20,116 mill.
General revenue . . . . $20,011 mill.
Per capita revenue $3,249
U.S. per capita average $3,689
Rank among states 36

Intergovernment revenue
Total . . . . $6,028 mill.
From federal government . . . . $5,886 mill.

Charges and miscellaneous
Total . . . . $3,782 mill.
Current charges . . . . $2,287 mill.
Misc. general income . . . . $1,495 mill.
Insurance trust revenue . . . . $106 mill.

Taxes
Total . . . . $10,201 mill.
Per capita taxes $1,657
Rank among states 35
Property taxes . . . . $6 mill.
Sales taxes . . . . $5,425 mill.
License taxes . . . . $377 mill.
Individual income taxes . . . . $3,541 mill.
Corporate income taxes . . . . $709 mill.
Other taxes . . . . $143 mill.

Total revenue figures include items not listed separately here.
Source: U.S. Bureau of the Census.

State government expenditures, 2002

General expenditures

Total state expenditures . . . . $22,205 mill.
Intergovernmental. . . . . $6,557 mill.

Per capita expenditures

State $3,343
Average of all states $3,859
Rank among states 41

Selected direct expenditures

Education. $4,146 mill.
Public welfare . . . . $4,805 mill.
Health, hospital . . . . $749 mill.
Highways . . . . $1,255 mill.
Police protection. . . . . $194 mill.
Corrections. . . . . $615 mill.
Natural resources . . . . $281 mill.
Parks and recreation . . . . $43 mill.
Government administration. . . . . $763 mill.
Interest on debt . . . . $397 mill.
Total direct expenditures. . . . . $14,028 mill.

Totals include items not listed separately.
Source: U.S. Census Bureau.

POLITICS

Governors since statehood

D = Democrat; R = Republican; O = other;
(r) resigned; (d) died in office; (i) removed from office

Jonathan Jennings (O) . . . . (r) 1816-1822
Ratliff Boon (O) 1822
William Hendricks (O) . . . . (r) 1822-1825
James B. Ray (O). 1825-1831
Noah Noble (O) 1831-1837
David Wallace (O) 1837-1840
Samuel Rigger (O). 1840-1843
James Whitcomb (D) . . . . (r) 1843-1848
Paris C. Dunning (D) 1848-1849
Joseph A. Wright (D) 1849-1857
Ashbel P. Willard (D) . . . . (d) 1857-1860
Abram A. Hammond (D) 1860-1861
Henry S. Lane (R). . . . . (r) 1861
Oliver H. P. T. Morton (R) . . . . (r) 1861-1865
Conrad Baker (R) 1865-1873
Thomas A. Hendricks (D). 1873-1877
James D. Williams (D). . . . . (d) 1877-1880
Isaac P. Gray (D) 1880-1881
Albert G. Porter (R) 1881-1885
Isaac P. Gray (D) 1885-1889
Alvin P. Hovey (R) . . . . (d) 1889-1891
Ira J. Chase (R). 1891-1893
Claude Matthews (D) 1893-1897
James A. Mount (R) 1897-1901
Winfield T. Durbin (R) 1901-1905
James Franklin Hanly (R) 1905-1909

Thomas R. Marshall (D). 1909-1913
Samuel M. Ralston (D) 1913-1917
James P. Goodrich (R). 1917-1921
Warren T. McCray (R) . . . . (i) 1921-1924
Emmett F. Branch (R) 1924-1925
Edward F. Jackson (R) 1925-1929
Harry G. Leslie (R) 1929-1933
Paul V. McNutt (D) 1933-1937
Maurice Clifford Townsend (D) 1937-1941
Henry F. Schricker (D) 1941-1945
Ralph F. Gates (R) 1945-1949
Henry F. Schricker (D) 1949-1953
George N. Craig (R). 1953-1957
Harold W. Handley (R) 1957-1961
Matthew E. Welsh (D) 1961-1965
Roger D. Branigan (D) 1965-1969
Edgar D. Whitcomb (R) 1969-1973
Otis R. Bowen (R) 1973-1981
Robert D. Orr (R) 1981-1989
Evan Bayh (D) 1989-1997
Frank O'Bannon (D) . . . . (d) 1997-2003
Joe Kernan (D) 2003-2005
Mitch Daniels (R) 2005-

Composition of congressional delegations, 1989-2007

	Dem	Rep	Total
House of Representatives			
101st Congress, 1989			
State delegates	6	3	9
Total U.S.	259	174	433
102d Congress, 1991			
State delegates	8	2	10
Total U.S.	267	167	434
103d Congress, 1993			
State delegates	7	3	10
Total U.S.	258	176	434
104th Congress, 1995			
State delegates	4	6	10
Total U.S.	197	236	433
105th Congress, 1997			
State delegates	4	6	10
Total U.S.	206	228	434
106th Congress, 1999			
State delegates	4	6	10
Total U.S.	211	222	433
107th Congress, 2001			
State delegates	4	6	10
Total U.S.	211	221	432
108th Congress, 2003			
State delegates	3	6	9
Total U.S.	205	229	434

(continued)

	Dem	Rep	Total
109th Congress, 2005			
State delegates	2	7	9
Total U.S.	202	231	433
110th Congress, 2007			
State delegates	5	4	9
Total U.S.	233	202	435
Senate			
101st Congress, 1989			
State delegates	0	2	2
Total U.S.	55	45	100
102d Congress, 1991			
State delegates	0	2	2
Total U.S.	56	44	100
103d Congress, 1993			
State delegates	0	2	2
Total U.S.	57	43	100
104th Congress, 1995			
State delegates	0	2	2
Total U.S.	46	53	99
105th Congress, 1997			
State delegates	0	2	2
Total U.S.	45	55	100
106th Congress, 1999			
State delegates	1	1	2
Total U.S.	45	54	99
107th Congress, 2001			
State delegates	1	1	2
Total U.S.	50	50	100
108th Congress, 2003			
State delegates	1	1	2
Total U.S.	48	51	99
109th Congress, 2005			
State delegates	1	1	2
Total U.S.	44	55	99
110th Congress, 2007			
State delegates	1	1	2
Total U.S.	49	49	98

Figures are for starts of first sessions. Totals are for Democrat (Dem.) and Republican (Rep.) members only. House membership totals under 435 and Senate totals under 100 reflect vacancies and seats held by independent party members. When the 110th Congress opened, the Senate's two independent members caucused with the Democrats, giving the Democrats control of the Senate.

Source: U.S. Congress, *Congressional Directory.*

Composition of state legislature, 1990-2006

	Democrats	Republicans
State House (100 seats)		
1990	52	48
1992	55	45
1994	44	56
1996	50	50
1998	53	47
2000	53	47
2002	51	49
2004	48	52
2006	51	49
State Senate (50 seats)		
1990	24	26
1992	22	28
1994	20	30
1996	19	31
1998	19	31
2000	19	31
2002	18	32
2004	17	33
2006	17	33

Figures for total seats may include independents and minor party members. Numbers reflect results of elections in listed years; elected members usually take their seats in the years that follow.

Source: Council of State Governments; *State Elective Officials and the Legislatures.*

Voter participation in presidential elections, 2000 and 2004

	2000	2004
Voting age population		
State	4,515,000	4,637,000
Total United States	209,831,000	220,377,000
State share of U.S. total	2.15	2.10
Rank among states	14	15
Portion of voting age population casting votes		
State	48.7%	53.2%
United States	50.3%	55.5%
Rank among states	34	38

Population figures are rounded to nearest thousand and include all residents, regardless of eligibility to vote.

Source: U.S. Census Bureau.

HEALTH AND MEDICAL CARE

Medical professionals
Physicians in 2003 and nurses in 2001

	U.S.	State
Physicians in 2003		
Total	774,849	13,346
Share of U.S. total		1.71%
Rate	266	215
Rank		38
Nurses in 2001		
Total	2,262,020	49,590
Share of U.S. total		2.19%
Rate	793	809
Rank		29

Rates are numbers of physicians and nurses per 100,000 resident population; ranks are based on rates.

Source: American Medical Association, *Physician Characteristics and Distribution in the U.S.*; U.S. Department of Health and Human Services, Health Resources and Services Administration.

Health insurance coverage, 2003

	State	U.S.
Total persons covered	5,296,000	243,320,000
Total persons not covered	853,000	44,961,000
Portion not covered	13.9%	15.6%
Rank among states	27	—
Children not covered	143,000	8,373,000
Portion not covered	9.0%	11.4%
Rank among states	24	—

Totals are rounded to nearest thousand. Ranks are from the highest to the lowest percentages of persons *not* insured.

Source: U.S. Census Bureau, Current Population Reports.

AIDS, syphilis, and tuberculosis cases, 2003

Disease	U.S. cases	State cases	Rank
AIDS	44,232	506	22
Syphilis	34,270	375	21
Tuberculosis	14,874	143	23

Source: U.S. Centers for Disease Control and Prevention.

Cigarette smoking, 2003
Residents over age 18 who smoke

	U.S.	State	Rank
All smokers	22.1%	26.1%	7
Male smokers	24.8%	28.6%	8
Female smokers	20.3%	23.8%	8

Cigarette smokers are defined as persons who reported having smoked at least 100 cigarettes during their lifetimes and who currently smoked at least occasionally.

Source: U.S. Centers for Disease Control and Prevention, *Morbidity and Mortality Weekly Report*, 53, no. 44 (November 12, 2004).

HOUSING

Home ownership rates, 1985-2004

	1985	1990	1995	2000	2004
State	67.6%	67.0%	71.0%	74.9%	75.8%
Total U.S.	63.9%	63.9%	64.7%	67.4%	69.0%
Rank among states	27	29	13	8	7

Net change in state home ownership rate,
1985-2004 . . . . +8.2%
Net change in U.S. home ownership rate,
1985-2004 . . . . +5.1%

Percentages represent the proportion of owner households to total occupied households.

Source: U.S. Census Bureau, 2006.

Home sales, 2000-2004
In thousands of units

Existing home sales	2000	2002	2003	2004
State sales	111.0	125.2	120.4	130.5
Total U.S. sales	5,171	5,631	6,183	6,784
State share of U.S. total	2.15%	2.22%	1.95%	1.92%
Sales rank among states	16	14	19	20

Units include single-family homes, condos, and co-ops.

Source: National Association of Realtors, Washington, D.C., *Real Estate Outlook: Market Trends & Insights*.

Values of owner-occupied homes, 2003

	State	U.S.
Total units	1,419,000	58,809,000
Value of units		
Under $100,000	45.5%	29.6%
$100,000-199,999	43.1%	36.9%
$200,000 or more	11.4%	33.5%
Median value	$106,840	$142,275
Rank among all states 37		

Units are owner-occupied one-family houses whose numbers are rounded to nearest thousand. Data are extrapolated from survey samples.
Source: U.S. Census Bureau, American Community Survey.

EDUCATION

Public school enrollment, 2002

Prekindergarten through grade 8
State enrollment 714,000
Total U.S. enrollment. 34,135,000
State share of U.S. total 2.09%

Grades 9 through 12
State enrollment 290,000
Total U.S. enrollment. 14,067,000
State share of U.S. total 2.06%

Enrollment rates
State public school enrollment rate. 85.9%
Overall U.S. rate 90.4%
Rank among states in 2002. 45
Rank among states in 1995. 33

Enrollment figures (which include unclassified students) are rounded to nearest thousand pupils during fall school term. Enrollment rates are based on enumerated resident population estimate for July 1, 2002.
Source: U.S. National Center for Education Statistics.

Public college finances, 2003-2004

FTE enrollment in public institutions of higher education
Students in state institutions 218,400
Students in all U.S. public institutions 9,916,600
State share of U.S. total 2.20
Rank among states 13

State and local government appropriations for higher education
State appropriation per FTE $5,103
National average. $5,716
Rank among states 32
State & local tax revenue going to higher
education 7.8%

FTE = full-time equivalent in public postsecondary programs, including summer sessions; student numbers are rounded to nearest hundred. Funding figures for 2003-2004 academic year include financial aid to students in state public institutions and exclude money for research, agriculture experiment stations, teaching hospitals, and medical schools; figures are rounded to nearest thousand dollars.
Source: Higher Education Executive Officers, Denver, Colorado.

TRANSPORTATION AND TRAVEL

Highway mileage, 2003

Interstate highways 1,169	
Other freeways and expressways 136	
Arterial roads 7,963	
Collector roads. 22,663	
Local roads. 62,666	
Urban roads 20,600	
Rural roads. 73,997	
Total state mileage. 94,597	
U.S. total 3,974,107	
State share 2.38%	
Rank among states 18	

Note that combined urban and rural road mileage matches the total of the other categories.
Source: U.S. Federal Highway Administration.

Motor vehicle registrations and driver licenses, 2003

Vehicle registrations	*State*	*U.S.*	*Share*	*Rank*
Autos, trucks, buses	5,739,000	231,390,000	2.48%	13
Autos only	3,252,000	135,670	2.40%	14
Motorcycles	144,000	5,328,000	2.70%	12
Driver licenses	4,536,000	196,166,000	2.31%	14

Figures, which do not include vehicles owned by military services, are rounded to the nearest thousand. Figures for automobiles include taxis.
Source: U.S. Federal Highway Administration.

Domestic travel expenditures, 2003

Spending by U.S. residents on overnight trips and
day trips of at least 50 miles from home

Total expenditures within state . . . . $6.69 bill.
Total expenditures within U.S. . . . . $490.87 bill.
State share of U.S. total 1.4%
Rank among states 27

Source: Travel Industry Association of America.

Retail gasoline prices, 2003-2007

Average price per gallon at the pump

Year	U.S.	State
2003	$1.267	$1.238
2004	$1.316	$1.273
2005	$1.644	$1.633
2007	$2.298	$2.353

Excise tax per gallon in 2004 . . . . 18.0¢
Rank among all states in 2007 prices 13

Prices are averages of all grades of gasoline sold at the pump
during March months in 2003-2005 and during February, 2007.
Averages for 2006, during which prices rose higher, are not
available.

Source: U.S. Energy Information Agency, *Petroleum Marketing
Monthly* (2003-2005 data); American Automobile Association
(2007 data).

CRIME AND LAW ENFORCEMENT

State and local police officers, 2000-2004

	2000	2002	2004
Total officers			
U.S.	654,601	665,555	675,734
State	10,163	10,742	10,769*
*Net change, 2000-2004			+5.96%
Officers per 1,000 residents			
U.S.	2.33	2.31	2.30
State	1.67	1.74	1.73
State rank	43	39	42

Totals include state and local police and sheriffs.
Source: Carsey Institute, University of New Hampshire.

Crime rates, 2003

Incidents per 100,000 residents

Crimes	State	U.S.
Violent crimes		
Total incidents	353	475
Murder	6	6
Forcible rape	28	32
Robbery	103	142
Aggravated assault	216	295
Property crimes		
Total incidents	3,358	3,588
Burglary	671	741
Larceny/theft	2,351	2,415
Motor vehicle theft	335	433
All crimes	3,711	4,063

Source: U.S. Federal Bureau of Investigation, *Crime in the United
States,* annual.

State prison populations, 1980-2003

	State	U.S.	State share
1980	6,683	305,458	2.19%
1990	12,736	708,393	1.80%
1996	16,960	1,025,624	1.65%
2000	20,125	1,391,261	1.45%
2003	23,069	1,470,045	1.57%

State figures exclude prisoners in federal penitentiaries.
Source: U.S. Bureau of Justice Statistics, *Prisoners in 2003.*

Iowa

Location: Midwest

Area and rank: 55,875 square miles (144,716 square kilometers); 56,276 square miles (145,755 square kilometers) including water; twenty-third largest state in area

Coastline: none

Population and rank: 2,954,000 (2004); thirtieth largest state in population

Capital and largest city: Des Moines (198,682 people in 2000 census)

Became territory: June 12, 1838

Entered Union and rank: December 28, 1846; twenty-ninth state

Present constitution adopted: 1857

Counties: 99

Iowa's state capitol building in Des Moines has the largest dome of any state capitol. (Greater Des Moines Convention and Visitors Bureau)

State name: "Iowa" probably derives from an Indian word meaning either "this is the place" or "the beautiful land"

State nickname: Hawkeye State

Motto: Our liberties we prize and our rights we will maintain

State flag: Red, white, and blue stripes with a detail from the state seal and the name "Iowa"

Highest point: Geographical survey section 29, T100N, R41W—1,670 feet (509 meters)

Lowest point: Mississippi River—480 feet (146 meters)

Highest recorded temperature: 118 degrees Fahrenheit (48 degrees Celsius)—Keokuk, 1934

Lowest recorded temperature: –47 degrees Fahrenheit (–44 degrees Celsius)—Washta, 1912

State songs: "Song of Iowa"; "Iowa State Fight Song"; "The Bells of Iowa State"

State flower: Wild prairie rose

State bird: Eastern goldfinch

Iowa History

Defined by the Mississippi River on the east and the Missouri River on the west, Iowa is a rolling stretch of lush, green prairie with rich, black soil and ample rainfall for growing crops. The fertility of the earth and the lack of trees make for excellent farmland, and as a result, Iowa has been and remains a state focused on agriculture.

Early History. The Paleo-Indians, nomadic hunters and gatherers, lived in the Iowa region more than ten thousand years ago. They were followed by other nomadic tribes and the mound builders. The Ioway, who controlled most of Iowa in the seventeenth century, left their name to the state and to one of its rivers but gave up all claim to land in the state in 1838, settling in Kansas and Nebraska. About seventeen different tribes are believed to have lived in what became Iowa.

In 1673, Father Jacques Marquette and mapmaker-explorer Louis Jolliet entered the Mississippi River from the Wisconsin River and gazed on Iowa, the "land across the river." They went ashore on June 25, finding members of the Illini tribe, who probably actually lived on the east side of the Mississippi. In 1682, France claimed all the lands along the Mississippi River, and in 1803, in the Louisiana Purchase, the United States bought the land from France. The following year, Meriwether Lewis and William Clark traveled up the Missouri River searching for a waterway that would take them to the Pacific Ocean.

In 1812, Iowa became part of the Territory of Missouri. Eight years later, Missouri became a state, and in 1834, the Territory of Michigan was expanded to include Iowa. In 1838, the Territory of Iowa was created.

The Native Americans. The U.S. government pushed the Sauk and the Mesquaki (Fox) tribes out of western Illinois and into Iowa, where the Sioux already lived. In 1832, Chief Black Hawk, a respected Sauk leader, sought to reclaim his tribe's land on the Illinois side of the Mississippi River. For three months, in what is known as the Black Hawk War, the Illinois militia pursued Black Hawk, chasing him to the mouth of the Bad Axe River in Wisconsin, where he gave up. In a treaty signed on September 21, 1832, the Mesquaki and Sauk were required to relinquish a strip of land along the Mississippi River and vacate the land by June 1, 1833. Large numbers of white settlers began to move into Iowa, pushing the tribes farther west or into Missouri. In 1842, the Sauk and Mesquaki signed a treaty agreeing to leave Iowa by May, 1845. By 1851 the Sioux had also been forced to give up all land in Iowa. In 1856, a few Mesquaki negotiated with the governor of Iowa to buy back a portion of their former land in modern-day Tama County, eventually buying back about 3,200 acres.

White Settlement and Statehood. In 1838, 23,000 people settled on land in the newly established Terri-

Usher's Ferry Historic Village, a re-creation of a turn-of-the-twentieth-century Iowa farming town in Cedar Rapids. (Paul Rehn)

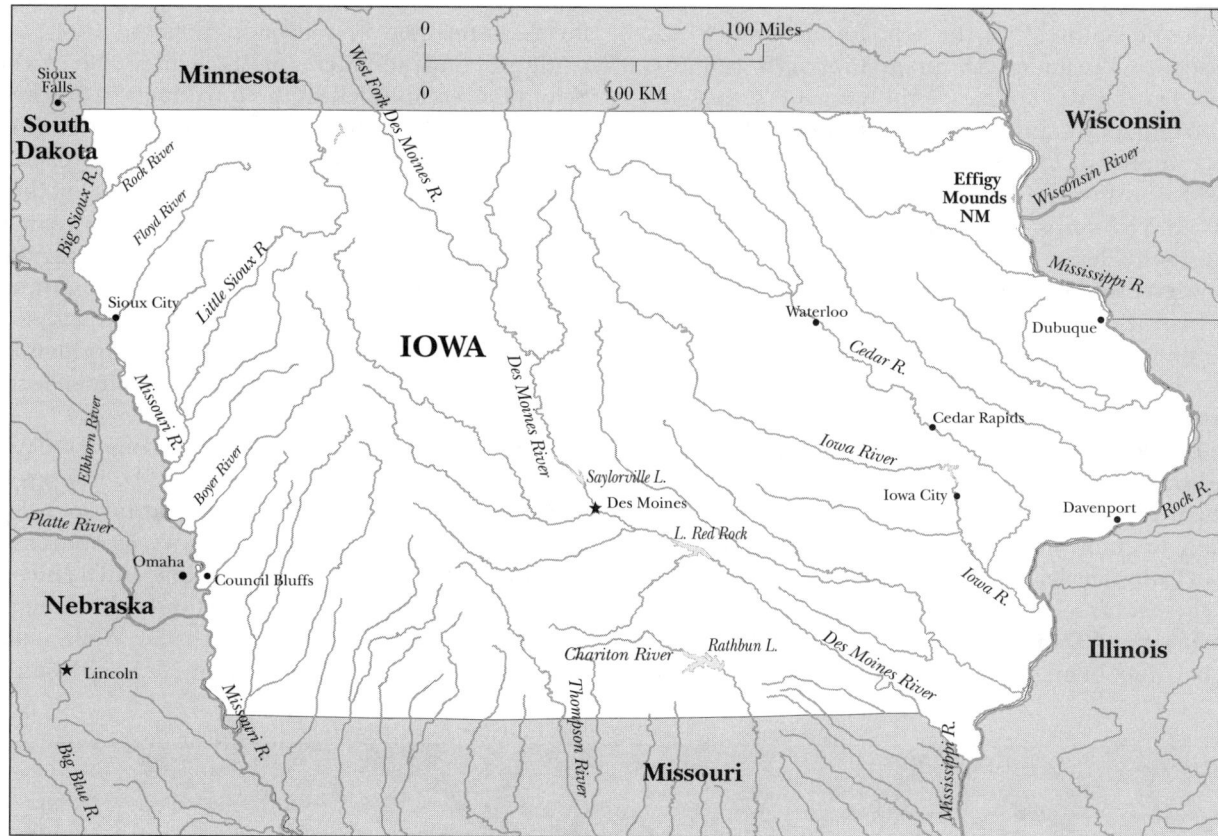

tory of Iowa, buying the land for $1.25 an acre. The first settlers were primarily of northern European ancestry. Many were families who had lived in eastern states such as New York, Pennsylvania, or Ohio, and many were originally from Germany. The 1840 census showed Iowa to have a population of 43,000, exclusive of American Indians. By 1846 the population of Iowa had reached 96,088. Iowa became the twenty-ninth state of the Union in 1846.

Industry, Education, and Religion. During the early 1850's, railroad companies sprung up in Iowa. The Chicago, Iowa, and Nebraska line became the first railroad to cross the state, in 1867. Soon tracks crisscrossed Iowa, providing year-round transportation to markets and giving birth to new industries such as an oat-processing plant that would come to be known as Quaker Oats.

Early settlers soon established township elementary schools, but high schools were not common until after 1900. State officials created the University of Iowa in 1855 to provide traditional and professional education, Iowa State College of Science and Technology (later Iowa State University) in 1858 for agricultural and technical training, and Iowa State Teachers' College (later University of Northern Iowa) in 1876 for teacher training. Many religious groups, including Congregationalists, Roman Catholics, and Methodists, which had come

to the state beginning during the 1830's, founded private colleges.

Although major religious denominations usually set up churches across the state, smaller religious groups tended to settle in specific areas. The Quakers settled in West Branch and Springdale, the Reorganized Church of the Latter-day Saints (a Mormon offshoot) in Lamoni, and the Mennonites in Johnson and Washington Counties. From 1855 to 1865, a group of German Pietists established the seven cities of Amana in Iowa County. The residents of the Amana colonies practiced communal living for about eighty years. The Amana name lives on in refrigerators, air-conditioners, and microwaves, although the colonies sold the business in 1937.

The Civil War. The biggest change the Civil War brought in Iowa was to create a one-party state. At the beginning of Iowa's statehood, the state was largely Democratic, although it contained some Whigs. However, many Iowans opposed slavery, and Iowa would later become an important station in the Underground Railroad. The identification of the Democratic Party with a proslavery stance, among other issues, caused many Iowans to turn to the new Republican Party. By the mid-1850's, the state was solidly Republican and would stay that way through the first half of the twentieth century.

After the outbreak of the war, Iowans quickly responded to President Abraham Lincoln's call for troops. During the course of the war, the state sent 70,000 soldiers, of whom 13,001 died and 8,500 were seriously wounded. Iowans fought at Wilson's Creek to keep Missouri in the Union, accompanied Ulysses S. Grant to Vicksburg, and participated in Sherman's March to the Sea.

Immigration. The population of Iowa grew from 674,913 in 1860 to 1,194,020 in 1870. The state encouraged immigration from northern Europe and attracted many Germans, Swedes, Norwegians, Danes, and Hollanders, as well as people from the British Isles. Many of these immigrant groups created rural neighborhoods with distinct ethnic identities and churches. The coal mines in central and southern Iowa, which promised immediate employment and required few skills, drew people from Italy and Wales and large numbers of former slaves, who formed camps near the mines.

Farming and Economic Growth. By the 1870's, Iowa had become blanketed by small towns and family farms, connected by railroads. Farmers were raising cattle and hogs and increasingly corn instead of wheat. Scientific research led to the introduction during the early twentieth century of soybeans, which eventually became second only to corn in terms of acreage and value. During World War I, farmers prospered, but after the war ended and farm subsidies were eliminated, farmers began to experience difficulties in paying off the money they had borrowed during boom times. A group of farmers formed the Farm Holiday Association, which attempted to withhold farm products from the market in order to force prices up, but the association's efforts had little impact.

Native Iowan Henry A. Wallace became secretary of agriculture under President Franklin D. Roosevelt in 1933. He believed that farmers would prosper if production was restricted and farmers were compensated for withholding land from production, and he incorporated these ideas into the Agricultural Adjustment Act of 1933, part of the New Deal. In 1926, Wallace and a partner founded what became Pioneer Seed Company,

Iowa's location along the Mississippi River has enhanced the value of its farm produce by providing easy access to relatively inexpensive bulk cargo carriage on the river. (PhotoDisc)

the first commercial company to produce hybrid seed corn, which led to increased yields and a more uniform plant that made mechanization of the harvest much easier. By 1944 nearly all corn planted in Iowa came from hybrid seed.

Farmers prospered when World War II and the Korean War boosted corn prices and again during the 1970's, when land prices rose and many farmers borrowed money to expand their operations. During the 1980's, however, land prices crashed, and many farmers lost their farms, initiating a trend away from family farms and toward farming corporations. In 1985, the Iowa legislature introduced legislation designed to help troubled farmers deal with creditors and keep their farms. During the 1990's, the family farm was challenged on another front as large-scale hog-producing corporations moved into the state, driving down hog prices and forcing small hog producers out of business.

Corn is an agricultural product with which Iowa has almost become synonymous. (PhotoDisc)

Although agriculture dominates Iowa's economy, the state has also supported business and manufacturing operations, some of which are farm-related. Major concerns include farm-implement producer John Deere, the washing machine and appliance company Maytag, Winnebago motorhomes, the Sheaffer pen company, and Iowa Beef Processors. In 1991, Iowa legalized riverboat gambling, creating a somewhat controversial source of revenue.

Middle America. Iowa is largely rural, an assemblage of small towns and family farms. In 1994, the state's population reached 2.8 million, and the population of its largest city, Des Moines, was 193,422. During the 1970's, 1980's, and to a lesser extent during the 1990's, the state became the focus of national attention early in each presidential election year during the Iowa caucuses. These early tests of presidential strength provided boosts to some candidates, including Jimmy Carter in 1976 and George H. W. Bush in 1980. Although the state is not a microcosm of the nation, its reputation as Middle America—a stable place where family values dominate—lends weight to its preferences. As more and more farm corporations are formed and the number of family farms decreases, the nature of Iowa, its character and makeup, which reflect this rural dominance, may undergo a transformation.

2000 Elections. The state of Iowa perennially gained national attention in the run-up to presidential elections through the institution of "Iowa caucuses," informal gatherings of Democratic and Republican state political party members, who cast votes on their choices for president. Because the caucuses are held early in election years, they have become a kind of barometer of political strength, attracting national candidates in profusion.

Thus, the results of the 2000 caucuses on January 24 were of some significance. Vice President Al Gore won the caucus over former senator Bill Bradley by a large margin, 63 to 35 percent, harming the former New Jersey senator's campaign and boosting his own. Similarly, Texas governor George W. Bush came in first in the Republican caucuses, gaining 41 percent of the vote to industrialist Steve Forbes's 30 percent, former diplomat Alan Keyes's 14 percent, and Senator John McCain's 5 percent.

In the general election later that year, the state went by a small margin to Vice President Gore, while all congressional incumbents, as well as state assembly incumbents, were victorious. The 4,144 margin was small enough for Governor Bush to threaten to demand a recount if Gore persisted in his calls for recounts in the wafer-thin Republican margin in Florida. Wildcard candidate Ralph Nader took 2 percent. The state's congressional delegation remained at four Republicans and one Democrat.

Controversies. In October and November, 2001, when anthrax attacks followed the September 11, 2001, terror attacks on New York City and the Pentagon, the national spotlight played on Iowa intermittently. The reason was that Iowa State University at Ames had first isolated a strain of anthrax that Tom Ridge, director of the Office of Homeland Security, said was the type used in all recent anthrax attacks. On November 9, however, the university reported that it had destroyed its anthrax samples after the first reported death from anthrax was identified as the Ames strain. The university did so because of security concerns but not before asking the Federal Bureau of Investigation (FBI) and the Centers for Disease Control (CDC) for their approval.

Another issue that affected Iowa, a premier farming state, concerned genetically modified crops (GM). In 2003, GM farming rules were reported to have been broken. Farmers were obligated to plant at least 20 percent of their crops in conventional seed, but a study showed that farmers in a number of midwestern states did not do so. Planting of crops, however, was a difficult matter to police in the absence of voluntary farmer compliance.

2004 Elections. John Kerry, destined to become the Democratic Party's presidential standard-bearer, won the Iowa caucuses in January, 2004. When Election Day arrived on November 2, another election cliff-hanger soon became evident. When Kerry conceded the election to President Bush, Iowa had not been called for either candidate. By morning, however, it was clear that the president had won by a small margin—33,500 votes—though not nearly as small as the margin that he had lost the state in 2000.

Rowena Wildin
Updated by the Editor

Iowa Time Line

1673	French explorers Jacques Marquette and Louis Jolliet are the first Europeans to reach Iowa.
1788	French trader Julien Dubuque begins mining lead near modern-day Dubuque, with the permission of the Mesquaki Indians.
Dec. 30, 1803	United States purchases the Louisiana Territory, which includes Iowa, from France.
1804	Explorers Meriwether Lewis and William Clark cross Iowa on their journey to the Pacific Ocean.
1832	Sauk chief Black Hawk signs a treaty in which the Sauk and Mesquaki agree to vacate a strip of land near the Mississippi River by June, 1833.
June 12, 1838	Territory of Iowa is created.
1838	Land offices begin to sell Iowa land for $1.25 per acre.
Oct. 11, 1842	Sauk and Fox agree to leave Iowa within three years.
1846	Mormons begin crossing Iowa on their trek to Utah from Navuvoo, Illinois.
Dec. 28, 1846	Iowa becomes the twenty-ninth state of the Union.
1851	The Sioux, the last Native Americans with land in the state, agree to leave Iowa.
1855	University of Iowa is founded.
1855-1865	German immigrants form the Amana colonies, a communal society that lasts for eighty years.
1857	Group of Mesquaki purchase land in Tama County, part of their former homeland.
1857	Group of Sioux kill thirty-four settlers along the shores of Spirit Lake and capture four women, two of whom are later ransomed.
1857	State capital moves from Iowa City to Des Moines.
1858	Iowa State University is founded.
1858	"Cardiff Giant," a prehistoric man, is found to be a hoax.
1861-1865	Iowa sends seventy thousand soldiers to the Civil War; thirteen thousand die.
1867	First railroad, the Chicago, Iowa, and Nebraska line, reaches the state's western edge.
1868	Iowa supreme court rules that segregated schools are unconstitutional in Iowa; African Americans are given voting rights.
1876	University of Northern Iowa is founded.
1880	Five major and spur railroad lines, more than five thousand miles of track, cover Iowa.
1896	Free rural mail delivery begins.
1900-1918	Buxton, a town in Monroe county inhabited predominantly by African American coal miners, flourishes until its coal mines are depleted.
1906-1920	Bicycle shop owner Fred Duesenberg and attorney Edward R. Mason build cars, designed by Duesenberg, in Iowa.
1910	Iowa State Experiment Station tests soybeans as a potential crop.
1912	Walter Sheaffer, a jeweler in Fort Madison, develops an easily inked fountain pen.
1926	Henry A. Wallace creates Pioneer Seed Corn, devoted to producing hybrid seed corn.
Mar. 4, 1929	Herbert Hoover, from Iowa, becomes president of the United States.
1935	Rural Electrification Administration brings electricity to Iowa farms.

Des Moines, Iowa's capital and largest city. (PhotoDisc)

1950's	Forrest City furniture dealer John Hanon creates the Winnebago motorhome.
1965	Des Moines students are suspended for wearing black armbands protesting the Vietnam War; four years later, the U.S. Supreme Court supports their right to protest.
1985	Country musician Willie Nelson holds Farm Aid benefit concert for farmers suffering from falling land values in Iowa.
1991	Iowa legalizes riverboat gambling.
1998	More than two hundred methamphetamine labs or dumpsites are found in Iowa, a record for the state.
Jan. 24, 2000	Presidential candidates Al Gore (Democrat) and George W. Bush (Republican) win Iowa caucuses.
Nov. 7, 2000	Gore wins Iowa's seven electoral votes by slightly more than four thousand votes.
Oct.-Nov., 2001	Iowa State University at Ames destroys its strain of anthrax samples after the same strain is said to be responsible for anthrax attacks in Washington, D.C., New York, New Jersey, and Connecticut.
2003	Study of midwestern states, including Iowa, shows that farmers fail to follow the rule providing that they plant at least 20 percent of their crops in conventional seed.
Nov. 2, 2004	President George W. Bush wins Iowa's electoral votes by a slim margin, 33,500 votes.

Notes for Further Study

Published Sources. *Iowa: The Middle Land* (1996) by Dorothy Schwieder presents a thorough history of Iowa from its earliest days to the mid-1990's. Allan Carpenter's *Between the Two Rivers: Iowa Year by Year, 1846-1996* (1997) examines the first 150 years of Iowa's statehood. Two older but still useful books on Iowa history are Joseph F. Wall's *Iowa, a Bicentennial History* (1978) and Leland L. Sage's *A History of Iowa* (1974). For young adults, David C. King and Rick Petreycik's *Iowa* (2006) offers an accessible account of the state's history. *Iowa History Reader* (1996), edited by Marvin Bergman, offers readings in Iowa history selected by the State Historical Society of Iowa. *Iowa's Ethnic Roots* (1993), edited by Ron E. Roberts, examines the ethnic history of Iowa. In *Iowa Letters: Dutch Immigrants on the American Frontier* (2005), compiled by Johan Stellingwerff and edited by Robert P. Swierenga, more than two hundred immigrant letters relating to the midwestern frontier and brought together from archives and private holdings provide insight into key issues in the minds of immigrants themselves and of their relatives in Holland. *Hook and Eye: A History of the Iowa Central Railway* (2005) by Don L. Hofsommer details the history of the Iowa Central Railway, a north-south route across the state which linked Minneapolis and St. Paul with St. Louis and provided transportation for the state's agricultural and industrial trade. Using primary sources that include memoirs, diaries, and census data, Patricia Riney-Kehrberg examines what life was like for rural children in Iowa and the greater Midwest between the end of the Civil War and the Progressive Era in *Childhood on the Farm: Work, Play, and Coming of Age in the Midwest* (2005). Charles O.

Musser's *Soldier Boy: The Civil War Letters of Charles O. Musser, 29th Iowa* (1995), edited by Barry Popchock, presents a look at the Civil War through the eyes of a soldier with the 29th Iowa Infantry Regiment. Although Iowa is not necessarily a sought-after tourist destination, Mike Whye argues in his *The Great Iowa Touring Book* (2004) that if travelers leave the major routes and take to the back roads, numerous intriguing attractions can be found in the state's rural and urban landscapes.

Web Resources. A good place to start searching for information about Iowa on the Internet is through the state of Iowa's site (www.iowa.gov/state/main/index.html). It provides current Iowa news and weather; information on tourism, travel, and special events; and links to many other sites. Another excellent source of information is the many links furnished by the Iowa secretary of state (www .sos.state.ia.us). The Iowa general assembly's site (www.legis.state.ia.us/) contains information about the assembly and legislation.

An essay found on the University of Iowa's Web site (www .uiowa.edu/~osa/learn/historic/hisper.htm) presents an interesting and informative look at various aspects of Iowa history, while the Iowa History Project (iagenweb.org/history/) brings together a number of pamphlets, newspaper articles, and journals related to the state's history. Another good source is the Iowa Tourism Bureau's site (www.iowa.tourism), which offers a brief history of Iowa, interesting facts, and travel-related information, including events and attractions. The online version of *Iowan* magazine (www.iowan.com) provides articles about the state and allows a search of back issues.

Counties

County	2000 pop.	Rank in pop.	Sq. miles	Rank in area	County	2000 pop.	Rank in pop.	Sq. miles	Rank in area
Adair	8,243	88	569.3	52	Clay	17,372	43	568.9	53
Adams	4,482	99	423.6	92	Clayton	18,678	39	778.8	5
Allamakee	14,675	56	639.6	18	Clinton	50,149	10	695.0	15
Appanoose	13,721	60	496.3	73	Crawford	16,942	46	714.4	13
Audubon	6,830	96	443.2	78	Dallas	40,750	14	586.5	26
Benton	25,308	24	716.5	11	Davis	8,541	87	503.3	70
Black Hawk	128,012	4	567.4	57	Decatur	8,689	85	532.3	65
Boone	26,224	23	571.5	44	Delaware	18,404	40	577.9	33
Bremer	23,325	26	437.9	80	Des Moines	42,351	12	416.2	93
Buchanan	21,093	31	571.3	45	Dickinson	16,424	49	381.1	99
Buena Vista	20,411	33	574.8	39	Dubuque	89,143	7	608.2	21
Butler	15,305	53	580.4	30	Emmet	11,027	75	395.8	98
Calhoun	11,115	74	570.2	48	Fayette	22,008	28	731.0	7
Carroll	21,421	29	569.3	51	Floyd	16,900	47	500.6	72
Cass	14,684	55	564.3	58	Franklin	10,704	77	582.5	28
Cedar	18,187	41	579.6	31	Fremont	8,010	90	511.3	68
Cerro Gordo	46,447	11	568.4	56	Greene	10,366	79	568.4	55
Cherokee	13,035	63	577.2	35	Grundy	12,369	64	502.6	71
Chickasaw	13,095	62	504.7	69	Guthrie	11,353	73	590.6	23
Clarke	9,133	84	431.2	88	Hamilton	16,438	48	576.7	36

County	2000 pop.	Rank in pop.	Sq. miles	Rank in area	County	2000 pop.	Rank in pop.	Sq. miles	Rank in area
Hancock	12,100	67	571.1	46	Osceola	7,003	94	398.8	97
Hardin	18,812	38	569.3	50	Page	16,976	45	534.9	63
Harrison	15,666	52	696.9	14	Palo Alto	10,147	80	563.9	59
Henry	20,336	34	434.5	83	Plymouth	24,849	25	863.6	4
Howard	9,932	82	473.4	75	Pocahontas	8,662	86	577.7	34
Humboldt	10,381	78	434.4	84	Polk	374,601	1	569.5	49
Ida	7,837	92	431.7	87	Pottawattamie	87,704	8	954.3	2
Iowa	15,671	51	586.5	25	Poweshiek	18,815	37	585.1	27
Jackson	20,296	35	636.1	19	Ringgold	5,469	98	537.7	62
Jasper	37,213	19	730.0	8	Sac	11,529	71	575.8	37
Jefferson	16,181	50	435.4	82	Scott	158,668	3	457.9	77
Johnson	111,006	5	614.5	20	Shelby	13,173	61	590.9	22
Jones	20,221	36	575.4	38	Sioux	31,589	22	767.9	6
Keokuk	11,400	72	579.2	32	Story	79,981	9	572.9	41
Kossuth	17,163	44	973.1	1	Tama	18,103	42	721.4	9
Lee	38,052	18	517.4	67	Taylor	6,958	95	534.0	64
Linn	191,701	2	717.5	10	Union	12,309	65	424.4	90
Louisa	12,183	66	401.9	94	Van Buren	7,809	93	485.3	74
Lucas	9,422	83	430.6	89	Wapello	36,051	20	431.8	86
Lyon	11,763	69	587.6	24	Warren	40,671	15	571.7	43
Madison	14,019	59	561.2	60	Washington	20,670	32	568.8	54
Mahaska	22,335	27	570.9	47	Wayne	6,730	97	525.6	66
Marion	32,052	21	554.3	61	Webster	40,235	16	715.3	12
Marshall	39,311	17	572.4	42	Winnebago	11,723	70	400.5	95
Mills	14,547	57	436.6	81	Winneshiek	21,310	30	689.7	17
Mitchell	10,874	76	469.0	76	Woodbury	103,877	6	872.7	3
Monona	10,020	81	693.2	16	Worth	7,909	91	400.0	96
Monroe	8,016	89	433.4	85	Wright	14,334	58	580.8	29
Montgomery	11,771	68	423.9	91					
Muscatine	41,722	13	438.7	79					
O'Brien	15,102	54	573.1	40					

Source: U.S. Census Bureau; National Association of Counties.

Cities
With 10,000 or more residents

Rank	City	Population
1	Des Moines (capital)	198,682
2	Cedar Rapids	120,758
3	Davenport	98,359
4	Sioux City	85,013
5	Waterloo	68,747
6	Iowa City	62,220
7	Council Bluffs	58,268
8	Dubuque	57,686
9	Ames	50,731
10	West Des Moines	46,403
11	Cedar Falls	36,145
12	Bettendorf	31,275
13	Mason City	29,172
14	Urbandale	29,072
15	Clinton	27,772
16	Ankeny	27,117
17	Burlington	26,839
18	Marion	26,294
19	Marshalltown	26,009

Rank	City	Population
20	Fort Dodge	25,136
21	Ottumwa	24,998
22	Muscatine	22,697
23	Newton	15,579
24	Coralville	15,123
25	Indianola	12,998
26	Clive	12,855
27	Boone	12,803
28	Keokuk	11,427
29	Spencer	11,317
30	Oskaloosa	10,938
31	Fort Madison	10,715
32	Altoona	10,345
33	Carroll	10,106
34	Storm Lake	10,076

Population figures are from 2000 census.
Source: U.S. Bureau of the Census.

Index to Tables

DEMOGRAPHICS

Resident state and national populations, 1970-2004

Population figures given in thousands

	State pop.	U.S. pop.	Share	Rank
1970	2,825	203,302	1.4%	25
1980	2,914	226,546	1.3%	27
1985	2,830	237,924	1.2%	29
1990	2,777	248,765	1.1%	30
1995	2,867	262,761	1.1%	30
2000	2,926	281,425	1.0%	30
2004	2,954	293,655	1.0%	30

Source: U.S. Census Bureau, Current Population Reports, 2006.

Resident population by age, 2004

Age Group	Total persons
Under 5 years	181,000
5 to 17 years	500,000
18 to 24 years	316,000
25 to 34 years	369,000
35 to 44 years	418,000
45 to 54 years	436,000
55 to 64 years	301,000
65 to 74 years	203,000
75 to 84 years	158,000
85 years and older	72,000
All age groups	2,954,000

Portion of residents 65 and older	14.7%
National rank in portion of oldest residents	5
National average	12.4%

Population figures are rounded to nearest thousand persons;
figures include armed forces personnel stationed in the state.
Source: U.S. Bureau of the Census, 2006.

Resident population by race, Hispanic origin, 2004

Category	State pop.	Share	U.S.
All residents	2,954	100.00%	100.00%
Non-Hispanic white	2,710	91.74%	67.37%
Hispanic white	97	3.28%	13.01%
Other Hispanic	7	0.24%	1.06%
African American	68	2.30%	12.77%
Native American	10	0.34%	0.96%
Asian, Pacific Islander	43	1.46%	4.37%
Two or more categories	26	0.88%	1.51%

Population figures are in thousands. Persons counted as "Hispanic" (Latino) may be of any race. Because of overlapping categories, categories may not add up to 100%. Shares in column 3 are percentages of each category within the state; these figures may be compared to the national percentages in column 4.
Source: U.S. Bureau of the Census, 2006.

Projected state population, 2000-2030

Year	Population
2000	2,926,000
2005	2,974,000
2010	3,010,000
2015	3,026,000
2020	3,020,000
2025	2,993,000
2030	2,955,000
Population increase, 2000-2030	29,000
Percentage increase, 2000-2030	1.0

Projections are based on data from the 2000 census.
Source: U.S. Census Bureau.

VITAL STATISTICS

Infant mortality rates, 1980-2002

	1980	1990	2000	2002
All state residents	11.8	8.1	6.5	5.3
All U.S. residents	12.6	9.2	9.4	9.1
All state white residents	11.5	7.9	6.0	5.1
All U.S. white residents	10.6	7.6	5.7	5.8
All state black residents	27.2	21.9	21.1	—
All U.S. black residents	22.2	18.0	14.1	14.4

Figures represent deaths per 1,000 live births of resident infants under 1 year old, exclusive of fetal deaths. Figures for all residents include members of other racial categories not listed separately. The Census Bureau considers the figures for black residents in 2002 to be too small to be statistically meaningful.
Source: U.S. Census Bureau, *Statistical Abstract of the United States,* 2006.

Abortion rates, 1990 and 2000

	1990	2000
Total abortions	7,000	6,000
Rate per 1,000 women	11.3	9.8
U.S. rate	25.7	21.3
Rank	44	38

Numbers of abortions are rounded to nearest thousand; ranks are based on rates.
Source: U.S. Census Bureau.

Marriages and divorces, 2004

Total marriages	20,500
Rate per 1,000 population	6.9
National rate per 1,000 population	7.4
Rank among all states	29
Total divorces	8,300
Rate per 1,000 population	2.8
National rate per 1,000 population	3.7
Rank among all states	39

Figures are for all marriages and divorces performed within the state, including those of nonresidents; totals are rounded to the nearest hundred. Ranks are for highest to lowest figures; note that divorce data are not available for five states.
Source: U.S. National Center for Health Statistics, *Vital Statistics of the United States,* 2006.

Death rates by leading causes, 2002
Deaths per 100,000 resident population

Cause	State	U.S.
Heart disease	278.6	241.7
Cancer	220.4	193.2
Cerebrovascular diseases	75.8	56.4
Accidents other than motor vehicle	37.2	37.0
Motor vehicle accidents	14.5	15.7
Chronic lower respiratory diseases	53.8	43.3
Diabetes mellitus	25.0	25.4
HIV	1.0	4.9
Suicide	10.7	11.0
Homicide	1.9	6.1
All causes	952.7	847.3
Rank in overall death rate among states		14

Figures exclude nonresidents who died in the state. Causes of death follow International Classification of Diseases. Rank is from highest to lowest death rate in the United States.
Source: U.S. National Center for Health Statistics, *National Vital Statistics Report,* 2006.

ECONOMY

Gross state product, 1990-2004
In current dollars

Year	State product	Nat'l product	State share
1990	$55.9 billion	$5.67 trillion	0.99%
2000	$90.8 billion	$9.75 trillion	0.93%
2002	$97.8 billion	$10.41 trillion	0.94%
2003	$102.4 billion	$10.92 trillion	0.94%
2004	$114.3 billion	$11.65 trillion	0.98%

Source: U.S. Bureau of Economic Analysis, *Survey of Current Business,* July, 2005.

Gross state product by industry, 2003
In billions of dollars

Construction	$3.5
Manufacturing	20.5
Wholesale trade	5.8
Retail trade	7.3
Finance & insurance	9.9
Information	3.3
Professional services	3.0
Health care & social assistance	6.2
Government	10.7
Total state product	$95.6
Total U.S. product	$10,289.2
State share of U.S. total	0.93%
Rank among all states	29

Total figures include industries not listed separately. Amounts are in chained 2000 dollars.
Source: U.S. Bureau of Economic Analysis, *Survey of Current Business,* July, 2005.

Personal income per capita, 1990-2004
In current dollars

	1990	2000	2004
Per capita income	$17,389	$26,554	$30,560
U.S. average	$19,477	$29,845	$32,937
Rank among states	32	33	31

Source: U.S. Bureau of Economic Analysis, *Survey of Current Business,* April, 2005.

Energy consumption, 2001
In trillions of British thermal units (BTU), except as noted

Total energy consumption

Total state energy consumption	1,151
Total U.S. energy consumption	96,275
State share of U.S. total	1.20%
Rank among states	29

Per capita consumption (In millions of BTU)

Total state per capita consumption	392
Total U.S. per capita consumption	338
Rank among states	14

End-use sectors

Residential	229
Commercial	179
Industrial	472
Transportation	270

Sources of energy

Petroleum	401
Natural gas	225
Coal	445
Hydroelectric power	9
Nuclear electric power	40

Figures for totals include categories not listed separately.
Source: U.S. Energy Information Administration, *State Energy Data Report,* 2001.

Nonfarm employment by sectors, 2004

Total	1,456,000
Construction	68,000
Manufacturing	223,000
Trade, transportation, utilities	306,000
Information	34,000
Finance, insurance, real estate	97,000
Professional & business services	107,000
Education & health services	191,000
Leisure, hospitality, arts, organizations	128,000
Other services, including repair & maintenance	56,000
Government	244,000

Figures are rounded to nearest thousand persons. "Total" includes mining and natural resources, not listed separately.
Source: U.S. Bureau of Labor Statistics, 2006.

Foreign exports, 1990-2004
In millions of dollars

Year	State	U.S.	State share
1990	2,189	394,045	0.56%
1996	4,400	624,767	0.70%
1997	5,118	688,896	0.74%
2000	4,466	712,055	0.57%
2003	5,236	724,006	0.77%
2004	6,394	769,332	0.83%

Rank among all states in 2004 28

U.S. total does not include U.S. dependencies.
Source: U.S. Census Bureau, *U.S. Merchandise Trade,* series FT 900, 2000; U.S. Census Bureau, *U.S. International Trade in Goods and Services,* Series FT 900, 2005.

LAND USE

Federally owned land, 2003
Areas in acres

	State	U.S.	State share
Total area	35,860,000	2,271,343,000	1.58%
Nonfederal land	35,558,000	1,599,584,000	2.22%
Federal land	302,000	671,759,000	0.05%
Federal share	0.8%	29.6%	—

Areas are rounded to nearest thousand acres. Figures for federally owned land do not include trust properties.
Source: U.S. General Services Administration, *Federal Real Property Profile,* 2006.

Land use, 1997
In acres, rounded to nearest thousand

Total surface area	36,017,000
Total nonfederal rural land.	33,673,000
Percentage rural land	93.5%
Cropland.	25,310,000
Conservation Reserve Program (CRP*) land . . .	1,739,000
Pastureland	3,572,000
Rangeland	(nil)
Forestland.	2,182,000
Other rural land	870,000

*CRP is a federal program begun in 1985 to assist private landowners to convert highly erodible cropland to vegetative cover for ten years. Note that some categories of land overlap.
Source: U.S. Department of Agriculture, Natural Resources and Conservation Service, and Iowa State University, Statistical Laboratory, S*ummary Report, 1997 National Resources Inventory,* revised December, 2000.

Farms and crop acreage, 2004

	State	U.S.	Share	Rank
Farms	90,000	2,113,000	4.26%	3
Acres (millions)	32	937	3.42%	10
Acres per farm	353	443	—	19

Source: U.S. Department of Agriculture, National Agricultural Statistics Service. Numbers of farms are rounded to nearest thousand units; acreage figures are rounded to nearest million. Rankings, including ties, are based on rounded figures.

GOVERNMENT AND FINANCE

Units of local government, 2002

	State	Total U.S.	Rank
All local governments	1,975	87,525	15
Counties	99	3,034	8
Municipalities	948	19,429	4
Townships	0	16,504	—
School districts	386	13,506	13
Special districts	542	35,052	25

Only 48 states have county governments, 20 states have township governments ("towns" in New England, Minnesota, New York, and Wisconsin), and 46 states have school districts. Special districts encompass such functions as natural resources, fire protection, and housing and community development.
Source: U.S. Census Bureau, *Census of Governments.*

State government revenue, 2002

Total revenue	$11,130 mill.
General revenue	$11,026 mill.
Per capita revenue	$3,757
U.S. per capita average	$3,689
Rank among states	29

Intergovernment revenue	
Total	$3,445 mill.
From federal government	$3,320 mill.

Charges and miscellaneous	
Total	$2,574 mill.
Current charges	$1,452 mill.
Misc. general income	$1,122 mill.
Insurance trust revenue	−$11 mill.

Taxes	
Total	$5,006 mill.
Per capita taxes	$1,705
Rank among states	31
Property taxes	(nil)
Sales taxes	$2,538 mill.
License taxes	$520 mill.
Individual income taxes	$1,769 mill.
Corporate income taxes.	$88 mill.
Other taxes	$90 mill.

Total revenue figures include items not listed separately here.
Source: U.S. Bureau of the Census.

State government expenditures, 2002

General expenditures
Total state expenditures . . . . $12,721 mill.
Intergovernmental . . . . $3,326 mill.

Per capita expenditures
State $3,895
Average of all states $3,859
Rank among states 26

Selected direct expenditures
Education . . . . $2,140 mill.
Public welfare . . . . $2,573 mill.
Health, hospital . . . . $865 mill.
Highways . . . . $939 mill.
Police protection . . . . $86 mill.
Corrections . . . . $233 mill.
Natural resources . . . . $239 mill.
Parks and recreation . . . . $18 mill.
Government administration . . . . $487 mill.
Interest on debt . . . . $123 mill.
Total direct expenditures . . . . $8,109 mill.

Totals include items not listed separately.
Source: U.S. Census Bureau.

POLITICS

Governors since statehood
D = Democrat; R = Republican; O = other;
(r) resigned; (d) died in office; (i) removed from office

Ansel Briggs (D) 1846-1850
Stephen P. Hempstead (D) 1850-1854
James W. Grimes (R) 1854-1858
Ralph P. Lowe (R) 1858-1860
Samuel J. Kirkwood (R) 1860-1864
William H. Stone (O) 1864-1868
Samuel Merrill (R) 1868-1872
Cyrus C. Carpenter (R) 1872-1876
Samuel J. Kirkwood (R) . . . . (r) 1876-1877
Joshua G. Newbold (R) 1877-1878
John H. Gear (R) 1878-1882
Buren R. Sherman (R) 1882-1886
William Larrabee (R) 1886-1890
Horace Boies (D) 1890-1894
Frank D. Jackson (R) 1894-1896
Francis M. Drake (R) 1896-1898
Leslie M. Shaw (R) 1898-1902
Albert B. Cummins (R) . . . . (r) 1902-1908
Warren Garst (R) 1908-1909
Beryl F. Carroll (R) 1909-1913
George W. Clarke (R) 1913-1917
William L. Harding (R) 1917-1921
Nathan E. Kendall (R) 1921-1925
John Hammill (R) 1925-1931
Daniel W. Turner (R) 1931-1933
Clyde L. Herring (D) 1933-1937

Nelson C. Kraschel (D) 1937-1939
George A. Wilson (R) 1939-1943
Bourke B. Hickenlooper (R) 1943-1945
Robert D. Blue (R) 1945-1949
William S. Beardsley (R) . . . . (d) 1949-1954
Leo Elthon (R) 1954-1955
Leo A. Hoegh (R) 1955-1957
Herschel C. Loveless (D) 1957-1961
Norman A. Erbe (R) 1961-1963
Harold E. Hughes (D) . . . . (r) 1963-1969
Robert D. Fulton (D) 1969
Robert D. Ray (R) 1969-1983
Terry E. Branstad (R) 1983-1999
Thomas Vilsack (D) 1999-2007
Chet Culver (D) 2007-

Composition of congressional delegations, 1989-2007

	Dem	Rep	Total
House of Representatives			
101st Congress, 1989			
State delegates	2	4	6
Total U.S.	259	174	433
102d Congress, 1991			
State delegates	2	4	6
Total U.S.	267	167	434
103d Congress, 1993			
State delegates	1	4	5
Total U.S.	258	176	434
104th Congress, 1995			
State delegates	1	4	5
Total U.S.	197	236	433
105th Congress, 1997			
State delegates	0	5	5
Total U.S.	206	228	434
106th Congress, 1999			
State delegates	1	4	5
Total U.S.	211	222	433
107th Congress, 2001			
State delegates	1	4	5
Total U.S.	211	221	432
108th Congress, 2003			
State delegates	1	4	5
Total U.S.	205	229	434
109th Congress, 2005			
State delegates	1	4	5
Total U.S.	202	231	433
110th Congress, 2007			
State delegates	3	2	5
Total U.S.	233	202	435

(continued)

	Dem	Rep	Total
Senate			
101st Congress, 1989			
State delegates	1	1	2
Total U.S.	55	45	100
102d Congress, 1991			
State delegates	1	1	2
Total U.S.	56	44	100
103d Congress, 1993			
State delegates	1	1	2
Total U.S.	57	43	100
104th Congress, 1995			
State delegates	1	1	2
Total U.S.	46	53	99
105th Congress, 1997			
State delegates	1	1	2
Total U.S.	45	55	100
106th Congress, 1999			
State delegates	1	1	2
Total U.S.	45	54	99
107th Congress, 2001			
State delegates	1	1	2
Total U.S.	50	50	100
108th Congress, 2003			
State delegates	1	1	2
Total U.S.	48	51	99
109th Congress, 2005			
State delegates	1	1	2
Total U.S.	44	55	99
110th Congress, 2007			
State delegates	1	1	2
Total U.S.	49	49	98

Figures are for starts of first sessions. Totals are for Democrat (Dem.) and Republican (Rep.) members only. House membership totals under 435 and Senate totals under 100 reflect vacancies and seats held by independent party members. When the 110th Congress opened, the Senate's two independent members caucused with the Democrats, giving the Democrats control of the Senate.

Source: U.S. Congress, *Congressional Directory.*

Composition of state legislature, 1990-2006

	Democrats	Republicans
State House (100 seats)		
1990	55	45
1992	49	51
1994	36	64
1996	46	54
1998	44	56
2000	44	56
2002	47	53
2004	49	51
2006	54	45
State Senate (50 seats)		
1990	29	21
1992	27	23
1994	27	23
1996	21	29
1998	20	30
2000	20	30
2002	21	29
2004	25	25
2006	30	20

Figures for total seats may include independents and minor party members. Numbers reflect results of elections in listed years; elected members usually take their seats in the years that follow.

Source: Council of State Governments; *State Elective Officials and the Legislatures.*

Voter participation in presidential elections, 2000 and 2004

	2000	2004
Voting age population		
State	2,198,000	2,274,000
Total United States	209,831,000	220,377,000
State share of U.S. total	1.05	1.03
Rank among states	30	30
Portion of voting age population casting votes		
State	61.5%	66.3%
United States	50.3%	55.5%
Rank among states	6	8

Population figures are rounded to nearest thousand and include all residents, regardless of eligibility to vote.

Source: U.S. Census Bureau.

HEALTH AND MEDICAL CARE

Medical professionals
Physicians in 2003 and nurses in 2001

	U.S.	State
Physicians in 2003		
Total	774,849	5,544
Share of U.S. total		0.71%
Rate	266	188
Rank		46
Nurses in 2001		
Total	2,262,020	30,190
Share of U.S. total		1.33%
Rate	793	1,030
Rank		6

Rates are numbers of physicians and nurses per 100,000 resident population; ranks are based on rates.
Source: American Medical Association, *Physician Characteristics and Distribution in the U.S.*; U.S. Department of Health and Human Services, Health Resources and Services Administration.

Health insurance coverage, 2003

	State	U.S.
Total persons covered	2,593,000	243,320,000
Total persons not covered	329,000	44,961,000
Portion not covered	11.3%	15.6%
Rank among states	35	—
Children not covered	60,000	8,373,000
Portion not covered	8.6%	11.4%
Rank among states	29	—

Totals are rounded to nearest thousand. Ranks are from the highest to the lowest percentages of persons *not* insured.
Source: U.S. Census Bureau, Current Population Reports.

AIDS, syphilis, and tuberculosis cases, 2003

Disease	U.S. cases	State cases	Rank
AIDS	44,232	75	40
Syphilis	34,270	46	39
Tuberculosis	14,874	40	38

Source: U.S. Centers for Disease Control and Prevention.

Cigarette smoking, 2003
Residents over age 18 who smoke

	U.S.	State	Rank
All smokers	22.1%	21.7%	30
Male smokers	24.8%	22.8%	35
Female smokers	20.3%	20.7%	21

Cigarette smokers are defined as persons who reported having smoked at least 100 cigarettes during their lifetimes and who currently smoked at least occasionally.
Source: U.S. Centers for Disease Control and Prevention, *Morbidity and Mortality Weekly Report*, 53, no. 44 (November 12, 2004).

HOUSING

Home ownership rates, 1985-2004

	1985	1990	1995	2000	2004
State	69.9%	70.7%	71.4%	75.2%	73.2%
Total U.S.	63.9%	63.9%	64.7%	67.4%	69.0%
Rank among states	14	7	9	6	17

Net change in state home ownership rate, 1985-2004 . . . . +3.3%
Net change in U.S. home ownership rate, 1985-2004 . . . . +5.1%

Percentages represent the proportion of owner households to total occupied households.
Source: U.S. Census Bureau, 2006.

Home sales, 2000-2004
In thousands of units

Existing home sales	2000	2002	2003	2004
State sales	53.3	58.4	62.4	71.1
Total U.S. sales	5,171	5,631	6,183	6,784
State share of U.S. total	1.03%	1.04%	1.01%	1.05%
Sales rank among states	30	32	32	32

Units include single-family homes, condos, and co-ops.
Source: National Association of Realtors, Washington, D.C., *Real Estate Outlook: Market Trends & Insights*.

Values of owner-occupied homes, 2003

	State	U.S.
Total units	688,000	58,809,000
Value of units		
Under $100,000	56.6%	29.6%
$100,000-199,999	34.5%	36.9%
$200,000 or more	8.9%	33.5%
Median value	$91,427	$142,275
Rank among all states 45		

Units are owner-occupied one-family houses whose numbers are rounded to nearest thousand. Data are extrapolated from survey samples.
Source: U.S. Census Bureau, American Community Survey.

EDUCATION

Public school enrollment, 2002

Prekindergarten through grade 8
State enrollment 326,000
Total U.S. enrollment. 34,135,000
State share of U.S. total 0.96%

Grades 9 through 12
State enrollment 156,000
Total U.S. enrollment. 14,067,000
State share of U.S. total 1.11%

Enrollment rates
State public school enrollment rate. 92.6%
Overall U.S. rate 90.4%
Rank among states in 2002. 10
Rank among states in 1995. 20

Enrollment figures (which include unclassified students) are rounded to nearest thousand pupils during fall school term. Enrollment rates are based on enumerated resident population estimate for July 1, 2002.
Source: U.S. National Center for Education Statistics.

Public college finances, 2003-2004

FTE enrollment in public institutions of higher education
Students in state institutions 117,700
Students in all U.S. public institutions 9,916,600
State share of U.S. total 1.19
Rank among states 30

State and local government appropriations for higher education
State appropriation per FTE $5,255
National average $5,716
Rank among states 30
State & local tax revenue going to higher education 9.8%

FTE = full-time equivalent in public postsecondary programs, including summer sessions; student numbers are rounded to nearest hundred. Funding figures for 2003-2004 academic year include financial aid to students in state public institutions and exclude money for research, agriculture experiment stations, teaching hospitals, and medical schools; figures are rounded to nearest thousand dollars.
Source: Higher Education Executive Officers, Denver, Colorado.

TRANSPORTATION AND TRAVEL

Highway mileage, 2003

Interstate highways	782
Arterial roads	9,680
Collector roads.	31,485
Local roads	71,569
Urban roads	10,705
Rural roads	102,811
Total state mileage	113,516
U.S. total	3,974,107
State share	2.86%
Rank among states	12

Note that combined urban and rural road mileage matches the total of the other categories.
Source: U.S. Federal Highway Administration.

Motor vehicle registrations and driver licenses, 2003

Vehicle registrations	State	U.S.	Share	Rank
Autos, trucks, buses	3,369,000	231,390,000	1.46%	25
Autos only	1,883,000	135,670	1.39%	26
Motorcycles	140,000	5,328,000	2.63%	14
Driver licenses	1,978,000	196,166,000	1.01%	32

Figures, which do not include vehicles owned by military services, are rounded to the nearest thousand. Figures for automobiles include taxis.
Source: U.S. Federal Highway Administration.

Domestic travel expenditures, 2003

Spending by U.S. residents on overnight trips and
day trips of at least 50 miles from home

Total expenditures within state	$4.63 bill.
Total expenditures within U.S.	$490.87 bill.
State share of U.S. total	0.9%
Rank among states	32

Source: Travel Industry Association of America.

Retail gasoline prices, 2003-2007

Average price per gallon at the pump

Year	U.S.	State
2003	$1.267	$1.201
2004	$1.316	$1.243
2005	$1.644	$1.598
2007	$2.298	$2.212

Excise tax per gallon in 2004	20.5¢
Rank among all states in 2007 prices	33

Prices are averages of all grades of gasoline sold at the pump
during March months in 2003-2005 and during February, 2007.
Averages for 2006, during which prices rose higher, are not
available.

Source: U.S. Energy Information Agency, *Petroleum Marketing
Monthly* (2003-2005 data); American Automobile Association
(2007 data).

CRIME AND LAW ENFORCEMENT

State and local police officers, 2000-2004

	2000	2002	2004
Total officers			
U.S.	654,601	665,555	675,734
State	5,043	5,053	4,959*
*Net change, 2000-2004			−1.67%
Officers per 1,000 residents			
U.S.	2.33	2.31	2.30
State	1.72	1.72	1.68
State rank	40	42	45

Totals include state and local police and sheriffs.
Source: Carsey Institute, University of New Hampshire.

Crime rates, 2003

Incidents per 100,000 residents

Crimes	State	U.S.
Violent crimes		
Total incidents	272	475
Murder	2	6
Forcible rape	26	32
Robbery	38	142
Aggravated assault	207	295
Property crimes		
Total incidents	2,961	3,588
Burglary	596	741
Larceny/theft	2,175	2,415
Motor vehicle theft	190	433
All crimes	3,233	4,063

Source: U.S. Federal Bureau of Investigation, *Crime in the United
States,* annual.

State prison populations, 1980-2003

	State	U.S.	State share
1980	2,481	305,458	0.81%
1990	3,967	708,393	0.56%
1996	6,342	1,025,624	0.62%
2000	7,955	1,391,261	0.57%
2003	8,546	1,470,045	0.58%

State figures exclude prisoners in federal penitentiaries.
Source: U.S. Bureau of Justice Statistics, *Prisoners in 2003.*

Kansas

Location: Midwest

Area and rank: 81,823 square miles (211,922 square kilometers); 82,282 square miles (213,110 square kilometers) including water; thirteenth largest state in area

Coastline: none

Population and rank: 2,736,000 (2004); thirty-third largest state in population

Capital city: Topeka (122,377 people in 2000 census)

Largest city: Wichita (344,284 people in 2000 census)

Became territory: May 30, 1854

State capitol building in Topeka. (©James Blank/Weststock)

Entered Union and rank: January 29, 1861; thirty-fourth state

Present constitution adopted: 1859

Counties: 105

State name: "Kansas" derives from a Sioux name for "people of the south wind"

State nickname: Sunflower State; Jayhawk State

Motto: *Ad astra per aspera* (To the stars through difficulties)

State flag: Blue field with state seal, state flower, and name "Kansas"

Highest point: Mount Sunflower—4,039 feet (1,231 meters)

Lowest point: Verdigris River—679 feet (207 meters)

Highest recorded temperature: 121 degrees Fahrenheit (49 degrees Celsius)—near Alton, 1936

Lowest recorded temperature: –40 degrees Fahrenheit (–40 degrees Celsius)—Lebanon, 1905

State song: "Home on the Range"

State tree: Cottonwood

State flower: Sunflower

State bird: Western meadowlark

State animal: Buffalo

Kansas History

Within Kansas, slightly northwest of Lebanon, is the geographical center of the forty-eight contiguous states. The Spanish explorer Francisco Vásquez de Coronado first ventured into the area in 1541 seeking gold. Native Americans had occupied the region since prehistoric times, possibly as early as 14,000 B.C.E. The Pawnee, Osage, Wichita, and Kansa Indians lived there during the early Spanish exploration. They were mostly hunters and farmers living along the Kansas River.

Later members of various seminomadic tribes, mainly the Kiowa, Cheyenne, Arapaho, and Comanche, also dwelled in the area. After 1830, however, the federal government forcibly moved many Native Americans from eastern tribes into the territory it had acquired through the Louisiana Purchase of 1803. Among the tribes whose members were relocated were the Cherokee, Miami, Potawatomi, Ottawa, Creek, Chickasaw, Choctaw, Delaware, and Shawnee. In all, about thirty tribes were assigned to Kansas for relocation.

French and American Settlement. The French moved into the area after the Spanish had been defeated by the Pawnee Indians in Nebraska. During the early eighteenth century, the French, attracted by the fur trade, built a trading post and military outpost, Fort Cavagnial, near present-day Leavenworth.

With the Louisiana Purchase, American exploration began. Meriwether Lewis and William Clark set out to explore the newly acquired area, which included all but a small part of southwestern Kansas bought in 1850 from Texas.

These explorers were followed in 1806 by Zebulon Pike, who made an east-west journey across the territory. As the eastern United States began to be developed, the federal government was under pressure to claim Native American lands for development. Relocating American Indians to the West provided the government with a convenient solution to a difficult problem. The Native Americans who were relocated are usually referred to as the emigrant tribes.

Between 1827 and 1853, Kansas was inhabited mostly

The building of the transcontinental railroad accelerated the development of Kansas, while also hastening the destruction of the region's once-great buffalo herds. (Library of Congress)

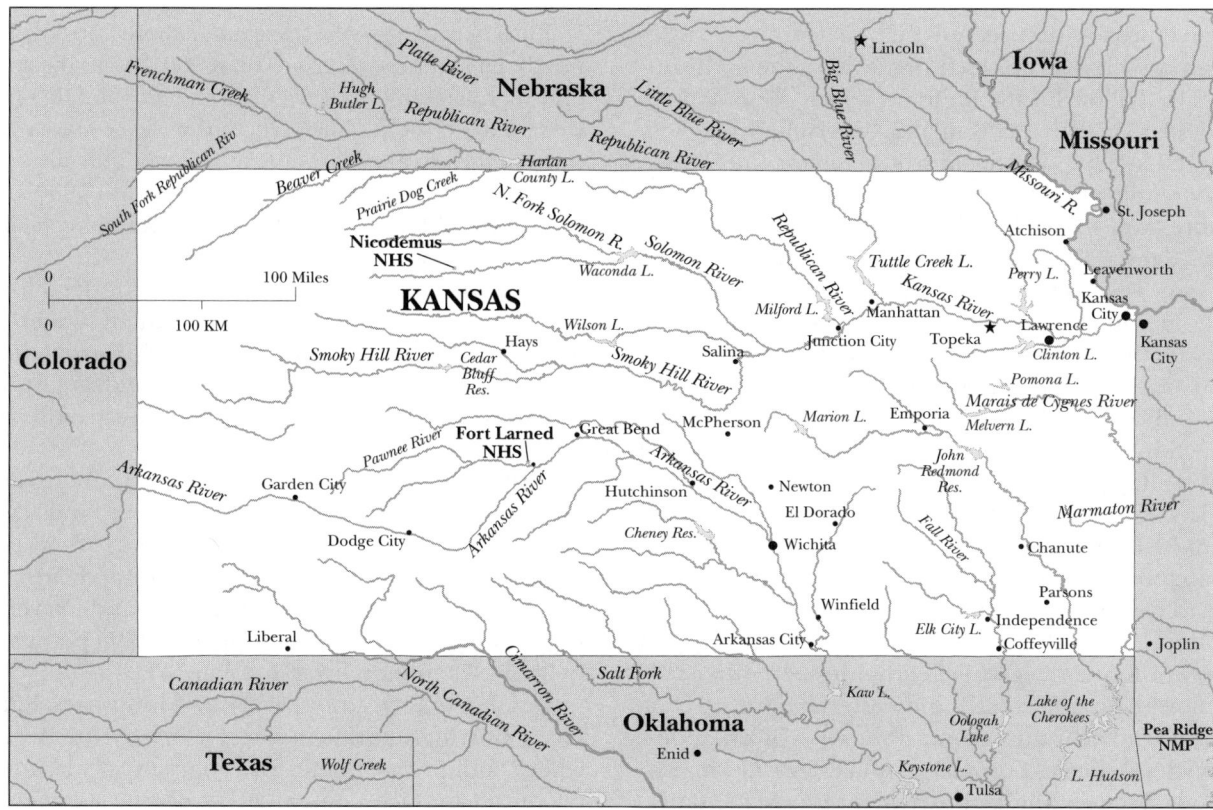

by Native Americans. Some thirty-four thousand Indians from over thirty tribes and only fifteen hundred white inhabitants, mostly missionaries and the personnel that maintained the government forts constructed at Leavenworth, Fort Scott, and Fort Riley, lived there.

The Kansas-Nebraska Act and Statehood. So great was the incursion of European settlers to the area after 1854 that the Native Americans who lived there, both original dwellers and the emigrant tribes, were removed from the state and settled elsewhere. In 1854, Kansas was created as a territory in the western part of what had previously been called the Missouri Territory. The early borders of the rectangular-shaped territory were much as they are today. Kansas is bounded by Missouri on the east and Colorado on the west. To the north, the boundary is Nebraska, and the southern border is Oklahoma. The only natural boundary is in the northeast, where the Missouri River constitutes part of the state line.

Soon after Kansas gained territorial status, the Kansas-Nebraska Act of 1854, which replaced the Missouri Compromise, opened the territory to settlement. Under the terms of this act, citizens of a territory decided whether it would be slave or free, whereas under the Missouri Compromise, an artificial balance between slave and free states was imposed.

Opinions were strongly divided about which choice Kansas should make. Its neighboring state, Missouri,

had slaves. Nebraska opted to be free, but proslavery sentiment was strong in Kansas. When the issue came to a vote, hundreds of land-hungry people who had come to Kansas stuffed the ballot boxes.

Kansas was plunged into controversy between the pro- and antislavery forces. Abolitionists were recruited to come to Kansas from New England and make it a free state. Abolitionist John Brown led the Pottawatomie Massacre in May of 1856. In 1863, an angry proslavery mob, led by William Clarke Quantrill, attacked Lawrence, Kansas, killing around 150 of its citizens.

With the pro- and antislavery forces fighting against each other, both sides drew up constitutions, neither of them acceptable to the United States Congress. Finally, in 1859, the antislavery Wyandotte Constitution was approved. This cleared the way for Kansas to achieve statehood on January 29, 1861, just as many southern states were seceding from the Union. Kansas was the thirty-fourth state admitted to the Union.

The Homestead Act of 1862. Following passage of the Homestead Act of 1862, Kansas grew rapidly. Under the terms of this act, upon the payment of a ten-dollar filing fee, heads of family or anyone over twenty-one years old could receive 160 acres of government land, which they would own if they lived on it for five years and improved the property. This opportunity was a magnet that drew thousands of easterners to Kansas.

The railroads that served the area received large land grants, chunks of which they sold to the early settlers. The Union Pacific Railroad began operating in Kansas in 1857, the Atchison and Topeka Railroad was chartered in 1859, and the Missouri, Kansas, and Texas line soon followed. Eventually twelve railroads operated on more than six thousand miles of track in Kansas.

The Kansas Economy. Because of the nature of its founding, Kansas was originally a rural state concentrating heavily on agriculture. During the Civil War, it sided with the North, and many of its citizens joined the Union army. Shortly after the war, cow towns began to develop in Kansas. These were towns that had railway connections, notably Abilene, Dodge City, Ellsworth, and Wichita.

Texas at this time had no railroad service, so until the mid-1880's, when rail service became available, Texan cattle ranchers drove their herds across Oklahoma to the railroad towns of Kansas, from which they were shipped to other destinations.

Eastern Kansas was settled early, but soon other settlers moved into the central and western regions, as far as Great Bend near the Colorado border. A diverse population developed as Europeans from Russia, Germany, Bohemia, France, England, and Italy came to the state, which also had a sizable African American population, being one of the free states that attracted freed slaves following the Civil War in what was called the "exodus movement."

Kansas, with a growing season of about 150 days in its northern reaches and more than 200 days in the southeast, is hospitable to agriculture. The rainfall ranges from sixteen inches annually in the west to more than forty inches in the east, although droughts are a frequent problem. During the early to mid-1930's, the dust bowls of Kansas and Oklahoma put many farmers out of business.

The state constructed more than twenty large reservoirs to control flooding, provide drinking water, and afford irrigation to farmers. Also, early Russian immigrants into Kansas brought with them a drought-resistant strain of wheat, Turkey Red, which is grown extensively in the state.

Although Kansas was originally rural, it increasingly moved toward manufacturing, commerce, and service occupations, causing a population shift to urban areas. Of its more than six hundred incorporated cites, fifty have populations exceeding five thousand. Nevertheless, more than two-thirds of the total 1990 population of about 2.5 million lived in urban areas.

Besides its agricultural and cattle industries, Kansas has a thriving aircraft industry centered in Wichita, where both private planes and commercial aircraft are produced by such companies as Boeing and Cessna. One of the nation's leading mental hospitals, the Menninger Neuropsychiatric Clinic, is located in Topeka. Kansas also has impressive oil reserves, as well as natural gas, coal, lead, salt, and zinc.

Arapaho and Comanche council in 1867 at Medicine Lodge Creek, where tribal leaders signed a treaty with the U.S. government designed to end their wars on the southern plains. (Library of Congress)

Kansas Conservatism. Kansas has traditionally been a conservative state, largely a Republican stronghold, although it has strong Populist leanings as well and has elected Populists as governors and representatives. It gave a moderate, Nancy Landon Kassebaum, three terms in the United States Senate.

In 1880, the state adopted prohibition and essentially remained a dry state. In 1899, Kansan Carry Nation single-handedly undertook the enforcement of Kansas's prohibition law by destroying saloons with her renowned axe.

The Twentieth Century Economy. The economy of Kansas had a significant resurgence during World War I, when the price of wheat escalated, bringing considerable money into the state's economy. The economy grew until the 1930's, when a drought that continued for several years devastated wheat farming.

The financial woes of the 1930's did not end until World War II again stimulated the economy and brought considerable industry into the state. The road building in the state during and after World War II resulted in one of the best road systems in the country. Kansas is served by 125 public and 250 private airports that provide excellent commercial air transport and encourage private ownership of airplanes.

Religion, Education, and Science. In 2000, controversy resulted from decisions of the Kansas State Board of Education. During 1999, the board had voted 6-4 to make teaching the theory of evolution optional for local school districts. Schools could also teach the biblical account of Creation or others in addition to or instead of evolution. In 2000, the board also rewrote state science standards to make the age of the earth ten thousand years, and it removed the "big bang" theory of the origin of the universe from its teaching standards. In the state's primary elections in 2000, some Democrats were said to have changed party affiliation in order to vote in the Republican primary for pro-evolution candidates. In the state's Republican primary, voters rejected three incumbent candidates for the state school board who rejected evolution. The outcome of the controversy was that the teaching of evolution was restored to the state curriculum in 2001, when the Kansas State Board of Education voted 7-3 to adopt new state science standards.

The new state education standards made provision for religious dissent from evolution among students and cautioned educators that students were free to ac-cept or reject the concepts presented. Teachers were not to ridicule dissenting students and were to suggest that students bring the subject up with parents or others. In 2004, however, conservatives won the board back, and controversial standards calling evolution into question were again in place. However, in August, 2006, voters elected one new science-oriented member to the school board that appeared to be split between the two camps.

Law and Public Policy Controversies. In other controversial issues in social policy, in mid-2002, a Kansas law barring alien Asian immigrants from inheriting real property was repealed. Florida and New Mexico were the only states left with such laws. The following year, the U.S. Supreme Court vacated a Kansas Court of Appeals decision that upheld a sentence of seventeen years for a developmentally disabled eighteen-year-old male, who was convicted of having consensual oral sex with a similarly disabled fourteen-year-old male. The court ordered Kansas to reconsider the case in the light of the court's decision in *Lawrence v. Texas* (2003), a case that struck down Texas antisodomy law. Late in 2005, the Kansas Supreme Court struck down the law under which the defendant was convicted.

Electoral Politics. In the 2000 general election, Kansas voted its six electoral votes for George W. Bush by a 58-37 percent margin; independent candidate Ralph Nader received thirty-five thousand votes, not nearly enough to make a difference in the outcome. All of the state's incumbent congressional delegation were reelected, but not all seats were easy wins. Democratic congressman Dennis Moore had a close call when his opponent, a state legislator, won 48 percent of the vote to Moore's 50 percent.

In the 2002 general election, Kansas voters elected a new governor. Democrat Kathleen Sebelius, the state insurance commissioner, won over Tim Shallenburger, a staunch conservative, by a margin of 53 to 45 percent.

In the 2004 election, U.S. senator Sam Brownback easily beat the challenger for his seat by a 62-27 percent margin. This was a wider margin in the popular vote than that of President Bush, who nevertheless handily took the state's six electoral votes by a 62-27 percent margin. Also in this election, former Olympic runner Jim Ryun won his fifth term in Congress by a 56-41 percent margin.

R. Baird Shuman
Updated by the Editor

Kansas Time Line

1541	Francisco Vásquez de Coronado explores central Kansas.
1723	Fort Orleans is built by French explorer Etienne de Bourgmont.
1744	French establish trading post at Fort Cavagnial, near Leavenworth.
1803	Area that becomes Kansas becomes part of the United States through the Louisiana Purchase.
1804	Meriwether Lewis and William Clark explore Kansas on their way to the Pacific Coast.
1806	Captain Zebulon Pike crosses Kansas from east to west.
June 4, 1812	Territory of Missouri is established, which includes Kansas.
Aug. 10, 1819	Stephen H. Long makes first steamboat expedition in Kansas.
1821	William Becknell establishes Santa Fe Trail.
1824	Founding of Presbyterian mission on Neosho River.
1827	Fort Leavenworth becomes the first permanent white settlement in Kansas.
1827	Daniel Boone establishes American Indian school in Jefferson County.
1830	United States government relocates Native Americans from the eastern states to Kansas.
1830	Shawnee Methodist Mission for Indians is established near Turner.
June 20, 1834	Kansas is declared Indian Country by Congress.
1839	Shawnee Methodist Mission moved to location near Shawnee.
1842	First of several expeditions by John C. Frémont passes through Kansas.
1842	Fort Scott is established.
1843	Great migration to Oregon begins.
1853	Fort Riley is established.
May 30, 1854	Kansas-Nebraska Act passed, giving Kansas territorial status.
July 2, 1855	First territorial legislature meeting at Pawnee and later at the Shawnee Mission legalizes slavery in Kansas.
1855	Free State antislavery party is established as conflict grows over slavery.
May 21, 1856	Lawrence Massacre results in 150 deaths when proslavery groups attack.
May 23-24, 1856	John Brown leads free-state massacre along Pottawatomie Creek.
1858	Congress rejects proslavery Lecompton Constitution.
1859	Atchison and Topeka Railroad chartered.
Oct. 4, 1859	Antislavery Wyandotte Constitution is adopted.
1860	First oil well drilled in Kansas near Paola.
Apr., 1860	Pony Express crosses Kansas.
Jan. 29, 1861	Kansas admitted to Union as thirty-fourth state.
1863	William Quantrill's Confederate troops attack Lawrence.
1864	University of Kansas opens at Lawrence.
1864	Confederate general Sterling Price leads his troops to Kansas.
1867	First Texas cattle run to Kansas.
1874	Mennonites from Russia introduce drought-resistant Turkey Red wheat to Kansas.
1878	Last Native American skirmish launched by Cheyenne Indians.
1880	Kansas imposes prohibition.
1899	Carry Nation begins her antisaloon raids.
1903	State capitol is completed.
1918	Economy bolstered by wheat sales during World War I.
1935	Dust storms devastate Kansas farmland.
1936	Alfred M. Landon is Republican candidate for president, losing with only 8 electoral votes.
1945	Growth of Kansas aircraft industry following World War II.
1948	Kanopolis Dam is completed on Smoky Hill River.
1949	Fall River Dam is completed.
1951	Cedar Bluff Dam on Smoky Hill River is completed.
1951	Kansas is devastated by floods.
1952	Kansan Dwight D. Eisenhower becomes thirty-fourth president of the United States.
1954	Eisenhower Museum opens in Abilene.

1954	U.S. Supreme Court rules against school board of Topeka in segregation case *Brown v. Board of Education of Topeka.*
1956	Kansas Turnpike is completed.
1965	Agricultural Hall of Fame and National Center opens near Kansas City.
1965	Fort Scott named a national historic monument.
1972	Terms of governor and other state officials increased from two to four years.
1976	Mid-American All-Indian Center opens in Wichita.
1988	Drought and wind erosion destroy more than 865,000 acres in Kansas.
1991	Largest remaining plot of Kansas prairie is plowed under.
Nov., 1991	Joan Finney is first woman elected governor of Kansas.
1999	Kansas State Board of Education votes 6-4 to make teaching the theory of evolution optional for local school districts.
2000	State Board of Education votes to replace the age of the earth in state education standards from three to four billion years to ten thousand years, a move that repudiates the theory of evolution. It also votes to remove the big bang as the prevailing theory of the origin of the universe.
2001	Newly seated members of the State Board of Education introduce new state science education standards that restore the theory of evolution to the curriculum.
2003	U.S. Supreme Court vacates conviction under Kansas law forbidding sex between consensual same-sex partners.
Nov. 2, 2004	Former world-record miler Jim Ryun wins fifth term in Congress.

Silhouette figures of cattle drivers erected near Caldwell, at Kansas's Oklahoma border, recall the days when great herds of cattle moved between Abilene, in east central Kansas, and Texas on the Chisholm Trail. (Kansas Department of Commerce & Housing, Travel and Tourism)

Notes for Further Study

Published Sources. *Natural Kansas* (1985), edited by Joseph T. Collins, provides interesting essays about biological, geological, geographical, and physical aspects of Kansas. Robert Richmond's *Kansas: A Land of Contrasts* (3d. ed., 1989) also presents varied information about the state, emphasizing that it is not entirely flat, soaring to an elevation of 4,039 feet at Mount Sunflower and having a mean elevation of 2,000 feet. *Kansas Archaeology* (2006) provides insight into the state's Native American past.

A thorough overview of the state's history can be found in *Kansas: The History of the Sunflower State, 1854-2000* (2002) by H. Craig Miner. *Bleeding Kansas: Contested Liberty in the Civil War Era* (2004) by Nicole Etcheson details the state's role in the struggle over slavery. Robert S. Bader's *Prohibition in Kansas: A History* (1986) offers interesting information about this phase of the state's history and the state's role in the passage of the Eighteenth Amendment to the U.S. Constitution. Thomas Goodrich relates details of the Lawrence Massacre of 1863 in *Bloody Dawn: The Story of the Lawrence Massacre* (1991). Pamela Riney-Kehrbert's *Rooted in Dust: Surviving Drought and Depression in Southwestern Kansas* (1994) offers the best coverage of how widespread droughts in the early 1930's led to a rapid deterioration of the Kansas economy, followed by the Great Depression. James R. Shortridge's *Cities on the Plains: The Evolution of Urban Kansas* (2004) offers a comparative history of the development of cities and the roles of railroads, the mining industry, and the cattle trade, among other factors.

Numerous books on Kansas are directed primarily to juvenile readers. Allen Carpenter's *Kansas* (1979) remains a useful resource despite being an older title. Zachary Kent's later *Kansas* (1990) is an excellent brief account of the state. Both of these books can be supplemented by Dennis Fradin's *Kansas: In Words and Pictures* (1980), Patricia D. Netzley's *Kansas* (2002), and Patricia K. Kummer's *Kansas* (Rev. ed., 2002).

Web Resources. The state of Kansas maintains a Web site (www.kansas.gov/) that provides useful information about the state and its government. The state's department of tourism has a Web site (www.travelks.com/) that includes information about tourist attractions, lodging, restaurants, and public transportation. The Web site of the University of Kansas (www.ku.edu/) offers information about the various branches of the university and their attractions. Various libraries around the state have Web sites through which their catalogs can be accessed. Chief among these are the libraries of Kansas City (www.kcpl.lib.mo.us) and (www.kcmlin.org), Manhattan (www.manhattan.lib.ks.us), Hutchinson (hutchpl.org/), Southeast Kansas (www.sekls.lib.ks.us), and Topeka (www.tscpl.org).

News developments that affect Kansas can be found on the *Wichita Eagle* site (www.kansas.com/mld/kansas/). For a wide range of historical information, visit Kansas History Online (www.kansashistoryonline.org/ksh/), the Kansas State Historical Society (www.kshs.org/research/topics/index.htm), and the History Gateway of Kansas (www.ku.edu/history/). Kansas Culture (www.davchi2000.addr.com/popup/kansas/kansas.html) acts as a portal site to all aspects of Kansas attractions, cities, geography, natural history, famous individuals, and much more.

Counties

County	2000 pop.	Rank in pop.	Sq. miles	Rank in area	County	2000 pop.	Rank in pop.	Sq. miles	Rank in area
Allen	14,385	35	503.1	97	Dickinson	19,344	28	848.4	43
Anderson	8,110	51	583.0	86	Doniphan	8,249	49	392.2	103
Atchison	16,774	32	432.4	102	Douglas	99,962	5	457.0	101
Barber	5,307	70	1,134.2	6	Edwards	3,449	86	622.1	81
Barton	28,205	20	894.0	30	Elk	3,261	89	647.9	74
Bourbon	15,379	34	637.1	79	Ellis	27,507	22	900.0	24
Brown	10,724	40	570.7	93	Ellsworth	6,525	60	715.9	66
Butler	59,482	9	1,428.2	1	Finney	40,523	11	1,300.2	2
Chase	3,030	93	775.9	50	Ford	32,458	17	1,098.6	8
Chautauqua	4,359	77	641.7	77	Franklin	24,784	24	573.9	91
Cherokee	22,605	26	587.2	85	Geary	27,947	21	384.3	104
Cheyenne	3,165	90	1,019.9	15	Gove	3,068	91	1,071.5	12
Clark	2,390	100	974.7	19	Graham	2,946	95	898.3	27
Clay	8,822	47	643.9	76	Grant	7,909	52	574.9	89
Cloud	10,268	43	715.7	67	Gray	5,904	66	868.9	39
Coffey	8,865	46	630.3	80	Greeley	1,534	105	778.1	49
Comanche	1,967	103	788.4	48	Greenwood	7,673	53	1,139.8	5
Cowley	36,291	13	1,126.3	7	Hamilton	2,670	97	996.5	17
Crawford	38,242	12	593.0	84	Harper	6,536	59	801.5	45
Decatur	3,472	84	893.6	31	Harvey	32,869	16	539.4	95

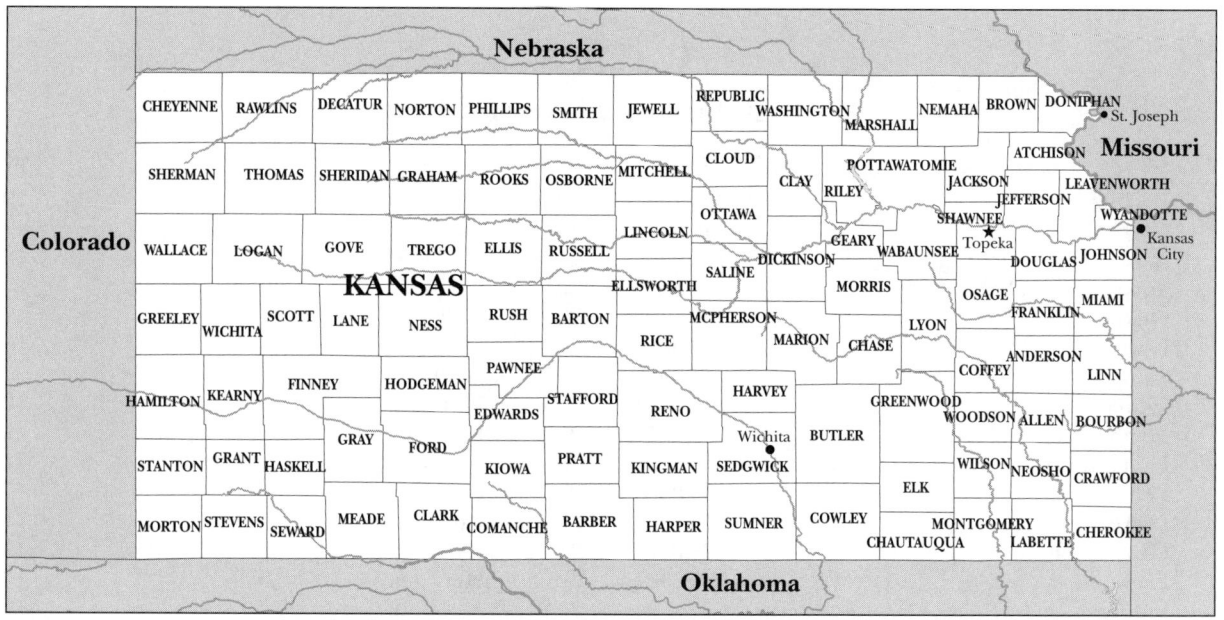

County	2000 pop.	Rank in pop.	Sq. miles	Rank in area	County	2000 pop.	Rank in pop.	Sq. miles	Rank in area
Haskell	4,307	78	577.4	87	Pottawatomie	18,209	30	844.3	44
Hodgeman	2,085	102	860.0	41	Pratt	9,647	44	735.0	52
Jackson	12,657	37	656.9	72	Rawlins	2,966	94	1,069.7	13
Jefferson	18,426	29	536.2	96	Reno	64,790	7	1,254.5	3
Jewell	3,791	79	909.2	22	Republic	5,835	67	716.5	65
Johnson	451,086	2	476.8	99	Rice	10,761	39	726.6	55
Kearny	4,531	75	870.0	38	Riley	62,843	8	609.6	82
Kingman	8,673	48	863.7	40	Rooks	5,685	68	888.4	34
Kiowa	3,278	88	722.4	56	Rush	3,551	82	718.2	62
Labette	22,835	25	648.9	73	Russell	7,370	54	884.7	36
Lane	2,155	101	717.3	64	Saline	53,597	10	719.6	58
Leavenworth	68,691	6	463.3	100	Scott	5,120	71	717.6	63
Lincoln	3,578	81	718.9	60	Sedgwick	452,869	1	1,000.2	16
Linn	9,570	45	598.8	83	Seward	22,510	27	639.6	78
Logan	3,046	92	1,073.1	11	Shawnee	169,871	3	549.9	94
Lyon	35,935	15	851.0	42	Sheridan	2,813	96	896.4	28
McPherson	29,554	18	899.8	25	Sherman	6,760	58	1,055.9	14
Marion	13,361	36	943.2	20	Smith	4,536	74	895.5	29
Marshall	10,965	38	902.6	23	Stafford	4,789	72	792.1	47
Meade	4,631	73	978.5	18	Stanton	2,406	99	680.1	71
Miami	28,351	19	576.8	88	Stevens	5,463	69	727.6	54
Mitchell	6,932	56	699.9	69	Sumner	25,946	23	1,181.9	4
Montgomery	36,252	14	645.3	75	Thomas	8,180	50	1,074.9	9
Morris	6,104	63	697.4	70	Trego	3,319	87	888.4	33
Morton	3,496	83	730.0	53	Wabaunsee	6,885	57	797.5	46
Nemaha	10,717	41	719.1	59	Wallace	1,749	104	914.1	21
Neosho	16,997	31	571.9	92	Washington	6,483	61	898.5	26
Ness	3,454	85	1,074.8	10	Wichita	2,531	98	718.6	61
Norton	5,953	65	877.9	37	Wilson	10,332	42	573.9	90
Osage	16,712	33	703.6	68	Woodson	3,788	80	500.7	98
Osborne	4,452	76	892.6	32	Wyandotte	157,882	4	151.4	105
Ottawa	6,163	62	721.2	57					
Pawnee	7,233	55	754.2	51					
Phillips	6,001	64	886.3	35					

Source: U.S. Census Bureau; National Association of Counties.

Cities
With 10,000 or more residents

Rank	City	Population	Rank	City	Population
1	Wichita	344,284	19	Liberal	19,666
2	Overland Park	149,080	20	Pittsburg	19,243
3	Kansas City	146,866	21	Junction City	18,886
4	Topeka (capital)	122,377	22	Derby	17,807
5	Olathe	92,962	23	Newton	17,190
6	Lawrence	80,098	24	Great Bend	15,345
7	Shawnee	47,996	25	McPherson	13,770
8	Salina	45,679	26	Winfield	12,206
9	Manhattan	44,831	27	El Dorado	12,057
10	Hutchinson	40,787	28	Arkansas City	11,963
11	Lenexa	40,238	29	Ottawa	11,921
12	Leavenworth	35,420	30	Parsons	11,514
13	Garden City	28,451	31	Coffeyville	11,021
14	Leawood	27,656	32	Merriam	11,008
15	Emporia	26,760	33	Atchison	10,232
16	Dodge City	25,176			
17	Prairie Village	22,072			
18	Hays	20,013			

Population figures are from 2000 census.
Source: U.S. Bureau of the Census.

Index to Tables

DEMOGRAPHICS

Resident state and national populations, 1970-2004

Population figures given in thousands

	State pop.	U.S. pop.	Share	Rank
1970	2,249	203,302	1.1%	28
1980	2,364	226,546	1.0%	32
1985	2,427	237,924	1.0%	32
1990	2,478	248,765	1.0%	32
1995	2,601	262,761	1.0%	32
2000	2,689	281,425	1.0%	32
2004	2,736	293,655	0.9%	33

Source: U.S. Census Bureau, Current Population Reports, 2006.

Resident population by age, 2004

Age Group	Total persons
Under 5 years	189,000
5 to 17 years	495,000
18 to 24 years	299,000
25 to 34 years	359,000
35 to 44 years	388,000
45 to 54 years	392,000
55 to 64 years	260,000
65 to 74 years	170,000
75 to 84 years	129,000
85 years and older	55,000
All age groups	2,736,000
Portion of residents 65 and older	13.0%
National rank in portion of oldest residents	20
National average	12.4%

Population figures are rounded to nearest thousand persons;
figures include armed forces personnel stationed in the state.
Source: U.S. Bureau of the Census, 2006.

Resident population by race, Hispanic origin, 2004

Category	State pop.	Share	U.S.
All residents	2,736	100.00%	100.00%
Non-Hispanic white	2,239	81.83%	67.37%
Hispanic white	206	7.53%	13.01%
Other Hispanic	14	0.51%	1.06%
African American	161	5.88%	12.77%
Native American	26	0.95%	0.96%
Asian, Pacific Islander	59	2.16%	4.37%
Two or more categories	44	1.61%	1.51%

Population figures are in thousands. Persons counted as
"Hispanic" (Latino) may be of any race. Because of overlapping
categories, categories may not add up to 100%. Shares in
column 3 are percentages of each category within the state;
these figures may be compared to the national percentages in
column 4.
Source: U.S. Bureau of the Census, 2006.

Projected state population, 2000-2030

Year	Population
2000	2,689,000
2005	2,752,000
2010	2,805,000
2015	2,853,000
2020	2,891,000
2025	2,919,000
2030	2,940,000
Population increase, 2000-2030	251,000
Percentage increase, 2000-2030	9.4

Projections are based on data from the 2000 census.
Source: U.S. Census Bureau.

VITAL STATISTICS

Infant mortality rates, 1980-2002

	1980	1990	2000	2002
All state residents	10.4	8.4	6.8	7.1
All U.S. residents	12.6	9.2	9.4	9.1
All state white residents	9.5	8.0	6.4	6.5
All U.S. white residents	10.6	7.6	5.7	5.8
All state black residents	20.6	17.7	12.2	15.2
All U.S. black residents	22.2	18.0	14.1	14.4

Figures represent deaths per 1,000 live births of resident infants
under 1 year old, exclusive of fetal deaths. Figures for all
residents include members of other racial categories not listed
separately.
Source: U.S. Census Bureau, *Statistical Abstract of the United States,*
2006.

Abortion rates, 1990 and 2000

	1990	2000
Total abortions	13,000	12,000
Rate per 1,000 women	22.4	21.4
U.S. rate	25.7	21.3
Rank	21	13

Numbers of abortions are rounded to nearest thousand; ranks are
based on rates.
Source: U.S. Census Bureau.

Marriages and divorces, 2004

Total marriages	19,100
Rate per 1,000 population	7.0
National rate per 1,000 population	7.4
Rank among all states	28
Total divorces	9,100
Rate per 1,000 population	3.3
National rate per 1,000 population	3.7
Rank among all states	30

Figures are for all marriages and divorces performed within the
state, including those of nonresidents; totals are rounded to the
nearest hundred. Ranks are for highest to lowest figures; note
that divorce data are not available for five states.
Source: U.S. National Center for Health Statistics, *Vital Statistics of
the United States,* 2006.

Death rates by leading causes, 2002
Deaths per 100,000 resident population

Cause	State	U.S.
Heart disease	246.0	241.7
Cancer	197.4	193.2
Cerebrovascular diseases	67.9	56.4
Accidents other than motor vehicle	41.9	37.0
Motor vehicle accidents	20.7	15.7
Chronic lower respiratory diseases	50.3	43.3
Diabetes mellitus	28.2	25.4
HIV	1.4	4.9
Suicide	12.7	11.0
Homicide	4.7	6.1
All causes	921.3	847.3
Rank in overall death rate among states		18

Figures exclude nonresidents who died in the state. Causes of
death follow International Classification of Diseases. Rank is
from highest to lowest death rate in the United States.
Source: U.S. National Center for Health Statistics, *National Vital
Statistics Report,* 2006.

ECONOMY

Gross state product, 1990-2004
In current dollars

Year	State product	Nat'l product	State share
1990	$51.3 billion	$5.67 trillion	0.90%
2000	$83.4 billion	$9.75 trillion	0.86%
2002	$89.9 billion	$10.41 trillion	0.86%
2003	$93.3 billion	$10.92 trillion	0.85%
2004	$99.1 billion	$11.65 trillion	0.85%

Source: U.S. Bureau of Economic Analysis, *Survey of Current Business,* July, 2005.

Gross state product by industry, 2003
In billions of dollars

Construction	$3.4
Manufacturing	12.9
Wholesale trade	5.7
Retail trade	7.3
Finance & insurance	5.5
Information	7.4
Professional services	3.9
Health care & social assistance	5.8
Government	11.5
Total state product	$86.8
Total U.S. product	$10,289.2
State share of U.S. total	0.84%
Rank among all states	31

Total figures include industries not listed separately. Amounts are in chained 2000 dollars.
Source: U.S. Bureau of Economic Analysis, *Survey of Current Business,* July, 2005.

Personal income per capita, 1990-2004
In current dollars

	1990	2000	2004
Per capita income	$18,085	$27,694	$30,811
U.S. average	$19,477	$29,845	$32,937
Rank among states	22	27	28

Source: U.S. Bureau of Economic Analysis, *Survey of Current Business,* April, 2005.

Energy consumption, 2001
In trillions of British thermal units (BTU), except as noted

Total energy consumption

Total state energy consumption	1,044
Total U.S. energy consumption	96,275
State share of U.S. total	1.08%
Rank among states	32

Per capita consumption (In millions of BTU)

Total state per capita consumption	387
Total U.S. per capita consumption	338
Rank among states	15

End-use sectors

Residential	215
Commercial	192
Industrial	385
Transportation	252

Sources of energy

Petroleum	391
Natural gas	274
Coal	355
Hydroelectric power	(z)
Nuclear electric power	108

Figures for totals include categories not listed separately.
(z) Indicates less than 0.5 trillion BTU.
Source: U.S. Energy Information Administration, *State Energy Data Report,* 2001.

Nonfarm employment by sectors, 2004

Total	1,323,000
Construction	63,000
Manufacturing	176,000
Trade, transportation, utilities	261,000
Information	42,000
Finance, insurance, real estate	70,000
Professional & business services	127,000
Education & health services	160,000
Leisure, hospitality, arts, organizations	110,000
Other services, including repair & maintenance	53,000
Government	252,000

Figures are rounded to nearest thousand persons. "Total" includes mining and natural resources, not listed separately.
Source: U.S. Bureau of Labor Statistics, 2006.

Foreign exports, 1990-2004
In millions of dollars

Year	State	U.S.	State share
1990	2,113	394,045	0.54%
1996	3,784	624,767	0.61%
1997	4,292	688,896	0.62%
2000	5,145	712,055	0.66%
2003	4,553	724,006	0.67%
2004	4,931	769,332	0.64%

Rank among all states in 2004 30

U.S. total does not include U.S. dependencies.
Source: U.S. Census Bureau, *U.S. Merchandise Trade,* series FT 900, 2000; U.S. Census Bureau, *U.S. International Trade in Goods and Services,* Series FT 900, 2005.

LAND USE

Federally owned land, 2003
Areas in acres

	State	U.S.	State share
Total area	52,511,000	2,271,343,000	2.31%
Nonfederal land	51,869,000	1,599,584,000	3.24%
Federal land	642,000	671,759,000	0.10%
Federal share	1.2%	29.6%	—

Areas are rounded to nearest thousand acres. Figures for federally owned land do not include trust properties.
Source: U.S. General Services Administration, *Federal Real Property Profile,* 2006.

Land use, 1997
In acres, rounded to nearest thousand

Total surface area 52,661,000
Total nonfederal rural land. 49,685,000
Percentage rural land 94.3%
Cropland. 26,524,000
Conservation Reserve Program (CRP*) land . . . 2,849,000
Pastureland 2,322,000
Rangeland 15,728,000
Forestland. 1,546,000
Other rural land 716,000

*CRP is a federal program begun in 1985 to assist private landowners to convert highly erodible cropland to vegetative cover for ten years. Note that some categories of land overlap.
Source: U.S. Department of Agriculture, Natural Resources and Conservation Service, and Iowa State University, Statistical Laboratory, *Summary Report, 1997 National Resources Inventory,* revised December, 2000.

Farms and crop acreage, 2004

	State	U.S.	Share	Rank
Farms	65,000	2,113,000	3.08%	12
Acres (millions)	47	937	5.02%	3
Acres per farm	732	443	—	12

Source: U.S. Department of Agriculture, National Agricultural Statistics Service. Numbers of farms are rounded to nearest thousand units; acreage figures are rounded to nearest million. Rankings, including ties, are based on rounded figures.

GOVERNMENT AND FINANCE

Units of local government, 2002

	State	Total U.S.	Rank
All local governments	3,887	87,525	5
Counties	104	3,034	5
Municipalities	627	19,429	8
Townships	1,299	16,504	6
School districts	324	13,506	16
Special districts	1,533	35,052	5

Only 48 states have county governments, 20 states have township governments ("towns" in New England, Minnesota, New York, and Wisconsin), and 46 states have school districts. Special districts encompass such functions as natural resources, fire protection, and housing and community development.
Source: U.S. Census Bureau, *Census of Governments.*

State government revenue, 2002

Total revenue . . . . $9,694 mill.
General revenue . . . . $9,179 mill.
Per capita revenue $3,384
U.S. per capita average $3,689
Rank among states 43

Intergovernment revenue
Total . . . . $2,992 mill.
From federal government . . . . $2,964 mill.

Charges and miscellaneous
Total . . . . $1,379 mill.
Current charges . . . . $669 mill.
Misc. general income . . . . $710 mill.
Insurance trust revenue . . . . $515 mill.

Taxes
Total . . . . $4,808 mill.
Per capita taxes $1,773
Rank among states 25
Property taxes . . . . $55 mill.
Sales taxes . . . . $2,432 mill.
License taxes . . . . $230 mill.
Individual income taxes . . . . $1,855 mill.
Corporate income taxes . . . . $122 mill.
Other taxes . . . . $115 mill.

Total revenue figures include items not listed separately here.
Source: U.S. Bureau of the Census.

State government expenditures, 2002

General expenditures
Total state expenditures . . . . $10,592 mill.
Intergovernmental . . . . $2,971 mill.

Per capita expenditures
State $3,546
Average of all states $3,859
Rank among states 36

Selected direct expenditures
Education . . . . $1,578 mill.
Public welfare . . . . $1,963 mill.
Health, hospital . . . . $542 mill.
Highways . . . . $967 mill.
Police protection . . . . $63 mill.
Corrections . . . . $268 mill.
Natural resources . . . . $175 mill.
Parks and recreation . . . . $5 mill.
Government administration . . . . $496 mill.
Interest on debt . . . . $127 mill.
Total direct expenditures . . . . $6,646 mill.

Totals include items not listed separately.
Source: U.S. Census Bureau.

POLITICS

Governors since statehood
D = Democrat; R = Republican; O = other;
(r) resigned; (d) died in office; (i) removed from office

Charles Robinson (R) 1861-1863
Thomas Carney (R) 1863-1865
Samuel J. Crawford (R) . . . . (r) 1865-1868
Nehemiah Green (R) 1868-1869
James M. Harvey (R) 1869-1873
Thomas A. Osborn (R) 1873-1877
George T. Anthony (R) 1877-1879
John P. St. John (R) 1879-1883
George W. Glick (D) 1883-1885
John A. Martin (R) 1885-1889
Lyman U. Humphrey (R) 1889-1893
Lorenzo D. Lewelling (O) 1893-1895
Edmund N. Morrill (R) 1895-1897
John W. Leedy (D) 1897-1899
William E. Stanley (R) 1899-1903
Willis J. Bailey (R) 1903-1905
Edward W. Hoch (R) 1905-1909
Walter R. Stubbs (R) 1909-1913
George H. Hodges (D) 1913-1915
Arthur Capper (R) 1915-1919
Henry J. Allen (R) 1919-1923
Jonathan M. Davis (D) 1923-1925
Benjamin S. Paulen (R) 1925-1929
Clyde M. Reed (R) 1929-1931
Harry H. Woodring (D) 1931-1933
Alfred M. Landon (R) 1933-1937
Walter A. Huxman (D) 1937-1939

Payne H. Ratner (R) 1939-1943
Andrew F. Schoeppel (R) 1943-1947
Frank Carlson (R) . . . . (r) 1947-1950
Frank L. Hagaman (R) 1950-1951
Edward F. Arn (R) 1951-1955
Fred L. Hall (R) . . . . (r) 1955-1957
John B. McCuish (R) 1957
George Docking (D) 1957-1961
John A. Anderson, Jr. (R) 1961-1965
William H. Avery (R) 1965-1967
Robert B. Docking (D) 1967-1973
Robert F. Bennett (R) 1973-1979
John W. Carlin (D) 1979-1987
Mike Hayden (R) 1987-1991
Joan Finney (D) 1991-1995
Bill Graves (R) 1995-2003
Kathleen Sebelius (D) 2003-

Composition of congressional delegations, 1989-2007

	Dem	Rep	Total
House of Representatives			
101st Congress, 1989			
State delegates	2	3	5
Total U.S.	259	174	433
102d Congress, 1991			
State delegates	2	3	5
Total U.S.	267	167	434
103d Congress, 1993			
State delegates	2	2	4
Total U.S.	258	176	434
104th Congress, 1995			
State delegates	0	4	4
Total U.S.	197	236	433
105th Congress, 1997			
State delegates	0	4	4
Total U.S.	206	228	434
106th Congress, 1999			
State delegates	1	3	4
Total U.S.	211	222	433
107th Congress, 2001			
State delegates	1	3	4
Total U.S.	211	221	432
108th Congress, 2003			
State delegates	1	3	4
Total U.S.	205	229	434
109th Congress, 2005			
State delegates	1	3	4
Total U.S.	202	231	433
110th Congress, 2007			
State delegates	2	2	4
Total U.S.	233	202	435

(continued)

	Dem	Rep	Total
Senate			
101st Congress, 1989			
State delegates	0	2	2
Total U.S.	55	45	100
102d Congress, 1991			
State delegates	0	2	2
Total U.S.	56	44	100
103d Congress, 1993			
State delegates	0	2	2
Total U.S.	57	43	100
104th Congress, 1995			
State delegates	0	2	2
Total U.S.	46	53	99
105th Congress, 1997			
State delegates	0	2	2
Total U.S.	45	55	100
106th Congress, 1999			
State delegates	0	2	2
Total U.S.	45	54	99
107th Congress, 2001			
State delegates	0	2	2
Total U.S.	50	50	100
108th Congress, 2003			
State delegates	0	2	2
Total U.S.	48	51	99
109th Congress, 2005			
State delegates	0	2	2
Total U.S.	44	55	99
110th Congress, 2007			
State delegates	0	2	2
Total U.S.	49	49	98

Figures are for starts of first sessions. Totals are for Democrat (Dem.) and Republican (Rep.) members only. House membership totals under 435 and Senate totals under 100 reflect vacancies and seats held by independent party members. When the 110th Congress opened, the Senate's two independent members caucused with the Democrats, giving the Democrats control of the Senate.

Source: U.S. Congress, *Congressional Directory.*

Composition of state legislature, 1990-2006

	Democrats	Republicans
State House (125 seats)		
1990	63	62
1992	59	66
1994	45	80
1996	48	77
1998	48	77
2000	48	77
2002	45	80
2004	42	83
2006	47	78
State Senate (50 seats)		
1990	18	22
1992	13	27
1994	13	27
1996	13	27
1998	13	27
2000	13	27
2002	10	30
2004	10	30
2006	10	30

Figures for total seats may include independents and minor party members. Numbers reflect results of elections in listed years; elected members usually take their seats in the years that follow.

Source: Council of State Governments; *State Elective Officials and the Legislatures.*

Voter participation in presidential elections, 2000 and 2004

	2000	2004
Voting age population		
State	1,981,000	2,052,000
Total United States	209,831,000	220,377,000
State share of U.S. total	0.94	0.93
Rank among states	33	33
Portion of voting age population casting votes		
State	54.1%	57.9%
United States	50.3%	55.5%
Rank among states	22	25

Population figures are rounded to nearest thousand and include all residents, regardless of eligibility to vote.

Source: U.S. Census Bureau.

HEALTH AND MEDICAL CARE

Medical professionals
Physicians in 2003 and nurses in 2001

	U.S.	State
Physicians in 2003		
Total	774,849	5,947
Share of U.S. total		0.76%
Rate	266	218
Rank		37
Nurses in 2001		
Total	2,262,020	24,680
Share of U.S. total		1.09%
Rate	793	913
Rank		14

Rates are numbers of physicians and nurses per 100,000 resident population; ranks are based on rates.
Source: American Medical Association, *Physician Characteristics and Distribution in the U.S.*; U.S. Department of Health and Human Services, Health Resources and Services Administration.

Health insurance coverage, 2003

	State	U.S.
Total persons covered	2,389,000	243,320,000
Total persons not covered	294,000	44,961,000
Portion not covered	11.0%	15.6%
Rank among states	38	—
Children not covered	45,000	8,373,000
Portion not covered	6.4%	11.4%
Rank among states	44	—

Totals are rounded to nearest thousand. Ranks are from the highest to the lowest percentages of persons *not* insured.
Source: U.S. Census Bureau, Current Population Reports.

AIDS, syphilis, and tuberculosis cases, 2003

Disease	U.S. cases	State cases	Rank
AIDS	44,232	111	34
Syphilis	34,270	77	35
Tuberculosis	14,874	75	33

Source: U.S. Centers for Disease Control and Prevention.

Cigarette smoking, 2003
Residents over age 18 who smoke

	U.S.	State	Rank
All smokers	22.1%	20.4%	38
Male smokers	24.8%	21.0%	40
Female smokers	20.3%	19.7%	31

Cigarette smokers are defined as persons who reported having smoked at least 100 cigarettes during their lifetimes and who currently smoked at least occasionally.
Source: U.S. Centers for Disease Control and Prevention, *Morbidity and Mortality Weekly Report*, 53, no. 44 (November 12, 2004).

HOUSING

Home ownership rates, 1985-2004

	1985	1990	1995	2000	2004
State	68.3%	69.0%	67.5%	69.3%	69.9%
Total U.S.	63.9%	63.9%	64.7%	67.4%	69.0%
Rank among states	23	14	24	31	35

Net change in state home ownership rate, 1985-2004 . . . . +1.6%
Net change in U.S. home ownership rate, 1985-2004 . . . . +5.1%

Percentages represent the proportion of owner households to total occupied households.
Source: U.S. Census Bureau, 2006.

Home sales, 2000-2004
In thousands of units

Existing home sales	2000	2002	2003	2004
State sales	52.6	60.0	65.3	73.4
Total U.S. sales	5,171	5,631	6,183	6,784
State share of U.S. total	1.02%	1.07%	1.06%	1.08%
Sales rank among states	31	31	30	30

Units include single-family homes, condos, and co-ops.
Source: National Association of Realtors, Washington, D.C., *Real Estate Outlook: Market Trends & Insights.*

Values of owner-occupied homes, 2003

	State	U.S.
Total units	611,000	58,809,000
Value of units		
Under $100,000	49.9%	29.6%
$100,000-199,999	37.0%	36.9%
$200,000 or more	13.1%	33.5%
Median value	$100,257	$142,275
Rank among all states 40		

Units are owner-occupied one-family houses whose numbers are rounded to nearest thousand. Data are extrapolated from survey samples.
Source: U.S. Census Bureau, American Community Survey.

EDUCATION

Public school enrollment, 2002

Prekindergarten through grade 8
State enrollment 322,000
Total U.S. enrollment. 34,135,000
State share of U.S. total 0.94%

Grades 9 through 12
State enrollment 149,000
Total U.S. enrollment. 14,067,000
State share of U.S. total 1.06%

Enrollment rates
State public school enrollment rate. 92.2%
Overall U.S. rate 90.4%
Rank among states in 2002. 13
Rank among states in 1995. 28

Enrollment figures (which include unclassified students) are rounded to nearest thousand pupils during fall school term. Enrollment rates are based on enumerated resident population estimate for July 1, 2002.
Source: U.S. National Center for Education Statistics.

Public college finances, 2003-2004

FTE enrollment in public institutions of higher education
Students in state institutions. 110,200
Students in all U.S. public institutions 9,916,600
State share of U.S. total 1.11
Rank among states 31

State and local government appropriations for higher education
State appropriation per FTE $5,940
National average. $5,716
Rank among states 19
State & local tax revenue going to higher education 10.1%

FTE = full-time equivalent in public postsecondary programs, including summer sessions; student numbers are rounded to nearest hundred. Funding figures for 2003-2004 academic year include financial aid to students in state public institutions and exclude money for research, agriculture experiment stations, teaching hospitals, and medical schools; figures are rounded to nearest thousand dollars.
Source: Higher Education Executive Officers, Denver, Colorado.

TRANSPORTATION AND TRAVEL

Highway mileage, 2003

Interstate highways 874
Other freeways and expressways 133
Arterial roads 9,197
Collector roads. 33,364
Local roads 91,444
Urban roads 10,593
Rural roads 124,419
Total state mileage 135,012
U.S. total 3,974,107
State share 3.40%
Rank among states. 4

Note that combined urban and rural road mileage matches the total of the other categories.
Source: U.S. Federal Highway Administration.

Motor vehicle registrations and driver licenses, 2003

Vehicle registrations	State	U.S.	Share	Rank
Autos, trucks, buses	2,314,000	231,390,000	1.00%	30
Autos only	834,000	135,670	0.61%	35
Motorcycles	56,000	5,328,000	1.05%	31
Driver licenses	1,987,000	196,166,000	1.01%	31

Figures, which do not include vehicles owned by military services, are rounded to the nearest thousand. Figures for automobiles include taxis.
Source: U.S. Federal Highway Administration.

Domestic travel expenditures, 2003
Spending by U.S. residents on overnight trips and day trips of at least 50 miles from home

Total expenditures within state . . . . $3.85 bill.
Total expenditures within U.S. . . . . $490.87 bill.
State share of U.S. total 0.8%
Rank among states 36

Source: Travel Industry Association of America.

Retail gasoline prices, 2003-2007
Average price per gallon at the pump

Year	U.S.	State
2003	$1.267	$1.193
2004	$1.316	$1.241
2005	$1.644	$1.645
2007	$2.298	$2.173

Excise tax per gallon in 2004 . . . . 24.0¢
Rank among all states in 2007 prices 38

Prices are averages of all grades of gasoline sold at the pump during March months in 2003-2005 and during February, 2007. Averages for 2006, during which prices rose higher, are not available.
Source: U.S. Energy Information Agency, *Petroleum Marketing Monthly* (2003-2005 data); American Automobile Association (2007 data).

CRIME AND LAW ENFORCEMENT

State and local police officers, 2000-2004

	2000	2002	2004
Total officers			
U.S.	654,601	665,555	675,734
State	6,556	6,787	7,144*
*Net change, 2000-2004			+8.97%
Officers per 1,000 residents			
U.S.	2.33	2.31	2.30
State	2.44	2.50	2.61
State rank	9	9	8

Totals include state and local police and sheriffs.
Source: Carsey Institute, University of New Hampshire.

Crime rates, 2003
Incidents per 100,000 residents

Crimes	State	U.S.
Violent crimes		
Total incidents	396	475
Murder	5	6
Forcible rape	38	32
Robbery	83	142
Aggravated assault	270	295
Property crimes		
Total incidents	3,994	3,588
Burglary	804	741
Larceny/theft	2,905	2,415
Motor vehicle theft	286	433
All crimes	4,390	4,063

Source: U.S. Federal Bureau of Investigation, *Crime in the United States,* annual.

State prison populations, 1980-2003

	State	U.S.	State share
1980	2,494	305,458	0.82%
1990	5,775	708,393	0.82%
1996	7,756	1,025,624	0.76%
2000	8,344	1,391,261	0.60%
2003	9,132	1,470,045	0.62%

State figures exclude prisoners in federal penitentiaries.
Source: U.S. Bureau of Justice Statistics, *Prisoners in 2003.*

Kentucky

Location: Eastern central United States

Area and rank: 39,732 square miles (102,907 square kilometers); 40,411 square miles (104,664 square kilometers) including water; thirty-sixth largest state in area

Coastline: none

Population and rank: 4,146,000 (2004); twenty-sixth largest state in population

Capital city: Frankfort (27,741 people in 2000 census)

Largest city: Lexington-Fayette (260,512 people in 2000 census)

Entered Union and rank: June 1, 1792; fifteenth state

Present constitution adopted: 1891

Counties: 120

Louisville, Kentucky's second-largest city, owes much of its historical growth to its position as a port on the Ohio River. (© Denise McQuillen/iStockphoto)

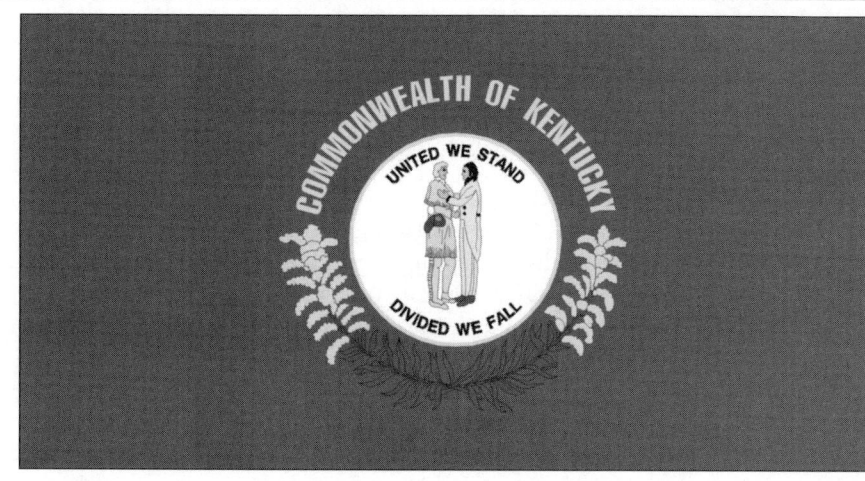

State name: "Kentucky" is derived from an Iroquoian word, "Ken-tah-ten," which means "land of tomorrow"

State nickname: Bluegrass State

Motto: United we stand, divided we fall

State flag: Blue field with state seal, goldenrod sprigs below, and legend "Commonwealth of Kentucky" above

Highest point: Black Mountain—4,139 feet (1,262 meters)

Lowest point: Mississippi River—257 feet (78 meters)

Highest recorded temperature: 114 degrees Fahrenheit (46 degrees Celsius)—Greensburg, 1930

Lowest recorded temperature: –34 degrees Fahrenheit (–37 degrees Celsius)—Cynthiana, 1963

State song: "My Old Kentucky Home"

State tree: Tulip poplar

State flower: Goldenrod

State bird: Kentucky cardinal

National parks: Mammoth Cave

Kentucky History

Popularly known as the Bluegrass State, Kentucky was the first state west of the Appalachian Mountains populated by settlers from the original thirteen English colonies. From its earliest days it served as a gateway from east to west and as a border state between the North and South. For most of its history an agricultural and mining state, during the second half of the twentieth century Kentucky began a rapid transformation into a modern industrial economy.

Early History and Settlement. Evidence suggests that Native Americans first entered the area of modern Kentucky as long as fifteen thousand years ago and were primarily hunters and gatherers. Later, agriculture and trade were established, leading to a period around 450 B.C.E. known as the Adena culture, when burial mounds were constructed in the northern Kentucky area. Around 1000 C.E. two distinct Native American cultures developed in the area, the Missippippian in the west and the Fort Ancient in the east; the two groups had many similarities, including the cultivation of beans and corn from the south and the use of agricultural implements including the hoe. The first European explorers found the Cherokee, Delaware, Iroquois, and Shawnee Indian tribes in the territory, although the central portion was not permanently settled by any of these groups. Instead, it seems to have been used as a common hunting ground by all of them. It may also have been reserved for a battlefield for their disputes.

During the mid-eighteenth century, English settlers from the colonies on the East Coast, in particular from Virginia, began to push over the mountains into the area known as Kentucky. The word itself is derived from an Indian word which most likely means "land of to-

President Abraham Lincoln is closely identified with Illinois, but he was born in what is now LaRue County, Kentucky, where this memorial marks his birthplace. (PhotoDisc)

morrow." Among these English explorers and settlers was Dr. Thomas Walker, who charted the Cumberland Gap, the entryway to Kentucky, and was the first European to build a permanent shelter in the area.

Another and more famous traveler was Daniel Boone, who explored the area first in 1767 and again in 1769. In his second journey, Boone reached as far as the central plateau of the state, soon known as "bluegrass country" from its distinctive vegetation. Boone's initial attempt at settlement in 1773 was a failure, but the following year James Harrod and colonists from Pennsylvania established Harrodstown. Boone returned the year after, and Fort Boonesborough was established in 1775. In 1776, the state of Virginia formally claimed the entire territory, giving it the name of the County of Kentucky.

Revolution and Statehood. Native Americans were bewildered and angered by the various treaties they had made with the settlers. The Native Americans felt that these treaties had robbed them of the use of the lands which had been common to all for generations; ownership, in the European sense of the word, was an alien concept to the American Indians. As a result, many tribes throughout the area beyond the mountains allied themselves with the British during the American Revolution, and their attacks on Kentucky threatened the entire American settlement. In response, pioneer George Rogers Clark launched an offensive against the British and Native American strongholds north of the Ohio River. In a campaign that pitted small forces against one another in extremely difficult terrain during the middle of winter, Clark won a crucial victory when he forced the besieged British to surrender the frontier fort of Vincennes in 1779. However, Kentucky remained under threat from British and Native American attack until the Battle of Blue Licks in 1782, which has been called "the last battle of the Revolution."

Shortly after the Revolution ended in American independence, Kentuckians began agitating for their own independence, with the creation of a state separate from Virginia. During the 1780's, ten separate conventions were held, which gradually drafted the provisions that eventually established Kentucky as a state in its own right. On June 1, 1792, Kentucky was admitted to the Union as the fifteenth state, with Frankfort as its capital. It was the first state of the new United States established west of the Alleghenies.

During the years that followed, Kentucky encouraged one struggle, the War of 1812 against England, and sought to avoid a second, the American Civil War. Kentucky's most famous statesman of the years before the Civil War, Henry Clay, played a key role in both efforts. As a War Hawk congressman during the early ninteenth century, Clay advocated a conflict with Great Britain that he and others hoped could lead to the United States acquiring Canada. Later, as a U.S. Senator, Clay helped craft the Missouri Compromise of 1820 and the Compromise of 1850, which delayed, if they did not prevent, war between the states over slavery.

The Civil War and Early Modern Times. As a border state, Kentucky shared qualities of both the North and South. The majority of its residents were small farmers who owned few or no slaves, and they were inclined to neutrality in the Civil War. There were a number of slaveholders in the broad central portion of the state, and while their sympathies were with the South, they also sought to remain aloof from the struggle. The northern part of the state shared in the developing commerce of the Ohio Valley, and crops of tobacco and cotton were often shipped south down the Mississippi to New Orleans; thus all parts of the state feared that war would disrupt this commerce. Along the eastern, more mountainous portions of the state, where slaves were few, pro-Union sentiment was strongest. Perhaps the fact that most dramatically illustrated the state's precariously balanced position was the fact that both Abraham Lincoln, president of the Union, and Jefferson Davis, president of the Confederacy, were born in Kentucky within a year of one another.

As the controversy over slavery grew more intense and the nation drifted toward war, Kentucky hoped to find yet one more compromise to avert struggle. When the Civil War finally erupted in 1861, Kentucky declared its official neutrality and was promptly invaded by both the Confederacy and the Union, which seized strategic points in the state. Some seventy thousand Kentuckians served with the Union forces; approximately thirty thousand rallied to the Confederacy. After a powerful Confederate thrust north was turned back in the summer of 1862, Kentucky was kept firmly in Union hands for the duration of the war.

Following the Civil War, Kentucky continued to develop its agriculture, most notably the tobacco industry. In addition, the state expanded its reputation for outstanding horse breeding and racing; the first Kentucky Derby was held in Louisville in 1875. Whiskey, especially bourbon, had been produced in the state since the 1820's and became world famous for its quality. The expansion of the railroads into the eastern, more mountainous portions of the state opened new coal fields for exploitation, often through the destructive process of strip-mining, which left a barren wasteland behind. Life for coal miners and their families was hard and often dangerous.

The Great Depression, which began in 1929, coupled with years of drought and then flood, caused enormous damage to Kentucky's economy. By 1940 Kentucky ranked last in the nation for per-capita income. President Franklin Roosevelt's New Deal and then the economic energy unleashed by World War II brought a measure of recovery to the state, including even parts of the Appalachian Mountains. However, poverty remained an endemic problem, especially in Appalachia, even through President Lyndon Johnson's Great Society programs of the mid-1960's.

The Modern Era. After World War II, northern Kentucky in particular experienced an economic boom, with growth in manufacturing companies, which supplied industries in fields such as chemicals, automotives, office supplies, electric appliances, and wood products. In addition, the state took the lead in fields such as health care, with Humana, a Kentucky-formed company and one of the largest health care corporations in the United States, having established its headquarters in Louisville. State government actively sought to recruit industry, especially "light industry" which can fit into the Kentucky environment with minimal impact on natural resources. Such concerns are important, as horse breeding and tourism are major parts of Kentucky's overall economic picture and depend on precisely these natural resources for their continued viability.

Kentucky also took its place in the developing automobile industry in the Southeast. Under Democratic governor Martha Layne Collins, the state recruited a $3.5 billion investment by Japanese automaker Toyota in Kentucky, which, by the early 1990's, was employing more than twenty thousand workers. The success of Toyota in Kentucky was one of the reasons that other international automobile makers chose to locate in the area, most notably BMW in South Carolina in 1993 and Mercedes-Benz in Alabama in 1994. In addition to the automobile manufacturing plants themselves, the companies also attracted large numbers of suppliers for the parts needed in the production of the finished vehicle.

Tobacco Politics. In 2000, Kentucky, like other major tobacco-producing states, enacted a Tobacco Industry Shield Law. The law addressed the substantial liability that the tobacco industry regularly faces, costing many billions of dollars. If tobacco companies were required to post the bond that would otherwise be required against court judgments against such liability, they would be bankrupted. Kentucky, therefore, passed a Shield Law stating that the companies must put up only $25 million against their tobacco suit liability.

In 2003, tobacco also figured in the civic life of one of Kentucky's principal cities. Situated in a principal tobacco-growing state, citizens of the city of Lexington voted to ban smoking in most public buildings.

State Politics. During the 2000 general election, Kentucky residents watched as the most contested and expensive electoral race in Kentucky history took place. The race was between incumbent Republican Congress member Ernie Fletcher and former Democratic Congress member Scotty Baesler. Fletcher won over his Democratic opponent by 53-35 percent. A reform party candidate took 12 percent of the vote. In the presidential race, Kentucky gave its eight electoral votes to Texas governor George W. Bush.

In 2002 and 2003, Kentucky's political order was shaken by a scandal involving the state's popular governor, Paul E. Patton. He was said to have abused his office by giving business opportunities and other benefits to a lover. He admitted two violations and was given a five-thousand-dollar fine, as well as a public reprimand. He left office in 2003 and was succeeded by Fletcher.

Kentucky's tilt to the political right continued in the

Barbaro, ridden by Edgar Parod, winning the 132d running of the Kentucky Derby in 2006. The most prestigious thoroughbred horse-racing event in the United States, the derby is held at Louisville's Churchill Downs in May. (AP/Wide World Photos)

2004 general election. The referendum on "gay marriage" that was on the ballot was credited with drawing conservative voters to the polls. As in a number of other states, Kentucky voted to ban same-sex marriages. Senator Jim Bunning, a former baseball star, was reelected despite his sometimes erratic behavior in the final weeks of the campaign. Voters also elected a Republican to Congress in a seat vacated by a Democrat when Geoff Davis defeated Nick Clooney, father of Hollywood actor George Clooney. The state then had among its political representatives five Republicans and one Democrat. Nationally, President Bush added the state to his win column.

Demise of Great Racehorses. Kentucky, home of the famed Kentucky Derby, held annually in Louisville, the state's largest city, is known for its fondness for racehorses. The 125th running of the race took place in 1999. Kentuckians were therefore disappointed to learn in 2001 that Affirmed, the 1978 Triple Crown winner, had to be euthanized at the age of twenty-six in Lexington as a result of serious illness. The following year, Seattle Slew—at the time the only living Triple Crown winner—died in his sleep at the age of twenty-eight. In 2006, thoroughbred racer Barbaro won the derby and was the heavy favorite for the Preakness Stakes soon after. However, the horse suffered a serious leg injury shortly after the beginning of that race which subsequently ended his racing career.

Michael Witkoski
Updated by the Editor

Kentucky Time Line

1671	Thomas Batts and Robert Fallam of Virginia reach Ohio Valley.
1682	René-Robert Cavalier, sieur de La Salle, claims Kentucky as part of Louisiana Territory for France.
1750	Dr. Thomas Walker discovers Cumberland Gap.
1751	Christopher Gist explores area along Ohio River.
1763	France cedes Louisiana Territory to Britain.
1769	Daniel Boone and John Finley explore Kentucky.
1774	James Harrod founds Harrodstown, later Harrodsburg.
1775	Daniel Boone blazes Wilderness Road and founds Boonesborough.
Dec. 6, 1776	Kentucky County is created by Virginia.
1778	Settlers break American Indian siege of Boonesborough.
1778	George Rogers Clark organizes expedition against British in Ohio valley.
Aug. 19, 1782	Last battle of American Revolution fought at Blue Licks, near Mount Olivet.
June 1, 1792	Kentucky ratifies Constitution to become fifteenth state.
1794	General "Mad Anthony" Wayne defeats Native Americans at Fallen Timbers, ending their attacks on settlers in Kentucky.
1796	Wilderness Road opens to wagons.
1798	Legislature passes Kentucky Resolutions, opposing Alien and Sedition Acts.
1811	Henry Clay is elected to Congress.
1819	While drilling for salt, Martin Beatty finds petroleum in Cumberland River.
1830	Louisville and Portland Canal opens.
1849	Zachary Taylor, a Kentucky native, is elected twelfth president of United States.
1861	Kentucky declares itself neutral in Civil War, but is invaded by both Union and Confederate troops.
1862	Union forces win victory over Confederates at Perryville.
1865	University of Kentucky is founded at Lexington.
May 17, 1875	First Kentucky Derby is held at Churchill Downs near Louisville.
1891	New state constitution is adopted.
1926	Mammoth Cave National Park is established.
1937	Worst recorded flood of Ohio River occurs.
1937	United States builds gold depository at Fort Knox.
1944	Tennessee Valley Authority completes Kentucky Dam on Tennessee River.
1950	Atomic energy plant is built near Paducah.
1959	Cumberland Gap National Historical Park is dedicated.
1962	Federal government gives Kentucky control of certain nuclear energy materials, making it the first state granted this power.
1966	Kentucky passes a wide-ranging civil rights law, making it the first southern state to do so.
1966	Barkley Dam on Cumberland River is dedicated.
1982	Martha Layne Collins becomes first woman elected governor of Kentucky.
1985	Toyota automotive company announces construction of manufacturing plant near Georgetown, Kentucky.
1988	Voters approve state lottery.
2000	Kentucky passes a Tobacco Industry Shield Law setting a limit of $25 million for bonds that tobacco companies in the state must post against tobacco suit liability.
2001-2002	Famed racehorses Triple Crown winners Affirmed and Seattle Slew die.
2003	City of Lexington bans smoking in most public buildings.
2003	Governor Paul E. Patton leaves office in disgrace after being fined and receiving a public reprimand over charges of corruption.
Nov. 2, 2004	In general election, Nick Clooney is rejected in bid for congressional seat; Jim Bunning, one-time baseball great, is reelected to the U.S. Senate.
May 20, 2006	Thoroughbred Barbaro injures his leg, ending his racing career.

Notes for Further Study

Published Sources. Two worthwhile books of introductory studies of Kentucky are M. Wharton's *Bluegrass Land and Life* (1992), which concentrates on the broad sweep of its historical development, economics, and popular culture, and Lowell H. Harrison and James C. Klotter's *A New History of Kentucky* (1997), a comprehensive survey of Kentucky from prehistoric to modern times, with a thorough review of developments in the twentieth century. Klotter further contributes to this discussion with his edited volume titled *Our Kentucky: A Study of the Bluegrass State* (1992), in which a variety of authors and scholars examine the state's historical development and current status. *Running Mad for Kentucky: Frontier Travel Accounts* (2004), edited by Ellen Eslinger, offers one dozen firsthand accounts of travelers as they crossed the Appalachian Mountains in the eighteenth century. A geographical analysis of military tactics and civilian involvement during the Civil War can be found in Brian D. McKnight's *Contested Borderland:*

The Civil War in Appalachian Kentucky and Virginia (2006). *Appalachians and Race: The Mountain South from Slavery to Segregation* (2001), edited by John C. Inscoe, examines the influences of African Americans on the region's economy, history, and culture.

The state's agriculture is discussed in Thomas D. Clark's *Agrarian Kentucky* (1977). *Kentucky Government and Politics* (1984), edited by Joel Goldstein, examines the state's political system. Economic difficulty in Kentucky's Appalachians is explored in *Poverty, Politics, and Health Care: An Appalachian Experience* (1975) by Richard A. Couto. Interesting Kentucky facts can be found in Ernie Couch and Jill Couch's *Kentucky Trivia* (1992). Readers will find nearly eight hundred pages of essays, statistics, photographs, and historical information about Kentucky's business and economy, the arts, sports, recreation, and family trends in *Clark's Kentucky Almanac and Book of Facts 2006*, edited by Sam Stephens (2006).

Web Resources. An excellent place to begin an Internet study of the state is the Commonwealth of Kentucky home page, the official site of the Kentucky state government (kentucky.gov/). This site is especially useful when supplemented with the home page of the Kentucky legislature (www.lrc.state.ky.us/home.htm) and the Kentucky State Government Links (www.govengine.com/stategov/kentucky .html), both of which are connected to a wealth of official information, statistics, and data. The Kentucky State History Center (history.ky.gov/) has a Web site worth visiting. Those interested in business conditions in the state should consult the Kentucky Chamber of Commerce (www.kychamber .com/kycchw/hw.dll?page&t=home page). For contemporary events, the Lexington *Herald-Leader Online* (www .kentuckyconnect .com/heraldleader) has outstanding resources. As one of Kentucky's premiere newspapers, the *Herald-Leader* offers excellent insights into the state's economic, political, and cultural events.

The cultural and scenic sides of Kentucky can be found at a number of Web sites. The Kentucky Department of Tourism (www .kentuckytourism.com/) gives visitors a good overview of what the state has to offer. Kentucky has a wealth of folk art, especially in its Appalachian region, which can be studied through the Folk Art Center Web site (www .kyfolkart.org) and on the University of Kentucky Art Museum page (www.uky.edu/ArtMuseum/luce/folkart.html). For western Kentucky, and indeed the entire Ohio Valley, one of the most important natural wonders is Mammoth Cave, the Web site of which can be visited at Mammoth Cave Online (www .mammothcave.com).

Kentucky has no major league baseball team, but Louisville is famous for manufacturing baseball bats. This giant bat stands outside the Louisville Slugger Museum in Louisville.

Counties

County	2000 pop.	Rank in pop.	Sq. miles	Rank in area	County	2000 pop.	Rank in pop.	Sq. miles	Rank in area
Adair	17,244	63	406.9	32	Fayette	260,512	2	284.5	72
Allen	17,800	60	346.1	50	Fleming	13,792	80	351.1	45
Anderson	19,111	56	202.7	101	Floyd	42,441	21	394.3	34
Ballard	8,286	105	251.2	84	Franklin	47,687	17	210.5	96
Barren	38,033	23	491.0	13	Fulton	7,752	111	209.0	98
Bath	11,085	95	279.4	75	Gallatin	7,870	110	98.8	120
Bell	30,060	36	360.8	42	Garrard	14,792	75	231.2	92
Boone	85,991	8	246.3	87	Grant	22,384	51	259.9	79
Bourbon	19,360	55	291.4	67	Graves	37,028	25	555.7	8
Boyd	49,752	16	160.2	115	Grayson	24,053	44	503.7	11
Boyle	27,697	38	181.6	111	Green	11,518	94	288.7	70
Bracken	8,279	106	203.2	100	Greenup	36,891	26	346.2	49
Breathitt	16,100	69	495.2	12	Hancock	8,392	104	188.8	109
Breckinridge	18,648	57	572.4	6	Hardin	94,174	4	628.0	4
Bullitt	61,236	13	299.1	66	Harlan	33,202	30	467.2	17
Butler	13,010	86	428.1	26	Harrison	17,983	59	309.7	59
Caldwell	13,060	85	347.0	46	Hart	17,445	62	416.0	30
Calloway	34,177	28	386.3	36	Henderson	44,829	20	440.2	24
Campbell	88,616	7	151.6	116	Henry	15,060	74	289.3	69
Carlisle	5,351	117	192.5	106	Hickman	5,262	118	244.5	88
Carroll	10,155	98	130.1	118	Hopkins	46,519	18	550.6	9
Carter	26,889	39	410.6	31	Jackson	13,495	81	346.3	48
Casey	15,447	72	445.6	20	Jefferson	693,604	1	385.1	37
Christian	72,265	9	721.4	2	Jessamine	39,041	22	173.2	113
Clark	33,144	31	254.3	81	Johnson	23,445	45	261.6	78
Clay	24,556	43	471.0	16	Kenton	151,464	3	162.6	114
Clinton	9,634	102	197.5	104	Knott	17,649	61	352.2	44
Crittenden	9,384	103	362.2	41	Knox	31,795	34	387.7	35
Cumberland	7,147	112	305.8	62	LaRue	13,373	82	263.4	77
Daviess	91,545	6	462.4	18	Laurel	52,715	15	435.7	25
Edmonson	11,644	93	302.6	64	Lawrence	15,569	71	418.9	29
Elliott	6,748	115	234.0	91	Lee	7,916	109	209.9	97
Estill	15,307	73	254.0	82	Leslie	12,401	89	404.0	33

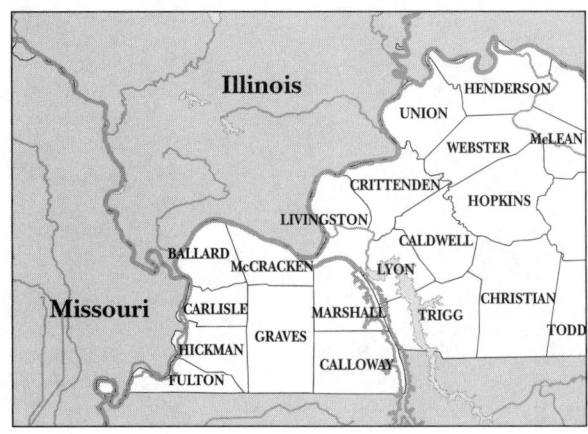

County	2000 pop.	Rank in pop.	Sq. miles	Rank in area
Letcher	25,277	42	339.1	53
Lewis	14,092	78	484.5	14
Lincoln	23,361	46	336.6	54
Livingston	9,804	101	316.1	58
Logan	26,573	40	555.7	7
Lyon	8,080	108	215.8	95
McCracken	65,514	12	251.1	85
McCreary	17,080	64	427.7	27
McLean	9,938	100	254.3	80
Madison	70,872	10	440.7	22
Magoffin	13,332	83	309.5	60
Marion	18,212	58	346.7	47
Marshall	30,125	35	304.9	63
Martin	12,578	88	230.7	93
Mason	16,800	65	241.1	89
Meade	26,349	41	308.5	61
Menifee	6,556	116	203.9	99
Mercer	20,817	53	250.9	86
Metcalfe	10,037	99	290.9	68
Monroe	11,756	92	330.8	56
Montgomery	22,554	50	198.6	102
Morgan	13,948	79	381.3	39
Muhlenberg	31,839	33	474.7	15
Nelson	37,477	24	422.7	28
Nicholas	6,813	114	196.6	105
Ohio	22,916	49	593.8	5
Oldham	46,178	19	189.2	108
Owen	10,547	97	352.2	43

County	2000 pop.	Rank in pop.	Sq. miles	Rank in area
Owsley	4,858	119	198.1	103
Pendleton	14,390	76	280.0	74
Perry	29,390	37	342.2	52
Pike	68,736	11	787.7	1
Powell	13,237	84	180.1	112
Pulaski	56,217	14	661.6	3
Robertson	2,266	120	100.1	119
Rockcastle	16,582	66	317.5	57
Rowan	22,094	52	280.8	73
Russell	16,315	68	253.5	83
Scott	33,061	32	285.2	71
Shelby	33,337	29	384.2	38
Simpson	16,405	67	236.2	90
Spencer	11,766	91	185.9	110
Taylor	22,927	48	269.8	76
Todd	11,971	90	376.4	40
Trigg	12,597	87	443.4	21
Trimble	8,125	107	148.9	117
Union	15,637	70	345.1	51
Warren	92,522	5	545.2	10
Washington	10,916	96	300.6	65
Wayne	19,923	54	459.4	19
Webster	14,120	77	334.7	55
Whitley	35,865	27	440.2	23
Wolfe	7,065	113	222.8	94
Woodford	23,208	47	190.7	107

Source: U.S. Census Bureau; National Association of Counties.

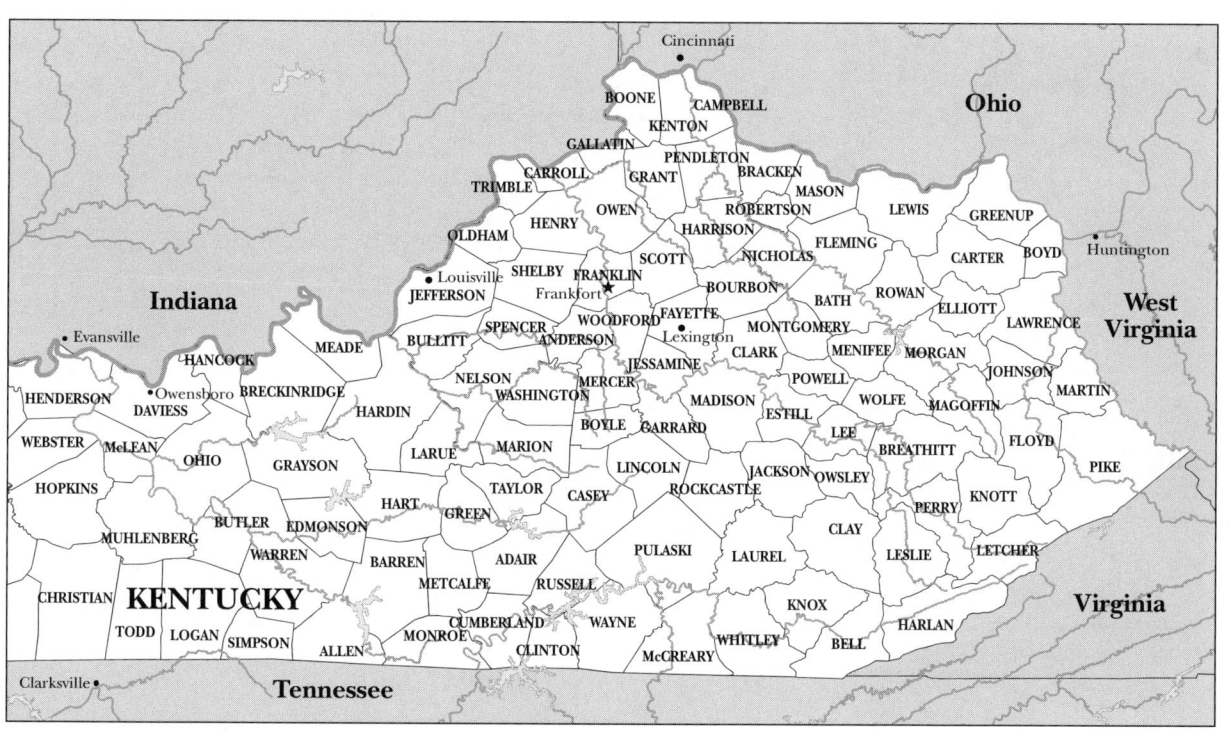

Cities

With 10,000 or more residents

Rank	City	Population	Rank	City	Population
1	Lexington-Fayette	260,512	24	Newport	17,048
2	Louisville	256,231	25	Winchester	16,724
3	Owensboro	54,067	26	Erlanger	16,676
4	Bowling Green	49,296	27	Fort Thomas	16,495
5	Covington	43,370	28	St. Matthews	15,852
6	Hopkinsville	30,089	29	Danville	15,477
7	Frankfort (capital)	27,741	30	Highview	15,161
8	Henderson	27,373	31	Shively	15,157
9	Richmond	27,152	32	Independence	14,982
10	Jeffersontown	26,633	33	Murray	14,950
11	Paducah	26,307	34	Fort Campbell North	14,338
12	Pleasure Ridge Park	25,776	35	Glasgow	13,019
13	Florence	23,551	36	Fort Knox	12,377
14	Valley Station	22,946	37	Somerset	11,352
15	Elizabethtown	22,542	38	Burlington	10,779
16	Ashland	21,981	39	Campbellsville	10,498
17	Radcliff	21,961	40	Middlesborough	10,384
18	Newburg	20,636	41	Bardstown	10,374
19	Nicholasville	19,680	42	Mayfield	10,349
20	Madisonville	19,307	43	Shelbyville	10,085
21	Georgetown	18,080			
22	Fern Creek	17,870			
23	Okolona	17,807			

Population figures are from 2000 census.

Source: U.S. Bureau of the Census.

Index to Tables

DEMOGRAPHICS

Resident state and national populations, 1970-2004

Population figures given in thousands

	State pop.	U.S. pop.	Share	Rank
1970	3,221	203,302	1.6%	23
1980	3,661	226,546	1.6%	23
1985	3,695	237,924	1.6%	23
1990	3,687	248,765	1.5%	23
1995	3,887	262,761	1.5%	24
2000	4,042	281,425	1.4%	25
2004	4,146	293,655	1.4%	26

Source: U.S. Census Bureau, Current Population Reports, 2006.

Resident population by age, 2004

Age Group	Total persons
Under 5 years	267,000
5 to 17 years	714,000
18 to 24 years	413,000
25 to 34 years	568,000
35 to 44 years	621,000
45 to 54 years	605,000
55 to 64 years	439,000
65 to 74 years	281,000
75 to 84 years	179,000
85 years and older	59,000
All age groups	4,146,000
Portion of residents 65 and older	12.5%
National rank in portion of oldest residents	27
National average	12.4%

Population figures are rounded to nearest thousand persons;
   figures include armed forces personnel stationed in the state.
Source: U.S. Bureau of the Census, 2006.

Resident population by race, Hispanic origin, 2004

Category	State pop.	Share	U.S.
All residents	4,146	100.00%	100.00%
Non-Hispanic white	3,678	88.71%	67.37%
Hispanic white	69	1.66%	13.01%
Other Hispanic	8	0.19%	1.06%
African American	311	7.50%	12.77%
Native American	9	0.22%	0.96%
Asian, Pacific Islander	39	0.94%	4.37%
Two or more categories	40	0.96%	1.51%

Population figures are in thousands. Persons counted as "Hispanic" (Latino) may be of any race. Because of overlapping categories, categories may not add up to 100%. Shares in column 3 are percentages of each category within the state; these figures may be compared to the national percentages in column 4.
Source: U.S. Bureau of the Census, 2006.

Projected state population, 2000-2030

Year	Population
2000	4,042,000
2005	4,163,000
2010	4,265,000
2015	4,351,000
2020	4,424,000
2025	4,490,000
2030	4,555,000
Population increase, 2000-2030	513,000
Percentage increase, 2000-2030	12.7

Projections are based on data from the 2000 census.
Source: U.S. Census Bureau.

VITAL STATISTICS

Infant mortality rates, 1980-2002

	1980	1990	2000	2002
All state residents	12.9	8.5	7.2	7.2
All U.S. residents	12.6	9.2	9.4	9.1
All state white residents	12.0	8.2	6.7	6.6
All U.S. white residents	10.6	7.6	5.7	5.8
All state black residents	22.0	14.3	12.7	14.2
All U.S. black residents	22.2	18.0	14.1	14.4

Figures represent deaths per 1,000 live births of resident infants under 1 year old, exclusive of fetal deaths. Figures for all residents include members of other racial categories not listed separately.
Source: U.S. Census Bureau, *Statistical Abstract of the United States,* 2006.

Abortion rates, 1990 and 2000

	1990	2000
Total abortions	10,000	5,000
Rate per 1,000 women	11.4	5.3
U.S. rate	25.7	21.3
Rank	43	49

Numbers of abortions are rounded to nearest thousand; ranks are based on rates.
Source: U.S. Census Bureau.

Marriages and divorces, 2004

Total marriages	36,800
Rate per 1,000 population	8.9
National rate per 1,000 population	7.4
Rank among all states	10
Total divorces	20,500
Rate per 1,000 population	4.9
National rate per 1,000 population	3.7
Rank among all states	6

Figures are for all marriages and divorces performed within the state, including those of nonresidents; totals are rounded to the nearest hundred. Ranks are for highest to lowest figures; note that divorce data are not available for five states.
Source: U.S. National Center for Health Statistics, *Vital Statistics of the United States,* 2006.

Death rates by leading causes, 2002
Deaths per 100,000 resident population

Cause	State	U.S.
Heart disease	285.8	241.7
Cancer	230.6	193.2
Cerebrovascular diseases	62.4	56.4
Accidents other than motor vehicle	51.1	37.0
Motor vehicle accidents	22.6	15.7
Chronic lower respiratory diseases	58.7	43.3
Diabetes mellitus	30.9	25.4
HIV	2.4	4.9
Suicide	13.2	11.0
Homicide	4.8	6.1
All causes	994.3	847.3
Rank in overall death rate among states		8

Figures exclude nonresidents who died in the state. Causes of death follow International Classification of Diseases. Rank is from highest to lowest death rate in the United States.
Source: U.S. National Center for Health Statistics, *National Vital Statistics Report,* 2006.

ECONOMY

Gross state product, 1990-2004
In current dollars

Year	State product	Nat'l product	State share
1990	$67.5 billion	$5.67 trillion	1.19%
2000	$112.7 billion	$9.75 trillion	1.16%
2002	$121.6 billion	$10.41 trillion	1.17%
2003	$128.3 billion	$10.92 trillion	1.17%
2004	$135.4 billion	$11.65 trillion	1.16%

Source: U.S. Bureau of Economic Analysis, *Survey of Current Business,* July, 2005.

Gross state product by industry, 2003
In billions of dollars

Construction	$4.8
Manufacturing	26.5
Wholesale trade	7.2
Retail trade	9.5
Finance & insurance	5.9
Information	3.3
Professional services	5.3
Health care & social assistance	8.8
Government	16.8
Total state product	$120.5
Total U.S. product	$10,289.2
State share of U.S. total	1.17%
Rank among all states	26

Total figures include industries not listed separately. Amounts are in chained 2000 dollars.

Source: U.S. Bureau of Economic Analysis, *Survey of Current Business,* July, 2005.

Personal income per capita, 1990-2004
In current dollars

	1990	2000	2004
Per capita income	$15,437	$24,412	$27,709
U.S. average	$19,477	$29,845	$32,937
Rank among states	44	40	41

Source: U.S. Bureau of Economic Analysis, *Survey of Current Business,* April, 2005.

Energy consumption, 2001
In trillions of British thermal units (BTU), except as noted

Total energy consumption

Total state energy consumption	1,880
Total U.S. energy consumption	96,275
State share of U.S. total	1.95%
Rank among states	18

Per capita consumption (In millions of BTU)

Total state per capita consumption	462
Total U.S. per capita consumption	338
Rank among states	6

End-use sectors

Residential	339
Commercial	246
Industrial	846
Transportation	449

Sources of energy

Petroleum	704
Natural gas	217
Coal	1,011
Hydroelectric power	39
Nuclear electric power	0

Figures for totals include categories not listed separately.
Source: U.S. Energy Information Administration, *State Energy Data Report,* 2001.

Nonfarm employment by sectors, 2004

Total	1,796,000
Construction	84,000
Manufacturing	264,000
Trade, transportation, utilities	372,000
Information	29,000
Finance, insurance, real estate	87,000
Professional & business services	162,000
Education & health services	231,000
Leisure, hospitality, arts, organizations	161,000
Other services, including repair & maintenance	78,000
Government	309,000

Figures are rounded to nearest thousand persons. "Total" includes mining and natural resources, not listed separately.
Source: U.S. Bureau of Labor Statistics, 2006.

Foreign exports, 1990-2004
In millions of dollars

Year	State	U.S.	State share
1990	3,175	394,045	0.81%
1996	6,385	624,767	1.02%
1997	7,953	688,896	1.15%
2000	9,612	712,055	1.23%
2003	10,734	724,006	1.59%
2004	12,992	769,332	1.69%

Rank among all states in 2004 19

U.S. total does not include U.S. dependencies.
Source: U.S. Census Bureau, *U.S. Merchandise Trade,* series FT 900, 2000; U.S. Census Bureau, *U.S. International Trade in Goods and Services,* Series FT 900, 2005.

LAND USE

Federally owned land, 2003
Areas in acres

	State	U.S.	State share
Total area	25,512,000	2,271,343,000	1.12%
Nonfederal land	23,806,000	1,599,584,000	1.49%
Federal land	1,706,000	671,759,000	0.25%
Federal share	6.7%	29.6%	—

Areas are rounded to nearest thousand acres. Figures for federally owned land do not include trust properties.
Source: U.S. General Services Administration, *Federal Real Property Profile,* 2006.

Land use, 1997
In acres, rounded to nearest thousand

Total surface area	25,863,000
Total nonfederal rural land.	22,327,000
Percentage rural land	86.3%
Cropland	5,178,000
Conservation Reserve Program (CRP*) land	332,000
Pastureland	5,686,000
Rangeland	(nil)
Forestland	10,667,000
Other rural land	465,000

*CRP is a federal program begun in 1985 to assist private landowners to convert highly erodible cropland to vegetative cover for ten years. Note that some categories of land overlap.
Source: U.S. Department of Agriculture, Natural Resources and Conservation Service, and Iowa State University, Statistical Laboratory, *Summary Report, 1997 National Resources Inventory,* revised December, 2000.

Farms and crop acreage, 2004

	State	U.S.	Share	Rank
Farms	85,000	2,113,000	4.02%	4
Acres (millions)	14	937	1.49%	22
Acres per farm	162	443	—	43

Source: U.S. Department of Agriculture, National Agricultural Statistics Service. Numbers of farms are rounded to nearest thousand units; acreage figures are rounded to nearest million. Rankings, including ties, are based on rounded figures.

GOVERNMENT AND FINANCE

Units of local government, 2002

	State	Total U.S.	Rank
All local governments	1,439	87,525	22
Counties	119	3,034	3
Municipalities	424	19,429	20
Townships	0	16,504	—
School districts	176	13,506	26
Special districts	720	35,052	15

Only 48 states have county governments, 20 states have township governments ("towns" in New England, Minnesota, New York, and Wisconsin), and 46 states have school districts. Special districts encompass such functions as natural resources, fire protection, and housing and community development.
Source: U.S. Census Bureau, *Census of Governments.*

State government revenue, 2002

Total revenue	$16,073 mill.
General revenue	$15,810 mill.
Per capita revenue	$3,866
U.S. per capita average	$3,689
Rank among states	22
Intergovernment revenue	
Total	$5,121 mill.
From federal government	$5,102 mill.
Charges and miscellaneous	
Total	$2,714 mill.
Current charges	$1,621 mill.
Misc. general income	$1,093 mill.
Insurance trust revenue	$263 mill.
Taxes	
Total	$7,975 mill.
Per capita taxes	$1,950
Rank among states	19
Property taxes	$438 mill.
Sales taxes	$3,741 mill.
License taxes	$539 mill.
Individual income taxes	$2,678 mill.
Corporate income taxes	$302 mill.
Other taxes	$276 mill.

Total revenue figures include items not listed separately here.
Source: U.S. Bureau of the Census.

State government expenditures, 2002

General expenditures

Total state expenditures . . . . $18,407 mill.
Intergovernmental . . . . $3,560 mill.

Per capita expenditures

State $4,004
Average of all states $3,859
Rank among states 22

Selected direct expenditures

Education. $2,981 mill.
Public welfare . . . . $4,762 mill.
Health, hospital . . . . $844 mill.
Highways . . . . $1,614 mill.
Police protection . . . . $163 mill.
Corrections . . . . $413 mill.
Natural resources . . . . $282 mill.
Parks and recreation . . . . $123 mill.
Government administration . . . . $636 mill.
Interest on debt . . . . $450 mill.
Total direct expenditures. . . . . $12,817 mill.

Totals include items not listed separately.
Source: U.S. Census Bureau.

POLITICS

Governors since statehood

D = Democrat; R = Republican; O = other;
(r) resigned; (d) died in office; (i) removed from office

Isaac Shelby (O) 1792-1796
James Garrard (O) 1796-1804
Christopher Greenup (O) 1804-1808
Charles Scott (O) 1808-1812
Isaac Shelby (O) 1812-1816
George Madison (O) . . . . (d) 1816
Gabriel Slaughter (O) 1816-1820
John Adair (O) 1820-1824
Joseph Desha (O) 1824-1828
Thomas Metcalfe (O) 1828-1832
John Breathitt (D) . . . . (d) 1832-1834
James T. Morehead (O) 1834-1836
James Clark (O) . . . . (d) 1836-1839
Charles A. Wickliffe (O) 1839-1840
Robert P. Letcher (O) 1840-1844
William Owsley (O) 1844-1848
John J. Crittenden (O) . . . . (r) 1848-1850
John L. Helm (O) 1850-1851
Lazarus W. Powell (D) 1851-1855
Charles S. Morehead (O) 1855-1859
Beriah Magoffin (D) . . . . (r) 1859-1862
James F. Robinson (O) 1862-1863
Thomas E. Bramlette (O) 1863-1867
John L. Helm (D) . . . . (d) 1867
John W. Stevenson (D) . . . . (r) 1867-1871
Preston H. Leslie (D) 1871-1875
James B. McCreary (D) 1875-1879
Luke P. Blackburn (D) 1879-1883

James Proctor Knott (D) 1883-1887
Simon B. Buckner (D) 1887-1891
John Young Brown (D) 1891-1895
William O. Bradley (R) . . . . (r) 1895-1899
William S. Taylor (R) . . . . (i) 1899-1900
William Goebel (D) . . . . (d) 1900
John C. W. Beckham (D) 1900-1907
Augustus E. Willson (R) 1907-1911
James B. McCreary (D) 1911-1915
Augustus O. Stanley (D) . . . . (r) 1915-1919
James D. Black (D) 1919
Edwin P. Morrow (R) 1919-1923
William J. Fields (D) 1923-1927
Flemon D. Sampson (R) 1927-1931
Ruby Laffoon (D) 1931-1935
Albert B. Chandler (D) . . . . (r) 1935-1939
Keen Johnson (D) 1939-1943
Simeon S. Willis (R) 1943-1947
Earle C. Clements (D) . . . . (r) 1947-1950
Lawrence W. Wetherby (D) 1950-1955
Albert B. Chandler (D) 1955-1959
Bert T. Combs (D) 1959-1963
Edward T. Breathitt (D) 1963-1967
Louis B. Nunn (R) 1967-1971
Wendell H. Ford (D) . . . . (r) 1971-1974
Julian M. Carroll (D) 1974-1980
John Y. Brown, Jr. (D) 1980-1984
Martha Layne Collins (D) 1984-1987
Wallace G. Wilkinson (D) 1987-1991
Brereton C. Jones (D) 1991-1995
Paul E. Patton (D) 1995-2003
Ernie Fletcher (R) 2003-

Composition of congressional delegations, 1989-2007

	Dem	Rep	Total
House of Representatives			
101st Congress, 1989			
State delegates	4	3	7
Total U.S.	259	174	433
102d Congress, 1991			
State delegates	4	3	7
Total U.S.	267	167	434
103d Congress, 1993			
State delegates	4	2	6
Total U.S.	258	176	434
104th Congress, 1995			
State delegates	1	5	6
Total U.S.	197	236	433
105th Congress, 1997			
State delegates	1	5	6
Total U.S.	206	228	434
106th Congress, 1999			
State delegates	1	5	6
Total U.S.	211	222	433

(continued)

	Dem	Rep	Total
107th Congress, 2001			
State delegates	1	5	6
Total U.S.	211	221	432
108th Congress, 2003			
State delegates	1	5	6
Total U.S.	205	229	434
109th Congress, 2005			
State delegates	1	5	6
Total U.S.	202	231	433
110th Congress, 2007			
State delegates	2	4	6
Total U.S.	233	202	435
Senate			
101st Congress, 1989			
State delegates	1	1	2
Total U.S.	55	45	100
102d Congress, 1991			
State delegates	1	1	2
Total U.S.	56	44	100
103d Congress, 1993			
State delegates	1	1	2
Total U.S.	57	43	100
104th Congress, 1995			
State delegates	1	1	2
Total U.S.	46	53	99
105th Congress, 1997			
State delegates	1	1	2
Total U.S.	45	55	100
106th Congress, 1999			
State delegates	0	2	2
Total U.S.	45	54	99
107th Congress, 2001			
State delegates	0	2	2
Total U.S.	50	50	100
108th Congress, 2003			
State delegates	0	2	2
Total U.S.	48	51	99
109th Congress, 2005			
State delegates	0	2	2
Total U.S.	44	55	99
110th Congress, 2007			
State delegates	0	2	2
Total U.S.	49	49	98

Figures are for starts of first sessions. Totals are for Democrat (Dem.) and Republican (Rep.) members only. House membership totals under 435 and Senate totals under 100 reflect vacancies and seats held by independent party members. When the 110th Congress opened, the Senate's two independent members caucused with the Democrats, giving the Democrats control of the Senate.

Source: U.S. Congress, *Congressional Directory.*

Composition of state legislature, 1990-2006

	Democrats	Republicans
State House (100 seats)		
1990	68	32
1992	71	29
1994	64	36
1996	64	36
1998	65	35
2000	65	35
2002	63	36
2004	57	43
2006	61	39
State Senate (38 seats)		
1990	27	11
1992	25	13
1994	21	17
1996	20	18
1998	18	20
2000	18	20
2002	16	22
2004	15	22
2006	16	21

Figures for total seats may include independents and minor party members. Numbers reflect results of elections in listed years; elected members usually take their seats in the years that follow.

Source: Council of State Governments; *State Elective Officials and the Legislatures.*

Voter participation in presidential elections, 2000 and 2004

	2000	2004
Voting age population		
State	3,055,000	3,166,000
Total United States	209,831,000	220,377,000
State share of U.S. total	1.46	1.44
Rank among states	25	25
Portion of voting age population casting votes		
State	50.5%	56.7%
United States	50.3%	55.5%
Rank among states	31	28

Population figures are rounded to nearest thousand and include all residents, regardless of eligibility to vote.

Source: U.S. Census Bureau.

HEALTH AND MEDICAL CARE

Medical professionals
Physicians in 2003 and nurses in 2001

	U.S.	State
Physicians in 2003		
Total	774,849	9,348
Share of U.S. total		1.20%
Rate	266	227
Rank		33
Nurses in 2001		
Total	2,262,020	34,920
Share of U.S. total		1.54%
Rate	793	858
Rank		21

Rates are numbers of physicians and nurses per 100,000 resident population; ranks are based on rates.
Source: American Medical Association, *Physician Characteristics and Distribution in the U.S.*; U.S. Department of Health and Human Services, Health Resources and Services Administration.

Health insurance coverage, 2003

	State	U.S.
Total persons covered	3,537,000	243,320,000
Total persons not covered	574,000	44,961,000
Portion not covered	14.0%	15.6%
Rank among states	25	—
Children not covered	107,000	8,373,000
Portion not covered	10.5%	11.4%
Rank among states	20	—

Totals are rounded to nearest thousand. Ranks are from the highest to the lowest percentages of persons *not* insured.
Source: U.S. Census Bureau, Current Population Reports.

AIDS, syphilis, and tuberculosis cases, 2003

Disease	U.S. cases	State cases	Rank
AIDS	44,232	220	28
Syphilis	34,270	160	29
Tuberculosis	14,874	138	24

Source: U.S. Centers for Disease Control and Prevention.

Cigarette smoking, 2003
Residents over age 18 who smoke

	U.S.	State	Rank
All smokers	22.1%	30.8%	1
Male smokers	24.8%	33.8%	1
Female smokers	20.3%	28.1%	1

Cigarette smokers are defined as persons who reported having smoked at least 100 cigarettes during their lifetimes and who currently smoked at least occasionally.
Source: U.S. Centers for Disease Control and Prevention, *Morbidity and Mortality Weekly Report*, 53, no. 44 (November 12, 2004).

HOUSING

Home ownership rates, 1985-2004

	1985	1990	1995	2000	2004
State	68.5%	65.8%	71.2%	73.4%	74.3%
Total U.S.	63.9%	63.9%	64.7%	67.4%	69.0%
Rank among states	20	31	11	13	11

Net change in state home ownership rate,
1985-2004 . . . . +5.8%
Net change in U.S. home ownership rate,
1985-2004 . . . . +5.1%

Percentages represent the proportion of owner households to total occupied households.
Source: U.S. Census Bureau, 2006.

Home sales, 2000-2004
In thousands of units

Existing home sales	2000	2002	2003	2004
State sales	66.0	73.5	81.1	89.3
Total U.S. sales	5,171	5,631	6,183	6,784
State share of U.S. total	1.28%	1.31%	1.31%	1.32%
Sales rank among states	26	25	26	28

Units include single-family homes, condos, and co-ops.
Source: National Association of Realtors, Washington, D.C., *Real Estate Outlook: Market Trends & Insights*.

Values of owner-occupied homes, 2003

	State	U.S.
Total units	812,000	58,809,000
Value of units		
Under $100,000	47.5%	29.6%
$100,000-199,999	39.5%	36.9%
$200,000 or more	13.0%	33.5%
Median value	$104,103	$142,275
Rank among all states 38		

Units are owner-occupied one-family houses whose numbers are rounded to nearest thousand. Data are extrapolated from survey samples.
Source: U.S. Census Bureau, American Community Survey.

EDUCATION

Public school enrollment, 2002

Prekindergarten through grade 8
State enrollment 477,000
Total U.S. enrollment. 34,135,000
State share of U.S. total 1.40%

Grades 9 through 12
State enrollment 184,000
Total U.S. enrollment. 14,067,000
State share of U.S. total 1.31%

Enrollment rates
State public school enrollment rate. 91.4%
Overall U.S. rate 90.4%
Rank among states in 2002. 18
Rank among states in 1995. 22

Enrollment figures (which include unclassified students) are rounded to nearest thousand pupils during fall school term. Enrollment rates are based on enumerated resident population estimate for July 1, 2002.
Source: U.S. National Center for Education Statistics.

Public college finances, 2003-2004

FTE enrollment in public institutions of higher education
Students in state institutions 144,700
Students in all U.S. public institutions 9,916,600
State share of U.S. total 1.46
Rank among states 24

State and local government appropriations for higher education
State appropriation per FTE $6,360
National average. $5,716
Rank among states 13
State & local tax revenue going to higher education 9.9%

FTE = full-time equivalent in public postsecondary programs, including summer sessions; student numbers are rounded to nearest hundred. Funding figures for 2003-2004 academic year include financial aid to students in state public institutions and exclude money for research, agriculture experiment stations, teaching hospitals, and medical schools; figures are rounded to nearest thousand dollars.
Source: Higher Education Executive Officers, Denver, Colorado.

TRANSPORTATION AND TRAVEL

Highway mileage, 2003

Interstate highways 763
Other freeways and expressways. 65
Arterial roads 5,850
Collector roads. 16,040
Local roads. 54,293
Urban roads 11,982
Rural roads. 65,029
Total state mileage. 77,011
U.S. total 3,974,107
State share 1.94%
Rank among states 26

Note that combined urban and rural road mileage matches the total of the other categories.
Source: U.S. Federal Highway Administration.

Motor vehicle registrations and driver licenses, 2003

Vehicle registrations	State	U.S.	Share	Rank
Autos, trucks, buses	3,389,000	231,390,000	1.46%	24
Autos only	1,959,000	135,670	1.44%	24
Motorcycles	51,000	5,328,000	0.96%	32
Driver licenses	2,800,000	196,166,000	1.43%	26

Figures, which do not include vehicles owned by military services, are rounded to the nearest thousand. Figures for automobiles include taxis.
Source: U.S. Federal Highway Administration.

Domestic travel expenditures, 2003

Spending by U.S. residents on overnight trips and
day trips of at least 50 miles from home

Total expenditures within state . . . . $5.43 bill.
Total expenditures within U.S. . . . . $490.87 bill.
State share of U.S. total 1.1%
Rank among states 30

Source: Travel Industry Association of America.

Retail gasoline prices, 2003-2007

Average price per gallon at the pump

Year	U.S.	State
2003	$1.267	$1.252
2004	$1.316	$1.297
2005	$1.644	$1.689
2007	$2.298	$2.226

Excise tax per gallon in 2004 . . . . 17.4¢
Rank among all states in 2007 prices 31

Prices are averages of all grades of gasoline sold at the pump
during March months in 2003-2005 and during February, 2007.
Averages for 2006, during which prices rose higher, are not
available.
Source: U.S. Energy Information Agency, *Petroleum Marketing
Monthly* (2003-2005 data); American Automobile Association
(2007 data).

CRIME AND LAW ENFORCEMENT

State and local police officers, 2000-2004

	2000	2002	2004
Total officers			
U.S.	654,601	665,555	675,734
State	7,531	7,719	7,655*
*Net change, 2000-2004			+1.65%
Officers per 1,000 residents			
U.S.	2.33	2.31	2.30
State	1.86	1.89	1.85
State rank	33	34	35

Totals include state and local police and sheriffs.
Source: Carsey Institute, University of New Hampshire.

Crime rates, 2003

Incidents per 100,000 residents

Crimes	State	U.S.
Violent crimes		
Total incidents	262	475
Murder	5	6
Forcible rape	26	32
Robbery	78	142
Aggravated assault	154	295
Property crimes		
Total incidents	2,682	3,588
Burglary	672	741
Larceny/theft	1,782	2,415
Motor vehicle theft	228	433
All crimes	2,944	4,063

Source: U.S. Federal Bureau of Investigation, *Crime in the United
States,* annual.

State prison populations, 1980-2003

	State	U.S.	State share
1980	3,588	305,458	1.17%
1990	9,023	708,393	1.27%
1996	12,910	1,025,624	1.26%
2000	14,919	1,391,261	1.07%
2003	16,622	1,470,045	1.13%

State figures exclude prisoners in federal penitentiaries.
Source: U.S. Bureau of Justice Statistics, *Prisoners in 2003.*

Louisiana

Location: Gulf coast

Area and rank: 43,566 square miles (112,836 square kilometers); 51,843 square miles (134,273 square kilometers) including water; thirty-third largest state in area

Coastline: 397 miles (639 kilometers) on the Gulf of Mexico

Shoreline: 7,721 miles (12,426 kilometers)

Population and rank: 4,516,000 (2004); twenty-fourth largest state in population

Capital city: Baton Rouge (227,818 people in 2000 census)

State capitol building in Baton Rouge. (Louisiana Office of Tourism)

Largest city: New Orleans (484,674 people in 2000 census, but population dropped by more than half after 2005 hurricane)

Became territory: March 26, 1804

Entered Union and rank: April 30, 1812; eighteenth state

Present constitution adopted: 1974

Parishes (counties): 64

State name: Louisiana takes its name from France's King Louis XIV

State nickname: Pelican State; Sportsman's Paradise; Creole State; Sugar State

Motto: Union, justice, and confidence

State flag: Blue field with state seal design and the state motto on a banner below

Highest point: Driskill Mountain—535 feet (163 meters)

Lowest point: New Orleans— –8 feet (–2 meters)

Highest recorded temperature: 114 degrees Fahrenheit (46 degrees Celsius)—Plain Dealing, 1936

Lowest recorded temperature: –16 degrees Fahrenheit (–27 degrees Celsius)—Minden, 1899

State songs: "Give Me Louisiana"; "You Are My Sunshine" ("Belle Louisiane" is an unofficial French song)

State tree: Bald cypress

State flower: Magnolia

State bird: Pelican

Louisiana History

Much of Louisiana lies in the Mississippi Alluvial Plain, flat lands that stretch from each side of the Mississippi River. As the river moves south to the Gulf of Mexico, the elevation of the land becomes progressively lower, and most of it is damp and swampy. Far western and northwestern Louisiana is part of the West Gulf Coastal Plain. In the northern area of this region, the land is hilly, and it becomes prairie farther south. On the eastern side, near Mississippi, lies the East Gulf Coastal Plain, which is similar to the territory in the west. These three regions correspond roughly to the historical and cultural divisions of Louisiana. The swampy south central and southwestern areas have corresponded to French Roman Catholic Louisiana. The western region and the eastern region have been home to mostly Protestant, English-speaking people.

Early History. During prehistoric times, Louisiana was populated by people who lived in highly organized farming societies. These societies are often known as the Mound Builders, after the great ceremonial earth mounds they constructed. The Mound Builders may be divided into the people of the Hopewell culture, who flourished from about the first century until about 800 C.E., and the people of the Mississippian culture, who were present from about 800 C.E. until about 1500.

When the Europeans arrived, Louisiana was inhabited by Native Americans of three language groups. Those of the Caddoan language group lived in the northwestern area. Those who spoke Muskogean languages lived in east central Louisiana near the Mississippi River. Speakers of the Tunican languages generally lived near the coast of the Gulf of Mexico. Louisiana's Native American population declined as a result of warfare, diseases introduced by the Europeans, and intermarriages with Americans of European and African descent. Some, such as the majority of the Choctaw nation, were forced westward into Indian ter-

The architecture of New Orleans's famous French Quarter reflects Louisiana's early history as a French colony. (PhotoDisc)

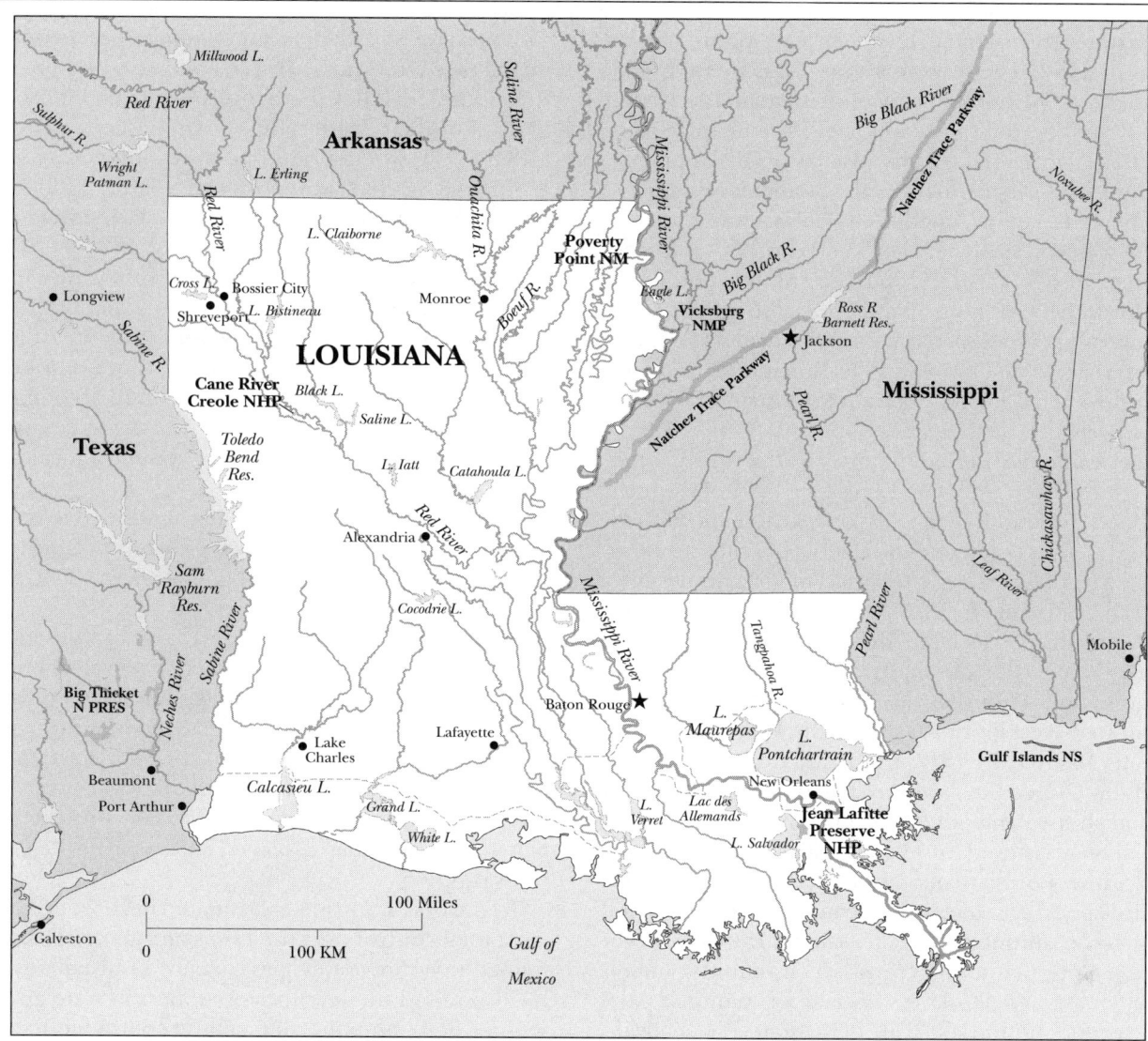

ritory in modern Oklahoma by the U.S. government during the 1830's. Contemporary Louisiana is home to communities of the Chitimacha, Houma, Tunica-Biloxi, Coushatta, and Choctaw.

Exploration and Settlement. The Spanish and the French were the first Europeans to explore the territory of the lower Mississippi River. In 1542, a Spanish expedition led by Hernando de Soto crossed through Louisiana. At the end of the seventeenth century, the French explorer René-Robert Cavelier, sieur de La Salle, journeyed down the Mississippi River to its mouth and claimed all of the land drained by the Mississippi in the name of France. La Salle named this huge expanse of territory Louisiana, in honor of King Louis XIV of France.

In 1718, the French explorer Jean-Baptiste Le Moyne de Bienville founded a settlement at a strategic location near the mouth of the Mississippi on the shores of the lake that the French had named Lake Pontchartrain.

Bienville named his settlement Nouvelle-Orléans (New Orleans) in honor of the regent of France, the duke of Orleans. In 1722, New Orleans would become the capital of Louisiana.

The Acadians, or Cajuns, one of Louisiana's best-known population groups, arrived in the region between 1763 and 1788. These were French-speaking people from the former French colony of Acadia in Canada expelled by British troops in the French and Indian Wars (1754-1763). The Acadians settled in the swampy areas of southwestern Louisiana and on the Mississippi just north of New Orleans. Isolation enabled them to keep the French language. Although the use of French largely disappeared in other parts of Louisiana after World War I, it would continue to be spoken in the Acadian region.

The British conquest of Canada also greatly reduced the strategic value of Louisiana for France. In order to entice the Spanish into entering the war against Britain, France transferred ownership of Louisiana to Spain in 1762. The following year, France and Spain lost the war. The Louisiana territories east of the Mississippi River became the property of Britain, and Spain was allowed to keep the lands west of the Mississippi, including New Orleans. Many of the French Louisianians had been born in America—Creoles—but they retained a devotion to France. The French Creoles revolted against Spanish rule, but Spanish troops quickly put down the rebellion. Spain, under the influence of French ruler Napoleon Bonaparte, returned the Louisiana territories to France in 1800. Bonaparte then sold the colony to the United States in 1803 in order to fund his own wars.

The American Period. The year after the United States purchased the huge Louisiana Territory, which extended the length of the Mississippi River, the United States split the region into the District of Louisiana and the District of Orleans. The District of Orleans became modern Louisiana. In 1810, American settlers in Spanish West Florida declared their independence from Spain and asked to join the United States. The American governor of Louisiana, William C. C. Claiborne, incorporated West Florida, as far as the Pearl River, into Orleans District. In 1812, the District of Orleans entered the United States as the state of Louisiana.

English-speaking settlers from other areas of the United States moved into Louisiana in large numbers. Most white Louisianians, both French-speaking and English-speaking, were small farmers. The most prosperous crops, though, were cotton and sugarcane. Both of these were plantation crops, which required intensive labor. As a result, slavery became a prominent part of the economic and social life of the state, especially in the southwestern bayou country, where the sugarcane flourished. Slave markets also became important to the economy of New Orleans.

One of the unique racial characteristics of Louisiana was the existence of a large group of free people of mixed race, known as the *gens de couleur libres,* or free people of color. Free people of color were sometimes quite prosperous and even owned slaves. According to historian John Hope Franklin, 3,000 of the 10,689 free people of color in New Orleans were slaveowners.

Civil War and Reconstruction. By the 1850's, the southern states, which were dependent on agriculture and slavery, were losing control of the U.S. Congress and presidency to the industrialized North. Many southerners believed that the southern way of life, including the institution of slavery, could only be preserved by seceding from the United States. In 1861, after the election of U.S. president Abraham Lincoln, southern states began declaring their independence. Louisiana withdrew from the union on April 12, 1861. One year later, though, the U.S. Navy captured New Orleans and soon afterward captured Baton Rouge.

Louisiana still had a large number of people of mixed race after the Civil War, and many of them were well educated. They made up the core of Louisiana's black political leadership during Reconstruction (1866-1877), when about one-third of the state's governmental leaders were black. In 1872, Louisiana's P. B. S. Pinchback became the first black governor in the United States.

After the withdrawal of Union troops, whites in the state reacted against Reconstruction violently. Taking control of the government, whites systematically excluded African Americans from many areas of public life. Legal segregation and the prevention of voting and political organization by African Americans continued until the 1960's, when Louisiana became a focal point of the Civil Rights movement.

Huey Long's Legacy. Louisiana continued to be a rural and agricultural state after the Civil War. During the 1920's, prices of agricultural goods, especially cotton, dropped. The charismatic politician Huey P. Long rose to power by championing the interests of workers and small farmers. One of Long's chief targets was Standard Oil Company, which had begun operating in Louisiana after the discovery of oil and gas deposits during the early twentieth century. Brilliant and ruthless, Long became governor in 1928. In 1930, he was elected U.S. senator, but he waited until 1932 to take his seat in the Senate, placing a hand-picked successor in the governor's position.

By the time Long was assassinated in 1935, he had almost total control over the Louisiana government. He helped to improve the lives of many Louisianians, but he also raised the level of corruption in state government. The Long political machine continued to operate under Huey's brother Earl Long through the 1950's, and the good and bad legacies of Huey Long would long remain with Louisiana politics.

Social and Economic Change. Although historically Louisiana has been a rural and agricultural state, the period after World War II saw substantial movement to cities. By 1990, 68 percent of Louisiana's people lived in urban areas. Sugarcane and rice farming continued to be economically important, but these agricultural activities became heavily mechanized and use only a small amount of human labor, mostly at planting and harvest times. Oil mining became increasingly important during the late twentieth century, and among the fifty states, Louisiana is second only to Texas in oil production.

Louisiana has one of the largest African American populations in the United States. About one out of every three Louisianians self-identified as African American in 1997. Despite the state's history of slavery and racial segregation, black Louisianians have made substantial progress toward political equality. During the 1990's, the state legislature was 16 percent black, and by 1992 two black Louisianians held elected office in the

More than a week after Hurricane Katrina tore through New Orleans, many sections of the city remained severely flooded. Many structures were irreparably damaged. (Jocelyn Augustino/FEMA)

U.S. House of Representatives. One of these representatives, Cleo Fields, made it into the runoffs for governor in 1996. Despite these advances, incomes and living conditions of African Americans in Louisiana lagged far behind those of white residents. It also appeared that racism was still prevalent. David Duke, a former leader of the Ku Klux Klan, won a majority of white votes in the 1991 election for governor. Duke was defeated only because black voters turned out in record numbers.

Politics and Elections. Aspects of the 2000 election in Louisiana illustrated general tensions in the national electoral system. In early October, the U.S. Justice Department dispatched eight observers to St. Joseph, Louisiana, to ensure the fairness of the municipal primary election, in compliance with the Voting Rights Act of 1965. Their presence was necessary to ensure fair treatment of African American voters. In the general election, all seven incumbents to the U.S. House of Representatives were easily reelected. In presidential polling, Republican George W. Bush defeated Democrat Al Gore by 53-45 percent.

In 2002, with divided opposition, U.S. senator and Democratic incumbent Mary Landrieu retained her seat with less than 50 percent of the vote. In 2003, the first round of voting found Republican Piyush "Bobby" Jindal in the lead (33 percent) and Lieutenant Governor Kathleen Blanco trailing in second (18 percent). In the November runoff, however, Blanco, who ran as a pro-life Democrat, beat Jindal by 52 to 48 percent to become the state's first woman governor. In 2004, George W. Bush again won the state in presidential polling, this time with 57 percent of the vote. Republican David Vitter won the U.S. Senate seat vacated by retiring senator John Breaux, with 51 percent against a divided opposition.

Hurricane Katrina. On August 29, 2005, Hurricane Katrina made landfall in Louisiana, near the city of Buras-Triumph. The storm, a strong Category 3 hurricane that had just been downgraded from Category 4, had already made landfall in Florida, where it did considerable damage and killed fourteen people. It proceeded to do catastrophic damage to Louisiana and neighboring states Mississippi and Alabama, killing more than eighteen hundred people, including nearly sixteen hundred in Louisiana. Soon after the storm struck, its storm surge caused Lake Pontchartrain, on the northern edge of New Orleans, to rise and flood communities along its shores. Bridges were destroyed and some 900,000 people in the state were left without power. The storm surge also caused breeches to the levees protecting the city of New Orleans. Since much of the city lay below the level of surrounding waters, the result was catastrophic flooding of about 80 percent of the city, as well as surrounding parishes. Although much of the city had been evacuated, thousands of residents who were unable, or in some cases unwilling, to leave were trapped inside their homes. About fifty-eight thousand National Guard members were deployed to keep order and rescue victims.

During the days that followed, thousands took refuge in the New Orleans Superdome, where terrible conditions added to the suffering. Looting and violence were commonplace in much of the city. Local, state, and federal government responses to the situation were inadequate. In the deluge of recriminations afterward, the Federal Emergency Management Agency (FEMA) was singled out for mismanagement. However, the City of New Orleans, its mayor, Ray Nagin, and Louisiana's state government led by Governor Blanco also shouldered much of the blame. Total damage was estimated at $150 billion.

FEMA spent hundreds of millions of dollars on relief, and by mid-2006 it was still housing 100,000 people in trailers. The Bush administration sought $105 billion for aid and reconstruction. The fallout from Katrina continued unabated, and by the one-year anniversary of the storm, tens of thousands of New Orleans residents had not returned and much of the city remained in ruin. Books and public conferences analyzed the catastrophe and spread copious amounts of blame and recrimination on all sides.

Carl L. Bankston III
Updated by the Editor

Louisiana Time Line

1500's	Mound Builder cultures flourish along the Mississippi River and in other areas of eastern North America.
1541-1542	Hernando de Soto discovers the Mississippi River.
Apr. 9, 1682	René-Robert Cavelier, sieur de La Salle, claims all territory drained by the Mississippi River for Louis XIV of France, for whom Louisiana is named.
1718	New Orleans is founded.
1722	France moves capital of the Louisiana colonies from Biloxi to New Orleans.
1763	Treaty of Paris transfers Louisiana to Spain.
1764	First Acadian families begin arriving in Louisiana.
Dec. 30, 1803	United States purchases the Louisiana Territory from France for fifteen million dollars.
Mar. 26, 1804	Louisiana is divided into the District of Orleans (modern Louisiana) and the District of Louisiana at 33 degrees latitude.
1810	American settlers in Spanish West Florida rebel against Spain; after a brief period of independence, West Florida becomes part of the District of Orleans.
Apr. 30, 1812	District of Orleans enters the United States as the state of Louisiana.
Jan. 8, 1815	U.S. general Andrew Jackson wins the Battle of New Orleans against the invading British.
1838	New Orleans holds its first Mardi Gras parade.
1849	State capital is moved from New Orleans to Baton Rouge.
Apr. 12, 1861	Louisiana votes to secede from the Union.
Apr. 25, 1862	U.S. Navy captures New Orleans.
1868	Louisiana ratifies a new state constitution, granting blacks social and civil rights, and is readmitted to the United States.
Nov., 1872	After the impeachment of Governor Henry C. Warmoth for corruption, Lieutenant Governor P. B. S. Pinchback becomes the first black governor in the United States.
1877	Reconstruction in Louisiana ends with the election of Democratic governor Francis T. Nicholls.
May 12, 1898	Louisiana adopts a new set of voting qualifications that take the vote away from almost all black Louisianians and many poor whites.
1901	First oil in Louisiana is discovered near the town of Jennings.
1915	New Orleans-style music becomes popularly known as "jazz."
1928	Huey P. Long is elected governor of Louisiana.
Sept. 8, 1935	Dr. Carl D. Weiss assassinates Long in Baton Rouge.
1947	Kerr-McGee Corporation drills the first deep-water, off-shore oil well off the Louisiana coast, with operations based in Morgan City.

1958	State legislature votes to close desegregated schools.
1963	In the midst of controversy over integration, Tulane University in New Orleans accepts its first black students.
1975	Super Dome in New Orleans is completed.
1977	Ernest N. (Dutch) Morial is elected the first black mayor of New Orleans.
1979	David Treen becomes the first Republican governor of Louisiana since Reconstruction.
1983	Edwin W. Edwards becomes the first Louisiana governor to be elected to three terms.
1988	Louisiana has the country's highest high school dropout rate.
1991	Edwards wins a historic fourth term in a runoff against former Ku Klux Klansman David Duke.
Nov. 7, 2000	George W. Bush wins state's nine electoral votes; all seven congressional incumbents easily retain their seats.
Oct. 21, 2002	Four-term Louisiana governor Edwin Edwards begins serving ten-year sentence in federal prison for racketeering and conspiracy.
May 9, 2003	Russell Long, scion of the Long political dynasty and the only senator in U.S. history to be preceded in the Senate by both parents, dies at eighty-four.
Nov. 15, 2003	Kathleen Blanco wins runoff election to become the state's first woman governor.
Aug. 29, 2005	Hurricane Katrina makes landfall in Louisiana; storm surge causes breeches in New Orleans levees, subsequently flooding and ruining the city and killing hundreds.

Notes for Further Study

Published Sources. Author Carl A. Brasseaux is one of the most prolific and respected authorities on Louisiana history, especially on the history of Acadian Louisiana. Brasseaux's *Acadian to Cajun: Transformation of a People, 1803-1877* (1992) is particularly recommended for its accurate, well-documented view of changing life in southwestern Louisiana. *Creoles of Color in the Bayou Country* (1996), also by Brasseaux, gives a fascinating account of Louisiana's free people of color. The *Historical Atlas of Louisiana* (1995) gives the places and facts of Louisiana history. For a short general overview of

Louisiana history, readers should consult *A Guide to the History of Louisiana* (1982), edited by Light Townsend Cummins and Glen Jeansonne. *Creole: The History and Legacy of Louisiana's Free People of Color* (2000), edited by Sybil Kein, examines the ethnic roots of the Creoles and analyzes their contributions to the state's history.

Although an older title, one of the best books on Louisiana's complicated political history is T. Harry Williams's biography *Huey Long* (1969). Another book that details Long's career is Richard D. White, Jr.'s, *Kingfish: The Reign of Huey P. Long* (2006). For later political history, two books by Louisiana political commentator John Maginnis are highly recommended. *The Last Hayride* (1984) looks at the controversial political career of three-term governor Edwin W. Edwards. In *Cross to Bear* (1992), Maginnis looks at the 1991 Louisiana gubernatorial campaign, in which Edwards, who was accused of massive corruption and frequently indicted by federal authorities, ran against David Duke, former Grand Wizard of the Ku Klux Klan and alleged neo-Nazi. Wayne Parent explores modern state politics with *Inside the Carnival: Unmasking Louisiana Politics* (2004). Historian and New Orleans resident Douglas Brinkley examines a preeminent social and political event in Louisiana's history—Hurricane Katrina—in *The Great Deluge: Hurricane Katrina, New Orleans, and the Mississippi Gulf Coast* (2006).

New Orleans is the subject of many books and articles. *Classic New Orleans* (1993), with text by William R. Mitchell and photographs by James R. Lockhart, is

Carnival masks in a New Orleans store foretoken the coming of the city's annual Mardi Gras, a festival with roots going back to 1838. (PhotoDisc)

a beautifully illustrated guide to the architecture and neighborhoods of the city. *Time and Place in New Orleans: Past Geographies in the Present Day* (2002) by Richard Campanella is an award-winning discussion of the way in which New Orleans's singular topography and geography influenced the city's growth and development. The second edition of the classic historical geography of New Orleans, Peirce F. Lewis's *New Orleans: The Making of an Urban Landscape*, was published in 2003.

Web Resources. A good starting place for obtaining information about Louisiana is Info Louisiana (portal.louisiana .gov/wps/wcm/connect/Louisiana.gov/Home/), which offers access to Louisiana state government sites. By clicking on About Louisiana, the Internet user can find sites on the state's people, culture, history, demographics and census informa-

tion, climate, and other topics. Those interested in the Civil War history of Louisiana should look at the Civil War in Louisiana site (www.crt.state.la.us/tourism/civilwar/civilwar.htm), which provides links to numerous short articles relating to the topic. American Civil War.com (www.americancivilwar .com/statepic/louisiana.html) also has a good map of critical battles fought within the state.

Louisiana.com (www.louisiana.com) offers updated news on entertainment and tourist attractions in the state. Louisiana is known for its unique culture, especially for its music. Both LouisianaRadio.com (www.louisianaradio.com) and New Orleans Music (www.louisianamusicfactory.com/) are devoted entirely to local and regional music of Louisiana. Zyde.com (members.aol.com/zydecom/page1.htm) is an online magazine devoted to the area's music.

Counties

County	2000 pop.	Rank in pop.	Sq. miles	Rank in area	County	2000 pop.	Rank in pop.	Sq. miles	Rank in area
Acadia	58,861	19	655.3	30	Natchitoches	39,080	30	1,256.4	4
Allen	25,440	38	764.6	23	Orleans	484,674	1	180.6	64
Ascension	76,627	16	291.6	58	Ouachita	147,250	8	611.0	39
Assumption	23,388	40	338.7	56	Plaquemines	26,757	36	844.6	17
Avoyelles	41,481	29	832.5	19	Pointe Coupee	22,763	42	557.4	45
Beauregard	32,986	33	1,160.2	7	Rapides	126,337	9	1,322.7	2
Bienville	15,752	52	810.7	20	Red River	9,622	62	388.6	54
Bossier	98,310	12	838.5	18	Richland	20,981	47	558.5	44
Caddo	252,161	4	882.1	12	Sabine	23,459	39	865.3	15
Calcasieu	183,577	7	1,071.2	9	St. Bernard	67,229	18	465.2	48
Caldwell	10,560	59	529.5	46	St. Charles	48,072	24	283.7	59
Cameron	9,991	61	1,313.0	3	St. Helena	10,525	60	408.4	52
Catahoula	10,920	58	703.7	26	St. James	21,216	46	246.1	61
Claiborne	16,851	51	754.7	24	St. John the Baptist	43,044	26	218.9	62
Concordia	20,247	48	696.4	27	St. Landry	87,700	15	928.7	11
DeSoto	25,494	37	877.3	14	St. Martin	48,583	23	739.9	25
East Baton Rouge	412,852	3	455.7	49	St. Mary	53,500	21	612.9	38
East Carroll	9,421	63	421.5	51	St. Tammany	191,268	5	854.4	16
East Feliciana	21,360	44	453.4	50	Tangipahoa	100,588	11	790.3	22
Evangeline	35,434	31	664.3	29	Tensas	6,618	64	602.5	40
Franklin	21,263	45	623.4	36	Terrebonne	104,503	10	1,255.1	5
Grant	18,698	49	645.1	33	Union	22,803	41	877.7	13
Iberia	73,266	17	575.2	42	Vermilion	53,807	20	1,173.9	6
Iberville	33,320	32	618.7	37	Vernon	52,531	22	1,328.5	1
Jackson	15,397	53	570.0	43	Washington	43,926	25	669.6	28
Jefferson	455,466	2	305.9	57	Webster	41,831	28	595.9	41
Jefferson Davis	31,435	34	652.4	31	West Baton Rouge	21,601	43	191.2	63
Lafayette	190,503	6	269.9	60	West Carroll	12,314	57	359.4	55
Lafourche	89,974	14	1,084.8	8	West Feliciana	15,111	54	406.0	53
LaSalle	14,282	55	623.9	35	Winn	16,894	50	950.6	10
Lincoln	42,509	27	471.4	47					
Livingston	91,814	13	648.1	32					
Madison	13,728	56	624.1	34					
Morehouse	31,021	35	794.3	21					

Louisiana's counties are called parishes.
Source: U.S. Census Bureau; National Association of Counties.

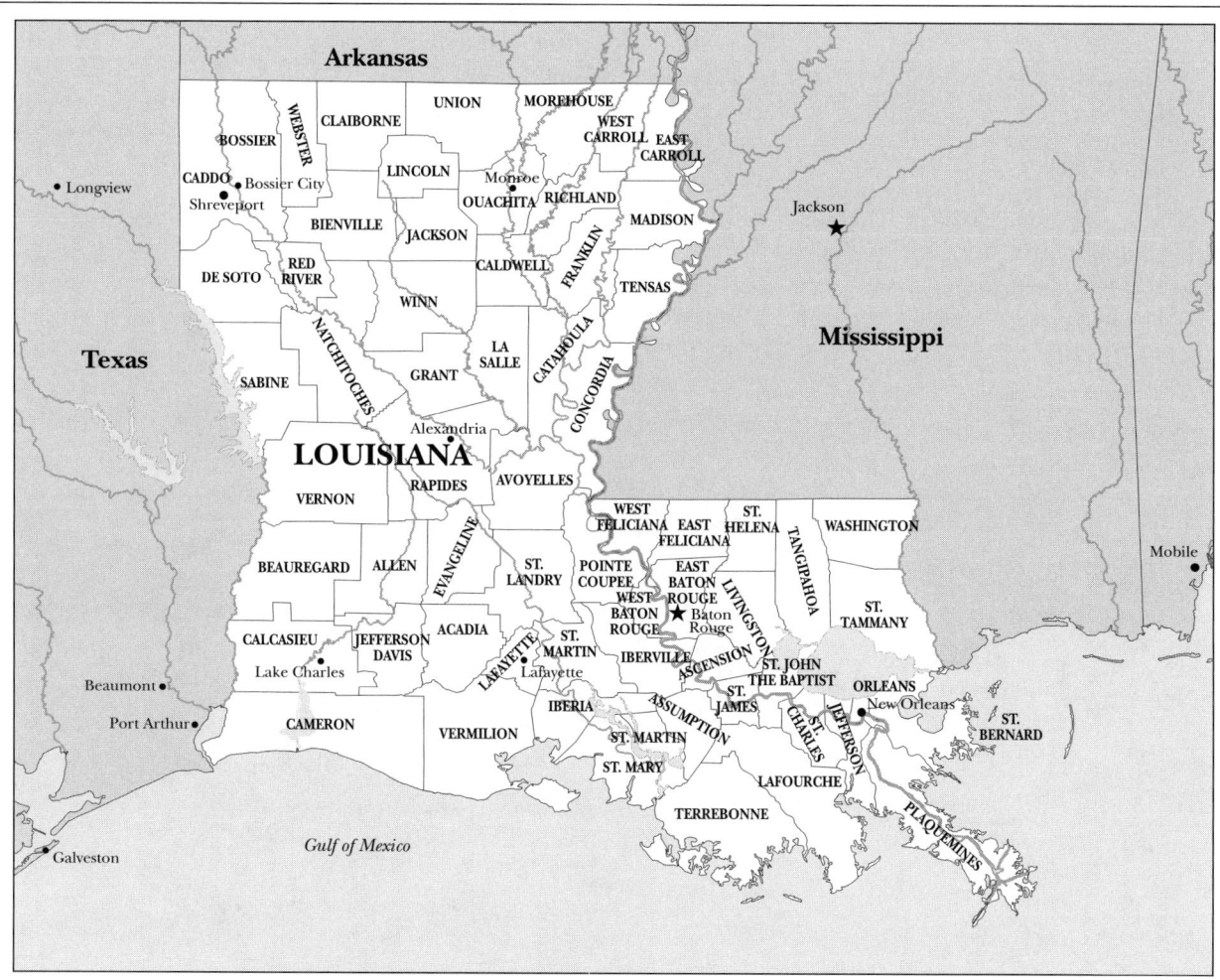

Cities
With 10,000 or more residents

Rank	City	Population	Rank	City	Population
1	New Orleans	484,674	20	Ruston	20,546
2	Baton Rouge (capital)	227,818	21	Sulphur	20,512
3	Shreveport	200,145	22	Natchitoches	17,865
4	Metairie	146,136	23	Hammond	17,639
5	Lafayette	110,257	24	Gretna	17,423
6	Lake Charles	71,757	25	Shenandoah	17,070
7	Kenner	70,517	26	Bayou Cane	17,046
8	Bossier City	56,461	27	Estelle	15,880
9	Monroe	53,107	28	River Ridge	14,588
10	Alexandria	46,342	29	Thibodaux	14,431
11	Marrero	36,165	30	Crowley	14,225
12	New Iberia	32,623	31	Pineville	13,829
13	Houma	32,393	32	Baker	13,793
14	Chalmette	32,069	33	Bogalusa	13,365
15	Laplace	27,684	34	West Monroe	13,250
16	Slidell	25,695	35	Woodmere	13,058
17	Terrytown	25,430	36	Minden	13,027
18	Opelousas	22,860	37	Bastrop	12,988
19	Harvey	22,226	38	Morgan City	12,703

(continued)

Rank	City	Population
39	Abbeville	11,887
40	Jefferson	11,843
41	Luling	11,512
42	Eunice	11,499
43	Timberlane	11,405
44	Zachary	11,275
45	Destrehan	11,260
46	Fort Polk South	11,000
47	Jennings	10,986
48	Westwego	10,763

Rank	City	Population
49	Moss Bluff	10,535
50	Mandeville	10,489
51	Merrydale	10,427
52	Raceland	10,224
53	Meraux	10,192

Population figures are from 2000 census. Note that the populations of many Louisiana cities—including Baton Rouge and New Orleans—dropped precipitously after Hurricane Katrina in 2005, and precise, recent figures are unavailable.

Source: U.S. Bureau of the Census.

Index to Tables

DEMOGRAPHICS

Resident state and national populations, 1970-2004

Population figures given in thousands

	State pop.	U.S. pop.	Share	Rank
1970	3,645	203,302	1.8%	20
1980	4,206	226,546	1.9%	19
1985	4,408	237,924	1.9%	19
1990	4,222	248,765	1.7%	21
1995	4,379	262,761	1.6%	21
2000	4,469	281,425	1.6%	22
2004	4,516	293,655	1.5%	24

Source: U.S. Census Bureau, Current Population Reports, 2006.

Resident population by age, 2004

Age Group	Total persons
Under 5 years	324,000
5 to 17 years	841,000
18 to 24 years	503,000
25 to 34 years	598,000
35 to 44 years	642,000
45 to 54 years	639,000
55 to 64 years	441,000
65 to 74 years	280,000
75 to 84 years	188,000
85 years and older	60,000
All age groups	4,516,000

Portion of residents 65 and older	11.7%
National rank in portion of oldest residents	39
National average	12.4%

Population figures are rounded to nearest thousand persons;
figures include armed forces personnel stationed in the state.
Source: U.S. Bureau of the Census, 2006.

Resident population by race, Hispanic origin, 2004

Category	State pop.	Share	U.S.
All residents	4,516	100.00%	100.00%
Non-Hispanic white	2,789	61.76%	67.37%
Hispanic white	107	2.37%	13.01%
Other Hispanic	17	0.38%	1.06%
African American	1,492	33.04%	12.77%
Native American	27	0.60%	0.96%
Asian, Pacific Islander	64	1.42%	4.37%
Two or more categories	37	0.82%	1.51%

Population figures are in thousands. Persons counted as "Hispanic" (Latino) may be of any race. Because of overlapping categories, categories may not add up to 100%. Shares in column 3 are percentages of each category within the state; these figures may be compared to the national percentages in column 4.
Source: U.S. Bureau of the Census, 2006.

Projected state population, 2000-2030

Year	Population
2000	4,469,000
2005	4,534,000
2010	4,613,000
2015	4,674,000
2020	4,719,000
2025	4,762,000
2030	4,803,000
Population increase, 2000-2030	334,000
Percentage increase, 2000-2030	7.5

Projections are based on data from the 2000 census.
Source: U.S. Census Bureau.

VITAL STATISTICS

Infant mortality rates, 1980-2002

	1980	1990	2000	2002
All state residents	14.3	11.1	9.0	10.3
All U.S. residents	12.6	9.2	9.4	9.1
All state white residents	10.5	8.1	5.9	6.9
All U.S. white residents	10.6	7.6	5.7	5.8
All state black residents	20.6	16.7	13.3	15.0
All U.S. black residents	22.2	18.0	14.1	14.4

Figures represent deaths per 1,000 live births of resident infants under 1 year old, exclusive of fetal deaths. Figures for all residents include members of other racial categories not listed separately.
Source: U.S. Census Bureau, *Statistical Abstract of the United States*, 2006.

Abortion rates, 1990 and 2000

	1990	2000
Total abortions	14,000	13,000
Rate per 1,000 women	13.4	13.0
U.S. rate	25.7	21.3
Rank	38	30

Numbers of abortions are rounded to nearest thousand; ranks are based on rates.
Source: U.S. Census Bureau.

Marriages and divorces, 2004

Total marriages	30,200
Rate per 1,000 population	6.7
National rate per 1,000 population	7.4
Rank among all states	31
Total divorces	n/a
National rate per 1,000 population	3.7
Rank among all states	n/a

Figures are for all marriages and divorces performed within the state, including those of nonresidents; totals are rounded to the nearest hundred. Ranks are for highest to lowest figures; note that no recent divorce data are available for Louisiana.
Source: U.S. National Center for Health Statistics, *Vital Statistics of the United States*, 2006.

Death rates by leading causes, 2002
Deaths per 100,000 resident population

Cause	State	U.S.
Heart disease	249.5	241.7
Cancer	210.6	193.2
Cerebrovascular diseases	57.9	56.4
Accidents other than motor vehicle	47.2	37.0
Motor vehicle accidents	21.4	15.7
Chronic lower respiratory diseases	37.8	43.3
Diabetes mellitus	39.6	25.4
HIV	8.1	4.9
Suicide	11.1	11.0
Homicide	13.5	6.1
All causes	936.6	847.3
Rank in overall death rate among states		15

Figures exclude nonresidents who died in the state. Causes of death follow International Classification of Diseases. Rank is from highest to lowest death rate in the United States.
Source: U.S. National Center for Health Statistics, *National Vital Statistics Report*, 2006.

ECONOMY

Gross state product, 1990-2004
In current dollars

Year	State product	Nat'l product	State share
1990	$93.6 billion	$5.67 trillion	1.65%
2000	$134.8 billion	$9.75 trillion	1.38%
2002	$134.4 billion	$10.41 trillion	1.29%
2003	$144.3 billion	$10.92 trillion	1.32%
2004	$152.0 billion	$11.65 trillion	1.30%

Source: U.S. Bureau of Economic Analysis, *Survey of Current Business,* July, 2005.

Gross state product by industry, 2003
In billions of dollars

Construction	$5.4
Manufacturing	14.1
Wholesale trade	7.3
Retail trade	10.8
Finance & insurance	5.2
Information	3.8
Professional services	6.1
Health care & social assistance	8.8
Government	16.6
Total state product	$130.7
Total U.S. product	$10,289.2
State share of U.S. total	1.27%
Rank among all states	24

Total figures include industries not listed separately. Amounts are in chained 2000 dollars.
Source: U.S. Bureau of Economic Analysis, *Survey of Current Business,* July, 2005.

Personal income per capita, 1990-2004
In current dollars

	1990	2000	2004
Per capita income	$15,173	$23,078	$27,581
U.S. average	$19,477	$29,845	$32,937
Rank among states	45	45	42

Source: U.S. Bureau of Economic Analysis, *Survey of Current Business,* April, 2005.

Energy consumption, 2001
In trillions of British thermal units (BTU), except as noted

Total energy consumption

Total state energy consumption	3,500
Total U.S. energy consumption	96,275
State share of U.S. total	3.64%
Rank among states	8

Per capita consumption (In millions of BTU)

Total state per capita consumption	784
Total U.S. per capita consumption	338
Rank among states	3

End-use sectors

Residential	348
Commercial	264
Industrial	2,135
Transportation	753

Sources of energy

Petroleum	1,491
Natural gas	1,340
Coal	240
Hydroelectric power	7
Nuclear electric power	181

Figures for totals include categories not listed separately.
Source: U.S. Energy Information Administration, *State Energy Data Report,* 2001.

Nonfarm employment by sectors, 2004

Total	1,920,000
Construction	117,000
Manufacturing	152,000
Trade, transportation, utilities	380,000
Information	29,000
Finance, insurance, real estate	103,000
Professional & business services	184,000
Education & health services	252,000
Leisure, hospitality, arts, organizations	204,000
Other services, including repair & maintenance	72,000
Government	383,000

Figures are rounded to nearest thousand persons. "Total" includes mining and natural resources, not listed separately.
Source: U.S. Bureau of Labor Statistics, 2006.

Foreign exports, 1990-2004
In millions of dollars

Year	State	U.S.	State share
1990	14,199	394,045	3.60%
1996	21,667	624,767	3.47%
1997	18,732	688,896	2.72%
2000	16,814	712,055	2.15%
2003	18,390	724,006	2.72%
2004	19,922	769,332	2.59%

Rank among all states in 2004 10

U.S. total does not include U.S. dependencies.
Source: U.S. Census Bureau, *U.S. Merchandise Trade*, series FT 900, 2000; U.S. Census Bureau, *U.S. International Trade in Goods and Services*, Series FT 900, 2005.

LAND USE

Federally owned land, 2003
Areas in acres

	State	U.S.	State share
Total area	28,868,000	2,271,343,000	1.27%
Nonfederal land	27,366,000	1,599,584,000	1.71%
Federal land	1,502,000	671,759,000	0.22%
Federal share	5.2%	29.6%	—

Areas are rounded to nearest thousand acres. Figures for federally owned land do not include trust properties.
Source: U.S. General Services Administration, *Federal Real Property Profile*, 2006.

Land use, 1997
In acres, rounded to nearest thousand

Total surface area	31,377,000
Total nonfederal rural land.	24,664,000
Percentage rural land	78.6%
Cropland	5,659,000
Conservation Reserve Program (CRP*) land. . . .	140,000
Pastureland	2,385,000
Rangeland	277,000
Forestland	13,226,000
Other rural land	2,976,000

*CRP is a federal program begun in 1985 to assist private landowners to convert highly erodible cropland to vegetative cover for ten years. Note that some categories of land overlap.
Source: U.S. Department of Agriculture, Natural Resources and Conservation Service, and Iowa State University, Statistical Laboratory, *Summary Report, 1997 National Resources Inventory*, revised December, 2000.

Farms and crop acreage, 2004

	State	U.S.	Share	Rank
Farms	27,000	2,113,000	1.28%	31
Acres (millions)	8	937	0.85%	33
Acres per farm	289	443	—	23

Source: U.S. Department of Agriculture, National Agricultural Statistics Service. Numbers of farms are rounded to nearest thousand units; acreage figures are rounded to nearest million. Rankings, including ties, are based on rounded figures.

GOVERNMENT AND FINANCE

Units of local government, 2002

	State	Total U.S.	Rank
All local governments	473	87,525	44
Parishes (counties)	60	3,034	25
Municipalities	302	19,429	26
Townships	0	16,504	—
School districts	66	13,506	37
Special districts	45	35,052	48

Only 48 states have county governments, 20 states have township governments ("towns" in New England, Minnesota, New York, and Wisconsin), and 46 states have school districts. Special districts encompass such functions as natural resources, fire protection, and housing and community development.
Source: U.S. Census Bureau, *Census of Governments*.

State government revenue, 2002

Total revenue	$18,079 mill.
General revenue	$17,659 mill.
Per capita revenue	$3,944
U.S. per capita average	$3,689
Rank among states	23

Intergovernment revenue	
Total	$6,049 mill.
From federal government	$5,994 mill.

Charges and miscellaneous	
Total	$4,253 mill.
Current charges	$2,218 mill.
Misc. general income	$2,035 mill.
Insurance trust revenue	$415 mill.

Taxes	
Total	$7,357 mill.
Per capita taxes	$1,644
Rank among states	37
Property taxes	$35 mill.
Sales taxes	$4,192 mill.
License taxes	$515 mill.
Individual income taxes	$1,789 mill.
Corporate income taxes	$264 mill.
Other taxes	$563 mill.

Total revenue figures include items not listed separately here.
Source: U.S. Bureau of the Census.

State government expenditures, 2002

General expenditures

Total state expenditures	$18,319 mill.
Intergovernmental	$4,168 mill.

Per capita expenditures

State	$3,611
Average of all states	$3,859
Rank among states	32

Selected direct expenditures

Education	$2,771 mill.
Public welfare	$3,311 mill.
Health, hospital	$1,932 mill.
Highways	$951 mill.
Police protection	$195 mill.
Corrections	$480 mill.
Natural resources	$317 mill.
Parks and recreation	$185 mill.
Government administration	$576 mill.
Interest on debt	$506 mill.
Total direct expenditures	$11,994 mill.

Totals include items not listed separately.
Source: U.S. Census Bureau.

POLITICS

Governors since statehood

D = Democrat; R = Republican; O = other;
(r) resigned; (d) died in office; (i) removed from office

William C. C. Claiborne		1812-1816
Jacques P. Villere		1816-1820
Thomas B. Robertson	(r)	1820-1824
Henry S. Thibodaux		1824
Henry Johnson		1824-1828
Pierre A. C. B. Derbigny	(d)	1828-1829
Armand Beauvais		1829-1830
Jacques Dupre		1830-1831
Andre B. Roman (O)		1831-1835
Edward D. White (O)		1835-1839
Andre B. Roman (O)		1839-1843
Alexandre Mouton (D)		1843-1846
Isaac Johnson (D)		1846-1850
Joseph M. Walker (D)		1850-1853
Paul O. Herbert (D)		1853
Robert C. Wickliffe (D)		1853-1860
Thomas O. Moore (D)		1860-1864
Henry W. Allen	(i)	1864
George Michael D. Hahn	(r)	1864-1865
J. Madison Wells (D)	(i)	1865-1867
Benjamin F. Flanders (D)	(i)	1867-1868
Joshua Baker (D)	(i)	1868
Henry C. Warmoth (R)	(r)	1868-1872
Pinckney B. S. Pinchback (R)		1872-1873
William P. Kellogg (R)		1873-1877
Francis R. T. Nicholls (D)		1877-1880

Louis A. Wiltz (D)	(d)	1880-1881
Samuel D. McEnery (D)		1881-1888
Francis R. T. Nicholls (D)		1888-1892
Murphy J. Foster (D)		1892-1900
William W. Heard (D)		1900-1904
Newton C. Blanchard (D)		1904-1908
Jared Y. Sanders (D)		1908-1912
Luther E. Hall (D)		1912-1916
Ruffin G. Pleasant (D)		1916-1920
John M. Parker (D)		1920-1924
Henry L. Fuqua (D)	(d)	1924-1926
Oramel H. Simpson (D)		1926-1928
Huey P. Long (D)	(r)	1928-1932
Alvin O. King (D)		1932
Oscar K. Allen (D)	(d)	1932-1936
James A. Noe (D)		1936
Richard W. Leche (D)	(r)	1936-1939
Earl K. Long (D)		1939-1940
Sam Houston Jones (D)		1940-1944
James H. (Jimmie) Davis (D)		1944-1948
Earl K. Long (D)		1948-1952
Robert F. Kennon (D)		1952-1956
Earl K. Long (D)		1956-1960
James H. (Jimmie) Davis (D)		1960-1964
John J. McKeithen (D)		1964-1972
Edwin W. Edwards (D)		1972-1988
Charles E. Roemer III (D)		1988-1992
Edwin W. Edwards (D)		1992-1996
Murphy J. (Mike) Foster (R)		1996-2004
Kathleen Blanco (D)		2004-

Composition of congressional delegations, 1989-2007

	Dem	Rep	Total
House of Representatives			
101st Congress, 1989			
State delegates	4	4	8
Total U.S.	259	174	433
102d Congress, 1991			
State delegates	4	4	8
Total U.S.	267	167	434
103d Congress, 1993			
State delegates	4	3	7
Total U.S.	258	176	434
104th Congress, 1995			
State delegates	2	5	7
Total U.S.	197	236	433
105th Congress, 1997			
State delegates	2	5	7
Total U.S.	206	228	434
106th Congress, 1999			
State delegates	2	5	7
Total U.S.	211	222	433

(continued)

	Dem	Rep	Total
107th Congress, 2001			
State delegates	2	5	7
Total U.S.	211	221	432
108th Congress, 2003			
State delegates	3	4	7
Total U.S.	205	229	434
109th Congress, 2005			
State delegates	2	5	7
Total U.S.	202	231	433
110th Congress, 2007			
State delegates	2	5	7
Total U.S.	233	202	435

Senate

	Dem	Rep	Total
101st Congress, 1989			
State delegates	2	0	2
Total U.S.	55	45	100
102d Congress, 1991			
State delegates	2	0	2
Total U.S.	56	44	100
103d Congress, 1993			
State delegates	2	0	2
Total U.S.	57	43	100
104th Congress, 1995			
State delegates	2	0	2
Total U.S.	46	53	99
105th Congress, 1997			
State delegates	2	0	2
Total U.S.	45	55	100
106th Congress, 1999			
State delegates	2	0	2
Total U.S.	45	54	99
107th Congress, 2001			
State delegates	2	0	2
Total U.S.	50	50	100
108th Congress, 2003			
State delegates	2	0	2
Total U.S.	48	51	99
109th Congress, 2005			
State delegates	1	1	2
Total U.S.	44	55	99
110th Congress, 2007			
State delegates	1	1	2
Total U.S.	49	49	98

Figures are for starts of first sessions. Totals are for Democrat (Dem.) and Republican (Rep.) members only. House membership totals under 435 and Senate totals under 100 reflect vacancies and seats held by independent party members. When the 110th Congress opened, the Senate's two independent members caucused with the Democrats, giving the Democrats control of the Senate.
Source: U.S. Congress, *Congressional Directory*.

Composition of state legislature, 1990-2006

	Democrats	Republicans
State House (105 seats)		
1990	89	16
1992	88	16
1994	86	17
1996	76	28
1998	74	28
2000	71	30
2002	68	37
2004	67	37
2006	62	41
State Senate (39 seats)		
1990	34	5
1992	33	6
1994	33	6
1996	25	14
1998	25	14
2000	26	13
2002	24	15
2004	24	15
2006	24	15

Figures for total seats may include independents and minor party members. Numbers reflect results of elections in listed years; elected members usually take their seats in the years that follow.
Source: Council of State Governments; *State Elective Officials and the Legislatures.*

Voter participation in presidential elections, 2000 and 2004

	2000	2004
Voting age population		
State	3,253,000	3,351,000
Total United States	209,831,000	220,377,000
State share of U.S. total	1.55	1.52
Rank among states	23	24
Portion of voting age population casting votes		
State	54.3%	58.0%
United States	50.3%	55.5%
Rank among states	21	24

Population figures are rounded to nearest thousand and include all residents, regardless of eligibility to vote.
Source: U.S. Census Bureau.

HEALTH AND MEDICAL CARE

Medical professionals
Physicians in 2003 and nurses in 2001

	U.S.	State
Physicians in 2003		
Total	774,849	11,904
Share of U.S. total		1.53%
Rate	266	265
Rank		15
Nurses in 2001		
Total	2,262,020	36,690
Share of U.S. total		1.62%
Rate	793	821
Rank		27

Rates are numbers of physicians and nurses per 100,000 resident population; ranks are based on rates.
Source: American Medical Association, *Physician Characteristics and Distribution in the U.S.*; U.S. Department of Health and Human Services, Health Resources and Services Administration.

Health insurance coverage, 2003

	State	U.S.
Total persons covered	3,517,000	243,320,000
Total persons not covered	912,000	44,961,000
Portion not covered	20.6%	15.6%
Rank among states	3	—
Children not covered	182,000	8,373,000
Portion not covered	15.2%	11.4%
Rank among states	6	—

Totals are rounded to nearest thousand. Ranks are from the highest to the lowest percentages of persons *not* insured.
Source: U.S. Census Bureau, Current Population Reports.

AIDS, syphilis, and tuberculosis cases, 2003

Disease	U.S. cases	State cases	Rank
AIDS	44,232	1,048	11
Syphilis	34,270	1,576	6
Tuberculosis	14,874	260	15

Source: U.S. Centers for Disease Control and Prevention.

Cigarette smoking, 2003
Residents over age 18 who smoke

	U.S.	State	Rank
All smokers	22.1%	26.6%	4
Male smokers	24.8%	30.3%	4
Female smokers	20.3%	23.2%	10

Cigarette smokers are defined as persons who reported having smoked at least 100 cigarettes during their lifetimes and who currently smoked at least occasionally.
Source: U.S. Centers for Disease Control and Prevention, *Morbidity and Mortality Weekly Report*, 53, no. 44 (November 12, 2004).

HOUSING

Home ownership rates, 1985-2004

	1985	1990	1995	2000	2004
State	70.2%	67.8%	65.3%	68.1%	70.6%
Total U.S.	63.9%	63.9%	64.7%	67.4%	69.0%
Rank among states	12	24	37	37	33

Net change in state home ownership rate,
1985-2004 . . . . +0.4%
Net change in U.S. home ownership rate,
1985-2004 . . . . +5.1%

Percentages represent the proportion of owner households to total occupied households.
Source: U.S. Census Bureau, 2006.

Home sales, 2000-2004
In thousands of units

Existing home sales	2000	2002	2003	2004
State sales	66.8	71.7	76.2	79.6
Total U.S. sales	5,171	5,631	6,183	6,784
State share of U.S. total	1.29%	1.27%	1.23%	1.17%
Sales rank among states	25	28	29	29

Units include single-family homes, condos, and co-ops.
Source: National Association of Realtors, Washington, D.C., *Real Estate Outlook: Market Trends & Insights*.

Values of owner-occupied homes, 2003

	State	U.S.
Total units	892,000	58,809,000
Value of units		
Under $100,000	50.6%	29.6%
$100,000-199,999	37.0%	36.9%
$200,000 or more	12.5%	33.5%
Median value	$99,215	$142,275
Rank among all states 41		

Units are owner-occupied one-family houses whose numbers are rounded to nearest thousand. Data are extrapolated from survey samples.
Source: U.S. Census Bureau, American Community Survey.

EDUCATION

Public school enrollment, 2002

Prekindergarten through grade 8
State enrollment 537,000
Total U.S. enrollment 34,135,000
State share of U.S. total 1.57%

Grades 9 through 12
State enrollment 194,000
Total U.S. enrollment 14,067,000
State share of U.S. total 1.38%

Enrollment rates
State public school enrollment rate 84.2%
Overall U.S. rate 90.4%
Rank among states in 2002 49
Rank among states in 1995 41

Enrollment figures (which include unclassified students) are rounded to nearest thousand pupils during fall school term. Enrollment rates are based on enumerated resident population estimate for July 1, 2002.
Source: U.S. National Center for Education Statistics.

Public college finances, 2003-2004

FTE enrollment in public institutions of higher education
Students in state institutions 183,300
Students in all U.S. public institutions 9,916,600
State share of U.S. total 1.85
Rank among states 18

State and local government appropriations for higher education
State appropriation per FTE $5,037
National average $5,716
Rank among states 36
State & local tax revenue going to higher education 8.7%

FTE = full-time equivalent in public postsecondary programs, including summer sessions; student numbers are rounded to nearest hundred. Funding figures for 2003-2004 academic year include financial aid to students in state public institutions and exclude money for research, agriculture experiment stations, teaching hospitals, and medical schools; figures are rounded to nearest thousand dollars.
Source: Higher Education Executive Officers, Denver, Colorado.

TRANSPORTATION AND TRAVEL

Highway mileage, 2003

Interstate highways 904
Other freeways and expressways 34
Arterial roads 5,246
Collector roads 10,132
Local roads 44,621
Urban roads 13,950
Rural roads 46,987
Total state mileage 60,937
U.S. total 3,974,107
State share 1.53%
Rank among states 33

Note that combined urban and rural road mileage matches the total of the other categories.
Source: U.S. Federal Highway Administration.

Motor vehicle registrations and driver licenses, 2003

Vehicle registrations	State	U.S.	Share	Rank
Autos, trucks, buses	3,714,000	231,390,000	1.61%	22
Autos only	1,997,000	135,670	1.47%	22
Motorcycles	57,000	5,328,000	1.07%	29
Driver licenses	3,120,000	196,166,000	1.59%	22

Figures, which do not include vehicles owned by military services, are rounded to the nearest thousand. Figures for automobiles include taxis.
Source: U.S. Federal Highway Administration.

Domestic travel expenditures, 2003

Spending by U.S. residents on overnight trips and
day trips of at least 50 miles from home

Total expenditures within state . . . . $9.06 bill.
Total expenditures within U.S. . . . . $490.87 bill.
State share of U.S. total 1.8%
Rank among states 19

Source: Travel Industry Association of America.

Retail gasoline prices, 2003-2007

Average price per gallon at the pump

Year	U.S.	State
2003	$1.267	$1.195
2004	$1.316	$1.223
2005	$1.644	$1.579
2007	$2.298	$2.181

Excise tax per gallon in 2004 . . . . 20.0¢
Rank among all states in 2007 prices 36

Prices are averages of all grades of gasoline sold at the pump
during March months in 2003-2005 and during February, 2007.
Averages for 2006, during which prices rose higher, are not
available.
Source: U.S. Energy Information Agency, *Petroleum Marketing
Monthly* (2003-2005 data); American Automobile Association
(2007 data).

CRIME AND LAW ENFORCEMENT

State and local police officers, 2000-2004

	2000	2002	2004
Total officers			
U.S.	654,601	665,555	675,734
State	16,874	16,957	16,563*
*Net change, 2000-2004			−1.84%
Officers per 1,000 residents			
U.S.	2.33	2.31	2.30
State	3.78	3.79	3.68
State rank	1	1	1

Totals include state and local police and sheriffs.
Source: Carsey Institute, University of New Hampshire.

Crime rates, 2003

Incidents per 100,000 residents

Crimes	State	U.S.
Violent crimes		
Total incidents	646	475
Murder	13	6
Forcible rape	41	32
Robbery	157	142
Aggravated assault	435	295
Property crimes		
Total incidents	4,350	3,588
Burglary	998	741
Larceny/theft	2,909	2,415
Motor vehicle theft	442	433
All crimes	4,996	4,063

Source: U.S. Federal Bureau of Investigation, *Crime in the United
States,* annual.

State prison populations, 1980-2003

	State	U.S.	State share
1980	8,889	305,458	2.91%
1990	18,599	708,393	2.63%
1996	26,779	1,025,624	2.61%
2000	35,207	1,391,261	2.53%
2003	36,047	1,470,045	2.45%

State figures exclude prisoners in federal penitentiaries.
Source: U.S. Bureau of Justice Statistics, *Prisoners in 2003.*

Maine

Location: New England

Area and rank: 30,865 square miles (79,939 square kilometers); 35,387 square miles (91,652 square kilometers) including water; thirty-ninth largest state in area

Coastline: 228 miles (367 kilometers) on the Atlantic Ocean

Shoreline: 3,478 miles (5,597 kilometers)

Population and rank: 1,317,000 (2004); thirty-ninth largest state in population

Capital city: Augusta (18,560 people in 2000 census)

Largest city: Portland (64,249 people in 2000 census)

Entered Union and rank: March 15, 1820; twenty-third state

Present constitution adopted: 1820

Counties: 16

State name: "Maine" was first used to distinguish the region's mainland from its offshore islands; the name was also considered a compliment to English king Charles I's consort, Henrietta Maria, of France's Mayne province

State nickname: Pine Tree State

Motto: *Dirigo* (I lead)

State flag: Blue field with the state coat of arms

Highest point: Mount Katahdin—5,267 feet (1,605 meters)

Lowest point: Atlantic Ocean—sea level

Highest recorded temperature: 105 degrees Fahrenheit (41 degrees Celsius)—North Bridgton, 1911

Lowest recorded temperature: –48 degrees Fahrenheit (–44 degrees Celsius)—Van Buren, 1925

State song: "State of Maine Song"

State tree: White pine tree

State flower: White pine cone and tassel

State bird: Chickadee

State fish: Landlocked salmon

State animal: Moose

National parks: Acadia

State capitol building in Augusta. (Maine Office of Tourism)

Maine History

Maine, the largest of the six New England states, is filled with natural wonder and beauty. It has more than five thousand lakes and ponds, woodlands cover almost 90 percent of the state, and more than 3,400 miles of its Atlantic shoreline twist from New Hampshire to Canada. The harsh, brutal winters have always made living there difficult, and the state remains relatively sparsely populated.

As far as it is known, the first Native Americans to settle in the area were members of the Abenaki (people of the dawnland) tribe. They, and the tribes that followed them, were hunters and gatherers, living on fish, deer, moose, beavers, and bears. Like many Native Americans of New England, they lived in wigwams and were generally peaceful—until European settlers began to come.

Early Exploration and Settlement. Viking leader Leif Eriksson and other Norse sailors most likely explored part of Maine during their travels in 1000. John Cabot, sent by King Henry VII of England, claimed Maine as territory for England in 1497. In 1524, explorer Giovanni da Verrazano claimed Maine for France. In 1605, British captain George Weymouth landed in Maine, kidnapped five Abenaki men, and took them back to England. Upon meeting the American Indians and hearing stories of the land, King James I agreed to sponsor a settlement there, sending Sir Ferdinando Gorges and Sir John Popham to lead the exhibition. In 1607, the British explorers reached the coast where the Kennebec River meets the ocean. There they began the Popham colony, where they built the *Virginia*—the first English ship built in North America. Success was short-lived, however, as a typically bitter Maine winter, combined with attacks from the Abenakis, drove the entire colony back to England in 1608.

Soon, however, both English and French explorers returned and claimed different parts of the state for their kings. The English fought with the Native Americans often. Englishman John Winter founded one of Maine's first shipyards in 1637, and Maine was on its way to becoming a major shipbuilding center. The ships built in Maine supplied fish, fur, lumber, and masts to England's navy. The empty ships returning brought more settlers, and as settlers moved inland, farming gained importance. As in most of New England, native corn was Maine's primary crop. Primarily because of the harsh winters, Maine did not grow as quickly as the other New England colonies. The small population and weak government motivated the colonists there to merge with Massachusetts in 1658, and they remained part of it for nearly 150 years.

Two Wars. In 1754, tension over the colonies between France, which ruled Canada, and England broke into the French and Indian War. Thousands of Maine settlers fought against the French. The French and Indians were eventually defeated, and many of the warring tribes fled to Canada. The victory was costly, however, and it left Great Britain deeply in debt. When the war ended in 1763, Maine was doing well. The colony had twenty-five thousand settlers and nearly fifty towns. Each year, Maine shipped millions of pounds of fish and lumber to cities in Europe. Like the other colonies, Maine started resenting Britain's meddling. Britain, trying to relieve its war debt, continually raised the taxes of the colonists.

In 1774, a group of men from York, Maine, burned English tea to protest the high taxes in what would be called the York Tea Party. In 1775, the Revolutionary War began in Massachusetts. On June 12 of that year, the first sea battle of the war occurred off Maine, when colonists from Machias rowed out and attacked an English ship. Soon after that the English retaliated, and the city of Falmouth (later Portland) was bombarded and burned. By the time the Union won the war, about one thousand colonists from Maine had given their lives.

After the war, the Massachusetts government sold Maine land to new settlers for less than a dollar an acre. Maine's population increased significantly, and by 1785 Maine started lobbying for statehood. The new and growing country had other problems, however. In 1812, the United States again went to war with Great Britain. Britain, at that time at war with France, would attack and capture American ships and conscript Americans into service. Maine's growing dominance as a shipbuilder played a major role in the American success, and after the war, it pushed even harder for statehood.

Statehood. In 1820, in an effort to defuse the hotly contested issue of slavery in America, it was proposed that Missouri be admitted as a slave state if Maine were admitted as a free state, thus keeping a balance of eleven proslavery states and eleven antislavery states. Known as the Missouri Compromise, this agreement is credited with postponing civil war. Maine then separated from Massachusetts and became the twenty-third state, and the last New England state accepted into the Union. Portland served as the state capital until 1832, when the more centrally located Augusta became the capital. By then, potatoes were replacing corn as the most profitable crop, and lumbering became the state's largest industry. The city of Bath became the leading shipbuilding city in the country.

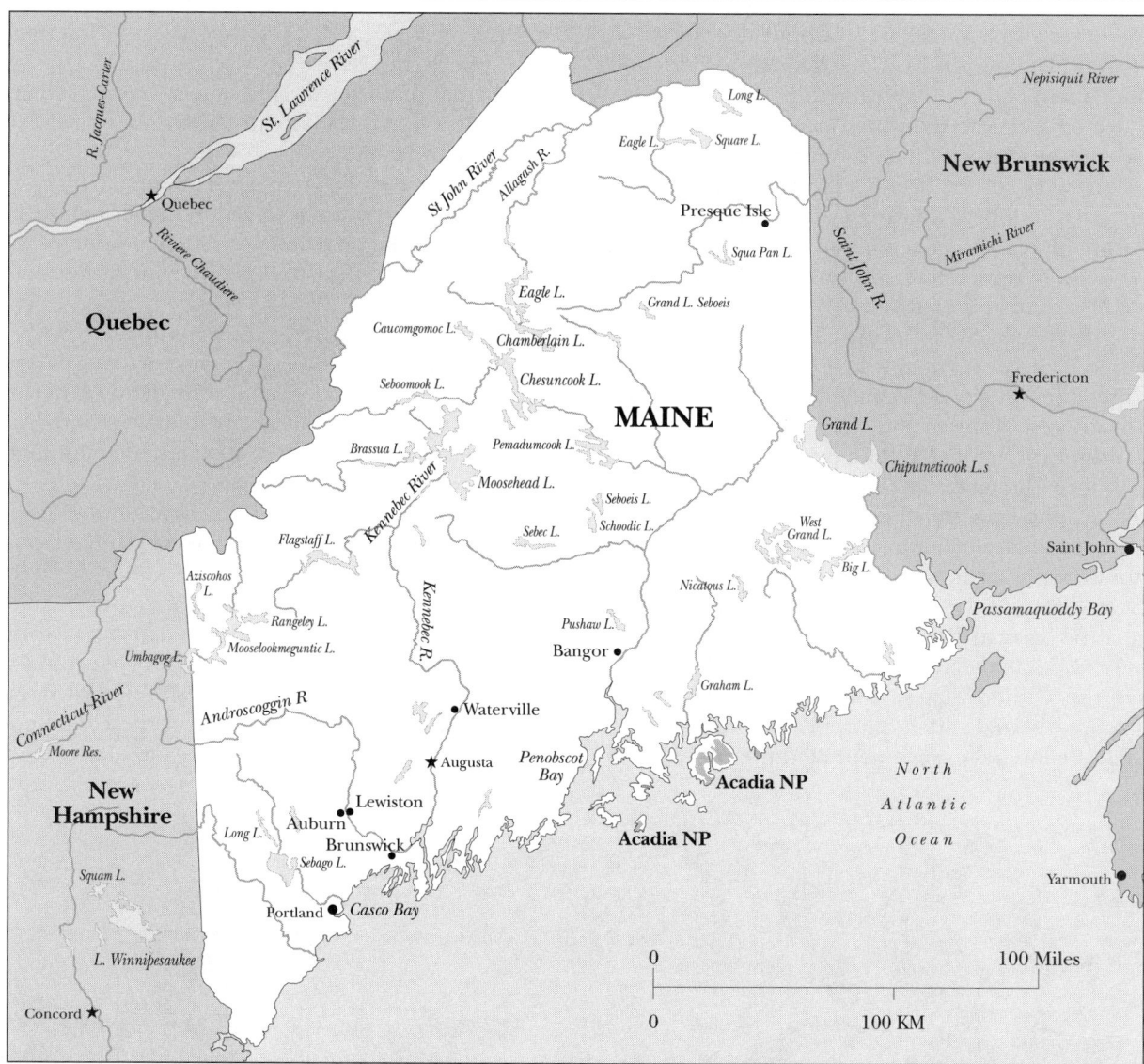

Maine was admitted to the Union as a free state, as it had a history of supporting people of African descent: When Bowdoin College opened in Brunswick in 1802, it was the first U.S. college to admit black students. John Russwurm, the college's first black graduate, co-founded *Freedom's Journal,* the country's first black-run newspaper, in 1827.

Antislavery Maine governor Hannibal Hamlin became President Abraham Lincoln's vice president in 1861. The Civil War erupted that year, and many Mainers heeded the call to arms. In the election of 1864, Lincoln was in political trouble, and he quietly allowed moderate southern Democrat Andrew Johnson to replace Hamlin as his vice president to ensure his re-election. By the time the Civil War ended in 1865, about 7,500 Maine soldiers had been killed fighting.

Industrial Revolution. During the 1850's, the Industrial Revolution began to influence American cities, and Maine came to operate textile and leather factories. Like the rest of New England, Maine was successful at building factories, and thousands of French Canadians crossed the border to find jobs. Many Irish escaped the horrible potato famine that began during the 1840's and came to Maine. In 1894, the Arrostock Railroad was completed, and trains began to move the wealth of Maine potatoes to the markets of other American cities. During this time Maine became one of the country's great potato-growing areas.

Economic Decline. During the twentieth century, tourists discovered Maine: its mystique, unspoiled beauty, and lack of crowded cities. The upsurge in tourists helped Maine's economy, as the state's other industries began to falter. The development of iron steamships damaged Maine's wooden-ship building industry, and the traditional activities of lumbering, fishing, and farming did not provide enough jobs for everyone.

There was a small break in economic decline when World War I began in 1914. Many Mainers did not wait for the United States to enter the war and joined Canada's armed forces to fight the Germans. The United States entered the war in 1917, and 35,000 Mainers joined the U.S. forces. Maine's shipbuilding industry sprang back to life, and farmers and fisherman saw a significant increase in price for their harvests. After the war ended, however, times were difficult in Maine. When the country entered World War II in 1941, Maine again sprang back to life. During the 1950's and 1960's, Air Force bases were built, which employed many locals, but unemployment remained higher in Maine than in the rest of the nation.

Modern Era. In 1954, Edmund Muskie became the first modern Democrat elected governor in the traditionally Republican state. In 1957, he was the first Maine Democrat elected to the Senate. The popular senator went on to run unsuccessfully for the vice presidency in 1968 and the presidential nomination of the Democratic party in 1972.

In 1972, Maine's Native Americans filed a lawsuit against the United States, claiming their lands had been wrongly seized and showing a 1794 treaty as proof. In 1980, the federal government paid the tribes $81.5 million for their land. It was the largest such settlement ever awarded to Native Americans.

During the 1980's, the state's economy became strong again, particularly in the largest city, Portland, although industry declined to the point that service industries represented 70 percent of the state's economy. Maine lobster is often referred to the best in the country, and the state produces 22 million pounds of it each year. Maine also produces 98 percent of the nation's blueberries.

The state is relatively underpopulated, with only about one million residents. In the northern part of the state, there are few developed cities. During the 1990's, less than 1 percent of the population was Native American, and most Mainers are descendants of emigrants from Great Britain, France, and Canada.

State politics. Although often considered a Republican state, Maine does not always stay true to that category when it comes to presidential politics. An old saying that "so Maine goes, so goes the nation" could not apply in the instances of Democratic Party victories in 2000. In that year, all of Maine's four electoral votes went to Democratic Party candidate Vice President Al Gore, by a margin of 49 percent to 44 percent. Republican U.S. senator Olympia Snowe was reelected, as were

With a population of fewer than twenty thousand people, Maine's capital city, Augusta, is only the ninth-largest city in the state. (PhotoDisc)

Although Maine ranks only thirty-ninth in area among the states, it has nearly 3,500 miles of shoreline and is famous for its numerous lighthouses. (PhotoDisc)

the state's two Democrats in the House of Representatives. The Maine state senate went to the Republican Party.

A number of important initiatives were on the ballot in 2000. Voters narrowly rejected a gay rights initiative that barred discrimination on the basis of sexual orientation by 51 percent to 49 percent. By the same margin, they also turned down an assisted suicide measure that would have allowed doctors to help certain patients to die at their own hands. For the third time in three years, Maine voters also were not interested in allowing a video-based lottery, with 61 percent dissenting. Finally, voters rejected curbs in cutting the state's timber by the lopsided margin of 71 percent to 29 percent.

In 2004, Maine voters repeated their year 2000 performance in presidential politics, voting the state's electoral votes to Democrat senator John Kerry from neighboring Massachusetts by a 53-45 percent margin. An initiative decided upon at the ballot box was a proposal to ban hunting bears with bait, traps, or dogs. Voters rejected the measure, which pitted animal rights activists against hunters, by a 54-46 percent margin. Voters also rejected a measure modeled after California's Proposition 13 that would have limited real estate taxes to 1 percent of assessed value.

Legal Disputes Settled. In 2001, the long border dispute between Maine and New Hampshire—sometimes called a "border war"—was finally settled by a decision of the U.S. Supreme Court. The border issue, which stretched back to 1827, revolved around whether the Portsmouth Navy Yard was in Maine or in New Hampshire. If it were in the latter, citizens of New Hampshire, which did not have a state income tax, would be able to stop paying Maine's state income tax. In an 8-0 decision, the Court ruled that New Hampshire could not change the border that had been agreed with Maine in 1977.

When asked at the polls on two occasions, Maine voters said that mentally ill people who are under guardianship should not be allowed to vote. In 2001, however, a federal judge overturned their decision, ruling that barring the mentally ill from voting violates the equal protection clause of the Fourteenth Amendment to the U.S. Constitution.

Kevin M. Mitchell
Updated by the Editor

Maine Time Line

1400	Abenaki tribe inhabits Maine area.
1497	John Cabot claims Maine for England.
1524	Explorer Giovanni da Verrazano claims Maine for France.
1605	Captain George Weymouth kidnaps five Native Americans and takes them to England.
1607	Gorge Popham establishes a settlement near Kennebec River; the first English ship, the *Virginia*, is built.
1620's	Smallpox wipes out many Abenaki.
1628	Plymouth Pilgrims establish several fur-trading posts in Maine territory.
1634	First sawmill in Maine begins operation.
1637	First shipyard in Maine opens.
1640's	French establish missions and begin converting Indians.
1649	Government grants all Christians the right to form churches.
1652	Maine becomes a part of the Massachusetts Bay Colony.
1690's	French and Indians from Canada pillage Maine until only four English settlements remain inhabited.
1774	Patriots burn English tea to protest high taxes in York Tea Party.
May 12, 1775	Maine patriots capture English ship in first naval battle of the American Revolution.
1778	Continental Congress divides Massachusetts into three districts, including one province called Maine.
1785	Maine's first newspaper, the *Falmouth Gazette*, is published.
1791	First lighthouse on the Atlantic Coast begins operation in Portland.
1801	First free public library opens in Castine.
1802	Bowdoin College opens in Brunswick.
1819	Maine state representatives vote to separate from Massachusetts and adopt a state constitution.
Mar. 15, 1820	Maine gains statehood under terms of Missouri Compromise, becoming the twenty-third state of the Union.
1832	State capital is moved to Augusta.
1834	Maine's Antislavery Society is formed in Augusta.
1850's	Most remaining Native Americans live on reservations.
1851	Antidrinking legislation passes making Maine the first dry state.
1855	State militia fires on civilians as they descend upon Portland's City Hall, looking for liquor; one man is killed.
1861	Maine Republican Hannibal Hamlin is elected vice president of the United States.
1894	Arrostock Railroad is completed; trains move potatoes to the markets of other American cities.
1912	Leon Bean founds clothing mail-order business L. L. Bean in Freeport.
1950	Margaret Chase Smith becomes the first woman elected to both houses of the U.S. Congress.
1957	Governor Edmund S. Muskie is first Maine Democrat elected to the U.S. Senate.
1979	Maine's three Indian reservations have a total population of 1,247.
1981	Tourism continues to lead all industries; more than $500 million is spent by out-of-state visitors in Maine.
1999	Children's Rights Council names Maine the best state in which to raise children.
Nov. 7, 2000	Maine voters give the state's four electoral votes to Al Gore and reelect Republican Olympia Snowe to the U.S. Senate.
May 29, 2001	Long-standing border dispute with New Hampshire is settled in Maine's favor by the U.S. Supreme Court.
Nov. 4, 2003	Voters reject a proposal by two Indian tribes, the Passamaquoddy Tribe and the Penobscot Nation, to build a $650 million casino resort.
Nov. 2, 2004	Maine voters choose Senator John Kerry for president, reject an initiative limiting the means by which bears are hunted, and also reject an initiative that would have limited real estate taxes to 1 percent of assessed value.

Notes for Further Study

Published Sources. For younger readers, information about Maine's history, culture, and social and political development can be found in Margaret Coull Phillips's *Maine* (2004), Terry Allan Hicks's *Maine* (2006), and *Maine History! Surprising Secrets About Our State's Founding Mothers, Fathers and Kids!* (1996) by Carole Marsh. *Maine: A Narrative History* (1990) by Neil Rolde offers a more in-depth view of the state. *Maine: Heads of Families at the First Census of the U.S. Taken in 1790* (1987), edited by Robert Danbury, offers insight to Maine's early settlers and the first families of the state. Gail Underwood Parker gives readers a lively narrative of Maine history from the first colony in the early seventeenth century to the modern era in *It Happened in Maine* (2004).

The French and Indian War (1997) by Christopher Collier and James Lincoln Collier covers the many battles that took place on Maine's soil, as well as the hundred years between initial colonization and the American Revolution. *The Maine Reader: The Down East Experience, 1614 to the Present* (1997), edited by Charles Shain and Samuella Shain, offers a sweeping history of the state through literature. Covering everything from ferry boats to the islands, in addition to coastal architecture, is *The Coast of Maine Book: A Complete Guide* (1999) by Rick Ackermann and Kathryn Buxton. *The Lobster Coast: Rebels, Rusticators, and the Struggle for a Forgotten Frontier* (2004) by Colin Woodard describes the political developments and environmental issues of the state by focusing on the coast's fishing and lobstering communities.

For those readers interested in all aspects of Maine's politics and politicians, author Christian P. Potholm covers these topics thoroughly with three books: *An Insider's Guide to Maine*

Founded in Freeport, Maine, in 1912, L. L. Bean is one of the largest mail-order clothing businesses in the United States. (Maine Office of Tourism)

Politics (1998), *This Splendid Game: Maine Campaigns and Elections, 1940-2002* (2003), and *Maine: The Dynamics of Political Change* (2006). Editor Richard Barringer, in *Changing Maine 1960-2010* (2004), brings together presentations from speakers in a 2003-2004 public lecture series presented by the Muskie School of Public Service University of Southern Maine. The lectures examine Maine's changing economic, political, and social landscape over several decades.

The Maine Handbook (1998) by Kathy Brandes provides information on all of Maine's natural beauty destinations, as does *Maine: An Explorer's Guide* (13th ed., 2006) by Christina Tree and Nancy English. *Maine Trivia* (1998), compiled by John N. Cole, is an entertaining, insightful, small volume of the facts, figures, and firsts of the Pine Tree State.

Web Resources. There are many Maine sites on the Internet, and those listed here often give valuable links to others. A good starting point is the Center for Maine History (www .mainehistory.org/). The center comprises the Maine Histor-ical Society Research Library, the Maine History Gallery, and the historic Wadsworth-Longfellow House. The official state of Maine home page (www.state.me.us/) is a collection of information and other Web sites on such topics as history, finance, and politics. Visit Maine (www.visitmaine.com/home .php) is the state's official tourism site. The U.S. Census Bureau provides its so-called QuickFacts for each of the fifty states; those for Maine can be found at quickfacts.census.gov/ qfd/states/23000.html. Information on Margaret Chase Smith and the organization that she inspired can be found at Margaret Chase Smith Library (www.mcslibrary.org/). The state's largest newspaper, the *Portland Press Herald* (pressherald.mainetoday.com/home.html), offers updated news on state happenings. The Portland Harbor Museum (www.portlandharbormuseum.org/) is a fascinating maritime museum with information on the city's port and working lighthouse.

Lobster boats tied up alongside a Portland pier piled high with traps used to catch the crustaceans for which the state is famous. (©Ben Thomas/iStockphoto.com)

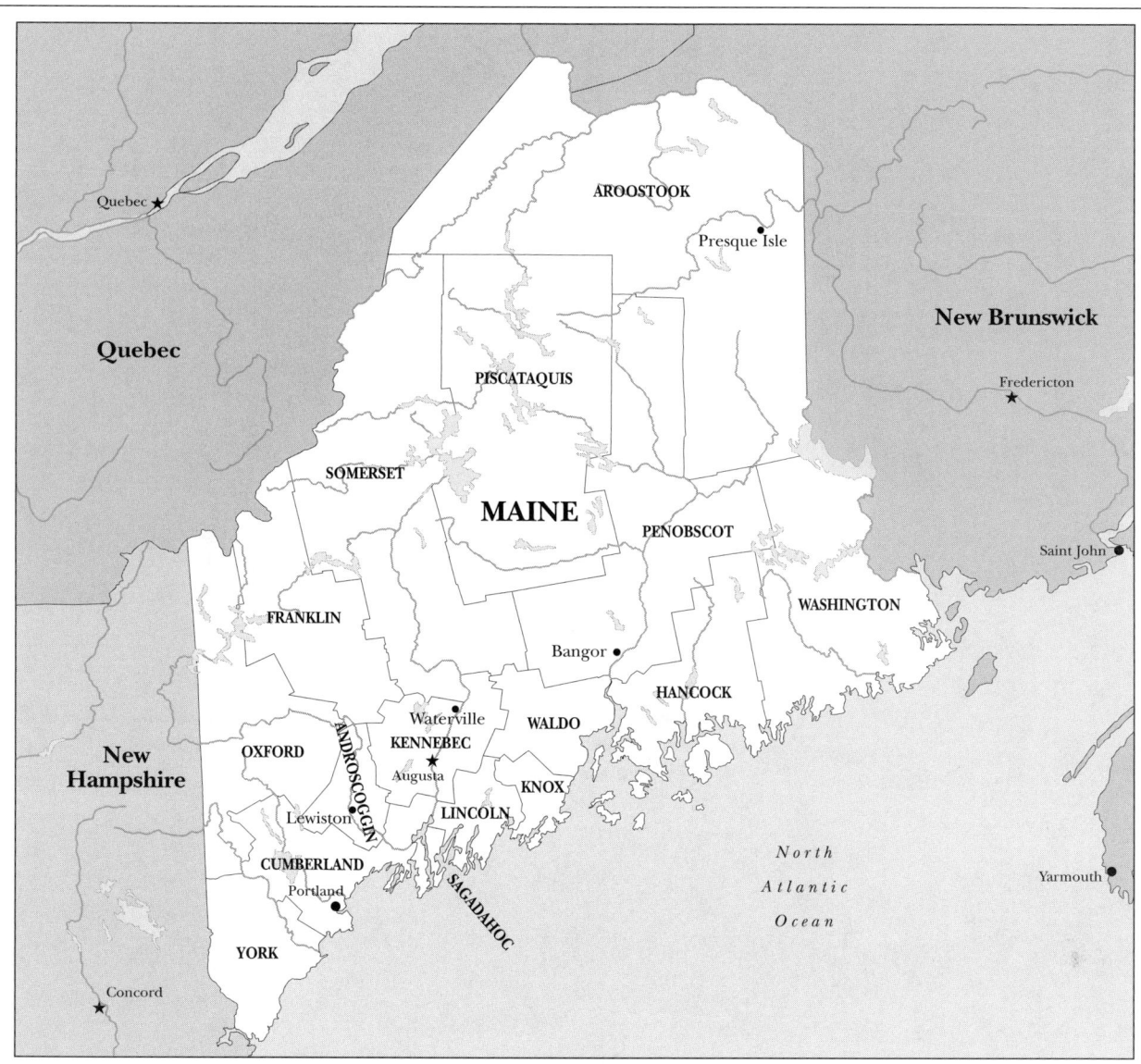

Counties

County	2000 pop.	Rank in pop.	Sq. miles	Rank in area
Androscoggin	103,793	5	470.3	13
Aroostook	73,938	6	6,671.9	1
Cumberland	265,612	1	835.6	11
Franklin	29,467	15	1,698.0	7
Hancock	51,791	8	1,589.1	8
Kennebec	117,114	4	867.5	10
Knox	39,618	10	365.6	15
Lincoln	33,616	14	455.6	14
Oxford	54,755	7	2,078.2	6
Penobscot	144,919	3	3,396.0	4
Piscataquis	17,235	16	3,966.5	2
Sagadahoc	35,214	12	254.0	16
Somerset	50,888	9	3,926.8	3
Waldo	36,280	11	729.8	12
Washington	33,941	13	2,568.6	5
York	186,742	2	991.0	9

Source: U.S. Census Bureau; National Association of Counties.

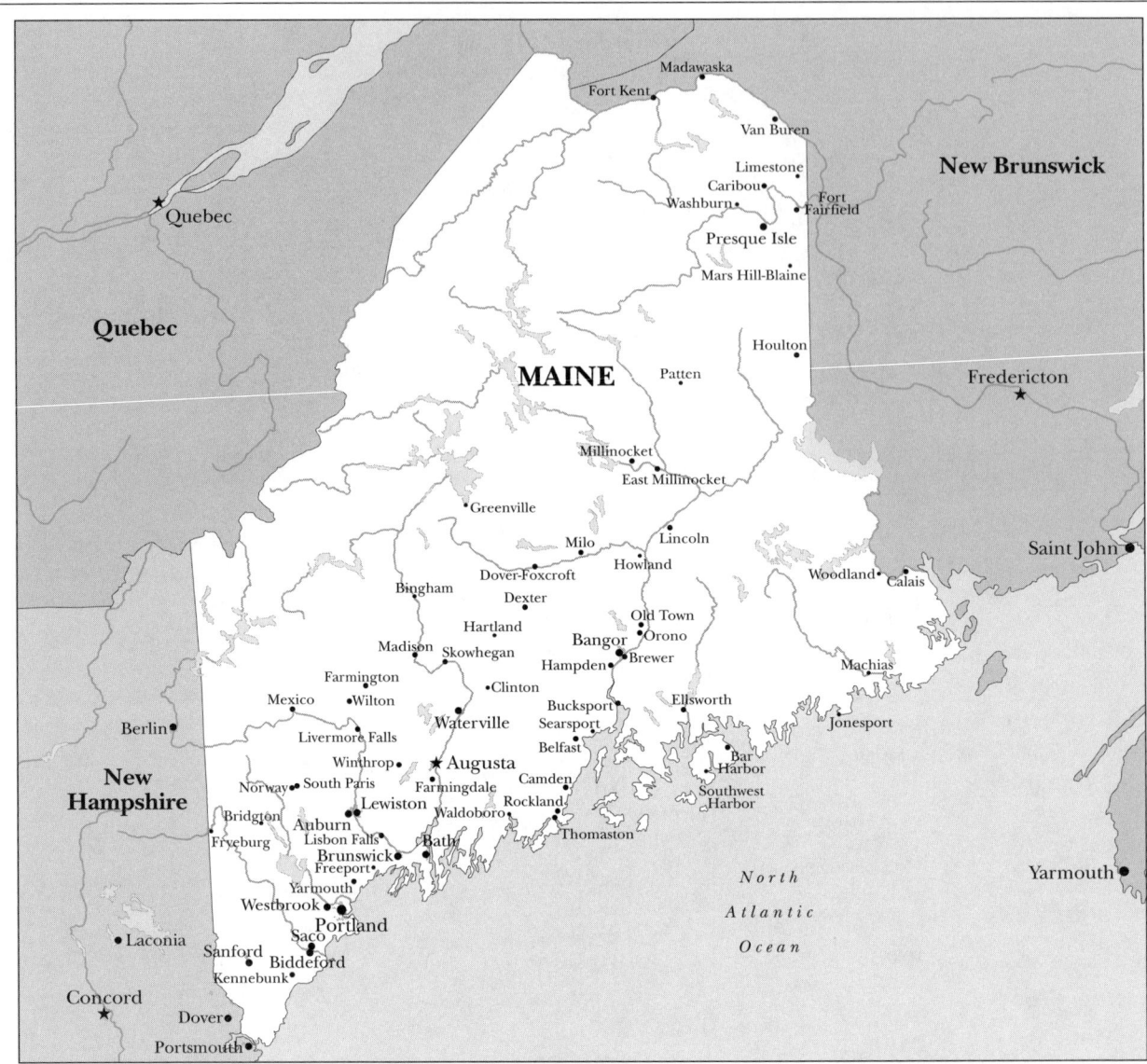

Cities

With 10,000 or more residents

Rank	City	Population	Rank	City	Population
1	Portland	64,249	13	Waterville	15,605
2	Lewiston	35,690	14	Windham	14,904
3	Bangor	31,473	15	Brunswick	14,816
4	South Portland	23,324	16	Gorham	14,141
5	Auburn	23,203	17	York	12,854
6	Brunswick	21,172	18	Kennebunk	10,476
7	Biddeford	20,942	19	Falmouth	10,310
8	Sanford	20,806	20	Sanford	10,133
9	Augusta (capital)	18,560			
10	Scarborough	16,970	Population figures are from 2000 census.		
11	Saco	16,822	*Source:* U.S. Bureau of the Census.		
12	Westbrook	16,142			

Index to Tables

DEMOGRAPHICS

Resident state and national populations, 1970-2004

Population figures given in thousands

	State pop.	U.S. pop.	Share	Rank
1970	994	203,302	0.5%	38
1980	1,125	226,546	0.5%	38
1985	1,163	237,924	0.5%	38
1990	1,228	248,765	0.5%	38
1995	1,243	262,761	0.5%	39
2000	1,275	281,425	0.5%	40
2004	1,317	293,655	0.5%	40

Source: U.S. Census Bureau, Current Population Reports, 2006.

Resident population by age, 2004

Age Group	Total persons
Under 5 years	68,000
5 to 17 years	215,000
18 to 24 years	124,000
25 to 34 years	146,000
35 to 44 years	205,000
45 to 54 years	216,000
55 to 64 years	155,000
65 to 74 years	95,000
75 to 84 years	69,000
85 years and older	25,000
All age groups	1,317,000

Portion of residents 65 and older	14.4%
National rank in portion of oldest residents	6
National average	12.4%

Population figures are rounded to nearest thousand persons;
figures include armed forces personnel stationed in the state.
Source: U.S. Bureau of the Census, 2006.

Resident population by race, Hispanic origin, 2004

Category	State pop.	Share	U.S.
All residents	1,317	100.00%	100.00%
Non-Hispanic white	1,266	96.13%	67.37%
Hispanic white	11	0.84%	13.01%
Other Hispanic	1	0.08%	1.06%
African American	10	0.76%	12.77%
Native American	7	0.53%	0.96%
Asian, Pacific Islander	11	0.84%	4.37%
Two or more categories	12	0.91%	1.51%

Population figures are in thousands. Persons counted as "Hispanic" (Latino) may be of any race. Because of overlapping categories, categories may not add up to 100%. Shares in column 3 are percentages of each category within the state; these figures may be compared to the national percentages in column 4.
Source: U.S. Bureau of the Census, 2006.

Projected state population, 2000-2030

Year	Population
2000	1,275,000
2005	1,319,000
2010	1,357,000
2015	1,389,000
2020	1,409,000
2025	1,414,000
2030	1,411,000
Population increase, 2000-2030	136,000
Percentage increase, 2000-2030	10.7

Projections are based on data from the 2000 census.
Source: U.S. Census Bureau.

VITAL STATISTICS

Infant mortality rates, 1980-2002

	1980	1990	2000	2002
All state residents	9.2	6.2	4.9	4.4
All U.S. residents	12.6	9.2	9.4	9.1
All state white residents	9.4	6.7	4.8	4.3
All U.S. white residents	10.6	7.6	5.7	5.8

Figures represent deaths per 1,000 live births of resident infants under 1 year old, exclusive of fetal deaths. Figures for all residents include members of other racial categories not listed separately. The Census Bureau considers the figures for black residents to be too small to be statistically meaningful.
Source: U.S. Census Bureau, *Statistical Abstract of the United States,* 2006.

Abortion rates, 1990 and 2000

	1990	2000
Total abortions	4,000	3,000
Rate per 1,000 women	14.9	9.9
U.S. rate	25.7	21.3
Rank	33	36

Numbers of abortions are rounded to nearest thousand; ranks are based on rates.
Source: U.S. Census Bureau.

Marriages and divorces, 2004

Total marriages	10,900
Rate per 1,000 population	8.3
National rate per 1,000 population	7.4
Rank among all states	13
Total divorces	4,700
Rate per 1,000 population	3.6
National rate per 1,000 population	3.7
Rank among all states	26

Figures are for all marriages and divorces performed within the state, including those of nonresidents; totals are rounded to the nearest hundred. Ranks are for highest to lowest figures; note that divorce data are not available for five states.
Source: U.S. National Center for Health Statistics, *Vital Statistics of the United States,* 2006.

Death rates by leading causes, 2002
Deaths per 100,000 resident population

Cause	State	U.S.
Heart disease	244.9	241.7
Cancer	247.7	193.2
Cerebrovascular diseases	63.6	56.4
Accidents other than motor vehicle	39.5	37.0
Motor vehicle accidents	16.6	15.7
Chronic lower respiratory diseases	61.1	43.3
Diabetes mellitus	31.2	25.4
HIV	n/a	4.9
Suicide	12.8	11.0
Homicide	n/a	6.1
All causes	980.6	847.3
Rank in overall death rate among states		10

Figures exclude nonresidents who died in the state. Causes of death follow International Classification of Diseases. Rank is from highest to lowest death rate in the United States.
Source: U.S. National Center for Health Statistics, *National Vital Statistics Report,* 2006.

ECONOMY

Gross state product, 1990-2004
In current dollars

Year	State product	Nat'l product	State share
1990	$23.3 billion	$5.67 trillion	0.41%
2000	$35.7 billion	$9.75 trillion	0.37%
2002	$39.0 billion	$10.41 trillion	0.37%
2003	$40.8 billion	$10.92 trillion	0.37%
2004	$43.3 billion	$11.65 trillion	0.37%

Source: U.S. Bureau of Economic Analysis, *Survey of Current Business,* July, 2005.

Gross state product by industry, 2003
In billions of dollars

Construction	$1.6
Manufacturing	4.9
Wholesale trade	2.1
Retail trade	4.0
Finance & insurance	2.6
Information	1.2
Professional services	1.7
Health care & social assistance	3.7
Government	5.2
Total state product	$38.1
Total U.S. product	$10,289.2
State share of U.S. total	0.37%
Rank among all states	43

Total figures include industries not listed separately. Amounts are in chained 2000 dollars.
Source: U.S. Bureau of Economic Analysis, *Survey of Current Business,* July, 2005.

Personal income per capita, 1990-2004
In current dollars

	1990	2000	2004
Per capita income	$17,376	$25,969	$30,566
U.S. average	$19,477	$29,845	$32,937
Rank among states	33	35	30

Source: U.S. Bureau of Economic Analysis, *Survey of Current Business,* April, 2005.

Energy consumption, 2001
In trillions of British thermal units (BTU), except as noted

Total energy consumption
Total state energy consumption	491
Total U.S. energy consumption	96,275
State share of U.S. total	0.51%
Rank among states	41

Per capita consumption (In millions of BTU)
Total state per capita consumption	382
Total U.S. per capita consumption	338
Rank among states	16

End-use sectors
Residential	111
Commercial	74
Industrial	199
Transportation	107

Sources of energy
Petroleum	233
Natural gas	101
Coal	8
Hydroelectric power	27
Nuclear electric power	0

Figures for totals include categories not listed separately.
Source: U.S. Energy Information Administration, *State Energy Data Report,* 2001.

Nonfarm employment by sectors, 2004

Total	614,000
Construction	31,000
Manufacturing	63,000
Trade, transportation, utilities	126,000
Information	12,000
Finance, insurance, real estate	35,000
Professional & business services	50,000
Education & health services	111,000
Leisure, hospitality, arts, organizations	59,000
Other services, including repair & maintenance	20,000
Government	105,000

Figures are rounded to nearest thousand persons. "Total" includes mining and natural resources, not listed separately.
Source: U.S. Bureau of Labor Statistics, 2006.

Foreign exports, 1990-2004
In millions of dollars

Year	State	U.S.	State share
1990	870	394,045	0.22%
1996	1,380	624,767	0.22%
1997	1,723	688,896	0.25%
2000	1,779	712,055	0.23%
2003	2,188	724,006	0.32%
2004	2,432	769,332	0.32%

Rank among all states in 2004 40

U.S. total does not include U.S. dependencies.
Source: U.S. Census Bureau, *U.S. Merchandise Trade,* series FT 900, 2000; U.S. Census Bureau, *U.S. International Trade in Goods and Services,* Series FT 900, 2005.

LAND USE

Federally owned land, 2003
Areas in acres

	State	U.S.	State share
Total area	19,848,000	2,271,343,000	0.87%
Nonfederal land	19,684,000	1,599,584,000	1.23%
Federal land	164,000	671,759,000	0.02%
Federal share	0.8%	29.6%	—

Areas are rounded to nearest thousand acres. Figures for federally owned land do not include trust properties.
Source: U.S. General Services Administration, *Federal Real Property Profile,* 2006.

Land use, 1997
In acres, rounded to nearest thousand

Total surface area	20,966,000
Total nonfederal rural land.	18,794,000
Percentage rural land	89.6%
Cropland	413,000
Conservation Reserve Program (CRP*) land	30,000
Pastureland	123,000
Rangeland	(nil)
Forestland	17,691,000
Other rural land	537,000

*CRP is a federal program begun in 1985 to assist private landowners to convert highly erodible cropland to vegetative cover for ten years. Note that some categories of land overlap.
Source: U.S. Department of Agriculture, Natural Resources and Conservation Service, and Iowa State University, Statistical Laboratory, *Summary Report, 1997 National Resources Inventory,* revised December, 2000.

Farms and crop acreage, 2004

	State	U.S.	Share	Rank
Farms	7,000	2,113,000	0.33%	41
Acres (millions)	1	937	0.11%	41
Acres per farm	190	443	—	36

Source: U.S. Department of Agriculture, National Agricultural Statistics Service. Numbers of farms are rounded to nearest thousand units; acreage figures are rounded to nearest million. Rankings, including ties, are based on rounded figures.

GOVERNMENT AND FINANCE

Units of local government, 2002

	State	Total U.S.	Rank
All local governments	826	87,525	34
Counties	16	3,034	40
Municipalities	22	19,429	46
Towns (townships)	467	16,504	12
School districts	99	13,506	32
Special districts	222	35,052	41

Only 48 states have county governments, 20 states have township governments ("towns" in New England, Minnesota, New York, and Wisconsin), and 46 states have school districts. Special districts encompass such functions as natural resources, fire protection, and housing and community development.
Source: U.S. Census Bureau, *Census of Governments.*

State government revenue, 2002

Total revenue	$5,451 mill.
General revenue	$5,600 mill.
Per capita revenue	$4,315
U.S. per capita average	$3,689
Rank among states	13
Intergovernment revenue	
Total	$1,830 mill.
From federal government	$1,817 mill.
Charges and miscellaneous	
Total	$1,143 mill.
Current charges	$438 mill.
Misc. general income	$706 mill.
Insurance trust revenue	−$231 mill.
Taxes	
Total	$2,627 mill.
Per capita taxes	$2,028
Rank among states	14
Property taxes	$48 mill.
Sales taxes	$1,237 mill.
License taxes	$149 mill.
Individual income taxes	$1,073 mill.
Corporate income taxes.	$77 mill.
Other taxes	$43 mill.

Total revenue figures include items not listed separately here.
Source: U.S. Bureau of the Census.

State government expenditures, 2002

General expenditures

Total state expenditures . . . . $6,265 mill.
Intergovernmental . . . . $1,010 mill.

Per capita expenditures

State $4,378
Average of all states $3,859
Rank among states 14

Selected direct expenditures

Education. $699 mill.
Public welfare . . . . $1,762 mill.
Health, hospital . . . . $413 mill.
Highways . . . . $439 mill.
Police protection . . . . $59 mill.
Corrections. . . . . $106 mill.
Natural resources . . . . $146 mill.
Parks and recreation . . . . $11 mill.
Government administration. . . . . $253 mill.
Interest on debt . . . . $238 mill.
Total direct expenditures . . . . $4,661 mill.

Totals include items not listed separately.
Source: U.S. Census Bureau.

POLITICS

Governors since statehood

D = Democrat; R = Republican; O = other;
(r) resigned; (d) died in office; (i) removed from office

William King (O) . . . . (r) 1820-1821
William D. Williamson (O) . . . . (r) 1821
Benjamin Ames (O) 1821-1822
Albion K. Parris (O) 1822-1827
Enoch Lincoln (O) . . . . (d) 1827-1829
Nathan Cutler (O) 1829-1830
Joshua Hall (O) 1830
Jonathan G. Hunton (O) 1830-1831
Samuel E. Smith (O) 1831-1834
Robert P. Dunlap (D) 1834-1838
Edward Kent (O) 1838-1839
John Fairfield (D) 1839-1841
Edward Kent (O) 1841-1842
John Fairfield (D) . . . . (r) 1842-1843
Edward Kavanagh (D) 1843-1844
Hugh J. Anderson (D) 1844-1847
John W. Dana (D) 1847-1850
John Hubbard (D) 1850-1853
William G. Crosby (O) 1853-1855
Anson P. Morrill (R) 1855-1856
Samuel Wells (D) 1856-1857
Hannibal Hamlin (R) 1857
Joseph H. Williams (R) 1857-1858
Lot M. Morrill (R) 1858-1861
Israel Washburn, Jr. (R) 1861-1863
Abner Coburn (R) 1863-1864
Samuel Cony (R) 1864-1867

Joshua L. Chamberlain (R) 1867-1871
Sidney Perham (R) 1871-1874
Nelson Dingley, Jr. (R) 1874-1876
Sheldon Connor (R) 1876-1879
Alonzo Garcelon (D) 1879-1880
Daniel F. Davis (R) 1880-1881
Harris M. Plaisted (O) 1881-1883
Frederick Robie (R) 1883-1887
Joseph R. Bodwell (R) . . . . (d) 1887
Sebastian S. Marble (R) 1887-1889
Edwin C. Burleigh (R) 1889-1893
Henry B. Cleaves (R) 1893-1897
Llewellyn Powers (R) 1897-1901
John F. Hill (R) 1901-1905
William T. Cobb (R) 1905-1909
Bert M. Fernald (R) 1909-1911
Frederick W. Plaisted (D) 1911-1913
William T. Haines (R) 1913-1915
Oakley C. Curtis (D) 1915-1917
Carl E. Milliken (R) 1917-1921
Frederic H. Parkhurst (R) . . . . (d) 1921
Percival P. Baxter (R) 1921-1925
Ralph O. Brewster (R) 1925-1929
William T. Gardiner (R) 1929-1933
Louis J. Brann (R) 1933-1937
Lewis O. Barrows (D) 1937-1941
Sumner Sewall (R) 1941-1945
Horace A. Hildreth (R) 1945-1949
Frederick G. Payne (R) . . . . (r) 1949-1952
Burton M. Cross (R) 1952-1955
Edmund S. Muskie (D) . . . . (r) 1955-1959
Robert N. Haskell (R) 1959
Clinton A. Clauson (D) . . . . (d) 1959
John H. Reed (R) 1959-1967
Kenneth M. Curtis (D) 1967-1975
James B. Longley (O) 1975-1979
Joseph E. Brennan (D) 1979-1987
John R. McKernan, Jr. (R) 1987-1995
Angus S. King, Jr. (O) 1995-2003
John Baldacci (D) 2003-

Composition of congressional delegations, 1989-2007

	Dem	Rep	Total
House of Representatives			
101st Congress, 1989			
State delegates	1	1	2
Total U.S.	259	174	433
102d Congress, 1991			
State delegates	1	1	2
Total U.S.	267	167	434
103d Congress, 1993			
State delegates	1	1	2
Total U.S.	258	176	434
104th Congress, 1995			
State delegates	2	0	2
Total U.S.	197	236	433
105th Congress, 1997			
State delegates	2	0	2
Total U.S.	206	228	434
106th Congress, 1999			
State delegates	2	0	2
Total U.S.	211	222	433
107th Congress, 2001			
State delegates	2	0	2
Total U.S.	211	221	432
108th Congress, 2003			
State delegates	2	0	2
Total U.S.	205	229	434
109th Congress, 2005			
State delegates	2	0	2
Total U.S.	202	231	433
110th Congress, 2007			
State delegates	2	0	2
Total U.S.	233	202	435
Senate			
101st Congress, 1989			
State delegates	1	1	2
Total U.S.	55	45	100
102d Congress, 1991			
State delegates	1	1	2
Total U.S.	56	44	100
103d Congress, 1993			
State delegates	1	1	2
Total U.S.	57	43	100
104th Congress, 1995			
State delegates	0	2	2
Total U.S.	46	53	99
105th Congress, 1997			
State delegates	0	2	2
Total U.S.	45	55	100

	Dem	Rep	Total
106th Congress, 1999			
State delegates	0	2	2
Total U.S.	45	54	99
107th Congress, 2001			
State delegates	0	2	2
Total U.S.	50	50	100
108th Congress, 2003			
State delegates	0	2	2
Total U.S.	48	51	99
109th Congress, 2005			
State delegates	0	2	2
Total U.S.	44	55	99
110th Congress, 2007			
State delegates	0	2	2
Total U.S.	49	49	98

Figures are for starts of first sessions. Totals are for Democrat (Dem.) and Republican (Rep.) members only. House membership totals under 435 and Senate totals under 100 reflect vacancies and seats held by independent party members. When the 110th Congress opened, the Senate's two independent members caucused with the Democrats, giving the Democrats control of the Senate.

Source: U.S. Congress, Congressional Directory.

Composition of state legislature, 1990-2006

	Democrats	Republicans
State House (151 seats)		
1990	97	54
1992	93	58
1994	77	74
1996	81	69
1998	79	71
2000	79	71
2002	80	67
2004	76	73
2006	89	60
State Senate (35 seats)		
1990	21	14
1992	20	15
1994	16	18
1996	19	15
1998	20	14
2000	20	14
2002	18	17
2004	19	16
2006	18	17

Figures for total seats may include independents and minor party members. Numbers reflect results of elections in listed years; elected members usually take their seats in the years that follow.

Source: Council of State Governments; State Elective Officials and the Legislatures.

Voter participation in presidential elections, 2000 and 2004

	2000	2004
Voting age population		
State	978,000	1,035,000
Total United States	209,831,000	220,377,000
State share of U.S. total	0.47	0.47
Rank among states	39	39
Portion of voting age population casting votes		
State	66.7%	71.6%
United States	50.3%	55.5%
Rank among states	2	2

Population figures are rounded to nearest thousand and include all residents, regardless of eligibility to vote.
Source: U.S. Census Bureau.

HEALTH AND MEDICAL CARE

Medical professionals
Physicians in 2003 and nurses in 2001

	U.S.	State
Physicians in 2003		
Total	774,849	3,485
Share of U.S. total		0.45%
Rate	266	267
Rank		13
Nurses in 2001		
Total	2,262,020	13,390
Share of U.S. total		0.59%
Rate	793	1,043
Rank		5

Rates are numbers of physicians and nurses per 100,000 resident population; ranks are based on rates.
Source: American Medical Association, *Physician Characteristics and Distribution in the U.S.*; U.S. Department of Health and Human Services, Health Resources and Services Administration.

Health insurance coverage, 2003

	State	U.S.
Total persons covered	1,150,000	243,320,000
Total persons not covered	133,000	44,961,000
Portion not covered	10.4%	15.6%
Rank among states	44	—
Children not covered	17,000	8,373,000
Portion not covered	6.0%	11.4%
Rank among states	46	—

Totals are rounded to nearest thousand. Ranks are from the highest to the lowest percentages of persons *not* insured.
Source: U.S. Census Bureau, Current Population Reports.

AIDS, syphilis, and tuberculosis cases, 2003

Disease	U.S. cases	State cases	Rank
AIDS	44,232	52	42
Syphilis	34,270	21	43
Tuberculosis	14,874	25	42

Source: U.S. Centers for Disease Control and Prevention.

Cigarette smoking, 2003
Residents over age 18 who smoke

	U.S.	State	Rank
All smokers	22.1%	23.6%	21
Male smokers	24.8%	23.1%	32
Female smokers	20.3%	24.0%	7

Cigarette smokers are defined as persons who reported having smoked at least 100 cigarettes during their lifetimes and who currently smoked at least occasionally.
Source: U.S. Centers for Disease Control and Prevention, *Morbidity and Mortality Weekly Report*, 53, no. 44 (November 12, 2004).

HOUSING

Home ownership rates, 1985-2004

	1985	1990	1995	2000	2004
State	73.7%	74.2%	76.7%	76.5%	74.7%
Total U.S.	63.9%	63.9%	64.7%	67.4%	69.0%
Rank among states	2	1	1	2	10

Net change in state home ownership rate,
1985-2004 . . . . +1.0%
Net change in U.S. home ownership rate,
1985-2004 . . . . +5.1%

Percentages represent the proportion of owner households to total occupied households.
Source: U.S. Census Bureau, 2006.

Home sales, 2000-2004
In thousands of units

Existing home sales	2000	2002	2003	2004
State sales	27.6	28.8	30.7	33.6
Total U.S. sales	5,171	5,631	6,183	6,784
State share of U.S. total	0.53%	0.51%	0.50%	0.50%
Sales rank among states	38	38	39	40

Units include single-family homes, condos, and co-ops.
Source: National Association of Realtors, Washington, D.C., *Real Estate Outlook: Market Trends & Insights.*

Values of owner-occupied homes, 2003

	State	U.S.
Total units	267,000	58,809,000
Value of units		
Under $100,000	31.6%	29.6%
$100,000-199,999	43.0%	36.9%
$200,000 or more	25.4%	33.5%
Median value	$134,846	$142,275
Rank among all states 25		

Units are owner-occupied one-family houses whose numbers are
  rounded to nearest thousand. Data are extrapolated from
  survey samples.
Source: U.S. Census Bureau, American Community Survey.

EDUCATION

Public school enrollment, 2002

Prekindergarten through grade 8
State enrollment 142,000
Total U.S. enrollment. 34,135,000
State share of U.S. total 0.42%

Grades 9 through 12
State enrollment 63,000
Total U.S. enrollment. 14,067,000
State share of U.S. total 0.45%

Enrollment rates
State public school enrollment rate 91.6%
Overall U.S. rate 90.4%
Rank among states in 2002 15
Rank among states in 1995 17

Enrollment figures (which include unclassified students) are
  rounded to nearest thousand pupils during fall school term.
  Enrollment rates are based on enumerated resident population
  estimate for July 1, 2002.
Source: U.S. National Center for Education Statistics.

Public college finances, 2003-2004

FTE enrollment in public institutions of higher education
Students in state institutions 34,500
Students in all U.S. public institutions 9,916,600
State share of U.S. total 0.35
Rank among states 44

**State and local government appropriations for higher
  education**
State appropriation per FTE $5,900
National average $5,716
Rank among states 20
State & local tax revenue going to higher
  education 5.2%

FTE = full-time equivalent in public postsecondary programs,
  including summer sessions; student numbers are rounded to
  nearest hundred. Funding figures for 2003-2004 academic year
  include financial aid to students in state public institutions and
  exclude money for research, agriculture experiment stations,
  teaching hospitals, and medical schools; figures are rounded to
  nearest thousand dollars.
Source: Higher Education Executive Officers, Denver, Colorado.

TRANSPORTATION AND TRAVEL

Highway mileage, 2003

Interstate highways 367
Other freeways and expressways 18
Arterial roads 2,288
Collector roads 5,975
Local roads 14,045
Urban roads 2,633
Rural roads 20,060
Total state mileage 22,693
U.S. total 3,974,107
State share 0.57%
Rank among states 43

Note that combined urban and rural road mileage matches the
  total of the other categories.
Source: U.S. Federal Highway Administration.

Motor vehicle registrations and driver licenses, 2003

Vehicle registrations	State	U.S.	Share	Rank
Autos, trucks, buses	1,052,000	231,390,000	0.45%	41
Autos only	619,000	135,670	0.46%	40
Motorcycles	35,000	5,328,000	0.66%	38
Driver licenses	932,000	196,166,000	0.48%	40

Figures, which do not include vehicles owned by military services,
  are rounded to the nearest thousand. Figures for automobiles
  include taxis.
Source: U.S. Federal Highway Administration.

Domestic travel expenditures, 2003

Spending by U.S. residents on overnight trips and
day trips of at least 50 miles from home

Total expenditures within state . . . . $1.99 bill.
Total expenditures within U.S. . . . . $490.87 bill.
State share of U.S. total 0.4%
Rank among states 42

Source: Travel Industry Association of America.

Retail gasoline prices, 2003-2007

Average price per gallon at the pump

Year	U.S.	State
2003	$1.267	$1.268
2004	$1.316	$1.344
2005	$1.644	$1.656
2007	$2.298	$2.327

Excise tax per gallon in 2004 . . . . 25.2¢
Rank among all states in 2007 prices 18

Prices are averages of all grades of gasoline sold at the pump
during March months in 2003-2005 and during February, 2007.
Averages for 2006, during which prices rose higher, are not
available.
Source: U.S. Energy Information Agency, *Petroleum Marketing
Monthly* (2003-2005 data); American Automobile Association
(2007 data).

CRIME AND LAW ENFORCEMENT

State and local police officers, 2000-2004

	2000	2002	2004
Total officers			
U.S.	654,601	665,555	675,734
State	2,172	2,195	2,194*
*Net change, 2000-2004			+1.01%
Officers per 1,000 residents			
U.S.	2.33	2.31	2.30
State	1.70	1.70	1.67
State rank	41	43	46

Totals include state and local police and sheriffs.
Source: Carsey Institute, University of New Hampshire.

Crime rates, 2003

Incidents per 100,000 residents

Crimes	State	U.S.
Violent crimes		
Total incidents	109	475
Murder	1	6
Forcible rape	27	32
Robbery	22	142
Aggravated assault	58	295
Property crimes		
Total incidents	2,457	3,588
Burglary	504	741
Larceny/theft	1,841	2,415
Motor vehicle theft	112	433
All crimes	2,566	4,063

Source: U.S. Federal Bureau of Investigation, *Crime in the United
States,* annual.

State prison populations, 1980-2003

	State	U.S.	State share
1980	814	305,458	0.27%
1990	1,523	708,393	0.21%
1996	1,426	1,025,624	0.14%
2000	1,679	1,391,261	0.12%
2003	2,013	1,470,045	0.14%

State figures exclude prisoners in federal penitentiaries.
Source: U.S. Bureau of Justice Statistics, *Prisoners in 2003.*

Maryland

Location: Atlantic coast

Area and rank: 9,775 square miles (25,316 square kilometers); 12,407 square miles (32,134 square kilometers) including water; forty-second largest state in area

Coastline: 31 miles (50 kilometers) on the Atlantic Ocean

Shoreline: 3,190 miles (5,134 kilometers)

Population and rank: 5,558,000 (2004); nineteenth largest state in population

Capital city: Annapolis (35,838 people in 2000 census)

Largest city: Baltimore (651,154 people in 2000 census)

Entered Union and rank: April 28, 1788; seventh state

State capitol building in Annapolis. (©Ken Cole/Dreamstime.com)

Present constitution adopted: 1867

Counties: 23, as well as 1 independent city

State name: Maryland was named to honor of Henrietta Maria, the queen of Charles I of England

State nicknames: Free State; Old Line State

Motto: *Fatti maschii, parole femine* (Manly deeds, womanly words; or, Strong deeds, gentle words)

State flag: Two quarters bear the arms of the Calvert family in gold and black; two quarters show the arms of the Crossland family in red and white

Highest point: Backbone Mountain—3,360 feet (1,024 meters)

Lowest point: Atlantic Ocean—sea level

Highest recorded temperature: 109 degrees Fahrenheit (43 degrees Celsius)—Cumberland and Frederick, 1936

Lowest recorded temperature: –40 degrees Fahrenheit (–40 degrees Celsius)—Oakland, 1912

State song: "Maryland! My Maryland!"

State tree: White oak

State flower: Black-eyed susan

State bird: Baltimore oriole

State fish: Rockfish

Maryland History

In many ways, Maryland is a microcosm of much of the United States, combining elements from the north, south, east, and west. Physically located in the middle of the English colonies, it was the center state of the new nation and thus the logical site for a capital, which is located in the District of Columbia. After the Revolution, Maryland led efforts to develop the nation westward; it remained in the Union during the Civil War but sent soldiers to both the North and the South during that conflict. After World War II, the state managed to preserve its historic traditions and environmental legacy while advancing into the future.

Early History and Settlement. It is uncertain when Native Americans first entered the area now known as Maryland, but tribes of the Iroquoian and Algonquian peoples were certainly present several hundred years prior to European arrival. The major Iroquoian tribe was the Susquehannock, sometimes known as Conestoga, who came south from the Pennsylvania area. The Algonquians included the Choptank, Portobago, and Wicomico, names which still survive on the map of Maryland. The major Algonquian tribes were the Piscataway on the western shore (the mainland) of the Chesapeake Bay, and the Nanticoke on the eastern shore (the peninsula between the Chesapeake Bay and the Atlantic coast). Both Iroquoian and Algonquian Indians lived and farmed in permanent settlements.

The Algonquian tribes welcomed the English settlers, but the Susquehannock proved hostile, although their attacks were aimed as much against Native American allies of the English as against the English themselves. In any event, the colonists successfully defended themselves and in 1652 concluded a peace with the Susquehannock, which included the American Indians' departure from Maryland. Between the 1690's and the mid-eighteenth century, first the Piscataway and then the other Native Americans also moved away from the area.

The Spanish were the first Europeans to explore the area, but the English were the first permanent settlers.

Antietam, the site of the single bloodiest battle fought during the Civil War. (PhotoDisc)

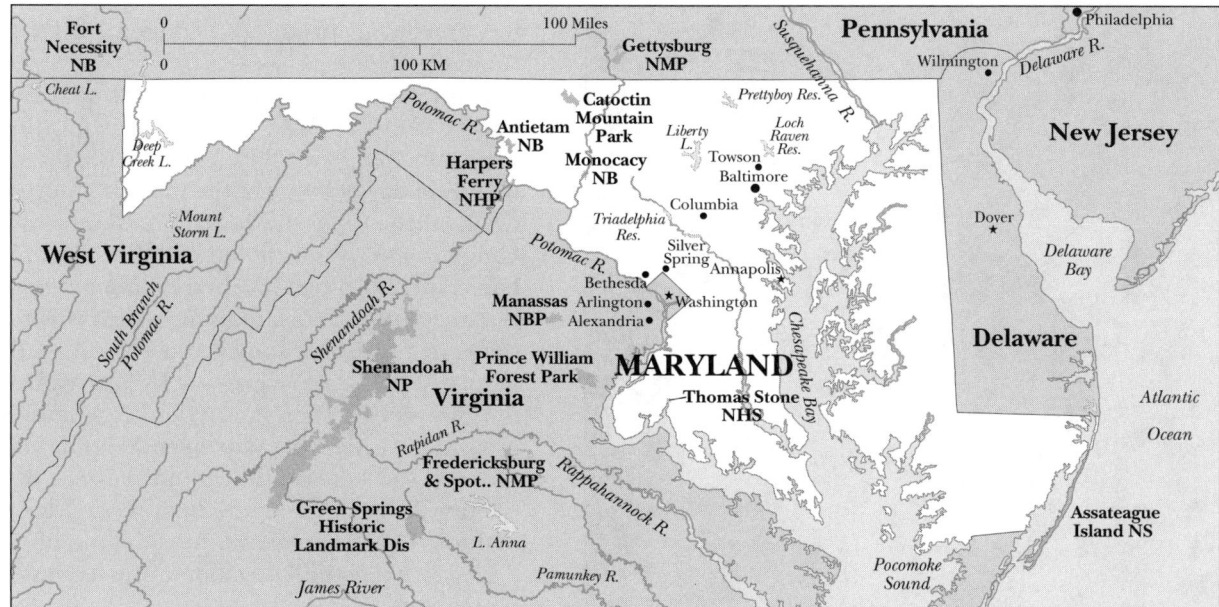

English colonists from Virginia under councilman William Claiborne established a trading post on Kent Island in Chesapeake Bay in 1631. The following year, King Charles I granted Baron Baltimore land north of the Potomac River, which included Maryland. It was on this land that Baltimore established a colony in 1634. Led by Leonard Calvert, half brother of Cecil, the colonists included many Roman Catholics, among them two priests. At this time Roman Catholics were forbidden by British law from voting or holding office. In part, Maryland was founded with the tacit understanding that it would be a refuge for English Catholics. In fact, the name of the colony, while officially honoring Queen Henrietta Maria of England, was often interpreted as referring to the Virgin Mary. In 1649, the colony adopted an "Act Concerning Religion," the first act of religious toleration in the colonies. Soon afterward, a group of Puritans arrived from Virginia.

In the meantime, Maryland settlers under Leonard Calvert disputed Virginia's claims to Kent Island. In 1654, Virginian Claiborne led the Puritans in a revolt that exiled Calvert, an action recognized by the English Commonwealth that had overthrown and executed Charles I. However, in 1658 Calvert and proprietary government were restored to Maryland. In 1692, Maryland became a royal colony, and the Church of England was declared the established, or official, church. In 1718, Roman Catholics were denied the right to vote.

By far the most important influence on Maryland's history has been the Chesapeake Bay, the largest inlet on the East Coast. The bay is nearly two hundred miles long from north to south and as wide as twenty-five miles and is important for commercial fishing, oystering, and crabbing. At the head of the bay is Baltimore, one of the major American ports since its founding in 1729 and Maryland's largest city.

Revolution and Growth. Marylanders joined with other colonists in their distaste for the high taxes imposed by Britain, and in 1774 a group of patriots boarded the *Peggy Stewart* in Annapolis Harbor and destroyed more than two thousand pounds of its cargo of tea. During the American Revolution, when the British threatened the capital of Philadelphia, the Continental Congress moved to Baltimore, then to Annapolis. Maryland troops were among the best in the Continental Army, and their straight ranks and orderly battle lines earned Maryland the nickname "The Old Line State" from General George Washington. After ratifying the Constitution of the newly independent United States, Maryland officially entered the Union in 1788.

In 1791, Maryland and Virginia ceded land to the United States to create the District of Columbia as the site of the new national capital. Construction of the White House began in 1793 and of the Capitol in 1794. In 1800, Congress moved to the new capital city from Philadelphia. During the War of 1812, British forces seized Washington and burned the White House but were unable to force their way past Fort McHenry to capture Baltimore. It was while watching this bombardment from Baltimore harbor that Francis Scott Key composed the poem "The Star Spangled Banner," which later became the national anthem of the United States.

In its key central position, Maryland took a leading role in the growth of the new nation, especially in its westward advancement. The Cumberland Road, also known as the National Pike, was a prime avenue for set-

Cadets lining up at the U.S. Naval Academy, which opened at Maryland's state capital, Annapolis, in 1845. (Middleton Evans/ Courtesy Maryland Office of Tourism)

was erected to protect Washington, D.C., from Confederate attack.

A number of battles were fought in Maryland during the Civil War, the largest being that of Antietam, fought in 1862. Antietam was the single bloodiest day of battle of the war, with more than twenty-three thousand casualties. It was a narrow Union victory, but enough for President Abraham Lincoln to feel justified in announcing the Emancipation Proclamation, which freed the slaves in the Confederacy and transformed the nature of the war to a crusade for liberty. During the summer of 1863, Confederate general Robert E. Lee's Army of Northern Virginia passed through the state on its way to the Battle of Gettysburg. In 1864, Confederate forces under General Jubal Early threatened Washington but were driven back at the last moment by federal reinforcements.

Post-Civil War Progress. Agriculture had been dominant in Maryland prior to the Civil War, with the major crop of tobacco being shipped through the port of Baltimore. However, after the war the state's economy shifted toward manufacturing. Baltimore remained a key shipbuilding and weaponry production center; in the twentieth century the city would make rockets and missiles for the U.S. military. Both shipbuilding and weapons manufacture were spurred by government purchases during the two world wars.

Education in the state received an infusion of resources during the second half of the nineteenth century, especially with donations from philanthropists such as Johns Hopkins, who provided the financial backing to create the prestigious university that bears his name. Later, during the 1960's, federal funds were allocated for the National Institutes of Health at Bethesda and the Goddard Space Flight Center.

Toward the Future. As the twentieth century advanced, Maryland's agriculture remained important, with the chief crops being tobacco, corn, hay, and soybeans. Manufacturing continued to expand, primarily in shipbuilding, transportation equipment, and modern technology such as electronics. Fishing in the renewed Chesapeake Bay provided much of the seafood sold nationally. However, it was commerce which led Maryland's revitalization, especially in its largest city.

Throughout most of Maryland's history, trade and commerce focused on Baltimore, which underwent a striking revival starting during the 1950's. Under Kurt Schmoke, the first African American elected mayor of the city, Baltimore completed an ambitious reconstruction of its inner harbor, with its centerpiece being the USS *Constellation*, the first warship commissioned by the

tlers heading into the interior of the continent; by 1818 it reached the Ohio River. Maryland was also active in the construction of canals, essential for transport of cargo during that period. Two vital waterways, the Chesapeake and Delaware and the Chesapeake and Ohio, connected the bay to those two rivers. The state also took the forefront in exploiting the new technology of the steam railroad, with the Baltimore and Ohio (B&O) starting operations in 1830 as the first American railroad to carry both passengers and freight.

Civil War. Slavery was legal in Maryland, and when the Civil War came there was considerable sentiment in the state for it to join others in the South in seceding from the Union. However, in 1861 the Maryland legislature rejected a bill of secession; still, many of the state's residents left to fight with the Confederate army, and many others were sympathizers. During the first months of the war mobs attacked Union troops as they marched through Baltimore. However, these disturbances were suppressed, and soon a ring of Union forts

U.S. Navy, in 1797. In 1992, the Baltimore Orioles opened their new stadium, Camden Yards, widely hailed as one of the best designed and most attractive of modern baseball parks.

Perhaps Maryland's most visible success is its reclaiming of Chesapeake Bay and its adoption of a policy of smart growth to combat urban sprawl. After decades of environmental neglect, including drainage of agriculture chemicals, unregulated dumping of waste, and overfishing, the bay was seriously endangered. Governor Marvin Mandel established a Chesapeake Bay Interagency Planning Committee, and a widespread Save the Bay organization was created—two parts of a comprehensive effort that linked grassroots activists, government, and the private sector in addressing the problem. Spurred by the growing success of this effort, an association of environmental and citizen groups known as the Thousand Friends of Maryland began to campaign for strategic planning and "smart growth" to control urban sprawl, save Maryland's traditional farmlands, and preserve its small towns and their unique character. Supported by Governor Parris Glendening, who made smart growth an issue in his reelection campaign, the Maryland smart growth program became a national trendsetter for the twenty-first century.

Politics and Politicians. In the 2000 election, Maryland, which leans to the Democratic Party, gave its electoral votes to Vice President Al Gore. Senator Paul Sarbanes, a popular Democrat, had little trouble being reelected, garnering 63 percent of the vote to his opponent's 37 percent. In a contested Maryland race, Republican representative Constance Morella defeated a former lobbyist who had been involved in questionable loan practices with a member of Congress.

A controversial issue in November, 2001, concerned legislation barring discriminatory treatment toward homosexuals in public accommodations, housing, and employment. The measure passed the Maryland legislature and became law. Opponents announced they could not force a referendum on the issue because they were unable to collect sufficient signatures. Passage of the measure had been a top priority of Governor Glendening.

On May 9, 2002, taking part in national soul-searching over the death penalty, Governor Glendening ordered a moratorium on the death penalty. The morato-

Few states have cities as dominant as Baltimore, whose population is more than seven times greater than that of Maryland's next-largest city, Columbia. (PhotoDisc)

rium was to remain in force at least until a study could be completed on whether racial bias was involved in its application.

In the 2002 midterm elections, Maryland's congressional delegation changed dramatically, as two Republicans seats were lost to Democrats, including the seat of eight-term member Constance Morella. At the same time, a new governor was elected, when Robert Ehrlich, Jr., defeated Kathleen Kennedy Townsend, ending thirty-six years of Democrat domination of the statehouse. In 2004, Maryland gave its ten electoral votes to Democratic challenger John Kerry by 56-43 percent. At the same time, it reelected Senator Barbara Mikulski. The $7 million spent on the Senate race set a record in the state.

Sniper Killings. Between October 2 and October 24, 2002, two persons, later identified as forty-one-year-old John Allen Muhammad and seventeen-year-old John Lee Malvo, perpetrated a series of fatal shootings in Washington, D.C., and its suburbs, including Maryland and Virginia. Residents were terrorized for weeks as the random attacks continued. Some motivation for the crimes, it was later said, was the men's plot to extort $10 million from the U.S. government. When the spree ended with the capture of the two, ten persons had been killed and three others critically wounded. Some fifteen hundred federal agents and thousands of state and local law enforcement personnel had hunted the snipers. More than seventy thousand calls from the public were received on a hotline by October 21. Most of the incidents occurred in Maryland, where six died and one was injured. The two snipers were apprehended at a Maryland highway rest stop.

Hurricane Isabel. In mid-September, 2003, the state was hit by Hurricane Isabel, which had been downgraded to a tropical storm when it arrived. The storm mainly affected coastal cities, where there was serious flooding. In Baltimore, the state's largest city, water was waist deep; in Annapolis, the state capital, water reached a depth of more than 7.5 feet in the city's streets.

Michael Witkoski
Updated by the Editor

Maryland Time Line

1608	English Captain John Smith charts Chesapeake Bay region.
1631	Councilman William Claiborne establishes trading post on Kent Island as outpost of Virginia.
June 20, 1632	English King Charles I grants Lord Baltimore the province of Maryland.
1634	Governor Leonard Calvert and settlers found St. Mary's City.
1635	St. Mary's City settlers fight Claiborne's colonists.
Apr. 21, 1649	Maryland enacts "Act Concerning Religion," the first act of religious toleration in the colonies.
1652	Peace treaty is made with Susquehannock Indians.
1654	English Commonwealth ends Maryland's proprietary government.
1658	Proprietary government is restored by English Parliament.
1692	Maryland becomes a royal colony; Church of England made state church.
1694	Capital is moved to Annapolis.
1718	Roman Catholics lose the right to vote.
Oct. 19, 1774	Patriots burn cargo of tea aboard *Peggy Stewart* in Annapolis Harbor.
1776	Maryland Provincial Convention votes for independence; adopts state constitution.
1776	Continental Congress, fearing capture by British, flees Philadelphia to Baltimore.
Jan. 14, 1784	Continental Congress meets at Annapolis to sign Treaty of Paris.
Apr. 28, 1788	Maryland ratifies U.S. Constitution, becoming seventh state.
1791	Maryland cedes land to District of Columbia.
1796	Baltimore City is incorporated.
1809	First Roman Catholic parochial school in Union opens in Baltimore.
1812	University of Maryland is founded at Baltimore.
1814	British are defeated in attack on Fort McHenry outside Baltimore; Francis Scott Key writes "The Star-Spangled Banner."
1818	Cumberland Road (National Pike) reaches Ohio River.
1824-1829	Chesapeake and Delaware Canal is constructed.
1827	Baltimore and Ohio Railroad is chartered.
1828-1850	Chesapeake and Ohio Canal is constructed.
1830	Locomotive *Tom Thumb* races on Baltimore and Ohio Railroad line, the first U.S. railroad to carry both passengers and freight.

May 24, 1844	First telegraph line in United States links Baltimore with Washington, D.C.
1845	U.S. Naval Academy opens at Annapolis.
1849	Edgar Allan Poe dies in Baltimore.
Apr. 19, 1861	Baltimore mob attacks Union troops passing through state; sixteen are killed.
Sept. 16-17, 1862	Union wins a bloody victory over Confederate army at Antietam.
1864	State adopts new constitution abolishing slavery.
1867	State adopts revised constitution.
1876	Johns Hopkins University opens in Baltimore.
1904	Great Baltimore Fire destroys downtown.
1920	Governor Albert Ritchie refuses to enforce national prohibition law.
1942	President Franklin D. Roosevelt establishes Shangri-La (now Camp David) as presidential retreat in Catoctin Mountains of Maryland.
1950	Friendship International Airport opens.
July, 1954	Chesapeake Bay Bridge is completed near Annapolis.
Sept., 1954	Baltimore desegregates public schools.
1957	Baltimore Harbor Tunnel opens.
1970	Perren Mitchell is elected to Congress, the first African American to represent Maryland.
1972	Maryland adopts state lottery.
1973	Parallel bridge of Chesapeake Bay Bridge is completed.
1980	Baltimore opens Harborplace, centerpiece of the renewed city.
1983	Chesapeake Bay Agreement to improve water quality and living resources of the bay is enacted.
1987	Updated and revised Chesapeake Bay Agreement to restore and protect the bay is enacted.
1987	Kurt Schmoke becomes first African American mayor of Baltimore.
1992	Baltimore Orioles open Camden Yards baseball stadium.
1992	Maryland is first state to require public high school students to perform community service to graduate.
1994	Maryland adopts Smart Growth initiative to control urban sprawl.
Nov. 22, 2001	Legislation barring various forms of discrimination against gays and lesbians becomes law when opponents concede they are unable to obtain the voter signatures required to force a referendum.
May 9, 2002	Governor Parris Glendening orders moratorium on use of the death penalty.
Oct. 2-24, 2002	Ten people were shot dead and three wounded by two men in a series of sniper incidents in the Washington, D.C., area. Most incidents took place in Maryland, where six died.
Nov. 5, 2002	Robert Ehrlich, Jr., becomes Maryland's governor.
Sept. 18-19, 2003	Maryland is hit by Tropical Storm Isabel.

Notes for Further Study

Published Sources. Maryland's history may best be studied in Robert J. Brugger's *Maryland: A Middle Temperament, 1684-1980* (1989), a traditional but solid history that examines the state's unique character and contributions from colonial times to the modern era. For young adults interested in the state's history and culture, *Maryland* (2006) by Michael Burgan, Roberta Wiener and James R. Arnold's *Maryland* (2004), and Liz Sonneborn's *Colony of Maryland* (2005) are good choices. *Maryland Lost and Found: People and Places from Chesapeake to Appalachia* (1986) by Eugene Meyer is a genial approach to the cultures, communities, and diversity found between Maryland's coast and mountains. Two excellent guides to the state are *Maryland: A New Guide to the Old Line State* (2d ed., 1999) by Earl Arnett with Robert J. Brugger and Edward C. Papenfuse and *The Chesapeake Bay Book: A Complete Guide* (4th ed., 2005) by Alison Blake and Tracy Sahler. Robert B. Harmon's *Government and Politics in Maryland* (1990) offers some excellent information and insights into Maryland's

economic, cultural, and historical trends, as does Theodore Sheckles's *Maryland Politics and Political Communication, 1950-2005* (2006). Readers interested in learning about the way in which the Civil Rights movement played out in Maryland will appreciate *Civil War on Race Street: The Civil Rights Movement in Cambridge, Maryland* (2003) by Peter B. Levy. It offers a detailed examination of a local protest by African Americans that had national ramifications. *African-American Leaders of Maryland: A Portrait Gallery* (2004) by Suzanne Ellery Chapelle and Glenn O. Phillips focuses both on Civil Rights leaders and on prominent African Americans from earlier decades and centuries.

Web Resources. A good starting point for information on the state is the Maryland Government page (www.maryland .gov/), which has links to various state agencies and departments and their wealth of resources. The state's office of tourism (www.mdisfun.org/home/index.asp) has an informative site for visitors. Of particular interest is the Maryland State Ar-

Counties

County	2000 pop.	Rank in pop.	Sq. miles	Rank in area
Allegany	74,930	14	425.3	12
Anne Arundel	489,656	4	416.0	13
Baltimore	754,292	3	598.6	3
Calvert	74,563	15	215.2	23
Caroline	29,772	21	320.2	19
Carroll	150,897	8	449.2	10
Cecil	85,951	12	348.2	17
Charles	120,546	10	461.1	8
Dorchester	30,674	19	557.6	4
Frederick	195,277	7	662.9	1
Garrett	29,846	20	648.1	2
Harford	218,590	6	440.4	11
Howard	247,842	5	252.2	22
Kent	19,197	23	279.4	20
Montgomery	873,341	1	494.6	5
Prince George's	801,515	2	486.4	6
Queen Anne's	40,563	17	372.2	15
St. Mary's	86,211	11	361.3	16
Somerset	24,747	22	327.2	18
Talbot	33,812	18	269.2	21
Washington	131,923	9	458.2	9
Wicomico	84,644	13	377.2	14
Worcester	46,543	16	473.2	7

The city of Baltimore is independent of all counties, including Baltimore County.

Source: U.S. Census Bureau; National Association of Counties.

chives site (www.mdarchives.state.md.us), which has much material on Maryland's history and development from its settlement. A good supplement to these two sites is that of the Maryland Historical Society (www.mdhs.org). Two generalized sites are Maryland Manual Online (www.mdsa.net/msa/mdmanual/html/mmtoc.html) and Maryland Online (www.maryland-online.com), both of which contain information about contemporary Maryland. More specialized are the sites devoted to Maryland's Eastern Shore (www.easternshore.com/) and to Maryland's Woman Citizen (www.mdarchives.state.md.us/msa/stagser/s1259/153/html/0044/womenhist/womentoc.html).

A Maryland horse farm. (Middleton Evans/Courtesy Maryland Office of Tourism)

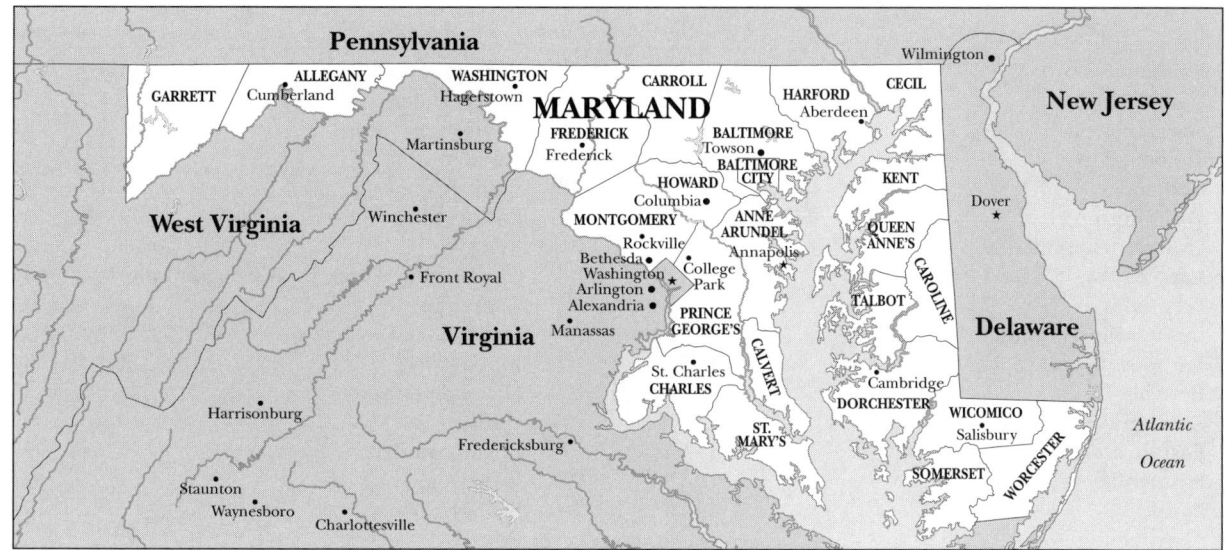

Cities
With 10,000 or more residents

Rank	City	Population	Rank	City	Population
1	Baltimore	651,154	35	South Gate	28,672
2	Columbia	88,254	36	Severna Park	28,507
3	Silver Spring	76,540	37	Carney	28,264
4	Dundalk	62,306	38	Eldersburg	27,741
5	Wheaton-Glenmont	57,694	39	Milford Mill	26,527
6	Ellicott City	56,397	40	Clinton	26,064
7	Germantown	55,419	41	Bel Air North	25,798
8	Bethesda	55,277	42	Lochearn	25,269
9	Frederick	52,767	43	College Park	24,657
10	Gaithersburg	52,613	44	Middle River	23,958
11	Towson	51,793	45	Fort Washington	23,845
12	Bowie	50,269	46	Salisbury	23,743
13	Aspen Hill	50,228	47	Arnold	23,422
14	Rockville	47,388	48	Edgewood	23,378
15	Potomac	44,822	49	North Potomac	23,044
16	Catonsville	39,820	50	Greater Landover	22,900
17	Bel Air South	39,711	51	Reisterstown	22,438
18	Essex	39,078	52	Waldorf	22,312
19	Glen Burnie	38,922	53	Elkridge	22,042
20	North Bethesda	38,610	54	Fairland	21,738
21	Montgomery Village	38,051	55	Cumberland	21,518
22	Hagerstown	36,687	56	Greenbelt	21,456
23	Woodlawn	36,079	57	White Oak	20,973
24	Annapolis (capital)	35,838	58	Odenton	20,534
25	Oxon Hill-Glassmanor	35,355	59	South Laurel	20,479
26	Severn	35,076	60	North Laurel	20,468
27	Chillum	34,252	61	Owings Mills	20,193
28	Suitland-Silver Hill	33,515	62	Arbutus	20,116
29	St. Charles	33,379	63	Crofton	20,091
30	Olney	31,438	64	Laurel	19,960
31	Parkville	31,118	65	Colesville	19,810
32	Randallstown	30,870	66	Cockeysville	19,388
33	Pikesville	29,123	67	Rosedale	19,199
34	Perry Hall	28,705	68	Greater Upper Marlboro	18,720

(continued)

Rank	City	Population
69	Lanham-Seabrook	18,190
70	Camp Springs	17,968
71	Green Haven	17,415
72	Takoma Park	17,299
73	Redland	16,998
74	Westminster	16,731
75	Hillcrest Heights	16,359
76	Langley Park	16,214
77	Ferndale	16,056
78	Lutherville-Timonium	15,814
79	Lansdowne-Baltimore Highlands	15,724
80	Beltsville	15,690
81	Adelphi	14,998
82	East Riverdale	14,961
83	Hyattsville	14,733
84	Parole	14,031
85	Aberdeen	13,842
86	Ballenger Creek	13,518
87	Lake Shore	13,065
88	Savage-Guilford	12,918
89	Forestville	12,707
90	Riviera Beach	12,695
91	Calverton	12,610
92	Glenn Dale	12,609
93	New Carrollton	12,589
94	Linganore-Bartonsville	12,529

Rank	City	Population
95	Rosaryville	12,322
96	Green Valley	12,262
97	Overlea	12,148
98	Pasadena	12,093
99	Elkton	11,893
100	Easton	11,708
101	Rossville	11,515
102	Chesapeake Ranch Estates-Drum Point	11,503
103	Damascus	11,430
104	Mays Chapel	11,427
105	Joppatowne	11,391
106	Havre de Grace	11,331
107	Walker Mill	11,104
108	Lexington Park	11,021
109	Kettering	11,008
110	Brooklyn Park	10,938
111	Friendly	10,938
112	Cambridge	10,911
113	Coral Hills	10,720
114	Ocean Pines	10,496
115	Bel Air	10,080
116	Halfway	10,065

Population figures are from 2000 census.

Source: U.S. Bureau of the Census.

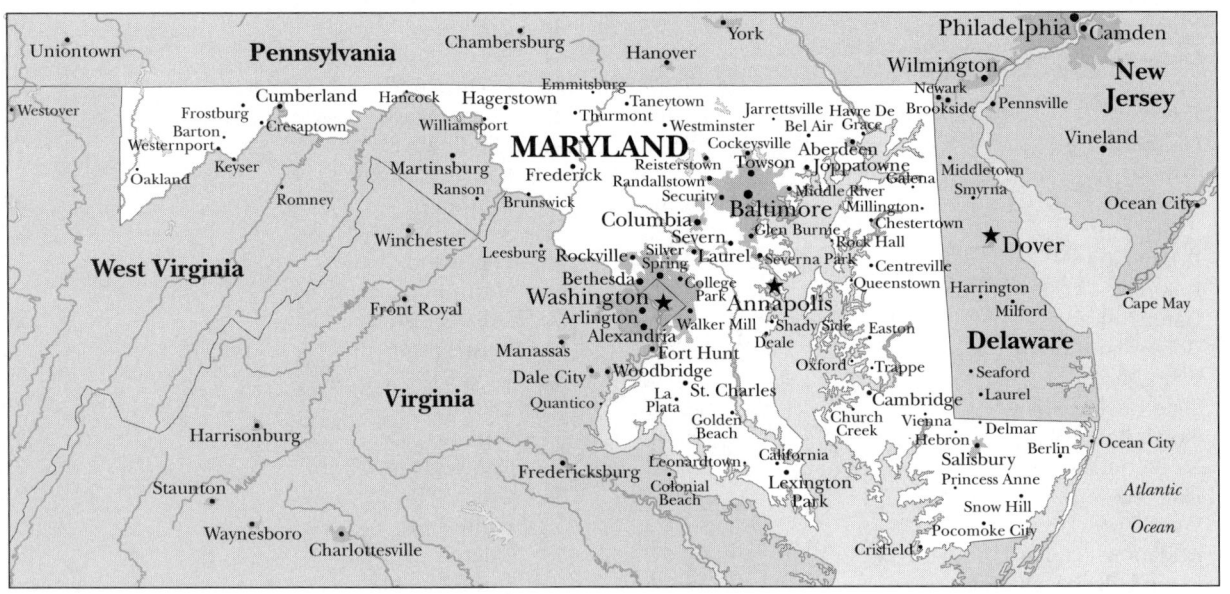

Index to Tables

DEMOGRAPHICS

Resident state and national populations, 1970-2004

Population figures given in thousands

	State pop.	U.S. pop.	Share	Rank
1970	3,924	203,302	1.9%	18
1980	4,217	226,546	1.9%	18
1985	4,413	237,924	1.9%	18
1990	4,781	248,765	1.9%	19
1995	5,070	262,761	1.9%	19
2000	5,297	281,425	1.9%	19
2004	5,558	293,655	1.9%	19

Source: U.S. Census Bureau, Current Population Reports, 2006.

Resident population by age, 2004

Age Group	Total persons
Under 5 years	375,000
5 to 17 years	1,020,000
18 to 24 years	521,000
25 to 34 years	711,000
35 to 44 years	895,000
45 to 54 years	829,000
55 to 64 years	573,000
65 to 74 years	326,000
75 to 84 years	226,000
85 years and older	83,000
All age groups	5,558,000
Portion of residents 65 and older	11.4%
National rank in portion of oldest residents	40
National average	12.4%

Population figures are rounded to nearest thousand persons;
figures include armed forces personnel stationed in the state.
Source: U.S. Bureau of the Census, 2006.

Resident population by race, Hispanic origin, 2004

Category	State pop.	Share	U.S.
All residents	5,558	100.00%	100.00%
Non-Hispanic white	3,325	59.82%	67.37%
Hispanic white	258	4.64%	13.01%
Other Hispanic	40	0.72%	1.06%
African American	1,615	29.06%	12.77%
Native American	18	0.32%	0.96%
Asian, Pacific Islander	261	4.70%	4.37%
Two or more categories	81	1.46%	1.51%

Population figures are in thousands. Persons counted as "Hispanic" (Latino) may be of any race. Because of overlapping categories, categories may not add up to 100%. Shares in column 3 are percentages of each category within the state; these figures may be compared to the national percentages in column 4.
Source: U.S. Bureau of the Census, 2006.

Projected state population, 2000-2030

Year	Population
2000	5,297,000
2005	5,601,000
2010	5,905,000
2015	6,208,000
2020	6,498,000
2025	6,763,000
2030	7,022,000
Population increase, 2000-2030	1,725,000
Percentage increase, 2000-2030	32.6

Projections are based on data from the 2000 census.
Source: U.S. Census Bureau.

VITAL STATISTICS

Infant mortality rates, 1980-2002

	1980	1990	2000	2002
All state residents	14.0	9.5	7.6	7.5
All U.S. residents	12.6	9.2	9.4	9.1
All state white residents	11.6	6.8	4.8	5.3
All U.S. white residents	10.6	7.6	5.7	5.8
All state black residents	20.4	17.1	13.2	12.3
All U.S. black residents	22.2	18.0	14.1	14.4

Figures represent deaths per 1,000 live births of resident infants under 1 year old, exclusive of fetal deaths. Figures for all residents include members of other racial categories not listed separately.
Source: U.S. Census Bureau, *Statistical Abstract of the United States,* 2006.

Abortion rates, 1990 and 2000

	1990	2000
Total abortions	31,000	35,000
Rate per 1,000 women	26.2	29.0
U.S. rate	25.7	21.3
Rank	11	7

Numbers of abortions are rounded to nearest thousand; ranks are based on rates.
Source: U.S. Census Bureau.

Marriages and divorces, 2004

Total marriages	37,700
Rate per 1,000 population	6.8
National rate per 1,000 population	7.4
Rank among all states	30
Total divorces	17,100
Rate per 1,000 population	3.1
National rate per 1,000 population	3.7
Rank among all states	33

Figures are for all marriages and divorces performed within the state, including those of nonresidents; totals are rounded to the nearest hundred. Ranks are for highest to lowest figures; note that divorce data are not available for five states.
Source: U.S. National Center for Health Statistics, *Vital Statistics of the United States,* 2006.

Death rates by leading causes, 2002
Deaths per 100,000 resident population

Cause	State	U.S.
Heart disease	220.0	241.7
Cancer	190.4	193.2
Cerebrovascular diseases	51.5	56.4
Accidents other than motor vehicle	24.4	37.0
Motor vehicle accidents	13.2	15.7
Chronic lower respiratory diseases	35.6	43.3
Diabetes mellitus	27.8	25.4
HIV	11.2	4.9
Suicide	8.7	11.0
Homicide	9.9	6.1
All causes	805.6	847.3
Rank in overall death rate among states		35

Figures exclude nonresidents who died in the state. Causes of death follow International Classification of Diseases. Rank is from highest to lowest death rate in the United States.
Source: U.S. National Center for Health Statistics, *National Vital Statistics Report,* 2006.

ECONOMY

Gross state product, 1990-2004
In current dollars

Year	State product	Nat'l product	State share
1990	$113.7 billion	$5.67 trillion	2.00%
2000	$180.0 billion	$9.75 trillion	1.85%
2002	$202.8 billion	$10.41 trillion	1.95%
2003	$213.1 billion	$10.92 trillion	1.95%
2004	$226.5 billion	$11.65 trillion	1.94%

Source: U.S. Bureau of Economic Analysis, *Survey of Current Business,* July, 2005.

Gross state product by industry, 2003
In billions of dollars

Construction	$10.3
Manufacturing	13.5
Wholesale trade	11.0
Retail trade	15.0
Finance & insurance	14.1
Information	7.9
Professional services	20.1
Health care & social assistance	14.0
Government	32.3
Total state product	$198.3
Total U.S. product	$10,289.2
State share of U.S. total	1.93%
Rank among all states	17

Total figures include industries not listed separately. Amounts are in chained 2000 dollars.
Source: U.S. Bureau of Economic Analysis, *Survey of Current Business,* July, 2005.

Personal income per capita, 1990-2004
In current dollars

	1990	2000	2004
Per capita income	$22,852	$34,257	$39,247
U.S. average	$19,477	$29,845	$32,937
Rank among states	5	5	4

Source: U.S. Bureau of Economic Analysis, *Survey of Current Business,* April, 2005.

Energy consumption, 2001
In trillions of British thermal units (BTU), except as noted

Total energy consumption

Total state energy consumption	1,420
Total U.S. energy consumption	96,275
State share of U.S. total	1.47%
Rank among states	25

Per capita consumption (In millions of BTU)

Total state per capita consumption	264
Total U.S. per capita consumption	338
Rank among states	41

End-use sectors

Residential	391
Commercial	372
Industrial	252
Transportation	405

Sources of energy

Petroleum	568
Natural gas	191
Coal	317
Hydroelectric power	12
Nuclear electric power	143

Figures for totals include categories not listed separately.
Source: U.S. Energy Information Administration, *State Energy Data Report,* 2001.

Nonfarm employment by sectors, 2004

Total	2,520,000
Construction	178,000
Manufacturing	143,000
Trade, transportation, utilities	468,000
Information	51,000
Finance, insurance, real estate	156,000
Professional & business services	373,000
Education & health services	348,000
Leisure, hospitality, arts, organizations	225,000
Other services, including repair & maintenance	114,000
Government	466,000

Figures are rounded to nearest thousand persons. "Total" includes mining and natural resources, not listed separately.
Source: U.S. Bureau of Labor Statistics, 2006.

Foreign exports, 1990-2004
In millions of dollars

Year	State	U.S.	State share
1990	2,592	394,045	0.66%
1996	5,019	624,767	0.80%
1997	5,214	688,896	0.76%
2000	4,593	712,055	0.59%
2003	4,941	724,006	0.73%
2004	5,746	769,332	0.75%

Rank among all states in 2004 29

U.S. total does not include U.S. dependencies.
Source: U.S. Census Bureau, *U.S. Merchandise Trade*, series FT 900, 2000; U.S. Census Bureau, *U.S. International Trade in Goods and Services*, Series FT 900, 2005.

LAND USE

Federally owned land, 2003
Areas in acres

	State	U.S.	State share
Total area	6,319,000	2,271,343,000	0.28%
Nonfederal land	6,127,000	1,599,584,000	0.38%
Federal land	192,000	671,759,000	0.03%
Federal share	3.0%	29.6%	—

Areas are rounded to nearest thousand acres. Figures for federally owned land do not include trust properties.
Source: U.S. General Services Administration, *Federal Real Property Profile*, 2006.

Land use, 1997
In acres, rounded to nearest thousand

Total surface area.	7,870,000
Total nonfederal rural land	4,808,000
Percentage rural land	61.1%
Cropland	1,616,000
Conservation Reserve Program (CRP*) land	19,000
Pastureland	478,000
Rangeland	(nil)
Forestland.	2,373,000
Other rural land	321,000

*CRP is a federal program begun in 1985 to assist private landowners to convert highly erodible cropland to vegetative cover for ten years. Note that some categories of land overlap.
Source: U.S. Department of Agriculture, Natural Resources and Conservation Service, and Iowa State University, Statistical Laboratory, *Summary Report, 1997 National Resources Inventory,* revised December, 2000.

Farms and crop acreage, 2004

	State	U.S.	Share	Rank
Farms	12,000	2,113,000	0.57%	37
Acres (millions)	2	937	0.21%	40
Acres per farm	169	443	—	42

Source: U.S. Department of Agriculture, National Agricultural Statistics Service. Numbers of farms are rounded to nearest thousand units; acreage figures are rounded to nearest million. Rankings, including ties, are based on rounded figures.

GOVERNMENT AND FINANCE

Units of local government, 2002

	State	Total U.S.	Rank
All local governments	265	87,525	46
Counties	23	3,034	37
Municipalities	157	19,429	36
Townships	0	16,504	—
School districts	0	13,506	—
Special districts	85	35,052	46

Only 48 states have county governments, 20 states have township governments ("towns" in New England, Minnesota, New York, and Wisconsin), and 46 states have school districts. Special districts encompass such functions as natural resources, fire protection, and housing and community development.
Source: U.S. Census Bureau, *Census of Governments.*

State government revenue, 2002

Total revenue	$20,788 mill.
General revenue	$19,909 mill.
Per capita revenue	$3,659
U.S. per capita average	$3,689
Rank among states	31
Intergovernment revenue	
Total	$5,453 mill.
From federal government	$5,260 mill.
Charges and miscellaneous	
Total	$3,635 mill.
Current charges	$1,967 mill.
Misc. general income	$1,668 mill.
Insurance trust revenue	$784 mill.
Taxes	
Total	$10,821 mill.
Per capita taxes	$1,985
Rank among states	16
Property taxes	$273 mill.
Sales taxes	$4,699 mill.
License taxes	$436 mill.
Individual income taxes	$4,704 mill.
Corporate income taxes	$359 mill.
Other taxes	$350 mill.

Total revenue figures include items not listed separately here.
Source: U.S. Bureau of the Census.

State government expenditures, 2002

General expenditures
Total state expenditures . . . . $23,317 mill.
Intergovernmental. . . . . $5,236 mill.

Per capita expenditures
State $3,798
Average of all states $3,859
Rank among states 29

Selected direct expenditures
Education. . . . . $3,414 mill.
Public welfare . . . . $4,625 mill.
Health, hospital . . . . $1,249 mill.
Highways . . . . $1,196 mill.
Police protection. . . . . $297 mill.
Corrections. $1,029 mill.
Natural resources . . . . $458 mill.
Parks and recreation. . . . . $167 mill.
Government administration. . . . . $840 mill.
Interest on debt . . . . $711 mill.
Total direct expenditures. . . . . $15,469 mill.

Totals include items not listed separately.
Source: U.S. Census Bureau.

POLITICS

Governors since statehood
D = Democrat; R = Republican; O = other;
(r) resigned; (d) died in office; (i) removed from office

Thomas Johnson. 1777-1779
Thomas Sim Lee. 1779-1782
William Paca 1782-1785
William Smallwood 1785-1788
John Eager Howard (O). 1788-1791
George Plater (O). . . . . (d) 1791-1792
James Brice (O) 1792
Thomas Sim Lee (O) 1792-1794
John Hoskins Stone (O). 1794-1797
John Henry (O) 1797-1798
Benjamin Ogle (O) 1798-1801
John Francis Mercer (O) 1801-1803
Robert Bowie (O) 1803-1806
Robert Wright (O). . . . . (r) 1806-1809
James Butcher (O). 1809
Edward Lloyd (O) 1809-1811
Robert Bowie (O) 1811-1812
Levin Winder (O) 1812-1816
Charles Carnan Ridgley (O) 1816-1819
Charles Goldsborough (O) 1819
Samuel Sprigg (O). 1819-1822
Samuel Stevens, Jr. (O) 1822-1826
Joseph Kent (O) 1826-1829
Daniel Martin (O) 1829-1830
Thomas King Carroll (O) 1830-1831
Daniel Martin (O). . . . . (d) 1831

George Howard (O) 1831-1833
James Thomas (O). 1833-1836
Thomas Ward Veazey (O) 1836-1839
William Grason (D) 1839-1842
Francis Thomas (D) 1842-1845
Thomas George Pratt (O). 1845-1848
Philip Francis Thomas (D) 1848-1851
Enoch Louis Lowe (D) 1851-1854
Thomas Watkins Ligon (D) 1854-1858
Thomas Holliday Hicks (O). 1858-1862
Augustus W. Bradford (O) 1862-1866
Thomas Swann (O) 1866-1869
Oden Bowie (D) 1869-1872
William Pinkney Whyte (D) . . . . (r) 1872-1874
James Black Groome (D) 1874-1876
John Lee Carroll (D) 1876-1880
William Thomas Hamilton (D) 1880-1884
Robert Milligan McLane (D) . . . . (r) 1884-1885
Henry Lloyd (D) 1885-1888
Elihu Emory Jackson (D) 1888-1892
Frank Brown (D). 1892-1896
Lloyd Lowndes (R) 1896-1900
John W. Smith (D). 1900-1904
Edwin Warfield (D) 1904-1908
Austin L. Crothers (D). 1908-1912
Phillips L. Goldsborough (R) 1912-1916
Emerson C. Harrington (D) 1916-1920
Albert C. Ritchie (D) 1920-1935
Harry W. Nice (R) 1935-1939
Herbert R. O'Conor (D) 1939-1947
William P. Lane, Jr. (D) 1947-1951
Theodore R. McKeldin (R) 1951-1959
J. Millard Tawes (D) 1959-1967
Spiro T. Agnew (R) . . . . (r) 1967-1969
Marvin Mandel (D) . . . . (i) 1969-1977
Blair Lee III (D) 1977-1979
Harry R. Hughes (D) 1979-1987
William Donald Schaefer (D) 1987-1991
Parris N. Glendening (D) 1995-2003
Robert L. Ehrlich (R) 2003-2007
Martin O'Malley (D). 2007-

Composition of congressional delegations, 1989-2007

	Dem	Rep	Total
House of Representatives			
101st Congress, 1989			
State delegates	6	2	8
Total U.S.	259	174	433
102d Congress, 1991			
State delegates	5	3	8
Total U.S.	267	167	434
103d Congress, 1993			
State delegates	4	4	8
Total U.S.	258	176	434
104th Congress, 1995			
State delegates	4	4	8
Total U.S.	197	236	433
105th Congress, 1997			
State delegates	4	4	8
Total U.S.	206	228	434
106th Congress, 1999			
State delegates	4	4	8
Total U.S.	211	222	433
107th Congress, 2001			
State delegates	4	4	8
Total U.S.	211	221	432
108th Congress, 2003			
State delegates	6	2	8
Total U.S.	205	229	434
109th Congress, 2005			
State delegates	6	2	8
Total U.S.	202	231	433
110th Congress, 2007			
State delegates	6	2	8
Total U.S.	233	202	435
Senate			
101st Congress, 1989			
State delegates	2	0	2
Total U.S.	55	45	100
102d Congress, 1991			
State delegates	2	0	2
Total U.S.	56	44	100
103d Congress, 1993			
State delegates	2	0	2
Total U.S.	57	43	100
104th Congress, 1995			
State delegates	2	0	2
Total U.S.	46	53	99
105th Congress, 1997			
State delegates	2	0	2
Total U.S.	45	55	100

	Dem	Rep	Total
106th Congress, 1999			
State delegates	2	0	2
Total U.S.	45	54	99
107th Congress, 2001			
State delegates	2	0	2
Total U.S.	50	50	100
108th Congress, 2003			
State delegates	2	0	2
Total U.S.	48	51	99
109th Congress, 2005			
State delegates	2	0	2
Total U.S.	44	55	99
110th Congress, 2007			
State delegates	2	0	2
Total U.S.	49	49	98

Figures are for starts of first sessions. Totals are for Democrat (Dem.) and Republican (Rep.) members only. House membership totals under 435 and Senate totals under 100 reflect vacancies and seats held by independent party members. When the 110th Congress opened, the Senate's two independent members caucused with the Democrats, giving the Democrats control of the Senate.

Source: U.S. Congress, *Congressional Directory.*

Composition of state legislature, 1990-2006

	Democrats	Republicans
State House (141 seats)		
1990	116	25
1992	116	25
1994	100	41
1996	100	41
1998	106	35
2000	106	35
2002	98	43
2004	98	43
2006	106	35
State Senate (47 seats)		
1990	38	9
1992	38	9
1994	32	15
1996	32	15
1998	32	15
2000	33	14
2002	33	14
2004	33	14
2006	33	14

Figures for total seats may include independents and minor party members. Numbers reflect results of elections in listed years; elected members usually take their seats in the years that follow.

Source: Council of State Governments; *State Elective Officials and the Legislatures.*

Voter participation in presidential elections, 2000 and 2004

	2000	2004
Voting age population		
State	3,953,000	4,163,000
Total United States	209,831,000	220,377,000
State share of U.S. total	1.88	1.89
Rank among states	19	20
Portion of voting age population casting votes		
State	51.2%	57.3%
United States	50.3%	55.5%
Rank among states	27	26

Population figures are rounded to nearest thousand and include all residents, regardless of eligibility to vote.
Source: U.S. Census Bureau.

HEALTH AND MEDICAL CARE

Medical professionals
Physicians in 2003 and nurses in 2001

	U.S.	State
Physicians in 2003		
Total	774,849	22,819
Share of U.S. total		2.93%
Rate	266	414
Rank		2
Nurses in 2001		
Total	2,262,020	43,340
Share of U.S. total		1.92%
Rate	793	805
Rank		30

Rates are numbers of physicians and nurses per 100,000 resident population; ranks are based on rates.
Source: American Medical Association, *Physician Characteristics and Distribution in the U.S.*; U.S. Department of Health and Human Services, Health Resources and Services Administration.

Health insurance coverage, 2003

	State	U.S.
Total persons covered	4,731,000	243,320,000
Total persons not covered	762,000	44,961,000
Portion not covered	13.9%	15.6%
Rank among states	27	—
Children not covered	114,000	8,373,000
Portion not covered	8.1%	11.4%
Rank among states	37	—

Totals are rounded to nearest thousand. Ranks are from the highest to the lowest percentages of persons *not* insured.
Source: U.S. Census Bureau, Current Population Reports.

AIDS, syphilis, and tuberculosis cases, 2003

Disease	U.S. cases	State cases	Rank
AIDS	44,232	1,572	8
Syphilis	34,270	974	10
Tuberculosis	14,874	268	13

Source: U.S. Centers for Disease Control and Prevention.

Cigarette smoking, 2003
Residents over age 18 who smoke

	U.S.	State	Rank
All smokers	22.1%	20.2%	39
Male smokers	24.8%	23.0%	34
Female smokers	20.3%	17.7%	45

Cigarette smokers are defined as persons who reported having smoked at least 100 cigarettes during their lifetimes and who currently smoked at least occasionally.
Source: U.S. Centers for Disease Control and Prevention, *Morbidity and Mortality Weekly Report*, 53, no. 44 (November 12, 2004).

HOUSING

Home ownership rates, 1985-2004

	1985	1990	1995	2000	2004
State	65.6%	64.9%	65.8%	69.9%	72.1%
Total U.S.	63.9%	63.9%	64.7%	67.4%	69.0%
Rank among states	34	35	36	29	24

Net change in state home ownership rate,
1985-2004 . . . . +6.5%
Net change in U.S. home ownership rate,
1985-2004 . . . . +5.1%

Percentages represent the proportion of owner households to total occupied households.
Source: U.S. Census Bureau, 2006.

Home sales, 2000-2004
In thousands of units

Existing home sales	2000	2002	2003	2004
State sales	100.5	117.6	120.8	140.6
Total U.S. sales	5,171	5,631	6,183	6,784
State share of U.S. total	1.94%	2.09%	1.95%	2.07%
Sales rank among states	19	16	18	18

Units include single-family homes, condos, and co-ops.
Source: National Association of Realtors, Washington, D.C., *Real Estate Outlook: Market Trends & Insights.*

Values of owner-occupied homes, 2003

	State	U.S.
Total units	1,255,000	58,809,000
Value of units		
Under $100,000	16.6%	29.6%
$100,000-199,999	38.1%	36.9%
$200,000 or more	45.3%	33.5%
Median value	$186,139	$142,275
Rank among all states 11		

Units are owner-occupied one-family houses whose numbers are
rounded to nearest thousand. Data are extrapolated from
survey samples.
Source: U.S. Census Bureau, American Community Survey.

EDUCATION

Public school enrollment, 2002

Prekindergarten through grade 8
State enrollment 610,000
Total U.S. enrollment 34,135,000
State share of U.S. total 1.79%

Grades 9 through 12
State enrollment 256,000
Total U.S. enrollment 14,067,000
State share of U.S. total 1.82%

Enrollment rates
State public school enrollment rate 85.6%
Overall U.S. rate 90.4%
Rank among states in 2002 47
Rank among states in 1995 37

Enrollment figures (which include unclassified students) are
rounded to nearest thousand pupils during fall school term.
Enrollment rates are based on enumerated resident population
estimate for July 1, 2002.
Source: U.S. National Center for Education Statistics.

Public college finances, 2003-2004

FTE enrollment in public institutions of higher education
Students in state institutions 165,500
Students in all U.S. public institutions 9,916,600
State share of U.S. total 1.67
Rank among states 21

**State and local government appropriations for higher
education**
State appropriation per FTE $5,378
National average $5,716
Rank among states 26
State & local tax revenue going to higher
education 7.2%

FTE = full-time equivalent in public postsecondary programs,
including summer sessions; student numbers are rounded to
nearest hundred. Funding figures for 2003-2004 academic year
include financial aid to students in state public institutions and
exclude money for research, agriculture experiment stations,
teaching hospitals, and medical schools; figures are rounded to
nearest thousand dollars.
Source: Higher Education Executive Officers, Denver, Colorado.

TRANSPORTATION AND TRAVEL

Highway mileage, 2003

Interstate highways	481
Other freeways and expressways	287
Arterial roads	3,732
Collector roads	4,825
Local roads	21,363
Urban roads	16,780
Rural roads	13,908
Total state mileage	30,688
U.S. total	3,974,107
State share	0.77%
Rank among states	41

Note that combined urban and rural road mileage matches the
total of the other categories.
Source: U.S. Federal Highway Administration.

Motor vehicle registrations and driver licenses, 2003

Vehicle registrations	State	U.S.	Share	Rank
Autos, trucks, buses	3,877,000	231,390,000	1.68%	21
Autos only	2,479,000	135,670	1.83%	20
Motorcycles	64,000	5,328,000	1.20%	26
Driver licenses	3,552,000	196,166,000	1.81%	21

Figures, which do not include vehicles owned by military services,
are rounded to the nearest thousand. Figures for automobiles
include taxis.
Source: U.S. Federal Highway Administration.

Domestic travel expenditures, 2003

Spending by U.S. residents on overnight trips and day trips of at least 50 miles from home

Total expenditures within state	$9.01 bill.
Total expenditures within U.S.	$490.87 bill.
State share of U.S. total	1.8%
Rank among states	20

Source: Travel Industry Association of America.

Retail gasoline prices, 2003-2007

Average price per gallon at the pump

Year	U.S.	State
2003	$1.267	$1.218
2004	$1.316	$1.280
2005	$1.644	$1.603
2007	$2.298	$2.258

Excise tax per gallon in 2004	23.5¢
Rank among all states in 2007 prices	26

Prices are averages of all grades of gasoline sold at the pump during March months in 2003-2005 and during February, 2007. Averages for 2006, during which prices rose higher, are not available.
Source: U.S. Energy Information Agency, *Petroleum Marketing Monthly* (2003-2005 data); American Automobile Association (2007 data).

CRIME AND LAW ENFORCEMENT

State and local police officers, 2000-2004

	2000	2002	2004
Total officers			
U.S.	654,601	665,555	675,734
State	14,404	14,827	14,897*
*Net change, 2000-2004			+3.42%
Officers per 1,000 residents			
U.S.	2.33	2.31	2.30
State	2.72	2.72	2.68
State rank	6	6	6

Totals include state and local police and sheriffs.
Source: Carsey Institute, University of New Hampshire.

Crime rates, 2003

Incidents per 100,000 residents

Crimes	State	U.S.
Violent crimes		
Total incidents	704	475
Murder	10	6
Forcible rape	25	32
Robbery	242	142
Aggravated assault	428	295
Property crimes		
Total incidents	3,801	3,588
Burglary	701	741
Larceny/theft	2,439	2,415
Motor vehicle theft	661	433
All crimes	4,505	4,063

Source: U.S. Federal Bureau of Investigation, *Crime in the United States,* annual.

State prison populations, 1980-2003

	State	U.S.	State share
1980	7,731	305,458	2.53%
1990	17,848	708,393	2.52%
1996	22,050	1,025,624	2.15%
2000	23,538	1,391,261	1.69%
2003	23,791	1,470,045	1.62%

State figures exclude prisoners in federal penitentiaries.
Source: U.S. Bureau of Justice Statistics, *Prisoners in 2003.*

Massachusetts

Location: New England

Area and rank: 7,838 square miles (20,300 square kilometers); 10,555 square miles (27,337 square kilometers) including water; forty-fifth largest state in area

Coastline: 192 miles (309 kilometers) on the Atlantic Ocean

Shoreline: 1,519 miles (2,445 kilometers)

Population and rank: 6,417,000 (2004); thirteenth largest state in population

Capital and largest city: Boston (589,141 people in 2000 census)

Entered Union and rank: February 6, 1788; sixth state

Present constitution adopted: 1780 (oldest U.S. state constitution in effect today)

Counties: 14

State name: "Massachusetts" is named after a Native American society of the same name

Known as Massachusetts State House, the state capitol building in Boston houses both the legislature and the offices of the governor. (Courtesy of MOTT)

State nicknames: Bay State; Old Colony State

Motto: *Ense petit placidam sub libertate quietem* (By the sword we seek peace, but peace only under liberty)

State flag: White field with state coat of arms in blue and yellow

Highest point: Mount Greylock—3,487 feet (1,063 meters)

Lowest point: Atlantic Ocean—sea level

Highest recorded temperature: 107 degrees Fahrenheit (42 degrees Celsius)—New Bedford and Chester, 1975

Lowest recorded temperature: –34 degrees Fahrenheit (–37 degrees Celsius)—Birch Hill Dam, 1957

State songs: "All Hail to Massachusetts"; "Massachusetts" (official folk song); "The Road to Boston" (official ceremonial march)

State tree: American elm

State flower: Trailing arbutus (Mayflower)

State bird: Chickadee

Massachusetts History

Massachusetts was one of the original thirteen colonies, and its capital, Boston, is considered the cradle of the American Revolution. The state was home to some of the greatest American leaders. Its reputation for excellent education is due to its many great universities and colleges, including the world-famous Harvard and Massachusetts Institute of Technology (MIT). Geographically, the state forms a narrow rectangle. Relatively small, it is forty-fifth in area among the states, yet thirteenth in state population.

Native American History. The Algonquians were a large family of tribes, related by language and customs, who lived throughout the northeastern United States. Several of these tribes made their homes in the fertile farming and hunting grounds of the area. The Nauset lived on Cape Cod, while the Wampanoag, the Massachusetts (for whom the state is named), and the Patuxet fished and hunted along the coast. Women played a central role in Algonquian society. They owned the tribe's land, which they cleared and farmed communally. When a young man married, he left home to become a member of his bride's family.

Early Exploration and the Pilgrims. In 1602, English navigator Bartholomew Gosnold visited Massachusetts Bay and named it Cape Cod. Two years later explorer Samuel de Champlain explored the coast, followed by Captain John Smith in 1614.

In September of 1620, an English merchant ship called the *Mayflower* set sail from the port of Southampton with 102 passengers bound for the Americas. Of these passengers, 41 were Separatists, members of a renegade congregation that had broken away from the Church of England. These people considered themselves religious pilgrims. Before the pilgrims and the others left England, the group leaders wrote and signed a document that became the foundation of American democracy, the Mayflower Compact. It decreed a representative government.

Despite legend, the ship did not land at Plymouth Rock, but rather at the tip of Cape Cod, the site of modern Provincetown. After a little exploring, Plymouth

The landing of English pilgrims at Plymouth Rock in 1620 is traditionally considered the beginning of British North America. (Library of Congress)

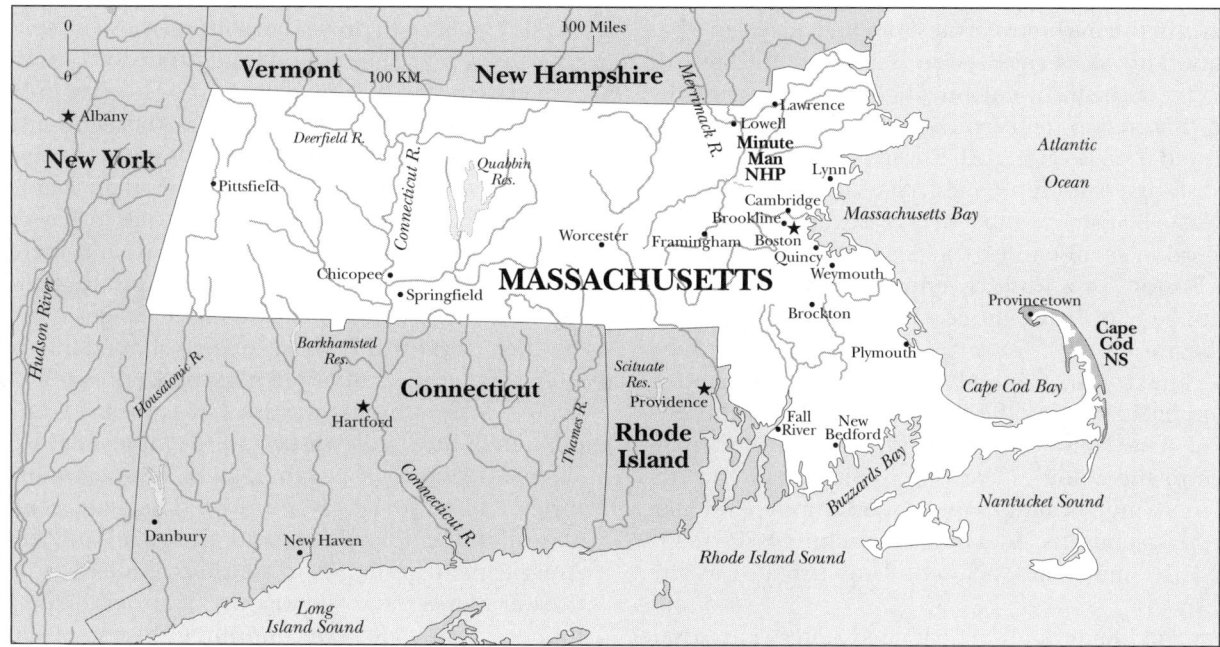

proved a better place to found a village. After the harsh winter of 1621, however, half the settlers were dead. Spring came, and the pilgrims met a Patuxet Indian named Squanto. Years earlier he had been captured by slave traders and sold in Spain. After escaping to England and becoming fluent in English, he made his way back to his homeland, only to find his tribe wiped out by disease. Squanto taught the pilgrims how to farm and served as an interpreter, making treaties with other tribes. After the first harvest in October, 1621, for three days the pilgrims hosted about ninety Native Americans in a feast. It became the first Thanksgiving, a tradition that would long be celebrated in the United States.

The colony began to prosper, and every year brought more colonists seeking religious freedom. In 1630, John Winthrop, with a charter for "The Governor and Company of the Massachusetts Bay in New England," landed at Salem with more than one thousand colonists. Winthrop and his followers did not want to separate from the church, but they believed it needed to be purified from within and thus were called Puritans. The Puritans felt the law must be strictly obeyed if the community were to be strong. A set of wooden stocks stood in the center of many towns, and wrongdoers were put there for crimes as small as swearing.

The Witch Trials. Ironically, while Winthrop and his followers left England to seek religious freedom, they had little tolerance of others' religious philosophies. During the 1660's, Puritan authorities hanged several Quakers as heretics. By 1692 this intolerance, mixed with superstition, turned into one of the New World's most shameful chapters, the Salem witch trials. Tituba, a West Indian slave woman, told locals tales of African magic. When some of the girls began to have fainting spells, they accused Tituba of casting spells over them. When Salem reverend Samuel Parris demanded to know who else had been practicing the evil arts, the girls started falsely accusing neighbors of witchery, and soon everyone was accusing everyone else. Nineteen men and women were burned as witches, and nearly 150 more were awaiting trail when authorities in Boston stopped the proceedings. Although the Puritans initiated an atmosphere of intolerance and fear in their society, they must also be remembered for their dedication to hard work and their respect for education; they founded Harvard, the first institution of higher learning in North America.

The American Revolution. By the mid-eighteenth century, Massachusetts was the center of shipbuilding and commerce in the British colonies. The people there were successful, well educated, and accustomed to managing their own affairs. The French and Indian War was won by the British, but at a great cost. To raise more money, Great Britain heavily taxed the colonies. The colonists were particularly upset about this because they were being taxed with no representation in Parliament: "No taxation without representation!" was the frequent cry of colonial protesters. The merchants of Boston led a boycott of British goods, and Britain responded by stationing troops in the city. One night in March of 1770, mounting tension exploded in a skirmish that became known as the Boston Massacre. Five were killed, the first being a young black man named Crispus Attucks.

On December 16, 1773, a group of Boston men crept aboard three British ships and dumped the tea cargoes in the harbor to protest the high taxes, in what became known as the Boston Tea Party. In April of 1775, the British, intent on quelling the patriots by force, planned to send armed men to Lexington, Concord, and then Boston. Paul Revere, among others, was able to warn the Minutemen, Massachusetts fighters. While the British were able to take Lexington and then Concord in small battles, the patriots were able to defend Boston for a while. Eventually, however, the city succumbed to British force. The Revolutionary War had begun.

The next year, General George Washington took Boston back, chasing the British out of Massachusetts forever. The Treaty of Paris of 1783 granted independence to the colonies. No other colony had contributed more men or money to the war for independence than Massachusetts. In 1788, Massachusetts formally joined the newly independent United States as the sixth state.

War and Immigration. The United States went to war with Britain again in 1812 for interfering with American trade, pirating U.S. ships, and forcing Americans to fight the British war with France. Boston, the largest American city of the time, suffered greatly. Boston developed industries to maintain the economy.

During the 1840's, the potato famine in Ireland sent more than one million Irish men and women to the United States, and hundreds of thousands settled in Massachusetts. They found work in the factories of Boston, Lawrence, Lowell, and Worcester. Many residents saw the flood of Irish Catholics as a threat to their Anglo-Protestant society. Discrimination against the Irish was prevalent, and it was not uncommon to see a Help Wanted sign include a No Irish Need Apply slogan. However, any labor was needed eventually as the state became a leader in the American Industrial Revolution. New mills producing textile, paper, boots, and shoes sprang up all over the state.

The Late Nineteenth Century. The Civil War began in 1861, and Massachusetts was the first state to respond, with a regiment of fifteen hundred soldiers. Throughout the war, the state supplied guns, uniforms, and boots to the Union army. When the war was over, the Irish, many of whom served in the war, began climbing the social ladder. They founded businesses, saved money, and bought their own homes. Still, they were discriminated against, and they looked to politics as a way to fight back. In 1880, Hugh O'Brien became Boston's first Irish mayor. In 1892, Patrick Joseph "P. J." Kennedy, son of an East Boston barrel maker, was elected to the state senate. Yet discrimination against the Irish, as well as all immigrants, continued.

During the 1880's and 1890's, fresh waves of immigrants poured in. In 1896, U.S. Senator Henry Cabot Lodge, a descendant of Boston's most elite families, sponsored a bill to restrict immigration. He claimed scientific evidence to prove that southern and eastern Europeans were racially inferior and prone to crime. It was vetoed by the U.S. president but signed into law in 1924.

Economic Hard Times. By 1900 Massachusetts was an industrial state, yet the large mills in the state would not always run smoothly. In 1912, more than twenty-two thousand textile workers staged a strike in Lawrence. There would be other labor problems, and men and women began to organize into unions to fight for better working conditions and higher wages.

After World War I, Massachusetts slipped into recession. When the country fell into the Depression of the 1930's, Massachusetts was hit hard. By 1931 only 44 percent of the state's workers were employed full-time. When World War II began in 1941, Massachusetts factories and shipyards rebounded. The state achieved almost full employment, and thousands of African Americans migrated from southern states to work in the war plants. After the war, the factories fell on hard times yet again. However, another industry, education, led by MIT and Harvard, proved to entice many great minds—and federal grants—to the state. Boston, meanwhile, emerged as a center for banking, insurance, and medicine.

The Kennedy Dynasty. Joseph Kennedy, the son of P. J. Kennedy, graduated from Harvard in 1912 and entered the world of banking. At twenty-five, he became the youngest bank president in the nation. He rose in stature and was eventually named ambassador to England. His political career was ruined, however, when he supported appeasement with German leader Adolf Hitler. Three of his nine children would fulfill his ambitions by going into politics.

In 1961, his son and Massachusetts senator John F. Kennedy became the first Irish Catholic president of the United States. He would not be allowed to finish out his term, however, and the nation grieved when the young president was assassinated in Dallas in 1963. His brother, Robert, was also killed when running for president, in 1968. Joseph Kennedy's youngest son, Edward "Ted" Kennedy, served in the U.S. Senate for many years, serving as the patriarch of the ill-fated family. Several of the next generation of Kennedys served in politics as well.

Great politicians and diversity continued to be strengths of the state. Michael S. Dukakis was the first Greek American to be elected governor, in 1972. He later won the Democratic nomination for U.S. president in 1988 but lost to George H. W. Bush.

Liberal Politics. Geographically small Massachusetts remained a major intellectual force in the nation, especially the area around Boston, where Harvard University, the Massachusetts Institute of Technology (MIT), and many other colleges and universities are located. Moreover, the state's representation in Congress, especially that of Senator Ted Kennedy, was a potent liberal

Now a picturesque resort region, Cape Cod is the actual site of the first pilgrim landing in 1620. (PhotoDisc)

influence in politics. The state's liberalism was manifest in May, 2004, as Massachusetts became the first state in the Union to issue official same-sex marriage licenses.

Massachusetts voters chose Vice President Al Gore for the state's twelve electoral votes in the 2000 presidential election. As expected, Senator Kennedy was reelected by a landslide margin, winning 73 percent of the vote. The state's voters declined to return a single Republican to Washington, as ten Democrats were reelected to the House of Representatives. Five of them ran unopposed. Similar electoral sentiment was apparent in 2002 and 2004, when Massachusetts's "favorite son," Democrat senator John Kerry, took the state's electoral votes for president by a lopsided 62-37 percent margin.

The liberal tradition suffered a hit in 2001, however, when Maxwell Kennedy, son of slain Senator Robert F. Kennedy, declined to run for public office. In another episode, which took place on May 4, 2006, Representative Patrick J. Kennedy, son of Ted and Joan Kennedy, crashed his car into a barricade on Capitol Hill at 2:45 A.M., after spending time in two bars. He later pleaded guilty to driving under the influence of prescription medicine.

The "Big Dig." The Central Artery/Tunnel Project, nicknamed the Big Dig, was designed to transform a limited-access highway running through the heart of Boston into a 3.5-mile tunnel. The project also included construction of a second tunnel and a bridge over the Charles River from Boston to Cambridge. Conceived during the 1970's, the project got underway officially in 1982, when planning began. Congress appropriated major funding in 1987, overriding President Ronald Reagan's veto. Work began in 1991, and by the end of 2004, it was 95 percent complete. Projected to cost $5.8 billion, its actual cost became more than $15 billion, the most expensive highway project in the nation's history.

The epic project spawned epic problems and scandals. Major obstacles delayed construction. Provision of substandard cement and evidence of doctored records led to arrests for those deemed responsible. In 2004, an official report found some four hundred leaks in the tunnels were found, but other sources said there were thousands. The city of Cambridge objected to the proposed bridge's design and sued. In 2006, the state demanded return of more than $100 million from companies accused of incompetence or worse.

On July 10, 2006, sections of the ceiling of a connector tunnel fell on a car, killing a passenger. The site of the collapse was treated as a crime scene and the possibility of criminal charges was suggested. The resignation of the state agency in charge of the project was demanded by the governor and others. A complete investigation into the safety of the entire project was also demanded.

"Curse of the Bambino" Broken. In 2004, the Boston Red Sox finally broke what had been called the "curse of the Bambino" and won baseball's World Series for the first time since 1918. For years it had been said that the team's fateful trade of George Herman "Babe" Ruth to the New York Yankees, where he blossomed into one of the greatest players in the game, had placed a curse on the team. Now, the team and its loyal followers in Boston and throughout the country, known as the Red Sox Nation, were free at last.

Kevin M. Mitchell
Updated by the Editor

Massachusetts Time Line

1620	*Mayflower* lands and begins settlement at Plymouth.
1621	Patuxet Indian named Squanto befriends the pilgrims and teaches them farming.
Oct., 1621	First Thanksgiving takes place.
1634	Boston Commons is established, making it the first city park in the nation.
1636	Harvard, America's first institution of higher learning, is founded.
1692	Salem witch trials begin, resulting in nineteen people being burned as witches.
Mar. 5, 1770	Five are killed, the first being Crispus Attucks, in Boston Massacre.
Dec. 16, 1773	Patriots sneak aboard a British cargo ship and dump tea into the harbor to protest the high taxes during the Boston Tea Party.
1775	First battle of the Revolutionary war occurs at Lexington; Paul Revere makes "midnight ride" to warn patriots.
1780	State constitution is adopted.
1783	Treaty of Paris is signed, ending the Revolutionary War and granting the thirteen colonies independence.
1783	Massachusetts abolishes slavery.
1786	Pelham farmer Daniel Shay leads an armed uprising protesting high taxes from Boston in Shay's Rebellion.
Feb. 6, 1788	Massachusetts, led by Samuel Adams and John Hancock, ratifies Constitution, becoming the sixth state.
1797	John Adams of Massachusetts becomes second president of the United States.
1815	Newburyport businessman Francis Cabot Lowell, inspired by England and Scotland's textile mills, opens the state's first mill at Waltham.
1825	John Quincy Adams, son of the second president, becomes the fifth president of the United States.
1829	Journalist William Lloyd Garrison begins publishing his antislavery newspaper, the *Liberator*, in Boston.
1832	Perkins Institute, the first school for the blind in the Union, is founded.
1881	Boston Symphony is founded.
1897	First Boston Marathon is held.
1908	P. J. Kennedy is elected to the state senate.
1912	More than twenty-two thousand textile workers stage a massive strike in Lawrence.
1919	Republican governor Calvin Coolidge sends in state police to restore order in the Boston Police strike.
1924	Newly installed U.S. president Coolidge signs into law Massachusetts senator Henry Cabot Lodge's bill limiting immigration.
1937	Joseph Kennedy is named ambassador to England, the first Irish American to represent the country in England's court.
1946	John F. Kennedy is elected to House of Representatives.
1956	Foster Furcolo becomes first Italian American governor of Massachusetts.
1966	Republican Edward Brooke is first black man elected U.S. senator in nearly a century.
1974	Federal judge orders Boston to start busing students in order to integrate its public schools, sparking years of turmoil.
July, 1999	John F. Kennedy, Jr., son of the slain president, is killed in a plane crash near Martha's Vineyard.
Sept. 11, 2001	Two jetliners from Boston's Logan Airport bound for California are hijacked by terrorists and crashed into the World Trade Center in Manhattan.

May, 2004   Massachusetts becomes first state to issue same-sex marriage licenses.
Oct. 27, 2004   Boston Red Sox win baseball's World Series for the first time since 1918.
Dec., 2004   Officials announce that 95 percent of Boston's Big Dig Project is complete.
Jul. 10, 2006   Sections of a tunnel ceiling in the Big Dig fall on automobile, killing one person.

Notes for Further Study

Published Sources. Those interested in learning about Massachusetts history will find a wealth of materials on all aspects of the state's early years. For short, informational histories, readers should consult *Massachusetts* (1998) by Sylvia McNair and *Massachusetts: From Sea to Shining Sea* (1994) by Dennis B. Fradin. *Massachusetts Bay Company and Its Predecessors* (1974) by Frances Rose-Troup offers an in-depth overview of the earliest European settlers and their trials and tribulations. *Massachusetts: A Concise History* (rev. and exp. ed., 2000) by Richard D. Brown and Jack Tager also provides a good overview of the state's history. Marcia Sewall's *The Pilgrims of Plymouth* (1996) chronicles in text and illustrations the day-to-day life of the early pilgrims of the Plymouth Colony. *Pilgrims and Puritans: 1620-1676* (1994) by Christopher Collier and James Lincoln Collier recounts the religious, political, and social history of the Massachusetts Bay Colony and its influence on modern life. Using as its basis the discovery of artifacts along what was once the colonists' line of defense at the northwest boundary of Massachusetts, Michael Coe's *The Line of Forts: Historical Archaeology on the Colonial Frontier of Mas-*

sachusetts (2006) weaves a narrative of eighteenth century American life. Although focused specifically on the Boston area, Jacqueline Barbara Carr's *After the Siege: A Social History of Boston, 1775-1800* (2005) allows the reader to discern the general aftereffects of the American Revolution and how state leaders attempted to bring the economy and daily life back to normalcy.

The Salem Witch Trials (1991) by Earle Rice covers the social, legal, and political realities surrounding the trials, as does *Salem Witch Trials: A Primary Source History of the Witchcraft Trials in Salem, Massachusetts* (2003) by Jenny Macbain. For a personal view of the American Revolution and such key events as the Tea Party and the Boston Massacre, a Boston shoemaker's account is available in *The Shoemaker and the Tea Party: Memory and the American Revolution* (1999), edited by Alfred F. Young. *Civil War Boston: Home Front and Battlefield* (1999) by Thomas H. O'Connor examines the dramatic ways that the Civil War affected Bostonians on the home front and discusses how residents contributed to the Union cause, focusing on businessmen, Irish Catholic immigrants, African

Harbor of Massachusetts's capital and largest city, Boston. (PhotoDisc)

Americans, and women. *The Boston Irish: A Political History* (1996), also by Thomas H. O'Connor, discusses how Irish political dominance in Boston grew out of generations of bitter and unyielding conflict between Yankees and Irish Catholic immigrants. Massachusetts political insider Richard A. Hogarty brings forth a discussion of the state's political arena, including the workings of the executive, legislative, and judicial branches, as well as the administrative bureaucracy, in *Massachusetts Politics and Public Policy: Studies in Power and Leadership* (2002). In *Extraordinary Tenure: Massachusetts and the Making of the Nation: From John Adams to Tip O'Neill* (2004) by Neil J. Savage, the lives and times of presidents, governors, senators, congress members, diplomats, and cabinet members who came out of Massachusetts to serve the interests of the nation are explored. There are a great deal of books available on the Kennedys, including *The Sins of the Father: Joseph P. Kennedy and the Dynasty He Founded* (1996) by Ronald Kessler.

Web Resources. There are many Massachusetts Internet sites, and those listed here often give valuable links to others. The state's official home page (www.mass.gov/) is a good launching point, providing comprehensive information about the state's government agencies, as well as information targeted to residents and visitors. Another good portal site is the Massachusetts home page (www.massachusetts.com), which lists a variety of sites, including links to all colleges and universities. A thorough overview of historical Massachusetts, as well as a Boston African American database, can be found at Massachusetts Historical Society (www.masshist.org/welcome/).

Massachusetts' early history can be accessed at Mayflower and Early Families (www.mayflowerfamilies.com/), the Massachusetts Bay Colony site (members.aol.com/ntgen/hrtg/mass.html), and the Wampanoag site (www.tolatsga.org/wampa.html). For information regarding the Salem witchcraft hysteria, visit Salem's city guide (www.salemweb.com/guide/witches.shtml), Destination Salem (www.salem.org/17th_Century.asp), and the University of Virginia's page about this period (etext.virginia.edu/salem/witchcraft/). The Kennedy Presidential Library and Museum, located in Boston, has a site (www.jfklibrary.org/) that is useful not only for learning more about the Kennedy political dynasty but also for keeping up with statewide travel information.

Counties

County	2000 pop.	Rank in pop.	Sq. miles	Rank in area
Barnstable	222,230	9	395.8	11
Berkshire	134,953	11	931.4	2
Bristol	534,678	6	556.0	7
Dukes	14,987	13	103.8	12
Essex	723,419	3	498.1	9
Franklin	71,535	12	702.1	4
Hampden	456,228	8	618.5	6
Hampshire	152,251	10	529.0	8

County	2000 pop.	Rank in pop.	Sq. miles	Rank in area
Middlesex	1,465,396	1	823.5	3
Nantucket	9,520	14	47.8	14
Norfolk	650,308	5	399.6	10
Plymouth	472,822	7	660.6	5
Suffolk	689,807	4	58.5	13
Worcester	750,963	2	1,513.2	1

Source: U.S. Census Bureau; National Association of Counties.

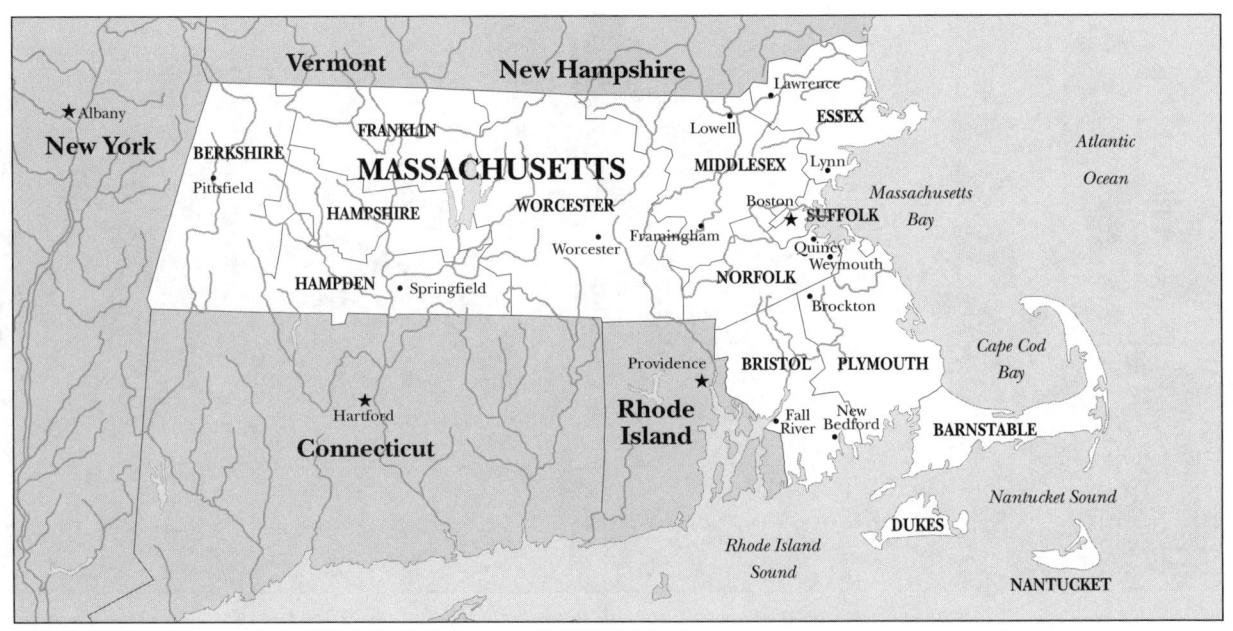

Cities
With 10,000 or more residents

Rank	City	Population	Rank	City	Population
1	Boston (capital)	589,141	56	Needham	28,911
2	Worcester	172,648	57	Tewksbury	28,851
3	Springfield	152,082	58	Norwood	28,587
4	Lowell	105,167	59	Dracut	28,562
5	Cambridge	101,355	60	Agawam	28,144
6	Brockton	94,304	61	West Springfield	27,899
7	New Bedford	93,768	62	North Andover	27,202
8	Fall River	91,938	63	Stoughton	27,149
9	Lynn	89,050	64	North Attleborough	27,143
10	Quincy	88,025	65	Melrose	27,134
11	Newton	83,829	66	Milford	26,799
12	Somerville	77,478	67	Wellesley	26,613
13	Lawrence	72,043	68	Saugus	26,078
14	Framingham	66,910	69	Milton	26,062
15	Waltham	59,226	70	Danvers	25,212
16	Haverhill	58,969	71	Bridgewater	25,185
17	Brookline	57,107	72	Yarmouth	24,807
18	Malden	56,340	73	Wakefield	24,804
19	Taunton	55,976	74	Marshfield	24,324
20	Medford	55,765	75	Belmont	24,194
21	Chicopee	54,653	76	Reading	23,708
22	Weymouth	53,988	77	Dedham	23,464
23	Plymouth	51,701	78	Burlington	22,876
24	Peabody	48,129	79	Walpole	22,824
25	Barnstable Town	47,821	80	Mansfield	22,414
26	Revere	47,283	81	Easton	22,299
27	Pittsfield	45,793	82	Stoneham	22,219
28	Methuen	43,789	83	Wilmington	21,363
29	Arlington	42,389	84	Ludlow	21,209
30	Attleboro	42,068	85	Winchester	20,810
31	Leominster	41,303	86	Canton	20,775
32	Salem	40,407	87	Gardner	20,770
33	Westfield	40,072	88	Westford	20,754
34	Beverly	39,862	89	Marblehead	20,377
35	Holyoke	39,838	90	Wareham	20,335
36	Fitchburg	39,102	91	Acton	20,331
37	Billerica	38,981	92	Sandwich	20,136
38	Everett	38,037	93	Middleborough	19,941
39	Woburn	37,258	94	Hingham	19,882
40	Marlborough	36,255	95	Bourne	18,721
41	Chelsea	35,080	96	Winthrop	18,303
42	Amherst	34,874	97	Somerset	18,234
43	Chelmsford	33,858	98	Norton	18,036
44	Braintree	33,698	99	Westborough	17,997
45	Watertown	32,986	100	Scituate	17,863
46	Falmouth	32,660	101	Rockland	17,670
47	Natick	32,170	102	Sharon	17,408
48	Shrewsbury	31,640	103	Southbridge	17,214
49	Andover	31,247	104	South Hadley	17,196
50	Randolph	30,963	105	Newburyport	17,189
51	Dartmouth	30,666	106	Amherst Center	17,050
52	Lexington	30,355	107	Concord	16,993
53	Gloucester	30,273	108	Pembroke	16,927
54	Franklin	29,560	109	Sudbury	16,841
55	Northampton	28,978	110	North Attleborough Center	16,796

(continued)

Rank	City	Population	Rank	City	Population
111	Webster	16,415	146	Belchertown	12,968
112	Foxborough	16,246	147	Mashpee	12,946
113	Fairhaven	16,159	148	Millbury	12,784
114	Easthampton	15,994	149	Bedford	12,595
115	Dennis	15,973	150	Palmer	12,497
116	Auburn	15,901	151	Medway	12,448
117	Swansea	15,901	152	Harwich	12,386
118	Longmeadow	15,633	153	Amesbury	12,327
119	Holden	15,621	154	Medfield	12,273
120	Bellingham	15,314	155	Kingston	11,780
121	Grafton	14,894	156	Raynham	11,739
122	North Adams	14,681	157	Spencer	11,691
123	Ashland	14,674	158	South Yarmouth	11,603
124	Abington	14,605	159	Lynnfield	11,542
125	Swampscott	14,412	160	Weston	11,469
126	Hudson	14,388	161	Athol	11,299
127	Duxbury	14,248	162	Charlton	11,263
128	Westport	14,183	163	Carver	11,163
129	Westwood	14,117	164	Uxbridge	11,156
130	East Longmeadow	14,100	165	Pepperell	11,142
131	Northborough	14,013	166	Tyngsborough	11,081
132	Whitman	13,882	167	Hull	11,050
133	North Reading	13,837	168	Holbrook	10,785
134	Holliston	13,801	169	Wrentham	10,554
135	Greenfield	13,716	170	Leicester	10,471
136	Wilbraham	13,473	171	Norfolk	10,460
137	Clinton	13,435	172	Maynard	10,433
138	Seekonk	13,425	173	Rehoboth	10,172
139	Oxford	13,352	174	Acushnet	10,161
140	Hopkinton	13,346	175	Brewster	10,094
141	Northbridge	13,182	176	Dudley	10,036
142	Hanover	13,164			
143	Wayland	13,100			
144	Ipswich	12,987			
145	East Bridgewater	12,974			

Population figures are from 2000 census.

Source: U.S. Bureau of the Census.

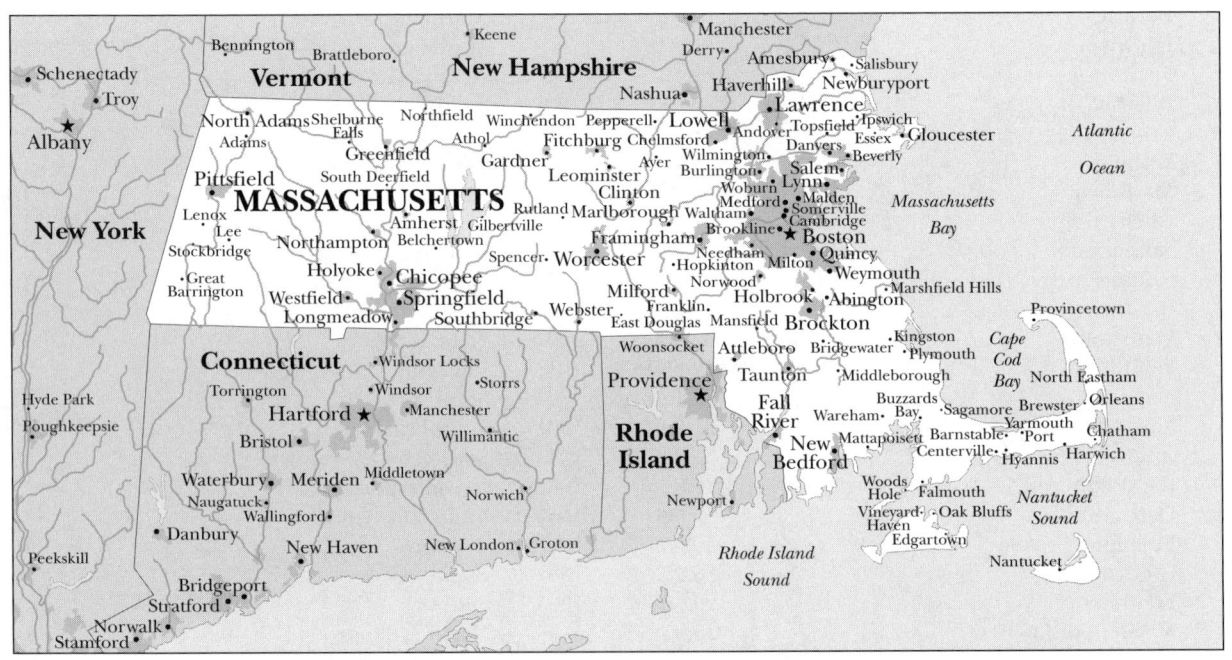

Index to Tables

DEMOGRAPHICS

Resident state and national populations, 1970-2004

Population figures given in thousands

	State pop.	U.S. pop.	Share	Rank
1970	5,689	203,302	2.8%	10
1980	5,737	226,546	2.5%	11
1985	5,881	237,924	2.5%	12
1990	6,016	248,765	2.4%	13
1995	6,141	262,761	2.3%	13
2000	6,349	281,425	2.3%	13
2004	6,417	293,655	2.2%	13

Source: U.S. Census Bureau, Current Population Reports, 2006.

Resident population by age, 2004

Age Group	Total persons
Under 5 years	396,000
5 to 17 years	1,069,000
18 to 24 years	598,000
25 to 34 years	880,000
35 to 44 years	1,030,000
45 to 54 years	937,000
55 to 64 years	652,000
65 to 74 years	396,000
75 to 84 years	322,000
85 years and older	136,000
All age groups	6,417,000

Portion of residents 65 and older	13.3%
National rank in portion of oldest residents	13
National average	12.4%

Population figures are rounded to nearest thousand persons;
  figures include armed forces personnel stationed in the state.
Source: U.S. Bureau of the Census, 2006.

Resident population by race, Hispanic origin, 2004

Category	State pop.	Share	U.S.
All residents	6,417	100.00%	100.00%
Non-Hispanic white	5,181	80.74%	67.37%
Hispanic white	400	6.23%	13.01%
Other Hispanic	94	1.46%	1.06%
African American	435	6.78%	12.77%
Native American	18	0.28%	0.96%
Asian, Pacific Islander	300	4.68%	4.37%
Two or more categories	83	1.29%	1.51%

Population figures are in thousands. Persons counted as "Hispanic" (Latino) may be of any race. Because of overlapping categories, categories may not add up to 100%. Shares in column 3 are percentages of each category within the state; these figures may be compared to the national percentages in column 4.
Source: U.S. Bureau of the Census, 2006.

Projected state population, 2000-2030

Year	Population
2000	6,349,000
2005	6,519,000
2010	6,649,000
2015	6,759,000
2020	6,856,000
2025	6,939,000
2030	7,012,000
Population increase, 2000-2030	663,000
Percentage increase, 2000-2030	10.4

Projections are based on data from the 2000 census.
Source: U.S. Census Bureau.

VITAL STATISTICS

Infant mortality rates, 1980-2002

	1980	1990	2000	2002
All state residents	10.5	7.0	4.6	4.9
All U.S. residents	12.6	9.2	9.4	9.1
All state white residents	10.1	6.1	4.0	4.5
All U.S. white residents	10.6	7.6	5.7	5.8
All state black residents	16.8	11.9	9.9	9.1
All U.S. black residents	22.2	18.0	14.1	14.4

Figures represent deaths per 1,000 live births of resident infants under 1 year old, exclusive of fetal deaths. Figures for all residents include members of other racial categories not listed separately.
Source: U.S. Census Bureau, *Statistical Abstract of the United States,* 2006.

Abortion rates, 1990 and 2000

	1990	2000
Total abortions	41,000	30,000
Rate per 1,000 women	28.1	21.4
U.S. rate	25.7	21.3
Rank	9	13

Numbers of abortions are rounded to nearest thousand; ranks are based on rates.
Source: U.S. Census Bureau.

Marriages and divorces, 2004

Total marriages	41,200
Rate per 1,000 population.	6.4
National rate per 1,000 population	7.4
Rank among all states	38
Total divorces	14,100
Rate per 1,000 population.	2.2
National rate per 1,000 population	3.7
Rank among all states	44

Figures are for all marriages and divorces performed within the state, including those of nonresidents; totals are rounded to the nearest hundred. Ranks are for highest to lowest figures; note that divorce data are not available for five states.
Source: U.S. National Center for Health Statistics, *Vital Statistics of the United States,* 2006.

Death rates by leading causes, 2002
Deaths per 100,000 resident population

Cause	State	U.S.
Heart disease	229.3	241.7
Cancer	216.5	193.2
Cerebrovascular diseases	55.4	56.4
Accidents other than motor vehicle	22.0	37.0
Motor vehicle accidents	8.8	15.7
Chronic lower respiratory diseases	42.7	43.3
Diabetes mellitus	22.1	25.4
HIV	3.6	4.9
Suicide	6.8	11.0
Homicide	2.9	6.1
All causes	885.7	847.3
Rank in overall death rate among states		23

Figures exclude nonresidents who died in the state. Causes of death follow International Classification of Diseases. Rank is from highest to lowest death rate in the United States.
Source: U.S. National Center for Health Statistics, *National Vital Statistics Report,* 2006.

ECONOMY

Gross state product, 1990-2004
In current dollars

Year	State product	Nat'l product	State share
1990	$158.9 billion	$5.67 trillion	2.80%
2000	$276.8 billion	$9.75 trillion	2.84%
2002	$287.2 billion	$10.41 trillion	2.76%
2003	$297.1 billion	$10.92 trillion	2.72%
2004	$317.7 billion	$11.65 trillion	2.73%

Source: U.S. Bureau of Economic Analysis, *Survey of Current Business,* July, 2005.

Gross state product by industry, 2003
In billions of dollars

Construction	$12.7
Manufacturing	38.0
Wholesale trade	17.5
Retail trade	17.5
Finance & insurance	33.2
Information	13.6
Professional services	27.7
Health care & social assistance	21.9
Government	23.3
Total state product	$284.3
Total U.S. product	$10,289.2
State share of U.S. total	2.76%
Rank among all states	12

Total figures include industries not listed separately. Amounts are in chained 2000 dollars.
Source: U.S. Bureau of Economic Analysis, *Survey of Current Business,* July, 2005.

Personal income per capita, 1990-2004
In current dollars

	1990	2000	2004
Per capita income	$23,043	$37,756	$41,801
U.S. average	$19,477	$29,845	$32,937
Rank among states	4	3	2

Source: U.S. Bureau of Economic Analysis, *Survey of Current Business,* April, 2005.

Energy consumption, 2001
In trillions of British thermal units (BTU), except as noted

Total energy consumption

Total state energy consumption	1,549
Total U.S. energy consumption	96,275
State share of U.S. total	1.61%
Rank among states	22

Per capita consumption (In millions of BTU)

Total state per capita consumption	242
Total U.S. per capita consumption	338
Rank among states	46

End-use sectors

Residential	461
Commercial	379
Industrial	261
Transportation	447

Sources of energy

Petroleum	762
Natural gas	364
Coal	109
Hydroelectric power	(z)
Nuclear electric power	54

Figures for totals include categories not listed separately.
  (z) Indicates less than 0.5 trillion BTU.
Source: U.S. Energy Information Administration, *State Energy Data Report,* 2001.

Nonfarm employment by sectors, 2004

Total	3,180,000
Construction	138,000
Manufacturing	314,000
Trade, transportation, utilities	573,000
Information	87,000
Finance, insurance, real estate	220,000
Professional & business services	449,000
Education & health services	582,000
Leisure, hospitality, arts, organizations	292,000
Other services, including repair & maintenance	116,000
Government	408,000

Figures are rounded to nearest thousand persons. "Total" includes mining and natural resources, not listed separately.
Source: U.S. Bureau of Labor Statistics, 2006.

Foreign exports, 1990-2004
In millions of dollars

Year	State	U.S.	State share
1990	9,501	394,045	2.41%
1996	14,524	624,767	2.32%
1997	16,526	688,896	2.40%
2000	20,514	712,055	2.62%
2003	18,663	724,006	2.76%
2004	21,837	769,332	2.84%

Rank among all states in 2004. 9

U.S. total does not include U.S. dependencies.
Source: U.S. Census Bureau, *U.S. Merchandise Trade,* series FT 900, 2000; U.S. Census Bureau, *U.S. International Trade in Goods and Services,* Series FT 900, 2005.

LAND USE

Federally owned land, 2003
Areas in acres

	State	U.S.	State share
Total area	5,035,000	2,271,343,000	0.22%
Nonfederal land	4,929,000	1,599,584,000	0.31%
Federal land	106,000	671,759,000	0.02%
Federal share	2.1%	29.6%	—

Areas are rounded to nearest thousand acres. Figures for federally owned land do not include trust properties.
Source: U.S. General Services Administration, *Federal Real Property Profile,* 2006.

Land use, 1997
In acres, rounded to nearest thousand

Total surface area.	5,339,000
Total nonfederal rural land	3,394,000
Percentage rural land	63.6%
Cropland	277,000
Conservation Reserve Program (CRP*) land	(nil)
Pastureland	119,000
Rangeland	(nil)
Forestland.	2,744,000
Other rural land	254,000

*CRP is a federal program begun in 1985 to assist private landowners to convert highly erodible cropland to vegetative cover for ten years. Note that some categories of land overlap.
Source: U.S. Department of Agriculture, Natural Resources and Conservation Service, and Iowa State University, Statistical Laboratory, *Summary Report, 1997 National Resources Inventory,* revised December, 2000.

Farms and crop acreage, 2004

	State	U.S.	Share	Rank
Farms	6,000	2,113,000	0.28%	42
Acres (millions)	1	937	0.11%	41
Acres per farm	85	443	—	48

Source: U.S. Department of Agriculture, National Agricultural Statistics Service. Numbers of farms are rounded to nearest thousand units; acreage figures are rounded to nearest million. Rankings, including ties, are based on rounded figures.

GOVERNMENT AND FINANCE

Units of local government, 2002

	State	Total U.S.	Rank
All local governments	841	87,525	33
Counties	5	3,034	46
Municipalities	45	19,429	44
Towns (townships)	306	16,504	15
School districts	82	13,506	36
Special districts	403	35,052	29

Only 48 states have county governments, 20 states have township governments ("towns" in New England, Minnesota, New York, and Wisconsin), and 46 states have school districts. Special districts encompass such functions as natural resources, fire protection, and housing and community development.
Source: U.S. Census Bureau, *Census of Governments.*

State government revenue, 2002

Total revenue	$26,885 mill.
General revenue	$26,476 mill.
Per capita revenue	$4,129
U.S. per capita average	$3,689
Rank among states.	8

Intergovernment revenue
Total	$5,431 mill.
From federal government	$5,061 mill.

Charges and miscellaneous
Total	$6,223 mill.
Current charges	$1,861 mill.
Misc. general income	$4,361 mill.
Insurance trust revenue	$297 mill.

Taxes
Total	$14,823 mill.
Per capita taxes	$2,308
Rank among states.	6
Property taxes.	$3 mill.
Sales taxes	$5,211 mill.
License taxes	$501 mill.
Individual income taxes	$7,913 mill.
Corporate income taxes	$812 mill.
Other taxes	$383 mill.

Total revenue figures include items not listed separately here.
Source: U.S. Bureau of the Census.

State government expenditures, 2002

General expenditures

Total state expenditures	$32,848 mill.
Intergovernmental	$6,284 mill.

Per capita expenditures

State	$4,433
Average of all states	$3,859
Rank among states	13

Selected direct expenditures

Education	$3,188 mill.
Public welfare	$5,665 mill.
Health, hospital	$2,399 mill.
Highways	$2,628 mill.
Police protection	$287 mill.
Corrections	$900 mill.
Natural resources	$243 mill.
Parks and recreation	$89 mill.
Government administration	$1,268 mill.
Interest on debt	$2,687 mill.
Total direct expenditures	$22,187 mill.

Totals include items not listed separately.
Source: U.S. Census Bureau.

POLITICS

Governors since statehood

D = Democrat; R = Republican; O = other;
(r) resigned; (d) died in office; (i) removed from office;
(a) acting

John Hancock	(r) 1780-1785
Thomas Cushing	1785
James Bowdoin	1785-1787
John Hancock	(d) 1787-1793
Samuel Adams (O)	1793-1797
Increase Sumner (O)	(d) 1797-1799
Moses Gill (O)	(d) 1799-1800
Thomas Dawes (O)	1800
Caleb Strong (O)	1800-1807
James Sullivan (O)	(d) 1807-1808
Levi Lincoln (O)	1808-1809
Christopher Gore (O)	1809-1810
Elbridge Gerry (O)	1810-1812
Caleb Strong (O)	1812-1816
John Brooks (O)	1816-1823
William Eustis (O)	(d) 1823-1825
Marcus Morton (O)	1825
Levi Lincoln, Jr. (O)	1825-1834
John Davis (O)	(r) 1834-1835
Samuel T. Armstrong (O)	1835-1836
Edward Everett (O)	1836-1840
Marcus Morton (D)	1840-1841
John Davis (O)	1841-1843
Marcus Morton (D)	1843-1844
George N. Briggs (O)	1844-1851
George S. Boutwell (D)	1851-1853
John H. Clifford (O)	1853-1854
Emory Washburn (O)	1854-1855
Henry J. Gardner (O)	1855-1858
Nathaniel P. Banks (R)	1858-1861
John A. Andrew (R)	1861-1866
Alexander H. Bullock (R)	1866-1869
William Claflin (R)	1869-1872
William B. Washburn (R)	(r) 1872-1874
William Talbot (R)	1874-1875
William Gaston (D)	1875-1876
Alexander H. Rice (R)	1876-1879
Thomas Talbot (R)	1879-1880
John D. Long (R)	1880-1883
Benjamin F. Butler (D)	1883-1884
George D. Robinson (R)	1884-1887
Oliver Ames (R)	1887-1890
John Q. A. Brackett (R)	1890-1891
William E. Russell (D)	1891-1894
Frederic T. Greenhalge (R)	(d) 1894-1896
Roger Wolcott (R)	1896-1900
Winthrop Murray Crane (R)	1900-1903
John L. Bates (R)	1903-1905
William L. Douglas (D)	1905-1906
Curtis Guild, Jr. (R)	1906-1909
Eben S. Draper (R)	1909-1911
Eugene N. Foss (D)	1911-1914
David T. Walsh (D)	1914-1916
Samuel W. McCall (R)	1916-1919
Calvin Coolidge (R)	1919-1921
Channing H. Cox (R)	1921-1925
Alvan T. Fuller (R)	1925-1929
Frank G. Allen (R)	1929-1931
Joseph B. Ely (D)	1931-1935
James M. Curley (D)	1935-1937
Charles F. Hurley (D)	1937-1939
Leverett Saltonstall (R)	1939-1945
Maurice J. Tobin (D)	1945-1947
Robert F. Bradford (R)	1947-1949
Paul A. Dever (D)	1949-1953
Christian A. Herter (R)	1953-1957
Foster Furcolo (D)	1957-1961
John A. Volpe (R)	1961-1963
Endicott Peabody (D)	1963-1965
John A. Volpe (R)	(r) 1965-1969
Francis W. Sargent (R)	1969-1975
Michael S. Dukakis (D)	1975-1979
Edward J. King (D)	1979-1983
Michael S. Dukakis (D)	1983-1991
William Weld (R)	(r) 1991-1997
Argeo Paul Cellucci (R)	(a) 1997-2001
Jane Swift (R)	(a) 2001-2003
W. Mitt Romney (R)	2003-2007
Deval Patrick (D)	2007-

Composition of congressional delegations, 1989-2007

	Dem	Rep	Total
House of Representatives			
101st Congress, 1989			
State delegates	10	1	11
Total U.S.	259	174	433
102d Congress, 1991			
State delegates	10	1	11
Total U.S.	267	167	434
103d Congress, 1993			
State delegates	8	2	10
Total U.S.	258	176	434
104th Congress, 1995			
State delegates	10	0	10
Total U.S.	197	236	433
105th Congress, 1997			
State delegates	10	0	10
Total U.S.	206	228	434
106th Congress, 1999			
State delegates	10	0	10
Total U.S.	211	222	433
107th Congress, 2001			
State delegates	10	0	10
Total U.S.	211	221	432
108th Congress, 2003			
State delegates	10	0	10
Total U.S.	205	229	434
109th Congress, 2005			
State delegates	10	0	10
Total U.S.	202	231	433
110th Congress, 2007			
State delegates	10	0	10
Total U.S.	233	202	435
Senate			
101st Congress, 1989			
State delegates	2	0	2
Total U.S.	55	45	100
102d Congress, 1991			
State delegates	2	0	2
Total U.S.	56	44	100
103d Congress, 1993			
State delegates	2	0	2
Total U.S.	57	43	100
104th Congress, 1995			
State delegates	2	0	2
Total U.S.	46	53	99
105th Congress, 1997			
State delegates	2	0	2
Total U.S.	45	55	100

	Dem	Rep	Total
106th Congress, 1999			
State delegates	2	0	2
Total U.S.	45	54	99
107th Congress, 2001			
State delegates	2	0	2
Total U.S.	50	50	100
108th Congress, 2003			
State delegates	2	0	2
Total U.S.	48	51	99
109th Congress, 2005			
State delegates	2	0	2
Total U.S.	44	55	99
110th Congress, 2007			
State delegates	2	0	2
Total U.S.	49	49	98

Figures are for starts of first sessions. Totals are for Democrat (Dem.) and Republican (Rep.) members only. House membership totals under 435 and Senate totals under 100 reflect vacancies and seats held by independent party members. When the 110th Congress opened, the Senate's two independent members caucused with the Democrats, giving the Democrats control of the Senate.

Source: U.S. Congress, Congressional Directory.

Composition of state legislature, 1990-2006

	Democrats	Republicans
State House (160 seats)		
1990	118	37
1992	123	34
1994	125	34
1996	134	25
1998	130	27
2000	131	27
2002	136	23
2004	136	21
2006	141	19
State Senate (40 seats)		
1990	25	15
1992	31	9
1994	30	10
1996	34	6
1998	33	7
2000	33	7
2002	34	6
2004	34	6
2006	35	5

Figures for total seats may include independents and minor party members. Numbers reflect results of elections in listed years; elected members usually take their seats in the years that follow.

Source: Council of State Governments; State Elective Officials and the Legislatures.

Voter participation in presidential elections, 2000 and 2004

	2000	2004
Voting age population		
State	4,864,000	4,952,000
Total United States	209,831,000	220,377,000
State share of U.S. total	2.32	2.25
Rank among states	13	13
Portion of voting age population casting votes		
State	56.2%	59.1%
United States	50.3%	55.5%
Rank among states	17	21

Population figures are rounded to nearest thousand and include all residents, regardless of eligibility to vote.
Source: U.S. Census Bureau.

HEALTH AND MEDICAL CARE

Medical professionals
Physicians in 2003 and nurses in 2001

	U.S.	State
Physicians in 2003		
Total	774,849	28,474
Share of U.S. total		3.66%
Rate	266	443
Rank		1
Nurses in 2001		
Total	2,262,020	75,580
Share of U.S. total		3.34%
Rate	793	1,181
Rank		1

Rates are numbers of physicians and nurses per 100,000 resident population; ranks are based on rates.
Source: American Medical Association, *Physician Characteristics and Distribution in the U.S.*; U.S. Department of Health and Human Services, Health Resources and Services Administration.

Health insurance coverage, 2003

	State	U.S.
Total persons covered	5,685,000	243,320,000
Total persons not covered	682,000	44,961,000
Portion not covered	10.7%	15.6%
Rank among states	43	—
Children not covered	118,000	8,373,000
Portion not covered	7.9%	11.4%
Rank among states	38	—

Totals are rounded to nearest thousand. Ranks are from the highest to the lowest percentages of persons *not* insured.
Source: U.S. Census Bureau, Current Population Reports.

AIDS, syphilis, and tuberculosis cases, 2003

Disease	U.S. cases	State cases	Rank
AIDS	44,232	757	16
Syphilis	34,270	644	15
Tuberculosis	14,874	261	14

Source: U.S. Centers for Disease Control and Prevention.

Cigarette smoking, 2003
Residents over age 18 who smoke

	U.S.	State	Rank
All smokers	22.1%	19.2%	44
Male smokers	24.8%	20.0%	44
Female smokers	20.3%	18.4%	38

Cigarette smokers are defined as persons who reported having smoked at least 100 cigarettes during their lifetimes and who currently smoked at least occasionally.
Source: U.S. Centers for Disease Control and Prevention, *Morbidity and Mortality Weekly Report,* 53, no. 44 (November 12, 2004).

HOUSING

Home ownership rates, 1985-2004

	1985	1990	1995	2000	2004
State	60.5%	58.6%	60.2%	59.9%	63.8%
Total U.S.	63.9%	63.9%	64.7%	67.4%	69.0%
Rank among states	45	44	45	47	46

Net change in state home ownership rate,
1985-2004 . . . . +3.3%
Net change in U.S. home ownership rate,
1985-2004 . . . . +5.1%

Percentages represent the proportion of owner households to total occupied households.
Source: U.S. Census Bureau, 2006.

Home sales, 2000-2004
In thousands of units

Existing home sales	2000	2002	2003	2004
State sales	112.3	115.9	118.3	141.7
Total U.S. sales	5,171	5,631	6,183	6,784
State share of U.S. total	2.17%	2.06%	1.91%	2.09%
Sales rank among states	14	18	20	17

Units include single-family homes, condos, and co-ops.
Source: National Association of Realtors, Washington, D.C., *Real Estate Outlook: Market Trends & Insights.*

Values of owner-occupied homes, 2003

	State	U.S.
Total units	1,259,000	58,809,000
Value of units		
Under $100,000	3.5%	29.6%
$100,000-199,999	19.9%	36.9%
$200,000 or more	76.7%	33.5%
Median value	$309,736	$142,275
Rank among all states 3		

Units are owner-occupied one-family houses whose numbers are rounded to nearest thousand. Data are extrapolated from survey samples.
Source: U.S. Census Bureau, American Community Survey.

EDUCATION

Public school enrollment, 2002

Prekindergarten through grade 8
State enrollment 701,000
Total U.S. enrollment. 34,135,000
State share of U.S. total 2.05%

Grades 9 through 12
State enrollment 282,000
Total U.S. enrollment. 14,067,000
State share of U.S. total 2.00%

Enrollment rates
State public school enrollment rate. 90.2%
Overall U.S. rate 90.4%
Rank among states in 2002. 29
Rank among states in 1995. 34

Enrollment figures (which include unclassified students) are rounded to nearest thousand pupils during fall school term. Enrollment rates are based on enumerated resident population estimate for July 1, 2002.
Source: U.S. National Center for Education Statistics.

Public college finances, 2003-2004

FTE enrollment in public institutions of higher education
Students in state institutions 137,500
Students in all U.S. public institutions 9,916,600
State share of U.S. total 1.39
Rank among states 26

State and local government appropriations for higher education
State appropriation per FTE $7,021
National average. $5,716
Rank among states. 9
State & local tax revenue going to higher
education 4.8%

FTE = full-time equivalent in public postsecondary programs, including summer sessions; student numbers are rounded to nearest hundred. Funding figures for 2003-2004 academic year include financial aid to students in state public institutions and exclude money for research, agriculture experiment stations, teaching hospitals, and medical schools; figures are rounded to nearest thousand dollars.
Source: Higher Education Executive Officers, Denver, Colorado.

TRANSPORTATION AND TRAVEL

Highway mileage, 2003

Interstate highways 569
Other freeways and expressways 288
Arterial roads 6,188
Collector roads 4,836
Local roads. 23,709
Urban roads 27,681
Rural roads 7,909
Total state mileage. 35,590
U.S. total 3,974,107
State share 0.90%
Rank among states 39

Note that combined urban and rural road mileage matches the total of the other categories.
Source: U.S. Federal Highway Administration.

Motor vehicle registrations and driver licenses, 2003

Vehicle registrations	State	U.S.	Share	Rank
Autos, trucks, buses	5,479,000	231,390,000	2.37%	14
Autos only	3,615,000	135,670	2.66%	13
Motorcycles	130,000	5,328,000	2.44%	16
Driver licenses	4,646,000	196,166,000	2.37%	13

Figures, which do not include vehicles owned by military services, are rounded to the nearest thousand. Figures for automobiles include taxis.
Source: U.S. Federal Highway Administration.

Domestic travel expenditures, 2003
Spending by U.S. residents on overnight trips and
day trips of at least 50 miles from home

Total expenditures within state . . . . $9.95 bill.
Total expenditures within U.S. . . . . $490.87 bill.
State share of U.S. total 2.0%
Rank among states 15

Source: Travel Industry Association of America.

Retail gasoline prices, 2003-2007
Average price per gallon at the pump

Year	U.S.	State
2003	$1.267	$1.282
2004	$1.316	$1.309
2005	$1.644	$1.582
2007	$2.298	$2.299

Excise tax per gallon in 2004 . . . . 21.0¢
Rank among all states in 2007 prices 22

Prices are averages of all grades of gasoline sold at the pump
during March months in 2003-2005 and during February, 2007.
Averages for 2006, during which prices rose higher, are not
available.
Source: U.S. Energy Information Agency, *Petroleum Marketing
Monthly* (2003-2005 data); American Automobile Association
(2007 data).

CRIME AND LAW ENFORCEMENT

State and local police officers, 2000-2004

	2000	2002	2004
Total officers			
U.S.	654,601	665,555	675,734
State	16,609	16,425	16,124*
*Net change, 2000-2004			−2.92%
Officers per 1,000 residents			
U.S.	2.33	2.31	2.30
State	2.62	2.58	2.51
State rank	7	8	12

Totals include state and local police and sheriffs.
Source: Carsey Institute, University of New Hampshire.

Crime rates, 2003
Incidents per 100,000 residents

Crimes	State	U.S.
Violent crimes		
Total incidents	469	475
Murder	2	6
Forcible rape	28	32
Robbery	124	142
Aggravated assault	315	295
Property crimes		
Total incidents	2,550	3,588
Burglary	540	741
Larceny/theft	1,613	2,415
Motor vehicle theft	397	433
All crimes	3,019	4,063

Source: U.S. Federal Bureau of Investigation, *Crime in the United
States*, annual.

State prison populations, 1980-2003

	State	U.S.	State share
1980	3,185	305,458	1.04%
1990	8,345	708,393	1.18%
1996	11,796	1,025,624	1.15%
2000	10,722	1,391,261	0.77%
2003	10,232	1,470,045	0.70%

State figures exclude prisoners in federal penitentiaries.
Source: U.S. Bureau of Justice Statistics, *Prisoners in 2003*.

Michigan

Location: Upper Midwest

Area and rank: 58,110 square miles (150,504 square kilometers); 96,810 square miles (250,738 square kilometers) including water; twenty-first largest state in area

Coastline: none

Population and rank: 10,113,000 (2004); eighth largest state in population

Capital city: Lansing (119,128 people in 2000 census)

Largest city: Detroit (951,270 people in 2000 census)

Became territory: January 11, 1805

State capitol building in Lansing. (Travel Michigan)

Entered Union and rank: January 26, 1837; twenty-sixth state

Present constitution adopted: April 1, 1963 (effective January 1, 1964)

Counties: 83

State name: "Michigan" comes from the Indian word "Michigana," meaning "great or large lake"

State nickname: Wolverine State

Motto: *Si quaeris peninsulam amoenam circumspice* (If you seek a pleasant peninsula, look around you)

State flag: Blue field with state coat of arms

Highest point: Mount Arvon—1,979 feet (603 meters)

Lowest point: Lake Erie—571 feet (174 meters)

Highest recorded temperature: 112 degrees Fahrenheit (44 degrees Celsius)—Mio, 1936

Lowest recorded temperature: –51 degrees Fahrenheit (–46 degrees Celsius)—Vanderbilt, 1934

State song: "Michigan, My Michigan"

State tree: White pine

State flower: Apple blossom

State bird: Robin

State fish: Trout; brook trout

National parks: Isle Royale

Michigan History

Michigan's abundant natural resources and access to major waterways, including four of the five Great Lakes, have made it an important area of human activity for more than ten thousand years. The unique geographic situation of Michigan, with the state divided into two separate land masses, has had a profound influence on its history. The southern land mass, known as the Lower Peninsula, developed into a heavily populated area of agriculture, forestry, and industry. The northern land mass, known as the Upper Peninsula, remained sparsely populated but provided important mineral resources.

Early History. The first inhabitants of the region hunted and fished about eleven thousand years ago. They also made tools from copper found in the Upper Peninsula. This is the earliest known use of metal in the New World. About three thousand years ago, agriculture began to develop in the southwestern part of the Lower Peninsula.

By the time Europeans arrived in North America, Michigan was primarily inhabited by Native Americans belonging to the Algonquian language group. These peoples included the Ottawa, the Ojibwa, the Miami, and the Potawatomi, mostly living in the northern regions. In the south lived the Huron, a Native American tribe belonging to the Iroquois language group. During the middle of the seventeenth century, conflict with other Iroquois peoples to the east drove the Huron and the Ottawa westward. At about the same time, the development of the French fur trade led many Native Americans in northern Michigan to move south.

Exploration and Settlement. The first European known to have visited the area was Étienne Brulé, who reached the Upper Peninsula from Canada in 1622. Another French explorer, Jean Nicolet, traveled through the narrow strait that separates the two peninsulas in 1634 during a journey from Canada to Wisconsin. The earliest permanent European settlements, located in the Upper Peninsula, were founded by the French missionary Jacques Marquette at Sault Sainte Marie in 1668 and St. Ignace in 1671. During the late seventeenth and early eighteenth centuries, several French missionary, fur trading, and military posts were established on both peninsulas. In 1701, Detroit was founded by Antoine Laumet de La Mothe, sieur de Cadillac. It soon became the most important French settlement in the Great Lakes region.

During the French and Indian War, a struggle between France and England for control of North America, Detroit was surrendered to the British in 1760. After the war, control of the region went to Great Britain.

Fearful that the British would bring many more settlers to the area, many Native Americans united under the Ottawa leader Pontiac. After capturing several British forts in the area, Pontiac's forces laid siege to Detroit for nearly six months in 1763. Pontiac was forced to abandon the siege in October, and the British remained in control.

Steps to Statehood. Although the end of the American Revolution officially brought the area under American control, the British did not leave Detroit and other military posts until 1796. Michigan was part of the Northwest Territory from 1787 to 1800, when it became part of the newly created Indiana Territory. The Michigan Territory was created in 1805. In the same year, a fire destroyed several buildings in Detroit.

After being rebuilt, Detroit was an important military objective in the War of 1812, a conflict between the United States and England. Detroit was captured by the British in August of 1812 but recaptured in September of 1813. Control of the Great Lakes region was restored to the United States the same month, when American naval forces commanded by Oliver Hazard Perry defeated the British in the Battle of Lake Erie.

Michigan began growing quickly after the war. Settlement was encouraged by the beginning of steamship transportation on Lake Erie from Buffalo to Detroit. The completion of the Erie Canal in 1825, linking the Hudson River to Lake Erie, also led to rapid population growth. From 1820 to 1840, the number of settlers, mostly from eastern states, increased from less than 9,000 to more than 200,000. During this time, many Native Americans gave up their lands or were forced to leave. However, some remained on reservations that still exist.

Michigan reached the population of sixty thousand required for statehood as early as 1833. Before statehood could be approved by Congress, however, a border dispute arose between Michigan and Ohio. Ohio claimed lands in the southeastern part of the Michigan Territory. In the Toledo War of 1835, Michigan militia prevented Ohio officials from occupying the area. Michigan eventually gave up the disputed region in return for a large increase in the size of its lands in the Upper Peninsula. It became the twenty-sixth state in 1837.

Economic Development. Despite an economic depression during the late 1830's, Michigan experienced rapid growth in the two decades after statehood. Many of the new residents were immigrants from Germany, Ireland, and the Netherlands. The vast majority of settlers were drawn to Michigan by the rich, productive soil found in the southern part of the Lower Peninsula.

During the 1850's, about 85 percent of the population was involved in agriculture.

The pine forests of the northern part of the Lower Peninsula and the mineral resources of the Upper Peninsula were also important parts of the state's economy. Iron, copper, and salt deposits began to be mined during the 1840's. Immigrants from Finland and Cornwall, a region of southwestern England, were involved in the development of the mining industry. An important stimulus to economic growth in the Upper Peninsula was the completion in 1855 of a series of locks at Sault Sainte Marie which allowed ships to travel from Lake Huron to Lake Superior. The growing importance of the northern regions of the state was a factor in the decision to move the capital from Detroit to Lansing in 1847.

Republicans and the Civil War. The Democratic Party dominated Michigan politics from before state-

hood until the national crisis over slavery during the 1850's. In 1854, antislavery members of the Democratic Party joined with members of the Whig Party and the Free-Soil Party to form the Republican Party in Jackson. The new party would dominate Michigan politics for the next eight decades.

During the Civil War about ninety thousand residents of Michigan fought for the Union, and around fourteen thousand were killed. Among the forces representing Michigan was a regiment of African Americans drawn from several states.

The Rise of Industry. The late nineteenth century saw the beginnings of modern manufacturing in Michigan. Grand Rapids became a center of furniture making. Kalamazoo dominated the paper industry. The Dow Chemical Company and the Upjohn Company made the chemical and pharmaceutical industries an important part of the state's economy. Perhaps the most distinctive industry to arise in Michigan at this time was the manufacture of breakfast cereal. This industry, which grew out of health resorts in the state that developed these products as part of a vegetarian diet, is centered in the city of Battle Creek.

By far the most important industry in Michigan during the twentieth century was automobile manufacturing. The industry began in 1901, when Ransom Eli Olds began marketing the Oldsmobile, the first successful American automobile. Inspired by this success, other automobile manufacturing companies soon appeared in the state. Henry Ford organized the Ford Motor Company in 1903 and began manufacturing the highly successful Model T in 1908. The same year, William C. Durant created the General Motors Corporation. Walter P. Chrysler founded the Chrysler Corporation in 1925. These and many other companies made the cities of Detroit, Flint, Pontiac, and Lansing dominant in the automobile industry.

The Twentieth Century. During the late nineteenth and early twentieth centuries, large numbers of immigrants from Ireland, Italy, Poland, and other European nations entered the state. At about the same time, African Americans from southern states began to arrive in large numbers. From 1900 to the late twentieth century, the number of African Americans in the state rose from less than sixteen thousand to well over one million. In the last few decades of the century, immigrants also arrived from Latin America, Asia, and the Middle East.

The Great Depression of the 1930's devastated the automobile industry. By 1932 half the industrial workers in Michigan were unemployed. This crisis ended the dominance of the Republican Party in the state. It also made organized labor an important force in Michigan. The entire automobile industry was unionized by the United Automobile Workers by 1941.

World War II revitalized industry in the state as automobile manufacturers turned to making military vehicles. Prosperity continued from the end of the war until the nationwide recession of the 1980's, which brought much higher unemployment to Michigan than to most other states. During the late 1980's and 1990's, the state made efforts to lessen its economic dependence on the

Ford Motor Company's Model T factory at Highland Park, Michigan, where assembly-line production began in 1913. (Library of Congress)

Renaissance Center in Michigan's largest city, Detroit. (Travel Michigan)

automobile industry, particularly by developing technological industries and tourism.

Economic Setbacks. As the twenty-first century neared, Michigan endured economic reverses in a mainstay of its economy, the automobile industry. In 2000, General Motors closed its production of Oldsmobiles, the oldest automobile make in the nation, with the loss of fifteen thousand jobs. The following year, DaimlerChrysler, a German-owned successor to the Chrysler Corporation, announced the closing of a Michigan plant and the layoff of twenty thousand workers in the process. In 2002, the Ford Motor Company announced the closing of five of its forty-four plants in North America.

Michigan was among the states losing jobs. Altogether, Ford laid off 10 percent of its workforce. The company also announced that it was discontinuing several of its models, including well-known cars such as the Ford Escort and the Lincoln Continental. At the same time, General Motors said it would lay off thousands more workers. Given such economic conditions, there was little surprise that, according to the 2000 census,

Michigan's population did not keep up national trends of population increase. As a result, the state lost one member of Congress.

Electoral Trends. In the 2000 presidential election, Michigan cast its eighteen electoral votes for Vice President Al Gore over Texas governor George W. Bush by a 51-47 percent margin. Democrats also took five seats in the Michigan state senate that were previously held by Republicans. Moreover, in the race for U.S. senator, Democrat Deborah Ann Stabenow unseated her Republican opponent, Senator Spencer Abraham, by 50 to 49 percent in a closely watched race. A Republican, however, took Stabenow's seat in the House.

In 2002, voters reelected Democrat Carl Levin to the U.S. Senate, but Republicans returned two new members to Congress. In the race for the statehouse, Democrat Jennifer Granholm, Michigan's attorney general, beat the state's Republican lieutenant governor to become the state's first female elected governor.

In 2004, Michigan again chose a Democrat to receive its electoral votes, as Senator John Kerry carried the state by a 51-48 percent margin. All fourteen incumbents were reelected, and a Republican victory in the fifteenth race retained a Republican seat when its holder retired.

Affirmative Action. Two University of Michigan lawsuits in 2003 (*Grutter v. Bollinger* and *Gratz v. Bollinger*) were important both for the state and for the nation. In December, 2000, a federal judge upheld a challenge to the University of Michigan's use of race in its admissions policies, which awarded undergraduate applicants points (20 points in a total of 150) for racial criteria. This policy differed from a previous policy of racial quotas that had been outlawed by the U.S. Supreme Court. When the case was appealed in 2003, the U.S. Supreme Court denied the validity of awarding such points since the policy did not use race in a "narrowly tailored" way. However, in a separate case decided the same day involving University of Michigan law school admissions, the Court, while continuing to ban admission quotas, upheld the use of race as a "plus" for applicants as individuals because the law school had a compelling state interest in attaining a diverse student body. The Court did ban any "mechanical" application of race that fails to consider each applicant as an individual.

Rose Secrest
Updated by the Editor

Michigan Time Line

1622	French explorer Étienne Brulé reaches the Upper Peninsula.
1634	Jean Nicolet journeys between the Upper and Lower Peninsulas.
1668	Father Jacques Marquette founds Sault Sainte Marie.
1671	Marquette founds St. Ignace.
July 24, 1701	Antoine Laumet de La Mothe, sieur de Cadillac, founds Detroit.
Nov. 29, 1760	Detroit surrenders to the British during the French and Indian War.
1763	Native American forces under Pontiac unsuccessfully lay siege to Detroit; end of the war brings the area under British control.
1783	End of the American Revolution brings the area under American control.
1787	Michigan becomes part of the Northwest Territory;
July 11, 1796	British leave Detroit.
1800	Michigan becomes part of the Indiana Territory.
Jan. 11, 1805	Michigan Territory is created with Detroit as the capital.
1805	Fire devastates Detroit.
1806	First post office in the state is established in Detroit.
Aug. 16, 1812	Detroit surrenders to the British during the War of 1812.
1813	Detroit is recaptured by the United States; Michigan returns to American control after the defeat of the British in the Battle of Lake Erie.
1818	Steamship travel begins between Buffalo and Detroit.
1820	Number of settlers reaches nearly nine thousand.
1825	Opening of the Erie Canal allows water transportation from New York City to Detroit.
1833	Population reaches sixty thousand.
1835	Toledo War, a border dispute between Michigan and Ohio, breaks out.
1836	First railroad is completed, linking Toledo and Arian.
Jan. 26, 1837	Michigan is admitted to the Union as the twenty-sixth state.
1837	University of Michigan is founded at Ann Arbor.
1840	Population reaches more than 200,000.
May 18, 1846	Michigan is first state to abolish the death penalty.
1847	Capital is moved to Lansing.
1854	Republican Party is founded at a convention in Jackson.
1855	Locks are completed at Sault Sainte Marie, linking Lake Huron and Lake Superior.
1901	Ransom Eli Olds begins selling the Oldsmobile.
1903	Henry Ford founds the Ford Motor Company.
1908	Ford begins manufacturing the Model T; William C. Durant founds the General Motors Corporation.
1914	Auto industry is responsible for 37 percent of state's manufacturing.
1920	For the first time, a majority of Michigan residents live in cities.

1925	Walter P. Chrysler founds the Chrysler Corporation.
1926	Commercial air travel from Detroit begins.
1932	Half of the state's industrial workers are unemployed due to the Great Depression.
1941	United Automobile Workers unionize the entire automobile industry.
June 20-21, 1943	Race riot breaks out in Detroit, leaving thirty-four dead.
1957	Mackinac Bridge connects the Upper and Lower Peninsulas.
1963	New state constitution is the first in the nation to create a Department of Civil Rights.
July 21-23, 1967	Race riot occurs in Detroit, leaving forty-three dead.
1973	Coleman Young is elected the first African American mayor of Detroit.
Aug. 9, 1974	Michigan resident Gerald R. Ford becomes president of United States.
1982	Due to a nationwide recession, unemployment reaches 17.3 percent.
1988	Less than one-quarter of all wage earners work in factories, a decline of 30 percent in ten years.
1998	Population reaches 9.8 million.
1998	Chrysler Corporation merges with German automaker Daimler-Benz to form DaimlerChrysler.
2000	General Motors announces discontinuation of the Oldsmobile, the oldest automobile make in the United States.
2002	Ford Motor Company announces major job reductions and discontinues manufacture of several major car models.
Nov. 5, 2002	Michigan attorney general Jennifer Granholm is elected the state's first woman governor.
June 23, 2003	In deciding two cases, the U.S. Supreme Court accepts the University of Michigan's use of race as one of many factors in determining admissions but bans any "mechanical" application of race.

Known as the Big House, the University of Michigan stadium is the world's largest facility built for American football. It regularly sells out to crowds of more than 100,000 people and on November 22, 2003, held a national record crowd of 112,118 when Michigan played Ohio State University.

Notes for Further Study

Published Sources. For students new to the subject, several books intended for a general audience provide a basic introduction to the state. *Michigan* (1998) by Martin Hintz is a good place to start, with a clear, simple account of the state's geography, plant and animal life, history, economy, culture, and people. Similar information about Michigan and its neighboring states is found in *Eastern Great Lakes: Indiana, Michigan, Ohio* (1995) by Thomas G. Aylesworth; *Michigan History* (2003) by Marcia Schonberg; and *Michigan, the Great Lakes State: An Illustrated History* (2005) by George S. May and Joellen Vinyard. General information, with an emphasis on tourist attractions, is also found in Tina Lassen's *Michigan Handbook* (1999) and in *Michigan* (2006) by David Lee Poremba, which offers readers good information about the people who have called the state home over the centuries, the state's industries and politics, and its cultural and political development.

An enjoyable way to learn about the state is *Michigan Trivia* (1995) by Ernie and Jill Couch. The importance of industry in the state is the subject of Burton W. Folsom's *Empire Builders: How Michigan Entrepreneurs Helped Make America Great* (1998). *Wheels for the World: Henry Ford, His Company, and a Century of Progress* (2003) by Douglas Brinkley provides a good survey of the life and work of Ford and the way in which the automobile industry transformed Detroit. Howard P. Seagal, in *Recasting the Machine Age: Henry Ford's Village Industries* (2005), details Ford's efforts to decentralize his automobile production from Detroit and into communities surrounding that city.

Of the many volumes concerning the state's past, *A Historical Album of Michigan* (1996) by Charles Wills is a good introduction. *Traveling Through Time: A Guide to Michigan's Historical Markers* (rev. ed., 2005), edited by Laura Rose Ashlee, introduces readers to nearly fifteen hundred historical sites in the state and provides information about each one's significance. A more scholarly account is found in *Michigan: A History of the Wolverine State* (1995) by Willis F. Dunbar and George S. May. The early history of the state's major city is the topic of Annick Hivert-Carthew's *Cadillac and the Dawn of Detroit* (1995). The important role of race relations in the city is the subject of Thomas J. Sugrue's *The Origins of the Urban Crisis: Race and Inequality in Postwar Detroit* (1996); the same subject is discussed in *Someone Else's House: America's Unfinished Struggle for Integration* (1998) by Tamar Jacoby, which compares the situation in Detroit to those in New York City and Atlanta.

In *William G. Milliken: Michigan's Passionate Moderate* (2006), Dave Dempsey argues that Milliken, a three-term governor, set in place a number of characteristics of modern-day politics in Michigan; the book gives readers good insight into state politics. *French Canadians of Michigan: Their Contribution to the Development of the Saginaw Valley and the Keweenaw Peninsula, 1840-1914* (2003) by Jean Lamarre (translated by Howard Keillor and Hermione Jack) details the French Canadians' substantial impact on the state's development.

Web Resources. An enormous variety of Internet resources exists with information about Michigan. A good place to begin exploring the many Web sites available is the state's official site (www.michigan.gov/), which covers government, travel and recreation, education and children's services, and business and economic growth, among other topics. The importance of farming to the state is studied at Michigan Department of Agriculture (www.michigan .gov/mda).

Statistical information is available in great detail from the U.S. Census Bureau State and County QuickFacts (quickfacts .census.gov/qfd/states/26000.html). Of the many sites devoted to the state's history, one of the best is Michigan Historical Center (www.michigan.gov/hal/0,1607,7-160-17445_19273—,00.html), which provides information on state archives and museums, as well as biographies of famous residents. Access Genealogy has a good Web page that describes Michigan tribes and allows users to research Native American ancestry (www.accessgenealogy.com/native/michigan/). The Saginaw-Chippewa tribe has its own Web page (www.sagchip.org/), as does the Sault tribe of the Chippewa (www.saulttribe.com/Michigan-Indian-Press.html).

Shelter Bay on Lake Superior. Almost surrounded by the Great Lakes, Michigan has thousands of miles of shoreline and vessels can reach its ports from the sea, by way of the St. Lawrence Seaway. (Travel Michigan)

Counties

County	2000 pop.	Rank in pop.	Sq. miles	Rank in area	County	2000 pop.	Rank in pop.	Sq. miles	Rank in area
Alcona	11,719	74	674.5	30	Cheboygan	26,448	54	715.6	25
Alger	9,862	77	917.9	12	Chippewa	38,543	42	1,561.1	2
Allegan	105,665	19	827.5	19	Clare	31,252	48	566.9	46
Alpena	31,314	47	574.2	39	Clinton	64,753	27	571.5	41
Antrim	23,110	62	476.9	76	Crawford	14,273	71	558.2	56
Arenac	17,269	66	366.9	81	Delta	38,520	43	1,170.2	5
Baraga	8,746	80	904.2	13	Dickinson	27,472	51	766.4	22
Barry	56,755	34	556.2	57	Eaton	103,655	20	576.5	37
Bay	110,157	18	444.3	79	Emmet	31,437	46	468.0	77
Benzie	15,998	68	321.3	83	Genesee	436,141	5	639.7	33
Berrien	162,453	13	571.0	42	Gladwin	26,023	56	506.8	71
Branch	45,787	38	507.4	70	Gogebic	17,370	65	1,101.9	7
Calhoun	137,985	17	708.9	27	Grand Traverse	77,654	24	465.1	78
Cass	51,104	35	492.2	74	Gratiot	42,285	40	570.2	43
Charlevoix	26,090	55	416.9	80	Hillsdale	46,527	37	598.9	36

(continued)

County	2000 pop.	Rank in pop.	Sq. miles	Rank in area
Houghton	36,016	45	1,011.7	10
Huron	36,079	44	836.6	18
Ingham	279,320	7	559.2	55
Ionia	61,518	31	573.2	40
Iosco	27,339	52	549.1	60
Iron	13,138	72	1,166.5	6
Isabella	63,351	29	574.3	38
Jackson	158,422	14	706.6	29
Kalamazoo	238,603	8	561.9	53
Kalkaska	16,571	67	561.0	54
Kent	574,335	4	856.2	16
Keweenaw	2,301	83	541.2	63
Lake	11,333	75	567.6	45
Lapeer	87,904	22	654.3	32
Leelanau	21,119	64	348.5	82
Lenawee	98,890	21	750.6	23
Livingston	156,951	15	568.4	44
Luce	7,024	82	903.1	14
Mackinac	11,943	73	1,021.6	9
Macomb	788,149	3	480.4	75
Manistee	24,527	59	543.9	62
Marquette	64,634	28	1,821.3	1
Mason	28,274	50	495.2	73
Mecosta	40,553	41	555.8	58
Menominee	25,326	58	1,043.7	8
Midland	82,874	23	521.2	67
Missaukee	14,478	69	566.8	47
Monroe	145,945	16	551.1	59

County	2000 pop.	Rank in pop.	Sq. miles	Rank in area
Montcalm	61,266	32	708.1	28
Montmorency	10,315	76	547.6	61
Muskegon	170,200	11	509.2	69
Newaygo	47,874	36	842.4	17
Oakland	1,194,156	2	872.7	15
Oceana	26,873	53	540.5	64
Ogemaw	21,645	63	564.4	52
Ontonagon	7,818	81	1,311.6	3
Osceola	23,197	61	566.1	48
Oscoda	9,418	78	565.0	51
Otsego	23,301	60	514.6	68
Ottawa	238,314	9	565.7	49
Presque Isle	14,411	70	660.1	31
Roscommon	25,469	57	521.4	66
Saginaw	210,039	10	809.0	21
St. Clair	164,235	12	724.5	24
St. Joseph	62,422	30	503.7	72
Sanilac	44,547	39	963.9	11
Schoolcraft	8,903	79	1,178.2	4
Shiawassee	71,687	26	538.8	65
Tuscola	58,266	33	812.6	20
Van Buren	76,263	25	611.0	35
Washtenaw	322,895	6	710.1	26
Wayne	2,061,162	1	614.1	34
Wexford	30,484	49	565.5	50

Source: U.S. Census Bureau; National Association of Counties.

Cities
With 10,000 or more residents

Rank	City	Population
1	Detroit	951,270
2	Grand Rapids	197,800
3	Warren	138,247
4	Flint	124,943
5	Sterling Heights	124,471
6	Lansing (capital)	119,128
7	Ann Arbor	114,024
8	Livonia	100,545
9	Dearborn	97,775
10	Clinton	95,648
11	Westland	86,602
12	Farmington Hills	82,111
13	Troy	80,959
14	Southfield	78,296
15	Kalamazoo	77,145
16	Canton	76,366
17	Waterford	73,150
18	Wyoming	69,368
19	Rochester Hills	68,825
20	Pontiac	66,337
21	Taylor	65,868

Rank	City	Population
22	Shelby	65,159
23	West Bloomfield Township	64,862
24	St. Clair Shores	63,096
25	Saginaw	61,799
26	Royal Oak	60,062
27	Dearborn Heights	58,264
28	Battle Creek	53,364
29	Redford	51,622
30	Roseville	48,129
31	Novi	47,386
32	East Lansing	46,525
33	Kentwood	45,255
34	Portage	44,897
35	Bloomfield Township	43,021
36	Midland	41,685
37	Muskegon	40,105
38	Lincoln Park	40,008
39	Bay City	36,817
40	Jackson	36,316
41	Holland	35,048
42	Eastpointe	34,077

Rank	City	Population	Rank	City	Population
43	Port Huron	32,338	63	Walker	21,842
44	Madison Heights	31,101	64	Adrian	21,574
45	Burton	30,308	65	Forest Hills	20,942
46	Southgate	30,136	66	Auburn Hills	19,837
47	Inkster	30,115	67	Marquette	19,661
48	Garden City	30,047	68	Trenton	19,584
49	Oak Park	29,793	69	Birmingham	19,291
50	Allen Park	29,376	70	Wayne	19,051
51	Wyandotte	28,006	71	Hazel Park	18,963
52	Plymouth Township	27,798	72	Mount Clemens	17,312
53	Mount Pleasant	25,946	73	Jenison	17,211
54	Saginaw Township North	24,994	74	Grosse Pointe Woods	17,080
55	Harrison	24,461	75	Highland Park	16,746
56	Romulus	22,979	76	Sault Ste. Marie	16,542
57	Hamtramck	22,976	77	Grandville	16,263
58	Okemos	22,805	78	Waverly	16,194
59	Norton Shores	22,527	79	Owosso	15,713
60	Ypsilanti	22,362	80	Berkley	15,531
61	Ferndale	22,105	81	Fraser	15,297
62	Monroe	22,076	82	Cutlerville	15,114

(continued)

Rank	City	Population
83	Northview	14,730
84	Traverse City	14,532
85	Harper Woods	14,254
86	Saginaw Township South	13,801
87	Riverview	13,272
88	Wixom	13,263
89	Escanaba	13,140
90	Beecher	12,793
91	Clawson	12,732
92	Coldwater	12,697
93	Woodhaven	12,530
94	Grosse Pointe Park	12,443
95	Niles	12,204
96	Muskegon Heights	12,049
97	Allendale	11,555
98	Holt	11,315
99	Alpena	11,304
100	Sturgis	11,285
101	Haslett	11,283

Rank	City	Population
102	Ecorse	11,229
103	Benton Harbor	11,182
104	Grand Haven	11,168
105	Grosse Ile	10,894
106	Big Rapids	10,849
107	East Grand Rapids	10,764
108	Melvindale	10,735
109	Comstock Park	10,674
110	Fenton	10,582
111	Ionia	10,569
112	Rochester	10,467
113	Beverly Hills	10,437
114	Farmington	10,423
115	South Lyon	10,036
116	Cadillac	10,000

Population figures are from 2000 census.
Source: U.S. Bureau of the Census.

Index to Tables

DEMOGRAPHICS

Resident state and national populations, 1970-2004

Population figures given in thousands

	State pop.	U.S. pop.	Share	Rank
1970	8,882	203,302	4.4%	7
1980	9,262	226,546	4.1%	8
1985	9,076	237,924	3.8%	8
1990	9,295	248,765	3.7%	8
1995	9,676	262,761	3.7%	8
2000	9,938	281,425	3.5%	8
2004	10,113	293,655	3.4%	8

Source: U.S. Census Bureau, Current Population Reports, 2006.

Resident population by age, 2004

Age Group	Total persons
Under 5 years	650,000
5 to 17 years	1,884,000
18 to 24 years	997,000
25 to 34 years	1,306,000
35 to 44 years	1,514,000
45 to 54 years	1,496,000
55 to 64 years	1,020,000
65 to 74 years	612,000
75 to 84 years	460,000
85 years and older	175,000
All age groups	10,113,000

Portion of residents 65 and older	12.3%
National rank in portion of oldest residents	31
National average	12.4%

Population figures are rounded to nearest thousand persons;
figures include armed forces personnel stationed in the state.
Source: U.S. Bureau of the Census, 2006.

Resident population by race, Hispanic origin, 2004

Category	State pop.	Share	U.S.
All residents	10,113	100.00%	100.00%
Non-Hispanic white	7,896	78.08%	67.37%
Hispanic white	336	3.32%	13.01%
Other Hispanic	39	0.39%	1.06%
African American	1,451	14.35%	12.77%
Native American	60	0.59%	0.96%
Asian, Pacific Islander	224	2.21%	4.37%
Two or more categories	146	1.44%	1.51%

Population figures are in thousands. Persons counted as "Hispanic" (Latino) may be of any race. Because of overlapping categories, categories may not add up to 100%. Shares in column 3 are percentages of each category within the state; these figures may be compared to the national percentages in column 4.
Source: U.S. Bureau of the Census, 2006.

Projected state population, 2000-2030

Year	Population
2000	9,938,000
2005	10,207,000
2010	10,429,000
2015	10,599,000
2020	10,696,000
2025	10,714,000
2030	10,694,000
Population increase, 2000-2030	756,000
Percentage increase, 2000-2030	7.6

Projections are based on data from the 2000 census.
Source: U.S. Census Bureau.

VITAL STATISTICS

Infant mortality rates, 1980-2002

	1980	1990	2000	2002
All state residents	12.8	10.7	8.2	8.1
All U.S. residents	12.6	9.2	9.4	9.1
All state white residents	10.6	7.4	6.0	6.0
All U.S. white residents	10.6	7.6	5.7	5.8
All state black residents	24.2	21.6	18.2	18.5
All U.S. black residents	22.2	18.0	14.1	14.4

Figures represent deaths per 1,000 live births of resident infants under 1 year old, exclusive of fetal deaths. Figures for all residents include members of other racial categories not listed separately.
Source: U.S. Census Bureau, *Statistical Abstract of the United States,* 2006.

Abortion rates, 1990 and 2000

	1990	2000
Total abortions	56,000	46,000
Rate per 1,000 women	25.1	21.6
U.S. rate	25.7	21.3
Rank	14	12

Numbers of abortions are rounded to nearest thousand; ranks are based on rates.
Source: U.S. Census Bureau.

Marriages and divorces, 2004

Total marriages	62,600
Rate per 1,000 population	6.2
National rate per 1,000 population	7.4
Rank among all states	40
Total divorces	35,000
Rate per 1,000 population	3.5
National rate per 1,000 population	3.7
Rank among all states	29

Figures are for all marriages and divorces performed within the state, including those of nonresidents; totals are rounded to the nearest hundred. Ranks are for highest to lowest figures; note that divorce data are not available for five states.
Source: U.S. National Center for Health Statistics, *Vital Statistics of the United States,* 2006.

Death rates by leading causes, 2002
Deaths per 100,000 resident population

Cause	State	U.S.
Heart disease	265.3	241.7
Cancer	198.8	193.2
Cerebrovascular diseases	57.8	56.4
Accidents other than motor vehicle	32.7	37.0
Motor vehicle accidents	13.8	15.7
Chronic lower respiratory diseases	44.1	43.3
Diabetes mellitus	27.7	25.4
HIV	2.4	4.9
Suicide	11.0	11.0
Homicide	6.9	6.1
All causes	873.5	847.3
Rank in overall death rate among states		25

Figures exclude nonresidents who died in the state. Causes of death follow International Classification of Diseases. Rank is from highest to lowest death rate in the United States.
Source: U.S. National Center for Health Statistics, *National Vital Statistics Report,* 2006.

ECONOMY

Gross state product, 1990-2004
In current dollars

Year	State product	Nat'l product	State share
1990	$189.7 billion	$5.67 trillion	3.34%
2000	$337.2 billion	$9.75 trillion	3.46%
2002	$347.0 billion	$10.41 trillion	3.33%
2003	$359.4 billion	$10.92 trillion	3.29%
2004	$372.8 billion	$11.65 trillion	3.20%

Source: U.S. Bureau of Economic Analysis, *Survey of Current Business,* July, 2005.

Gross state product by industry, 2003
In billions of dollars

Construction	$13.5
Manufacturing	76.4
Wholesale trade	20.3
Retail trade	26.0
Finance & insurance	19.8
Information	10.0
Professional services	27.1
Health care & social assistance	22.2
Government	33.5
Total state product	$341.0
Total U.S. product	$10,289.2
State share of U.S. total	3.31%
Rank among all states	9

Total figures include industries not listed separately. Amounts are in chained 2000 dollars.
Source: U.S. Bureau of Economic Analysis, *Survey of Current Business,* July, 2005.

Personal income per capita, 1990-2004
In current dollars

	1990	2000	2004
Per capita income	$18,922	$29,552	$31,954
U.S. average	$19,477	$29,845	$32,937
Rank among states	20	17	22

Source: U.S. Bureau of Economic Analysis, *Survey of Current Business,* April, 2005.

Energy consumption, 2001
In trillions of British thermal units (BTU), except as noted

Total energy consumption

Total state energy consumption	3,120
Total U.S. energy consumption	96,275
State share of U.S. total	3.24%
Rank among states	9

Per capita consumption (In millions of BTU)

Total state per capita consumption	312
Total U.S. per capita consumption	338
Rank among states	34

End-use sectors

Residential	790
Commercial	598
Industrial	928
Transportation	804

Sources of energy

Petroleum	1,042
Natural gas	929
Coal	797
Hydroelectric power	4
Nuclear electric power	279

Figures for totals include categories not listed separately.
Source: U.S. Energy Information Administration, *State Energy Data Report,* 2001.

Nonfarm employment by sectors, 2004

Total	4,391,000
Construction	190,000
Manufacturing	696,000
Trade, transportation, utilities	810,000
Information	68,000
Finance, insurance, real estate	218,000
Professional & business services	584,000
Education & health services	553,000
Leisure, hospitality, arts, organizations	403,000
Other services, including repair & maintenance	179,000
Government	682,000

Figures are rounded to nearest thousand persons. "Total" includes mining and natural resources, not listed separately.
Source: U.S. Bureau of Labor Statistics, 2006.

Foreign exports, 1990-2004
In millions of dollars

Year	State	U.S.	State share
1990	18,474	394,045	4.69%
1996	27,553	624,767	4.41%
1997	32,254	688,896	4.68%
2000	33,845	712,055	4.33%
2003	32,941	724,006	4.87%
2004	35,625	769,332	4.63%

Rank among all states in 2004. 4

U.S. total does not include U.S. dependencies.
Source: U.S. Census Bureau, *U.S. Merchandise Trade,* series FT 900, 2000; U.S. Census Bureau, *U.S. International Trade in Goods and Services,* Series FT 900, 2005.

LAND USE

Federally owned land, 2003
Areas in acres

	State	U.S.	State share
Total area	36,492,000	2,271,343,000	1.61%
Nonfederal land	32,854,000	1,599,584,000	2.05%
Federal land	3,638,000	671,759,000	0.54%
Federal share	10.0%	29.6%	—

Areas are rounded to nearest thousand acres. Figures for federally owned land do not include trust properties.
Source: U.S. General Services Administration, *Federal Real Property Profile,* 2006.

Land use, 1997
In acres, rounded to nearest thousand

Total surface area	37,349,000
Total nonfederal rural land.	29,426,000
Percentage rural land	78.8%
Cropland	8,540,000
Conservation Reserve Program (CRP*) land. . . .	321,000
Pastureland.	2,032,000
Rangeland	(nil)
Forestland.	16,354,000
Other rural land	2,178,000

*CRP is a federal program begun in 1985 to assist private landowners to convert highly erodible cropland to vegetative cover for ten years. Note that some categories of land overlap.
Source: U.S. Department of Agriculture, Natural Resources and Conservation Service, and Iowa State University, Statistical Laboratory, S*ummary Report, 1997 National Resources Inventory,* revised December, 2000.

Farms and crop acreage, 2004

	State	U.S.	Share	Rank
Farms	53,000	2,113,000	2.51%	15
Acres (millions)	10	937	1.07%	29
Acres per farm	190	443	—	36

Source: U.S. Department of Agriculture, National Agricultural Statistics Service. Numbers of farms are rounded to nearest thousand units; acreage figures are rounded to nearest million. Rankings, including ties, are based on rounded figures.

GOVERNMENT AND FINANCE

Units of local government, 2002

	State	Total U.S.	Rank
All local governments	2,804	87,525	12
Counties	83	3,034	15
Municipalities	533	19,429	14
Townships	1,242	16,504	8
School districts	580	13,506	6
Special districts	366	35,052	33

Only 48 states have county governments, 20 states have township governments ("towns" in New England, Minnesota, New York, and Wisconsin), and 46 states have school districts. Special districts encompass such functions as natural resources, fire protection, and housing and community development.
Source: U.S. Census Bureau, *Census of Governments.*

State government revenue, 2002

Total revenue . . . . $43,950 mill.
General revenue . . . . $40,886 mill.
Per capita revenue $4,071
U.S. per capita average $3,689
Rank among states 14

Intergovernment revenue
Total . . . . $11,507 mill.
From federal government . . . . $11,241 mill.

Charges and miscellaneous
Total . . . . $7,515 mill.
Current charges . . . . $4,620 mill.
Misc. general income . . . . $2,895 mill.
Insurance trust revenue . . . . $2,457 mill.

Taxes
Total . . . . $21,864 mill.
Per capita taxes $2,177
Rank among states 10
Property taxes . . . . $1,891 mill.
Sales taxes . . . . $10,069 mill.
License taxes . . . . $1,297 mill.
Individual income taxes . . . . $6,125 mill.
Corporate income taxes . . . . $2,065 mill.
Other taxes . . . . $416 mill.

Total revenue figures include items not listed separately here.
Source: U.S. Bureau of the Census.

State government expenditures, 2002

General expenditures
Total state expenditures . . . . $49,184 mill.
Intergovernmental . . . . $19,067 mill.

Per capita expenditures
State $4,364
Average of all states $3,859
Rank among states 15

Selected direct expenditures
Education. . . . . $6,590 mill.
Public welfare . . . . $9,069 mill.
Health, hospital . . . . $2,318 mill.
Highways . . . . $1,250 mill.
Police protection. . . . . $307 mill.
Corrections. . . . . $1,613 mill.
Natural resources . . . . $484 mill.
Parks and recreation . . . . $174 mill.
Government administration . . . . $820 mill.
Interest on debt . . . . $1,064 mill.
Total direct expenditures. . . . . $24,760 mill.

Totals include items not listed separately.
Source: U.S. Census Bureau.

POLITICS

Governors since statehood

D = Democrat; R = Republican; O = other;
(r) resigned; (d) died in office; (i) removed from office

Stevens T. Mason (D) 1835-1840
William Woodbridge (O) . . . . (r) 1840-1841
James Wright Gordon (O). 1841-1842
John S. Barry (D) 1842-1846
Alpheus Felch (D) . . . . (r) 1846-1847
William L. Greely (D) 1847-1848
Epaphroditus Ransom (D) 1848-1850
John S. Barry (D) 1850-1852
Robert McClelland (D) . . . . (r) 1852-1853
Andrew Parsons (D) 1853-1855
Kinsley S. Bingham (R) 1855-1859
Moses Wisner (R) 1859-1861
Austin Blair (R) 1861-1865
Henry H. Crapo (R) 1865-1869
Henry P. Baldwin (R) 1869-1873
John J. Bagley (R) 1873-1877
Charles M. Crosswell (R) 1877-1881
David H. Jerome (R). 1881-1883
Josiah W. Begole (O) 1883-1885
Russell A. Alger (R) 1885-1887
Cyrus G. Luce (R) 1887-1891
Edwin B. Winans (D) 1891-1893
John T. Rich (R) 1893-1897
Hazen S. Pingree (R) 1897-1901
Aaron T. Bliss (R) 1901-1905
Fred M. Warner (R) 1905-1911
Chase M. Osborn (R) 1911-1913

Woodbridge N. Ferris (D) 1913-1917
Albert E. Sleeper (R) 1917-1921
Alexander J. Groesbeck (R) 1921-1927
Fred W. Green (R). 1927-1931
Wilbur M. Brucker (R) 1931-1933
William A. Comstock (D) 1933-1935
Frank D. Fitzgerald (R) 1935-1937
Frank Murphy (D) 1937-1939
Frank D. Fitzgerald (R) . . . . (d) 1939
Luren D. Dickinson (R) 1939-1941
Murray D. Van Wagoner (D) 1941-1943
Harry F. Kelly (R) 1943-1947
Kim Sigler (R) 1947-1949
Gerhard Mennon Williams (D) 1949-1961
John B. Swainson (D) 1961-1963
George W. Romney (R) . . . . (r) 1963-1969
William G. Milliken (R) 1969-1983
James J. Blanchard (D) 1983-1991
John Engler (R) 1991-2003
Jennifer Granholm (D) 2003-

Composition of congressional delegations, 1989-2007

	Dem	Rep	Total
House of Representatives			
101st Congress, 1989			
State delegates	11	7	18
Total U.S.	259	174	433
102d Congress, 1991			
State delegates	11	7	18
Total U.S.	267	167	434
103d Congress, 1993			
State delegates	10	6	16
Total U.S.	258	176	434
104th Congress, 1995			
State delegates	10	6	16
Total U.S.	197	236	433
105th Congress, 1997			
State delegates	10	6	16
Total U.S.	206	228	434
106th Congress, 1999			
State delegates	10	6	16
Total U.S.	211	222	433
107th Congress, 2001			
State delegates	9	7	16
Total U.S.	211	221	432
108th Congress, 2003			
State delegates	6	9	15
Total U.S.	205	229	434
109th Congress, 2005			
State delegates	6	9	15
Total U.S.	202	231	433

(continued)

	Dem	Rep	Total
110th Congress, 2007			
State delegates	6	9	15
Total U.S.	233	202	435
Senate			
101st Congress, 1989			
State delegates	2	0	2
Total U.S.	55	45	100
102d Congress, 1991			
State delegates	2	0	2
Total U.S.	56	44	100
103d Congress, 1993			
State delegates	2	0	2
Total U.S.	57	43	100
104th Congress, 1995			
State delegates	1	1	2
Total U.S.	46	53	99
105th Congress, 1997			
State delegates	1	1	2
Total U.S.	45	55	100
106th Congress, 1999			
State delegates	1	1	2
Total U.S.	45	54	99
107th Congress, 2001			
State delegates	2	0	2
Total U.S.	50	50	100
108th Congress, 2003			
State delegates	2	0	2
Total U.S.	48	51	99
109th Congress, 2005			
State delegates	2	0	2
Total U.S.	44	55	99
110th Congress, 2007			
State delegates	2	0	2
Total U.S.	49	49	98

Figures are for starts of first sessions. Totals are for Democrat (Dem.) and Republican (Rep.) members only. House membership totals under 435 and Senate totals under 100 reflect vacancies and seats held by independent party members. When the 110th Congress opened, the Senate's two independent members caucused with the Democrats, giving the Democrats control of the Senate.

Source: U.S. Congress, *Congressional Directory.*

Composition of state legislature, 1990-2006

	Democrats	Republicans
State House (110 seats)		
1990	61	49
1992	55	55
1994	53	56
1996	58	52
1998	52	58
2000	52	58
2002	63	47
2004	52	58
2006	58	52
State Senate (38 seats)		
1990	18	20
1992	16	22
1994	16	22
1996	16	22
1998	15	23
2000	15	23
2002	16	22
2004	16	22
2006	17	21

Figures for total seats may include independents and minor party members. Numbers reflect results of elections in listed years; elected members usually take their seats in the years that follow.

Source: Council of State Governments; *State Elective Officials and the Legislatures.*

Voter participation in presidential elections, 2000 and 2004

	2000	2004
Voting age population		
State	7,362,000	7,579,000
Total United States	209,831,000	220,377,000
State share of U.S. total	3.51	3.44
Rank among states	8	8
Portion of voting age population casting votes		
State	57.5%	63.8%
United States	50.3%	55.5%
Rank among states	12	11

Population figures are rounded to nearest thousand and include all residents, regardless of eligibility to vote.

Source: U.S. Census Bureau.

HEALTH AND MEDICAL CARE

Medical professionals
Physicians in 2003 and nurses in 2001

	U.S.	State
Physicians in 2003		
Total	774,849	24,004
Share of U.S. total		3.08%
Rate	266	238
Rank		30
Nurses in 2001		
Total	2,262,020	83,950
Share of U.S. total		3.71%
Rate	793	839
Rank		25

Rates are numbers of physicians and nurses per 100,000 resident population; ranks are based on rates.

Source: American Medical Association, *Physician Characteristics and Distribution in the U.S.*; U.S. Department of Health and Human Services, Health Resources and Services Administration.

Health insurance coverage, 2003

	State	U.S.
Total persons covered	8,838,000	243,320,000
Total persons not covered	1,080,000	44,961,000
Portion not covered	10.9%	15.6%
Rank among states	40	—
Children not covered	147,000	8,373,000
Portion not covered	5.8%	11.4%
Rank among states	47	—

Totals are rounded to nearest thousand. Ranks are from the highest to the lowest percentages of persons *not* insured.

Source: U.S. Census Bureau, Current Population Reports.

AIDS, syphilis, and tuberculosis cases, 2003

Disease	U.S. cases	State cases	Rank
AIDS	44,232	676	18
Syphilis	34,270	860	12
Tuberculosis	14,874	243	19

Source: U.S. Centers for Disease Control and Prevention.

Cigarette smoking, 2003
Residents over age 18 who smoke

	U.S.	State	Rank
All smokers	22.1%	26.2%	6
Male smokers	24.8%	30.2%	6
Female smokers	20.3%	22.3%	14

Cigarette smokers are defined as persons who reported having smoked at least 100 cigarettes during their lifetimes and who currently smoked at least occasionally.

Source: U.S. Centers for Disease Control and Prevention, *Morbidity and Mortality Weekly Report,* 53, no. 44 (November 12, 2004).

HOUSING

Home ownership rates, 1985-2004

	1985	1990	1995	2000	2004
State	70.7%	72.3%	72.2%	77.2%	77.1%
Total U.S.	63.9%	63.9%	64.7%	67.4%	69.0%
Rank among states	8	4	4	1	4

Net change in state home ownership rate, 1985-2004 . . . . +6.4%

Net change in U.S. home ownership rate, 1985-2004 . . . . +5.1%

Percentages represent the proportion of owner households to total occupied households.

Source: U.S. Census Bureau, 2006.

Home sales, 2000-2004
In thousands of units

Existing home sales	2000	2002	2003	2004
State sales	185.0	203.5	207.4	213.4
Total U.S. sales	5,171	5,631	6,183	6,784
State share of U.S. total	3.58%	3.61%	3.35%	3.15%
Sales rank among states	8	8	8	9

Units include single-family homes, condos, and co-ops.

Source: National Association of Realtors, Washington, D.C., *Real Estate Outlook: Market Trends & Insights.*

Values of owner-occupied homes, 2003

	State	U.S.
Total units	2,417,000	58,809,000
Value of units		
Under $100,000	28.6%	29.6%
$100,000-199,999	45.5%	36.9%
$200,000 or more	25.9%	33.5%
Median value	$141,413	$142,275
Rank among all states 22		

Units are owner-occupied one-family houses whose numbers are
rounded to nearest thousand. Data are extrapolated from
survey samples.
Source: U.S. Census Bureau, American Community Survey.

EDUCATION

Public school enrollment, 2002

Prekindergarten through grade 8
State enrollment 1,254,000
Total U.S. enrollment. 34,135,000
State share of U.S. total 3.67%

Grades 9 through 12
State enrollment 531,000
Total U.S. enrollment. 14,067,000
State share of U.S. total 3.77%

Enrollment rates
State public school enrollment rate. 93.7%
Overall U.S. rate 90.4%
Rank among states in 2002 7
Rank among states in 1995. 38

Enrollment figures (which include unclassified students) are
rounded to nearest thousand pupils during fall school term.
Enrollment rates are based on enumerated resident population
estimate for July 1, 2002.
Source: U.S. National Center for Education Statistics.

Public college finances, 2003-2004

FTE enrollment in public institutions of higher education
Students in state institutions 357,600
Students in all U.S. public institutions 9,916,600
State share of U.S. total 3.61
Rank among states. 7

**State and local government appropriations for higher
education**
State appropriation per FTE $5,950
National average. $5,716
Rank among states 17
State & local tax revenue going to higher
education 8.5%

FTE = full-time equivalent in public postsecondary programs,
including summer sessions; student numbers are rounded to
nearest hundred. Funding figures for 2003-2004 academic year
include financial aid to students in state public institutions and
exclude money for research, agriculture experiment stations,
teaching hospitals, and medical schools; figures are rounded to
nearest thousand dollars.
Source: Higher Education Executive Officers, Denver, Colorado.

TRANSPORTATION AND TRAVEL

Highway mileage, 2003

Interstate highways 1,243
Other freeways and expressways 306
Arterial roads. 12,101
Collector roads. 25,814
Local roads. 82,758
Urban roads 35,088
Rural roads. 87,134
Total state mileage 122,222
U.S. total 3,974,107
State share 3.08%
Rank among states. 8

Note that combined urban and rural road mileage matches the
total of the other categories.
Source: U.S. Federal Highway Administration.

Motor vehicle registrations and driver licenses, 2003

Vehicle registrations	State	U.S.	Share	Rank
Autos, trucks, buses	8,540,000	231,390,000	3.69%	8
Autos only	4,805,000	135,670	3.54%	8
Motorcycles	214,000	5,328,000	4.02%	8
Driver licenses	7,065,000	196,166,000	3.60%	8

Figures, which do not include vehicles owned by military services,
are rounded to the nearest thousand. Figures for automobiles
include taxis.
Source: U.S. Federal Highway Administration.

Domestic travel expenditures, 2003
Spending by U.S. residents on overnight trips and
day trips of at least 50 miles from home

Total expenditures within state . . . . $11.99 bill.
Total expenditures within U.S. . . . . $490.87 bill.
State share of U.S. total 2.4%
Rank among states 13

Source: Travel Industry Association of America.

Retail gasoline prices, 2003-2007
Average price per gallon at the pump

Year	U.S.	State
2003	$1.267	$1.241
2004	$1.316	$1.287
2005	$1.644	$1.666
2007	$2.298	$2.337

Excise tax per gallon in 2004 . . . . 19.0¢
Rank among all states in 2007 prices 15

Prices are averages of all grades of gasoline sold at the pump
during March months in 2003-2005 and during February, 2007.
Averages for 2006, during which prices rose higher, are not
available.
Source: U.S. Energy Information Agency, *Petroleum Marketing
Monthly* (2003-2005 data); American Automobile Association
(2007 data).

CRIME AND LAW ENFORCEMENT

State and local police officers, 2000-2004

	2000	2002	2004
Total officers			
U.S.	654,601	665,555	675,734
State	20,958	21,006	20,220*
*Net change, 2000-2004			−3.52%
Officers per 1,000 residents			
U.S.	2.33	2.31	2.30
State	2.11	2.09	2.00
State rank	25	27	27

Totals include state and local police and sheriffs.
Source: Carsey Institute, University of New Hampshire.

Crime rates, 2003
Incidents per 100,000 residents

Crimes	State	U.S.
Violent crimes		
Total incidents	511	475
Murder	6	6
Forcible rape	54	32
Robbery	112	142
Aggravated assault	339	295
Property crimes		
Total incidents	3,277	3,588
Burglary	677	741
Larceny/theft	2,067	2,415
Motor vehicle theft	533	433
All crimes	3,788	4,063

Source: U.S. Federal Bureau of Investigation, *Crime in the United
States,* annual.

State prison populations, 1980-2003

	State	U.S.	State share
1980	15,124	305,458	4.95%
1990	34,267	708,393	4.84%
1996	42,349	1,025,624	4.13%
2000	47,718	1,391,261	3.43%
2003	49,358	1,470,045	3.36%

State figures exclude prisoners in federal penitentiaries.
Source: U.S. Bureau of Justice Statistics, *Prisoners in 2003.*

Minnesota

Location: Upper Midwest

Area and rank: 79,617 square miles (206,207 square kilometers); 86,943 square miles (225,182 square kilometers) including water; fourteenth largest state in area

Coastline: none

Population and rank: 5,101,000 (2004); twenty-first largest state in population

Capital city: St. Paul (287,151 people in 2000 census)

Largest city: Minneapolis (382,618 people in 2000 census)

Became territory: March 3, 1849

Entered Union and rank: May 11, 1858; thirty-second state

State capitol building at St. Paul. (©James Blank/Weststock)

Present constitution adopted: 1858

Counties: 87

State name: "Minnesota" is derived from a Dakota Indian word that means "sky-tinted water"

State nickname: North Star State; Gopher State; Land of 10,000 Lakes

Motto: *L'Etoile du nord* (The North Star)

State flag: Blue field with detail from state seal, name "Minnesota," and nineteen stars

Highest point: Eagle Mountain—2,301 feet (701 meters)

Lowest point: Lake Superior—602 feet (183 meters)

Highest recorded temperature: 114 degrees Fahrenheit (46 degrees Celsius)—Moorhead, 1936

Lowest recorded temperature: –59 degrees Fahrenheit (–51 degrees Celsius)—Pokegama Dam, 1903

State song: "Hail! Minnesota"

State tree: Red (or Norway) pine

State flower: Pink-and-white lady's slipper

State bird: Common loon (also known as great northern diver)

State fish: Walleye

National parks: Voyageurs

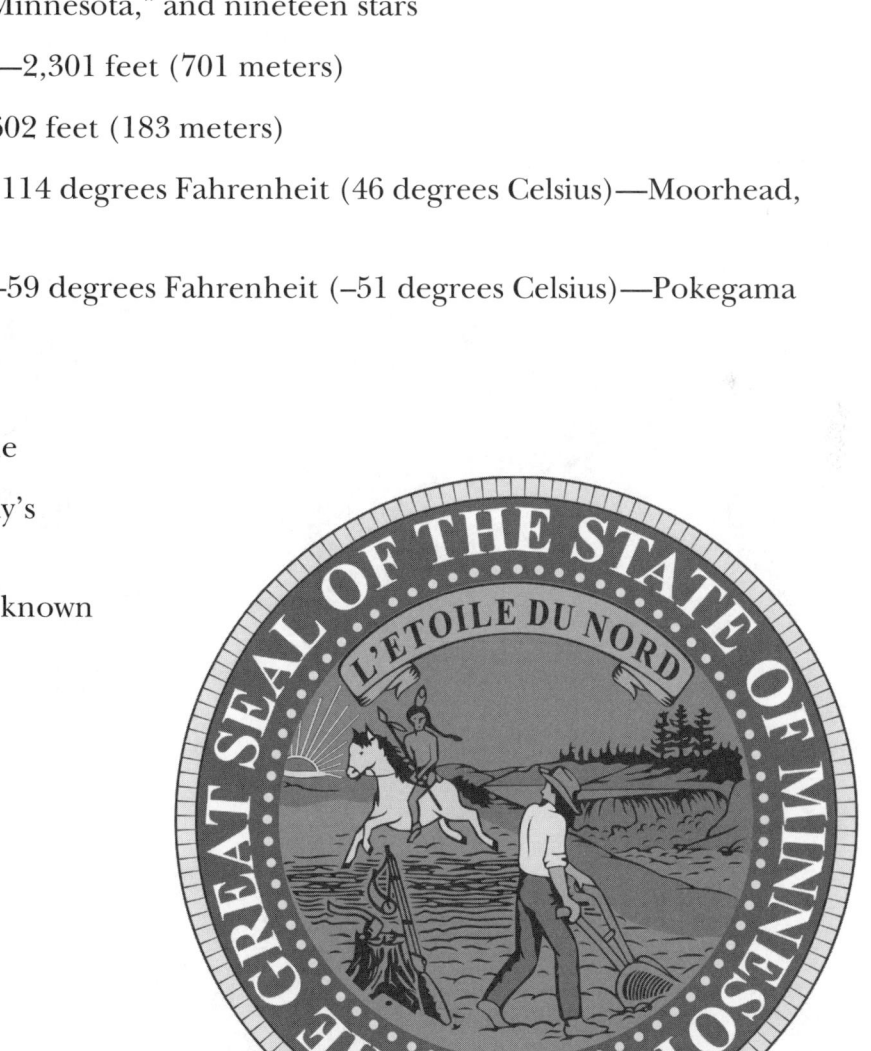

Minnesota History

Reaching farther north than any other state except Alaska, Minnesota was settled more slowly than other states in the center of the United States, which were more accessible to heavily populated eastern states. Despite its isolation, the fertile soils of the south and west, the pine forests of the northeast, and the hardwood forests between these regions eventually attracted settlers. The state's access to Lake Superior, numerous rivers, and countless lakes also brought economic growth to the area. Much of Minnesota remains rural, in sharp contrast to the Twin Cities of Minneapolis and St. Paul near the eastern edge of the state.

Early History. The earliest people to inhabit the area, known as the Paleo-Indian culture, hunted bison and other large animals more than ten thousand years ago. About seven thousand years ago, the people of the Eastern Archaic culture hunted small and large animals and made tools from copper. The Woodland culture, starting about three thousand years ago, introduced the use of pottery and burial mounds. Starting about one thousand years ago, the Mississippian culture built large, permanent villages located in fertile river valleys and raised corn, beans, and squash.

Both the Woodland culture and Mississippian culture lifestyles lasted until Europeans arrived about three hundred years ago. Until the middle of the nineteenth century, Minnesota was primarily inhabited by the Ojibwa in the north and east and the Dakota in the south and west. Conflicts between these peoples led to the Ojibwa forcing the Dakota to move farther southwest during the middle of the eighteenth century.

Located near the confluence of Minnehaha Creek and the Mississippi River, Minnehaha Falls is a popular tourist attraction because of its association with Henry Wadsworth Longfellow's 1855 poem The Song of Hiawatha. *During the winter months, the falls often freeze solid.*

Exploration and Settlement. The first European explorers to reach the area were the French fur traders Pierre Esprit Radisson and Médard Chouart des Groseilliers, who traveled from Canada through Wisconsin and into eastern Minnesota in 1658. In September of 1679, Daniel Greysolon, sieur du Lhut, met with Native Americans near Mille Lacs Lake near the center of the region. As a result of this meeting, peaceful relations were established among the French, the Ojibwa, and the Dakota. Du Lhut also claimed the area for King Louis XIV of France.

In January of 1680, the French missionary Louis Hennepin began a journey north along the Mississippi River into eastern Minnesota. In April, Hennepin was captured by the Dakota. During his captivity, Hennepin named a waterfall on the Mississippi River the Falls of St. Anthony, near the future site of the Twin Cities. Hennepin was rescued by Du Lhut in July.

In 1682, the French explorer René-Robert Cavelier, sieur de La Salle, claimed the entire valley of the Mississippi River for France. He named this vast area, including western Minnesota, Louisiana. Meanwhile, French fur traders had established the first permanent European settlement in the region in the far north, at Grand Portage. Grand Portage soon became the center of the prosperous fur trade. Among the many noted French explorers who established settlements in the area were Nicolas Perrot, who founded Fort Antoine in 1686, and Pierre Gaultier de Varennes, sieur de La Vérendrye, who founded Fort Saint Charles in 1731.

The British and Americans. The wealth generated by the fur trade was part of the struggle for control of

North America between France and England that led to the French and Indian War (1754-1763). The British took control of Minnesota east of the Mississippi River after the war. Western Minnesota, with the rest of Louisiana, had been ceded to Spain in 1762 but was returned to France in 1800.

Spain did little to settle the area, but England quickly established the North West Company at Grand Portage to take advantage of the lucrative fur trade. At the end of the American Revolution (1775-1783), eastern Minnesota officially became part of the United States. The North West Company did not leave Grand Portage until 1803, when it moved to Canada. It was replaced by the American Fur Company, established in 1808.

Eastern Minnesota became part of the newly created Northwest Territory in 1787. It became part of several different territories as the vast Northwest Territory was reorganized during the early nineteenth century. Between 1800 and 1858, it was part of Indiana Territory, Illinois Territory, Michigan Territory, Wisconsin Territory, and Minnesota Territory.

Meanwhile, the United States purchased Louisiana, including western Minnesota, from France in 1803. From 1834 to 1849, western Minnesota was part of Michigan Territory, Wisconsin Territory, the Iowa Territory, again Wisconsin Territory, and Minnesota Territory.

Becoming a State. During this time, Minnesota remained a sparsely populated area isolated from the rest of the United States. In 1805, a military expedition led by Zebulon Pike failed to locate the source of the Mississippi but did manage to secure lands along a river from the Dakota Indians. In 1818, a treaty with England added a large area of land to northern Minnesota. In 1819, Fort Saint Anthony was established as the first permanent American settlement in the area. The site was renamed Fort Snelling in 1825 and went on to become the most important settlement in the area until the middle of the century.

The fur trade began to decline in 1837, with the first in a series of treaties with the Dakota and Ojibwa Indians that ceded large amounts of land to the United States. This encouraged settlers to enter the region and eventually made the lumber industry and agriculture more important than the fur trade.

The Minnesota Territory had about four thousand settlers in 1849, mostly near Fort Snelling. Most of these early settlers were from New England, although many had entered Minnesota from Canada. Within one year, the population jumped to more than six thousand. As the lumber industry grew more important, the pop-

Mass execution of participants in the Minnesota Dakota Sioux uprising of 1862. (Library of Congress)

ulation grew even more quickly. By 1857 the number of Minnesota residents, mostly from eastern states, reached more than 150,000.

The majority of new residents settled in the southeast part of the territory, near Fort Snelling. In the same area, St. Paul was founded in 1838 and became the territory capital in 1849. The nearby city of Minneapolis was founded in 1855. Minnesota became the thirty-second state, with much of its western lands removed and added to the Nebraska Territory, in 1858.

Wars and Industry. Minnesota was the first state to send volunteers to fight for the Union during the Civil War. More than twenty thousand residents of the state served in the war. Meanwhile, Minnesota faced its own violent conflict. In 1862, a rebellion by the Dakotas, confined to reservations within the state, eventually led to more than five hundred deaths within a few weeks. The defeated Dakotas were forced into reservations in western territories. The Ojibwas remained on reservations created for them in the north of the state.

After the Civil War, growth continued at a rapid pace. Germans, Swedes, and Norwegians arrived in large numbers. Other important sources of new immigrants were Finland, Poland, Bohemia, Ireland, France, Canada, the Netherlands, Belgium, Iceland, Denmark, Wales, and Switzerland. During the 1880's, the period of the state's fastest growth, most settlers were homesteaders in western Minnesota or worked in the lumber industry. Flour milling was also a major industry in the Twin Cities, both of which tripled in population during this decade. Mining of iron ore began in 1884 and soon became a major source of income.

The Twentieth Century. Immigration during the early twentieth century was mostly to the Twin Cities and included Finns, Italians, Slovakians, Croatians, Serbs, Greeks, Jews, Ukrainians, Russians, and Hispanics. African Americans from southern states moved to the Twin Cities also. In later years, Asians also immigrated.

Throughout the twentieth century Minnesota tended to be politically independent. It traditionally supported a wide variety of small political parties that influenced the policies of the major parties. The modern Democratic Party in Minnesota incorporates many of the ideas of the Farmer-Labor Party, while the modern Republican Party in the state is influenced by independents.

Loss of natural resources led to changes in the state's economy during the twentieth century. Much of the most valuable lumber was cut by 1920, forcing the industry to turn to other trees. At about the same time, flour milling was moved from Minneapolis to Buffalo. The best iron ore was depleted by the late 1950's. New techniques for using lower-grade iron ore led to a revitalization of the industry during the 1960's, but low-cost imports led to another decline during the 1980's. Despite a decline in agriculture after World War II, agriculture was still the state's largest industry.

The early 1980's brought a drop in crop prices, bringing hardship to farmers throughout the state. However, the nationwide recession of the late 1980's had only a minimal effect on Minnesota. During the 1990's, the state's economy turned to industries such as printing, health care, scientific instruments, chemicals, and recreational equipment.

Governor Ventura. From January, 1999, until January, 2003, Minnesota's governor was a colorful and sometimes controversial figure, Jesse Ventura. The name was his stage name as a professional wrestler and actor. Ventura was elected as a third-party reformer and gained office when the vote was split three ways. Describing himself as "fiscally conservative and socially liberal," Ventura achieved remarkable levels of public approval, which at one point soared to nearly 75 percent, despite his holding of sometimes-divisive views. As governor, he supported property tax reform, gay rights, medical marijuana, and abortion rights and was outspoken in his preference for atheism. He was also an outspoken advocate of a light rail system for the state. He vetoed many pieces of legislation, but his vetoes were frequently overridden and he was given derisive treatment by the media. In 2002, he refused to run for reelection, complaining about the focus of the press on politicians' private lives.

Hmong Citizenship. In 2000, an issue from Minnesota's past finally reached a climax. The issue involved the citizenship status of the many of the Hmong, a people mainly from Laos in Southeast Asia. Some 160,000 Hmong immigrated after the Vietnam War to the United States, and among them, about 60,000 settled in Minnesota. Tens of thousands had assisted the U.S. Army fighting and wished their sacrifices to be recompensed with lower barriers to citizenship. They wished to become citizens but found the language requirement daunting. They were vigorously supported in this regard by Democratic senator Paul Wellstone. On May 26, 2000, President Bill Clinton signed into law a measure exempting up to 45,000 Hmong immigrants from the English requirement for citizenship.

2002 Elections. Just before the 2002 general election, a tragic accident aggrieved many Minnesotans. Senator Wellstone, who had held office since 1991, was killed with his wife and daughter in a small plane crash. Wellstone, a former political science professor, was campaigning for reelection. The televised memorial service for him was turned into a political rally by his supporters. Others in attendance, such as Governor Ventura, who were not always allied with Wellstone's politics, decried being part of an impromptu rally, since they believed the event had a different purpose.

In the 2002 general election, the death of Senator

Wellstone left the Democratic Party without a candidate. Implored to fill the position, former senator and vice president Walter Mondale agreed to assume the vacancy. He was not successful at the election, however. St. Paul mayor Norm Coleman, a Republican, in one of the closest observed and contested races in the country, defeated him by 50 to 47 percent. At the same election, Republican Tim Pawlenty, a Minnesota House of Representatives leader, was elected governor in a three-way race. Two years later, Democrat John Kerry defeated George W. Bush 51 to 48 percent to win the state's ten electoral votes.

Rose Secrest
Updated by the Editor

Minnesota Time Line

1658	Pierre Esprit Radisson and Médard Chouart des Groseilliers are the first Europeans to explore the region.
1679	Daniel Greysolon, sieur Du Lhut, meets with Native Americans and claims the area for France.
1680	Father Louis Hennepin explores the area, is captured by the Dakota, and is rescued by Du Lhut.
1682	René-Robert Cavelier, sieur de La Salle, claims the entire valley of the Mississippi River for France, naming it Louisiana.
1686	Nicolas Perrot founds Fort Antoine.
1731	Pierre Gaultier de Varennes, sieur de La Vérendrye, founds Fort Saint Charles.
1762	Louisiana is ceded to Spain.
1763	End of the French and Indian War brings eastern Minnesota under British control.
1783	End of the American Revolution brings eastern Minnesota under American control.
1787	Eastern Minnesota becomes part of the Northwest Territory.
1800	Louisiana is returned to France.
1800	Eastern Minnesota becomes part of Indiana Territory.
1803	United States purchases Louisiana Territory from France.
1805	Explorer Zebulon Pike leads a military expedition to the region.
1808	American Fur Company is established.
1809	Eastern Minnesota becomes part of Illinois Territory.
1818	Eastern Minnesota becomes part of Michigan Territory.
1818	Part of Canada is ceded to the United States by England and is incorporated into Minnesota.
1819	Fort Saint Anthony (later Fort Snelling) is established.
1834	Western Minnesota becomes part of Michigan Territory
1836	Minnesota becomes part of Wisconsin Territory.
1837	Treaties with Native Americans open new lands for settlers.
1838	St. Paul is founded.
1838	Western Minnesota becomes part of Iowa Territory.
1846	Western Minnesota is returned to Wisconsin Territory.
Mar. 3, 1849	Minnesota Territory is created, with St. Paul as the capital.
1849	Population is about four thousand.
1850	Population is more than six thousand.
1851	University of Minnesota is established.
1855	Minneapolis is founded.
1857	Population reaches 150,000.
May 11, 1858	Minnesota is admitted to the Union as the thirty-second state.
1862	Rebellion by the Dakota Indians leads to five hundred deaths.
1862	First railroad, linking the Twin Cities, is built.
1867	Railroads link the Twin Cities to Chicago.
1880's	Minnesota experiences its period of fastest growth.
1880	Minneapolis surpasses St. Paul in population.
1884	Mining of iron ore begins.
1890's	Immigration shifts from rural areas to the Twin Cities.
1920's	Flour milling and lumber industries decline in importance.

Minnesota's largest city, Minneapolis, is separated from the capital city, St. Paul, by the Mississippi River. The side-by-side cities are popularly known as the Twin Cities. (PhotoDisc)

1950's	High-grade iron ore is depleted.
1959	Great Lakes are opened to oceangoing vessels.
1960's	Methods are developed to use low-grade iron ore.
1970's	Asian immigrants begin to arrive in Minnesota.
1980's	Crop prices decline, leading to economic hardship.
1980's	Low-cost foreign iron ore leads to a decline in the iron business.
1990	Population reaches nearly 4.4 million; more than half live in the Minneapolis-St. Paul metropolitan area.
1998	Population reaches 4.7 million.
1998	In a campaign that draws national attention, former professional wrestler Jesse Ventura is elected governor, the first Reform Party member to win a statewide office.
May 26, 2000	President Bill Clinton signs bill exempting up to 45,000 Hmong immigrants from the English language requirement for citizenship.
Oct. 25, 2002	Senator Paul Wellstone is killed in an airplane crash while campaigning.
Nov. 5, 2002	St. Paul mayor Norm Coleman defeats Walter Mondale for the U.S. Senate; Tim Pawlenty is elected governor with 44 percent of the vote.
Jan. 6, 2003	Controversial Governor Jesse Ventura, who reached the highest level of public approval of any governor in U.S. history, leaves office.
2004	Light-rail Hiawatha Line advocated by Governor Ventura in 1999 is completed; public use exceeds all estimates.

Notes for Further Study

Published Sources. Of the many books that offer general information about the state, one of the most enjoyable for beginning students may be *Minnesota Trivia* (1990) by Laurel Winter. Minnesota's scenic beauty has led to the publications of many books about the land and the living things that reside there. Two of the best are *Minnesota's Natural Heritage: An Ecological Perspective* (1995), edited by John R. Tester and Mary Keinstead, and *Natural Wonders of Minnesota: Parks, Preserves, and Wild Places* (1997) by Martin Hintz. An interesting look at new ways of influencing political decisions, using the issue of school choice in Minnesota as an example, can be found in *Transforming Public Policy: Dynamics of Policy Entrepreneurship and Innovation* (1996) by Nancy C. Roberts and Paula J. King. Jennifer A. Delton, in *Making Minnesota Liberal: Civil Rights and the Transformation of the Democratic Party* (2002), delves into the roots of Minnesota political culture to answer why a largely white state became a springboard for civil rights and social justice movements.

For students of the state's history, an excellent starting place is *A Historical Album of Minnesota* (1993) by Jeffrey D. Carlson or *A Popular History of Minnesota* (2005) by Norman K. Risjord. A more scholarly account is found in *Minnesota: A History* (1998) by William E. Lass. An interesting account of Native Americans in the state is offered in Samuel W. Pond's *The Dakota or Sioux in Minnesota as They Were in 1834* (1986). A colorful account of the early days of fur trading can be found in *The Grand Portage Story* (1992) by Carolyn Gilman. Kurt D. Bergemann's *Battalion: Minnesota Cavalry in the Civil War and Dakota War* (2004) details how a modestly trained group of volunteers from Minnesota lived to serve longer and see more action than any other Minnesota unit engaged in the Civil War; it later played a pivotal role during the uprising of the Dakota Indians. The Minnesota Historical Society has published a number of excellent books in its People of Minnesota Series, which explore the ethnic roots of the state, including *African Americans in Minnesota* (2002) by David Vassar, *Jews in Minnesota* (2002) by Hyman Berman and Linda Mack Schloff, and *Chinese in Minnesota* (2004) by Sherri Gebert Fuller. The modern history of the state is discussed in detail in *Minnesota in a Century of Change: The State and Its People Since 1900* (1989), edited by Cliford E. Clark.

Web Resources. A wide variety of Web sites dealing with all aspects of Minnesota can be found on the Internet. Many of these are associated with the state government, which maintains a large number of informative sites. Minnesota North Star (www.state.mn.us/portal/mn/jsp/home.do?agency=NorthStar) serves as a general portal to a wide range of information about the state, including government, business, health and safety, and travel and leisure. Explore Minnesota (www.exploreminnesota.com/) is a good place to begin the search for tourist-related information. At the Minnesota Department of Natural Resources site (www.dnr.state.mn.us/index.html), users can study native plants, see photos of state wildlife, and learn about the region's climate, among many other features. On the University of Minnesota's Geological Survey page (www.geo.umn.edu/mgs/) users can view topographical maps or regional rocks. Statistical information from the U.S. Census Bureau can be found at Minnesota QuickFacts (quickfacts.census.gov/qfd/states/27000.html).

Detailed information on economic activity in the state is available at Minnesota's Department of Employment and Economic Development (www.deed.state.mn.us/index.htm). An unusual Web site, dealing with public policy issues such as crime and the environment, can be found at Minnesota Planning (www.mnplan.state.mn.us). Of the many Web sites devoted to the state's past, a good starting place is Minnesota Historical Society (www.mnhs.org/index.htm), which offers information about the state's historical museums, archives, and libraries. Minnesota Genealogy (www.rootsweb.com/~mngenweb/) allows users to search for ancestor information by county. Information about the state's political process can be found at Minnesota's State Legislature (www.leg.state.mn.us/).

Counties

County	2000 pop.	Rank in pop.	Sq. miles	Rank in area	County	2000 pop.	Rank in pop.	Sq. miles	Rank in area
Aitkin	15,301	57	1,819.4	9	Chisago	41,101	22	417.7	82
Anoka	298,084	4	424.0	80	Clay	51,229	17	1,045.3	19
Becker	30,000	34	1,310.5	15	Clearwater	8,423	75	994.8	21
Beltrami	39,650	23	2,505.4	4	Cook	5,168	84	1,450.7	12
Benton	34,226	26	408.3	83	Cottonwood	12,167	63	640.0	47
Big Stone	5,820	81	497.0	68	Crow Wing	55,099	16	996.7	20
Blue Earth	55,941	15	752.4	33	Dakota	355,904	3	569.7	57
Brown	26,911	37	610.9	51	Dodge	17,731	51	439.5	74
Carlton	31,671	31	860.4	28	Douglas	32,821	28	634.3	48
Carver	70,205	11	357.1	85	Faribault	16,181	55	713.7	38
Cass	27,150	36	2,017.7	6	Fillmore	21,122	46	861.3	27
Chippewa	13,088	62	582.8	54	Freeborn	32,584	29	707.7	41

(continued)

County	2000 pop.	Rank in pop.	Sq. miles	Rank in area
Goodhue	44,127	19	758.6	31
Grant	6,289	80	546.5	62
Hennepin	1,116,200	1	556.6	60
Houston	19,718	48	558.4	59
Hubbard	18,376	50	922.6	24
Isanti	31,287	33	439.1	75
Itasca	43,992	20	2,665.3	3
Jackson	11,268	66	701.9	43
Kanabec	14,996	58	525.0	66
Kandiyohi	41,203	21	796.2	29
Kittson	5,285	82	1,097.1	18
Koochiching	14,355	59	3,102.4	2
Lac qui Parle	8,067	76	764.9	30
Lake	11,058	69	2,099.4	5
Lake of the Woods	4,522	85	1,296.7	16
Le Sueur	25,426	39	448.5	73
Lincoln	6,429	79	537.1	63
Lyon	25,425	40	714.2	37
McLeod	34,898	25	491.9	69
Mahnomen	5,190	83	556.2	61
Marshall	10,155	70	1,772.3	10
Martin	21,802	44	709.4	40
Meeker	22,644	42	608.6	52
Mille Lacs	22,330	43	574.5	55
Morrison	31,712	30	1,124.5	17
Mower	38,603	24	711.5	39
Murray	9,165	74	704.5	42
Nicollet	29,771	35	452.3	72
Nobles	20,832	47	715.5	36
Norman	7,442	77	876.3	26
Olmsted	124,277	8	653.0	46
Otter Tail	57,159	13	1,979.8	7
Pennington	13,584	61	616.6	50

County	2000 pop.	Rank in pop.	Sq. miles	Rank in area
Pine	26,530	38	1,411.2	13
Pipestone	9,895	72	465.9	71
Polk	31,369	32	1,970.5	8
Pope	11,236	67	670.2	44
Ramsey	511,035	2	155.8	87
Red Lake	4,299	86	432.4	78
Redwood	16,815	53	879.9	25
Renville	17,154	52	983.0	22
Rice	56,665	14	497.6	67
Rock	9,721	73	482.6	70
Roseau	16,338	54	1,662.6	11
St. Louis	200,528	6	6,225.7	1
Scott	89,498	10	356.8	86
Sherburne	64,417	12	436.6	76
Sibley	15,356	56	588.7	53
Stearns	133,166	7	1,344.6	14
Steele	33,680	27	429.6	79
Stevens	10,053	71	562.1	58
Swift	11,956	64	743.6	35
Todd	24,426	41	942.1	23
Traverse	4,134	87	574.1	56
Wabasha	21,610	45	525.0	65
Wadena	13,713	60	535.5	64
Waseca	19,526	49	423.3	81
Washington	201,130	5	391.7	84
Watonwan	11,876	65	434.5	77
Wilkin	7,138	78	751.5	34
Winona	49,985	18	626.3	49
Wright	89,986	9	660.8	45
Yellow Medicine	11,080	68	758.0	32

Source: U.S. Census Bureau; National Association of Counties.

Cities
With 10,000 or more residents

Rank	City	Population
1	Minneapolis	382,618
2	St. Paul (capital)	287,151
3	Duluth	86,918
4	Rochester	85,806
5	Bloomington	85,172
6	Brooklyn Park	67,388
7	Plymouth	65,894
8	Eagan	63,557
9	Coon Rapids	61,607
10	Burnsville	60,220
11	St. Cloud	59,107
12	Eden Prairie	54,901
13	Minnetonka	51,301
14	Maple Grove	50,365
15	Edina	47,425

Rank	City	Population
16	Woodbury	46,463
17	Apple Valley	45,527
18	Blaine	44,942
19	St. Louis Park	44,126
20	Lakeville	43,128
21	Maplewood	34,947
22	Richfield	34,439
23	Roseville	33,690
24	Mankato	32,427
25	Moorhead	32,177
26	Cottage Grove	30,582
27	Inver Grove Heights	29,751
28	Brooklyn Center	29,172
29	Fridley	27,449
30	Winona	27,069

Rank	City	Population	Rank	City	Population
31	Oakdale	26,653	48	Columbia Heights	18,520
32	Andover	26,588	49	Ramsey	18,510
33	Shoreview	25,924	50	Albert Lea	18,356
34	White Bear Lake	24,325	51	Willmar	18,351
35	Austin	23,314	52	Hastings	18,204
36	Crystal	22,698	53	Anoka	18,076
37	Owatonna	22,434	54	Chaska	17,449
38	New Brighton	22,206	55	Northfield	17,147
39	Champlin	22,193	56	Hopkins	17,145
40	Savage	21,115	57	Hibbing	17,071
41	New Hope	20,873	58	Lino Lakes	16,791
42	Faribault	20,818	59	Elk River	16,447
43	Shakopee	20,568	60	Red Wing	16,116
44	Chanhassen	20,321	61	Prior Lake	15,917
45	Golden Valley	20,281	62	Stillwater	15,143
46	South St. Paul	20,167	63	Rosemount	14,619
47	West St. Paul	19,405	64	Robbinsdale	14,123

(continued)

Rank	City	Population
65	New Ulm	13,594
66	Fergus Falls	13,471
67	Brainerd	13,178
68	Hutchinson	13,080
69	Vadnais Heights	13,069
70	Mounds View	12,738
71	Marshall	12,735
72	Ham Lake	12,710
73	Farmington	12,365
74	North St. Paul	11,929
75	Bemidji	11,917

Rank	City	Population
76	North Mankato	11,798
77	Mendota Heights	11,434
78	Worthington	11,283
79	Cloquet	11,201
80	East Bethel	10,941
81	Fairmont	10,889
82	Sauk Rapids	10,213
83	Buffalo	10,097

Population figures are from 2000 census.
Source: U.S. Bureau of the Census.

Index to Tables

DEMOGRAPHICS

Resident state and national populations, 1970-2004

Population figures given in thousands

	State pop.	U.S. pop.	Share	Rank
1970	3,806	203,302	1.9%	19
1980	4,076	226,546	1.8%	21
1985	4,184	237,924	1.8%	21
1990	4,376	248,765	1.8%	20
1995	4,660	262,761	1.8%	20
2000	4,919	281,425	1.8%	21
2004	5,101	293,655	1.7%	21

Source: U.S. Census Bureau, Current Population Reports, 2006.

Resident population by age, 2004

Age Group	Total persons
Under 5 years	332,000
5 to 17 years	908,000
18 to 24 years	531,000
25 to 34 years	678,000
35 to 44 years	793,000
45 to 54 years	755,000
55 to 64 years	488,000
65 to 74 years	300,000
75 to 84 years	217,000
85 years and older	98,000
All age groups	5,101,000

Portion of residents 65 and older	12.1%
National rank in portion of oldest residents	33
National average	12.4%

Population figures are rounded to nearest thousand persons;
figures include armed forces personnel stationed in the state.
Source: U.S. Bureau of the Census, 2006.

Resident population by race, Hispanic origin, 2004

Category	State pop.	Share	U.S.
All residents	5,101	100.00%	100.00%
Non-Hispanic white	4,421	86.67%	67.37%
Hispanic white	162	3.18%	13.01%
Other Hispanic	17	0.33%	1.06%
African American	212	4.16%	12.77%
Native American	59	1.16%	0.96%
Asian, Pacific Islander	175	3.43%	4.37%
Two or more categories	72	1.41%	1.51%

Population figures are in thousands. Persons counted as "Hispanic" (Latino) may be of any race. Because of overlapping categories, categories may not add up to 100%. Shares in column 3 are percentages of each category within the state; these figures may be compared to the national percentages in column 4.
Source: U.S. Bureau of the Census, 2006.

Projected state population, 2000-2030

Year	Population
2000	4,919,000
2005	5,175,000
2010	5,421,000
2015	5,668,000
2020	5,901,000
2025	6,109,000
2030	6,306,000
Population increase, 2000-2030	1,387,000
Percentage increase, 2000-2030	28.2

Projections are based on data from the 2000 census.
Source: U.S. Census Bureau.

VITAL STATISTICS

Infant mortality rates, 1980-2002

	1980	1990	2000	2002
All state residents	10.0	7.3	5.6	5.4
All U.S. residents	12.6	9.2	9.4	9.1
All state white residents	9.6	6.7	4.8	5.0
All U.S. white residents	10.6	7.6	5.7	5.8
All state black residents	20.0	23.7	14.6	10.3
All U.S. black residents	22.2	18.0	14.1	14.4

Figures represent deaths per 1,000 live births of resident infants under 1 year old, exclusive of fetal deaths. Figures for all residents include members of other racial categories not listed separately.
Source: U.S. Census Bureau, *Statistical Abstract of the United States,* 2006.

Abortion rates, 1990 and 2000

	1990	2000
Total abortions	16,000	15,000
Rate per 1,000 women	15.6	13.5
U.S. rate	25.7	21.3
Rank	31	28

Numbers of abortions are rounded to nearest thousand; ranks are based on rates.
Source: U.S. Census Bureau.

Marriages and divorces, 2004

Total marriages	30,100
Rate per 1,000 population	5.9
National rate per 1,000 population	7.4
Rank among all states	45
Total divorces	14,200
Rate per 1,000 population	2.8
National rate per 1,000 population	3.7
Rank among all states	39

Figures are for all marriages and divorces performed within the state, including those of nonresidents; totals are rounded to the nearest hundred. Ranks are for highest to lowest figures; note that divorce data are not available for five states.
Source: U.S. National Center for Health Statistics, *Vital Statistics of the United States,* 2006.

Death rates by leading causes, 2002
Deaths per 100,000 resident population

Cause	State	U.S.
Heart disease	171.4	241.7
Cancer	183.5	193.2
Cerebrovascular diseases	53.9	56.4
Accidents other than motor vehicle	38.4	37.0
Motor vehicle accidents	14.8	15.7
Chronic lower respiratory diseases	39.3	43.3
Diabetes mellitus	26.2	25.4
HIV	1.1	4.9
Suicide	9.9	11.0
Homicide	2.5	6.1
All causes	767.2	847.3
Rank in overall death rate among states		41

Figures exclude nonresidents who died in the state. Causes of death follow International Classification of Diseases. Rank is from highest to lowest death rate in the United States.
Source: U.S. National Center for Health Statistics, *National Vital Statistics Report,* 2006.

ECONOMY

Gross state product, 1990-2004
In current dollars

Year	State product	Nat'l product	State share
1990	$100.3 billion	$5.67 trillion	1.77%
2000	$185.4 billion	$9.75 trillion	1.90%
2002	$199.3 billion	$10.41 trillion	1.91%
2003	$210.2 billion	$10.92 trillion	1.92%
2004	$225.6 billion	$11.65 trillion	1.94%

Source: U.S. Bureau of Economic Analysis, *Survey of Current Business,* July, 2005.

Gross state product by industry, 2003
In billions of dollars

Construction $9.1
Manufacturing 28.8
Wholesale trade. 14.3
Retail trade 14.7
Finance & insurance 20.9
Information 7.4
Professional services 11.7
Health care & social assistance. 14.7
Government 19.3

Total state product. $198.5
Total U.S. product $10,289.2
State share of U.S. total 1.93%
Rank among all states 16

Total figures include industries not listed separately. Amounts are in chained 2000 dollars.
Source: U.S. Bureau of Economic Analysis, *Survey of Current Business,* July, 2005.

Personal income per capita, 1990-2004
In current dollars

	1990	2000	2004
Per capita income	$19,891	$32,017	$35,861
U.S. average	$19,477	$29,845	$32,937
Rank among states	15	10	8

Source: U.S. Bureau of Economic Analysis, *Survey of Current Business,* April, 2005.

Energy consumption, 2001
In trillions of British thermal units (BTU), except as noted

Total energy consumption
Total state energy consumption 1,745
Total U.S. energy consumption 96,275
State share of U.S. total 1.81%
Rank among states 21

Per capita consumption (In millions of BTU)
Total state per capita consumption 350
Total U.S. per capita consumption. 338
Rank among states 23

End-use sectors
Residential. 381
Commercial 336
Industrial 526
Transportation 502

Sources of energy
Petroleum 674
Natural gas. 345
Coal 353
Hydroelectric power 9
Nuclear electric power 123

Figures for totals include categories not listed separately.
Source: U.S. Energy Information Administration, *State Energy Data Report,* 2001.

Nonfarm employment by sectors, 2004

Total. 2,678,000
Construction 127,000
Manufacturing 343,000
Trade, transportation, utilities. 523,000
Information 60,000
Finance, insurance, real estate. 176,000
Professional & business services 302,000
Education & health services 377,000
Leisure, hospitality, arts, organizations 235,000
Other services, including repair &
    maintenance 118,000
Government 411,000

Figures are rounded to nearest thousand persons. "Total" includes mining and natural resources, not listed separately.
Source: U.S. Bureau of Labor Statistics, 2006.

Foreign exports, 1990-2004
In millions of dollars

Year	State	U.S.	State share
1990	5,091	394,045	1.29%
1996	8,992	624,767	1.44%
1997	9,447	688,896	1.37%
2000	10,303	712,055	1.32%
2003	11,266	724,006	1.67%
2004	12,678	769,332	1.65%

Rank among all states in 2004 21

U.S. total does not include U.S. dependencies.
Source: U.S. Census Bureau, *U.S. Merchandise Trade*, series FT 900, 2000; U.S. Census Bureau, *U.S. International Trade in Goods and Services*, Series FT 900, 2005.

LAND USE

Federally owned land, 2003
Areas in acres

	State	U.S.	State share
Total area	51,206,000	2,271,343,000	2.25%
Nonfederal land	47,671,000	1,599,584,000	2.98%
Federal land	3,535,000	671,759,000	0.53%
Federal share	6.9%	29.6%	—

Areas are rounded to nearest thousand acres. Figures for federally owned land do not include trust properties.
Source: U.S. General Services Administration, *Federal Real Property Profile*, 2006.

Land use, 1997
In acres, rounded to nearest thousand

Total surface area	54,010,000
Total nonfederal rural land.	45,356,000
Percentage rural land	84.0%
Cropland.	21,414,000
Conservation Reserve Program (CRP*) land . . .	1,544,000
Pastureland	3,434,000
Rangeland	(nil)
Forestland	16,248,000
Other rural land	2,716,000

*CRP is a federal program begun in 1985 to assist private landowners to convert highly erodible cropland to vegetative cover for ten years. Note that some categories of land overlap.
Source: U.S. Department of Agriculture, Natural Resources and Conservation Service, and Iowa State University, Statistical Laboratory, *Summary Report, 1997 National Resources Inventory*, revised December, 2000.

Farms and crop acreage, 2004

	State	U.S.	Share	Rank
Farms	80,000	2,113,000	3.79%	7
Acres (millions)	28	937	2.99%	13
Acres per farm	346	443	—	21

Source: U.S. Department of Agriculture, National Agricultural Statistics Service. Numbers of farms are rounded to nearest thousand units; acreage figures are rounded to nearest million. Rankings, including ties, are based on rounded figures.

GOVERNMENT AND FINANCE

Units of local government, 2002

	State	Total U.S.	Rank
All local governments	3,482	87,525	7
Counties	87	3,034	14
Municipalities	854	19,429	7
Towns (townships)	1,793	16,504	1
School districts	345	13,506	15
Special districts	403	35,052	29

Only 48 states have county governments, 20 states have township governments ("towns" in New England, Minnesota, New York, and Wisconsin), and 46 states have school districts. Special districts encompass such functions as natural resources, fire protection, and housing and community development.
Source: U.S. Census Bureau, *Census of Governments.*

State government revenue, 2002

Total revenue . . . . $22,439 mill.
General revenue . . . . $21,910 mill.
Per capita revenue $4,360
U.S. per capita average $3,689
Rank among states 12

Intergovernment revenue
Total . . . . $5,427 mill.
From federal government . . . . $5,282 mill.

Charges and miscellaneous
Total . . . . $3,259 mill.
Current charges . . . . $1,539 mill.
Misc. general income . . . . $1,720 mill.
Insurance trust revenue . . . . $529 mill.

Taxes
Total . . . . $13,224 mill.
Per capita taxes $2,632
Rank among states 3
Property taxes . . . . $306 mill.
Sales taxes . . . . $5,767 mill.
License taxes . . . . $864 mill.
Individual income taxes . . . . $5,443 mill.
Corporate income taxes . . . . $534 mill.
Other taxes . . . . $310 mill.

Total revenue figures include items not listed separately here.
Source: U.S. Bureau of the Census.

State government expenditures, 2002

General expenditures
Total state expenditures . . . . $26,693 mill.
Intergovernmental. . . . . $8,271 mill.

Per capita expenditures
State $4,672
Average of all states $3,859
Rank among states. 9

Selected direct expenditures
Education. . . . . $3,496 mill.
Public welfare . . . . $6,071 mill.
Health, hospital . . . . $541 mill.
Highways . . . . $1,080 mill.
Police protection. . . . . $178 mill.
Corrections. . . . . $335 mill.
Natural resources . . . . $453 mill.
Parks and recreation . . . . $111 mill.
Government administration. . . . . $659 mill.
Interest on debt . . . . $354 mill.
Total direct expenditures. . . . . $15,206 mill.

Totals include items not listed separately.
Source: U.S. Census Bureau.

POLITICS

Governors since statehood
D = Democrat; R = Republican; O = other;
(r) resigned; (d) died in office; (i) removed from office

Henry H. Sibley (D) 1858-1860
Alexander Ramsey (R). . . . . (r) 1860-1863
Henry A. Swift (R) 1863-1864
Stephen Miller (R). 1864-1868
William R. Marshall (R) 1868-1870
Horace Austin (R) 1870-1874
Cushman K. Davis (R) 1874-1876
John S. Pillsbury (R). 1876-1882
Lucius F. Hubbard (R). 1882-1887
Andrew R. McGill (R) 1887-1889
William R. Merriam (R) 1889-1893
Knute Nelson (R) . . . . (r) 1893-1895
David M. Clough (R) 1895-1899
John Lind (D) 1899-1901
Samuel R. Van Sant (R) 1901-1905
John A. Johnson (D) . . . . (d) 1905-1909
Adolph O. Eberhart (R). 1909-1915
Winfield S. Hammond (D) . . . . (d) 1915
Joseph A. A. Burnquist (R) 1915-1921
Jacob A. O. Preus (R) 1921-1925
Theodore Christianson (R) 1925-1931
Floyd B. Olson (O) . . . . (d) 1931-1936
Hjalmar Petersen (O) 1936-1937
Elmer A. Benson (O) 1937-1939
Harold E. Stassen (R) . . . . (r) 1939-1943
Edward J. Thye (R) 1943-1947
Luther W. Youngdahl (R) . . . . (r) 1947-1951

Clyde Elmer Anderson (R) 1951-1955
Orville L. Freeman (O) 1955-1961
Elmer L. Anderson (R) 1961-1963
Karl F. Rolvaag (O) 1963-1967
Harold P. LeVander (R) 1967-1971
Wendell R. Anderson (O) . . . . (r) 1971-1976
Rudy Perpich (O) 1976-1979
Albert H. Quie (R). 1979-1983
Rudolph Perpich (O) 1983-1991
Arne Carlson (R) 1991-1999
Jesse Ventura (O) 1999-2003
Tim Pawlenty (R) 2003-

Composition of congressional delegations, 1989-2007

	Dem	Rep	Total
House of Representatives			
101st Congress, 1989			
State delegates	5	3	8
Total U.S.	259	174	433
102d Congress, 1991			
State delegates	6	2	8
Total U.S.	267	167	434
103d Congress, 1993			
State delegates	6	2	8
Total U.S.	258	176	434
104th Congress, 1995			
State delegates	6	2	8
Total U.S.	197	236	433
105th Congress, 1997			
State delegates	6	2	8
Total U.S.	206	228	434
106th Congress, 1999			
State delegates	6	2	8
Total U.S.	211	222	433
107th Congress, 2001			
State delegates	5	3	8
Total U.S.	211	221	432
108th Congress, 2003			
State delegates	4	4	8
Total U.S.	205	229	434
109th Congress, 2005			
State delegates	4	4	8
Total U.S.	202	231	433
110th Congress, 2007			
State delegates	5	3	8
Total U.S.	233	202	435
Senate			
101st Congress, 1989			
State delegates	0	2	2
Total U.S.	55	45	100

(continued)

	Dem	Rep	Total
102d Congress, 1991			
State delegates	1	1	2
Total U.S.	56	44	100
103d Congress, 1993			
State delegates	1	1	2
Total U.S.	57	43	100
104th Congress, 1995			
State delegates	1	1	2
Total U.S.	46	53	99
105th Congress, 1997			
State delegates	1	1	2
Total U.S.	45	55	100
106th Congress, 1999			
State delegates	1	1	2
Total U.S.	45	54	99
107th Congress, 2001			
State delegates	2	0	2
Total U.S.	50	50	100
108th Congress, 2003			
State delegates	1	1	2
Total U.S.	48	51	99
109th Congress, 2005			
State delegates	1	1	2
Total U.S.	44	55	99
110th Congress, 2007			
State delegates	1	1	2
Total U.S.	49	49	98

Figures are for starts of first sessions. Totals are for Democrat (Dem.) and Republican (Rep.) members only. House membership totals under 435 and Senate totals under 100 reflect vacancies and seats held by independent party members. When the 110th Congress opened, the Senate's two independent members caucused with the Democrats, giving the Democrats control of the Senate.

Source: U.S. Congress, *Congressional Directory.*

Composition of state legislature, 1990-2006

	Democrats	Republicans
State House (134 seats)		
1990	78	56
1992	85	49
1994	71	63
1996	70	64
1998	62	70
2000	63	70
2002	53	81
2004	66	68
2006	85	49
State Senate (67 seats)		
1990	46	21
1992	45	22
1994	43	21
1996	42	24
1998	40	26
2000	41	25
2002	35	31
2004	35	31
2006	44	23

Figures for total seats may include independents and minor party members. Numbers reflect results of elections in listed years; elected members usually take their seats in the years that follow.

Source: Council of State Governments; *State Elective Officials and the Legislatures.*

Voter participation in presidential elections, 2000 and 2004

	2000	2004
Voting age population		
State	3,650,000	3,861,000
Total United States	209,831,000	220,377,000
State share of U.S. total	1.74	1.75
Rank among states	21	21
Portion of voting age population casting votes		
State	66.8%	73.3%
United States	50.3%	55.5%
Rank among states	1	1

Population figures are rounded to nearest thousand and include all residents, regardless of eligibility to vote.

Source: U.S. Census Bureau.

HEALTH AND MEDICAL CARE

Medical professionals
Physicians in 2003 and nurses in 2001

	U.S.	State
Physicians in 2003		
Total	774,849	14,088
Share of U.S. total		1.81%
Rate	266	278
Rank		10
Nurses in 2001		
Total	2,262,020	46,990
Share of U.S. total		2.08%
Rate	793	943
Rank		10

Rates are numbers of physicians and nurses per 100,000 resident population; ranks are based on rates.
Source: American Medical Association, *Physician Characteristics and Distribution in the U.S.*; U.S. Department of Health and Human Services, Health Resources and Services Administration.

Health insurance coverage, 2003

	State	U.S.
Total persons covered	4,633,000	243,320,000
Total persons not covered	444,000	44,961,000
Portion not covered	8.7%	15.6%
Rank among states	50	—
Children not covered	77,000	8,373,000
Portion not covered	6.2%	11.4%
Rank among states	45	—

Totals are rounded to nearest thousand. Ranks are from the highest to the lowest percentages of persons *not* insured.
Source: U.S. Census Bureau, Current Population Reports.

AIDS, syphilis, and tuberculosis cases, 2003

Disease	U.S. cases	State cases	Rank
AIDS	44,232	179	33
Syphilis	34,270	195	28
Tuberculosis	14,874	214	21

Source: U.S. Centers for Disease Control and Prevention.

Cigarette smoking, 2003
Residents over age 18 who smoke

	U.S.	State	Rank
All smokers	22.1%	21.1%	34
Male smokers	24.8%	22.4%	36
Female smokers	20.3%	19.9%	30

Cigarette smokers are defined as persons who reported having smoked at least 100 cigarettes during their lifetimes and who currently smoked at least occasionally.
Source: U.S. Centers for Disease Control and Prevention, *Morbidity and Mortality Weekly Report*, 53, no. 44 (November 12, 2004).

HOUSING

Home ownership rates, 1985-2004

	1985	1990	1995	2000	2004
State	70.0%	68.0%	73.3%	76.1%	76.4%
Total U.S.	63.9%	63.9%	64.7%	67.4%	69.0%
Rank among states	13	22	2	4	5

Net change in state home ownership rate,
1985-2004 . . . . +6.4%
Net change in U.S. home ownership rate,
1985-2004 . . . . +5.1%

Percentages represent the proportion of owner households to total occupied households.
Source: U.S. Census Bureau, 2006.

Home sales, 2000-2004
In thousands of units

Existing home sales	2000	2002	2003	2004
State sales	96.3	122.6	126.7	137.4
Total U.S. sales	5,171	5,631	6,183	6,784
State share of U.S. total	1.86%	2.18%	2.05%	2.03%
Sales rank among states	21	15	17	19

Units include single-family homes, condos, and co-ops.
Source: National Association of Realtors, Washington, D.C., *Real Estate Outlook: Market Trends & Insights.*

Values of owner-occupied homes, 2003

	State	U.S.
Total units	1,259,000	58,809,000
Value of units		
Under $100,000	20.0%	29.6%
$100,000-199,999	44.3%	36.9%
$200,000 or more	35.7%	33.5%
Median value	$169,778	$142,275
Rank among all states		15

Units are owner-occupied one-family houses whose numbers are rounded to nearest thousand. Data are extrapolated from survey samples.
Source: U.S. Census Bureau, American Community Survey.

EDUCATION

Public school enrollment, 2002

Prekindergarten through grade 8
State enrollment 568,000
Total U.S. enrollment. 34,135,000
State share of U.S. total 1.66%

Grades 9 through 12
State enrollment 279,000
Total U.S. enrollment. 14,067,000
State share of U.S. total 1.98%

Enrollment rates
State public school enrollment rate 90.6%
Overall U.S. rate 90.4%
Rank among states in 2002. 24
Rank among states in 1995. 32

Enrollment figures (which include unclassified students) are rounded to nearest thousand pupils during fall school term. Enrollment rates are based on enumerated resident population estimate for July 1, 2002.
Source: U.S. National Center for Education Statistics.

Public college finances, 2003-2004

FTE enrollment in public institutions of higher education
Students in state institutions 189,800
Students in all U.S. public institutions 9,916,600
State share of U.S. total 1.91
Rank among states 17

State and local government appropriations for higher education
State appropriation per FTE $5,564
National average $5,716
Rank among states 23
State & local tax revenue going to higher education 7.2%

FTE = full-time equivalent in public postsecondary programs, including summer sessions; student numbers are rounded to nearest hundred. Funding figures for 2003-2004 academic year include financial aid to students in state public institutions and exclude money for research, agriculture experiment stations, teaching hospitals, and medical schools; figures are rounded to nearest thousand dollars.
Source: Higher Education Executive Officers, Denver, Colorado.

TRANSPORTATION AND TRAVEL

Highway mileage, 2003

Interstate highways 912
Other freeways and expressways 153
Arterial roads. 12,702
Collector roads. 29,602
Local roads 88,524
Urban roads 16,209
Rural roads 115,684
Total state mileage 131,893
U.S. total 3,974,107
State share 3.32%
Rank among states 5

Note that combined urban and rural road mileage matches the total of the other categories.
Source: U.S. Federal Highway Administration.

Motor vehicle registrations and driver licenses, 2003

Vehicle registrations	State	U.S.	Share	Rank
Autos, trucks, buses	4,525,000	231,390,000	1.96%	18
Autos only	2,502,000	135,670	1.84%	19
Motorcycles	174,000	5,328,000	3.27%	10
Driver licenses	3,036,000	196,166,000	1.55%	23

Figures, which do not include vehicles owned by military services, are rounded to the nearest thousand. Figures for automobiles include taxis.
Source: U.S. Federal Highway Administration.

Domestic travel expenditures, 2003

Spending by U.S. residents on overnight trips and
day trips of at least 50 miles from home

Total expenditures within state . . . . $7.95 bill.
Total expenditures within U.S. . . . . $490.87 bill.
State share of U.S. total 1.6%
Rank among states 22

Source: Travel Industry Association of America.

Retail gasoline prices, 2003-2007

Average price per gallon at the pump

Year	U.S.	State
2003	$1.267	$1.244
2004	$1.316	$1.332
2005	$1.644	$1.669
2007	$2.298	$2.149

Excise tax per gallon in 2004 . . . . 20.0¢
Rank among all states in 2007 prices 43

Prices are averages of all grades of gasoline sold at the pump
during March months in 2003-2005 and during February, 2007.
Averages for 2006, during which prices rose higher, are not
available.
Source: U.S. Energy Information Agency, *Petroleum Marketing
Monthly* (2003-2005 data); American Automobile Association
(2007 data).

CRIME AND LAW ENFORCEMENT

State and local police officers, 2000-2004

	2000	2002	2004
Total officers			
U.S.	654,601	665,555	675,734
State	7,904	8,104	8,147*
*Net change, 2000-2004			+3.07%
Officers per 1,000 residents			
U.S.	2.33	2.31	2.30
State	1.61	1.61	1.60
State rank	46	47	47

Totals include state and local police and sheriffs.
Source: Carsey Institute, University of New Hampshire.

Crime rates, 2003

Incidents per 100,000 residents

Crimes	State	U.S.
Violent crimes		
Total incidents	263	475
Murder	3	6
Forcible rape	41	32
Robbery	77	142
Aggravated assault	142	295
Property crimes		
Total incidents	3,117	3,588
Burglary	547	741
Larceny/theft	2,297	2,415
Motor vehicle theft	272	433
All crimes	3,380	4,063

Source: U.S. Federal Bureau of Investigation, *Crime in the United
States,* annual.

State prison populations, 1980-2003

	State	U.S.	State share
1980	2,001	305,458	0.66%
1990	3,176	708,393	0.45%
1996	5,158	1,025,624	0.50%
2000	6,238	1,391,261	0.45%
2003	7,865	1,470,045	0.54%

State figures exclude prisoners in federal penitentiaries.
Source: U.S. Bureau of Justice Statistics, *Prisoners in 2003.*

Mississippi

Location: Gulf coast

Area and rank: 46,914 square miles (121,506 square kilometers); 48,434 square miles (125,444 square kilometers) including water; thirty-first largest state in area

Coastline: 44 miles (71 kilometers) on the Gulf of Mexico

Shoreline: 359 miles (578 kilometers)

Population and rank: 2,903,000 (2004); thirty-first largest state in population

Capital and largest city: Jackson (184,256 people in 2000 census)

Became territory: April 7, 1798

Entered Union and rank: December 10, 1817; twentieth state

Present constitution adopted: 1890

This modern Mississippi riverboat recalls the great age of nineteenth century steamboating on the Mississippi River. (Photo-Disc)

Counties: 82

State name: Mississippi takes its name from an Indian expression for "father of waters"

State nickname: Magnolia State

Motto: *Virtute et armis* (By valor and arms)

State flag: Modified Confederate flag in upper left corner, over red, white, and blue stripes

Highest point: Woodall Mountain—806 feet (246 meters)

Lowest point: Gulf of Mexico—sea level

Highest recorded temperature: 115 degrees Fahrenheit (46 degrees Celsius)—Holly Springs, 1930

Lowest recorded temperature: –19 degrees Fahrenheit (–28 degrees Celsius)—Corinth, 1966

State song: "Go, Mississippi"

State tree: Magnolia

State flower: Magnolia

State bird: Mockingbird

State fish: Largemouth or black bass

Mississippi History

Mississippi's climate has greatly influenced its history. Located in the Deep South of the United States, just above the Gulf of Mexico, Mississippi has long, humid summers and generally short, mild winters. Consequently the growing season throughout the state is more than two hundred days long. In the far South, the growing season can be as long as 280 days. This long growing period, combined with abundant rain, has made agriculture a prominent economic activity. Outside the hilly region in the north, the soils are finely textured, composed of clays, sands, and other components.

In the nineteenth century, when cotton became a major export crop for the United States, climate and soil tended to make the state heavily dependent on production of cotton. The prominence of cotton, a plantation crop requiring heavy investment of labor, contributed to the development of slavery as a major feature of life before the Civil War. Slavery gave Mississippi a large African American population, and the legacy of slavery produced racial inequality and troubled race relations. Continuing reliance on agriculture also tended to make Mississippi one of the least industrialized and poorest states in the United States throughout the twentieth century.

Early History. During prehistoric times, the area of Mississippi was populated by people who lived in highly organized farming societies. These societies are known as the Mound Builders, after the great ceremonial earth mounds they constructed. The Mound Builders may be divided into the people of the Hopewell culture, who flourished from about the first century until about 800 C.E., and the people of the Mississippian culture, who lived from about 800 C.E. until about 1500. When the earliest French settlers arrived in what is now the southwestern part of Mississippi, the Natchez Indians were still building mounds, which were used for burials and as sites for public buildings.

Modern machine harvesting cotton, the product on which Mississippi's agricultural economy was built during the nineteenth century. (Mississippi Division of Tourism Development)

By the time of European settlement in this area of North America, there were three major Native American nations in the Mississippi region, as well as a host of small Native American groups. The nation of the Choctaw was the largest of the three. The Choctaw controlled most of central and southern Mississippi. In southwestern Mississippi, the Natchez nation was dominant. In the northern part of what is now the state of Mississippi, the Chickasaw were the largest and most powerful group.

The Choctaw were an agricultural people who lived in thatched-roof cabins made of mud and bark. The Chickasaw were closely related to the Choctaw, and both groups spoke languages of the Muskogean family, but they were traditional enemies before European settlement. The Natchez were the largest and most unified group in the area. However, war broke out between the Natchez and French settlers during the early eighteenth century. The French joined with the Choctaw to destroy the Natchez in 1729. Some Natchez were sold into slavery, and others were absorbed into other tribes. The Choctaw and Chickasaw continued to live in the Mississippi region, adopting many of the ways of European society. By 1842 though, the U.S. government, under pressure from land-hungry white settlers, forced most of the Native Americans of the Southeast to relocate to Indian Territory in Oklahoma.

Exploration and Settlement. The Spanish and the French were the first Europeans to explore the territory of the lower Mississippi River. From 1539 to 1543, the Spaniard Hernando de Soto led an expedition that is believed to have crossed the northern part of the modern state of Mississippi. At the end of the seventeenth century, the French explorer René-Robert Cavelier, sieur de La Salle, journeyed down the Mississippi River to its mouth and claimed all of the land drained by the Mississippi in the name of France. La Salle named this huge expanse of territory Louisiana, in honor of King Louis XIV of France.

After the French and Indian War between France and Great Britain, from 1754 to 1763, France ceded all of the French land east of the Mississippi River to Great Britain. Although the British attempted to reserve the land of northern Mississippi for Native Americans and forbade white settlement in that region, white Ameri-

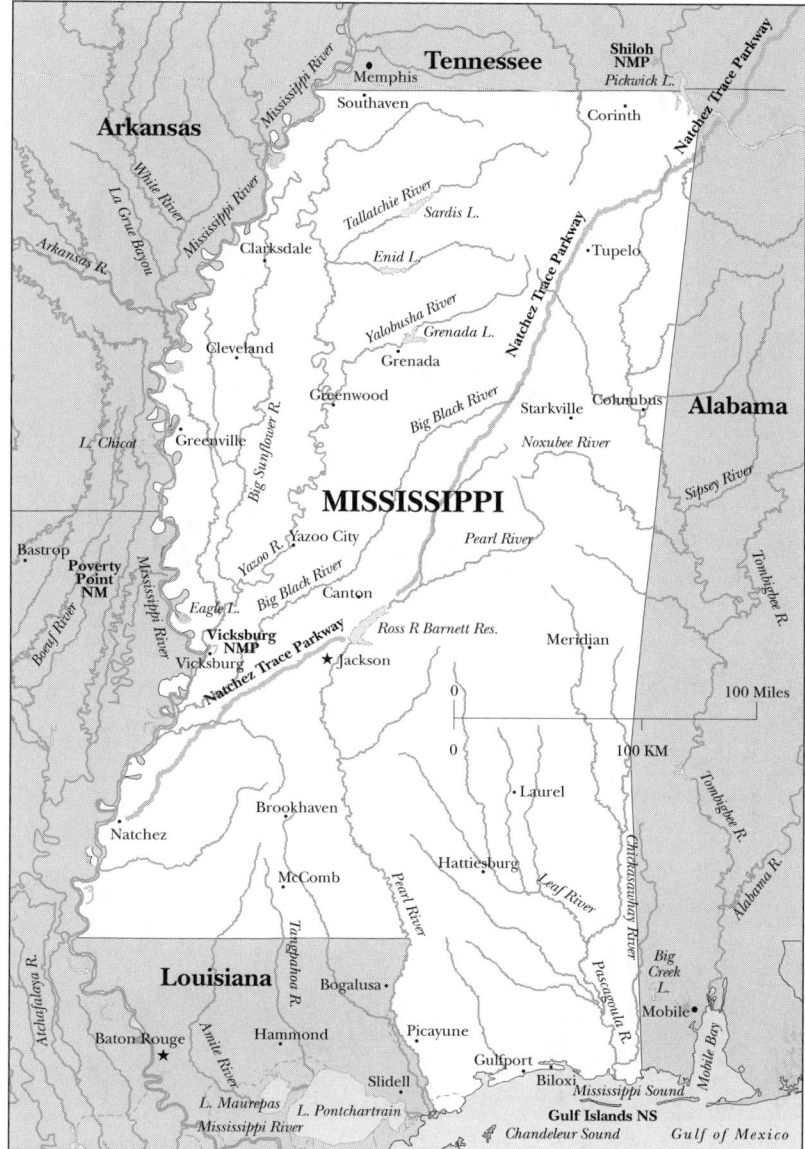

cans were drawn to the region for its rich soil. In 1783, the Spanish, who had acquired the Louisiana territories from France, took southern Mississippi from the British. In 1798, Spain recognized the northern part of modern Mississippi as territory of the new United States. That same year, the U.S. Congress organized this region as the Mississippi Territory.

American colonists in West Florida, the areas of modern Louisiana and southern Mississippi still under Spanish rule, revolted against Spain in 1810. West Florida became independent briefly, then it was annexed to the United States. In 1817, Mississippi was admitted to the United States as the twentieth state.

Cotton and the Civil War. In 1800, there were only 7,600 settlers in Mississippi. By 1820 this number had grown to 75,448. Ten years later, the U.S. Census put the state's population at 136,621. The 1860 census

State capitol building in Jackson. (Mississippi Division of Tourism Development)

showed a population of 791,305. Much of this rapid growth was due to the immigration of farmers who were looking for land to grow cotton. Cotton was Mississippi's most important crop, and, by the eve of the Civil War, Mississippi produced more cotton than any other state. Although only a small minority of the whites in the state were large plantation owners, owners of the big plantations held most of the economic and political power. Reliance on slave labor meant that the state had a huge slave population, with slaves of African descent outnumbering whites. Because there were so many people held in bondage, Mississippi's slave laws were among the harshest in the South.

By the 1850's the southern states, which were dependent on agriculture and slavery, were losing control over the U.S. Congress and presidency to the industrialized North. Many southerners believed that the south-

ern way of life, including the institution of slavery, could be preserved only by seceding from the United States. In 1861, after the election of U.S. president Abraham Lincoln, southern states began declaring their independence. Mississippi was the second state to secede, and Mississippi planter and former U.S. senator Jefferson Davis became president of the Confederate States of America.

About eighty thousand Mississippians fought for the Confederacy, and almost one-third of them died in the Civil War. Many counties in Mississippi also saw internal civil wars, as small farmers who opposed secession organized themselves to fight against the Confederacy. Fighting ravaged the state, and the forces of U.S. general William T. Sherman were especially destructive in their efforts to defeat the rebellious southerners.

The Legacy of War and Slavery. Mississippi's history of slavery and civil war led to continuing problems of racial inequality. During Reconstruction, the period following the Civil War when northern troops occupied the defeated lands of the Confederacy, the state's freed slaves entered political life, although few had sufficient education or experience to hold more than minor offices. By 1875, though, the whites of Mississippi began to retake power. They instituted segregation and, by the early twentieth century, excluded African Americans from public life by laws and terrorism. In some of the counties of the Mississippi Delta, the region where the Mississippi and Yazoo Rivers join together, 80 to 90 percent of the people were African American. Most of them worked as sharecroppers, farmers working the land for a share of the crop, on land owned by whites.

As a consequence of this legacy of slavery, Mississippi became a central battleground of the Civil Rights movement. In 1964, black and white college students working with civil rights organizations traveled to the state for Freedom Summer, to provide educational opportunities to local African Americans and to encourage minority voter registration. After the passage of the Civil Rights Act of 1964 and the Voting Rights Act of 1965, segregation became illegal in the United States, and black Mississippians began to enter public life. By the 1990's, the Mississippi legislature had the highest percentage of African Americans of any state legislature in the nation. Nevertheless, racial prejudice and poverty in Mississippi's black population continued to be problems.

Economy and Population After the War. Mississippi continued to have an economy based on agriculture well into the twentieth century. However, declining prices for cotton and other agricultural goods contributed to making it the poorest state in the nation by many measures. In 1936, Governor Hugh L. White began an effort to bring industry into the state with his Balance Agriculture with Industry (BAWI) program. World War II helped industrialization, especially in the shipbuilding industry along the Gulf Coast. The period following World War II saw rapid industrialization. By 1990 less than 3 percent of Mississippi's labor force were employed in agriculture, while almost 23 percent were employed in factories. The state's largest areas of employment during the late twentieth century were lumber and wood products, furniture, food products, and the manufacture of clothing.

With the disappearance of agricultural jobs, many black Mississippians left the state. The state's African American population declined from 60 percent of all Mississippians in 1900 to 36 percent in 1990. Most small towns and villages grew smaller or even disappeared after World War II. Most of the state's population growth in this period took place in the urban areas of Jackson, Biloxi-Gulfport, and Pascagoula-Moss Point. By 1990 nearly half of all the people in the state lived in cities.

History and Tradition. Despite economic and social progress in the state, issues from the past arose from time to time as a new decade began. When students at the University of Mississippi waved Confederate flags at football games in 2000, the university banned them. Students took the university to court for the right to wave the flags, but a state appeals court sided with the university. The Confederate flag issue resurfaced the following year in a referendum, and two-thirds of the state's voters chose to approve retaining the symbol of the Old South as the official flag of the state. At that, the National Association for the Advancement of Colored People (NAACP) announced a boycott of the state.

In 2001, another public issue tugged at the public's sense of traditionalism. Governor Ronnie Musgrove signed a law requiring schools to show the motto In God We Trust in classrooms, auditoriums, and cafeterias. In response, the American Civil Liberties Union (ACLU) threatened to sue. Backers of the law countered that the display of the motto was justified by its being a national motto of the United States, found on U.S. currency.

In April of the same year, Mississippi reached a $500 million settlement to end a twenty-six-year-old class action suit to desegregate the state's public colleges and universities. Plaintiffs said that the state's three historically black colleges were chronically underfunded. Nearly all of the settlement funds went to those colleges.

Early in December, 2002, Mississippi senator Trent Lott, majority leader in the Senate, raised a national furor for remarks he made at an event for South Carolina senator Strom Thurmond. Lott said that the nation "wouldn't have had all these problems over the years" if it had elected Thurmond in 1948, when the South Carolina senator ran for president on a segregationist platform. The torrent of criticism that followed caused Lott to make profuse public apologies, calling Mississippi segregation "wrong and wicked." Nevertheless, just before Christmas he resigned as Senate majority leader.

Another echo of the state's racist past was heard when, in 2003, a seventy-two-year-old man, Ernest Avants, was convicted in federal court of aiding and abetting the murder of a black sharecropper, sixty-seven-year-old Ben Chester White, in 1966. Avants had been tried and found innocent in 1967, but the case was reopened in 1999 when it was found that the murder had taken place on federal land. Avants was sentenced to life in prison and died there in June, 2004.

Hurricane Katrina. The state's coast suffered catastrophic damage when Hurricane Katrina made landfall on August 29, 2005. The Category 3 storm, with sustained winds of 120 miles per hour, was responsible for the deaths of 238 people; 67 remained missing. The hurricane's damage in Mississippi, which occurred throughout the state, amounted to billions of dollars. Officials determined that 90 percent of the buildings and other structures within one-half mile of the coast were destroyed.

Carl L. Bankston III
Updated by the Editor

Mississippi Time Line

1500's	Mound Builder cultures flourish along the Mississippi River and in other areas of eastern North America
1540	Spanish explorer Hernando de Soto's expedition enters the northern part of modern Mississippi.
1682	René-Robert Cavalier, sieur de La Salle, travels down the Mississippi to its mouth and claims all lands along the river in the name of France.
1699	French found Biloxi, the first permanent European settlement in Mississippi.
1729	French and the Choctaw together destroy the Natchez nation.
1763	Great Britain takes control of the Mississippi region after the French and Indian Wars.

(continued)

Apr. 7, 1798	Spain recognizes northern Mississippi as part of the United States; U.S. Congress organizes the Mississippi Territory.
1816	Chickasaw sign a treaty ceding their lands to the United States.
Dec. 10, 1817	Mississippi is admitted to the United States as the twentieth state.
1822	Capital of Mississippi is moved from Columbia to Jackson.
1830	Choctaw sign a treaty ceding their lands in Mississippi to the United States.
1844	University of Mississippi is chartered by the state legislature.
Jan. 9, 1861	Mississippi is the second state to secede from the Union, joining the Confederacy.
Apr. 12, 1861	Civil War begins when Confederate forces attack Fort Sumter, South Carolina.
Feb. 22, 1862	Former U.S. senator Jefferson Davis of Mississippi is made Confederate president.
July 4, 1863	Vicksburg, Mississippi, falls to Union forces.
Feb. 23, 1870	Mississippi is readmitted to the Union.
1875	Democratic Party takes control of the Mississippi legislature from the Republicans, essentially ending Reconstruction in Mississippi.
1890	Mississippi legislature adopts a constitution that formally establishes racial segregation in the state and effectively takes the vote away from most black citizens.
1908	Mississippi state legislature prohibits the sale and consumption of alcohol.
1926	Public schools are forbidden to teach evolution.
Apr. 21, 1927	Mississippi River floods and devastates many areas of Mississippi.
1936	Governor Hugh L. White begins attempting to industrialize Mississippi with the Balance Agriculture with Industry (BAWI) program.
Apr. 5, 1955	Governor White signs a bill providing fines and a jail sentence for white students who attend schools with African Americans.
Sept. 28, 1962	U.S. Court of Appeals orders Mississippi governor Ross R. Barnett to stop interfering with desegregation at the University of Mississippi.

James Meredith's admission to the University of Mississippi in 1962 marked a turning point in the Civil Rights movement. (Library of Congress)

Oct. 1, 1962	James Meredith is admitted to the University of Mississippi after riots that result in two deaths.
June 12, 1963	Medgar N. Evers, a Mississippi official of the National Association for the Advancement of Colored People, is shot to death.
June, 1964	Three young civil rights workers are murdered in Mississippi.
1969	Charles Evers, brother of Medgar Evers, becomes mayor of Fayette, making him the first black mayor in Mississippi.
1973	U.S. Supreme Court rules unconstitutional a Mississippi law enabling the state to purchase textbooks and distribute them free to segregated private schools.
1978	Mississippi elects its first Republican senator since Reconstruction.
1983	Unemployment is at a record high of 13.8 percent.
1988	Three southern governors, including Mississippi's, agree to improve conditions in the extremely impoverished Mississippi Delta.
1991	Kirk Fordice is elected the first Republican governor in Mississippi since Reconstruction.
June 30, 1992	U.S. Supreme Court rules that Mississippi has still not sufficiently erased segregation from its state university system.
2000	University of Mississippi wins law suit allowing it to ban the waving of Confederate flags at football games.
2001	Mississippians vote in referendum to retain the Confederate flag as the state's official flag.
Jan., 2001	Byron De La Beckwith, convicted in 1994 of murdering civil rights activist Medgar Evers in 1963, dies in prison at the age of eighty.
Dec. 20, 2002	Mississippi senator Trent Lott resigns as majority leader of the U.S. Senate after furor erupts at his comments about the segregationist policies advocated in 1948 by Senator Strom Thurmond of South Carolina.
Feb. 2, 2003	Ernest Avants is convicted in Jackson of the 1966 murder of black sharecropper Ben Chester White and is later sentenced to life in prison.
Aug. 29, 2005	Hurricane Katrina savages Mississippi's Gulf Coast, with 238 dead, 67 missing, and billions of dollars in damage.

Notes for Further Study

Published Sources. One of the most readable introductions to Mississippi history and the legacy of this history is Anthony Walton's *Mississippi: An American Journey* (1997). Walton, from a Mississippi family, weaves the story of his own family together with the history of the state and gives a moving and sympathetic account of Mississippi's past and present. *Mississippi: A Documentary History* (2003) by Bradley G. Bond also offeres a scholarly survey of the state's history. Those interested in Mississippi's pre-European past would do well to consult *Archeology of Mississippi* (1992) by Calvin S. Brown. *Mississippi Women: Their Histories, Their Lives* (2003), edited by Martha H. Swain, Elizabeth Anne Payne, and Marjorie Julian Spruill, brings together seventeen biographies of historically important women.

Readers interested in the Civil War period will want to look at *A Mississippi Rebel in the Army of Northern Virginia: The Civil War Memoirs of Private David Holt* (1995), written by war veteran David Holt and edited by Thomas D. Cockrell and Michael B. Ballard. Holt's memoirs begin well before the Civil War, so they provide an excellent view of middle-class life in Mississippi in the antebellum years. *Jefferson Davis: The Man and His Hour* (1991) by William C. Davis is a good biography of the Mississippian who led the Confederacy. *Jefferson Davis: The Essential Writings* (2003), edited by William J. Cooper, brings together Davis's letters and speeches.

The literature on the civil rights era in Mississippi is vast. Eric R. Burner's *And Gently He Shall Lead Them: Robert Parris Moses and Civil Rights in Mississippi* (1994) tells the story of the organization of civil rights activists in Mississippi by relating the story of one of the central organizers. *Have No Fear: The Charles Evers Story* (1996) is the autobiography of Charles Evers, a prominent black Mississippi civil rights activist and brother of Medgar Evers, who was murdered by a white supremacist in 1963. *I've Got the Light of Freedom: The Organizing Tradition and the Mississippi Freedom Struggle* (1995) by Charles M. Payne uses archives and interviews with participants in the Civil Rights movement to present a social history of the struggle. J. Todd Moye, in his use of extensive oral history interviews and archival research, provides a window into how struggles over civil rights and democracy in Mississippi played out against national developments in the Civil Rights movement with *Let the People Decide: Black Freedom and White Resistance Movements in Sunflower County, Mississippi* (2004). Paul Hendrickson's award-winning book *Sons of Mississippi: A Story of Race and Its Legacy* (2003) uses a racist event that occurred in 1962 to expose the wider issues surrounding race in the state.

Web Resources. One of the best online sources for general information about Mississippi is the home page of the state (www.state.ms.us). This offers connections to all of the Mississippi state government Web sites, sites for federal government officials and agencies in Mississippi, educational institution home pages, and a variety of other sites. For students of state government, the Mississippi Legislature site (www.ls .state.ms.us/) provides links to elected officials, the legislative calendar, and a good graphic showing how a bill becomes a law in Mississippi. For outdoor enthusiasts, the Mississippi Wildlife, Fisheries, and Parks site (www.mdwfp.com/) has information on a range of recreational activities and natural attractions. Those interested in detailed information about Mississippi history should go to the site of the Mississippi Department of Archives and History (www.mdah.state.ms .us), which gives material on historical landmarks in the state, as well as genealogical records and primary historical sources. The Visit Mississippi site (www.visitmississippi.org/ cultural%5Fhistorical/) has an extensive and well-designed collection of historical information, including links to the state's experiences with the Civil War and the Civil Rights movement, as well as narratives on the Native American and African American heritage within the region.

Counties

County	2000 pop.	Rank in pop.	Sq. miles	Rank in area	County	2000 pop.	Rank in pop.	Sq. miles	Rank in area
Adams	34,340	26	460.3	57	Lincoln	33,166	28	585.8	37
Alcorn	34,558	24	400.0	82	Lowndes	61,586	12	502.3	47
Amite	13,599	62	729.7	12	Madison	74,674	8	719.1	15
Attala	19,661	49	735.2	11	Marion	25,595	36	542.4	44
Benton	8,026	80	406.8	78	Marshall	34,993	23	706.4	17
Bolivar	40,633	17	876.3	2	Monroe	38,014	21	764.2	9
Calhoun	15,069	58	586.6	36	Montgomery	12,189	67	406.9	77
Carroll	10,769	71	627.8	30	Neshoba	28,684	31	570.0	41
Chickasaw	19,440	50	501.6	48	Newton	21,838	43	578.1	40
Choctaw	9,758	76	419.1	68	Noxubee	12,548	66	694.9	19
Claiborne	11,831	69	486.8	51	Oktibbeha	42,902	16	457.8	59
Clarke	17,955	55	691.3	22	Panola	34,274	27	684.3	23
Clay	21,979	42	408.6	75	Pearl River	48,621	14	811.5	4
Coahoma	30,622	29	554.2	43	Perry	12,138	68	647.2	26
Copiah	28,757	30	776.7	6	Pike	38,940	19	408.9	74
Covington	19,407	51	413.8	72	Pontotoc	26,726	35	497.4	49
DeSoto	107,199	5	478.3	53	Prentiss	25,556	37	415.0	71
Forrest	72,604	9	466.7	56	Quitman	10,117	75	404.9	79
Franklin	8,448	79	564.6	42	Rankin	115,327	4	774.6	7
George	19,144	53	478.3	52	Scott	28,423	32	609.1	31
Greene	13,299	63	712.9	16	Sharkey	6,580	81	427.7	64
Grenada	23,263	40	421.9	67	Simpson	27,639	34	588.8	34
Hancock	42,967	15	476.9	54	Smith	16,182	56	635.9	28
Harrison	189,601	2	581.0	39	Stone	13,622	61	445.4	62
Hinds	250,800	1	869.3	3	Sunflower	34,369	25	693.8	21
Holmes	21,609	44	756.1	10	Tallahatchie	14,903	59	644.0	27
Humphreys	11,206	70	418.1	69	Tate	25,370	38	404.5	80
Issaquena	2,274	82	413.0	73	Tippah	20,826	47	457.9	58
Itawamba	22,770	41	532.4	45	Tishomingo	19,163	52	424.2	65
Jackson	131,420	3	726.6	13	Tunica	9,227	78	454.8	60
Jasper	18,149	54	676.0	25	Union	25,362	39	415.5	70
Jefferson	9,740	77	519.4	46	Walthall	15,156	57	403.8	81
Jefferson Davis	13,962	60	408.4	76	Warren	49,644	13	586.7	35
Jones	64,958	10	693.9	20	Washington	62,977	11	724.0	14
Kemper	10,453	72	766.2	8	Wayne	21,216	45	810.4	5
Lafayette	38,744	20	631.2	29	Webster	10,294	74	422.8	66
Lamar	39,070	18	497.4	50	Wilkinson	10,312	73	676.8	24
Lauderdale	78,161	6	703.6	18	Winston	20,160	48	607.0	32
Lawrence	13,258	64	430.6	63	Yalobusha	13,051	65	467.2	55
Leake	20,940	46	582.7	38	Yazoo	28,149	33	919.6	1
Lee	75,755	7	449.7	61					
Leflore	37,947	22	592.0	33					

Source: U.S. Census Bureau; National Association of Counties.

Cities

With 10,000 or more residents

Rank	City	Population	Rank	City	Population
1	Jackson (capital)	184,256	14	Starkville	21,869
2	Gulfport	71,127	15	Olive Branch	21,054
3	Biloxi	50,644	16	Clarksdale	20,645
4	Hattiesburg	44,779	17	Ridgeland	20,173
5	Greenville	41,633	18	Natchez	18,464
6	Meridian	39,968	19	Greenwood	18,425
7	Tupelo	34,211	20	Laurel	18,393
8	Southaven	28,977	21	Long Beach	17,320
9	Vicksburg	26,407	22	Ocean Springs	17,225
10	Pascagoula	26,200	23	Brandon	16,436
11	Columbus	25,944	24	Moss Point	15,851
12	Clinton	23,347	25	Grenada	14,879
13	Pearl	21,961	26	Madison	14,692

(continued)

Rank	City	Population	Rank	City	Population
27	Yazoo City	14,550	34	Indianola	12,066
28	Horn Lake	14,099	35	Oxford	11,756
29	Corinth	14,054	36	Gautier	11,681
30	Cleveland	13,841	37	Picayune	10,535
31	McComb	13,337			
32	Canton	12,911			
33	West Point	12,145			

Population figures are from 2000 census.

Source: U.S. Bureau of the Census.

Index to Tables

DEMOGRAPHICS

Resident state and national populations, 1970-2004

Population figures given in thousands

	State pop.	U.S. pop.	Share	Rank
1970	2,217	203,302	1.1%	29
1980	2,521	226,546	1.1%	31
1985	2,588	237,924	1.1%	31
1990	2,575	248,765	1.0%	31
1995	2,773	262,761	1.0%	31
2000	2,845	281,425	1.0%	31
2004	2,903	293,655	1.0%	31

Source: U.S. Census Bureau, Current Population Reports, 2006.

Resident population by age, 2004

Age Group	Total persons
Under 5 years	208,000
5 to 17 years	541,000
18 to 24 years	323,000
25 to 34 years	391,000
35 to 44 years	405,000
45 to 54 years	397,000
55 to 64 years	284,000
65 to 74 years	193,000
75 to 84 years	121,000
85 years and older	40,000
All age groups	2,903,000
Portion of residents 65 and older	12.2%
National rank in portion of oldest residents	32
National average	12.4%

Population figures are rounded to nearest thousand persons; figures include armed forces personnel stationed in the state.
Source: U.S. Bureau of the Census, 2006.

Resident population by race, Hispanic origin, 2004

Category	State pop.	Share	U.S.
All residents	2,903	100.00%	100.00%
Non-Hispanic white	1,739	59.90%	67.37%
Hispanic white	41	1.41%	13.01%
Other Hispanic	8	0.28%	1.06%
African American	1,069	36.82%	12.77%
Native American	13	0.45%	0.96%
Asian, Pacific Islander	22	0.76%	4.37%
Two or more categories	18	0.62%	1.51%

Population figures are in thousands. Persons counted as
"Hispanic" (Latino) may be of any race. Because of overlapping
categories, categories may not add up to 100%. Shares in
column 3 are percentages of each category within the state;
these figures may be compared to the national percentages in
column 4.
Source: U.S. Bureau of the Census, 2006.

Projected state population, 2000-2030

Year	Population
2000	2,845,000
2005	2,916,000
2010	2,971,000
2015	3,014,000
2020	3,045,000
2025	3,069,000
2030	3,092,000
Population increase, 2000-2030	247,000
Percentage increase, 2000-2030	8.7

Projections are based on data from the 2000 census.
Source: U.S. Census Bureau.

VITAL STATISTICS

Infant mortality rates, 1980-2002

	1980	1990	2000	2002
All state residents	17.0	12.1	10.7	10.3
All U.S. residents	12.6	9.2	9.4	9.1
All state white residents	11.1	7.4	6.8	6.9
All U.S. white residents	10.6	7.6	5.7	5.8
All state black residents	23.7	16.2	15.3	14.8
All U.S. black residents	22.2	18.0	14.1	14.4

Figures represent deaths per 1,000 live births of resident infants
under 1 year old, exclusive of fetal deaths. Figures for all
residents include members of other racial categories not listed
separately.
Source: U.S. Census Bureau, *Statistical Abstract of the United States,*
2006.

Abortion rates, 1990 and 2000

	1990	2000
Total abortions	8,000	4,000
Rate per 1,000 women	12.4	5.9
U.S. rate	25.7	21.3
Rank	40	47

Numbers of abortions are rounded to nearest thousand; ranks are
based on rates.
Source: U.S. Census Bureau.

Marriages and divorces, 2004

Total marriages	17,800
Rate per 1,000 population	6.1
National rate per 1,000 population	7.4
Rank among all states	42
Total divorces	13,100
Rate per 1,000 population	4.5
National rate per 1,000 population	3.7
Rank among all states	12

Figures are for all marriages and divorces performed within the
state, including those of nonresidents; totals are rounded to the
nearest hundred. Ranks are for highest to lowest figures; note
that divorce data are not available for five states.
Source: U.S. National Center for Health Statistics, *Vital Statistics of
the United States,* 2006.

Death rates by leading causes, 2002
Deaths per 100,000 resident population

Cause	State	U.S.
Heart disease	315.5	241.7
Cancer	211.3	193.2
Cerebrovascular diseases	67.1	56.4
Accidents other than motor vehicle	57.2	37.0
Motor vehicle accidents	30.6	15.7
Chronic lower respiratory diseases	48.0	43.3
Diabetes mellitus	23.4	25.4
HIV	6.4	4.9
Suicide	11.9	11.0
Homicide	10.6	6.1
All causes	1,004.7	847.3
Rank in overall death rate among states		6

Figures exclude nonresidents who died in the state. Causes of
death follow International Classification of Diseases. Rank is
from highest to lowest death rate in the United States.
Source: U.S. National Center for Health Statistics, *National Vital
Statistics Report,* 2006.

ECONOMY

Gross state product, 1990-2004
In current dollars

Year	State product	Nat'l product	State share
1990	$38.8 billion	$5.67 trillion	0.68%
2000	$64.1 billion	$9.75 trillion	0.66%
2002	$68.6 billion	$10.41 trillion	0.66%
2003	$71.9 billion	$10.92 trillion	0.66%
2004	$76.2 billion	$11.65 trillion	0.65%

Source: U.S. Bureau of Economic Analysis, *Survey of Current Business,* July, 2005.

Gross state product by industry, 2003
In billions of dollars

Construction	$2.6
Manufacturing	10.9
Wholesale trade	3.6
Retail trade	6.6
Finance & insurance	2.9
Information	1.9
Professional services	2.3
Health care & social assistance	4.6
Government	11.1
Total state product	$66.6
Total U.S. product	$10,289.2
State share of U.S. total	0.65%
Rank among all states	35

Total figures include industries not listed separately. Amounts are in chained 2000 dollars.

Source: U.S. Bureau of Economic Analysis, *Survey of Current Business,* July, 2005.

Personal income per capita, 1990-2004
In current dollars

	1990	2000	2004
Per capita income	$13,089	$21,005	$24,650
U.S. average	$19,477	$29,845	$32,937
Rank among states	50	50	50

Source: U.S. Bureau of Economic Analysis, *Survey of Current Business,* April, 2005.

Energy consumption, 2001
In trillions of British thermal units (BTU), except as noted

Total energy consumption

Total state energy consumption	1,173
Total U.S. energy consumption	96,275
State share of U.S. total	1.22%
Rank among states	28

Per capita consumption (In millions of BTU)

Total state per capita consumption	410
Total U.S. per capita consumption	338
Rank among states	12

End-use sectors

Residential	234
Commercial	163
Industrial	427
Transportation	349

Sources of energy

Petroleum	486
Natural gas	341
Coal	198
Hydroelectric power	0
Nuclear electric power	104

Figures for totals include categories not listed separately.

Source: U.S. Energy Information Administration, *State Energy Data Report,* 2001.

Nonfarm employment by sectors, 2004

Total	1,125,000
Construction	49,000
Manufacturing	179,000
Trade, transportation, utilities	220,000
Information	15,000
Finance, insurance, real estate	46,000
Professional & business services	83,000
Education & health services	119,000
Leisure, hospitality, arts, organizations	125,000
Other services, including repair & maintenance	38,000
Government	243,000

Figures are rounded to nearest thousand persons. "Total" includes mining and natural resources, not listed separately.

Source: U.S. Bureau of Labor Statistics, 2006.

Foreign exports, 1990-2004
In millions of dollars

Year	State	U.S.	State share
1990	1,605	394,045	0.41%
1996	2,623	624,767	0.42%
1997	2,290	688,896	0.33%
2000	2,726	712,055	0.35%
2003	2,558	724,006	0.38%
2004	3,179	769,332	0.41%

Rank among all states in 2004 35

U.S. total does not include U.S. dependencies.
Source: U.S. Census Bureau, *U.S. Merchandise Trade,* series FT 900, 2000; U.S. Census Bureau, *U.S. International Trade in Goods and Services,* Series FT 900, 2005.

LAND USE

Federally owned land, 2003
Areas in acres

	State	U.S.	State share
Total area	30,223,000	2,271,343,000	1.33%
Nonfederal land	28,122,000	1,599,584,000	1.76%
Federal land	2,101,000	671,759,000	0.31%
Federal share	7.0%	29.6%	—

Areas are rounded to nearest thousand acres. Figures for federally owned land do not include trust properties.
Source: U.S. General Services Administration, *Federal Real Property Profile,* 2006.

Land use, 1997
In acres, rounded to nearest thousand

Total surface area	30,527,000
Total nonfederal rural land.	26,429,000
Percentage rural land	86.6%
Cropland	5,352,000
Conservation Reserve Program (CRP*) land	799,000
Pastureland	3,679,000
Rangeland	(nil)
Forestland	16,209,000
Other rural land	389,000

*CRP is a federal program begun in 1985 to assist private landowners to convert highly erodible cropland to vegetative cover for ten years. Note that some categories of land overlap.
Source: U.S. Department of Agriculture, Natural Resources and Conservation Service, and Iowa State University, Statistical Laboratory, *Summary Report, 1997 National Resources Inventory,* revised December, 2000.

Farms and crop acreage, 2004

	State	U.S.	Share	Rank
Farms	42,000	2,113,000	1.99%	23
Acres (millions)	11	937	1.17%	27
Acres per farm	262	443	—	25

Source: U.S. Department of Agriculture, National Agricultural Statistics Service. Numbers of farms are rounded to nearest thousand units; acreage figures are rounded to nearest million. Rankings, including ties, are based on rounded figures.

GOVERNMENT AND FINANCE

Units of local government, 2002

	State	Total U.S.	Rank
All local governments	1,000	87,525	29
Counties	82	3,034	16
Municipalities	296	19,429	27
Townships	0	16,504	—
School districts	164	13,506	29
Special districts	458	35,052	28

Only 48 states have county governments, 20 states have township governments ("towns" in New England, Minnesota, New York, and Wisconsin), and 46 states have school districts. Special districts encompass such functions as natural resources, fire protection, and housing and community development.
Source: U.S. Census Bureau, *Census of Governments.*

State government revenue, 2002

Total revenue	$11,052 mill.
General revenue	$11,044 mill.
Per capita revenue	$3,851
U.S. per capita average	$3,689
Rank among states	27

Intergovernment revenue	
Total	$4,535 mill.
From federal government	$4,374 mill.

Charges and miscellaneous	
Total	$1,780 mill.
Current charges	$1,193 mill.
Misc. general income	$587 mill.
Insurance trust revenue	−$167 mill.

Taxes	
Total	$4,729 mill.
Per capita taxes	$1,649
Rank among states	36
Property taxes.	$1 mill.
Sales taxes	$3,183 mill.
License taxes	$301 mill.
Individual income taxes	$985 mill.
Corporate income taxes	$196 mill.
Other taxes	$62 mill.

Total revenue figures include items not listed separately here.
Source: U.S. Bureau of the Census.

State government expenditures, 2002

General expenditures
Total state expenditures . . . . $12,742 mill.
Intergovernmental. . . . . $3,457 mill.

Per capita expenditures
State $3,998
Average of all states $3,859
Rank among states 23

Selected direct expenditures
Education. $1,698 mill.
Public welfare . . . . $3,214 mill.
Health, hospital . . . . $894 mill.
Highways . . . . $776 mill.
Police protection . . . . $67 mill.
Corrections. . . . . $249 mill.
Natural resources . . . . $198 mill.
Parks and recreation . . . . $37 mill.
Government administration. . . . . $202 mill.
Interest on debt . . . . $211 mill.
Total direct expenditures . . . . $8,005 mill.

Totals include items not listed separately.
Source: U.S. Census Bureau.

POLITICS

Governors since statehood
D = Democrat; R = Republican; O = other;
(r) resigned; (d) died in office; (i) removed from office

David Holmes (O) 1817-1820
George Poindexter (O) 1820-1822
Walter Leake (O) . . . . (d) 1822-1825
Gerard C. Brandon (O) 1825-1826
David Holmes(O) . . . . (r) 1826
Gerard C. Brandon (O) 1826-1832
Abram M. Scott (O) . . . . (d) 1832-1833
Charles Lynch (O) 1833
Hiram G. Runnells (O) 1833-1835
John A. Quitman (O) 1835-1836
Charles Lynch (O) 1836-1838
Alexander G. McNutt (D) 1838-1842
Tilghman M. Tucker (D) 1842-1844
Albert G. Brown (D) 1844-1848
Joseph M. Matthews (D) 1848-1850
John A. Quitman (D) . . . . (r) 1850-1851
John I. Guion (D) 1851
James Whitfield (D) 1851-1852
Henry S. Foote (D) . . . . (r) 1852-1854
John J. Pettus (D) 1854
John J. McRae (D) 1854-1857
William McWillie (D) 1857-1859
John J. Pettus (D) 1859-1863
Charles Clark (D) . . . . (i) 1863-1865
William L. Sharkey (D) . . . . (i) 1865

Benjamin G. Humphreys (D) . . . . (i) 1865-1868
Adelbert Ames (R). 1868-1870
James L. Alcorn (R) . . . . (r) 1870-1871
Ridgely C. Powers (R) 1871-1874
Adelbert Ames (R) . . . . (r) 1874-1876
John M. Stone (D) 1876-1882
Robert Lowry, Jr. (D) 1882-1890
John M. Stone (D) 1890-1896
Anselm J. McLaurin (D) 1896-1900
Andrew H. Longbird (D) 1900-1904
James K. Vardman (D) 1904-1908
Edmund F. Noel (D) 1908-1912
Earl L. Brewer (D) 1912-1916
Theodore G. Bilbo (D) 1916-1920
Lee M. Russell (D) 1920-1924
Henry L. Whitfield (D) . . . . (d) 1924-1927
Dennis Murphree (D) 1927-1928
Theodore G. Bilbo (D) 1928-1932
Martin S. Conner (D) 1932-1936
Hugh L. White (D) 1936-1940
Paul B. Johnson (D) . . . . (d) 1940-1943
Dennis Murphree (D) 1943-1944
Thomas L. Bailey (D) . . . . (d) 1944-1946
Fielding L. Wright (D) 1946-1952
Hugh L. White (D) 1952-1956
James F. Coleman (D) 1956-1960
Ross R. Barnett (D) 1960-1964
Paul B. Johnson, Jr. (D) 1964-1968
John Bell Williams (D) 1968-1972
William L. Waller (D) 1972-1976
Cliff Finch (D) 1976-1980
William Winter (D) 1980-1984
Bill Allain (D) 1984-1988
Ray Mabus (D) 1988-1992
Kirk Fordice (R) 1992-2000
Ronnie Musgrove (D) 2000-2004
Haley Barbour (R) 2004-

Composition of congressional delegations, 1989-2007

	Dem	Rep	Total
House of Representatives			
101st Congress, 1989			
State delegates	4	1	5
Total U.S.	259	174	433
102d Congress, 1991			
State delegates	5	0	5
Total U.S.	267	167	434
103d Congress, 1993			
State delegates	5	0	5
Total U.S.	258	176	434
104th Congress, 1995			
State delegates	2	3	5
Total U.S.	197	236	433
105th Congress, 1997			
State delegates	2	3	5
Total U.S.	206	228	434
106th Congress, 1999			
State delegates	3	2	5
Total U.S.	211	222	433
107th Congress, 2001			
State delegates	3	2	5
Total U.S.	211	221	432
108th Congress, 2003			
State delegates	2	2	4
Total U.S.	205	229	434
109th Congress, 2005			
State delegates	2	2	4
Total U.S.	202	231	433
110th Congress, 2007			
State delegates	2	2	4
Total U.S.	233	202	435
Senate			
101st Congress, 1989			
State delegates	0	2	2
Total U.S.	55	45	100
102d Congress, 1991			
State delegates	0	2	2
Total U.S.	56	44	100
103d Congress, 1993			
State delegates	0	2	2
Total U.S.	57	43	100
104th Congress, 1995			
State delegates	0	2	2
Total U.S.	46	53	99
105th Congress, 1997			
State delegates	0	2	2
Total U.S.	45	55	100

	Dem	Rep	Total
106th Congress, 1999			
State delegates	0	2	2
Total U.S.	45	54	99
107th Congress, 2001			
State delegates	0	2	2
Total U.S.	50	50	100
108th Congress, 2003			
State delegates	0	2	2
Total U.S.	48	51	99
109th Congress, 2005			
State delegates	0	2	2
Total U.S.	44	55	99
110th Congress, 2007			
State delegates	0	2	2
Total U.S.	49	49	98

Figures are for starts of first sessions. Totals are for Democrat (Dem.) and Republican (Rep.) members only. House membership totals under 435 and Senate totals under 100 reflect vacancies and seats held by independent party members. When the 110th Congress opened, the Senate's two independent members caucused with the Democrats, giving the Democrats control of the Senate.

Source: U.S. Congress, *Congressional Directory.*

Composition of state legislature, 1990-2006

	Democrats	Republicans
State House (121 seats)		
1990	98	23
1992	91	29
1994	89	31
1996	86	33
1998	83	37
2000	86	33
2002	80	42
2004	75	46
2006	74	47
State Senate (52 seats)		
1990	43	9
1992	37	15
1994	36	14
1996	34	18
1998	34	18
2000	34	18
2002	30	22
2004	28	24
2006	26	26

Figures for total seats may include independents and minor party members. Numbers reflect results of elections in listed years; elected members usually take their seats in the years that follow.

Source: Council of State Governments; *State Elective Officials and the Legislatures.*

Voter participation in presidential elections, 2000 and 2004

	2000	2004
Voting age population		
State	2,076,000	2,153,000
Total United States	209,831,000	220,377,000
State share of U.S. total	0.99	0.98
Rank among states	31	31
Portion of voting age population casting votes		
State	47.9%	52.9%
United States	50.3%	55.5%
Rank among states	39	39

Population figures are rounded to nearest thousand and include all residents, regardless of eligibility to vote.
Source: U.S. Census Bureau.

HEALTH AND MEDICAL CARE

Medical professionals
Physicians in 2003 and nurses in 2001

	U.S.	State
Physicians in 2003		
Total	774,849	5,240
Share of U.S. total		0.67%
Rate	266	182
Rank		48
Nurses in 2001		
Total	2,262,020	22,290
Share of U.S. total		0.99%
Rate	793	779
Rank		32

Rates are numbers of physicians and nurses per 100,000 resident population; ranks are based on rates.
Source: American Medical Association, *Physician Characteristics and Distribution in the U.S.*; U.S. Department of Health and Human Services, Health Resources and Services Administration.

Health insurance coverage, 2003

	State	U.S.
Total persons covered	2,343,000	243,320,000
Total persons not covered	511,000	44,961,000
Portion not covered	17.9%	15.6%
Rank among states	11	—
Children not covered	92,000	8,373,000
Portion not covered	12.1%	11.4%
Rank among states	16	—

Totals are rounded to nearest thousand. Ranks are from the highest to the lowest percentages of persons *not* insured.
Source: U.S. Census Bureau, Current Population Reports.

AIDS, syphilis, and tuberculosis cases, 2003

Disease	U.S. cases	State cases	Rank
AIDS	44,232	509	21
Syphilis	34,270	435	20
Tuberculosis	14,874	128	26

Source: U.S. Centers for Disease Control and Prevention.

Cigarette smoking, 2003
Residents over age 18 who smoke

	U.S.	State	Rank
All smokers	22.1%	25.6%	9
Male smokers	24.8%	31.1%	3
Female smokers	20.3%	20.7%	21

Cigarette smokers are defined as persons who reported having smoked at least 100 cigarettes during their lifetimes and who currently smoked at least occasionally.
Source: U.S. Centers for Disease Control and Prevention, *Morbidity and Mortality Weekly Report*, 53, no. 44 (November 12, 2004).

HOUSING

Home ownership rates, 1985-2004

	1985	1990	1995	2000	2004
State	69.6%	69.4%	71.1%	75.2%	74.0%
Total U.S.	63.9%	63.9%	64.7%	67.4%	69.0%
Rank among states	16	11	12	6	12

Net change in state home ownership rate,
1985-2004 . . . . +4.4%
Net change in U.S. home ownership rate,
1985-2004 . . . . +5.1%

Percentages represent the proportion of owner households to total occupied households.
Source: U.S. Census Bureau, 2006.

Home sales, 2000-2004
In thousands of units

Existing home sales	2000	2002	2003	2004
State sales	38.7	48.0	51.5	58.1
Total U.S. sales	5,171	5,631	6,183	6,784
State share of U.S. total	0.75%	0.85%	0.83%	0.86%
Sales rank among states	34	34	34	34

Units include single-family homes, condos, and co-ops.
Source: National Association of Realtors, Washington, D.C., *Real Estate Outlook: Market Trends & Insights.*

Values of owner-occupied homes, 2003

	State	*U.S.*
Total units	560,000	58,809,000
Value of units		
Under $100,000	61.3%	29.6%
$100,000-199,999	30.3%	36.9%
$200,000 or more	8.4%	33.5%
Median value	$85,142	$142,275
Rank among all states 48		

Units are owner-occupied one-family houses whose numbers are
rounded to nearest thousand. Data are extrapolated from
survey samples.
Source: U.S. Census Bureau, American Community Survey.

EDUCATION

Public school enrollment, 2002

Prekindergarten through grade 8
State enrollment 360,000
Total U.S. enrollment. 34,135,000
State share of U.S. total 1.05%

Grades 9 through 12
State enrollment 132,000
Total U.S. enrollment. 14,067,000
State share of U.S. total 0.94%

Enrollment rates
State public school enrollment rate. 88.9%
Overall U.S. rate 90.4%
Rank among states in 2002. 31
Rank among states in 1995. 27

Enrollment figures (which include unclassified students) are
rounded to nearest thousand pupils during fall school term.
Enrollment rates are based on enumerated resident population
estimate for July 1, 2002.
Source: U.S. National Center for Education Statistics.

Public college finances, 2003-2004

FTE enrollment in public institutions of higher education
Students in state institutions. 145,900
Students in all U.S. public institutions 9,916,600
State share of U.S. total 1.47
Rank among states 23

**State and local government appropriations for higher
education**
State appropriation per FTE $3,980
National average. $5,716
Rank among states 46
State & local tax revenue going to higher
education 11.9%

FTE = full-time equivalent in public postsecondary programs,
including summer sessions; student numbers are rounded to
nearest hundred. Funding figures for 2003-2004 academic year
include financial aid to students in state public institutions and
exclude money for research, agriculture experiment stations,
teaching hospitals, and medical schools; figures are rounded to
nearest thousand dollars.
Source: Higher Education Executive Officers, Denver, Colorado.

TRANSPORTATION AND TRAVEL

Highway mileage, 2003

Interstate highways	685
Other freeways and expressways.	46
Arterial roads	7,372
Collector roads.	15,286
Local roads.	50,716
Urban roads	10,661
Rural roads.	63,444
Total state mileage.	74,105
U.S. total	3,974,107
State share	1.86%
Rank among states	27

Note that combined urban and rural road mileage matches the
total of the other categories.
Source: U.S. Federal Highway Administration.

Motor vehicle registrations and driver licenses, 2003

Vehicle registrations	*State*	*U.S.*	*Share*	*Rank*
Autos, trucks, buses	1,951,000	231,390,000	0.84%	33
Autos only	1,139,000	135,670	0.84%	30
Motorcycles	27,000	5,328,000	0.51%	41
Driver licenses	1,886,000	196,166,000	0.96%	33

Figures, which do not include vehicles owned by military services,
are rounded to the nearest thousand. Figures for automobiles
include taxis.
Source: U.S. Federal Highway Administration.

Domestic travel expenditures, 2003

Spending by U.S. residents on overnight trips and day trips of at least 50 miles from home

Total expenditures within state . . . . $5.43 bill.
Total expenditures within U.S. . . . . $490.87 bill.
State share of U.S. total 1.1%
Rank among states 30

Source: Travel Industry Association of America.

Retail gasoline prices, 2003-2007

Average price per gallon at the pump

Year	U.S.	State
2003	$1.267	$1.244
2004	$1.316	$1.293
2005	$1.644	$1.646
2007	$2.298	$2.148

Excise tax per gallon in 2004 . . . . 18.4¢
Rank among all states in 2007 prices 44

Prices are averages of all grades of gasoline sold at the pump during March months in 2003-2005 and during February, 2007. Averages for 2006, during which prices rose higher, are not available.
Source: U.S. Energy Information Agency, *Petroleum Marketing Monthly* (2003-2005 data); American Automobile Association (2007 data).

CRIME AND LAW ENFORCEMENT

State and local police officers, 2000-2004

	2000	2002	2004
Total officers			
U.S.	654,601	665,555	675,734
State	5,000	5,277	5,527*
*Net change, 2000-2004			+10.54%
Officers per 1,000 residents			
U.S.	2.33	2.31	2.30
State	1.76	1.84	1.90
State rank	38	36	31

Totals include state and local police and sheriffs.
Source: Carsey Institute, University of New Hampshire.

Crime rates, 2003

Incidents per 100,000 residents

Crimes	State	U.S.
Violent crimes		
Total incidents	326	475
Murder	9	6
Forcible rape	37	32
Robbery	105	142
Aggravated assault	174	295
Property crimes		
Total incidents	3,720	3,588
Burglary	1,036	741
Larceny/theft	2,374	2,415
Motor vehicle theft	311	433
All crimes	4,046	4,063

Source: U.S. Federal Bureau of Investigation, *Crime in the United States*, annual.

State prison populations, 1980-2003

	State	U.S.	State share
1980	3,902	305,458	1.28%
1990	8,375	708,393	1.18%
1996	13,859	1,025,624	1.35%
2000	20,241	1,391,261	1.45%
2003	23,182	1,470,045	1.58%

State figures exclude prisoners in federal penitentiaries.
Source: U.S. Bureau of Justice Statistics, *Prisoners in 2003*.

Missouri

Location: Midwest

Area and rank: 68,898 square miles (178,446 square kilometers); 69,709 square miles (180,546 square kilometers) including water; eighteenth largest state in area

Coastline: none

Population and rank: 5,755,000 (2004); seventeenth largest state in population

Capital city: Jefferson City (39,636 people in 2000 census)

Largest city: Kansas City (441,545 people in 2000 census)

Became territory: June 4, 1812

Entered Union and rank: August 10, 1821; twenty-fourth state

Present constitution adopted: 1945

Counties: 114, as well as 1 independent city

State name: Missouri takes its name from the Missouri Indians, whose name means "town of the large canoes"

State nickname: Show-Me State

Motto: *Salus populi suprema lex esto* (The welfare of the people shall be the supreme law)

State capitol building in Jefferson City. (Missouri Division of Tourism)

State flag: Red, white, and blue stripes with state coat of arms surrounded by twenty-four stars

Highest point: Taum Sauk Mountain—1,772 feet (540 meters)

Lowest point: St. Francis River—230 feet (70 meters)

Highest recorded temperature: 118 degrees Fahrenheit (48 degrees Celsius)—Warsaw and Union, 1954

Lowest recorded temperature: –40 degrees Fahrenheit (–40 degrees Celsius)—Warsaw, 1905

State song: "Missouri Waltz"

State tree: Flowering dogwood

State flower: Hawthorn

State bird: Bluebird

State fish: Paddlefish; channel catfish

State animal: Mule

Missouri History

Missouri lies almost in the center of the forty-eight contiguous states. It is the southernmost midwestern state. Its eastern boundary is the Mississippi River, its western boundary the Missouri River. It is bordered by eight states: west of Missouri are Nebraska, Kansas, and Oklahoma. To its east are Illinois and Kentucky. Iowa borders it on the north, and Arkansas and Tennessee are on the south. Missouri is about 300 miles from east to west and about 280 miles from north to south.

The earliest settlers in the area probably lived there more than twelve thousand years ago. By the seventeenth century, the Missouri and Osage Indian tribes were there. The first Europeans in the region were Jacques Marquette, a French missionary, and Louis Jolliet, a fur trader, known to be there in 1673. In 1683, René-Robert Cavelier, sieur de La Salle, claimed a vast expanse of land, including present-day Missouri, for France, calling it Louisiana after King Louis XIV.

Early Settlements. The first permanent French settlement in Missouri was Sainte Genevieve, on the Mississippi River south of present-day St. Louis, established in 1735. In 1764, Pierre Laclède and René Auguste Chouteau founded St. Louis, also on the Mississippi River.

In 1762, Spain claimed France's Louisiana territory and futilely attempted to coerce Spaniards to move there. When the United States became independent in 1776, Spain invited Americans east of the Mississippi to move into Missouri. Substantial numbers of farmers and miners accepted. By 1799 groups of settlers inhabited the area.

In 1800, France reclaimed the Louisiana territory, which, through the Louisiana Purchase, it sold to the United States for fifteen million dollars in 1803. The Missouri Territory, which included Kansas, had a population of about twenty thousand by 1812. Most settled on land that had been the property of Native Americans, who sought to reclaim it. Various treaties were signed between the indigenous people and the new arrivals, but by 1825, almost no American Indians remained in Missouri.

The Missouri Compromise. Black slaves came to Missouri as early as 1720, owned by French miners searching for gold and other minerals. These slaves were involved in building Missouri's first cities. Soon

Modern depiction of a wagon train leaving Missouri to follow the Oregon Trail to the West. (Library of Congress)

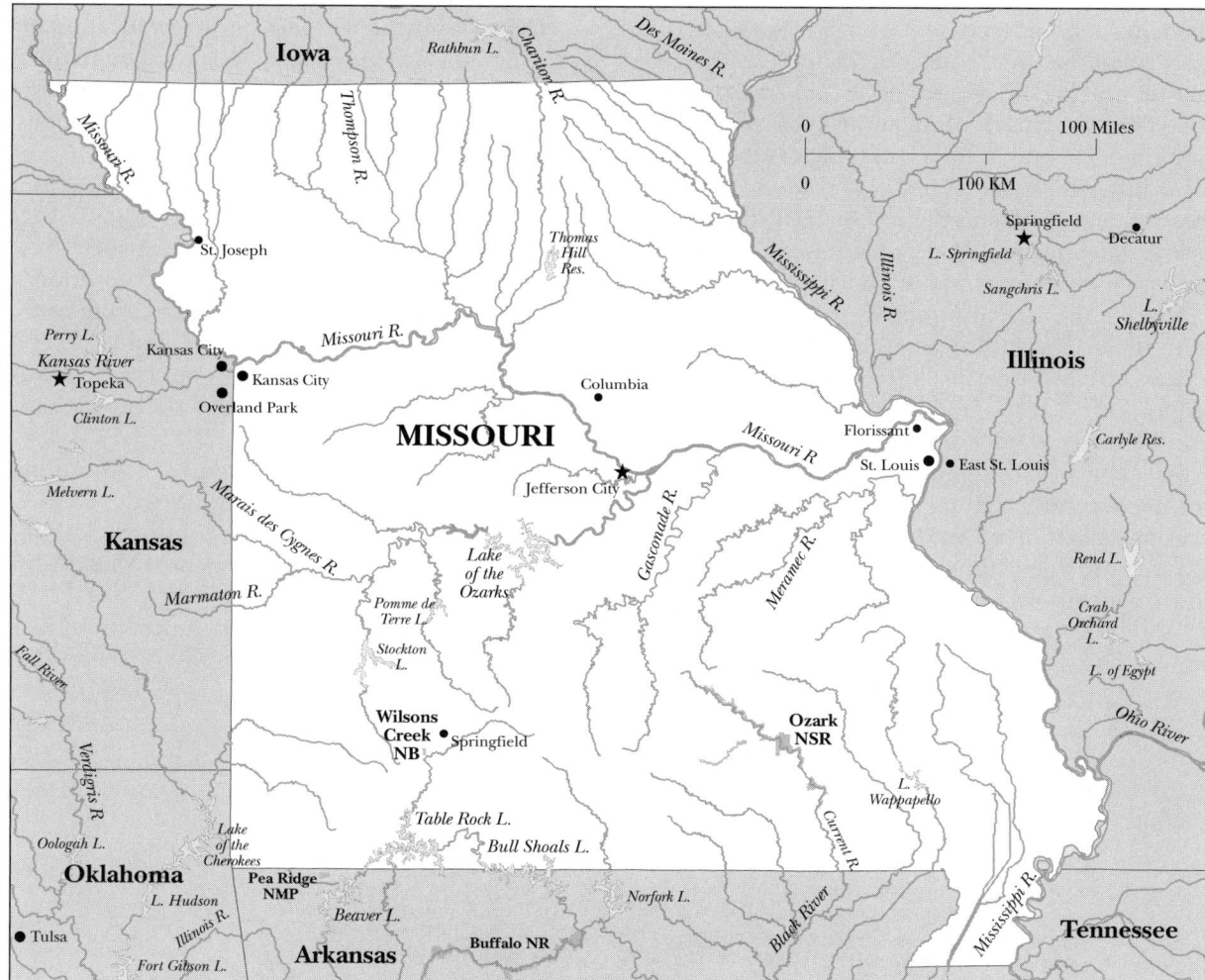

southern farmers and plantation owners relocated in Missouri, bringing their slaves with them.

Missouri applied to join the United States in 1818, coming in as a slave state. This would have made for one extra slave state in the country, and the federal government could not sanction an imbalance between slave and free states. The solution was the Missouri Compromise of 1821, which assured that the number of slave states and free states would remain equal. Maine was to be admitted as a free state, thereby permitting Missouri statehood as a slave state. In 1821, Missouri became the twenty-fourth state.

Early Economy. Missouri's land became fertile when advancing glaciers deposited rich topsoil upon it thousands of years ago. The state also has excellent river transportation in the east and the west. Steamboats carried their cargos to points along the rivers that eventually became thriving ports. Trails running west from Missouri led into the Rocky Mountains, where independent fur traders lived.

Soon there were permanent settlements and thriving towns along the river banks and trade routes. In 1822, the Santa Fe Trail was opened between Independence, in western Missouri, and Santa Fe, New Mexico, then a possession of Mexico. The beginning of the two-thousand-mile-long Oregon Trail was in Independence. When the Gold Rush to California began in 1848, thousands of prospectors passed through Missouri.

The potato famine in Ireland during the mid-1840's resulted in an influx of Irish into Missouri, where they worked on railroad construction or as day laborers. Missouri was growing so fast that extra hands were welcome. By the late 1840's, a wave of Germans seeking a better life came to the area around St. Louis.

Slavery. Slavery was a contentious matter in Missouri. By 1860, nearly 115,000 slaves were held in servitude in Missouri, many of them working on farms in the western part of the state. Some 3,600 free African Americans also lived in the state prior to the Civil War, most of them settling around St. Louis.

Dred Scott and his wife, Harriet, were slaves in Missouri. In 1846, the Scotts sued for their freedom, claming that they were humans, not chattel. Their case reached the U.S. Supreme Court in 1857. The Court ultimately ruled that the Scotts were property owned by the master who had bought them. As such, they had no rights as citizens. This decision enraged northern abolitionists and was one of the crucial factors that led to the Civil War, which started in 1861.

Missouri and the Confederacy. In 1861, the southern slave states formed the Confederacy, a separate nation with its own government. As a border state, Missouri, despite pressure from many of its slave owners, voted to remain in the Union, although nearly thirty-five thousand Missourians joined the Confederate armed forces.

Months before the war ended, Missouri freed all of its slaves, many of whom remained in the state. At the end of the twentieth century, Missouri had an African American population of nearly 11 percent. During the Civil War, more than a thousand battles were fought in Missouri, which sent more than 150,000 of its men to fight. About 115,000 of these fought in the Union forces.

Urban Growth. Missouri's strategic location and access to waterways and major trails resulted in the establishment of towns and cities along trade routes and encouraged urban development. The two cities that emerged as preeminent were St. Louis in the east and Kansas City on the western border with Kansas. Both cities became railroad centers, and Kansas City was known for its stockyards, first established in 1870, which still contribute substantially to its economy.

St. Louis became a major manufacturing center. In 1904, the city held a World's Fair that attracted people from around the world. In the same year, St. Louis also became the first U.S. city chosen as the site of the Olympic Games.

By 1990, 75 percent of Missouri's residents lived in urban areas. Chief among these, besides Kansas City and St. Louis, were Springfield, Joplin, St. Joseph, and Columbia, the site of the University of Missouri's main campus, established in 1841.

Other Factors in the Economy. Agriculture is a major contributor to Missouri's economy. Soybeans are the

Ornate buildings constructed for the 1904 St. Louis World's Fair. Scenes from the fair were re-created in the 1944 film Meet Me in St. Louis. *(Courtesy, Missouri Historical Society)*

St. Louis's skyline is dramatically framed by the Gateway Arch, which opened in 1965. The arch was built to symbolize the city's history as the gateway through which the American West was developed. (Courtesy, St. Louis Convention & Visitors Commission)

state's most lucrative crop, but Missouri farms produce sorghum, wheat, and hay as well. Cattle, hogs, and turkeys are also raised.

Its agricultural production nothwithstanding, manufacturing became the largest and most important factor in Missouri's economy. Among the major industries located in the state are General Motors and Ford, whose plants produce automobiles and trucks, McDonnell-Douglas, which makes commercial and private airplanes, and the Hallmark Card Company.

Tourism and commerce are also major factors in the economy. Tourists bring more than five billion dollars per year into the state, coming there to sightsee, gamble in the riverboat casinos, and attend the many shows in Branson, where nearly thirty well-known singers own theaters.

Missouri's Attractions. Besides the riverboat casinos and Branson's theaters, tourists are drawn to the state to view such attractions as the Gateway Arch in St. Louis, designed by Eero Saarinen and opened in 1965, which commemorates St. Louis as the jumping-off point for many pioneers heading into the western frontier.

Tourists also flock into New Madrid, a town on the Mississippi River that in 1811 and 1812 was rocked by three of the worst earthquakes ever recorded in North America. The New Madrid Museum provides detailed information about these earthquakes, which were so destructive they were felt as far away as Washington, D.C., and changed the course of the Mississippi River.

The Ozark Mountains and Lake of the Ozarks in southern Missouri offer excellent recreational facilities. This area attracts both tourists and retirees in large numbers. Tourists also flock into Florida and Hannibal in the north to visit the birthplace of Mark Twain and the town in which he grew up and used as the setting for some of his most popular stories.

Electoral Politics and Controversies. As the year 2000 arrived, Missouri politics were bifurcated, leaning right of center and to left of center. In presidential politics, the state leaned slightly to the right, as Republican candidate George W. Bush took Missouri's eleven electoral votes by 51-47 percent over Vice President Al Gore. On the other hand, the Democrats won a seat in the U.S. Senate previously held by Republican John Ashcroft, who lost the race to a deceased candidate, the late governor, Mel Carnahan. Voters chose Carnahan despite his death on October 16 in a plane crash amid the campaign; Senator Ashcroft lost the vote by two percentage points. The interim governor, Roger B. Wilson, appointed Carnahan's widow Jean in her late husband's place. A critical factor in the election was the stance of each candidate regarding gun control. Ashcroft made an issue of Carnahan's opposition to a proposed law that would allow carrying concealed weapons.

A controversial measure on the ballot that went down to defeat by a wide margin was a proposal to tax large businesses in order to help candidates who voluntarily agree to limit their acceptance of special interest contributions. Two-thirds of the voters opposed it. The election was marred by the inability to vote by some voters in largely African American St. Louis precincts. Crowds were so large as the polls' closing time approached that it was clear that some would be unable to vote. The Democratic Party proposed that the polls be allowed to remain open until 10:00 P.M. The Republican Party opposed this, and in the end the polls closed forty-five minutes later than their usual time. It was later determined that votes of those unable to cast their ballots would not have changed the electoral outcome.

After the election, a suit was filed and four members of the St. Louis Election Board were ousted by the governor. He explained that he was replacing them because of charges of irregularities that excluded hundreds of black voters from voting, mainly on account of crowding. In the governor's race, the outcome was decided by a hair, as the Democratic candidate Bob Holden edged out Republican Jim Talent by fewer than 22,000 votes among more than 2.3 million votes cast.

Third-party candidates played a possibly decisive role in collecting more than 60,000 votes. Two years later, when Talent ran for U.S. Senate, however, he won the very close race. Running against Jean Carnahan for a full Senate term, Talent won by fewer than 23,000 out of some 1.87 million votes cast.

By 2004, however, Missouri voters made a clear choice, though by no means of landslide proportions. This time, George W. Bush won the state by 53-46 percent over challenger John Kerry. In the governor's race, Republican Matt Blunt defeated his opponent by nearly 84,000 votes; and in the race for U.S. Senate, Republican Kit Bond won by 13 percent, which translated into more than 360,000 votes. In races for House seats, all incumbents were reelected. No incumbent received less than 59 percent of the vote; most had more than 60 percent and up to 75 percent, a huge margin. A newly elected member of the House was Democrat Russ Carnahan, son of the late governor and Jean Carnahan. He ran for the seat vacated by long-time congressional leader and presidential candidate Richard Gephardt, who opted for retirement. One key factor in the shift to the right of public opinion was the impact of the terrorist attacks in September, 2001. While this effect was felt everywhere in the nation, it was especially felt in Missouri because the Gateway Arch in St. Louis was closed as a possible terrorist target.

R. Baird Shuman
Updated by the Editor

Missouri Time Line

1673	Jacques Marquette, a missionary, and Louis Jolliet, a fur trader, sail the Mississippi, exploring Missouri and Tennessee.
1682	René-Robert Cavelier, sieur de La Salle, claims the Mississippi River Valley for France, naming it Louisiana.
1720	Philip Renault, searching for silver, brings black slaves to Missouri.
1724	Fort Orleans is built to protect French settlers from Spanish.
1750	Founding of Sainte Genevieve, the first permanent French settlement.
1763	Treaty of Paris cedes all of Canada and land west of the Mississippi River to Britain.
1764	René Auguste Chouteau and Pierre Laclède found St. Louis.
1799	Spanish encourage Americans to settle in Missouri.
1800	Spain returns western Louisiana territory to France.
1803	France sells area to the United States in Louisiana Purchase.
1804	Meriwether Lewis and William Clark leave St. Louis on their cross-country exploration.
1811	First of three earthquakes rocks New Madrid area.
June 4, 1812	Missouri becomes a territory.
1815	Indians in Missouri sign peace treaty with the United States.
1818	Missouri applies for statehood as a slave state.
1819	Steamship *Independence* sails the Missouri River, proving its navigability.
1820	Henry Clay brings the Missouri Compromise before Congress, which approves it.

Aug. 10, 1821	Missouri admitted to Union as twenty-fourth state.
1834	*St. Louis Herald*, first daily paper in the state, published in St. Louis.
1836	Missouri gains six northern counties from American Indians in Platte Purchase.
1839	University of Missouri chartered.
1841	University of Missouri opens in Columbia.
1847	St. Louis linked to eastern United States by telegraph.
1849	Major fire devastates much of the center of St. Louis.
1853	State opens first public high school in St. Louis.
1857	U.S. Supreme Court renders Dred Scott decision, denying him freedom.
1859	First railroad across Missouri links St. Joseph and Hannibal.
Apr. 3, 1860	First Pony Express service begins in St. Joseph.
Mar. 6, 1861	Missouri votes against seceding from Union.
1865	Civil War ends; new Missouri constitution bans slavery.
1866	Lincoln Institute is founded for recently freed slaves.
1867	First women admitted to University of Missouri.
1869	First bridge across Missouri River opens at Kansas City.
1875	New constitution restores voting rights to Confederate sympathizers.
1880	First newspaper in Missouri for African Americans, the *Advocate*, is established.
1904	St. Louis hosts Olympic Games and World's Fair.
1908	University of Missouri launches first journalism school in the United States.
1921	Missouri's first radio station, WEW, begins broadcasting at St. Louis University.
1931	Bagnell Dam on Osage River opens and forms Lake of the Ozarks.
1945	Harry S. Truman of Independence becomes the thirty-third president of the United States.
1945	Missouri's present constitution is adopted.
1952	Drought ravishes Missouri.
1955	Tornados kill 115 people in Missouri and Kansas.
1957	Harry S Truman Library opens in Independence.
1959	Tornadoes kill 22 and injure 5,350 in St. Louis.
1965	Gateway Arch opens in St. Louis.
1973	Floods devastate Missouri, causing $100 million in damage.
1982	Dioxin contamination closes Times Beach, threatens fifty other localities.
1986	State, suffering economic recession, institutes lottery.
1988	Court orders desegregation of Kansas City public schools.
1990	Governor signs educational bill allowing parental choice in public schools their children will attend.
1991	Kansas City elects its first black mayor, Emanuel Cleaver.
1993	St. Louis elects its first black mayor, Freeman Bosley, Jr.
1993	Floods cause five billion dollars damage in eastern Missouri.
Oct. 16, 2000	Governor Mel Carnahan, a candidate for U.S. Senate, is killed in airplane crash.
Nov. 7, 2000	Governor Carnahan is elected posthumously to the U.S. Senate; the state's interim governor appoints his widow to the seat.
Sept. 11, 2001	Gateway Arch in St. Louis is temporarily closed as a suspected terrorist target.
Jan., 2005	Richard Gephardt, longtime congressional member and House Democratic leader, retires from Congress after failing in bid for presidential nomination.

Notes for Further Study

Published Sources. P. C. Nagel's *Missouri: A History* (1988) is useful and readable. It should be read in conjunction with M. D. Rafferty's *Missouri: A Geography* (1982), which gives graphic descriptions of the state's topography. Michael J. O'Brien delves into Missouri's distant past in *Paradigms of the Past: The Story of Missouri Archeology* (1996). W. E. Foley views the development of Missouri from a wilderness to a state in

The Genesis of Missouri: From Wilderness to Statehood (1989), while Walter D. Kamphoefner considers the nineteenth century German immigration into the state in *The Westphalians: From Germany to Missouri* (1987). More specialized is John E. Farley's *Earthquake Fears, Predictions, and Preparations in Mid-America* (1998), which offers a detailed account of the New Madrid earthquakes and explains the underlying geological structure that makes Missouri earthquake prone. Also somewhat specialized but of exceeding importance is Paul Finkelman's *Dred Scott v. Sandford: A Brief History with Documents* (1997). It offers a explanation of the case that helped to start the Civil War.

David Thelen's *Paths of Resistance: Tradition and Dignity in Industrializing Missouri* (1996) offers information about the industrialization of the state and the obstacles that the shift from agriculture to industry involved. *Dino, Godzilla, and the Pigs: My Life on Our Missouri Hog Farm* (1993) by Mary Elizabeth Fricke is a beguiling memoir that chronicles the author's growing up on a Missouri farm. It is interesting when read along with R. Douglas Hurt's *Agriculture and Slavery in Missouri's Little Dixie* (1992), focusing on the matter of what slavery meant to Missouri's agricultural economy. Joan Gilbert in *The Trail of Tears Across Missouri* (1996) deals with the dispossession of the Cherokee Indians from North Carolina and Tennessee, who were forced to go west to Missouri and Oklahoma. *American Confluence: The Missouri Frontier from Borderland to Border State* (2006) by Stephen Aron provides a window to frontier and pioneer life in the Missouri River region. *The Other Missouri History: Populists, Prostitutes, and Regular Folk* (2004), edited by Thomas M. Spencer, is a fascinating narrative of the state's social history. *Women in Missouri History: In Search of Power and Influence* (2004), edited by LeeAnn Whites, Mary C. Neth, and Gary R. Kremer, offers a collection of lively essays profiling several important women from the period of colonial settlement through the mid-twentieth century.

The Off the Beaten Path series typically delivers a solid blend of photographs and interesting text designed to guide travelers through the state; the series' *Missouri* (7th ed., 2004) by Patti DeLano is a worthwhile read. Among the best accounts of the state aimed at juvenile readers are Patricia K. Kummer's *Missouri* (Rev. ed., 2002), Dennis B. and Judith Bloom Fradin's *Missouri* (1994), Rita C. LaDoux's *Missouri* (Rev. ed., 2001), and William R. Sanford's *America the Beautiful: Missouri* (1990).

Web Resources. The state of Missouri Web site (www.state .mo.us) offers comprehensive information about Missouri and its economy and leads users to other pertinent Web sites. The state's tourist bureau provides a site (www.visitmo.com/) offering voluminous information about tourism in Missouri and will direct viewers to lodgings, restaurants, and tourist attractions, including the twenty-two caves in the state open to tourists. People interested in Branson and its offerings should consult some of its fourteen Web sites, among them Bransom.com (www.branson.com) and BransomInfo.com (www.bransoninfo.com). Lake of the Ozarks Web sites include Lake of the Ozarks (www.funlake.com/) and Lake of the Ozarks State Park (www.mostateparks.com/lakeozark .htm).

The Missouri Historical Society (www.mohistory.org/content/Homepage/Homepage.aspx) should be the first stop

Kansas City, Missouri's largest city. (PhotoDisc)

for a wide range of information regarding the state's past. The State History Guide Web page for Missouri (www .shgresources.com/mo/timeline/) offers a detailed historical time line. Access Genealogy maintains pages that detail states' Indian tribes; those of Missouri can be found at www .accessgenealogy.com/native/missouri/index.htm. Web sites that detail cultural attractions include the St. Louis Art Museum (www.slam.org) and the Kansas City Museum (www

.unionstation.org/kcmuseum.cfm). The Harry S. Truman site (www.nps.gov/hstr) provides information about Truman, his home, and the Truman Library. Information about higher education in the state is best obtained from the Missouri Department of Higher Education site (www.dhe.mo.gov/). The state's Department of Natural Resources (www.dnr.mo.gov/index.html) provides visitors with information about state parks, conservation, and environmental issues.

Counties

County	2000 pop.	Rank in pop.	Sq. miles	Rank in area	County	2000 pop.	Rank in pop.	Sq. miles	Rank in area
Adair	24,977	40	567.7	61	Holt	5,351	108	461.9	94
Andrew	16,492	64	435.2	100	Howard	10,212	88	465.8	92
Atchison	6,430	106	544.7	69	Howell	37,238	27	927.8	3
Audrain	25,853	39	693.4	30	Iron	10,697	83	551.4	66
Barry	34,010	30	779.1	15	Jackson	654,880	2	604.8	54
Barton	12,541	78	594.3	56	Jasper	104,686	8	639.8	43
Bates	16,653	63	848.5	6	Jefferson	198,099	5	656.8	39
Benton	17,180	61	705.6	25	Johnson	48,258	18	830.6	9
Bollinger	12,029	80	620.8	50	Knox	4,361	111	505.7	80
Boone	135,454	7	685.4	31	Laclede	32,513	33	765.9	16
Buchanan	85,998	10	409.8	109	Lafayette	32,960	32	629.4	48
Butler	40,867	20	697.6	28	Lawrence	35,204	29	613.1	52
Caldwell	8,969	93	429.4	102	Lewis	10,494	84	505.1	81
Callaway	40,766	21	839.1	7	Lincoln	38,944	26	630.5	46
Camden	37,051	28	655.2	40	Linn	13,754	71	620.4	51
Cape Girardeau	68,693	14	578.7	59	Livingston	14,558	70	534.6	73
Carroll	10,285	87	694.6	29	McDonald	21,681	51	539.5	71
Carter	5,941	107	507.6	78	Macon	15,762	65	803.8	13
Cass	82,092	11	699.1	27	Madison	11,800	81	496.8	84
Cedar	13,733	72	476.0	89	Maries	8,903	95	527.8	74
Chariton	8,438	97	755.9	19	Marion	28,289	37	438.1	98
Christian	54,285	16	563.2	64	Mercer	3,757	113	454.5	95
Clark	7,416	101	507.3	79	Miller	23,564	44	592.3	58
Clay	184,006	6	396.5	111	Mississippi	13,427	74	413.2	108
Clinton	18,979	56	418.8	106	Moniteau	14,827	69	416.5	107
Cole	71,397	13	391.6	112	Monroe	9,311	92	646.0	42
Cooper	16,670	62	565.1	63	Montgomery	12,136	79	538.7	72
Crawford	22,804	48	742.6	23	Morgan	19,309	55	597.5	55
Dade	7,923	100	490.4	87	New Madrid	19,760	54	678.1	34
Dallas	15,661	66	541.6	70	Newton	52,636	17	626.5	49
Daviess	8,016	99	567.0	62	Nodaway	21,912	50	876.7	5
DeKalb	11,597	82	424.2	103	Oregon	10,344	86	791.5	14
Dent	14,927	68	753.6	21	Osage	13,062	77	606.1	53
Douglas	13,084	76	814.6	11	Ozark	9,542	91	746.8	22
Dunklin	33,155	31	545.6	68	Pemiscot	20,047	53	493.1	85
Franklin	93,807	9	922.1	4	Perry	18,132	58	474.7	90
Gasconade	15,342	67	519.5	75	Pettis	39,403	25	685.0	32
Gentry	6,861	103	491.6	86	Phelps	39,825	23	672.9	38
Greene	240,391	4	675.0	36	Pike	18,351	57	672.9	37
Grundy	10,432	85	435.9	99	Platte	73,781	12	420.4	105
Harrison	8,850	96	725.2	24	Polk	26,992	38	637.2	44
Henry	21,997	49	702.5	26	Pulaski	41,165	19	547.1	67
Hickory	8,940	94	398.7	110	Putnam	5,223	109	518.0	76

(continued)

County	2000 pop.	Rank in pop.	Sq. miles	Rank in area
Ralls	9,626	90	471.0	91
Randolph	24,663	41	482.4	88
Ray	23,354	45	569.5	60
Reynolds	6,689	105	811.3	12
Ripley	13,509	73	629.5	47
St. Charles	283,883	3	561.4	65
St. Clair	9,652	89	676.7	35
St. Francois	55,641	15	449.5	96
St. Genevieve	17,842	60	502.4	82
St. Louis	1,016,315	1	507.8	77
Saline	23,756	43	755.6	20
Schuyler	4,170	112	307.9	113
Scotland	4,983	110	438.5	97
Scott	40,422	22	421.0	104
Shannon	8,324	98	1,003.9	2
Shelby	6,799	104	500.9	83

County	2000 pop.	Rank in pop.	Sq. miles	Rank in area
Stoddard	29,705	35	827.2	10
Stone	28,658	36	463.3	93
Sullivan	7,219	102	651.0	41
Taney	39,703	24	632.4	45
Texas	23,003	47	1,178.6	1
Vernon	20,454	52	834.0	8
Warren	24,525	42	431.7	101
Washington	23,344	46	759.8	18
Wayne	13,259	75	761.1	17
Webster	31,045	34	593.4	57
Worth	2,382	114	266.5	114
Wright	17,955	59	682.3	33

Note: The city of St. Louis is independent of all counties.
Source: U.S. Census Bureau; National Association of Counties.

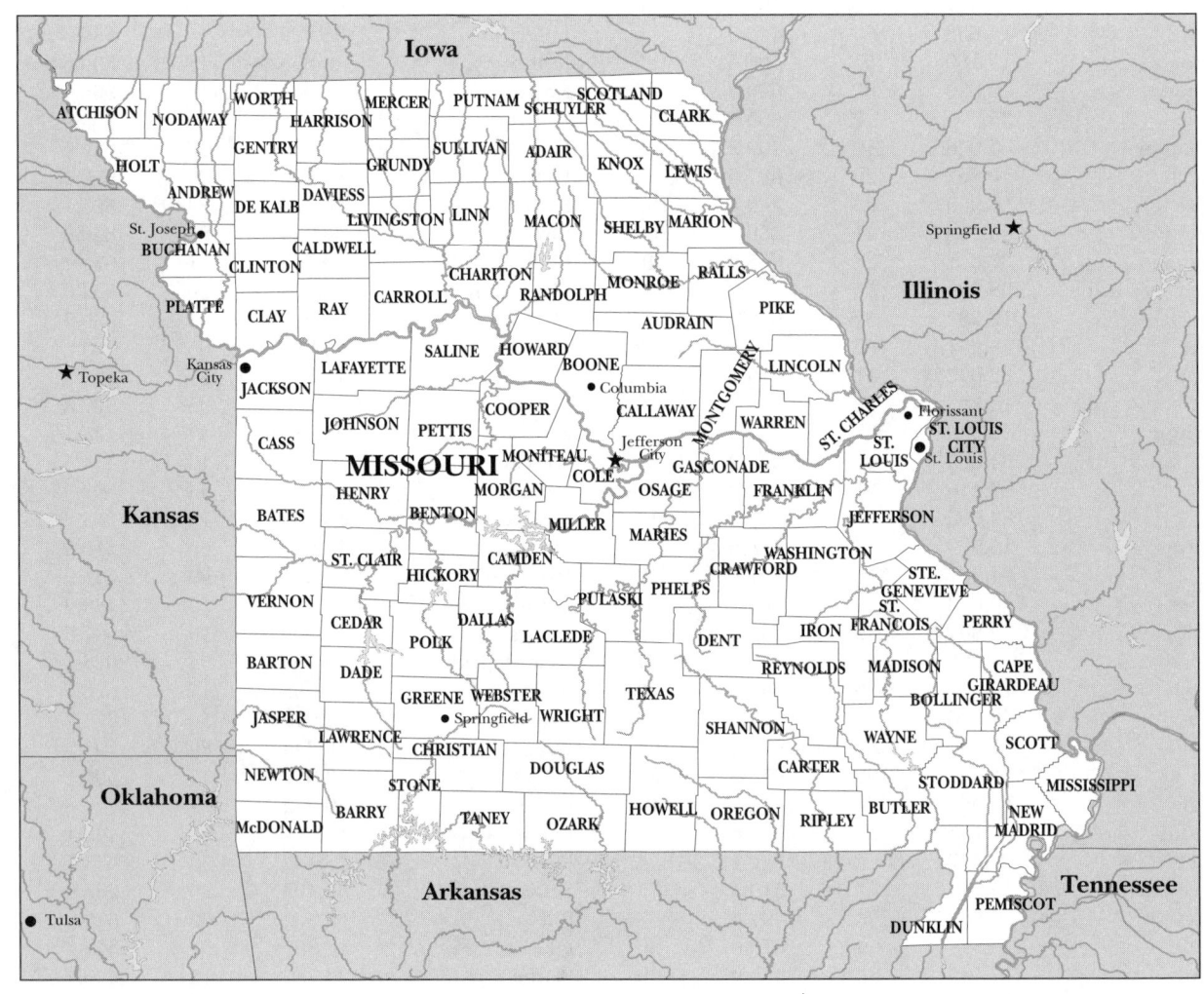

Cities
With 10,000 or more residents

Rank	City	Population	Rank	City	Population
1	Kansas City	441,545	18	Oakville	35,309
2	St. Louis	348,189	19	Wildwood	32,884
3	Springfield	151,580	20	Ballwin	31,283
4	Independence	113,288	21	Raytown	30,388
5	Columbia	84,531	22	Mehlville	28,822
6	St. Joseph	73,990	23	Kirkwood	27,324
7	Lee's Summit	70,700	24	Gladstone	26,365
8	St. Charles	60,321	25	Liberty	26,232
9	St. Peters	51,381	26	Hazelwood	26,206
10	Florissant	50,497	27	Maryland Heights	25,756
11	Blue Springs	48,080	28	Grandview	24,881
12	Chesterfield	46,802	29	Webster Groves	23,230
13	O'Fallon	46,169	30	Ferguson	22,406
14	Joplin	45,504	31	Belton	21,730
15	Jefferson City (capital)	39,636	32	Spanish Lake	21,337
16	University City	37,428	33	Affton	20,535
17	Cape Girardeau	35,349	34	Sedalia	20,339

(continued)

Rank	City	Population
35	Arnold	19,965
36	Manchester	19,161
37	Hannibal	17,757
38	Lemay	17,215
39	Sikeston	16,992
40	Kirksville	16,988
41	Overland	16,838
42	Concord	16,689
43	Poplar Bluff	16,651
44	Creve Coeur	16,500
45	Rolla	16,367
46	Warrensburg	16,340
47	Bridgeton	15,550
48	Jennings	15,469
49	Farmington	13,924
50	Fort Leonard Wood	13,666
51	St. Ann	13,607
52	Washington	13,243
53	Clayton	12,825
54	Carthage	12,668
55	Marshall	12,433

Rank	City	Population
56	Lebanon	12,155
57	Fulton	12,128
58	Nixa	12,124
59	Jackson	11,947
60	Moberly	11,945
61	Crestwood	11,863
62	Mexico	11,320
63	Bellefontaine Neighbors	11,271
64	Kennett	11,260
65	Raymore	11,146
66	Town and Country	10,894
67	West Plains	10,866
68	Excelsior Springs	10,847
69	Maryville	10,581
70	Neosho	10,505
71	Lake St. Louis	10,169
72	Berkeley	10,063

Population figures are from 2000 census.

Source: U.S. Bureau of the Census.

Index to Tables

DEMOGRAPHICS

Resident state and national populations, 1970-2004

Population figures given in thousands

	State pop.	U.S. pop.	Share	Rank
1970	4,678	203,302	2.3%	13
1980	4,917	226,546	2.2%	15
1985	5,000	237,924	2.1%	15
1990	5,117	248,765	2.1%	15
1995	5,378	262,761	2.0%	16
2000	5,597	281,425	2.0%	17
2004	5,755	293,655	2.0%	17

Source: U.S. Census Bureau, Current Population Reports, 2006.

Resident population by age, 2004

Age Group	Total persons
Under 5 years	371,000
5 to 17 years.	1,013,000
18 to 24 years	589,000
25 to 34 years	751,000
35 to 44 years	845,000
45 to 54 years	826,000
55 to 64 years	592,000
65 to 74 years	392,000
75 to 84 years	274,000
85 years and older	100,000
All age groups.	5,755,000

Portion of residents 65 and older	13.3%
National rank in portion of oldest residents	13
National average	12.4%

Population figures are rounded to nearest thousand persons;
figures include armed forces personnel stationed in the state.
Source: U.S. Bureau of the Census, 2006.

Resident population by race, Hispanic origin, 2004

Category	State pop.	Share	U.S.
All residents	5,755	100.00%	100.00%
Non-Hispanic white	4,781	83.08%	67.37%
Hispanic white	135	2.35%	13.01%
Other Hispanic	13	0.23%	1.06%
African American	661	11.49%	12.77%
Native American	26	0.45%	0.96%
Asian, Pacific Islander	79	1.37%	4.37%
Two or more categories	73	1.27%	1.51%

Population figures are in thousands. Persons counted as "Hispanic" (Latino) may be of any race. Because of overlapping categories, categories may not add up to 100%. Shares in column 3 are percentages of each category within the state; these figures may be compared to the national percentages in column 4.
Source: U.S. Bureau of the Census, 2006.

Projected state population, 2000-2030

Year	Population
2000	5,597,000
2005	5,765,000
2010	5,922,000
2015	6,070,000
2020	6,200,000
2025	6,315,000
2030	6,430,000
Population increase, 2000-2030	833,000
Percentage increase, 2000-2030	14.9

Projections are based on data from the 2000 census.
Source: U.S. Census Bureau.

VITAL STATISTICS

Infant mortality rates, 1980-2002

	1980	1990	2000	2002
All state residents	12.4	9.4	7.2	8.5
All U.S. residents	12.6	9.2	9.4	9.1
All state white residents	11.1	7.9	5.9	7.1
All U.S. white residents	10.6	7.6	5.7	5.8
All state black residents	20.7	18.2	14.7	17.1
All U.S. black residents	22.2	18.0	14.1	14.4

Figures represent deaths per 1,000 live births of resident infants under 1 year old, exclusive of fetal deaths. Figures for all residents include members of other racial categories not listed separately.
Source: U.S. Census Bureau, *Statistical Abstract of the United States,* 2006.

Abortion rates, 1990 and 2000

	1990	2000
Total abortions	14,000	8,000
Rate per 1,000 women	11.5	6.6
U.S. rate	25.7	21.3
Rank	42	45

Numbers of abortions are rounded to nearest thousand; ranks are based on rates.
Source: U.S. Census Bureau.

Marriages and divorces, 2004

Total marriages	36,500
Rate per 1,000 population	6.3
National rate per 1,000 population	7.4
Rank among all states	39
Total divorces	21,900
Rate per 1,000 population	3.8
National rate per 1,000 population	3.7
Rank among all states	22

Figures are for all marriages and divorces performed within the state, including those of nonresidents; totals are rounded to the nearest hundred. Ranks are for highest to lowest figures; note that divorce data are not available for five states.
Source: U.S. National Center for Health Statistics, *Vital Statistics of the United States,* 2006.

Death rates by leading causes, 2002
Deaths per 100,000 resident population

Cause	State	U.S.
Heart disease	294.5	241.7
Cancer	217.2	193.2
Cerebrovascular diseases	68.5	56.4
Accidents other than motor vehicle	46.6	37.0
Motor vehicle accidents	21.4	15.7
Chronic lower respiratory diseases	50.5	43.3
Diabetes mellitus	28.6	25.4
HIV	2.2	4.9
Suicide	12.2	11.0
Homicide	6.5	6.1
All causes	986.1	847.3
Rank in overall death rate among states		9

Figures exclude nonresidents who died in the state. Causes of death follow International Classification of Diseases. Rank is from highest to lowest death rate in the United States.
Source: U.S. National Center for Health Statistics, *National Vital Statistics Report,* 2006.

ECONOMY

Gross state product, 1990-2004
In current dollars

Year	State product	Nat'l product	State share
1990	$104.1 billion	$5.67 trillion	1.83%
2000	$176.4 billion	$9.75 trillion	1.81%
2002	$187.1 billion	$10.41 trillion	1.80%
2003	$193.8 billion	$10.92 trillion	1.77%
2004	$203.2 billion	$11.65 trillion	1.74%

Source: U.S. Bureau of Economic Analysis, *Survey of Current Business,* July, 2005.

Gross state product by industry, 2003
In billions of dollars

Construction	$7.9
Manufacturing	28.8
Wholesale trade	11.8
Retail trade	14.7
Finance & insurance	11.6
Information	9.2
Professional services	10.4
Health care & social assistance	12.7
Government	20.1
Total state product	$181.6
Total U.S. product	$10,289.2
State share of U.S. total	1.76%
Rank among all states	20

Total figures include industries not listed separately. Amounts are in chained 2000 dollars.
Source: U.S. Bureau of Economic Analysis, *Survey of Current Business,* July, 2005.

Personal income per capita, 1990-2004
In current dollars

	1990	2000	2004
Per capita income	$17,627	$27,241	$30,608
U.S. average	$19,477	$29,845	$32,937
Rank among states	28	30	29

Source: U.S. Bureau of Economic Analysis, *Survey of Current Business,* April, 2005.

Energy consumption, 2001

In trillions of British thermal units (BTU), except as noted

Total energy consumption

Total state energy consumption	1,815
Total U.S. energy consumption	96,275
State share of U.S. total	1.89%
Rank among states	20

Per capita consumption (In millions of BTU)

Total state per capita consumption	322
Total U.S. per capita consumption	338
Rank among states	29

End-use sectors

Residential	496
Commercial	389
Industrial	374
Transportation	556

Sources of energy

Petroleum	719
Natural gas	289
Coal	716
Hydroelectric power	9
Nuclear electric power	88

Figures for totals include categories not listed separately.
Source: U.S. Energy Information Administration, *State Energy Data Report,* 2001.

Nonfarm employment by sectors, 2004

Total	2,693,000
Construction	138,000
Manufacturing	312,000
Trade, transportation, utilities	533,000
Information	64,000
Finance, insurance, real estate	163,000
Professional & business services	303,000
Education & health services	359,000
Leisure, hospitality, arts, organizations	267,000
Other services, including repair & maintenance	119,000
Government	429,000

Figures are rounded to nearest thousand persons. "Total" includes mining and natural resources, not listed separately.
Source: U.S. Bureau of Labor Statistics, 2006.

Foreign exports, 1990-2004
In millions of dollars

Year	State	U.S.	State share
1990	3,130	394,045	0.79%
1996	5,404	624,767	0.86%
1997	6,724	688,896	0.98%
2000	6,497	712,055	0.83%
2003	7,234	724,006	1.07%
2004	8,997	769,332	1.17%

Rank among all states in 2004 25

U.S. total does not include U.S. dependencies.
Source: U.S. Census Bureau, *U.S. Merchandise Trade,* series FT 900,
2000; U.S. Census Bureau, *U.S. International Trade in Goods and
Services,* Series FT 900, 2005.

LAND USE

Federally owned land, 2003
Areas in acres

	State	U.S.	State share
Total area	44,248,000	2,271,343,000	1.95%
Nonfederal land	42,010,000	1,599,584,000	2.63%
Federal land	2,238,000	671,759,000	0.33%
Federal share	5.1%	29.6%	—

Areas are rounded to nearest thousand acres. Figures for federally
owned land do not include trust properties.
Source: U.S. General Services Administration, *Federal Real Property
Profile,* 2006.

Land use, 1997
In acres, rounded to nearest thousand

Total surface area	44,614,000
Total nonfederal rural land.	39,358,000
Percentage rural land	88.2%
Cropland.	13,751,000
Conservation Reserve Program (CRP*) land . . .	1,606,000
Pastureland	10,849,000
Rangeland	88,000
Forestland	12,431,000
Other rural land	634,000

*CRP is a federal program begun in 1985 to assist private
landowners to convert highly erodible cropland to vegetative
cover for ten years. Note that some categories of land overlap.
Source: U.S. Department of Agriculture, Natural Resources and
Conservation Service, and Iowa State University, Statistical
Laboratory, S*ummary Report, 1997 National Resources Inventory,*
revised December, 2000.

Farms and crop acreage, 2004

	State	U.S.	Share	Rank
Farms	106,000	2,113,000	5.02%	2
Acres (millions)	30	937	3.20%	12
Acres per farm	284	443	—	24

Source: U.S. Department of Agriculture, National Agricultural
Statistics Service. Numbers of farms are rounded to nearest
thousand units; acreage figures are rounded to nearest million.
Rankings, including ties, are based on rounded figures.

GOVERNMENT AND FINANCE

Units of local government, 2002

	State	Total U.S.	Rank
All local governments	3,422	87,525	8
Counties	114	3,034	4
Municipalities	946	19,429	5
Townships	312	16,504	14
School districts	536	13,506	10
Special districts	1,514	35,052	6

Only 48 states have county governments, 20 states have township
governments ("towns" in New England, Minnesota, New York,
and Wisconsin), and 46 states have school districts. Special
districts encompass such functions as natural resources, fire
protection, and housing and community development.
Source: U.S. Census Bureau, *Census of Governments.*

State government revenue, 2002

Total revenue	$19,085 mill.
General revenue	$18,654 mill.
Per capita revenue	$3,284
U.S. per capita average	$3,689
Rank among states	41

Intergovernment revenue	
Total	$6,819 mill.
From federal government	$6,693 mill.

Charges and miscellaneous	
Total	$3,106 mill.
Current charges	$1,444 mill.
Misc. general income	$1,662 mill.
Insurance trust revenue	$432 mill.

Taxes	
Total	$8,729 mill.
Per capita taxes	$1,539
Rank among states	41
Property taxes	$21 mill.
Sales taxes	$4,140 mill.
License taxes	$518 mill.
Individual income taxes	$3,615 mill.
Corporate income taxes	$300 mill.
Other taxes	$134 mill.

Total revenue figures include items not listed separately here.
Source: U.S. Bureau of the Census.

State government expenditures, 2002

General expenditures

Total state expenditures	$20,841 mill.
Intergovernmental	$5,073 mill.

Per capita expenditures

State	$3,299
Average of all states	$3,859
Rank among states	42

Selected direct expenditures

Education.	$2,556 mill.
Public welfare	$5,377 mill.
Health, hospital	$1,361 mill.
Highways	$1,609 mill.
Police protection	$172 mill.
Corrections	$606 mill.
Natural resources	$261 mill.
Parks and recreation	$49 mill.
Government administration	$513 mill.
Interest on debt	$568 mill.
Total direct expenditures	$13,634 mill.

Totals include items not listed separately.
Source: U.S. Census Bureau.

POLITICS

Governors since statehood

D = Democrat; R = Republican; O = other;
(r) resigned; (d) died in office; (i) removed from office

Alexander McNair (O)	1820-1824
Frederick Bates (O) . . . . (d)	1824-1825
Abraham J. Williams (O)	1825-1826
John Miller (O)	1826-1832
Daniel Dunkin (D) . . . . (r)	1832-1836
Lillburn W. Boggs (D)	1836-1840
Thomas Reynolds (D) . . . . (d)	1840-1844
Meredith M. Marmaduke (D)	1844
John C. Edwards (D)	1844-1848
Austin A. King (D)	1848-1853
Sterling Price (D)	1853-1857
Truston Polk (D)	1857
Hancock L. Jackson (D)	1857
Robert M. Stewart (D)	1857-1861
Claiborne F. Jackson (D) . . . . (i)	1861
Hamilton R. Gamble (O) . . . . (d)	1861-1864
Willard P. Hall (O)	1864-1865
Thomas C. Fletcher (R)	1865-1869
Joseph W. McClurg (R)	1869-1871
Benjamin Gratz Brown (R)	1871-1873
Silas Woodson (D)	1873-1875
Charles H. Hardin (D)	1875-1877
John S. Phelps (D)	1877-1881
Thomas T. Crittenden (D)	1881-1885
John S. Marmaduke (D) . . . . (d)	1885-1887
Albert P. Morehouse (D)	1887-1889
David R. Francis (D)	1889-1893

William J. Stone (D)	1893-1897
Lon V. Stephens (D)	1897-1901
Alexander M. Dockery (D)	1901-1905
Joseph W. Polk (D)	1905-1909
Herbert S. Hadley (R)	1909-1913
Elliott W. Major (D)	1913-1917
Frederick D. Gardner (D)	1917-1921
Arthur M. Hyde (R)	1921-1925
Samuel A. Baker (R)	1925-1929
Henry S. Caulfield (R)	1929-1933
Guy B. Park (D)	1933-1937
Lloyd C. Stark (D)	1937-1941
Forrest C. Donnell (R)	1941-1945
Phillip M. Donnelly (D)	1945-1949
Forest Smith (D)	1949-1953
Phillip M. Donnelly (D)	1953-1957
James T. Blair, Jr. (D)	1957-1961
John M. Dalton (D)	1961-1965
Warren E. Hearnes (D)	1965-1973
Christopher S. Bond (R)	1973-1977
Joseph P. Teasdale (D)	1977-1981
Christopher S. Bond (R)	1981-1985
John D. Ashcroft (R)	1985-1993
Mel Carnahan (D) . . . . (d)	1993-2000
Roger B. Wilson (D)	2000-2001
Robert Lee Holden, Jr. (D)	2001-2005
Matthew Roy Blunt (R)	2005-

Composition of congressional delegations, 1989-2007

	Dem	Rep	Total
House of Representatives			
101st Congress, 1989			
State delegates	5	4	9
Total U.S.	259	174	433
102d Congress, 1991			
State delegates	6	3	9
Total U.S.	267	167	434
103d Congress, 1993			
State delegates	6	3	9
Total U.S.	258	176	434
104th Congress, 1995			
State delegates	5	4	9
Total U.S.	197	236	433
105th Congress, 1997			
State delegates	5	4	9
Total U.S.	206	228	434
106th Congress, 1999			
State delegates	5	4	9
Total U.S.	211	222	433
107th Congress, 2001			
State delegates	4	5	9
Total U.S.	211	221	432

(continued)

	Dem	Rep	Total
108th Congress, 2003			
State delegates	4	5	9
Total U.S.	205	229	434
109th Congress, 2005			
State delegates	4	5	9
Total U.S.	202	231	433
110th Congress, 2007			
State delegates	4	5	9
Total U.S.	233	202	435
Senate			
101st Congress, 1989			
State delegates	0	2	2
Total U.S.	55	45	100
102d Congress, 1991			
State delegates	0	2	2
Total U.S.	56	44	100
103d Congress, 1993			
State delegates	0	2	2
Total U.S.	57	43	100
104th Congress, 1995			
State delegates	0	2	2
Total U.S.	46	53	99
105th Congress, 1997			
State delegates	0	2	2
Total U.S.	45	55	100
106th Congress, 1999			
State delegates	0	2	2
Total U.S.	45	54	99
107th Congress, 2001			
State delegates	1	1	2
Total U.S.	50	50	100
108th Congress, 2003			
State delegates	0	2	2
Total U.S.	48	51	99
109th Congress, 2005			
State delegates	0	2	2
Total U.S.	44	55	99
110th Congress, 2007			
State delegates	1	1	2
Total U.S.	49	49	98

Figures are for starts of first sessions. Totals are for Democrat (Dem.) and Republican (Rep.) members only. House membership totals under 435 and Senate totals under 100 reflect vacancies and seats held by independent party members. When the 110th Congress opened, the Senate's two independent members caucused with the Democrats, giving the Democrats control of the Senate.

Source: U.S. Congress, *Congressional Directory.*

Composition of state legislature, 1990-2006

	Democrats	Republicans
State House (163 seats)		
1990	99	64
1992	98	65
1994	87	76
1996	88	75
1998	85	76
2000	84	76
2002	73	90
2004	66	97
2006	71	92
State Senate (34 seats)		
1990	23	11
1992	20	14
1994	19	15
1996	19	15
1998	18	16
2000	18	16
2002	14	20
2004	11	23
2006	13	21

Figures for total seats may include independents and minor party members. Numbers reflect results of elections in listed years; elected members usually take their seats in the years that follow.

Source: Council of State Governments; *State Elective Officials and the Legislatures.*

Voter participation in presidential elections, 2000 and 2004

	2000	2004
Voting age population		
State	4,182,000	4,370,000
Total United States	209,831,000	220,377,000
State share of U.S. total	1.99	1.98
Rank among states	17	17
Portion of voting age population casting votes		
State	56.4%	62.5%
United States	50.3%	55.5%
Rank among states	16	15

Population figures are rounded to nearest thousand and include all residents, regardless of eligibility to vote.

Source: U.S. Census Bureau.

HEALTH AND MEDICAL CARE

Medical professionals
Physicians in 2003 and nurses in 2001

	U.S.	State
Physicians in 2003		
Total	774,849	13,732
Share of U.S. total		1.76%
Rate	266	241
Rank		27
Nurses in 2001		
Total	2,262,020	52,970
Share of U.S. total		2.34%
Rate	793	940
Rank		11

Rates are numbers of physicians and nurses per 100,000 resident population; ranks are based on rates.
Source: American Medical Association, *Physician Characteristics and Distribution in the U.S.*; U.S. Department of Health and Human Services, Health Resources and Services Administration.

Health insurance coverage, 2003

	State	U.S.
Total persons covered	5,004,000	243,320,000
Total persons not covered	620,000	44,961,000
Portion not covered	11.0%	15.6%
Rank among states	38	—
Children not covered	103,000	8,373,000
Portion not covered	7.3%	11.4%
Rank among states	42	—

Totals are rounded to nearest thousand. Ranks are from the highest to the lowest percentages of persons *not* insured.
Source: U.S. Census Bureau, Current Population Reports.

AIDS, syphilis, and tuberculosis cases, 2003

Disease	U.S. cases	State cases	Rank
AIDS	44,232	404	24
Syphilis	34,270	207	26
Tuberculosis	14,874	131	25

Source: U.S. Centers for Disease Control and Prevention.

Cigarette smoking, 2003
Residents over age 18 who smoke

	U.S.	State	Rank
All smokers	22.1%	27.3%	3
Male smokers	24.8%	31.2%	2
Female smokers	20.3%	23.8%	8

Cigarette smokers are defined as persons who reported having smoked at least 100 cigarettes during their lifetimes and who currently smoked at least occasionally.
Source: U.S. Centers for Disease Control and Prevention, *Morbidity and Mortality Weekly Report*, 53, no. 44 (November 12, 2004).

HOUSING

Home ownership rates, 1985-2004

	1985	1990	1995	2000	2004
State	69.2%	64.0%	69.4%	74.2%	72.4%
Total U.S.	63.9%	63.9%	64.7%	67.4%	69.0%
Rank among states	18	39	18	10	21

Net change in state home ownership rate,
1985-2004 . . . . +3.2%
Net change in U.S. home ownership rate,
1985-2004 . . . . +5.1%

Percentages represent the proportion of owner households to total occupied households.
Source: U.S. Census Bureau, 2006.

Home sales, 2000-2004
In thousands of units

Existing home sales	2000	2002	2003	2004
State sales	110.2	115.2	131.1	141.8
Total U.S. sales	5,171	5,631	6,183	6,784
State share of U.S. total	2.13%	2.05%	2.12%	2.09%
Sales rank among states	17	19	15	16

Units include single-family homes, condos, and co-ops.
Source: National Association of Realtors, Washington, D.C., *Real Estate Outlook: Market Trends & Insights.*

Values of owner-occupied homes, 2003

	State	U.S.
Total units	1,256,000	58,809,000
Value of units		
Under $100,000	45.2%	29.6%
$100,000-199,999	39.8%	36.9%
$200,000 or more	15.0%	33.5%
Median value	$108,625	$142,275
Rank among all states		36

Units are owner-occupied one-family houses whose numbers are rounded to nearest thousand. Data are extrapolated from survey samples.
Source: U.S. Census Bureau, American Community Survey.

EDUCATION

Public school enrollment, 2002

Prekindergarten through grade 8
State enrollment. 653,000
Total U.S. enrollment 34,135,000
State share of U.S. total 1.91%

Grades 9 through 12
State enrollment. 272,000
Total U.S. enrollment 14,067,000
State share of U.S. total 1.93%

Enrollment rates
State public school enrollment rate 88.9%
Overall U.S. rate. 90.4%
Rank among states in 2002 31
Rank among states in 1995 46

Enrollment figures (which include unclassified students) are rounded to nearest thousand pupils during fall school term. Enrollment rates are based on enumerated resident population estimate for July 1, 2002.
Source: U.S. National Center for Education Statistics.

Public college finances, 2003-2004

FTE enrollment in public institutions of higher education
Students in state institutions. 138,100
Students in all U.S. public institutions 9,916,600
State share of U.S. total 1.39
Rank among states 25

State and local government appropriations for higher education
State appropriation per FTE $7,031
National average. $5,716
Rank among states. 8
State & local tax revenue going to higher education 7.0%

FTE = full-time equivalent in public postsecondary programs, including summer sessions; student numbers are rounded to nearest hundred. Funding figures for 2003-2004 academic year include financial aid to students in state public institutions and exclude money for research, agriculture experiment stations, teaching hospitals, and medical schools; figures are rounded to nearest thousand dollars.
Source: Higher Education Executive Officers, Denver, Colorado.

TRANSPORTATION AND TRAVEL

Highway mileage, 2003

Interstate highways	1,181
Other freeways and expressways	326
Arterial roads	9,414
Collector roads.	24,976
Local roads.	88,788
Urban roads	17,576
Rural roads	107,109
Total state mileage	124,685
U.S. total	3,974,107
State share	3.14%
Rank among states.	6

Note that combined urban and rural road mileage matches the total of the other categories.
Source: U.S. Federal Highway Administration.

Motor vehicle registrations and driver licenses, 2003

Vehicle registrations	State	U.S.	Share	Rank
Autos, trucks, buses	4,460,000	231,390,000	1.93%	19
Autos only	2,600,000	135,670	1.92%	17
Motorcycles	74,000	5,328,000	1.39%	21
Driver licenses	3,966,000	196,166,000	2.02%	17

Figures, which do not include vehicles owned by military services, are rounded to the nearest thousand. Figures for automobiles include taxis.
Source: U.S. Federal Highway Administration.

Domestic travel expenditures, 2003

Spending by U.S. residents on overnight trips and day trips of at least 50 miles from home

Total expenditures within state . . . . $9.18 bill.
Total expenditures within U.S. . . . . $490.87 bill.
State share of U.S. total 1.9%
Rank among states 17

Source: Travel Industry Association of America.

Retail gasoline prices, 2003-2007

Average price per gallon at the pump

Year	U.S.	State
2003	$1.267	$1.206
2004	$1.316	$1.266
2005	$1.644	$1.633
2007	$2.298	$2.084

Excise tax per gallon in 2004 . . . . 17.0¢
Rank among all states in 2007 prices 50

Prices are averages of all grades of gasoline sold at the pump during March months in 2003-2005 and during February, 2007. Averages for 2006, during which prices rose higher, are not available.
Source: U.S. Energy Information Agency, *Petroleum Marketing Monthly* (2003-2005 data); American Automobile Association (2007 data).

CRIME AND LAW ENFORCEMENT

State and local police officers, 2000-2004

	2000	2002	2004
Total officers			
U.S.	654,601	665,555	675,734
State	11,167	13,202	13,450*
*Net change, 2000-2004			+20.44%
Officers per 1,000 residents			
U.S.	2.33	2.31	2.30
State	2.00	2.33	2.34
State rank	31	14	15

Totals include state and local police and sheriffs.
Source: Carsey Institute, University of New Hampshire.

Crime rates, 2003

Incidents per 100,000 residents

Crimes	State	U.S.
Violent crimes		
Total incidents	473	475
Murder	5	6
Forcible rape	24	32
Robbery	109	142
Aggravated assault	335	295
Property crimes		
Total incidents	4,015	3,588
Burglary	717	741
Larceny/theft	2,795	2,415
Motor vehicle theft	502	433
All crimes	4,488	4,063

Source: U.S. Federal Bureau of Investigation, *Crime in the United States,* annual.

State prison populations, 1980-2003

	State	U.S.	State share
1980	5,726	305,458	1.87%
1990	14,943	708,393	2.11%
1996	22,003	1,025,624	2.15%
2000	27,543	1,391,261	1.98%
2003	30,303	1,470,045	2.06%

State figures exclude prisoners in federal penitentiaries.
Source: U.S. Bureau of Justice Statistics, *Prisoners in 2003.*

Montana

Location: Northwestern United States

Area and rank: 145,556 square miles (376,991 square kilometers); 147,046 square miles (380,849 square kilometers) including water; fourth largest state in area

Coastline: none

Population and rank: 927,000 (2004); forty-fourth largest state in population

Capital city: Helena (25,780 people in 2000 census)

Largest city: Billings (89,847 people in 2000 census)

Became territory: May 26, 1864

State capitol building in Helena. (Travel Montana/Donnie Sexton)

Entered Union and rank: November 8, 1889; forty-first state

Present constitution adopted: 1972

Counties: 56, as well as a small part of Yellowstone National Park

State name: "Montana" is a Latinized form for a Spanish word meaning "mountainous."

State nickname: Treasure State

Motto: *Oro y plata* (Gold and silver)

State flag: Dark blue field with the state seal emblem and name "Montana" above

Highest point: Granite Peak—12,799 feet (244 meters)

Lowest point: Kootenai River—1,800 feet (549 meters)

Highest recorded temperature: 117 degrees Fahrenheit (47 degrees Celsius)—Medicine Lake, 1937

Lowest recorded temperature: –70 degrees Fahrenheit (–57 degrees Celsius)—Rogers Pass, 1954

State songs: "Montana"; "Montana Melody"

State tree: Ponderosa pine

State flower: Bitterroot

State bird: Western meadowlark

National parks: Glacier, Yellowstone

Montana History

One of the six Rocky Mountain states, Montana lies directly south of the Canadian provinces of Saskatchewan and Alberta. To its east are North and South Dakota. Wyoming lies south of it, and Idaho borders it to the south and west. It is 570 miles from east to west. From Canada in the north to Wyoming in the south is 315 miles.

With an area exceeding 147,000 square miles, it ranks fourth in size among the fifty states. With a population density of 5.5 people per square mile, Montana ranks forty-fourth among the states in population. Montana lost population between 1980 and 1990 but experienced a slight population upsurge during the 1990's.

The Rocky Mountains dominate the western two-fifths of the state. The eastern three-fifths consist mostly of rolling hills and plains. The climate is dry and, in winter, extremely cold. Summers are hot. The rich soil of the plains, the hot summers, and the long summer days in this latitude are ideal for agriculture.

Early History. When French Canadian explorers first visited the area, it had already been inhabited by humans for more than nine thousand years. Evidence exists of cultures that date to 8000 B.C.E. Among the native tribes in the area were the Arapaho, Assiniboine, Blackfoot, Cheyenne, Crow, Kalispel, Kutenai, and Salish Indians.

In prehistoric times, dinosaurs roamed Montana. A nest of duck-billed dinosaur fossils was discovered there in 1978. In 1988, the most complete skeleton of a tyrannosaur ever unearthed was discovered. The earliest human inhabitants hunted bison and other indigenous animals with spears.

Early Exploration. The earliest known explorers to reach Montana were François and Louis Joseph de La

Decision Point, at the confluence of the Marias and Missouri Rivers—a key site in Meriwether Lewis and William Clark's exploration of the Louisiana Territory during the early nineteenth century. (Travel Montana/Victor Bjornberg)

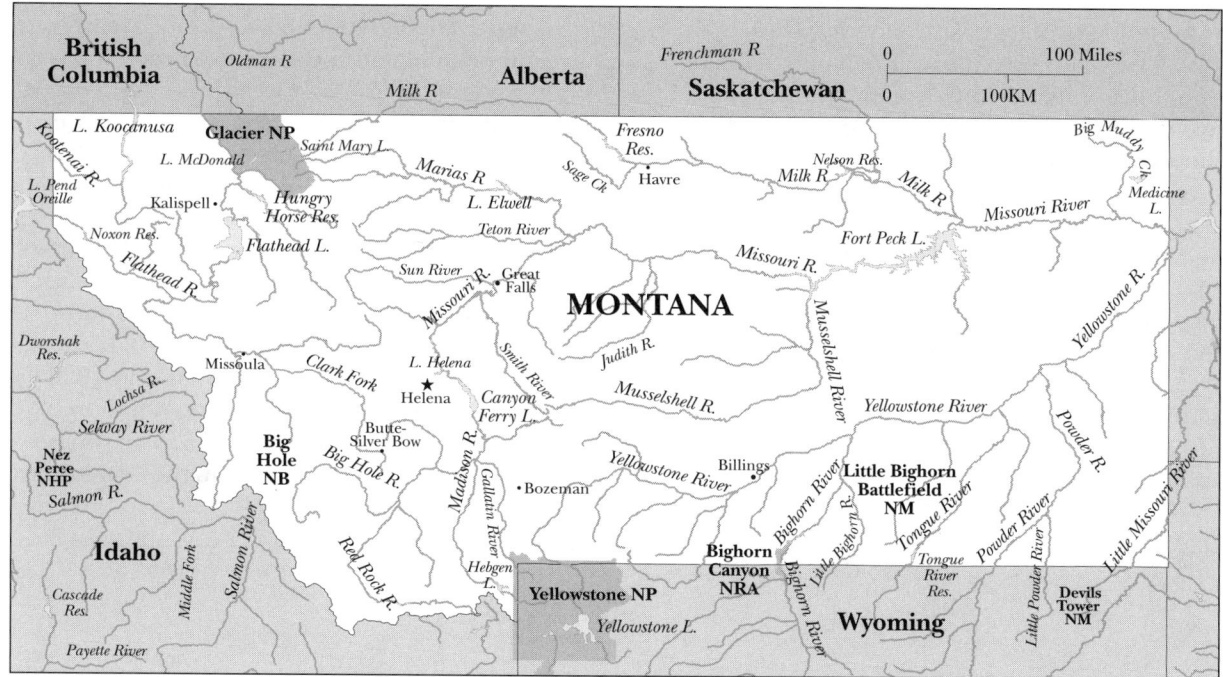

Vérendrye, French Canadian brothers who arrived in 1743. Montana became part of the United States in 1803 through the Louisiana Purchase.

Explorers Meriwether Lewis and William Clark, guided by a young American Indian woman, Sacagawea, crossed the territory in 1805 en route to America's northwest coast. They returned in 1806 on their trip east. A Spanish trader, Manuel Lisa, established the Missouri Fur Company and went on a trading expedition up the Yellowstone River. In 1807, he established Montana's first trading post, Fort Manuel.

The following year Canadian David Thompson established a trading post on the Kootenai River and, in 1809, founded Salish House near Thompson Falls. By 1829, both the Hudson Bay Company and the American Fur Company traded in this area.

Montana's rivers and low mountain passes encouraged transportation. The second longest river in the United States, the 2,315-mile-long Missouri, begins in Montana. Other rivers—including the Madison, the Gallatin, and the Yellowstone—criss-cross the state.

By 1850 fur traders had overhunted and exploited Montana to the extent that most of the fur-bearing animals had been killed. Whole herds of bison, fox, and deer were wiped out by voracious traders.

The Discovery of Gold. When gold was discovered in California in 1848, thousands of easterners rushed across the country seeking instant wealth. Meanwhile, residents of Montana searched for gold in their area. In 1862, John White discovered small gold deposits at Grasshopper Creek. By 1863 more than five hundred miners had come there.

Soon a gold strike was made nearby. A settlement, Virginia City, which by 1865 had ten thousand inhabitants, sprang into being. Gold was discovered at Last Chance Gulch, where its discovery spawned another city, Helena. Meanwhile, rich veins of copper and silver were found around Butte in the Rocky Mountains.

Lawlessness soon became a considerable problem. Gangsters robbed stagecoaches of the gold and silver they transported. During 1863 one gang killed more than one hundred people. In the following year, vigilantes captured and hanged more than twenty such criminals, thereby reducing crime substantially.

Miners flocked into the area as well as merchants, who arrived with their families to open stores and to establish an infrastructure. Cattle ranchers came to eastern Montana. In 1863, schools were opened in Bannack and Nevada City.

The Road to Statehood. Congress created the Montana Territory in 1864. In 1875, Helena became its capital. American Indian uprisings raged. In 1876, the Sioux and Cheyenne Indians killed Lieutenant Colonel George Custer in the Battle of the Little Bighorn, but in 1877, Chief Joseph of the Nez Perce tribe surrendered, ending the American Indian wars that plagued the territory. By 1880, Montana's Native American population was deployed to seven American Indian reservations within the territory.

In 1880, the Utah and Northern Railroad laid tracks across Montana, enabling Montanans to ship produce and cattle to eastern markets. Montana's first bid for statehood in 1866 was premature because the state had a very small population, little access to eastern markets, and continuing problems with American Indian wars. Because the expansion of the railroad into the state resulted in the population quadrupling within a decade, a constitutional convention was called in 1884, and statehood was again requested but refused for political reasons.

In 1889, President Grover Cleveland signed an enabling bill guaranteeing that if North Dakota, South Dakota, Washington, and Montana submitted acceptable constitutions, statehood would be granted. Montana held a constitutional convention in July of that year, offered a constitution to its electorate, and was granted statehood in November, 1889, becoming the forty-first state. In 1894, Montana voters chose Helena as the capital.

Copper Mining in Montana. Although early prospectors found gold and silver around Butte, it was copper that brought the greatest wealth to Montana. Marcus Daly, seeking silver in the area, discovered one of the richest copper deposits in the world and in 1881 opened his copper mine in Anaconda. William Clark soon opened a copper operation nearby in Butte.

The copper found here was so abundant that Butte Hill was nicknamed "the Richest Hill on Earth." The copper industry attracted immigrants, mostly from Great Britain, to work in the mines. Daly established the Anaconda Copper Company, and in 1926 Clark's Butte holdings were sold to that corporation.

Montana Politics and Education. The two powerful copper barons who emerged from the Butte-Anaconda

Little Bighorn, the battlefield on which the Sioux and their allies annihilated the U.S. cavalry troops commanded by George Armstrong Custer, has been consecrated as a national monument. (PhotoDisc)

Located on Montana's border with Canada, Glacier National Park was established by the U.S. Congress in 1910. (PhotoDisc)

area, Marcus Daly and William Clark, were business and political rivals. They engaged in a heated campaign to have their own towns declared capital of the state, with Clark prevailing. Each owned the newspaper in his respective town.

Clark was elected to the U.S. Senate in 1891 but resigned when a scandal, perpetrated by reports accusing him of bribery in Daly's newspaper, the *Anaconda Standard*, cast doubt upon Clark's integrity. He was, nevertheless, elected to the Senate when he ran again in 1900.

Montana was the first state to elect a woman to Congress. Jeanette Rankin was elected in 1917 and served for two years. She served again from 1941 to 1943. Rankin was the only member of Congress to vote against the U.S. entry into World War I in 1917 and into World War II in 1941.

Montana's first constitution, ratified in 1889, was replaced when a constitutional convention called in 1972 produced a new constitution, narrowly ratified by the electorate and put into effect in 1973. This constitution combined more than one hundred state agencies into fifteen departments, whose heads report to the governor. In 1974, the constitution was amended to change the annual sixty-day legislative session to a ninety-day session to meet in odd-numbered years.

Montana prides itself on valuing education. Its 1990 literacy rate of 92 percent is 5 percent above the national average. Seventy-five percent of Montanans are high school graduates, whereas the national average is 67 percent.

Industrial Expansion. Natural gas was discovered in Glendive, near Montana's eastern border, in 1913. This was an important discovery because where there is natural gas, there is usually oil. It was not until 1950, however, that vast oil deposits were discovered on the Montana-North Dakota border. Oil revenues spurred the state's faltering economy. The strip mining of bituminous coal in the eastern part of the state also helped to advance Montana's economy, changing the nature of the plains considerably. Nevertheless, the Montana plains are among the most prolific producers of wheat in the United States.

In 1955, the Anaconda Aluminum Company began operation in Columbia Falls in northwestern Montana. In 1983, however, the once-powerful Anaconda Copper Company, having mined out the area around Butte, suspended operations.

Natural Disasters. Between 1917 and 1920, Montana suffered greatly from droughts that caused many farmers and cattle ranchers in eastern Montana to fail. In 1929, another drought began that again devastated eastern Montana and lasted for several years, during which the economic contractions of the Great Depression also affected that state's economy. During 1935 Helena was struck by more than one hundred earthquakes. Although no lives were lost, property damage was severe.

With federal aid, Montana strove to avert the devastation earlier droughts had inflicted upon the state. Although Flathead Lake, which covers two hundred square miles, is the largest freshwater lake west of the Mississippi River, it proved insufficient to provide irrigation during droughts. In 1934, Montana began a dam-building project that, in 1940, culminated in the creation of the four-hundred-square-mile Lake Peck and several other artificial lakes that provide irrigation and hydroelectric power for Montana's farms and cattle ranches.

Elections. During the year 2000 elections, Montana voters chose Republican candidate George W. Bush for its three electoral votes by a wide margin, 58 percent to 34 percent. Republican victories set the tone for other races, as a Republican retained the state's at-large member of Congress, Senator Conrad Burns retained his seat in the U.S. Senate, and Lieutenant Governor Judy Martz, also a Republican, took the governor's mansion by 51 percent to 48 percent vote. Voters also decided to repeal the state's inheritance taxes.

In the 2004 presidential race, Montana again chose Republican candidate George W. Bush. In the race for governor, however, Brian Schweitzer, a Democrat, beat Republican Bob Brown, Montana's secretary of state, by a 50-46 percent margin. A principal campaign issue was whether Montanans should be able to import inexpensive prescription drugs from Canada, a position that Schweitzer strongly backed.

Cultural and Environmental Issues. The state's reputation for conservatism suffered a setback the following year, however, when voters in the state's capital, Helena, decided to ban indoor smoking in public places within the city, including bars and restaurants. Other issues that captured public attention during the early years of the new millennium was a 2002 proposal to drill for oil at Sacred Valley, a site of rock drawings thought to be among the most significant in the area. The proposal was not approved. Another issue was the environmental impact of the use of snowmobiles in Yellowstone National Park, a part of which lies in Montana and which is frequently visited by Montanans. In this case, the U.S. House of Representatives rejected a proposal for a complete snowmobile ban in the park. In 2004, a further environmental issue came to the fore as oil and gas exploration companies planned drilling in the state's Rocky Mountain Front, the largest concentration of wilderness in the nation except for Alaska. Most Montanans opposed the exploration plans, and in October of that year, the federal Bureau of Land Management suspended its plan for drilling.

Wildfires. In common with a number of other Western states, Montana endured tremendous damage from wildfires that burned out of control in the summer of 2000 and in succeeding years. In 2000, at least thirty-three major wildfires burned across the West, affecting 380,000 acres—a Level 5 condition, the worst on the standard scale. Some 22,600 firefighters fought the blazes. In 2003, two firefighters were killed near Missoula, and the fires consumed great portions of Glacier National Park. In July, 2006, five major fires burned in the southern and eastern parts of the state, engulfing about 294 square miles.

R. Baird Shuman
Updated by the Editor

Montana Time Line

c. 8000 B.C.E.	People first settle Montana.
1743 C.E.	French Canadians Francois and Louis de La Vérendrye explore the area.
1803	United States gains most of Montana through the Louisiana Purchase.
1805	Explorers Meriwether Lewis and William Clark are guided through Montana by American Indian Sacagawea.
1807	Spanish trader Manuel Lisa establishes Montana's first fur-trading post.
1846	Fort Benton is built.
1862	John White discovers gold at Grasshopper Creek.
1863	Virginia City is established near Grasshopper Creek gold strike.
May 26, 1864	Montana Territory is created.
1875	Helena becomes capital of the territory.
June 25, 1876	Battle of the Little Bighorn takes place between Sioux and U.S. Army; Lieutenant Colonel George Custer is killed.
Oct. 5, 1877	Chief Joseph of the Nez Perce surrenders, ending the American Indian wars.
1880	Most of Montana's Native Americans are placed on reservations.
Nov. 8, 1889	Montana becomes the forty-first state.
1893	Four public institutions of higher learning open in Montana.
1910	Congress establishes Glacier National Park.
1917	Jeannette Rankin becomes the first female member of Congress.
1917-1918	More than forty thousand Montanans serve in World War I.
1917-1920	Severe droughts devastate Montana farms and ranches.
1934	Work begins on Fort Peck Dam.
1935	Helena is hit by more than one hundred earthquakes.
1940	Jeannette Rankin is elected to a second term in Congress.
1941-1945	Some fifty-seven thousand Montanans serve in World War II.
1950	Large oil strike is made in eastern Montana.
1955	Anaconda Aluminum Company begins operation.
1959	Huge earthquake creates Quake Lake on Madison River.
1973	New state constitution is instituted.
1983	Anaconda Copper Company closes its Butte mining operations.
1984	Forest fires ravage state.
1996	Native Americans sue state over voting precinct districting.
1997	Montana farmers seek right to kill buffalo outside Yellowstone Park to control brucellosis.
1998	Montana farmers block border point to protest low Canadian produce prices.
1999	Montana replaces "reasonable and prudent" speed limit with one of 75 miles per hour on most highways.
2000	Wildfires devastate thousands of acres of Montana along with similar devastation across the West.
2004	Secretary of Agriculture Ann Veneman announces repeal of the "roadless rule" under which roads could not be built in any of the nearly sixty million acres of federal lands.
Oct. 1, 2004	Federal Bureau of Land Management suspends plans for oil drilling along Montana's Rocky Mountain Front.
Nov. 2, 2004	Democrat Brian Schweitzer defeats Republican Bob Brown for governorship.
July, 2006	Five wildfires engulf some 294 square miles of the southern and eastern parts of the state, mostly east of Billings.

Notes for Further Study

Published Sources. The most comprehensive study of Montana is *Montana: A History of Two Centuries* (Rev. ed., 2003) by Michael P. Malone, Richard B. Roeder, and William L. Lang. This richly illustrated book presents the history of the state, considering its cultural, educational, and economic development. *Montana Legacy: Essays on History, People, and Place* (2002), edited by Harry W. Fritz, Mary Murphy, and Robert R. Swartout, Jr., brings together sixteen essays that detail the people, cultures, places, and events that shaped present-day Montana. Donald Spritzer's *Roadside History of Montana* (1999) is divided into chapters corresponding to the state's six geographical areas and follows highway routes as a device to reveal the state's history. Readers interested in statistical and demographic data might enjoy perusing *Montana: 2000, Summary Social, Economic, and Housing Characteristics* (2003), published by the U.S. Census Bureau.

Janice Cohn in *The Christmas Menorahs: How a Town Fought Hate* (1995) explains how citizens of Billings, Montana, defended a Jewish family that fell victim to hate crimes. R. E. Mather in *Vigilante Victims: Montana's Hanging Spree* (1991) discusses the vigilantes who broke the Montana crime wave of the 1860's. Laura Ross focuses on America's dealings with Montana's Native Americans in *Inventing the Savage: The Social Construction of Native American Criminality* (1998). In *The Mechanics of Optimism: Mining Companies, Technology, and the Hot Spring Gold Rush* (2004), Jeffrey J. Safford examines the boom-bust cycles of mining in nineteenth century Montana by focusing on the failed Hot Springs District, a gold-mining camp.

Richard Allan Fox, Jr., discusses the Battle of the Little Bighorn and George Custer's defeat in *Archeology, History, and Custer's Last Battle: The Little Big Horn Reexamined* (1993), updating *Archeological Insights into the Custer Battle: The Assessment of the 1984 Field Season* (1987) by Douglas D. Scott and Richard A. Fox, Jr. Duane A. Smith's *Rocky Mountain West: Colorado, Wyoming, and Montana* (1991) emphasizes the western part of the state, in which most of its mining occurs.

General audiences will enjoy *Hidden Montana* (5th ed.,

2005); John Gottberg provides detailed maps, Internet information for each listing, suggested itineraries, and walking and driving tours, among other features. Younger readers will find Ann Heinrichs's *Montana* (2005) clear, well written, and detailed. Rita Ladoux's *Montana* (Rev. and exp. ed., 2002) is written for a teenage audience.

Web Resources. The best Internet source for information about the government of Montana is its home page (www.mt.gov). For tourist information, consult the Web sites of the tourist service (www.travel.mt.gov), Glacier National Park (www.glacierparkinc.com/), and Yellowstone National Park (www.nps.gov/yell). Information about hunting and fishing can be found at the state's Fish, Wildlife, and Parks Web site (fwp.mt.gov/default.html) or the Montana Bowhunters site (www.mtba.org). *Montana Outdoors* (fwp.mt.gov/mtoutdoors/) provides a number of online articles from its back issues, and *Big Sky Outdoor News and Adventure* (www.outdoorsmontana.com/) brings together articles about the state's outdoor recreational opportunities.

Links directing users to a range of business and commerce sites can be found at Montana Business Connections (www.mbc.umt.edu/). For information about legal matters, the Montana Bar Association's Web site (www.montanabar.org) is useful. The Montana Education Association maintains a Web site (www.mea-mft.org/), as does the Montana Medical Association (www.mmaoffice.org/).

For those interested in the state's historical and cultural past, several sites offer valuable information. Montana History (visitmt.com/tripplanner/thingstodo/history.htm), the Montana History Web Site (www.metnet.state.mt.us/teachmthistory/), and Montana History.net (www.montanahistory.net/) are all good starting points. Indian Nations of Montana (indiannations.visitmt.com/) is an attractive site that details the history and culture of tribes such as the Blackfeet and Crow, as well as locales that are important to these communities. For young Web users, Montana Is for Kids (montanakids.com/) is an entertaining site that discusses plants and animals, cultural history, and regional attractions.

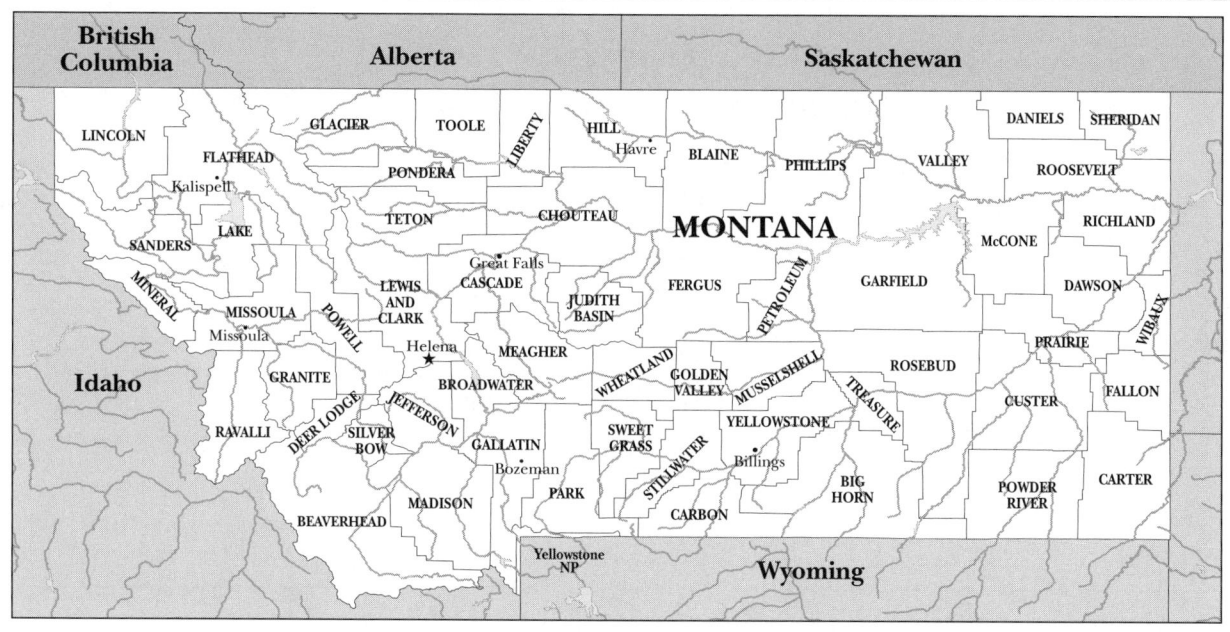

Counties

County	2000 pop.	Rank in pop.	Sq. miles	Rank in area	County	2000 pop.	Rank in pop.	Sq. miles	Rank in area
Beaverhead	9,202	24	5,542.6	1	Meagher	1,932	48	2,391.9	27
Big Horn	12,671	14	4,994.9	5	Mineral	3,884	39	1,219.9	50
Blaine	7,009	29	4,226.2	9	Missoula	95,802	2	2,598.2	24
Broadwater	4,385	37	1,191.5	51	Musselshell	4,497	36	1,867.2	36
Carbon	9,552	21	2,048.1	33	Park	15,694	12	2,656.2	21
Carter	1,360	50	3,339.7	15	Petroleum	493	56	1,653.9	43
Cascade	80,357	3	2,698.0	20	Phillips	4,601	35	5,139.9	2
Chouteau	5,970	33	3,973.4	10	Pondera	6,424	32	1,624.7	44
Custer	11,696	16	3,783.3	11	Powder River	1,858	49	3,297.3	16
Daniels	2,017	46	1,426.1	48	Powell	7,180	28	2,326.0	30
Dawson	9,059	25	2,373.3	28	Prairie	1,199	52	1,736.6	39
Deer Lodge	9,417	22	736.9	55	Ravalli	36,070	7	2,394.3	26
Fallon	2,837	41	1,620.4	45	Richland	9,667	20	2,084.2	32
Fergus	11,893	15	4,339.3	8	Roosevelt	10,620	17	2,355.7	29
Flathead	74,471	4	5,098.6	3	Rosebud	9,383	23	5,012.4	4
Gallatin	67,831	5	2,506.9	25	Sanders	10,227	18	2,762.3	19
Garfield	1,279	51	4,668.2	7	Sheridan	4,105	38	1,676.7	41
Glacier	13,247	13	2,994.7	17	Silver Bow	34,606	8	718.3	56
Golden Valley	1,042	54	1,175.3	52	Stillwater	8,195	26	1,794.7	38
Granite	2,830	42	1,727.5	40	Sweet Grass	3,609	40	1,855.2	37
Hill	16,673	11	2,896.4	18	Teton	6,445	31	2,272.6	31
Jefferson	10,049	19	1,656.7	42	Toole	5,267	34	1,910.9	34
Judith Basin	2,329	43	1,869.9	35	Treasure	861	55	978.9	53
Lake	26,507	9	1,493.8	46	Valley	7,675	27	4,920.9	6
Lewis and Clark	55,716	6	3,461.0	14	Wheatland	2,259	44	1,423.2	49
Liberty	2,158	45	1,429.8	47	Wibaux	1,068	53	889.3	54
Lincoln	18,837	10	3,612.8	12	Yellowstone	129,352	1	2,635.2	23
McCone	1,977	47	2,642.6	22					
Madison	6,851	30	3,586.6	13					

Source: U.S. Census Bureau; National Association of Counties.

Cities

With 6,000 or more residents

Rank	City	Population
1	Billings	89,847
2	Missoula	57,053
3	Great Falls	56,690
4	Butte-Silver Bow	33,892
5	Bozeman	27,509
6	Helena (capital)	25,780
7	Kalispell	14,223
8	Havre	9,621
9	Anaconda-Deer Lodge County	9,417

Rank	City	Population
10	Miles City	8,487
11	Helena Valley Southeast	7,141
12	Helena Valley West Central	6,983
13	Livingston	6,851
14	Laurel	6,255
15	Evergreen	6,215

Population figures are from 2000 census.
Source: U.S. Bureau of the Census.

Index to Tables

DEMOGRAPHICS

Resident state and national populations, 1970-2004

Population figures given in thousands

	State pop.	U.S. pop.	Share	Rank
1970	694	203,302	0.3%	43
1980	787	226,546	0.3%	44
1985	822	237,924	0.3%	44
1990	799	248,765	0.3%	44
1995	877	262,761	0.3%	44
2000	902	281,425	0.3%	44
2004	927	293,655	0.3%	44

Source: U.S. Census Bureau, Current Population Reports, 2006.

Resident population by age, 2004

Age Group	Total persons
Under 5 years	53,000
5 to 17 years	156,000
18 to 24 years	99,000
25 to 34 years	107,000
35 to 44 years	128,000
45 to 54 years	152,000
55 to 64 years	107,000
65 to 74 years	66,000
75 to 84 years	42,000
85 years and older	18,000
All age groups	927,000

Portion of residents 65 and older	13.7%
National rank in portion of oldest residents	10
National average	12.4%

Population figures are rounded to nearest thousand persons;
figures include armed forces personnel stationed in the state.
Source: U.S. Bureau of the Census, 2006.

Resident population by race, Hispanic origin, 2004

Category	State pop.	Share	U.S.
All residents	927	100.00%	100.00%
Non-Hispanic white	826	89.10%	67.37%
Hispanic white	18	1.94%	13.01%
Other Hispanic	4	0.43%	1.06%
African American	3	0.32%	12.77%
Native American	60	6.47%	0.96%
Asian, Pacific Islander	6	0.65%	4.37%
Two or more categories	14	1.51%	1.51%

Population figures are in thousands. Persons counted as "Hispanic" (Latino) may be of any race. Because of overlapping categories, categories may not add up to 100%. Shares in column 3 are percentages of each category within the state; these figures may be compared to the national percentages in column 4.
Source: U.S. Bureau of the Census, 2006.

Projected state population, 2000-2030

Year	Population
2000	902,000
2005	933,000
2010	969,000
2015	999,000
2020	1,023,000
2025	1,037,000
2030	1,045,000
Population increase, 2000-2030	143,000
Percentage increase, 2000-2030	15.8

Projections are based on data from the 2000 census.
Source: U.S. Census Bureau.

VITAL STATISTICS

Infant mortality rates, 1980-2002

	1980	1990	2000	2002
All state residents	12.4	9.0	6.1	7.5
All U.S. residents	12.6	9.2	9.4	9.1
All state white residents	11.8	6.0	5.5	7.1
All U.S. white residents	10.6	7.6	5.7	5.8

Figures represent deaths per 1,000 live births of resident infants under 1 year old, exclusive of fetal deaths. Figures for all residents include members of other racial categories not listed separately. The Census Bureau considers the figures for black residents to be too small to be statistically meaningful.
Source: U.S. Census Bureau, *Statistical Abstract of the United States,* 2006.

Abortion rates, 1990 and 2000

	1990	2000
Total abortions	3,000	3,000
Rate per 1,000 women	18.4	13.5
U.S. rate	25.7	21.3
Rank	26	28

Numbers of abortions are rounded to nearest thousand; ranks are based on rates.
Source: U.S. Census Bureau.

Marriages and divorces, 2004

Total marriages	6,800
Rate per 1,000 population	7.4
National rate per 1,000 population	7.4
Rank among all states	23
Total divorces	3,500
Rate per 1,000 population	3.8
National rate per 1,000 population	3.7
Rank among all states	22

Figures are for all marriages and divorces performed within the state, including those of nonresidents; totals are rounded to the nearest hundred. Ranks are for highest to lowest figures; note that divorce data are not available for five states.
Source: U.S. National Center for Health Statistics, *Vital Statistics of the United States,* 2006.

Death rates by leading causes, 2002
Deaths per 100,000 resident population

Cause	State	U.S.
Heart disease	213.8	241.7
Cancer	210.1	193.2
Cerebrovascular diseases	70.3	56.4
Accidents other than motor vehicle	57.6	37.0
Motor vehicle accidents	28.0	15.7
Chronic lower respiratory diseases	63.3	43.3
Diabetes mellitus	23.1	25.4
HIV	n/a	4.9
Suicide	20.2	11.0
Homicide	2.5	6.1
All causes	935.3	847.3
Rank in overall death rate among states		16

Figures exclude nonresidents who died in the state. Causes of death follow International Classification of Diseases. Rank is from highest to lowest death rate in the United States.
Source: U.S. National Center for Health Statistics, *National Vital Statistics Report,* 2006.

ECONOMY

Gross state product, 1990-2004
In current dollars

Year	State product	Nat'l product	State share
1990	$13.4 billion	$5.67 trillion	0.24%
2000	$21.4 billion	$9.75 trillion	0.22%
2002	$23.9 billion	$10.41 trillion	0.23%
2003	$25.6 billion	$10.92 trillion	0.23%
2004	$27.7 billion	$11.65 trillion	0.24%

Source: U.S. Bureau of Economic Analysis, *Survey of Current Business,* July, 2005.

Gross state product by industry, 2003
In billions of dollars

Construction	$1.3
Manufacturing	1.2
Wholesale trade	1.4
Retail trade	2.1
Finance & insurance	1.2
Information	0.8
Professional services	1.2
Health care & social assistance	2.0
Government	3.8
Total state product	$23.5
Total U.S. product	$10,289.2
State share of U.S. total	0.23%
Rank among all states	47

Total figures include industries not listed separately. Amounts are in chained 2000 dollars.
Source: U.S. Bureau of Economic Analysis, *Survey of Current Business,* July, 2005.

Personal income per capita, 1990-2004
In current dollars

	1990	2000	2004
Per capita income	$15,448	$22,929	$26,857
U.S. average	$19,477	$29,845	$32,937
Rank among states	43	46	45

Source: U.S. Bureau of Economic Analysis, *Survey of Current Business,* April, 2005.

Energy consumption, 2001
In trillions of British thermal units (BTU), except as noted

Total energy consumption
Total state energy consumption	366
Total U.S. energy consumption	96,275
State share of U.S. total	0.38%
Rank among states	44

Per capita consumption (In millions of BTU)
Total state per capita consumption	404
Total U.S. per capita consumption	338
Rank among states	13

End-use sectors
Residential	70
Commercial	60
Industrial	128
Transportation	108

Sources of energy
Petroleum	168
Natural gas	67
Coal	184
Hydroelectric power	67
Nuclear electric power	0

Figures for totals include categories not listed separately.
Source: U.S. Energy Information Administration, *State Energy Data Report,* 2001.

Nonfarm employment by sectors, 2004

Total	412,000
Construction	25,000
Manufacturing	19,000
Trade, transportation, utilities	86,000
Information	8,000
Finance, insurance, real estate	21,000
Professional & business services	33,000
Education & health services	54,000
Leisure, hospitality, arts, organizations	55,000
Other services, including repair & maintenance	17,000
Government	87,000

Figures are rounded to nearest thousand persons. "Total" includes mining and natural resources, not listed separately.
Source: U.S. Bureau of Labor Statistics, 2006.

Foreign exports, 1990-2004
In millions of dollars

Year	State	U.S.	State share
1990	229	394,045	0.06%
1996	440	624,767	0.07%
1997	530	688,896	0.08%
2000	541	712,055	0.07%
2003	361	724,006	0.05%
2004	565	769,332	0.07%
Rank among all states in 2004 49			

U.S. total does not include U.S. dependencies.
Source: U.S. Census Bureau, *U.S. Merchandise Trade*, series FT 900, 2000; U.S. Census Bureau, *U.S. International Trade in Goods and Services*, Series FT 900, 2005.

LAND USE

Federally owned land, 2003
Areas in acres

	State	U.S.	State share
Total area	93,271,000	2,271,343,000	4.11%
Nonfederal land	64,032,000	1,599,584,000	4.00%
Federal land	29,239,000	671,759,000	4.35%
Federal share	31.3%	29.6%	—

Areas are rounded to nearest thousand acres. Figures for federally owned land do not include trust properties.
Source: U.S. General Services Administration, *Federal Real Property Profile*, 2006.

Land use, 1997
In acres, rounded to nearest thousand

Total surface area	94,110,000
Total nonfederal rural land.	64,958,000
Percentage rural land	69.0%
Cropland.	15,171,000
Conservation Reserve Program (CRP*) land . . .	2,721,000
Pastureland	3,443,000
Rangeland	36,751,000
Forestland.	5,431,000
Other rural land	1,443,000

*CRP is a federal program begun in 1985 to assist private landowners to convert highly erodible cropland to vegetative cover for ten years. Note that some categories of land overlap.
Source: U.S. Department of Agriculture, Natural Resources and Conservation Service, and Iowa State University, Statistical Laboratory, *Summary Report, 1997 National Resources Inventory,* revised December, 2000.

Farms and crop acreage, 2004

	State	U.S.	Share	Rank
Farms	28,000	2,113,000	1.33%	30
Acres (millions)	60	937	6.40%	2
Acres per farm	2,146	443	—	4

Source: U.S. Department of Agriculture, National Agricultural Statistics Service. Numbers of farms are rounded to nearest thousand units; acreage figures are rounded to nearest million. Rankings, including ties, are based on rounded figures.

GOVERNMENT AND FINANCE

Units of local government, 2002

	State	Total U.S.	Rank
All local governments	1,127	87,525	28
Counties	54	3,034	29
Municipalities	129	19,429	38
Townships	0	16,504	—
School districts	352	13,506	14
Special districts	592	35,052	21

Only 48 states have county governments, 20 states have township governments ("towns" in New England, Minnesota, New York, and Wisconsin), and 46 states have school districts. Special districts encompass such functions as natural resources, fire protection, and housing and community development.
Source: U.S. Census Bureau, *Census of Governments.*

State government revenue, 2002

Total revenue	$4,033 mill.
General revenue	$3,721 mill.
Per capita revenue	$4,086
U.S. per capita average	$3,689
Rank among states	20
Intergovernment revenue	
Total	$1,427 mill.
From federal government	$1,419 mill.
Charges and miscellaneous	
Total	$852 mill.
Current charges	$387 mill.
Misc. general income	$464 mill.
Insurance trust revenue	$266 mill.
Taxes	
Total	$1,443 mill.
Per capita taxes	$1,585
Rank among states	39
Property taxes	$182 mill.
Sales taxes	$371 mill.
License taxes	$199 mill.
Individual income taxes	$518 mill.
Corporate income taxes.	$68 mill.
Other taxes	$105 mill.

Total revenue figures include items not listed separately here.
Source: U.S. Bureau of the Census.

State government expenditures, 2002

General expenditures

Total state expenditures	$4,265 mill.
Intergovernmental	$911 mill.

Per capita expenditures

State	$4,159
Average of all states	$3,859
Rank among states	19

Selected direct expenditures

Education.	$637 mill.
Public welfare	$643 mill.
Health, hospital	$287 mill.
Highways	$436 mill.
Police protection	$28 mill.
Corrections.	$106 mill.
Natural resources	$181 mill.
Parks and recreation	$6 mill.
Government administration.	$207 mill.
Interest on debt	$143 mill.
Total direct expenditures	$2,874 mill.

Totals include items not listed separately.
Source: U.S. Census Bureau.

POLITICS

Governors since statehood

D = Democrat; R = Republican; O = other;
(r) resigned; (d) died in office; (i) removed from office

Joseph K. Toole (D)	1889-1893
John E. Rickards (R).	1893-1897
Robert B. Smith (O)	1897-1901
Joseph K. Toole (D) . . . . (r)	1901-1908
Edwin L. Norris (D)	1908-1913
Samuel V. Stewart (D)	1913-1921
Joseph M. Dixon (R).	1921-1925
John E. Erickson (D) . . . . (r)	1925-1933
Frank H. Cooney (D) . . . . (d)	1933-1935
William Elmer Hoyt (D).	1935-1937
Roy E. Ayers (D)	1937-1941
Samuel C. Ford (R)	1941-1949
John W. Bonner (D)	1949-1953
John Hugo Aronson (R).	1953-1961
Donald G. Nutter (R) . . . . (d)	1961-1962
Tim M. Babcock (R)	1962-1969
Forrest H. Anderson (D)	1969-1973
Thomas L. Judge (D)	1973-1981
Ted Schwinden (D)	1981-1989
Stan Stephens (R)	1989-1993
Marc Racicot (R).	1993-2001
Judy Martz (R)	2001-2005
Brian Schweitzer (D)	2005-

Composition of congressional delegations, 1989-2007

	Dem	Rep	Total
House of Representatives			
101st Congress, 1989			
State delegates	1	1	2
Total U.S.	259	174	433
102d Congress, 1991			
State delegates	1	1	2
Total U.S.	267	167	434
103d Congress, 1993			
State delegates	1	0	1
Total U.S.	258	176	434
104th Congress, 1995			
State delegates	0	1	1
Total U.S.	197	236	433
105th Congress, 1997			
State delegates	0	1	1
Total U.S.	206	228	434
106th Congress, 1999			
State delegates	0	1	1
Total U.S.	211	222	433
107th Congress, 2001			
State delegates	0	1	1
Total U.S.	211	221	432
108th Congress, 2003			
State delegates	0	1	1
Total U.S.	205	229	434
109th Congress, 2005			
State delegates	0	1	1
Total U.S.	202	231	433
110th Congress, 2007			
State delegates	0	1	1
Total U.S.	233	202	435
Senate			
101st Congress, 1989			
State delegates	1	1	2
Total U.S.	55	45	100
102d Congress, 1991			
State delegates	1	1	2
Total U.S.	56	44	100
103d Congress, 1993			
State delegates	1	1	2
Total U.S.	57	43	100
104th Congress, 1995			
State delegates	1	1	2
Total U.S.	46	53	99
105th Congress, 1997			
State delegates	1	1	2
Total U.S.	45	55	100

(continued)

	Dem	Rep	Total
106th Congress, 1999			
State delegates	1	1	2
Total U.S.	45	54	99
107th Congress, 2001			
State delegates	1	1	2
Total U.S.	50	50	100
108th Congress, 2003			
State delegates	1	1	2
Total U.S.	48	51	99
109th Congress, 2005			
State delegates	1	1	2
Total U.S.	44	55	99
110th Congress, 2007			
State delegates	2	0	2
Total U.S.	49	49	98

Figures are for starts of first sessions. Totals are for Democrat (Dem.) and Republican (Rep.) members only. House membership totals under 435 and Senate totals under 100 reflect vacancies and seats held by independent party members. When the 110th Congress opened, the Senate's two independent members caucused with the Democrats, giving the Democrats control of the Senate.

Source: U.S. Congress, *Congressional Directory.*

Composition of state legislature, 1990-2006

	Democrats	Republicans
State House (100 seats)		
1990	61	39
1992	47	53
1994	33	67
1996	35	65
1998	41	59
2000	41	59
2002	47	53
2004	50	50
2006	49	50
State Senate (50 seats)		
1990	29	21
1992	30	20
1994	19	31
1996	16	34
1998	18	32
2000	18	32
2002	21	29
2004	27	23
2006	26	24

Figures for total seats may include independents and minor party members. Numbers reflect results of elections in listed years; elected members usually take their seats in the years that follow.

Source: Council of State Governments; *State Elective Officials and the Legislatures.*

Voter participation in presidential elections, 2000 and 2004

	2000	2004
Voting age population		
State	675,000	719,000
Total United States	209,831,000	220,377,000
State share of U.S. total	0.32	0.33
Rank among states	44	44
Portion of voting age population casting votes		
State	60.9%	62.7%
United States	50.3%	55.5%
Rank among states	8	13

Population figures are rounded to nearest thousand and include all residents, regardless of eligibility to vote.

Source: U.S. Census Bureau.

HEALTH AND MEDICAL CARE

Medical professionals
Physicians in 2003 and nurses in 2001

	U.S.	State
Physicians in 2003		
Total	774,849	2,079
Share of U.S. total		0.27%
Rate	266	227
Rank		33
Nurses in 2001		
Total	2,262,020	7,620
Share of U.S. total		0.34%
Rate	793	842
Rank		23

Rates are numbers of physicians and nurses per 100,000 resident population; ranks are based on rates.

Source: American Medical Association, *Physician Characteristics and Distribution in the U.S.;* U.S. Department of Health and Human Services, Health Resources and Services Administration.

Health insurance coverage, 2003

	State	U.S.
Total persons covered	739,000	243,320,000
Total persons not covered	177,000	44,961,000
Portion not covered	19.4%	15.6%
Rank among states	5	—
Children not covered	38,000	8,373,000
Portion not covered	17.7%	11.4%
Rank among states	3	—

Totals are rounded to nearest thousand. Ranks are from the highest to the lowest percentages of persons *not* insured.

Source: U.S. Census Bureau, Current Population Reports.

AIDS, syphilis, and tuberculosis cases, 2003

Disease	U.S. cases	State cases	Rank
AIDS	44,232	7	49
Syphilis	34,270	0	50
Tuberculosis	14,874	7	48

Source: U.S. Centers for Disease Control and Prevention.

Cigarette smoking, 2003
Residents over age 18 who smoke

	U.S.	State	Rank
All smokers	22.1%	19.9%	40
Male smokers	24.8%	19.5%	48
Female smokers	20.3%	20.3%	26

Cigarette smokers are defined as persons who reported having smoked at least 100 cigarettes during their lifetimes and who currently smoked at least occasionally.
Source: U.S. Centers for Disease Control and Prevention, *Morbidity and Mortality Weekly Report,* 53, no. 44 (November 12, 2004).

HOUSING

Home ownership rates, 1985-2004

	1985	1990	1995	2000	2004
State	66.5%	69.1%	68.7%	70.2%	72.4%
Total U.S.	63.9%	63.9%	64.7%	67.4%	69.0%
Rank among states	33	13	20	26	21

Net change in state home ownership rate,
1985-2004 . . . . +5.9%
Net change in U.S. home ownership rate,
1985-2004 . . . . +5.1%

Percentages represent the proportion of owner households to total occupied households.
Source: U.S. Census Bureau, 2006.

Home sales, 2000-2004
In thousands of units

Existing home sales	2000	2002	2003	2004
State sales	17.4	22.6	23.2	24.2
Total U.S. sales	5,171	5,631	6,183	6,784
State share of U.S. total	0.34%	0.40%	0.38%	0.36%
Sales rank among states	43	43	43	43

Units include single-family homes, condos, and co-ops.
Source: National Association of Realtors, Washington, D.C., *Real Estate Outlook: Market Trends & Insights.*

Values of owner-occupied homes, 2003

	State	U.S.
Total units	173,000	58,809,000
Value of units		
Under $100,000	38.8%	29.6%
$100,000-199,999	45.7%	36.9%
$200,000 or more	15.5%	33.5%
Median value	$118,887	$142,275
Rank among all states 30		

Units are owner-occupied one-family houses whose numbers are rounded to nearest thousand. Data are extrapolated from survey samples.
Source: U.S. Census Bureau, American Community Survey.

EDUCATION

Public school enrollment, 2002

Prekindergarten through grade 8
State enrollment 101,000
Total U.S. enrollment. 34,135,000
State share of U.S. total 0.30%

Grades 9 through 12
State enrollment. 49,000
Total U.S. enrollment. 14,067,000
State share of U.S. total 0.35%

Enrollment rates
State public school enrollment rate. 90.6%
Overall U.S. rate 90.4%
Rank among states in 2002. 24
Rank among states in 1995. 16

Enrollment figures (which include unclassified students) are rounded to nearest thousand pupils during fall school term. Enrollment rates are based on enumerated resident population estimate for July 1, 2002.
Source: U.S. National Center for Education Statistics.

Public college finances, 2003-2004

FTE enrollment in public institutions of higher education

Students in state institutions	35,800
Students in all U.S. public institutions	9,916,600
State share of U.S. total	0.36
Rank among states	42

State and local government appropriations for higher education

State appropriation per FTE	$3,915
National average	$5,716
Rank among states	47
State & local tax revenue going to higher education	7.0%

FTE = full-time equivalent in public postsecondary programs, including summer sessions; student numbers are rounded to nearest hundred. Funding figures for 2003-2004 academic year include financial aid to students in state public institutions and exclude money for research, agriculture experiment stations, teaching hospitals, and medical schools; figures are rounded to nearest thousand dollars.

Source: Higher Education Executive Officers, Denver, Colorado.

TRANSPORTATION AND TRAVEL

Highway mileage, 2003

Interstate highways	1,192
Arterial roads	6,038
Collector roads	16,368
Local roads	45,852
Urban roads	2,753
Rural roads	66,697
Total state mileage	69,450
U.S. total	3,974,107
State share	1.75%
Rank among states	29

Note that combined urban and rural road mileage matches the total of the other categories.

Source: U.S. Federal Highway Administration.

Motor vehicle registrations and driver licenses, 2003

Vehicle registrations	State	U.S.	Share	Rank
Autos, trucks, buses	1,010,000	231,390,000	0.44%	42
Autos only	437,000	135,670	0.32%	44
Motorcycles	66,000	5,328,000	1.24%	25
Driver licenses	705,000	196,166,000	0.36%	44

Figures, which do not include vehicles owned by military services, are rounded to the nearest thousand. Figures for automobiles include taxis.

Source: U.S. Federal Highway Administration.

Domestic travel expenditures, 2003

Spending by U.S. residents on overnight trips and day trips of at least 50 miles from home

Total expenditures within state	$2.06 bill.
Total expenditures within U.S.	$490.87 bill.
State share of U.S. total	0.4%
Rank among states	41

Source: Travel Industry Association of America.

Retail gasoline prices, 2003-2007

Average price per gallon at the pump

Year	U.S.	State
2003	$1.267	$1.234
2004	$1.316	$1.232
2005	$1.644	$1.608
2007	$2.298	$2.157

Excise tax per gallon in 2004	27.0¢
Rank among all states in 2007 prices	41

Prices are averages of all grades of gasoline sold at the pump during March months in 2003-2005 and during February, 2007. Averages for 2006, during which prices rose higher, are not available.

Source: U.S. Energy Information Agency, *Petroleum Marketing Monthly* (2003-2005 data); American Automobile Association (2007 data).

CRIME AND LAW ENFORCEMENT

State and local police officers, 2000-2004

	2000	2002	2004
Total officers			
U.S.	654,601	665,555	675,734
State	1,401	1,581	1,626*
*Net change, 2000-2004			+16.06%
Officers per 1,000 residents			
U.S.	2.33	2.31	2.30
State	1.50	1.74	1.75
State rank	49	39	41

Totals include state and local police and sheriffs.
Source: Carsey Institute, University of New Hampshire.

Crime rates, 2003
Incidents per 100,000 residents

Crimes	State	U.S.
Violent crimes		
Total incidents	365	475
Murder	3	6
Forcible rape	27	32
Robbery	33	142
Aggravated assault	303	295
Property crimes		
Total incidents	3,098	3,588
Burglary	406	741
Larceny/theft	2,485	2,415
Motor vehicle theft	208	433
All crimes	3,463	4,063

Source: U.S. Federal Bureau of Investigation, *Crime in the United States*, annual.

State prison populations, 1980-2003

	State	U.S.	State share
1980	739	305,458	0.24%
1990	1,425	708,393	0.20%
1996	2,293	1,025,624	0.22%
2000	3,105	1,391,261	0.22%
2003	3,620	1,470,045	0.25%

State figures exclude prisoners in federal penitentiaries.
Source: U.S. Bureau of Justice Statistics, *Prisoners in 2003.*

Nebraska

Location: Midwest

Area and rank: 76,644 square miles (198,508 square kilometers); 77,358 square miles (200,357 square kilometers) including water; fifteenth largest state in area

Coastline: none

Population and rank: 1,747,000 (2004); thirty-eighth largest state in population

Capital city: Lincoln (225,581 people in 2000 census)

Largest city: Omaha (390,007 people in 2000 census)

Became territory: May 30, 1854

Nebraska's largest city, Omaha. (PhotoDisc)

Entered Union and rank: March 1, 1867; thirty-seventh state

Present constitution adopted: October 12, 1875 (extensively amended 1919-1920)

Counties: 93

State name: "Nebraska" is derived from an Oto Indian word meaning "flat water"

State nicknames: Cornhusker State; Beef State

Motto: Equality before the law

State flag: Blue field with state seal in gold and silver

Highest point: Johnson Township—5,424 feet (1,653 meters)

Lowest point: Missouri River—840 feet (256 meters)

Highest recorded temperature: 118 degrees Fahrenheit (48 degrees Celsius)—Minden, 1936

Lowest recorded temperature: –47 degrees Fahrenheit (–44 degrees Celsius)—Camp Clarke, 1899

State song: "Beautiful Nebraska"

State tree: Cottonwood

State flower: Goldenrod

State bird: Western meadowlark

Nebraska History

Nebraska's eastern and northeastern borders are defined by the Missouri River, across which lie Iowa to the east and South Dakota to the north. It is 462 miles across Iowa to its extreme western border at the Wyoming state line. West and south of the state is Colorado. From the northern border at the South Dakota line to the southern border at the Kansas line is 210 miles. With a land mass of 77,358 square miles, Nebraska ranks sixteenth in size of the states, although, with 1,656,870 residents in 1997, it ranked thirty-eighth in population. In 1990, it had a population density of about twenty people per square mile.

Nebraska is considered one of the midwestern states, although it is at the western extreme of the Midwest. Its climate is semi-arid, with hot, dry summers and very cold winters. Because glaciers pushed topsoil into the area as they advanced south more than two million years ago, the soil, called till, is fertile. However, droughts sometimes lead to dust storms that blow away some of the richest topsoil from thousands of acres.

Early History. Human habitation of the Nebraska area is estimated to have begun more than ten thousand years ago. Ancestors of the bison roamed the plains, supplying settlers with food and fur, from which they fashioned clothing and shelters in the form of tepees. They used animal bones to make buttons and such instruments as knives.

The largest mammoth skeleton ever recovered was found near North Platte. This animal, resembling an elephant, was nearly fourteen feet tall. When the Ice Age arrived more than two million years ago, many of these animals disappeared and eventually became extinct. At the end of the Ice Age, however, some animals, including bison and mammoths, survived, and the ancient people who lived in the area hunted them with spears. These people also farmed and made pottery.

Eerily reminiscent of the Statue of Liberty, which later welcomed immigrants to New York Harbor, Chimney Rock in western Nebraska's North Platte River Valley served as a beacon to early nineteenth century settlers moving west along the Oregon, California, and Mormon Trails. The natural formation rises almost three hundred feet above the surrounding plain, to an altitude of 4,226 feet above sea level. (Courtesy, Nebraska State Historical Society)

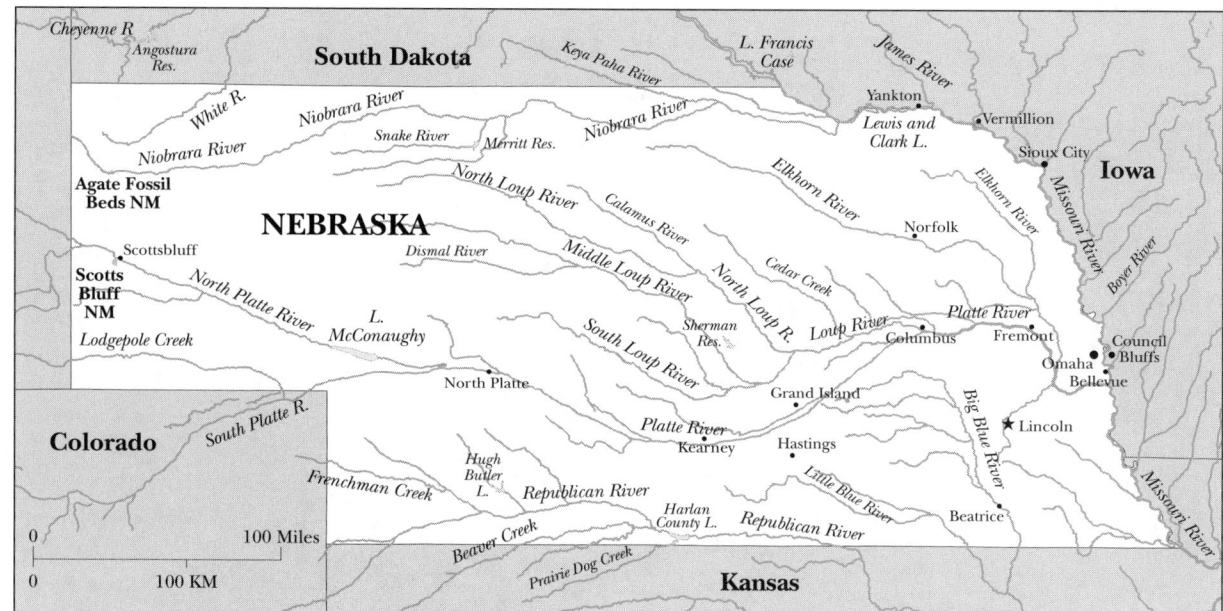

By the sixteenth century, Native Americans, notably the Omaha, Oto, Pawnee, and Ponca, occupied the area, living in villages and raising crops of beans, corn, and squash. The Arapaho, Cheyenne, Comanche, and Sioux were more hunters than farmers. Living in tepees, they roved the plains hunting for animals, mostly bison. The largest Native American group at this time was the Pawnee.

Early European Exploration. Even before Europeans reached what is now Nebraska, Spanish explorers who had traveled to Texas, Oklahoma, Kansas, and Missouri had claimed for Spain all of the land they had visited and a great deal of land north and west of it that they had not seen. By 1541 both Francisco Vásquez de Coronado and Hernando de Soto had laid claim to much of this land for Spain.

In 1682, René-Robert Cavelier, sieur de La Salle, had claimed much of the same land for France, naming the whole vast area between the Mississippi River and the Rocky Mountains Louisiana, in honor of King Louis XIV of France. It was not until 1803 that the United States, through the Louisiana Purchase, bought all of this land from France for fifteen million dollars.

Meanwhile, in 1714 Etienne Veniard de Bourgmont, a French explorer, made his way into the Missouri River Valley of Nebraska. Spanish forces were known to have been in the state in 1720, when they clashed with some of the natives, who soundly defeated them. Almost two decades later, in 1739, brothers Paul and Pierre Mallet crossed Nebraska, following the course of the Platte River.

The area was so sparsely populated that its development was slow. It was not until 1823 that the first white settlement was established at Bellevue on the Missouri River in the eastern part of the region. The United States Army had built Fort Atkinson on the Missouri's west bank four years earlier.

The Oregon Trail passed through Nebraska, so a steady stream of people who set out during the 1840's to seek their fortunes in the West passed through the area. These early travelers, however, had to keep moving because the government had designated Nebraska as an Indian territory and, at that time, would not permit further white settlement there.

The Homestead Act. By 1854 the federal government, in enacting the Kansas-Nebraska Act, made Kansas and Nebraska territories. Nebraska was now opened to anyone, mostly Europeans, who wished to settle there. In the same year, Omaha was founded.

The Homestead Act of 1862 gave families or any male over age twenty-one 160 acres of land that would become theirs after five years if they settled on it and improved it. This bonanza attracted so many people that by 1867 Nebraska had sufficient population numbers to justify statehood. With many of its residents still living on the prairie in sod houses, Nebraska became the thirty-seventh state in 1867. Lincoln became its capital. In 1871, the University of Nebraska was founded at Lincoln.

Early Homesteaders. Life was not easy for most of the homesteaders who were given land in Nebraska. The winters were long and harsh. Driving winds howled outside as residents huddled in drafty homes, many of which had been fashioned from squares of sod cut from the prairie. Wood for stoves was scarce.

During the long winters, hungry animals, particu-

Contemporary illustration of Crazy Horse's Sioux riding from Camp Sheridan to surrender to the U.S. Cavalry in 1877. (Library of Congress)

larly wolves, roved the prairie looking for food and putting the settlers, particularly small children, at risk. Until the late 1870's, there was the added threat of attacks by hostile American Indians, which subsided somewhat after the Sioux chief Crazy Horse surrendered at Fort Robinson, where he was murdered in 1877. These were difficult times for people living on the prairie.

Water Problems. The eastern part of Nebraska always received more precipitation than the west, but droughts were common throughout the state, ruining agriculture. Permanent damage was done to the land as dust storms blew valuable topsoil away. A particularly devastating blizzard in 1888 resulted in the deaths of more than two hundred people in Nebraska. Floods in springtime plagued the areas along the Missouri and Platte Rivers.

It was not until late in the nineteenth century that Nebraska farmers began to irrigate their fields with water obtained from great reservoirs that had been constructed along the Platte. In 1895, largely at the instigation of the Populist Party that had been established three years earlier, the state set up a Board of Irrigation. In 1902, the U.S. government passed the Reclamation Act, which provided money for the development of irrigation projects.

Modern Nebraska faces significant water problems: On their way to Nebraska the state's rivers are siphoned by other states, depriving Nebraska of much-needed water. So great has been the problem that Nebraska has had to tap its aquifer, the subterranean water in porous rocks and gravel, that is not renewable. The use of pesticides and other agricultural chemicals has polluted much of Nebraska's water, including its aquifer.

Nebraska's Economy. Nebraska is known for having the lowest unemployment rate of any state in the United States for many years. During World War I, Nebraska farms supplied much of the food that the armed forces required, and 48,000 Nebraskans went off to serve their country in the war. Wheat and corn production was strong, as was the production of sorghum and soybeans. The state was prosperous until the late 1920's, when two coincident factors ruined the economy.

The stock market crash late in 1929 changed the economic picture all over the United States. Banks and businesses failed. People lost their life savings and their homes. Factories closed and armies of people were unemployed nationwide. Despite this economic chaos, farmers, who were usually self-sufficient, might have been expected to survive economically.

During the early 1930's, however, severe droughts plagued the Midwest, reducing farm production to all-time lows. Nebraska, like many other midwestern states, found itself hit hard by the Great Depression. In 1934, Nebraskans voted to establish a one-house legislature to speed up legislation and to cut costs. This unicameral system persisted.

More than sixty thousand desperate Nebraskans were forced by the economic meltdown to leave the state and find work elsewhere. By the end of the 1930's, Nebraska's weather had improved measurably, so farming again became profitable. War industries came into the state during World War II, bringing factory jobs. As

State capitol building in Lincoln. (P. Michael Whye/Department of Economic Development, Nebraska Division of Travel and Tourism)

rainfall increased substantially during the 1940's, farmers were again producing record crops.

The Move Away from Farms. After World War II, Nebraska's farms were bigger, but there were fewer of them. Many independent farmers sold their land and moved into cities and towns. Large agricultural corporations moved into the state, swallowing up small farms and turning agriculture into a much more specialized and scientific pursuit than it had once been. Omaha became a center for food processing. In 1953, the first frozen dinners in America were produced there.

By 1960 Nebraska had more city dwellers than rural inhabitants. By 1994 Omaha and Lincoln had only about a 2 percent unemployment rate. During the 1990's, about half of Nebraska's work force of 800,000 were employed in sales or service occupations. Some 200,000 people were employed in sales and telemarketing, centered in Omaha. Another 200,000 worked as doctors, nurses, lawyers, bankers, insurance agents, automotive repair people, and other service personnel. The local, state, and federal governments offered employment to another 150,000. The state had one public school teacher for every fourteen students enrolled, which is much higher than the national average.

Despite the move to urban areas, Nebraska still has more than fifty thousand farms; farms and ranches occupy 90 percent of the state's land. In the western part of Nebraska, which is not suited to farming, the great grasslands provide excellent grazing for cattle, which are produced there in large numbers.

Elections. As the twenty-first century approached, Nebraska's politics reflected its rural roots and moderate conservative leanings, despite the fact that most Nebraskans are employed in nonfarm settings in cities and towns. In the 2000 presidential election, for example, George W. Bush received the state's five electoral votes. Unlike all other states (except for Maine), in Nebraska candidates do not necessarily receive all the state's electoral votes if they win a majority of the vote. Instead, electoral votes are distributed proportionally to the votes received by each candidate. However, Bush's victory was so resounding—he defeated Al Gore 63-33 percent—that he was awarded all the votes.

The state's political moderation was reflected in the race for U.S. Senate. Ben Nelson, a Democrat, won the seat being vacated by Democrat senator Bob Kerrey, who declined to run. Nelson won his seat with just 51 percent of the vote. In 2002, the state's three members of Congress, all of them Republicans, were reelected, as was Senator Chuck Hagel, also a Republican. Hagel, however, was elected by a landslide, with 83 percent of the votes cast. At the same time, Republican governor Mike Johanns was reelected by the considerable margin of 69-28 percent.

In the Nebraska, 2004, presidential election, Bush again handily defeated his opponent, this time by a 2-1 margin. Shortly afterward, Governor Johanns was nominated to be secretary of agriculture in Washington, D.C. When he resigned in January, 2005, Lieutenant Governor David Heineman, a Nebraska native who graduated from the U.S. Military Academy at West Point, took Johanns's place as governor. He was elected to a four-year term later in the year, after narrowly defeating former University of Nebraska football coach Tom Osborne by a 49-46 percent margin.

Headlines. In May, 2002, Nebraska was victim of a series of homegrown terrorist incidents. A disturbed person placed a total of eighteen homemade bombs in rural mailboxes in five midwestern states. Seven of them were planted in Nebraska. Included with the bombs were notes that decried government power and threatened more attacks. None of the bombs went off, however, and a twenty-one-year-old college student eventually confessed to the crimes.

In 2003, issues before the public included the breaking of the rules for planting genetically modified (GM) seeds. Farmers were to plant at least 20 percent of unmodified seed but instead exceeded their GM seed planting allowance. Another issue was the *Escherichia coli* bacteria found in the beef of the Omaha slaughterhouse Nebraska Beef, Ltd. The company settled a lawsuit arising out of the contamination.

In another headline, a federal judge found that the height of the waters of the Missouri River would have to be lowered because the high level of the river was harming three endangered species of fish. While the Bush administration argued that high waters were needed by the barge industry, the judge disagreed. The result was that navigation on the river was disrupted for six weeks.

R. Baird Shuman
Updated by the Editor

Monument to the famous shelter for boys founded at Omaha in 1917. (Department of Economic Development, Nebraska Division of Travel and Tourism)

Nebraska Time Line

1541	Francisco Vásquez de Coronado claims America's Southwest, including present-day Nebraska, for Spain.
1682	René-Robert Cavelier, sieur de La Salle, claims all lands that drain into the Mississippi River, including modern Nebraska, for France.
1714	Etienne Veniard sails up the Missouri River to the Platte.
Aug. 13, 1720	Pawnee Indians defeat Spanish forces led by Pedro de Villasur.
1739	Paul and Pierre Mallet sail on the Missouri and Platte Rivers.
Apr. 30, 1803	United States buys the area that includes present-day Nebraska from France for fifteen million dollars in the Louisiana Purchase.
1806	Zebulon Pike visits south central Nebraska on his journey west.
1809	Manuel Lisa builds first trading posts along the Missouri River.
1813	Robert Stuart crosses Nebraska on his trek from Oregon to New York on what becomes the Oregon Trail.
1819	Fort Atkinson is built.
1823	Bellevue, the first permanent non-Indian settlement in the area, is established as a trading post on the west bank of the Missouri River.
1843	Early travelers along the Oregon Trail pass through Nebraska, now designated an Indian territory.
May 30, 1854	Kansas-Nebraska Act establishes Kansas and Nebraska as territories.
1862	Congress passes the Homestead Act, increasing settlement in Nebraska and other parts of the Midwest.
1865	Union Pacific Railroad lays tracks west from Omaha.
Mar. 1, 1867	Nebraska becomes the thirty-seventh state.
1872	Nebraska initiates the nation's first Arbor Day to encourage the planting of trees on the prairie.
1877	Sioux Chief Crazy Horse surrenders at Fort Robinson.
1888	Huge blizzard kills more than two hundred Nebraskans.
1892	Populist Party is formed.
1895	Nebraska establishes Board of Irrigation.
1896	Nebraskan William Jennings Bryan runs unsuccessfully for president of the United States.
1902	Congress passes the Reclamation Act, providing money for irrigation.
1917	Near Omaha, Father Edward Flanagan begins shelter for boys that becomes Boys Town.
1917	United States enters World War I; 48,000 Nebraskans serve in armed forces.
1919	Law prohibits teaching of any subject in any foreign language; U.S. Supreme Court strikes it down in 1923.
1934	Nebraskans vote to have a unicameral state legislature, the only one in America.
1935	Severe dust storms turn state into "Great American Desert."
1939	Oil is discovered in southeastern Nebraska.
1941	United States enters World War II; 140,000 Nebraskans serve in armed forces.
1944	United States Congress approves Missouri River Basin Project.
1952	Missouri River floods devastate eastern Nebraska.
1953	First frozen dinner processed in Omaha.
1960	Census reveals more Nebraskans live in cities than in rural areas.
1967	Nebraska Department of Economic development is established to attract new industry into the state.
1974	Nebraska-born Gerald R. Ford becomes thirty-eighth president of the United States.
1982	Constitutional amendment passed prohibiting further corporate farming.
1986	Both the Republican and Democratic candidates for governor are women; Republican Kay Orr wins.
1992	Omaha is telemarketing capital of the world.
1993	President Bill Clinton declares parts of Nebraska disaster areas after devastating Missouri River floods.
1994	Nebraska has record harvest of corn and soybeans.
Nov. 7, 2000	George W. Bush is awarded all of Nebraska's five electoral votes.

(continued)

May 4-5, 2002	Homemade bombs are planted in seven rural mailboxes but do not explode.
Dec. 2, 2004	President Bush nominates Governor Mike Johanns to be U.S. secretary of agriculture.
Jan. 20, 2005	David Heineman is sworn in as Nebraska governor.

Notes for Further Study

Published Sources. One of the most complete histories of Nebraska is James C. Olson and Ronald C. Naugle's *History of Nebraska* (3d ed., 1997), which covers the history of the state from prehistoric times to the date of publication, offering valuable illustrations, maps, and statistical tables. It is especially strong in its presentation of the growth of the Populist movement in Nebraska. A less formal offering is Donald R. Hickey's *Nebraska Moments: Glimpses of Nebraska's Past* (1992). It provides insightful vignettes which help readers understand Nebraska's people, especially the homesteaders. *Nebraska: An Illustrated History* (2d ed., 2005) by Frederick C. Luebke presents fifty-eight short topical chapters on Nebraska history, which are paired with detailed illustrations.

For information about Nebraska's Native Americans, one should turn to Mildred Mott Wedel's *The Wichita Indians, 1541-1750: Ethnohistorical Essays* (1988), which reproduces many essays relating to the state and its development. The dislocation of Nebraska's Indians is revealed in heart-rending terms in David J. Wishart's *An Unspeakable Sadness: The Dispossession of the Nebraska Indians* (1994). Donald Worster, in *Under Western Stars: A Nature and History of the American West* (1992), writes with feeling about its nature, prairies, and grasslands. *Dunwoody Pond: Reflections on the High Plains Wetlands and the Cultivation of Naturalists* (1994) by John Janovy, Jr., offers a well-considered ecological presentation that is nicely supplemented by Robert Hanna's *A Nebraska Portfolio* (1992), the photographs in which provide a sensitive visual record of the state. Paul A. Johnsgard brings forth a similar book with *The Nature of Nebraska: Ecology and Biodiversity* (2001), which details the historical geology, biology, botany, and ecology of the state.

Juvenile readers should turn to A. P. Porter's *Nebraska* (2d. rev. ed., 2002) or Dean Galiano's *Nebraska* (2006), while general audiences will enjoy *Nebraska Off the Beaten Path* (5th ed., 2005) by Hannah McNally.

Web Resources. The Nebraska state government's Web site (www.state.ne.us) and its travel and tourism Web site (www.visitnebraska.org/) provide essential information about the state and its attractions. These sites also refer users to additional relevant sites, including the Western Nebraska Web site (www.westnebraska.com). The Nebraska Department of Economic Development site (assist.neded.org/neweb.html/) offers considerable information and statistics about Nebraska communities. Related supplemental information is available on the Department of Labor's Web site (www.dol.state.ne.us).

The Missouri River Web site (www.nps.gov/mnrr), part of the National Parks series of Web pages, is frequently updated and gives information about the river, including flood warnings and information about irrigation projects. Omaha and Lincoln both have Web sites (www.visitomaha.com/, www.lincoln.org), which focus on their respective cities. The library systems of Omaha (www.omaha.lib.ne.us) and Lincoln (www.lcl.lib.ne.us) are both online. The Girls and Boys Town Web site (www.girlsandboystown.org/home.asp) offers details about that establishment and photographs of the events. The Nebraska Historical Society (www.nebraskahistory.org/) allows users to pursue genealogical research, learn about historical sites, and access the state's historical photograph archives, among other features. Nebraska Studies (www.nebraskastudies.org/), a resource designed for teachers, provides an excellent interactive time line and a section called Notable Nebraskans.

Counties

County	2000 pop.	Rank in pop.	Sq. miles	Rank in area	County	2000 pop.	Rank in pop.	Sq. miles	Rank in area
Adams	31,151	11	563.4	66	Cass	24,334	13	559.3	67
Antelope	7,452	43	857.1	24	Cedar	9,615	31	740.3	31
Arthur	444	93	715.4	36	Chase	4,068	62	894.5	21
Banner	819	85	746.3	30	Cherry	6,148	53	5,960.7	1
Blaine	583	91	710.8	39	Cheyenne	9,830	29	1,196.4	11
Boone	6,259	51	686.7	41	Clay	7,039	45	573.1	56
Box Butte	12,158	22	1,075.4	13	Colfax	10,441	26	413.2	86
Boyd	2,438	74	540.1	72	Cuming	10,203	27	572.0	58
Brown	3,525	67	1,221.4	10	Custer	11,793	23	2,575.8	2
Buffalo	42,259	5	968.1	18	Dakota	20,253	15	264.0	92
Burt	7,791	41	492.8	76	Dawes	9,060	35	1,396.3	9
Butler	8,767	37	583.6	44	Dawson	24,365	12	1,012.9	15

County	2000 pop.	Rank in pop.	Sq. miles	Rank in area	County	2000 pop.	Rank in pop.	Sq. miles	Rank in area
Deuel	2,098	78	439.9	82	Merrick	8,204	39	484.6	77
Dixon	6,339	50	476.4	78	Morrill	5,440	56	1,423.9	8
Dodge	36,160	7	534.5	74	Nance	4,038	64	441.3	81
Douglas	463,585	1	331.0	91	Nemaha	7,576	42	409.3	87
Dundy	2,292	76	919.9	20	Nuckolls	5,057	58	575.3	49
Fillmore	6,634	47	576.5	45	Otoe	15,396	19	615.9	43
Franklin	3,574	66	575.9	46	Pawnee	3,087	72	431.7	84
Frontier	3,099	71	974.6	17	Perkins	3,200	69	883.2	22
Furnas	5,324	57	718.1	34	Phelps	9,747	30	540.0	73
Gage	22,993	14	855.3	25	Pierce	7,857	40	574.0	54
Garden	2,292	75	1,704.6	7	Platte	31,662	10	678.1	42
Garfield	1,902	79	570.1	60	Polk	5,639	55	439.1	83
Gosper	2,143	77	458.2	79	Red Willow	11,448	25	716.7	35
Grant	747	88	776.3	27	Richardson	9,531	32	553.5	68
Greeley	2,714	73	569.9	61	Rock	1,756	80	1,008.5	16
Hall	53,534	4	546.4	70	Saline	13,843	21	575.4	48
Hamilton	9,403	33	543.7	71	Sarpy	122,595	3	240.7	93
Harlan	3,786	65	552.8	69	Saunders	19,830	16	754.1	29
Hayes	1,068	82	713.1	37	Scotts Bluff	36,951	6	739.3	32
Hitchcock	3,111	70	710.1	40	Seward	16,496	18	574.8	52
Holt	11,551	24	2,412.8	5	Sheridan	6,198	52	2,441.2	4
Hooker	783	86	721.2	33	Sherman	3,318	68	565.9	65
Howard	6,567	48	569.5	63	Sioux	1,475	81	2,066.7	6
Jefferson	8,333	38	573.1	55	Stanton	6,455	49	429.9	85
Johnson	4,488	60	376.2	90	Thayer	6,055	54	574.6	53
Kearney	6,882	46	516.1	75	Thomas	729	89	712.9	38
Keith	8,875	36	1,061.3	14	Thurston	7,171	44	393.8	88
Keya Paha	983	83	773.3	28	Valley	4,647	59	568.1	64
Kimball	4,089	61	951.8	19	Washington	18,780	17	390.5	89
Knox	9,374	34	1,108.2	12	Wayne	9,851	28	443.5	80
Lancaster	250,291	2	838.9	26	Webster	4,061	63	574.9	51
Lincoln	34,632	9	2,564.2	3	Wheeler	886	84	575.2	50
Logan	774	87	570.7	59	York	14,598	20	575.7	47
Loup	712	90	569.7	62					
McPherson	533	92	859.0	23					
Madison	35,226	8	572.6	57					

Source: U.S. Census Bureau; National Association of Counties.

Cities
With 10,000 or more residents

Rank	City	Population
1	Omaha	390,007
2	Lincoln (capital)	225,581
3	Bellevue	44,382
4	Grand Island	42,940
5	Kearney	27,431
6	Fremont	25,174
7	Hastings	24,064
8	North Platte	23,878
9	Norfolk	23,516
10	Columbus	20,971

Rank	City	Population
11	Papillion	16,363
12	Scottsbluff	14,732
13	Beatrice	12,496
14	South Sioux City	11,925
15	La Vista	11,699
16	Chalco	10,736
17	Lexington	10,011

Population figures are from 2000 census.
Source: U.S. Bureau of the Census.

Index to Tables

DEMOGRAPHICS

Resident state and national populations, 1970-2004

Population figures given in thousands

	State pop.	U.S. pop.	Share	Rank
1970	1,485	203,302	0.7%	35
1980	1,570	226,546	0.7%	35
1985	1,585	237,924	0.7%	36
1990	1,578	248,765	0.6%	36
1995	1,657	262,761	0.6%	37
2000	1,711	281,425	0.6%	38
2004	1,747	293,655	0.6%	38

Source: U.S. Census Bureau, Current Population Reports, 2006.

Resident population by age, 2004

Age Group	Total persons
Under 5 years	122,000
5 to 17 years	313,000
18 to 24 years	191,000
25 to 34 years	229,000
35 to 44 years	244,000
45 to 54 years	249,000
55 to 64 years	167,000
65 to 74 years	111,000
75 to 84 years	85,000
85 years and older	36,000
All age groups	1,747,000

Portion of residents 65 and older	13.3%
National rank in portion of oldest residents	13
National average	12.4%

Population figures are rounded to nearest thousand persons;
figures include armed forces personnel stationed in the state.
Source: U.S. Bureau of the Census, 2006.

Resident population by race, Hispanic origin, 2004

Category	State pop.	Share	U.S.
All residents	1,747	100.00%	100.00%
Non-Hispanic white	1,497	85.69%	67.37%
Hispanic white	112	6.41%	13.01%
Other Hispanic	8	0.46%	1.06%
African American	75	4.29%	12.77%
Native American	17	0.97%	0.96%
Asian, Pacific Islander	28	1.60%	4.37%
Two or more categories	19	1.09%	1.51%

Population figures are in thousands. Persons counted as "Hispanic" (Latino) may be of any race. Because of overlapping categories, categories may not add up to 100%. Shares in column 3 are percentages of each category within the state; these figures may be compared to the national percentages in column 4.
Source: U.S. Bureau of the Census, 2006.

Projected state population, 2000-2030

Year	Population
2000	1,711,000
2005	1,744,000
2010	1,769,000
2015	1,789,000
2020	1,803,000
2025	1,813,000
2030	1,820,000
Population increase, 2000-2030	109,000
Percentage increase, 2000-2030	6.4

Projections are based on data from the 2000 census.
Source: U.S. Census Bureau.

VITAL STATISTICS

Infant mortality rates, 1980-2002

	1980	1990	2000	2002
All state residents	11.5	8.3	7.3	7.0
All U.S. residents	12.6	9.2	9.4	9.1
All state white residents	10.7	6.9	6.4	6.1
All U.S. white residents	10.6	7.6	5.7	5.8
All state black residents	25.2	18.9	20.3	20.8
All U.S. black residents	22.2	18.0	14.1	14.4

Figures represent deaths per 1,000 live births of resident infants under 1 year old, exclusive of fetal deaths. Figures for all residents include members of other racial categories not listed separately.
Source: U.S. Census Bureau, *Statistical Abstract of the United States,* 2006.

Abortion rates, 1990 and 2000

	1990	2000
Total abortions	6,000	4,000
Rate per 1,000 women	15.6	11.6
U.S. rate	25.7	21.3
Rank	32	33

Numbers of abortions are rounded to nearest thousand; ranks are based on rates.
Source: U.S. Census Bureau.

Marriages and divorces, 2004

Total marriages	12,900
Rate per 1,000 population	7.4
National rate per 1,000 population	7.4
Rank among all states	23
Total divorces	6,400
Rate per 1,000 population	3.6
National rate per 1,000 population	3.7
Rank among all states	26

Figures are for all marriages and divorces performed within the state, including those of nonresidents; totals are rounded to the nearest hundred. Ranks are for highest to lowest figures; note that divorce data are not available for five states.
Source: U.S. National Center for Health Statistics, *Vital Statistics of the United States,* 2006.

Death rates by leading causes, 2002
Deaths per 100,000 resident population

Cause	State	U.S.
Heart disease	245.3	241.7
Cancer	198.5	193.2
Cerebrovascular diseases	63.8	56.4
Accidents other than motor vehicle	44.1	37.0
Motor vehicle accidents	19.5	15.7
Chronic lower respiratory diseases	54.0	43.3
Diabetes mellitus	22.7	25.4
HIV	1.2	4.9
Suicide	11.6	11.0
Homicide	2.9	6.1
All causes	910.1	847.3
Rank in overall death rate among states		20

Figures exclude nonresidents who died in the state. Causes of death follow International Classification of Diseases. Rank is from highest to lowest death rate in the United States.
Source: U.S. National Center for Health Statistics, *National Vital Statistics Report,* 2006.

ECONOMY

Gross state product, 1990-2004
In current dollars

Year	State product	Nat'l product	State share
1990	$33.8 billion	$5.67 trillion	0.60%
2000	$55.7 billion	$9.75 trillion	0.57%
2002	$60.6 billion	$10.41 trillion	0.58%
2003	$65.4 billion	$10.92 trillion	0.60%
2004	$67.9 billion	$11.65 trillion	0.58%

Source: U.S. Bureau of Economic Analysis, *Survey of Current Business,* July, 2005.

Gross state product by industry, 2003
In billions of dollars

Construction	$2.4
Manufacturing	7.8
Wholesale trade	4.1
Retail trade	4.5
Finance & insurance	5.0
Information	2.3
Professional services	2.6
Health care & social assistance	4.1
Government	8.5
Total state product	$60.7
Total U.S. product	$10,289.2
State share of U.S. total	0.59%
Rank among all states	36

Total figures include industries not listed separately. Amounts are in chained 2000 dollars.
Source: U.S. Bureau of Economic Analysis, *Survey of Current Business,* July, 2005.

Personal income per capita, 1990-2004
In current dollars

	1990	2000	2004
Per capita income	$17,983	$27,625	$31,339
U.S. average	$19,477	$29,845	$32,937
Rank among states	26	29	25

Source: U.S. Bureau of Economic Analysis, *Survey of Current Business,* April, 2005.

Energy consumption, 2001
In trillions of British thermal units (BTU), except as noted

Total energy consumption

Total state energy consumption	627
Total U.S. energy consumption	96,275
State share of U.S. total	0.65%
Rank among states	39

Per capita consumption (In millions of BTU)

Total state per capita consumption	365
Total U.S. per capita consumption	338
Rank among states	22

End-use sectors

Residential	152
Commercial	130
Industrial	182
Transportation	163

Sources of energy

Petroleum	218
Natural gas	124
Coal	228
Hydroelectric power	11
Nuclear electric power	91

Figures for totals include categories not listed separately.
Source: U.S. Energy Information Administration, *State Energy Data Report,* 2001.

Nonfarm employment by sectors, 2004

Total	923,000
Construction	48,000
Manufacturing	101,000
Trade, transportation, utilities	196,000
Information	22,000
Finance, insurance, real estate	63,000
Professional & business services	94,000
Education & health services	127,000
Leisure, hospitality, arts, organizations	78,000
Other services, including repair & maintenance	35,000
Government	160,000

Figures are rounded to nearest thousand persons. "Total" includes mining and natural resources, not listed separately.
Source: U.S. Bureau of Labor Statistics, 2006.

Foreign exports, 1990-2004
In millions of dollars

Year	State	U.S.	State share
1990	693	394,045	0.18%
1996	1,907	624,767	0.31%
1997	1,971	688,896	0.29%
2000	2,511	712,055	0.32%
2003	2,724	724,006	0.40%
2004	2,316	769,332	0.30%

Rank among all states in 2004 41

U.S. total does not include U.S. dependencies.
Source: U.S. Census Bureau, *U.S. Merchandise Trade,* series FT 900, 2000; U.S. Census Bureau, *U.S. International Trade in Goods and Services,* Series FT 900, 2005.

LAND USE

Federally owned land, 2003
Areas in acres

	State	U.S.	State share
Total area	49,032,000	2,271,343,000	2.16%
Nonfederal land	47,573,000	1,599,584,000	2.97%
Federal land	1,459,000	671,759,000	0.22%
Federal share	3.0%	29.6%	—

Areas are rounded to nearest thousand acres. Figures for federally owned land do not include trust properties.
Source: U.S. General Services Administration, *Federal Real Property Profile,* 2006.

Land use, 1997
In acres, rounded to nearest thousand

Total surface area	49,510,000
Total nonfederal rural land.	47,187,000
Percentage rural land	95.3%
Cropland.	19,469,000
Conservation Reserve Program (CRP*) land . . .	1,245,000
Pastureland	1,801,000
Rangeland	23,089,000
Forestland.	826,000
Other rural land	757,000

*CRP is a federal program begun in 1985 to assist private landowners to convert highly erodible cropland to vegetative cover for ten years. Note that some categories of land overlap.
Source: U.S. Department of Agriculture, Natural Resources and Conservation Service, and Iowa State University, Statistical Laboratory, *Summary Report, 1997 National Resources Inventory,* revised December, 2000.

Farms and crop acreage, 2004

	State	U.S.	Share	Rank
Farms	48,000	2,113,000	2.27%	18
Acres (millions)	46	937	4.91%	4
Acres per farm	950	443	—	10

Source: U.S. Department of Agriculture, National Agricultural Statistics Service. Numbers of farms are rounded to nearest thousand units; acreage figures are rounded to nearest million. Rankings, including ties, are based on rounded figures.

GOVERNMENT AND FINANCE

Units of local government, 2002

	State	Total U.S.	Rank
All local governments	2,791	87,525	13
Counties	93	3,034	10
Municipalities	531	19,429	15
Townships	446	16,504	13
School districts	575	13,506	7
Special districts	1,146	35,052	9

Only 48 states have county governments, 20 states have township governments ("towns" in New England, Minnesota, New York, and Wisconsin), and 46 states have school districts. Special districts encompass such functions as natural resources, fire protection, and housing and community development.
Source: U.S. Census Bureau, *Census of Governments.*

State government revenue, 2002

Total revenue	$6,002 mill.
General revenue	$5,987 mill.
Per capita revenue	$3,468
U.S. per capita average	$3,689
Rank among states	33

Intergovernment revenue
Total	$1,823 mill.
From federal government	$1,780 mill.

Charges and miscellaneous
Total	$1,172 mill.
Current charges	$559 mill.
Misc. general income	$613 mill.
Insurance trust revenue	$15 mill.

Taxes
Total	$2,993 mill.
Per capita taxes	$1,732
Rank among states	30
Property taxes	$6 mill.
Sales taxes	$1,505 mill.
License taxes	$196 mill.
Individual income taxes	$1,153 mill.
Corporate income taxes	$108 mill.
Other taxes	$24 mill.

Total revenue figures include items not listed separately here.
Source: U.S. Bureau of the Census.

State government expenditures, 2002

General expenditures
Total state expenditures . . . . $6,537 mill.
Intergovernmental . . . . $1,820 mill.

Per capita expenditures
State $3,599
Average of all states $3,859
Rank among states 34

Selected direct expenditures
Education. . . . . $1,116 mill.
Public welfare . . . . $1,647 mill.
Health, hospital . . . . $274 mill.
Highways . . . . $526 mill.
Police protection . . . . $52 mill.
Corrections. . . . . $176 mill.
Natural resources . . . . $142 mill.
Parks and recreation . . . . $29 mill.
Government administration. . . . . $165 mill.
Interest on debt . . . . $110 mill.
Total direct expenditures . . . . $4,399 mill.

Totals include items not listed separately.
Source: U.S. Census Bureau.

POLITICS

Governors since statehood
D = Democrat; R = Republican; O = other;
(r) resigned; (d) died in office; (i) removed from office

David Butler (R) . . . . (i) 1867-1871
William H. James (R) 1871-1873
Robert W. Furnas (R) 1873-1875
Silas Garber (R) 1875-1879
Albinus Nance (R) 1879-1883
James W. Dawes (R) 1883-1887
John M. Thayer (R) 1887-1891
James E. Boyd (D) . . . . (i) 1891
John M. Thayer (R) . . . . (i) 1891-1892
James E. Boyd (D) 1892-1893
Lorenzo Crounse (R) 1893-1895
Silas A. Holcomb (O) 1895-1899
William A. Poynter (O) 1899-1901
Charles H. Dietrich (R) . . . . (r) 1901
Ezra P. Savage (R) 1901-1903
John H. Mickey (R) 1903-1907
George L. Sheldon (R) 1907-1909
Ashton C. Shallenberger (D) 1909-1911
Chester H. Aldrich (R) 1911-1913
John H. Morehead (D) 1913-1917
Keith Neville (D) 1917-1919
Samuel R. McKelvie (R) 1919-1923
Charles W. Bryan (D) 1923-1925
Adam McMullen (R). 1925-1929
Arthur J. Weaver (R). 1929-1931
Charles W. Bryan (D) 1931-1935

Robert L. Cochran (D) 1935-1941
Dwight P. Griswold (R) 1941-1947
Frederick Val Peterson (R) 1947-1953
Robert B. Crosby (R) 1953-1955
Victor E. Anderson (R) 1955-1959
Ralph G. Brooks (D) . . . . (d) 1959-1960
Dwight W. Burney (R) 1960-1961
Frank B. Morrison (D) 1961-1967
Norbert T. Tiemann (R) 1967-1971
John James Exon (D) 1971-1979
Charles Thone (R). 1979-1983
Robert Kerrey (D) 1983-1987
Kay A. Orr (R) 1987-1991
Ben Nelson (D) 1991-1999
Mike Johanns (R) . . . . (r) 1999-2005
Dave Heineman (R) 2005-

Composition of congressional delegations, 1989-2007

	Dem	Rep	Total
House of Representatives			
101st Congress, 1989			
State delegates	1	2	3
Total U.S.	259	174	433
102d Congress, 1991			
State delegates	1	2	3
Total U.S.	267	167	434
103d Congress, 1993			
State delegates	1	2	3
Total U.S.	258	176	434
104th Congress, 1995			
State delegates	0	3	3
Total U.S.	197	236	433
105th Congress, 1997			
State delegates	0	3	3
Total U.S.	206	228	434
106th Congress, 1999			
State delegates	0	3	3
Total U.S.	211	222	433
107th Congress, 2001			
State delegates	0	3	3
Total U.S.	211	221	432
108th Congress, 2003			
State delegates	0	3	3
Total U.S.	205	229	434
109th Congress, 2005			
State delegates	0	3	3
Total U.S.	202	231	433
110th Congress, 2007			
State delegates	0	3	3
Total U.S.	233	202	435

(continued)

	Dem	Rep	Total
Senate			
101st Congress, 1989			
State delegates	2	0	2
Total U.S.	55	45	100
102d Congress, 1991			
State delegates	2	0	2
Total U.S.	56	44	100
103d Congress, 1993			
State delegates	2	0	2
Total U.S.	57	43	100
104th Congress, 1995			
State delegates	1	1	2
Total U.S.	46	53	99
105th Congress, 1997			
State delegates	1	1	2
Total U.S.	45	55	100
106th Congress, 1999			
State delegates	1	1	2
Total U.S.	45	54	99
107th Congress, 2001			
State delegates	1	1	2
Total U.S.	50	50	100
108th Congress, 2003			
State delegates	1	1	2
Total U.S.	48	51	99
109th Congress, 2005			
State delegates	1	1	2
Total U.S.	44	55	99
110th Congress, 2007			
State delegates	1	1	2
Total U.S.	49	49	98

Figures are for starts of first sessions. Totals are for Democrat (Dem.) and Republican (Rep.) members only. House membership totals under 435 and Senate totals under 100 reflect vacancies and seats held by independent party members. When the 110th Congress opened, the Senate's two independent members caucused with the Democrats, giving the Democrats control of the Senate.
Source: U.S. Congress, *Congressional Directory.*

Composition of state legislature, 1990-2006

Nebraska has a unicameral legislature of 49 members who are elected without party affiliations.

Source: Council of State Governments; *State Elective Officials and the Legislatures.*

Voter participation in presidential elections, 2000 and 2004

	2000	2004
Voting age population		
State	1,264,000	1,313,000
Total United States	209,831,000	220,377,000
State share of U.S. total	0.60	0.60
Rank among states	38	38
Portion of voting age population casting votes		
State	55.1%	59.3%
United States	50.3%	55.5%
Rank among states	20	19

Population figures are rounded to nearest thousand and include all residents, regardless of eligibility to vote.
Source: U.S. Census Bureau.

HEALTH AND MEDICAL CARE

Medical professionals
Physicians in 2003 and nurses in 2001

	U.S.	State
Physicians in 2003		
Total	774,849	4,216
Share of U.S. total		0.54%
Rate	266	242
Rank		26
Nurses in 2001		
Total	2,262,020	15,970
Share of U.S. total		0.71%
Rate	793	928
Rank		12

Rates are numbers of physicians and nurses per 100,000 resident population; ranks are based on rates.
Source: American Medical Association, *Physician Characteristics and Distribution in the U.S.*; U.S. Department of Health and Human Services, Health Resources and Services Administration.

Health insurance coverage, 2003

	State	U.S.
Total persons covered	1,532,000	243,320,000
Total persons not covered	195,000	44,961,000
Portion not covered	11.3%	15.6%
Rank among states	35	—
Children not covered	31,000	8,373,000
Portion not covered	7.0%	11.4%
Rank among states	43	—

Totals are rounded to nearest thousand. Ranks are from the highest to the lowest percentages of persons *not* insured.
Source: U.S. Census Bureau, Current Population Reports.

AIDS, syphilis, and tuberculosis cases, 2003

Disease	U.S. cases	State cases	Rank
AIDS	44,232	60	41
Syphilis	34,270	27	42
Tuberculosis	14,874	28	41

Source: U.S. Centers for Disease Control and Prevention.

Cigarette smoking, 2003
Residents over age 18 who smoke

	U.S.	State	Rank
All smokers	22.1%	21.3%	32
Male smokers	24.8%	23.6%	30
Female smokers	20.3%	19.0%	33

Cigarette smokers are defined as persons who reported having smoked at least 100 cigarettes during their lifetimes and who currently smoked at least occasionally.
Source: U.S. Centers for Disease Control and Prevention, *Morbidity and Mortality Weekly Report,* 53, no. 44 (November 12, 2004).

HOUSING

Home ownership rates, 1985-2004

	1985	1990	1995	2000	2004
State	68.5%	67.3%	67.1%	70.2%	71.2%
Total U.S.	63.9%	63.9%	64.7%	67.4%	69.0%
Rank among states	21	27	29	26	29

Net change in state home ownership rate,
1985-2004 . . . . +2.7%
Net change in U.S. home ownership rate,
1985-2004 . . . . +5.1%

Percentages represent the proportion of owner households to total occupied households.
Source: U.S. Census Bureau, 2006.

Home sales, 2000-2004
In thousands of units

Existing home sales	2000	2002	2003	2004
State sales	32.3	34.3	38.0	39.8
Total U.S. sales	5,171	5,631	6,183	6,784
State share of U.S. total	0.62%	0.61%	0.61%	0.59%
Sales rank among states	36	37	37	37

Units include single-family homes, condos, and co-ops.
Source: National Association of Realtors, Washington, D.C., *Real Estate Outlook: Market Trends & Insights.*

Values of owner-occupied homes, 2003

	State	U.S.
Total units	389,000	58,809,000
Value of units		
Under $100,000	49.6%	29.6%
$100,000-199,999	39.8%	36.9%
$200,000 or more	10.6%	33.5%
Median value	$100,539	$142,275
Rank among all states 39		

Units are owner-occupied one-family houses whose numbers are rounded to nearest thousand. Data are extrapolated from survey samples.
Source: U.S. Census Bureau, American Community Survey.

EDUCATION

Public school enrollment, 2002

Prekindergarten through grade 8
State enrollment 195,000
Total U.S. enrollment. 34,135,000
State share of U.S. total 0.57%

Grades 9 through 12
State enrollment. 90,000
Total U.S. enrollment. 14,067,000
State share of U.S. total 0.64%

Enrollment rates
State public school enrollment rate. 88.1%
Overall U.S. rate 90.4%
Rank among states in 2002. 37
Rank among states in 1995. 39

Enrollment figures (which include unclassified students) are rounded to nearest thousand pupils during fall school term. Enrollment rates are based on enumerated resident population estimate for July 1, 2002.
Source: U.S. National Center for Education Statistics.

Public college finances, 2003-2004

FTE enrollment in public institutions of higher education

Students in state institutions 71,300
Students in all U.S. public institutions 9,916,600
State share of U.S. total 0.72
Rank among states 35

State and local government appropriations for higher education

State appropriation per FTE $5,475
National average $5,716
Rank among states 25
State & local tax revenue going to higher
  education 11.1%

FTE = full-time equivalent in public postsecondary programs,
  including summer sessions; student numbers are rounded to
  nearest hundred. Funding figures for 2003-2004 academic year
  include financial aid to students in state public institutions and
  exclude money for research, agriculture experiment stations,
  teaching hospitals, and medical schools; figures are rounded to
  nearest thousand dollars.
Source: Higher Education Executive Officers, Denver, Colorado.

TRANSPORTATION AND TRAVEL

Highway mileage, 2003

Interstate highways 482
Other freeways and expressways 21
Arterial roads 8,007
Collector roads 20,778
Local roads 63,910
Urban roads 5,767
Rural roads 87,431
Total state mileage 93,198
U.S. total 3,974,107
State share 2.35%
Rank among states 20

Note that combined urban and rural road mileage matches the
  total of the other categories.
Source: U.S. Federal Highway Administration.

Motor vehicle registrations and driver licenses, 2003

Vehicle registrations	State	U.S.	Share	Rank
Autos, trucks, buses	1,677,000	231,390,000	0.72%	35
Autos only	855,000	135,670	0.63%	34
Motorcycles	27,000	5,328,000	0.51%	41
Driver licenses	1,311,000	196,166,000	0.67%	36

Figures, which do not include vehicles owned by military services,
  are rounded to the nearest thousand. Figures for automobiles
  include taxis.
Source: U.S. Federal Highway Administration.

Domestic travel expenditures, 2003

Spending by U.S. residents on overnight trips and
day trips of at least 50 miles from home

Total expenditures within state . . . . $2.77 bill.
Total expenditures within U.S. . . . . $490.87 bill.
State share of U.S. total 0.6%
Rank among states 38

Source: Travel Industry Association of America.

Retail gasoline prices, 2003-2007

Average price per gallon at the pump

Year	U.S.	State
2003	$1.267	$1.187
2004	$1.316	$1.250
2005	$1.644	$1.646
2007	$2.298	$2.256

Excise tax per gallon in 2004 . . . . 25.4¢
Rank among all states in 2007 prices 27

Prices are averages of all grades of gasoline sold at the pump
  during March months in 2003-2005 and during February, 2007.
  Averages for 2006, during which prices rose higher, are not
  available.
Source: U.S. Energy Information Agency, *Petroleum Marketing
  Monthly* (2003-2005 data); American Automobile Association
  (2007 data).

CRIME AND LAW ENFORCEMENT

State and local police officers, 2000-2004

	2000	2002	2004
Total officers			
U.S.	654,601	665,555	675,734
State	3,251	3,386	3,443*
*Net change, 2000-2004			+5.91%
Officers per 1,000 residents			
U.S.	2.33	2.31	2.30
State	1.90	1.96	1.97
State rank	32	32	29

Totals include state and local police and sheriffs.
Source: Carsey Institute, University of New Hampshire.

Crime rates, 2003
Incidents per 100,000 residents

Crimes	State	U.S.
Violent crimes		
Total incidents	289	475
Murder	3	6
Forcible rape	29	32
Robbery	67	142
Aggravated assault	191	295
Property crimes		
Total incidents	3,711	3,588
Burglary	579	741
Larceny/theft	2,780	2,415
Motor vehicle theft	352	433
All crimes	4,000	4,063

Source: U.S. Federal Bureau of Investigation, *Crime in the United States*, annual.

State prison populations, 1980-2003

	State	U.S.	State share
1980	1,446	305,458	0.47%
1990	2,403	708,393	0.34%
1996	3,287	1,025,624	0.32%
2000	3,895	1,391,261	0.28%
2003	4,040	1,470,045	0.27%

State figures exclude prisoners in federal penitentiaries.
Source: U.S. Bureau of Justice Statistics, *Prisoners in 2003*.

Nevada

Location: Western United States

Area and rank: 109,806 square miles (284,397 square kilometers); 110,567 square miles (286,369 square kilometers) including water; seventh largest state in area

Coastline: none

Population and rank: 2,335,000 (2004); thirty-fifth largest state in population

Capital city: Carson City (52,457 people in 2000 census)

Largest city: Las Vegas (478,434 people in 2000 census)

Became territory: March 2, 1861

Nevada's legalization of gambling during the Great Depression made possible the post-World War II transformation of Las Vegas into a world center of casino gambling and entertainment. By the early twenty-first century, the city was undergoing a new transformation, into a travel destination for families that offered diverse amusement park-type attractions. (Jon Sullivan/PDPhoto.org)

Entered Union and rank: October 31, 1864; thirty-sixth state

Present constitution adopted: 1864

Counties: 16, as well as 1 independent city

State name: "Nevada" is the Spanish word for "snowcapped"

State nicknames: Sagebrush State; Silver State; Battle Born State

Motto: All for Our Country

State flag: Cobalt field with silver star above sagebrush in the upper left, with name "Nevada" below and legend "Battle Born" on a scroll above

Highest point: Boundary Peak—13,140 feet (4,005 meters)

Lowest point: Colorado River—479 feet (146 meters)

Highest recorded temperature: 122 degrees Fahrenheit (50 degrees Celsius)—Overton, 1954

Lowest recorded temperature: –50 degrees Fahrenheit (–46 degrees Celsius)—San Jacinto, 1937

State song: "Home Means Nevada"

State trees: Single-leaf pinon; bristlecone pine

State flower: Sagebrush

State bird: Mountain bluebird

State fish: Lahontan cutthroat trout

State animal: Desert bighorn sheep

National parks: Great Basin

Nevada History

Nevada is mostly arid, its desert terrain broken up by a series of mountain ranges. Part of the Great Basin region, it lies between Utah to the east and California to the west. Nevada's geography has deeply influenced nearly every principal aspect of its economy and society. Nevada's history would hardly have been the same without its laws, all influenced by geography, governing gambling, personal and corporate taxation, and marriage and divorce—even prostitution, which, unique among American states, it permits in sparsely populated counties.

The role of the state's geography is most apparent in that, unlike its neighbors, especially California, Nevada has few hospitable natural areas for human settlement. The proximity of populous, wealthy California, however, provides an abundant source of tourism. This fact gave legalized gambling in Nevada an irresistible appeal. Gambling revenues, in turn, allow the state to dispense with state income tax, which now helps to persuade large numbers of retirees, many of them Californians, to settle in the state, especially in the Las Vegas area.

Nevada has had incredible wealth beneath its surface, though virtually all of its mining bonanzas have turned to busts, at least temporarily. Even with the precious metals and other minerals in the state, Nevada's population did not exceed one million until the 1980's; at the end of the twentieth century its population was still fewer than two million.

Early History. Human society in Nevada extends as much as ten thousand years into the past. Before the arrival of white settlers, American Indian peoples, in-

The scenic splendors of Nevada are often overshadowed by the glitz and glamor of the state's gambling centers. Not far from downtown Las Vegas are striking sandstone formations, such as those pictured here, of Red Rock Canyon. (Jon Sullivan/PD Photo.org)

cluding the Shoshone, Northern Paiute, and Washoe tribes, inhabited the region. In the eighteenth century, Spanish explorers were the first Europeans to visit the area. Spanish interest in the territory waned, however, after the report of Father Francisco Silvestre Vélez de Escalante, who accompanied an expedition, commented negatively on the area's steep, dry character.

By the early nineteenth century, Canadian and American explorers had arrived. Some were seeking animal furs, and others led scientific expeditions, such as John C. Frémont during the 1840's. Frémont's systematic research of the area and reports on his findings provided the federal government its first systematic account of the region and stimulated interest in the West among easterners. However, the harsh terrain was inhospitable to settlers, and those who passed through Nevada's deserts and mountains were usually on their way to kinder environs. One of the immigrant parties that crossed Nevada was the Donner party, which in 1846-1847 became snowbound while attempting to cross the Sierra Nevada range west of Reno, resorting to cannibalism to survive.

There appear to have been fewer conflicts between settlers and American Indians than in neighboring territories. The settler population was sparse and grouped in only a few locations, so that contacts with American Indians were fewer. That did not mean there was no conflict, however. For example, in 1855 when Mormons arrived in Las Vegas (Spanish for "the meadows") to convert Paiute Indians and supply travelers on their way to Salt Lake City from the Pacific, they found themselves attacked by American Indian raiding parties. Three years later, they abandoned their adobe fort.

During the 1870's, in accordance with federal American Indian policy, reservations were established, the largest of which were the Pyramid Lake Reservation, north of Reno, and the Walker River Reservation, southeast of Reno. These and a number of other smaller reservations, numbering fewer than a dozen, are scattered around the state.

From Territory to Statehood. The United States acquired the land of modern Nevada, along with other territory in 1848, after the signing of the Treaty of Guadalupe Hidalgo ended the Mexican-American War. In 1850, when New Mexico and Utah were estab-

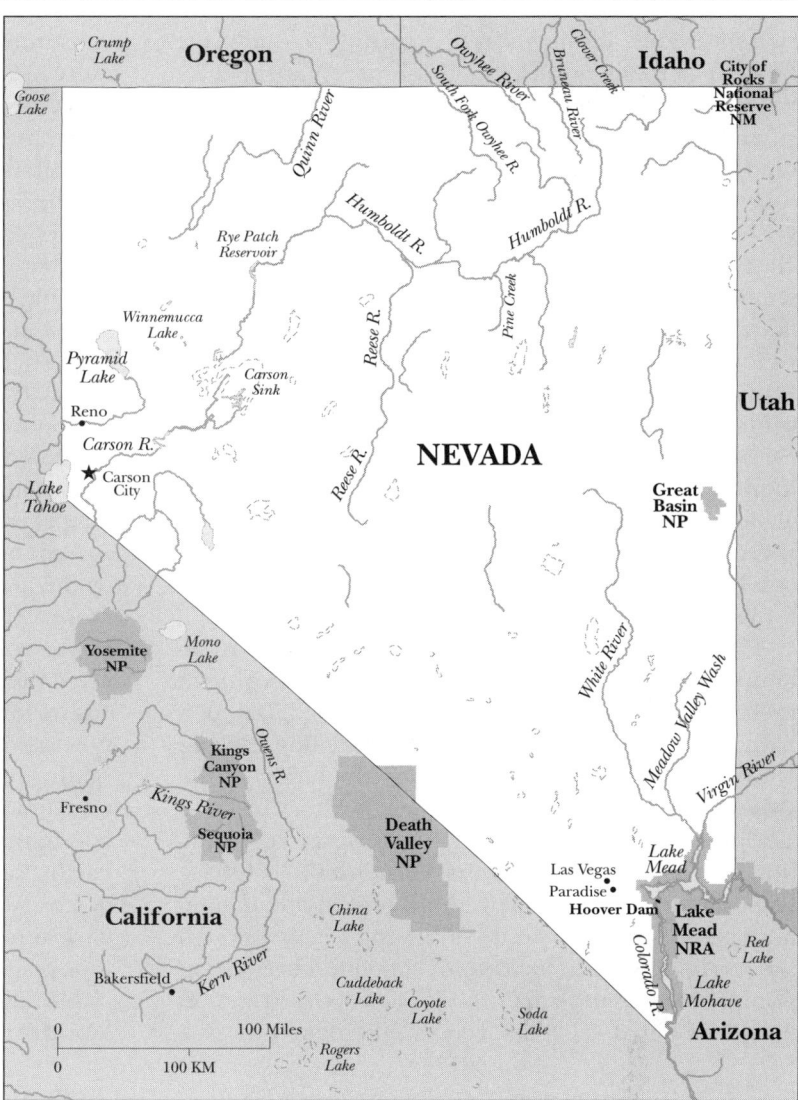

lished as territories, Nevada's land was incorporated into the new Utah Territory, administered from Salt Lake City by the Mormon regime.

Those seeking their fortunes in the gold fields of California undertook the first great trek through Nevada in 1849-1850. Their numbers led to the first white settlement in present Nevada, when Mormons from Salt Lake City established Mormon Station (later called Genoa), southeast of Carson City. The establishment was obliged to close in 1857, when Mormon leader Brigham Young recalled them, fearful of an attack by U.S. Army troops during a dispute with the federal government. Young had proposed a new state to be formed called "Deseret" but was turned down in Washington. Non-Mormons who flocked to the area two years later, who generally opposed living under Mormon rule, tried to set up a provisional territorial government, but Washington refused to recognize it.

Miners began pouring into Nevada in 1859, when a

rich silver lode was discovered, according to one story, by siblings Ethan and Hosea Grosh near Virginia City but credited to Henry Tompkins Comstock, who assumed the brothers' claims after they mysteriously died. This strike, which resulted in the extraction of some $400 million in silver, brought thousands of adventurers into Comstock and the surrounding area. Nearby Virginia City became the site's de facto capital, scene of fabulous luxury as well as lawless behavior, as fantastic fortunes were extracted from the ground. Among the invaders from California was the young Samuel Clemens, better known later as Mark Twain, who had become a reporter for Virginia City's *Territorial Enterprise*. Twain chronicled the raucous life of the era in his book *Roughing It* (1872). By the 1870's, however, wasteful mining methods and the demonetization of silver by the U.S. government, which lowered its price, combined to diminish the silver rush, and by 1898, Comstock was all but abandoned.

Although settlers were unsuccessful in their first attempt at establishing a territory, events were moving in their favor. Lawlessness needed to be curbed, but, perhaps more important, the Civil War looming early in 1861 directed Washington to ensure the loyalty of the West. Accordingly, Nevada became a territory in 1861. The next step to statehood was the writing of a constitution. After voters rejected a first constitution in 1863, a second version—this time without objectionable mining taxes—was accepted the following year. Although the territory was unqualified for statehood because its population was too small (6,857 in 1860), President Abraham Lincoln needed votes in the Senate to pass constitutional amendments and was anxious to add more. Accordingly, the entire text of the new constitution was sent to Washington for approval in the longest telegram up to then ever sent, at the astronomical cost of $3,416.77. The territory was made a state in 1864.

The formal institutions of government followed the lead of other states in splitting executive powers into a number of elective offices. This policy had the effect of keeping power out of the hands of a single chief executive, and it reflected traditional American, especially western, distrust of executives, whether kings or presidents. The legislature is bicameral. Five justices sit on the Supreme Court of Nevada, all elected to six-year staggered terms. Nine district courts, with thirty-five district judges serving six-year terms, and a series of municipal courts complete the judicial system.

Economy and Society. Life in the new state improved by the arrival in 1868 of a transcontinental railroad, a more satisfactory communications link than the Pony Express. During the 1870's, the economy went sour when the nation turned to the gold standard and silver was no longer used in coins. Cattle and sheep ranching now assumed prominence in the state's economy. Mining in the state revived after 1900 with new gold, silver, and copper discoveries. Moreover, the mining boom stimulated railroad building. In 1905, the Union Pacific Railroad constructed tracks from Salt Lake City to Los Angeles through Las Vegas. Prosperity had its dark side, too, as early in the century violent strikes took place, pitting workers against mining companies.

Mining boomed again when the nation entered World War I in 1917, but after the war demand fell off and declined during the 1920's. When the Depression came in 1930, to stimulate the economy the state legalized gambling, which had been outlawed since 1909. To attract more visitors, it also relaxed marriage and divorce laws, in time making a "Nevada divorce" a household term. Mining revived once more during the late 1930's and 1940's, as federal spending for war materiel increased.

Postwar Developments. After World War II, society and economy in Nevada changed dramatically. Contrary to some expectations, the demand for minerals remained high in the postwar years. First, big-time gambling was inaugurated with the opening in Las Vegas of the Flamingo Hotel, built and financed by organized crime. By the mid-1950's dozens of large casinos had opened in Las Vegas and Reno, drawing gamblers and vacationers from throughout the nation with headline entertainment and inexpensive food and accommodations.

Although it was one of the most prosperous cities of the Far West during the peak of western Nevada's nineteenth century mining boom, Virginia City is now little more than a curiosity for tourists. (Nevada Commission on Tourism)

Second, the federal government dramatically increased spending in the state, opening an Air Force base north of Las Vegas and a bombing range, including a site for testing atomic weapons. In addition, irrigation projects brought water to make the desert bloom. By the 1980's a controversy had broken out between the state and the federal government, which owns 87 percent of the state's domain, over use of federal land for storing atomic waste. During the 1990's, the state lost key court decisions over the matter, and the federal government began creating storage facilities for nuclear waste.

Recreational Mecca. During the 1960's, the threat of organized crime to the state's gaming industry led Nevada to change its laws, allowing public companies to open casinos in the state. The advent of well-financed commercial gaming in the state was to revolutionize the industry. Gamblers, some of them very rich, began to arrive from all over the world. By the 1980's and 1990's casinos had adopted a policy of attracting families, and significant expansion of the tourist industry took place. Reno and neighboring Lake Tahoe prospered, and Las Vegas became an international center of postmodern architecture. Its cavernous casino-hotels, some designed with a touch of whimsy, often made thematic reference to lost civilizations, such as ancient Egypt and Rome, or to contemporary cities, such as New York and Paris.

The state also attracts increasing numbers of retirees. Las Vegas in particular, with its mild winter climate and proximity to Southern California, became a mecca for retirees. Other factors attracting retirees and others was housing made inexpensive by an inexhaustible supply of cheap land, stretching endlessly into the desert and the absence of a state income tax, made unnecessary by gambling revenues.

Environmental Issues. As 2001 and a new century approached, Nevada continued its growth and prosperity but found itself involved in environmental issues. As a magnet for tourists and a site of burgeoning population growth, the state also attracted pollution-producing vehicles. In 2000, Nevada was one of fourteen states to set exhaust emissions curbs on trucks and buses.

A potential pollution problem of a different kind produced a major and continuing controversy in the state, especially in southern Nevada: the selection by the federal government of a southern Nevada location for underground storage of nuclear waste. Selection of a site for nuclear waste disposal was the topic of a twenty-year national debate. In 2000, approval of the Yucca Mountain waste site cleared Congress. Although the project was shelved when President Bill Clinton vetoed the measure, the nuclear waste storage issue was soon revisited by the new Republican administration. In July, 2002, Congress again overrode Nevada's objections to the Yucca Mountain site, and President George W. Bush signed the congressional resolution. While lawsuits filed by the state continued to seek termination of the project, if none is successful, the Department of Energy (DOE) has designated March 31, 2017, as the date when the facility will accept nuclear waste. In 2006, the DOE was preparing an application for a license from a federal regulatory agency to construct the waste depository.

Supporting Freedom of Expression. As the twenty-first century was beginning, Nevada found itself affected by the age of terrorism and continuing political repression in various parts of the world. To support freedom of expression, Las Vegas Valley was designated as a refuge for persecuted writers by an agreement between Las Vegas and the International Parliament of Writers in 2000. Las Vegas became the first North American city to join the program, thanks to sponsorship by a local hotel-casino company. Early in October, Syl Cheney-Coker, who barely escaped alive from his native Sierra Leone, arrived to become the region's first resident-writer-in-asylum. Less positively, in August, 2002, a federal indictment of six accused terrorists gave evidence that they videotaped the MGM Grand Hotel in Las Vegas as a potential terrorist-attack target.

Politics. Politically, Nevada's population increase was translated into an additional seat in Congress. In 2002, voters elected Republican Jon Porter to the new seat. Republican presidential candidate George W. Bush took the state's four electoral votes in 2000 and its five electoral votes in 2004, in both cases by a narrow margin. The 2002 gubernatorial election was so one-sided that a prominent newspaper described it as largely uncontested; months before the election, Governor Kenny Guinn's lead was so large that he stopped raising funds and returned to donors part of what had been raised. Guinn won over his opponent by a 68-22 percent margin. In 2004, Democratic senator Harry Reid, who had been promoted to minority leader of the U.S. Senate, was reelected by the landslide proportions of 61 to 35 percent.

Charles F. Bahmueller

Nevada Time Line

1775	Spanish missionary Francisco Garces is the first white person to enter Nevada.
1826	Explorer and fur trader Jedediah Smith leads a party across southern Nevada and recrosses the region while returning east the following year.
c. 1830	Fur trader Peter S. Ogden discovers Humboldt River in northeastern Nevada.
1843-1846	Explorer John C. Frémont with scout Kit Carson leads three exploratory expeditions through Nevada.
1848	Nevada and other lands are acquired from Mexico by the United States through the Treaty of Guadalupe Hidalgo.
1849	Thousands of speculators cross northern Nevada on their way to the California gold fields near Sacramento.
1849	Mormon Station (later Genoa), Nevada's first non-American Indian settlement, is established in the Carson Valley to supply the forty-niners.
1850	Utah Territory, including most of modern Nevada, is established.
1855	First Mormon settlement is established in Las Vegas.
1859	Silver strike is made at Comstock, near Virginia City.
1860	Population of Nevada is 6,700, nearly all around the Carson City and Virginia City areas.
1861	Nevada Territory is formed, with capital at Carson City.
1862	Voters reject first Nevada constitution.
Oct. 31, 1864	Nevada enters the Union as the thirty-sixth state.
1868	Transcontinental railroad crosses Nevada; is completed in Utah the following year.
1869	Legislature legalizes gambling.
1874	University of Nevada is founded at Elko.
1877-1881	Drop in the price of silver leaves many unemployed.
1880	Population reaches 62,266.
1881-1890	Depopulation occurs due to unemployment.

Completion of Hoover Dam in 1936 harnessed the Colorado River waters, which are vital to the Southwest, and created Nevada's Lake Mead, now a major recreational area. (Nevada Commission on Tourism)

1900	Population falls to 42,335.
1900	Silver deposits found at Tonopah, gold at Goldfield, and copper at Ely revive state's mining industry.
1907	Construction begun on Newlands irrigation project to irrigate Fallon area, east of Reno.
1909	Gambling is made illegal.
1911	City of Las Vegas is incorporated.
1917-1918	U.S. entrance into World War I gives rise to short-lived mining boom.
1931	Gambling is legalized; residency required for divorce is reduced to six weeks.
1936	Boulder (later Hoover) Dam is completed.
1939-1945	World War II creates great demand for Nevada minerals.
1941	First casino-hotels open in Las Vegas.
1942-1945	Federal government establishes military installations in Nevada, stimulating economy and population growth.
1946	Flamingo Hotel on Las Vegas Strip is opened by mobster "Bugsy" Siegel; first state gambling taxes levied.
1950	Population is 160,083.
1951	U.S. Atomic Energy Commission inaugurates above-ground atomic testing in southern Nevada.
1963	U.S. Supreme Court settles long-standing dispute over water among Nevada and neighboring states.
1969	Corporate Gaming Act allows publicly traded companies to open casinos.
1971	Robert B. Griffith Water Project is completed.
1975	Nevada gaming revenues top $1 billion mark.
1980	Legislature acts to counter pollution of Lake Tahoe.
1990	State population is 1,206,152.
1990	Excaliber Hotel opens with 4,032 rooms as the world's largest hotel, beginning decade-long hotel-casino building boom.
1994	Visitors top 40 million, including 28.2 million to Las Vegas.
1998	State population estimated at 1,746,898.
1999	Metropolitan Las Vegas is one of the fastest growing urban areas in America, adding from four thousand to six thousand people monthly.
Oct. 3, 2000	Sierra Leone writer Syl Cheney-Coker arrives in Las Vegas as first participant in the international City of Asylum program.
July, 2002	Congress overrides Nevada's objections to the designation of Yucca Mountain as a future nuclear waste site.
Aug. 28, 2002	Federal terrorism indictment identifies Las Vegas as a potential target.
Oct. 3, 2003	Roy Horn, of famed magic act Siegfried & Roy, is injured on stage in Las Vegas by a 600-pound tiger, closing the show.
July 18, 2006	Department of Energy agrees upon March 31, 2017, as the date when the new nuclear waste facility will open and will receive waste material.

Notes for Further Study

Published Sources. For an overview of Nevada history, see Robert Laxalt's *Nevada: A Bicentennial History* (1991). A lively history of the rowdy frontier territory before it became a state can be found in Sally Zanjani's *Devils Will Reign: How Nevada Began* (2003). In *The Silver State: Nevada's Heritage Reinterpreted* (3d ed., 2004), James W. Hulse examines the economic, social, and political events that shaped the state, paying particular attention to events that occurred both in the last decade of the twentieth century and in the early twenty-first century. The story of the Comstock silver bonanza is chronicled in Grant H. Smith and Joseph V. Tingley's *The History of the Comstock Lode* (1998). Another resource on Nevada's mining history is *Nevada's Twentieth-Century Mining Boom: Tonopah,*

Goldfield, Ely (1966) by Russell R. Elliott. For information about the Donner Party tragedy, *The Donner Party Chronicles: A Day-by-Day Account of a Doomed Wagon Train, 1846-1847* (1997) by Frank Mullen and Will Bagley is a good reference. Michael W. Bowers's *The Sagebrush State: Nevada's History, Government, and Politics* (2d ed., 2002) serves as a textbook for students of state government, offering the full text of the state constitution and exploring how Nevada government operates and how the area's history has shaped its political culture. An entertaining way to learn about the state's history, culture, and attractions is with Richard Moreno's *Nevada Trivia* (3d ed., 2005).

For an example of the state's ethnic history, students

State capitol building in Carson City. (Nevada Commission on Tourism)

should begin with Malvin Miranda's *A History of Hispanics in Southern Nevada* (1997). An excellent resource on Native American history in the state is *The Washoe, Paiute, and Shoshone Indians of Nevada* (1961) by E. Haglund. In the Nevada Studies in History and Political Science series, see, for example, James W. Hulse, *Forty Years in the Wilderness: Impressions of Nevada, 1940-1980* (1986), and *East of Eden, West of Zion: Essays on Nevada* (1989), edited by Wilbur S. Shepperson.

For a sense of the state's natural beauty, readers should consult Sessions S. Wheeler, a professional biologist and conservationist, who discusses the prehistory and geology of the desert regions and, with photographs and text, brings the reader to the present day in *The Nevada Desert* (2003). Photographs and essays depict the state's rugged and stunning ranch culture in *Fifty Miles from Home: Riding the Long Circle on a Nevada Family Ranch* (2002), with photographs by Linda Dufurrena and text by Carolyn Dufurrena.

Web Resources. Web resources on Nevada begin with the state's home page (www.nv.gov/). The state legislature maintains its own home page (www.leg.state.nv.us/), where information on pending or existing legislation may be found. The Law Library of Congress site (www.loc.gov/law/guide/us-nv .html) is also a good reference. A variety of history links may

be found in the Encyclopaedia Nevadaca (www.nevadaweb .com/nevadaca/historylinks.html).

The Nevada State Library (dmla.clan.lib.nv.us/docs/ nsla/) allows users to search state archives, view lists of important Nevadans, and view historical sites and attractions, among many other features.

Individual cities maintain sites that give a range of information relevant to tourists or to residents. The City Guide (www.wowworks.com/wowcity/nv.htm) provides links to nearly all of the state's city and county Web sites. The Nevada Index (www.nevadaindex.com/3ref2.htm) includes a detailed set of links to politics, public interest groups, and similar sites, some of which are specific to Nevada, such as the National Organization for Women of Southern Nevada and Law Officers from Nevada. The City of Las Vegas home page (www.lasvegasnevada.gov/) is also helpful. Nevada universities' Web sites include, for example, those of the University of Nevada at Las Vegas (www.unlv.edu) and its counterpart at Reno (www.unr.edu). For resources on Native Americans, see the site on Nevada tribes (www.unr.edu/nnap/NT/nt_main .htm). Visitors can find a wealth of travel information at the Nevada Commission on Tourism (www.travelnevada.com/) or at (www.chiff.com/travel/nevada.htm).

Counties

County	2000 pop.	Rank in pop.	Sq. miles	Rank in area
Churchill	23,982	7	4,929.3	10
Clark	1,375,765	1	7,910.7	6
Douglas	41,259	4	709.9	15
Elko	45,291	3	17,181.6	2
Esmeralda	971	16	3,588.7	13
Eureka	1,651	15	4,176.0	11
Humboldt	16,106	8	9,648.3	4
Lander	5,794	11	5,493.5	9
Lincoln	4,165	13	10,634.7	3
Lyon	34,501	5	1,993.8	14

County	2000 pop.	Rank in pop.	Sq. miles	Rank in area
Mineral	5,071	12	3,756.6	12
Nye	32,485	6	18,147.2	1
Pershing	6,693	10	6,009.1	8
Storey	3,399	14	263.5	16
Washoe	339,486	2	6,342.5	7
White Pine	9,181	9	8,876.6	5

Carson City is independent of all counties.

Source: U.S. Census Bureau; National Association of Counties.

Cities
With 10,000 or more residents

Rank	City	Population
1	Las Vegas	478,434
2	Paradise	186,070
3	Reno	180,480
4	Henderson	175,381
5	Sunrise Manor	156,120
6	Spring Valley	117,390
7	North Las Vegas	115,488
8	Sparks	66,346
9	Carson City (capital)	52,457
10	Winchester	26,958
11	Pahrump	24,631

Rank	City	Population
12	Sun Valley	19,461
13	Whitney	18,273
14	Elko	16,708
15	Boulder City	14,966
16	Enterprise	14,676
17	Gardnerville Ranchos	11,054
18	Spring Creek	10,548

Population figures are from 2000 census.
Source: U.S. Bureau of the Census.

Index to Tables

DEMOGRAPHICS

Resident state and national populations, 1970-2004

Population figures given in thousands

	State pop.	U.S. pop.	Share	Rank
1970	489	203,302	0.2%	47
1980	800	226,546	0.4%	43
1985	951	237,924	0.4%	43
1990	1,202	248,765	0.5%	39
1995	1,582	262,761	0.6%	38
2000	1,998	281,425	0.7%	35
2004	2,335	293,655	0.8%	35

Source: U.S. Census Bureau, Current Population Reports, 2006.

Resident population by age, 2004

Age Group	Total persons
Under 5 years	169,000
5 to 17 years	435,000
18 to 24 years	210,000
25 to 34 years	355,000
35 to 44 years	355,000
45 to 54 years	310,000
55 to 64 years	239,000
65 to 74 years	154,000
75 to 84 years	84,000
85 years and older	24,000
All age groups	2,335,000
Portion of residents 65 and older	11.2%
National rank in portion of oldest residents	44
National average	12.4%

Population figures are rounded to nearest thousand persons;
figures include armed forces personnel stationed in the state.
Source: U.S. Bureau of the Census, 2006.

Resident population by race, Hispanic origin, 2004

Category	State pop.	Share	U.S.
All residents	2,335	100.00%	100.00%
Non-Hispanic white	1,429	61.20%	67.37%
Hispanic white	498	21.33%	13.01%
Other Hispanic	34	1.46%	1.06%
African American	176	7.54%	12.77%
Native American	33	1.41%	0.96%
Asian, Pacific Islander	140	6.00%	4.37%
Two or more categories	58	2.48%	1.51%

Population figures are in thousands. Persons counted as "Hispanic" (Latino) may be of any race. Because of overlapping categories, categories may not add up to 100%. Shares in column 3 are percentages of each category within the state; these figures may be compared to the national percentages in column 4.
Source: U.S. Bureau of the Census, 2006.

Projected state population, 2000-2030

Year	Population
2000	1,998,000
2005	2,352,000
2010	2,691,000
2015	3,058,000
2020	3,452,000
2025	3,863,000
2030	4,282,000
Population increase, 2000-2030	2,284,000
Percentage increase, 2000-2030	114.3

Projections are based on data from the 2000 census.
Source: U.S. Census Bureau.

VITAL STATISTICS

Infant mortality rates, 1980-2002

	1980	1990	2000	2002
All state residents	10.7	8.4	6.5	6.0
All U.S. residents	12.6	9.2	9.4	9.1
All state white residents	10.0	8.2	6.0	5.1
All U.S. white residents	10.6	7.6	5.7	5.8
All state black residents	20.6	14.2	12.7	18.4
All U.S. black residents	22.2	18.0	14.1	14.4

Figures represent deaths per 1,000 live births of resident infants under 1 year old, exclusive of fetal deaths. Figures for all residents include members of other racial categories not listed separately.
Source: U.S. Census Bureau, Statistical Abstract of the United States, 2006.

Abortion rates, 1990 and 2000

	1990	2000
Total abortions	13,000	14,000
Rate per 1,000 women	43.3	32.2
U.S. rate	25.7	21.3
Rank	3	3

Numbers of abortions are rounded to nearest thousand; ranks are based on rates.
Source: U.S. Census Bureau.

Marriages and divorces, 2004

Total marriages	145,800
Rate per 1,000 population	62.4
National rate per 1,000 population	7.4
Rank among all states	1
Total divorces	14,800
Rate per 1,000 population	6.4
National rate per 1,000 population	3.7
Rank among all states	1

Figures are for all marriages and divorces performed within the state, including those of nonresidents; totals are rounded to the nearest hundred. Ranks are for highest to lowest figures; note that divorce data are not available for five states.
Source: U.S. National Center for Health Statistics, Vital Statistics of the United States, 2006.

Death rates by leading causes, 2002
Deaths per 100,000 resident population

Cause	State	U.S.
Heart disease	203.4	241.7
Cancer	181.1	193.2
Cerebrovascular diseases	44.9	56.4
Accidents other than motor vehicle	39.6	37.0
Motor vehicle accidents	17.8	15.7
Chronic lower respiratory diseases	54.0	43.3
Diabetes mellitus	15.8	25.4
HIV	3.5	4.9
Suicide	19.5	11.0
Homicide	8.1	6.1
All causes	778.8	847.3
Rank in overall death rate among states		38

Figures exclude nonresidents who died in the state. Causes of death follow International Classification of Diseases. Rank is from highest to lowest death rate in the United States.
Source: U.S. National Center for Health Statistics, National Vital Statistics Report, 2006.

ECONOMY

Gross state product, 1990-2004
In current dollars

Year	State product	Nat'l product	State share
1990	$31.8 billion	$5.67 trillion	0.56%
2000	$74.8 billion	$9.75 trillion	0.77%
2002	$82.4 billion	$10.41 trillion	0.79%
2003	$89.7 billion	$10.92 trillion	0.82%
2004	$99.4 billion	$11.65 trillion	0.85%

Source: U.S. Bureau of Economic Analysis, *Survey of Current Business,* July, 2005.

Gross state product by industry, 2003
In billions of dollars

Construction $7.3
Manufacturing 3.1
Wholesale trade 3.5
Retail trade 7.5
Finance & insurance 6.9
Information 2.3
Professional services 4.3
Health care & social assistance 4.0
Government 8.1

Total state product $83.6
Total U.S. product $10,289.2
State share of U.S. total 0.81%
Rank among all states 32

Total figures include industries not listed separately. Amounts are in chained 2000 dollars.
Source: U.S. Bureau of Economic Analysis, *Survey of Current Business,* July, 2005.

Personal income per capita, 1990-2004
In current dollars

	1990	2000	2004
Per capita income	$20,346	$30,437	$33,405
U.S. average	$19,477	$29,845	$32,937
Rank among states	13	14	17

Source: U.S. Bureau of Economic Analysis, *Survey of Current Business,* April, 2005.

Energy consumption, 2001
In trillions of British thermal units (BTU), except as noted

Total energy consumption
Total state energy consumption 629
Total U.S. energy consumption 96,275
State share of U.S. total 0.65%
Rank among states 38

Per capita consumption (In millions of BTU)
Total state per capita consumption 301
Total U.S. per capita consumption 338
Rank among states 37

End-use sectors
Residential 147
Commercial 108
Industrial 169
Transportation 205

Sources of energy
Petroleum 250
Natural gas 181
Coal 189
Hydroelectric power 26
Nuclear electric power 0

Figures for totals include categories not listed separately.
Source: U.S. Energy Information Administration, *State Energy Data Report,* 2001.

Nonfarm employment by sectors, 2004

Total 1,152,000
Construction 118,000
Manufacturing 46,000
Trade, transportation, utilities 205,000
Information 15,000
Finance, insurance, real estate 62,000
Professional & business services 133,000
Education & health services 80,000
Leisure, hospitality, arts, organizations 313,000
Other services, including repair & maintenance . . . 35,000
Government 139,000

Figures are rounded to nearest thousand persons. "Total" includes mining and natural resources, not listed separately.
Source: U.S. Bureau of Labor Statistics, 2006.

Foreign exports, 1990-2004
In millions of dollars

Year	State	U.S.	State share
1990	394	394,045	0.10%
1996	1,268	624,767	0.20%
1997	1,075	688,896	0.16%
2000	1,482	712,055	0.19%
2003	2,033	724,006	0.30%
2004	2,907	769,332	0.38%

Rank among all states in 2004 39

U.S. total does not include U.S. dependencies.
Source: U.S. Census Bureau, *U.S. Merchandise Trade*, series FT 900, 2000; U.S. Census Bureau, *U.S. International Trade in Goods and Services*, Series FT 900, 2005.

LAND USE

Federally owned land, 2003
Areas in acres

	State	U.S.	State share
Total area	70,264,000	2,271,343,000	3.09%
Nonfederal land	5,675,000	1,599,584,000	0.35%
Federal land	64,589,000	671,759,000	9.61%
Federal share	91.9%	29.6%	—

Areas are rounded to nearest thousand acres. Figures for federally owned land do not include trust properties.
Source: U.S. General Services Administration, *Federal Real Property Profile*, 2006.

Land use, 1997
In acres, rounded to nearest thousand

Total surface area 70,763,000
Total nonfederal rural land. 10,079,000
Percentage rural land 14.2%
Cropland 701,000
Conservation Reserve Program (CRP*) land 2,000
Pastureland 279,000
Rangeland 8,372,000
Forestland. 305,000
Other rural land 420,000

*CRP is a federal program begun in 1985 to assist private landowners to convert highly erodible cropland to vegetative cover for ten years. Note that some categories of land overlap.
Source: U.S. Department of Agriculture, Natural Resources and Conservation Service, and Iowa State University, Statistical Laboratory, S*ummary Report, 1997 National Resources Inventory*, revised December, 2000.

Farms and crop acreage, 2004

	State	U.S.	Share	Rank
Farms	3,000	2,113,000	0.14%	46
Acres (millions)	6	937	0.64%	37
Acres per farm	2,100	443	—	5

Source: U.S. Department of Agriculture, National Agricultural Statistics Service. Numbers of farms are rounded to nearest thousand units; acreage figures are rounded to nearest million. Rankings, including ties, are based on rounded figures.

GOVERNMENT AND FINANCE

Units of local government, 2002

	State	Total U.S.	Rank
All local governments	210	87,525	47
Counties	16	3,034	40
Municipalities	19	19,429	47
Townships	0	16,504	—
School districts	17	13,506	42
Special districts	158	35,052	43

Only 48 states have county governments, 20 states have township governments ("towns" in New England, Minnesota, New York, and Wisconsin), and 46 states have school districts. Special districts encompass such functions as natural resources, fire protection, and housing and community development.
Source: U.S. Census Bureau, *Census of Governments*.

State government revenue, 2002

Total revenue. $6,888 mill.
General revenue . . . . $6,167 mill.
Per capita revenue $2,844
U.S. per capita average $3,689
Rank among states 44

Intergovernment revenue
Total . . . . $1,338 mill.
From federal government . . . . $1,281 mill.

Charges and miscellaneous
Total . . . . $884 mill.
Current charges . . . . $513 mill.
Misc. general income . . . . $370 mill.
Insurance trust revenue . . . . $557 mill.

Taxes
Total . . . . $3,945 mill.
Per capita taxes $1,821
Rank among states 22
Property taxes . . . . $113 mill.
Sales taxes . . . . $3,338 mill.
License taxes . . . . $439 mill.
Individual income taxes . . . . (nil)
Corporate income taxes . . . . (nil)
Other taxes . . . . $56 mill.

Total revenue figures include items not listed separately here.
Source: U.S. Bureau of the Census.

State government expenditures, 2002

General expenditures

Total state expenditures	$7,348 mill.
Intergovernmental	$2,433 mill.

Per capita expenditures

State	$2,881
Average of all states	$3,859
Rank among states	48

Selected direct expenditures

Education	$904 mill.
Public welfare	$1,004 mill.
Health, hospital	$310 mill.
Highways	$568 mill.
Police protection	$64 mill.
Corrections	$225 mill.
Natural resources	$82 mill.
Parks and recreation	$17 mill.
Government administration	$198 mill.
Interest on debt	$150 mill.
Total direct expenditures	$3,809 mill.

Totals include items not listed separately.
Source: U.S. Census Bureau.

POLITICS

Governors since statehood

D = Democrat; R = Republican; O = other;
(r) resigned; (d) died in office; (i) removed from office

Henry G. Blasdel (R)	1864-1871
Lewis R. Bradley (D)	1871-1879
John H. Kinkead (R)	1879-1883
Jewett W. Adams (D)	1883-1887
Charles C. Stevenson (R)	(r) 1887-1890
Frank Bell (R)	1890-1891
Roswell K. Colcord (R)	1891-1895
John E. Jones (O)	(d) 1895-1896
Reinhold Sadler (O)	1896-1903
John Sparks (D)	(d) 1903-1908
Denver S. Dickerson (D)	1908-1911
Tasker L. Oddie (R)	1911-1915
Emmet D. Boyle (D)	1915-1923
James G. Scrugham (D)	1923-1927
Frederick B. Balzer (R)	(d) 1927-1934
Morley I. Griswold (R)	1934-1935
Richard Kirman (D)	1935-1939
Edward P. Carville (D)	(r) 1939-1945
Vail M. Pittman (D)	1945-1951
Charles H. Russell (R)	1951-1959
Grant Sawyer (R)	1959-1967
Paul D. Laxalt (R)	1967-1971
Mike O'Callaghan (D)	1971-1979
Robert F. List (R)	1979-1983
Richard H. Bryan (D)	1983-1991

Robert Miller (D)	1991-1999
Kenny C. Guinn (R)	1999-2007
Jim Gibbons (R)	2007-

Composition of congressional delegations, 1989-2007

	Dem	Rep	Total
House of Representatives			
101st Congress, 1989			
State delegates	1	1	2
Total U.S.	259	174	433
102d Congress, 1991			
State delegates	1	1	2
Total U.S.	267	167	434
103d Congress, 1993			
State delegates	1	1	2
Total U.S.	258	176	434
104th Congress, 1995			
State delegates	0	2	2
Total U.S.	197	236	433
105th Congress, 1997			
State delegates	0	2	2
Total U.S.	206	228	434
106th Congress, 1999			
State delegates	1	1	2
Total U.S.	211	222	433
107th Congress, 2001			
State delegates	1	1	2
Total U.S.	211	221	432
108th Congress, 2003			
State delegates	1	2	3
Total U.S.	205	229	434
109th Congress, 2005			
State delegates	1	2	3
Total U.S.	202	231	433
110th Congress, 2007			
State delegates	1	2	3
Total U.S.	233	202	435
Senate			
101st Congress, 1989			
State delegates	2	0	2
Total U.S.	55	45	100
102d Congress, 1991			
State delegates	2	0	2
Total U.S.	56	44	100
103d Congress, 1993			
State delegates	2	0	2
Total U.S.	57	43	100
104th Congress, 1995			
State delegates	2	0	2
Total U.S.	46	53	99

(continued)

	Dem	Rep	Total
105th Congress, 1997			
State delegates	2	0	2
Total U.S.	45	55	100
106th Congress, 1999			
State delegates	2	0	2
Total U.S.	45	54	99
107th Congress, 2001			
State delegates	1	1	2
Total U.S.	50	50	100
108th Congress, 2003			
State delegates	1	1	2
Total U.S.	48	51	99
109th Congress, 2005			
State delegates	1	1	2
Total U.S.	44	55	99
110th Congress, 2007			
State delegates	1	1	2
Total U.S.	49	49	98

Figures are for starts of first sessions. Totals are for Democrat (Dem.) and Republican (Rep.) members only. House membership totals under 435 and Senate totals under 100 reflect vacancies and seats held by independent party members. When the 110th Congress opened, the Senate's two independent members caucused with the Democrats, giving the Democrats control of the Senate.
Source: U.S. Congress, *Congressional Directory.*

Composition of state legislature, 1990-2006

	Democrats	Republicans
State Assembly (42 seats)		
1990	22	19
1992	27	12
1994	21	21
1996	25	17
1998	28	14
2000	27	14
2002	23	19
2004	26	16
2006	27	15
State Senate (21 seats)		
1990	10	10
1992	10	11
1994	8	13
1996	9	12
1998	9	12
2000	9	12
2002	8	13
2004	9	12
2006	10	11

Figures for total seats may include independents and minor party members. Numbers reflect results of elections in listed years; elected members usually take their seats in the years that follow.
Source: Council of State Governments; *State Elective Officials and the Legislatures.*

Voter participation in presidential elections, 2000 and 2004

	2000	2004
Voting age population		
State	1,500,000	1,731,000
Total United States	209,831,000	220,377,000
State share of U.S. total	0.71	0.79
Rank among states	35	34
Portion of voting age population casting votes		
State	40.6%	47.9%
United States	50.3%	55.5%
Rank among states	48	47

Population figures are rounded to nearest thousand and include all residents, regardless of eligibility to vote.
Source: U.S. Census Bureau.

HEALTH AND MEDICAL CARE

Medical professionals
Physicians in 2003 and nurses in 2001

	U.S.	State
Physicians in 2003		
Total	774,849	4,152
Share of U.S. total		0.53%
Rate	266	185
Rank		47
Nurses in 2001		
Total	2,262,020	10,840
Share of U.S. total		0.48%
Rate	793	517
Rank		50

Rates are numbers of physicians and nurses per 100,000 resident population; ranks are based on rates.
Source: American Medical Association, *Physician Characteristics and Distribution in the U.S.;* U.S. Department of Health and Human Services, Health Resources and Services Administration.

Health insurance coverage, 2003

	State	U.S.
Total persons covered	1,824,000	243,320,000
Total persons not covered	426,000	44,961,000
Portion not covered	18.9%	15.6%
Rank among states	6	—
Children not covered	103,000	8,373,000
Portion not covered	17.4%	11.4%
Rank among states	4	—

Totals are rounded to nearest thousand. Ranks are from the highest to the lowest percentages of persons *not* insured.
Source: U.S. Census Bureau, Current Population Reports.

AIDS, syphilis, and tuberculosis cases, 2003

Disease	U.S. cases	State cases	Rank
AIDS	44,232	279	26
Syphilis	34,270	149	30
Tuberculosis	14,874	107	31

Source: U.S. Centers for Disease Control and Prevention.

Cigarette smoking, 2003
Residents over age 18 who smoke

	U.S.	State	Rank
All smokers	22.1%	25.2%	14
Male smokers	24.8%	29.0%	7
Female smokers	20.3%	21.3%	19

Cigarette smokers are defined as persons who reported having
smoked at least 100 cigarettes during their lifetimes and who
currently smoked at least occasionally.
Source: U.S. Centers for Disease Control and Prevention, *Morbidity
and Mortality Weekly Report*, 53, no. 44 (November 12, 2004).

HOUSING

Home ownership rates, 1985-2004

	1985	1990	1995	2000	2004
State	57.0%	55.8%	58.6%	64.0%	65.7%
Total U.S.	63.9%	63.9%	64.7%	67.4%	69.0%
Rank among states	47	47	46	43	44

Net change in state home ownership rate,
1985-2004 . . . . +8.7%
Net change in U.S. home ownership rate,
1985-2004 . . . . +5.1%

Percentages represent the proportion of owner households to total
occupied households.
Source: U.S. Census Bureau, 2006.

Home sales, 2000-2004
In thousands of units

Existing home sales	2000	2002	2003	2004
State sales	44.6	63.5	80.9	99.8
Total U.S. sales	5,171	5,631	6,183	6,784
State share of U.S. total	0.86%	1.13%	1.31%	1.47%
Sales rank among states	33	30	27	24

Units include single-family homes, condos, and co-ops.
Source: National Association of Realtors, Washington, D.C., *Real
Estate Outlook: Market Trends & Insights.*

Values of owner-occupied homes, 2003

	State	U.S.
Total units	433,000	58,809,000
Value of units		
Under $100,000	9.3%	29.6%
$100,000-199,999	54.3%	36.9%
$200,000 or more	36.4%	33.5%
Median value	$170,333	$142,275
Rank among all states 14		

Units are owner-occupied one-family houses whose numbers are
rounded to nearest thousand. Data are extrapolated from
survey samples.
Source: U.S. Census Bureau, American Community Survey.

EDUCATION

Public school enrollment, 2002

Prekindergarten through grade 8
State enrollment 271,000
Total U.S. enrollment. 34,135,000
State share of U.S. total 0.79%

Grades 9 through 12
State enrollment. 99,000
Total U.S. enrollment. 14,067,000
State share of U.S. total 0.70%

Enrollment rates
State public school enrollment rate. 90.8%
Overall U.S. rate 90.4%
Rank among states in 2002. 22
Rank among states in 1995 7

Enrollment figures (which include unclassified students) are
rounded to nearest thousand pupils during fall school term.
Enrollment rates are based on enumerated resident population
estimate for July 1, 2002.
Source: U.S. National Center for Education Statistics.

Public college finances, 2003-2004

FTE enrollment in public institutions of higher education

Students in state institutions 57,200
Students in all U.S. public institutions 9,916,600
State share of U.S. total 0.58
Rank among states 38

State and local government appropriations for higher education

State appropriation per FTE $7,834
National average $5,716
Rank among states 7
State & local tax revenue going to higher
education 5.6%

FTE = full-time equivalent in public postsecondary programs,
including summer sessions; student numbers are rounded to
nearest hundred. Funding figures for 2003-2004 academic year
include financial aid to students in state public institutions and
exclude money for research, agriculture experiment stations,
teaching hospitals, and medical schools; figures are rounded to
nearest thousand dollars.
Source: Higher Education Executive Officers, Denver, Colorado.

TRANSPORTATION AND TRAVEL

Highway mileage, 2003

Interstate highways 560
Other freeways and expressways 52
Arterial roads 2,875
Collector roads 5,210
Local roads 25,280

Urban roads 5,727
Rural roads 28,250

Total state mileage 33,977
U.S. total 3,974,107
State share 0.85%
Rank among states 40

Note that combined urban and rural road mileage matches the
total of the other categories.
Source: U.S. Federal Highway Administration.

Motor vehicle registrations and driver licenses, 2003

Vehicle registrations	State	U.S.	Share	Rank
Autos, trucks, buses	1,222,000	231,390,000	0.53%	39
Autos only	624,000	135,670	0.46%	39
Motorcycles	37,000	5,328,000	0.69%	37
Driver licenses	1,488,000	196,166,000	0.76%	35

Figures, which do not include vehicles owned by military services,
are rounded to the nearest thousand. Figures for automobiles
include taxis.
Source: U.S. Federal Highway Administration.

Domestic travel expenditures, 2003
Spending by U.S. residents on overnight trips and day trips of at least 50 miles from home

Total expenditures within state . . . . $19.32 bill.
Total expenditures within U.S. . . . . $490.87 bill.
State share of U.S. total 3.9%
Rank among states 6

Source: Travel Industry Association of America.

Retail gasoline prices, 2003-2007
Average price per gallon at the pump

Year	U.S.	State
2003	$1.267	$1.518
2004	$1.316	$1.617
2005	$1.644	$1.806
2007	$2.298	$2.581

Excise tax per gallon in 2004 . . . . 23.0¢
Rank among all states in 2007 prices 3

Prices are averages of all grades of gasoline sold at the pump
during March months in 2003-2005 and during February, 2007.
Averages for 2006, during which prices rose higher, are not
available.
Source: U.S. Energy Information Agency, *Petroleum Marketing
Monthly* (2003-2005 data); American Automobile Association
(2007 data).

CRIME AND LAW ENFORCEMENT

State and local police officers, 2000-2004

	2000	2002	2004
Total officers			
U.S.	654,601	665,555	675,734
State	4,814	4,907	4,758*
*Net change, 2000-2004			−1.16%
Officers per 1,000 residents			
U.S.	2.33	2.31	2.30
State	2.41	2.26	2.04
State rank	11	17	26

Totals include state and local police and sheriffs.
Source: Carsey Institute, University of New Hampshire.

Crime rates, 2003
Incidents per 100,000 residents

Crimes	State	U.S.
Violent crimes		
Total incidents	614	475
Murder	9	6
Forcible rape	39	32
Robbery	230	142
Aggravated assault	336	295
Property crimes		
Total incidents	4,288	3,588
Burglary	981	741
Larceny/theft	2,378	2,415
Motor vehicle theft	930	433
All crimes	4,902	4,063

Source: U.S. Federal Bureau of Investigation, *Crime in the United States*, annual.

State prison populations, 1980-2003

	State	U.S.	State share
1980	1,839	305,458	0.60%
1990	5,322	708,393	0.75%
1996	8,439	1,025,624	0.82%
2000	10,063	1,391,261	0.72%
2003	10,543	1,470,045	0.72%

State figures exclude prisoners in federal penitentiaries.
Source: U.S. Bureau of Justice Statistics, *Prisoners in 2003.*

New Hampshire

Location: New England coast

Area and rank: 8,969 square miles (23,231 square kilometers); 9,351 square miles (24,219 square kilometers) including water; forty-fourth largest state in area

Coastline: 13 miles (21 kilometers) on the Atlantic Ocean

Shoreline: 131 miles (211 kilometers)

Population and rank: 1,300,000 (2004); forty-first largest state in population

Capital city: Concord (40,687 people in 2000 census)

Largest city: Manchester (107,006 people in 2000 census)

New Hampshire's State House in Concord serves as the state capitol, housing both the executive and the legislative branches of the government. (©Mary Lane/Dreamstime.com)

Entered Union and rank:
June 21, 1788; ninth
state

**Present constitution
adopted:** 1784

Counties: 10

State name: New
Hampshire was named
after England's
Hampshire county

State nickname: Granite
State

Motto: Live free or die

State flag: Blue field with state seal bordered with laurel leaves and stars

Highest point: Mount Washington—6,288 feet (1,917 meters)

Lowest point: Atlantic Ocean—sea level

Highest recorded temperature: 106 degrees Fahrenheit (41 degrees Celsius)—Nashua, 1911

Lowest recorded temperature: –46 degrees Fahrenheit (–43 degrees Celsius)—Pittsburg,
1925

State song: "Old New Hampshire"

State tree: White birch

State flower: Purple lilac

State bird: Purple finch

State fish: Striped bass (saltwater);
brook trout (freshwater)

State animal: White-tailed deer

New Hampshire History

Part of New England, New Hampshire is one of the original thirteen states. When the glaciers that once covered the North American continent retreated in the area now known as New Hampshire, they left behind a hard, gray granite rock called gneiss, which is why New Hampshire is called the Granite State. The state is relatively small: Its longest distance is 180 miles from north to south, and it is ranked forty-fourth in land area among states. Bounded by Canada in the north, its other borders are the New England states of Massachusetts, Maine, and Vermont. New Hampshire has a small coastline, stretching only eighteen miles, with Portsmouth serving as the state's only harbor. Because of the state's relatively small amount of arable land, farms produce mostly dairy and poultry products. The impressive water power available made New Hampshire attractive to Industrialists during the early twentieth century, and manufacturing is still an important segment of the state's economy. A fiercely independent people whose state motto is "Live free or die," this traditionally conservative state is one of the few without a state income tax.

Before 1800, New Hampshire was home to the Ossipee, Nashua, Pennacook, Piscataqua, Sqamscot, and Winnipesaukee Indians. These people, known collectively as the western Abenaki, belonged to the eastern branch of the Algonquian family, a large group of tribes related by similar languages and customs. They lived in wigwams and were primarily hunters and gatherers, living off the area's fertile fishing waters and hunting grounds. The encroaching European settlements drove most of the early settlers off the land by the eighteenth century. Native Americans comprised 0.2 percent of the population in 1990.

Early Exploration. Viking Leif Eriksson and other Norse sailors most likely explored some of New Hampshire during their travels in 1000. Explorer Martin Pring was at the mouth of the Piscataqua in 1603. In 1605, British captain George Weymouth landed in Maine, kidnapped five Abenaki men, and took them back to England. Upon meeting the tribesmen, King James I agreed to sponsor a settlement there. In 1620, he formed the Council for New England which gave out land grants, the first going to Captain John Mason, "the founder of New Hampshire." The following year, David Thomson started the first known English settlement in New Hampshire, now known as Rye. He headed a company that organized fishing and trading.

Religious Conflict. In 1636, the Reverend John Wheelwright was banished from Massachusetts for his religious beliefs. Wheelwright was an Antinomian who believed that Christians do not need to observe moral laws if they are saved by God. Ironically, the Puritans, who had fled England because they were persecuted for their religious beliefs, had little tolerance of other religious philosophies.

Wheelwright turned down an offer from Roger Williams to come to Rhode Island because he wanted to establish a new colony. He went by boat as far as the site of present day Portsmouth, New

Until centuries of weathering caused it to collapse in 2003, the natural granite formation known as "Old Man of the Mountain" was New Hampshire's best-known landmark. The jagged, facelike formation appeared on the state's official emblem, the New Hampshire quarter dollar, and a U.S. postage stamp. This photograph is a composite image, showing the formation before and after its collapse. (Rob Gallagher)

Hampshire. It was there that he and a settler named John explored farther west and established the village of Exeter and the Laconia Company, a joint-stock company.

In the same year, Massachusetts encouraged Puritans to settle nearby Hampton. Tension quickly erupted between the Antinomians and the Puritans. Both New Hampshire and Massachusetts granted townships within New Hampshire territory. It took the Revolutionary War against Great Britain to unite the two factions for a greater cause.

The Wentworth Family. The Wentworths were New Hampshire's most influential family throughout much of the eighteenth century. In 1717, the king of England appointed John Wentworth, a wealthy, self-made merchant, lieutenant governor of New Hampshire. At the time a single royal governor administered both Massachusetts and New Hampshire.

When John Wentworth died in 1730, his son Benning worked to separate from Massachusetts. In 1740, the King's Council established a boundary and the following year appointed Benning Wentworth as the first independent governor of the province. Like his father, he was a loyal representative of the Crown. His devotion to England was unpopular with most citizens, who found the king's taxes unjust, and he resigned from office in 1766. His nephew, John Wentworth, was the new royal appointee. He too tried to keep New Hampshire on the side of Britain, and in 1774, he dissolved the assembly for speaking of revolution. The colonists took matters into their own hands, and in June of 1775, Governor Wentworth was forced from office, ending 160 years of colonial rule in New Hampshire.

Revolution. In what some historians consider the first revolutionary act against Britain, four hundred New Hampshire men stormed the British fort at New Castle and carried off arms and ammunition in 1774. The following year the Revolutionary War began, and New Hampshire was represented in every important battle. Portsmouth's shipbuilding industry naturally grew significantly as naval vessels were needed to aid the war.

About four thousand of the state's men fought in the war. Another three thousand served the cause by privateering: These men sailed the coast capturing British

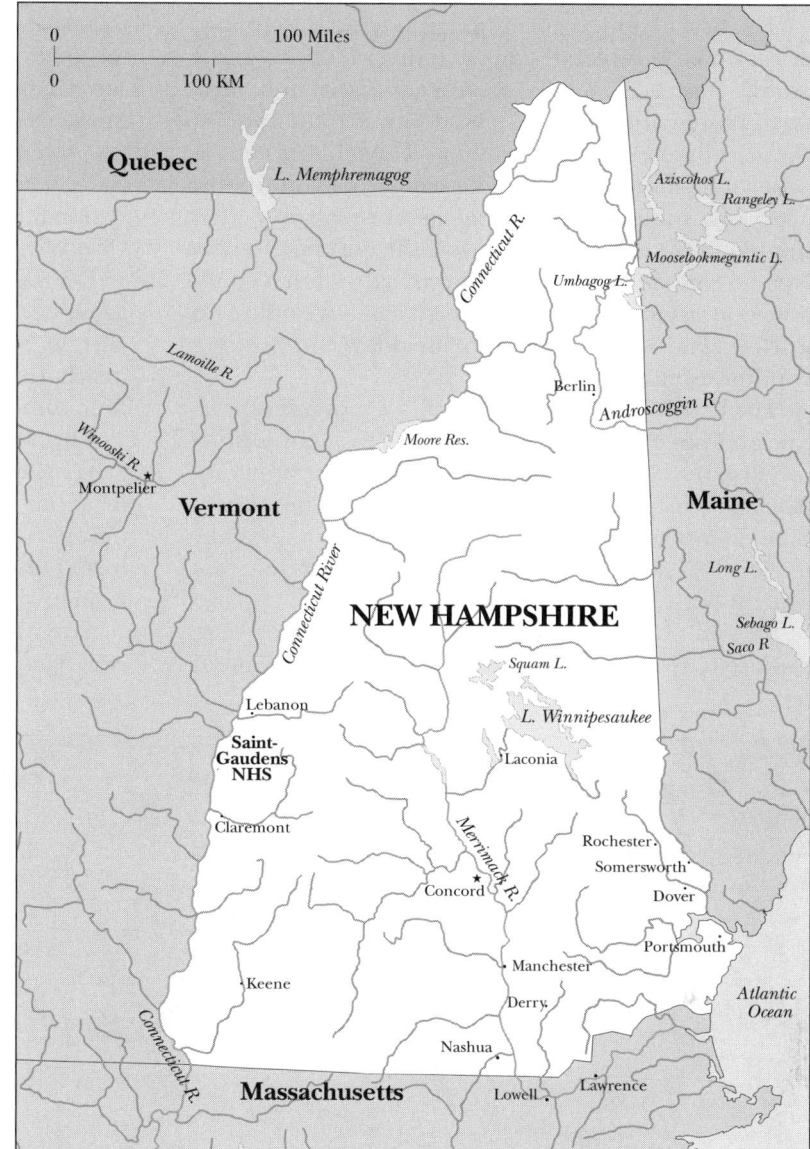

supply ships and seized their cargoes for the American army. Those at home did not have to suffer invasions—New Hampshire was the only one of the original thirteen states British armies never attacked.

The New State. New Hampshire was the first state to adopt its own constitution, in 1776, and also the first of the original thirteen states to call a convention to write a better one. In 1784, the permanent state constitution was adopted, and on June 21, 1788, New Hampshire became the ninth state.

In 1808, the state's seat of government moved to Concord. Like most of the country's population, New Hampshire's at this time was mainly made up of farmers. When the Industrial Revolution came to New England during the 1830's, it caused an upsurge in economic activity downriver from Concord in Manchester, which soon became the economic center of the state.

The first commercial buildings to appear were sawmills, which processed lumber, and gristmills to grind grain. The rivers in the Merrimack Valley provided great power, and soon the area developed into one of the world's leading textile centers. The mill workers labored long hours, usually under dangerous conditions. The workers had no bargaining power to speak of, as in the 1840's the mill owners had an influx of cheap labor: Ireland's potato famine had driven many of that country's poorest to the shores of America, many ending up in New Hampshire. Wages remained low and working conditions harsh.

The Civil War. One of the country's most gifted orators and famous politicians, Daniel Webster, was born in Salisbury, New Hampshire, in 1782. After graduating from Dartmouth College, he was New Hampshire's state representative from 1813 to 1817. He eventually moved to Massachusetts, however, representing that state in both houses of Congress.

In 1852, New Hampshire lawyer and former state representative Franklin Pierce came out of retirement to become the Democratic nominee for president. He was elected and was then the youngest president ever to serve. His inexperience led to several botched political moves, and in 1854 he backed the Kansas-Nebraska Act, which repealed the Missouri Compromise. Many historians believe that this act reignited the slavery issue on a national level and pushed the country quickly toward Civil War, which began in 1860.

During the Civil War, New Hampshire was fortunate again because no battles were fought on its soil. Yet the citizens were staunch defenders of the Union, and nearly half the state's population at the time, thirty-nine thousand men, fought in the war.

The Twentieth Century. When the new century began, more people in New Hampshire made their living from manufacturing than from agriculture. Labor unions began forming in the factories, and a labor reform bill passed in 1907 that limited the workweek for women and children to fifty-eight hours.

The United States entered World War I in 1917, and New Hampshire citizens fought again in large num-

A characteristic New Hampshire scene, with the spire of a Protestant church rising above a small town. (PhotoDisc)

The Mount Washington Cog Railway. (State of New Hampshire Office of Travel and Tourism)

bers. The Portsmouth Naval Shipyard built warships, including submarines. After the war, the 1920's brought the beginning of years of decline for New England textile milling, and the state began an economic slump that would worsen through the Depression and only start to get better at the beginning of World War II.

Frank Knox, publisher of Manchester's *Union Leader,* was appointed secretary of the Navy. Production rapidly went into high gear at the Portsmouth Naval Shipyard making U.S. submarines—at one point during the war, two a week. About twenty thousand men and women worked in the yard.

The Primary State. In 1913, New Hampshire state legislators moved the date of their election year primary and began a long tradition of being the first primary of every political season. After World War II, presidential primaries became more important, as they were seen as a testing ground for potential candidates. The eyes of the nation focus on New Hampshire during this time every four years. Other states, jealous of the attention, have tried to move up their primaries, and New Hampshire has responded by passing a law dictating that their primary will be held the Tuesday before any other state's. After 1952, no president was elected with-

out first winning the New Hampshire primary—until 1992, when U.S. senator Paul Tsongas won that primary but later lost the nomination to Bill Clinton.

Controversies and Headlines. In 2000, New Hampshire found itself in a controversy over whether the death penalty should be repealed. At the time, no state had repealed capital punishment following its reinstatement by the U.S. Supreme Court in 1976. New Hampshire had not executed anyone since 1939 and no one was on death row waiting for execution. The state legislature nevertheless voted to ban the practice by votes of 14-10 in the Senate and by 191-163 in the lower house. Governor Jeanne Shaheen vetoed the bill, however, arguing that there are murders so heinous that the death penalty is an appropriate punishment.

A second controversy in 2000 involved the chief justice of the state's supreme court, David Brock, who was accused of perjury and of allowing a fellow judge to influence the selection of judges in his divorce case. Brock's impeachment on these charges was the first in the state since 1790 and the first ever impeachment of a chief justice. The state senate, however, found him innocent.

In 2001, New Hampshire was horrified by a sensational crime when two Dartmouth College professors were found murdered. Soon afterward, two young men—one eighteen and the other seventeen—were arrested for the crimes. Tried and found guilty, the older of the two was sentenced to life without parole, while the younger received a sentence of twenty-five years to life.

Politics. The 2000 general election found New Hampshire's voters divided and, perhaps, ambivalent. On one hand, George W. Bush gained the state's four electoral votes in a narrow victory over Al Gore. Bush won with 48 percent to Gore's 47 percent of the vote, which translated into a 7,200-vote plurality. Independent candidate Ralph Nader, however, won 4 percent of the vote, leading analysts to believe that he saved Bush from defeat. On the other hand, Governor Shaheen, a Democrat, defeated former U.S. senator Gordon Humphrey, a Republican, by 49-44 percent. She won despite refusing to pledge that she would not seek a state income tax, a thirty-year tradition in the state. However, when the same issue arose in the 2002 governor's race with two new candidates, Republican Craig Benson, who opposed the tax, won by 59 to 38 percent over an opponent who proposed a state income tax to pay for public schools. Shaheen relinquished the governorship to run for the U.S. Senate against John E.

Sununu—son of a former governor and presidential chief of staff—who defeated the former governor by 51-47 percent.

In 2004, without a Nader candidacy, Democrat John Kerry from neighboring Massachusetts beat Bush in the presidential poll by fewer than 10,000 votes among 671,000 votes cast. Republican U.S. senator Judd Greg was reelected, as were the state's two members of Congress. However, as if to demonstrate the state's political ambivalence, Democrat John Lynch unseated Republican governor Benson.

Old Man of the Mountain. In 2003, an environmental event saddened the state when the famed Old Man of the Mountain, a rock formation in the likeness of a man's profile thought to be thousands of years old, collapsed. The formation was said to symbolize the steadfastness of the state's Yankee character and the resolve of its people. Experts said the collapse was the result of erosion and other natural factors, such as the cycle of freezing and thawing, which eventually severely weakened the rock. In response, an Old Man of the Mountain Revitalization Taskforce was established to restore the iconic formation that drew thousands of tourists annually.

Kevin M. Mitchell
Updated by the Editor

New Hampshire Time Line

1500's	Western Abenaki Indians inhabit New Hampshire.
1603	England's Martin Pring explores mouth of the Piscataqua River.
1605	French explorer Samuel de Champlain enters Piscataqua Bay.
1623	First English settlements are founded at Dover and at Little Harbor (later Rye).
1629	England's Captain John Mason receives a grant of land in the area and names it New Hampshire after England's Hampshire.
1630	Dover settlement is established.
1634	Dover becomes site of the first church built in New Hampshire.
1641	Because of religious disagreements among Anglicans, Puritans, and Quakers, communities are unable to decide on a government and thus become part of Massachusetts.
1647	New Hampshire colonists pass an education act requiring towns to provide public education.
1679	New Hampshire becomes a royal province, separate from Massachusetts.
1693	New school law requires each town to provide a schoolmaster.
1756	*New Hampshire Gazette*, the state's first paper, is published.
1763	French and Indian War ends; most Native Americans are driven into Canada, and the French are driven out completely.
1768	Dartmouth College opens in Hanover.
1774	Colonists raid England's Fort William and Mary in Portsmouth, taking ammunition and gunpowder.
1776	New Hampshire becomes first colony to declare independence from Great Britain.
1784	Revised state constitution is adopted.
1785	Two-party political system begins.
June 21, 1788	New Hampshire becomes ninth state.

One of New Hampshire's many covered bridges. (PhotoDisc)

1804	State's first cotton factory begins operation.
1819	Amoskeag Mills, in Manchester, introduces the power loom for weaving cloth.
1838	State's first railroad begins operation.
1847	First ten-hour-day law for factory workers is enacted.
1853	New Hampshire politician Franklin Pierce becomes fourteenth president of the United States.
1865	Fifth New Hampshire Regiment ends Civil War service with more casualties than any other regiment in the Union.
1871	School attendance is made compulsory.
1877	Law requiring that state's governor, senators, and representatives be Protestants is repealed.
1891	New Hampshire's Library Commission provides free public libraries with state aid.
1909	New Hampshire adopts direct primary law.
1922	State's first radio station begins operation.
1961	New Hampshire-born Alan B. Shepard, Jr., becomes first American to travel in space.
1963	John W. King becomes first Democrat to be elected governor in fifty years.
1972	State ratifies Equal Rights Amendment.
1977	Two thousand demonstrators march on construction site of nuclear plant at Seabrook.
1980-1990	Median household income jumps 27.4 percent, the greatest increase in the nation.
1986	Concord teacher Christa McAuliffe is among crew members killed when the space shuttle *Challenger* explodes.
1999	New Hampshire senator Bob Smith leaves the Republican Party, which he says has become too liberal, to pursue an independent presidential bid.

(continued)

2000	Governor Jeanne Shaheen vetoes legislative bill banning capital punishment.
2000	State senate finds Chief Justice David Brock innocent in impeachment trial.
2001	Border dispute with Maine is settled by U.S. Supreme Court's 8-0 decision in Maine's favor.
May 3, 2003	Old Man of the Mountain rock formation in Franconia Notch State Park collapses.
Nov. 2, 2004	Republican U.S. senator Judd Greg is reelected; Democrat John Lynch defeats sitting governor Craig Benson.

Notes for Further Study

Published Sources. Those looking for short historical and social overviews will find material in *New Hampshire: From Sea to Shining Sea* (2002) by Terry Miller Shannon and *New Hampshire* (2004) by Michael Teitelbaum. Deeper analysis is found in *New Hampshire: Crosscurrents in Its Development* (3d ed., 2004) by Nancy Coffeey Heffernan and Ann P. Stecker. The book covers the state's industry, from the prosperous shipbuilding trade to high-tech industry, and tells about its colorful political figures and the New Hampshire political primary. *The New Hampshire Primary and the American Electoral Process* (1997) studies the peculiar role and history of the state primary in American presidential elections. The work reviews the primary's history and analyzes the media's treatment of New Hampshire results, including the role played by local media.

New Hampshire: Disaster and Catastrophes (1990) by Carole Marsh provides coverage of the floods, fires, and other disasters which the state's residents have had to endure. *New Hampshire: An Explorer's Guide* (Rev. ed., 2006) by Christina Tree and Christine Hamm covers the state's recreation and natural world, as does *New Hampshire Off the Beaten Path: A Guide to Unique Places* (6th ed., 2004) by Barbara Radcliffe Rogers and Stillman Rogers. Books on the American Industrial Revolution and the textile industry revealing life in nineteenth century New England include *The Growth of Manufacturing in Early Nineteenth Century New England* (1975) by Robert Brooke Zevin and *The Lowell Offering: Writings by New England Mill Women, 1840-1845* (1997), edited by Benita Eisler. Based on a magazine produced at the time, it comprises personal essays of the first women to work in American mills. An interesting approach to the state's more modern history is Felice Belman and Mike Pride's *The New Hampshire Century* (2001), an illustrated account of twentieth century New Hampshire told through the lives of those who contributed to its development.

David R. Starbuck's *Archeology of New Hampshire: Exploring 10,000 Years in the Granite State* (2006) is a diversion from many books focusing on archaeology in that, along with discussing prehistoric sites, Starbuck also devotes equal time to historic, industrial, and nautical sites. A collection of reprints of journal articles, edited by Thaddeus Piotrowski and presented as *The Indian Heritage of New Hampshire and Northern New England* (2002), preserves historical accounts of the state's native peoples and includes archaeological investigations of prehistoric sites and listings of collections of artifacts, places, names, and trails associated with New Hampshire Indians.

Web Resources. There are many New Hampshire sites on the Internet, and those listed here often give worthwhile links to others. Perhaps the best starting point is the state's official Web site, sponsored by the state's largest newspaper, the *Union Leader* (www.newhampshire.com) or the state's government portal site (www.nh.gov/). A brief history of New Hampshire (www.nh.gov/markers/brief.html) offers details emphasizing the state's beginnings. The New Hampshire Primary site (www.newhampshireprimary.com) provides updates to the beginning of the nation's presidential race. Those planning a visit to the state should visit the official tourism Web site (www.visitnh.gov/), the White Mountains site (www.visitwhitemountains.com/), or Roadside America's New Hampshire page (www.roadsideamerica.com/map/nh.html).

Counties

County	2000 pop.	Rank in pop.	Sq. miles	Rank in area
Belknap	56,325	7	401.3	9
Carroll	43,666	8	933.9	4
Cheshire	73,825	6	707.5	6
Coos	33,111	10	1,800.6	1
Grafton	81,743	5	1,713.5	2
Hillsborough	380,841	1	876.5	5

County	2000 pop.	Rank in pop.	Sq. miles	Rank in area
Merrimack	136,225	3	934.5	3
Rockingham	277,359	2	695.2	7
Strafford	112,233	4	368.8	10
Sullivan	40,458	9	537.4	8

Source: U.S. Census Bureau; National Association of Counties.

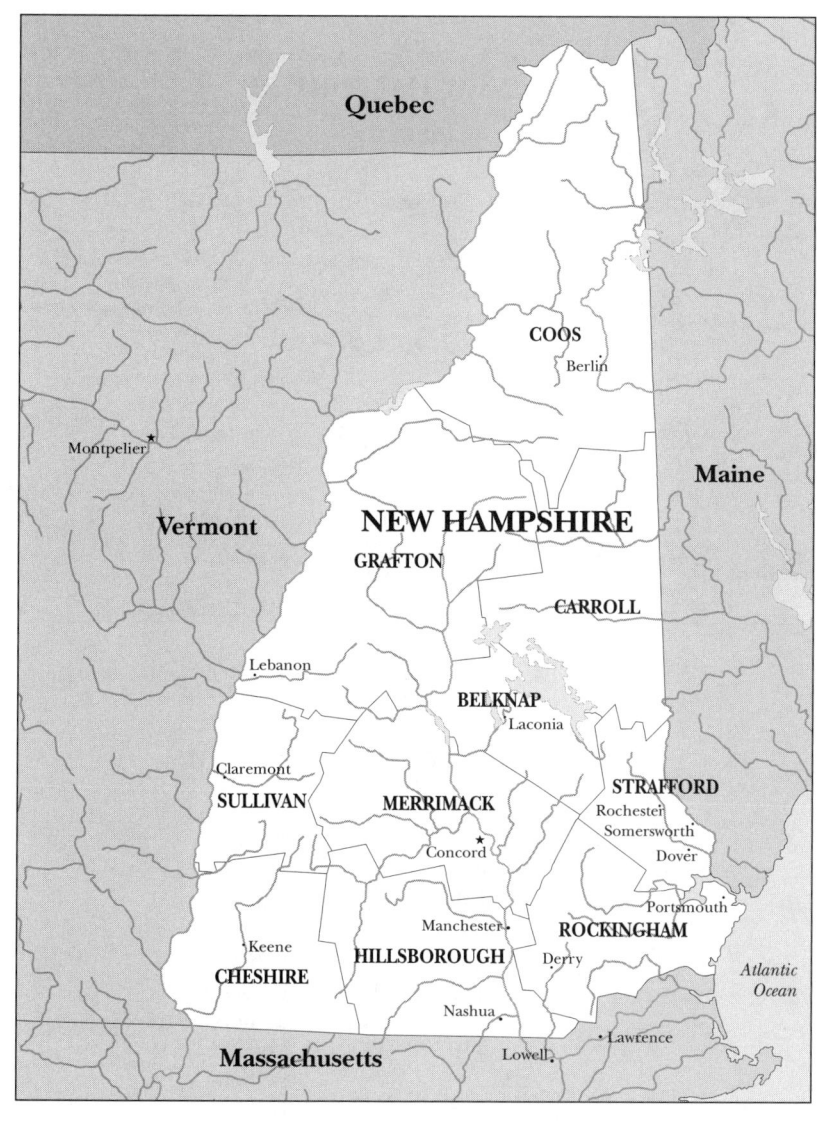

Cities

With 10,000 or more residents

Rank	City	Population	Rank	City	Population
1	Manchester	107,006	18	Exeter	14,058
2	Nashua	86,605	19	Milford	13,535
3	Concord (capital)	40,687	20	Claremont	13,151
4	Derry	34,021	21	Durham	12,664
5	Rochester	28,461	22	Lebanon	12,568
6	Salem	28,112	23	Hooksett	11,721
7	Dover	26,884	24	Somersworth	11,477
8	Merrimack	25,119	25	Londonderry	11,417
9	Londonderry	23,236	26	Pelham	10,914
10	Hudson	22,928	27	Hanover	10,850
11	Derry	22,661	28	Amherst	10,769
12	Keene	22,563	29	Windham	10,709
13	Portsmouth	20,784	30	Berlin	10,331
14	Bedford	18,274			
15	Goffstown	16,929			
16	Laconia	16,411			
17	Hampton	14,937			

Population figures are from 2000 census.

Source: U.S. Bureau of the Census.

Index to Tables

DEMOGRAPHICS

Resident state and national populations, 1970-2004

Population figures given in thousands

	State pop.	U.S. pop.	Share	Rank
1970	738	203,302	0.4%	41
1980	921	226,546	0.4%	42
1985	997	237,924	0.4%	40
1990	1,109	248,765	0.4%	40
1995	1,158	262,761	0.4%	42
2000	1,236	281,425	0.4%	41
2004	1,300	293,655	0.4%	41

Source: U.S. Census Bureau, Current Population Reports, 2006.

Resident population by age, 2004

Age Group	Total persons
Under 5 years	73,000
5 to 17 years	232,000
18 to 24 years	122,000
25 to 34 years	149,000
35 to 44 years	216,000
45 to 54 years	209,000
55 to 64 years	141,000
65 to 74 years	79,000
75 to 84 years	56,000
85 years and older	22,000
All age groups	1,300,000

Portion of residents 65 and older	12.1%
National rank in portion of oldest residents	33
National average	12.4%

Population figures are rounded to nearest thousand persons;
  figures include armed forces personnel stationed in the state.
Source: U.S. Bureau of the Census, 2006.

Resident population by race, Hispanic origin, 2004

Category	State pop.	Share	U.S.
All residents	1,300	100.00%	100.00%
Non-Hispanic white	1,225	94.23%	67.37%
Hispanic white	25	1.92%	13.01%
Other Hispanic	3	0.23%	1.06%
African American	12	0.92%	12.77%
Native American	3	0.23%	0.96%
Asian, Pacific Islander	23	1.77%	4.37%
Two or more categories	12	0.92%	1.51%

Population figures are in thousands. Persons counted as
"Hispanic" (Latino) may be of any race. Because of overlapping
categories, categories may not add up to 100%. Shares in
column 3 are percentages of each category within the state;
these figures may be compared to the national percentages in
column 4.
Source: U.S. Bureau of the Census, 2006.

Projected state population, 2000-2030

Year	Population
2000	1,236,000
2005	1,315,000
2010	1,386,000
2015	1,457,000
2020	1,525,000
2025	1,586,000
2030	1,646,000
Population increase, 2000-2030	410,000
Percentage increase, 2000-2030	33.2

Projections are based on data from the 2000 census.
Source: U.S. Census Bureau.

VITAL STATISTICS

Infant mortality rates, 1980-2002

	1980	1990	2000	2002
All state residents	9.9	7.1	5.7	5.0
All U.S. residents	12.6	9.2	9.4	9.1
All state white residents	9.9	6.0	5.5	5.3
All U.S. white residents	10.6	7.6	5.7	5.8
All state black residents	22.5	—	—	—
All U.S. black residents	22.2	18.0	14.1	14.4

Figures represent deaths per 1,000 live births of resident infants
under 1 year old, exclusive of fetal deaths. Figures for all
residents include members of other racial categories not listed
separately. The Census Bureau considers the post-1980 figures
for black residents to be too small to be statistically meaningful.
Source: U.S. Census Bureau, *Statistical Abstract of the United States,*
2006.

Abortion rates, 1990 and 2000

	1990	2000
Total abortions	4,000	3,000
Rate per 1,000 women	14.6	11.2
U.S. rate	25.7	21.3
Rank	34	34

Numbers of abortions are rounded to nearest thousand; ranks are
based on rates.
Source: U.S. Census Bureau.

Marriages and divorces, 2004

Total marriages	9,800
Rate per 1,000 population	7.6
National rate per 1,000 population	7.4
Rank among all states	20
Total divorces	5,000
Rate per 1,000 population	3.9
National rate per 1,000 population	3.7
Rank among all states	19

Figures are for all marriages and divorces performed within the
state, including those of nonresidents; totals are rounded to the
nearest hundred. Ranks are for highest to lowest figures; note
that divorce data are not available for five states.
Source: U.S. National Center for Health Statistics, *Vital Statistics of
the United States,* 2006.

Death rates by leading causes, 2002
Deaths per 100,000 resident population

Cause	State	U.S.
Heart disease	217.7	241.7
Cancer	198.3	193.2
Cerebrovascular diseases	49.2	56.4
Accidents other than motor vehicle	28.0	37.0
Motor vehicle accidents	9.8	15.7
Chronic lower respiratory diseases	45.3	43.3
Diabetes mellitus	24.4	25.4
HIV	n/a	4.9
Suicide	10.4	11.0
Homicide	n/a	6.1
All causes	772.8	847.3
Rank in overall death rate among states		40

Figures exclude nonresidents who died in the state. Causes of
death follow International Classification of Diseases. Rank is
from highest to lowest death rate in the United States.
Source: U.S. National Center for Health Statistics, *National Vital
Statistics Report,* 2006.

ECONOMY

Gross state product, 1990-2004
In current dollars

Year	State product	Nat'l product	State share
1990	$23.8 billion	$5.67 trillion	0.42%
2000	$43.6 billion	$9.75 trillion	0.45%
2002	$46.1 billion	$10.41 trillion	0.44%
2003	$48.2 billion	$10.92 trillion	0.44%
2004	$52.1 billion	$11.65 trillion	0.45%

Source: U.S. Bureau of Economic Analysis, *Survey of Current Business,* July, 2005.

Gross state product by industry, 2003
In billions of dollars

Construction	$2.2
Manufacturing	6.6
Wholesale trade	3.0
Retail trade	4.6
Finance & insurance	3.9
Information	1.5
Professional services	2.8
Health care & social assistance	3.5
Government	4.0
Total state product	$45.9
Total U.S. product	$10,289.2
State share of U.S. total	0.45%
Rank among all states	39

Total figures include industries not listed separately. Amounts are in chained 2000 dollars.

Source: U.S. Bureau of Economic Analysis, *Survey of Current Business,* July, 2005.

Personal income per capita, 1990-2004
In current dollars

	1990	2000	2004
Per capita income	$20,512	$33,396	$37,040
U.S. average	$19,477	$29,845	$32,937
Rank among states	11	6	6

Source: U.S. Bureau of Economic Analysis, *Survey of Current Business,* April, 2005.

Energy consumption, 2001
In trillions of British thermal units (BTU), except as noted

Total energy consumption

Total state energy consumption	322
Total U.S. energy consumption	96,275
State share of U.S. total	0.33%
Rank among states	45

Per capita consumption (In millions of BTU)

Total state per capita consumption	256
Total U.S. per capita consumption	338
Rank among states	42

End-use sectors

Residential	87
Commercial	65
Industrial	68
Transportation	102

Sources of energy

Petroleum	178
Natural gas	25
Coal	40
Hydroelectric power	10
Nuclear electric power	91

Figures for totals include categories not listed separately.
Source: U.S. Energy Information Administration, *State Energy Data Report,* 2001.

Nonfarm employment by sectors, 2004

Total	627,000
Construction	30,000
Manufacturing	80,000
Trade, transportation, utilities	140,000
Information	13,000
Finance, insurance, real estate	38,000
Professional & business services	57,000
Education & health services	95,000
Leisure, hospitality, arts, organizations	64,000
Other services, including repair & maintenance	21,000
Government	90,000

Figures are rounded to nearest thousand persons. "Total" includes mining and natural resources, not listed separately.
Source: U.S. Bureau of Labor Statistics, 2006.

Foreign exports, 1990-2004
In millions of dollars

Year	State	U.S.	State share
1990	973	394,045	0.25%
1996	1,481	624,767	0.24%
1997	1,597	688,896	0.23%
2000	2,373	712,055	0.30%
2003	1,931	724,006	0.29%
2004	2,286	769,332	0.30%

Rank among all states in 2004 42

U.S. total does not include U.S. dependencies.
Source: U.S. Census Bureau, *U.S. Merchandise Trade,* series FT 900, 2000; U.S. Census Bureau, *U.S. International Trade in Goods and Services,* Series FT 900, 2005.

LAND USE

Federally owned land, 2003
Areas in acres

	State	U.S.	State share
Total area	5,769,000	2,271,343,000	0.25%
Nonfederal land	4,939,000	1,599,584,000	0.31%
Federal land	830,000	671,759,000	0.12%
Federal share	14.4%	29.6%	—

Areas are rounded to nearest thousand acres. Figures for federally owned land do not include trust properties.
Source: U.S. General Services Administration, *Federal Real Property Profile,* 2006.

Land use, 1997
In acres, rounded to nearest thousand

Total surface area.	5,941,000
Total nonfederal rural land	4,353,000
Percentage rural land	73.3%
Cropland	134,000
Conservation Reserve Program (CRP*) land	(nil)
Pastureland.	94,000
Rangeland	(nil)
Forestland.	3,932,000
Other rural land	193,000

*CRP is a federal program begun in 1985 to assist private landowners to convert highly erodible cropland to vegetative cover for ten years. Note that some categories of land overlap.
Source: U.S. Department of Agriculture, Natural Resources and Conservation Service, and Iowa State University, Statistical Laboratory, S*ummary Report, 1997 National Resources Inventory,* revised December, 2000.

Farms and crop acreage, 2004

	State	U.S.	Share	Rank
Farms	3,000	2,113,000	0.14%	46
Acres (millions)	0.4*	937	0.00%	48
Acres per farm	132	443	—	45

Source: U.S. Department of Agriculture, National Agricultural Statistics Service. Numbers of farms are rounded to nearest thousand units; acreage figures are rounded to nearest million; *New Hampshire has fewer than 500,000 acres of farmland. Rankings, including ties, are based on rounded figures.

GOVERNMENT AND FINANCE

Units of local government, 2002

	State	Total U.S.	Rank
All local governments	559	87,525	42
Counties	10	3,034	45
Municipalities	13	19,429	48
Towns (townships)	221	16,504	18
School districts	167	13,506	28
Special districts	148	35,052	45

Only 48 states have county governments, 20 states have township governments ("towns" in New England, Minnesota, New York, and Wisconsin), and 46 states have school districts. Special districts encompass such functions as natural resources, fire protection, and housing and community development.
Source: U.S. Census Bureau, *Census of Governments.*

State government revenue, 2002

Total revenue. . . . . $4,636 mill.
General revenue . . . . $4,391 mill.
Per capita revenue $3,442
U.S. per capita average $3,689
Rank among states 50

Intergovernment revenue
Total . . . . $1,389 mill.
From federal government . . . . $1,189 mill.

Charges and miscellaneous
Total . . . . $1,104 mill.
Current charges . . . . $506 mill.
Misc. general income . . . . $598 mill.
Insurance trust revenue . . . . −$81 mill.

Taxes
Total . . . . $1,897 mill.
Per capita taxes $1,489
Rank among states 44
Property taxes . . . . $502 mill.
Sales taxes . . . . $605 mill.
License taxes . . . . $185 mill.
Individual income taxes. . . . . $71 mill.
Corporate income taxes . . . . $377 mill.
Other taxes . . . . $157 mill.

Total revenue figures include items not listed separately here.
Source: U.S. Bureau of the Census.

State government expenditures, 2002

General expenditures
Total state expenditures . . . . $4,823 mill.
Intergovernmental . . . . $1,179 mill.

Per capita expenditures
State $3,278
Average of all states $3,859
Rank among states 43

Selected direct expenditures
Education. . . . . $630 mill.
Public welfare . . . . $879 mill.
Health, hospital . . . . $162 mill.
Highways . . . . $347 mill.
Police protection . . . . $37 mill.
Corrections . . . . $80 mill.
Natural resources . . . . $40 mill.
Parks and recreation . . . . $5 mill.
Government administration. . . . . $187 mill.
Interest on debt . . . . $322 mill.
Total direct expenditures . . . . $2,998 mill.

Totals include items not listed separately.
Source: U.S. Census Bureau.

POLITICS

Governors since statehood
D = Democrat; R = Republican; O = other;
(r) resigned; (d) died in office; (i) removed from office

Meshech Weare 1776-1785
John Langdon 1785-1786
John Sullivan 1786-1788
John Langdon . . . . (r) 1788-1789
John Pickering 1789
John Sullivan 1789-1790
Josiah Bartlett 1790-1794
John T. Gilman (O) 1794-1805
John Langdon (O) 1805-1809
Jeremiah Smith (O) 1809-1810
John Langdon (O) 1810-1812
William Plumer (O) 1812-1813
John T. Gilman (O) 1813-1816
William Plumer (O) 1816-1819
Samuel Bell (O) 1819-1823
Levi Woodbury (O) 1823-1824
David L. Morril (O) 1824-1827
Benjamin Pierce (O) 1827-1828
John Bell (O) 1828-1829
Benjamin Pierce (O) 1829-1830
Matthew Harvey (O). . . . . (r) 1830-1831
Joseph M. Harper (O) 1831
Samuel Dinsmoor (O) 1831-1834
William Badger (D) 1834-1836
Isaac Hill (D) 1836-1839
John Page (D) 1839-1842
Henry Hubbard (D) 1842-1844
John H. Steele (D) 1844-1846

Anthony Colby (O) 1846-1847
Jared W. Williams (D) 1847-1849
Samuel Dinsmoor, Jr. (D) 1849-1852
Noah Martin (D). 1852-1854
Nathaniel B. Baker (D) 1854-1855
Ralph Metcalf (O) 1855-1857
William Haile (R) 1857-1859
Ichabod Goodwin (R) 1859-1861
Nathaniel S. Berry (R). 1861-1863
Joseph A. Gilmore (R) 1863-1865
Frederick Smith (R) 1865-1867
Walter Harriman (R) 1867-1869
Onslow Stearns (R) 1869-1871
James A. Weston (D). 1871-1872
Ezekiel A. Straw (R) 1872-1874
James A. Weston (D) 1874-1875
Person C. Cheney (R) 1875-1877
Benjamin F. Prescott (R) 1877-1879
Nathaniel Head (R) 1879-1881
Charles H. Bell (R) 1881-1883
Samuel W. Hale (R) 1883-1885
Moody Currier (R). 1885-1887
Charles H. Sawyer (R) 1887-1889
David H. Goodell (R) 1889-1891
Hiram A. Tuttle (R) 1891-1893
John B. Smith (R) 1893-1895
Charles A. Busiel (R) 1895-1897
George A. Ramsdell (R) 1897-1899
Frank W. Rollins (R). 1899-1901
Chester B. Jordan (R) 1901-1903
Nahum J. Bachelder (R) 1903-1905
John McLane (R) 1905-1907
Charles M. Floyd (R) 1907-1909
Henry B. Quimby (R) 1909-1911
Robert P. Bass (R) 1911-1913
Samuel D. Felker (D) 1913-1915
Rolland H. Spaulding (R) 1915-1917
Henry W. Keyes (R) 1917-1919
John H. Bartlett (R) 1919-1921
Albert O. Brown (R) 1921-1923
Fred H. Brown (D). 1923-1925
John G. Winant (R) 1925-1927
Huntley N. Spaulding (R) 1927-1929
Charles W. Tobey (R) 1929-1931
John G. Winant (R) 1931-1935
Henry Styles Bridges (R) 1935-1937
Francis P. Murphy (R) 1937-1941
Robert O. Blood (R). 1941-1945
Charles M. Dale (R) 1945-1949
Sherman Adams (R) 1949-1953
Hugh Gregg (R) 1953-1955
Lane Dwinell (R) 1955-1959
Wesley Powell (R) 1959-1963
John W. King (D) 1963-1969
Walter R. Peterson, Jr. (R) 1969-1973
Meldrim Thomson, Jr. (R) 1973-1979
Hugh J. Gallen (D) 1979-1982
Vesta Roy (R). 1982-1983
John H. Sununu (R) 1983-1989
Judd Gregg (R) 1989-1993
Steve Merrill (R) 1993-1997

(continued)

Jeanne Shaheen (D) 1997-2003
Craig Benson (R) 2003-2005
John Lynch (D) 2005-

Governors were called state presidents before 1792.

Composition of congressional delegations, 1989-2007

	Dem	Rep	Total
House of Representatives			
101st Congress, 1989			
State delegates	0	2	2
Total U.S.	259	174	433
102d Congress, 1991			
State delegates	1	1	2
Total U.S.	267	167	434
103d Congress, 1993			
State delegates	1	1	2
Total U.S.	258	176	434
104th Congress, 1995			
State delegates	0	2	2
Total U.S.	197	236	433
105th Congress, 1997			
State delegates	0	2	2
Total U.S.	206	228	434
106th Congress, 1999			
State delegates	0	2	2
Total U.S.	211	222	433
107th Congress, 2001			
State delegates	0	2	2
Total U.S.	211	221	432
108th Congress, 2003			
State delegates	0	2	2
Total U.S.	205	229	434
109th Congress, 2005			
State delegates	0	2	2
Total U.S.	202	231	433
110th Congress, 2007			
State delegates	2	0	2
Total U.S.	233	202	435
Senate			
101st Congress, 1989			
State delegates	0	2	2
Total U.S.	55	45	100
102d Congress, 1991			
State delegates	0	2	2
Total U.S.	56	44	100
103d Congress, 1993			
State delegates	0	2	2
Total U.S.	57	43	100
104th Congress, 1995			
State delegates	0	2	2
Total U.S.	46	53	99

	Dem	Rep	Total
105th Congress, 1997			
State delegates	0	2	2
Total U.S.	45	55	100
106th Congress, 1999			
State delegates	0	1	2
Total U.S.	45	54	99
107th Congress, 2001			
State delegates	0	2	2
Total U.S.	50	50	100
108th Congress, 2003			
State delegates	0	2	2
Total U.S.	48	51	99
109th Congress, 2005			
State delegates	0	2	2
Total U.S.	44	55	99
110th Congress, 2007			
State delegates	0	2	2
Total U.S.	49	49	98

Figures are for starts of first sessions. Totals are for Democrat (Dem.) and Republican (Rep.) members only. House membership totals under 435 and Senate totals under 100 reflect vacancies and seats held by independent party members. When the 110th Congress opened, the Senate's two independent members caucused with the Democrats, giving the Democrats control of the Senate.

Source: U.S. Congress, *Congressional Directory.*

Composition of state legislature, 1990-2006

	Democrats	Republicans
State House (398 seats)		
1990	125	268
1992	136	258
1994	112	286
1996	143	255
1998	154	244
2000	152	241
2002	119	281
2004	147	250
2006	239	161
State Senate (24 seats)		
1990	11	13
1992	11	13
1994	6	18
1996	9	15
1998	13	11
2000	12	12
2002	6	18
2004	8	16
2006	14	10

Figures for total seats may include independents and minor party members. Numbers reflect results of elections in listed years; elected members usually take their seats in the years that follow.

Source: Council of State Governments; *State Elective Officials and the Legislatures.*

Voter participation in presidential elections, 2000 and 2004

	2000	2004
Voting age population		
State	931,000	995,000
Total United States	209,831,000	220,377,000
State share of U.S. total	0.44	0.45
Rank among states	40	41
Portion of voting age population casting votes		
State	61.1%	68.2%
United States	50.3%	55.5%
Rank among states	7	4

Population figures are rounded to nearest thousand and include all residents, regardless of eligibility to vote.
Source: U.S. Census Bureau.

HEALTH AND MEDICAL CARE

Medical professionals
Physicians in 2003 and nurses in 2001

	U.S.	State
Physicians in 2003		
Total	774,849	3,392
Share of U.S. total		0.44%
Rate	266	263
Rank		16
Nurses in 2001		
Total	2,262,020	11,190
Share of U.S. total		0.49%
Rate	793	889
Rank		17

Rates are numbers of physicians and nurses per 100,000 resident population; ranks are based on rates.
Source: American Medical Association, *Physician Characteristics and Distribution in the U.S.*; U.S. Department of Health and Human Services, Health Resources and Services Administration.

Health insurance coverage, 2003

	State	U.S.
Total persons covered	1,133,000	243,320,000
Total persons not covered	131,000	44,961,000
Portion not covered	10.3%	15.6%
Rank among states	46	—
Children not covered	17,000	8,373,000
Portion not covered	5.5%	11.4%
Rank among states	48	—

Totals are rounded to nearest thousand. Ranks are from the highest to the lowest percentages of persons *not* insured.
Source: U.S. Census Bureau, Current Population Reports.

AIDS, syphilis, and tuberculosis cases, 2003

Disease	U.S. cases	State cases	Rank
AIDS	44,232	37	43
Syphilis	34,270	37	41
Tuberculosis	14,874	15	45

Source: U.S. Centers for Disease Control and Prevention.

Cigarette smoking, 2003
Residents over age 18 who smoke

	U.S.	State	Rank
All smokers	22.1%	21.2%	33
Male smokers	24.8%	22.4%	36
Female smokers	20.3%	20.2%	28

Cigarette smokers are defined as persons who reported having smoked at least 100 cigarettes during their lifetimes and who currently smoked at least occasionally.
Source: U.S. Centers for Disease Control and Prevention, *Morbidity and Mortality Weekly Report*, 53, no. 44 (November 12, 2004).

HOUSING

Home ownership rates, 1985-2004

	1985	1990	1995	2000	2004
State	65.5%	65.0%	66.0%	69.2%	73.3%
Total U.S.	63.9%	63.9%	64.7%	67.4%	69.0%
Rank among states	35	33	35	32	15

Net change in state home ownership rate,
1985-2004 . . . . +7.8%
Net change in U.S. home ownership rate,
1985-2004 . . . . +5.1%

Percentages represent the proportion of owner households to total occupied households.
Source: U.S. Census Bureau, 2006.

Home sales, 2000-2004
In thousands of units

Existing home sales	2000	2002	2003	2004
State sales	26.7	23.8	25.4	27.2
Total U.S. sales	5,171	5,631	6,183	6,784
State share of U.S. total	0.52%	0.42%	0.41%	0.40%
Sales rank among states	39	42	42	42

Units include single-family homes, condos, and co-ops.
Source: National Association of Realtors, Washington, D.C., *Real Estate Outlook: Market Trends & Insights.*

Values of owner-occupied homes, 2003

	State	U.S.
Total units	280,000	58,809,000
Value of units		
Under $100,000	9.3%	29.6%
$100,000-199,999	37.4%	36.9%
$200,000 or more	53.3%	33.5%
Median value	$208,403	$142,275
Rank among all states 7		

Units are owner-occupied one-family houses whose numbers are
    rounded to nearest thousand. Data are extrapolated from
    survey samples.
Source: U.S. Census Bureau, American Community Survey.

EDUCATION

Public school enrollment, 2002

Prekindergarten through grade 8
State enrollment 144,000
Total U.S. enrollment. 34,135,000
State share of U.S. total 0.42%

Grades 9 through 12
State enrollment. 64,000
Total U.S. enrollment. 14,067,000
State share of U.S. total 0.45%

Enrollment rates
State public school enrollment rate. 88.7%
Overall U.S. rate 90.4%
Rank among states in 2002. 33
Rank among states in 1995. 36

Enrollment figures (which include unclassified students) are
    rounded to nearest thousand pupils during fall school term.
    Enrollment rates are based on enumerated resident population
    estimate for July 1, 2002.
Source: U.S. National Center for Education Statistics.

Public college finances, 2003-2004

FTE enrollment in public institutions of higher education
Students in state institutions 30,500
Students in all U.S. public institutions 9,916,600
State share of U.S. total 0.31
Rank among states 46

**State and local government appropriations for higher
    education**
State appropriation per FTE $3,316
National average. $5,716
Rank among states 48
State & local tax revenue going to higher
    education 3.0%

FTE = full-time equivalent in public postsecondary programs,
    including summer sessions; student numbers are rounded to
    nearest hundred. Funding figures for 2003-2004 academic year
    include financial aid to students in state public institutions and
    exclude money for research, agriculture experiment stations,
    teaching hospitals, and medical schools; figures are rounded to
    nearest thousand dollars.
Source: Higher Education Executive Officers, Denver, Colorado.

TRANSPORTATION AND TRAVEL

Highway mileage, 2003

Interstate highways 235
Other freeways and expressways. 37
Arterial roads 1,609
Collector roads 2,789
Local roads. 10,960
Urban roads 3,036
Rural roads. 12,594
Total state mileage. 15,630
U.S. total 3,974,107
State share 0.39%
Rank among states 45

Note that combined urban and rural road mileage matches the
    total of the other categories.
Source: U.S. Federal Highway Administration.

Motor vehicle registrations and driver licenses, 2003

Vehicle registrations	State	U.S.	Share	Rank
Autos, trucks, buses	1,145,000	231,390,000	0.49%	40
Autos only	656,000	135,670	0.48%	38
Motorcycles	60,000	5,328,000	1.13%	28
Driver licenses	968,000	196,166,000	0.49%	39

Figures, which do not include vehicles owned by military services,
    are rounded to the nearest thousand. Figures for automobiles
    include taxis.
Source: U.S. Federal Highway Administration.

Domestic travel expenditures, 2003
Spending by U.S. residents on overnight trips and
day trips of at least 50 miles from home

Total expenditures within state . . . . $2.69 bill.
Total expenditures within U.S. . . . . $490.87 bill.
State share of U.S. total 0.5%
Rank among states 39

Source: Travel Industry Association of America.

Retail gasoline prices, 2003-2007
Average price per gallon at the pump

Year	U.S.	State
2003	$1.267	$1.267
2004	$1.316	$1.317
2005	$1.644	$1.617
2007	$2.298	$2.292

Excise tax per gallon in 2004 . . . . 19.5¢
Rank among all states in 2007 prices 24

Prices are averages of all grades of gasoline sold at the pump
during March months in 2003-2005 and during February, 2007.
Averages for 2006, during which prices rose higher, are not
available.
Source: U.S. Energy Information Agency, *Petroleum Marketing
Monthly* (2003-2005 data); American Automobile Association
(2007 data).

CRIME AND LAW ENFORCEMENT

State and local police officers, 2000-2004

	2000	2002	2004
Total officers			
U.S.	654,601	665,555	675,734
State	1,865	1,917	2,005*
*Net change, 2000-2004			+7.51%
Officers per 1,000 residents			
U.S.	2.33	2.31	2.30
State	1.51	1.50	1.54
State rank	48	50	49

Totals include state and local police and sheriffs.
Source: Carsey Institute, University of New Hampshire.

Crime rates, 2003
Incidents per 100,000 residents

Crimes	State	U.S.
Violent crimes		
Total incidents	149	475
Murder	1	6
Forcible rape	33	32
Robbery	37	142
Aggravated assault	77	295
Property crimes		
Total incidents	2,054	3,588
Burglary	354	741
Larceny/theft	1,552	2,415
Motor vehicle theft	149	433
All crimes	2,203	4,063

Source: U.S. Federal Bureau of Investigation, *Crime in the United
States,* annual.

State prison populations, 1980-2003

	State	U.S.	State share
1980	326	305,458	0.11%
1990	1,342	708,393	0.19%
1996	2,062	1,025,624	0.20%
2000	2,257	1,391,261	0.16%
2003	2,434	1,470,045	0.17%

State figures exclude prisoners in federal penitentiaries.
Source: U.S. Bureau of Justice Statistics, *Prisoners in 2003.*

New Jersey

Location: Atlantic coast

Area and rank: 7,419 square miles (19,215 square kilometers); 8,722 square miles (22,590 square kilometers) including water; forty-sixth largest state in area

Coastline: 130 miles (209 kilometers) on the Atlantic Ocean

Shoreline: 1,792 miles (2,884 kilometers)

Population and rank: 8,699,000 (2004); tenth largest state in population

Capital city: Trenton (85,403 people in 2000 census)

Largest city: Newark (273,546 people in 2000 census)

Nassau Hall, the administration building of Princeton University, which has long ranked as one of the finest institutions of higher learning in the entire United States. Built in 1756, Nassau Hall itself housed the first session of the New Jersey state legislature in 1776 and also served as the headquarters of the Continental Congress in 1783. (Robert Merkel)

Entered Union and rank:
December 18, 1787;
third state

**Present constitution
adopted:** 1947

Counties: 21

State name: New Jersey was
named after the Channel
Isle of Jersey

State nickname: Garden
State

Motto: Liberty and
prosperity

State flag: Buff field with state coat of arms

Highest point: High Point—1,803 feet (550 meters)

Lowest point: Atlantic Ocean—sea level

Highest recorded temperature: 110 degrees Fahrenheit (43 degrees Celsius)—Runyon, 1936

Lowest recorded temperature: –34 degrees Fahrenheit (–37 degrees Celsius)—River Vale,
1904

State song: (no official song; "Born to Run" and "Who Says You Can't Go Home" are both
associated with the state)

State tree: Red oak

State flower: Purple violet

State bird: Eastern goldfinch

State fish: Brook trout

State animal: Horse

New Jersey History

Situated on a relatively narrow strip of land between the Atlantic Ocean and the Delaware River, New Jersey has been one of the most densely populated areas of the nation since the early years of the United States. Bordering the large cities of New York City to the northeast and Philadelphia to the southwest, New Jersey was heavily urbanized and industrialized at an early date but still retains scenic seacoasts and wilderness areas.

Early History. About six thousand years ago, the Delaware, a Native American people also known as the Lenni Lenape, arrived in the region between the Hudson River and the Delaware River. The Delaware practiced agriculture, hunted, fished in the rivers, and gathered shellfish from the Atlantic Ocean. Not long after European colonists established settlements in the area, the Delaware, reduced greatly in numbers by newly introduced European diseases, sold their native lands and moved westward. By the middle of the nineteenth century, the Delaware were removed to Oklahoma, where many of their descendants reside today.

The first European to reach New Jersey was the Italian navigator Giovanni da Verrazano. Working for the French, Verrazano explored the Atlantic coast from North Carolina to Canada in 1524. During this voyage, Verrazano entered what is now Newark Bay. In 1609, the English navigator Henry Hudson, working for the Dutch, explored what is now Sandy Hook Bay.

Colonization. Despite this early exploration, settlement of the area began slowly. Although Dutch trading posts were founded on the Hudson River as early as 1618, and Swedish trading posts on the Delaware River by 1638, the first permanent European settlement was not founded until 1660. This settlement, known as Bergen, was founded by the Dutch at the present site of Jersey City. The Dutch, who had taken control of the Swedish trading posts in 1655, retained ownership of the colony until 1664, when an English fleet sailed into New York Harbor and took control of the Dutch colonies of New York and New Jersey without a fight.

King Charles II of England granted all the lands between the Connecticut River and the Delaware River, including New York and New Jersey, to his brother, the Duke of York and Albany. The duke (later King James II) in turn granted the region between the Hudson River and the Delaware River to John Berkeley and George Carteret, two friends and allies of the king. This area was divided into East Jersey and West Jersey in 1676, when Berkeley sold his share of the land to a group of Quakers. The Quakers took possession of West Jersey, while Carteret retained control of East Jersey.

East Jersey was mostly settled by Puritans from Long Island and New England. The Quakers purchased East Jersey in 1682. In 1702, English Queen Anne united the two colonies under royal rule and placed them under the administration of the governor of New York. In 1738, New Jersey became a separate colony from New York, with Lewis Morris serving as its first governor.

Revolution. Located between the two important colonial cities of New York City and Philadelphia, New Jersey soon became an important area of transportation, with more roads than any other colony. During the American Revolution (1775-1783), New Jersey's strategic position between these two vital cities led to more than one hundred battles in the area.

The British, who had captured New York City in late 1776, drove American troops commanded by General George Washington out of New York and New Jersey into Pennsylvania. Early on the morning of December 26, 1776, Washington crossed the Delaware River into New Jersey and captured Trenton. Although Trenton was recaptured by the British on January 2, 1777, Washington won another victory at Princeton the next day. These early successes, although not decisive, prevented the American war effort from failing during the early years of the Revolution. A later American victory on June 28, 1778, when Washington attacked British forces withdrawing from Philadelphia at Monmouth Court House, helped maintain a stalemate in the northern states, allowing the Revolution to continue until more critical victories in the southern states led to the end of the war.

After the war, Princeton served as the capital of the United States for brief periods in 1783 and 1784. New Jersey played a key role during the convention in Philadelphia in 1787 that created the U.S. Constitution. The New Jersey Plan, which advocated equal representation for each state, was combined with the Virginia Plan, which advocated representation based on population, to create the Senate and the House of Representatives. New Jersey ratified the Constitution on December 18, 1787, officially becoming the third state. It was the first state to ratify the first ten amendments to the Constitution, known as the Bill of Rights, on November 20, 1789.

Industry and Transportation. Although first noted in colonial days as a highly productive area for agriculture, hence the nickname of the "Garden State," New Jersey quickly became one of the first states to develop an industrial economy. The process began during the American Revolution, when New Jersey supplied much of the iron needed for cannons and ammunition. In

1791, Alexander Hamilton founded the nation's first industrial town at Paterson, located at the Great Falls of the Passaic River, which supplied water power.

Much of the success of industrial growth during the early nineteenth century was due to improvements in transportation. During the 1830's, a series of canals linked the Hudson River and the Delaware River, allowing easier transport of goods between New York City and Philadelphia. During the same period, railroads began to appear in the state. An early industry that developed in New Jersey due to the transportation revolution was the dyeing and weaving of cloth. The textile industry would remain important to the state's economy.

The Civil War and Immigration. Its central position between northern states and southern states, combined with economic ties to southern states, made New Jersey one of the most divided states during the Civil War (1861-1865). The Democratic Party in the state included many Peace Democrats, who advocated an end to the war through negotiation with the Confederacy. The Republican Party demanded complete victory over the Confederacy. This early struggle was reflected in later years, when the two parties continued to share almost equal power in the state. Although the military draft was strongly opposed in 1863, New Jersey supplied large numbers of troops and manufactured goods to the Union. After the war, many politicians opposed granting civil rights to African Americans, who were not allowed to vote in New Jersey until 1870.

Meanwhile, the first of many waves of immigration to the state brought many Germans and Irish to New Jersey during the 1840's. Immigrants during the late nineteenth century mostly arrived from southern and eastern Europe, particularly Italy, Russia, Poland, and Hungary. The increase in population, particularly in urban areas, combined with an increased demand for manufactured goods, continued the industrialization of the state. One of the largest factories in New Jersey was founded by Isaac M. Singer, who opened a sewing machine plant in Elizabeth in 1871. Other thriving industries at this time included oil refining along the Hudson River and pottery manufacturing in Trenton. Newark became one of the most prominent indus-

trial cities in the state, with a variety of manufacturers as well as an important insurance industry.

The Age of Wilson. New Jersey rose to prominence in national politics during the early years of the twentieth century. Woodrow Wilson, president of Princeton University since 1902, was elected governor in 1910. The success of his progressive policies led to his election as president of the United States in 1912. During his first term in office, Wilson was active in promoting legislation that reformed national economic policies. Reelected in 1916, Wilson helped to establish the League of Nations after World War I, winning him the Nobel Peace Prize in 1920.

In sharp contrast to Wilson's idealism, local politics in New Jersey were often highly corrupt. The most notorious of the state's political bosses was Frank Hague, who ruled Jersey City from 1917 to 1947. Hague was fa-

mous for his boast that "I am the law." Although reforms diminished the power of political bosses, New Jersey continued to have a reputation for political corruption and organized crime.

The Twentieth Century. World War I made New Jersey a center of shipbuilding and munitions manufacturing. The war also prevented German chemicals and pharmaceuticals from reaching the United States, and New Jersey became a leader in these industries. Chemical production continued to be the most important industry in the state. After the Great Depression of the 1930's, New Jersey's economy recovered during World War II, when aircraft manufacturing became a major industry in the state, along with a revival in the making of ships and armaments.

World War II also brought many African Americans to New Jersey. The 1950's and 1960's saw large numbers of Puerto Ricans enter the state. After Fidel Castro established a Communist government in Cuba in 1959, many Cubans immigrated to New Jersey. Later decades saw an increase in the number of immigrants from Asia and the Middle East.

After a recession during the 1970's and early 1980's, New Jersey's economy shifted from manufacturing to service industries. Unemployment dropped from 10 percent during the mid-1970's to 4 percent in 1988. Despite a strong economy during the 1990's, New Jersey faced the problems of crime, poverty, and pollution, which were inevitable for any heavily urbanized state.

Political Scandals. The political scene in New Jersey at the opening of the twenty-first century was marred by a succession of scandals. In 2002, following the September 11, 2001, terrorist attacks, furor arose when New Jersey's poet laureate, sixty-eight-year-old Amiri Baraka, issued poems insinuating that Israel was responsible for the attacks on the World Trade Center. Governor Jim McGreevey asked him to resign, but he refused. On July 1, 2003, however, the New Jersey legislature voted to abolish the post, effectively ending Baraka's tenure.

In 2002, Democrat Robert Torricelli dropped out of his race for reelection to the U.S. Senate after charges of financial improprieties surfaced, he was severely rebuked by the Senate Ethics Committee, and a poll showed him behind by 49-34 percent. To run in his place, Democrats prevailed upon retired U.S. senator Frank Lautenberg to campaign for the seat.

The following year, former mayor of Camden Milton Milan received a seven-year prison sentence for fraud committed while in public office. At the same time, the trial of former Newark mayor Kenneth Gibson on corruption charges ended in a hung jury.

In 2004, Governor McGreevy resigned. At a news conference on August 12, McGreevy, accompanied by his wife, announced that he is "a gay American" and would resign from office effective on November 15. Opponents tried to have the resignation effective earlier but were unsuccessful. Critics also claimed that his dramatic announcement was an attempt to deflect attention from the many scandals of his administration.

Anthrax Attacks and Power Outage. New Jersey also figured in the nation's struggle against terrorism. Beginning on September 18, 2001, a week after the terrorist attacks on the World Trade Center and the Pentagon, letters laced with deadly anthrax were mailed from New Jersey addresses to news media offices and the offices of two U.S. senators. In 2002, investigators found anthrax in a Princeton, New Jersey, mailbox, which might have been used to mail one or more of the anthrax letters. Some anthrax letters used New Jersey return addresses that were found to be fictitious. Although five per-

The Atlantic City Boardwalk at the end of the nineteenth century. (Library of Congress)

sons died from the attacks, none was from New Jersey.

New Jersey was also adversely affected by the Blackout of 2003. On August 14, 2003, a massive power outage caused by overloaded lines in Ohio hit New Jersey, seven other eastern states, and Ontario, Canada. Power was not restored until August 16.

General Elections. New Jersey gave Democrat Al Gore a substantial victory and fifteen electoral votes in the 2000 presidential election, allowing Gore to win the state by a 56-41 percent margin. In the same election, Democrat Jon Corzine, former head of famed Wall Street investment firm Goldman Sachs, was elected U.S. senator by the closer margin of 50-47 percent. After McGreevey resigned as governor in 2004, Corzine decided to run for the position. Without serious opposition, he won the June 7, 2005, Democratic primary election, spending more than $35 million of his own funds. In the general election held on November 8, Corzine defeated his Republican opponent by a 55-44 percent margin. Altogether, Corzine spent $62.9 million on his campaign, the most expensive political campaign in American history.

In the 2004 presidential election, the Democratic Party again claimed New Jersey's fifteen electoral votes, as John Kerry took the state by a 53-46 percent margin. At the same time, former senator Frank Lautenberg, called upon by his party to return to politics, once more won a seat in the U.S. Senate.

Rose Secrest
Updated by the Editor

The Statue of Liberty stands on an island claimed by both New York and New Jersey. (©Andrew Carter/Dreamstime.com)

New Jersey Time Line

1524	Explorer Giovanni da Verrazano, sailing for the French, reaches Newark Bay.
1609	English navigator Henry Hudson, working for the Dutch, reaches Sandy Hook Bay.
1618	Dutch trading posts are established on the Hudson River.
1638	Swedish trading posts are established on the Delaware River.
1655	Dutch take control of the Swedish trading posts.
1660	Dutch establish the first permanent European settlement at Bergen, at the modern site of Jersey City.
1664	English take control of New Jersey.
1676	New Jersey is divided into East Jersey and West Jersey, with Quakers purchasing West Jersey.
1682	Quakers purchase East Jersey.
1702	East Jersey and West Jersey are united under the control of English Queen Anne, who places them under the same administration as New York.
1738	Lewis Morris becomes the first governor of New Jersey after its administration is separated from that of New York.

(continued)

1746	Princeton University is founded.
1758	American Indians sell all New Jersey lands to the state; first Indian reservation in the Union is established in Burlington County.
1766	Queens College, later known as Rutgers University, is founded.
Dec. 26, 1776	American forces led by General George Washington capture Trenton during the Revolution.
Jan. 4, 1777	British recapture Trenton but are defeated by Washington at Princeton.
1778	Washington defeats British at Monmouth Court House.
1783-1784	Princeton serves briefly twice as the national capital.
Dec. 18, 1787	New Jersey ratifies the U.S. Constitution, becoming the third state.
1789	New Jersey becomes the first state to ratify the Bill of Rights.
1791	Alexander Hamilton establishes the nation's first industrial town at Paterson.
1830's	Canals and railroads improve transportation in the state.
1840's	German and Irish immigrants arrive.
1850	Population reaches 500,000.
1863	Opposition to the military draft in the Civil War breaks out.
1870	African Americans are allowed to vote.
1870	First boardwalk is erected in Atlantic City.
1873	Isaac M. Singer establishes a sewing machine factory in Elizabeth.
1876	Thomas Edison establishes a research laboratory in Menlo Park.
1880	Population reaches one million.
1890's	Immigrants arrive from southern and eastern Europe.
1910	Woodrow Wilson is elected governor.
Nov. 5, 1912	Wilson is elected president of the United States; is reelected in 1916.
1917	Political boss Frank Hague takes control of Jersey City.
1921	New York and New Jersey form the Port of New York Authority, operating transportation facilities near New York City in both states.
1940's	Large numbers of African Americans migrate to New Jersey.
1946	State takes control of Rutgers University, establishing the State University of New Jersey.
1947	New state constitution is adopted.
1950's-60's	Many Puerto Ricans and Cubans enter the state.
July, 1967	Four days of rioting take place in slums; twenty-three die.
1968	Amphitheater for drama, music, and dance opens at the Garden State Arts Center.
1970's	Economic recession leads to unemployment rate of 10 percent.
1976	Gambling is legalized in Atlantic City.
1978	Pinelands National Reserve, the nation's first national reserve, is established.
1988	Economic recovery reduces the unemployment rate to 4 percent.
1991	State prohibits ocean dumping after beaches become contaminated with medical waste.
1999	Severe drought leads to mandatory water rationing.
Sept., 2001	Anthrax-laced letters are mailed from New Jersey addresses as part of terrorist attacks.
Aug. 14-16, 2003	Blackout of 2003 hits New Jersey, seven other eastern states, and Ontario, Canada.
Aug. 12, 2004	Governor Jim McGreevey announces he has had a gay affair and will resign from office effective on November 15.
Nov. 8, 2005	Special election for governor is won by Senator Jon Corzine.

Notes for Further Study

Published Sources. Of the many books dealing with New Jersey, one of the best for students new to the subject is *New Jersey* (1998) by R. Conrad Stein, which discusses the state's geography, plant and animal life, history, economy, and people in a clear and concise manner. The ecology of one of the most unusual wilderness areas in the state is presented in detail in *Pine Barrens: Ecosystem and Landscape* (1998), edited by Richard T. T. Forman. A useful account of the foundations of the

state government is provided by *The New Jersey Constitution: A Reference Guide* (1997) by Robert F. Williams. More details on the state government can be found in *New Jersey Politics and Government: Suburban Politics Come of Age* (1998) by Barbara G. Salmore and Stephen A. Salmore.

The state's early history is detailed in *New Jersey: The History of New Jersey Colony, 1644-1776* (2004) by Roberta Wiener and James R. Arnold, as well as in *These Daring Disturbers of the Pub-*

lic Peace: The Struggle for Property and Power in Early New Jersey (2000) by Brendan McConville, who depicts the bitter conflicts that occurred over control of the land tenure system in the century before the American Revolution. Mark Di Ionno provides an extraordinary textual tour to American Revolution sites in New Jersey with *Guide to New Jersey's Revolutionary War Trail: For Families and History Buffs* (2000).

An excellent description of the many different ethnic groups in the state is provided in *Keys to Successful Immigration: Implications of the New Jersey Experience* (1997) by Thomas J. Espenshade. A book that supplies a dramatic account of the serious problem of race relations in New Jersey is *Our Town: Race, Housing, and the Soul of Suburbia* (1995) by David L. Kirp, John P. Dwyer, and Larry A. Rosenthal. Paul Mattingly also focuses on suburbanization by examining the way in which some New Jersey towns developed into thriving bedroom communities for New York City in *Suburban Landscapes: Culture and Politics in a New York Metropolitan Community* (2001). Using the city of Camden as a case study, Howard Gillette explores the process of deindustrialization and the interaction of politics, economic restructuring, and racial bias in *Camden After the Fall: Decline and Renewal in a Post-Industrial City* (2005).

An unusual guidebook, with a great deal of information on lesser-known attractions in the state, is provided in *Discover the Hidden New Jersey* (1995) by Russell Roberts. A lively history of New Jersey's most famous tourist attraction is found in Vicki Gold Levi's *Atlantic City: 125 Years of Ocean Madness* (1994).

Web Resources. A good starting point for exploring Internet resources dedicated to New Jersey is the state's official Web site (www.state.nj.us), which supplies general information and a guide to the state government. Other general Web sites include New Jersey Online (www.nj.com) and the *Asbury Park Press* (www.app.com/apps/pbcs.dll/frontpage). A guide

Harvesting cranberries, a major New Jersey crop. (Courtesy of New Jersey Commerce & Economic Growth Commission)

to tourism in the state is supplied by New Jersey Travel and Tourism (www.state.nj.us/travel/index.html). A detailed account of transportation in New Jersey, vital to the state's economy, is found at Welcome to NJ Transit's Web site (www.njtransit.state.nj.us). Detailed weather information is provided by Rutgers University at the Office of the NJ State Climatologist site (climate.rutgers.edu/stateclim/).

Of the many Web sites dedicated to New Jersey history, one of the best for a clear introduction to the subject is found at New Jersey History (www.state.nj.us/hangout/history.html).

Links to archives, museums, and other historical resources are provided by New Jersey Historical Commission (www.state.nj.us/state/history/hisidx.html). An excellent account of the vital role New Jersey played in the American Revolution is provided by New Jersey in the Revolution (www.doublegv.com/ggv/NJrev.html).

Counties

County	2000 pop.	Rank in pop.	Sq. miles	Rank in area
Atlantic	252,552	15	561.2	3
Bergen	884,118	1	234.2	15
Burlington	423,394	11	804.8	1
Camden	508,932	8	222.3	17
Cape May	102,326	20	255.2	14
Cumberland	146,438	16	489.3	5
Essex	793,633	2	126.3	19
Gloucester	254,673	14	324.9	11
Hudson	608,975	5	46.7	21
Hunterdon	121,989	18	430.1	8
Mercer	350,761	12	226.0	16
Middlesex	750,162	3	310.6	12
Monmouth	615,301	4	471.9	6
Morris	470,212	10	469.1	7
Ocean	510,916	7	636.3	2
Passaic	489,049	9	185.0	18
Salem	64,285	21	337.8	10
Somerset	297,490	13	304.7	13
Sussex	144,166	17	521.2	4
Union	522,541	6	103.3	20
Warren	102,437	19	357.9	9

Source: U.S. Census Bureau; National Association of Counties.

Cities

With 10,000 or more residents

Rank	City	Population	Rank	City	Population
1	Newark	273,546	18	New Brunswick	48,573
2	Jersey City	240,055	19	Plainfield	47,829
3	Paterson	149,222	20	Bloomfield	47,683
4	Elizabeth	120,568	21	Perth Amboy	47,303
5	Edison	97,687	22	East Brunswick	46,756
6	Toms River	86,327	23	West New York	45,768
7	Trenton (capital)	85,403	24	West Orange	44,943
8	Camden	79,904	25	Hackensack	42,677
9	Clifton	78,672	26	Atlantic City	40,517
10	East Orange	69,824	27	Kearny	40,513
11	Passaic	67,861	28	Sayreville	40,377
12	Union City	67,088	29	Linden	39,394
13	Bayonne	61,842	30	Teaneck	39,260
14	Irvington	60,695	31	Montclair	38,977
15	Vineland	56,271	32	Hoboken	38,577
16	Union	54,405	33	North Brunswick Township	36,287
17	Wayne	54,069	34	Lakewood	36,065

Rank	City	Population	Rank	City	Population
35	Belleville	35,928	94	North Arlington	15,181
36	Pennsauken	35,737	95	Phillipsburg	15,166
37	Ewing	35,707	96	Tinton Falls	15,053
38	Fort Lee	35,461	97	Fords	15,032
39	Orange	32,868	98	Clark	14,597
40	Fair Lawn	31,637	99	Springfield	14,429
41	Long Branch	31,340	100	Harrison	14,424
42	Garfield	29,786	101	Springdale	14,409
43	Westfield	29,644	102	Ramsey	14,351
44	Livingston	27,391	103	Collingswood	14,326
45	Nutley	27,362	104	Princeton	14,203
46	Millville	26,847	105	Eatontown	14,008
47	Rahway	26,500	106	Highland Park	13,999
48	Mercerville-Hamilton Square	26,419	107	Holiday City-Berkeley	13,884
49	West Milford	26,410	108	Moorestown-Lenola	13,860
50	Bergenfield	26,247	109	Tenafly	13,806
51	Englewood	26,203	110	Middlesex	13,717
52	Paramus	25,737	111	Verona	13,533
53	Ridgewood	24,936	112	Princeton Meadows	13,436
54	Lodi	23,971	113	Berkeley Heights	13,407
55	Maplewood	23,868	114	Roselle Park	13,281
56	Somerset	23,040	115	Fairview	13,255
57	Cliffside Park	23,007	116	Cherry Hill Mall	13,238
58	Old Bridge	22,833	117	Saddle Brook	13,155
59	Bridgeton	22,771	118	Ocean Acres	13,155
60	Scotch Plains	22,732	119	Ventnor City	12,910
61	Cranford	22,578	120	Ridgefield Park	12,873
62	South Plainfield	21,810	121	Metuchen	12,840
63	Hillside	21,747	122	Hammonton	12,604
64	Roselle	21,274	123	Brigantine	12,594
65	Summit	21,131	124	Succasunna-Kenvil	12,569
66	North Plainfield	21,103	125	West Freehold	12,498
67	Carteret	20,709	126	Oakland	12,466
68	Millburn	19,765	127	Somerville	12,423
69	Lyndhurst	19,383	128	Ringwood	12,396
70	Point Pleasant	19,306	129	Cedar Grove	12,300
71	Glassboro	19,068	130	New Providence	11,907
72	Pleasantville	19,012	131	Red Bank	11,844
73	Elmwood Park	18,925	132	Williamstown	11,812
74	Morristown	18,544	133	Hasbrouck Heights	11,662
75	Woodbridge	18,309	134	Haddonfield	11,659
76	Hawthorne	18,218	135	Pennsville	11,657
77	Dover	18,188	136	Somers Point	11,614
78	Rutherford	18,110	137	Wallington	11,583
79	Colonia	17,811	138	Glen Rock	11,546
80	Avenel	17,552	139	Greentree	11,536
81	Dumont	17,503	140	Gloucester City	11,484
82	Lindenwold	17,414	141	Bellmawr	11,262
83	Palisades Park	17,073	142	Browns Mills	11,257
84	South Orange	16,964	143	Morganville	11,255
85	Asbury Park	16,930	144	West Caldwell	11,233
86	Iselin	16,698	145	Leisure Village West-Pine Lake Park	11,085
87	Madison	16,530	146	Westwood	10,999
88	Wyckoff	16,508	147	West Paterson	10,987
89	New Milford	16,400	148	Freehold	10,976
90	Secaucus	15,931	149	River Edge	10,946
91	Hopatcong	15,888	150	Lincoln Park	10,930
92	Ocean City	15,378	151	Pine Hill	10,880
93	South River	15,322	152	Little Falls	10,855

(continued)

Rank	City	Population
153	Ridgefield	10,830
154	Guttenberg	10,807
155	Little Ferry	10,800
156	Keansburg	10,732
157	Barclay-Kingston	10,728
158	Pompton Lakes	10,640
159	Echelon	10,440
160	Franklin Lakes	10,422
161	Hackettstown	10,403
162	Beachwood	10,375

Rank	City	Population
163	Manville	10,343
164	Woodbury	10,307
165	Wanaque	10,266
166	Marlton	10,260
167	Bound Brook	10,155
168	Hillsdale	10,087

Population figures are from 2000 census.

Source: U.S. Bureau of the Census.

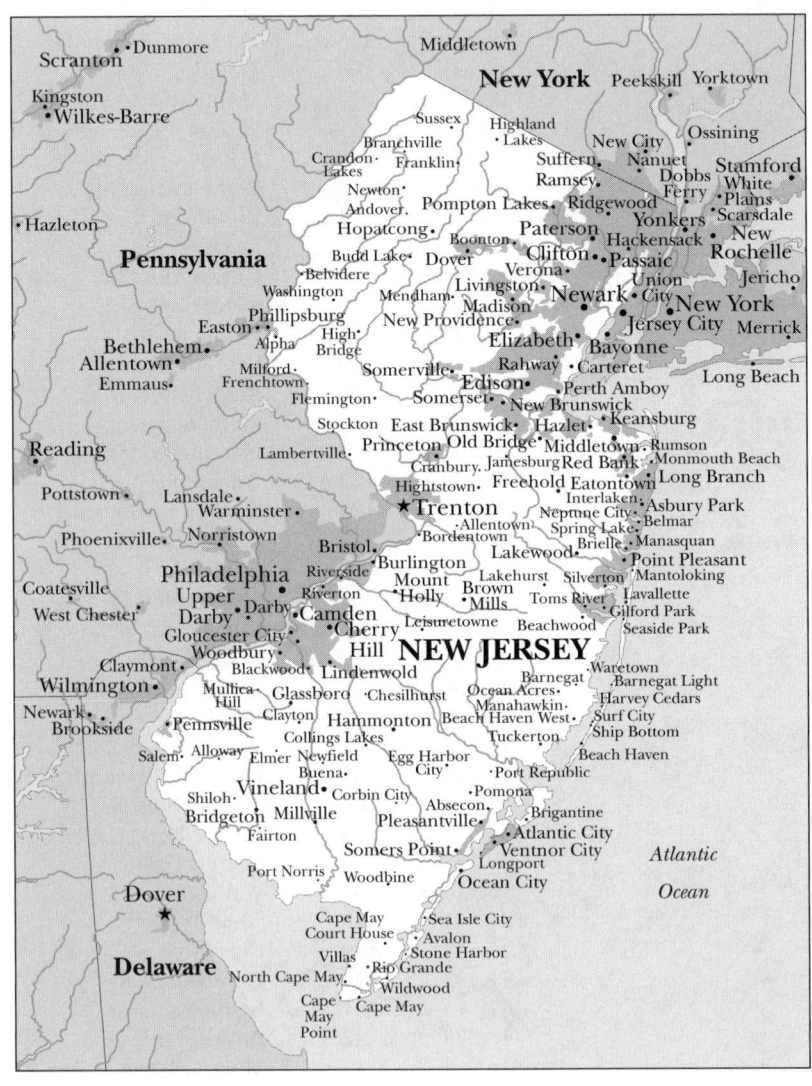

Index to Tables

DEMOGRAPHICS

Resident state and national populations, 1970-2004

Population figures given in thousands

	State pop.	U.S. pop.	Share	Rank
1970	7,171	203,302	3.5%	8
1980	7,365	226,546	3.3%	9
1985	7,566	237,924	3.2%	9
1990	7,748	248,765	3.1%	9
1995	8,083	262,761	3.0%	9
2000	8,414	281,425	3.0%	9
2004	8,699	293,655	3.0%	10

Source: U.S. Census Bureau, Current Population Reports, 2006.

Resident population by age, 2004

Age Group	Total persons
Under 5 years	581,000
5 to 17 years	1,575,000
18 to 24 years	744,000
25 to 34 years	1,095,000
35 to 44 years	1,416,000
45 to 54 years	1,275,000
55 to 64 years	886,000
65 to 74 years	543,000
75 to 84 years	420,000
85 years and older	163,000
All age groups	8,699,000

Portion of residents 65 and older	12.9%
National rank in portion of oldest residents	24
National average	12.4%

Population figures are rounded to nearest thousand persons;
    figures include armed forces personnel stationed in the state.
Source: U.S. Bureau of the Census, 2006.

Resident population by race, Hispanic origin, 2004

Category	State pop.	Share	U.S.
All residents	8,699	100.00%	100.00%
Non-Hispanic white	5,549	63.79%	67.37%
Hispanic white	1,141	13.12%	13.01%
Other Hispanic	153	1.76%	1.06%
African American	1,260	14.48%	12.77%
Native American	27	0.31%	0.96%
Asian, Pacific Islander	614	7.06%	4.37%
Two or more categories	108	1.24%	1.51%

Population figures are in thousands. Persons counted as
"Hispanic" (Latino) may be of any race. Because of overlapping
categories, categories may not add up to 100%. Shares in
column 3 are percentages of each category within the state;
these figures may be compared to the national percentages in
column 4.
Source: U.S. Bureau of the Census, 2006.

Projected state population, 2000-2030

Year	Population
2000	8,414,000
2005	8,745,000
2010	9,018,000
2015	9,256,000
2020	9,462,000
2025	9,637,000
2030	9,802,000
Population increase, 2000-2030	1,388,000
Percentage increase, 2000-2030	16.5

Projections are based on data from the 2000 census.
Source: U.S. Census Bureau.

VITAL STATISTICS

Infant mortality rates, 1980-2002

	1980	1990	2000	2002
All state residents	12.5	9.0	6.3	5.7
All U.S. residents	12.6	9.2	9.4	9.1
All state white residents	10.3	6.4	5.0	4.5
All U.S. white residents	10.6	7.6	5.7	5.8
All state black residents	21.9	18.4	13.6	12.8
All U.S. black residents	22.2	18.0	14.1	14.4

Figures represent deaths per 1,000 live births of resident infants
under 1 year old, exclusive of fetal deaths. Figures for all
residents include members of other racial categories not listed
separately.
Source: U.S. Census Bureau, *Statistical Abstract of the United States*,
2006.

Abortion rates, 1990 and 2000

	1990	2000
Total abortions	55,000	66,000
Rate per 1,000 women	30.4	36.3
U.S. rate	25.7	21.3
Rank	6	2

Numbers of abortions are rounded to nearest thousand; ranks are
based on rates.
Source: U.S. Census Bureau.

Marriages and divorces, 2004

Total marriages	50,100
Rate per 1,000 population.	5.8
National rate per 1,000 population	7.4
Rank among all states	46
Total divorces	26,000
Rate per 1,000 population.	3.0
National rate per 1,000 population	3.7
Rank among all states	35

Figures are for all marriages and divorces performed within the
state, including those of nonresidents; totals are rounded to the
nearest hundred. Ranks are for highest to lowest figures; note
that divorce data are not available for five states.
Source: U.S. National Center for Health Statistics, *Vital Statistics of
the United States*, 2006.

Death rates by leading causes, 2002
Deaths per 100,000 resident population

Cause	State	U.S.
Heart disease	262.0	241.7
Cancer	207.5	193.2
Cerebrovascular diseases	46.8	56.4
Accidents other than motor vehicle	30.3	37.0
Motor vehicle accidents	9.1	15.7
Chronic lower respiratory diseases	33.6	43.3
Diabetes mellitus	29.5	25.4
HIV	8.9	4.9
Suicide	6.4	11.0
Homicide	3.9	6.1
All causes	861.5	847.3
Rank in overall death rate among states		29

Figures exclude nonresidents who died in the state. Causes of
death follow International Classification of Diseases. Rank is
from highest to lowest death rate in the United States.
Source: U.S. National Center for Health Statistics, *National Vital
Statistics Report*, 2006.

ECONOMY

Gross state product, 1990-2004
In current dollars

Year	State product	Nat'l product	State share
1990	$214.8 billion	$5.67 trillion	3.79%
2000	$344.0 billion	$9.75 trillion	3.53%
2002	$377.8 billion	$10.41 trillion	3.63%
2003	$394.0 billion	$10.92 trillion	3.61%
2004	$415.9 billion	$11.65 trillion	3.57%

Source: U.S. Bureau of Economic Analysis, *Survey of Current Business,* July, 2005.

Gross state product by industry, 2003
In billions of dollars

Construction	$14.0
Manufacturing	43.3
Wholesale trade	32.0
Retail trade	27.5
Finance & insurance	32.5
Information	18.0
Professional services	30.3
Health care & social assistance	23.7
Government	35.4
Total state product	$371.8
Total U.S. product	$10,289.2
State share of U.S. total	3.61%
Rank among all states	8

Total figures include industries not listed separately. Amounts are in chained 2000 dollars.
Source: U.S. Bureau of Economic Analysis, *Survey of Current Business,* July, 2005.

Personal income per capita, 1990-2004
In current dollars

	1990	2000	2004
Per capita income	$24,572	$38,365	$41,332
U.S. average	$19,477	$29,845	$32,937
Rank among states	2	2	3

Source: U.S. Bureau of Economic Analysis, *Survey of Current Business,* April, 2005.

Energy consumption, 2001
In trillions of British thermal units (BTU), except as noted

Total energy consumption
Total state energy consumption	2,500
Total U.S. energy consumption	96,275
State share of U.S. total	2.60%
Rank among states	13

Per capita consumption (In millions of BTU)
Total state per capita consumption	294
Total U.S. per capita consumption	338
Rank among states	38

End-use sectors
Residential	573
Commercial	554
Industrial	491
Transportation	882

Sources of energy
Petroleum	1,246
Natural gas	586
Coal	112
Hydroelectric power	−1
Nuclear electric power	318

Figures for totals include categories not listed separately. The negative figure for hydroelectric power resulted from pumped storage for which more electricity was expended than created during peak demand periods.
Source: U.S. Energy Information Administration, *State Energy Data Report,* 2001.

Nonfarm employment by sectors, 2004

Total	4,002,000
Construction	166,000
Manufacturing	339,000
Trade, transportation, utilities	876,000
Information	99,000
Finance, insurance, real estate	278,000
Professional & business services	582,000
Education & health services	547,000
Leisure, hospitality, arts, organizations	327,000
Other services, including repair & maintenance	154,000
Government	634,000

Figures are rounded to nearest thousand persons. "Total" includes mining and natural resources, not listed separately.
Source: U.S. Bureau of Labor Statistics, 2006.

Foreign exports, 1990-2004
In millions of dollars

Year	State	U.S.	State share
1990	7,633	394,045	1.94%
1996	13,119	624,767	2.10%
1997	15,167	688,896	2.20%
2000	18,638	712,055	2.38%
2003	16,818	724,006	2.49%
2004	19,192	769,332	2.49%
Rank among all states in 2004 12			

U.S. total does not include U.S. dependencies.
Source: U.S. Census Bureau, *U.S. Merchandise Trade,* series FT 900, 2000; U.S. Census Bureau, *U.S. International Trade in Goods and Services,* Series FT 900, 2005.

LAND USE

Federally owned land, 2003
Areas in acres

	State	U.S.	State share
Total area	4,813,000	2,271,343,000	0.21%
Nonfederal land	4,633,000	1,599,584,000	0.29%
Federal land	180,000	671,759,000	0.03%
Federal share	3.7%	29.6%	—

Areas are rounded to nearest thousand acres. Figures for federally owned land do not include trust properties.
Source: U.S. General Services Administration, *Federal Real Property Profile,* 2006.

Land use, 1997
In acres, rounded to nearest thousand

Total surface area.	5,216,000
Total nonfederal rural land	2,766,000
Percentage rural land	53.0%
Cropland	589,000
Conservation Reserve Program (CRP*) land	1,000
Pastureland	111,000
Rangeland	(nil)
Forestland.	1,698,000
Other rural land	367,000

*CRP is a federal program begun in 1985 to assist private landowners to convert highly erodible cropland to vegetative cover for ten years. Note that some categories of land overlap.
Source: U.S. Department of Agriculture, Natural Resources and Conservation Service, and Iowa State University, Statistical Laboratory, S*ummary Report, 1997 National Resources Inventory,* revised December, 2000.

Farms and crop acreage, 2004

	State	U.S.	Share	Rank
Farms	10,000	2,113,000	0.47%	38
Acres (millions)	1	937	0.11%	41
Acres per farm	83	443	—	49

Source: U.S. Department of Agriculture, National Agricultural Statistics Service. Numbers of farms are rounded to nearest thousand units; acreage figures are rounded to nearest million. Rankings, including ties, are based on rounded figures.

GOVERNMENT AND FINANCE

Units of local government, 2002

	State	Total U.S.	Rank
All local governments	1,412	87,525	24
Counties	21	3,034	39
Municipalities	324	19,429	24
Townships	242	16,504	16
School districts	549	13,506	9
Special districts	276	35,052	39

Only 48 states have county governments, 20 states have township governments ("towns" in New England, Minnesota, New York, and Wisconsin), and 46 states have school districts. Special districts encompass such functions as natural resources, fire protection, and housing and community development.
Source: U.S. Census Bureau, *Census of Governments.*

State government revenue, 2002

Total revenue	$32,709 mill.
General revenue	$33,897 mill.
Per capita revenue	$3,952
U.S. per capita average	$3,689
Rank among states	16

Intergovernment revenue
Total	$8,677 mill.
From federal government	$8,235 mill.

Charges and miscellaneous
Total	$6,891 mill.
Current charges	$3,682 mill.
Misc. general income	$3,209 mill.
Insurance trust revenue	−$1,734 mill.

Taxes
Total	$18,329 mill.
Per capita taxes	$2,137
Rank among states	12
Property taxes	$3 mill.
Sales taxes	$8,777 mill.
License taxes	$957 mill.
Individual income taxes	$6,837 mill.
Corporate income taxes	$1,101 mill.
Other taxes	$653 mill.

Total revenue figures include items not listed separately here.
Source: U.S. Bureau of the Census.

State government expenditures, 2002

General expenditures

Total state expenditures	$41,988 mill.
Intergovernmental	$9,320 mill.

Per capita expenditures

State	$3,841
Average of all states	$3,859
Rank among states	27

Selected direct expenditures

Education	$4,558 mill.
Public welfare	$5,663 mill.
Health, hospital	$2,135 mill.
Highways	$1,977 mill.
Police protection	$343 mill.
Corrections	$1,139 mill.
Natural resources	$382 mill.
Parks and recreation	$506 mill.
Government administration	$1,346 mill.
Interest on debt	$1,199 mill.
Total direct expenditures	$23,616 mill.

Totals include items not listed separately.
Source: U.S. Census Bureau.

POLITICS

Governors since statehood

D = Democrat; R = Republican; O = other;
(r) resigned; (d) died in office; (i) removed from office;
(a) acting

William Livingston	(d) 1776-1790
Elisha Lawrence	1790
William Paterson (O)	(r) 1790-1793
Thomas Henderson (O)	1793
Richard Howell (O)	1793-1801
Joseph Bloomfield (O)	1801-1802
John Lambert (O)	1802-1803
Joseph Bloomfield (O)	(r) 1803-1812
Charles Clark (O)	1812
Aaron Ogden (O)	1812-1813
William S. Pennington (O)	(r) 1813-1815
William Kennedy (O)	1815
Mahlon Dickerson (O)	(r) 1815-1817
Isaac H. Williamson (O)	1817-1829
Peter D. Vroom (O)	1829-1832
Samuel L. Southard (O)	(r) 1832-1833
Elias P. Seeley (O)	1833
Peter D. Vroom (O)	1833-1836
Philemon Dickerson (D)	1836-1837
William Pennington (O)	1837-1843
Daniel Haines (D)	1843-1845
Charles C. Stratton (O)	1845-1848
Daniel Haines (D)	1848-1851
George F. Fort (D)	1851-1854
Rodman M. Price (D)	1854-1857

William A. Newell (R)	1857-1860
Charles S. Olden (R)	1860-1863
Joel Parker (D)	1863-1866
Marcus L. Ward (R)	1866-1869
Theodore F. Randolph (D)	1869-1872
Joel Parker (D)	1872-1875
Joseph D. Bedle (D)	1875-1878
George B. McClellan (D)	1878-1881
George C. Ludlow (D)	1881-1884
Leon Abbett (D)	1884-1887
Robert S. Green (D)	1887-1890
Leon Abbett (D)	1890-1893
George T. Werts (D)	1893-1896
John W. Griggs (R)	(r) 1896-1898
Foster M. Voorhees (R)	(r) 1898
David O. Watkins (R)	1898-1899
Foster M. Voorhees (R)	1899-1902
Franklin Murphy (R)	1902-1905
Edward C. Stokes (R)	1905-1908
John F. Fort (R)	1908-1911
Woodrow Wilson (D)	(r) 1911-1913
James F. Fielder (D)	(r) 1913
Leon R. Taylor (D)	1913-1914
James F. Fielder (D)	1914-1917
Walter E. Edge (R)	(r) 1917-1919
William N. Runyon (R)	1919-1920
Clarence E. Case (R)	1920
Edward I. Edwards (D)	1920-1923
George S. Silzer (D)	1923-1926
Arthur Harry Moore (D)	1926-1929
Morgan F. Larson (R)	1929-1932
Arthur Henry Moore (D)	(r) 1932-1935
Clifford R. Powell (D)	1935
Horace G. Prall (R)	1935
Harold G. Hoffman (R)	1935-1938
Arthur Henry Moore (D)	1938-1941
Charles Edison (D)	1941-1944
Walter E. Edge (R)	1944-1947
Alfred E. Driscoll (R)	1947-1954
Robert B. Meyner (D)	1954-1962
Richard J. Hughes (D)	1962-1970
William T. Cahill (D)	1970-1974
Brendan T. Byrne (D)	1974-1982
Thomas H. Kean (R)	1982-1990
James Florio (D)	1990-1994
Christine Todd Whitman (R)	(r) 1994-2001
Donald DiFrancesco (R)	(a) 2001-2002
John O. Bennett (R)	(a) 2002
Richard Codey (D)	(a) 2002
Jim McGreevey (D)	(r) 2002-2004
Richard Codey (D)	2004-2006
Jon Corzine (D)	2006-

Composition of congressional delegations, 1989-2007

	Dem	Rep	Total
House of Representatives			
101st Congress, 1989			
State delegates	8	6	14
Total U.S.	259	174	433
102d Congress, 1991			
State delegates	8	6	14
Total U.S.	267	167	434
103d Congress, 1993			
State delegates	7	6	13
Total U.S.	258	176	434
104th Congress, 1995			
State delegates	6	7	13
Total U.S.	197	236	433
105th Congress, 1997			
State delegates	6	7	13
Total U.S.	206	228	434
106th Congress, 1999			
State delegates	7	6	13
Total U.S.	211	222	433
107th Congress, 2001			
State delegates	7	6	13
Total U.S.	211	221	432
108th Congress, 2003			
State delegates	7	6	13
Total U.S.	205	229	434
109th Congress, 2005			
State delegates	7	6	13
Total U.S.	202	231	433
110th Congress, 2007			
State delegates	7	6	13
Total U.S.	233	202	435
Senate			
101st Congress, 1989			
State delegates	2	0	2
Total U.S.	55	45	100
102d Congress, 1991			
State delegates	2	0	2
Total U.S.	56	44	100
103d Congress, 1993			
State delegates	2	0	2
Total U.S.	57	43	100
104th Congress, 1995			
State delegates	2	0	2
Total U.S.	46	53	99
105th Congress, 1997			
State delegates	2	0	2
Total U.S.	45	55	100

	Dem	Rep	Total
106th Congress, 1999			
State delegates	2	0	2
Total U.S.	45	54	99
107th Congress, 2001			
State delegates	2	0	2
Total U.S.	50	50	100
108th Congress, 2003			
State delegates	2	0	2
Total U.S.	48	51	99
109th Congress, 2005			
State delegates	2	0	2
Total U.S.	44	55	99
110th Congress, 2007			
State delegates	2	0	2
Total U.S.	49	49	98

Figures are for starts of first sessions. Totals are for Democrat (Dem.) and Republican (Rep.) members only. House membership totals under 435 and Senate totals under 100 reflect vacancies and seats held by independent party members. When the 110th Congress opened, the Senate's two independent members caucused with the Democrats, giving the Democrats control of the Senate.

Source: U.S. Congress, *Congressional Directory.*

Composition of state legislature, 1990-2006

	Democrats	Republicans
State Assembly (80 seats)		
1990	22	58
1992	27	53
1994	28	52
1996	30	50
1998	32	48
2000	35	45
2002	47	33
2004	47	33
2006	49	31
State Senate (40 seats)		
1990	13	27
1992	16	24
1994	16	24
1996	16	24
1998	16	24
2000	16	24
2002	22	18
2004	22	18
2006	22	18

Figures for total seats may include independents and minor party members. Numbers reflect results of elections in listed years; elected members usually take their seats in the years that follow.

Source: Council of State Governments; *State Elective Officials and the Legislatures.*

Voter participation in presidential elections, 2000 and 2004

	2000	2004
Voting age population		
State	6,342,000	6,543,000
Total United States	209,831,000	220,377,000
State share of U.S. total	3.02	2.97
Rank among states	9	9
Portion of voting age population casting votes		
State	50.3%	55.2%
United States	50.3%	55.5%
Rank among states	32	32

Population figures are rounded to nearest thousand and include all residents, regardless of eligibility to vote.
Source: U.S. Census Bureau.

HEALTH AND MEDICAL CARE

Medical professionals
Physicians in 2003 and nurses in 2001

	U.S.	State
Physicians in 2003		
Total	774,849	26,804
Share of U.S. total		3.44%
Rate	266	310
Rank		7
Nurses in 2001		
Total	2,262,020	71,500
Share of U.S. total		3.16%
Rate	793	840
Rank		24

Rates are numbers of physicians and nurses per 100,000 resident population; ranks are based on rates.
Source: American Medical Association, *Physician Characteristics and Distribution in the U.S.*; U.S. Department of Health and Human Services, Health Resources and Services Administration.

Health insurance coverage, 2003

	State	U.S.
Total persons covered	7,378,000	243,320,000
Total persons not covered	1,201,000	44,961,000
Portion not covered	14.0%	15.6%
Rank among states	26	—
Children not covered	237,000	8,373,000
Portion not covered	11.0%	11.4%
Rank among states	18	—

Totals are rounded to nearest thousand. Ranks are from the highest to the lowest percentages of persons *not* insured.
Source: U.S. Census Bureau, Current Population Reports.

AIDS, syphilis, and tuberculosis cases, 2003

Disease	U.S. cases	State cases	Rank
AIDS	44,232	1,514	9
Syphilis	34,270	1,089	9
Tuberculosis	14,874	495	7

Source: U.S. Centers for Disease Control and Prevention.

Cigarette smoking, 2003
Residents over age 18 who smoke

	U.S.	State	Rank
All smokers	22.1%	19.5%	42
Male smokers	24.8%	21.2%	39
Female smokers	20.3%	17.9%	43

Cigarette smokers are defined as persons who reported having smoked at least 100 cigarettes during their lifetimes and who currently smoked at least occasionally.
Source: U.S. Centers for Disease Control and Prevention, *Morbidity and Mortality Weekly Report*, 53, no. 44 (November 12, 2004).

HOUSING

Home ownership rates, 1985-2004

	1985	1990	1995	2000	2004
State	62.3%	65.0%	64.9%	66.2%	68.8%
Total U.S.	63.9%	63.9%	64.7%	67.4%	69.0%
Rank among states	40	33	38	41	39

Net change in state home ownership rate, 1985-2004 . . . . . . +6.5%
Net change in U.S. home ownership rate, 1985-2004 . . . . . . +5.1%

Percentages represent the proportion of owner households to total occupied households.
Source: U.S. Census Bureau, 2006.

Home sales, 2000-2004
In thousands of units

Existing home sales	2000	2002	2003	2004
State sales	160.8	166.8	174.3	188.7
Total U.S. sales	5,171	5,631	6,183	6,784
State share of U.S. total	3.11%	2.96%	2.82%	2.78%
Sales rank among states	9	10	9	11

Units include single-family homes, condos, and co-ops.
Source: National Association of Realtors, Washington, D.C., *Real Estate Outlook: Market Trends & Insights.*

Values of owner-occupied homes, 2003

	State	U.S.
Total units	1,795,000	58,809,000
Value of units		
Under $100,000	8.1%	29.6%
$100,000-199,999	28.4%	36.9%
$200,000 or more	63.5%	33.5%
Median value	$245,573	$142,275
Rank among all states 4		

Units are owner-occupied one-family houses whose numbers are rounded to nearest thousand. Data are extrapolated from survey samples.
Source: U.S. Census Bureau, American Community Survey.

EDUCATION

Public school enrollment, 2002

Prekindergarten through grade 8
State enrollment 979,000
Total U.S. enrollment. 34,135,000
State share of U.S. total 2.87%

Grades 9 through 12
State enrollment 389,000
Total U.S. enrollment. 14,067,000
State share of U.S. total 2.77%

Enrollment rates
State public school enrollment rate. 87.9%
Overall U.S. rate 90.4%
Rank among states in 2002. 38
Rank among states in 1995. 49

Enrollment figures (which include unclassified students) are rounded to nearest thousand pupils during fall school term. Enrollment rates are based on enumerated resident population estimate for July 1, 2002.
Source: U.S. National Center for Education Statistics.

Public college finances, 2003-2004

FTE enrollment in public institutions of higher education
Students in state institutions. 195,500
Students in all U.S. public institutions 9,916,600
State share of U.S. total 1.97
Rank among states 16

State and local government appropriations for higher education
State appropriation per FTE $8,326
National average. $5,716
Rank among states. 5
State & local tax revenue going to higher education 5.7%

FTE = full-time equivalent in public postsecondary programs, including summer sessions; student numbers are rounded to nearest hundred. Funding figures for 2003-2004 academic year include financial aid to students in state public institutions and exclude money for research, agriculture experiment stations, teaching hospitals, and medical schools; figures are rounded to nearest thousand dollars.
Source: Higher Education Executive Officers, Denver, Colorado.

TRANSPORTATION AND TRAVEL

Highway mileage, 2003

Interstate highways	431
Other freeways and expressways	402
Arterial roads	5,538
Collector roads	3,839
Local roads.	28,742
Urban roads	31,541
Rural roads	7,411
Total state mileage.	38,952
U.S. total	3,974,107
State share	0.98%
Rank among states	37

Note that combined urban and rural road mileage matches the total of the other categories.
Source: U.S. Federal Highway Administration.

Motor vehicle registrations and driver licenses, 2003

Vehicle registrations	State	U.S.	Share	Rank
Autos, trucks, buses	6,712,000	231,390,000	2.90%	10
Autos only	4,449,000	135,670	3.28%	9
Motorcycles	140,000	5,328,000	2.63%	14
Driver licenses	5,729,000	196,166,000	2.92%	11

Figures, which do not include vehicles owned by military services, are rounded to the nearest thousand. Figures for automobiles include taxis.
Source: U.S. Federal Highway Administration.

Domestic travel expenditures, 2003
Spending by U.S. residents on overnight trips and
day trips of at least 50 miles from home

Total expenditures within state . . . . $14.73 bill.
Total expenditures within U.S. . . . . $490.87 bill.
State share of U.S. total 3.0%
Rank among states 8

Source: Travel Industry Association of America.

Retail gasoline prices, 2003-2007
Average price per gallon at the pump

Year	U.S.	State
2003	$1.267	$1.270
2004	$1.316	$1.335
2005	$1.644	$1.586
2007	$2.298	$2.148

Excise tax per gallon in 2004 . . . . 10.5¢
Rank among all states in 2007 prices 44

Prices are averages of all grades of gasoline sold at the pump
during March months in 2003-2005 and during February, 2007.
Averages for 2006, during which prices rose higher, are not
available.
Source: U.S. Energy Information Agency, *Petroleum Marketing
Monthly* (2003-2005 data); American Automobile Association
(2007 data).

CRIME AND LAW ENFORCEMENT

State and local police officers, 2000-2004

	2000	2002	2004
Total officers			
U.S.	654,601	665,555	675,734
State	30,166	30,483	31,313*
*Net change, 2000-2004			+3.80%
Officers per 1,000 residents			
U.S.	2.33	2.31	2.30
State	3.59	3.55	3.60
State rank	2	2	2

Totals include state and local police and sheriffs.
Source: Carsey Institute, University of New Hampshire.

Crime rates, 2003
Incidents per 100,000 residents

Crimes	State	U.S.
Violent crimes		
Total incidents	366	475
Murder	5	6
Forcible rape	15	32
Robbery	155	142
Aggravated assault	191	295
Property crimes		
Total incidents	2,544	3,588
Burglary	503	741
Larceny/theft	1,641	2,415
Motor vehicle theft	400	433
All crimes	2,910	4,063

Source: U.S. Federal Bureau of Investigation, *Crime in the United
States,* annual.

State prison populations, 1980-2003

	State	U.S.	State share
1980	5,884	305,458	1.93%
1990	21,128	708,393	2.98%
1996	27,490	1,025,624	2.68%
2000	29,784	1,391,261	2.14%
2003	27,246	1,470,045	1.85%

State figures exclude prisoners in federal penitentiaries.
Source: U.S. Bureau of Justice Statistics, *Prisoners in 2003.*

New Mexico

Location: Southwest

Area and rank: 121,365 square miles (314,334 square kilometers); 121,598 square miles (314,939 square kilometers) including water; fifth largest state in area

Coastline: none

Population and rank: 1,903,000 (2004); thirty-sixth largest state in population

Capital city: Santa Fe (62,203 people in 2000 census)

Largest city: Albuquerque (448,607 people in 2000 census)

Became territory: September 9, 1850

Entered Union and rank: January 6, 1912; forty-seventh state

Known as the Roundhouse, New Mexico's state capitol in Santa Fe is built in the form of a circle with four rectangular wings projecting from the center. Viewed from above, the structure has the appearance of the Zia sun symbol, which is also depicted on the state flag.

Present constitution adopted: 1911

Counties: 33

State name: New Mexico is named after neighboring Mexico

State nicknames: Land of Enchantment; Sunshine State

Motto: *Crescit eundo* (It grows as it goes)

State flag: Yellow field with red circle with four rays emanating from it

Highest point: Wheeler Peak—13,161 feet (4,011 meters)

Lowest point: Red Bluff Reservoir—2,842 feet (866 meters)

Highest recorded temperature: 116 degrees Fahrenheit (47 degrees Celsius)—Orogrande, 1936

Lowest recorded temperature: –50 degrees Fahrenheit (–46 degrees Celsius)—Gavilan, 1951

State song: "O Fair New Mexico" (English); "Asi Es Nuevo Méjico" (Spanish)

State tree: Pinon

State flower: Yucca flower

State bird: Roadrunner

State fish: Cutthroat trout

State animal: Black bear

National parks: Carlsbad Caverns

New Mexico History

New Mexico's arid climate and southwestern geographical position have deeply influenced its history. It is nicknamed the "Land of Enchantment." Its high altitudes, clear air, and colorful mountains and deserts attract artists and tourists alike. Its lack of water, however, makes large-scale settlement difficult, and its proximity to Mexico has long been a factor in making its culture a Spanish-American hybrid. Added to these ingredients, the state's large American Indian population and late—1912—entry to statehood give New Mexico a unique flavor.

Early History. American Indians have lived in New Mexico for perhaps twenty-five thousand years. Evidence shows that they hunted in northeastern New Mexico about ten thousand years ago. Later, the Mogollons settled near the modern Arizona border, eventually building villages. The Anasazis, another ancient people, lived in "Four Corners," where Colorado, Arizona, New Mexico, and Utah meet, and created one of the most developed civilizations of the time. The Pueblo Indians are descendants of the Anasazis. In about 1500 B.C.E. the Navaho and Apache Indians arrived; Ute and Comanche tribes arrived shortly afterward.

Exploration. The Spanish conquistador Hernán Cortés invaded Mexico in 1519. Nine years later, another Spaniard, explorer Alvar Núñez Cabeza de Vaca, became shipwrecked off the Texas coast. When he finally made it to Mexico City in 1536, his reports of large wealthy cities sparked interest in further exploration. In early 1539, Franciscan friar Marcos de Niza set out exploring and within a year returned with tales of golden cities larger than Mexico City.

Spanish authorities chose Franciso de Coronado, then twenty-nine, to explore the region. He set out in 1540 with more than 1,600 men but in two years had found no opulent cities. His travels did increase Spain's geographical knowledge of the region, however, and profoundly influenced the future.

After later expeditions, the Spanish finally decided

With hundreds of fine Pueblo ruins such as this, New Mexico has one of the richest collections of major archaeological sites in North America. (PhotoDisc)

in 1598 to found a colony in the region, with the capital at San Juan de los Caballeros, near the Chama River. In 1609, the capital was moved to Santa Fe ("holy faith"). The Spanish treated the American Indians harshly. Missionaries made inroads into their traditional culture, while secular rulers set up a system of forced labor tantamount to slavery. A revolt in1680 left hundreds of Spaniards killed; the remainder fled. Twelve years later the Spanish reconquered the region, and for the next 125 years, the two sides lived in relative peace.

After 1821, however, Mexico gained its independence from Spain. Traders and trappers had been making uninvited forays into the New Mexico area, but now, with the suspicious Spanish gone, they were welcome. Also in 1821 American trader William Becknell established the Santa Fe Trail, over which millions of dollars of goods would travel until it was replaced by transcontinental railroads. New Mexico's Indians and the Mexicans themselves rebelled against the government in 1837 but were crushed. In 1841, Texas, which had become an independent republic, invaded the region, but that attempt also failed.

Matters changed again, this time decisively, after the United States and Mexico went to war in 1846. Troops led by General Stephen W. Kearny occupied New Mexico with little difficulty. After American victory in 1848, New Mexico, along with a huge swathe of territory that included much of California, Colorado, Utah, Nevada, and Arizona, came under American rule. The stage was set for the future state to emerge.

Becoming a Territory. It took sixty-four years for New Mexico to join the American Union as a separate and equal state. Much conflict and agonizing over statehood lay ahead. First, in 1850, New Mexico, which then included Arizona, was organized into a territory. In 1853, the Gadsden Purchase added new land on the southern border. Yet statehood was little more than a dream. The region had too few inhabitants—about sixty thousand in 1850—to become part of the Union. And, while in time thousands of Americans came to live there, the territory's Mexican character drew hostility from certain forces in Congress. The fact that most inhabitants were Roman Catholic added to the distrust of the suspicious East.

Moreover, New Mexico, along with Arizona and other western regions, was a violent place, plagued with serious American Indian problems and often equally serious Anglo-American problems, in the form of range wars and general lawlessness. From the 1850's to the 1880's, when the last dangerous American Indian menace succumbed to peace and outlaws such as Billy the Kid were laid to rest, New Mexico was truly the Wild West.

Civil War. The territory experienced the Civil War in 1862, when an army of Texas Confederates commanded by General Henry J. Sibley invaded from the east. Sibley defeated a Union force at Valverde, more than one hundred miles south of Albuquerque on the east side of the Rio Grande, and advanced north toward Santa Fe and Albuquerque. His army was then to head north to Colorado and its gold regions around Pike's Peak and Denver. They never made it, however, because when they reached Glorietta Pass and Apache Canyon, near Santa Fe, Union soldiers turned them back in a battle sometimes called "the Gettysburg of the West."

Conflict. In 1863, Congress organized the territories of Arizona and Colorado, in the process reducing the size of New Mexico. After the Civil War ended in 1865, cattle ranchers, sheepherders, and others flocked to the state in search of prosperity or adventure. Affairs were hardly fit for the pursuit of wealth, however, since conflicts broke out repeatedly among settlers. Some of the worst of the hostilities came during the late 1870's in a county southeast of Albuquerque. The Lincoln County War saw cattlemen and others battling for political control. In this "war" Billy the Kid, a teenage bandit who survived only until age twenty-one, murdered twenty-one men before being shot by Sheriff Pat Garrett. To end the bloodshed, in 1878 the territorial governor pardoned the fighters. The next decade other territorial governors helped establish order.

Establishing peace between settlers and American Indians, however, was another matter. Apache chief Victorio led many murderous raids against his enemies until his death in 1880. Control was passed to Geronimo, last of the warring Apache warrior chiefs. Geronimo surrendered repeatedly, only to escape and regroup his army. In September, 1886, he finally surrendered after receiving personal assurances of safety from President Grover Cleveland. Geronimo lived on to convert to Christianity and participate in President Theodore Roosevelt's inauguration in 1905.

New Mexico Economy. With peace established, economic progress could proceed. Without American In-

dian depredations, cattle ranching prospered. Mineral wealth had been discovered and would continue to be discovered well into the next century. Between 1880 and 1890 the population swelled by more than one-third, to just more than 160,000. By 1910, though New Mexico was still not a state, the population had more than doubled again, to 325,000.

As in much of the West, the advent of the transcontinental railroad changed life in New Mexico. When the first train entered in 1878, products such as cattle could be easily and cheaply transported east. The territory experienced a boom in cattle and mining products. New Mexico's economy, however, was handicapped by a lack of water; annual rainfall is less than ten inches. Sheriff Pat Garrett inaugurated far-reaching irrigation projects.

Statehood. New Mexicans desired statehood, but by 1901 this goal had not been accomplished, despite many attempts. Congress feared allowing a seemingly foreign territory to gain precious votes in the Senate. The territory appeared too Mexican for full membership. The Spanish-American War (1898) allowed the

J. Robert Oppenheimer (wearing wide-brimmed light hat) with military and government officials examining the rubble at "ground zero" left by the first atomic bomb blast at Trinity, New Mexico, some time after the actual test. (Courtesy, U.S. Department of Energy)

territory to demonstrate its loyalty. Lieutenant Colonel Theodore Roosevelt recruited many of his Rough Riders in New Mexico, and they proved their trustworthiness. Finally, in 1910 Congress passed a statehood bill, and two years later New Mexico entered the Union.

The state constitution, adopted in 1911, is considered conservative in comparison to other western states, since it omits the initiative, referendum, and recall, which allot extra powers to the electorate. Instead, all legislative power lies in the bicameral legislature. Along with a governor, a lieutenant governor, and five other executive officers, officials are elected to four-year terms. They may hold office for no more than two successive terms. Members of the upper house serve four-year terms; lower-house members serve two-year terms. Provisions guaranteeing voting rights and education for Spanish-speaking people can be changed only by the support of three-fourths of the legislature and three-fourths of the electorate.

Two World Wars. The state was soon called upon again for military service, and its soldiers fought in World Wars I and II. The postwar period proved problematic, however, as a long drought wreaked havoc with the state's economy. Livestock prices sank, ranchers went bankrupt, and banks collapsed. Providentially, however, new mineral wealth was discovered, and new businesses appeared. When Carlsbad Caverns became a national park in 1930, a focal point for tourism was born. Water projects begun during the 1920's eventually brought significant acreage under cultivation. While there was limited capacity for these supplies to be increased, New Deal projects during the Depression continued making inroads into this chronic problem.

Like neighboring states, New Mexico's economy gained considerably during World War II, when federal spending increased dramatically. A secret project begun at Los Alamos turned out to be development of the world's first atomic bombs. The first atomic explosion lighted up the New Mexico desert at Trinity, near Alamogordo, in 1945.

Postindustrial Society. Mexico's postwar economy grew on the strength of federal spending, especially for defense. Key areas were research on the military, peacetime uses of nuclear power, and experiments with rockets. This effort was assisted when uranium was discovered in the state in 1950. During the 1960's, coal production rose markedly; the state's power supply is generated primarily from coal burning.

New Mexico's economy and society dramatically changed with its passage from an industrial to a postindustrial and high-tech economy, with service industries far outweighing manufacturing, construction, agriculture, and mining in both income produced (70 percent) and number of employees (81 percent). During the 1990's, the state ranked among the nation's leaders in nuclear and space research.

Suspected Espionage. A sensational and complex case of suspected espionage began roiling New Mexico and the nation in December, 1999, when Wen Ho Lee, a Taiwanese American working at the Los Alamos National Laboratory as a scientist, was arrested. American intelligence had found that China had a copy of an American atomic bomb design. Investigators locked their attention on Lee, since he had access to the information, was of Chinese ethnicity, and had met with fellow scientists at professional meetings in China. After losing his security clearance, he was able to place classified data on a network that had been accessed more than forty times from the Student Union of the University of California at Berkeley.

After his arrest, Lee spent 278 days in solitary confinement until he agreed to plead guilty to one felony count of improperly downloading restricted data. Lee then accused the federal government and news organizations of violating his privacy. He was never charged with or convicted of espionage. He claimed that his Chinese ethnicity was the reason the government investigated and punished him. Others, he said, who had illegally downloaded data were not fired and charged. In the end, in June, 2006, the federal government and several news organizations agreed to pay him $1.6 million in damages for violation of his privacy by government leaks. Reporters were held in contempt of court for refusing to name the source of the leaks.

Wildfires. Like other Western states around the beginning of the twenty-first century, New Mexico experienced destructive wildfires. One such fire that occurred in 2000, however, was especially devastating. The Cerro Grande fire burned forty-eight thousand acres, more than eighty square miles, from May 4 until July 20. At the time, the fire was the largest and most destructive in the state's history. Having its origin in a controlled burn by the National Park Service, the fire forced the evacuation of Los Alamos and Los Alamos Laboratory and burned more 230 homes, leaving 400 families homeless. It also burned more than one hundred minor structures of the Los Alamos National Laboratory. Altogether the fire did about $1 billion damage. The federal government admitted responsibility, and Congress appropriated $661 million for compensation.

Politics. In 2000, New Mexico gave its electoral votes to Al Gore but only after a recount that determined that the vice president was the victor by a scant 366 votes. In 2004, however, George W. Bush took the state by 6,000 votes. In 2002, Bill Richardson, former secretary of education, ambassador to the United Nations, and presidential candidate, was elected governor by a 59-39 percent margin. Richardson's election brought an element of international involvement to the state—in the summer of 2003, he was called upon to hold talks with North Korea and later met with Mexican president

Nearly one quarter of New Mexico's residents live in Albuquerque, which has more people than the state's next ten largest cities combined. (PhotoDisc)

Vicente Fox. One of Richardson's important public acts occurred in 2005, when he declared an emergency in four counties on the state's border with Mexico over a continuing influx of illegal immigrants. The region, he said, had been devastated by human smuggling, drug smuggling, kidnapping, murder, and the destruction of property and livestock.

Charles F. Bahmueller

New Mexico Time Line

300 C.E.-1400 C.E.	Mogollon and Anasazi Indian cultures flourish.
1200-1500	Pueblo Indians establish villages along the Rio Grande and its tributaries.
1539	Franciscan friar Marcos de Niza leads expedition to find fabled cities of Cíbola.
1540-1542	Francisco de Coronado explores the Southwest.
1598	Juan de Onate establishes the first capital, San Juan de los Caballeros.
1599	Battle at Aroma occurs between Native Americans and Spaniards.
1600	San Gabriel, second capital, is founded.
1601	Mass desertion of San Gabriel by colonists takes place; new recruits from Spain and Mexico are sent.
1626	Spanish Inquisition is established in New Mexico.
Aug., 1680	During Pueblo Indian Revolt, Spanish survivors flee to El Paso del Norte.
1696	Second Pueblo Indian Revolt against Spanish occurs.
1706	Albuquerque is founded.
1743	French trappers reach Santa Fe and begin trade with Spanish.

1807	Zebulon Pike leads first American expedition to New Mexico.
1821	Mexico declares independence from Spain.
Sept., 1821	Santa Fe Trail is opened to trade.
1828	First major gold discovery in West made south of Santa Fe.
1841	Texas soldiers invade New Mexico but are stopped by Mexican troops.
1846	Mexican-American War begins; Stephen Kearny declares New Mexico annexed to United States
1848	Treaty of Guadalupe Hidalgo ends Mexican-American War.
Sept. 9, 1850	New Mexico Territory is organized.
Dec. 30, 1853	Gadsden Purchase from Mexico adds land to southern New Mexico.
1861	Confederacy invades New Mexico during Civil War.
1862	Battles of Apache Canyon and Glorieta Pass end intrusion of Confederate troops.
1863	Navajos and Apaches are relocated to Bosque Redondo in the Long Walk from Arizona; they return five years later.
1863	Creation of Arizona Territory halves New Mexico's area.
1878	Lincoln County War erupts in southeast.
July 14, 1881	Outlaw Billy the Kid is shot by Sheriff Pat Garrett in Fort Sumner.
1886	Geronimo makes final surrender; American Indian hostilities cease in the Southwest.
1906	Joint statehood is approved by New Mexico but rejected by Arizona.
1911	New Mexico Constitution is adopted.
Jan. 6, 1912	New Mexico is admitted to the Union as forty-seventh state.
Mar. 9, 1916	Mexican bandit Pancho Villa raids Columbus, killing eighteen.
1923	Oil is discovered on Navajo Reservation.
July 16, 1945	First atomic bomb is detonated near Alamogordo after development at Los Alamos.
1947	Rumors of unidentified flying object crash between Roswell and Corona; believers claim U.S. government covers up the incident.
1948	Native Americans gain right to vote in state elections.
1950	Uranium is discovered near Grants.
1969	Voters reject proposed new state constitution.
1970	U.S. Senate votes to return forty-eight thousand acres to Taos Indians.
mid-1970's	San Juan-Chama Project brings water to north-central area.
1977	First U.S. fusion reaction using electron beams is conducted in Albuquerque.
1988	Severe drought damages 1.4 million acres of the state.
1999	Scandal rocks research laboratories at Los Alamos when lax security is blamed for loss of nuclear secrets to China.
May-July, 2000	Cerro Grande wildfire near Los Alamos burns 48,000 acres and causes $1 billion in damage.
Sept. 13, 2000	Wen Ho Lee, Los Alamos scientist accused of espionage, is released from prison after pleading guilty to a felony as part of a plea bargain.
Nov. 7, 2000	Presidential election, too close to call on election night, is later declared for Al Gore with a slim 366-vote margin.
Nov. 5, 2002	Bill Richardson is elected governor.
May 10, 2004	Wildfire in Lincoln National Forest burns 59,000 acres.
Nov. 2, 2004	George W. Bush wins New Mexico with a 1 percent margin.
Aug. 13, 2005	Governor Richardson declares an emergency on the Mexican border over consequences of large-scale illegal immigration.

Notes for Further Study

Published Sources. Those interested in New Mexican government should consult Paul L. Hain et al. *New Mexico Government* (1994) and Maurilo E. Virgil et al. *New Mexico Government and Politics* (1990). Of numerous historical resources, a good general history is Susan A. Roberts and Calvin A. Roberts's *History of New Mexico* (3d rev. ed., 2004); Marc Simmons's *New Mexico: An Interpretive History* (1988) and Thomas E. Chávez's

An Illustrated History of New Mexico (2002) are also helpful. Robert J. Tórrez, in *UFO's Over Galisteo and Other Stories of New Mexico's History* (2004), uses collections from the New Mexico State Archives to create thirty-six vivid essays about the hardships and leisure of New Mexico's historical residents.

The Lincoln County War is treated in Maurice Garland Fulton et al. *History of the Lincoln County War* (1997). New Mexico's Spanish past is discussed in Marc Simmons's *Coronado's Land: Essays on Daily Life in Colonial New Mexico* (1996). Civil War history in the state is covered in Steve Cottrell's *Civil War in Texas and New Mexico Territory* (1998). For information on the state's Native American peoples, readers should consult Edmund J. Ladd's *The Zuni* (1999); *Indian Tribes of the Americas* (1999), edited by Fred L. Israel; and *Native Resistance and the Pax Colonial in New Spain* (1998), edited by Susan Schroeder. A good resource on natural history is *The Smithsonian Guide to Natural America: The Southwest, Arizona and New Mexico* (1995) by Jake Page and George H. H. Huey (photographer). Julie Kirgo's *New Mexico: Portrait of the Land and the People* (1990) presents a geographer's perspective.

New Mexico can count among its early residents and settlers a wide range of ethnicities. In *The Taos Trappers: The Fur Trade in the Far Southwest, 1540-1846* (2005), David J. Weber details the early penetration of the area by French and American trappers and the wealth of goods that traveled along the Santa Fe Trail. *Contested Homeland: A Chicano History of New Mexico* (2000), edited by Erlinda Gonzales-Berry and David Maciel, details the history and ethnic relations of Mexican Americans within the state. John L. Kessell's *Spain in the Southwest: A Narrative History of Colonial New Mexico, Arizona, Texas, and California* (2002) is an abundantly illustrated history of the Spanish colonies that eventually became the Southwest American states. *A History of the Jews in New Mexico* (1992) by Henry J. Tobias explores the role of Jews in the state's development.

Web Resources. The New Mexico state government home page (www.newmexico.gov/) contains a great deal of information on varied topics. The state legislation site (legis.state.nm.us/lcs/) offers information about New Mexico law and elected officials. New Mexico's geography is surveyed at New Mexico Geography (www.netstate.com/states/geography/nm_geography.htm) and at Kidport (www.kidport.com/REFLIB/UsaGeography/Facts/NewMexico.htm). For an account of the state's history with an emphasis on the era prior to statehood, see the Cuarto Centennial History of New Mexico (nmgs.org/artcuarto.htm), written by a state historian.

The sites for the history of the state's northeast (www.nenewmexico.com/index.php) and for the Santa Fe Trail (www.sangres.com/history/santafetrail01.htm) give background and valuable links to other sites. Examples of sites dealing with the state's American Indian population include two dealing with all tribes—New Mexico Indians (www.kstrom.net/isk/maps/nm/nmmap.html) and Indigenous Peoples of New Mexico (cybergata.com/native.htm). Other sites include Indian Pueblo Cultural Center (www.indianpueblo.org/intro/index.cfm); and the Center of Southwest Studies (swcenter.fortlewis.edu/index.html).

New Mexico's clear and dry air and open spaces have made it an ideal site for this large array of radio telescopes.

Counties

County	2000 pop.	Rank in pop.	Sq. miles	Rank in area
Bernalillo	556,678	1	1,166.2	31
Catron	3,543	31	6,928.3	1
Chaves	61,382	9	6,071.4	4
Cibola	25,595	17	4,539.6	10
Colfax	14,189	24	3,756.9	17
Curry	45,044	12	1,406.1	30
DeBaca	2,240	32	2,325.1	25
Dona Ana	174,682	2	3,807.4	16
Eddy	51,658	11	4,182.2	12
Grant	31,002	14	3,966.2	14
Guadalupe	4,680	29	3,030.6	21
Harding	810	33	2,125.5	27
Hidalgo	5,932	27	3,445.9	19
Lea	55,511	10	4,393.3	11
Lincoln	19,411	19	4,831.4	8
Los Alamos	18,343	20	109.4	33
Luna	25,016	18	2,965.3	22
McKinley	74,798	6	5,449.1	7
Mora	5,180	28	1,931.2	28
Otero	62,298	8	6,626.9	3
Quay	10,155	26	2,875.1	23
Rio Arriba	41,190	13	5,858.1	5
Roosevelt	18,018	22	2,448.7	24
San Juan	89,908	5	5,514.4	6
San Miguel	113,801	4	4,717.4	9
Sandoval	30,126	15	3,709.7	18
Santa Fe	129,292	3	1,909.4	29
Sierra	13,270	25	4,180.5	13
Socorro	18,078	21	6,647.1	2
Taos	29,979	16	2,203.3	26
Torrance	16,911	23	3,345.1	20
Union	4,174	30	3,830.2	15
Valencia	66,152	7	1,067.6	32

Source: U.S. Census Bureau; National Association of Counties.

Cities
With 10,000 or more residents

Rank	City	Population
1	Albuquerque	448,607
2	Las Cruces	74,267
3	Santa Fe (capital)	62,203
4	Rio Rancho	51,765
5	Roswell	45,293
6	South Valley	39,060
7	Farmington	37,844
8	Alamogordo	35,582
9	Clovis	32,667
10	Hobbs	28,657
11	Carlsbad	25,625
12	Gallup	20,209

Rank	City	Population
13	Las Vegas	14,565
14	Deming	14,116
15	Sunland Park	13,309
16	North Valley	11,923
17	Los Alamos	11,909
18	Portales	11,131
19	Artesia	10,692
20	Silver City	10,545
21	Los Lunas	10,034

Population figures are from 2000 census.

Source: U.S. Bureau of the Census.

Index to Tables

DEMOGRAPHICS

Resident state and national populations, 1970-2004
Population figures given in thousands

	State pop.	U.S. pop.	Share	Rank
1970	1,017	203,302	0.5%	37
1980	1,303	226,546	0.6%	37
1985	1,438	237,924	0.6%	37
1990	1,515	248,765	0.6%	37
1995	1,720	262,761	0.6%	36
2000	1,819	281,425	0.7%	36
2004	1,903	293,655	0.7%	36

Source: U.S. Census Bureau, Current Population Reports, 2006.

Resident population by age, 2004

Age Group	Total persons
Under 5 years	133,000
5 to 17 years	359,000
18 to 24 years	206,000
25 to 34 years	236,000
35 to 44 years	266,000
45 to 54 years	275,000
55 to 64 years	199,000
65 to 74 years	126,000
75 to 84 years	77,000
85 years and older	27,000
All age groups	1,903,000

Portion of residents 65 and older	12.1%
National rank in portion of oldest residents	33
National average	12.4%

Population figures are rounded to nearest thousand persons;
figures include armed forces personnel stationed in the state.
Source: U.S. Bureau of the Census, 2006.

Resident population by race, Hispanic origin, 2004

Category	State pop.	Share	U.S.
All residents	1,903	100.00%	100.00%
Non-Hispanic white	827	43.46%	67.37%
Hispanic white	785	41.25%	13.01%
Other Hispanic	38	2.00%	1.06%
African American	45	2.36%	12.77%
Native American	192	10.09%	0.96%
Asian, Pacific Islander	26	1.37%	4.37%
Two or more categories	28	1.47%	1.51%

Population figures are in thousands. Persons counted as "Hispanic" (Latino) may be of any race. Because of overlapping categories, categories may not add up to 100%. Shares in column 3 are percentages of each category within the state; these figures may be compared to the national percentages in column 4.
Source: U.S. Bureau of the Census, 2006.

Projected state population, 2000-2030

Year	Population
2000	1,819,000
2005	1,902,000
2010	1,980,000
2015	2,042,000
2020	2,084,000
2025	2,107,000
2030	2,100,000
Population increase, 2000-2030	281,000
Percentage increase, 2000-2030	15.4

Projections are based on data from the 2000 census.
Source: U.S. Census Bureau.

VITAL STATISTICS

Infant mortality rates, 1980-2002

	1980	1990	2000	2002
All state residents	11.5	9.0	6.6	6.3
All U.S. residents	12.6	9.2	9.4	9.1
All state white residents	11.3	7.6	6.3	5.7
All U.S. white residents	10.6	7.6	5.7	5.8
All state black residents	23.1	—	—	—
All U.S. black residents	22.2	18.0	14.1	14.4

Figures represent deaths per 1,000 live births of resident infants under 1 year old, exclusive of fetal deaths. Figures for all residents include members of other racial categories not listed separately. The Census Bureau considers the post-1980 figures for black residents to be too small to be statistically meaningful.
Source: U.S. Census Bureau, *Statistical Abstract of the United States,* 2006.

Abortion rates, 1990 and 2000

	1990	2000
Total abortions	6,000	6,000
Rate per 1,000 women	17.6	14.7
U.S. rate	25.7	21.3
Rank	28	25

Numbers of abortions are rounded to nearest thousand; ranks are based on rates.
Source: U.S. Census Bureau.

Marriages and divorces, 2004

Total marriages	14,100
Rate per 1,000 population	7.4
National rate per 1,000 population	7.4
Rank among all states	23
Total divorces	8,800
Rate per 1,000 population	4.6
National rate per 1,000 population	3.7
Rank among all states	11

Figures are for all marriages and divorces performed within the state, including those of nonresidents; totals are rounded to the nearest hundred. Ranks are for highest to lowest figures; note that divorce data are not available for five states.
Source: U.S. National Center for Health Statistics, *Vital Statistics of the United States,* 2006.

Death rates by leading causes, 2002
Deaths per 100,000 resident population

Cause	State	U.S.
Heart disease	181.1	241.7
Cancer	165.3	193.2
Cerebrovascular diseases	38.5	56.4
Accidents other than motor vehicle	59.6	37.0
Motor vehicle accidents	22.8	15.7
Chronic lower respiratory diseases	46.2	43.3
Diabetes mellitus	31.4	25.4
HIV	1.9	4.9
Suicide	18.8	11.0
Homicide	8.7	6.1
All causes	773.2	847.3
Rank in overall death rate among states		39

Figures exclude nonresidents who died in the state. Causes of death follow International Classification of Diseases. Rank is from highest to lowest death rate in the United States.
Source: U.S. National Center for Health Statistics, *National Vital Statistics Report,* 2006.

ECONOMY

Gross state product, 1990-2004
In current dollars

Year	State product	Nat'l product	State share
1990	$26.9 billion	$5.67 trillion	0.47%
2000	$50.4 billion	$9.75 trillion	0.52%
2002	$53.4 billion	$10.41 trillion	0.51%
2003	$57.1 billion	$10.92 trillion	0.52%
2004	$60.9 billion	$11.65 trillion	0.52%

Source: U.S. Bureau of Economic Analysis, *Survey of Current Business,* July, 2005.

Gross state product by industry, 2003
In billions of dollars

Construction	$2.1
Manufacturing	7.1
Wholesale trade	2.0
Retail trade	4.3
Finance & insurance	2.0
Information	1.7
Professional services	3.6
Health care & social assistance	3.4
Government	10.1
Total state product	$54.2
Total U.S. product	$10,289.2
State share of U.S. total	0.53%
Rank among all states	37

Total figures include industries not listed separately. Amounts are in chained 2000 dollars.

Source: U.S. Bureau of Economic Analysis, *Survey of Current Business,* July, 2005.

Personal income per capita, 1990-2004
In current dollars

	1990	2000	2004
Per capita income	$14,924	$22,135	$26,191
U.S. average	$19,477	$29,845	$32,937
Rank among states	46	47	47

Source: U.S. Bureau of Economic Analysis, *Survey of Current Business,* April, 2005.

Energy consumption, 2001
In trillions of British thermal units (BTU), except as noted

Total energy consumption

Total state energy consumption	679
Total U.S. energy consumption	96,275
State share of U.S. total	0.71%
Rank among states	37

Per capita consumption (In millions of BTU)

Total state per capita consumption	371
Total U.S. per capita consumption	338
Rank among states	20

End-use sectors

Residential	107
Commercial	122
Industrial	220
Transportation	230

Sources of energy

Petroleum	251
Natural gas	262
Coal	297
Hydroelectric power	2
Nuclear electric power	0

Figures for totals include categories not listed separately.

Source: U.S. Energy Information Administration, *State Energy Data Report,* 2001.

Nonfarm employment by sectors, 2004

Total persons	791,000
Construction	50,000
Manufacturing	36,000
Trade, transportation, utilities	138,000
Information	15,000
Finance, insurance, real estate	35,000
Professional & business services	90,000
Education & health services	103,000
Leisure, hospitality, arts, organizations	83,000
Other services, including repair & maintenance	29,000
Government	198,000

Figures are rounded to nearest thousand persons. "Total" includes mining and natural resources, not listed separately.

Source: U.S. Bureau of Labor Statistics, 2006.

Foreign exports, 1990-2004
In millions of dollars

Year	State	U.S.	State share
1990	249	394,045	0.06%
1996	931	624,767	0.15%
1997	1,776	688,896	0.26%
2000	2,391	712,055	0.31%
2003	2,326	724,006	0.34%
2004	2,046	769,332	0.27%
Rank among all states in 2004 44			

U.S. total does not include U.S. dependencies.
Source: U.S. Census Bureau, *U.S. Merchandise Trade*, series FT 900, 2000; U.S. Census Bureau, *U.S. International Trade in Goods and Services*, Series FT 900, 2005.

LAND USE

Federally owned land, 2003
Areas in acres

	State	U.S.	State share
Total area	77,766,000	2,271,343,000	3.42%
Nonfederal land	51,248,000	1,599,584,000	3.20%
Federal land	26,518,000	671,759,000	3.95%
Federal share	34.1%	29.6%	—

Areas are rounded to nearest thousand acres. Figures for federally owned land do not include trust properties.
Source: U.S. General Services Administration, *Federal Real Property Profile*, 2006.

Land use, 1997
In acres, rounded to nearest thousand

Total surface area	77,823,000
Total nonfederal rural land.	50,071,000
Percentage rural land	64.3%
Cropland	1,875,000
Conservation Reserve Program (CRP*) land. . . .	467,000
Pastureland	231,000
Rangeland	39,990,000
Forestland.	5,467,000
Other rural land	2,041,000

*CRP is a federal program begun in 1985 to assist private landowners to convert highly erodible cropland to vegetative cover for ten years. Note that some categories of land overlap.
Source: U.S. Department of Agriculture, Natural Resources and Conservation Service, and Iowa State University, Statistical Laboratory, S*ummary Report, 1997 National Resources Inventory,* revised December, 2000.

Farms and crop acreage, 2004

	State	U.S.	Share	Rank
Farms	18,000	2,113,000	0.85%	35
Acres (millions)	45	937	4.80%	5
Acres per farm	2,554	443	—	3

Source: U.S. Department of Agriculture, National Agricultural Statistics Service. Numbers of farms are rounded to nearest thousand units; acreage figures are rounded to nearest million. Rankings, including ties, are based on rounded figures.

GOVERNMENT AND FINANCE

Units of local government, 2002

	State	Total U.S.	Rank
All local governments	858	87,525	32
Counties	33	3,034	35
Municipalities	101	19,429	39
Townships	0	16,504	—
School districts	96	13,506	33
Special districts	628	35,052	19

Only 48 states have county governments, 20 states have township governments ("towns" in New England, Minnesota, New York, and Wisconsin), and 46 states have school districts. Special districts encompass such functions as natural resources, fire protection, and housing and community development.
Source: U.S. Census Bureau, *Census of Governments.*

State government revenue, 2002

Total revenue	$8,746 mill.
General revenue	$8,478 mill.
Per capita revenue	$4,570
U.S. per capita average	$3,689
Rank among states	9
Intergovernment revenue	
Total	$2,855 mill.
From federal government	$2,760 mill.
Charges and miscellaneous	
Total	$1,995 mill.
Current charges	$696 mill.
Misc. general income	$1,299 mill.
Insurance trust revenue	$268 mill.
Taxes	
Total	$3,628 mill.
Per capita taxes	$1,959
Rank among states	18
Property taxes	$53 mill.
Sales taxes	$1,823 mill.
License taxes	$171 mill.
Individual income taxes	$983 mill.
Corporate income taxes	$124 mill.
Other taxes	$474 mill.

Total revenue figures include items not listed separately here.
Source: U.S. Bureau of the Census.

State government expenditures, 2002

General expenditures

Total state expenditures . . . . $10,084 mill.
Intergovernmental. . . . . $2,768 mill.

Per capita expenditures

State $4,975
Average of all states $3,859
Rank among states. 8

Selected direct expenditures

Education. . . . . $1,468 mill.
Public welfare . . . . $2,028 mill.
Health, hospital . . . . $739 mill.
Highways . . . . $925 mill.
Police protection . . . . $89 mill.
Corrections. . . . . $241 mill.
Natural resources . . . . $138 mill.
Parks and recreation . . . . $49 mill.
Government administration. . . . . $349 mill.
Interest on debt . . . . $192 mill.
Total direct expenditures . . . . $6,445 mill.

Totals include items not listed separately.
Source: U.S. Census Bureau.

POLITICS

Governors since statehood

D = Democrat; R = Republican; O = other;
(r) resigned; (d) died in office; (i) removed from office

William C. McDonald (D) 1912-1917
Ezequiel Cabeza DeBaca (D) . . . . (d) 1917
Washington E. Lindsay (R) 1917-1919
Octaviano A. Larrazolo (R) 1919-1921
Merritt C. Mechem (R) 1921-1923
James F. Hinkle (D) 1923-1925
Arthur T. Hannett (D). 1925-1927
Richard C. Dillon (R) 1927-1931
Arthur Seligman (D) . . . . (d) 1931-1933
Andrew W. Hockenbull (D). 1933-1935
Clyde Tingley (D) 1935-1939
John E. Miles (D) 1939-1943
John J. Dempsey (D). 1943-1947
Thomas L. Mabry (D) 1947-1951
Edwin L. Mechem (R) 1951-1955
John F. Sims, Jr. (D) 1955-1957
Edwin L. Mechem (R) 1957-1959
John Burroughs (D) 1959-1961
Edwin L. Mechem (R) . . . . (r) 1961-1962
Thomas F. Bolack (R) 1962-1963
Jack M. Campbell (D) 1963-1967
David F. Cargo (R). 1967-1971
Bruce King (D) 1971-1975
Raymond S. (Jerry) Apodaca (D). 1975-1979
Bruce King (D) 1979-1983
Toney Anaya (D). 1983-1987
Garrey E. Carruthers (R) 1987-1991
Bruce King (D) 1991-1995
Gary E. Johnson (R) 1995-2003
Bill Richardson (D) 2003-

Composition of congressional delegations, 1989-2007

	Dem	Rep	Total
House of Representatives			
101st Congress, 1989			
State delegates	1	2	3
Total U.S.	259	174	433
102d Congress, 1991			
State delegates	1	2	3
Total U.S.	267	167	434
103d Congress, 1993			
State delegates	1	2	3
Total U.S.	258	176	434
104th Congress, 1995			
State delegates	0	3	3
Total U.S.	197	236	433
105th Congress, 1997			
State delegates	1	2	3
Total U.S.	206	228	434
106th Congress, 1999			
State delegates	1	2	3
Total U.S.	211	222	433
107th Congress, 2001			
State delegates	1	2	3
Total U.S.	211	221	432
108th Congress, 2003			
State delegates	1	2	3
Total U.S.	205	229	434
109th Congress, 2005			
State delegates	1	2	3
Total U.S.	202	231	433
110th Congress, 2007			
State delegates	1	2	3
Total U.S.	233	202	435
Senate			
101st Congress, 1989			
State delegates	1	1	2
Total U.S.	55	45	100
102d Congress, 1991			
State delegates	1	1	2
Total U.S.	56	44	100
103d Congress, 1993			
State delegates	1	1	2
Total U.S.	57	43	100
104th Congress, 1995			
State delegates	1	1	2
Total U.S.	46	53	99

(continued)

	Dem	Rep	Total
105th Congress, 1997			
State delegates	1	1	2
Total U.S.	45	55	100
106th Congress, 1999			
State delegates	1	1	2
Total U.S.	45	54	99
107th Congress, 2001			
State delegates	1	1	2
Total U.S.	50	50	100
108th Congress, 2003			
State delegates	1	1	2
Total U.S.	48	51	99
109th Congress, 2005			
State delegates	1	1	2
Total U.S.	44	55	99
110th Congress, 2007			
State delegates	1	1	2
Total U.S.	49	49	98

Figures are for starts of first sessions. Totals are for Democrat (Dem.) and Republican (Rep.) members only. House membership totals under 435 and Senate totals under 100 reflect vacancies and seats held by independent party members. When the 110th Congress opened, the Senate's two independent members caucused with the Democrats, giving the Democrats control of the Senate.
Source: U.S. Congress, *Congressional Directory.*

Composition of state legislature, 1990-2006

	Democrats	Republicans
State House (70 seats)		
1990	49	21
1992	53	17
1994	46	24
1996	42	28
1998	40	30
2000	40	30
2002	43	27
2004	42	28
2006	42	28
State Senate (42 seats)		
1990	26	16
1992	27	15
1994	27	15
1996	25	17
1998	25	17
2000	25	17
2002	24	18
2004	24	18
2006	24	18

Figures for total seats may include independents and minor party members. Numbers reflect results of elections in listed years; elected members usually take their seats in the years that follow.
Source: Council of State Governments; *State Elective Officials and the Legislatures.*

Voter participation in presidential elections, 2000 and 2004

	2000	2004
Voting age population		
State	1,315,000	1,411,000
Total United States	209,831,000	220,377,000
State share of U.S. total	0.63	0.64
Rank among states	37	37
Portion of voting age population casting votes		
State	45.5%	53.6%
United States	50.3%	55.5%
Rank among states	44	37

Population figures are rounded to nearest thousand and include all residents, regardless of eligibility to vote.
Source: U.S. Census Bureau.

HEALTH AND MEDICAL CARE

Medical professionals
Physicians in 2003 and nurses in 2001

	U.S.	State
Physicians in 2003		
Total	774,849	4,473
Share of U.S. total		0.58%
Rate	266	239
Rank		29
Nurses in 2001		
Total	2,262,020	11,630
Share of U.S. total		0.51%
Rate	793	635
Rank		46

Rates are numbers of physicians and nurses per 100,000 resident population; ranks are based on rates.
Source: American Medical Association, *Physician Characteristics and Distribution in the U.S.*; U.S. Department of Health and Human Services, Health Resources and Services Administration.

Health insurance coverage, 2003

	State	U.S.
Total persons covered	1,457,000	243,320,000
Total persons not covered	414,000	44,961,000
Portion not covered	22.1%	15.6%
Rank among states	2	—
Children not covered	65,000	8,373,000
Portion not covered	13.2%	11.4%
Rank among states	12	—

Totals are rounded to nearest thousand. Ranks are from the highest to the lowest percentages of persons *not* insured.
Source: U.S. Census Bureau, Current Population Reports.

AIDS, syphilis, and tuberculosis cases, 2003

Disease	U.S. cases	State cases	Rank
AIDS	44,232	111	34
Syphilis	34,270	205	27
Tuberculosis	14,874	49	36

Source: U.S. Centers for Disease Control and Prevention.

Cigarette smoking, 2003
Residents over age 18 who smoke

	U.S.	State	Rank
All smokers	22.1%	22.0%	28
Male smokers	24.8%	23.6%	30
Female smokers	20.3%	20.5%	24

Cigarette smokers are defined as persons who reported having smoked at least 100 cigarettes during their lifetimes and who currently smoked at least occasionally.
Source: U.S. Centers for Disease Control and Prevention, *Morbidity and Mortality Weekly Report,* 53, no. 44 (November 12, 2004).

HOUSING

Home ownership rates, 1985-2004

	1985	1990	1995	2000	2004
State	68.2%	68.6%	67.0%	73.7%	71.5%
Total U.S.	63.9%	63.9%	64.7%	67.4%	69.0%
Rank among states	24	18	30	12	28

Net change in state home ownership rate, 1985-2004 . . . . +3.3%
Net change in U.S. home ownership rate, 1985-2004 . . . . +5.1%

Percentages represent the proportion of owner households to total occupied households.
Source: U.S. Census Bureau, 2006.

Home sales, 2000-2004
In thousands of units

Existing home sales	2000	2002	2003	2004
State sales	29.9	38.9	43.3	50.6
Total U.S. sales	5,171	5,631	6,183	6,784
State share of U.S. total	0.58%	0.69%	0.70%	0.75%
Sales rank among states	37	36	36	35

Units include single-family homes, condos, and co-ops.
Source: National Association of Realtors, Washington, D.C., *Real Estate Outlook: Market Trends & Insights.*

Values of owner-occupied homes, 2003

	State	U.S.
Total units	363,000	58,809,000
Value of units		
Under $100,000	38.1%	29.6%
$100,000-199,999	45.6%	36.9%
$200,000 or more	16.4%	33.5%
Median value	$118,764	$142,275
Rank among all states 31		

Units are owner-occupied one-family houses whose numbers are rounded to nearest thousand. Data are extrapolated from survey samples.
Source: U.S. Census Bureau, American Community Survey.

EDUCATION

Public school enrollment, 2002

Prekindergarten through grade 8
State enrollment 224,000
Total U.S. enrollment. 34,135,000
State share of U.S. total 0.66%

Grades 9 through 12
State enrollment 96,000
Total U.S. enrollment. 14,067,000
State share of U.S. total 0.68%

Enrollment rates
State public school enrollment rate. 86.5%
Overall U.S. rate 90.4%
Rank among states in 2002. 43
Rank among states in 1995. 28

Enrollment figures (which include unclassified students) are rounded to nearest thousand pupils during fall school term. Enrollment rates are based on enumerated resident population estimate for July 1, 2002.
Source: U.S. National Center for Education Statistics.

Public college finances, 2003-2004

FTE enrollment in public institutions of higher education

Students in state institutions 79,600
Students in all U.S. public institutions 9,916,600
State share of U.S. total 0.80
Rank among states 34

State and local government appropriations for higher education

State appropriation per FTE $5,586
National average $5,716
Rank among states 22
State & local tax revenue going to higher
    education 14.5%

FTE = full-time equivalent in public postsecondary programs,
    including summer sessions; student numbers are rounded to
    nearest hundred. Funding figures for 2003-2004 academic year
    include financial aid to students in state public institutions and
    exclude money for research, agriculture experiment stations,
    teaching hospitals, and medical schools; figures are rounded to
    nearest thousand dollars.
Source: Higher Education Executive Officers, Denver, Colorado.

TRANSPORTATION AND TRAVEL

Highway mileage, 2003

Interstate highways 1,000
Other freeways and expressways 5
Arterial roads 5,028
Collector roads 7,234
Local roads 50,686

Urban roads 6,814
Rural roads 57,139

Total state mileage 63,953
U.S. total 3,974,107
State share 1.61%
Rank among states 32

Note that combined urban and rural road mileage matches the
    total of the other categories.
Source: U.S. Federal Highway Administration.

Motor vehicle registrations and driver licenses, 2003

Vehicle registrations	State	U.S.	Share	Rank
Autos, trucks, buses	1,509,000	231,390,000	0.65%	36
Autos only	694,000	135,670	0.51%	37
Motorcycles	32,000	5,328,000	0.60%	39
Driver licenses	1,236,000	196,166,000	0.63%	38

Figures, which do not include vehicles owned by military services,
    are rounded to the nearest thousand. Figures for automobiles
    include taxis.
Source: U.S. Federal Highway Administration.

Domestic travel expenditures, 2003
Spending by U.S. residents on overnight trips and
day trips of at least 50 miles from home

Total expenditures within state . . . . $4.08 bill.
Total expenditures within U.S. . . . . $490.87 bill.
State share of U.S. total 0.8%
Rank among states 34

Source: Travel Industry Association of America.

Retail gasoline prices, 2003-2007
Average price per gallon at the pump

Year	U.S.	State
2003	$1.267	$1.261
2004	$1.316	$1.317
2005	$1.644	$1.703
2007	$2.298	$2.265

Excise tax per gallon in 2004 . . . . 18.9¢
Rank among all states in 2007 prices 25

Prices are averages of all grades of gasoline sold at the pump
    during March months in 2003-2005 and during February, 2007.
    Averages for 2006, during which prices rose higher, are not
    available.
Source: U.S. Energy Information Agency, *Petroleum Marketing
    Monthly* (2003-2005 data); American Automobile Association
    (2007 data).

CRIME AND LAW ENFORCEMENT

State and local police officers, 2000-2004

	2000	2002	2004
Total officers			
U.S.	654,601	665,555	675,734
State	3,925	4,142	3,944*
*Net change, 2000-2004			+0.48%
Officers per 1,000 residents			
U.S.	2.33	2.31	2.30
State	2.16	2.24	2.07
State rank	24	20	24

Totals include state and local police and sheriffs.
Source: Carsey Institute, University of New Hampshire.

Crime rates, 2003
Incidents per 100,000 residents

Crimes	State	U.S.
Violent crimes		
Total incidents	665	475
Murder	6	6
Forcible rape	50	32
Robbery	104	142
Aggravated assault	505	295
Property crimes		
Total incidents	4,124	3,588
Burglary	1,025	741
Larceny/theft	2,711	2,415
Motor vehicle theft	387	433
All crimes	4,789	4,063

Source: U.S. Federal Bureau of Investigation, *Crime in the United States*, annual.

State prison populations, 1980-2003

	State	U.S.	State share
1980	1,279	305,458	0.42%
1990	3,187	708,393	0.45%
1996	4,724	1,025,624	0.46%
2000	5,342	1,391,261	0.38%
2003	6,223	1,470,045	0.42%

State figures exclude prisoners in federal penitentiaries.
Source: U.S. Bureau of Justice Statistics, *Prisoners in 2003.*

New York

Location: Northeast Atlantic coast

Area and rank: 47,224 square miles (122,310 square kilometers); 54,475 square miles (141,090 square kilometers) including water; thirtieth largest state in area

Coastline: 127 miles (204 kilometers) on the Atlantic Ocean

Shoreline: 1,850 miles (2,978 kilometers)

Population and rank: 19,227,000 (2004); third largest state in population

Capital city: Albany (95,658 people in 2000 census)

Largest city: New York City (8,008,278 people in 2000 census)

Entered Union and rank: July 26, 1788; eleventh state

Present constitution adopted: 1777 (last revised 1938)

Lower Manhattan, with Brooklyn in the background. With more than eight million residents, New York City has a larger population than that of all but eleven states. (David Raboin/iStockphoto)

Counties: 62

State name: New York takes its name from the duke of York

State nickname: Empire State

Motto: *Excelsior* (Ever upward)

State flag: Blue field with state coat of arms

Highest point: Mount Marcy—5,344 feet (1,629 meters)

Lowest point: Atlantic Ocean—sea level

Highest recorded temperature: 108 degrees Fahrenheit (42 degrees Celsius)—Troy, 1926

Lowest recorded temperature: –52 degrees Fahrenheit (–47 degrees Celsius)—Old Forge, 1979

State song: "I Love New York"

State tree: Sugar maple

State flower: Rose

State bird: Bluebird

State fish: Brook trout

State animal: Beaver

New York History

Dominated by the nation's most heavily populated city, New York has been an area of economic and political importance since the earliest years of the United States. Its position between the Atlantic Ocean and the Great Lakes made it a major area of population movement to the west, and New York City attracts emigrants from around the world.

Early History. The first humans to reside in the area arrived about ten thousand years ago and hunted bison and other large game. Thousands of years later, the culture known as the Mound Builders grew crops in southwestern New York. By the time Europeans arrived in the New World, the Atlantic coast was inhabited by the Mohegans and the Munsees, members of the Algonquian language group. Farther inland resided the Onondaga, the Oneida, the Seneca, the Cayuga, and the Mohawk tribes, members of the Iroquois language group. In 1570, these five peoples united into the Iroquois League, a powerful confederation that dominated the area for two centuries.

Exploration and Settlement. The first European to visit the area was the Italian navigator Giovanni da Verrazano. Working for the French, Verrazano explored the Atlantic coast from North Carolina to Canada, including New York Harbor, in 1524. The French explorer Samuel de Champlain journeyed from Canada to northern New York and reached Lake Champlain in 1609. The same year, the English navigator Henry Hudson, working for the Dutch, sailed up the Hudson River about as far as the modern site of Albany.

Despite this early exploration, settlement of New York began slowly. The Dutch established Fort Orange,

State capitol building in Albany. (©NYS Department of Economic Development)

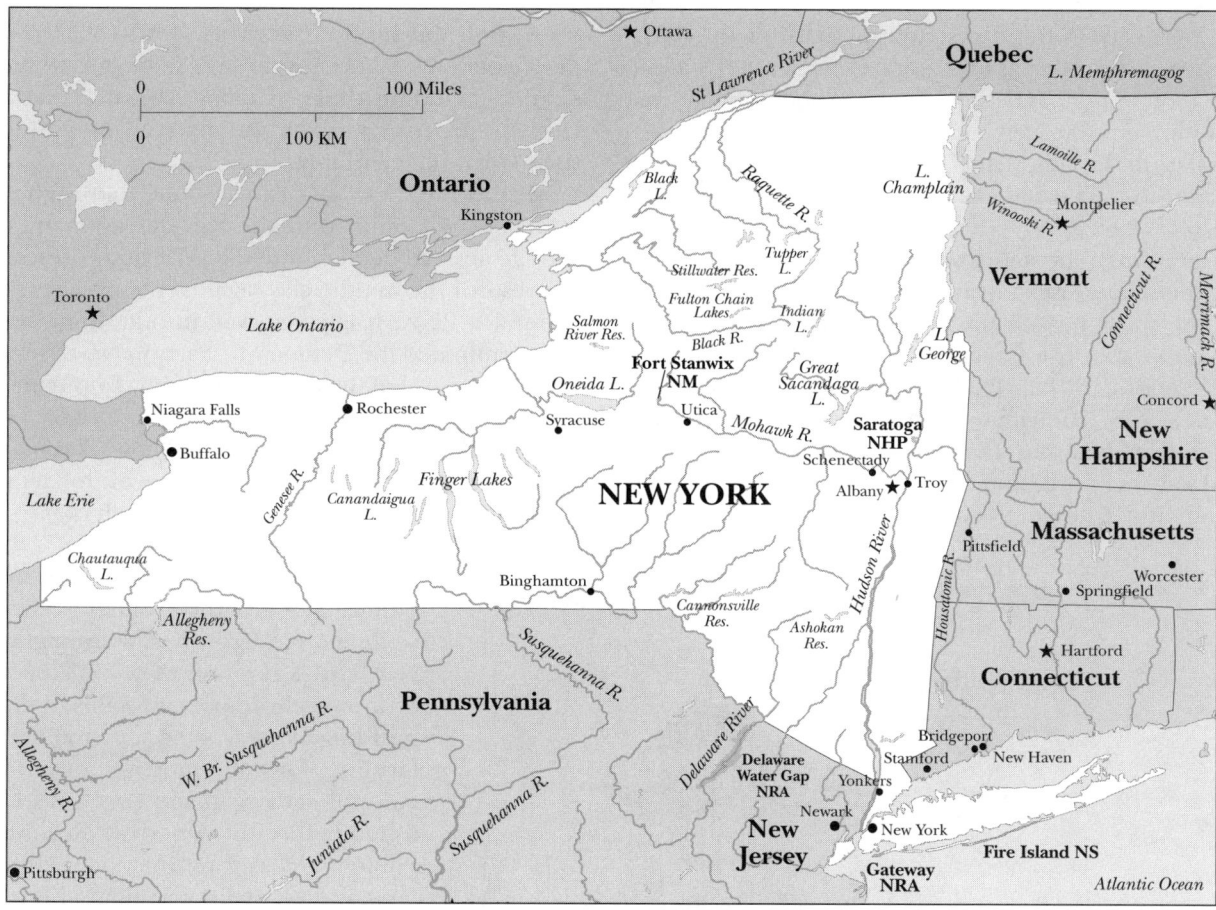

later known as Albany, in 1624 as the first permanent European settlement in the area. The next year they established New Amsterdam, later known as New York City, on Manhattan Island. By 1650, the Dutch colony had about one thousand residents. In 1664, an English fleet sailed into New York Harbor and captured the colony without a fight. At this time the area had about eight thousand colonists, including Dutch, English, French, Germans, Finns, Swedes, Jews, and African slaves.

The colony was granted by English King Charles II to his brother, the duke of York and Albany, later King James II. After approving a charter adopted by the colonists in 1683, James II revoked it after he became king in 1685. Instead, he united New York and the colonies of New England to the north under a single administration. Strong resistance to the unification of the colonies led to a rebellion in 1689, after a political crisis in England forced James II to abdicate. Jacob Leisler, the leader of the rebellion, controlled New York until 1691, when the new king, William II, sent in a new royal governor, who had Leisler hanged for treason.

The next several decades brought conflict between the French and the English in the area. The French made a number of raids from Canada into central and northern New York, limiting settlement beyond Albany. An important factor in England's ability to retain control of the colony was an alliance with the Iroquois League. The struggle for control of North America led to the French and Indian War (1754-1763), which ended with the English in firm control of New York. The war also weakened the power of the Iroquois League, which ceded much of its land to the colonists.

Revolution and Population Growth. The British victory in the war encouraged settlement of the area. By the start of the American Revolution (1775-1783), New York had a population of 163,000. About one-third of the battles of the Revolution took place in New York. American forces under Ethan Allen captured Fort Ticonderoga, in the northeastern part of the colony, in 1775. The British captured New York City in 1776 and recaptured Fort Ticonderoga in 1777. One of the most important events in the war took place in New York on October 17, 1777, when British general John Burgoyne surrendered his army at Saratoga, between Fort Ticonderoga and Albany. This American victory, often considered the turning point in the Revolution, helped bring France into the war against the British.

New York adopted its first state constitution on April 20, 1777, with Kingston, located between Albany and

New York City, as the first state capital. After the war, New York City served as the capital of the United States from 1785 to 1790. It became the most populous city in the nation in 1790. New York officially became the eleventh state of the Union in 1788, when it ratified the U.S. Constitution. The state capital was moved to Albany nine years later.

Migration to the state from New England made New York the second most heavily populated state in 1800 and the most heavily populated state in 1810. The opening of the Erie Canal between the Hudson River and Lake Erie in 1825, linking New York to new territories in the west, contributed to the state's rapid growth.

The Civil War and Tammany Hall. New York abolished slavery in 1827 and was a center of the antislavery movement. Although the state was firmly on the side of the Union during the Civil War (1861-1865), violent draft riots in New York City in 1863 led to two thousand deaths, including those of many African Americans. Despite this crisis, the war was generally good for the state's growing economy.

Meanwhile, New York City became a stronghold of political corruption with the rise of Tammany Hall. This group had been founded in 1789 to represent the interests of the middle class against the policies of the Federalist Party. It later evolved into an organization that dominated the Democratic Party in New York City, giving it control of the city government. Tammany Hall reached its greatest power during the middle of the nineteenth century, when William "Boss" Tweed took control in 1857. Tweed stole millions of dollars from the city treasury. Tammany Hall lost much of its power when Tweed was arrested in 1872, but it continued to have an influence in city politics well into the twentieth century.

Economic Growth and Immigration. New York's position as one of the most economically important states in the nation began soon after statehood. Dairy farming, long the most important agricultural activity in the state, was established before the American Revolution. Poultry and egg production, as well as fruit and vegetable farming, also began at an early date and would remain important parts of the state's economy.

Investment and finance, which began with the founding of the New York Stock Exchange in 1817, would remain centered in New York City's Wall Street. The textile industry began during the 1820's. International trade was also established at an early date, with New York handling half of the nation's imported goods as early as 1831.

The first railroad in the state was completed in 1831. The growth of the New York Central Railroad Company throughout the nineteenth century was a major factor in the rise of industry in the state. After the Civil War, during the so-called Gilded Age, rapid economic growth created many millionaires and led to the founding of nationally important companies such as Westinghouse, General Electric, and Eastman Kodak.

Meanwhile, the first of many waves of immigration brought large numbers of Germans and Irish to New York during the 1840's. During the late nineteenth century, new residents from around the world arrived, particularly from eastern

New York City's Empire State Building nearing completion in 1930. (Library of Congress)

New York City's Manhattan is the most densely populated major residential area in the nation, but its crowding is relieved by Central Park, which stretches from Fifty-ninth Street in the south to 110th Street in the north and from Fifth Avenue in the east to Eighth Avenue in the west. (Corbis)

and southern Europe. New York's Ellis Island was the center of immigration in the United States from 1892 to 1943.

Large numbers of African Americans began to arrive in New York during World War I, followed by an even larger number during and after World War II. New York's African American population rose from less than 5 percent during the early 1940's to more than 20 percent by the end of the century. During the 1950's and 1960's, large numbers of Puerto Ricans arrived in the state. Later decades brought an increase in immigration from Asia and the Middle East.

The Twentieth Century. New York, long dominant in national politics, began a new era with the election of Franklin Delano Roosevelt as governor in 1928. Roosevelt's policy of increased government spending on social services, particularly after the stock market crash of 1929 and the Great Depression, continued when he served as president of the United States from 1933 to 1945. This trend continued in New York City after World War II, leading to a financial crisis in 1975, when federal funds of $4.5 billion were needed to protect the city from bankruptcy.

In 1970, California surpassed New York in population. Between 1970 and 1980, New York was one of the few states to decrease in population. Despite a decline in manufacturing during the same decade, the rise of service industries led to economic growth during the late 1970's and 1980's. This growth came to a sudden halt in late 1987, when a stock market crash led to a recession. In addition to economic problems, New York City faced an increase in racial violence during the late 1980's and early 1990's. Although New York City managed to lessen its image as a center of crime and poverty during the late 1990's, it still faced numerous challenges in the twenty-first century.

2000 General Elections. The most sensational political development in New York in 2000 was undoubtedly the victory of First Lady Hillary Rodham Clinton in her race for the U.S. Senate. This victory fed speculation that she would eventually make a bid for the presidency. In the simultaneous presidential polling, New York went solidly for Al Gore over George W. Bush by a 60-35 percent victory, with Ralph Nader taking 5 percent.

Also in 2000, New York experienced a number of unexpected negative surprises. In February, a small bomb exploded near Wall Street in lower Manhattan. In July, a gunman seized a plane at John F. Kennedy International Airport on Long Island and took two hostages, surrendering the next day. The same month, the West Nile virus reappeared in Manhattan after its original appearance in August, 1999.

9/11. On the morning of September 11, 2001, several coordinated terrorist attacks and one attempted attack on iconic targets in Manhattan, northern Virginia, and Washington, D.C., took place involving hijacked passenger jets that were crashed into the intended targets. These attacks included two planes, each of which hit one of the 110-floor Twin Towers of the World Trade Center (WTC) in lower Manhattan, destroying both. In the WTC attacks, 2,749 persons died, including 343 New York City firefighters and 23 police officers, as well as 37 Port Authority police. Some two hundred persons jumped to their deaths from the burning towers, but most of those in the towers at the time of the attacks were successfully evacuated. In the wake of the WTC attacks, five other buildings at the site were destroyed or badly damaged; in all, twenty-five buildings were damaged. The attacks caused widespread terror and confu-

sion. In the New York City area, most schools and many businesses closed for the day. New Yorkers, however, were soon rallied by Mayor Rudi Giuliani.

Giuliani's leadership role catapulted him into national prominence and soon earned him the honorific title "America's mayor." *Time* magazine named him the 2001 Person of the Year. He became a constant and reassuring public presence during the crisis. Paying little attention to his own security, he modeled courage and grace under fire. He managed the response of the agencies of city government and made or delegated hundreds of key decisions. He also coordinated efforts of the city and with those of state and federal governments. He reassured New Yorkers that their city would be rebuilt and would literally and figuratively "stand tall" again. A work by composer John Adams commemorating the tragedy, "On the Transmigration of Souls," debuted on September 19, 2002. In 2003, new plans for a "freedom tower" to be built on the WTC site were unveiled, though to mixed reviews.

Anthrax Attacks. New acts of terrorism began on September 18, 2001, a week after the 9/11 attacks. Anthrax-laced letters were sent to the news organizations of several major television networks, as well as the

Smoke billowing out of both towers of the World Trade Center shortly after the two buildings were struck by hijacked airliners carrying large quantities of jet fuel. Both buildings later collapsed. (www.bigfoto.com)

New York Post. Another was sent to Florida, and other such letters were later sent to two senators in Washington, D.C. One of the five persons to die of the anthrax-caused disease was a New Yorker. Despite extensive efforts, the persons responsible were not identified. To make matters worse, on November 12, 2001, only two months after the 9/11 attacks, an American Airlines Airbus crashed on takeoff from Kennedy International Airport, killing all on board and five on the ground—some 260 persons in all. Despite initial fears that foul play was involved, after exhaustive investigation, the crash was ruled in 2004 to have been caused by pilot error.

Elections. The election for mayor of New York City was held in the wake of the September 11 terrorist attacks. Mayor Giuliani, who could not run again because of term limits, endorsed billionaire businessman Michael Bloomberg for the job. Bloomberg, a liberal Republican, narrowly defeated Democrat Mark Green 50-48 percent. Bloomberg was reelected to the post in 2005, gaining 57 percent of the vote. In the gubernatorial election of 2002, Governor George Pataki was reelected with 48 percent of the vote, over two opponents, one of whom—billionaire Blaise Thomas Golisano—spent $70 million of his fortune but gained just 14 percent of the ballots cast. In 2004, John Kerry swept the state with 58 percent of the vote for U.S. president to George W. Bush's 41 percent, while Democratic senator Chuck Schumer trounced his Republican opponent, 71-25 percent.

Rose Secrest
Updated by the Editor

New York Time Line

Apr. 17, 1524	Italian navigator Giovanni da Verrazano enters New York Harbor.
1570	Five Native American peoples unite into the Iroquois League.
1609	French explorer Samuel de Champlain reaches Lake Champlain; English navigator Henry Hudson, working for the Dutch, explores the Hudson River.
1624	Dutch establish Fort Orange, later known as Albany.
1625	Dutch establish New Amsterdam, later known as New York City, on Manhattan Island.
1650	Dutch colony has about one thousand residents.
Sept. 9, 1664	English fleet captures the colony, which now has about eight thousand residents.
1683	General assembly of colonists adopts a charter, which King James II revokes two years later.
1686	James II dissolves the assembly and unites New York and New England under a single administration.
1689	James II abdicates, leading to a rebellion against the administration led by Jacob Leisler.
1754	King's College, later known as Columbia University, is established in New York City.
1763	End of the French and Indian War ends French attempts to win control of the area.
1776	British forces capture New York City.
Apr. 20, 1777	New York adopts its first state constitution, with the state capital located at Kingston.
Oct. 17, 1777	British general John Burgoyne surrenders his army at Saratoga.
1784	University of the State of New York is founded.
1785	New York City becomes the capital of the United States.
July 26, 1788	New York ratifies the U.S. Constitution, becoming the eleventh state.
1789	Tammany Hall is created.
1790	New York City is the most populous city in the nation.
1790	National capital is moved to the newly created Washington, D.C.
1791	First public school is established.
1797	State capital is moved to Albany.
1800	New York is the second most populous state.
1810	New York is the most populous state.
1817	New York Stock Exchange is established.
1825	Erie Canal opens.
July 4, 1827	New York abolishes slavery.
1831	New York handles half the nation's imports.
1831	First railroad in the state is completed.
July 19, 1848	First women's rights convention in the nation is held at Seneca Falls.

(continued)

1857	William Tweed takes control of Tammany Hall.
July 13-16, 1863	Antidraft riots in New York City lead to two thousand deaths.
1872	Tweed is arrested for stealing millions of dollars in state funds.
1892	Ellis Island begins serving as the center of immigration for the United States.
1918	New York State Barge Canal System, the nation's largest inland waterway, is completed.
1928	Franklin Delano Roosevelt is elected governor.
1929	Stock market crashes, leading to the Great Depression.
1933	Roosevelt takes office as president of the United States.
Nov. 8, 1966	State lottery legalized.
1970	California surpasses New York in population.
1975	$4.5 billion in federal funds save New York City from bankruptcy.
1987	Stock market crashes, leading to a recession.
1989	One-quarter of lakes and ponds in Adirondacks polluted by acid rain.
Feb. 26, 1993	World Trade Center is bombed by terrorists, killing six.
1999	First Lady Hillary Rodham Clinton announces her candidacy for U.S. senator from New York, becoming the first presidential wife to do so.
July 19, 1999	Manhattanite John F. Kennedy, Jr., son of the late president, dies in crash of airplane that he was piloting.
Aug., 1999	West Nile virus-carrying mosquitoes are discovered in New York and reappear the following July.
Nov. 7, 2000	First Lady Hillary Rodham Clinton wins one of New York's U.S. Senate seats; Democrat Al Gore wins the state's electoral votes for president despite losing nationally.
Sept. 11, 2001	Terrorists attack and destroy the World Trade Center in lower Manhattan with hijacked commercial airliners; New York Stock Exchange closes for a week.
Sept. 18, 2001	In another terrorist attack, anthrax-laced letters are sent to news outlets and the *New York Post*.
Nov. 1, 2001	Liberal Republican billionaire Michael Bloomberg is elected mayor of New York City.
Nov. 12, 2001	An American Airlines Airbus crashes after takeoff from New York's JFK International Airport, killing all aboard.
Nov. 5, 2002	George Pataki is reelected governor with 48 percent of the vote.
Nov. 8, 2005	Bloomberg is reelected mayor of New York City
Mar., 2006	Construction on World Trade Center Memorial begins.

Notes for Further Study

Published Sources. A good, basic source of information on the state is *New York* (2005) by Ann Heinrichs, which discusses New York's geography, plants, animals, history, economy, and people. A broad discussion of the many issues facing New York in the future, including education, the environment, and the economy, can be found in *New York State in the Twenty-first Century* (1999), edited by Thomas A. Hirschl and Tim B. Heaton. *The Empire State: A History of New York* (2001), edited by Milton M. Klein, begins in the early seventeenth century, when the region was still populated solely by Native Americans, and concludes at the year 2000.

By far the largest number of books available deal with New York City. Two excellent histories of the city are *American Metropolis: A History of New York City* (1998) by George J. Lankevich and *Gotham: A History of New York City to 1898* (1999) by Edwin G. Burrows and Mike Wallace. *A History of New York* (2004) by Françoise Weil (translated by Jody Gladding) provides a fascinating look at the cultural, economic, and social development of New York City from the early seventeenth century and into the twenty-first century. *New York: An Illustrated History* (Rev. ed., 2003) by Ric Burns,

Lisa Ades, and James Sanders serves as the companion text to the 1999 Public Broadcasting System (PBS) network series on America's iconic city. Hundreds of rare photographs, paintings, lithographs, prints, and period maps complement the narrative. An updated version of a classic work dealing with the many different ethnic groups in the city is found in *Beyond the Melting Pot: The Negroes, Puerto Ricans, Jews, Italians, and Irish of New York City* (1990) by Nathan Glazer. A detailed account of the attempt in the 1990's to transform the city's most famous area from a place of crime and poverty to a tourist attraction is provided by Alexander J. Reichl in *Reconstructing Times Square: Politics and Culture in Urban Development* (1999).

Aimed at middle-school students, *The Natural History of New York* (2002) by Stan Freeman and Mike Nasuti is also appropriate for general audiences interested in the state's flora and fauna.

New York Politics: A Tale of Two States (2001) by Edward Schneier and John Brian Murtaugh and *Governing New York State* (5th ed., 2006), edited by Robert F. Pecorella and Jeffrey M. Stonecash, both offer solid discussions on the state's political process and institutions.

Looking north over the Hudson River from Bear Mountain Bridge. Linked to the Erie Canal, the Hudson was an important transportation route during the nineteenth and early twentieth centuries. (Rolf Müller)

Web Resources. As might be expected for a state with the largest city in the United States, an enormous variety of Web sites exist relating to New York. A good place to start is with the state government's official Web site, Welcome to New York State (www.state.ny.us), which provides information about government services and discussions of important issues such as crime, education, the economy, the environment, health care, and welfare. A large number of relevant Web sites can be reached through the New York State Links Page (www.historyoftheworld.com/usa/nyork.htm). A similar site, with information for each county, is found at New York GenWeb Project (www.rootsweb.com/~nygenweb/). Tourist attractions in the state are the subject of I Love New York (www.iloveny.state.ny.us).

Statistical information for the state can be found at New York QuickFacts (quickfacts.census.gov/qfd/states/36000 .html), provided by the U.S. Census Bureau. A concise guide to the state's government is found at New York State Law and Government Information Resources (www.law.cuny.edu/ library/libwebsites/nygovinfo.html). Of the many Web sites dealing with the state's history, one of the best for the student new to the subject is New York History and Genealogy (www .usgennet.org/usa/ny/state/). To find more historical details, search the New York State Archives site (www.archives .nysed.gov/aindex.shtml).

Among the countless Web sites dealing with New York City, the official New York City site (www.ci.nyc.ny.us/portal/ index.jsp?front_door=true) is the best place to start, while the Gotham Center for New York City History (www .gothamcenter.org/) provides many sections on the city's history. Sites dealing with two of the city's most famous institutions are the New York Stock Exchange (www.nyse.com) and *The New York Times* on the Web (nytimes.com).

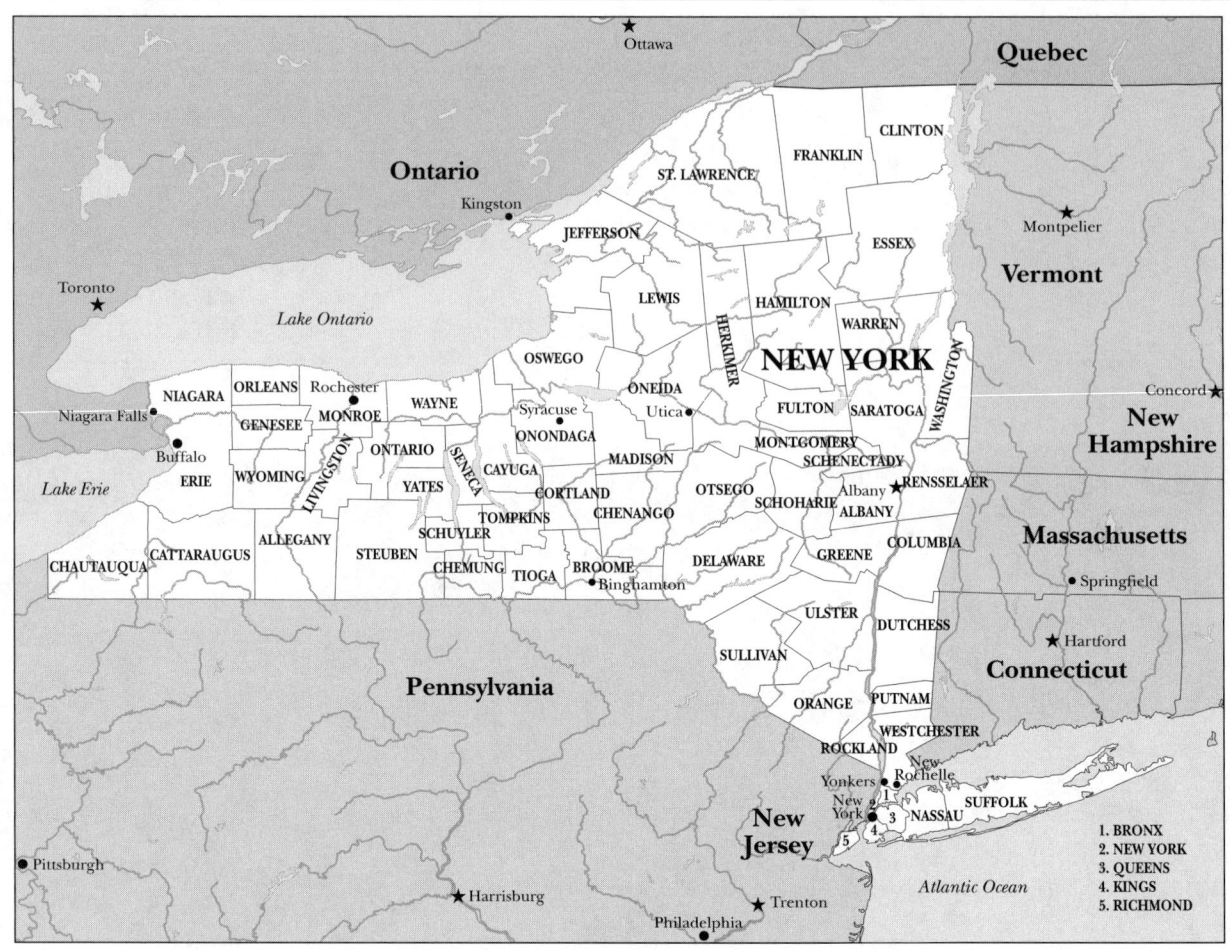

Counties

County	2000 pop.	Rank in pop.	Sq. miles	Rank in area	County	2000 pop.	Rank in pop.	Sq. miles	Rank in area
Albany	294,565	13	523.8	41	Hamilton	5,379	62	1,720.7	4
Allegany	49,927	49	1,030.3	17	Herkimer	64,427	38	1,411.8	7
Bronx*	1,332,650	6	42.0	61	Jefferson	111,738	26	1,272.3	11
Broome	200,536	19	706.9	29	Kings*	2,465,326	1	26,796	1
Cattaraugus	83,955	33	1,309.9	9	Lewis	26,944	59	1,275.6	10
Cayuga	81,963	34	693.3	30	Livingston	64,328	39	632.2	37
Chautauqua	139,750	23	1,062.1	14	Madison	69,441	37	655.9	32
Chemung	91,070	32	408.2	49	Monroe	735,343	9	659.3	31
Chenango	51,401	47	894.4	22	Montgomery	49,708	50	404.8	50
Clinton	79,894	35	1,039.4	16	Nassau	1,334,544	5	286.8	55
Columbia	63,094	41	635.8	36	New York*	1,537,195	3	28.4	62
Cortland	48,599	51	499.7	44	Niagara	219,846	17	523.0	42
Delaware	48,055	53	1,446.4	6	Oneida	235,469	16	1,212.8	12
Dutchess	280,150	15	801.7	27	Onondaga	458,336	10	780.3	28
Erie	950,265	7	1,044.7	15	Ontario	100,224	27	644.4	35
Essex	38,851	56	1,797.0	3	Orange	341,367	12	816.4	25
Franklin	51,134	48	1,631.6	5	Orleans	44,171	54	391.4	51
Fulton	55,073	45	496.2	45	Oswego	122,377	24	953.3	20
Genesee	60,370	44	494.1	46	Otsego	61,676	42	1,002.9	18
Greene	48,195	52	647.9	34	Putnam	95,745	30	231.5	56

County	2000 pop.	Rank in pop.	Sq. miles	Rank in area
Queens*	2,229,379	2	109.4	59
Rensselaer	152,538	21	654.0	33
Richmond*	443,728	11	58.6	60
Rockland	286,753	14	174.2	58
St. Lawrence	111,931	25	2,685.7	2
Saratoga	200,635	18	811.9	26
Schenectady	146,555	22	206.1	57
Schoharie	31,582	58	621.8	38
Schuyler	19,224	61	328.7	53
Seneca	33,342	57	324.9	54
Steuben	98,726	28	1,392.7	8
Suffolk	1,419,369	4	911.2	21
Sullivan	73,966	36	969.8	19
Tioga	51,784	46	518.7	43

County	2000 pop.	Rank in pop.	Sq. miles	Rank in area
Tompkins	96,501	29	476.1	47
Ulster	177,749	20	1,126.6	13
Warren	63,303	40	869.7	23
Washington	61,042	43	835.5	24
Wayne	93,765	31	604.2	39
Westchester	923,459	8	432.9	48
Wyoming	43,424	55	593.0	40
Yates	24,621	60	338.2	52

*Each of New York City's five boroughs is coterminous with a county: Bronx, Brooklyn (Kings County), Manhattan (New York County), Queens, and Staten Island (Richmond County).

Source: U.S. Census Bureau; National Association of Counties.

Cities
With 10,000 or more residents

Rank	City	Population
1	New York	8,008,278
2	Hempstead (town)	755,924
3	Brookhaven	448,248
4	Islip (town)	322,612
5	Oyster Bay	293,925
6	Buffalo	292,648
7	North Hempstead	222,611
8	Rochester	219,773
9	Babylon (town)	211,792
10	Yonkers	196,086
11	Huntington (town)	195,289
12	Syracuse	147,306
13	Amherst	116,510
14	Smithtown (town)	115,715
15	Ramapo	108,905
16	Albany (capital)	95,658
17	Greece (town)	94,141
18	Cheektowaga (town)	94,019
19	Greenburgh	86,764
20	Clarkstown	82,082
21	Cheektowaga (CDP)	79,988
22	Colonie	79,258
23	Tonawanda (town)	78,155
24	New Rochelle	72,182
25	Mount Vernon	68,381
26	Schenectady	61,821
27	Tonawanda (CDP)	61,729
28	Utica	60,651
29	Clay	58,805
30	Hempstead (village)	56,554
31	Union	56,298
32	Hamburg (town)	56,259
33	Niagara Falls	55,593

Rank	City	Population
34	Southampton	54,712
35	Brentwood	53,917
36	White Plains	53,077
37	Levittown	53,067
38	Irondequoit	52,354
39	Troy	49,170
40	Orangetown	47,711
41	Binghamton	47,380
42	Perinton	46,090
43	West Seneca	45,920
44	Rye (town)	43,880
45	Freeport	43,783
46	West Babylon	43,452
47	Mount Pleasant	43,221
48	Poughkeepsie (town)	42,777
49	Hicksville	41,260
50	Henrietta	39,028
51	Lancaster (town)	39,019
52	Cortlandt	38,467
53	Webster	37,926
54	East Meadow	37,461
55	Ossining (town)	36,534
56	Valley Stream	36,368
57	Commack	36,367
58	Yorktown	36,318
59	Brighton	35,588
60	Long Beach	35,462
61	Rome	34,950
62	Coram	34,923
63	Penfield	34,645
64	New City	34,038
65	Haverstraw (town)	33,811
66	Salina	33,290

(continued)

Rank	City	Population	Rank	City	Population
67	North Tonawanda	33,262	91	Newburgh (city)	28,259
68	Carmel	33,006	92	Glenville	28,183
69	Clifton Park	32,995	93	Cicero	27,982
70	Oceanside	32,733	94	Port Chester	27,867
71	Guilderland	32,688	95	Lindenhurst	27,819
72	Elmont	32,657	96	Riverhead (town)	27,680
73	Central Islip	31,950	97	Chili	27,638
74	Manlius	31,872	98	Orchard Park	27,637
75	Jamestown	31,730	99	Newburgh (town)	27,568
76	Monroe	31,407	100	Holbrook	27,512
77	Eastchester (town)	31,318	101	Centereach	27,285
78	Bethlehem	31,304	102	Pittsford	27,219
79	Elmira	30,940	103	Smithtown (CDP)	26,901
80	Warwick	30,764	104	Watertown	26,705
81	Huntington Station	29,910	105	Glen Cove	26,622
82	Poughkeepsie (city)	29,871	106	Vestal	26,535
83	Franklin Square	29,342	107	Wappinger	26,274
84	Ithaca (city)	29,287	108	Saratoga Springs	26,186
85	Gates	29,275	109	Clarence	26,123
86	Mamaroneck (town)	28,967	110	Dix Hills	26,024
87	West Islip	28,907	111	Plainview	25,637
88	Auburn	28,574	112	East Fishkill	25,589
89	Deer Park	28,316	113	Spring Valley	25,464
90	Rotterdam (town)	28,316	114	Queensbury	25,441

Rank	City	Population	Rank	City	Population
115	Shirley	25,395	174	Huntington (village)	18,403
116	Middletown	25,388	175	Amsterdam	18,355
117	Wallkill	24,659	176	Somers	18,346
118	Rockville Centre	24,568	177	Ithaca (town)	18,198
119	Harrison	24,154	178	Bedford	18,133
120	De Witt	24,071	179	Oswego	17,954
121	Ossining (village)	24,010	180	North Babylon	17,877
122	Bay Shore	23,852	181	Scarsdale	17,823
123	Kingston	23,456	182	Geddes	17,740
124	Baldwin	23,455	183	Evans	17,594
125	Camillus	23,152	184	Massapequa Park	17,499
126	Uniondale	23,011	185	New Castle	17,491
127	New Windsor	22,866	186	Blooming Grove	17,351
128	Merrick	22,764	187	Southeast	17,316
129	Massapequa	22,652	188	Milton	17,103
130	Peekskill	22,441	189	Holtsville	17,006
131	Lockport (city)	22,279	190	Sayville	16,735
132	Medford	21,985	191	Nanuet	16,707
133	Copiague	21,922	192	Depew	16,629
134	Selden	21,861	193	North Amityville	16,572
135	Garden City	21,672	194	Bethpage	16,543
136	New Hartford	21,172	195	Farmingville	16,458
137	Onondaga	21,063	196	Woodmere	16,447
138	Montgomery	20,891	197	Bellmore	16,441
139	Hyde Park	20,851	198	Kenmore	16,426
140	East Northport	20,845	199	Lewiston	16,257
141	East Patchogue	20,824	200	Batavia	16,256
142	Southold	20,599	201	Kings Park	16,146
143	Islip (CDP)	20,575	202	Tonawanda (city)	16,136
144	Rotterdam (CDP)	20,536	203	Floral Park	15,967
145	Owego	20,365	204	Potsdam	15,957
146	Niskayuna	20,295	205	Setauket-East Setauket	15,931
147	Fishkill	20,258	206	Roosevelt	15,854
148	Hauppauge	20,100	207	Seaford	15,791
149	North Bellmore	20,079	208	North Valley Stream	15,789
150	Ronkonkoma	20,029	209	East Greenbush	15,560
151	Lynbrook	19,911	210	Pearl River	15,553
152	Saugerties	19,868	211	Johnson City	15,535
153	Le Ray	19,836	212	Cohoes	15,521
154	East Hampton	19,719	213	Mastic	15,436
155	Lake Ronkonkoma	19,701	214	Gloversville	15,413
156	Lockport (town)	19,653	215	Olean	15,347
157	East Massapequa	19,565	216	Port Washington	15,215
158	Horseheads	19,561	217	Gates-North Gates	15,138
159	Lysander	19,285	218	South Farmingdale	15,061
160	Mineola	19,234	219	North Bay Shore	14,992
161	North Massapequa	19,152	220	Sullivan	14,991
162	Lackawanna	19,064	221	Malone	14,981
163	Wantagh	18,971	222	Rye (city)	14,955
164	Plattsburgh (city)	18,816	223	La Grange	14,928
165	Mamaroneck (village)	18,752	224	Jefferson Valley-Yorktown	14,891
166	Cortland	18,740	225	Arcadia	14,889
167	West Hempstead	18,713	226	Parma	14,822
168	Whitestown	18,635	227	Pomfret	14,703
169	Grand Island	18,621	228	Greece (village)	14,614
170	Eastchester (CDP)	18,564	229	North New Hyde Park	14,542
171	Syosset	18,544	230	Melville	14,533
172	Ogden	18,492	231	Monsey	14,504
173	Halfmoon	18,474	232	Glens Falls	14,354

(continued)

Rank	City	Population
233	Westbury	14,263
234	Stony Point (town)	14,244
235	Thompson	14,189
236	Wheatfield	14,086
237	East Islip	14,078
238	Kent	14,009
239	Aurora	13,996
240	Moreau	13,826
241	Beacon	13,808
242	Stony Brook	13,727
243	Sweden	13,716
244	German Flatts	13,629
245	Geneva	13,617
246	Dryden	13,532
247	Ridge	13,380
248	New Cassel	13,298
249	Oneonta	13,292
250	Greenlawn	13,286
251	St. James	13,268
252	Kiryas Joel	13,138
253	Dunkirk	13,131
254	Massena (town)	13,121
255	Jericho	13,045
256	Endicott	13,038
257	Malta	13,005
258	Goshen	12,913
259	Wawarsing	12,889
260	New Paltz	12,830
261	Van Buren	12,667
262	Babylon (village)	12,615
263	Ulster	12,544
264	Schodack	12,536
265	Wilton	12,511
266	Highlands	12,484
267	Arlington	12,481
268	Ogdensburg	12,364
269	Salisbury	12,341
270	Lewisboro	12,324
271	Cornwall	12,307
272	Hampton Bays	12,236
273	Fallsburg	12,234
274	North Wantagh	12,156
275	Chester	12,140
276	Fort Drum	12,123
277	Bath	12,097
278	Shawangunk	12,022
279	Nesconset	11,992
280	Patchogue	11,919
281	Pelham	11,866
282	Fulton	11,855
283	Catskill	11,849
284	North Merrick	11,844
285	North Lindenhurst	11,767
286	Stony Point (village)	11,744

Rank	City	Population
287	Endwell	11,706
288	Brunswick	11,664
289	Mastic Beach	11,543
290	Chenango	11,454
291	Beekman	11,452
292	Patterson	11,306
293	Elma	11,304
294	Canandaigua	11,264
295	Massena (village)	11,209
296	Plattsburgh (town)	11,190
297	Lancaster (village)	11,188
298	Southport	11,185
299	Kingsbury	11,171
300	Manorville	11,131
301	Tarrytown	11,090
302	Suffern	11,006
303	Mamakating	11,002
304	Oneida	10,987
305	Elwood	10,916
306	North Castle	10,849
307	Corning	10,842
308	North Greenbush	10,805
309	Fairmount	10,795
310	Fredonia	10,706
311	Putnam Valley	10,686
312	Dobbs Ferry	10,622
313	Terryville	10,589
314	Farmington	10,585
315	Miller Place	10,580
316	Wyandanch	10,546
317	Lansing	10,521
318	Riverhead (village)	10,513
319	Alden	10,470
320	East Rockaway	10,414
321	Red Hook	10,408
322	Canton	10,334
323	West Haverstraw	10,295
324	Lake Grove	10,250
325	Watervliet	10,207
326	Rocky Point	10,185
327	Kirkland	10,138
328	Haverstraw (village)	10,117
329	Hamburg (village)	10,116

Population figures are from 2000 census. Note that this list
  contains the names of many "cities," "towns," "villages," and
  "census-designated places" (CDP) that share the same names. In
  some instances, the smaller entities—although legally
  incorporated—are wholly or partly within the boundaries of the
  large entities with the same names. Many larger entities also
  encompass other entities with other names. In cases in which
  two or more entities share the same name (such as Tonawanda),
  designations such as "city" and "town do not necessarily indicate
  which has the largest population.
Source: U.S. Bureau of the Census.

Index to Tables

DEMOGRAPHICS

Resident state and national populations, 1970-2004

Population figures given in thousands

	State pop.	U.S. pop.	Share	Rank
1970	18,241	203,302	9.0%	2
1980	17,558	226,546	7.8%	2
1985	17,792	237,924	7.5%	2
1990	17,991	248,765	7.2%	2
1995	18,524	262,761	6.9%	3
2000	18,977	281,425	6.7%	3
2004	19,227	293,655	6.6%	3

Source: U.S. Census Bureau, Current Population Reports, 2006.

Resident population by age, 2004

Age Group	Total persons
Under 5 years	1,246,000
5 to 17 years	3,326,000
18 to 24 years	1,825,000
25 to 34 years	2,633,000
35 to 44 years	2,993,000
45 to 54 years	2,741,000
55 to 64 years	1,970,000
65 to 74 years	1,226,000
75 to 84 years	913,000
85 years and older	354,000
All age groups	19,227,000

Portion of residents 65 and older	13.0%
National rank in portion of oldest residents	20
National average	12.4%

Population figures are rounded to nearest thousand persons;
figures include armed forces personnel stationed in the state.
Source: U.S. Bureau of the Census, 2006.

Resident population by race, Hispanic origin, 2004

Category	State pop.	Share	U.S.
All residents	19,227	100.00%	100.00%
Non-Hispanic white	11,746	61.09%	67.37%
Hispanic white	2,470	12.85%	13.01%
Other Hispanic	607	3.16%	1.06%
African American	3,361	17.48%	12.77%
Native American	103	0.54%	0.96%
Asian, Pacific Islander	1,267	6.59%	4.37%
Two or more categories	279	1.45%	1.51%

Population figures are in thousands. Persons counted as "Hispanic" (Latino) may be of any race. Because of overlapping categories, categories may not add up to 100%. Shares in column 3 are percentages of each category within the state; these figures may be compared to the national percentages in column 4.
Source: U.S. Bureau of the Census, 2006.

Projected state population, 2000-2030

Year	Population
2000	18,977,000
2005	19,258,000
2010	19,444,000
2015	19,547,000
2020	19,577,000
2025	19,540,000
2030	19,477,000
Population increase, 2000-2030	500,000
Percentage increase, 2000-2030	2.6

Projections are based on data from the 2000 census.
Source: U.S. Census Bureau.

VITAL STATISTICS

Infant mortality rates, 1980-2002

	1980	1990	2000	2002
All state residents	12.5	9.6	6.4	6.0
All U.S. residents	12.6	9.2	9.4	9.1
All state white residents	10.8	7.4	5.4	5.4
All U.S. white residents	10.6	7.6	5.7	5.8
All state black residents	20.0	18.1	10.9	9.9
All U.S. black residents	22.2	18.0	14.1	14.4

Figures represent deaths per 1,000 live births of resident infants under 1 year old, exclusive of fetal deaths. Figures for all residents include members of other racial categories not listed separately.
Source: U.S. Census Bureau, *Statistical Abstract of the United States*, 2006.

Abortion rates, 1990 and 2000

	1990	2000
Total abortions	195,000	165,000
Rate per 1,000 women	45.6	39.1
U.S. rate	25.7	21.3
Rank	2	1

Numbers of abortions are rounded to nearest thousand; ranks are based on rates.
Source: U.S. Census Bureau.

Marriages and divorces, 2004

Total marriages	124,400
Rate per 1,000 population.	6.5
National rate per 1,000 population	7.4
Rank among all states	32
Total divorces	57,800
Rate per 1,000 population.	3.0
National rate per 1,000 population	3.7
Rank among all states	35

Figures are for all marriages and divorces performed within the state, including those of nonresidents; totals are rounded to the nearest hundred. Ranks are for highest to lowest figures; note that divorce data are not available for five states.
Source: U.S. National Center for Health Statistics, *Vital Statistics of the United States*, 2006.

Death rates by leading causes, 2002
Deaths per 100,000 resident population

Cause	State	U.S.
Heart disease	295.8	241.7
Cancer	191.4	193.2
Cerebrovascular diseases	39.8	56.4
Accidents other than motor vehicle	24.3	37.0
Motor vehicle accidents	8.8	15.7
Chronic lower respiratory diseases	36.4	43.3
Diabetes mellitus	20.5	25.4
HIV	10.3	4.9
Suicide	6.4	11.0
Homicide	4.8	6.1
All causes	825.4	847.3
Rank in overall death rate among states		33

Figures exclude nonresidents who died in the state. Causes of death follow International Classification of Diseases. Rank is from highest to lowest death rate in the United States.
Source: U.S. National Center for Health Statistics, *National Vital Statistics Report*, 2006.

ECONOMY

Gross state product, 1990-2004
In current dollars

Year	State product	Nat'l product	State share
1990	$503.6 billion	$5.67 trillion	8.88%
2000	$769.4 billion	$9.75 trillion	7.89%
2002	$802.9 billion	$10.41 trillion	7.71%
2003	$838.0 billion	$10.92 trillion	7.67%
2004	$899.7 billion	$11.65 trillion	7.72%

Source: U.S. Bureau of Economic Analysis, *Survey of Current Business,* July, 2005.

Gross state product by industry, 2003
In billions of dollars

Construction	$23.5
Manufacturing	60.6
Wholesale trade	43.8
Retail trade	48.6
Finance & insurance	138.3
Information	57.0
Professional services	66.0
Health care & social assistance	58.5
Government	78.5
Total state product	$801.0
Total U.S. product	$10,289.2
State share of U.S. total	7.78%
Rank among all states	2

Total figures include industries not listed separately. Amounts are in chained 2000 dollars.
Source: U.S. Bureau of Economic Analysis, *Survey of Current Business,* July, 2005.

Personal income per capita, 1990-2004
In current dollars

	1990	2000	2004
Per capita income	$23,523	$34,897	$38,228
U.S. average	$19,477	$29,845	$32,937
Rank among states	3	4	5

Source: U.S. Bureau of Economic Analysis, *Survey of Current Business,* April, 2005.

Energy consumption, 2001
In trillions of British thermal units (BTU), except as noted

Total energy consumption

Total state energy consumption	4,135
Total U.S. energy consumption	96,275
State share of U.S. total	4.29%
Rank among states	3

Per capita consumption (In millions of BTU)

Total state per capita consumption	217
Total U.S. per capita consumption	338
Rank among states	49

End-use sectors

Residential	1,194
Commercial	1,303
Industrial	667
Transportation	970

Sources of energy

Petroleum	1,713
Natural gas	1,206
Coal	315
Hydroelectric power	225
Nuclear electric power	422

Figures for totals include categories not listed separately.
Source: U.S. Energy Information Administration, *State Energy Data Report,* 2001.

Nonfarm employment by sectors, 2004

Total persons	8,447,000
Construction	318,000
Manufacturing	596,000
Trade, transportation, utilities	1,483,000
Information	271,000
Finance, insurance, real estate	702,000
Professional & business services	1,054,000
Education & health services	1,521,000
Leisure, hospitality, arts, organizations	662,000
Other services, including repair & maintenance	352,000
Government	1,483,000

Figures are rounded to nearest thousand persons. "Total" includes mining and natural resources, not listed separately.
Source: U.S. Bureau of Labor Statistics, 2006.

Foreign exports, 1990-2004
In millions of dollars

Year	State	U.S.	State share
1990	22,072	394,045	5.60%
1996	34,230	624,767	5.48%
1997	37,979	688,896	5.51%
2000	42,846	712,055	5.48%
2003	39,181	724,006	5.80%
2004	44,401	769,332	5.77%

Rank among all states in 2004. 3

U.S. total does not include U.S. dependencies.
Source: U.S. Census Bureau, *U.S. Merchandise Trade,* series FT 900, 2000; U.S. Census Bureau, *U.S. International Trade in Goods and Services,* Series FT 900, 2005.

LAND USE

Federally owned land, 2003
Areas in acres

	State	U.S.	State share
Total area	30,681,000	2,271,343,000	1.35%
Nonfederal land	30,439,000	1,599,584,000	1.90%
Federal land	242,000	671,759,000	0.04%
Federal share	0.8%	29.6%	—

Areas are rounded to nearest thousand acres. Figures for federally owned land do not include trust properties.
Source: U.S. General Services Administration, *Federal Real Property Profile,* 2006.

Land use, 1997
In acres, rounded to nearest thousand

Total surface area	31,361,000
Total nonfederal rural land.	26,702,000
Percentage rural land	85.1%
Cropland	5,417,000
Conservation Reserve Program (CRP*) land	54,000
Pastureland	2,722,000
Rangeland	(nil)
Forestland	17,702,000
Other rural land	808,000

*CRP is a federal program begun in 1985 to assist private landowners to convert highly erodible cropland to vegetative cover for ten years. Note that some categories of land overlap.
Source: U.S. Department of Agriculture, Natural Resources and Conservation Service, and Iowa State University, Statistical Laboratory, *Summary Report, 1997 National Resources Inventory,* revised December, 2000.

Farms and crop acreage, 2004

	State	U.S.	Share	Rank
Farms	36,000	2,113,000	1.70%	25
Acres (millions)	8	937	0.85%	33
Acres per farm	211	443	—	31

Source: U.S. Department of Agriculture, National Agricultural Statistics Service. Numbers of farms are rounded to nearest thousand units; acreage figures are rounded to nearest million. Rankings, including ties, are based on rounded figures.

GOVERNMENT AND FINANCE

Units of local government, 2002

	State	Total U.S.	Rank
All local governments	3,420	87,525	9
Counties	57	3,034	26
Municipalities	616	19,429	9
Towns (townships)	929	16,504	11
School districts	683	13,506	4
Special districts	1,135	35,052	10

Only 48 states have county governments, 20 states have township governments ("towns" in New England, Minnesota, New York, and Wisconsin), and 46 states have school districts. Special districts encompass such functions as natural resources, fire protection, and housing and community development.
Source: U.S. Census Bureau, *Census of Governments.*

State government revenue, 2002

Total revenue	$104,534 mill.
General revenue	$92,897 mill.
Per capita revenue	$4,851
U.S. per capita average	$3,689
Rank among states	7
Intergovernment revenue	
Total	$37,730 mill.
From federal government	$32,197 mill.
Charges and miscellaneous	
Total	$11,905 mill.
Current charges	$5,198 mill.
Misc. general income	$6,707 mill.
Insurance trust revenue	$6,272 mill.
Taxes	
Total	$43,262 mill.
Per capita taxes	$2,261
Rank among states	7
Property taxes	(nil)
Sales taxes	$13,121 mill.
License taxes	$1,040 mill.
Individual income taxes	$25,574 mill.
Corporate income taxes	$2,258 mill.
Other taxes	$1,270 mill.

Total revenue figures include items not listed separately here.
Source: U.S. Bureau of the Census.

State government expenditures, 2002

General expenditures

Total state expenditures. . . . . $119,199 mill.
Intergovernmental . . . . $38,982 mill.

Per capita expenditures

State $5,045
Average of all states $3,859
Rank among states 7

Selected direct expenditures

Education. . . . . $7,619 mill.
Public welfare . . . . $23,328 mill.
Health, hospital . . . . $4,756 mill.
Highways . . . . $3,222 mill.
Police protection . . . . $568 mill.
Corrections . . . . $2,371 mill.
Natural resources . . . . $346 mill.
Parks and recreation . . . . $430 mill.
Government administration . . . . $4,037 mill.
Interest on debt . . . . $3,647 mill.
Total direct expenditures. . . . . $57,547 mill.

Totals include items not listed separately.
Source: U.S. Census Bureau.

POLITICS

Governors since statehood

D = Democrat; R = Republican; O = other;
(r) resigned; (d) died in office; (i) removed from office

George Clinton	1777-1795
John Jay	1795-1801
George Clinton (O)	1801-1804
Morgan Lewis (O)	1804-1807
Daniel D. Tompkins (O)	1807-1817
John Tayler (O)	1817
DeWitt Clinton (O)	1817-1822
Joseph C. Yates (O)	1823-1824
DeWitt Clinton (O)	1825-1828
Nathaniel Pitcher (O)	1828
Martin Van Buren (D)	1829
Enos T. Throop (D)	1829-1832
William L. Marcy (D)	1833-1838
William H. Seward (O)	1839-1842
William C. Bouck (D)	1843-1844
Silas Wright (D)	1845-1846
John Young (O)	1847-1848
Hamilton Fish (O)	1849-1850
Washington Hunt (O)	1851-1852
Horatio Seymour (D)	1853-1854
Myron H. Clark (O)	1855-1856
John A. King (R)	1857-1858
Edwin D. Morgan (R)	1859-1862
Horatio Seymour (D)	1863-1864
Reuben E. Fenton (R)	1865-1868
John T. Hoffman (D)	1869-1872
John Adams Dix (R)	1873-1874
Samuel J. Tilden (D)	1875-1876
Lucius Robinson (D)	1877-1879
Alonzo B. Cornell (R)	1880-1882
Grover Cleveland (D)	1883-1885
David B. Hill (D)	1885-1891
Roswell P. Flower (D)	1892-1894
Levi P. Morton (R)	1895-1896
Frank S. Black (R)	1897-1898
Theodore Roosevelt (R)	1899-1900
Benjamin B. Odell, Jr. (R)	1901-1904
Frank W. Higgins (R)	1905-1906
Charles Evans Hughes (R)	1907-1910
Horace White (R)	1910
John Alden Dix (D)	1911-1912
William Sulzer (D)	1913
Martin Glynn (D)	1913-1914
Charles S. Whitman (R)	1915-1918
Alfred E. Smith (D)	1919-1920
Nathan L. Miller (R)	1921-1922
Alfred E. Smith (D)	1923-1928
Franklin D. Roosevelt (D)	1929-1932
Herbert H. Lehman (D)	1933-1942
Charles Poletti (D)	1942
Thomas E. Dewey (R)	1943-1954
Averell Harriman (D)	1955-1958
Nelson Rockefeller (R)	1959-1973
Malcolm Wilson (R)	1973-1974
Hugh J. Carey (D)	1975-1982
Mario M. Cuomo (D)	1983-1994
George E. Pataki (R)	1995-2006
Eliot Spitzer (D)	2007-

Composition of congressional delegations, 1989-2007

	Dem	Rep	Total
House of Representatives			
101st Congress, 1989			
State delegates	21	13	34
Total U.S.	259	174	433
102d Congress, 1991			
State delegates	21	13	34
Total U.S.	267	167	434
103d Congress, 1993			
State delegates	18	13	31
Total U.S.	258	176	434
104th Congress, 1995			
State delegates	18	13	31
Total U.S.	197	236	433
105th Congress, 1997			
State delegates	18	12	30
Total U.S.	206	228	434
106th Congress, 1999			
State delegates	19	12	31
Total U.S.	211	222	433
107th Congress, 2001			
State delegates	19	12	31
Total U.S.	211	221	432
108th Congress, 2003			
State delegates	19	10	29
Total U.S.	205	229	434
109th Congress, 2005			
State delegates	20	9	29
Total U.S.	202	231	433
110th Congress, 2007			
State delegates	23	6	29
Total U.S.	233	202	435
Senate			
101st Congress, 1989			
State delegates	1	1	2
Total U.S.	55	45	100
102d Congress, 1991			
State delegates	1	1	2
Total U.S.	56	44	100
103d Congress, 1993			
State delegates	1	1	2
Total U.S.	57	43	100
104th Congress, 1995			
State delegates	1	1	2
Total U.S.	46	53	99
105th Congress, 1997			
State delegates	1	1	2
Total U.S.	45	55	100

	Dem	Rep	Total
106th Congress, 1999			
State delegates	2	0	2
Total U.S.	45	54	99
107th Congress, 2001			
State delegates	2	0	2
Total U.S.	50	50	100
108th Congress, 2003			
State delegates	2	0	2
Total U.S.	48	51	99
109th Congress, 2005			
State delegates	2	0	2
Total U.S.	44	55	99
110th Congress, 2007			
State delegates	2	0	2
Total U.S.	49	49	98

Figures are for starts of first sessions. Totals are for Democrat (Dem.) and Republican (Rep.) members only. House membership totals under 435 and Senate totals under 100 reflect vacancies and seats held by independent party members. When the 110th Congress opened, the Senate's two independent members caucused with the Democrats, giving the Democrats control of the Senate.
Source: U.S. Congress, *Congressional Directory.*

Composition of state legislature, 1990-2006

	Democrats	Republicans
State Assembly (150 seats)		
1990	95	55
1992	100	50
1994	94	56
1996	96	54
1998	98	52
2000	98	51
2002	103	47
2004	104	46
2006	108	42
State Senate (61 seats)		
1990	26	35
1992	26	35
1994	25	36
1996	26	35
1998	24	36
2000	25	36
2002	25	37
2004	28	34
2006	28	34

Figures for total seats may include independents and minor party members. Numbers reflect results of elections in listed years; elected members usually take their seats in the years that follow.
Source: Council of State Governments; *State Elective Officials and the Legislatures.*

Voter participation in presidential elections, 2000 and 2004

	2000	2004
Voting age population		
State	14,314,000	14,655,000
Total United States	209,831,000	220,377,000
State share of U.S. total	6.82	6.65
Rank among states	3	3
Portion of voting age population casting votes		
State	48.6%	50.8%
United States	50.3%	55.5%
Rank among states	35	43

Population figures are rounded to nearest thousand and include all residents, regardless of eligibility to vote.
Source: U.S. Census Bureau.

HEALTH AND MEDICAL CARE

Medical professionals
Physicians in 2003 and nurses in 2001

	U.S.	State
Physicians in 2003		
Total	774,849	75,048
Share of U.S. total		9.64%
Rate	266	391
Rank		3
Nurses in 2001		
Total	2,262,020	165,580
Share of U.S. total		7.32%
Rate	793	868
Rank		20

Rates are numbers of physicians and nurses per 100,000 resident population; ranks are based on rates.
Source: American Medical Association, *Physician Characteristics and Distribution in the U.S.*; U.S. Department of Health and Human Services, Health Resources and Services Administration.

Health insurance coverage, 2003

	State	U.S.
Total persons covered	16,104,000	243,320,000
Total persons not covered	2,866,000	44,961,000
Portion not covered	15.1%	15.6%
Rank among states	21	—
Children not covered	432,000	8,373,000
Portion not covered	9.4%	11.4%
Rank among states	23	—

Totals are rounded to nearest thousand. Ranks are from the highest to the lowest percentages of persons *not* insured.
Source: U.S. Census Bureau, Current Population Reports.

AIDS, syphilis, and tuberculosis cases, 2003

Disease	U.S. cases	State cases	Rank
AIDS	44,232	5,133	2
Syphilis	34,270	3,825	3
Tuberculosis	14,874	1,140	3

Source: U.S. Centers for Disease Control and Prevention.

Cigarette smoking, 2003
Residents over age 18 who smoke

	U.S.	State	Rank
All smokers	22.1%	21.6%	31
Male smokers	24.8%	24.8%	25
Female smokers	20.3%	18.8%	36

Cigarette smokers are defined as persons who reported having smoked at least 100 cigarettes during their lifetimes and who currently smoked at least occasionally.
Source: U.S. Centers for Disease Control and Prevention, *Morbidity and Mortality Weekly Report*, 53, no. 44 (November 12, 2004).

HOUSING

Home ownership rates, 1985-2004

	1985	1990	1995	2000	2004
State	50.3%	53.3%	52.7%	53.4%	54.8%
Total U.S.	63.9%	63.9%	64.7%	67.4%	69.0%
Rank among states	50	50	49	50	50

Net change in state home ownership rate, 1985-2004 . . . . . . +4.5%
Net change in U.S. home ownership rate, 1985-2004 . . . . . . +5.1%

Percentages represent the proportion of owner households to total occupied households.
Source: U.S. Census Bureau, 2006.

Home sales, 2000-2004
In thousands of units

Existing home sales	2000	2002	2003	2004
State sales	273.3	290.4	282.6	307.5
Total U.S. sales	5,171	5,631	6,183	6,784
State share of U.S. total	5.29%	5.16%	4.57%	4.53%
Sales rank among states	4	4	4	4

Units include single-family homes, condos, and co-ops.
Source: National Association of Realtors, Washington, D.C., *Real Estate Outlook: Market Trends & Insights*.

Values of owner-occupied homes, 2003

	State	U.S.
Total units	2,804,000	58,809,000
Value of units		
Under $100,000	26.9%	29.6%
$100,000-199,999	23.3%	36.9%
$200,000 or more	49.8%	33.5%
Median value	$198,883	$142,275
Rank among all states 10		

Units are owner-occupied one-family houses whose numbers are rounded to nearest thousand. Data are extrapolated from survey samples.

Source: U.S. Census Bureau, American Community Survey.

EDUCATION

Public school enrollment, 2002

Prekindergarten through grade 8
State enrollment 2,017,000
Total U.S. enrollment. 34,135,000
State share of U.S. total 5.91%

Grades 9 through 12
State enrollment 871,000
Total U.S. enrollment. 14,067,000
State share of U.S. total 6.19%

Enrollment rates
State public school enrollment rate. 85.8%
Overall U.S. rate 90.4%
Rank among states in 2002. 46
Rank among states in 1995. 39

Enrollment figures (which include unclassified students) are rounded to nearest thousand pupils during fall school term. Enrollment rates are based on enumerated resident population estimate for July 1, 2002.

Source: U.S. National Center for Education Statistics.

Public college finances, 2003-2004

FTE enrollment in public institutions of higher education
Students in state institutions 487,300
Students in all U.S. public institutions 9,916,600
State share of U.S. total 4.91
Rank among states. 4

State and local government appropriations for higher education
State appropriation per FTE $6,663
National average. $5,716
Rank among states 12
State & local tax revenue going to higher education 5.1%

FTE = full-time equivalent in public postsecondary programs, including summer sessions; student numbers are rounded to nearest hundred. Funding figures for 2003-2004 academic year include financial aid to students in state public institutions and exclude money for research, agriculture experiment stations, teaching hospitals, and medical schools; figures are rounded to nearest thousand dollars.

Source: Higher Education Executive Officers, Denver, Colorado.

TRANSPORTATION AND TRAVEL

Highway mileage, 2003

Interstate highways 1,674
Other freeways and expressways 798
Arterial roads. 13,502
Collector roads. 20,557
Local roads. 76,593
Urban roads 41,145
Rural roads. 71,979
Total state mileage 113,124
U.S. total 3,974,107
State share 2.85%
Rank among states 14

Note that combined urban and rural road mileage matches the total of the other categories.

Source: U.S. Federal Highway Administration.

Motor vehicle registrations and driver licenses, 2003

Vehicle registrations	State	U.S.	Share	Rank
Autos, trucks, buses	10,802,000	231,390,000	4.67%	4
Autos only	8,313,000	135,670	6.13%	3
Motorcycles	150,000	5,328,000	2.82%	11
Driver licenses	11,357,000	196,166,000	5.79%	4

Figures, which do not include vehicles owned by military services, are rounded to the nearest thousand. Figures for automobiles include taxis.

Source: U.S. Federal Highway Administration.

Domestic travel expenditures, 2003

Spending by U.S. residents on overnight trips and day trips of at least 50 miles from home

Total expenditures within state	$27.73 bill.
Total expenditures within U.S.	$490.87 bill.
State share of U.S. total	5.6%
Rank among states	4

Source: Travel Industry Association of America.

Retail gasoline prices, 2003-2007

Average price per gallon at the pump

Year	U.S.	State
2003	$1.267	$1.240
2004	$1.316	$1.333
2005	$1.644	$1.583
2007	$2.298	$2.499

Excise tax per gallon in 2004	23.2¢
Rank among all states in 2007 prices	6

Prices are averages of all grades of gasoline sold at the pump during March months in 2003-2005 and during February, 2007. Averages for 2006, during which prices rose higher, are not available.
Source: U.S. Energy Information Agency, *Petroleum Marketing Monthly* (2003-2005 data); American Automobile Association (2007 data).

CRIME AND LAW ENFORCEMENT

State and local police officers, 2000-2004

	2000	2002	2004
Total officers			
U.S.	654,601	665,555	675,734
State	65,527	59,654	63,108*
*Net change, 2000-2004			−3.69%
Officers per 1,000 residents			
U.S.	2.33	2.31	2.30
State	3.45	3.12	3.28
State rank	3	3	3

Totals include state and local police and sheriffs.
Source: Carsey Institute, University of New Hampshire.

Crime rates, 2003

Incidents per 100,000 residents

Crimes	State	U.S.
Violent crimes		
Total incidents	465	475
Murder	5	6
Forcible rape	20	32
Robbery	186	142
Aggravated assault	254	295
Property crimes		
Total incidents	2,248	3,588
Burglary	393	741
Larceny/theft	1,619	2,415
Motor vehicle theft	236	433
All crimes	2,713	4,063

Source: U.S. Federal Bureau of Investigation, *Crime in the United States,* annual.

State prison populations, 1980-2003

	State	U.S.	State share
1980	21,815	305,458	7.14%
1990	54,895	708,393	7.75%
1996	69,709	1,025,624	6.80%
2000	70,199	1,391,261	5.05%
2003	65,198	1,470,045	4.44%

State figures exclude prisoners in federal penitentiaries.
Source: U.S. Bureau of Justice Statistics, *Prisoners in 2003.*

North Carolina

Location: Atlantic coast

Area and rank: 48,718 square miles (126,180 square kilometers); 53,821 square miles (139,396 square kilometers) including water; twenty-ninth largest state in area

Coastline: 301 miles (484 kilometers) on the Atlantic Ocean

Shoreline: 3,375 miles (5,432 kilometers)

Population and rank: 8,541,000 (2004); eleventh largest state in population

Capital city: Raleigh (276,093 people in 2000 census)

Largest city: Charlotte (540,828 people in 2000 census)

Entered Union and rank: November 21, 1789; twelfth state

Present constitution adopted: 1971

State capitol building in Raleigh. (Courtesy of the North Carolina Division of Tourism, Film & Sports Development)

Counties: 100

State name: North Carolina was named after Charles I of England

State nickname: Tar Heel State

Motto: *Esse quam videri* (To be rather than to seem)

State flag: One-third is blue with a white star surrounded by letters N and C, with gold scrolls above and below reading "May 20th, 1775" and "April 12th, 1776"; other two-thirds are red and white

Highest point: Mount Mitchell—6,684 feet (2,037 meters)

Lowest point: Atlantic Ocean—sea level

Highest recorded temperature: 110 degrees Fahrenheit (43 degrees Celsius)—Fayetteville, 1983

Lowest recorded temperature: −34 degrees Fahrenheit (−37 degrees Celsius)—Mount Mitchell, 1985

State song: "The Old North State"

State tree: Pine

State flower: American dogwood

State bird: Cardinal

National parks: Great Smoky Mountains

North Carolina History

Although sometimes historically overshadowed by its neighbors Virginia and South Carolina, North Carolina has contributed much to the development of the United States. A relatively narrow state, it stretches from the Great Smoky Mountains, a part of the Appalachian system, through the Piedmont Plateau to the coastal plain, which terminates at the long, narrow islands known as the Outer Banks, where Europeans first attempted to settle the land during the late sixteenth century.

Native Americans and Early Europeans. Sometime around 8000 B.C.E., Native Americans began settling what is now North Carolina. By the period 500 B.C.E., what is known as the Woodland culture had developed throughout much of the area, with cultivation of corn, beans, and squash and the hunting of game. By the time Europeans arrived there were around thirty tribes in the area belonging to three basic linguistic groups, the Algonquian, Iroquoian, and Siouan. The five most powerful and important tribes were the Hatteras (also known as Croatoan), Chowanoe, Tuscarora, Catawba, and Cherokee. The relationship between these Native Americans and the Europeans, especially the English, would have a major impact on the development of North Carolina.

Giovanni da Verrazano, an Italian explorer in the service of France, was the first European to chart the Carolina coast. He was followed by the Spanish in 1526 with an unsuccessful attempt at settlement and in 1540 with Spanish explorer Hernando de Soto's travel through the state. The first serious attempts at European settlement came through England's Sir Walter Raleigh, who had been granted land by Queen Elizabeth. In 1585 and 1586, the first two expeditions sponsored, but not led, by Raleigh were unsuccessful. However, in 1587 a third group established itself on Roanoke Island on the Outer Banks. A few weeks after the colony was founded, Eleanor Dare gave birth to a daughter named Virginia, the first English child born in the New World. John White, father of Eleanor Dare and the colony's governor, sailed to England for supplies. Hostile Spanish fleets prevented his return until 1590, when he found the colony deserted and the word "Croatoan" carved into a tree. Although this may have signaled the community's move to Croatoan Island, south of Cape Hatteras, the mystery of the so-called Lost Colony was never solved.

English Settlement and Revolution. In 1663, King Charles II of England granted a charter to eight Lord Proprietors for a colony to be called Carolina, after himself. A northern county, known as Albemarle, be-

came the foundation of North Carolina. Settlers came from England and Virginia. Initial growth was slow, marked by frequent disputes, sometimes breaking into open rebellion, between settlers and representatives of the Proprietors. The colony faced numerous dangers, including the ravages of pirates, such as Edward Teach or Blackbeard, and the colony was hard-pressed during the Tuscarora War with that tribe, which raged from 1711 through 1715. However, it overcame these difficulties, and in 1712 North and South Carolina were officially recognized as two separate and distinct colonies. In 1729, North Carolina became a royal province.

After an initially slow start, North Carolina's population grew steadily, and its economy prospered from the production of naval staples such as turpentine and tar. It was during this period that "Tarheel" became a popular nickname for the state and its residents, because of the abundance of that material. As British high taxes and unfair treatment pushed the colonies toward rebellion, North Carolina joined the movement for independence and took a dramatic step in advance of other American colonies: In 1775, citizens of Mecklenburg County adopted a set of "resolves," which declared North Carolina independent of Great Britain. In Halifax in April, 1776, a provincial congress again voted in favor of independence.

Revolution and Statehood. The only two battles during the Revolution in North Carolina were those of Moore's Creek Bridge in 1776 and Guilford Courthouse in 1781. However, there was a vicious partisan struggle during the Revolution between loyalists and rebels, as well as uprisings by Cherokee Indians in the mountain areas throughout the conflict.

North Carolina initially rejected the proposed U.S. Constitution from fear of a strong central government but ratified it in 1789, after the Bill of Rights was proposed. Until the mid-1830's, it lagged behind the new nation in economic development, educational initiatives, and overall prosperity. During this time, North Carolina was sometimes scornfully referred to as the "Rip Van Winkle State" because of its stagnation. However, state leaders pushed through important changes, writing a new state constitution and making the state capital Raleigh, near the center of the state. Railroads, canals, public schools, and other civic improvements led to economic development and population growth.

Civil War. When the Civil War was brewing, North Carolina resisted joining other southern states in seceding from the Union. There was strong antislavery and pro-Union sentiment in North Carolina, especially in the western portion of the state, and efforts were made to find a peaceful solution to the conflict. It was not until Confederate forces fired on Fort Sumter and President Abraham Lincoln issued a call for troops to put down the rebellion that North Carolina left the Union, in 1861.

Despite coming late to the conflict, North Carolina sent more troops to the Confederate army than any other southern state, and more than one-quarter of its soldiers were killed. During the war, Union forces quickly captured the Outer Banks and much of the coastline, with only the port of Wilmington remaining open for Confederate blockade runners until the spring of 1865. The last major battle of the war was fought at Bentonville on March 19-21, 1865, between the forces of Union General William T. Sherman and Confederate Joseph E. Johnston. Johnston's defeat and surrender to Sherman shortly after Confederate general Robert E. Lee's effectively ended the Civil War.

Reconstruction. The Reconstruction period in North Carolina was one of intense struggle between defenders of the old order against newly freed African Americans and whites who had not been slave owners before the war. Under a new constitution, North Carolina was readmitted to the Union in 1868, and a series of reforms were enacted, which benefited both whites and blacks. However, conservative forces regained power in the state legislature in 1870, and in 1876, when federal troops left and Reconstruction ended, blacks and poor whites found themselves again under the domination of landlords and the rich.

Antebellum North Carolina's economy had relied primarily upon agriculture, with the state split between larger farms and plantations dependent upon slave labor in the east and smaller farms in the west. Following the Civil War, small farms leased out to sharecroppers became a dominant pattern, with tobacco and cotton the primary cash crops. Textile mills, many of them us-

ing the water power abundant in the state's piedmont area, were established. Tobacco became a major crop, and North Carolina a major manufacturer of tobacco products. In 1890, James B. Duke founded the American Tobacco Company, and his rival, Richard Joshua Reynolds, made his company, R. J. Reynolds, one of the nation's leading industries. Meanwhile, the abundant forests and water power of western North Carolina and the woodworking technology it powered caused furniture making to become a growth industry that remained important throughout the twentieth century. Technology of another kind was literally launched on December 17, 1903, when Wilbur and Orville Wright made the first powered flight of an aircraft at Kitty Hawk on the windswept Outer Banks.

Modern North Carolina. North Carolina, like so much of the South, was hard hit by the Great Depression, but Franklin Roosevelt's New Deal and the economic mobilization brought about by World War II began massive changes in the state. By offering tax breaks and other incentives, North Carolina was highly successful in recruiting new business, including high-technology firms. Research Triangle Park, located in the Raleigh-Durham-Chapel Hill area, became the site of research and development efforts by many national and international companies, often in conjunction with North Carolina's colleges and universities. During the 1980's, North Carolina became a major player in the financial world as regional and national banks located their headquarters in the state.

Under Governor Terry Sanford, from 1961 to 1965, North Carolina developed a progressive attitude toward education and the arts. Many community and technical colleges were established to provide training and education for workers in high-tech industries, and the nation's first state-supported school for the performing arts was launched in Winston-Salem. During

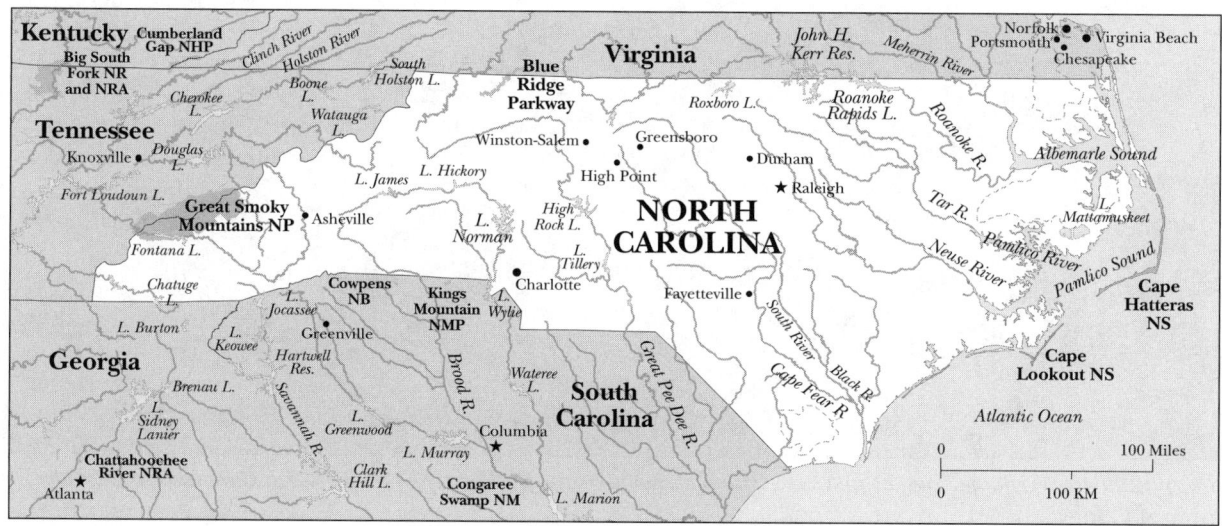

this time North Carolina's institutions of higher education, such as the University of North Carolina at Chapel Hill, Duke University, and Wake Forest, became recognized as among the finest in the United States.

However, economic development and academic achievement were not always evenly matched by social progress. The nation's first sit-in to protest racial segregation occurred in Greensboro in 1960 and provoked reactions from the Ku Klux Klan and other white supremacist groups, including the murder of five protesters at an anti-Klan rally in 1979. At the same time, the Republican Party grew in strength in North Carolina, at times by appealing to the "white backlash" vote. In 1972, Jesse Helms became the first Republican elected to the U.S. Senate from North Carolina in the twentieth century.

The state was also battered by natural disasters during the 1980's and 1990's. In March, 1984, a series of tornadoes in the state's eastern counties killed forty-four people. Only six months later, Hurricane Diana caused more than $65 million in damage. In 1989, Hurricane Hugo, one of the strongest storms ever to come ashore in the United States, caused millions of dollars of damage in Charlotte, hundreds of miles inland. In 1996, two hurricanes, Bertha in July and Fran in September, left massive destruction behind them, and twenty-one people died in Fran's fury. With potential prosperity and growth on one hand, and unresolved racial tensions on the other, North Carolina is ever more mindful of its motto, *Esse quam videri*—"To be rather than to seem."

Politics. Around the beginning of the twenty-first century, North Carolina experienced several political firsts. In the November, 2000, general election, Democrat Beverly Eaves Perdue was elected the state's first female lieutenant governor; she was reelected in 2004. Also in 2004, Democratic senator John Edwards became the first North Carolinian to run for vice president of the United States. During the year following, Terry Bellamy, a two-term city council member, was elected the first black mayor of the city of Asheville, the economic hub of the state's western region. She became one of the nation's forty-seven African American mayors of cities with populations over fifty thousand. She was preceded by Leni Sitnick, who was elected Asheville's first female mayor in 1997.

By 2006, the partisan dimensions of North Carolina politics seemed somewhat bifurcated between state government and representation in Washington, D.C. State government leaned decidedly to the Democratic

Orville and Wilbur Wright making the first successful powered airplane flight at Kittyhawk, North Carolina, in December, 1903. (Library of Congress)

North Carolina's largest city, Charlotte has a population more than double that of its nearest rival, Raleigh. (Courtesy of the North Carolina Division of Tourism, Film & Sports Development)

side, as the offices of governor, lieutenant governor, secretary of state, treasurer, and attorney general were all held by Democrats. On the other hand, Republican George W. Bush had won the state's electoral votes in the elections of 2000 and 2004, and seven of the state's thirteen members of the House of Representatives were Republicans in 2004. Both of the state's U.S. senators were also Republicans. In 2002, Republican Elizabeth Dole was elected to the U.S. Senate, assuming the seat of North Carolina's long-serving, staunchly conservative Senator Helms. Dole was elected by a 54-45 percent margin in the state's most expensive race of the year, as candidates spent a combined $24 million. The second Republican senator, Richard Burr, was elected in 2004 to the seat vacated by vice presidential candidate Edwards.

Questions Surrounding Race. In April, 2001, the U.S. Supreme Court decided a case important to the state. In *Easley v. Cromartie,* the Court ruled on allegations by minority white voters that North Carolina's Twelfth Congressional District was racially gerrymandered. The district notoriously straddles a highway along which black voters constitute a large majority. The Court held, however, that the district's boundaries were drawn on the basis of voters' party preferences,

not on their race, and were therefore constitutionally permissible. Another contentious racial issue was whether the state's judicial system applied capital punishment with racial bias. While this question was to be investigated, a moratorium on capital punishment was declared by the state legislature in 2003, lasting until June 1, 2005.

Hurricane Seasons. In 2003 and 2004, the weather was a factor in North Carolina's history, as a succession of hurricanes and tropical storms invaded the state. In 2003, Hurricane Isabel hit the state in mid-September with one-hundred-mile-per-hour winds, doing $5 billion in damage; only $1 billion was insured. In 2004, Tropical Storm Bonnie, which killed three persons, was followed by the remnants of Hurricane Charley, much weakened by its destructive adventures in Florida. Tropical Storm Gaston followed and was itself followed by Hurricane Ivan, which resulted in parts of the state being declared disaster areas. Even then the storms were not at an end, as Tropical Storm Jeanne hit the state. In 2005, Hurricane Ophelia ravaged coastal areas, though causing no direct deaths.

Michael Witkoski
Updated by the Editor

North Carolina Time Line

1524	Giovanni da Verrazano commands French expedition along coast of North Carolina.
1540	Hernando de Soto leads Spanish exploration through North Carolina mountains.
1584	Queen Elizabeth grants Sir Walter Raleigh right to found colony; English explore Roanoke Island.
Aug., 1585	Raleigh establishes first English colony in America on Roanoke Island.
1586	English abandon Roanoke colony.
1587	English found second colony on Roanoke Island.
Aug. 18, 1587	Virginia Dare is born, first English child born in North America.
1590	Governor John White returns from England to find colony deserted under mysterious circumstances.
1629	King Charles I of England grants territory to Sir Robert Heath, who names it "Carolina" after the king.
1663	Charles II of England grants region to Lord Proprietors.
1705	First school opens in Pasquotank County.
1706	Bath is incorporated as first town.
1710	New Bern is founded.
Sept., 1711	Tuscarora War begins with massacre of settlers by Native Americans.
1712	Carolina is divided into two colonies, North and South Carolina.
Feb., 1715	Tuscarora War ends with defeat of Native Americans.
1729	North Carolina becomes royal province.
1768	Backcountry farmers known as "Regulators" oppose British rule and threaten to rebel.
May 17, 1771	Regulators are defeated by colonial militia at battle of Alamance Creek.
Aug. 25, 1774	Provincial congress is organized at New Bern.
May 20, 1775	Mecklenburg Resolves are adopted, effectively declaring North Carolina independent.
Feb. 27, 1776	Rebels defeat Loyalists at Moore's Creek Bridge.
Apr. 12, 1776	Halifax Resolves instruct North Carolina delegates to Continental Congress to vote for independence.
Dec. 18, 1776	First state constitution is adopted.
1780	British General Charles Cornwallis occupies Charlotte.
Mar. 15, 1781	Cornwallis wins Battle of Guilford Courthouse but is forced to retreat.
Nov. 21, 1789	North Carolina enters the Union as the twelfth state to ratify the Constitution.
1789	University of North Carolina is chartered.
1792	Raleigh is made the capital.
1795	University of North Carolina becomes first state university to open, at Chapel Hill.
Early 1800's	First gold rush in United States in North Carolina piedmont.
1813	First cotton mill in North Carolina opens.
1830's	Cherokees forcibly removed to western territories along "Trail of Tears."
1835	Changes in state constitution give more representation to western part of state and disenfranchise free blacks.
1840	State's first railroad opens.
May 20, 1861	North Carolina secedes from Union.
1865	Confederate general Joseph E. Johnston surrenders to General William T. Sherman.
1865	Washington Duke begins packaging tobacco near Durham.
June 25, 1868	North Carolina is readmitted to Union.
1890	James B. Duke founds American Tobacco Company.
Dec. 17, 1903	Wright brothers make first successful powered flight near Kitty Hawk.
1920	Tobacco becomes the state's major crop.
1924	Duke University is founded.
1936	Intracoastal Waterway is completed.
1944	Fontana Dam, the largest in the Tennessee Valley Authority system, is completed.
1958	Research Triangle Park is established.
Feb. 1, 1960	First sit-in to protest segregation takes place in Greensboro.
1965	Nation's first state-supported school for the performing arts opens in Winston-Salem.

1966	Cape Lookout National Seashore is established.
1971	New state constitution is adopted.
1972	Jesse Helms becomes first Republican in the twentieth century elected to U.S. Senate from North Carolina.
1972	James E. Holshouser, Jr., becomes first Republican in the twentieth century elected governor of North Carolina.
1976	Section of historic New River designated a "scenic river" to prevent construction of a dam.
1979	Ku Klux Klan members murder five protesters at anti-Klan rally in Greensboro.
1980's	Charlotte becomes one of the largest banking centers in the United States.
1984	Severe tornadoes strike eastern counties, killing forty-four; Hurricane Diana strikes, causing millions in damages.
1988	Drought disaster declared worst since heat wave of the 1930's.
1989	Hurricane Hugo cripples Charlotte.
1996	Hurricanes Bertha and Fran strike state, causing billions in damage and twenty-one deaths.
1999	Cape Hatteras Lighthouse is moved to protect it from erosion.
Nov. 7, 2000	Beverly Eaves Perdue is elected first female lieutenant governor in North Carolina's history.
Apr. 18, 2001	U.S. Supreme Court allows North Carolina's Twelfth Congressional District to remain in its present configuration.
Nov. 5, 2002	Elizabeth Dole, wife of former senator Robert Dole, is elected to the U.S. Senate.
Sept. 18, 2003	Hurricane Isabel strikes North Carolina coast, killing four and doing massive damage.
Nov. 2, 2004	John Edwards becomes first North Carolinian to run for vice president of the United States; Governor Mike Easley is reelected by a 55-43 percent margin.
Nov. 8, 2005	Terry Bellamy is elected first black female mayor of Asheville.

Notes for Further Study

Published Sources. The beginning student should consult the older but still useful *North Carolina: A History* (1988) by William S. Powell, which begins in prehistoric times and includes original documents. Powell's *North Carolina Through Four Centuries* (1990) is the definitive history of the state from European colonization to the twentieth century; it offers excellent discussions of all aspects of the state's development, including the colonial and Civil War periods. *Discovering North Carolina: A Tar Heel Reader* (1991), edited by Jack Claiborne and William Price, contains a sampling of North Carolina scenes and personalities, presented by North Carolina writers. *Tar Heel State: A History of North Carolina* (2005) by Milton Ready offers a comprehensive view of the state's geography, its roles in the American Revolution and Civil War, the early history of the Cherokees, the rise of industrial mills, and socioeconomic and political changes brought forth in the last decades of the twentieth century.

Jack Fleer's *North Carolina Government and Politics* (1994) is a serious study of the changing nature of North Carolina government from colonial times to the modern era and how the political landscape has shifted during that period. Paul Luebke's *Tar Heel Politics 2000* (1998) is another study of North Carolina politics from the colonial days with its "east versus west" rivalry to the rise of the Republican Party.

Focusing on everyday life in a mountain community, Nannie Greene and Catherine Stokes Shepperd's *Community and Change in the North Carolina Mountains: Oral Histories and Profiles of People, from Western Watauga County* (2006) is a good source for those seeking insight into the state's rural history in the decades from 1930 to 1960. Presented in "reverse history," Gerald M. Sider's *Living Indian Histories: The Lumbee and Tuscarora People in North Carolina* (Rev. ed., 2003) focuses on five violent incidents in 1973 that took place among or against the Indian people of Robeson County. Using these events as a point of reference, the book then examines the colonial origins of the tensions underlying each of these issues and then moves forward to examine how the tribes have endured social and political changes in the modern era.

Two books are worthwhile for their focus on the natural beauty of the state and its culture and people. *Insiders' Guide to North Carolina's Outer Banks* (2006) by Karen Bachman brings together beautiful photographs and interesting text to introduce the reader to the state's barrier islands. Hugh Morton, a photojournalist for more than sixty years, captures the state's history and culture with photographs in *Hugh Morton's North Carolina* (2003), a book divided into three sections: scenes, people and events, and sports.

Web Resources. Many Web sites provide information on North Carolina, and a good place to start is the North Carolina Government portal site (www.ncgov.com/), which provides a range of information categorized for citizen, business, and state employee users. The North Carolina Encyclopedia (statelibrary.dcr.state.nc.us/nc/cover.htm) site is also quite good, offering links to counties and communities, history, geography, health, and state government. The secretary of state offers a page for children that provides a good interactive time line of the state's history (www.secretary.state.nc.us/kidspg/history.htm). Both the North Carolina Humanities

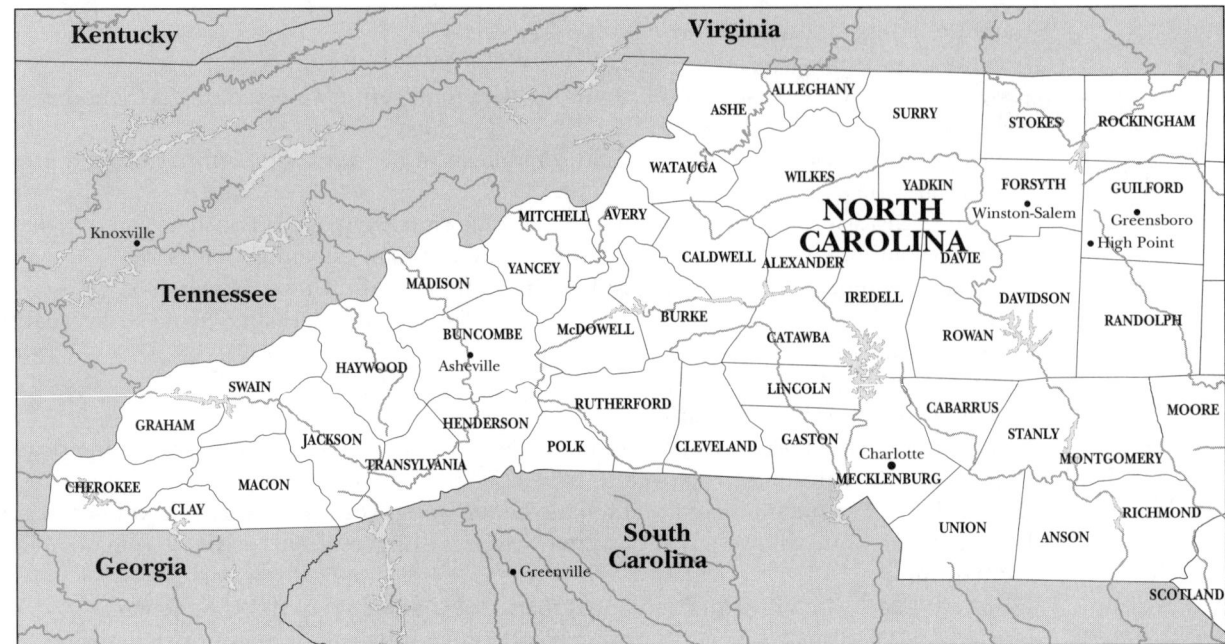

Council (www.nchumanities.org/home.html) and the North Carolina Department of Cultural Resources (www.ncdcr .gov/) are good destinations for those interested in the state's cultural offerings. The state's Cherokee community has its own Web page (www.cherokee-nc.com/), and Access Genealogy (www.accessgenealogy.com/native/northcarolina/ index.htm) provides a page that details many of the state's tribes.

Counties

County	2000 pop.	Rank in pop.	Sq. miles	Rank in area	County	2000 pop.	Rank in pop.	Sq. miles	Rank in area
Alamance	130,800	15	430.7	56	Craven	91,436	26	695.6	17
Alexander	33,603	65	260.3	88	Cumberland	302,963	5	653.1	20
Alleghany	10,677	93	234.7	95	Currituck	18,190	84	261.7	87
Anson	25,275	73	531.6	35	Dare	29,967	68	381.7	68
Ashe	24,384	74	426.2	58	Davidson	147,246	11	552.2	31
Avery	17,167	86	247.0	92	Davie	34,835	63	265.2	86
Beaufort	44,958	53	827.6	8	Duplin	49,063	48	817.8	9
Bertie	19,773	80	699.2	15	Durham	223,314	6	290.6	84
Bladen	32,278	67	875.0	4	Edgecombe	55,606	44	505.1	43
Brunswick	73,143	34	854.9	6	Forsyth	306,067	4	409.7	60
Buncombe	206,330	7	656.3	19	Franklin	47,260	51	491.6	44
Burke	89,148	29	506.7	42	Gaston	190,365	8	356.5	73
Cabarrus	131,063	14	364.4	72	Gates	10,516	94	340.6	76
Caldwell	77,415	31	471.7	49	Graham	7,993	97	292.1	83
Camden	6,885	98	240.7	93	Granville	48,498	50	531.2	37
Carteret	59,383	41	531.4	36	Greene	18,974	82	265.4	85
Caswell	23,501	76	425.7	59	Guilford	421,048	3	650.1	22
Catawba	141,685	12	400.0	61	Halifax	57,370	43	725.4	14
Chatham	49,329	47	683.1	18	Harnett	91,025	27	595.0	25
Cherokee	24,298	75	455.2	52	Haywood	54,033	46	553.9	29
Chowan	14,526	88	172.6	100	Henderson	89,173	28	373.8	70
Clay	8,775	96	214.7	98	Hertford	22,601	77	353.7	74
Cleveland	96,287	24	464.3	50	Hoke	33,646	64	391.2	66
Columbus	54,749	45	936.8	3	Hyde	5,826	99	612.8	24

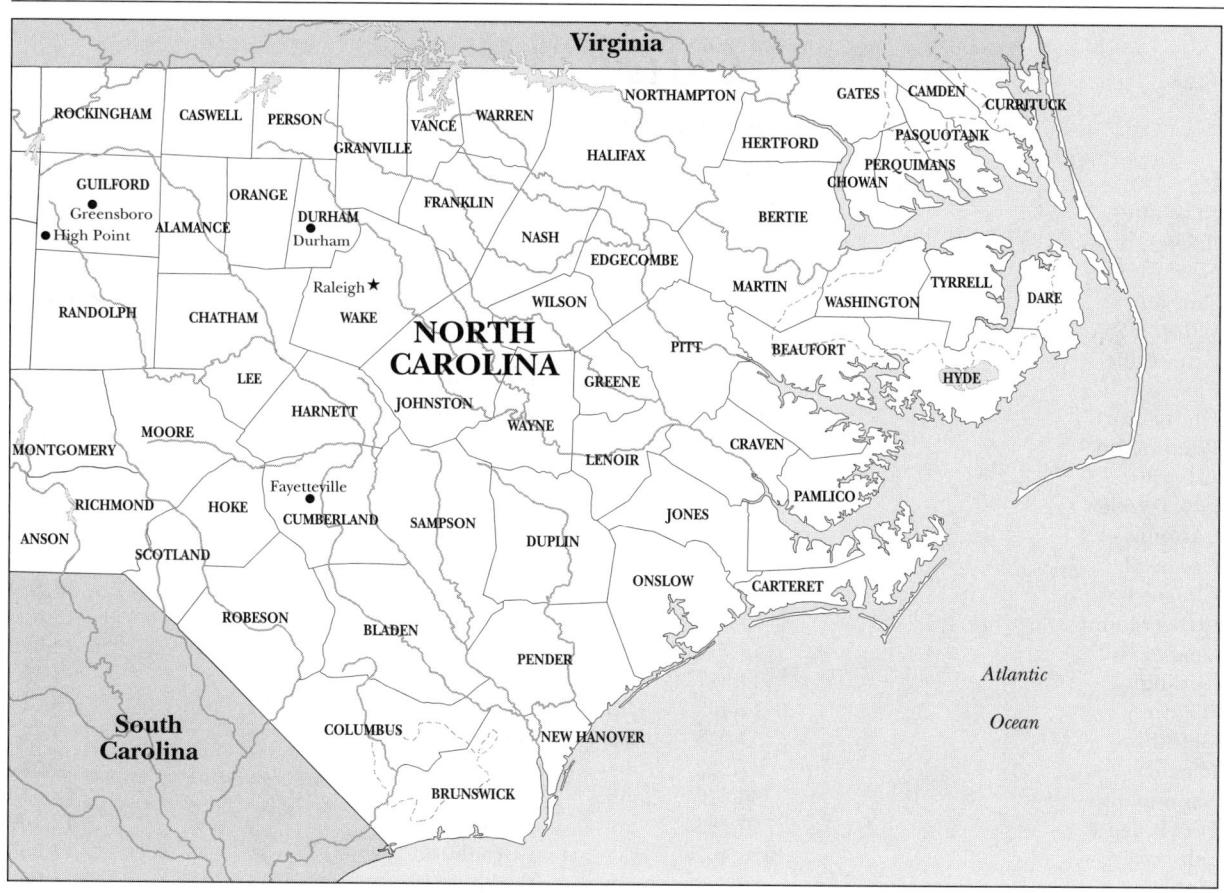

County	2000 pop.	Rank in pop.	Sq. miles	Rank in area	County	2000 pop.	Rank in pop.	Sq. miles	Rank in area
Iredell	122,660	20	574.4	26	Randolph	130,454	16	787.5	11
Jackson	33,121	66	490.6	46	Richmond	46,564	52	474.0	47
Johnston	121,965	21	792.0	10	Robeson	123,339	19	948.9	1
Jones	10,381	95	473.3	48	Rockingham	91,928	25	566.5	27
Lee	49,040	49	257.3	89	Rowan	130,340	17	511.4	41
Lenoir	59,648	40	399.9	62	Rutherford	62,899	38	564.2	28
Lincoln	63,780	37	298.8	82	Sampson	60,161	39	945.5	2
McDowell	42,151	57	441.7	55	Scotland	35,998	60	319.2	79
Macon	29,811	69	516.5	40	Stanly	58,100	42	395.1	64
Madison	19,635	81	449.4	54	Stokes	44,711	54	451.9	53
Martin	25,593	72	462.6	51	Surry	71,219	35	536.6	33
Mecklenburg	695,454	1	527.4	39	Swain	12,968	90	528.1	38
Mitchell	15,687	87	221.5	97	Transylvania	29,334	70	378.4	69
Montgomery	26,822	71	491.1	45	Tyrrell	4,149	100	389.9	67
Moore	74,769	32	698.8	16	Union	123,677	18	637.4	23
Nash	87,420	30	540.3	32	Vance	42,954	55	253.5	90
New Hanover	160,307	9	198.9	99	Wake	627,846	2	833.9	7
Northampton	22,086	78	536.1	34	Warren	19,972	79	428.7	57
Onslow	150,355	10	766.9	12	Washington	13,723	89	347.8	75
Orange	118,227	22	399.8	63	Watauga	42,695	56	312.5	80
Pamlico	12,934	91	336.9	77	Wayne	113,329	23	552.6	30
Pasquotank	34,897	62	226.9	96	Wilkes	65,632	36	757.2	13
Pender	41,082	58	870.7	5	Wilson	73,814	33	371.1	71
Perquimans	11,368	92	247.2	91	Yadkin	36,348	59	335.6	78
Person	35,623	61	392.3	65	Yancey	17,774	85	312.4	81
Pitt	133,798	13	651.6	21					
Polk	18,324	83	237.8	94					

Source: U.S. Census Bureau; National Association of Counties.

Cities

With 10,000 or more residents

Rank	City	Population	Rank	City	Population
1	Charlotte	540,828	35	Lexington	19,953
2	Raleigh (capital)	276,093	36	Thomasville	19,788
3	Greensboro	223,891	37	Shelby	19,477
4	Durham	187,035	38	Mooresville	18,823
5	Winston-Salem	185,776	39	Garner	17,757
6	Fayetteville	121,015	40	Morganton	17,310
7	Cary	94,536	41	Elizabeth City	17,188
8	High Point	85,839	42	Kernersville	17,126
9	Wilmington	75,838	43	Roanoke Rapids	16,957
10	Asheville	68,889	44	Lenoir	16,793
11	Jacksonville	66,715	45	Carrboro	16,782
12	Gastonia	66,277	46	Henderson	16,095
13	Greenville	60,476	47	Eden	15,908
14	Concord	55,977	48	Laurinburg	15,874
15	Rocky Mount	55,893	49	Albemarle	15,680
16	Chapel Hill	48,715	50	Mint Hill	14,922
17	Burlington	44,917	51	Reidsville	14,485
18	Wilson	44,405	52	Clemmons	13,827
19	Goldsboro	39,043	53	Boone	13,472
20	Hickory	37,222	54	Graham	12,833
21	Kannapolis	36,910	55	Wake Forest	12,588
22	Fort Bragg	29,183	56	Newton	12,560
23	Salisbury	26,462	57	Cornelius	11,969
24	Monroe	26,228	58	Indian Trail	11,905
25	Huntersville	24,960	59	Masonboro	11,812
26	Kinston	23,688	60	Piney Green	11,658
27	Statesville	23,320	61	Smithfield	11,510
28	Sanford	23,220	62	Hope Mills	11,237
29	New Bern	23,128	63	Tarboro	11,138
30	Havelock	22,442	64	Southern Pines	10,918
31	Matthews	22,127	65	Hendersonville	10,420
32	Asheboro	21,672			
33	Lumberton	20,795			
34	Apex	20,212			

Population figures are from 2000 census.

Source: U.S. Bureau of the Census.

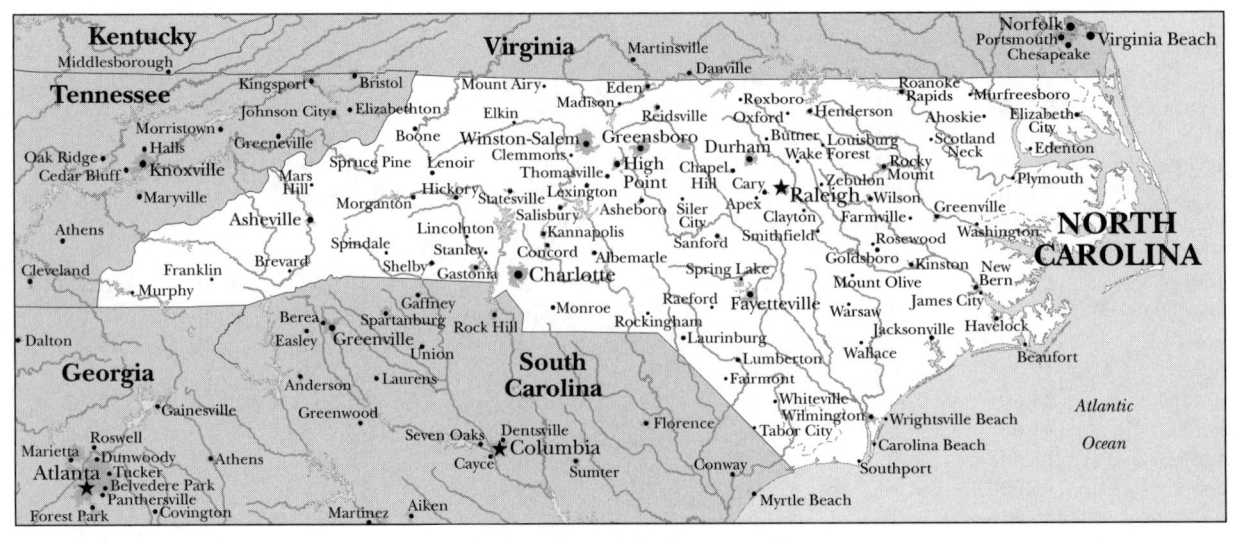

Index to Tables

DEMOGRAPHICS

Resident state and national populations, 1970-2004

Population figures given in thousands

	State pop.	U.S. pop.	Share	Rank
1970	5,084	203,302	2.5%	12
1980	5,882	226,546	2.6%	10
1985	6,254	237,924	2.6%	10
1990	6,632	248,765	2.7%	10
1995	7,345	262,761	2.7%	11
2000	8,046	281,425	2.9%	11
2004	8,541	293,655	2.9%	11

Source: U.S. Census Bureau, Current Population Reports, 2006.

Resident population by age, 2004

Age Group	Total persons
Under 5 years	600,000
5 to 17 years.	1,518,000
18 to 24 years	828,000
25 to 34 years	1,242,000
35 to 44 years	1,289,000
45 to 54 years	1,175,000
55 to 64 years	856,000
65 to 74 years	555,000
75 to 84 years	356,000
85 years and older	121,000
All age groups.	8,541,000

Portion of residents 65 and older	12.1%
National rank in portion of oldest residents	33
National average	12.4%

Population figures are rounded to nearest thousand persons;
figures include armed forces personnel stationed in the state.
Source: U.S. Bureau of the Census, 2006.

Resident population by race, Hispanic origin, 2004

Category	State pop.	Share	U.S.
All residents	8,541	100.00%	100.00%
Non-Hispanic white	5,861	68.62%	67.37%
Hispanic white	471	5.51%	13.01%
Other Hispanic	47	0.55%	1.06%
African American	1,861	21.79%	12.77%
Native American	110	1.29%	0.96%
Asian, Pacific Islander	154	1.80%	4.37%
Two or more categories	83	0.97%	1.51%

Population figures are in thousands. Persons counted as "Hispanic" (Latino) may be of any race. Because of overlapping categories, categories may not add up to 100%. Shares in column 3 are percentages of each category within the state; these figures may be compared to the national percentages in column 4.
Source: U.S. Bureau of the Census, 2006.

Projected state population, 2000-2030

Year	Population
2000	8,046,000
2005	8,702,000
2010	9,346,000
2015	10,011,000
2020	10,709,000
2025	11,449,000
2030	12,228,000
Population increase, 2000-2030	4,182,000
Percentage increase, 2000-2030	51.9

Projections are based on data from the 2000 census.
Source: U.S. Census Bureau.

VITAL STATISTICS

Infant mortality rates, 1980-2002

	1980	1990	2000	2002
All state residents	14.5	10.6	8.6	8.2
All U.S. residents	12.6	9.2	9.4	9.1
All state white residents	12.1	8.0	6.3	5.9
All U.S. white residents	10.6	7.6	5.7	5.8
All state black residents	20.0	16.5	15.7	15.6
All U.S. black residents	22.2	18.0	14.1	14.4

Figures represent deaths per 1,000 live births of resident infants under 1 year old, exclusive of fetal deaths. Figures for all residents include members of other racial categories not listed separately.
Source: U.S. Census Bureau, *Statistical Abstract of the United States,* 2006.

Abortion rates, 1990 and 2000

	1990	2000
Total abortions	36,000	38,000
Rate per 1,000 women	22.2	21.0
U.S. rate	25.7	21.3
Rank	22	16

Numbers of abortions are rounded to nearest thousand; ranks are based on rates.
Source: U.S. Census Bureau.

Marriages and divorces, 2004

Total marriages	65,900
Rate per 1,000 population	7.7
National rate per 1,000 population	7.4
Rank among all states	19
Total divorces	37,700
Rate per 1,000 population	4.4
National rate per 1,000 population	3.7
Rank among all states	13

Figures are for all marriages and divorces performed within the state, including those of nonresidents; totals are rounded to the nearest hundred. Ranks are for highest to lowest figures; note that divorce data are not available for five states.
Source: U.S. National Center for Health Statistics, *Vital Statistics of the United States,* 2006.

Death rates by leading causes, 2002
Deaths per 100,000 resident population

Cause	State	U.S.
Heart disease	222.6	241.7
Cancer	194.8	193.2
Cerebrovascular diseases	63.2	56.4
Accidents other than motor vehicle	44.5	37.0
Motor vehicle accidents	20.3	15.7
Chronic lower respiratory diseases	44.2	43.3
Diabetes mellitus	26.5	25.4
HIV	5.8	4.9
Suicide	11.9	11.0
Homicide	7.7	6.1
All causes	865.7	847.3
Rank in overall death rate among states		27

Figures exclude nonresidents who died in the state. Causes of death follow International Classification of Diseases. Rank is from highest to lowest death rate in the United States.
Source: U.S. National Center for Health Statistics, *National Vital Statistics Report,* 2006.

ECONOMY

Gross state product, 1990-2004
In current dollars

Year	State product	Nat'l product	State share
1990	$140.3 billion	$5.67 trillion	2.47%
2000	$274.3 billion	$9.75 trillion	2.81%
2002	$301.3 billion	$10.41 trillion	2.89%
2003	$315.5 billion	$10.92 trillion	2.89%
2004	$335.4 billion	$11.65 trillion	2.88%

Source: U.S. Bureau of Economic Analysis, *Survey of Current Business,* July, 2005.

Gross state product by industry, 2003
In billions of dollars

Construction	$11.4
Manufacturing	68.7
Wholesale trade	16.8
Retail trade	21.8
Finance & insurance	29.1
Information	9.9
Professional services	13.9
Health care & social assistance	16.5
Government	35.4
Total state product	$295.9
Total U.S. product	$10,289.2
State share of U.S. total	2.88%
Rank among all states	11

Total figures include industries not listed separately. Amounts are in chained 2000 dollars.

Source: U.S. Bureau of Economic Analysis, *Survey of Current Business,* July, 2005.

Personal income per capita, 1990-2004
In current dollars

	1990	2000	2004
Per capita income	$17,246	$27,068	$29,246
U.S. average	$19,477	$29,845	$32,937
Rank among states	34	32	37

Source: U.S. Bureau of Economic Analysis, *Survey of Current Business,* April, 2005.

Energy consumption, 2001
In trillions of British thermal units (BTU), except as noted

Total energy consumption

Total state energy consumption	2,591
Total U.S. energy consumption	96,275
State share of U.S. total	2.69%
Rank among states	12

Per capita consumption (In millions of BTU)

Total state per capita consumption	316
Total U.S. per capita consumption	338
Rank among states	33

End-use sectors

Residential	641
Commercial	513
Industrial	743
Transportation	694

Sources of energy

Petroleum	950
Natural gas	216
Coal	757
Hydroelectric power	26
Nuclear electric power	395

Figures for totals include categories not listed separately.
Source: U.S. Energy Information Administration, *State Energy Data Report,* 2001.

Nonfarm employment by sectors, 2004

Total persons	3,830,000
Construction	217,000
Manufacturing	580,000
Trade, transportation, utilities	724,000
Information	72,000
Finance, insurance, real estate	192,000
Professional & business services	429,000
Education & health services	446,000
Leisure, hospitality, arts, organizations	345,000
Other services, including repair & maintenance	168,000
Government	651,000

Figures are rounded to nearest thousand persons. "Total" includes mining and natural resources, not listed separately.
Source: U.S. Bureau of Labor Statistics, 2006.

Foreign exports, 1990-2004
In millions of dollars

Year	State	U.S.	State share
1990	8,010	394,045	2.03%
1996	15,734	624,767	2.52%
1997	16,402	688,896	2.38%
2000	17,946	712,055	2.29%
2003	16,199	724,006	2.40%
2004	18,115	769,332	2.35%

Rank among all states in 2004 15

U.S. total does not include U.S. dependencies.
Source: U.S. Census Bureau, *U.S. Merchandise Trade,* series FT 900, 2000; U.S. Census Bureau, *U.S. International Trade in Goods and Services,* Series FT 900, 2005.

LAND USE

Federally owned land, 2003
Areas in acres

	State	U.S.	State share
Total area	31,403,000	2,271,343,000	1.38%
Nonfederal land	27,801,000	1,599,584,000	1.74%
Federal land	3,602,000	671,759,000	0.54%
Federal share	11.5%	29.6%	—

Areas are rounded to nearest thousand acres. Figures for federally owned land do not include trust properties.
Source: U.S. General Services Administration, *Federal Real Property Profile,* 2006.

Land use, 1997
In acres, rounded to nearest thousand

Total surface area 33,709,000
Total nonfederal rural land. 24,592,000
Percentage rural land 73.0%
Cropland 5,639,000
Conservation Reserve Program (CRP*) land 131,000
Pastureland 2,039,000
Rangeland . . . . (nil)
Forestland 15,959,000
Other rural land 824,000

*CRP is a federal program begun in 1985 to assist private landowners to convert highly erodible cropland to vegetative cover for ten years. Note that some categories of land overlap.
Source: U.S. Department of Agriculture, Natural Resources and Conservation Service, and Iowa State University, Statistical Laboratory, *Summary Report, 1997 National Resources Inventory,* revised December, 2000.

Farms and crop acreage, 2004

	State	U.S.	Share	Rank
Farms	52,000	2,113,000	2.46%	16
Acres (millions)	9	937	0.96%	31
Acres per farm	173	443	—	40

Source: U.S. Department of Agriculture, National Agricultural Statistics Service. Numbers of farms are rounded to nearest thousand units; acreage figures are rounded to nearest million. Rankings, including ties, are based on rounded figures.

GOVERNMENT AND FINANCE

Units of local government, 2002

	State	Total U.S.	Rank
All local governments	960	87,525	30
Counties	100	3,034	7
Municipalities	541	19,429	13
Townships	0	16,504	—
School districts	0	13,506	—
Special districts	319	35,052	35

Only 48 states have county governments, 20 states have township governments ("towns" in New England, Minnesota, New York, and Wisconsin), and 46 states have school districts. Special districts encompass such functions as natural resources, fire protection, and housing and community development.
Source: U.S. Census Bureau, *Census of Governments.*

State government revenue, 2002

Total revenue . . . . $31,524 mill.
General revenue . . . . $29,972 mill.
Per capita revenue $3,606
U.S. per capita average $3,689
Rank among states 25

Intergovernment revenue
Total . . . . $10,202 mill.
From federal government . . . . $9,466 mill.

Charges and miscellaneous
Total . . . . $4,233 mill.
Current charges . . . . $2,722 mill.
Misc. general income . . . . $1,512 mill.
Insurance trust revenue . . . . $1,551 mill.

Taxes
Total . . . . $15,537 mill.
Per capita taxes $1,871
Rank among states 21
Property taxes . . . . (nil)
Sales taxes . . . . $6,565 mill.
License taxes . . . . $884 mill.
Individual income taxes . . . . $7,265 mill.
Corporate income taxes . . . . $668 mill.
Other taxes . . . . $155 mill.

Total revenue figures include items not listed separately here.
Source: U.S. Bureau of the Census.

State government expenditures, 2002

General expenditures

Total state expenditures . . . . $33,124 mill.
Intergovernmental . . . . $9,451 mill.

Per capita expenditures

State $3,556
Average of all states $3,859
Rank among states 35

Selected direct expenditures

Education . . . . $4,602 mill.
Public welfare . . . . $6,522 mill.
Health, hospital . . . . $1,921 mill.
Highways . . . . $2,574 mill.
Police protection . . . . $329 mill.
Corrections . . . . $914 mill.
Natural resources . . . . $524 mill.
Parks and recreation . . . . $125 mill.
Government administration . . . . $781 mill.
Interest on debt . . . . $583 mill.
Total direct expenditures . . . . $20,087 mill.

Totals include items not listed separately.
Source: U.S. Census Bureau.

POLITICS

Governors since statehood

D = Democrat; R = Republican; O = other;
(r) resigned; (d) died in office; (i) removed from office

Richard Caswell	1777-1780
Abner Nash	1780-1781
Thomas Burke	1781
Alexander Martin	1781-1782
Thomas Burke	1782
Alexander Martin	1782-1785
Richard Caswell	1785-1787
Samuel Johnston	1787-1789
Alexander Martin (O)	1789-1792
Richard D. Spaight (O)	1792-1795
Samuel Ashe (O)	1795-1798
William R. Davie (O)	1798-1799
Benjamin Williams (O)	1799-1802
James Turner (O)	1802-1805
Nathaniel Alexander (O)	1805-1807
Benjamin Williams (O)	1807-1808
David Stone (O)	1808-1810
Benjamin Smith (O)	1810-1811
William Hawkins (O)	1811-1814
William Miller (O)	1814-1817
John Branch (O)	1817-1820
Jesse Franklin (O)	1820-1821
Gabriel Holmes (O)	1821-1824
Hutchins G. Burton (O)	1824-1827
James Iredell, Jr. (O)	1827-1828
John Owen (D)	1828-1830
Montfort Stokes (D)	1830-1832
David L. Swain (D)	1832-1835
Richard D. Spaight, Jr. (D)	1835-1836
Edward B. Dudley (O)	1836-1841
John M. Morehead (O)	1841-1845
William A. Graham (O)	1845-1849
Charles Manly (O)	1849-1851
David S. Reid (D)	(r) 1851-1854
Warren Winslow (D)	1854-1855
Thomas Bragg (D)	1855-1859
John W. Ellis (D)	(d) 1859-1861
Henry T. Clark (D)	1861-1862
Zebulon B. Vance (D)	(i) 1862-1865
William W. Holden	1865
Jonathan Worth (D)	1865-1868
William W. Holden (R)	(i) 1868-1870
Tod R. Caldwell (R)	(d) 1870-1874
Curtis H. Brogden (R)	1874-1877
Zebulon B. Vance (D)	(r) 1877-1879
Thomas J. Jarvis (D)	1879-1885
Alfred M. Scales (D)	1885-1889
Daniel G. Fowle (D)	(d) 1889-1891
Thomas M. Holt (D)	1891-1893
Elias Carr (D)	1893-1897
Daniel L. Russell (D)	1897-1901
Charles B. Aycock (D)	1901-1905
Robert B. Glenn (D)	1905-1909
William W. Kitchen (D)	1909-1913
Locke Craig (D)	1913-1917
Thomas W. Bickett (D)	1917-1921
Cameron Morrison (D)	1921-1925
Angus W. McLean (D)	1925-1929
Oliver Max Gardner (D)	1929-1933
John C. B. Ehringhouse (D)	1933-1937
Clyde R. Hoey (D)	1937-1941
Joseph Melville Broughton (D)	1941-1945
Robert Gregg Cherry (D)	1945-1949
William Kerr Scott (D)	1949-1953
William B. Umstead (D)	(d) 1953-1954
Luther H. Hodges (D)	1954-1961
Terry Sanford (D)	1961-1965
Daniel K. Moore (D)	1965-1969
Robert W. Scott (D)	1969-1973
James E. Holshouser, Jr. (R)	1973-1977
James Baxter Hunt, Jr. (R)	1977-1985
James G. Martin (R)	1985-1993
James Baxter Hunt, Jr. (R)	1993-2001
Mike Easley (D)	2001-

Composition of congressional delegations, 1989-2007

	Dem	Rep	Total
House of Representatives			
101st Congress, 1989			
State delegates	8	3	11
Total U.S.	259	174	433
102d Congress, 1991			
State delegates	7	4	11
Total U.S.	267	167	434
103d Congress, 1993			
State delegates	8	4	12
Total U.S.	258	176	434
104th Congress, 1995			
State delegates	6	6	12
Total U.S.	197	236	433
105th Congress, 1997			
State delegates	6	6	12
Total U.S.	206	228	434
106th Congress, 1999			
State delegates	5	7	12
Total U.S.	211	222	433
107th Congress, 2001			
State delegates	5	7	12
Total U.S.	211	221	432
108th Congress, 2003			
State delegates	6	7	13
Total U.S.	205	229	434
109th Congress, 2005			
State delegates	6	7	13
Total U.S.	202	231	433
110th Congress, 2007			
State delegates	7	6	13
Total U.S.	233	202	435
Senate			
101st Congress, 1989			
State delegates	1	1	2
Total U.S.	55	45	100
102d Congress, 1991			
State delegates	1	1	2
Total U.S.	56	44	100
103d Congress, 1993			
State delegates	0	2	2
Total U.S.	57	43	100
104th Congress, 1995			
State delegates	0	2	2
Total U.S.	46	53	99
105th Congress, 1997			
State delegates	0	2	2
Total U.S.	45	55	100

	Dem	Rep	Total
106th Congress, 1999			
State delegates	1	1	2
Total U.S.	45	54	99
107th Congress, 2001			
State delegates	1	1	2
Total U.S.	50	50	100
108th Congress, 2003			
State delegates	1	1	2
Total U.S.	48	51	99
109th Congress, 2005			
State delegates	0	2	2
Total U.S.	44	55	99
110th Congress, 2007			
State delegates	0	2	2
Total U.S.	49	49	98

Figures are for starts of first sessions. Totals are for Democrat (Dem.) and Republican (Rep.) members only. House membership totals under 435 and Senate totals under 100 reflect vacancies and seats held by independent party members. When the 110th Congress opened, the Senate's two independent members caucused with the Democrats, giving the Democrats control of the Senate.

Source: U.S. Congress, *Congressional Directory.*

Composition of state legislature, 1990-2006

	Democrats	Republicans
State House (120 seats)		
1990	81	39
1992	78	42
1994	52	68
1996	59	61
1998	66	54
2000	66	53
2002	59	61
2004	63	57
2006	68	52
State Senate (50 seats)		
1990	36	14
1992	39	11
1994	26	24
1996	30	20
1998	35	15
2000	35	15
2002	28	22
2004	29	21
2006	31	19

Figures for total seats may include independents and minor party members. Numbers reflect results of elections in listed years; elected members usually take their seats in the years that follow.

Source: Council of State Governments; *State Elective Officials and the Legislatures.*

Voter participation in presidential elections, 2000 and 2004

	2000	2004
Voting age population		
State	6,104,000	6,423,000
Total United States	209,831,000	220,377,000
State share of U.S. total	2.91	2.91
Rank among states	10	11
Portion of voting age population casting votes		
State	47.8%	54.5%
United States	50.3%	55.5%
Rank among states	40	35

Population figures are rounded to nearest thousand and include all residents, regardless of eligibility to vote.
Source: U.S. Census Bureau.

HEALTH AND MEDICAL CARE

Medical professionals
Physicians in 2003 and nurses in 2001

	U.S.	State
Physicians in 2003		
Total	774,849	21,287
Share of U.S. total		2.73%
Rate	266	253
Rank		22
Nurses in 2001		
Total	2,262,020	72,050
Share of U.S. total		3.19%
Rate	793	878
Rank		19

Rates are numbers of physicians and nurses per 100,000 resident population; ranks are based on rates.
Source: American Medical Association, *Physician Characteristics and Distribution in the U.S.*; U.S. Department of Health and Human Services, Health Resources and Services Administration.

Health insurance coverage, 2003

	State	U.S.
Total persons covered	6,829,000	243,320,000
Total persons not covered	1,424,000	44,961,000
Portion not covered	17.3%	15.6%
Rank among states	13	—
Children not covered	249,000	8,373,000
Portion not covered	11.9%	11.4%
Rank among states	17	—

Totals are rounded to nearest thousand. Ranks are from the highest to the lowest percentages of persons *not* insured.
Source: U.S. Census Bureau, Current Population Reports.

AIDS, syphilis, and tuberculosis cases, 2003

Disease	U.S. cases	State cases	Rank
AIDS	44,232	1,102	10
Syphilis	34,270	848	13
Tuberculosis	14,874	374	8

Source: U.S. Centers for Disease Control and Prevention.

Cigarette smoking, 2003
Residents over age 18 who smoke

	U.S.	State	Rank
All smokers	22.1%	24.8%	16
Male smokers	24.8%	28.0%	12
Female smokers	20.3%	21.9%	18

Cigarette smokers are defined as persons who reported having smoked at least 100 cigarettes during their lifetimes and who currently smoked at least occasionally.
Source: U.S. Centers for Disease Control and Prevention, *Morbidity and Mortality Weekly Report*, 53, no. 44 (November 12, 2004).

HOUSING

Home ownership rates, 1985-2004

	1985	1990	1995	2000	2004
State	68.0%	69.0%	70.1%	71.1%	69.8%
Total U.S.	63.9%	63.9%	64.7%	67.4%	69.0%
Rank among states	25	14	15	21	36

Net change in state home ownership rate, 1985-2004 . . . . . . +1.8%
Net change in U.S. home ownership rate, 1985-2004 . . . . . . +5.1%

Percentages represent the proportion of owner households to total occupied households.
Source: U.S. Census Bureau, 2006.

Home sales, 2000-2004
In thousands of units

Existing home sales	2000	2002	2003	2004
State sales	134.2	142.1	156.3	192.6
Total U.S. sales	5,171	5,631	6,183	6,784
State share of U.S. total	2.60%	2.52%	2.53%	2.84%
Sales rank among states	11	12	12	10

Units include single-family homes, condos, and co-ops.
Source: National Association of Realtors, Washington, D.C., *Real Estate Outlook: Market Trends & Insights*.

Values of owner-occupied homes, 2003

	State	U.S.
Total units	1,678,000	58,809,000
Value of units		
Under $100,000	34.9%	29.6%
$100,000-199,999	44.9%	36.9%
$200,000 or more	20.2%	33.5%
Median value	$125,428	$142,275
Rank among all states 27		

Units are owner-occupied one-family houses whose numbers are rounded to nearest thousand. Data are extrapolated from survey samples.
Source: U.S. Census Bureau, American Community Survey.

EDUCATION

Public school enrollment, 2002

Prekindergarten through grade 8
State enrollment 964,000
Total U.S. enrollment. 34,135,000
State share of U.S. total 2.82%

Grades 9 through 12
State enrollment 372,000
Total U.S. enrollment. 14,067,000
State share of U.S. total 2.64%

Enrollment rates
State public school enrollment rate. 90.3%
Overall U.S. rate 90.4%
Rank among states in 2002. 28
Rank among states in 1995. 26

Enrollment figures (which include unclassified students) are rounded to nearest thousand pupils during fall school term. Enrollment rates are based on enumerated resident population estimate for July 1, 2002.
Source: U.S. National Center for Education Statistics.

Public college finances, 2003-2004

FTE enrollment in public institutions of higher education
Students in state institutions. 315,200
Students in all U.S. public institutions 9,916,600
State share of U.S. total 3.18
Rank among states. 9

State and local government appropriations for higher education
State appropriation per FTE $6,699
National average. $5,716
Rank among states 11
State & local tax revenue going to higher education 11.4%

FTE = full-time equivalent in public postsecondary programs, including summer sessions; student numbers are rounded to nearest hundred. Funding figures for 2003-2004 academic year include financial aid to students in state public institutions and exclude money for research, agriculture experiment stations, teaching hospitals, and medical schools; figures are rounded to nearest thousand dollars.
Source: Higher Education Executive Officers, Denver, Colorado.

TRANSPORTATION AND TRAVEL

Highway mileage, 2003

Interstate highways	1,019
Other freeways and expressways	299
Arterial roads	8,937
Collector roads.	17,621
Local roads.	74,284
Urban roads	24,410
Rural roads.	77,750
Total state mileage	102,160
U.S. total	3,974,107
State share	2.57%
Rank among states	16

Note that combined urban and rural road mileage matches the total of the other categories.
Source: U.S. Federal Highway Administration.

Motor vehicle registrations and driver licenses, 2003

Vehicle registrations	State	U.S.	Share	Rank
Autos, trucks, buses	6,119,000	231,390,000	2.64%	12
Autos only	3,654,000	135,670	2.69%	12
Motorcycles	95,000	5,328,000	1.78%	18
Driver licenses	6,015,000	196,166,000	3.07%	9

Figures, which do not include vehicles owned by military services, are rounded to the nearest thousand. Figures for automobiles include taxis.
Source: U.S. Federal Highway Administration.

Domestic travel expenditures, 2003
Spending by U.S. residents on overnight trips and
day trips of at least 50 miles from home

Total expenditures within state	$12.63 bill.
Total expenditures within U.S.	$490.87 bill.
State share of U.S. total	2.6%
Rank among states	11

Source: Travel Industry Association of America.

Retail gasoline prices, 2003-2007
Average price per gallon at the pump

Year	U.S.	State
2003	$1.267	$1.207
2004	$1.316	$1.244
2005	$1.644	$1.575
2007	$2.298	$2.238

Excise tax per gallon in 2004	26.6¢
Rank among all states in 2007 prices	29

Prices are averages of all grades of gasoline sold at the pump
during March months in 2003-2005 and during February, 2007.
Averages for 2006, during which prices rose higher, are not
available.
Source: U.S. Energy Information Agency, *Petroleum Marketing
Monthly* (2003-2005 data); American Automobile Association
(2007 data).

CRIME AND LAW ENFORCEMENT

State and local police officers, 2000-2004

	2000	2002	2004
Total officers			
U.S.	654,601	665,555	675,734
State	19,330	19,691	20,769*
*Net change, 2000-2004			+7.44%
Officers per 1,000 residents			
U.S.	2.33	2.31	2.30
State	2.40	2.37	2.43
State rank	14	13	13

Totals include state and local police and sheriffs.
Source: Carsey Institute, University of New Hampshire.

Crime rates, 2003
Incidents per 100,000 residents

Crimes	State	U.S.
Violent crimes		
Total incidents	455	475
Murder	6	6
Forcible rape	25	32
Robbery	146	142
Aggravated assault	278	295
Property crimes		
Total incidents	4,278	3,588
Burglary	1,198	741
Larceny/theft	2,761	2,415
Motor vehicle theft	320	433
All crimes	4,733	4,063

Source: U.S. Federal Bureau of Investigation, *Crime in the United
States,* annual.

State prison populations, 1980-2003

	State	U.S.	State share
1980	15,513	305,458	5.08%
1990	18,411	708,393	2.60%
1996	30,647	1,025,624	2.99%
2000	31,266	1,391,261	2.25%
2003	33,560	1,470,045	2.28%

State figures exclude prisoners in federal penitentiaries.
Source: U.S. Bureau of Justice Statistics, *Prisoners in 2003.*

North Dakota

Location: North-central United States

Area and rank: 68,994 square miles (178,695 square kilometers); 70,704 square miles (183,123 square kilometers) including water; seventeenth largest state in area

Coastline: none

Population and rank: 634,000 (2004); forty-eighth largest state in population

Capital city: Bismarck (55,532 people in 2000 census)

Largest city: Fargo (90,599 people in 2000 census)

Became territory: March 2, 1861

Entered Union and rank: November 2, 1889; thirty-ninth state

State capitol building in Bismarck. (North Dakota Tourism Department)

Present constitution adopted: 1889

Counties: 53

State name: "Dakota" is a Sioux word meaning "allies"

State nickname: Sioux State; Flickertail State; Peace Garden State

Motto: Liberty and union, now and forever: one and inseparable

State flag: Blue field with eagle holding olive branch, arrows, and scroll reading "*E pluribus unum*," bearing shield of the Stars and Stripes on its breast; double arch of thirteen stars with a sunburst above, scroll with name "North Dakota" below

Highest point: White Butte—3,506 feet (1,069 meters)

Lowest point: Red River—750 feet (229 meters)

Highest recorded temperature: 121 degrees Fahrenheit (49 degrees Celsius)—Steele, 1936

Lowest recorded temperature: –60 degrees Fahrenheit (–51 degrees Celsius)—Parshall, 1936

State song: "North Dakota Hymn"

State tree: American elm

State flower: Wild prairie rose

State bird: Western meadowlark

State fish: Northern pike

National parks: Theodore Roosevelt

North Dakota History

With a 2004 population estimated at about 634,000, North Dakota ranked forty-eighth among the fifty states in population and was growing smaller. Its total area of almost 71,000 square miles makes it the seventeenth largest state in land mass. Its population density of 9.3 people per square mile is among America's lowest.

Bordered on the north by the Canadian provinces of Saskatchewan and Manitoba, on the east by Minnesota, on the south by South Dakota, and on the west by Montana, North Dakota runs 360 miles from east to west and 210 miles from north to south.

Early History. North Dakota had human inhabitants more than ten thousand years ago. Millions of years earlier, dinosaurs and mastodons roamed the area. During the Ice Age, the Dakotas were covered by glaciers, which melted around 10,000 B.C.E., leaving a huge lake in what is now the Red River Valley in eastern North Da-

kota. Topsoil trapped in the glacier was deposited in the lake as the ice melted. When the lake evaporated, that topsoil created fertile fields.

Prehistoric settlers lived beside the Red and Missouri Rivers. The Mandan Indians around 1300 C.E. were the earliest of the Native American settlers, followed some three hundred years later by the Hidatsa and Arikara, all groups that created settlements and engaged in farming, growing mostly squash, sunflowers, corn, and beans. They hunted indigenous animals, particularly bison, for their meat and fur.

The more migratory Sioux and Chippewa entered the area in pursuit of bison. Other tribes lived in North Dakota for short periods, notably the Assiniboine, Cheyenne, Cree, and Crow. The first Europeans in the area were Pierre Gaultier de Varennes, sieur de La Vérendrye, his sons, and a nephew, who visited Mandan villages in 1738.

This blockhouse at Fort Lincoln, North Dakota, is a vestige of the federal government's nineteenth century wars with Native Americans. (North Dakota Tourism Department)

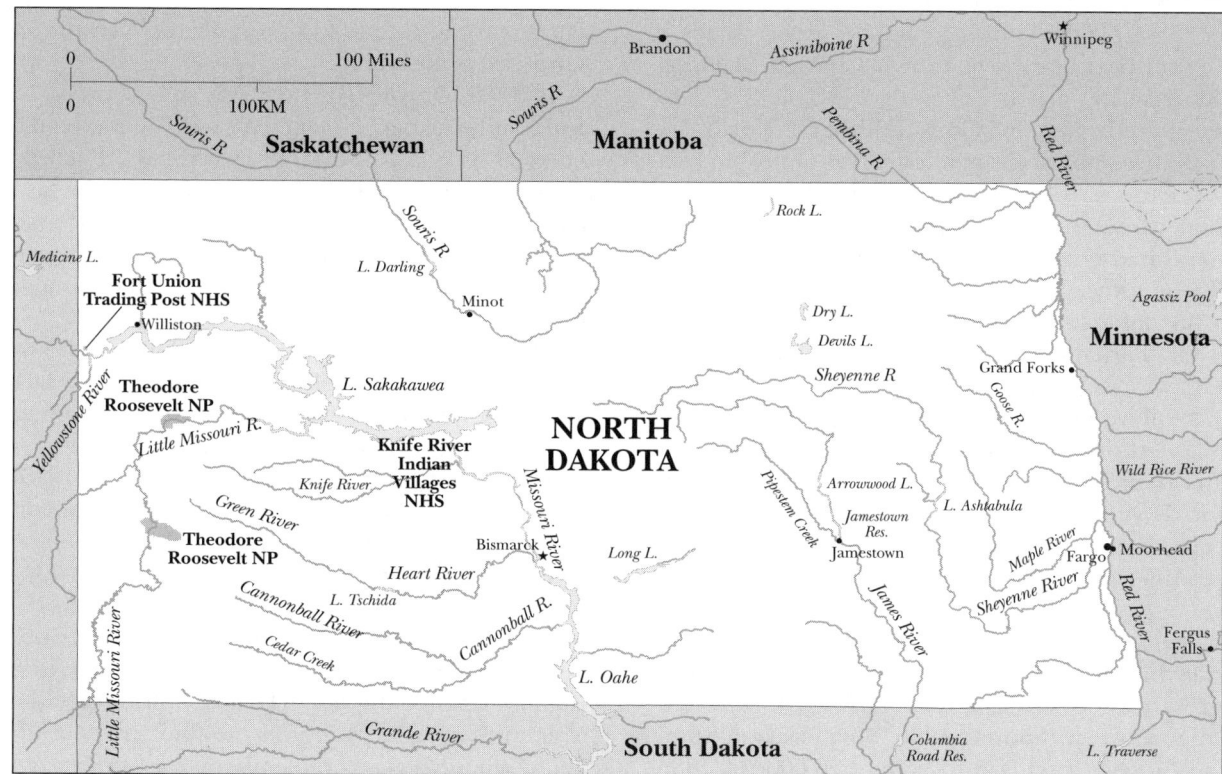

The Fur Trade.

Relations between North Dakota's Native Americans and visiting Europeans were amicable initially. The American Indians had an abundance of furs, and the European traders had ready markets for these furs. By the 1780's, a thriving fur trade flourished in the region, largely stimulated by the Hudson Bay Company, headquartered in Manitoba. In 1801, Alexander Henry established a fur-trading post at Pembina, the first European settlement in the area.

In 1713, the French gave England the northern part of North Dakota, which bordered Canada. In 1812, a group of Canadians started a town at the Pembina trading post, building a school and some permanent buildings. In 1818, however, the United States, through a treaty with Great Britain, was given Britain's section of North Dakota, establishing the territory's northern border. Canadians living there returned to Canada.

Early Growth.

Few non-American Indians came to North Dakota in its early days, although Congress established the Dakota Territory in 1861. By 1870, the territory had 2,405 inhabitants. By 1880, however, the population had ballooned to about 37,000.

Three major factors brought this increase. The Homestead Act of 1862, designed to encourage settlement of the sparsely inhabited territory west of the Mississippi, permitted people to stake claims for the 160 acres allotted to each homesteader, to improve the land and live on it for five years, and then to receive a clear title to that land. Although homesteading became more prevalent during the 1870's, there was no immediate rush of homesteaders to the Dakotas. Homesteading was difficult. In a land bereft of forests, timber was scarce, forcing early settlers to build sod houses made by cutting square chunks of sod from the prairie for roofs and walls. Sod houses extended below ground; these small houses offered adequate shelter and were warm in winter but were quite unlike the dwellings to which homesteaders were accustomed.

The establishment of towns in the area also spurred population growth. Fargo and Grand Forks were established in 1871, and the following year Bismarck was founded in the middle of the state. By 1874 Bismarck was publishing its own newspaper, the Bismarck *Tribune*. Concurrent with the establishment of towns was the spread of railroads, first from Minnesota to Fargo in 1872 and, in 1873, to Bismarck. Railroad service enabled farmers and cattle ranchers to send their products to eastern markets.

By 1875 farmers in the Red River Valley of eastern North Dakota were producing huge amounts of wheat on their fertile soil. North Dakota eventually ranked second only to Kansas in the amount of wheat it produces, and it now ranks first in its production of sunflower seed and barley. Long, hot summer days and abundant topsoil make the eastern half of the state agriculturally productive.

In 1878, large-scale cattle ranching began in the western Dakota Territory, whose stubby grasses proved perfect for grazing. Growing railroad service made it easy to transport cattle to markets in Chicago, St. Louis, and Kansas City.

American Indian Relations. Although North Dakota's Native Americans generally had amicable relations with the early European traders, relations became strained when the federal government reneged on treaties it had entered into with Native Americans. In 1875, when the government permitted white settlement on American Indian lands in abrogation of the 1868 Fort Laramie Treaty, major Indian uprisings occurred.

The following year, in neighboring Montana, the Sioux killed many American settlers, including Lieutenant Colonel George Custer, in the Battle of the Little Bighorn. In 1877, the federal government confiscated Sioux lands in the Dakotas. Within a year, most of the Native American population was deployed to reservations.

Achieving Statehood. The Dakotas were growing and moving irrevocably toward statehood, although Congress resisted admitting the entire territory as a single state. Between 1880 and 1900, North Dakota's population increased tenfold to about 320,000. In 1883,

the territorial capital was moved from Yankton in the southeast to Bismarck.

In 1889, Dakota Territory was split between North and South Dakota, and each part was guaranteed statehood as soon as each territory submitted acceptable constitutions. North Dakota drew up a constitution that the electorate approved, and late in 1889 President Benjamin Harrison signed papers admitting North Dakota as the thirty-ninth state and South Dakota as the fortieth.

The Early Twentieth Century. Between 1900 and 1915, inequities existed for North Dakota's farmers and cattle ranchers. Their labors were enriching the state's banks, flour mills, and railroads, but life was difficult for those providing the basic labor. In 1915, discouraged by these inequities, thirty thousand farmers joined the Nonpartisan League, which later helped to elect Lynn Frazier, a reform candidate, governor.

Frazier helped establish the Bank of North Dakota in Bismarck in 1919. This state-operated bank offered farmers and cattle ranchers low-interest loans. In 1922, the state opened the North Dakota Mill and Elevator, in which wheat farmers could store their crops until they could sell them at favorable prices. Farmers' taxes were

The Badlands of western North Dakota's Theodore Roosevelt National Park resemble a lunar landscape during an Earth winter. (Courtesy, NPS)

Contrary to what some people believe, the city of Fargo takes its name, not from the fact that it lies "far" to the north, but from William Fargo, the founder of the Wells Fargo Express Company. (Courtesy, City of Fargo)

North Dakota's farmers lost their farms. Nearly forty thousand people had left the state by 1940.

In 1937, realizing the need for water conservation, North Dakota established the Water Conservation Commission. All its fifty-three counties embarked upon water-conservation projects. It was not until 1960, however, that the Garrison Dam was completed, creating Lake Sakakawea, which provides irrigation and whose dam generates hydroelectric power.

Recovery. During the 1950's, many farmers moved to cities, entering new walks of life. The state's first television station opened in Minot in 1953. Interstate Highway 94 crossed the state in 1956. Air transportation to became more accessible, and North Dakota, which had suffered from isolation, was now linked more closely to mainstream America.

Oil was discovered in Tioga in 1951, but not until 1978 did an enormous oil boom begin around Williston. In the same general area is substantial mining of lignite, which is burned to fuel electrical generating plants.

2000 Elections. North Dakota, a state that often leans Republican in presidential politics, cast its three electoral votes for Texas governor George W. Bush by a wide margin, 61-33 percent. At the same time, however, voters reelected Democrat senator Kent Conrad. They also elected a Democrat to the state's single at-large congressional seat. In the governor's race, the incumbent, a Republican, declined to run, leaving the field to fellow Republican John Hoeven. Hoeven defeated the state's attorney general, a Democrat, by a margin of 55-45 percent. At the same time, North Dakotans voted for tradition when they passed a referendum by the landslide proportions of 77-23 percent. The measure asked if voters wished to make hunting, fishing, and trapping constitutional rights and "a valued part of our heritage."

When the results of the 2000 census were announced, it seemed unlikely that the state's traditions would be endangered by population growth. However, the state had grown at the snail's pace of just 0.5 percent—one half of one percent. The state's 642,200 pop-

lowered, and an increased percentage of state revenues were earmarked for rural schools, which extended educational opportunities to farm children.

During World Wars I and II, North Dakota provided produce to feed members of the armed forces. Although North Dakota opposed entry into both of these wars, the citizens served valiantly in the armed forces.

During the 1920's, agriculture boomed in North Dakota. Sugar beets and red potatoes became profitable crops. The upsurge in agriculture caused the population to more than double between 1900 and 1930.

No state was more severely damaged by the Great Depression than North Dakota. During most of the 1930's, widespread droughts and dust storms that blew away precious topsoil plagued the state. By 1936 half the state's citizens required public assistance. A third of

Remnants of the immense herds of buffalo that once roamed the Great Plains grazing near a modern North Dakota power plant. (North Dakota Tourism Department)

ulation was 91.2 percent white, 4.9 percent American Indian, 1.2 percent Hispanic, and a minute percentage of African American and Asian residents.

Economy and Social Issues. In 2002, North Dakota, a wheat producing state, could celebrate a ruling by the U.S. International Trade Commission. On November 19, the body issued a preliminary ruling that the Canadian Wheat Board was a monopoly and for that reason could set lower prices. The ruling later allowed the U.S. Department of Commerce to impose preliminary duties on two types of Canadian wheat entering the country. In response, Canada launched an appeal to the North American Free Trade Association (NAFTA).

The health of North Dakota society was evident in a national study of high school dropout rates. North Dakota led the nation with the lowest high school dropout rate. Some 89 percent of North Dakota high school students were found to graduate, the highest percentage in the nation.

The state's conservative character with regard to certain social issues was also evident during this period. The state's senate defeated a proposal to repeal an 1890 law against cohabitation. Thus, cohabiting remained a sex crime punishable by a 30-day jail sentence and a $1,000 fine for opposite-sex couples living together "openly and notoriously."

Economic Prosperity. In the first years of the twenty-first century, North Dakota, like neighboring states such as Wyoming and Montana, experienced a substantial increase in prosperity. Unemployment rates fell to very low percentages, and tax receipts were significant and expanding. The state's budget surplus was estimated at well over $500 million. Employment growth rates in cities such as Bismark and Fargo far outshine those of the large metropolitan areas on the coasts. The changes are partly the result of the ability of business service firms to move away from the congested coasts, thanks to the Internet. Perhaps an even greater reason is that the dramatic rise in energy prices made states such as North Dakota energy exporters to the rest of the country. Vast coal deposits and synthetic gas exports have brought the state to the edge of an energy boom.

2004 Election. In the presidential-year elections, the state again gave its electoral votes to Republican Bush and running mate Dick Cheney, by a 63-35 percent margin. Voters also reelected by comfortable margins both Democratic senator Byron Dorgan and its at-large member of Congress, Earl Pomeroy, also a Democrat.

R. Baird Shuman
Updated by the Editor

North Dakota Time Line

c. 9000 B.C.E.	Early human habitation of the North Dakota area begins.
c. 550-400 B.C.E.	Woodlands people live in southeastern North Dakota.
c. 100 B.C.E.	Inhabitants build burial mounds.
c. 1200 C.E.	Jamestown mounds are abandoned.
c. 1610	Explorer Henry Hudson claims northeastern Dakota for England.
1682	René-Robert Cavelier, sieur de La Salle, claims area as part of France's Louisiana Territory.
Dec. 3, 1738	Pierre Gaultier de Varennes, sieur de La Vérendrye, visits American Indian villages along the Missouri River.
1762	Louisiana Territory ceded by France to Spain.
1801	Alexander Henry establishes fur-trading post at Pembina, spawning the first white settlement in North Dakota.
Dec. 20, 1803	United States gains major portion of North Dakota through the Louisiana Purchase.
1804-1805	Meriwether Lewis and William Clark spend winter in North Dakota en route to the Pacific Northwest.
1812	Canadians attempt to establish town at Pembina.
1818	Treaty with Great Britain establishes northern border of North Dakota.
1829	Fort Union Trading Post is founded on the Upper Missouri River.
1842	Road opens between eastern North Dakota and St. Paul, Minnesota.
1857	Fort Abercrombie is established on the Red River.
Mar. 2, 1861	Congress establishes the Dakota Territory.
1863	North Dakota opens for homesteading.
1867	Sioux Indians accept treaty to cede lands to the federal government.
1868	Standing Rock Indian Reservation is established.
1868	Montana and Wyoming are separated from Dakota Territory.
1870's	Increased homesteading spawns a land boom.
1872	Railway service from Minnesota to Fargo begins.
July 11, 1873	Bismarck *Tribune* begins publication.
1875	American Indian uprisings occur, caused by federal government's violation of the Fort Laramie Treaty.
1880	Population grows from 2,405 in 1870 to 36,909.
1882	Turtle Mountain Indian Reservation is established.
1883	Territorial capital is moved from Yankton to Bismarck.
1883	University of North Dakota is established at Grand Forks.
Nov. 2, 1889	North Dakota becomes thirty-ninth state.
1890	North Dakota State University opens at Fargo.
1897	State's first public library opens in Grafton.
1915	Nonpartisan League is established to aid farmers.
1919	Bank of North Dakota begins operation in Bismarck.
1920	Electorate adds recall measure to state constitution.
1921	Lynn J. Frazier is first state governor to be recalled in U.S. history.
1930's	Prolonged drought and the Great Depression devastate North Dakota.
1937	North Dakota Water Conservation Commission is established.
1944	Congress passes Pick-Sloan Plan to build dams on Missouri River.
Apr. 4, 1951	Oil is discovered in northwestern North Dakota.
1960	Garrison Dam is completed.
1979	Oil boom occurs in western North Dakota.
1980	Beulah's coal gasification plant is built, the first in the United States.
1988	Devastating drought bankrupts many farmers and cattle ranchers.
1989	Legislature passes bill legalizing home schooling.
1997	Severe floods devastate Red River Valley.
1998	Per capita income rises 7.8 percent in one year.

(continued)

Nov. 7, 2000	Voters give the state's three electoral votes to Republican presidential candidate George W. Bush and elect Republican John Hoeven governor. They also reelect Democrat Kent Conrad to the U.S. Senate.
Nov. 19, 2002	U.S. International Trade Commission issues preliminary ruling that prices of Canadian wheat entering the United States are set by monopoly power; ruling later paves the way for U.S. wheat tariffs benefiting North Dakota farmers.
Nov. 2, 2004	Voters reelect one Democrat to the U.S. Senate and another to the U.S. House of Representatives. The state's Republican governor is reelected.

Notes for Further Study

Published Sources. John C. Hudson's *Plains Country Towns* (1985) contains well-presented information about small-town North Dakota. For a sensitive rendering of North Dakota's educational development, consult Esther Burnett Horne and Sally McBeth's *Essie's Story: The Life and Legacy of a Shoshone Teacher* (1998), in which Horne relates her early experiences as a teacher in North Dakota. Her material on off-reservation boarding schools is valuable, particularly if read in conjunction with Brenda J. Child's *Boarding School Seasons: American Indian Families, 1900-1940* (1998). Carrie Young's *Nothing to Do but Stay: My Pioneer Mother* (1991) is very interesting anecdotally. *Rachel Calof's Story: Jewish Homesteader on the Northern Plains* (1995) tells how a member of a religious and ethnic minority was treated in early North Dakota, offering an interesting sociological treatment in a book written many years ago but later translated and edited by Jacob Calof and Molly Shaw. Young adults will find Martin Hintz and Janet Daily's *North Dakota* (2005) from the America the Beautiful series informative.

Kathleen Norris's *Dakota: A Spiritual Geography* (1993) offers insights into the varied cultures of the area. Catherine McNicol Stock's *Main Street in Crisis: The Great Depression and the Old Middle Class on the Northern Plains* (1992) provides the best socioeconomic analysis of the Plains states during the 1930's. Two books expertly explore the state's natural landscapes and wildlife while also including some discussion of the region's history: *North Dakota Wildlife Portfolio* (2005) by Daphne Kinzler and *Geology of the Lewis and Clark Trail in North Dakota* (2003) by John W. Hoganson and Edward C. Murphy.

North Dakota's indigenous people's history is both rich and complex. For younger audiences, Carole Marsh's *North Dakota Native Americans* (2004) provides valuable information on the state's tribes, reservations, history, and lore. *The Last Days of the Sioux Nation* (2d ed., 2004) by Robert M. Utley details the struggle of the Sioux tribes to keep their lands in the mid-eighteenth century and their subsequent forced move to reservations farther west.

Web Resources. The Web site of North Dakota's state government (www.state.nd.us) provides information about the state's history, economy, industry, population, and political organization. Information about tourism is available on several Web sites, including those of the state tourist office (www.ndtourism.com/) and Dickinson Visitors' Bureau (www.dickinsoncvb.com/). The North Dakota League of Cities (www.ndlc.org/) serves as a resource for cities and park districts; users can find good information about individual North Dakota towns and counties there. To learn more about North Dakota geography and its susceptibility to floods, visit www.netstate.com/states/geography/nd_geography.htm or the Fargo Flood home page (www.ndsu.nodak.edu/fargo flood/).

The North Dakota Art Museum Web site (www.ndmoa .com) is well illustrated and informative. The State University Library's Web site (www.lib.ndsu.nodak.edu) provides access to its resources. Agricultural information is available through the Web sites of the North Dakota Corn Growers (www .ndcorn.com) and the North Dakota Wheat Association (www.ndwheat.com). Access Genealogy has a good page detailing the Native American communities in the state (www .accessgenealogy.com/native/northdakota/index.htm), while the State Historical Society of North Dakota offers an extensive essay detailing the state's history (www.state.nd.us/ hist/ndhist.htm).

Counties

County	2000 pop.	Rank in pop.	Sq. miles	Rank in area
Adams	2,593	44	988.0	40
Barnes	11,775	13	1,491.8	15
Benson	6,964	19	1,388.6	19
Billings	888	52	1,151.5	28
Bottineau	7,149	18	1,668.7	11
Bowman	3,242	36	1,162.1	27
Burke	2,242	48	1,103.6	33
Burleigh	69,416	2	1,633.2	13
Cass	123,138	1	1,765.7	10
Cavalier	4,831	26	1,489.1	16
Dickey	5,757	23	1,131.1	31
Divide	2,283	46	1,259.4	24
Dunn	3,600	34	2,010.0	6
Eddy	2,757	39	632.1	53
Emmons	4,331	30	1,510.0	14
Foster	3,759	32	635.3	52
Golden Valley	1,924	50	1,002.0	38
Grand Forks	66,109	3	1,437.9	17
Grant	2,841	38	1,659.6	12
Griggs	2,754	40	708.5	51
Hettinger	2,715	42	1,132.3	30
Kidder	2,753	41	1,351.6	20
LaMoure	4,701	27	1,147.2	29
Logan	2,308	45	992.7	39
McHenry	5,987	21	1,874.2	8
McIntosh	3,390	35	975.3	42
McKenzie	5,737	24	2,742.2	1
McLean	9,311	14	2,110.4	3

County	2000 pop.	Rank in pop.	Sq. miles	Rank in area
Mercer	8,644	15	1,045.4	35
Morton	25,303	5	1,926.4	7
Mountrail	6,631	20	1,824.0	9
Nelson	3,715	33	981.7	41
Oliver	2,065	49	723.6	49
Pembina	8,585	16	1,118.8	32
Pierce	4,675	28	1,017.9	37
Ramsey	12,066	12	1,186.2	26
Ransom	5,890	22	862.8	46
Renville	2,610	43	874.8	45
Richland	17,998	9	1,436.9	18
Rolette	13,674	10	902.5	44
Sargent	4,366	29	858.8	48
Sheridan	1,710	51	971.8	43
Sioux	4,044	31	1,094.2	34
Slope	767	53	1,218.0	25
Stark	22,636	6	1,338.3	21
Steele	2,258	47	712.4	50
Stutsman	21,908	7	2,221.5	2
Towner	2,876	37	1,025.4	36
Traill	8,477	17	861.9	47
Walsh	12,389	11	1,282.0	22
Ward	58,795	4	2,013.0	5
Wells	5,102	25	1,271.4	23
Williams	19,761	8	2,070.6	4

Source: U.S. Census Bureau; National Association of Counties.

Cities

With 6,000 or more residents

Rank	City	Population
1	Fargo	90,599
2	Bismarck (capital)	55,532
3	Grand Forks	49,321
4	Minot	36,567
5	Mandan	16,718
6	Dickinson	16,010
7	Jamestown	15,527
8	West Fargo	14,940

Rank	City	Population
9	Williston	12,512
10	Wahpeton	8,586
11	Minot Air Force Base	7,599
12	Devils Lake	7,222
13	Valley City	6,826

Population figures are from 2000 census.
Source: U.S. Bureau of the Census.

Index to Tables

DEMOGRAPHICS

Resident state and national populations, 1970-2004

Population figures given in thousands

	State pop.	U.S. pop.	Share	Rank
1970	618	203,302	0.3%	45
1980	653	226,546	0.3%	46
1985	677	237,924	0.3%	46
1990	639	248,765	0.3%	47
1995	648	262,761	0.2%	47
2000	642	281,425	0.2%	47
2004	634	293,655	0.2%	48

Source: U.S. Census Bureau, Current Population Reports, 2006.

Resident population by age, 2004

Age Group	Total persons
Under 5 years	36,000
5 to 17 years	103,000
18 to 24 years	77,000
25 to 34 years	81,000
35 to 44 years	85,000
45 to 54 years	97,000
55 to 64 years	63,000
65 to 74 years	43,000
75 to 84 years	34,000
85 years and older	16,000
All age groups	634,000

Portion of residents 65 and older	14.7%
National rank in portion of oldest residents	4
National average	12.4%

Population figures are rounded to nearest thousand persons;
figures include armed forces personnel stationed in the state.
Source: U.S. Bureau of the Census, 2006.

Resident population by race, Hispanic origin, 2004

Category	State pop.	Share	U.S.
All residents	634	100.00%	100.00%
Non-Hispanic white	578	91.17%	67.37%
Hispanic white	8	1.26%	13.01%
Other Hispanic	2	0.32%	1.06%
African American	5	0.79%	12.77%
Native American	33	5.21%	0.96%
Asian, Pacific Islander	4	0.63%	4.37%
Two or more categories	6	0.95%	1.51%

Population figures are in thousands. Persons counted as "Hispanic" (Latino) may be of any race. Because of overlapping categories, categories may not add up to 100%. Shares in column 3 are percentages of each category within the state; these figures may be compared to the national percentages in column 4.
Source: U.S. Bureau of the Census, 2006.

Projected state population, 2000-2030

Year	Population
2000	642,000
2005	635,000
2010	637,000
2015	635,000
2020	630,000
2025	621,000
2030	607,000
Population decrease, 2000-2030	−35,000
Percentage decrease, 2000-2030	−5.5

Projections are based on data from the 2000 census.
Source: U.S. Census Bureau.

VITAL STATISTICS

Infant mortality rates, 1980-2002

	1980	1990	2000	2002
All state residents	12.1	8.0	8.1	6.3
All U.S. residents	12.6	9.2	9.4	9.1
All state white residents	11.7	7.2	7.5	5.6
All U.S. white residents	10.6	7.6	5.7	5.8
All state black residents	27.5	—	—	—
All U.S. black residents	22.2	18.0	14.1	14.4

Figures represent deaths per 1,000 live births of resident infants under 1 year old, exclusive of fetal deaths. Figures for all residents include members of other racial categories not listed separately. The Census Bureau considers the post-1980 figures for black residents to be too small to be statistically meaningful.
Source: U.S. Census Bureau, *Statistical Abstract of the United States,* 2006.

Abortion rates, 1990 and 2000

	1990	2000
Total abortions	1,000	1,000
Rate per 1,000 women	10.7	9.9
U.S. rate	25.7	21.3
Rank	45	36

Numbers of abortions are rounded to nearest thousand; ranks are based on rates.
Source: U.S. Census Bureau.

Marriages and divorces, 2004

Total marriages	4,100
Rate per 1,000 population	6.5
National rate per 1,000 population	7.4
Rank among all states	32
Total divorces	1,800
Rate per 1,000 population	2.8
National rate per 1,000 population	3.7
Rank among all states	39

Figures are for all marriages and divorces performed within the state, including those of nonresidents; totals are rounded to the nearest hundred. Ranks are for highest to lowest figures; note that divorce data are not available for five states.
Source: U.S. National Center for Health Statistics, *Vital Statistics of the United States,* 2006.

Death rates by leading causes, 2002
Deaths per 100,000 resident population

Cause	State	U.S.
Heart disease	255.9	241.7
Cancer	203.9	193.2
Cerebrovascular diseases	74.0	56.4
Accidents other than motor vehicle	38.8	37.0
Motor vehicle accidents	17.5	15.7
Chronic lower respiratory diseases	50.8	43.3
Diabetes mellitus	33.7	25.4
HIV	n/a	4.9
Suicide	14.4	11.0
Homicide	n/a	6.1
All causes	929.2	847.3
Rank in overall death rate among states		17

Figures exclude nonresidents who died in the state. Causes of death follow International Classification of Diseases. Rank is from highest to lowest death rate in the United States.
Source: U.S. National Center for Health Statistics, *National Vital Statistics Report,* 2006.

ECONOMY

Gross state product, 1990-2004
In current dollars

Year	State product	Nat'l product	State share
1990	$11.5 billion	$5.67 trillion	0.20%
2000	$18.1 billion	$9.75 trillion	0.19%
2002	$20.0 billion	$10.41 trillion	0.19%
2003	$21.6 billion	$10.92 trillion	0.20%
2004	$23.6 billion	$11.65 trillion	0.20%

Source: U.S. Bureau of Economic Analysis, *Survey of Current Business,*
July, 2005.

Gross state product by industry, 2003
In billions of dollars

Construction	$0.8
Manufacturing	2.1
Wholesale trade	1.6
Retail trade	1.7
Finance & insurance	1.3
Information	0.7
Professional services	0.8
Health care & social assistance	1.7
Government	3.0
Total state product	$19.9
Total U.S. product	$10,289.2
State share of U.S. total	0.19%
Rank among all states	49

Total figures include industries not listed separately. Amounts are
in chained 2000 dollars.
Source: U.S. Bureau of Economic Analysis, *Survey of Current Business,*
July, 2005.

Personal income per capita, 1990-2004
In current dollars

	1990	2000	2004
Per capita income	$15,943	$25,106	$31,398
U.S. average	$19,477	$29,845	$32,937
Rank among states	39	38	24

Source: U.S. Bureau of Economic Analysis, *Survey of Current Business,*
April, 2005.

Energy consumption, 2001
In trillions of British thermal units (BTU), except as noted

Total energy consumption

Total state energy consumption	407
Total U.S. energy consumption	96,275
State share of U.S. total	0.42%
Rank among states	43

Per capita consumption (In millions of BTU)

Total state per capita consumption	640
Total U.S. per capita consumption	338
Rank among states	4

End-use sectors

Residential	61
Commercial	56
Industrial	203
Transportation	88

Sources of energy

Petroleum	138
Natural gas	63
Coal	420
Hydroelectric power	14
Nuclear electric power	0

Figures for totals include categories not listed separately.
Source: U.S. Energy Information Administration, *State Energy Data
Report,* 2001.

Nonfarm employment by sectors, 2004

Total persons	337,000
Construction	17,000
Manufacturing	25,000
Trade, transportation, utilities	73,000
Information	8,000
Finance, insurance, real estate	19,000
Professional & business services	24,000
Education & health services	49,000
Leisure, hospitality, arts, organizations	31,000
Other services, including repair & maintenance	15,000
Government	75,000

Figures are rounded to nearest thousand persons. "Total" includes
mining and natural resources, not listed separately.
Source: U.S. Bureau of Labor Statistics, 2006.

Foreign exports, 1990-2004
In millions of dollars

Year	State	U.S.	State share
1990	360	394,045	0.09%
1996	707	624,767	0.11%
1997	778	688,896	0.11%
2000	626	712,055	0.08%
2003	854	724,006	0.13%
2004	1,008	769,332	0.13%

Rank among all states in 2004 46

U.S. total does not include U.S. dependencies.
Source: U.S. Census Bureau, *U.S. Merchandise Trade,* series FT 900, 2000; U.S. Census Bureau, *U.S. International Trade in Goods and Services,* Series FT 900, 2005.

LAND USE

Federally owned land, 2003
Areas in acres

	State	U.S.	State share
Total area	44,452,000	2,271,343,000	1.96%
Nonfederal land	43,119,000	1,599,584,000	2.70%
Federal land	1,333,000	671,759,000	0.20%
Federal share	3.0%	29.6%	—

Areas are rounded to nearest thousand acres. Figures for federally owned land do not include trust properties.
Source: U.S. General Services Administration, *Federal Real Property Profile,* 2006.

Land use, 1997
In acres, rounded to nearest thousand

Total surface area 45,251,000
Total nonfederal rural land. 41,442,000
Percentage rural land 91.6%
Cropland. 25,004,000
Conservation Reserve Program (CRP*) land . . . 2,802,000
Pastureland 1,129,000
Rangeland 10,689,000
Forestland. 454,000
Other rural land 1,363,000

*CRP is a federal program begun in 1985 to assist private landowners to convert highly erodible cropland to vegetative cover for ten years. Note that some categories of land overlap.
Source: U.S. Department of Agriculture, Natural Resources and Conservation Service, and Iowa State University, Statistical Laboratory, *Summary Report, 1997 National Resources Inventory,* revised December, 2000.

Farms and crop acreage, 2004

	State	U.S.	Share	Rank
Farms	30,000	2,113,000	1.42%	29
Acres (millions)	39	937	4.16%	7
Acres per farm	1,300	443	—	8

Source: U.S. Department of Agriculture, National Agricultural Statistics Service. Numbers of farms are rounded to nearest thousand units; acreage figures are rounded to nearest million. Rankings, including ties, are based on rounded figures.

GOVERNMENT AND FINANCE

Units of local government, 2002

	State	Total U.S.	Rank
All local governments	2,735	87,525	14
Counties	53	3,034	30
Municipalities	360	19,429	22
Townships	1,332	16,504	4
School districts	226	13,506	23
Special districts	764	35,052	14

Only 48 states have county governments, 20 states have township governments ("towns" in New England, Minnesota, New York, and Wisconsin), and 46 states have school districts. Special districts encompass such functions as natural resources, fire protection, and housing and community development.
Source: U.S. Census Bureau, *Census of Governments.*

State government revenue, 2002

Total revenue. . . . . $3,017 mill.
General revenue . . . . $2,868 mill.
Per capita revenue $4,526
U.S. per capita average $3,689
Rank among states 11

Intergovernment revenue
Total . . . . $1,043 mill.
From federal government . . . . $1,022 mill.

Charges and miscellaneous
Total . . . . $708 mill.
Current charges . . . . $506 mill.
Misc. general income . . . . $202 mill.
Insurance trust revenue . . . . $148 mill.

Taxes
Total . . . . $1,117 mill.
Per capita taxes $1,762
Rank among states 27
Property taxes. . . . . $1 mill.
Sales taxes . . . . $620 mill.
License taxes . . . . $103 mill.
Individual income taxes . . . . $200 mill.
Corporate income taxes. . . . . $50 mill.
Other taxes . . . . $144 mill.

Total revenue figures include items not listed separately here.
Source: U.S. Bureau of the Census.

State government expenditures, 2002

General expenditures

Total state expenditures . . . . $3,020 mill.
Intergovernmental . . . . $586 mill.

Per capita expenditures

State $4,436
Average of all states $3,859
Rank among states 12

Selected direct expenditures

Education. . . . . $563 mill.
Public welfare . . . . $626 mill.
Health, hospital . . . . $80 mill.
Highways . . . . $311 mill.
Police protection . . . . $14 mill.
Corrections . . . . $37 mill.
Natural resources . . . . $101 mill.
Parks and recreation . . . . $13 mill.
Government administration. . . . . $103 mill.
Interest on debt . . . . $87 mill.
Total direct expenditures . . . . $2,227 mill.

Totals include items not listed separately.
Source: U.S. Census Bureau.

POLITICS

Governors since statehood

D = Democrat; R = Republican; O = other;
(r) resigned; (d) died in office; (i) removed from office

John Miller (R). 1889-1891
Andrew H. Burke (R) 1891-1893
Eli C. D. Shortridge (O) 1893-1895
Roger Allin (R) 1895-1897
Frank A. Briggs (R) 1897-1898
Joseph N. Devine (R) 1898-1899
Frederick B. Fancher (R) 1899-1901
Frank White (R) 1901-1905
Elmore Y. Sarles (R) 1905-1907
John Burke (D) 1907-1913
Louis B. Hanna (R) 1913-1917
Lynn J. Frazier (R) . . . . (i) 1917-1921
Ragnvald A. Nestos (R) 1921-1925
Arthur C. Sorlie (R) . . . . (d) 1925-1928
Walter J. Maddock (R). 1928-1929
George F. Shafer (R). 1929-1933
William Langer (R) . . . . (i) 1933-1934
Ole H. Olson (R) 1934-1935
Thomas Moodie (D). . . . . (i) 1935
Walter H. Welford (R). 1935-1937
William Langer (O) 1937-1939
John Moses (D) 1939-1945
Fred G. Aandahl (R). 1945-1951
Norman Brunsdale (R) 1951-1957
John E. Davis (R) 1957-1961

William L. Guy (D) 1961-1973
Arthur A. Link (D). 1973-1981
Allen I. Olson (R) 1981-1985
George A. Sinner (D) 1985-1992
Edward T. Schafer (R) 1992-2000
John Hoeven (R). 2000-

Composition of congressional delegations, 1989-2007

	Dem	Rep	Total
House of Representatives			
101st Congress, 1989			
State delegates	1	0	1
Total U.S.	259	174	433
102d Congress, 1991			
State delegates	1	0	1
Total U.S.	267	167	434
103d Congress, 1993			
State delegates	1	0	1
Total U.S.	258	176	434
104th Congress, 1995			
State delegates	1	0	1
Total U.S.	197	236	433
105th Congress, 1997			
State delegates	1	0	1
Total U.S.	206	228	434
106th Congress, 1999			
State delegates	1	0	1
Total U.S.	211	222	433
107th Congress, 2001			
State delegates	1	0	1
Total U.S.	211	221	432
108th Congress, 2003			
State delegates	1	0	1
Total U.S.	205	229	434
109th Congress, 2005			
State delegates	1	0	1
Total U.S.	202	231	433
110th Congress, 2007			
State delegates	1	0	1
Total U.S.	233	202	435
Senate			
101st Congress, 1989			
State delegates	2	0	2
Total U.S.	55	45	100
102d Congress, 1991			
State delegates	2	0	2
Total U.S.	56	44	100

	Dem	Rep	Total
103d Congress, 1993			
State delegates	2	0	2
Total U.S.	57	43	100
104th Congress, 1995			
State delegates	2	0	2
Total U.S.	46	53	99
105th Congress, 1997			
State delegates	2	0	2
Total U.S.	45	55	100
106th Congress, 1999			
State delegates	2	0	2
Total U.S.	45	54	99
107th Congress, 2001			
State delegates	2	0	2
Total U.S.	50	50	100
108th Congress, 2003			
State delegates	2	0	2
Total U.S.	48	51	99
109th Congress, 2005			
State delegates	2	0	2
Total U.S.	44	55	99
110th Congress, 2007			
State delegates	2	0	2
Total U.S.	49	49	98

Figures are for starts of first sessions. Totals are for Democrat (Dem.) and Republican (Rep.) members only. House membership totals under 435 and Senate totals under 100 reflect vacancies and seats held by independent party members. When the 110th Congress opened, the Senate's two independent members caucused with the Democrats, giving the Democrats control of the Senate.

Source: U.S. Congress, *Congressional Directory.*

Composition of state legislature, 1990-2006

	Democrats	Republicans
State House (106 seats in 1990; 98 seats thereafter)		
1990	48	58
1992	33	65
1994	23	75
1996	26	72
1998	34	64
2000	34	62
2002	28	66
2004	27	67
2006	33	61
State Senate (49 seats)		
1990	27	26
1992	25	24
1994	20	29
1996	19	30
1998	18	31
2000	18	31
2002	16	31
2004	15	32
2006	21	26

Figures for total seats may include independents and minor party members. Numbers reflect results of elections in listed years; elected members usually take their seats in the years that follow.

Source: Council of State Governments; *State Elective Officials and the Legislatures.*

Voter participation in presidential elections, 2000 and 2004

	2000	2004
Voting age population		
State	482,000	495,000
Total United States	209,831,000	220,377,000
State share of U.S. total	0.23	0.22
Rank among states	47	47
Portion of voting age population casting votes		
State	59.8%	63.1%
United States	50.3%	55.5%
Rank among states	9	12

Population figures are rounded to nearest thousand and include all residents, regardless of eligibility to vote.

Source: U.S. Census Bureau.

HEALTH AND MEDICAL CARE

Medical professionals
Physicians in 2003 and nurses in 2001

	U.S.	State
Physicians in 2003		
Total	774,849	1,529
Share of U.S. total		0.20%
Rate	266	241
Rank		27
Nurses in 2001		
Total	2,262,020	6,460
Share of U.S. total		0.29%
Rate	793	1,014
Rank		7

Rates are numbers of physicians and nurses per 100,000 resident population; ranks are based on rates.
Source: American Medical Association, *Physician Characteristics and Distribution in the U.S.*; U.S. Department of Health and Human Services, Health Resources and Services Administration.

Health insurance coverage, 2003

	State	U.S.
Total persons covered	563,000	243,320,000
Total persons not covered	69,000	44,961,000
Portion not covered	10.9%	15.6%
Rank among states	40	—
Children not covered	11,000	8,373,000
Portion not covered	7.5%	11.4%
Rank among states	40	—

Totals are rounded to nearest thousand. Ranks are from the highest to the lowest percentages of persons *not* insured.
Source: U.S. Census Bureau, Current Population Reports.

AIDS, syphilis, and tuberculosis cases, 2003

Disease	U.S. cases	State cases	Rank
AIDS	44,232	2	50
Syphilis	34,270	2	48
Tuberculosis	14,874	6	49

Source: U.S. Centers for Disease Control and Prevention.

Cigarette smoking, 2003
Residents over age 18 who smoke

	U.S.	State	Rank
All smokers	22.1%	20.5%	37
Male smokers	24.8%	22.0%	38
Female smokers	20.3%	19.0%	33

Cigarette smokers are defined as persons who reported having smoked at least 100 cigarettes during their lifetimes and who currently smoked at least occasionally.
Source: U.S. Centers for Disease Control and Prevention, *Morbidity and Mortality Weekly Report*, 53, no. 44 (November 12, 2004).

HOUSING

Home ownership rates, 1985-2004

	1985	1990	1995	2000	2004
State	69.9%	67.2%	67.3%	70.7%	70.0%
Total U.S.	63.9%	63.9%	64.7%	67.4%	69.0%
Rank among states	14	28	27	24	34

Net change in state home ownership rate, 1985-2004 . . . . +0.1%
Net change in U.S. home ownership rate, 1985-2004 . . . . +5.1%

Percentages represent the proportion of owner households to total occupied households.
Source: U.S. Census Bureau, 2006.

Home sales, 2000-2004
In thousands of units

Existing home sales	2000	2002	2003	2004
State sales	10.8	12.3	12.9	14.5
Total U.S. sales	5,171	5,631	6,183	6,784
State share of U.S. total	0.21%	0.22%	0.21%	0.21%
Sales rank among states	49	49	49	48

Units include single-family homes, condos, and co-ops.
Source: National Association of Realtors, Washington, D.C., *Real Estate Outlook: Market Trends & Insights*.

Values of owner-occupied homes, 2003

	State	U.S.
Total units	129,000	58,809,000
Value of units		
Under $100,000	64.3%	29.6%
$100,000-199,999	30.6%	36.9%
$200,000 or more	5.1%	33.5%
Median value	$81,796	$142,275
Rank among all states 50		

Units are owner-occupied one-family houses whose numbers are
rounded to nearest thousand. Data are extrapolated from
survey samples.
Source: U.S. Census Bureau, American Community Survey.

EDUCATION

Public school enrollment, 2002

Prekindergarten through grade 8
State enrollment. 69,000
Total U.S. enrollment. 34,135,000
State share of U.S. total 0.20%

Grades 9 through 12
State enrollment. 35,000
Total U.S. enrollment. 14,067,000
State share of U.S. total 0.25%

Enrollment rates
State public school enrollment rate. 92.9%
Overall U.S. rate 90.4%
Rank among states in 2002 9
Rank among states in 1995. 20

Enrollment figures (which include unclassified students) are
rounded to nearest thousand pupils during fall school term.
Enrollment rates are based on enumerated resident population
estimate for July 1, 2002.
Source: U.S. National Center for Education Statistics.

Public college finances, 2003-2004

FTE enrollment in public institutions of higher education
Students in state institutions 36,200
Students in all U.S. public institutions 9,916,600
State share of U.S. total 0.37
Rank among states 41

**State and local government appropriations for higher
education**
State appropriation per FTE $4,345
National average. $5,716
Rank among states 43
State & local tax revenue going to higher
education 11.8%

FTE = full-time equivalent in public postsecondary programs,
including summer sessions; student numbers are rounded to
nearest hundred. Funding figures for 2003-2004 academic year
include financial aid to students in state public institutions and
exclude money for research, agriculture experiment stations,
teaching hospitals, and medical schools; figures are rounded to
nearest thousand dollars.
Source: Higher Education Executive Officers, Denver, Colorado.

TRANSPORTATION AND TRAVEL

Highway mileage, 2003

Interstate highways 572	
Arterial roads 5,879	
Collector roads. 11,736	
Local roads. 68,595	
Urban roads 1,834	
Rural roads. 84,948	
Total state mileage. 86,782	
U.S. total 3,974,107	
State share 2.18%	
Rank among states 23	

Note that combined urban and rural road mileage matches the
total of the other categories.
Source: U.S. Federal Highway Administration.

Motor vehicle registrations and driver licenses, 2003

Vehicle registrations	State	U.S.	Share	Rank
Autos, trucks, buses	694,000	231,390,000	0.30%	46
Autos only	346,000	135,670	0.26%	47
Motorcycles	19,000	5,328,000	0.36%	47
Driver licenses	460,000	196,166,000	0.23%	49

Figures, which do not include vehicles owned by military services,
are rounded to the nearest thousand. Figures for automobiles
include taxis.
Source: U.S. Federal Highway Administration.

Domestic travel expenditures, 2003
Spending by U.S. residents on overnight trips and
day trips of at least 50 miles from home

Total expenditures within state . . . . $1.24 bill.
Total expenditures within U.S. . . . . $490.87 bill.
State share of U.S. total 0.3%
Rank among states 49

Source: Travel Industry Association of America.

Retail gasoline prices, 2003-2007
Average price per gallon at the pump

Year	U.S.	State
2003	$1.267	$1.283
2004	$1.316	$1.352
2005	$1.644	$1.707
2007	$2.298	$2.201

Excise tax per gallon in 2004 . . . . 21.0¢
Rank among all states in 2007 prices 34

Prices are averages of all grades of gasoline sold at the pump
during March months in 2003-2005 and during February, 2007.
Averages for 2006, during which prices rose higher, are not
available.
Source: U.S. Energy Information Agency, *Petroleum Marketing
Monthly* (2003-2005 data); American Automobile Association
(2007 data).

CRIME AND LAW ENFORCEMENT

State and local police officers, 2000-2004

	2000	2002	2004
Total officers			
U.S.	654,601	665,555	675,734
State	1,092	1,104	1,182*
*Net change, 2000-2004			+8.24%
Officers per 1,000 residents			
U.S.	2.33	2.31	2.30
State	1.70	1.74	1.86
State rank	41	39	34

Totals include state and local police and sheriffs.
Source: Carsey Institute, University of New Hampshire.

Crime rates, 2003
Incidents per 100,000 residents

Crimes	State	U.S.
Violent crimes		
Total incidents	78	475
Murder	2	6
Forcible rape	24	32
Robbery	8	142
Aggravated assault	44	295
Property crimes		
Total incidents	2,096	3,588
Burglary	306	741
Larceny/theft	1,620	2,415
Motor vehicle theft	170	433
All crimes	2,174	4,063

Source: U.S. Federal Bureau of Investigation, *Crime in the United
States*, annual.

State prison populations, 1980-2003

	State	U.S.	State share
1980	253	305,458	0.08%
1990	483	708,393	0.07%
1996	722	1,025,624	0.07%
2000	1,076	1,391,261	0.08%
2003	1,239	1,470,045	0.08%

State figures exclude prisoners in federal penitentiaries.
Source: U.S. Bureau of Justice Statistics, *Prisoners in 2003.*

Ohio

Location: Midwest

Area and rank: 40,953 square miles (106,067 square kilometers); 44,828 square miles (116,105 square kilometers) including water; thirty-fifth largest state in area

Coastline: none

Population and rank: 11,459,000 (2004); seventh largest state in population

Capital and largest city: Columbus (711,470 people in 2000 census)

Entered Union and rank: March 1, 1803; seventeenth state

Present constitution adopted: 1951

Counties: 88

Rising in front of the Statehouse in Columbus is a statue of former governor William McKinley, one of the eight presidents of the United States from Ohio. (Courtesy, Ohio Division of Travel and Tourism)

State name: "Ohio" derives from an Iroquoian word for "great river"

State nickname: Buckeye State

Motto: With God, all things are possible

State flag: Red and white stripes on a double-pointed pennant with a blue triangle at the staff end bearing a red circle bordered by seventeen stars

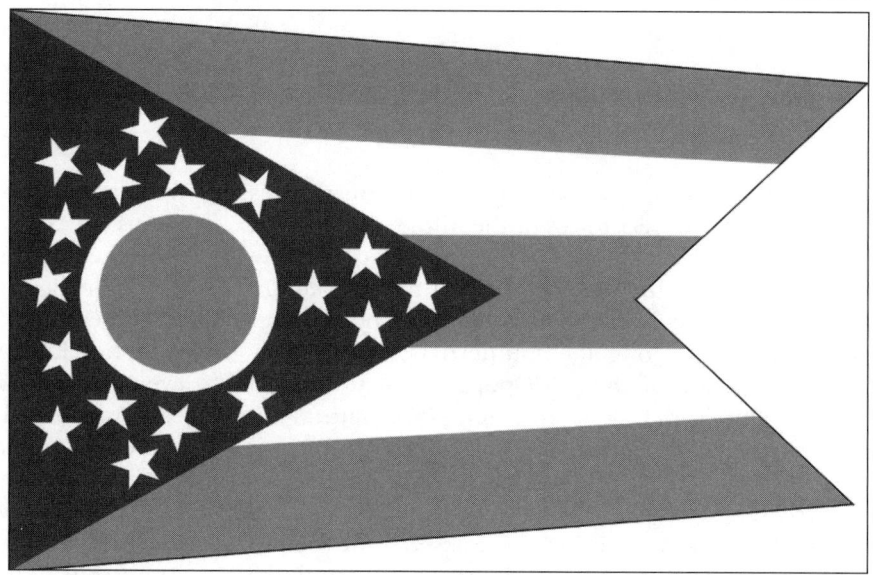

Highest point: Campbell Hill—1,549 feet (472 meters)

Lowest point: Ohio River—455 feet (139 meters)

Highest recorded temperature: 113 degrees Fahrenheit (45 degrees Celsius)—near Gallipolis, 1934

Lowest recorded temperature: –39 degrees Fahrenheit (–39.4 degrees Celsius)—Milligan, 1899

State song: "Beautiful Ohio"

State tree: Buckeye

State flower: Scarlet carnation

State bird: Cardinal

National parks: Cuyahoga Valley

Ohio History

Located between previously settled eastern states and newer territories in the Midwest, Ohio was one of the first states to be established after the creation of the United States. Ease of transportation, supplied by Lake Erie along the northern border and the Ohio River along the southern border, quickly made Ohio one of the most populous states in the Union. Ohio's rich soils and abundant natural resources have made it one of the most important areas of agricultural and industrial activity in the nation.

Early History. About eleven thousand years ago, the earliest humans to reside in the area used stone tools to hunt bison as well as extinct species such as mammoths and mastodons. About 2,500 years ago, the people of the Adena culture, located in southern Ohio, built mounds, lived in villages, made pottery, and subsisted by hunting, fishing, and gathering wild plant foods. About five hundred years later, the people of the Hopewell culture, living in the same area, established agriculture with the growing of corn. They also produced the most advanced metal artifacts, mostly made

from copper, found in North America until the Europeans arrived. About fifteen hundred years ago, the Hopewell culture began to decline. By the time Europeans first arrived in the region during the late seventeenth century, Ohio was mostly uninhabited.

Before Europeans were established in the area, however, Native Americans returned to Ohio during the early eighteenth century. The Wyandot, originally residing in Ontario, were driven south into northern Ohio by the devastation caused by newly introduced European diseases and by their enemies, the Iroquois League, a powerful confederation of eastern Native Americans. The Delaware, originally residing along the Atlantic coast, were driven west into northern Ohio by the Iroquois League and European settlers. The Miami, originally residing in eastern Wisconsin, expanded south and east into many areas, including southern Ohio. The Shawnee, who had originally resided along the Ohio River, were driven out by the Iroquois League but returned to southern Ohio in 1725.

Ohio is rich in Native American archaeological sites, such as this pyramid-shaped mound at Miamisburg. (Ohio Division of Travel and Tourism)

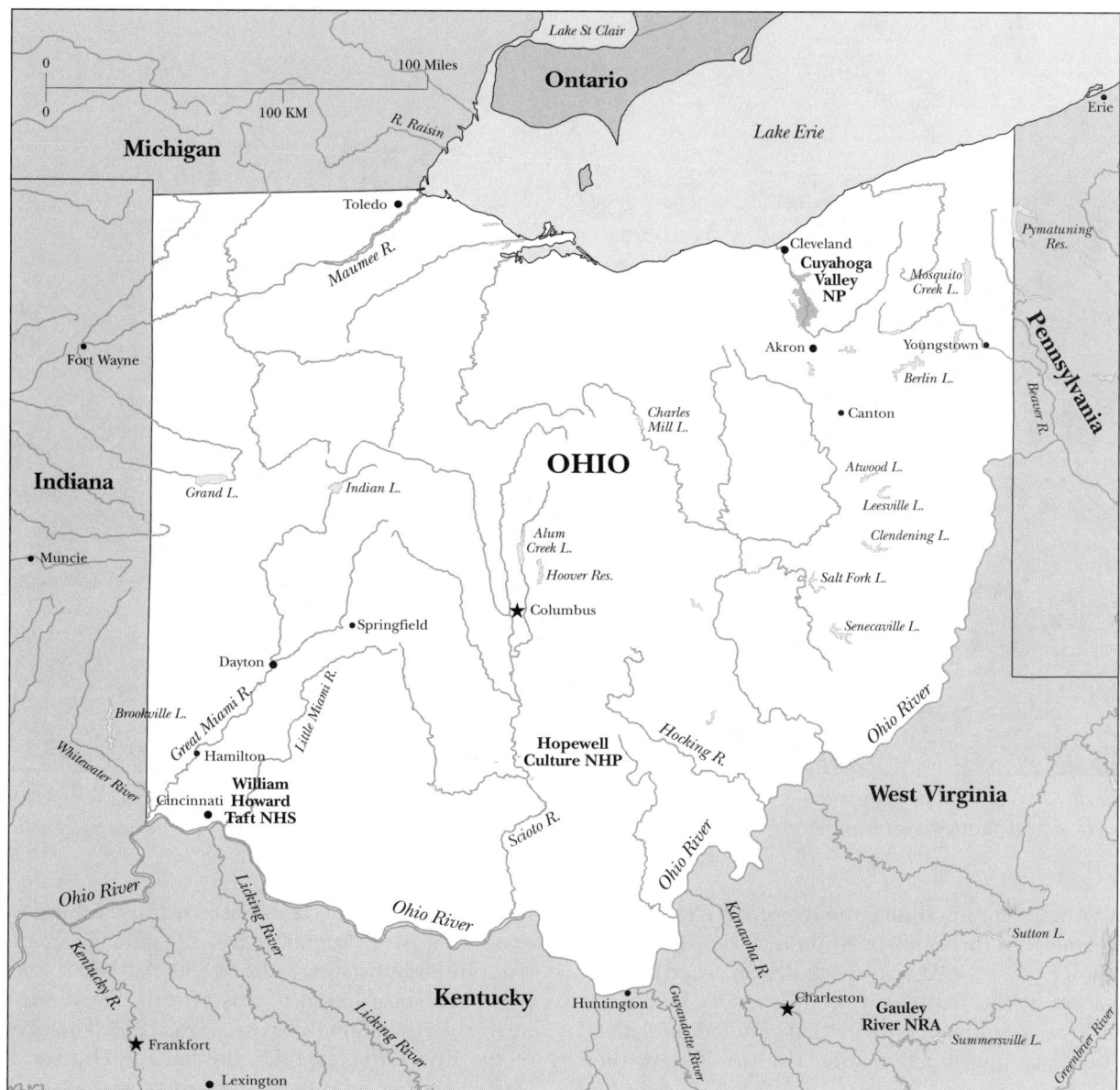

Exploration and Settlement. The first European known to have visited the area was the French explorer René-Robert Cavelier, sieur de La Salle, who journeyed southwest from Canada along the Saint Lawrence River, past Lake Ontario and Lake Erie, and into Ohio in 1670. During the first half of the eighteenth century, French traders from Canada and British traders from eastern colonies provided manufactured goods to the Native Americans in the area in exchange for deer and beaver skins. The lucrative fur trade led both sides to attempt to win control of the area. In 1749, the French sent an expedition led by Celeron de Bienville from Canada into Ohio, in order to make trade agreements with the inhabitants. The next year, the British sent a similar expedition, led by Christopher Gist, from Virginia to Ohio.

The conflict between France and England for control of North America led to the French and Indian War (1754-1763), which ended with the British in control of the area. During the American Revolution, American forces led by George Rogers Clark seized British outposts in Ohio. Clark also destroyed villages of the Shawnee, who were allied with the British. The war ended with the United States in control of the region. It became part of the newly created Northwest Territory in 1787.

The first permanent settlement in Ohio was founded in 1788 at Marietta by veterans of the Revolutionary War. The next year, settlers from New Jersey led by John Cleves Symes established a settlement at the future site of Cincinnati. These and other early settlements, located along the Ohio River, caused conflicts with the

Put-in-Bay on Lake Erie, near the site of Commodore Perry's naval victory over a British fleet during the war of 1812. The bay is on the north side of South Bass Island, north of Sandusky. (Ohio Division of Travel and Tourism)

Native Americans inhabiting the region. On August 20, 1794, American forces led by Anthony Wayne defeated an alliance of Native Americans under Shawnee leader Bluejacket at the Battle of Fallen Timbers. The next year Wayne negotiated a treaty that resulted in Native Americans ceding much of their land in Ohio to the United States.

Statehood. Settlements continued to be located almost entirely in the southern part of Ohio until 1796, when settlers from Connecticut arrived in northeast Ohio. By 1802 Ohio had the sixty thousand white adult male residents required for statehood, and it became the seventeenth state the next year. The capital was located at Chillicothe until 1810, when it was briefly moved to Zanesville. After returning to Chillicothe in 1812, the capital was moved to the newly founded city of Columbus in 1816.

During the early years of statehood, Shawnee leader Tecumseh organized an alliance of Native Americans that attempted to win back control of the region from the United States. During the War of 1812 Tecumseh was allied with the British against the Americans. Tecumseh and British general Henry A. Proctor led an invasion of Ohio in 1812 but were driven back into Canada the next year.

After the war, the population of Ohio grew rapidly.

In addition to settlers from eastern and southern states, emigrants from England, Ireland, and Germany arrived in large numbers after 1830. Advances in transportation contributed to this growth. Steamboats appeared on the Ohio River as early as 1811. The opening of the Erie Canal in 1825, linking the Hudson River with Lake Erie, improved transportation to Ohio and the territories beyond it. From 1825 to 1841, a series of canals linked the Ohio River and Lake Erie. The first railroad in the state was established in 1832. Between 1825 and 1838, the federal government extended the National Road across Ohio, linking the state to Pennsylvania and Maryland. By 1850, Ohio was the third most populous state in the Union.

At this time, agriculture was the most important part of the state's economy. In 1850, Ohio had a larger agricultural output than any other state. Coal was discovered in Ohio in 1808 and was later of great importance to the iron and steel industry. Other important mineral resources developed at this time included limestone, sandstone, clay, shale, and rock salt.

The Civil War. During the Civil War, Ohio was divided in loyalty. The strongest support for the Union was found in northern Ohio. Southern Ohio, bordering on Kentucky and Virginia, was more sympathetic to the Confederacy. Ohio supplied 320,000 volunteers for the Union. Three of the Union's most important generals, Ulysses S. Grant, William T. Sherman, and Philip H. Sheridan, were from Ohio.

Ohio was an important center of the Peace Democrats, known to their opponents as Copperheads. The Peace Democrats advocated an end to the war through negotiation with the Confederacy. Clement L. Vallandigham, a leader of the Peace Democrats, was nominated for governor of Ohio in 1863 but was defeated by Union supporter John Brough. The same year, Confederate soldiers led by John Hunt Morgan raided southern Ohio, reaching farther north than any other Confederate forces.

Industry and Immigration. The demand for manufactured goods during the war led to the growth of industry in Ohio, particularly in the northern part of the state. Iron ore from states to the northwest was transported via the Great Lakes to the steelmaking cities of Toldeo, Cleveland, and Youngstown. During the 1870's, Akron became a center of the rubber industry. Oil and natural gas were discovered in 1860. The Standard Oil Company, founded in Cleveland in 1870, soon controlled almost all oil production in the United States.

Immigrants from Italy, Poland, Hungary, and Russia arrived in large numbers after 1880. Cleveland was particularly diverse in the ethnic origins of its new residents, with immigrants arriving from Austria, the Netherlands, Portugal, Greece, China, Japan, Turkey, and Mexico. A large number of African Americans moved into the state at this time also, increasing the black population from about twenty-five thousand in 1850 to more than sixty-three thousand in 1870.

The Twentieth Century. Ohio was dominant in national politics during the turn of the century. Of the twelve U.S. presidents who held office from 1869 to 1923, seven were born in Ohio. Ohio was also the birthplace of Victoria Woodhull, who became the first woman to run for president, in 1872.

The state's economy expanded during World War I. The increase in automobile manufacturing after the war strengthened Ohio's oil, rubber, and glass industries. The Great Depression of the 1930's led to widespread unemployment, and the economy did not recover until World War II. Although economic conditions were generally favorable until the late 1970's, Ohio faced serious problems, including pollution in Lake Erie, race riots in Cleveland, poverty in the cities, and a decline in the quality of education.

A recession during the late 1970's and 1980's led to Ohio having 14 percent unemployment in 1982. During the 1980's and 1990's, Ohio shifted much of its economy away from manufacturing to the service and technology industries. The state also took steps to encourage new businesses, provide vocational training, and protect the environment.

Cincinnati's location as a port on the Ohio River contributed greatly to its development during the nineteenth century. At the center of this view of the city's modern skyline, Paul Brown Stadium—the home of the Cincinnati Bengals football team—can be seen. (Rick Dikeman)

Though perhaps less famous than Cleveland or Cincinnati, Columbus is both Ohio's largest city and its capital, and is almost as big as Cleveland and Cincinnati combined. (PhotoDisc)

Riots and Scandal. Public life in Ohio was marked in the opening years of the new millennium by public disturbances in one city and criminal accusations against a sitting member of Congress. In 2001, serious rioting erupted in Cincinnati's African American community after an incident on April 7, when a police officer killed nineteen-year-old Timothy Thomas. The city had recently been through a number of police killings and alleged abuse of black residents. During the prior six years, fifteen black males had been killed by police; the black community was simmering with resentment.

The death of Thomas ignited the black community. The result was the worst rioting in Cincinnati since the 1960's, lasting the three nights of April 10-12 and ending only with a curfew and heavy rain. A federal lawsuit over the death ensued, resulting in an agreement directed at changing police-community relations. In September, 2001, a judge found the police officer who killed Thomas innocent of all charges. Thomas's mother subsequently filed a separate wrongful death suit; it was settled after the trial began. Following the riots, Cincinnati set new records for murder rates. The city's police began a "work slowdown" to protest new measures to scrutinize their behavior and a perceived lack of support from city hall.

Scandal involved a well-known congressman, James Traficant, Jr. In 2002, Traficant, a Democrat, was indicted on federal charges of bribery, tax evasion, and racketeering, accused of misappropriating campaign funds for his own use. In April, 2002, he was convicted of ten felony counts. On July 25, by a vote of 420-1, he became the first person expelled from the House of Representatives since 1980. Sentenced to eight years in federal prison, he continued his political activities from prison, running for Congress in 2002. He received more than 27,000 votes, about 15 percent of the votes cast.

Blackout of 2003. On August 14, 2003, a massive power outage swept across eight eastern states and Ontario, Canada, including Ohio. While most states regained power on August 15, power was not restored in the northern part of Ohio until August 16. An investigation showed that the outage was caused by the overloaded lines of troubled Akron-based FirstEnergy Corp., the nation's fourth largest utility holding company. Shortly after the restoration of power, a class action lawsuit was filed against the company; the suit was later settled for $90 million, with no admission of wrongdoing by the company.

Electoral Politics. In 2000, Ohio gave its twenty-one electoral votes to George W. Bush, who won the state by a narrow margin of 177,000 votes among more than 4.3

million votes cast. Mike DeWine was reelected U.S. senator, and all congressional incumbents were returned to Washington. The state's congressional delegation was composed of eleven Republicans and eight Democrats. Two years later, matters were slightly different. The state had lost a congressional seat after the 2000 census, and after the 2002 election there were twelve Republicans and six Democrats in Congress.

Two years later, in 2004, Ohio determined the cliffhanger election between President Bush and Senator John Kerry of Massachusetts. On the morning after the election, the two candidates were virtually tied, with Ohio undetermined. If Iowa, Nevada, and New Mexico, which were still undecided, went to Kerry, then there would be a tie in the electoral college. In that case, the presidency would be decided in the House of Representatives, each state having one vote, resulting in a Bush victory.

Thus, Ohio was the key to either candidate's victory. Because Ohio was a "battleground" (hotly contested and evenly divided) state in a close national election, there were hundreds of observers from both parties watching the polling process and looking for legal infractions. The eligibility to vote of certain voters was disputed, and federal courts were brought into the fray. Contested voters cast "provisional" ballots, but standards for counting these contested votes were vigorously disputed. In the end, on the morning of November 3, Democrats' hopes lay in provisional ballots that had not been counted. Later that morning, however, Ohio's secretary of state announced that it was statistically impossible for Kerry to win, no matter how contested votes were counted. At that, Senator Kerry conceded the election.

Rose Secrest
Updated by the Editor

Ohio Time Line

1670	French explorer René-Robert Cavelier, sieur de La Salle, reaches Ohio.
1725	Shawnee, previously driven out by the Iroquois League, return to southern Ohio.
1749	French explorer Celeron de Bienville leads a trade expedition to Ohio.
1750	British explorer Christopher Gist leads a trade expedition to Ohio.
1754-1763	French and Indian War.
1763	End of the French and Indian War brings the area under British control.
1783	End of the American Revolution brings the area under American control.
1787	Ohio becomes part of the newly created Northwest Territory.
Apr. 7, 1788	First permanent settlement in Ohio is founded at Marietta.
1789	Settlement is founded at the future site of Cincinnati.
Aug. 20, 1794	United States defeats an alliance of Native Americans at the Battle of Fallen Timbers.
Aug. 3, 1795	Treaty of Greenville results in Native Americans ceding most of their lands in Ohio to the United States.
1796	First permanent settlement in northern Ohio is founded.
1800	*Chillicothe Gazette*, Ohio's oldest newspaper, is founded.
Mar. 1, 1803	Ohio is admitted to the Union as the seventeenth state.
1804	Ohio University is founded in Athens.
1808	Coal is discovered in Ohio.
1810	State capital is moved to Zanesville.
1811	Steamboat travel begins on the Ohio River.
1812	Capital is moved back to Chillicothe.
1812-1813	Allied British and Native American forces invade Ohio.
1816	State capital is moved to Columbus.
1825	Erie Canal, linking the Hudson River to Lake Erie, is opened, increasing water traffic to Ohio.
1825-1838	National Road is extended through Ohio, increasing land traffic into the state.
1832	First railroad in Ohio is established.
1850	With two million residents, Ohio becomes the third most populous state in the Union; ranks first among the states in agricultural production.
1860	Oil and natural gas production begin in Ohio.
July, 1863	Confederate forces under John Hunt Morgan raid Ohio.
1870	Standard Oil Company is founded in Cleveland.

(continued)

1872	Ohio native Victoria Woodhull becomes the first woman to run for U.S. president.
1934	State sales tax is enacted.
1951	Ohio adopts its fourth constitution.
1959	Completion of the Saint Lawrence Seaway, linking the Great Lakes to the Atlantic Ocean, allows ocean vessels to reach Ohio.
1968	Carl B. Stokes of Cleveland becomes the first African American mayor of a major city.
May 4, 1970	Four students are killed in a confrontation with the National Guard during a protest against the Vietnam War at Kent State University.
1980	Unemployment reaches 14 percent.
1998	Population reaches more than eleven million.
1999	Federal judge stops the state of Ohio from providing tax-funded tuition vouchers to students attending religious schools.
Apr. 7, 2001	Cincinnati police kill African American Timothy Thomas, setting off days of rioting and far-reaching consequences for the city.
Nov. 5, 2002	Republican Robert A. Taft II is reelected governor.
2003	Cincinnati opens Contemporary Arts Museum, the first major U.S. arts museum designed by a woman.
Aug. 14-16, 2003	Massive power outage caused by overloaded lines of Akron-based FirstEnergy Corp. hits Ohio, seven other eastern states, and Ontario, Canada.
Nov. 2-3, 2004	Ohio plays key role in presidential election, which hinges on its vote. The morning after the election, Ohio swings into the column of President George W. Bush, sealing his reelection.

Notes for Further Study

Published Sources. An excellent resource for the student new to the subject of Ohio is *Eastern Great Lakes: Indiana, Michigan, Ohio* (1995) by Thomas G. Aylesworth, which provides basic information on the state and compares it to other states in the region. A similar work, with an emphasis on the culture and society of Ohio, is George W. Knepper's *Ohio and Its People* (3d ed., 2003).

The physical geography of the state is presented in a popular style in *Natural Wonders of Ohio: Exploring Wild and Scenic Places* (1998) by Gordon and Janet Groene. A more scholarly discussion of the same subject is found in *A Geography of Ohio* (1996), edited by Leonard Peacefull. An entertaining way to learn about many different locations in the state is Larry L. Miller's *Ohio Place Names* (1996). Nearly 350 photographs, original artworks, maps, time lines, and graphics help to tell the fascinating story of the region's Native American history in *Ohio Archaeology: An Illustrated Chronicle of Ohio's Ancient American Indian Cultures* (2005) by Bradley Thomas Lepper. Six chronological chapters based on the major archaeological periods are supplemented with twenty-eight feature articles written by top regional scholars.

Of the many different books that discuss Ohio's history, one of the most dramatic is Allan W. Eckert's *That Dark and Bloody River: Chronicles of the Ohio River Valley* (1995). An outstanding discussion of the early history of the state is found in *The Ohio Frontier: Crucible of the Old Northwest, 1720-1830* (1996) by R. Douglas Hurt. *The Center of a Great Empire: The Ohio Country in the Early Republic* (2005), edited by Andrew R. L. Cayton and Stuart D. Hobbs, takes a sweeping look at the conquest of Native Americans, the emergence of a democratic political culture, the origins of capitalism, and the for-

mation of public culture, among other topics, during the late eighteenth and early nineteenth centuries. The role that Ohio played in the Civil War is included in *Rebel Raider: The Life of General John Hunt Morgan* (1986) by James A. Ramage. An excellent review of racial tensions in Ohio is found in Joseph Watras's *Politics, Race, and Schools: Racial Integration, 1954-1994* (1997), which uses the city of Dayton as a case study. The state's second-largest city is the topic of *Cleveland: A Concise History, 1796-1990* (1997) by Carol Poh Miller. George Zimmermann and Carol Zimmermann's *Ohio Off the Beaten Path: A Guide to Unique Places* (2004) is a good for those interested in the unique locales and history of the state. For young audiences, both Joyce Hart's *Ohio* (2006) from the It's My State series and *Ohio History* (2003) by Marcia Schonberg provide accessible information about many aspects of the state's history and culture.

Web Resources. As one of the most heavily populated states in the Union, Ohio provides an enormous variety of Web sites with information on the state. A good place to start is the state of Ohio Government Information and Services (www.state.oh.us), the official site for the state government. Besides the information on government services usually provided by similar Web sites, this site also provides links to a large number of sites with general information about the state. For a concise but clear and accurate overview of Ohio, InfoPlease's page on Ohio (www.infoplease.com/ipa/a0108258.htm) gives an excellent summary of basic facts. Numerous links are also found at Ohio.com (www.ohio.com), provided by the *Akron Beacon Journal*. This site emphasizes news events and Ohio businesses.

Statistical information on the state is provided by the U.S.

Census Bureau at Ohio QuickFacts (quickfacts.census.gov/ qfd/states/39000.html). A guide to attractions and events within Ohio can be found at Discover Ohio Tourism (www .ohiotourism.com). The flora and fauna of the state are discussed in detail at Ohio Biological Survey (www.ohio biologicalsurvey.org/), an ambitious project involving ninety-one colleges, universities, museums, and other organizations. The complete text of the state's constitution, with all amendments, can be found at Anderson's Ohio Online Documents (onlinedocs.andersonpublishing.com/oh/lpExt .dll?f=templates&fn=titlepage.htm).

Counties

County	2000 pop.	Rank in pop.	Sq. miles	Rank in area	County	2000 pop.	Rank in pop.	Sq. miles	Rank in area
Adams	27,330	80	584.0	10	Logan	46,005	52	458.5	38
Allen	108,473	26	404.5	75	Lorain	284,664	9	492.6	28
Ashland	52,523	48	424.4	49	Lucas	455,054	6	340.4	85
Ashtabula	102,728	27	702.7	1	Madison	40,213	62	465.2	35
Athens	62,223	41	506.8	23	Mahoning	257,555	10	415.3	58
Auglaize	46,611	51	401.3	80	Marion	66,217	38	403.9	77
Belmont	70,226	37	537.3	18	Medina	151,095	16	421.6	53
Brown	42,285	54	491.8	30	Meigs	23,072	81	429.5	46
Butler	332,807	8	467.3	34	Mercer	40,924	57	463.3	36
Carroll	28,836	76	394.7	84	Miami	98,868	28	407.0	70
Champaign	38,890	66	428.6	47	Monroe	15,180	85	455.6	40
Clark	144,742	19	400.0	81	Montgomery	559,062	4	461.7	37
Clermont	177,977	13	452.1	42	Morgan	14,897	86	417.7	55
Clinton	40,543	61	410.9	63	Morrow	31,628	72	405.5	74
Columbiana	112,075	23	532.5	19	Muskingum	84,585	31	664.6	4
Coshocton	36,655	67	564.1	13	Noble	14,058	87	399.0	83
Crawford	46,966	50	402.3	79	Ottawa	40,985	56	255.1	86
Cuyahoga	1,393,978	1	458.3	39	Paulding	20,293	83	416.3	57
Darke	53,309	46	599.9	9	Perry	34,078	69	410.0	65
Defiance	39,500	63	411.2	62	Pickaway	52,727	47	502.2	25
Delaware	109,989	25	442.5	43	Pike	27,695	79	441.5	44
Erie	79,551	32	254.5	87	Portage	152,061	15	492.4	29
Fairfield	122,759	21	505.7	24	Preble	42,337	53	424.8	48
Fayette	28,433	77	406.6	72	Putnam	34,726	68	483.9	31
Franklin	1,068,978	2	540.0	17	Richland	128,852	20	497.0	26
Fulton	42,084	55	406.8	71	Ross	73,345	35	688.5	2
Gallia	31,069	73	468.8	33	Sandusky	61,792	42	409.2	68
Geauga	90,895	30	404.1	76	Scioto	79,195	33	612.3	8
Greene	147,886	17	414.9	59	Seneca	58,683	44	550.6	16
Guernsey	40,792	60	522.0	22	Shelby	47,910	49	409.3	67
Hamilton	845,303	3	407.4	69	Stark	378,098	7	576.2	11
Hancock	71,295	36	531.4	20	Summit	542,899	5	412.8	61
Hardin	31,945	71	470.3	32	Trumbull	225,116	12	615.8	7
Harrison	15,856	84	403.6	78	Tuscarawas	90,914	29	567.6	12
Henry	29,210	75	416.5	56	Union	40,909	58	436.7	45
Highland	40,875	59	553.3	15	Van Wert	29,659	74	410.1	64
Hocking	28,241	78	422.8	51	Vinton	12,806	88	414.1	60
Holmes	38,943	65	423.0	50	Warren	158,383	14	399.9	82
Huron	59,487	43	493.1	27	Washington	63,251	39	635.2	5
Jackson	32,641	70	420.3	54	Wayne	111,564	24	555.4	14
Jefferson	73,894	34	409.6	66	Williams	39,188	64	421.8	52
Knox	54,500	45	527.2	21	Wood	121,065	22	617.4	6
Lake	227,511	11	228.2	88	Wyandot	22,908	82	405.6	73
Lawrence	62,319	40	455.4	41					
Licking	145,491	18	686.5	3					

Source: U.S. Census Bureau; National Association of Counties.

Cities

With 10,000 or more residents

Rank	City	Population	Rank	City	Population
1	Columbus (capital)	711,470	19	Cleveland Heights	49,958
2	Cleveland	478,403	20	Cuyahoga Falls	49,374
3	Cincinnati	331,285	21	Mansfield	49,346
4	Toledo	313,619	22	Warren	46,832
5	Akron	217,074	23	Newark	46,279
6	Dayton	166,179	24	Strongsville	43,858
7	Parma	85,655	25	Fairfield	42,097
8	Youngstown	82,026	26	Lima	40,081
9	Canton	80,806	27	Findlay	38,967
10	Lorain	68,652	28	Huber Heights	38,212
11	Springfield	65,358	29	Beavercreek	37,984
12	Hamilton	60,690	30	Boardman	37,215
13	Kettering	57,502	31	Lancaster	35,335
14	Lakewood	56,646	32	Westerville	35,318
15	Elyria	55,953	33	Marion	35,318
16	Euclid	52,717	34	North Olmsted	34,113
17	Middletown	51,605	35	Upper Arlington	33,686
18	Mentor	50,278	36	Brunswick	33,388

Rank	City	Population		Rank	City	Population
37	Gahanna	32,636		55	Maple Heights	26,156
38	Stow	32,139		56	Zanesville	25,586
39	Reynoldsburg	32,069		57	Delaware	25,243
40	Fairborn	32,052		58	Medina	25,139
41	Westlake	31,719		59	Wooster	24,811
42	Austintown	31,627		60	Hilliard	24,230
43	Dublin	31,392		61	Xenia	24,164
44	Massillon	31,325		62	Riverside	23,545
45	Garfield Heights	30,734		63	South Euclid	23,537
46	Bowling Green	29,636		64	Alliance	23,253
47	Shaker Heights	29,405		65	Centerville	23,024
48	North Royalton	28,648		66	Green	22,817
49	Kent	27,906		67	Willoughby	22,621
50	Barberton	27,899		68	Hudson	22,439
51	Sandusky	27,844		69	North Ridgeville	22,338
52	Trotwood	27,420		70	Mason	22,016
53	East Cleveland	27,217		71	Troy	21,999
54	Grove City	27,075		72	Oxford	21,943

(continued)

Rank	City	Population	Rank	City	Population
73	Solon	21,802	127	Washington	13,524
74	Chillicothe	21,796	128	Finneytown	13,492
75	Norwood	21,675	129	Circleville	13,485
76	Parma Heights	21,659	130	Wickliffe	13,484
77	Athens	21,342	131	Brecksville	13,382
78	Ashland	21,249	132	Clayton	13,347
79	Brook Park	21,218	133	Greenville	13,294
80	Ashtabula	20,962	134	White Oak	13,277
81	Niles	20,932	135	Bucyrus	13,224
82	Portsmouth	20,909	136	Bexley	13,203
83	Piqua	20,738	137	East Liverpool	13,089
84	Rocky River	20,735	138	Bellefontaine	13,069
85	Eastlake	20,255	139	Landen	12,766
86	Sidney	20,211	140	Bridgetown North	12,569
87	Miamisburg	19,489	141	Blue Ash	12,513
88	Forest Park	19,463	142	Conneaut	12,485
89	Mayfield Heights	19,386	143	Springboro	12,380
90	Oregon	19,355	144	Streetsboro	12,311
91	Whitehall	19,201	145	Englewood	12,235
92	Steubenville	19,015	146	Dover	12,210
93	Berea	18,970	147	Salem	12,197
94	Sylvania	18,670	148	Beachwood	12,186
95	Wadsworth	18,437	149	Seven Hills	12,080
96	Avon Lake	18,145	150	Wilmington	11,921
97	Tiffin	18,135	151	Amherst	11,797
98	Fairview Park	17,572	152	Ravenna	11,771
99	Painesville	17,503	153	Struthers	11,756
100	Fremont	17,375	154	Coshocton	11,682
101	New Philadelphia	17,056	155	Loveland	11,677
102	Twinsburg	17,006	156	Urbana	11,613
103	Lebanon	16,962	157	Brooklyn	11,586
104	Perrysburg	16,945	158	Norton	11,523
105	Defiance	16,465	159	Cambridge	11,520
106	Tallmadge	16,390	160	Avon	11,446
107	North Canton	16,369	161	Franklin	11,396
108	Norwalk	16,238	162	Bedford Heights	11,375
109	Bay Village	16,087	163	Galion	11,341
110	Broadview Heights	15,967	164	Reading	11,292
111	Marysville	15,942	165	Shiloh	11,272
112	Middleburg Heights	15,542	166	Ironton	11,211
113	Lyndhurst	15,279	167	Northbrook	11,076
114	Maumee	15,237	168	Forestville	10,978
115	Warrensville Heights	15,109	169	Richmond Heights	10,944
116	Vandalia	14,603	170	Vermilion	10,927
117	Marietta	14,515	171	Girard	10,902
118	Mount Vernon	14,375	172	Van Wert	10,690
119	Willowick	14,361	173	Springdale	10,563
120	Bedford	14,214	174	Celina	10,303
121	University Heights	14,146	175	Pataskala	10,249
122	Worthington	14,125	176	Montgomery	10,163
123	Fostoria	13,931	177	North College Hill	10,082
124	West Carrollton City	13,818			
125	Sharonville	13,804			
126	Aurora	13,556			

Population figures are from 2000 census.
Source: U.S. Bureau of the Census.

Index to Tables

DEMOGRAPHICS

Resident state and national populations, 1970-2004

Population figures given in thousands

	State pop.	U.S. pop.	Share	Rank
1970	10,657	203,302	5.2%	6
1980	10,798	226,546	4.8%	6
1985	10,735	237,924	4.5%	7
1990	10,847	248,765	4.4%	7
1995	11,203	262,761	4.2%	7
2000	11,353	281,425	4.0%	7
2004	11,459	293,655	3.9%	7

Source: U.S. Census Bureau, Current Population Reports, 2006.

Resident population by age, 2004

Age Group	Total persons
Under 5 years	730,000
5 to 17 years	2,049,000
18 to 24 years	1,128,000
25 to 34 years	1,464,000
35 to 44 years	1,684,000
45 to 54 years	1,702,000
55 to 64 years	1,177,000
65 to 74 years	747,000
75 to 84 years	570,000
85 years and older	208,000
All age groups	11,459,000

Portion of residents 65 and older	13.3%
National rank in portion of oldest residents	13
National average	12.4%

Population figures are rounded to nearest thousand persons;
figures include armed forces personnel stationed in the state.
Source: U.S. Bureau of the Census, 2006.

Resident population by race, Hispanic origin, 2004

Category	State pop.	Share	U.S.
All residents	11,459	100.00%	100.00%
Non-Hispanic white	9,547	83.31%	67.37%
Hispanic white	221	1.93%	13.01%
Other Hispanic	31	0.27%	1.06%
African American	1,362	11.89%	12.77%
Native American	26	0.23%	0.96%
Asian, Pacific Islander	163	1.42%	4.37%
Two or more categories	140	1.22%	1.51%

Population figures are in thousands. Persons counted as "Hispanic" (Latino) may be of any race. Because of overlapping categories, categories may not add up to 100%. Shares in column 3 are percentages of each category within the state; these figures may be compared to the national percentages in column 4.
Source: U.S. Bureau of the Census, 2006.

Projected state population, 2000-2030

Year	Population
2000	11,353,000
2005	11,478,000
2010	11,576,000
2015	11,635,000
2020	11,644,000
2025	11,606,000
2030	11,551,000
Population increase, 2000-2030	198,000
Percentage increase, 2000-2030	1.7

Projections are based on data from the 2000 census.
Source: U.S. Census Bureau.

VITAL STATISTICS

Infant mortality rates, 1980-2002

	1980	1990	2000	2002
All state residents	12.8	9.8	7.6	7.9
All U.S. residents	12.6	9.2	9.4	9.1
All state white residents	11.2	7.8	6.3	6.2
All U.S. white residents	10.6	7.6	5.7	5.8
All state black residents	23.0	19.5	15.4	17.7
All U.S. black residents	22.2	18.0	14.1	14.4

Figures represent deaths per 1,000 live births of resident infants under 1 year old, exclusive of fetal deaths. Figures for all residents include members of other racial categories not listed separately.
Source: U.S. Census Bureau, *Statistical Abstract of the United States,* 2006.

Abortion rates, 1990 and 2000

	1990	2000
Total abortions	50,000	40,000
Rate per 1,000 women	19.5	16.5
U.S. rate	25.7	21.3
Rank	24	21

Numbers of abortions are rounded to nearest thousand; ranks are based on rates.
Source: U.S. Census Bureau.

Marriages and divorces, 2004

Total marriages	75,900
Rate per 1,000 population	6.6
National rate per 1,000 population	7.4
Rank among all states	32
Total divorces	42,400
Rate per 1,000 population	3.7
National rate per 1,000 population	3.7
Rank among all states	24

Figures are for all marriages and divorces performed within the state, including those of nonresidents; totals are rounded to the nearest hundred. Ranks are for highest to lowest figures; note that divorce data are not available for five states.
Source: U.S. National Center for Health Statistics, *Vital Statistics of the United States,* 2006.

Death rates by leading causes, 2002
Deaths per 100,000 resident population

Cause	State	U.S.
Heart disease	274.8	241.7
Cancer	220.4	193.2
Cerebrovascular diseases	63.5	56.4
Accidents other than motor vehicle	36.3	37.0
Motor vehicle accidents	14.0	15.7
Chronic lower respiratory diseases	53.1	43.3
Diabetes mellitus	33.7	25.4
HIV	2.1	4.9
Suicide	11.3	11.0
Homicide	4.8	6.1
All causes	961.1	847.3
Rank in overall death rate among states		12

Figures exclude nonresidents who died in the state. Causes of death follow International Classification of Diseases. Rank is from highest to lowest death rate in the United States.
Source: U.S. National Center for Health Statistics, *National Vital Statistics Report,* 2006.

ECONOMY

Gross state product, 1990-2004
In current dollars

Year	State product	Nat'l product	State share
1990	$228.3 billion	$5.67 trillion	4.02%
2000	$371.2 billion	$9.75 trillion	3.81%
2002	$385.7 billion	$10.41 trillion	3.70%
2003	$398.9 billion	$10.92 trillion	3.65%
2004	$418.3 billion	$11.65 trillion	3.59%

Source: U.S. Bureau of Economic Analysis, *Survey of Current Business,* July, 2005.

Gross state product by industry, 2003
In billions of dollars

Construction	$13.6
Manufacturing	80.8
Wholesale trade	23.4
Retail trade	30.3
Finance & insurance	28.0
Information	11.6
Professional services	20.1
Health care & social assistance	27.6
Government	39.4
Total state product	$375.7
Total U.S. product	$10,289.2
State share of U.S. total	3.65%
Rank among all states	7

Total figures include industries not listed separately. Amounts are in chained 2000 dollars.
Source: U.S. Bureau of Economic Analysis, *Survey of Current Business,* July, 2005.

Personal income per capita, 1990-2004
In current dollars

	1990	2000	2004
Per capita income	$18,743	$28,207	$31,322
U.S. average	$19,477	$29,845	$32,937
Rank among states	21	24	26

Source: U.S. Bureau of Economic Analysis, *Survey of Current Business,* April, 2005.

Energy consumption, 2001
In trillions of British thermal units (BTU), except as noted

Total energy consumption

Total state energy consumption	3,982
Total U.S. energy consumption	96,275
State share of U.S. total	4.14%
Rank among states	5

Per capita consumption (In millions of BTU)

Total state per capita consumption	350
Total U.S. per capita consumption	338
Rank among states	23

End-use sectors

Residential	892
Commercial	682
Industrial	1,429
Transportation	979

Sources of energy

Petroleum	1,305
Natural gas	836
Coal	1,343
Hydroelectric power	5
Nuclear electric power	162

Figures for totals include categories not listed separately.
Source: U.S. Energy Information Administration, *State Energy Data Report,* 2001.

Nonfarm employment by sectors, 2004

Total persons	5,407,000
Construction	235,000
Manufacturing	825,000
Trade, transportation, utilities	1,038,000
Information	93,000
Finance, insurance, real estate	312,000
Professional & business services	624,000
Education & health services	744,000
Leisure, hospitality, arts, organizations	495,000
Other services, including repair & maintenance	227,000
Government	802,000

Figures are rounded to nearest thousand persons. "Total" includes mining and natural resources, not listed separately.
Source: U.S. Bureau of Labor Statistics, 2006.

Foreign exports, 1990-2004
In millions of dollars

Year	State	U.S.	State share
1990	13,378	394,045	3.40%
1996	22,677	624,767	3.63%
1997	24,903	688,896	3.61%
2000	26,322	712,055	3.36%
2003	29,764	724,006	4.40%
2004	31,208	769,332	4.06%

Rank among all states in 2004. 6

U.S. total does not include U.S. dependencies.
Source: U.S. Census Bureau, *U.S. Merchandise Trade,* series FT 900, 2000; U.S. Census Bureau, *U.S. International Trade in Goods and Services,* Series FT 900, 2005.

LAND USE

Federally owned land, 2003
Areas in acres

	State	U.S.	State share
Total area	26,222,000	2,271,343,000	1.15%
Nonfederal land	25,764,000	1,599,584,000	1.61%
Federal land	458,000	671,759,000	0.07%
Federal share	1.7%	29.6%	—

Areas are rounded to nearest thousand acres. Figures for federally owned land do not include trust properties.
Source: U.S. General Services Administration, *Federal Real Property Profile,* 2006.

Land use, 1997
In acres, rounded to nearest thousand

Total surface area	26,445,000
Total nonfederal rural land.	22,070,000
Percentage rural land	83.5%
Cropland.	11,627,000
Conservation Reserve Program (CRP*) land. . . .	324,000
Pastureland	2,006,000
Rangeland	(nil)
Forestland.	7,081,000
Other rural land	1,032,000

*CRP is a federal program begun in 1985 to assist private landowners to convert highly erodible cropland to vegetative cover for ten years. Note that some categories of land overlap.
Source: U.S. Department of Agriculture, Natural Resources and Conservation Service, and Iowa State University, Statistical Laboratory, *Summary Report, 1997 National Resources Inventory,* revised December, 2000.

Farms and crop acreage, 2004

	State	U.S.	Share	Rank
Farms	77,000	2,113,000	3.64%	8
Acres (millions)	15	937	1.60%	19
Acres per farm	189	443	—	38

Source: U.S. Department of Agriculture, National Agricultural Statistics Service. Farm totals are rounded to nearest thousand units; acreage figures are rounded to nearest million. Rankings, including ties, are based on rounded figures.

GOVERNMENT AND FINANCE

Units of local government, 2002

	State	Total U.S.	Rank
All local governments	3,636	87,525	6
Counties	88	3,034	13
Municipalities	942	19,429	6
Townships	1,308	16,504	5
School districts	667	13,506	5
Special districts	631	35,052	18

Only 48 states have county governments, 20 states have township governments ("towns" in New England, Minnesota, New York, and Wisconsin), and 46 states have school districts. Special districts encompass such functions as natural resources, fire protection, and housing and community development.
Source: U.S. Census Bureau, *Census of Governments.*

State government revenue, 2002

Total revenue	$45,439 mill.
General revenue	$40,232 mill.
Per capita revenue	$3,526
U.S. per capita average	$3,689
Rank among states	38

Intergovernment revenue
Total	$12,654 mill.
From federal government	$12,328 mill.

Charges and miscellaneous
Total	$7,447 mill.
Current charges	$4,134 mill.
Misc. general income	$3,314 mill.
Insurance trust revenue	$4,682 mill.

Taxes
Total	$20,130 mill.
Per capita taxes	$1,764
Rank among states	26
Property taxes	$18 mill.
Sales taxes	$9,328 mill.
License taxes	$1,562 mill.
Individual income taxes	$8,336 mill.
Corporate income taxes	$761 mill.
Other taxes	$125 mill.

Total revenue figures include items not listed separately here.
Source: U.S. Bureau of the Census.

State government expenditures, 2002

General expenditures

Total state expenditures	$52,594 mill.
Intergovernmental	$15,052 mill.

Per capita expenditures

State	$3,713
Average of all states	$3,859
Rank among states	30

Selected direct expenditures

Education	$6,515 mill.
Public welfare	$9,723 mill.
Health, hospital	$2,234 mill.
Highways	$2,255 mill.
Police protection	$233 mill.
Corrections	$1,297 mill.
Natural resources	$366 mill.
Parks and recreation	$91 mill.
Government administration	$1,911 mill.
Interest on debt	$1,135 mill.
Total direct expenditures	$27,310 mill.

Totals include items not listed separately.
Source: U.S. Census Bureau.

POLITICS

Governors since statehood

D = Democrat; R = Republican; O = other;
(r) resigned; (d) died in office; (i) removed from office

Edward Tiffin (O)	(r) 1803-1807
Thomas Kirker (O)	1807-1808
Samuel Huntington (O)	1808-1810
Return J. Meigs, Jr. (O)	(r) 1810-1814
Othniel Looker (O)	1814
Thomas Worthington (O)	1814-1818
Ethen A. Brown (O)	(r) 1818-1822
Allen Trimble (O)	1822
Jeremiah Morrow (O)	1822-1826
Allen Trimble (O)	1826-1830
Duncan McArthur (O)	1830-1832
Robert Lucas (D)	1832-1836
Joseph Vance (O)	1836-1838
Wilson Shannon (D)	1838-1840
Thomas Corwin (O)	1840-1842
Wilson Shannon (D)	(r) 1842-1844
Thomas W. Bartley (D)	1844
William Bebb (O)	1844-1846
Seabury Ford (O)	1846-1849
Reuben Wood (O)	(r) 1849-1850
William Medill (D)	1850-1856
Salmon P. Chase (R)	1856-1860
William Dennison (R)	1860-1862
David Tod (O)	1862-1864
John Brough (O)	(d) 1864-1865
Charles Anderson (O)	1865-1866
Jacob D. Cox (O)	1866-1868
Rutherford B. Hayes (R)	1868-1872
Edward F. Noyes (R)	1872-1874
William Allen (D)	1874-1876
Rutherford B. Hayes (R)	(r) 1876-1877
Thomas L. Young (R)	1877-1878
Richard M. Bishop (D)	1878-1880
Charles Foster (R)	1880-1884
George Hoadly (D)	1884-1886
Joseph B. Foraker (R)	1886-1890
James E. Campbell (D)	1890-1892
William McKinley (R)	1892-1896
Asa S. Bushnell (R)	1896-1900
George E. Nash (R)	1900-1904
Myron T. Merrick (R)	1904-1906
John M. Pattison (D)	(d) 1906
Andrew L. Harris (R)	1906-1909
Judson Harmon (D)	1909-1913
James M. Cox (D)	1913-1915
Frank B. Willis (R)	1915-1917
James M. Cox (D)	1917-1921
Harry L. Davis (R)	1921-1923
Alvin Victor Donahey (D)	1923-1929
Myers T. Cooper (R)	1929-1931
George White (D)	1931-1935
Martin L. Davey (D)	1935-1939
John W. Bricker (R)	1939-1945
Frank J. Lausche (D)	1945-1947
Thomas J. Herbert (R)	1947-1949
Frank J. Lausche (D)	(r) 1949-1957
John W. Brown (R)	1957
Crone William O'Neill (R)	1957-1959
Michael V. Disalle (D)	1959-1963
James A. Rhodes (R)	1963-1971
John J. Gilligan (D)	1971-1975
James A. Rhodes (R)	1975-1983
Richard F. Celeste (D)	1983-1991
George Voinovich (R)	1991-1999
Bob Taft (R)	1999-2007
Ted Strickland (D)	2007-

Composition of congressional delegations, 1989-2007

	Dem	Rep	Total
House of Representatives			
101st Congress, 1989			
State delegates	11	10	21
Total U.S.	259	174	433
102d Congress, 1991			
State delegates	11	10	21
Total U.S.	267	167	434
103d Congress, 1993			
State delegates	10	9	20
Total U.S.	258	176	434
104th Congress, 1995			
State delegates	8	11	19
Total U.S.	197	236	433
105th Congress, 1997			
State delegates	8	11	19
Total U.S.	206	228	434
106th Congress, 1999			
State delegates	8	11	19
Total U.S.	211	222	433
107th Congress, 2001			
State delegates	8	11	19
Total U.S.	211	221	432
108th Congress, 2003			
State delegates	6	12	18
Total U.S.	205	229	434
109th Congress, 2005			
State delegates	6	11	17
Total U.S.	202	231	433
110th Congress, 2007			
State delegates	7	11	18
Total U.S.	233	202	435
Senate			
101st Congress, 1989			
State delegates	2	0	2
Total U.S.	55	45	100
102d Congress, 1991			
State delegates	2	0	2
Total U.S.	56	44	100
103d Congress, 1993			
State delegates	2	0	2
Total U.S.	57	43	100
104th Congress, 1995			
State delegates	1	1	2
Total U.S.	46	53	99
105th Congress, 1997			
State delegates	1	1	2
Total U.S.	45	55	100

	Dem	Rep	Total
106th Congress, 1999			
State delegates	0	2	2
Total U.S.	45	54	99
107th Congress, 2001			
State delegates	0	2	2
Total U.S.	50	50	100
108th Congress, 2003			
State delegates	0	2	2
Total U.S.	48	51	99
109th Congress, 2005			
State delegates	0	2	2
Total U.S.	44	55	99
110th Congress, 2007			
State delegates	1	1	2
Total U.S.	49	49	98

Figures are for starts of first sessions. Totals are for Democrat (Dem.) and Republican (Rep.) members only. House membership totals under 435 and Senate totals under 100 reflect vacancies and seats held by independent party members. When the 110th Congress opened, the Senate's two independent members caucused with the Democrats, giving the Democrats control of the Senate.

Source: U.S. Congress, *Congressional Directory.*

Composition of state legislature, 1990-2006

	Democrats	Republicans
State House (99 seats)		
1990	61	38
1992	53	46
1994	43	56
1996	39	60
1998	39	58
2000	40	59
2002	37	62
2004	40	59
2006	46	53
State Senate (33 seats)		
1990	12	21
1992	13	20
1994	13	20
1996	12	21
1998	12	21
2000	12	21
2002	11	22
2004	11	22
2006	12	21

Figures for total seats may include independents and minor party members. Numbers reflect results of elections in listed years; elected members usually take their seats in the years that follow.

Source: Council of State Governments; *State Elective Officials and the Legislatures.*

Voter participation in presidential elections, 2000 and 2004

	2000	2004
Voting age population		
State	8,480,000	8,680,000
Total United States	209,831,000	220,377,000
State share of U.S. total	4.04	3.94
Rank among states	7	7
Portion of voting age population casting votes		
State	55.4%	64.8%
United States	50.3%	55.5%
Rank among states	18	9

Population figures are rounded to nearest thousand and include all residents, regardless of eligibility to vote.
Source: U.S. Census Bureau.

HEALTH AND MEDICAL CARE

Medical professionals
Physicians in 2003 and nurses in 2001

	U.S.	State
Physicians in 2003		
Total	774,849	29,153
Share of U.S. total		3.75%
Rate	266	255
Rank		20
Nurses in 2001		
Total	2,262,020	103,870
Share of U.S. total		4.59%
Rate	793	912
Rank		16

Rates are numbers of physicians and nurses per 100,000 resident population; ranks are based on rates.
Source: American Medical Association, *Physician Characteristics and Distribution in the U.S.*; U.S. Department of Health and Human Services, Health Resources and Services Administration.

Health insurance coverage, 2003

	State	U.S.
Total persons covered	9,885,000	243,320,000
Total persons not covered	1,362,000	44,961,000
Portion not covered	12.1%	15.6%
Rank among states	33	—
Children not covered	236,000	8,373,000
Portion not covered	8.3%	11.4%
Rank among states	35	—

Totals are rounded to nearest thousand. Ranks are from the highest to the lowest percentages of persons *not* insured.
Source: U.S. Census Bureau, Current Population Reports.

AIDS, syphilis, and tuberculosis cases, 2003

Disease	U.S. cases	State cases	Rank
AIDS	44,232	775	15
Syphilis	34,270	481	19
Tuberculosis	14,874	229	20

Source: U.S. Centers for Disease Control and Prevention.

Cigarette smoking, 2003
Residents over age 18 who smoke

	U.S.	State	Rank
All smokers	22.1%	25.4%	12
Male smokers	24.8%	26.9%	18
Female smokers	20.3%	24.0%	6

Cigarette smokers are defined as persons who reported having smoked at least 100 cigarettes during their lifetimes and who currently smoked at least occasionally.
Source: U.S. Centers for Disease Control and Prevention, *Morbidity and Mortality Weekly Report*, 53, no. 44 (November 12, 2004).

HOUSING

Home ownership rates, 1985-2004

	1985	1990	1995	2000	2004
State	67.9%	68.7%	67.9%	71.3%	73.1%
Total U.S.	63.9%	63.9%	64.7%	67.4%	69.0%
Rank among states	26	17	23	19	18

Net change in state home ownership rate,
1985-2004 . . . . +5.2%
Net change in U.S. home ownership rate,
1985-2004 . . . . +5.1%

Percentages represent the proportion of owner households to total occupied households.
Source: U.S. Census Bureau, 2006.

Home sales, 2000-2004
In thousands of units

Existing home sales	2000	2002	2003	2004
State sales	216.4	237.0	253.1	275.7
Total U.S. sales	5,171	5,631	6,183	6,784
State share of U.S. total	4.18%	4.21%	4.09%	4.06%
Sales rank among states	6	6	6	6

Units include single-family homes, condos, and co-ops.
Source: National Association of Realtors, Washington, D.C., *Real Estate Outlook: Market Trends & Insights.*

Values of owner-occupied homes, 2003

	State	U.S.
Total units	2,727,000	58,809,000
Value of units		
Under $100,000	37.8%	29.6%
$100,000-199,999	45.4%	36.9%
$200,000 or more	16.8%	33.5%
Median value	$118,956	$142,275
Rank among all states		29

Units are owner-occupied one-family houses whose numbers are rounded to nearest thousand. Data are extrapolated from survey samples.

Source: U.S. Census Bureau, American Community Survey.

EDUCATION

Public school enrollment, 2002

Prekindergarten through grade 8
State enrollment 1,284,000
Total U.S. enrollment. 34,135,000
State share of U.S. total 3.76%

Grades 9 through 12
State enrollment 554,000
Total U.S. enrollment. 14,067,000
State share of U.S. total 3.94%

Enrollment rates
State public school enrollment rate. 87.8%
Overall U.S. rate 90.4%
Rank among states in 2002. 40
Rank among states in 1995. 42

Enrollment figures (which include unclassified students) are rounded to nearest thousand pupils during fall school term. Enrollment rates are based on enumerated resident population estimate for July 1, 2002.

Source: U.S. National Center for Education Statistics.

Public college finances, 2003-2004

FTE enrollment in public institutions of higher education
Students in state institutions 378,700
Students in all U.S. public institutions 9,916,600
State share of U.S. total 3.82
Rank among states. 5

State and local government appropriations for higher education
State appropriation per FTE $4,680
National average $5,716
Rank among states 40
State & local tax revenue going to higher
  education 6.0%

FTE = full-time equivalent in public postsecondary programs, including summer sessions; student numbers are rounded to nearest hundred. Funding figures for 2003-2004 academic year include financial aid to students in state public institutions and exclude money for research, agriculture experiment stations, teaching hospitals, and medical schools; figures are rounded to nearest thousand dollars.

Source: Higher Education Executive Officers, Denver, Colorado.

TRANSPORTATION AND TRAVEL

Highway mileage, 2003

Interstate highways	1,574
Other freeways and expressways	484
Arterial roads.	10,868
Collector roads.	22,518
Local roads.	88,078
Urban roads	43,262
Rural roads.	80,260
Total state mileage	123,522
U.S. total	3,974,107
State share	3.11%
Rank among states.	7

Note that combined urban and rural road mileage matches the total of the other categories.

Source: U.S. Federal Highway Administration.

Motor vehicle registrations and driver licenses, 2003

Vehicle registrations	State	U.S.	Share	Rank
Autos, trucks, buses	10,536,000	231,390,000	4.55%	5
Autos only	6,519,000	135,670	4.81%	5
Motorcycles	285,000	5,328,000	5.35%	3
Driver licenses	7,656,000	196,166,000	3.90%	7

Figures, which do not include vehicles owned by military services, are rounded to the nearest thousand. Figures for automobiles include taxis.

Source: U.S. Federal Highway Administration.

Domestic travel expenditures, 2003

Spending by U.S. residents on overnight trips and day trips of at least 50 miles from home

Total expenditures within state	$12.43 bill.
Total expenditures within U.S.	$490.87 bill.
State share of U.S. total	2.5%
Rank among states	12

Source: Travel Industry Association of America.

Retail gasoline prices, 2003-2007

Average price per gallon at the pump

Year	U.S.	State
2003	$1.267	$1.241
2004	$1.316	$1.294
2005	$1.644	$1.642
2007	$2.298	$2.355

Excise tax per gallon in 2004	26.0¢
Rank among all states in 2007 prices	12

Prices are averages of all grades of gasoline sold at the pump during March months in 2003-2005 and during February, 2007. Averages for 2006, during which prices rose higher, are not available.
Source: U.S. Energy Information Agency, *Petroleum Marketing Monthly* (2003-2005 data); American Automobile Association (2007 data).

CRIME AND LAW ENFORCEMENT

State and local police officers, 2000-2004

	2000	2002	2004
Total officers			
U.S.	654,601	665,555	675,734
State	22,893	23,664	19,589*
*Net change, 2000-2004			−4.43%
Officers per 1,000 residents			
U.S.	2.33	2.31	2.30
State	2.02	2.07	1.71
State rank	29	28	44

Totals include state and local police and sheriffs.
Source: Carsey Institute, University of New Hampshire.

Crime rates, 2003

Incidents per 100,000 residents

Crimes	State	U.S.
Violent crimes		
Total incidents	333	475
Murder	5	6
Forcible rape	40	32
Robbery	148	142
Aggravated assault	141	295
Property crimes		
Total incidents	3,641	3,588
Burglary	830	741
Larceny/theft	2,452	2,415
Motor vehicle theft	359	433
All crimes	3,974	4,063

Source: U.S. Federal Bureau of Investigation, *Crime in the United States,* annual.

State prison populations, 1980-2003

	State	U.S.	State share
1980	13,489	305,458	4.42%
1990	31,822	708,393	4.49%
1996	46,174	1,025,624	4.50%
2000	45,833	1,391,261	3.29%
2003	44,778	1,470,045	3.05%

State figures exclude prisoners in federal penitentiaries.
Source: U.S. Bureau of Justice Statistics, *Prisoners in 2003.*

Oklahoma

Location: Midwest

Area and rank: 68,679 square miles (177,877 square kilometers); 69,903 square miles (181,049 square kilometers) including water; nineteenth largest state in area

Coastline: none

Population and rank: 3,524,000 (2004); twenty-eighth largest state in population

Capital and largest city: Oklahoma City (506,132 people in 2000 census)

Became territory: May 2, 1890

Entered Union and rank: November 16, 1907; forty-sixth state

Present constitution adopted: 1907

Counties: 77

State name: "Oklahoma" derives from two Choctaw Indian words meaning "red people"

State nickname: Sooner State

Motto: *Labor omnia vincit* (Labor conquers all things)

State flag: Blue field with American Indian shield bearing six red crosses, seven eagle feathers, a peace pipe, and an olive branch, with the name "Oklahoma" below

Highest point: Black Mesa—4,973 feet (1,516 meters)

Lowest point: Little River—289 feet (88 meters)

Highest recorded temperature: 120 degrees Fahrenheit (49 degrees Celsius)—Tishomingo, 1943

Lowest recorded temperature: −27 degrees Fahrenheit (−33 degrees Celsius)—Watts, 1930

State song: "Oklahoma!"

State tree: Redbud

State flower: Mistletoe

State bird: Scissor-tailed flycatcher

State fish: White or sand bass

State animal: Bison

State capitol building in Oklahoma City.

Oklahoma History

Oklahoma is almost square except for its north-western extreme, called the Panhandle, a strip about 40 miles wide and 120 miles long that reaches to Colorado, which, with Kansas, forms the state's northern border. To the west lie New Mexico and Texas, which also forms its southern boundary. On the east are Missouri and Arkansas. Although some geographers consider Oklahoma a southwestern state, along with New Mexico, Arizona, and Nevada, others call it a south-central state.

Early History. The first humans probably settled in the Oklahoma region more than twenty thousand years ago, living in caves, where their drawings have been discovered on cave walls near Kenton. These early dwellers lived on roots and berries as well as the meat they obtained from the animals they hunted.

When Spanish explorer Francisco Vásquez de Coronado first came to the area in 1541, he found a place in which few people lived, although a few Native American tribes, notably the Plains Indians, eked out an existence there. Chief among these were the Apache, Comanche, and Kiowa, although the area also had some

village-dwelling Indians, notably the Caddo, Pawnee, and Wichita, who had inhabited the area prior to 1500. These Native American groups were joined between 1815 and 1840 by the Cherokee, Chickasaw, Choctaw, Creek, and Seminole Indians, known as the Five Civilized Tribes. The federal government had driven them from their homes and forcibly relocated them in large enclaves in Oklahoma and other nearby areas, called Indian Territory.

The Earliest Explorers. It has been speculated that Vikings from Greenland reached Oklahoma as early as 1012. The evidence for this, however—a huge stone found at Heavener in eastern Oklahoma with the date carved into it in the kind of runic letters used by the Vikings—has not been authenticated. It is known that Spanish explorers crossed the Oklahoma Panhandle in 1541, coming from Mexico in search of gold. In the same year, Hernando de Soto, also seeking gold, came into the area from the east, traveling along the Arkansas River. All explorers claimed the area for Spain.

In 1682, René-Robert Cavelier, sieur de La Salle, explored the Mississippi River, claiming for France all the

Titled Trail of Tears, *this 1942 painting by Robert Lindneux is a romanticized depiction of the forced removal of the Cherokee from Georgia to what later became Oklahoma during the 1830's. Most Cherokee actually made the arduous journey on foot.* (Woolaroc Museum, Bartlesville, Oklahoma)

lands drained by the Mississippi and naming it Louisiana in honor of his king, Louis XIV. The vast area he claimed included most of present-day Oklahoma. The early explorers traded trinkets with the native dwellers for furs.

The Louisiana Territory changed hands several times. In 1762, Spain took it from France. In 1800, Spain returned it to France, and in 1803, the United States, in the Louisiana Purchase, bought it from France for fifteen million dollars. It must be remembered that at the time of the Louisiana Purchase, fewer than five hundred Europeans lived in the entire area called Louisiana, which included parts of Texas, Oklahoma, Arkansas, Kansas, and Missouri.

The first non-Indian settlement in Oklahoma, near present-day Salina, was established in 1823 by Auguste Pierre Chouteau, whose trading post served the area's fur traders. In 1830, the U.S. Congress passed the Indian Removal Act, under which the government was permitted to relocate Native Americans from the East Coast of the United States. Between 1830 and 1842, around 75,000 Native Americans were deployed to the area, many dying en route. Those who survived lived much as white people in the east did, creating villages, building schools and churches, farming, and raising cattle and poultry. Some became so affluent that they owned slaves.

The government promised the relocated tribes that the land they were given in the eastern and southern parts of the area, known as the Indian Territory, would always be theirs. The various tribes set up their own governments and functioned as separate nations.

The Civil War. Because the Indian Territory had not achieved statehood, it could not secede from the Union during the Civil War. Many of the Native Americans who dwelled there owned slaves, and about six thousand of the Indians fought for the Confederacy during the war, although some joined the Union forces. Most of these people held a grudge against the federal government for having taken them from their native lands and relocated them. This caused many who were not slave owners to side with the South.

After the war, in 1866, representatives of the Indian Territory were forced to sign the Reconstruction Treaty. The government retaliated against the Native Americans for their support of the Confederacy by taking back much of their land and by forcing them to permit railroads to cross their property.

Land Disputes. During the 1870's, Texan cattlemen drove their herds to Kansas railroad towns from which livestock could be shipped to market, crossing Oklahoma. Irritated, Kansans tried to pressure the government into opening more land in the area to white settlement. The Missouri-Kansas-Texas Railroad crossed eastern Oklahoma by 1872 and brought many people into the region.

Many white farmers rented the land they tilled from the Native Americans. In time the federal government bought five thousand square miles of the Indian Territory and, in 1889, opened it to settlers on a first come, first served basis. Each family could claim 160 acres merely by placing themselves upon it. About fifty thousand land-hungry people arrived. At noon, the great Land Run of 1889 began, marking an important phase in Oklahoma's development. A tent city in Guthrie housed fifteen thousand people temporarily. On that single day, the settlements of Kingfisher, Norman, Oklahoma City, and Stillwater were started.

After development started there, the U.S. Congress established the Oklahoma Territory, which lay west of the Indian Territory. The two areas were called the Twin Territories. The federal purchase of more Indian land was followed by more land runs, so that by the early twentieth century, the area had a substantial white population. The Native Americans wanted to establish their own state, but their desires were overlooked. In 1907, the Twin Territories were admitted to the Union as the state of Oklahoma, the forty-sixth of the United States, with Guthrie as its capital. Three years later, the capital was moved to Oklahoma City.

The Discovery of Oil. In 1901, Oklahoma began its journey toward affluence. Oil was discovered near Tulsa. An oil rush began, with many petroleum companies establishing offices in Tulsa. As oil was discovered in other parts of the state, many boomtowns grew, and the entire state experienced an economic upsurge.

The decade following World War I was a time of considerable prosperity for the state. Oil fueled the economy, but agriculture was also important. The state's prosperity, based on these two enterprises, was not to last, however.

Dust Bowls and the Great Depression. The economic chaos following the collapse of the stock market in 1929 affected the entire United States. Oklahoma, however, suffered more than most other states because, combined with a national economic downturn that devastated the oil industry, a continued drought resulted in huge dust storms and reduced agriculture production to below the subsistence level.

The Great Depression was so devastating to Oklahoma that more than sixty thousand of its citizens, labeled "Okies," left the state, many of them heading for the West Coast, particularly to California.

World War II and After. World War II brought renewed prosperity to Oklahoma. The weather improved to the point that agriculture again contributed significantly to the economy. War industries came into the state, notably aeronautical and munitions factories. The state's oil wells produced much-needed petroleum products for the war effort. Some two hundred thousand Oklahomans served in the nation's armed forces.

Shortly after the war, in 1947, the McClellan-Kerr Arkansas River Navigation Project was begun. When it was completed in 1970, the Arkansas River had been made navigable by widening and deepening. The system of dams and locks on the river made it possible for large ships to navigate it. Muskogee and Tulsa became important port cities once the waterway was opened.

Other dams were built on rivers throughout Oklahoma as a means of flood control and irrigation. The lakes these dams formed offer visitors extensive recreational facilities and attracted many tourists. The hydroelectric power the dams generate stimulated industrial growth.

This industrial growth, mainly in companies that make airplanes, rockets, automobile parts, and computers, brought an influx of new people into the state, which, from 1970 to 1980, attracted 466,000 new residents. During the 1970's, three groups of Oklahoma Indians, the Cherokee, the Choctaw, and the Chickasaw, regained ninety-six miles of the Arkansas River, increasing their prosperity.

In 1971, the voters of Oklahoma City elected Patience Latting mayor, making

Oklahoma City, the state's capital and largest city. (Oklahoma Tourism/ Fred W. Marvel)

Dedicated in 2000 to honor the victims, survivors, and rescuers of the 1995 bombing of the Murrah Federal Office Building, on whose former site it is built, the Oklahoma City National Memorial is the largest memorial of its kind in the United States. The center of the memorial contains 168 empty chairs, each of which has a glass base on which a bombing victim's name is etched. (Dustin M. Ramsey)

her the first female mayor of a major metropolis. Three years later, the state selected thirty-three-year-old David Boren as governor, making him the youngest governor in the United States.

The Federal Building Bombing. The 1990's were marked by tragedy in Oklahoma. In a horrible act of domestic terrorism, on April 19, 1995, Timothy McVeigh loaded a rental truck with explosives, parked it outside the Alfred P. Murrah Federal Building in Oklahoma City, retreated a safe distance, and detonated the explosives.

The Murrah Building collapsed, killing 168 people and seriously injuring scores of others, among them many young children in a day-care center housed in the building. The city and state were devastated by this crime and erected a memorial on the site of the demolished building. Timothy McVeigh, granted a change of venue for his court case, was tried in Denver, Colorado. He was convicted of first-degree murder, for which he received the death sentence.

Shadows of the Federal Building Bombing. Near the beginning of the twenty-first century, the ghost of the Oklahoma Federal Building, blown up five years prior,

still hung over the state. In 2000, however, a significant measure of closure came in sight, as the principal bomber, Timothy McVeigh, ended his appeals, which had begun after his 1997 conviction, and sought execution. On June 11, 2001, McVeigh was executed by lethal injection at 7:00 A.M. at the U.S. federal penitentiary in Terre Haute, Indiana. The Oklahoma City National Memorial, largest of its kind in the nation, had already been constructed and opened by the time McVeigh was put to death. The memorial, operated by the U.S. National Park Service and set on more than six acres, was established in 1997. On February 19, 2001, it opened and was dedicated by President George W. Bush and First Lady Laura Bush. Four years later, in 2005, the tenth anniversary of the bombing was marked by a National Week of Hope from April 17 to April 24, with a series of events at the memorial. On April 19, Vice President Dick Cheney, former president Bill Clinton, and other dignitaries attended a memorial service for the victims.

In a related matter, Terry Nichols, on December 23, 1997, had been convicted in federal court of conspiring with McVeigh in the Oklahoma City bombing. On

June 4, 1998, he was sentenced in federal court to life imprisonment without parole, the jury having spared his life. This was not the end of the matter, however, since Nichols was returned to Oklahoma in January, 2000, for trial on capital charges by the state. His trial began more than four years later, in June, 2004. On August 9, 2004, he was convicted of 161 counts of first-degree murder; again, his life was spared by the jury. While no others have been arrested for the bombing, many believe that co-conspirators remain at large.

Elections. In the presidential election of 2000, Oklahoma gave its eight electoral votes to George W. Bush and Dick Cheney. In the midterm election two years later, the state's voters elected James Inhofe to the U.S. Senate for a second term. They also elected a new Republican to the House of Representatives and a new governor, Brad Henry, a Democrat, who campaigned as an "education governor." In a three-way race, Henry won with about 43 percent of the vote, just ahead of his Republican opponent. Missing from the ballot, however, was J. C. Watts, Oklahoma's prominent black Republican congress member, a handsome and articulate star of the party. Despite entreaties by President Bush, Watts, a four-term member and the only black Republican in Congress, opted to return to private life.

In 2004, Oklahoma again voted for George W. Bush. This election, however, saw the exit of a longtime member of the U.S. Senate, Don Nickles, who retired. In his place, Tom Coburn, a conservative medical doctor who had already spent some years in politics, was elected. Coburn, elected to the U.S. House of Representatives in 1994, had promised to leave after three terms. In 2001, he kept his word.

R. Baird Shuman
Updated by the Editor

Oklahoma Time Line

1541	Spanish explorer Francisco Vásquez de Coronado crosses the Oklahoma Panhandle.
1541	Spanish explorer Hernando de Soto travels to eastern Oklahoma.
1682	René-Robert Cavelier, sieur de La Salle, claims the Louisiana Territory, which includes much of Oklahoma, for France.
1762	France cedes Louisiana, including Oklahoma, to Spain.
1800	Spain returns Louisiana to France.
1803	United States buys the area from France in the Louisiana Purchase.
1823	Auguste Pierre Chouteau establishes a trading post and the first permanent non-Indian settlement near present-day Salina.
1830	U.S. Congress passes the Indian Removal Act, through which Native American tribes are brought to Oklahoma between 1830 and 1842.
1834	U.S. government creates the Indian Territory in eastern Oklahoma.
1844	Relocated Cherokees publish Oklahoma's first newspaper, the *Cherokee Advocate.*
1861	Six thousand Oklahomans support the Confederacy during the Civil War.
1865	Oklahoma's black slaves are freed at the conclusion of the Civil War.
1866	Government retaliates against Indians by taking back some of their land.
1880	Pressure exerted for the government to open more land for white settlement.
Apr. 22, 1889	Great Land Run brings more than fifty thousand people to the area to compete for the newly available land.
1890	Congress creates the Oklahoma Territory, calling it and the Indian Territory the Twin Territories.
May 2, 1890	U.S. government buys more Indian land for redistribution to white settlers.
1892	University of Oklahoma opens at Norman.
Sept. 16, 1893	Great Land Run draws 100,000 participants.
1901	Oil is discovered near Tulsa.
1905	Indians try to create their own separate state, Sequoyah.
Nov. 16, 1907	Twin Territories admitted to the Union as Oklahoma, the forty-sixth state, with Guthrie as its capital.
1910	Oklahoma City named state capital.
1917	Ninety thousand Oklahomans join armed forces in World War I.
1930's	Oklahoma's agriculture devastated by extended drought; thousands leave the state.
1941	United States enters World War II; defense industries bring renewed prosperity to Oklahoma.

Port of Muskogee on the Arkansas River, which links Oklahoma to the Mississippi River and the world's oceans. (Oklahoma Tourism/Fred W. Marvel)

1953	Toll road, the Turner Turnpike, is completed between Tulsa and Oklahoma City.
1970	McClellan-Kerr Arkansas River Navigation System is completed.
1971	Patience Latting is elected mayor of Oklahoma City, the first woman mayor of a city of more than 200,000.
1974	David Boren, age thirty-three, is elected governor, becoming the youngest governor in the United States.
1980	Oklahoma suffers devastating drought.
Sept.-Oct., 1986	Severe floods lead to great property damage.
1991	University of Oklahoma law professor Anita F. Hill accuses U.S. Supreme Court nominee Clarence Thomas of sexual harassment.
Apr. 19, 1995	Timothy McVeigh bombs the Alfred P. Murrah Federal Building in Oklahoma City, killing 168.
June 3, 1997	Timothy McVeigh convicted on eleven counts of murder and on June 13 is sentenced to death.
2001	President George W. Bush dedicates the museum in Oklahoma City that memorializes the victims of the Alfred P. Murrah Federal Building bombing.
June 11, 2001	Timothy McVeigh is put to death by lethal injection at 7:00 A.M. at the federal penitentiary in Terre Haute, Indiana.
Nov. 2, 2004	Senator Don Nickles retires, and prominent Republican congressman J. C. Watts declines to run for a fifth term. Nickles is replaced by former congress member Tom Coburn.
Apr. 17-24, 2005	Oklahoma National Memorial holds series of events to commemorate the tenth anniversary of the 1995 bombing.

Notes for Further Study

Published Sources. Two older but worthwhile titles cover the state's history quite well: Arrel M. Gibson's *Oklahoma: A History of Five Centuries* (2d ed., 1989) provides an encompassing history of the state through its various stages of development; *Oklahoma: The Story of Its Past and Present* (Rev. ed., 1985) by Edwin C. McReynolds et al. covers the essentials of the state's development accurately and thoroughly. Claudette Marie Gilbert and Robert L. Brooks's *From Mounds to Mammoths: A Field Guide to Oklahoma Prehistory* (2d ed., 2000) provides a thorough discussion of the state's antiquities and archaeology. In *American Outback: The Oklahoma Panhandle in the Twentieth Century* (2006), Richard Lowitt provides an in-depth history of the Oklahoma Panhandle region. Although a fictional account of the land rush, *Dreams to Dust: A Tale of the Oklahoma Land Rush* (2006) by Sheldon Russell nonetheless uses a great deal of factual information in its telling and gives the reader an accurate description of this period in the state's history.

Rennard Strickland's *The Indians in Oklahoma* (1980) reviews the convoluted history of the various Native American tribes in Oklahoma with special and valuable emphasis on the Five Civilized Tribes that were relocated in the state. W. Dale Mason focuses on some of the problems of Native Americans in Oklahoma and their solutions in *Interest Group Federalism: Indian Gaming and the Status of Indian Tribes in the American Political System* (1992). In *Professors, Presidents, and Politicians: Civil Rights and the University of Oklahoma, 1890-1968* (1981), George Lynn Cross considers the broad question of human rights in Oklahoma. *Acres of Aspiration: The All-Black Towns in Oklahoma* (2002) by Hannibal B. Johnson and Michael Eric Dyson details the more than sixty all-African American towns that developed within the state during the frontier era. Murray Wickett, in *Contested Territory: Whites, Native Americans and African Americans in Oklahoma* (2000), uses sources including government records, newspapers, diaries, oral history interviews, poems, and anecdotes to tell of the interactions between three ethnic groups in the Indian and Oklahoma Territories from the end of the Civil War until statehood in 1907.

Written specifically for juvenile readers are Doug Sanders's *Oklahoma* (2006) from the It's My State series and Ann Heinrichs and Ann Hamilton's *Oklahoma* (2005). Kendra Fox and Deborah Bouziden's *Oklahoma off the Beaten Path* (5th ed., 2005) serves as an accessible guide to the unique locales of the state. Although quite specialized, Bradford Koplowitz's *Guide to the Historical Records of Oklahoma* (1998) is an indispensable guide to those wishing to undertake research on the state.

Web Resources. The state of Oklahoma's Web site (www.state.ok.us) and the Oklahoma Department of Tourism's Web site (www.oklatourism.gov/) both provide extensive information about the state and its attractions. Information about the state's American Indian population is available at Access Genealogy (www.accessgenealogy.com/native/oklahoma/), the Chickasaw Nation Web site (www.chickasaw.com), and the Oklahoma City site (www.okccvb.org/special/native_am_history.htm). Economic information is available on the Oklahoma Small Business Web site (www.osbdc.org) and the state's Department of Commerce Web site (www.okcommerce.gov/). The U.S. Census Bureau provides a range of demographic statistics for the state with its QuickFacts section (quickfacts.census.gov/qfd/states/40000.html).

Among the individual municipal Web sites, the most useful are those for Oklahoma City (www.okccvb.org and www.okconline.com), Norman (www.ci.norman.ok.us), and Stillwater (www.stillwater.org/). Tulsa's Chamber of Commerce also maintains a Web site (www.tulsachamber.com), which provides varied information about that city. For a good overview of the state's history, visit the state's history page (www.state.ok.us/osfdocs/stinfo2.html) or the Oklahoma Historical Society (www.ok-history.mus.ok.us/).

Counties

County	2000 pop.	Rank in pop.	Sq. miles	Rank in area	County	2000 pop.	Rank in pop.	Sq. miles	Rank in area
Adair	21,038	38	575.7	64	Cimarron	3,148	77	1,835.1	4
Alfalfa	6,105	67	866.7	35	Cleveland	208,016	3	536.2	71
Atoka	13,879	48	978.4	23	Coal	6,031	69	518.2	72
Beaver	5,857	70	1,814.5	5	Comanche	114,996	4	1,069.4	15
Beckham	19,799	40	901.9	31	Cotton	6,614	66	636.7	59
Blaine	11,976	51	928.6	27	Craig	14,950	45	761.1	43
Bryan	36,534	26	908.9	29	Creek	67,367	9	955.6	26
Caddo	30,150	32	1,278.4	10	Custer	26,142	36	986.6	22
Canadian	87,697	5	899.9	32	Delaware	37,077	25	740.7	47
Carter	45,621	16	823.9	36	Dewey	4,743	72	1,000.2	21
Cherokee	42,521	21	751.1	45	Ellis	4,075	73	1,229.2	12
Choctaw	15,342	44	774.0	42	Garfield	57,813	11	1,058.5	16

County	2000 pop.	Rank in pop.	Sq. miles	Rank in area
Garvin	27,210	35	809.2	38
Grady	45,516	17	1,101.0	14
Grant	5,144	71	1,000.6	20
Greer	6,061	68	639.4	58
Harmon	3,283	76	537.9	70
Harper	3,562	74	1,039.1	17
Haskell	11,792	53	577.1	63
Hughes	14,154	46	806.8	39
Jackson	28,439	33	802.8	40
Jefferson	6,818	65	758.9	44
Johnston	10,513	59	644.6	57
Kay	48,080	15	918.8	28
Kingfisher	13,926	47	903.1	30
Kiowa	10,227	60	1,014.7	18
Latimer	10,692	57	722.2	49
Le Flore	48,109	14	1,586.0	6
Lincoln	32,080	31	958.6	24
Logan	33,924	29	744.6	46
Love	8,831	63	515.4	73
McClain	27,740	34	569.7	66
McCurtain	34,402	28	1,852.4	3
McIntosh	19,456	41	620.0	62
Major	7,545	64	956.8	25
Marshall	13,184	49	371.1	77
Mayes	38,369	24	656.2	56
Murray	12,623	50	418.3	75
Muskogee	69,451	7	813.9	37
Noble	11,411	56	732.0	48

County	2000 pop.	Rank in pop.	Sq. miles	Rank in area
Nowata	10,569	58	565.0	68
Okfuskee	11,814	52	624.8	61
Oklahoma	660,448	1	709.2	51
Okmulgee	39,685	22	697.0	52
Osage	44,437	18	2,251.0	1
Ottawa	33,194	30	471.4	74
Pawnee	16,612	43	569.5	67
Payne	68,190	8	686.4	53
Pittsburg	43,953	19	1,306.0	8
Pontotoc	35,143	27	719.7	50
Pottawatomie	65,521	10	787.9	41
Pushmataha	11,667	54	1,397.4	7
Roger Mills	3,436	75	1,141.9	13
Rogers	70,641	6	675.0	54
Seminole	24,894	37	632.5	60
Sequoyah	38,972	23	673.9	55
Stephens	43,182	20	877.2	33
Texas	20,107	39	2,037.3	2
Tillman	9,287	61	872.4	34
Tulsa	563,299	2	570.3	65
Wagoner	57,491	12	563.1	69
Washington	48,996	13	416.9	76
Washita	11,508	55	1,003.5	19
Woods	9,089	62	1,286.6	9
Woodward	18,486	42	1,242.4	11

Source: U.S. Census Bureau; National Association of Counties.

Cities
With 10,000 or more residents

Rank	City	Population
1	Oklahoma City (capital)	506,132
2	Tulsa	393,049
3	Norman	95,694
4	Lawton	92,757
5	Broken Arrow	74,859
6	Edmond	68,315
7	Midwest City	54,088
8	Enid	47,045
9	Moore	41,138
10	Stillwater	39,065
11	Muskogee	38,310
12	Bartlesville	34,748
13	Shawnee	28,692
14	Ponca City	25,919
15	Ardmore	23,711
16	Duncan	22,505
17	Del City	22,128
18	Altus	21,447
19	Yukon	21,043
20	Bethany	20,307
21	Sapulpa	19,166

Rank	City	Population
22	Owasso	18,502
23	McAlester	17,783
24	Sand Springs	17,451
25	El Reno	16,212
26	Claremore	15,873
27	Chickasha	15,850
28	Ada	15,691
29	Tahlequah	14,458
30	Miami	13,704
31	Durant	13,549
32	Bixby	13,336
33	Mustang	13,156
34	Okmulgee	13,022
35	Woodward	11,853
36	Elk City	10,510
37	Guymon	10,472
38	The Village	10,157

Population figures are from 2000 census.
Source: U.S. Bureau of the Census.

Index to Tables

DEMOGRAPHICS

Resident state and national populations, 1970-2004
Population figures given in thousands

	State pop.	U.S. pop.	Share	Rank
1970	2,559	203,302	1.3%	27
1980	3,025	226,546	1.3%	26
1985	3,271	237,924	1.4%	25
1990	3,146	248,765	1.3%	28
1995	3,308	262,761	1.2%	27
2000	3,451	281,425	1.2%	27
2004	3,524	293,655	1.2%	28

Source: U.S. Census Bureau, Current Population Reports, 2006.

Resident population by age, 2004

Age Group	Total persons
Under 5 years	242,000
5 to 17 years	618,000
18 to 24 years	385,000
25 to 34 years	470,000
35 to 44 years	488,000
45 to 54 years	493,000
55 to 64 years	363,000
65 to 74 years	249,000
75 to 84 years	161,000
85 years and older	54,000
All age groups	3,524,000

Portion of residents 65 and older	13.2%
National rank in portion of oldest residents	17
National average	12.4%

Population figures are rounded to nearest thousand persons;
figures include armed forces personnel stationed in the state.
Source: U.S. Bureau of the Census, 2006.

Resident population by race, Hispanic origin, 2004

Category	State pop.	Share	U.S.
All residents	3,524	100.00%	100.00%
Non-Hispanic white	2,570	72.93%	67.37%
Hispanic white	200	5.68%	13.01%
Other Hispanic	23	0.65%	1.06%
African American	272	7.72%	12.77%
Native American	284	8.06%	0.96%
Asian, Pacific Islander	57	1.62%	4.37%
Two or more categories	140	3.97%	1.51%

Population figures are in thousands. Persons counted as "Hispanic" (Latino) may be of any race. Because of overlapping categories, categories may not add up to 100%. Shares in column 3 are percentages of each category within the state; these figures may be compared to the national percentages in column 4.
Source: U.S. Bureau of the Census, 2006.

Projected state population, 2000-2030

Year	Population
2000	3,451,000
2005	3,521,000
2010	3,592,000
2015	3,662,000
2020	3,736,000
2025	3,821,000
2030	3,913,000
Population increase, 2000-2030	462,000
Percentage increase, 2000-2030	13.4

Projections are based on data from the 2000 census.
Source: U.S. Census Bureau.

VITAL STATISTICS

Infant mortality rates, 1980-2002

	1980	1990	2000	2002
All state residents	12.7	9.2	8.5	8.1
All U.S. residents	12.6	9.2	9.4	9.1
All state white residents	12.1	9.1	7.9	7.1
All U.S. white residents	10.6	7.6	5.7	5.8
All state black residents	21.8	14.3	16.9	17.2
All U.S. black residents	22.2	18.0	14.1	14.4

Figures represent deaths per 1,000 live births of resident infants under 1 year old, exclusive of fetal deaths. Figures for all residents include members of other racial categories not listed separately.
Source: U.S. Census Bureau, *Statistical Abstract of the United States,* 2006.

Abortion rates, 1990 and 2000

	1990	2000
Total abortions	9,000	7,000
Rate per 1,000 women	12.5	10.1
U.S. rate	25.7	21.3
Rank	39	35

Numbers of abortions are rounded to nearest thousand; ranks are based on rates.
Source: U.S. Census Bureau.

Marriages and divorces

Total marriages in 2004	22,800
Rate per 1,000 population.	6.5
National rate per 1,000 population	7.4
Rank among all states	32
Total divorces in 2000	12,400
Rate per 1,000 population in 2000	3.7
National rate per 1,000 population in 2004	3.7
Rank among all states in 2004	n/a

Figures are for all marriages and divorces performed within the state, including those of nonresidents; totals are rounded to the nearest hundred. Ranks are for highest to lowest figures; note that 2004 divorce data are not available for Oklahoma and four other states.
Source: U.S. National Center for Health Statistics, *Vital Statistics of the United States,* 2006.

Death rates by leading causes, 2002
Deaths per 100,000 resident population

Cause	State	U.S.
Heart disease	321.4	241.7
Cancer	213.9	193.2
Cerebrovascular diseases	69.5	56.4
Accidents other than motor vehicle	45.2	37.0
Motor vehicle accidents	21.9	15.7
Chronic lower respiratory diseases	56.9	43.3
Diabetes mellitus	30.5	25.4
HIV	2.6	4.9
Suicide	14.3	11.0
Homicide	5.6	6.1
All causes	1,016.2	847.3
Rank in overall death rate among states		5

Figures exclude nonresidents who died in the state. Causes of death follow International Classification of Diseases. Rank is from highest to lowest death rate in the United States.
Source: U.S. National Center for Health Statistics, *National Vital Statistics Report,* 2006.

ECONOMY

Gross state product, 1990-2004
In current dollars

Year	State product	Nat'l product	State share
1990	$57.7 billion	$5.67 trillion	1.02%
2000	$89.9 billion	$9.75 trillion	0.92%
2002	$95.3 billion	$10.41 trillion	0.92%
2003	$101.2 billion	$10.92 trillion	0.93%
2004	$107.2 billion	$11.65 trillion	0.92%

Source: U.S. Bureau of Economic Analysis, *Survey of Current Business,* July, 2005.

Gross state product by industry, 2003
In billions of dollars

Construction	$3.6
Manufacturing	11.2
Wholesale trade	5.1
Retail trade	8.4
Finance & insurance	4.9
Information	4.2
Professional services	4.4
Health care & social assistance	6.3
Government	15.3
Total state product	$93.8
Total U.S. product	$10,289.2
State share of U.S. total	0.91%
Rank among all states	30

Total figures include industries not listed separately. Amounts are in chained 2000 dollars.
Source: U.S. Bureau of Economic Analysis, *Survey of Current Business,* July, 2005.

Personal income per capita, 1990-2004
In current dollars

	1990	2000	2004
Per capita income	$16,187	$24,407	$28,089
U.S. average	$19,477	$29,845	$32,937
Rank among states	37	41	39

Source: U.S. Bureau of Economic Analysis, *Survey of Current Business,* April, 2005.

Energy consumption, 2001
In trillions of British thermal units (BTU), except as noted

Total energy consumption

Total state energy consumption	1,540
Total U.S. energy consumption	96,275
State share of U.S. total	1.60%
Rank among states	24

Per capita consumption (In millions of BTU)

Total state per capita consumption	444
Total U.S. per capita consumption	338
Rank among states	8

End-use sectors

Residential	298
Commercial	233
Industrial	544
Transportation	466

Sources of energy

Petroleum	588
Natural gas	548
Coal	377
Hydroelectric power	23
Nuclear electric power	0

Figures for totals include categories not listed separately.
Source: U.S. Energy Information Administration, *State Energy Data Report,* 2001.

Nonfarm employment by sectors, 2004

Total persons	1,470,000
Construction	62,000
Manufacturing	142,000
Trade, transportation, utilities	276,000
Information	31,000
Finance, insurance, real estate	84,000
Professional & business services	161,000
Education & health services	179,000
Leisure, hospitality, arts, organizations	129,000
Other services, including repair & maintenance	74,000
Government	302,000

Figures are rounded to nearest thousand persons. "Total" includes mining and natural resources, not listed separately.
Source: U.S. Bureau of Labor Statistics, 2006.

Foreign exports, 1990-2004
In millions of dollars

Year	State	U.S.	State share
1990	1,646	394,045	0.42%
1996	2,365	624,767	0.38%
1997	2,728	688,896	0.40%
2000	3,072	712,055	0.39%
2003	2,660	724,006	0.39%
2004	3,178	769,332	0.41%

Rank among all states in 2004 36

U.S. total does not include U.S. dependencies.
Source: U.S. Census Bureau, *U.S. Merchandise Trade,* series FT 900, 2000; U.S. Census Bureau, *U.S. International Trade in Goods and Services,* Series FT 900, 2005.

LAND USE

Federally owned land, 2003
Areas in acres

	State	U.S.	State share
Total area	44,088,000	2,271,343,000	1.94%
Nonfederal land	42,756,000	1,599,584,000	2.67%
Federal land	1,332,000	671,759,000	0.20%
Federal share	3.0%	29.6%	—

Areas are rounded to nearest thousand acres. Figures for federally owned land do not include trust properties.
Source: U.S. General Services Administration, *Federal Real Property Profile,* 2006.

Land use, 1997
In acres, rounded to nearest thousand

Total surface area	44,738,000
Total nonfederal rural land.	40,610,000
Percentage rural land	90.8%
Cropland	9,737,000
Conservation Reserve Program (CRP*) land . . .	1,138,000
Pastureland	7,963,000
Rangeland	14,033,000
Forestland.	7,281,000
Other rural land	459,000

*CRP is a federal program begun in 1985 to assist private landowners to convert highly erodible cropland to vegetative cover for ten years. Note that some categories of land overlap.
Source: U.S. Department of Agriculture, Natural Resources and Conservation Service, and Iowa State University, Statistical Laboratory, *Summary Report, 1997 National Resources Inventory,* revised December, 2000.

Farms and crop acreage, 2004

	State	U.S.	Share	Rank
Farms	84,000	2,113,000	3.98%	6
Acres (millions)	34	937	3.63%	8
Acres per farm	404	443	—	17

Source: U.S. Department of Agriculture, National Agricultural Statistics Service. Numbers of farms are rounded to nearest thousand units; acreage figures are rounded to nearest million. Rankings, including ties, are based on rounded figures.

GOVERNMENT AND FINANCE

Units of local government, 2002

	State	Total U.S.	Rank
All local governments	1,798	87,525	18
Counties	77	3,034	17
Municipalities	590	19,429	10
Townships	0	16,504	—
School districts	571	13,506	8
Special districts	560	35,052	23

Only 48 states have county governments, 20 states have township governments ("towns" in New England, Minnesota, New York, and Wisconsin), and 46 states have school districts. Special districts encompass such functions as natural resources, fire protection, and housing and community development.
Source: U.S. Census Bureau, *Census of Governments.*

State government revenue, 2002

Total revenue	$13,134 mill.
General revenue	$12,761 mill.
Per capita revenue	$3,658
U.S. per capita average	$3,689
Rank among states	42

Intergovernment revenue

Total	$4,120 mill.
From federal government	$4,044 mill.

Charges and miscellaneous

Total	$2,588 mill.
Current charges	$1,583 mill.
Misc. general income	$1,005 mill.
Insurance trust revenue.	$55 mill.

Taxes

Total	$6,053 mill.
Per capita taxes	$1,734
Rank among states	29
Property taxes	(nil)
Sales taxes	$2,273 mill.
License taxes	$823 mill.
Individual income taxes	$2,286 mill.
Corporate income taxes	$174 mill.
Other taxes	$497 mill.

Total revenue figures include items not listed separately here.
Source: U.S. Bureau of the Census.

State government expenditures, 2002

General expenditures

Total state expenditures	$14,727 mill.
Intergovernmental	$3,377 mill.

Per capita expenditures

State	$3,697
Average of all states	$3,859
Rank among states	31

Selected direct expenditures

Education	$2,520 mill.
Public welfare	$3,156 mill.
Health, hospital	$527 mill.
Highways	$1,010 mill.
Police protection	$92 mill.
Corrections	$506 mill.
Natural resources	$174 mill.
Parks and recreation	$66 mill.
Government administration	$458 mill.
Interest on debt	$258 mill.
Total direct expenditures	$9,527 mill.

Totals include items not listed separately.
Source: U.S. Census Bureau.

POLITICS

Governors since statehood

D = Democrat; R = Republican; O = other;
(r) resigned; (d) died in office; (i) removed from office

Charles N. Haskell (D)	1907-1911
Lee Cruce (D)	1911-1915
Robert L. Williams (D)	1915-1919
James B. A. Robertson (D)	1919-1923
John C. Walton (D)	(i) 1923
Martin E. Trapp (D)	1923-1927
Henry S. Johnston (D)	(i) 1927-1929
William J. Holloway (D)	1929-1931
William H. Murray (D)	1931-1935
Ernest W. Marland (D)	1935-1939
Leon C. Phillips (D)	1939-1943
Robert S. Kerr (D)	1943-1947
Roy J. Turner (D)	1947-1951
Johnston Murray (D)	1951-1955
Raymond D. Gary (D)	1955-1959
James Howard Edmondson (D)	(r) 1959-1963
George P. Nigh (D)	1963
Henry L. Bellmon (R)	1963-1967
Dewey F. Bartlett (R)	1967-1971
David Hall (D)	1971-1975
David L. Boren (D)	1975-1979
George P. Nigh (D)	1979-1987
Henry Bellmon (R)	1987-1991
David Walters (D)	1991-1995
Frank Keating (R)	1995-2003
Brad Henry (D)	2003-

Composition of congressional delegations, 1989-2007

	Dem	Rep	Total
House of Representatives			
101st Congress, 1989			
State delegates	4	2	6
Total U.S.	259	174	433
102d Congress, 1991			
State delegates	4	2	6
Total U.S.	267	167	434
103d Congress, 1993			
State delegates	4	2	6
Total U.S.	258	176	434
104th Congress, 1995			
State delegates	0	6	6
Total U.S.	197	236	433
105th Congress, 1997			
State delegates	0	5	5
Total U.S.	206	228	434
106th Congress, 1999			
State delegates	0	6	6
Total U.S.	211	222	433
107th Congress, 2001			
State delegates	1	5	6
Total U.S.	211	221	432
108th Congress, 2003			
State delegates	1	4	5
Total U.S.	205	229	434
109th Congress, 2005			
State delegates	1	4	5
Total U.S.	202	231	433
110th Congress, 2007			
State delegates	1	4	5
Total U.S.	233	202	435
Senate			
101st Congress, 1989			
State delegates	1	1	2
Total U.S.	55	45	100
102d Congress, 1991			
State delegates	1	1	2
Total U.S.	56	44	100
103d Congress, 1993			
State delegates	1	1	2
Total U.S.	57	43	100
104th Congress, 1995			
State delegates	0	2	2
Total U.S.	46	53	99
105th Congress, 1997			
State delegates	0	2	2
Total U.S.	45	55	100

(continued)

	Dem	Rep	Total
106th Congress, 1999			
State delegates	0	2	2
Total U.S.	45	54	99
107th Congress, 2001			
State delegates	0	2	2
Total U.S.	50	50	100
108th Congress, 2003			
State delegates	0	2	2
Total U.S.	48	51	99
109th Congress, 2005			
State delegates	0	2	2
Total U.S.	44	55	99
110th Congress, 2007			
State delegates	0	2	2
Total U.S.	49	49	98

Figures are for starts of first sessions. Totals are for Democrat (Dem.) and Republican (Rep.) members only. House membership totals under 435 and Senate totals under 100 reflect vacancies and seats held by independent party members. When the 110th Congress opened, the Senate's two independent members caucused with the Democrats, giving the Democrats control of the Senate.
Source: U.S. Congress, *Congressional Directory.*

Composition of state legislature, 1990-2006

	Democrats	Republicans
State House (101 seats)		
1990	68	33
1992	70	31
1994	65	36
1996	65	36
1998	61	40
2000	61	40
2002	53	48
2004	44	57
2006	44	57
State Senate (48 seats)		
1990	37	11
1992	37	11
1994	35	13
1996	33	15
1998	33	15
2000	33	15
2002	28	20
2004	26	22
2006	24	24

Figures for total seats may include independents and minor party members. Numbers reflect results of elections in listed years; elected members usually take their seats in the years that follow.
Source: Council of State Governments; *State Elective Officials and the Legislatures.*

Voter participation in presidential elections, 2000 and 2004

	2000	2004
Voting age population		
State	2,565,000	2,664,000
Total United States	209,831,000	220,377,000
State share of U.S. total	1.22	1.21
Rank among states	28	28
Portion of voting age population casting votes		
State	48.1%	55.0%
United States	50.3%	55.5%
Rank among states	38	33

Population figures are rounded to nearest thousand and include all residents, regardless of eligibility to vote.
Source: U.S. Census Bureau.

HEALTH AND MEDICAL CARE

Medical professionals
Physicians in 2003 and nurses in 2001

	U.S.	State
Physicians in 2003		
Total	774,849	6,034
Share of U.S. total		0.78%
Rate	266	172
Rank		49
Nurses in 2001		
Total	2,262,020	22,890
Share of U.S. total		1.01%
Rate	793	660
Rank		43

Rates are numbers of physicians and nurses per 100,000 resident population; ranks are based on rates.
Source: American Medical Association, *Physician Characteristics and Distribution in the U.S.*; U.S. Department of Health and Human Services, Health Resources and Services Administration.

Health insurance coverage, 2003

	State	U.S.
Total persons covered	2,737,000	243,320,000
Total persons not covered	701,000	44,961,000
Portion not covered	20.4%	15.6%
Rank among states	4	—
Children not covered	154,000	8,373,000
Portion not covered	17.9%	11.4%
Rank among states	2	—

Totals are rounded to nearest thousand. Ranks are from the highest to the lowest percentages of persons *not* insured.
Source: U.S. Census Bureau, Current Population Reports.

AIDS, syphilis, and tuberculosis cases, 2003

Disease	U.S. cases	State cases	Rank
AIDS	44,232	214	30
Syphilis	34,270	353	22
Tuberculosis	14,874	163	22

Source: U.S. Centers for Disease Control and Prevention.

Cigarette smoking, 2003
Residents over age 18 who smoke

	U.S.	State	Rank
All smokers	22.1%	25.2%	14
Male smokers	24.8%	27.8%	13
Female smokers	20.3%	22.7%	12

Cigarette smokers are defined as persons who reported having smoked at least 100 cigarettes during their lifetimes and who currently smoked at least occasionally.

Source: U.S. Centers for Disease Control and Prevention, *Morbidity and Mortality Weekly Report,* 53, no. 44 (November 12, 2004).

HOUSING

Home ownership rates, 1985-2004

	1985	1990	1995	2000	2004
State	70.5%	70.3%	69.8%	72.7%	71.1%
Total U.S.	63.9%	63.9%	64.7%	67.4%	69.0%
Rank among states	9	8	17	15	30

Net change in state home ownership rate, 1985-2004 . . . . +0.6%

Net change in U.S. home ownership rate, 1985-2004 . . . . +5.1%

Percentages represent the proportion of owner households to total occupied households.

Source: U.S. Census Bureau, 2006.

Home sales, 2000-2004
In thousands of units

Existing home sales	2000	2002	2003	2004
State sales	67.3	79.5	85.1	93.6
Total U.S. sales	5,171	5,631	6,183	6,784
State share of U.S. total	1.30%	1.41%	1.38%	1.38%
Sales rank among states	23	24	24	26

Units include single-family homes, condos, and co-ops.

Source: National Association of Realtors, Washington, D.C., *Real Estate Outlook: Market Trends & Insights.*

Values of owner-occupied homes, 2003

	State	U.S.
Total units	749,000	58,809,000
Value of units		
Under $100,000	63.3%	29.6%
$100,000-199,999	30.2%	36.9%
$200,000 or more	6.5%	33.5%
Median value	$85,502	$142,275
Rank among all states 47		

Units are owner-occupied one-family houses whose numbers are rounded to nearest thousand. Data are extrapolated from survey samples.

Source: U.S. Census Bureau, American Community Survey.

EDUCATION

Public school enrollment, 2002

Prekindergarten through grade 8

State enrollment 449,000

Total U.S. enrollment. 34,135,000

State share of U.S. total 1.32%

Grades 9 through 12

State enrollment 176,000

Total U.S. enrollment. 14,067,000

State share of U.S. total 1.25%

Enrollment rates

State public school enrollment rate. 97.8%

Overall U.S. rate 90.4%

Rank among states in 2002 1

Rank among states in 1995 9

Enrollment figures (which include unclassified students) are rounded to nearest thousand pupils during fall school term. Enrollment rates are based on enumerated resident population estimate for July 1, 2002.

Source: U.S. National Center for Education Statistics.

Public college finances, 2003-2004

FTE enrollment in public institutions of higher education

Students in state institutions.	133,400
Students in all U.S. public institutions	9,916,600
State share of U.S. total	1.35
Rank among states	28

State and local government appropriations for higher education

State appropriation per FTE	$4,872
National average.	$5,716
Rank among states	37
State & local tax revenue going to higher education	9.9%

FTE = full-time equivalent in public postsecondary programs, including summer sessions; student numbers are rounded to nearest hundred. Funding figures for 2003-2004 academic year include financial aid to students in state public institutions and exclude money for research, agriculture experiment stations, teaching hospitals, and medical schools; figures are rounded to nearest thousand dollars.
Source: Higher Education Executive Officers, Denver, Colorado.

TRANSPORTATION AND TRAVEL

Highway mileage, 2003

Interstate highways	930
Other freeways and expressways	186
Arterial roads	8,163
Collector roads.	25,305
Local roads.	77,994
Urban roads	14,991
Rural roads.	97,587
Total state mileage	112,578
U.S. total	3,974,107
State share	2.83%
Rank among states	15

Note that combined urban and rural road mileage matches the total of the other categories.
Source: U.S. Federal Highway Administration.

Motor vehicle registrations and driver licenses, 2003

Vehicle registrations	State	U.S.	Share	Rank
Autos, trucks, buses	3,074,000	231,390,000	1.33%	27
Autos only	1,623,000	135,670	1.20%	28
Motorcycles	72,000	5,328,000	1.35%	23
Driver licenses	2,348,000	196,166,000	1.20%	29

Figures, which do not include vehicles owned by military services, are rounded to the nearest thousand. Figures for automobiles include taxis.
Source: U.S. Federal Highway Administration.

Domestic travel expenditures, 2003

Spending by U.S. residents on overnight trips and day trips of at least 50 miles from home

Total expenditures within state	$4.21 bill.
Total expenditures within U.S.	$490.87 bill.
State share of U.S. total	0.9%
Rank among states	33

Source: Travel Industry Association of America.

Retail gasoline prices, 2003-2007

Average price per gallon at the pump

Year	U.S.	State
2003	$1.267	$1.156
2004	$1.316	$1.217
2005	$1.644	$1.617
2007	$2.298	$2.086

Excise tax per gallon in 2004.	17.0¢
Rank among all states in 2007 prices	49

Prices are averages of all grades of gasoline sold at the pump during March months in 2003-2005 and during February, 2007. Averages for 2006, during which prices rose higher, are not available.
Source: U.S. Energy Information Agency, *Petroleum Marketing Monthly* (2003-2005 data); American Automobile Association (2007 data).

CRIME AND LAW ENFORCEMENT

State and local police officers, 2000-2004

	2000	2002	2004
Total officers			
U.S.	654,601	665,555	675,734
State	6,957	7,108	6,997*
*Net change, 2000-2004			+0.57%
Officers per 1,000 residents			
U.S.	2.33	2.31	2.30
State	2.02	2.04	1.99
State rank	29	29	28

Totals include state and local police and sheriffs.
Source: Carsey Institute, University of New Hampshire.

Crime rates, 2003
Incidents per 100,000 residents

Crimes	State	U.S.
Violent crimes		
Total incidents	506	475
Murder	6	6
Forcible rape	43	32
Robbery	92	142
Aggravated assault	365	295
Property crimes		
Total incidents	4,306	3,588
Burglary	992	741
Larceny/theft	2,945	2,415
Motor vehicle theft	369	433
All crimes	4,812	4,063

Source: U.S. Federal Bureau of Investigation, *Crime in the United States,* annual.

State prison populations, 1980-2003

	State	U.S.	State share
1980	4,796	305,458	1.57%
1990	12,285	708,393	1.73%
1996	19,593	1,025,624	1.91%
2000	23,181	1,391,261	1.67%
2003	22,821	1,470,045	1.55%

State figures exclude prisoners in federal penitentiaries.
Source: U.S. Bureau of Justice Statistics, *Prisoners in 2003.*

Oregon

Location: Northwest Pacific coast

Area and rank: 96,003 square miles (248,647 square kilometers); 98,386 square miles (254,820 square kilometers) including water; tenth largest state in area

Coastline: 296 miles (476 kilometers) on the Pacific Ocean

Shoreline: 1,410 miles (2,269 kilometers)

Population and rank: 3,595,000 (2004); twenty-seventh largest state in population

Capital city: Salem (136,924 people in 2000 census)

Largest city: Portland (529,121 people in 2000 census)

Became territory: August 14, 1848

Entered Union and rank: February 14, 1859; thirty-third state

Present constitution adopted: 1859

Counties: 36

State name: The derivation of "Oregon" is uncertain; the name was first used by Jonathan Carver in 1778 and taken from the writings of Major Robert Rogers, an English army officer.

State nickname: Beaver State

Motto: *Alis volat propriis* (She flies with her own wings)

State flag: Navy blue field with, on one side, coat of arms and legends "State of Oregon" and "1859" below; gold beaver on other side

Highest point: Mount Hood—11,239 feet (3,426 meters)

Lowest point: Pacific Ocean—sea level

Highest recorded temperature: 119 degrees Fahrenheit (48 degrees Celsius)— Pendleton, 1898

Lowest recorded temperature:
–54 degrees Fahrenheit (–48 degrees Celsius)—Seneca, 1933

State song: "Oregon, My Oregon"

State tree: Douglas fir

State flower: Oregon grape

State bird: Western meadowlark

State fish: Chinook salmon

State animal: Beaver

National parks: Crater Lake

Mall of Oregon's state capitol building in Salem. (Oregon Tourism Commission)

Oregon History

Oregon's special character, like that of every state, was formed from its geography and geographical position in the nation combined with the formative events of its history. Oregon's character marries the independent spirit of the frontier West inherited from the nineteenth century with modern, urban America, the result of the economic development of the World War II era and the years of steady growth that followed. The cool, wet western portion of the state coexists with a semi-arid eastern segment in whose economy irrigation has played a major role. Oregon's society and politics exhibit a unique blend of liberalism and conservatism, making it a fascinating laboratory of democracy.

Early History. Before the arrival of white settlers, the region of Oregon was inhabited by numerous Native Americans. These included the Clackma, the Multnomah, the Tillamook, and the Kalapuya in the northwest. Also present were the Bannock, Cayuse, Nez Perce, Paiute, and Umatilla, who lived east of the Cascade Mountains. Near today's California border were the Klamath and the Rogue peoples.

Exploration. Oregon was explored by a succession of European nations before Americans arrived. In the sixteenth century, Spanish adventurers first explored the region. Two centuries later English and more Spaniards searched for the Northwest Passage linking eastern North America to the Pacific, eliminating a voyage around South America. In 1774, Juan Pérez sailed the coast, and the following year Bruno Heceta was the first European to find the Columbia River.

In 1778, the famed English navigator Captain James

A natural lake in the caldera of an extinct volcano in southern Oregon, Crater Lake is one of North America's scenic wonders. It is also the deepest lake in the world whose water is entirely above sea level. (PhotoDisc)

Cook, also searching for the Northwest Passage and the twenty-thousand-pound finders' reward, sailed up the coast to Yaqina Bay. In 1788, the first American ships arrived, including those of John Kendrick and Robert Gray. In 1792, Gray became the first white man to sail up the Columbia River, which he named after his ship. Soon afterwards, William Brougham, a lieutenant of British Captain George Vancouver, who was exploring the region, sailed into the Columbia and continued well inland. At this time, too, Russian traders were pushing south from posts in Alaska, and British fur traders were exploring the West, since Oregon furs were seen as a promising component of the growing trade with China.

American Exploration and Settlement. Spain abandoned exploration of the area after 1795, leaving it to the British and Americans. In 1805, Meriwether Lewis and William Clark, leading the expedition sent by President Thomas Jefferson to explore the territory of the Louisiana Purchase, arrived at Fort Clatsop, where the Columbia River meets the Pacific Ocean.

A more permanent American presence first appeared in the form of fur trappers and traders, and only later in the form of agricultural settlers. The first American fur company was established in the region by John Jacob Astor, who brought his Pacific Fur Company to Oregon, basing it in Astoria in 1811. Two years later, during the War of 1812, he sold it to the North West

Company, which in turn sold it to Hudson's Bay Company in 1821. By then, however, Britain and the United States had signed a treaty establishing joint occupation of the region by both countries.

Joint occupation brought both British and American influence. By the 1820's, Britain's Hudson's Bay Company was a dominant force in the region, guided by Dr. John McLoughlin at Fort Vancouver, on the Columbia River. Americans were also arriving: Mountain men such as Jedediah S. Smith rivaled the trappers of Hudson's Bay Company in the southeast of the region. In 1829, Hall J. Kelley founded the American Society for the Settlement of Oregon Territory. One of his followers, Nathaniel J. Wyeth, attempted to establish a permanent post on the Columbia River.

Missionaries added their numbers to the fur trappers and traders, especially after Marcus Whitman arrived in the region in 1836. The missionaries awakened American interest in the region. Two years after Whitman, the first Roman Catholic missionaries, François N. Blanchet and Modeste Demers, arrived, and others followed.

The 1840's saw the advent of the "Great Migration" of Americans moving steadily westward in covered wagons across the Great Plains. In 1842 and 1843, enormous wagon trains braved American Indian attacks and hardship to cross the prairies and mountain chains of the Oregon Trail. Friction soon arose between Americans and the British. It had not been so long, after all, since Britain had attempted to undo the results of the American Revolution in the War of 1812. American leaders such as Jesse Applegate advocated establishment of an American government in the area. Thus, in 1843 about one hundred settlers, missionaries, and retired fur traders met at Champoeg and created an Oregon provisional government, modeled on American lines, despite objections by the British-oriented among them.

Conflict with Native Americans and Statehood. The national spirit of the young American republic was now sufficiently stirred to demand removal of British authority in its entirely from the area. The 1844 election slogan "Fifty-four Forty or Fight" expressed American

demands for ousting the British up to that latitude. Fighting proved unnecessary, however, since in 1846 the two nations agreed on borders dividing the Oregon Country.

The next year, the slaughter by American Indians of Marcus Whitman and thirteen others near present-day Walla Walla, Washington, brought demands for protection. The massacre led to the Cayuse War of 1847-1848 and the execution in 1850 of five Indians found guilty of its perpetration. Demands for protection from Indians also led to the establishment of Oregon Territory. The territory embraced far more than the present state but was reduced in 1853 with the creation of a separate Washington Territory. Finally, in 1859 Oregon became the nation's thirty-third state.

The discovery of gold in Oregon's southwest led to fighting with the Rogue Indians, who resisted abuse at the hands of miners. Conflict with Indians often arose on account of settlers' abuse or Native American resistance to their forcible removal to reservations, as occurred with the Modoc tribe during the early 1870's.

Economic Development. The period from 1850 to 1880 was marked by Indian wars. Nevertheless, Oregon's economy was developing. The California gold rush brought thousands of people to nearby Oregon. Discovery of gold in Oregon had a similar effect.

In 1867-1868 a bumper wheat crop made it possible to ship grain to England, beginning a large wheat export industry in the state. The most important stimulus came later in the century, however, with the arrival of the transcontinental railroad. Under the direction of Henry Villard, the North Pacific Railroad was completed during the 1880's, bringing with it new trade and the onset of manufacturing. The lumber industry was already important to the state's economy, much of the timber being shipped overseas. Australian newspapers of the period invariably carried advertisements for Oregon lumber. With the arrival of the transcontinental railroad from the East, however, wood could be shipped throughout the United States, and for a time timber dominated the state's economy. The railroad was also extended to California, facilitating transport of Oregon goods to the growing state to the south.

Political Developments. After 1900, with the state's growing prosperity, Oregon's politics tended to conservatism. This conservatism, however, has long been punctuated with a pronounced streak of reformism and a taste for grassroots democracy. The latter is illus-

Located on Columbia River Gorge, Oregon's Multnomah Falls is a spectacular two-level waterfall with a total height of about 620 feet. During the winter its waters occasionally freeze solid. (Kelvin Kay)

Oregon's largest city, Portland has access to the Pacific Ocean on the Columbia River. (PhotoDisc)

trated by a series of measures enacted early in the century, designed to ensure the influence of popular will over government. In 1902, the initiative and referendum were adopted. The former gave the right of citizens to propose laws to be voted upon in general elections. The referendum secured the electorate's right to reject certain laws passed by the state legislature. In 1904, direct primary elections were instituted. These empowered the electorate at the expense of political party organizations, since candidates for office at general elections were to be chosen directly by the electorate at "primary" elections. In 1908, the state adopted the "recall" election, whereby officeholders can be voted from office in special elections. Finally, in 1912, woman suffrage was adopted, after a long and difficult struggle led by Abigail Jane Scott Duniway.

Depression and War. Oregon's twentieth century economic and social life saw continued emigration from the East. Electric power and irrigation projects propelled agriculture and manufacturing to the fore. The Great Depression of the 1930's dramatically increased the role of the federal government in economic affairs. Federal law allowed the lumber industry to set production quotas and prices. Farmers were paid to lower crop production. The federal government also completed the Bonneville Dam on the Columbia River

in 1937, bringing important economic benefits as well as flood control to the region.

After the economic hardships of the 1930's, World War II saw a tremendous lift to the state's manufacturing industries. The war brought the state an aluminum industry and revitalized Portland's shipbuilding industry. The city also became an important port for shipping war material to U.S. forces and the Soviet Union. Thousands of workers migrated from the East to work in wartime industries, and many stayed after the war. The federal government built and operated an entire city in the Portland-Vancouver, Washington, area to house the huge influx of wartime workers. The city was not well situated, however, and was washed away in the great Columbia River floods of 1948.

Postwar Developments. Growing prosperity punctuated by a thriving tourist industry marked the postwar era. Visitors flocked to see the state's scenic wonders, including Crater Lake National Park. Cheap hydroelectric power became more plentiful from a series of federally funded dams, such as The Dalles and McNary projects on the Columbia River. By 1956 natural gas became available, adding to the energy supply. Mechanization and diversification of products aided the state's farms and agricultural industries. During the 1960's, forest products also became more diversified, as new uses were found for previously discarded refuse.

The postwar state's population also became predominantly urban. In 1880, only 15 percent lived in towns. In 1910, the figure was 44 percent, but by 1993, 62 percent of the population lived in incorporated cities and towns. These demographic changes were reflected in the state's politics. The state's early history was marked by domination of the Republican Party. With the urbanization of the 1950's and 1960's and the influx of migrants from other parts of the country, the pattern was reversed and a majority of voters were Democrats. From the 1970's to the end of the 1990's reformist politics were prominent. Oregonians, however, showed themselves independent minded, repeatedly electing Independent Wayne Morse, an outspoken critic of the Vietnam War, to the U.S. Senate. Indicative of this spirit was Oregon's passage of the nation's first "bottle law," requiring deposits on disposable bottles and cans. The state's century-long tradition of conservation continued, and in 1998, the nation's first "right to die" law, which passed as an initiative in 1994, went into effect.

Wildfires. Around the beginning of the twenty-first century, Oregon, like other western states, was beset by annual wildfires that destroyed thousands of acres of the state's natural habitats. In 2001, for example, thirteen fires, several of them very large, ravaged the landscape from mid-July until the end of September. The largest of the fires, which burned in the Lakeview area for ten days in mid-August, scorched 127,552 acres. In 2002, smoke from an immense wildfire at the southwestern Oregon-California border known as the Biscuit Fires, composing three fires that joined together, was dramatically visible in satellite photographs. The fire, which began on July 15 and was contained on September 6, burned nearly 500,000 acres. Wildfires, such as the 2004 B&B Complex, the largest wildfire complex in the history of the Oregon Cascade Mountains, and the Dear Creek fire of 2005, continued in succeeding years.

Right-to-Die Law. The state's Physician Assisted Suicide law, also called the "right-to-die" law, continued to attract national attention following 2000. An annual report to the electorate published during that year showed that in the first three years of the law's operation, ninety-six prescriptions for lethal drugs were written and seventy persons died after taking the drugs. Others either failed to take the drugs or died of disease. A study of those who died through the prescribed lethal medicines showed that they were much more likely to have a college education than the overall population. After the federal government announced it would revoke licenses of participating physicians, an Oregon man sued. On January 17, 2006, the U.S. Supreme Court ruled that Oregon's suicide law was constitutional and that the actions of the Bush administration had criminalized the practice under the law without congressional authorization.

Terrorists Arrested. On October 4, 2002, U.S. Attorney General John Ashcroft, in what he called a "defining day" in America's fight against terrorism, announced that six persons, five of whom were American-born U.S. citizens, had been charged with terrorism. Three of those charged appeared in federal court in Portland the same day, and two brothers appeared in court the following week. On September 18, 2003, the brothers, Ahmed and Muhammad Bilal, pleaded guilty to terrorism charges. One was sentenced to eight to fourteen years and the other to a ten-to-fourteen-year sentence.

Then, in 2004, cleric Abu Hamza al-Masri was arrested in London on charges of conspiring to set up a terrorist training camp in Oregon during 1999-2000. In January, 2005, the Oregon bureau chief of the Federal Bureau of Investigation (FBI) told an interviewer that "jihadists" (Muslim extremists who believe in jihad or holy war) who had trained in Afghanistan terrorist camps were living in Oregon.

Politics. In political matters, Oregon cast its electoral votes for the Democratic Party candidates, Al Gore and John Kerry, in the presidential elections of 2000 and 2004. In 2002, Oregon voters reelected Democrat Ted Kulongoski governor in the closest race in fifty years after a Libertarian Party candidate took 4 percent of the vote, enough to allow the defeat of the Republican candidate. In a contentious ballot measure in 2004, voters refused to endorse a system of licensed nonprofit dispensaries for medical marijuana.

Charles F. Bahmueller

Oregon Time Line

1542	Spanish explorers sail near Oregon coast.
1579	English explorer Sir Francis Drake may have landed on Oregon coast.
1774	Spanish explorer Juan Pérez, seeking Northwest Passage, arrives in Oregon; other Spaniards follow.
Mar. 7, 1778	Captain James Cook explores Oregon coast.
1788	First American ships arrive off Oregon coast.
May 11, 1792	Captain Robert Gray sails into Columbia River.

1795	George Vancouver, a British officer, explores much of the region.
1805-1806	Expedition of Meriwether Lewis and William Clark reaches mouth of Columbia via land, establishing strong American claim to the land.
1811	Britain-United States treaty allows citizens of both countries to trade and live in the region.
Apr. 12, 1811	John Jacob Astor establishes fur trading post at Astoria, the first white settlement of Oregon.
1824-1825	Russia cedes claims south of 54 degrees, 40 minutes.
1834	Methodist missionaries establish first American settlement in Willamette Valley.
1843	Nine hundred settlers arrive in Oregon.
1843	Acts passed to prohibit slavery and to exclude blacks and mulattoes from Oregon.
May 2, 1843	Willamette Valley settlers organize provisional government based on the laws of Iowa.
1846	Forty-ninth parallel is established as principal border between British and American territories in the Pacific Northwest.
1847	Massacre by Cayuse Indians of fourteen American settlers leads to war.
1847	Congress passes Oregon Donation Land Law; ensuing increase in settler migration sparks Indian-white hostilities.
Aug. 14, 1848	Oregon Territory created.
1850's	Discovery of gold leads to conflict with American Indians.
1850-1855	Indian agents sign more than twenty treaties with Oregon Indians, but none is ratified in the Senate.
1856	Rogue River Indian War begins with Indian resistance to abuse by miners, ends with removal of Indians to distant reservations.
Feb. 14, 1859	Oregon becomes thirty-third state.
1860's	Cattle becomes significant part of state's economy.
1861-1862	Gold strikes worth tens of millions of dollars achieved; state economy vitalized.
1870's	Indian wars break out; Modoc Indians, dissatisfied with forced removal and mistreatment on Klamath Reserve, are defeated and sent permanently to Oklahoma.
1877	Nez Perce War; defeated tribal members are sent to Oklahoma, but most eventually return to the Northwest.
1890	Population reaches 300,000, rising from about 52,000 in 1860.
1902	Crater Lake National Park is established.
1912	Woman suffrage is adopted.
1937	Completion of Bonneville Dam.
1940	Population exceeds one million.
1942-1945	World War II raises prosperity of state; Portland is major transshipment point for war material.
May 30, 1948	City of Vanport is swept away in massive flood.
1950's	McNary and The Dalles Dams make available cheap, plentiful electric power.
1950's	Oregon industry prospers; marked increase in urbanization.
1960's	Oregon's timber industry transformed by new uses for forestry products and large replantation projects.
1964	Heavy floods ravage western part of the state.
1973	Establishment of Land Conservation and Development Commission.
1982	Completion of second powerhouse at Bonneville Dam more than doubles its electric power production.
1994	Passage of nation's first assisted suicide law.
1998	Assisted suicide law becomes effective.
July-Sept., 2001	Wildfire in the Lakeview area burns for ten days, consuming 127,552 acres.
July 15-Sept. 6, 2002	Biscuit Fires, the largest wildfire complex in Oregon history, burn 499,968 acres.
Oct. 4, 2002	Six Oregonians, including two brothers, Ahmed and Muhammad Bilal, are charged with terrorism.
Nov. 5, 2002	Ted Kulongoski is reelected governor in the closest gubernatorial race in fifty years.
Jan. 17, 2006	U.S. Supreme Court upholds the constitutionality of Oregon's right-to-die law.

Notes for Further Study

Published Sources. A detailed discussion of state and local government in Oregon is found in Richard Sanders's *Government in Oregon* (1991). Place names are examined in *Oregon Geographic Names* (7th ed., 2003), a work originating in 1928, comprising more than 5,400 entries. *The Oregon Atlas and Gazetteer* (4th ed., 2001), published by the Delorme Mapping Company, is one of a series of imaginative atlases and encompasses information about the state's parks, forests, wilderness areas, campgrounds, cycling routes, hiking, and fishing.

Comprehensive histories are Gordon B. Dobbs's *Oregon: A Bicentennial History* (1977) and Herman Leonard's *History of the Oregon Territory from Its First Discovery Up to the Present Time* (1980). The story of the state's first American settlers is told in *Blazing a Wagon Trail to Oregon: A Weekly Chronicle of the Great Migration of 1843* (1993) by Lloyd W. Coffman. *The Oregon Trail: An American Saga* (2004) by David Dary gives a vivid account, using diaries, journals, recollections, reports, and newspaper accounts, of the first European peopling of the Oregon area. Using stories taken from trail diaries and memoirs, *Oregon Trail Stories: True Accounts of Life in a Covered Wagon* (2003) by David Klausmeier documents this pioneer period in American history. Using historical photographs and engaging stories to document the state's history, the staff of *The Oregonian* newspaper compiled The *Oregon Story: 1850-2000* (2002). For insight into modern-era state politics, consult *Oregon Politics and Government: Progressives Versus Conservative Populists* (2005), edited by Richard A. Clucas, Mark Henkels, and Brent S. Steel.

For a history of Oregon's indigenous peoples, see Jeff Zucker et al. *Oregon Indians* (1983) and Bert Webber's *Indians Along the Oregon Trail: The Tribes of Nebraska, Wyoming, Idaho, Oregon, and Washington Identified* (1992). The relationship between the state's history and its geography is treated in *Making Oregon: A Study in Historical Geography* (1981) by Samuel Dicken. Finally, for Oregon's wildlife, see *Atlas of Oregon's Wildlife: Distribution, Habitat, and Natural History* (1997), edited by Blair A. Csuti et al. Ellen Morris Bishop's well-researched text is paired with high-quality photographs in her *In Search of Ancient Oregon: A Geological and Natural History* (2003), which details the state's present and past landscapes, plants, animals, and climates.

Web Resources. A starting place on the Web for those seeking information on the state's politics and government is the official state Web site (www.oregon .gov/), supplemented by the Oregon Law and Government site (www.lawresearch .com/csor.htm), which contains links to each branch of state government, including individual agencies, government documents, and general information. It also has links to county and city government, as well as to Oregon law sites. Another excellent site for broad information about the state is Oregon Blue Book (bluebook.state.or.us/ default.htm). The Oregon Historical Society (www.ohs.org/) is the best place to start for any research related to the state's past. The Oregon Historic Photograph Collection (photos .salemhistory.org/), hosted by the Salem Public Library, is extensive and fascinating.

A number of sites are dedicated to Oregon's Native Americans. An interactive map of the state providing good information of the state's tribes can be found on Native Americans of Oregon (www.chenowith.k12.or.us/tech/subject/social/ natam_or.html).

The Oregon Native American Chamber of Commerce (www.onacc.org/) is also a good destination for research on indigenous communities. An informative site on the state's coastal regions, including an events calendar, maps, and information on whale watching and lodging, is Oregon Coast (www.oregoncoast.com).

Gorge of the Columbia River, which separates Oregon and Washington. (Photo-Disc)

Counties

County	2000 pop.	Rank in pop.	Sq. miles	Rank in area
Baker	16,741	28	3,068.3	10
Benton	78,153	11	676.5	33
Clackamas	338,391	3	1,868.3	18
Clatsop	35,630	19	827.3	28
Columbia	43,560	18	656.8	34
Coos	62,779	15	1,600.5	23
Crook	19,182	26	2,979.5	12
Curry	21,137	24	1,627.4	22
Deschutes	115,367	7	3,018.3	11
Douglas	100,399	9	5,036.8	5
Gilliam	1,915	35	1,204.1	24
Grant	7,935	30	4,528.8	7
Harney	7,609	31	10,134.9	1
Hood River	20,411	25	522.4	35
Jackson	181,269	6	2,785.4	13
Jefferson	19,009	27	1,780.9	19
Josephine	75,726	12	1,639.5	21
Klamath	63,775	14	5,944.6	4
Lake	7,422	32	8,136.3	3
Lane	322,959	4	4,554.2	6
Lincoln	44,479	17	979.7	27
Linn	103,069	8	2,291.4	15
Malheur	31,615	20	9,887.7	2
Marion	284,834	5	1,185.0	25
Morrow	10,995	29	2,032.8	17
Multnomah	660,486	1	435.3	36
Polk	62,380	16	741.1	30
Sherman	1,934	34	823.3	29
Tillamook	24,262	22	1,102.2	26
Umatilla	70,548	13	3,215.3	8
Union	24,530	21	2,036.7	16
Wallowa	7,226	33	3,145.4	9
Wasco	23,791	23	2,381.2	14
Washington	445,342	2	723.8	31
Wheeler	1,547	36	1,715.0	20
Yamhill	84,992	10	715.6	32

Source: U.S. Census Bureau; National Association of Counties.

Cities

With 10,000 or more residents

Rank	City	Population	Rank	City	Population
1	Portland	529,121	27	Hayesville	18,222
2	Eugene	137,893	28	Newberg	18,064
3	Salem (capital)	136,924	29	Forest Grove	17,708
4	Gresham	90,205	30	Pendleton	16,354
5	Beaverton	76,129	31	Oatfield	15,750
6	Hillsboro	70,186	32	Coos Bay	15,374
7	Medford	63,154	33	Wilsonville	13,991
8	Springfield	52,864	34	Four Corners	13,922
9	Bend	52,029	35	Troutdale	13,777
10	Corvallis	49,322	36	Redmond	13,481
11	Aloha	41,741	37	Hermiston	13,154
12	Tigard	41,223	38	Lebanon	12,950
13	Albany	40,852	39	Oak Grove	12,808
14	Lake Oswego	35,278	40	Canby	12,790
15	Keizer	32,203	41	Cedar Mill	12,597
16	McMinnville	26,499	42	Central Point	12,493
17	Oregon City	25,754	43	Dallas	12,459
18	Grants Pass	23,003	44	La Grande	12,327
19	Tualatin	22,791	45	City of The Dalles	12,156
20	West Linn	22,261	46	Sherwood	11,791
21	Milwaukie	20,490	47	Gladstone	11,438
22	Woodburn	20,100	48	Ontario	10,985
23	Roseburg	20,017	49	St. Helens	10,019
24	Altamont	19,603			
25	Ashland	19,522			
26	Klamath Falls	19,462			

Population figures are from 2000 census.

Source: U.S. Bureau of the Census.

Index to Tables

DEMOGRAPHICS

Resident state and national populations, 1970-2004

Population figures given in thousands

	State pop.	U.S. pop.	Share	Rank
1970	2,092	203,302	1.0%	31
1980	2,633	226,546	1.2%	30
1985	2,673	237,924	1.1%	30
1990	2,842	248,765	1.1%	29
1995	3,184	262,761	1.2%	29
2000	3,421	281,425	1.2%	28
2004	3,595	293,655	1.2%	27

Source: U.S. Census Bureau, Current Population Reports, 2006.

Resident population by age, 2004

Age Group	Total persons
Under 5 years	226,000
5 to 17 years	626,000
18 to 24 years	350,000
25 to 34 years	506,000
35 to 44 years	511,000
45 to 54 years	537,000
55 to 64 years	379,000
65 to 74 years	227,000
75 to 84 years	163,000
85 years and older	70,000
All age groups	3,595,000

Portion of residents 65 and older 12.8%
National rank in portion of oldest residents 25
National average 12.4%

Population figures are rounded to nearest thousand persons;
figures include armed forces personnel stationed in the state.
Source: U.S. Bureau of the Census, 2006.

Resident population by race, Hispanic origin, 2004

Category	State pop.	Share	U.S.
All residents	3,595	100.00%	100.00%
Non-Hispanic white	2,948	82.00%	67.37%
Hispanic white	319	8.87%	13.01%
Other Hispanic	24	0.67%	1.06%
African American	64	1.78%	12.77%
Native American	49	1.36%	0.96%
Asian, Pacific Islander	132	3.67%	4.37%
Two or more categories	83	2.31%	1.51%

Population figures are in thousands. Persons counted as "Hispanic" (Latino) may be of any race. Because of overlapping categories, categories may not add up to 100%. Shares in column 3 are percentages of each category within the state; these figures may be compared to the national percentages in column 4.
Source: U.S. Bureau of the Census, 2006.

Projected state population, 2000-2030

Year	Population
2000	3,421,000
2005	3,596,000
2010	3,791,000
2015	4,013,000
2020	4,260,000
2025	4,536,000
2030	4,834,000
Population increase, 2000-2030	1,413,000
Percentage increase, 2000-2030	41.3

Projections are based on data from the 2000 census.
Source: U.S. Census Bureau.

VITAL STATISTICS

Infant mortality rates, 1980-2002

	1980	1990	2000	2002
All state residents	12.2	8.3	5.6	5.8
All U.S. residents	12.6	9.2	9.4	9.1
All state white residents	12.2	7.0	5.5	5.6
All U.S. white residents	10.6	7.6	5.7	5.8
All state black residents	15.9	—	—	—
All U.S. black residents	22.2	18.0	14.1	14.4

Figures represent deaths per 1,000 live births of resident infants under 1 year old, exclusive of fetal deaths. Figures for all residents include members of other racial categories not listed separately. The Census Bureau considers the post-1980 figures for black residents to be too small to be statistically meaningful.
Source: U.S. Census Bureau, *Statistical Abstract of the United States,* 2006.

Abortion rates, 1990 and 2000

	1990	2000
Total abortions	16,000	17,000
Rate per 1,000 women	23.9	23.5
U.S. rate	25.7	21.3
Rank	15	9

Numbers of abortions are rounded to nearest thousand; ranks are based on rates.
Source: U.S. Census Bureau.

Marriages and divorces, 2004

Total marriages	29,000
Rate per 1,000 population	8.1
National rate per 1,000 population	7.4
Rank among all states	16
Total divorces	14,800
Rate per 1,000 population	4.1
National rate per 1,000 population	3.7
Rank among all states	16

Figures are for all marriages and divorces performed within the state, including those of nonresidents; totals are rounded to the nearest hundred. Ranks are for highest to lowest figures; note that divorce data are not available for five states.
Source: U.S. National Center for Health Statistics, *Vital Statistics of the United States,* 2006.

Death rates by leading causes, 2002
Deaths per 100,000 resident population

Cause	State	U.S.
Heart disease	206.2	241.7
Cancer	205.8	193.2
Cerebrovascular diseases	75.1	56.4
Accidents other than motor vehicle	39.7	37.0
Motor vehicle accidents	13.1	15.7
Chronic lower respiratory diseases	52.4	43.3
Diabetes mellitus	29.6	25.4
HIV	2.6	4.9
Suicide	14.7	11.0
Homicide	3.0	6.1
All causes	883.7	847.3
Rank in overall death rate among states		24

Figures exclude nonresidents who died in the state. Causes of death follow International Classification of Diseases. Rank is from highest to lowest death rate in the United States.
Source: U.S. National Center for Health Statistics, *National Vital Statistics Report,* 2006.

ECONOMY

Gross state product, 1990-2004
In current dollars

Year	State product	Nat'l product	State share
1990	$57.3 billion	$5.67 trillion	1.01%
2000	$113.0 billion	$9.75 trillion	1.16%
2002	$115.1 billion	$10.41 trillion	1.11%
2003	$120.0 billion	$10.92 trillion	1.10%
2004	$128.1 billion	$11.65 trillion	1.10%

Source: U.S. Bureau of Economic Analysis, *Survey of Current Business,* July, 2005.

Gross state product by industry, 2003
In billions of dollars

Construction	$4.8
Manufacturing	21.4
Wholesale trade	8.1
Retail trade	7.9
Finance & insurance	6.5
Information	4.0
Professional services	5.7
Health care & social assistance	8.1
Government	13.8
Total state product	$116.1
Total U.S. product	$10,289.2
State share of U.S. total	1.13%
Rank among all states	28

Total figures include industries not listed separately. Amounts are in chained 2000 dollars.
Source: U.S. Bureau of Economic Analysis, *Survey of Current Business,* July, 2005.

Personal income per capita, 1990-2004
In current dollars

	1990	2000	2004
Per capita income	$18,010	$28,097	$29,971
U.S. average	$19,477	$29,845	$32,937
Rank among states	24	25	36

Source: U.S. Bureau of Economic Analysis, *Survey of Current Business,* April, 2005.

Energy consumption, 2001
In trillions of British thermal units (BTU), except as noted

Total energy consumption

Total state energy consumption	1,064
Total U.S. energy consumption	96,275
State share of U.S. total	1.11%
Rank among states	31

Per capita consumption (In millions of BTU)

Total state per capita consumption	307
Total U.S. per capita consumption	338
Rank among states	36

End-use sectors

Residential	252
Commercial	208
Industrial	298
Transportation	307

Sources of energy

Petroleum	368
Natural gas	236
Coal	43
Hydroelectric power	291
Nuclear electric power	0

Figures for totals include categories not listed separately.
Source: U.S. Energy Information Administration, *State Energy Data Report,* 2001.

Nonfarm employment by sectors, 2004

Total persons	1,594,000
Construction	82,000
Manufacturing	200,000
Trade, transportation, utilities	320,000
Information	33,000
Finance, insurance, real estate	97,000
Professional & business services	177,000
Education & health services	193,000
Leisure, hospitality, arts, organizations	156,000
Other services, including repair & maintenance	57,000
Government	270,000

Figures are rounded to nearest thousand persons. "Total" includes mining and natural resources, not listed separately.
Source: U.S. Bureau of Labor Statistics, 2006.

Foreign exports, 1990-2004
In millions of dollars

Year	State	U.S.	State share
1990	4,065	394,045	1.03%
1996	8,948	624,767	1.43%
1997	9,151	688,896	1.33%
2000	11,441	712,055	1.46%
2003	10,357	724,006	1.53%
2004	11,172	769,332	1.45%

Rank among all states in 2004 23

U.S. total does not include U.S. dependencies.
Source: U.S. Census Bureau, *U.S. Merchandise Trade*, series FT 900, 2000; U.S. Census Bureau, *U.S. International Trade in Goods and Services*, Series FT 900, 2005.

LAND USE

Federally owned land, 2003
Areas in acres

	State	U.S.	State share
Total area	61,599,000	2,271,343,000	2.71%
Nonfederal land	30,960,000	1,599,584,000	1.94%
Federal land	30,639,000	671,759,000	4.56%
Federal share	49.7%	29.6%	—

Areas are rounded to nearest thousand acres. Figures for federally owned land do not include trust properties.
Source: U.S. General Services Administration, *Federal Real Property Profile*, 2006.

Land use, 1997
In acres, rounded to nearest thousand

Total surface area	62,161,000
Total nonfederal rural land.	28,858,000
Percentage rural land	46.4%
Cropland	3,762,000
Conservation Reserve Program (CRP*) land	483,000
Pastureland	1,961,000
Rangeland	9,286,000
Forestland	12,643,000
Other rural land	724,000

*CRP is a federal program begun in 1985 to assist private landowners to convert highly erodible cropland to vegetative cover for ten years. Note that some categories of land overlap.
Source: U.S. Department of Agriculture, Natural Resources and Conservation Service, and Iowa State University, Statistical Laboratory, *Summary Report, 1997 National Resources Inventory,* revised December, 2000.

Farms and crop acreage, 2004

	State	U.S.	Share	Rank
Farms	40,000	2,113,000	1.89%	24
Acres (millions)	17	937	1.81%	17
Acres per farm	430	443	—	16

Source: U.S. Department of Agriculture, National Agricultural Statistics Service. Farm totals are rounded to nearest thousand units; acreage figures are rounded to nearest million. Rankings, including ties, are based on rounded figures.

GOVERNMENT AND FINANCE

Units of local government, 2002

	State	Total U.S.	Rank
All local governments	1,439	87,525	22
Counties	36	3,034	34
Municipalities	240	19,429	31
Townships	0	16,504	—
School districts	236	13,506	21
Special districts	927	35,052	12

Only 48 states have county governments, 20 states have township governments ("towns" in New England, Minnesota, New York, and Wisconsin), and 46 states have school districts. Special districts encompass such functions as natural resources, fire protection, and housing and community development.
Source: U.S. Census Bureau, *Census of Governments.*

State government revenue, 2002

Total revenue	$14,815 mill.
General revenue	$14,305 mill.
Per capita revenue	$4,060
U.S. per capita average	$3,689
Rank among states	19
Intergovernment revenue	
Total	$5,710 mill.
From federal government	$5,625 mill.
Charges and miscellaneous	
Total	$3,431 mill.
Current charges	$1,878 mill.
Misc. general income	$1,552 mill.
Insurance trust revenue	$256 mill.
Taxes	
Total	$5,164 mill.
Per capita taxes	$1,467
Rank among states	46
Property taxes	$24 mill.
Sales taxes	$650 mill.
License taxes	$496 mill.
Individual income taxes	$3,675 mill.
Corporate income taxes	$196 mill.
Other taxes	$121 mill.

Total revenue figures include items not listed separately here.
Source: U.S. Bureau of the Census.

State government expenditures, 2002

General expenditures

Total state expenditures	$18,029 mill.
Intergovernmental	$4,213 mill.

Per capita expenditures

State	$4,228
Average of all states	$3,859
Rank among states	17

Selected direct expenditures

Education.	$2,040 mill.
Public welfare	$3,796 mill.
Health, hospital	$1,401 mill.
Highways	$587 mill.
Police protection	$141 mill.
Corrections.	$494 mill.
Natural resources	$315 mill.
Parks and recreation	$46 mill.
Government administration	$897 mill.
Interest on debt	$251 mill.
Total direct expenditures	$10,671 mill.

Totals include items not listed separately.
Source: U.S. Census Bureau.

POLITICS

Governors since statehood

D = Democrat; R = Republican; O = other;
(r) resigned; (d) died in office; (i) removed from office

John Whiteaker (D)	1859-1862
Addison C. Gibbs (O)	1862-1866
George L. Woods (R)	1866-1870
LaFayette Grover (D) . . . . (r)	1870-1877
Stephen F. Chadwick (D)	1877-1878
William W. Thayer (D)	1878-1882
Zenas F. Moody (R)	1882-1887
Sylvester Pennoyer (D)	1887-1895
William P. Lord (R)	1895-1899
Theodore T. Geer (R)	1899-1903
George E. Chamberlain (R) . . . . (r)	1903-1909
Frank W. Benson (R) . . . . (r)	1909-1910
Jay Bowerman (R)	1910-1911
Oswald West (D)	1911-1915
James Withycombe (R) . . . . (d)	1915-1919
Benjamin W. Olcott (R)	1919-1923
Walter M. Pierce (D).	1923-1927
Isaac L. Patterson (R) . . . . (d)	1927-1929
Albin W. Norblad (R)	1929-1931
Julius L. Meier (O).	1931-1935
Charles H. Martin (D)	1935-1939
Charles A. Sprague (R)	1939-1943
Earl W. Snell (R). . . . . (d)	1943-1947
John H. Hall (R)	1947-1949
Douglas McKay (R) . . . . (r)	1949-1952
Paul L. Patterson (R) . . . . (d)	1952-1956
Elmo Smith (R)	1956-1957

Robert D. Holmes (D)	1957-1959
Mark O. Hatfield (R)	1959-1967
Tom L. McCall (R)	1967-1975
Robert W. Straub (D)	1975-1979
Victor Atiyeh (R)	1979-1987
Neil Goldschmidt (D)	1987-1991
Barbara Roberts (D)	1991-1995
John A. Kitzhaber (D)	1995-2003
Ted Kulongoski (D)	2003-

Composition of congressional delegations, 1989-2007

	Dem	Rep	Total
House of Representatives			
101st Congress, 1989			
State delegates	3	2	5
Total U.S.	259	174	433
102d Congress, 1991			
State delegates	4	1	5
Total U.S.	267	167	434
103d Congress, 1993			
State delegates	4	1	5
Total U.S.	258	176	434
104th Congress, 1995			
State delegates	4	1	5
Total U.S.	197	236	433
105th Congress, 1997			
State delegates	4	1	5
Total U.S.	206	228	434
106th Congress, 1999			
State delegates	4	1	5
Total U.S.	211	222	433
107th Congress, 2001			
State delegates	4	1	5
Total U.S.	211	221	432
108th Congress, 2003			
State delegates	4	1	5
Total U.S.	205	229	434
109th Congress, 2005			
State delegates	4	1	5
Total U.S.	202	231	433
110th Congress, 2007			
State delegates	4	1	5
Total U.S.	233	202	435
Senate			
101st Congress, 1989			
State delegates	0	2	2
Total U.S.	55	45	100
102d Congress, 1991			
State delegates	0	2	2
Total U.S.	56	44	100

(continued)

	Dem	Rep	Total
103d Congress, 1993			
State delegates	0	2	2
Total U.S.	57	43	100
104th Congress, 1995			
State delegates	1	1	2
Total U.S.	46	53	99
105th Congress, 1997			
State delegates	1	1	2
Total U.S.	45	55	100
106th Congress, 1999			
State delegates	1	1	2
Total U.S.	45	54	99
107th Congress, 2001			
State delegates	1	1	2
Total U.S.	50	50	100
108th Congress, 2003			
State delegates	1	1	2
Total U.S.	48	51	99
109th Congress, 2005			
State delegates	1	1	2
Total U.S.	44	55	99
110th Congress, 2007			
State delegates	1	1	2
Total U.S.	49	49	98

Figures are for starts of first sessions. Totals are for Democrat (Dem.) and Republican (Rep.) members only. House membership totals under 435 and Senate totals under 100 reflect vacancies and seats held by independent party members. When the 110th Congress opened, the Senate's two independent members caucused with the Democrats, giving the Democrats control of the Senate.

Source: U.S. Congress, *Congressional Directory.*

Composition of state legislature, 1990-2006

	Democrats	Republicans
State House (60 seats)		
1990	28	32
1992	28	32
1994	26	34
1996	29	31
1998	25	34
2000	25	35
2002	25	35
2004	27	33
2006	31	29
State Senate (30 seats)		
1990	20	10
1992	16	14
1994	11	19
1996	10	20
1998	13	17
2000	13	17
2002	14	15
2004	18	12
2006	17	11

Figures for total seats may include independents and minor party members. Numbers reflect results of elections in listed years; elected members usually take their seats in the years that follow.

Source: Council of State Governments; *State Elective Officials and the Legislatures.*

Voter participation in presidential elections, 2000 and 2004

	2000	2004
Voting age population		
State	2,583,000	2,742,000
Total United States	209,831,000	220,377,000
State share of U.S. total	1.23	1.24
Rank among states	27	27
Portion of voting age population casting votes		
State	59.4%	67.0%
United States	50.3%	55.5%
Rank among states	10	5

Population figures are rounded to nearest thousand and include all residents, regardless of eligibility to vote.

Source: U.S. Census Bureau.

HEALTH AND MEDICAL CARE

Medical professionals
Physicians in 2003 and nurses in 2001

	U.S.	State
Physicians in 2003		
Total	774,849	9,342
Share of U.S. total		1.20%
Rate	266	262
Rank		17
Nurses in 2001		
Total	2,262,020	26,040
Share of U.S. total		1.15%
Rate	793	750
Rank		38

Rates are numbers of physicians and nurses per 100,000 resident population; ranks are based on rates.
Source: American Medical Association, *Physician Characteristics and Distribution in the U.S.*; U.S. Department of Health and Human Services, Health Resources and Services Administration.

Health insurance coverage, 2003

	State	U.S.
Total persons covered	2,957,000	243,320,000
Total persons not covered	613,000	44,961,000
Portion not covered	17.2%	15.6%
Rank among states	14	—
Children not covered	113,000	8,373,000
Portion not covered	13.5%	11.4%
Rank among states	11	—

Totals are rounded to nearest thousand. Ranks are from the highest to the lowest percentages of persons *not* insured.
Source: U.S. Census Bureau, Current Population Reports.

AIDS, syphilis, and tuberculosis cases, 2003

Disease	U.S. cases	State cases	Rank
AIDS	44,232	242	27
Syphilis	34,270	118	32
Tuberculosis	14,874	106	32

Source: U.S. Centers for Disease Control and Prevention.

Cigarette smoking, 2003
Residents over age 18 who smoke

	U.S.	State	Rank
All smokers	22.1%	21.0%	35
Male smokers	24.8%	23.1%	32
Female smokers	20.3%	18.9%	35

Cigarette smokers are defined as persons who reported having smoked at least 100 cigarettes during their lifetimes and who currently smoked at least occasionally.
Source: U.S. Centers for Disease Control and Prevention, *Morbidity and Mortality Weekly Report*, 53, no. 44 (November 12, 2004).

HOUSING

Home ownership rates, 1985-2004

	1985	1990	1995	2000	2004
State	61.5%	64.4%	63.2%	65.3%	69.0%
Total U.S.	63.9%	63.9%	64.7%	67.4%	69.0%
Rank among states	41	37	40	42	38

Net change in state home ownership rate, 1985-2004 . . . . +7.5%
Net change in U.S. home ownership rate, 1985-2004 . . . . +5.1%

Percentages represent the proportion of owner households to total occupied households.
Source: U.S. Census Bureau, 2006.

Home sales, 2000-2004
In thousands of units

Existing home sales	2000	2002	2003	2004
State sales	62.6	72.1	78.3	90.7
Total U.S. sales	5,171	5,631	6,183	6,784
State share of U.S. total	1.21%	1.28%	1.27%	1.34%
Sales rank among states	28	27	28	27

Units include single-family homes, condos, and co-ops.
Source: National Association of Realtors, Washington, D.C., *Real Estate Outlook: Market Trends & Insights*.

Values of owner-occupied homes, 2003

	State	U.S.
Total units	709,000	58,809,000
Value of units		
Under $100,000	9.2%	29.6%
$100,000-199,999	54.7%	36.9%
$200,000 or more	36.1%	33.5%
Median value	$171,039	$142,275
Rank among all states 13		

Units are owner-occupied one-family houses whose numbers are rounded to nearest thousand. Data are extrapolated from survey samples.
Source: U.S. Census Bureau, American Community Survey.

EDUCATION

Public school enrollment, 2002

Prekindergarten through grade 8
State enrollment 382,000
Total U.S. enrollment. 34,135,000
State share of U.S. total 1.12%

Grades 9 through 12
State enrollment 172,000
Total U.S. enrollment. 14,067,000
State share of U.S. total 1.22%

Enrollment rates
State public school enrollment rate. 88.2%
Overall U.S. rate 90.4%
Rank among states in 2002. 36
Rank among states in 1995. 35

Enrollment figures (which include unclassified students) are rounded to nearest thousand pupils during fall school term. Enrollment rates are based on enumerated resident population estimate for July 1, 2002.
Source: U.S. National Center for Education Statistics.

Public college finances, 2003-2004

FTE enrollment in public institutions of higher education
Students in state institutions. 124,400
Students in all U.S. public institutions 9,916,600
State share of U.S. total 1.25
Rank among states 29

State and local government appropriations for higher education
State appropriation per FTE $4,772
National average. $5,716
Rank among states 38
State & local tax revenue going to higher education 6.8%

FTE = full-time equivalent in public postsecondary programs, including summer sessions; student numbers are rounded to nearest hundred. Funding figures for 2003-2004 academic year include financial aid to students in state public institutions and exclude money for research, agriculture experiment stations, teaching hospitals, and medical schools; figures are rounded to nearest thousand dollars.
Source: Higher Education Executive Officers, Denver, Colorado.

TRANSPORTATION AND TRAVEL

Highway mileage, 2003

Interstate highways	728
Other freeways and expressways.	53
Arterial roads	6,818
Collector roads.	17,503
Local roads.	40,849
Urban roads	11,067
Rural roads.	54,884
Total state mileage.	65,951
U.S. total	3,974,107
State share	1.66%
Rank among states	31

Note that combined urban and rural road mileage matches the total of the other categories.
Source: U.S. Federal Highway Administration.

Motor vehicle registrations and driver licenses, 2003

Vehicle registrations	*State*	*U.S.*	*Share*	*Rank*
Autos, trucks, buses	3,061,000	231,390,000	1.32%	28
Autos only	1,545,000	135,670	1.14%	29
Motorcycles	75,000	5,328,000	1.41%	20
Driver licenses	2,590,000	196,166,000	1.32%	28

Figures, which do not include vehicles owned by military services, are rounded to the nearest thousand. Figures for automobiles include taxis.
Source: U.S. Federal Highway Administration.

Domestic travel expenditures, 2003

Spending by U.S. residents on overnight trips and
day trips of at least 50 miles from home

Total expenditures within state . . . . $5.56 bill.
Total expenditures within U.S. . . . . $490.87 bill.
State share of U.S. total 1.1%
Rank among states 28

Source: Travel Industry Association of America.

Retail gasoline prices, 2003-2007

Average price per gallon at the pump

Year	U.S.	State
2003	$1.267	$1.442
2004	$1.316	$1.385
2005	$1.644	$1.717
2007	$2.298	$2.525

Excise tax per gallon in 2004 . . . . 24.0¢
Rank among all states in 2007 prices 5

Prices are averages of all grades of gasoline sold at the pump
during March months in 2003-2005 and during February, 2007.
Averages for 2006, during which prices rose higher, are not
available.
Source: U.S. Energy Information Agency, *Petroleum Marketing
Monthly* (2003-2005 data); American Automobile Association
(2007 data).

CRIME AND LAW ENFORCEMENT

State and local police officers, 2000-2004

	2000	2002	2004
Total officers			
U.S.	654,601	665,555	675,734
State	5,584	5,617	4,920*
*Net change, 2000-2004			−1.89%
Officers per 1,000 residents			
U.S.	2.33	2.31	2.30
State	1.63	1.60	1.37
State rank	44	48	50

Totals include state and local police and sheriffs.
Source: Carsey Institute, University of New Hampshire.

Crime rates, 2003

Incidents per 100,000 residents

Crimes	State	U.S.
Violent crimes		
Total incidents	296	475
Murder	2	6
Forcible rape	34	32
Robbery	80	142
Aggravated assault	179	295
Property crimes		
Total incidents	4,782	3,588
Burglary	804	741
Larceny/theft	3,445	2,415
Motor vehicle theft	534	433
All crimes	5,078	4,063

Source: U.S. Federal Bureau of Investigation, *Crime in the United
States,* annual.

State prison populations, 1980-2003

	State	U.S.	State share
1980	3,177	305,458	1.04%
1990	6,492	708,393	0.92%
1996	8,661	1,025,624	0.84%
2000	10,580	1,391,261	0.76%
2003	12,715	1,470,045	0.86%

State figures exclude prisoners in federal penitentiaries.
Source: U.S. Bureau of Justice Statistics, *Prisoners in 2003.*

Pennsylvania

Location: Northeast

Area and rank: 44,820 square miles (116,083 square kilometers); 46,058 square miles (119,290 square kilometers) including water; thirty-second largest state in area

Shoreline: 89 miles (143 kilometers) on the Delaware River

Population and rank: 12,406,000 (2004); sixth largest state in population

Capital city: Harrisburg (48,950 people in 2000 census)

Largest city: Philadelphia (1,517,550 people in 2000 census)

Entered Union and rank: December 12, 1787; second state

Present constitution adopted: 1968

Counties: 67

State name: Meaning "Penn's Woodland," Pennsylvania was named for Admiral Sir William Penn, the father of William Penn, who founded the state's first English colony

Long dismissed as a gritty industrial city, Pittsburgh now has one of the most attractive city centers in the United States. Point State Park, pictured here, marks the confluence of the Allegheny (upper left) and Monongahela (right) rivers, which join to form the Ohio River (lower left). (Bobak Ha 'Eri)

State nickname: Keystone State

Motto: Virtue, liberty, and independence

State flag: Blue field with state coat of arms

Highest point: Mount Davis—3,213 feet (979 meters)

Lowest point: Delaware River—sea level

Highest recorded temperature: 111 degrees Fahrenheit (44 degrees Celsius)—Phoenixville, 1936

Lowest recorded temperature: −42 degrees Fahrenheit (−41 degrees Celsius)—Smethport, 1904

State song: "Pennsylvania"

State tree: Hemlock

State flower: Mountain laurel

State bird: Ruffed grouse

Pennsylvania History

Even though Pennsylvania is located in the northeastern part of the United States and is called a mid-Atlantic state, it is not on the Atlantic Ocean, as are Delaware, New Jersey, and New York. It has access to the Atlantic Ocean's important shipping routes from the Delaware River, which marks Pennsylvania's eastern boundary. New York is east and north of it, New Jersey east, and Delaware east and south. Maryland borders it to the south, and West Virginia lies both south and west of it. Its western boundary is eastern Ohio.

Located in the middle the original thirteen colonies, Pennsylvania is known as the Keystone State. The state is quite mountainous, with the Appalachian Mountains running through much of it. In the east are the Pocono Mountains and to the south the Blue Ridge. These mountains have more than two hundred lakes, the largest of which is Lake Wallenpaupack in northeastern Pennsylvania, between Milford and Scranton.

Early History. Humans lived in Pennsylvania as much as twelve thousand years ago, probably drawn there by its network of rivers. Besides the Delaware, Susquehanna, Schuylkill, and Lackawanna Rivers in the east, the Monongahela, Ohio, Juniata, and Allegheny Rivers run through the western part of the state. The northwestern section of Pennsylvania borders on Lake Erie, one of the five Great Lakes. These waterways afforded the earliest settlers mobility, food, and water.

Among the people who originally inhabited the area were Algonquian, Delaware, Erie, Lenape, Monongahela, and Susquehannock Indians. The state's Native American peoples during the 1990's of about fourteen thousand were mostly descendants of the Algonquians.

The first Europeans in the area were led by Dutch explorers Cornelius Mey, who sailed into the Delaware River in 1614. By 1638, Swedish immigrants had built the first European settlement, New Sweden, establishing Fort New Gothenburg on Tinicum Island south of present-day Philadelphia. The Dutch captured New Sweden in 1655. In 1664, the British took it from the Dutch. Shortly thereafter, in 1681, King Charles II of England granted William Penn's father the area which today is Pennsylvania. The following year, William Penn, Jr., founded the Pennsylvania colony and the city of Philadelphia, after making peace with the American Indians who lived in the region.

As modern as this Amish farm near Lancaster, Pennsylvania, appears to be, it lacks such modern advances as electricity. (©Commonwealth Media Services)

The Importance of Philadelphia. Pennsylvania lay midway between the New England colonies and those in the south. When official business was to be transacted, Philadelphia, a well-developed colonial city, was the logical meeting place. Benjamin Franklin had settled there in 1723 and established a library in 1731. The State House, later renamed Independence Hall, provided a good venue for delegates from the other colonies. Its famed bell, later known as the Liberty Bell, was placed in its tower in 1753.

England was engaged in war against France during the period immediately before the Revolutionary War. To finance the war, the English raised the colonies' taxes. The outcry against taxation without representation became strident. Beginning in 1774, the leaders of the thirteen original colonies met in Philadelphia. In 1775, they named George Washington to head the Continental army, and on July 4, 1776, they approved the Declaration of Independence, which was read publicly four days later.

In effect, this declaration began England's war against the colonies. Although they were clearly the underdogs in this conflict, the colonists ultimately prevailed. England surrendered in 1781 and signed a peace treaty in 1783. A Constitutional Convention was called and met in Philadelphia in 1787, out of which the United States Constitution, ratified on December 12, 1787, evolved. Pennsylvania became the second of the United States. Philadelphia, because of its central location, was the capital of the country from 1790 to 1800.

Pennsylvania's Growth. From 1732, although England laid claim to the whole of Pennsylvania, the French were building forts in the western part of Penn's land grant. Conflicts over the ownership of western Pennsylvania resulted in a war between England and France, and it was the financing of this war that led indirectly to the Revolutionary War.

By 1763 England controlled all of Pennsylvania. The English raised Fort Pitt beside the Monongahela River, where modern Pittsburgh stands. This area, because of its geographical isolation, was slower to develop than the eastern region of Penn's grant, but its rivers and Lake Erie provided it with the potential to grow quickly.

The Pennsylvania colony was quite progressive. It had a circulating library as early as 1731 and a volunteer fire department by 1736. The first hospital in the colonies opened in Philadelphia in 1751. With the discovery of bituminous coal near Pittsburgh in 1759 and anthracite coal in the Wyoming Valley in 1762, ready sources of power became available. This, combined with navigable waterways throughout the state, led to rapid development. The state decreed in 1780 that no black person born in Pennsylvania would be a slave. It remained a free state throughout its existence.

By 1812 steamboats transported people and goods down the Ohio River. Canals and roads were being built. In 1829, the state's first commercial railroad was functioning. The state became a trading center. In 1859, the first commercially successful oil well in the United States was drilled at Titusville in western Pennsylvania.

With plentiful oil, coal, and iron ore available in the western part of the state, it was clear that steel manufacturing would become a major enterprise in and around Pittsburgh, where the first steel mill was established in

Philadelphia's population of more than 1.5 million people makes it larger than Pennsylvania's next twenty-five largest cities combined. (PhotoDisc)

1873. Later the Bethlehem Steel Company was established in the eastern part of the state.

The Civil War. A free state since its inception, Pennsylvania was a staunch supporter of the Union during the Civil War. Many towns in the state had, since the early ninteenth century, been significant way stations along the Underground Railroad, an informal complex of safe havens for slaves escaping from the South and heading to either New England or Canada. Safe houses throughout Pennsylvania offered shelter and food to runaway slaves.

Following President Abraham Lincoln's call for volunteers to fight in the war, Pennsylvanians, in two weeks, created twenty-five regiments to fight against the Confederate forces. A total of more than 340,000 men from Pennsylvania served in the Union forces between 1861 and 1865.

General Robert E. Lee's army invaded Pennsylvania in 1863. As Lee made his incursions into the state, the Army of the Potomac stood between his army and Washington, D.C., in an attempt to protect the nation's capital. On July 1, 1863, the two armies met outside Gettysburg in the southern part of the state and, for three days, engaged in the bloodiest battle of the Civil War, leaving more than fifty thousand dead or wounded soldiers on the battlefield. This battle was the turning point in the war, although before it ended, Confederate forces attacked Chambersburg in July, 1864.

Pennsylvania's People. Most Pennsylvanians are descendants of early settlers from Europe. More than 70 percent of all Pennsylvanians live in cities, chief among them Philadelphia, Pittsburgh, Allentown, Easton, Bethlehem, Scranton, Lancaster, Williamsport, Erie, and Harrisburg, the state's capital since 1812. Nearly four million Pennsylvanians live on farms or in small towns, giving the state the largest rural population in the nation.

The earliest European settlers were from Germany, France, the Netherlands, Scandinavia, and Britain. Immigrants from Ireland arrived during the 1840's. During the 1880's, people began arriving in large numbers from central Europe, notably Czechoslovakia, Poland, and Russia.

Unique among Pennsylvanians are the Pennsylvania Dutch, German immigrants who live mostly in Lancaster County. These Amish farmers lead simple lives, eschewing electricity, telephones, and automobiles.

About 9 percent of Pennsylvanians are of African American descent. Some lived there as free men before the Civil War, but many flooded into Pennsylvania after the war and again during World Wars I and II, when the defense industries offered them ready work.

The Pennsylvania Economy. About four million Pennsylvanians work in such service industries as banking, insurance, and retail. John Wanamaker established the first American department store in Philadelphia in 1876, mostly to serve visitors to the United States Centennial Exposition, which was held in Philadelphia's Fairmount Park.

Manufacturing industries, mainly of steel, food products, and chemicals, employ almost one million people. Another hundred thousand work on farms. Mining, which was once a major industry, now, because of mechanization, employs around twenty thousand miners. Philadelphia, Pittsburgh, and Erie are thriving ports that employ many people, and Hershey has the world's largest chocolate factory. Tourism, which brings in ten billion dollars annually, also contributes significantly to the state's economy.

Dairy products are the leading farm product. The state's leading agricultural crop is mushrooms. Pennsylvania also has a large timber industry that produces wood for building.

Politics. Following 1999, Pennsylvania politics was almost evenly split between the two major parties. In the 2000 election, the state's twenty-three electoral votes went to Vice President Al Gore by a 51-47 percent margin. On the other hand, Senator Rick Santorum, a right-of-center politician, was reelected by a 53-46 percent majority, and both new members of Congress were Republicans. A year later, on September 20, 2001, the state lost its Republican governor, Tom Ridge, who was tapped by President George W. Bush to be director of Homeland Security after the September 11 terrorist attacks. In 2002, Pennsylvania's statehouse was won by a Democrat, Ed Rendell, the former mayor of Philadelphia.

In 2004, Pennsylvania voted its twenty-one electoral votes for Senator John Kerry by a 51-40 percent margin. It also reelected Republican Arlen Specter to the U.S. Senate and sent seven Democrats and twelve Republicans to the House. A Republican suit to block the counting of Philadelphia's twelve thousand absentee ballots was successful but became moot after Bush was elected president.

9/11 Crash. On September 11, 2001, Pennsylvania became the site of a tragedy when United Airlines Flight 93, which had been hijacked by terrorists, crashed into a field near Shanksville in southwestern Somerset County, killing all on board. Parts and debris were found scattered up to eight miles from the crash site. The local community soon established a tempo-

Architect Frank Lloyd Wright's Fallingwater house in Fayette County, Pennsylvania, is one of North America's most famous examples of residential architectural design. (©Commonwealth Media Services/Terry Way)

rary memorial at the crash site. The mining company that owned the field later sold it, and a professionally designed permanent memorial, superintended by the National Park Service, was planned.

New Concert Hall. Later in 2001, the state's cultural life gained a fine new facility when the $65 million Kimmel Center for the Performing Arts opened in Philadelphia, after twenty years of planning and construction. In December, the 2,500-seat concert hall became the new home of world-renowned Philadelphia Orchestra, often placed among the world's four best symphony orchestras, with more than three hundred concerts and other presentations a year. In 2003, Christoph Eschenbach took up the helm as the orchestra's seventh music director in its then-103-year history.

Mine Rescue. In 2002, an event captivated the nation. Near the southwest Pennsylvania town of Quecreek (ten miles from the Shanksville crash site), nine coal miners became trapped for nearly eighty hours in a chamber 240 feet underground. Several human-led rescue attempts, as well as the use of drilling equipment, failed, and fears grew that the men might drown. On July 28, however, a national television audience watched as rescuers, who had to guess where the men were trapped, pulled the miners from the chamber through a thirty-inch-wide hole. The mining company was blamed for the accident and in 2004 was fined $14,100 for maintaining inaccurate maps.

R. Baird Shuman
Updated by the Editor

Pennsylvania Time Line

1614	Dutch explorer Cornelius Mey sails up the Delaware River.
1615	French explorer Etienne Brule sails the Susquehanna River from its source to its mouth.
1616	Dutch explorer Cornelius Hendrickson sails up the Delaware to the Schuylkill.
1638	Swedish settlers found New Sweden on the Delaware River.
1655	Dutch forces from New Netherland (New York) take possession of New Sweden.
1664	British forces overwhelm Dutch, driving them from Pennsylvania.
Mar. 4, 1681	King Charles II of England gives 45,000 square miles of Pennsylvania to Admiral William Penn.
1682	William Penn, Jr., founds the colony of Pennsylvania.
Mar. 19, 1683	First Pennsylvania Assembly meets in Philadelphia and enacts Penn's Charter of Liberties, an early constitution.
1723	Benjamin Franklin, age seventeen, arrives in Philadelphia.
1731	First colonial circulating library is opened by Benjamin Franklin.
1732	Benjamin Franklin publishes first issue of *Poor Richard's Almanac.*
1751	Benjamin Rush establishes the first colonial hospital, in Philadelphia.
1753	Liberty Bell placed in State House tower.
1754	General George Washington builds Fort Necessity near Uniontown.
1759	British build Fort Pitt at Pittsburgh.
1759	Bituminous coal found in western Pennsylvania.
1762	Anthracite coal found in the Wyoming Valley of northeastern Pennsylvania.
1767	Mason-Dixon line sets boundary between Pennsylvania and Maryland, essentially the boundary between North and South.
1768	Pennsylvania Assembly renounces British imposition of taxation without representation.
Sept. 5, 1774	First Continental Congress meets in Philadelphia.
1775	Second Continental Congress meets in Philadelphia, names George Washington commander of the Continental army.
July 4, 1776	Declaration of Independence is adopted.
1776	Washington defeats the British at Trenton.
1777	British occupy Philadelphia, defeat Continental army at Germantown.
1777	Washington's Continental army winters at Valley Forge.
1778	British leave Philadelphia, intimidated by Washington's regenerated army.
1780	Pennsylvania declares that no black person born in the state shall be a slave.
Dec. 12, 1787	Pennsylvania ratifies the Constitution during the Constitutional Convention and joins the Union as the second state.
1792	U.S. Mint is established in Philadelphia.
1792	Purchase of the Erie Triangle completes Pennsylvania's boundaries.

1800	U.S. capital moved from Philadelphia to Washington, D.C.
1812	Harrisburg becomes state capital.
1829	First commercial railway in state begins operation.
1857	Pennsylvanian James Buchanan becomes fifteenth president of the United States.
Aug. 2, 1859	First discovery of oil in United States at Titusville.
July 1-3, 1863	Battle of Gettysburg marks turning point in Civil War.
1873	Andrew Carnegie opens first steel mill in Pittsburgh.
May 31, 1889	Johnstown flood kills 2,200 people.
Jan. 1, 1901	Philadelphia holds first annual Mummers' Parade.
1920	First public radio broadcast in the United States is made by KDKA in Pittsburgh.
1951	Pennsylvania Turnpike, running from Philadelphia to the Ohio border, is completed.
1957	First nuclear power plant in the United States opens at Shippingport.
1967	Long, violent steelworkers strike disrupts state's economy.
1968	Pennsylvania adopts new state constitution.
June, 1972	Hurricane Agnes devastates eastern Pennsylvania.
Mar. 28, 1979	Dangerous nuclear accident occurs at Three Mile Island, near Harrisburg.
1984	W. Wilson Goode is elected Philadelphia's first black mayor.
1988	Collapse of oil storage tank south of Pittsburgh spills a million gallons of diesel oil into the Monongahela and Ohio Rivers.
Nov. 18, 1989	Pennsylvania is first state to pass law restricting abortion.
1998	Democrats and Republicans in Pennsylvania's legislature pass bill to make it difficult for third-party candidates to get on ballot; Governor Tom Ridge vetoes the bill.
Sept. 11, 2001	Commercial jetliner hijacked by terrorists crashes in a field near Shanksville, Somerset County.
Sept. 20, 2001	Governor Tom Ridge leaves office to become head to the newly formed Office of Homeland Security in Washington.
Dec. 15, 2001	Philadelphia Orchestra gives its first concert in the new Kimmel Center for the Performing Arts in Philadelphia.
July 28, 2002	Nine coal miners are rescued from an underground chamber where they were trapped for eighty hours.
Nov. 2, 2002	Former Philadelphia mayor Ed Rendell is elected governor.
Aug. 14-15, 2003	Pennsylvania is one of eight states in which millions experience a power blackout.

Notes for Further Study

Published Sources. A solid overall history of Pennsylvania is Dennis B. Downey and Francis J. Bremer's *A Guide to the History of Pennsylvania* (1993). Also informative are P. S. Klein and Ari Hoogenboom's *A History of Pennsylvania* (1980) and T. C. Cochran's *Pennsylvania: A Bicentennial History* (1978). *Pennsylvania: A History of the Commonwealth* (2002), edited by Randall M. Miller and William Pencak, chronicles the political, cultural, and economic developments that have shaped the state.

Richard Ammon's *Growing up Amish* (1989) presents an inside view of the Pennsylvania Dutch in Lancaster County. Charles L. Blockson's *The Underground Railroad in Pennsylvania* (1981) provides a fascinating account of how Pennsylvanians helped slaves escape from the South. Two provocative books, Gary B. Nash's *Freedom by Degrees: Emancipation in Pennsylvania and Its Aftermath* (1991) and Edward Raymond Turner's *The Negro in Pennsylvania: Slavery, Servitude, Freedom, 1639-1861* (1969), focus on the slavery question, emancipation, and Pennsylvania's role in dealing with runaway slaves. *African Americans in Pennsylvania: Above Ground and Underground* (2001) by Charles L. Blockson explores sites significant to the African American experience in Pennsylvania and includes maps with highlighted events from each part of the state.

James T. Lemon's *The Best Poor Man's Country: A Geographical Study of Early Southeastern Pennsylvania* (1972) and R. Eugene Harper's *The Transformation of Western Pennsylvania, 1770-1800* (1991) present contrasting views of the settlements of the two major portions of Pennsylvania, the east, dominated by Philadelphia and the west, dominated by Pittsburgh. John Bodnar's *Steelton: Immigration and Industrialization* (1990) discusses the growth of the steel industry in western Pennsylvania and the people who came to that part of the state to work. Gerald G. Eggert's *Harrisburg Industrializes: The Coming of Factories to an American Community* (1993) shows how the state's capital, in need of industrial development, achieved its ends. In *The Face of Decline: The Pennsylvania Anthracite Region in the Twentieth Century* (2005), Thomas Dublin and Walter Licht focus on the varied impact of economic decline across generations of mining families by using oral histories and survey questionnaires, documentary photographs, and community newspapers, among other sources.

An interesting twist on the tourist guidebook is Lorett Treese's *Railroads of Pennsylvania: Fragments of the Past in the Keystone Landscape* (2003). Because of its geography, Pennsylvania was very important in the pioneering of railroads, and Treese seeks out traces of these early railroads in order to cover each of the state's tourism regions. Directed toward juvenile readers are Craig A. Doherty and Katharine M. Doherty's *Pennsylvania* (2005), part of the Thirteen Colonies series, and *Pennsylvania* (2004) by Roberta Wiener and James R. Arnold, which should appeal to teenage readers.

Web Resources. The state of Pennsylvania Web site (www.state.pa.us/) and the official state tourism site (www.visitpa.com/visitpa/home.pa) are the best starting places for information about the state. The *Philadelphia Inquirer* (www.philly.com/mld/inquirer/) online is a good destination for contemporary events and issues affecting the state. A thorough description of the state's history can be found at a site spon-sored by the state legislature (www.legis.state.pa.us/WU01/VC/visitor_info/pa_history/pa_history.htm). Find links and information about historical societies and museums on the Pennsylvania Historical and Museum Commission site (www.phmc.state.pa.us/). Explore PA History (www.explorepahistory.com/) is also an attractive and useful site.

Information about tourist attractions in Gettysburg, including comprehensive data about the famed Civil War battleground, is available on two Gettysburg Web sites (www.gettysburgguide.com and www.gettysburg.com). The best overall Web sites for individual cities or areas are those of Pittsburgh (www.pghguide.com), Philadelphia (www.philanet.com), and Lancaster County (www.co.lancaster.pa.us). The Wow Works site provides links to states' city, county, and regional Web sites; Pennsylvania's can be found at www.wowworks.com/wowcity/pa.htm.

Counties

County	2000 pop.	Rank in pop.	Sq. miles	Rank in area	County	2000 pop.	Rank in pop.	Sq. miles	Rank in area
Adams	91,292	33	520.1	45	Lancaster	470,658	6	949.1	12
Allegheny	1,281,666	2	730.2	29	Lawrence	94,643	31	360.5	61
Armstrong	72,392	38	654.0	35	Lebanon	120,327	28	361.8	60
Beaver	181,412	19	435.3	52	Lehigh	312,090	12	346.7	62
Bedford	49,984	43	1,014.6	9	Luzerne	319,250	11	891.0	14
Berks	373,638	9	859.2	18	Lycoming	120,044	30	1,234.9	1
Blair	129,144	27	525.8	43	McKean	45,936	47	981.6	11
Bradford	62,761	40	1,150.7	2	Mercer	120,293	29	671.9	33
Bucks	597,635	4	607.6	36	Mifflin	46,486	45	410.7	54
Butler	174,083	20	788.6	25	Monroe	138,687	24	607.3	37
Cambria	152,598	21	688.1	31	Montgomery	750,097	3	483.1	47
Cameron	5,974	66	397.2	56	Montour	18,236	62	130.8	67
Carbon	58,802	41	382.6	58	Northampton	267,066	14	373.9	59
Centre	135,758	25	1,107.6	5	Northumberland	94,556	32	459.9	48
Chester	433,501	7	756.0	28	Perry	43,602	51	553.6	40
Clarion	41,765	53	602.5	38	Philadelphia	1,517,550	1	135.1	66
Clearfield	83,382	36	1,147.4	3	Pike	46,302	46	547.1	42
Clinton	37,914	57	890.9	15	Potter	18,080	63	1,081.2	6
Columbia	64,151	39	485.6	46	Schuylkill	150,336	22	778.6	26
Crawford	90,366	34	1,012.9	10	Snyder	37,546	58	331.2	63
Cumberland	213,674	16	550.2	41	Somerset	80,023	37	1,074.8	7
Dauphin	251,798	15	525.3	44	Sullivan	6,556	65	450.0	50
Delaware	550,864	5	184.2	65	Susquehanna	42,238	52	823.0	22
Elk	35,112	59	828.7	21	Tioga	41,373	55	1,133.8	4
Erie	280,843	13	802.0	23	Union	41,624	54	316.8	64
Fayette	148,644	23	790.1	24	Venango	57,565	42	675.1	32
Forest	4,946	67	428.1	53	Warren	43,863	50	883.5	16
Franklin	129,313	26	772.0	27	Washington	202,897	18	857.1	19
Fulton	14,261	64	437.6	51	Wayne	47,722	44	729.4	30
Greene	40,672	56	575.9	39	Westmoreland	369,993	10	1,022.6	8
Huntingdon	45,586	49	875.4	17	Wyoming	28,080	60	397.2	55
Indiana	89,605	35	829.5	20	York	381,751	8	904.6	13
Jefferson	45,932	48	655.5	34					
Juniata	22,821	61	391.6	57					
Lackawanna	213,295	17	458.8	49					

Source: U.S. Census Bureau; National Association of Counties.

Cities

With 10,000 or more residents

Rank	City	Population	Rank	City	Population
1	Philadelphia	1,517,550	29	New Castle	26,309
2	Pittsburgh	334,563	30	Easton	26,263
3	Allentown	106,632	31	Lebanon	24,461
4	Erie	103,717	32	McKeesport	24,040
5	Reading	81,207	33	Johnstown	23,906
6	Scranton	76,415	34	Springfield	23,677
7	Bethlehem	71,329	35	Hazleton	23,329
8	Lancaster	56,348	36	West Mifflin	22,464
9	Levittown	53,966	37	Pottstown	21,859
10	Altoona	49,523	38	Upper St. Clair	20,053
11	Harrisburg (capital)	48,950	39	Baldwin	19,999
12	Penn Hills	46,809	40	Wilkinsburg	19,196
13	Wilkes-Barre	43,123	41	Municipality of Murrysville	18,872
14	York	40,862	42	King of Prussia	18,511
15	State College	38,420	43	Carlisle	17,970
16	Chester	36,854	44	Chambersburg	17,862
17	Bethel Park	33,556	45	West Chester	17,861
18	Mount Lebanon	33,017	46	Hampton Township	17,526
19	Ross Township	32,551	47	Scott Township	17,288
20	Norristown	31,282	48	Sharon	16,328
21	Radnor Township	30,878	49	Willow Grove	16,234
22	Williamsport	30,706	50	Hermitage	16,157
23	Shaler Township	29,757	51	Lansdale	16,071
24	Drexel Hill	29,364	52	Greensburg	15,889
25	Municipality of Monroeville	29,349	53	Pottsville	15,549
26	McCandless Township	29,022	54	Mountain Top	15,269
27	Plum	26,940	55	Washington	15,268
28	Back Mountain	26,690	56	Butler	15,121

(continued)

Rank	City	Population
57	West Norriton	14,901
58	Indiana	14,895
59	Phoenixville	14,788
60	Horsham	14,779
61	New Kensington	14,701
62	Hanover	14,535
63	St. Marys	14,502
64	Whitehall	14,444
65	South Park Township	14,340
66	Fullerton	14,268
67	Dunmore	14,018
68	Kingston	13,855
69	Meadville	13,685
70	Nether Providence Township	13,456
71	Colonial Park	13,259
72	Ephrata	13,213
73	East Norriton	13,211
74	Hershey	12,771
75	Ardmore	12,616
76	Lower Burrell	12,608
77	Uniontown	12,422
78	Bloomsburg	12,375
79	Robinson Township	12,289
80	Munhall	12,264
81	Fernway	12,188
82	Montgomeryville	12,031
83	Elizabethtown	11,887

Rank	City	Population
84	Yeadon	11,762
85	Aliquippa	11,734
86	Oil City	11,504
87	Franklin Park	11,364
88	Emmaus	11,313
89	North Versailles	11,125
90	Broomall	11,046
91	Lansdowne	11,044
92	Nanticoke	10,955
93	Harrison Township	10,934
94	Coatesville	10,838
95	Berwick	10,774
96	Jeannette	10,654
97	Carnot-Moon	10,637
98	Sunbury	10,610
99	Upper Providence Township	10,509
100	Brentwood	10,466
101	Columbia	10,311
102	Darby	10,299
103	Warren	10,259
104	Shiloh	10,192
105	Weigelstown	10,117
106	Woodlyn	10,036
107	Morrisville	10,023

Population figures are from 2000 census.
Source: U.S. Bureau of the Census.

Index to Tables

DEMOGRAPHICS

Resident state and national populations, 1970-2004

Population figures given in thousands

	State pop.	U.S. pop.	Share	Rank
1970	11,801	203,302	5.8%	3
1980	11,864	226,546	5.2%	4
1985	11,771	237,924	5.0%	4
1990	11,883	248,765	4.8%	5
1995	12,198	262,761	4.6%	5
2000	12,281	281,425	4.4%	6
2004	12,406	293,655	4.2%	6

Source: U.S. Census Bureau, Current Population Reports, 2006.

Resident population by age, 2004

Age Group	Total persons
Under 5 years	719,000
5 to 17 years	2,118,000
18 to 24 years	1,185,000
25 to 34 years	1,471,000
35 to 44 years	1,823,000
45 to 54 years	1,869,000
55 to 64 years	1,325,000
65 to 74 years	864,000
75 to 84 years	742,000
85 years and older	291,000
All age groups	12,406,000

Portion of residents 65 and older	15.3%
National rank in portion of oldest residents	2
National average	12.4%

Population figures are rounded to nearest thousand persons; figures include armed forces personnel stationed in the state.
Source: U.S. Bureau of the Census, 2006.

Resident population by race, Hispanic origin, 2004

Category	State pop.	Share	U.S.
All residents	12,406	100.00%	100.00%
Non-Hispanic white	10,288	82.93%	67.37%
Hispanic white	405	3.26%	13.01%
Other Hispanic	71	0.57%	1.06%
African American	1,304	10.51%	12.77%
Native American	22	0.18%	0.96%
Asian, Pacific Islander	272	2.19%	4.37%
Two or more categories	115	0.93%	1.51%

Population figures are in thousands. Persons counted as "Hispanic" (Latino) may be of any race. Because of overlapping categories, categories may not add up to 100%. Shares in column 3 are percentages of each category within the state; these figures may be compared to the national percentages in column 4.
Source: U.S. Bureau of the Census, 2006.

Projected state population, 2000-2030

Year	Population
2000	12,281,000
2005	12,427,000
2010	12,584,000
2015	12,711,000
2020	12,787,000
2025	12,802,000
2030	12,768,000
Population increase, 2000-2030	487,000
Percentage increase, 2000-2030	4.0

Projections are based on data from the 2000 census.
Source: U.S. Census Bureau.

VITAL STATISTICS

Infant mortality rates, 1980-2002

	1980	1990	2000	2002
All state residents	13.2	9.6	7.1	7.6
All U.S. residents	12.6	9.2	9.4	9.1
All state white residents	11.9	7.4	5.8	6.6
All U.S. white residents	10.6	7.6	5.7	5.8
All state black residents	23.1	20.5	15.7	15.1
All U.S. black residents	22.2	18.0	14.1	14.4

Figures represent deaths per 1,000 live births of resident infants under 1 year old, exclusive of fetal deaths. Figures for all residents include members of other racial categories not listed separately.
Source: U.S. Census Bureau, *Statistical Abstract of the United States*, 2006.

Abortion rates, 1990 and 2000

	1990	2000
Total abortions	50,000	37,000
Rate per 1,000 women	18.6	14.3
U.S. rate	25.7	21.3
Rank	25	26

Numbers of abortions are rounded to nearest thousand; ranks are based on rates.
Source: U.S. Census Bureau.

Marriages and divorces, 2004

Total marriages	65,100
Rate per 1,000 population	5.3
National rate per 1,000 population	7.4
Rank among all states	48
Total divorces	30,700
Rate per 1,000 population	2.5
National rate per 1,000 population	3.7
Rank among all states	43

Figures are for all marriages and divorces performed within the state, including those of nonresidents; totals are rounded to the nearest hundred. Ranks are for highest to lowest figures; note that divorce data are not available for five states.
Source: U.S. National Center for Health Statistics, *Vital Statistics of the United States*, 2006.

Death rates by leading causes, 2002
Deaths per 100,000 resident population

Cause	State	U.S.
Heart disease	315.0	241.7
Cancer	242.0	193.2
Cerebrovascular diseases	69.5	56.4
Accidents other than motor vehicle	38.3	37.0
Motor vehicle accidents	14.1	15.7
Chronic lower respiratory diseases	48.8	43.3
Diabetes mellitus	30.1	25.4
HIV	4.0	4.9
Suicide	10.9	11.0
Homicide	5.2	6.1
All causes	1,055.7	847.3
Rank in overall death rate among states		2

Figures exclude nonresidents who died in the state. Causes of death follow International Classification of Diseases. Rank is from highest to lowest death rate in the United States.
Source: U.S. National Center for Health Statistics, *National Vital Statistics Report*, 2006.

ECONOMY

Gross state product, 1990-2004
In current dollars

Year	State product	Nat'l product	State share
1990	$248.3 billion	$5.67 trillion	4.38%
2000	$391.5 billion	$9.75 trillion	4.02%
2002	$424.8 billion	$10.41 trillion	4.08%
2003	$443.7 billion	$10.92 trillion	4.06%
2004	$468.8 billion	$11.65 trillion	4.02%

Source: U.S. Bureau of Economic Analysis, *Survey of Current Business,* July, 2005.

Gross state product by industry, 2003
In billions of dollars

Construction	$16.3
Manufacturing	72.2
Wholesale trade	24.2
Retail trade	31.7
Finance & insurance	31.0
Information	17.2
Professional services	27.9
Health care & social assistance	34.7
Government	38.4
Total state product	$415.3
Total U.S. product	$10,289.2
State share of U.S. total	4.04%
Rank among all states	6

Total figures include industries not listed separately. Amounts are in chained 2000 dollars.
Source: U.S. Bureau of Economic Analysis, *Survey of Current Business,* July, 2005.

Personal income per capita, 1990-2004
In current dollars

	1990	2000	2004
Per capita income	$19,687	$29,695	$33,348
U.S. average	$19,477	$29,845	$32,937
Rank among states	17	16	18

Source: U.S. Bureau of Economic Analysis, *Survey of Current Business,* April, 2005.

Energy consumption, 2001
In trillions of British thermal units (BTU), except as noted

Total energy consumption
Total state energy consumption	3,923
Total U.S. energy consumption	96,275
State share of U.S. total	4.07%
Rank among states	6

Per capita consumption (In millions of BTU)
Total state per capita consumption	319
Total U.S. per capita consumption	338
Rank among states	31

End-use sectors
Residential	931
Commercial	709
Industrial	1,286
Transportation	997

Sources of energy
Petroleum	1,454
Natural gas	669
Coal	1,379
Hydroelectric power	11
Nuclear electric power	770

Figures for totals include categories not listed separately.
Source: U.S. Energy Information Administration, *State Energy Data Report,* 2001.

Nonfarm employment by sectors, 2004

Total persons	5,640,000
Construction	248,000
Manufacturing	691,000
Trade, transportation, utilities	1,121,000
Information	112,000
Finance, insurance, real estate	336,000
Professional & business services	633,000
Education & health services	996,000
Leisure, hospitality, arts, organizations	476,000
Other services, including repair & maintenance	263,000
Government	745,000

Figures are rounded to nearest thousand persons. "Total" includes mining and natural resources, not listed separately.
Source: U.S. Bureau of Labor Statistics, 2006.

Foreign exports, 1990-2004
In millions of dollars

Year	State	U.S.	State share
1990	8,491	394,045	2.15%
1996	14,364	624,767	2.30%
1997	16,069	688,896	2.33%
2000	18,792	712,055	2.40%
2003	16,299	724,006	2.41%
2004	18,487	769,332	2.40%
Rank among all states in 2004 14			

U.S. total does not include U.S. dependencies.
Source: U.S. Census Bureau, *U.S. Merchandise Trade,* series FT 900, 2000; U.S. Census Bureau, *U.S. International Trade in Goods and Services,* Series FT 900, 2005.

LAND USE

Federally owned land, 2003
Areas in acres

	State	U.S.	State share
Total area	28,804,000	2,271,343,000	1.27%
Nonfederal land	28,080,000	1,599,584,000	1.76%
Federal land	724,000	671,759,000	0.11%
Federal share	2.5%	29.6%	—

Areas are rounded to nearest thousand acres. Figures for federally owned land do not include trust properties.
Source: U.S. General Services Administration, *Federal Real Property Profile,* 2006.

Land use, 1997
In acres, rounded to nearest thousand

Total surface area	28,995,000
Total nonfederal rural land.	23,816,000
Percentage rural land	82.1%
Cropland	5,471,000
Conservation Reserve Program (CRP*) land	90,000
Pastureland	1,845,000
Rangeland	(nil)
Forestland	15,478,000
Other rural land	932,000

*CRP is a federal program begun in 1985 to assist private landowners to convert highly erodible cropland to vegetative cover for ten years. Note that some categories of land overlap.
Source: U.S. Department of Agriculture, Natural Resources and Conservation Service, and Iowa State University, Statistical Laboratory, *Summary Report, 1997 National Resources Inventory,* revised December, 2000.

Farms and crop acreage, 2004

	State	U.S.	Share	Rank
Farms	58,000	2,113,000	2.74%	14
Acres (millions)	8	937	0.85%	33
Acres per farm	132	443	—	45

Source: U.S. Department of Agriculture, National Agricultural Statistics Service. Numbers of farms are rounded to nearest thousand units; acreage figures are rounded to nearest million. Rankings, including ties, are based on rounded figures.

GOVERNMENT AND FINANCE

Units of local government, 2002

	State	Total U.S.	Rank
All local governments	5,031	87,525	2
Counties	66	3,034	21
Municipalities	1,018	19,429	3
Townships	1,546	16,504	2
School districts	516	13,506	11
Special districts	1,885	35,052	4

Only 48 states have county governments, 20 states have township governments ("towns" in New England, Minnesota, New York, and Wisconsin), and 46 states have school districts. Special districts encompass such functions as natural resources, fire protection, and housing and community development.
Source: U.S. Census Bureau, *Census of Governments.*

State government revenue, 2002

Total revenue	$46,165 mill.
General revenue	$46,544 mill.
Per capita revenue	$3,775
U.S. per capita average	$3,689
Rank among states	28
Intergovernment revenue	
Total	$13,734 mill.
From federal government	$13,685 mill.
Charges and miscellaneous	
Total	$10,675 mill.
Current charges	$6,305 mill.
Misc. general income	$4,370 mill.
Insurance trust revenue	−$1,339 mill.
Taxes	
Total	$22,136 mill.
Per capita taxes	$1,795
Rank among states	23
Property taxes	$51 mill.
Sales taxes	$10,948 mill.
License taxes	$2,078 mill.
Individual income taxes	$6,735 mill.
Corporate income taxes	$1,198 mill.
Other taxes	$1,125 mill.

Total revenue figures include items not listed separately here.
Source: U.S. Bureau of the Census.

State government expenditures, 2002

General expenditures

Total state expenditures	$55,171 mill.
Intergovernmental	$12,788 mill.

Per capita expenditures

State	$3,824
Average of all states	$3,859
Rank among states	28

Selected direct expenditures

Education	$7,304 mill.
Public welfare	$12,160 mill.
Health, hospital	$2,749 mill.
Highways	$4,066 mill.
Police protection	$893 mill.
Corrections	$1,456 mill.
Natural resources	$528 mill.
Parks and recreation	$149 mill.
Government administration	$1,300 mill.
Interest on debt	$1,073 mill.
Total direct expenditures	$34,360 mill.

Totals include items not listed separately.
Source: U.S. Census Bureau.

POLITICS

Governors since statehood

D = Democrat; R = Republican; O = other;
(r) resigned; (d) died in office; (i) removed from office

Thomas Wharton, Jr.	(d) 1777-1778
George Bryan	1778
Joseph Reed	1778-1781
William Moore	1781-1782
John Dickinson	1782-1785
Benjamin Franklin	1785-1788
Thomas Mifflin	1788-1799
Thomas McKean (O)	1799-1808
Simon Snyder (O)	1808-1817
William Findlay (O)	1817-1820
Joseph Hiester (O)	1820-1823
John A. Schulze (O)	1823-1829
George Wolf (O)	1829-1835
Joseph Ritner (D)	1835-1839
David R. Porter (D)	1839-1845
Francis R. Shunk (D)	(r) 1845-1848
William F. Johnston (O)	1848-1852
William Bigler (D)	1852-1855
James Pollock (O)	1855-1858
William F. Packer (D)	1858-1861
Andrew G. Curtin (R)	1861-1867
John W. Geary (R)	1867-1873
John F. Hartranft (R)	1873-1879
Henry M. Hoyt (R)	1879-1883
Robert E. Pattison (D)	1883-1887
James A. Beaver (R)	1887-1891
Robert E. Pattison (D)	1891-1895

Daniel W. Hastings (R)	1895-1899
William A. Stone (R)	1899-1903
Samuel W. Pennypacker (R)	1903-1907
Edwin S. Stuart (R)	1907-1911
John K. Tener (R)	1911-1915
Martin G. Brumbaugh (R)	1915-1919
William C. Sproul (R)	1919-1923
Gifford Pinchot (R)	1923-1927
John S. Fisher (R)	1927-1931
Gifford Pinchot (R)	1931-1935
George H. Earle III (D)	1935-1939
Arthur H. James (R)	1939-1943
Edward Martin (R)	(r) 1943-1947
John C. Bell (R)	1947
James H. Duff (R)	1947-1951
John S. Fine (R)	1951-1955
George M. Leader (D)	1955-1959
David L. Lawrence (D)	1959-1963
William W. Scranton (R)	1963-1967
Raymond P. Shafer (R)	1967-1971
Milton J. Shapp (D)	1971-1979
Richard L. Thornburgh (R)	1979-1987
Robert P. Casey (D)	1987-1995
Tom Ridge (R)	(r) 1995-2001
Mark Stephen Schweiker (R)	2001-2003
Edward Gene Rendell (D)	2003-

Governors were called state council presidents before 1790.

Composition of congressional delegations, 1989-2007

	Dem	Rep	Total
House of Representatives			
101st Congress, 1989			
State delegates	12	11	23
Total U.S.	259	174	433
102d Congress, 1991			
State delegates	11	12	23
Total U.S.	267	167	434
103d Congress, 1993			
State delegates	11	10	21
Total U.S.	258	176	434
104th Congress, 1995			
State delegates	11	10	21
Total U.S.	197	236	433
105th Congress, 1997			
State delegates	12	10	21
Total U.S.	206	228	434
106th Congress, 1999			
State delegates	11	10	21
Total U.S.	211	222	433
107th Congress, 2001			
State delegates	10	11	21
Total U.S.	211	221	432

(continued)

	Dem	Rep	Total
108th Congress, 2003			
State delegates	7	12	19
Total U.S.	205	229	434
109th Congress, 2005			
State delegates	7	12	19
Total U.S.	202	231	433
110th Congress, 2007			
State delegates	11	8	19
Total U.S.	233	202	435

Senate

	Dem	Rep	Total
101st Congress, 1989			
State delegates	0	2	2
Total U.S.	55	45	100
102d Congress, 1991			
State delegates	0	2	2
Total U.S.	56	44	100
103d Congress, 1993			
State delegates	1	1	2
Total U.S.	57	43	100
104th Congress, 1995			
State delegates	0	2	2
Total U.S.	46	53	99
105th Congress, 1997			
State delegates	0	2	2
Total U.S.	45	55	100
106th Congress, 1999			
State delegates	0	2	2
Total U.S.	45	54	99
107th Congress, 2001			
State delegates	0	2	2
Total U.S.	50	50	100
108th Congress, 2003			
State delegates	0	2	2
Total U.S.	48	51	99
109th Congress, 2005			
State delegates	0	2	2
Total U.S.	44	55	99
110th Congress, 2007			
State delegates	1	1	2
Total U.S.	49	49	98

Figures are for starts of first sessions. Totals are for Democrat (Dem.) and Republican (Rep.) members only. House membership totals under 435 and Senate totals under 100 reflect vacancies and seats held by independent party members. When the 110th Congress opened, the Senate's two independent members caucused with the Democrats, giving the Democrats control of the Senate.

Source: U.S. Congress, *Congressional Directory.*

Composition of state legislature, 1990-2006

	Democrats	Republicans
State House (203 seats)		
1990	107	94
1992	105	98
1994	101	102
1996	99	104
1998	100	103
2000	100	100
2002	94	108
2004	93	110
2006	102	101
State Senate (50 seats)		
1990	24	26
1992	24	25
1994	21	29
1996	20	30
1998	20	30
2000	20	30
2002	21	29
2004	18	29
2006	21	29

Figures for total seats may include independents and minor party members. Numbers reflect results of elections in listed years; elected members usually take their seats in the years that follow.

Source: Council of State Governments; *State Elective Officials and the Legislatures.*

Voter participation in presidential elections, 2000 and 2004

	2000	2004
Voting age population		
State	9,371,000	9,569,000
Total United States	209,831,000	220,377,000
State share of U.S. total	4.47	4.34
Rank among states	5	5
Portion of voting age population casting votes		
State	52.4%	60.3%
United States	50.3%	55.5%
Rank among states	25	18

Population figures are rounded to nearest thousand and include all residents, regardless of eligibility to vote.

Source: U.S. Census Bureau.

HEALTH AND MEDICAL CARE

Medical professionals
Physicians in 2003 and nurses in 2001

	U.S.	State
Physicians in 2003		
Total	774,849	36,421
Share of U.S. total		4.68%
Rate	266	295
Rank		9
Nurses in 2001		
Total	2,262,020	132,120
Share of U.S. total		5.84%
Rate	793	1,074
Rank		3

Rates are numbers of physicians and nurses per 100,000 resident population; ranks are based on rates.

Source: American Medical Association, *Physician Characteristics and Distribution in the U.S.*; U.S. Department of Health and Human Services, Health Resources and Services Administration.

Health insurance coverage, 2003

	State	U.S.
Total persons covered	10,771,000	243,320,000
Total persons not covered	1,384,000	44,961,000
Portion not covered	11.4%	15.6%
Rank among states	34	—
Children not covered	239,000	8,373,000
Portion not covered	8.4%	11.4%
Rank among states	31	—

Totals are rounded to nearest thousand. Ranks are from the highest to the lowest percentages of persons *not* insured.

Source: U.S. Census Bureau, Current Population Reports.

AIDS, syphilis, and tuberculosis cases, 2003

Disease	U.S. cases	State cases	Rank
AIDS	44,232	1,906	6
Syphilis	34,270	705	14
Tuberculosis	14,874	336	9

Source: U.S. Centers for Disease Control and Prevention.

Cigarette smoking, 2003
Residents over age 18 who smoke

	U.S.	State	Rank
All smokers	22.1%	25.5%	10
Male smokers	24.8%	27.1%	17
Female smokers	20.3%	24.1%	4

Cigarette smokers are defined as persons who reported having smoked at least 100 cigarettes during their lifetimes and who currently smoked at least occasionally.

Source: U.S. Centers for Disease Control and Prevention, *Morbidity and Mortality Weekly Report*, 53, no. 44 (November 12, 2004).

HOUSING

Home ownership rates, 1985-2004

	1985	1990	1995	2000	2004
State	71.6%	73.8%	71.5%	74.7%	74.9%
Total U.S.	63.9%	63.9%	64.7%	67.4%	69.0%
Rank among states	5	2	7	9	8

Net change in state home ownership rate, 1985-2004	+3.3%
Net change in U.S. home ownership rate, 1985-2004	+5.1%

Percentages represent the proportion of owner households to total occupied households.

Source: U.S. Census Bureau, 2006.

Home sales, 2000-2004
In thousands of units

Existing home sales	2000	2002	2003	2004
State sales	194.0	204.7	219.6	244.6
Total U.S. sales	5,171	5,631	6,183	6,784
State share of U.S. total	3.75%	3.64%	3.55%	3.61%
Sales rank among states	7	7	7	7

Units include single-family homes, condos, and co-ops.

Source: National Association of Realtors, Washington, D.C., *Real Estate Outlook: Market Trends & Insights*.

Values of owner-occupied homes, 2003

	State	U.S.
Total units	3,002,000	58,809,000
Value of units		
Under $100,000	45.0%	29.6%
$100,000-199,999	37.0%	36.9%
$200,000 or more	18.1%	33.5%
Median value	$110,020	$142,275
Rank among all states		34

Units are owner-occupied one-family houses whose numbers are rounded to nearest thousand. Data are extrapolated from survey samples.
Source: U.S. Census Bureau, American Community Survey.

EDUCATION

Public school enrollment, 2002

Prekindergarten through grade 8
State enrollment 1,242,000
Total U.S. enrollment. 34,135,000
State share of U.S. total 3.64%

Grades 9 through 12
State enrollment 575,000
Total U.S. enrollment. 14,067,000
State share of U.S. total 4.09%

Enrollment rates
State public school enrollment rate. 84.6%
Overall U.S. rate 90.4%
Rank among states in 2002. 48
Rank among states in 1995. 50

Enrollment figures (which include unclassified students) are rounded to nearest thousand pupils during fall school term. Enrollment rates are based on enumerated resident population estimate for July 1, 2002.
Source: U.S. National Center for Education Statistics.

Public college finances, 2003-2004

FTE enrollment in public institutions of higher education
Students in state institutions. 322,700
Students in all U.S. public institutions 9,916,600
State share of U.S. total 3.25
Rank among states. 8

State and local government appropriations for higher education
State appropriation per FTE $5,355
National average. $5,716
Rank among states 27
State & local tax revenue going to higher education 5.6%

FTE = full-time equivalent in public postsecondary programs, including summer sessions; student numbers are rounded to nearest hundred. Funding figures for 2003-2004 academic year include financial aid to students in state public institutions and exclude money for research, agriculture experiment stations, teaching hospitals, and medical schools; figures are rounded to nearest thousand dollars.
Source: Higher Education Executive Officers, Denver, Colorado.

TRANSPORTATION AND TRAVEL

Highway mileage, 2003

Interstate highways 1,758
Other freeways and expressways 516
Arterial roads. 13,194
Collector roads. 19,802
Local roads. 85,153
Urban roads 37,689
Rural roads 82,734
Total state mileage 120,423
U.S. total 3,974,107
State share 3.03%
Rank among states. 9

Note that combined urban and rural road mileage matches the total of the other categories.
Source: U.S. Federal Highway Administration.

Motor vehicle registrations and driver licenses, 2003

Vehicle registrations	State	U.S.	Share	Rank
Autos, trucks, buses	9,724,000	231,390,000	4.20%	6
Autos only	6,121,000	135,670	4.51%	6
Motorcycles	268,000	5,328,000	5.03%	4
Driver licenses	8,370,000	196,166,000	4.27%	5

Figures, which do not include vehicles owned by military services, are rounded to the nearest thousand. Figures for automobiles include taxis.
Source: U.S. Federal Highway Administration.

Domestic travel expenditures, 2003

Spending by U.S. residents on overnight trips and
day trips of at least 50 miles from home

Total expenditures within state . . . . $15.24 bill.
Total expenditures within U.S. . . . . $490.87 bill.
State share of U.S. total 3.1%
Rank among states 7

Source: Travel Industry Association of America.

Retail gasoline prices, 2003-2007

Average price per gallon at the pump

Year	U.S.	State
2003	$1.267	$1.189
2004	$1.316	$1.258
2005	$1.644	$1.565
2007	$2.298	$2.329

Excise tax per gallon in 2004 . . . . 30.0¢
Rank among all states in 2007 prices 17

Prices are averages of all grades of gasoline sold at the pump
during March months in 2003-2005 and during February, 2007.
Averages for 2006, during which prices rose higher, are not
available.
Source: U.S. Energy Information Agency, *Petroleum Marketing
Monthly* (2003-2005 data); American Automobile Association
(2007 data).

CRIME AND LAW ENFORCEMENT

State and local police officers, 2000-2004

	2000	2002	2004
Total officers			
U.S.	654,601	665,555	675,734
State	22,763	23,713	22,756*
*Net change, 2000-2004			−0.03%
Officers per 1,000 residents			
U.S.	2.33	2.31	2.30
State	1.85	1.92	1.83
State rank	34	33	37

Totals include state and local police and sheriffs.
Source: Carsey Institute, University of New Hampshire.

Crime rates, 2003

Incidents per 100,000 residents

Crimes	State	U.S.
Violent crimes		
Total incidents	398	475
Murder	5	6
Forcible rape	29	32
Robbery	145	142
Aggravated assault	219	295
Property crimes		
Total incidents	2,431	3,588
Burglary	436	741
Larceny/theft	1,725	2,415
Motor vehicle theft	270	433
All crimes	2,829	4,063

Source: U.S. Federal Bureau of Investigation, *Crime in the United
States,* annual.

State prison populations, 1980-2003

	State	U.S.	State share
1980	8,171	305,458	2.67%
1990	22,290	708,393	3.15%
1996	34,537	1,025,624	3.37%
2000	36,847	1,391,261	2.65%
2003	40,890	1,470,045	2.78%

State figures exclude prisoners in federal penitentiaries.
Source: U.S. Bureau of Justice Statistics, *Prisoners in 2003.*

Rhode Island

Location: New England

Area and rank: 1,045 square miles (2,706 square kilometers); 1,545 square miles (4,002 square kilometers) including water; fiftieth largest state in area

Coastline: 40 miles (64 kilometers) on the Atlantic Ocean

Shoreline: 384 miles (618 kilometers)

Population and rank: 1,081,000 (2004); forty-third largest state in population

Capital and largest city: Providence (173,618 people in 2000 census)

Entered Union and rank: May 29, 1790; thirteenth state

Present constitution adopted: 1843

Rhode Island's State House in Providence. (Frederick E. D'Andrea)

Counties: 5

State name: Rhode Island took its name from the Greek island of Rhodes

State nickname: Ocean State

Motto: Hope

State flag: White field with state coat of arms

Highest point: Jerimoth Hill— 812 feet (247 meters)

Lowest point: Atlantic Ocean— sea level

Highest recorded temperature: 104 degrees Fahrenheit (40 degrees Celsius)—Providence, 1975

Lowest recorded temperature: –23 degrees Fahrenheit (–31 degrees Celsius)—Kingston, 1942

State song: "Rhode Island, It's for Me"

State tree: Red maple

State flower: Violet

State bird: Rhode Island Red hen

Rhode Island History

Though the smallest state in the Union in area, Rhode Island has the longest name: Rhode Island and Providence Plantations. Rhode Island, though it is only 48 miles long and 37 miles wide, has 384 miles of shoreline, which earned for it the nickname the Ocean State. The state is practically divided by Narragansett Bay, which extends twenty-eight miles into the interior. As a result, every town in Rhode Island is no more than twenty-five miles from water. The state's geography played a major role in its development, with fishing, shipbuilding, and international trade being its early major industries. The numerous and swift rivers running through the state also shaped industry, being harnessed for power to the nation's first mills. Due to its small size, Rhode Island has always been intimately linked to its neighbors, Connecticut on the west and Massachusetts on the east and north.

Native American Presence. Archaeological evidence shows that Rhode Island has been inhabited for at least eight thousand years. During the seventeenth century, the area of Rhode Island, Connecticut, and Massachusetts was inhabited by about thirty thousand American Indians of the Algonquian family, roughly split into five tribes: Narragansetts, Wampanoags, Niantics, Nipmucs, and Pequots. They farmed the land for corn, squash, beans, and tobacco.

The first European settlers of the state during the 1630's lived peaceably among the Native Americans; Indians even gave portions of their land to the English. Eventually, however, discord among the groups arose, when whites began taking American Indian land. During the 1637 Pequot War, Pequots unsuccessfully tried to drive out the colonists who had taken over their land. The continued disintegration of ties led to King Philip's War in 1675. The Wampanoags, their leader King Philip, and their violent behavior provoked Connecticut and Massachusetts to declare war against them. The Rhode Island Narragansetts joined with the Wampanoags eventually, but the Native Americans were defeated, with thousands of Indians and more than six hundred whites killed and most of the city of Providence burned. After the war, Native Americans were shipped to the South or to the West Indies as slaves. Most eventually left the state, and by the year

The Cliffwalk-Breakers mansion reflects the wealthy and aristocratic lifestyle for which Newport, Rhode Island, has long been known. (Rhode Island Tourism Division)

2000, Native Americans made up less than 0.5 percent of Rhode Island's population.

Discovery and Colonization. Rhode Island may have been visited by Norwegian Vikings as early as 1000 C.E. In 1524, the Italian explorer Giovanni da Verrazano, sailing for France, found Narragansett Bay. He may have named the state, comparing it to the Greek island of Rhodes. The state's name is also often attributed to Dutch trader Adriaen Block, who visited the region in 1614 and called it *roodt eylandt* (red island).

Rhode Island was first settled by Europeans in 1636, when the city of Providence was founded by religious dissenter Roger Williams. Williams was about to be exiled from the Massachusetts Bay Colony to England due to his unpopular view that religion and state should be separate. He escaped, and his Native American friends, the Narragansetts, gave him land that he named Providence. He declared the region "a shelter for persons distressed of conscience."

In 1638, Anne Hutchinson was banished from the Massachusetts Bay Colony for preaching against the established church. She settled in Portsmouth, at the north end of Aquidneck Island. A year later William Coddington broke from Hutchinson's group and founded Newport. After Warwick was founded by Samuel Gorton in 1642, the four towns received a charter from England to become one colony, with freedom of religion guaranteed to all. Soon all those seeking asylum from persecution—including Quakers, Jews, Congregationalists, Baptists—made their homes there, and the region became known for its tolerance. Because of its open-mindedness, the colony was considered by outsiders a haven for misfits and was thus scorned.

Although the first antislavery law in the Union was signed in Rhode Island in 1652, Rhode Island, especially Newport and Bristol, was a hub of the so-called "triangle trade" during the eighteenth century. Rum, which Rhode Islanders manufactured, was traded in Africa for slaves, who were traded in the West Indies for molasses, which was used in New England to make more rum. Slavery was abolished in 1784, and the triangle trade ended by 1800.

Steps to Revolution. By 1750 the main industries in Rhode Island were fishing, rum manufacture, and rum trade. After Great Britain imposed taxes on trade, Rhode Islanders became smugglers to maintain their livelihoods. In 1764, they fired on a British ship, one of the first acts of aggression and rebellion against England. In 1772, the British ship *Gaspee* was burned by Providence residents, in an act thought to be the first of the Revolution.

Always progressive, Rhode Island's general assembly voted to end allegiance to Britain on May 4, 1776—two months before the rest of the colonies. Rhode Island played an active part in the fighting; the Battle of Rhode Island took place in Newport in 1778. A com-

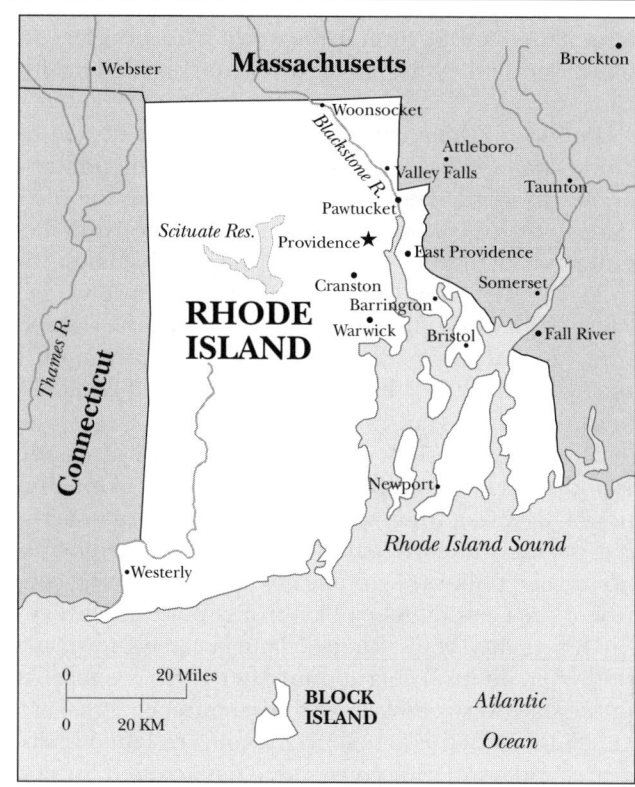

pany of freed slaves, known as the Black Regiment, fought with the colonists, becoming the first such regiment to fight in America. After winning independence, Rhode Island was the last of the original thirteen colonies to ratify the Constitution, in 1790, refusing to sign until the Bill of Rights was added. Desiring a balance of power, until 1854 Rhode Island had five capital cities: Providence, Newport, East Greenwich, Bristol, and South Kingstown. From 1854 to 1900, Providence and Newport shared capital status, and in 1900 Providence became the sole capital.

Industry. The American Industrial Revolution began in Pawtucket, Rhode Island, in 1790. Harnessing the power of the mighty Blackstone River, resident Samuel Slater built the first water-powered cotton mill in the Union. Later, in 1827, Slater erected the first steam-powered cotton mill. Rhode Island thrived during the nineteenth century due to the prosperity of its mills. Though the state's land was arable, by 1860 about 50 percent of Rhode Islanders worked in industrial jobs, while only 10 percent were farmers.

Production remained steady during the Civil War, and after the war the state's industry shifted from production of textiles to that of metals and jewelry. By the second half of the twentieth century an estimated 85 percent of U.S. costume jewelry was produced in Providence, though many factories faced difficulties when low-cost imports from Asia threatened to bankrupt them. Rhode Island is also home to Hasbro, the second-largest toy manufacturer in the world. The three largest employers in the state are industry, tourism, and health care.

Political, Ethnic, and Religious Makeup. Rhode Island expanded its trend of tolerance into the political arena. In 1842, Thomas Dorr founded the People's Party to try to give all citizens the right to vote. After illegitimately claiming governorship during what is known as Dorr's Rebellion, he was suppressed. However, because of his work, all adult males were given the right to vote, regardless of color. Rhode Island was the only state in which black and white citizens voted as equals before the Civil War.

Until the twentieth century, the majority of Rhode Island voters were Republicans. Democrats came into power, however, when diverse immigrants began arriving during the early part of the century. Democrats dominated politics beginning in 1935, never losing control of the General Assembly throughout the century.

During the 1980's, Rhode Island became known as a hotbed of political corruption. After 1986, two mayors in the state were convicted on corruption charges, two chief justices of the state supreme court resigned in disgrace, and a superior court judge was arrested for taking bribes. Possible reasons for the state's scandals include the longtime dominance of one political party,

the small size of the state, and the fact that Rhode Island is considered the New England headquarters of the Mafia. Residents hoping for a turn for the better elected Patrick Kennedy, the son of Senator Ted Kennedy, to the Rhode Island State Assembly in 1988. Although Kennedy was just a twenty-one-year-old attending Providence College, he proved himself worthy of reelection twice.

Italian Americans make up a large percentage of the Rhode Island population, second only to Irish Americans. Irish and Italian immigrants helped make Roman Catholicism the prevalent religion in the state. Rhode Island is about 70 percent Catholic, making it the state with the largest percentage of Catholics.

Revitalization of Providence. Though at the turn of the twentieth century Providence was one of the nation's richest and most thriving cities, after 1925 residents began fleeing to suburban and rural areas. Mayor Vincent "Buddy" Cianci, Jr., was mostly responsible for bringing the city back to life beginning during the 1970's. During the 1990's, the two downtown rivers that had been covered by pavement were uncovered, and bridges, walkways, and an amphitheater highlighted the center of the city, replacing unused train tracks and freight yards. Providence became a haven for artists and attracted multitudes with the building of new ho-

From 1930 until the mid-1980's, the world's premier yachting race, the America's Cup, was held off the coast of Newport, Rhode Island. (Rhode Island Tourism Division)

Rhode Island Red chickens—the official bird of the state. (©Tom Oliveira/Dreamstime.com)

tels, a convention center, a giant mall, and an outdoor ice rink. The city experienced a 40 percent drop in crime during the early 1990's, providing more reason for residents to return to the once-empty downtown area.

Politics. In 2000, Rhode Island chose Vice President Al Gore by a 61-32 percent margin as the recipient of its four electoral votes in the November presidential election. At the same time, the state's electorate voted to send Lincoln Chafee to the U.S. Senate for a full six-year term by a 57-42 percent margin. During 1999, Chafee, a liberal Republican, was appointed by then-governor Lincoln Almond to the Senate seat held by Chafee's father, John Chafee, who had died in office. Chaffe's political liberalism is such that he is known among conservatives as a "RINO"—"Republican in name only."

Also reelected was Democrat congress member Patrick Kennedy, who received 67 percent of the vote.

Kennedy, originally elected to his national seat in 1994, was urged both in 2000 and in 2006 to run for the U.S. Senate against Chafee; he declined. On May 4, 2006, Kennedy came to public attention when he crashed his car into a security barrier on Capitol Hill during the early morning hours. The following day, he announced he would enter a rehabilitation program. He had previously acknowledged drug use as a teen, addiction to prescription drugs, and clinical depression.

Political corruption was brought to public notice in 2001 when Providence mayor Cianci was indicted for corruption. In the election of the following year, occupancy of Rhode Island's statehouse changed as Governor Almond was barred by term limits legislation from seeking reelection. Elected in his place was Republican Don Carcieri, a onetime high school mathematics teacher and later business executive. Carcieri ran on a platform of ethical government and job creation.

In the 2004 presidential election, Senator John Kerry, from neighboring Massachusetts, received 60 percent of the vote and Rhode Island's four electoral votes. The state's members of Congress, both Democrats, were reelected.

Freedom of the Press at Brown. One of the state's most prominent universities, Ivy League member Brown University, was the site of controversial events in 2001. On March 13, the university newspaper, *The Brown Daily Herald*, ran an advertisement denouncing reparations to black Americans for slavery. The advertisement incensed a group of Brown students, who seized and destroyed copies of the paper. The students then attempted to force their way into the paper's offices to destroy remaining copies but were stopped by newspaper staff. To thwart the attackers' intent, the paper reprinted the offending issue and put it on newsstands a day late. The advertisement was printed in nine of the fifty-one college newspapers to which it was submitted.

Tragic Fire. In 2003, Rhode Island was the scene of tragedy of national dimensions. On February 20, a fire at the Station, a nightclub in West Warwick, killed one hundred persons and injured two hundred others, many of them badly. Fireworks set off by a live band ignited soundproofing material, and the fire quickly spread. It was the fourth worst such fire in U.S. history.

Lauren M. Mitchell
Updated by the Editor

Rhode Island Time Line

1500's	Algonquian Indians are dominant society throughout New England area.
1524	Italian navigator Giovanni da Verrazano explores Narragansett Bay.
1614	Dutch explorer Adriaen Block lands at Block Island.
1636	Roger Williams founds Providence.

(continued)

1638	Anne Hutchinson settles Portsmouth.
1639	Williams and Ezekiel Holliman found the first Baptist church in the New World, in Providence.
1639	William Coddington settles Newport.
1642	Samuel Gorton founds Shawomet (later Warwick).
1644	Williams is granted a charter for Rhode Island.
1652	Union's first antislavery law is passed in Rhode Island.
July 8, 1663	King Charles II grants Rhode Island a charter guaranteeing religious freedom and self-governance.
1675	King Philip's War begins as Massachusetts and Connecticut fight American Indians, eventually bringing Rhode Island into the war.
1732	First Rhode Island newspaper, *Rhode Island Gazette*, is published.
1763	Rhode Island College is established (becomes Brown University in 1804).
1763	Touro Synagogue, the first Jewish house of worship in the colonies, is built in Newport.
June 9, 1772	Colonists burn the British ship *Gaspee* to protest trade restrictions.
1774	Rhode Island outlaws the importation of slaves.
May 4, 1776	Rhode Island is first colony to declare independence from Great Britain.
Aug. 29, 1778	British seize Newport during Battle of Rhode Island.
1778	Black Regiment, the nation's first battalion of freed slaves, begins fighting in the Revolution.
1784	Colony abolishes slavery.
May 29, 1790	Rhode Island ratifies U.S. Constitution, becoming the thirteenth state in the Union.
1790	Samuel Slater builds the first water-powered cotton mill in the Union, in Pawtucket.
1827	Samuel Slater builds first steam-powered cotton mill.
1828	Providence Arcade, the first enclosed shopping mall in the Union, is opened.
1835	Train line connects Boston and Providence.
1842	Dorr's Rebellion results in voting rights for all adult males in the state.
1843	Present state constitution is adopted.
1861	More than 24,000 Rhode Islanders serve on Union side in Civil War.
1880	Nearly half the population of the state is of Irish ancestry.
1882	Public schooling is made mandatory.
1883	U.S. Navy opens station at Newport.
1890's	Italian Americans become the state's second-largest ethnic group.
1900	Providence becomes the sole capital of the state.
1910	Roman Catholicism becomes the major religion in the state.
1917-1918	Almost 28,000 Rhode Islanders serve in World War I.
1920	Rhode Island refuses to ratify national prohibition amendment.
1935	Democrats take control of state's General Assembly, which they will retain throughout twentieth century.
1938	Severe hurricane causes 317 deaths and more than $100 million in damage.
1946	Rhode Island legislates equal pay rates for women and men.
1969	Newport Bridge is completed across Narragansett Bay.
1971	First state income tax is enacted.
1983	After general depression, state's economy improves.
Aug. 8, 1988	Rhode Island celebrates first V-J Day; is the only state to commemorate victory over Japan in World War II.
1990	Prominent banker steals $13 million from bank, causing forty-five banks and credit unions to close temporarily.
1991	Sewage pollution in Narragansett Bay declines 13 percent from 1990.
Nov. 7, 2000	Rhode Island chooses Al Gore for president by a two-to-one margin.
2001	Providence mayor Vincent Cianci is sentenced to more than five years in prison for accepting bribes and racketeering.
Nov. 5, 2002	Republican businessman Don Carcieri is elected governor.
Feb. 20, 2003	Fire in West Warwick nightclub kills one hundred persons and injures two hundred.

Notes for Further Study

Published Sources. Those interested in learning about Rhode Island's history will find a wealth of materials on all aspects of the state's early years. For information on the founding of the colony, Edwin S. Gaustad's *Liberty of Conscience: Roger Williams in America* (1991) is excellent. *Flintlock and Tomahawk: New England in King Philip's War* (1992) by Douglas Edward Leach describes the conflict between Native Americans and white settlers. *Inventing New England's Slave Paradise: Master/Slave Relations in Eighteenth-Century Narragansett, Rhode Island* (1998) by Robert K. Fitts is one of two excellent books on the subject of slavery in the state; the other title is Deborah Bingham Van Broekhoven's *The Devotion of These Women: Rhode Island in the Antislavery Network* (2002), which provides a fascinating account of the way in which a network of women revived the state's waning abolitionist movement and kept it running for another ten years. *The Colonial Metamorphoses in Rhode Island: A Study of Institutions in Change* (2000), by Sydney V. James and edited by Sheila L. Skemp and Bruce C. Daniels, details the state's colonial history between 1600 and 1775.

Rhode Island's role in the American Revolution is discussed in *The Documentary History of the Destruction of the Gaspee* (1990) by William R. Staples. Barbara Tucker analyzes the American Industrial Revolution in *Samuel Slater and the Origins of the American Textile Industry, 1790-1860* (1984). Carole Marsh's *Rhode Island Bandits, Bushwackers, Outlaws, Crooks, Devils, Ghosts, Desperadoes, and Other Assorted and Sundry Characters!* (1994) describes the colorful individuals who have inhabited the state throughout its history. For younger readers, two good overviews of the state can be found in *Rhode Island: The Ocean State* (2003) by Joanne Mattern and *Colony of Rhode Island* (2001) by Susan Whitehurst.

Some good books for visitors to the state include *The Smithsonian Guides to Historic America: Southern New England* (1998) by Henry Wiencek, *Compass American Guide: Connecticut and Rhode Island* (2004) by Anna Mundow and James Marshall (photographer), and *Rhode Island: An Explorer's Guide* (4th ed., 2004) by Phyllis Méras and Katherine Imbrie. *Providence, the Renaissance City* (2004) by Francis J. Leazes, Jr., and Mark T. Motte reveals the ideas, opportunities, people, and projects behind the twenty-five-year revitalization of Providence.

Web Resources. There are many Rhode Island sites on the Internet, and those listed here often give links to others. A good starting point is the Rhode Island Home Page (www.ri .gov/), which gives information on state government and history as well as visitor information. It is especially valuable when paired with the official tourism site (www .visitrhodeisland.com/). Rhode Island History (www.rilin .state.ri.us/studteaguide/RhodeIslandHistory/rodehist .html) provides a lengthy look at the state's past, from the Indian and explorer age through the year 2000. The state of Rhode Island Parks and Recreation site (www.riparks.com) offers details about the state's many nature areas and history, as well as maps and information on park events. The Narragansett Bay site (www.narrbay.org/) gives information on location and trails available to nature lovers. The 500 Nations site (500nations.com/Rhode_Island_ Tribes.asp) has a good page detailing the state's Native American communities.

Good sites for information about Newport include Newport Notables (www.redwood1747.org/notables/nntitle .htm#h), which offers biographies of prominent Newport citizens from the colony's earliest years. The Web site of the *Providence Journal*, the state's main newspaper (www.projo .com), offers daily news on events in and around the state. Brown University (www.brown.edu) and the University of Rhode Island (www.uri.edu) maintain updated sites about the respective schools.

Counties

County	2000 pop.	Rank in pop.	Sq. miles	Rank in area
Bristol	50,648	5	24.7	5
Kent	167,090	2	170.1	3
Newport	85,433	4	104.1	4
Providence	621,602	1	413.3	1
Washington	123,546	3	332.9	2

Source: U.S. Census Bureau; National Association of Counties.

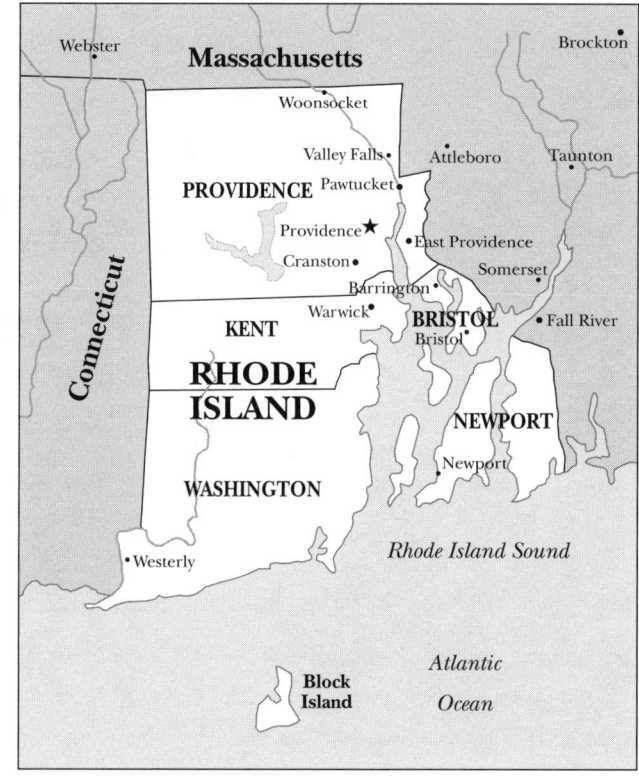

Cities
With 10,000 or more residents

Rank	City	Population	Rank	City	Population
1	Providence (capital)	173,618	19	Central Falls	18,928
2	Warwick	85,808	20	Westerly	17,682
3	Cranston	79,269	21	Middletown	17,334
4	Pawtucket	72,958	22	Portsmouth	17,149
5	East Providence	48,688	23	Barrington	16,819
6	Woonsocket	43,224	24	Narragansett	16,361
7	Coventry	33,668	25	Burrillville	15,796
8	North Providence	32,411	26	Tiverton	15,260
9	Cumberland	31,840	27	East Greenwich	12,948
10	West Warwick	29,581	28	Valley Falls	11,599
11	Johnston	28,195	29	Newport East	11,463
12	South Kingstown	27,921	30	Warren	11,360
13	Newport	26,475	31	North Smithfield	10,618
14	North Kingstown	26,326	32	Scituate	10,324
15	Westerly	22,966			
16	Bristol	22,469			
17	Lincoln	20,898			
18	Smithfield	20,613			

Population figures are from 2000 census.
Source: U.S. Bureau of the Census.

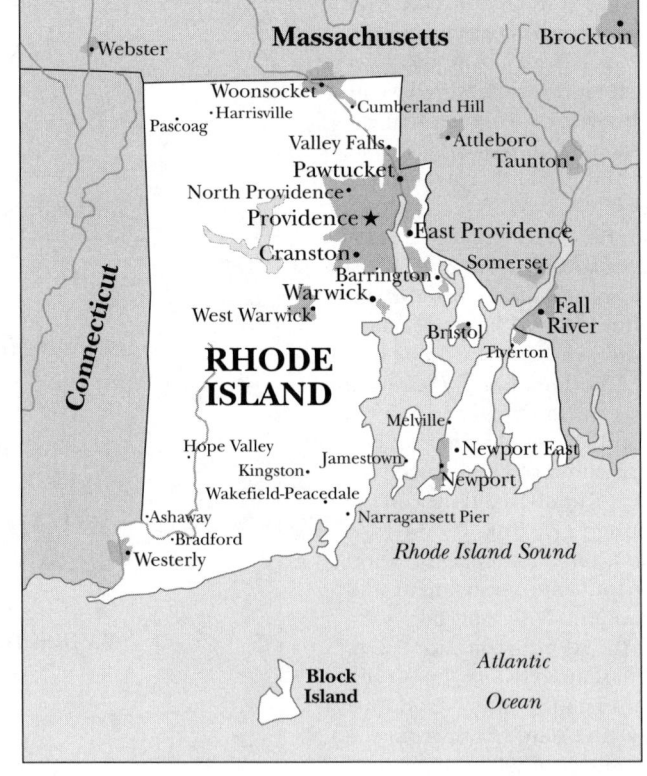

Index to Tables

DEMOGRAPHICS

Resident state and national populations, 1970-2004

Population figures given in thousands

	State pop.	U.S. pop.	Share	Rank
1970	950	203,302	0.5%	39
1980	947	226,546	0.4%	40
1985	969	237,924	0.4%	42
1990	1,003	248,765	0.4%	43
1995	1,017	262,761	0.4%	43
2000	1,048	281,425	0.4%	43
2004	1,081	293,655	0.4%	43

Source: U.S. Census Bureau, Current Population Reports, 2006.

Resident population by age, 2004

Age Group	Total persons
Under 5 years	62,000
5 to 17 years	182,000
18 to 24 years	112,000
25 to 34 years	139,000
35 to 44 years	166,000
45 to 54 years	159,000
55 to 64 years	110,000
65 to 74 years	65,000
75 to 84 years	60,000
85 years and older	26,000
All age groups	1,081,000

Portion of residents 65 and older	13.9%
National rank in portion of oldest residents	8
National average	12.4%

Population figures are rounded to nearest thousand persons;
figures include armed forces personnel stationed in the state.
Source: U.S. Bureau of the Census, 2006.

Resident population by race, Hispanic origin, 2004

Category	State pop.	Share	U.S.
All residents	1,081	100.00%	100.00%
Non-Hispanic white	870	80.48%	67.37%
Hispanic white	92	8.51%	13.01%
Other Hispanic	20	1.85%	1.06%
African American	66	6.11%	12.77%
Native American	6	0.56%	0.96%
Asian, Pacific Islander	30	2.78%	4.37%
Two or more categories	16	1.48%	1.51%

Population figures are in thousands. Persons counted as "Hispanic" (Latino) may be of any race. Because of overlapping categories, categories may not add up to 100%. Shares in column 3 are percentages of each category within the state; these figures may be compared to the national percentages in column 4.
Source: U.S. Bureau of the Census, 2006.

Projected state population, 2000-2030

Year	Population
2000	1,048,000
2005	1,087,000
2010	1,117,000
2015	1,140,000
2020	1,154,000
2025	1,158,000
2030	1,153,000
Population increase, 2000-2030	105,000
Percentage increase, 2000-2030	10.0

Projections are based on data from the 2000 census.
Source: U.S. Census Bureau.

VITAL STATISTICS

Infant mortality rates, 1980-2002

	1980	1990	2000	2002
All state residents	11.0	8.1	6.3	7.0
All U.S. residents	12.6	9.2	9.4	9.1
All state white residents	10.9	7.0	5.9	6.4
All U.S. white residents	10.6	7.6	5.7	5.8

Figures represent deaths per 1,000 live births of resident infants under 1 year old, exclusive of fetal deaths. Figures for all residents include members of other racial categories not listed separately. The Census Bureau considers the figures for black residents to be too small to be statistically meaningful.
Source: U.S. Census Bureau, *Statistical Abstract of the United States,* 2006.

Abortion rates, 1990 and 2000

	1990	2000
Total abortions	7,000	6,000
Rate per 1,000 women	29.5	24.1
U.S. rate	25.7	21.3
Rank	7	8

Numbers of abortions are rounded to nearest thousand; ranks are based on rates.
Source: U.S. Census Bureau.

Marriages and divorces, 2004

Total marriages	8,200
Rate per 1,000 population	7.6
National rate per 1,000 population	7.4
Rank among all states	20
Total divorces	3,300
Rate per 1,000 population	3.0
National rate per 1,000 population	3.7
Rank among all states	35

Figures are for all marriages and divorces performed within the state, including those of nonresidents; totals are rounded to the nearest hundred. Ranks are for highest to lowest figures; note that divorce data are not available for five states.
Source: U.S. National Center for Health Statistics, *Vital Statistics of the United States,* 2006.

Death rates by leading causes, 2002
Deaths per 100,000 resident population

Cause	State	U.S.
Heart disease	290.6	241.7
Cancer	224.7	193.2
Cerebrovascular diseases	56.6	56.4
Accidents other than motor vehicle	25.9	37.0
Motor vehicle accidents	8.9	15.7
Chronic lower respiratory diseases	48.7	43.3
Diabetes mellitus	24.6	25.4
HIV	2.2	4.9
Suicide	8.0	11.0
Homicide	4.0	6.1
All causes	957.8	847.3
Rank in overall death rate among states		13

Figures exclude nonresidents who died in the state. Causes of death follow International Classification of Diseases. Rank is from highest to lowest death rate in the United States.
Source: U.S. National Center for Health Statistics, *National Vital Statistics Report,* 2006.

ECONOMY

Gross state product, 1990-2004
In current dollars

Year	State product	Nat'l product	State share
1990	$21.5 billion	$5.67 trillion	0.38%
2000	$33.8 billion	$9.75 trillion	0.35%
2002	$37.0 billion	$10.41 trillion	0.36%
2003	$39.4 billion	$10.92 trillion	0.36%
2004	$41.9 billion	$11.65 trillion	0.36%

Source: U.S. Bureau of Economic Analysis, *Survey of Current Business,* July, 2005.

Gross state product by industry, 2003
In billions of dollars

Construction	$2.0
Manufacturing	3.9
Wholesale trade	1.9
Retail trade.	2.8
Finance & insurance.	4.9
Information	1.5
Professional services.	1.9
Health care & social assistance	3.1
Government	4.2
Total state product	$36.5
Total U.S. product	$10,289.2
State share of U.S. total	0.35%
Rank among all states	44

Total figures include industries not listed separately. Amounts are in chained 2000 dollars.

Source: U.S. Bureau of Economic Analysis, *Survey of Current Business,* July, 2005.

Personal income per capita, 1990-2004
In current dollars

	1990	2000	2004
Per capita income	$20,006	$29,214	$33,733
U.S. average	$19,477	$29,845	$32,937
Rank among states	14	18	16

Source: U.S. Bureau of Economic Analysis, *Survey of Current Business,* April, 2005.

Energy consumption, 2001
In trillions of British thermal units (BTU), except as noted

Total energy consumption

Total state energy consumption	227
Total U.S. energy consumption	96,275
State share of U.S. total	0.24%
Rank among states	49

Per capita consumption (In millions of BTU)

Total state per capita consumption	215
Total U.S. per capita consumption	338
Rank among states	50

End-use sectors

Residential	73
Commercial.	63
Industrial	26
Transportation	66

Sources of energy

Petroleum	100
Natural gas	99
Coal	(z)
Hydroelectric power.	(z)
Nuclear electric power.	0

Figures for totals include categories not listed separately.
  (z) Indicates less than 0.5 trillion BTU.

Source: U.S. Energy Information Administration, *State Energy Data Report,* 2001.

Nonfarm employment by sectors, 2004

Total persons	488,000
Construction	21,000
Manufacturing	57,000
Trade, transportation, utilities	80,000
Information	11,000
Finance, insurance, real estate	34,000
Professional & business services.	54,000
Education & health services.	93,000
Leisure, hospitality, arts, organizations	50,000
Other services, including repair & maintenance. . .	23,000
Government	66,000

Figures are rounded to nearest thousand persons. "Total" includes mining and natural resources, not listed separately.

Source: U.S. Bureau of Labor Statistics, 2006.

Foreign exports, 1990-2004
In millions of dollars

Year	State	U.S.	State share
1990	595	394,045	0.15%
1996	919	624,767	0.15%
1997	1,088	688,896	0.16%
2000	1,186	712,055	0.15%
2003	1,178	724,006	0.17%
2004	1,286	769,332	0.17%
Rank among all states in 2004 45			

U.S. total does not include U.S. dependencies.
Source: U.S. Census Bureau, *U.S. Merchandise Trade,* series FT 900, 2000; U.S. Census Bureau, *U.S. International Trade in Goods and Services,* Series FT 900, 2005.

LAND USE

Federally owned land, 2003
Areas in acres

	State	U.S.	State share
Total area	677,000	2,271,343,000	0.03%
Nonfederal land	672,000	1,599,584,000	0.04%
Federal land	5,000	671,759,000	0.00%
Federal share	0.8%	29.6%	—

Areas are rounded to nearest thousand acres. Figures for federally owned land do not include trust properties.
Source: U.S. General Services Administration, *Federal Real Property Profile,* 2006.

Land use, 1997
In acres, rounded to nearest thousand

Total surface area.	813,000
Total nonfederal rural land	458,000
Percentage rural land	56.3%
Cropland	22,000
Conservation Reserve Program (CRP*) land	(nil)
Pastureland.	25,000
Rangeland	(nil)
Forestland.	387,000
Other rural land	24,000

*CRP is a federal program begun in 1985 to assist private landowners to convert highly erodible cropland to vegetative cover for ten years. Note that some categories of land overlap.
Source: U.S. Department of Agriculture, Natural Resources and Conservation Service, and Iowa State University, Statistical Laboratory, *Summary Report, 1997 National Resources Inventory,* revised December, 2000.

Farms and crop acreage, 2004

	State	U.S.	Share	Rank
Farms	1,000	2,113,000	0.05%	49
Acres (millions)	0.1*	937	0.00%	48
Acres per farm	71	443	—	50

Source: U.S. Department of Agriculture, National Agricultural Statistics Service. Numbers of farms are rounded to nearest thousand units; acreage figures are rounded to nearest million; *Rhode Island has fewer than 500,000 acres of farmland. Rankings, including ties, are based on rounded figures.

GOVERNMENT AND FINANCE

Units of local government, 2002

	State	Total U.S.	Rank
All local governments	118	87,525	49
Counties	0	3,034	—
Municipalities	8	19,429	49
Towns (townships)	31	16,504	20
School districts	4	13,506	45
Special districts	75	35,052	47

Only 48 states have county governments, 20 states have township governments ("towns" in New England, Minnesota, New York, and Wisconsin), and 46 states have school districts. Special districts encompass such functions as natural resources, fire protection, and housing and community development.
Source: U.S. Census Bureau, *Census of Governments.*

State government revenue, 2002

Total revenue.	$4,891 mill.
General revenue	$4,836 mill.
Per capita revenue	$4,524
U.S. per capita average	$3,689
Rank among states	10

Intergovernment revenue

Total	$1,720 mill.
From federal government	$1,637 mill.

Charges and miscellaneous

Total	$988 mill.
Current charges	$385 mill.
Misc. general income	$603 mill.
Insurance trust revenue.	$43 mill.

Taxes

Total	$2,128 mill.
Per capita taxes	$1,992
Rank among states	15
Property taxes.	$1 mill.
Sales taxes	$1,161 mill.
License taxes.	$92 mill.
Individual income taxes	$824 mill.
Corporate income taxes.	$28 mill.
Other taxes	$22 mill.

Total revenue figures include items not listed separately here.
Source: U.S. Bureau of the Census.

State government expenditures, 2002

General expenditures

Total state expenditures . . . . $5,767 mill.
Intergovernmental . . . . $749 mill.

Per capita expenditures

State $4,534
Average of all states $3,859
Rank among states 10

Selected direct expenditures

Education. $672 mill.
Public welfare . . . . $1,659 mill.
Health, hospital . . . . $295 mill.
Highways . . . . $260 mill.
Police protection . . . . $48 mill.
Corrections. . . . . $158 mill.
Natural resources . . . . $47 mill.
Parks and recreation . . . . $25 mill.
Government administration . . . . $260 mill.
Interest on debt . . . . $257 mill.
Total direct expenditures . . . . $4,094 mill.

Totals include items not listed separately.
Source: U.S. Census Bureau.

POLITICS

Governors since statehood

D = Democrat; R = Republican; O = other;
(r) resigned; (d) died in office; (i) removed from office

Nicholas Cooke 1776-1778
William Greene 1778-1786
John Collins 1786-1790
Arthur Fenner (O) . . . . (d) 1790-1805
Henry Smith (O) 1805-1806
Isaac Wilbour (O) 1806-1807
James Fenner (O) 1807-1811
William Jones (O) 1811-1817
Nehemiah Knight (O) 1817-1821
Edward Wilcox (O) 1821
William C. Gibbs (O) 1821-1824
James Fenner (O) 1824-1831
Lemuel H. Arnold (D) 1831-1833
John B. Francis (D) 1833-1838
William Sprague (O) 1838-1839
Samuel W. King (O) 1839-1843
James Fenner (O) 1843-1845
Charles Jackson (O) 1845-1846
Byron Diman (O) 1846-1847
Elisha Harris (O) 1847-1849
Henry B. Anthony (O) 1849-1851
Philip Allen (D) . . . . (r) 1851-1853
Francis M. Dimond (D) 1853-1854
William W. Hoppin (O) 1854-1857
Elisha Dyer II (R) 1857-1859
Thomas G. Turner (R) 1859-1860

William Sprague II (O) . . . . (r) 1860-1863
William C. Cozzens (O) 1863
James Y. Smith (O). 1863-1866
Ambrose E. Burnside (R) 1866-1869
Seth Padelford (R) 1869-1873
Henry Howard (R) 1873-1875
Henry Lippitt (R) 1875-1877
Charles C. Van Zandt (R) 1877-1880
Alfred H. Littlefield (R) 1880-1883
Augustus O. Bourne (R). 1883-1885
George P. Wetmore (R) 1885-1887
John W. Davis (D) 1887-1888
Royal C. Taft (R) 1888-1889
Herbert W. Ladd (R) 1889-1890
John W. Davis (D) 1890-1891
Herbert W. Ladd (R) 1891-1892
Daniel Russell Brown (R) 1892-1895
Charles W. Lippitt (R) 1895-1897
Elisha Dyer III (R) 1897-1900
William Gregory (R) . . . . (d) 1900-1901
Charles D. Kimball (R) 1901-1903
Lucius F. C. Garvin (D) 1903-1905
George H. Utter (R). 1905-1907
James H. Higgins (D) 1907-1909
Aram J. Pothier (R) 1909-1915
Robert Livingston Beeckman (R). 1915-1921
Emery J. San Souci (R) 1921-1923
William S. Flynn (D). 1923-1925
Aram J. Pothier (R) . . . . (d) 1925-1928
Norman S. Case (R) 1928-1933
Theodore F. Green (D) 1933-1937
Robert E. Quinn (D) 1937-1939
William H. Vanderbilt (R). 1939-1941
James Howard McGrath (D) . . . . (r) 1941-1945
John O. Pastore (D) . . . . (r) 1945-1950
John S. McKiernan (D) 1950-1951
Dennis J. Roberts (D) 1951-1959
Christopher Del Sesto (R). 1959-1961
John A. Notte, Jr. (D) 1961-1963
John H. Chafee (R) 1963-1969
Frank R. Licht (D) 1969-1973
Philip W. Noel (D). 1973-1977
J. Joseph Garrahy (D) 1977-1985
Edward D. DiPrete (R) 1985-1991
Bruce Sundlun (D) 1991-1995
Lincoln Almond (R). 1995-2003
Donald Carcieri (R) 2003-

Composition of congressional delegations, 1989-2007

	Dem	Rep	Total
House of Representatives			
101st Congress, 1989			
State delegates	0	2	2
Total U.S.	259	174	433
102d Congress, 1991			
State delegates	1	1	2
Total U.S.	267	167	434
103d Congress, 1993			
State delegates	1	1	2
Total U.S.	258	176	434
104th Congress, 1995			
State delegates	2	0	2
Total U.S.	197	236	433
105th Congress, 1997			
State delegates	2	0	2
Total U.S.	206	228	434
106th Congress, 1999			
State delegates	2	0	2
Total U.S.	211	222	433
107th Congress, 2001			
State delegates	2	0	2
Total U.S.	211	221	432
108th Congress, 2003			
State delegates	2	0	2
Total U.S.	205	229	434
109th Congress, 2005			
State delegates	2	0	2
Total U.S.	202	231	433
110th Congress, 2007			
State delegates	2	0	2
Total U.S.	233	202	435
Senate			
101st Congress, 1989			
State delegates	1	1	2
Total U.S.	55	45	100
102d Congress, 1991			
State delegates	1	1	2
Total U.S.	56	44	100
103d Congress, 1993			
State delegates	1	1	2
Total U.S.	57	43	100
104th Congress, 1995			
State delegates	1	1	2
Total U.S.	46	53	99
105th Congress, 1997			
State delegates	1	1	2
Total U.S.	45	55	100

	Dem	Rep	Total
106th Congress, 1999			
State delegates	1	1	2
Total U.S.	45	54	99
107th Congress, 2001			
State delegates	1	1	2
Total U.S.	50	50	100
108th Congress, 2003			
State delegates	1	1	2
Total U.S.	48	51	99
109th Congress, 2005			
State delegates	1	1	2
Total U.S.	44	55	99
110th Congress, 2007			
State delegates	2	0	2
Total U.S.	49	49	98

Figures are for starts of first sessions. Totals are for Democrat (Dem.) and Republican (Rep.) members only. House membership totals under 435 and Senate totals under 100 reflect vacancies and seats held by independent party members. When the 110th Congress opened, the Senate's two independent members caucused with the Democrats, giving the Democrats control of the Senate.

Source: U.S. Congress, *Congressional Directory.*

Composition of state legislature, 1990-2006

	Democrats	Republicans
State House (100 seats until 2000; 75 seats thereafter)		
1990	89	11
1992	85	15
1994	84	16
1996	84	16
1998	86	13
2000	86	13
2002	63	11
2004	60	15
2006	60	15
State Senate (50 seats until 2000; 38 seats thereafter)		
1990	45	5
1992	39	11
1994	40	10
1996	41	9
1998	42	8
2000	42	8
2002	32	6
2004	33	5
2006	33	5

Figures for total seats may include independents and minor party members. Numbers reflect results of elections in listed years; elected members usually take their seats in the years that follow.

Source: Council of State Governments; *State Elective Officials and the Legislatures.*

Voter participation in presidential elections, 2000 and 2004

	2000	2004
Voting age population		
State	803,000	837,000
Total United States	209,831,000	220,377,000
State share of U.S. total	0.38	0.38
Rank among states	43	43
Portion of voting age population casting votes		
State	50.9%	52.2%
United States	50.3%	55.5%
Rank among states	29	41

Population figures are rounded to nearest thousand and include all residents, regardless of eligibility to vote.
Source: U.S. Census Bureau.

HEALTH AND MEDICAL CARE

Medical professionals
Physicians in 2003 and nurses in 2001

	U.S.	State
Physicians in 2003		
Total	774,849	3,770
Share of U.S. total		0.48%
Rate	266	350
Rank		6
Nurses in 2001		
Total	2,262,020	11,160
Share of U.S. total		0.49%
Rate	793	1,053
Rank		4

Rates are numbers of physicians and nurses per 100,000 resident population; ranks are based on rates.
Source: American Medical Association, *Physician Characteristics and Distribution in the U.S.*; U.S. Department of Health and Human Services, Health Resources and Services Administration.

Health insurance coverage, 2003

	State	U.S.
Total persons covered	946,000	243,320,000
Total persons not covered	108,000	44,961,000
Portion not covered	10.2%	15.6%
Rank among states	47	—
Children not covered	13,000	8,373,000
Portion not covered	5.2%	11.4%
Rank among states	49	—

Totals are rounded to nearest thousand. Ranks are from the highest to the lowest percentages of persons *not* insured.
Source: U.S. Census Bureau, Current Population Reports.

AIDS, syphilis, and tuberculosis cases, 2003

Disease	U.S. cases	State cases	Rank
AIDS	44,232	102	37
Syphilis	34,270	90	34
Tuberculosis	14,874	46	37

Source: U.S. Centers for Disease Control and Prevention.

Cigarette smoking, 2003
Residents over age 18 who smoke

	U.S.	State	Rank
All smokers	22.1%	22.4%	24
Male smokers	24.8%	23.8%	28
Female smokers	20.3%	21.1%	20

Cigarette smokers are defined as persons who reported having smoked at least 100 cigarettes during their lifetimes and who currently smoked at least occasionally.
Source: U.S. Centers for Disease Control and Prevention, *Morbidity and Mortality Weekly Report*, 53, no. 44 (November 12, 2004).

HOUSING

Home ownership rates, 1985-2004

	1985	1990	1995	2000	2004
State	61.4%	58.5%	57.9%	61.5%	61.5%
Total U.S.	63.9%	63.9%	64.7%	67.4%	69.0%
Rank among states	42	45	47	46	47

Net change in state home ownership rate,
1985-2004 . . . . +0.1%
Net change in U.S. home ownership rate,
1985-2004 . . . . +5.1%

Percentages represent the proportion of owner households to total occupied households.
Source: U.S. Census Bureau, 2006.

Home sales, 2000-2004
In thousands of units

Existing home sales	2000	2002	2003	2004
State sales	17.0	17.1	16.9	19.2
Total U.S. sales	5,171	5,631	6,183	6,784
State share of U.S. total	0.33%	0.30%	0.27%	0.28%
Sales rank among states	44	45	45	45

Units include single-family homes, condos, and co-ops.
Source: National Association of Realtors, Washington, D.C., *Real Estate Outlook: Market Trends & Insights.*

Values of owner-occupied homes, 2003

	State	U.S.
Total units	212,000	58,809,000
Value of units		
Under $100,000	4.6%	29.6%
$100,000-199,999	43.4%	36.9%
$200,000 or more	52.1%	33.5%
Median value	$205,244	$142,275
Rank among all states		8

Units are owner-occupied one-family houses whose numbers are rounded to nearest thousand. Data are extrapolated from survey samples.

Source: U.S. Census Bureau, American Community Survey.

EDUCATION

Public school enrollment, 2002

Prekindergarten through grade 8

State enrollment	113,000
Total U.S. enrollment	34,135,000
State share of U.S. total	0.33%

Grades 9 through 12

State enrollment	47,000
Total U.S. enrollment	14,067,000
State share of U.S. total	0.33%

Enrollment rates

State public school enrollment rate	87.2%
Overall U.S. rate	90.4%
Rank among states in 2002	42
Rank among states in 1995	44

Enrollment figures (which include unclassified students) are rounded to nearest thousand pupils during fall school term. Enrollment rates are based on enumerated resident population estimate for July 1, 2002.

Source: U.S. National Center for Education Statistics.

Public college finances, 2003-2004

FTE enrollment in public institutions of higher education

Students in state institutions	27,800
Students in all U.S. public institutions	9,916,600
State share of U.S. total	0.28
Rank among states	48

State and local government appropriations for higher education

State appropriation per FTE	$6,180
National average	$5,716
Rank among states	14
State & local tax revenue going to higher education	4.7%

FTE = full-time equivalent in public postsecondary programs, including summer sessions; student numbers are rounded to nearest hundred. Funding figures for 2003-2004 academic year include financial aid to students in state public institutions and exclude money for research, agriculture experiment stations, teaching hospitals, and medical schools; figures are rounded to nearest thousand dollars.

Source: Higher Education Executive Officers, Denver, Colorado.

TRANSPORTATION AND TRAVEL

Highway mileage, 2003

Interstate highways	71
Other freeways and expressways	85
Arterial roads	832
Collector roads	879
Local roads	4,548
Urban roads	5,193
Rural roads	1,222
Total state mileage	6,415
U.S. total	3,974,107
State share	0.16%
Rank among states	48

Note that combined urban and rural road mileage matches the total of the other categories.

Source: U.S. Federal Highway Administration.

Motor vehicle registrations and driver licenses, 2003

Vehicle registrations	State	U.S.	Share	Rank
Autos, trucks, buses	806,000	231,390,000	0.35%	45
Autos only	549,000	135,670	0.40%	42
Motorcycles	25,000	5,328,000	0.47%	44
Driver licenses	731,000	196,166,000	0.37%	43

Figures, which do not include vehicles owned by military services, are rounded to the nearest thousand. Figures for automobiles include taxis.

Source: U.S. Federal Highway Administration.

Domestic travel expenditures, 2003

Spending by U.S. residents on overnight trips and day trips of at least 50 miles from home

Total expenditures within state	$1.43 bill.
Total expenditures within U.S.	$490.87 bill.
State share of U.S. total	0.3%
Rank among states	46

Source: Travel Industry Association of America.

Retail gasoline prices, 2003-2007

Average price per gallon at the pump

Year	U.S.	State
2003	$1.267	$1.234
2004	$1.316	$1.279
2005	$1.644	$1.558
2007	$2.298	$2.302

Excise tax per gallon in 2004	30.0¢
Rank among all states in 2007 prices	21

Prices are averages of all grades of gasoline sold at the pump during March months in 2003-2005 and during February, 2007. Averages for 2006, during which prices rose higher, are not available.

Source: U.S. Energy Information Agency, *Petroleum Marketing Monthly* (2003-2005 data); American Automobile Association (2007 data).

CRIME AND LAW ENFORCEMENT

State and local police officers, 2000-2004

	2000	2002	2004
Total officers			
U.S.	654,601	665,555	675,734
State	2,450	2,485	2,473*
*Net change, 2000-2004			+0.94%
Officers per 1,000 residents			
U.S.	2.33	2.31	2.30
State	2.34	2.33	2.29
State rank	17	15	17

Totals include state and local police and sheriffs.
Source: Carsey Institute, University of New Hampshire.

Crime rates, 2003

Incidents per 100,000 residents

Crimes	State	U.S.
Violent crimes		
Total incidents	286	475
Murder	2	6
Forcible rape	47	32
Robbery	77	142
Aggravated assault	159	295
Property crimes		
Total incidents	2,995	3,588
Burglary	513	741
Larceny/theft	2,074	2,415
Motor vehicle theft	408	433
All crimes	3,281	4,063

Source: U.S. Federal Bureau of Investigation, *Crime in the United States,* annual.

State prison populations, 1980-2003

	State	U.S.	State share
1980	813	305,458	0.27%
1990	2,392	708,393	0.34%
1996	3,271	1,025,624	0.32%
2000	3,286	1,391,261	0.24%
2003	3,527	1,470,045	0.24%

State figures include jail inmates but exclude prisoners in federal penitentiaries.
Source: U.S. Bureau of Justice Statistics, *Prisoners in 2003.*

South Carolina

Location: Southeast Atlantic coast

Area and rank: 30,111 square miles (77,988 square kilometers); 32,007 square miles (82,898 square kilometers) including water; fortieth largest state in area

Coastline: 187 miles (301 kilometers) on the Atlantic Ocean

Shoreline: 2,876 miles (4,628 kilometers)

Population and rank: 4,198,000 (2004); twenty-fifth largest state in population

Capital and largest city: Columbia (116,278 people in 2000 census)

Entered Union and rank: May 23, 1788; eighth state

Present constitution adopted: 1895

Located near historic Fort Sumter, Charleston's Battery district is famed for its stately old homes. (South Carolina Department of Parks, Recreation & Tourism)

Counties: 46

State name: South Carolina was named after Charles I of England

State nickname: Palmetto State

Mottoes: *Animis opibusque parati* (Prepared in mind and resources); *Dum spiro spero* (While I breathe, I hope)

State flag: Blue field with palmetto tree and crescent moon

Highest point: Sassafras Mountain—3,560 feet (1,085 meters)

Lowest point: Atlantic Ocean—sea level

Highest recorded temperature: 111 degrees Fahrenheit (44 degrees Celsius)—Camden, 1954

Lowest recorded temperature: –19 degrees Fahrenheit (–28 degrees Celsius)—Caesar's Head, 1985

State song: "Carolina"

State tree: Palmetto tree

State flower: Carolina yellow jessamine

State bird: Carolina wren

National parks: Congaree

South Carolina History

South Carolina, known as the Palmetto State, is the smallest of the southeastern states and is one of the richest in history and enduring influence on national events and development. A blend of diverse cultures, including European, Native American, and African American, produced notable social, artistic, political, military, and cultural accomplishments. The state has been among the richest and the poorest in the United States and has known both victory and harsh defeat.

Early History. The first human inhabitants of what is now South Carolina arrived around 13,000 B.C.E. as hunters of the large animals, including elephants, that inhabited the region. During the period from 8000 to 1500 B.C.E., the area's climate changed, bringing hardwood trees and more easily huntable animals such as deer, turkey, and squirrel. Many inhabitants became largely migratory, moving through the seasons to follow their prey. Along the coast, shellfish provided a major diet staple for more settled groups.

Around 1150 B.C.E. a new group, the Mississippians, moved into the area. They built large villages with earthen mounds for temples along river bluffs. These villages established a nation known as Cofitachequi, after its capital, located on the banks of the Wateree River in central South Carolina. In 1540, the Spanish explorer Hernando de Soto was greeted by the "queen" of Cofitachequi during his expedition across the Southeast.

At the time of the arrival of the Europeans, there were thirty to forty separate Native American nations in the region, including Cherokee, Saluda, Catawba, Wateree, Congaree, Wando, Waccamaw, and Coosaw. All of these names, and many others, were preserved in place names in South Carolina.

Exploration and Settlement. By 1521 the Spanish had explored the Carolina coast, and on August 18, 1525, Saint Helena's feast day, they sighted and named an island and a sound in her honor; both would retain the name Saint Helena. Lucas Vásquez de Ayllón

Reenactment of a Revolutionary War battle in Kings Mountain State Park, where Tennessee pioneers turned back a British force trying to occupy South Carolina in 1780. (South Carolina Department of Parks, Recreation & Tourism)

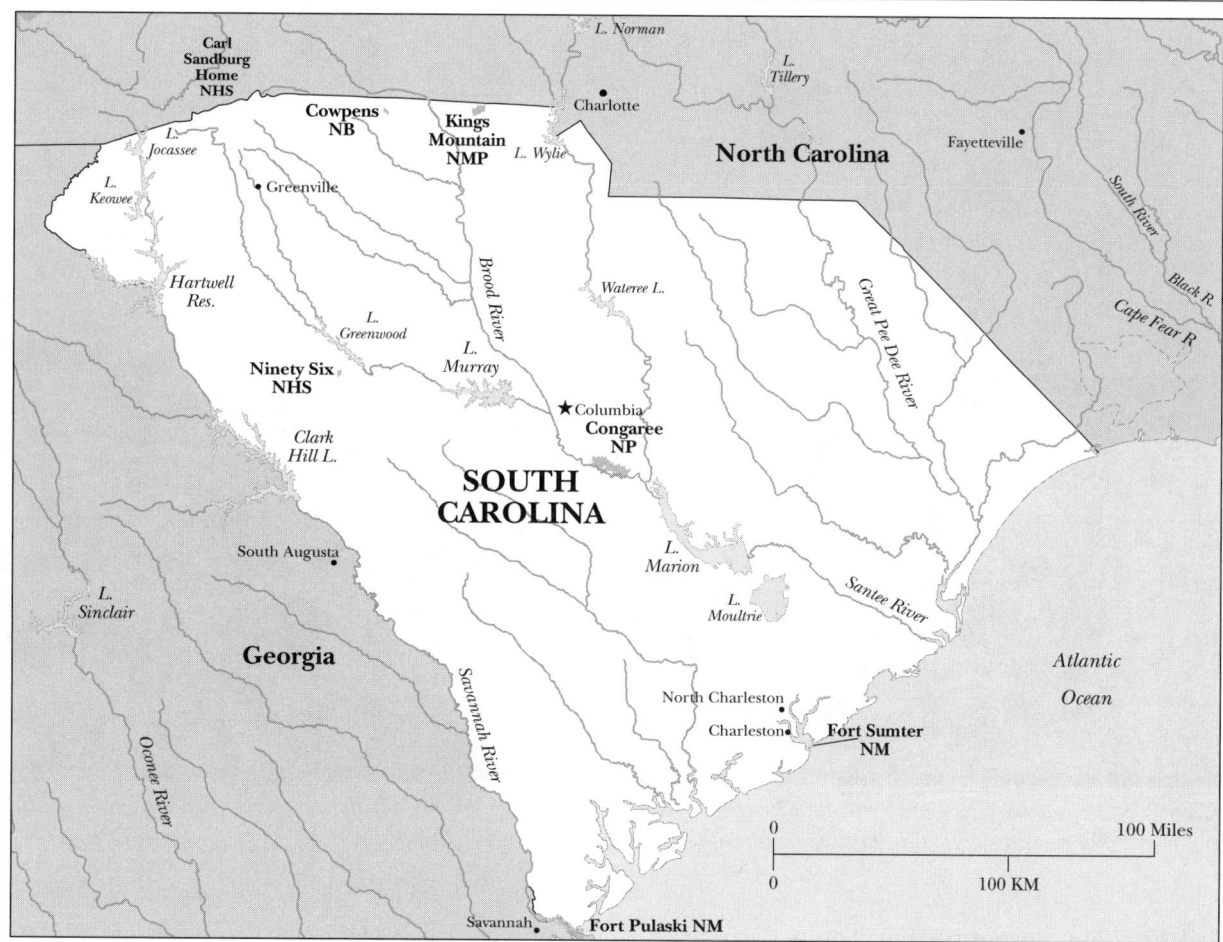

founded a short-lived Spanish settlement on Winyah Bay near modern Georgetown in 1526, and in 1562, the French under Jean Ribaut challenged the Spanish by establishing a small fort on an island in what they named Port Royal Sound.

The Spanish returned in 1566 and established Santa Elena, also on Port Royal Sound, which grew into a settlement of considerable size and was for a time the capital of all Spanish colonies in North America. However, under increasing pressure from the Native Americans and the English, the Spanish abandoned Santa Elena in 1587 to consolidate their position at St. Augustine in northern Florida.

Colonization and Revolution. In 1663, King Charles II of England granted extensive lands, named "Carolina" after himself, to eight Lord Proprietors, chief among them Anthony Ashley Cooper, earl of Shaftesbury. Cooper, along with English philosopher John Locke, drafted an elaborate Fundamental Constitution for the colony. In 1670, the first settlers arrived. Within ten years they had re-established the city of Charleston at the confluence of the Ashley and Cooper rivers. Settled largely by English inhabitants of Barbados, the new colony prospered from the production of crops includ-

ing rice, indigo, and cotton. The wealth of these crops, and the plantation systems they fostered, was gained only through the knowledge and labor of large numbers of African slaves. Long before the American Revolution, there were more blacks than whites in the colony. Along the South Carolina Sea Islands, they created their own distinctive culture, including the Gullah language, a mixture of African, Caribbean, and English languages.

Early threats to the colony included struggles with the Native Americans and raids by pirates such as the notorious Blackbeard (Edward Teach). These dangers were increased by proprietary incompetence, and in 1729 South Carolina became a royal colony. South Carolina was a leader in the move for American independence, and during the American Revolution more than 130 battles and skirmishes were fought in the state. In June, 1776, British naval forces were repulsed from Charleston but returned and captured the city in 1780. The battles of Kings Mountain in 1780 and Cowpens in 1781 helped turn the tide of the war in favor of the Americans. Partisan leaders such as Francis Marion, known as the Swamp Fox, played an essential role in the struggle for independence.

The Civil War is traditionally regarded as having begun on April 12, 1861, when Confederate troops fired on Union soldiers defending Fort Sumter on a small island at the mouth of Charleston's harbor. (Corbis)

Civil War and Reconstruction. South Carolinians Charles Pinckney and John Rutledge were highly influential in drafting the U.S. Constitution, and they were instrumental in having it adopted by the state legislature in 1788. However, as with many others in the state and throughout the South, they wished to restrain the powers of the federal government, especially regarding the highly sensitive issue of slavery.

In was because of this concern that South Carolina, along with other southern states, increasingly insisted upon the doctrine of states' rights. Senator John C. Calhoun became the chief spokesperson for the South, and while he helped to fashion compromises that kept South Carolina in the Union, he also advocated nullification, the doctrine that a state could declare invalid within its borders an act of the national government. During the Nullification Crisis of 1832-1833 President Andrew Jackson ordered U.S. Navy ships to Charleston to enforce federal law. The election of President Abraham Lincoln in 1860 prompted South Carolina to become the first state to secede from the Union on December 20, 1860.

On April 12, 1861, the Civil War began, when Confederate troops fired on Union-held Fort Sumter in Charleston harbor. During the war, Union troops quickly captured the sea islands around Port Royal Sound, liberating thousands of slaves and placing Charleston under a four-year siege. After General Wil-

liam T. Sherman's Union army completed its March to the Sea from Atlanta to Savannah, it "let South Carolina howl" as it swept through the state, forcing the Confederates to abandon Charleston and Columbia, the state capital. Sherman largely blamed South Carolina for the war because it was the first state to secede, and he punished it harshly.

South Carolina was readmitted to the Union in 1868, and a Reconstruction government mingled social and educational reforms with blatant corruption. In 1876, under the leadership of former Confederate general Wade Hampton, white South Carolinians reclaimed their hold on the state. For almost a hundred years, the memory of the Civil War and Reconstruction ensured that South Carolina would remain a solidly Democratic state. It was only during the civil rights era of the 1960's, when the Democratic Party became closely associated with that effort, that many white South Carolinians turned to the Republican Party. Senator Strom Thurmond, who had run as a Dixiecrat in 1948 to protest the Democrats' civil rights platform, became a Republican in 1964. In 1974, James Edwards was the first Republican elected governor after Reconstruction.

A Modern Economy. After the Civil War, agriculture remained South Carolina's primary source of income. During the 1880's, the textile industry greatly increased, due in large part to the hydroelectric power available upstate. Textile plants drew workers from the farms and rural areas to create a new and thriving industry, until the Great Depression brought economic disaster during the 1930's. The New Deal of President Franklin Delano Roosevelt sought to remedy these problems in part by the creation of the Santee Cooper project, one of the largest hydroelectric and navigational efforts in North America, which helped advance South Carolina's economy into the twentieth century. During and after World War II, large military bases throughout the state provided additional economic benefits.

However, agriculture and textiles remained the state's major sources of income until the early 1970's, when modern industry and technology took hold, best exemplified by BMW's 1993 decision to locate its first car-manufacturing plant outside Germany in South Carolina. By that time, manufacturing had become the state's number-one industry in terms of employees and included more than two hundred international companies. Tourism became a major source of income, with visitors flocking to South Carolina's coastline and beaches; historic cities such as Camden, Charleston, and Beaufort; and three hundred golf courses, many of them world class and the site of prestigious tournaments.

Modernization in the economy brought increased attention to both an old problem and a new concern: the issue of resolving racial differences among the state's population and the need to protect the state's natural environment. South Carolina, with its long and often troubled history, and its abundant natural resources threatened by rapid development and population growth, faced the delicate task of balancing past, present, and future.

Confederate Flag Controversy. The year 2000 found South Carolina embroiled in an issue dating back to the Old South and the Civil War. The long-simmering controversy was over the flying of the Confederate flag, a widely recognized symbol of the organization of Southern states that seceded from the Union in 1861 to form the Confederate States of America; the confederation lasted until its defeat in 1865. In 2000, the Confederate flag flew on South Carolina's statehouse dome; however, many, especially black South Carolinians, who form 30 percent of the state's population, found it objectionable as symbolic of slavery and racism. Others saw the flag as a symbol of tradition rather than racism.

In April, 2000, the state senate voted to remove the flag from the statehouse dome and to fly a traditional version of the flag next to an existing memorial to

State capitol building in Columbia.

fallen Confederate soldiers in front of the Capitol. This bill was sent to the state's House of Representatives, where it received a less than enthusiastic reception. However, on May 18, by a 66-43 vote, the House approved a modified bill agreeing to move the flag as the senate had decided but stipulating that the flag be flown on a pole ten feet higher than in the senate version.

Significantly, only four of twenty-six black members of the House voted for the bill. Since the state did not entirely dispense with the flag, the controversy continued. The National Association for the Advancement of Colored People (NAACP) instituted a boycott of the state over the flag issue in late 1999 and has refused to abandon it over the next eight years. However, public interest in the boycott faded.

Perhaps also indicative of movement on racial issues was a policy at one of the state's most conservative institutions. In 2000, fundamentalist Christian Bob Jones University, reversing a policy dating back to the 1950's, announced lifting a ban on interracial dating among its student body.

Senator Strom Thurmond. In 2003, one of the state's most controversial but also beloved figures, U.S. senator Strom Thurmond, died at age one hundred. At the time, before Senator Robert Byrd surpassed his record on June 10, 2006, Thurmond was the longest-serving member ever of the Senate. First elected to the Senate in 1954, Thurmond, who started his career in politics as a Democrat, became a Republican a decade later. He was notorious for having run for president in 1948 on a segregationist ticket. However, by the 1970's, Thurmond changed course and endorsed racial integration. He enrolled his daughter in an integrated public school and hired African American staffers. Upon his retirement in 2003, Thurmond was succeeded by Lindsey Graham.

Politics. South Carolina voted for George W. Bush in both the 2000 and the 2004 presidential elections by substantial margins, the first time by 57 to 41 percent, the second time by a 58-41 percent margin. In 2004, the U.S. Senate seat vacated by retiring Democratic senator Ernest "Fritz" Hollings was won by Republican Jim DeMint, who defeated his opponent by a 54-44 percent margin.

Michael Witkoski
Updated by the Editor

South Carolina Time Line

1500-1600	Native American nation of Cofitachequi is powerful in Southeast.
1521	Spanish explore South Carolina coast.
1525	Spanish explore and name Saint Helena Island and Sound.
1526	Lucas Vásquez de Ayllón establishes Spanish settlement on Winyah Bay.
1540	Spanish explorer Hernando de Soto passes through area.
1562	Jean Ribaut establishes short-lived French colony on Port Royal Sound.
1566	Spanish establish Santa Elena on Port Royal Sound.
1587	Spanish abandon Santa Elena.
1663	King Charles II of England grants Carolina to eight Lord Proprietors.
1670	English establish Charles Town (later Charleston).
1670	First African slaves arrive from the West Indies.
1680	Charleston moved to peninsula between Ashley and Cooper rivers.
1680	Rice introduced as a crop.
1715	War rages between English settlers and Yamasee Indians.
1718	Colonists end threat of pirates.
1729	Carolina becomes a royal colony.
1730	North and South Carolina become separate colonies.
1742	Indigo introduced as a crop.
1760	Cherokees defeated in conflicts with colonists.
1776	British defeated in attack on Charleston.
1778	South Carolina declares independence from Great Britain.
1780	British capture Charleston.
1786	State capital moved to Columbia.
May 23, 1788	South Carolina becomes eighth state to join the Union.
1801	University of South Carolina is established in Columbia.
1820	Cotton begins to replace rice and indigo as the major crop.
1822	Denmark Vesey leads abortive slave revolt in Charleston.

1832	Legislature passes Ordinance of Nullification.
1833	President Andrew Jackson orders U.S. Navy fleet to South Carolina to enforce federal laws.
Dec. 20, 1860	South Carolina becomes first state to secede from the Union.
Apr. 12, 1861	Confederate assault on Charleston's Fort Sumter begins the Civil War.
1865	Union forces under General William T. Sherman march through state; Columbia is burned.
1866-1876	South Carolina undergoes Reconstruction period.
June 25, 1868	South Carolina is readmitted to the Union.
1880	Textile industry begins rapid expansion.
1895	New state constitution is adopted.
1942	Santee Cooper hydroelectric project is completed.
1948	Governor Strom Thurmond runs for president as a Dixiecrat to protest civil rights plank in Democratic Party platform.
1950	Site in Aiken and Barnwell counties selected for plutonium-making project known as the Savannah River Plant.
1952	U.S. Supreme Court upholds segregation in South Carolina.
1963	Integration of state's public school system begins in Charleston.
1964	U.S. Senator Strom Thurmond switches from Democratic to Republican Party, beginning realignment of state's political structure.
1970	State begins to attract modern industrial and technological companies.
1974	James Edwards is first Republican elected governor after Reconstruction.
1989	Hurricane Hugo sweeps through state, leaving $6 billion in damage and twenty-nine dead.
1993	BMW locates its first manufacturing facility outside Germany in upstate South Carolina.
May 18, 2000	State legislature approves removing Confederate flag from statehouse dome and placing it near a Confederate soldiers' memorial.
Nov. 7, 2000	South Carolina chooses George W. Bush for president.
June 26, 2003	Senator Strom Thurmond dies at the age of one hundred.
Nov. 2, 2004	George W. Bush again gains the state's presidential electoral votes.

Notes for Further Study

Published Sources. One of South Carolina's most distinguished historians, Walter Edgar, has written several excellent studies of the state and its people. *South Carolina: A History* (1998) is the definitive state history presented in a cleanly written and engaging narrative. It is well illustrated and amply annotated. His *South Carolina in the Modern Age* (1992) is a study of the years following the Civil War, focusing on the transformation from an agricultural to a textile and then industrial economic base. His *South Carolina Encyclopedia* (2006) provides an excellent overview of numerous aspects of the state's history, culture, and character. *South Carolina Native Americans* (2004) by Carole Marsh is a good introductory text about the state's indigenous cultures. *Mary Chestnut's Civil War* (1981), edited by C. Vann Woodward, is an acclaimed presentation of a key historical document, the wartime diary of Mary Chestnut of Charleston, which is fundamental for understanding the Civil War's impact on the state. Edward Miller's *Gullah Statesman: Robert Smalls, from Slavery to Congress, 1835-1915* (1995) is a comprehensive biography of the man who became one of the outstanding African American leaders of the post-Civil War era. Hyman Rubin III's *South Carolina Scalawags* (2006) provides insight into the era of Reconstruction within the state and explores the role of white Southerners who supported the newly freed slaves.

South Carolina Politics and Government (1994) by Cole Blease Graham, Jr., and William V. Moore presents the intricate nature of South Carolina political life clearly and engagingly. Peter A. Coclanis's *The Shadow of a Dream: Economic Life and Death in the South Carolina Low Country, 1670-1920* (1989) is a review of economic developments throughout most of the state's history. It is especially valuable for its discussion of the major cash crops of the antebellum era. *From New Babylon to Eden: The Huguenots and Their Migration to Colonial South Carolina* (2006) by Bertrand Van Ruymbeke details the history of the French-speaking Huguenots and their eventual ascendance as among the most influential and successful colonists, leaving a legacy throughout Charleston and the state's low country. A text that explores the state's Civil Rights era is Philip G. Grose's *South Carolina at the Brink: Robert McNair and the Politics of Civil Rights, 1965-1971* (2006).

Web Resources. The best place to begin a search for information on South Carolina, with links to state government sites, educational institutions, and other organizations, is the state of South Carolina Public Information home page (www.sc.gov/). This site can be supplemented with a visit to the home page of the South Carolina State Library (www.scstatelibrary.org/), which is valuable because the library provides extensive resources for those interested in all aspects of South Carolina, from contemporary events to its earliest history. An excellent source for historical information is

This tree-shaded entrance to one of South Carolina's great old farm homes recalls the opulence of the state's nineteenth century plantation economy. (PhotoDisc)

the South Carolina Department of Archives and History (www.state.sc.us/scdah/homepage.htm). As the holder of the state's official records, papers, and documents, the archives's site is very useful to any student of South Carolina and its history. Those in search of historical information should also visit the South Carolina Historical Society (www.schistory.org). The state's rich history has encouraged study by professional, independent, and amateur scholars; this site is an excellent place to sample their research and to find links to additional Web pages.

Another excellent source for a variety of Web sites is SCIWay (South Carolina Information Highway; www.sciway.net), a frequently updated site that directs users to Web resources. Finally, the most famous city in South Carolina has its own Web site, the Charleston Connection (www.segetaway.com/Charleston/index.html). This site is devoted to information on one of the most historic cities in South Carolina and the nation. Several of the state's cities and towns have a Web presence, and the South Carolina Reference Room (www.state.sc.us/scsl/cities.html) directs users to the specific URLs. For those in need of demographic statistics, the U.S. Census Bureau's QuickFacts about the state (quickfacts.census.gov/qfd/index.html) are quite helpful.

Counties

County	2000 pop.	Rank in pop.	Sq. miles	Rank in area	County	2000 pop.	Rank in pop.	Sq. miles	Rank in area
Abbeville	26,167	35	508.0	33	Calhoun	15,185	44	380.3	45
Aiken	142,552	10	1,073.1	4	Charleston	309,969	3	917.4	7
Allendale	11,211	45	408.2	41	Cherokee	52,537	24	392.7	44
Anderson	165,740	7	718.0	15	Chester	34,068	30	580.6	26
Bamberg	16,658	43	393.3	43	Chesterfield	42,768	25	798.8	11
Barnwell	23,478	37	548.5	31	Clarendon	32,502	31	607.2	24
Beaufort	120,937	12	587.0	25	Colleton	38,264	26	1,056.5	5
Berkeley	142,651	9	1,099.5	3	Darlington	67,394	18	562.1	28

County	2000 pop.	Rank in pop.	Sq. miles	Rank in area
Dillon	30,722	32	404.9	42
Dorchester	96,413	15	574.8	27
Edgefield	24,595	36	501.9	34
Fairfield	23,454	38	686.6	18
Florence	125,761	11	799.2	10
Georgetown	55,797	22	814.9	8
Greenville	379,616	1	792.1	12
Greenwood	66,271	19	455.5	38
Hampton	21,386	39	559.9	29
Horry	196,629	6	1,133.7	1
Jasper	20,678	40	654.3	21
Kershaw	52,647	23	726.3	14
Lancaster	61,351	21	549.0	30
Laurens	69,567	17	713.2	16
Lee	20,119	41	410.3	40
Lexington	216,014	5	700.8	17

County	2000 pop.	Rank in pop.	Sq. miles	Rank in area
McCormick	9,958	46	359.6	46
Marion	35,466	29	489.1	36
Marlboro	28,818	34	479.7	37
Newberry	36,108	28	630.8	22
Oconee	66,215	20	625.1	23
Orangeburg	91,582	16	1,106.0	2
Pickens	110,757	13	496.9	35
Richland	320,677	2	756.5	13
Saluda	19,181	42	451.4	39
Spartanburg	253,791	4	811.0	9
Sumter	104,646	14	665.5	20
Union	29,881	33	514.2	32
Williamsburg	37,217	27	934.0	6
York	164,614	8	682.5	19

Source: U.S. Census Bureau; National Association of Counties.

Cities

With 10,000 or more residents

Rank	City	Population	Rank	City	Population
1	Columbia (capital)	116,278	25	Simpsonville	14,352
2	Charleston	96,650	26	Socastee	14,295
3	North Charleston	79,641	27	Berea	14,158
4	Greenville	56,002	28	Gantt	13,962
5	Rock Hill	49,765	29	Ladson	13,264
6	Mount Pleasant	47,609	30	West Columbia	13,064
7	Spartanburg	39,673	31	Dentsville	13,009
8	Sumter	39,643	32	Gaffney	12,968
9	Hilton Head Island	33,862	33	Beaufort	12,950
10	Florence	30,248	34	Hanahan	12,937
11	Goose Creek	29,208	35	Orangeburg	12,765
12	Summerville	27,752	36	Cayce	12,150
13	Anderson	25,514	37	Clemson	11,939
14	Aiken	25,337	38	Conway	11,788
15	Myrtle Beach	22,759	39	Irmo	11,039
16	Greenwood	22,071	40	North Myrtle Beach	10,974
17	St. Andrews	21,814	41	Parker	10,760
18	Wade Hampton	20,458	42	Newberry	10,580
19	Taylors	20,125	43	Forest Acres	10,558
20	Easley	17,754	44	Red Hill	10,509
21	North Augusta	17,574			
22	Greer	16,843			
23	Seven Oaks	15,755			
24	Mauldin	15,224			

Population figures are from 2000 census.

Source: U.S. Bureau of the Census.

Index to Tables

DEMOGRAPHICS

Resident state and national populations, 1970-2004

Population figures given in thousands

	State pop.	U.S. pop.	Share	Rank
1970	2,591	203,302	1.3%	26
1980	3,122	226,546	1.4%	24
1985	3,303	237,924	1.4%	24
1990	3,486	248,765	1.4%	25
1995	3,749	262,761	1.4%	26
2000	4,012	281,425	1.4%	26
2004	4,198	293,655	1.4%	25

Source: U.S. Census Bureau, Current Population Reports, 2006.

Resident population by age, 2004

Age Group	Total persons
Under 5 years	280,000
5 to 17 years	744,000
18 to 24 years	429,000
25 to 34 years	568,000
35 to 44 years	611,000
45 to 54 years	594,000
55 to 64 years	451,000
65 to 74 years	286,000
75 to 84 years	175,000
85 years and older	59,000
All age groups	4,198,000

Portion of residents 65 and older	12.4%
National rank in portion of oldest residents	29
National average	12.4%

Population figures are rounded to nearest thousand persons;
figures include armed forces personnel stationed in the state.
Source: U.S. Bureau of the Census, 2006.

Resident population by race, Hispanic origin, 2004

Category	State pop.	Share	U.S.
All residents	4,198	100.00%	100.00%
Non-Hispanic white	2,753	65.58%	67.37%
Hispanic white	115	2.74%	13.01%
Other Hispanic	15	0.36%	1.06%
African American	1,233	29.37%	12.77%
Native American	16	0.38%	0.96%
Asian, Pacific Islander	46	1.10%	4.37%
Two or more categories	35	0.83%	1.51%

Population figures are in thousands. Persons counted as "Hispanic" (Latino) may be of any race. Because of overlapping categories, categories may not add up to 100%. Shares in column 3 are percentages of each category within the state; these figures may be compared to the national percentages in column 4.
Source: U.S. Bureau of the Census, 2006.

Projected state population, 2000-2030

Year	Population
2000	4,012,000
2005	4,239,000
2010	4,447,000
2015	4,642,000
2020	4,823,000
2025	4,990,000
2030	5,149,000
Population increase, 2000-2030	1,137,000
Percentage increase, 2000-2030	28.3

Projections are based on data from the 2000 census.
Source: U.S. Census Bureau.

VITAL STATISTICS

Infant mortality rates, 1980-2002

	1980	1990	2000	2002
All state residents	15.6	11.7	8.7	9.3
All U.S. residents	12.6	9.2	9.4	9.1
All state white residents	10.8	8.1	5.4	6.0
All U.S. white residents	10.6	7.6	5.7	5.8
All state black residents	22.9	17.3	14.8	15.8
All U.S. black residents	22.2	18.0	14.1	14.4

Figures represent deaths per 1,000 live births of resident infants under 1 year old, exclusive of fetal deaths. Figures for all residents include members of other racial categories not listed separately.
Source: U.S. Census Bureau, *Statistical Abstract of the United States,* 2006.

Abortion rates, 1990 and 2000

	1990	2000
Total abortions	12,000	8,000
Rate per 1,000 women	14.2	9.3
U.S. rate	25.7	21.3
Rank	35	42

Numbers of abortions are rounded to nearest thousand; ranks are based on rates.
Source: U.S. Census Bureau.

Marriages and divorces, 2004

Total marriages	34,500
Rate per 1,000 population	8.2
National rate per 1,000 population	7.4
Rank among all states	15
Total divorces	13,400
Rate per 1,000 population	3.2
National rate per 1,000 population	3.7
Rank among all states	31

Figures are for all marriages and divorces performed within the state, including those of nonresidents; totals are rounded to the nearest hundred. Ranks are for highest to lowest figures; note that divorce data are not available for five states.
Source: U.S. National Center for Health Statistics, *Vital Statistics of the United States,* 2006.

Death rates by leading causes, 2002
Deaths per 100,000 resident population

Cause	State	U.S.
Heart disease	235.2	241.7
Cancer	202.9	193.2
Cerebrovascular diseases	68.7	56.4
Accidents other than motor vehicle	48.0	37.0
Motor vehicle accidents	24.9	15.7
Chronic lower respiratory diseases	46.0	43.3
Diabetes mellitus	27.1	25.4
HIV	7.3	4.9
Suicide	10.7	11.0
Homicide	7.9	6.1
All causes	918.8	847.3
Rank in overall death rate among states		19

Figures exclude nonresidents who died in the state. Causes of death follow International Classification of Diseases. Rank is from highest to lowest death rate in the United States.
Source: U.S. National Center for Health Statistics, *National Vital Statistics Report,* 2006.

ECONOMY

Gross state product, 1990-2004
In current dollars

Year	State product	Nat'l product	State share
1990	$65.7 billion	$5.67 trillion	1.16%
2000	$112.8 billion	$9.75 trillion	1.16%
2002	$122.3 billion	$10.41 trillion	1.17%
2003	$128.0 billion	$10.92 trillion	1.17%
2004	$135.3 billion	$11.65 trillion	1.16%

Source: U.S. Bureau of Economic Analysis, *Survey of Current Business,* July, 2005.

Gross state product by industry, 2003
In billions of dollars

Construction	$6.1
Manufacturing	24.8
Wholesale trade	6.8
Retail trade	10.7
Finance & insurance	5.8
Information	3.4
Professional services	5.1
Health care & social assistance	6.5
Government	17.6
Total state product	$120.0
Total U.S. product	$10,289.2
State share of U.S. total	1.17%
Rank among all states	27

Total figures include industries not listed separately. Amounts are in chained 2000 dollars.

Source: U.S. Bureau of Economic Analysis, *Survey of Current Business,* July, 2005.

Personal income per capita, 1990-2004
In current dollars

	1990	2000	2004
Per capita income	$15,894	$24,424	$27,172
U.S. average	$19,477	$29,845	$32,937
Rank among states	40	39	43

Source: U.S. Bureau of Economic Analysis, *Survey of Current Business,* April, 2005.

Energy consumption, 2001
In trillions of British thermal units (BTU), except as noted

Total energy consumption

Total state energy consumption	1,549
Total U.S. energy consumption	96,275
State share of U.S. total	1.61%
Rank among states	22

Per capita consumption (In millions of BTU)

Total state per capita consumption	382
Total U.S. per capita consumption	338
Rank among states	16

End-use sectors

Residential	322
Commercial	235
Industrial	609
Transportation	383

Sources of energy

Petroleum	470
Natural gas	147
Coal	414
Hydroelectric power	2
Nuclear electric power	521

Figures for totals include categories not listed separately.
Source: U.S. Energy Information Administration, *State Energy Data Report,* 2001.

Nonfarm employment by sectors, 2004

Total persons	1,823,000
Construction	113,000
Manufacturing	269,000
Trade, transportation, utilities	353,000
Information	26,000
Finance, insurance, real estate	93,000
Professional & business services	192,000
Education & health services	176,000
Leisure, hospitality, arts, organizations	201,000
Other services, including repair & maintenance	68,000
Government	328,000

Figures are rounded to nearest thousand persons. "Total" includes mining and natural resources, not listed separately.
Source: U.S. Bureau of Labor Statistics, 2006.

Foreign exports, 1990-2004
In millions of dollars

Year	State	U.S.	State share
1990	3,116	394,045	0.79%
1996	6,698	624,767	1.07%
1997	7,517	688,896	1.09%
2000	8,565	712,055	1.09%
2003	11,773	724,006	1.74%
2004	13,376	769,332	1.74%

Rank among all states in 2004 18

U.S. total does not include U.S. dependencies.
Source: U.S. Census Bureau, *U.S. Merchandise Trade,* series FT 900, 2000; U.S. Census Bureau, *U.S. International Trade in Goods and Services,* Series FT 900, 2005.

LAND USE

Federally owned land, 2003
Areas in acres

	State	U.S.	State share
Total area	19,374,000	2,271,343,000	0.85%
Nonfederal land	18,138,000	1,599,584,000	1.13%
Federal land	1,236,000	671,759,000	0.18%
Federal share	6.4%	29.6%	—

Areas are rounded to nearest thousand acres. Figures for federally owned land do not include trust properties.
Source: U.S. General Services Administration, *Federal Real Property Profile,* 2006.

Land use, 1997
In acres, rounded to nearest thousand

Total surface area 19,939,000
Total nonfederal rural land. 16,018,000
Percentage rural land 80.3%
Cropland 2,574,000
Conservation Reserve Program (CRP*) land 263,000
Pastureland 1,197,000
Rangeland . . . . (nil)
Forestland 11,188,000
Other rural land 797,000

*CRP is a federal program begun in 1985 to assist private landowners to convert highly erodible cropland to vegetative cover for ten years. Note that some categories of land overlap.
Source: U.S. Department of Agriculture, Natural Resources and Conservation Service, and Iowa State University, Statistical Laboratory, *Summary Report, 1997 National Resources Inventory,* revised December, 2000.

Farms and crop acreage, 2004

	State	U.S.	Share	Rank
Farms	24,000	2,113,000	1.14%	33
Acres (millions)	5	937	0.53%	38
Acres per farm	199	443	—	33

Source: U.S. Department of Agriculture, National Agricultural Statistics Service. Numbers of farms are rounded to nearest thousand units; acreage figures are rounded to nearest million. Rankings, including ties, are based on rounded figures.

GOVERNMENT AND FINANCE

Units of local government, 2002

	State	Total U.S.	Rank
All local governments	701	87,525	37
Counties	46	3,034	31
Municipalities	269	19,429	30
Townships	0	16,504	—
School districts	85	13,506	35
Special districts	301	35,052	37

Only 48 states have county governments, 20 states have township governments ("towns" in New England, Minnesota, New York, and Wisconsin), and 46 states have school districts. Special districts encompass such functions as natural resources, fire protection, and housing and community development.
Source: U.S. Census Bureau, *Census of Governments.*

State government revenue, 2002

Total revenue . . . . $16,997 mill.
General revenue . . . . $14,477 mill.
Per capita revenue $3,526
U.S. per capita average $3,689
Rank among states 30

Intergovernment revenue
Total . . . . $5,434 mill.
From federal government . . . . $5,028 mill.

Charges and miscellaneous
Total . . . . $2,954 mill.
Current charges . . . . $2,136 mill.
Misc. general income . . . . $818 mill.
Insurance trust revenue . . . . $1,534 mill.

Taxes
Total . . . . $6,088 mill.
Per capita taxes $1,483
Rank among states 45
Property taxes . . . . $13 mill.
Sales taxes . . . . $3,158 mill.
License taxes . . . . $311 mill.
Individual income taxes . . . . $2,349 mill.
Corporate income taxes . . . . $160 mill.
Other taxes . . . . $97 mill.

Total revenue figures include items not listed separately here.
Source: U.S. Bureau of the Census.

State government expenditures, 2002

General expenditures
Total state expenditures . . . . $20,009 mill.
Intergovernmental . . . . $4,241 mill.

Per capita expenditures
State $4,154
Average of all states $3,859
Rank among states 20

Selected direct expenditures
Education . . . . $2,763 mill.
Public welfare . . . . $4,360 mill.
Health, hospital . . . . $1,542 mill.
Highways . . . . $1,276 mill.
Police protection . . . . $205 mill.
Corrections . . . . $423 mill.
Natural resources . . . . $225 mill.
Parks and recreation . . . . $60 mill.
Government administration . . . . $540 mill.
Interest on debt . . . . $652 mill.
Total direct expenditures . . . . $12,807 mill.

Totals include items not listed separately.
Source: U.S. Census Bureau.

POLITICS

Governors since statehood
D = Democrat; R = Republican; O = other;
(r) resigned; (d) died in office; (i) removed from office

John Rutledge . . . . (r) 1776-1777
Rawlins Lowndes 1777-1779
John Rutledge 1779-1782
John Mathews 1782-1783
Benjamin Guerand 1783-1785
William Moultrie 1785-1787
Thomas Pinckney 1787-1789
Charles Pinckney 1789-1792
William Moultrie (O) 1792-1794
Arnoldus Vanderhorst (O) 1794-1796
Charles Pinckney (O) 1796-1798
Edward Rutledge (O) . . . . (d) 1798-1800
John Drayton (O) 1800-1802
James B. Richardson (O) 1802-1804
Paul Hamilton (O) 1804-1806
Charles Pinckney (O) 1806-1808
John Drayton (O) 1808-1810
Henry Middleton (O) 1810-1812
Joseph Alston (O) 1812-1814
David R. Williams (O) 1814-1816
Andrew Pickens (O) 1816-1818
John Geddes (O) 1818-1820
Thomas Bennett (O) 1820-1822
John L. Wilson (O) 1822-1824
Richard I. Manning (O) 1824-1826
John Taylor (O) 1826-1828
Stephen D. Miller (D) 1828-1830

James Hamilton, Jr. (D) 1830-1832
Robert Y. Hayne (D) 1832-1834
George McDuffie (D) 1834-1836
Pierce M. Butler (D) 1836-1838
Patrick Noble (D) . . . . (d) 1838-1840
Barnabas K. Henagan (D) 1840
John P. Richardson (D) 1840-1842
James H. Hammond (D) 1842-1844
William Aiken (D) 1844-1846
David Johnson (D) 1846-1848
Whitemarsh B. Seabrook (D) 1848-1850
John H. Means (D) 1850-1852
John L. Manning (D) 1852-1854
James H. Adams (D) 1854-1856
Robert F. W. Allston (D) 1856-1858
William W. Gist (D) 1858-1860
Francis W. Pickens (D) 1860-1862
Milledge L. Bonham (D) 1862-1864
Andrew G. Magrath (D) . . . . (i) 1864-1865
Benjamin F. Perry 1865
James L. Orr 1865-1868
Robert K. Scott (R) 1868-1872
Franklin J. Moses, Jr. (R) 1872-1874
Daniel H. Chamberlain (R) 1874-1876
Wade Hampton (D) . . . . (r) 1876-1879
William D. Sampson (D) . . . . (r) 1879-1880
Thomas B. Jeter (D) 1880
Johnson Hagood (D) 1880-1882
Hugh S. Thompson (D) . . . . (r) 1882-1886
John C. Sheppard (D) 1886
John P. Richardson, Jr. (D) 1886-1890
Benjamin R. Tillman (D) 1890-1894
John G. Evans (D) 1894-1897
William H. Ellerbe (D) . . . . (d) 1897-1899
Miles B. McSweeney (D) 1899-1903
Duncan C. Heyward (D) 1903-1907
Martin F. Ansel (D) 1907-1911
Coleman L. Blease (D) . . . . (r) 1911-1915
Charles A. Smith (D) 1915
Richard I. Manning III (D) 1915-1919
Robert A. Cooper (D) . . . . (r) 1919-1922
William G. Harvey (D) 1922-1923
Thomas G. McLeod (D) 1923-1927
John G. Richards (D) 1927-1931
Ibra C. Blackwood (D) 1931-1935
Olin D. T. Johnston (D) 1935-1939
Burnet R. Maybank (D) . . . . (r) 1939-1941
Joseph E. Harley (D) . . . . (d) 1941-1942
Richard M. Jeffries (D) 1942-1943
Olin D. T. Johnston (D) . . . . (r) 1943-1945
Ransome J. Williams (D) 1945-1947
J. Strom Thurmond (D) 1947-1951
James F. Byrnes (D) 1951-1955
George B. Timmerman, Jr. (D) 1955-1959
Ernest F. Hollings (D) 1959-1963
Donald S. Russell (D) . . . . (r) 1963-1965
Robert E. McNair (D) 1965-1971
John C. West (D) 1971-1975
James B. Edwards (R) 1975-1979
Richard W. Riley (D) 1979-1987
Carroll A. Campbell, Jr. (R) 1987-1995

(continued)

David M. Beasley (R) 1995-1999
Jim Hodges (D) 1999-2003
Mark Sanford (R) 2003-

Governors were called state presidents before 1778.

Composition of congressional delegations, 1989-2007

	Dem	Rep	Total
House of Representatives			
101st Congress, 1989			
State delegates	4	2	6
Total U.S.	259	174	433
102d Congress, 1991			
State delegates	4	2	6
Total U.S.	267	167	434
103d Congress, 1993			
State delegates	3	3	6
Total U.S.	258	176	434
104th Congress, 1995			
State delegates	2	4	6
Total U.S.	197	236	433
105th Congress, 1997			
State delegates	2	4	6
Total U.S.	206	228	434
106th Congress, 1999			
State delegates	2	4	6
Total U.S.	211	222	433
107th Congress, 2001			
State delegates	2	4	6
Total U.S.	211	221	432
108th Congress, 2003			
State delegates	2	4	6
Total U.S.	205	229	434
109th Congress, 2005			
State delegates	2	4	6
Total U.S.	202	231	433
110th Congress, 2007			
State delegates	2	4	6
Total U.S.	233	202	435
Senate			
101st Congress, 1989			
State delegates	1	1	2
Total U.S.	55	45	100
102d Congress, 1991			
State delegates	1	1	2
Total U.S.	56	44	100
103d Congress, 1993			
State delegates	1	1	2
Total U.S.	57	43	100
104th Congress, 1995			
State delegates	1	1	2
Total U.S.	46	53	99

	Dem	Rep	Total
105th Congress, 1997			
State delegates	1	1	2
Total U.S.	45	55	100
106th Congress, 1999			
State delegates	1	1	2
Total U.S.	45	54	99
107th Congress, 2001			
State delegates	1	1	2
Total U.S.	50	50	100
108th Congress, 2003			
State delegates	1	1	2
Total U.S.	48	51	99
109th Congress, 2005			
State delegates	0	2	2
Total U.S.	44	55	99
110th Congress, 2007			
State delegates	0	2	2
Total U.S.	49	49	98

Figures are for starts of first sessions. Totals are for Democrat (Dem.) and Republican (Rep.) members only. House membership totals under 435 and Senate totals under 100 reflect vacancies and seats held by independent party members. When the 110th Congress opened, the Senate's two independent members caucused with the Democrats, giving the Democrats control of the Senate.

Source: U.S. Congress, *Congressional Directory.*

Composition of state legislature, 1990-2006

	Democrats	Republicans
State House (124 seats)		
1990	79	43
1992	71	52
1994	58	62
1996	53	70
1998	57	66
2000	59	64
2002	51	73
2004	50	74
2006	51	73
State Senate (46 seats)		
1990	33	13
1992	30	16
1994	29	17
1996	26	20
1998	24	22
2000	24	22
2002	20	25
2004	20	26
2006	20	26

Figures for total seats may include independents and minor party members. Numbers reflect results of elections in listed years; elected members usually take their seats in the years that follow.

Source: Council of State Governments; *State Elective Officials and the Legislatures.*

Voter participation in presidential elections, 2000 and 2004

	2000	2004
Voting age population		
State	3,014,000	3,173,000
Total United States	209,831,000	220,377,000
State share of U.S. total	1.44	1.44
Rank among states	26	25
Portion of voting age population casting votes		
State	45.9%	51.0%
United States	50.3%	55.5%
Rank among states	43	42

Population figures are rounded to nearest thousand and include all residents, regardless of eligibility to vote.
Source: U.S. Census Bureau.

HEALTH AND MEDICAL CARE

Medical professionals
Physicians in 2003 and nurses in 2001

	U.S.	State
Physicians in 2003		
Total	774,849	9,521
Share of U.S. total		1.22%
Rate	266	230
Rank		31
Nurses in 2001		
Total	2,262,020	28,130
Share of U.S. total		1.24%
Rate	793	693
Rank		42

Rates are numbers of physicians and nurses per 100,000 resident population; ranks are based on rates.
Source: American Medical Association, *Physician Characteristics and Distribution in the U.S.*; U.S. Department of Health and Human Services, Health Resources and Services Administration.

Health insurance coverage, 2003

	State	U.S.
Total persons covered	3,481,000	243,320,000
Total persons not covered	584,000	44,961,000
Portion not covered	14.4%	15.6%
Rank among states	22	—
Children not covered	92,000	8,373,000
Portion not covered	8.9%	11.4%
Rank among states	26	—

Totals are rounded to nearest thousand. Ranks are from the highest to the lowest percentages of persons *not* insured.
Source: U.S. Census Bureau, Current Population Reports.

AIDS, syphilis, and tuberculosis cases, 2003

Disease	U.S. cases	State cases	Rank
AIDS	44,232	778	14
Syphilis	34,270	548	18
Tuberculosis	14,874	254	17

Source: U.S. Centers for Disease Control and Prevention.

Cigarette smoking, 2003
Residents over age 18 who smoke

	U.S.	State	Rank
All smokers	22.1%	25.5%	10
Male smokers	24.8%	28.5%	9
Female smokers	20.3%	22.8%	11

Cigarette smokers are defined as persons who reported having smoked at least 100 cigarettes during their lifetimes and who currently smoked at least occasionally.
Source: U.S. Centers for Disease Control and Prevention, *Morbidity and Mortality Weekly Report*, 53, no. 44 (November 12, 2004).

HOUSING

Home ownership rates, 1985-2004

	1985	1990	1995	2000	2004
State	72.0%	71.4%	71.3%	76.5%	76.2%
Total U.S.	63.9%	63.9%	64.7%	67.4%	69.0%
Rank among states	4	6	10	2	6

Net change in state home ownership rate,
1985-2004 . . . . +4.2%
Net change in U.S. home ownership rate,
1985-2004 . . . . +5.1%

Percentages represent the proportion of owner households to total occupied households.
Source: U.S. Census Bureau, 2006.

Home sales, 2000-2004
In thousands of units

Existing home sales	2000	2002	2003	2004
State sales	64.3	72.7	83.0	99.3
Total U.S. sales	5,171	5,631	6,183	6,784
State share of U.S. total	1.24%	1.29%	1.34%	1.46%
Sales rank among states	27	26	25	25

Units include single-family homes, condos, and co-ops.
Source: National Association of Realtors, Washington, D.C., *Real Estate Outlook: Market Trends & Insights*.

Values of owner-occupied homes, 2003

	State	U.S.
Total units	818,000	58,809,000
Value of units		
Under $100,000	37.4%	29.6%
$100,000-199,999	40.9%	36.9%
$200,000 or more	21.6%	33.5%
Median value	$121,290	$142,275
Rank among all states 28		

Units are owner-occupied one-family houses whose numbers are rounded to nearest thousand. Data are extrapolated from survey samples.
Source: U.S. Census Bureau, American Community Survey.

EDUCATION

Public school enrollment, 2002

Prekindergarten through grade 8
State enrollment 501,000
Total U.S. enrollment. 34,135,000
State share of U.S. total 1.47%

Grades 9 through 12
State enrollment 194,000
Total U.S. enrollment. 14,067,000
State share of U.S. total 1.38%

Enrollment rates
State public school enrollment rate. 93.2%
Overall U.S. rate 90.4%
Rank among states in 2002 8
Rank among states in 1995. 11

Enrollment figures (which include unclassified students) are rounded to nearest thousand pupils during fall school term. Enrollment rates are based on enumerated resident population estimate for July 1, 2002.
Source: U.S. National Center for Education Statistics.

Public college finances, 2003-2004

FTE enrollment in public institutions of higher education
Students in state institutions. 137,100
Students in all U.S. public institutions 9,916,600
State share of U.S. total 1.38
Rank among states 27

State and local government appropriations for higher education
State appropriation per FTE $5,053
National average. $5,716
Rank among states 34
State & local tax revenue going to higher
education 7.0%

FTE = full-time equivalent in public postsecondary programs, including summer sessions; student numbers are rounded to nearest hundred. Funding figures for 2003-2004 academic year include financial aid to students in state public institutions and exclude money for research, agriculture experiment stations, teaching hospitals, and medical schools; figures are rounded to nearest thousand dollars.
Source: Higher Education Executive Officers, Denver, Colorado.

TRANSPORTATION AND TRAVEL

Highway mileage, 2003

Interstate highways 842	
Other freeways and expressways 71	
Arterial roads 6,876	
Collector roads. 13,378	
Local roads. 45,063	
Urban roads 10,685	
Rural roads. 55,545	
Total state mileage. 66,230	
U.S. total 3,974,107	
State share 1.67%	
Rank among states 30	

Note that combined urban and rural road mileage matches the total of the other categories.
Source: U.S. Federal Highway Administration.

Motor vehicle registrations and driver licenses, 2003

Vehicle registrations	State	U.S.	Share	Rank
Autos, trucks, buses	3,162,000	231,390,000	1.37%	26
Autos only	1,915,000	135,670	1.41%	25
Motorcycles	57,000	5,328,000	1.07%	29
Driver licenses	2,919,000	196,166,000	1.49%	25

Figures, which do not include vehicles owned by military services, are rounded to the nearest thousand. Figures for automobiles include taxis.
Source: U.S. Federal Highway Administration.

Domestic travel expenditures, 2003
Spending by U.S. residents on overnight trips and
day trips of at least 50 miles from home

Total expenditures within state . . . . $7.22 bill.
Total expenditures within U.S. . . . . $490.87 bill.
State share of U.S. total 1.5%
Rank among states 24

Source: Travel Industry Association of America.

Retail gasoline prices, 2003-2007
Average price per gallon at the pump

Year	U.S.	State
2003	$1.267	$1.208
2004	$1.316	$1.269
2005	$1.644	$1.603
2007	$2.298	$2.110

Excise tax per gallon in 2004 . . . . 16.0¢
Rank among all states in 2007 prices 48

Prices are averages of all grades of gasoline sold at the pump
during March months in 2003-2005 and during February, 2007.
Averages for 2006, during which prices rose higher, are not
available.
Source: U.S. Energy Information Agency, *Petroleum Marketing
Monthly* (2003-2005 data); American Automobile Association
(2007 data).

CRIME AND LAW ENFORCEMENT

State and local police officers, 2000-2004

	2000	2002	2004
Total officers			
U.S.	654,601	665,555	675,734
State	9,476	8,787	10,567*
*Net change, 2000-2004			+11.51%
Officers per 1,000 residents			
U.S.	2.33	2.31	2.30
State	2.36	2.14	2.52
State rank	16	23	11

Totals include state and local police and sheriffs.
Source: Carsey Institute, University of New Hampshire.

Crime rates, 2003
Incidents per 100,000 residents

Crimes	State	U.S.
Violent crimes		
Total incidents	794	475
Murder	7	6
Forcible rape	44	32
Robbery	137	142
Aggravated assault	605	295
Property crimes		
Total incidents	4,477	3,588
Burglary	1,051	741
Larceny/theft	3,046	2,415
Motor vehicle theft	380	433
All crimes	5,271	4,063

Source: U.S. Federal Bureau of Investigation, *Crime in the United
States*, annual.

State prison populations, 1980-2003

	State	U.S.	State share
1980	7,862	305,458	2.57%
1990	17,319	708,393	2.44%
1996	20,446	1,025,624	1.99%
2000	21,778	1,391,261	1.57%
2003	23,719	1,470,045	1.61%

State figures exclude prisoners in federal penitentiaries.
Source: U.S. Bureau of Justice Statistics, *Prisoners in 2003.*

South Dakota

Location: Upper Midwest

Area and rank: 75,898 square miles (196,575 square kilometers); 77,121 square miles (199,743 square kilometers) including water; sixteenth largest state in area

Coastline: none

Population and rank: 771,000 (2004); forty-sixth largest state in population

Capital city: Pierre (13,876 people in 2000 census)

Largest city: Sioux Falls (123,975 people in 2000 census)

Became territory: March 2, 1861

Entered Union and rank: November 2, 1889; fortieth state

Present constitution adopted: 1889

Counties: 66

State name: "South Dakota" comes from a Sioux word meaning "allies"

The monumental relief of four U.S. presidents on southwestern South Dakota's Mount Rushmore took nearly fifteen years to carve during the early twentieth century. (Photo Disc)

State nicknames: Mount Rushmore State; Coyote State; Sunshine State

Motto: Under God the people rule

State flag: Blue field with state seal and sunburst, with words "South Dakota" above and "The Mount Rushmore State" below

Highest point: Harney Peak—7,242 feet (2,207 meters)

Lowest point: Big Stone Lake—966 feet (294 meters)

Highest recorded temperature: 120 degrees Fahrenheit (49 degrees Celsius)—Gannvalley, 1936

Lowest recorded temperature: –58 degrees Fahrenheit (–50 degrees Celsius)—McIntosh, 1936

State song: "Hail! South Dakota"

State tree: Black Hills spruce

State flower: Pasque flower

State bird: Ring-necked pheasant

State fish: Walleye

State animal: Coyote

National parks: Badlands, Wind Cave

South Dakota History

One of the plains states in America's Midwest, South Dakota is bounded on the north by North Dakota, on the east by Iowa and Minnesota, on the south by Nebraska, and on the west by Montana and Wyoming. It stretches 360 miles from east to west and 240 miles from north to south. The state is the sixteenth largest of the United States but ranks forty-sixth in population. Its capital is Pierre (pronounced "Peer"). Temperatures in South Dakota are extreme—low in winter and high in summer—with minimal precipitation and low humidity.

South Dakota's terrain, with more than three hundred natural lakes and four huge reservoirs created by the damming of its rivers, has considerable variety. Sparsely wooded, it consists largely of rolling plains marked occasionally by buttes rising dramatically from the landscape. In the western part of the plains, well before the towering Black Hills, are the Badlands, with deep canyons and formations carved into the red rocks over eons by wind and water erosion.

Early History. Humans inhabited the Dakotas more than twenty-five thousand years ago. Forty million years ago, dinosaurs roamed the landscape. Dinosaur bones have been unearthed in South Dakota as well as shells of archela, the largest known turtles, which were ten feet long.

The earliest settlers hunted the abundant big game in the area. By 500 C.E., a society of seminomadic Mound Builders thrived in the area and remained for about three hundred years, leaving behind valuable artifacts.

The Arikara Indians moved north from Nebraska during the sixteenth century and settled along the eastern banks of the Missouri River, where they farmed and fished, prospering to the extent that, by the late eighteenth century, they had established thirty earth-lodge settlements. During the early nineteenth century, however, the Sioux, a powerful tribe that entered the area from the east, drove the Arikara away.

Exploration and Settlement. The Dakotas became part of France's vast Louisiana Territory in 1682. The first white explorers in the region were French Canadian brothers, François and Louis Joseph de La Vérendrye. While seeking a water route to the Pacific, they

The rugged canyons and mountains of western South Dakota's Badlands were carved by eons of powerful winds and erosion. (PhotoDisc)

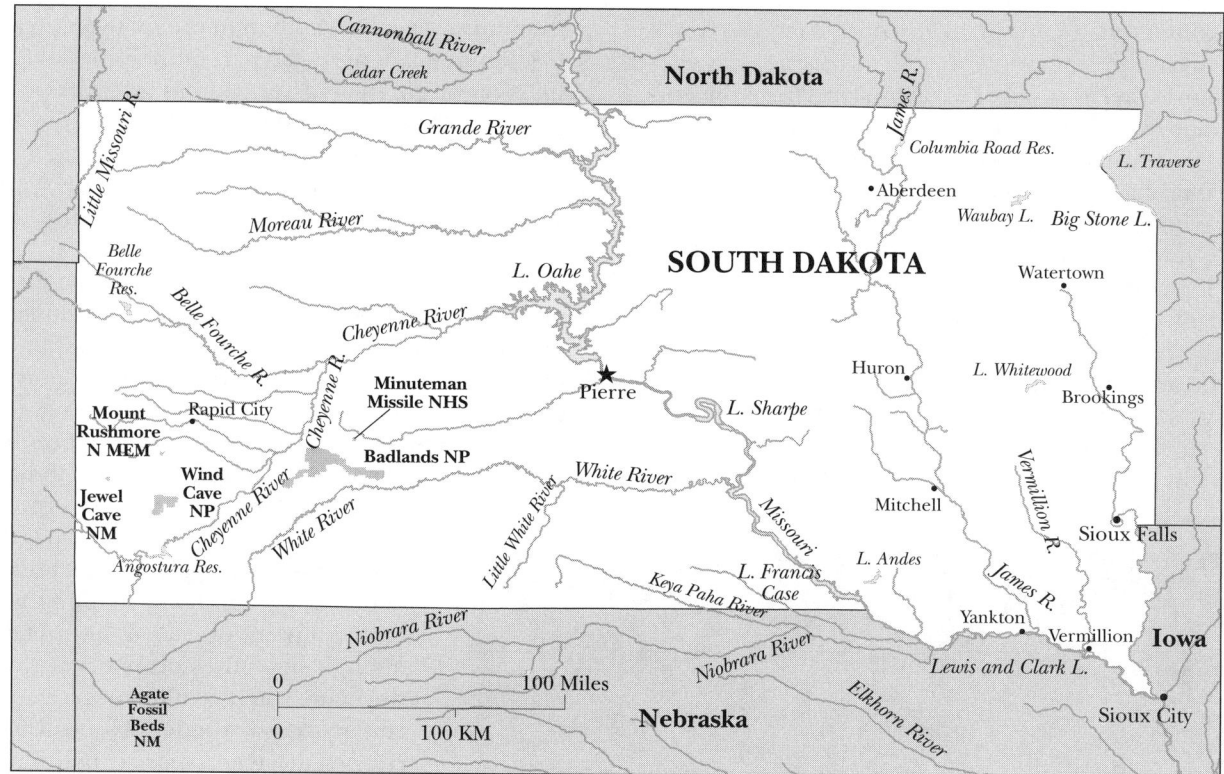

entered the area in 1743 and claimed it for France, burying a lead plate near Fort Pierre—the plate was found in 1913.

In 1762, France ceded all its land west of the Mississippi River to Spain, so when the French Canadian fur trader Pierre Dorion became the first permanent white resident in the Dakotas in 1775, the Spanish were in control. The Louisiana Territory was returned to France in 1800 and, in 1803 as a result of the Louisiana Purchase, became the property of the United States.

Explorers Meriwether Lewis and William Clark passed through the area in 1804, bound for the Pacific Northwest, and again in 1806 on their return. A Spanish trader, Manuel Lisa, began trading with the American Indians along the Missouri River in 1809. In 1812, the entire area became part of the Missouri Territory. In the same year, the Sioux Indians, whose property rights were being severely infringed by the United States, sided with the British in the War of 1812.

Relations between the Native Americans and whites in the area were marked by peace treaties that the federal government, with its substantial economic stake in the lands of the Missouri Territory, soon broke. When the Missouri River proved navigable by steamboat in 1831, the commercial viability of the areas along the river became obvious.

Government Relations with the Sioux. In 1857, the modern-day city of Sioux Falls on the Missouri River was planned. Development began in the area, which in

1861 was declared the Dakota Territory, encompassing all of contemporary North and South Dakota, as well as parts of Wyoming and Montana. The southeastern town of Yankton became the territory's capital.

In 1862, the government, frequently warring with the Sioux, forced the Santee Sioux from Minnesota into the Dakota Territory. Strife between the Sioux and the federal government continued until 1890, when, at Wounded Knee, government forces massacred more than two hundred Sioux, including women and children who were attempting to surrender. As late as 1973, two hundred armed members of the American Indian Movement occupied Wounded Knee for seventy-one days demanding reparations.

In 1979, the U.S. Court of Claims ordered the U.S. government to pay the Sioux $100 million for the land it confiscated in 1877. The Sioux, however, refused to accept a monetary settlement, insisting instead on the return of their land, which has great spiritual significance to them.

Moving Toward Statehood. With the formation of the Montana Territory in 1864 and the Wyoming Territory in 1868, the Dakota Territory was downsized to what has become North and South Dakota. In 1872, railroad service began in the territory. In 1874, Lieutenant Colonel George Custer discovered gold in the Black Hills, triggering a gold rush. In 1876, when the Sioux attacked prospectors, trying to expel them from Sioux property in the Black Hills, the federal government intervened and, in 1877, confiscated the Black Hills from the Sioux.

Many easterners, eager to obtain land from the government under the Homestead Act of 1862, came to the Dakotas to obtain their allotted 160 acres, for which they filed claims. They cultivated the land and, after living on it for five years, it became theirs. With the discovery of gold, miners flocked into the Black Hills, swelling the population by 1879 to the point that the territory was large enough to warrant consideration for statehood.

The area was wracked by floods in 1881. The devastating blizzard of 1888 killed hundreds of Dakotans. Nevertheless, development continued with the establishment of Yankton College in 1881 and the University of South Dakota at Vermillion in the following year. In 1888, Republicans urged, as part of their platform, the admission of the Dakota Territory as two states.

In 1889, Congress voted to divide the Dakota Territory evenly into North Dakota and South Dakota and admitted them as the thirty-ninth and fortieth states in the Union. North Dakota was designated the thirty-ninth state because of its alphabetical position.

South Dakota was plagued by the worst drought in its history through the next decaade. It was another half century before the federal government assisted the state in mounting a concerted effort to build dams to irrigate farms and provide hydroelectric power.

Political Progressivism and the Economy. South Dakota's voters consistently elected reform candidates from the Populist and Progressive Republican parties. In 1898, South Dakota became the first state to pass initiative and referendum laws, enabling voters to pass any law directly if they obtained enough signatures on petitions to put the matter on the ballot or to reject any laws passed by the legislature if 5 percent of the voters signed petitions requesting that their repeal be placed on the ballot and the repeal is supported by the electorate.

Agriculture and mining were the two most important industries in South Dakota during its early days. In 1909, the Morrell Company opened a large meat processing and packing plant in Sioux Falls, thereby launching an important industry in the state. South Dakota became a major national supplier of meat.

The state needed a dependable railway system to transport its cattle and produce to eastern markets. In 1917, Governor Peter Norbeck spearheaded a movement to end railroad monopolies and to stabilize rates. Under Norbeck's progressive leadership, the legislature voted to extend loans to farmers.

The droughts during the early years of the Great Depression ravaged South Dakota agriculture. Plagues of grasshoppers ate the few crops that survived the drought. The economic situation deteriorated so badly that, in 1932, voters for the first time elected Democratic candidates to every state office in what had long been a Republican state.

In 1954, the state's first productive oil well was drilled in western South Dakota, producing more than two million barrels annually. Strip mining of bitu-

State capitol building in Pierre. (South Dakota Tourism)

minous coal contributes to the economy of western South Dakota, which also has a large gold-mining industry. Despite the mineral wealth of its western region, South Dakota's non-American Indians have settled largely in the eastern region, where manufacturing and service industries flourish.

The electronics industry brings considerable revenue into the state and employs many of its citizens. In 1982, Citicorp, the largest bank holding company in the United States, transferred its credit-card division to Sioux Falls, which underwent a substantial increase in population.

The Native American Population. During the 1990's, more than 7 percent of South Dakotans were Native Americans. Most of them lived on eight major reservations, the largest of them being the Rosebud, the Pine Ridge, the Cheyenne River, and the Standing Rock Indian Reservations in the central or western regions of the state.

Life for South Dakota's Native Americans remains difficult. Stripped of much of their most fertile and mineral-rich land, they have often been forced during difficult economic times to sell the land remaining to them.

Electoral Politics. As the twenty-first century opened, South Dakota continued its tradition of splitting its congressional representation in Washington between the two major parties. Both senators, long-serving senator Tom Daschle and Tim Johnson were Democrats, while John Thune, the state's sole congress member, was a Republican, winning reelection in 2000 with a resounding 74 percent of the vote. Electoral competition between Thune and each of the Democratic senators was to make South Dakota political history over the next four years. In the 2000 presidential election, George W. Bush took the state's three electoral votes by a 60-38 percent margin.

In competition for state public office, preparation for the 2002 midterm elections, popular state senator Mike Rounds won a stunning upset victory in the Republican gubernatorial primary election. He did so against two opponents, each of whom outspent his campaign by a ten-to-one margin. Their negative campaigning, however, soured the electorate on both of them. In the primary election, Rounds, who had run a consistently positive campaign, won a remarkable victory, winning 44.3 percent of the vote. He went on to win the general election by a 57-42 percent margin.

The elections for representation in Washington in 2002 and 2004 were climactic. In 2002, Representative Thune, who had promised to serve only three terms in the House of Representatives, took on Senator Johnson in a nationally watched race. Senator Daschle devoted much time and energy campaigning for Johnson, who managed to beat Thune by the tiny margin of 524 votes. This razor-thin defeat for Thune set up the key battle in 2004 to unseat Daschle. Daschle was majority leader in the Senate, a prominent national figure, and vigorous opponent of the Republican president. The campaign thus was viewed as a proxy fight between anti-Bush forces and the president's defenders. In the event, Thune defeated Daschle by 4,500 votes. Thune was aided by the victory of President Bush, who easily carried the state, by his identical 60-38 percent margin of 2000.

Janklow Accident. In 2002, Bill Janklow, former governor and state attorney general, won a close race for the state's sole seat in the House of Representatives in Washington. A tragedy, however, soon cost him his seat and his political career. On August 16, 2003, Janklow struck a motorcyclist with his automobile as he drove through a rural intersection. Janklow was injured, but the cyclist was killed. It was later established that he had been speeding and ran the stop sign at the intersection. In December, a jury found him guilty of second-degree manslaughter. He resigned his seat in Congress, effective January 20, 2004. He was then jailed for one hundred days, his political career at an end.

Abortion Rights. In 2006, with Governor Rounds still in office, the state became involved in an intense controversy over abortion rights. In February, the state legislature passed a comprehensive abortion ban bill, with a threat to a woman's life the only exception to the ban. Rounds signed the law, due to take effect on July 1 of that year. The ban, however, greatly displeased the public. Rounds, who had enjoyed the remarkable approval rating of 73 percent, saw his popularity plummet by 14 percent after he approved the abortion bill. Moreover, a public opinion poll found that 57 percent of the electorate wanted the abortion ban removed. As a result of public opposition, sufficient enough referendum signatures were collected by a June deadline to enable the question to be placed on the November, 2006, ballot, and the ban was voted down in a referendum.

R. Baird Shuman
Updated by the Editor

South Dakota Time Line

500 to 800 C.E.	Seminomadic Mound Builders flourish in South Dakota.
c. 1500	Arikara, the first native settlers of whom there are written records, arrive.
1682	René-Robert Cavelier, Sieur de La Salle, claims area for France.
c. 1700	Sioux Indians move into South Dakota from the east.
1743	French Canadian brothers François and Louis Joseph de La Vérendrye claim area for France.
1762	France cedes land west of the Mississippi River to Spain.
1800	France regains possession of the Dakotas.
1803	United States acquires the area through the Louisiana Purchase.
1804	Meriwether Lewis and William Clark pass through South Dakota on journey to the Pacific Northwest.
1809	Spanish trader Manuel Lisa organizes St. Louis Fur Company to trade in Upper Missouri Valley.
1812	Region becomes part of Missouri Territory.
1817	First permanent white settlement is established at Fort Pierre.
1831	Steamboat service begins to Upper Missouri Valley on the Missouri River.
Mar. 2, 1861	Congress creates Dakota Territory.
1868	Sioux are promised the Black Hills in Fort Laramie Treaty.
1872	First railroad service begins.
1874	George Custer discovers gold in the Black Hills; prospectors descend on territory.
1877	Gold rush intensifies, causing federal confiscation of the Black Hills from the Sioux.
1878	Homesteaders arrive during South Dakota land boom.
1888	Severe blizzard kills hundreds in South Dakota.
Nov. 2, 1889	South Dakota becomes fortieth state.
Dec. 29, 1890	Federal cavalry massacre Sioux at Wounded Knee Creek.
1897	South Dakota's nine-year drought ends.
1898	South Dakota is first state to enact a referendum law.
1910	State capital is established at Pierre.
1927	Mount Rushmore National Memorial is begun by Gutzon Borglum; is completed in 1941.
1929-1939	Droughts and the Great Depression devastate South Dakota.
1944	Congress passes Flood Control Act to build dams.
1948	Korczak Ziolkowski begins work on Crazy Horse sculpture, the world's largest statue of a person.
1972	Collapse of Rapid City Canyon Dam kills 236 people.
1973	American Indians occupy site of Wounded Knee for seventy-one days.
1979	U.S. Court of Claims orders U.S. government to pay Sioux $100 million for land seized in 1877.
1980	U.S. Supreme Court grants $22.5 million to Sioux for their confiscated lands; Sioux decline monetary settlement.
1982	Citicorp moves its credit-card operation to Sioux City.
1987	South Dakota establishes state lottery.
1988	Casino gambling legalized in South Dakota; National Indian Gaming Act legalizes tribal casinos.
1996	U.S. Supreme Court overturns South Dakota law requiring parental permission for teenage abortions.
1998	Tornado devastates Spencer, injuring more than three hundred.
Nov. 7, 2000	George W. Bush wins the state's three electoral votes for president.
Nov. 5, 2002	John Thune loses race for U.S. Senate to Tim Johnson by 527 votes; Republican Mike Rounds is elected governor by nearly fifteen percentage points.
Nov. 2, 2004	Thune narrowly defeats Senate Majority Leader Tom Daschle for U.S. senate seat. President Bush again takes the state's three electoral votes.
Mar. 6, 2006	Governor Rounds signs into law a legislative an act banning abortions, except when the mother's life is at risk.
Nov. 7, 2006	Legislative ban on abortions is overturned in a referendum.

When completed, South Dakota's Chief Crazy Horse Monument, which was begun in 1948, will be the world's largest sculpture. The finished monument will include Crazy Horse's head, arms, and torso and the head, neck, and forelegs of the horse on which he sits. The project is funded entirely by private donations. (Courtesy, Crazy Horse Memorial Foundation)

Notes for Further Study

Published Sources. A good overview study is *History of South Dakota* (4th ed., 2004) by Herbert Samuel Schell and John E. Miller. Catherine McNicol Stock's *Main Street in Crisis: The Great Depression and the Old Middle Class on the Northern Plains* (1992) and Paula Nelson's *The Prairie Winnows out Its Own: The West River Country of South Dakota in the Years of the Depression and Dust* (1996) focus on the Great Depression and the accompanying droughts in South Dakota during the 1930's. Native American-white relations are examined in *The Politics of the Hallowed Ground: Wounded Knee and the Struggle for Indian Sovereignty* (1999) by Mario Gonzalez and Elizabeth Cook-Lynn and in *Boarding School Seasons: American Indian Families, 1900-1940* (1998) by Brenda Child. Mikael Kurkiala focuses on the Pine Ridge Reservation in *Building the Nation Back Up: The Politics of Identity on the Pine Ridge Indian Reservation* (1997). In *Life of Elaine Goodale Eastman* (2005), Theodore D. Sargent provides a biography of the woman who established a school on the Great Sioux Reserva-

tion in South Dakota in the 1880's and witnessed many of the monumental events that affected the Lakotas during that period.

Aimed at adolescent readers, *South Dakota* (2d ed., 2006) by Melissa McDaniel investigates the state's geography, history, government, people, achievements, and landmarks, while Carole Marsh's *South Dakota Native Americans* (2004) examines the state's indigenous peoples. *South Dakota: Every Town on the Map and More* (1998) by Vernell Johnson and Louise Johnson explores the variety of towns in the state. An accessible traveler's guide to one of the state's best-known regions can be found with the *Insiders' Guide to South Dakota's Black Hills and Badlands* (3d ed., 2004) by Bert Gildart, Jane Gildart, and Thomas D. Griffith.

Web Resources. The most complete Web site on South Dakota is the state government's site (www.state.sd.us), offering information about the state's history, economy, industries, and population. Those seeking tourist information should

One of South Dakota's most popular tourist attractions is the Corn Palace in Mitchell, a city on the James River in the southeastern part of the state. The combination sports arena and concert hall was built in 1921, but the original first Corn Palace was erected on the same site in 1892 as a showcase for South Dakota's agricultural industry. The chief attraction of the current building is its exterior decorations, which are made entirely from corn and other grains. Every year, the exterior murals are redesigned with a new theme. (Patrick Bolduan)

turn to various tourist Web sites, including those of the State Tourist Office (www.state.sd.us/tourism), the Badlands (www.blackhillsbadlands.com/), Big Stone Lake (www.bigstonelake.com), Black Hills Information (theblackhills.com/), the Missouri River (www.nps.gov/mnrr), Mount Rushmore (www.nps.gov/moru/), and Wind Cave (www.nps.gov/wica). For history information, visit the South Dakota State Historical Society (www.sdhistory.org/) or the South Dakota State Library for Kids (www.sdstatelibrary.com/forkids/southdakota.htm).

South Dakota's communities maintain individual Web sites, and many of them can be accessed by using the U.S. Cities Online Web page for South Dakota (www.usacitieson line.com/sd.htm). South Dakota's institutions of higher learning maintain informative Web sites. Among these are Augustana College (www.augie.edu), Black Hills University (www.bhsu.edu), Dakota State University (www.dsu.edu), Dakota Wesleyan University (www.dwu.edu), South Dakota University (www.sdstate.edu), the University of Sioux Falls (www.thecoo.edu), and the University of South Dakota (www.usd.edu).

Counties

County	2000 pop.	Rank in pop.	Sq. miles	Rank in area	County	2000 pop.	Rank in pop.	Sq. miles	Rank in area
Aurora	3,058	49	708.2	45	Brookings	28,220	4	794.5	42
Beadle	17,023	11	1,259.4	22	Brown	35,460	3	1,712.8	13
Bennett	3,574	45	1,185.4	23	Brule	5,364	36	819.0	38
Bon Homme	7,260	27	563.4	55	Buffalo	2,032	61	470.6	61

County	2000 pop.	Rank in pop.	Sq. miles	Rank in area
Butte	9,094	19	2,248.6	7
Campbell	1,782	62	735.8	44
Charles Mix	9,350	18	1,098.3	27
Clark	4,143	42	958.0	33
Clay	13,537	13	411.6	66
Codington	25,897	5	687.8	47
Corson	4,181	41	2,473.1	5
Custer	7,275	26	1,557.8	16
Davison	18,741	10	435.5	63
Day	6,267	30	1,028.6	28
Deuel	4,498	39	623.6	49
Dewey	5,972	32	2,302.8	6
Douglas	3,458	46	433.6	65
Edmunds	4,367	40	1,145.7	24
Fall River	7,453	25	1,739.9	12
Faulk	2,640	56	1,000.2	31
Grant	7,847	23	682.5	48
Gregory	4,792	37	1,016.0	29
Haakon	2,196	59	1,813.1	11
Hamlin	5,540	35	511.2	60
Hand	3,741	44	1,436.7	19
Hanson	3,139	48	434.7	64
Harding	1,353	65	2,670.6	4
Hughes	16,481	12	741.0	43
Hutchinson	8,075	22	813.0	39
Hyde	1,671	63	861.1	35
Jackson	2,930	50	1,869.3	10
Jerauld	2,295	58	530.3	57
Jones	1,193	66	970.6	32
Kingsbury	5,815	34	838.4	37

County	2000 pop.	Rank in pop.	Sq. miles	Rank in area
Lake	11,276	16	563.3	56
Lawrence	21,802	8	800.1	41
Lincoln	24,131	7	578.1	51
Lyman	3,895	43	1,640.1	14
McCook	5,832	33	574.6	52
McPherson	2,904	51	1,137.0	25
Marshall	4,576	38	838.9	36
Meade	24,253	6	3,470.8	1
Mellette	2,083	60	1,306.6	21
Miner	2,884	52	570.4	53
Minnehaha	148,281	1	809.2	40
Moody	6,595	28	519.7	59
Pennington	88,565	2	2,776.4	3
Perkins	3,363	47	2,871.8	2
Potter	2,693	54	866.5	34
Roberts	10,016	17	1,101.3	26
Sanborn	2,675	55	569.0	54
Shannon	12,466	15	2,094.0	8
Spink	7,454	24	1,504.0	17
Stanley	2,772	53	1,443.4	18
Sully	1,556	64	1,007.0	30
Todd	9,050	20	1,388.2	20
Tripp	6,430	29	1,613.6	15
Turner	8,849	21	616.9	50
Union	12,584	14	460.4	62
Walworth	5,974	31	707.8	46
Yankton	21,652	9	521.6	58
Ziebach	2,519	57	1,962.5	9

Source: U.S. Census Bureau; National Association of Counties.

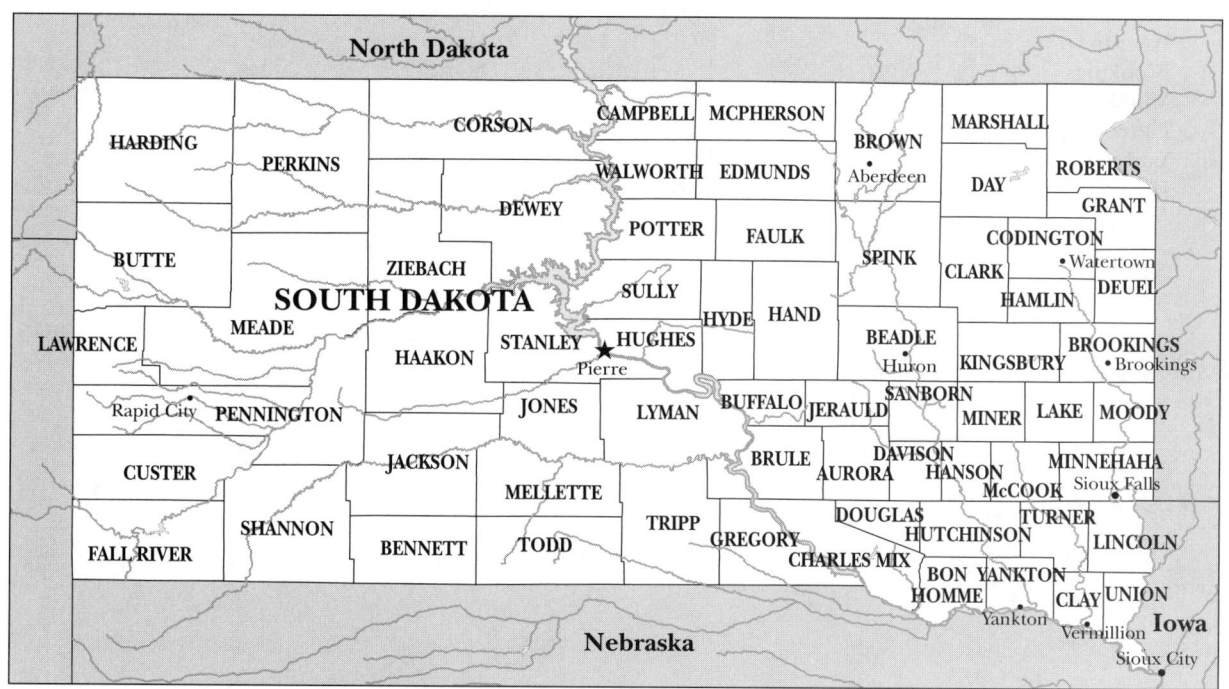

Cities

With 6,000 or more residents

Rank	City	Population
1	Sioux Falls	123,975
2	Rapid City	59,607
3	Aberdeen	24,658
4	Watertown	20,237
5	Brookings	18,504
6	Mitchell	14,558
7	Pierre (capital)	13,876
8	Yankton	13,528
9	Huron	11,893

Rank	City	Population
10	Vermillion	9,765
11	Spearfish	8,606
12	Rapid Valley	7,043
13	Madison	6,540
14	Sturgis	6,442

Population figures are from 2000 census.
Source: U.S. Bureau of the Census.

Index to Tables

DEMOGRAPHICS

Resident state and national populations, 1970-2004

Population figures given in thousands

	State pop.	U.S. pop.	Share	Rank
1970	666	203,302	0.3%	44
1980	691	226,546	0.3%	45
1985	698	237,924	0.3%	45
1990	696	248,765	0.3%	45
1995	738	262,761	0.3%	45
2000	755	281,425	0.3%	46
2004	771	293,655	0.3%	46

Source: U.S. Census Bureau, Current Population Reports, 2006.

Resident population by age, 2004

Age Group	Total persons
Under 5 years	52,000
5 to 17 years.	139,000
18 to 24 years.	87,000
25 to 34 years.	93,000
35 to 44 years	106,000
45 to 54 years	111,000
55 to 64 years.	74,000
65 to 74 years.	52,000
75 to 84 years.	39,000
85 years and older	18,000
All age groups.	771,000

Portion of residents 65 and older 14.2%
National rank in portion of oldest residents 7
National average 12.4%

Population figures are rounded to nearest thousand persons;
figures include armed forces personnel stationed in the state.
Source: U.S. Bureau of the Census, 2006.

Resident population by race, Hispanic origin, 2004

Category	State pop.	Share	U.S.
All residents	771	100.00%	100.00%
Non-Hispanic white	671	87.03%	67.37%
Hispanic white	13	1.69%	13.01%
Other Hispanic	2	0.26%	1.06%
African American	6	0.78%	12.77%
Native American	67	8.69%	0.96%
Asian, Pacific Islander	5	0.65%	4.37%
Two or more categories	9	1.17%	1.51%

Population figures are in thousands. Persons counted as "Hispanic" (Latino) may be of any race. Because of overlapping categories, categories may not add up to 100%. Shares in column 3 are percentages of each category within the state; these figures may be compared to the national percentages in column 4.
Source: U.S. Bureau of the Census, 2006.

Projected state population, 2000-2030

Year	Population
2000	755,000
2005	772,000
2010	786,000
2015	797,000
2020	802,000
2025	802,000
2030	800,000
Population increase, 2000-2030	45,000
Percentage increase, 2000-2030	6.0

Projections are based on data from the 2000 census.
Source: U.S. Census Bureau.

VITAL STATISTICS

Infant mortality rates, 1980-2002

	1980	1990	2000	2002
All state residents	10.9	10.1	5.5	6.5
All U.S. residents	12.6	9.2	9.4	9.1
All state white residents	9.0	8.0	4.3	4.9
All U.S. white residents	10.6	7.6	5.7	5.8

Figures represent deaths per 1,000 live births of resident infants under 1 year old, exclusive of fetal deaths. Figures for all residents include members of other racial categories not listed separately. The Census Bureau considers the figures for black residents to be too small to be statistically meaningful.
Source: U.S. Census Bureau, *Statistical Abstract of the United States,* 2006.

Abortion rates, 1990 and 2000

	1990	2000
Total abortions	1,000	1,000
Rate per 1,000 women	6.9	5.5
U.S. rate	25.7	21.3
Rank	49	48

Numbers of abortions are rounded to nearest thousand; ranks are based on rates.
Source: U.S. Census Bureau.

Marriages and divorces, 2004

Total marriages	6,500
Rate per 1,000 population	8.4
National rate per 1,000 population	7.4
Rank among all states	11
Total divorces	2,500
Rate per 1,000 population	3.2
National rate per 1,000 population	3.7
Rank among all states	31

Figures are for all marriages and divorces performed within the state, including those of nonresidents; totals are rounded to the nearest hundred. Ranks are for highest to lowest figures; note that divorce data are not available for five states.
Source: U.S. National Center for Health Statistics, *Vital Statistics of the United States,* 2006.

Death rates by leading causes, 2002

Deaths per 100,000 resident population

Cause	State	U.S.
Heart disease	254.5	241.7
Cancer	205.2	193.2
Cerebrovascular diseases	68.1	56.4
Accidents other than motor vehicle	45.7	37.0
Motor vehicle accidents	24.4	15.7
Chronic lower respiratory diseases	50.3	43.3
Diabetes mellitus	25.6	25.4
HIV	n/a	4.9
Suicide	12.4	11.0
Homicide	2.9	6.1
All causes	906.4	847.3
Rank in overall death rate among states		21

Figures exclude nonresidents who died in the state. Causes of death follow International Classification of Diseases. Rank is from highest to lowest death rate in the United States.
Source: U.S. National Center for Health Statistics, *National Vital Statistics Report,* 2006.

ECONOMY

Gross state product, 1990-2004
In current dollars

Year	State product	Nat'l product	State share
1990	$12.8 billion	$5.67 trillion	0.23%
2000	$23.2 billion	$9.75 trillion	0.24%
2002	$25.8 billion	$10.41 trillion	0.25%
2003	$27.3 billion	$10.92 trillion	0.25%
2004	$29.4 billion	$11.65 trillion	0.25%

Source: U.S. Bureau of Economic Analysis, *Survey of Current Business,* July, 2005.

Gross state product by industry, 2003
In billions of dollars

Construction	$1.0
Manufacturing	3.2
Wholesale trade	1.4
Retail trade	2.3
Finance & insurance	4.4
Information	0.7
Professional services	0.6
Health care & social assistance	2.1
Government	3.1
Total state product	$25.6
Total U.S. product	$10,289.2
State share of U.S. total	0.25%
Rank among all states	46

Total figures include industries not listed separately. Amounts are in chained 2000 dollars.
Source: U.S. Bureau of Economic Analysis, *Survey of Current Business,* July, 2005.

Personal income per capita, 1990-2004
In current dollars

	1990	2000	2004
Per capita income	$16,172	$25,720	$30,856
U.S. average	$19,477	$29,845	$32,937
Rank among states	38	36	27

Source: U.S. Bureau of Economic Analysis, *Survey of Current Business,* April, 2005.

Energy consumption, 2001
In trillions of British thermal units (BTU), except as noted

Total energy consumption
Total state energy consumption	248
Total U.S. energy consumption	96,275
State share of U.S. total	0.26%
Rank among states	48

Per capita consumption (In millions of BTU)
Total state per capita consumption	327
Total U.S. per capita consumption	338
Rank among states	28

End-use sectors
Residential	60
Commercial	50
Industrial	54
Transportation	83

Sources of energy
Petroleum	112
Natural gas	37
Coal	44
Hydroelectric power	35
Nuclear electric power	0

Figures for totals include categories not listed separately.
Source: U.S. Energy Information Administration, *State Energy Data Report,* 2001.

Nonfarm employment by sectors, 2004

Total persons	383,000
Construction	20,000
Manufacturing	39,000
Trade, transportation, utilities	77,000
Information	7,000
Finance, insurance, real estate	28,000
Professional & business services	24,000
Education & health services	57,000
Leisure, hospitality, arts, organizations	41,000
Other services, including repair & maintenance	16,000
Government	74,000

Figures are rounded to nearest thousand persons. "Total" includes mining and natural resources, not listed separately.
Source: U.S. Bureau of Labor Statistics, 2006.

Foreign exports, 1990-2004
In millions of dollars

Year	State	U.S.	State share
1990	205	394,045	0.05%
1996	443	624,767	0.07%
1997	517	688,896	0.08%
2000	679	712,055	0.09%
2003	672	724,006	0.10%
2004	826	769,332	0.11%

Rank among all states in 2004 47

U.S. total does not include U.S. dependencies.
Source: U.S. Census Bureau, *U.S. Merchandise Trade,* series FT 900, 2000; U.S. Census Bureau, *U.S. International Trade in Goods and Services,* Series FT 900, 2005.

LAND USE

Federally owned land, 2003
Areas in acres

	State	U.S.	State share
Total area	48,882,000	2,271,343,000	2.15%
Nonfederal land	46,568,000	1,599,584,000	2.91%
Federal land	2,314,000	671,759,000	0.34%
Federal share	4.7%	29.6%	—

Areas are rounded to nearest thousand acres. Figures for federally owned land do not include trust properties.
Source: U.S. General Services Administration, *Federal Real Property Profile,* 2006.

Land use, 1997
In acres, rounded to nearest thousand

Total surface area	49,358,000
Total nonfederal rural land.	44,411,000
Percentage rural land	90.0%
Cropland.	16,738,000
Conservation Reserve Program (CRP*) land . . .	1,686,000
Pastureland	2,108,000
Rangeland	21,876,000
Forestland.	518,000
Other rural land	1,484,000

*CRP is a federal program begun in 1985 to assist private landowners to convert highly erodible cropland to vegetative cover for ten years. Note that some categories of land overlap.
Source: U.S. Department of Agriculture, Natural Resources and Conservation Service, and Iowa State University, Statistical Laboratory, S*ummary Report, 1997 National Resources Inventory,* revised December, 2000.

Farms and crop acreage, 2004

	State	U.S.	Share	Rank
Farms	32,000	2,113,000	1.51%	27
Acres (millions)	44	937	4.70%	6
Acres per farm	1,386	443	—	7

Source: U.S. Department of Agriculture, National Agricultural Statistics Service. Numbers of farms are rounded to nearest thousand units; acreage figures are rounded to nearest million. Rankings, including ties, are based on rounded figures.

GOVERNMENT AND FINANCE

Units of local government, 2002

	State	Total U.S.	Rank
All local governments	1,866	87,525	17
Counties	66	3,034	21
Municipalities	308	19,429	25
Townships	940	16,504	10
School districts	176	13,506	26
Special districts	376	35,052	32

Only 48 states have county governments, 20 states have township governments ("towns" in New England, Minnesota, New York, and Wisconsin), and 46 states have school districts. Special districts encompass such functions as natural resources, fire protection, and housing and community development.
Source: U.S. Census Bureau, *Census of Governments.*

State government revenue, 2002

Total revenue . . . . $2,491 mill.
General revenue . . . . $2,604 mill.
Per capita revenue $3,424
U.S. per capita average $3,689
Rank among states 37

Intergovernment revenue
Total . . . . $1,063 mill.
From federal government . . . . $1,045 mill.

Charges and miscellaneous
Total . . . . $564 mill.
Current charges . . . . $177 mill.
Misc. general income . . . . $388 mill.
Insurance trust revenue . . . . −$113 mill.

Taxes
Total . . . . $977 mill.
Per capita taxes $1,285
Rank among states 50
Property taxes . . . . (nil)
Sales taxes . . . . $777 mill.
License taxes . . . . $133 mill.
Individual income taxes . . . . (nil)
Corporate income taxes. . . . . $41 mill.
Other taxes . . . . $26 mill.

Total revenue figures include items not listed separately here.
Source: U.S. Bureau of the Census.

State government expenditures, 2002

General expenditures

Total state expenditures . . . . $2,772 mill.
Intergovernmental . . . . $506 mill.

Per capita expenditures

State $3,361
Average of all states $3,859
Rank among states 40

Selected direct expenditures

Education . . . . $377 mill.
Public welfare . . . . $593 mill.
Health, hospital . . . . $125 mill.
Highways . . . . $390 mill.
Police protection . . . . $22 mill.
Corrections . . . . $67 mill.
Natural resources . . . . $91 mill.
Parks and recreation . . . . $26 mill.
Government administration . . . . $103 mill.
Interest on debt . . . . $120 mill.
Total direct expenditures . . . . $2,048 mill.

Totals include items not listed separately.
Source: U.S. Census Bureau.

POLITICS

Governors since statehood

D = Democrat; R = Republican; O = other;
(r) resigned; (d) died in office; (i) removed from office

Arthur C. Mellette (R) 1889-1893
Charles H. Sheldon (R) 1893-1897
Andrew E. Lee (R) 1897-1901
Charles N. Herreid (R) 1901-1905
Samuel H. Elrod (R) 1905-1907
Coe (Corie I.) Crawford (R) 1907-1909
Robert S. Vessey (R) 1909-1913
Frank M. Byrne (R) 1913-1917
Peter Norbeck (R) 1917-1921
William H. McMaster (R) 1921-1925
Carl Gunderson (R) 1925-1927
William J. Bulow (D) 1927-1931
Warren E. Green (R) 1931-1933
Thomas M. Berry (D) 1933-1937
Leslie Jensen (R) 1937-1939
Harlan J. Bushfield (R) 1939-1943
Merrell Q. Sharpe (R) 1943-1947
George T. Mickelson (R) 1947-1951
Sigurd Anderson (R) 1951-1955
Joseph J. Foss, Jr. (R) 1955-1959
Ralph Herseth (D) 1959-1961
Archie M. Gubbrud (R) 1961-1965
Nils A. Boe (R) 1965-1969
Frank L. Farrar (R) 1969-1971
Richard F. Kneip (D) 1971-1979
William J. Janklow (R) 1979-1987

George S. Mickelson (R) 1987-1993
Walter Dale Miller (R) 1993-1995
William J. Janklow (R) 1995-2003
M. Michael Rounds (R) 2003-

Composition of congressional delegations, 1989-2007

	Dem	Rep	Total
House of Representatives			
101st Congress, 1989			
State delegates	1	0	1
Total U.S.	259	174	433
102d Congress, 1991			
State delegates	1	0	1
Total U.S.	267	167	434
103d Congress, 1993			
State delegates	1	0	1
Total U.S.	258	176	434
104th Congress, 1995			
State delegates	0	1	1
Total U.S.	197	236	433
105th Congress, 1997			
State delegates	0	1	1
Total U.S.	206	228	434
106th Congress, 1999			
State delegates	0	1	1
Total U.S.	211	222	433
107th Congress, 2001			
State delegates	0	1	1
Total U.S.	211	221	432
108th Congress, 2003			
State delegates	0	1	1
Total U.S.	205	229	434
109th Congress, 2005			
State delegates	1	0	1
Total U.S.	202	231	433
110th Congress, 2007			
State delegates	1	0	1
Total U.S.	233	202	435
Senate			
101st Congress, 1989			
State delegates	1	1	2
Total U.S.	55	45	100
102d Congress, 1991			
State delegates	1	1	2
Total U.S.	56	44	100
103d Congress, 1993			
State delegates	1	1	2
Total U.S.	57	43	100

(continued)

	Dem	Rep	Total
104th Congress, 1995			
State delegates	2	0	2
Total U.S.	46	53	99
105th Congress, 1997			
State delegates	2	0	2
Total U.S.	45	55	100
106th Congress, 1999			
State delegates	2	0	2
Total U.S.	45	54	99
107th Congress, 2001			
State delegates	2	0	2
Total U.S.	50	50	100
108th Congress, 2003			
State delegates	2	0	2
Total U.S.	48	51	99
109th Congress, 2005			
State delegates	1	1	2
Total U.S.	44	55	99
110th Congress, 2007			
State delegates	1	1	2
Total U.S.	49	49	98

Figures are for starts of first sessions. Totals are for Democrat (Dem.) and Republican (Rep.) members only. House membership totals under 435 and Senate totals under 100 reflect vacancies and seats held by independent party members. When the 110th Congress opened, the Senate's two independent members caucused with the Democrats, giving the Democrats control of the Senate.

Source: U.S. Congress, *Congressional Directory.*

Composition of state legislature, 1990-2006

	Democrats	Republicans
State House (70 seats)		
1990	25	45
1992	28	42
1994	24	46
1996	23	47
1998	19	51
2000	19	51
2002	21	49
2004	19	51
2006	20	50
State Senate (35 seats)		
1990	17	18
1992	20	15
1994	16	19
1996	13	22
1998	13	22
2000	13	22
2002	9	26
2004	10	25
2006	15	20

Figures for total seats may include independents and minor party members. Numbers reflect results of elections in listed years; elected members usually take their seats in the years that follow.

Source: Council of State Governments; *State Elective Officials and the Legislatures.*

Voter participation in presidential elections, 2000 and 2004

	2000	2004
Voting age population		
State	554,000	580,000
Total United States	209,831,000	220,377,000
State share of U.S. total	0.26	0.26
Rank among states	46	46
Portion of voting age population casting votes		
State	57.1%	66.9%
United States	50.3%	55.5%
Rank among states	13	6

Population figures are rounded to nearest thousand and include all residents, regardless of eligibility to vote.

Source: U.S. Census Bureau.

HEALTH AND MEDICAL CARE

Medical professionals
Physicians in 2003 and nurses in 2001

	U.S.	State
Physicians in 2003		
Total	774,849	1,640
Share of U.S. total		0.21%
Rate	266	215
Rank		40
Nurses in 2001		
Total	2,262,020	8,440
Share of U.S. total		0.37%
Rate	793	1,114
Rank		2

Rates are numbers of physicians and nurses per 100,000 resident population; ranks are based on rates.
Source: American Medical Association, *Physician Characteristics and Distribution in the U.S.*; U.S. Department of Health and Human Services, Health Resources and Services Administration.

Health insurance coverage, 2003

	State	U.S.
Total persons covered	659,000	243,320,000
Total persons not covered	91,000	44,961,000
Portion not covered	12.2%	15.6%
Rank among states	32	—
Children not covered	16,000	8,373,000
Portion not covered	8.4%	11.4%
Rank among states	31	—

Totals are rounded to nearest thousand. Ranks are from the highest to the lowest percentages of persons *not* insured.
Source: U.S. Census Bureau, Current Population Reports.

AIDS, syphilis, and tuberculosis cases, 2003

Disease	U.S. cases	State cases	Rank
AIDS	44,232	13	47
Syphilis	34,270	5	46
Tuberculosis	14,874	20	44

Source: U.S. Centers for Disease Control and Prevention.

Cigarette smoking, 2003
Residents over age 18 who smoke

	U.S.	State	Rank
All smokers	22.1%	22.7%	23
Male smokers	24.8%	24.7%	26
Female smokers	20.3%	20.7%	21

Cigarette smokers are defined as persons who reported having smoked at least 100 cigarettes during their lifetimes and who currently smoked at least occasionally.
Source: U.S. Centers for Disease Control and Prevention, *Morbidity and Mortality Weekly Report*, 53, no. 44 (November 12, 2004).

HOUSING

Home ownership rates, 1985-2004

	1985	1990	1995	2000	2004
State	67.6%	66.2%	67.5%	71.2%	68.5%
Total U.S.	63.9%	63.9%	64.7%	67.4%	69.0%
Rank among states	27	30	24	20	41

Net change in state home ownership rate, 1985-2004 . . . . . +0.9%
Net change in U.S. home ownership rate, 1985-2004 . . . . . +5.1%

Percentages represent the proportion of owner households to total occupied households.
Source: U.S. Census Bureau, 2006.

Home sales, 2000-2004
In thousands of units

Existing home sales	2000	2002	2003	2004
State sales	12.6	14.9	15.6	17.3
Total U.S. sales	5,171	5,631	6,183	6,784
State share of U.S. total	0.24%	0.26%	0.25%	0.26%
Sales rank among states	47	46	47	47

Units include single-family homes, condos, and co-ops.
Source: National Association of Realtors, Washington, D.C., *Real Estate Outlook: Market Trends & Insights*.

Values of owner-occupied homes, 2003

	State	U.S.
Total units	146,000	58,809,000
Value of units		
Under $100,000	52.7%	29.6%
$100,000-199,999	38.3%	36.9%
$200,000 or more	8.9%	33.5%
Median value	$96,977	$142,275
Rank among all states		43

Units are owner-occupied one-family houses whose numbers are
   rounded to nearest thousand. Data are extrapolated from
   survey samples.
Source: U.S. Census Bureau, American Community Survey.

EDUCATION

Public school enrollment, 2002

Prekindergarten through grade 8
State enrollment 87,000
Total U.S. enrollment 34,135,000
State share of U.S. total 0.25%

Grades 9 through 12
State enrollment 41,000
Total U.S. enrollment 14,067,000
State share of U.S. total 0.29%

Enrollment rates
State public school enrollment rate 87.7%
Overall U.S. rate 90.4%
Rank among states in 2002 41
Rank among states in 1995 15

Enrollment figures (which include unclassified students) are
   rounded to nearest thousand pupils during fall school term.
   Enrollment rates are based on enumerated resident population
   estimate for July 1, 2002.
Source: U.S. National Center for Education Statistics.

Public college finances, 2003-2004

FTE enrollment in public institutions of higher education
Students in state institutions 28,100
Students in all U.S. public institutions 9,916,600
State share of U.S. total 0.28
Rank among states 47

**State and local government appropriations for higher
   education**
State appropriation per FTE $4,408
National average $5,716
Rank among states 42
State & local tax revenue going to higher
   education 8.2%

FTE = full-time equivalent in public postsecondary programs,
   including summer sessions; student numbers are rounded to
   nearest hundred. Funding figures for 2003-2004 academic year
   include financial aid to students in state public institutions and
   exclude money for research, agriculture experiment stations,
   teaching hospitals, and medical schools; figures are rounded to
   nearest thousand dollars.
Source: Higher Education Executive Officers, Denver, Colorado.

TRANSPORTATION AND TRAVEL

Highway mileage, 2003

Interstate highways	679
Arterial roads	6,352
Collector roads	19,234
Local roads	57,423
Urban roads	2,264
Rural roads	81,424
Total state mileage	83,688
U.S. total	3,974,107
State share	2.11%
Rank among states	24

Note that combined urban and rural road mileage matches the
   total of the other categories.
Source: U.S. Federal Highway Administration.

Motor vehicle registrations and driver licenses, 2003

Vehicle registrations	State	U.S.	Share	Rank
Autos, trucks, buses	827,000	231,390,000	0.36%	44
Autos only	388,000	135,670	0.29%	46
Motorcycles	38,000	5,328,000	0.71%	34
Driver licenses	555,000	196,166,000	0.28%	46

Figures, which do not include vehicles owned by military services,
   are rounded to the nearest thousand. Figures for automobiles
   include taxis.
Source: U.S. Federal Highway Administration.

Domestic travel expenditures, 2003
Spending by U.S. residents on overnight trips and
day trips of at least 50 miles from home

Total expenditures within state	$1.52 bill.
Total expenditures within U.S.	$490.87 bill.
State share of U.S. total	0.3%
Rank among states	45

Source: Travel Industry Association of America.

Retail gasoline prices, 2003-2007
Average price per gallon at the pump

Year	U.S.	State
2003	$1.267	$1.230
2004	$1.316	$1.311
2005	$1.644	$1.668
2007	$2.298	$2.237

Excise tax per gallon in 2004	22.0¢
Rank among all states in 2007 prices	30

Prices are averages of all grades of gasoline sold at the pump
during March months in 2003-2005 and during February, 2007.
Averages for 2006, during which prices rose higher, are not
available.
Source: U.S. Energy Information Agency, *Petroleum Marketing
Monthly* (2003-2005 data); American Automobile Association
(2007 data).

CRIME AND LAW ENFORCEMENT

State and local police officers, 2000-2004

	2000	2002	2004
Total officers			
U.S.	654,601	665,555	675,734
State	1,195	1,267	1,362*
*Net change, 2000-2004			+13.97%
Officers per 1,000 residents			
U.S.	2.33	2.31	2.30
State	1.58	1.67	1.77
State rank	47	45	38

Totals include state and local police and sheriffs.
Source: Carsey Institute, University of New Hampshire.

Crime rates, 2003
Incidents per 100,000 residents

Crimes	State	U.S.
Violent crimes		
Total incidents	173	475
Murder	1	6
Forcible rape	46	32
Robbery	14	142
Aggravated assault	112	295
Property crimes		
Total incidents	2,002	3,588
Burglary	376	741
Larceny/theft	1,511	2,415
Motor vehicle theft	114	433
All crimes	2,175	4,063

Source: U.S. Federal Bureau of Investigation, *Crime in the United
States*, annual.

State prison populations, 1980-2003

	State	U.S.	State share
1980	635	305,458	0.21%
1990	1,341	708,393	0.19%
1996	2,063	1,025,624	0.20%
2000	2,616	1,391,261	0.19%
2003	3,026	1,470,045	0.21%

State figures exclude prisoners in federal penitentiaries.
Source: U.S. Bureau of Justice Statistics, *Prisoners in 2003*.

Tennessee

Location: South

Area and rank: 41,220 square miles (106,759 square kilometers); 42,146 square miles (109,158 square kilometers) including water; thirty-fourth largest state in area

Coastline: none

Population and rank: 5,901,000 (2004); sixteenth largest state in population

Capital city: Nashville-Davidson (545,524 people in 2000 census)

Largest city: Memphis (650,100 people in 2000 census)

Entered Union and rank: June 1, 1796; sixteenth state

Present constitution adopted: 1870; amended 1953, 1960, 1966, 1972, 1978

Counties: 95

Nashville's full-sized replica of Greece's Parthenon building was originally built for Tennessee's centennial exposition in 1876. During the 1920's, the original, mostly plaster-of-paris, structure was replaced by a concrete-and-steel building, which now houses an art gallery and a monumental statue of the Greek goddess Athena. (Ryan Kaldari)

State name: "Tennessee" is derived from a Cherokee word

State nickname: Volunteer State

Motto: Agriculture and Commerce

State flag: Red field with two vertical stripes of white and blue on the end, with a blue circle in the center containing three white stars

Highest point: Clingmans Dome—6,643 feet (2,025 meters)

Lowest point: Mississippi River—178 feet (54 meters)

Highest recorded temperature: 113 degrees Fahrenheit (45 degrees Celsius)—Perryville, 1930

Lowest recorded temperature: −32 degrees Fahrenheit (−36 degrees Celsius)—Mountain City, 1917

State songs: "Tennessee Waltz"; "My Homeland, Tennessee"; "When It's Iris Time in Tennessee"; "My Tennessee"; "Rocky Top"; "Tennessee"

State tree: Tulip poplar

State flower: Iris

State bird: Mockingbird

State animal: Raccoon

National parks: Great Smoky Mountains

Tennessee History

Tennessee is one of the south-central states, strategically located along the Mississippi River on the west and the Unaka range of the Appalachian Mountains on the east. To its north lie Kentucky and Virginia; to its south Georgia, Alabama, and Mississippi; to its east North Carolina; and to its west Arkansas and Missouri. The state, which runs 120 miles from north to south and 430 miles from east to west, has dense forests in the portions that lie within the Great Smoky Mountains. In its lower regions in the west are cypress swamps much like those found in parts of southern Georgia.

Early History. Ancient burial mounds and archaeological artifacts verify the presence of inhabitants in Tennessee prior to recorded history and long before European explorers made their ways into the area. Paleo-Indians are thought to have lived in this region as long as fifteen thousand years ago. These prehistoric inhabitants were followed by other early American Indians.

The early British and Spanish explorers in the area encountered several Indian tribes, notably the Cherokee, the Chickasaw, the Shawnee, the Creek, and the Yuchi. Of these, the Cherokee were the most sophisticated, living in their own well-developed enclaves in the southeastern part of Tennessee in the Appalachian Mountains. The Chickasaw lived to the west toward the Mississippi River and were considered a belligerent tribe.

By 1714 the Cherokee and the Chickasaw had driven the Shawnee out of the Cumberland Valley, which they inhabited, through the Kentucky area, to north of the Ohio River. At about the same time, these two dominant tribes drove the Creek and Yuchi Indians south to Georgia, leaving the area very much in their hands.

Exploration and Settlement. It is known that a group of explorers led by the Spanish explorer Hernando de Soto, presumably the first Europeans to enter the area, were in southeastern Tennessee in 1540. By the following year, this group had pushed west and had reached the Mississippi River. By 1566-1567, another Spanish group, led by Juan Pardo, had carried out two expeditions in the southeastern part of Tennessee and had erected a fortification near modern Chattanooga.

During the 1930's, the federal Resettlement Administration produced films such as The River *(1937) to win public support for the construction of the Tennessee Valley Authority, part of whose purpose was to combat flooding. (Museum of Modern Art, Films Stills Archive)*

It was not until 1673 that both French and British explorers arrived, at almost the same time, in the area. Two Virginia traders of British descent, James Needham and Gabriel Arthur, made their way into eastern Tennessee at about this time. In the western extreme of the area, two Frenchmen, Father Jacques Marquette, a missionary, and Louis Jolliet, a fur trader, arrived, having sailed down the Mississippi from the north. A decade later, in 1682, another famous French explorer, René-Robert Cavelier, Sieur de La Salle, and his band of followers constructed Fort Prud'Homme on the Natchez (Hatchie) River.

Early Tennessee. The territory into which many of the explorers pressed was a part of the large Cherokee nation in eastern Tennessee. The French and British competed for control of the Cherokee, with the French initially emerging as the victors. At the end of the French and Indian War, however, the Treaty of Paris, enacted in 1763, ceded the area to the British.

Daniel Boone explored this territory, and, in 1769, permanent settlement by whites began, with four parts of the state attracting residents. One settlement was in eastern Tennessee near the Virginia border, a town that eventually was to lie partly in Virginia and partly in Tennessee. Another settlement grew up along the Watauga River near Elizabethtown. West of the Holston River near Rogersville, a settlement was established, while a fourth settlement developed near Erwin along the banks of the Nolichuky River.

When it was discovered in 1771 that all the land on which the white inhabitants had settled except that north of the Holston River belonged legally to the Cherokee, the white settlers were forced to lease the land from them. These settlers finally bought it in 1775 under the Treaty of Sycamore Shoals.

The Revolutionary War. Although this area was remote from the major battlefields of the Revolutionary War, people from the Tennessee region engaged in some combat against the British and the Loyalists. In October, 1780, the Battle of King's Mountain marked one of the most severe British defeats in the South. Shortly before this battle, North Carolina annexed the eastern region of Tennessee into its western territory and held it until 1784, when it gave the territory over to the U.S. government. The people in this territory established a separate state, called Franklin, with John Sevier as governor. This state existed for four years. North Carolina, however, attempted to retrieve the territory and finally succeeded in 1788 but soon again ceded it to the United States. In 1790, it officially came to be known as the Territory South of the River Ohio; its governor was William Blount. By 1794 the Tennessee region became the first territory to achieve the representative-government stage under the recently enacted Northwest Ordinance. The first territory to have a delegate in the U.S. Congress, Tennessee, in 1796, became the sixteenth state to enter the Union.

Slavery and the Civil War. Tennessee had few of the sprawling plantations found in parts of the Deep South, although in its eastern lowlands and central area, where cotton was grown, there was considerable slave labor. In eastern Tennessee, however, the agricultural economy was on a small scale. Farmers raised their own food, hunted, and were essentially self-sufficient. What help they had usually came from their children and other family members.

Before the Civil War, significant road building took place in Tennessee. Turnpikes were constructed, railroad tracks were laid, and waterways were improved for river navigation. Some industry developed, mainly ironworks, but the chief occupation was farming.

Naturally, where slave labor was used, mainly in the western and middle parts of the state, people favored slavery, but in its eastern extremes, Tennesseans were resolutely antislavery. After South Carolina and other southern states left the Union, Tennessee refused to call a convention to consider secession. In April, 1861, however, Tennessee's governor refused to send troops to join the Union Army, and on June 8, Tennesseans voted to secede.

Tennessee's largest city, Memphis owes its development to its port location on the Mississippi River. Clearly visible behind the city center is the Pyramid Arena, home to the National Basketball Association's Memphis Grizzlies and the University of Memphis men's basketball team.

Aside from Virginia, Tennessee had more battles fought on its land than any other southern state—more than four hundred. Of its 145,000 soldiers, however, more than 30,000, mostly from eastern Tennessee, joined the Union Army. In 1865, Tennesseans voted to abolish slavery, although in 1870 they voted to ban interracial marriages and in 1875 enacted the first Jim Crow laws that strictly limited the freedom of African Americans.

Postwar Tennessee. Tennessee was readmitted to the Union on July 25, 1866. It was spared many of the punitive programs that Reconstruction imposed on other southern states. The war left Tennessee impoverished to the point that it was unable to meet its financial obligations and in 1883 settled with its lenders for fifty to eighty cents on the dollar. Farmers were extremely strained financially. In 1891 and 1892, coal miners, protesting the use of convicts leased to Tennessee's coal mines, revolted in the Coal Miners War.

Tennessee gained national attention in 1925, when charges were leveled against schoolteacher John Scopes for teaching the theory of evolution in his high school classes. The Scopes Trial, known as the Monkey Trial, focused attention on the state, and the outcome, which favored Tennessee's religious conservatives, was decried by much of the nation.

The Tennessee Valley Authority. Rich in natural resources, Tennessee did not profit significantly from its natural wealth until the years following 1933, when Congress established the Tennessee Valley Authority (TVA) as a flood control and power project of President Franklin Roosevelt's New Deal. The TVA harnessed rivers and created lakes. It enhanced the power output that private industry had already begun to finance by building dams on the Little Tennessee, Ocoee, and Pigeon Rivers during the 1920's.

By the mid-1990's, Tennessee was generating some seventy-two billion kilowatt-hours of electricity annually. Besides serving its stated purposes, the TVA created attractive recreational areas in parts of the state. Moreover, the lakes created by the TVA, combined with the Mississippi, Tennessee, and Cumberland rivers, give Tennessee more than a thousand miles of inland waterways. These navigational routes are supplemented by more than 1,100 miles of interstate highways and 154,000 miles of public roads. With 155 airports, Tennessee has ample provision for air transport.

Other Commercial Enterprises. One of the longstanding commercial enterprises in Tennessee is lumbering. The forests of the Appalachian Mountains provide a great deal of hardwood, and the central area of the state is known for its red cedar.

Manufacturing is centered mostly in eastern Tennessee, which produces grain mill products, inorganic chemicals, drugs, and plastics. A major nuclear research facility at Oak Ridge has brought many scientists into the state, enhancing some of its manufacturing enterprises.

Rich in minerals, Tennessee produces a great deal of gravel, zinc, coal, and clay. It ranks first in the nation for its production of ball clay and gemstones. Although coal production dropped off significantly after 1980, two of the most important zinc-producing operations are in Mascot and Jefferson City, Tennessee.

Politics and Elections. As the 2000 presidential election loomed, Tennessee, reflecting the condition of much of the nation, was badly divided along partisan lines. On one hand, Democratic candidate Al Gore was a "favorite son," or native of the state. Such status is often a considerable benefit to presidential candidates. On the other hand, Republican popularity was on the increase. When the election was held, George W. Bush won the state by the narrow margin of 51 to 48 percent, a key victory on the road to the White House. Republican senator Bill Frist was reelected by a two-to-one margin. Gore's liability was that he was seen as having more roots in Washington, D.C., than in Tennessee. After the election, however, he returned at least temporarily to teach courses at several universities in the state.

In the 2004 presidential race, Bush had a much easier time adding the state to his win column than in 2000. He easily overwhelmed Democrat John Kerry with 57 percent of the vote to the challenger's 43 percent. In congressional contests, the results exemplified the lack of real competition typical of House races across the country. In Tennessee, among the state's nine congressional districts, no challenger received more than 43 percent of the vote, one incumbent was unopposed, and the remainder garnered percentages in the 60 and 70 percent range, except for Democratic congressman Harold Ford, Jr., who won 82 percent of the vote.

Among the most colorful politicians in the state was Republican Fred Dalton Thompson, a nationally known film and television actor, who successfully sought a U.S. Senate seat in 1994 for a partial term and was easily reelected in 1996. Urged to run again in 2002, Thompson hesitated, then declined. In his place, voters chose former governor and U.S. secretary of education Lamar Alexander, son of Tennessee teachers.

The Memphis home of rock and roll legend Elvis Presley, Graceland has become one of Tennessee's major tourist draws. (©Kent Knudson/Westock)

The governor's race pitted Democrat Phil Bredesen against Republican congress member Van Hilleary. Bredesen was born in New Jersey and raised in upstate New York; he held a degree in physics from Harvard. After early political defeats, he overcame these handicaps to take the statehouse with a narrow win, aided by his reputation for moderation and administrative competence.

Country Music Hall of Fame. Tennessee is perhaps better known for its whiskey and its music than for politics, and during the early months of the new century its musical heritage came to the fore. The state capital, Nashville, had long enjoyed a reputation as the nation's epicenter of country music. The original Country Music Hall of Fame and Museum (CMF) opened its doors there in 1961. On May 17, 2001, it was time for the inauguration of a new CMF, built at a cost of $37 million. It included a performance hall and a vast exhibition space. A featured exhibit is "Sing Me Back Home: A Journey Through Country Music."

R. Baird Shuman
Updated by the Editor

Tennessee Time Line

1540	Spanish explorer Hernando de Soto comes to the Tennessee region.
1566	Juan Pardo and his men build a fort near Chattanooga.
1673	First British explorers, James Needham and Gabriel Arthur, arrive in eastern Tennessee.
1673	First French explorers, missionary Jacques Marquette and fur trader Louis Jolliet, travel down the Mississippi River to western Tennessee.
1682	French explorer René-Robert Cavelier, Sieur de La Salle, and his men build Fort Prud'Homme on the Natchez (Hatchie) River.
1757	Fort Loudon, the westernmost fort of the British, is built by Loyalists from South Carolina.
1769	First permanent white settlement is established near the Watauga River.
1772	Early settlers establish the Watauga Association.
1779	Nashville is founded in Middle Tennessee.
1780	Tennesseans deliver a stunning defeat to the British in the Battle of King's Mountain.
Dec., 1784	Eastern Tennesseans create the state of Franklin.
1788	State of Franklin is disbanded.
May 26, 1790	Territory is officially designated "Territory South of the River Ohio," also called the Southwest Territory.
1794	Founding of Blount College, which eventually becomes the University of Tennessee at Knoxville.
June 1, 1796	Tennessee joins the Union as the sixteenth state.
1818	Jackson Purchase buys western Tennessee from the Chickasaw.
1829	Tennessean Andrew Jackson becomes seventh president of the United States.
1835	Charter of 1796 is replaced by new state constitution.
1838	Cherokee Indians involuntarily relocated to Oklahoma.
1843	Nashville becomes Tennessee's state capital.
1845	Tennessean James Knox Polk becomes seventeenth president of the United States.
1854	Railroad is completed to join Nashville and Chattanooga.
1860	Tennessee refuses to call convention to consider secession.
June 8, 1861	Tennessee secedes from the Union, joining the Confederacy.
1863	Eastern Tennessee cleared of Confederates.
1864	Andrew Johnson becomes vice president of the United States.
Jan. 9, 1865	Union Convention to restore civil government and abolish slavery meets in Nashville.
Feb. 22, 1865	Tennesseans vote to abolish slavery.
1865	Civil government restored and slavery abolished.
Apr. 15, 1865	Andrew Johnson becomes president of the United States the day after President Abraham Lincoln is assassinated.
July 25, 1866	Tennessee is readmitted to the Union.
1867	Tennesseans vote to extend the franchise to African Americans.
1870	New state constitution is written and adopted; interracial marriages banned.

1875	Tennessee passes the first Jim Crow laws, which limit the rights of blacks and deny them considerable public access.
1891	First Coal Miner War takes place.
1925	John Scopes tried and found guilty of teaching evolution in the famed Monkey Trial.
1926	Great Smoky Mountains National Park is established.
1933	Congress approves the Tennessee Valley Authority (TVA).
1942	Manhattan Project is established at Oak Ridge for nuclear and atomic research.
1954	State constitution of 1870 amended.
1960	Downtown lunch counters are integrated after "sit-ins."
1964	Tennessee Space Institute is established at Tullahoma.
Nov. 7, 2000	In the presidential election, favorite son Al Gore narrowly loses his home state.
May 17, 2001	$37 million Country Music Hall of Fame and Museum opens in Nashville.
Nov. 2, 2002	Former governor Lamar Alexander is elected to the U.S. Senate; former Nashville mayor Phil Bredesen is narrowly elected governor.

Notes for Further Study

Published Sources. Two of the most accessible resources for Tennessee history, both by Wilma Dykeman, are *The French Broad* (1974) and *Tennessee: A Bicentennial History* (Rev. ed., 1984). Two books give readers insight into how the Civil War was experienced within the state. *All Right Let Them Come: The Civil War Diary of an East Tennessee Confederate* (2003), edited by Charles Swift Northen III and part of the Voices of the Civil War series published by the University of Tennessee, presents the diary of a young man in the 60th Tennessee Infantry. Jack H. Lepa's *Breaking the Confederacy: The Georgia and Tennessee Campaigns of 1864* (2005) details the locales, conditions, personnel, strategies, tactics, and battles in the Tennessee region in an important period during the Civil War. Edited by Carol Van West in association with the Tennessee Historical Society, *Tennessee Encyclopedia of History and Culture* (1998) brings together more than fifteen hundred articles and thirty-two topical essays which discuss primary aspects of Tennessee's history and culture.

Aimed at younger readers, *Tennessee* (2d rev. ed., 2002) by Karen Sirvaitis and *Tennessee* (2006) by Rick Petreycik both offer a good overview of the state's geography, history, people, places, and economy. John Chimprich's *Slavery's End in Tennessee: Eighteen Sixty-One to Eighteen Sixty-Five* (1985) discusses in detail one of the most divisive questions in Tennessee history, a question that pitted eastern Tennessee against the middle and western parts of the state. Bobby L. Lovett draws on special collections from libraries across the state, personal papers, manuscript collections, scholarly articles, and newspa-

pers to explore how African Americans struggled for their rights in *The Civil Rights Movement in Tennessee: A Narrative History* (2005). Volume 2 of Donald Davidson's *The Tennessee*, titled *The New River: Civil War to TVA* (1992), is a thoroughly researched and well-written account of Tennessee history from 1861 to 1940. Margaret E. Dick and Amy Lynch offer an informative study of the economic history of Nashville in *Nashville: Upbeat and Down to Business* (1990). Two guidebooks are quite competent in highlighting the states's history, attractions, and natural beauty: *Moon Handbooks Tennessee* (2005) by Jeff

Tennessee's capital and second-largest city, Nashville-Davidson. (Corbis)

Bradley and *Compass American Guides: Tennessee* (2d ed., 2006) by Robert Brandt (revised by Monique Peterson).

Web Resources. The first stop for an online study of the state should be the state's official site (www.state.tn.us/). Another useful Web site is the Tennessee Chamber of Commerce (www.tncoc.com). The Tennessee Blue Book (state.tn .us/sos/bluebook/) is a good destination for those researching the state's government agencies and branches of the state government. The Tennessee Encyclopedia of History and Culture (tennesseeencyclopedia.net/) provides galleries of images, multimedia, and maps and is organized so that users can find articles about state locations, historical events, or notable figures by alphabetical order.

Some cities, such as Nashville (www.nashvillecvb.com/) have their own Web sites which provide local information about various aspects of the city. The Nashville site is particularly strong in listing entertainment and tourist attractions. Among its features are news, chat rooms, forums, and polls. It also lists all of the print media, numbering some sixteen publications, in Nashville as well as the city's six television stations. Many people visit Nashville for its music scene; the Grand Ole Opry (www.opry.com/) and the Country Music Hall of Fame (www.countrymusichalloffame.com/site/) have excellent and attractive Web sites.

Counties

County	2000 pop.	Rank in pop.	Sq. miles	Rank in area	County	2000 pop.	Rank in pop.	Sq. miles	Rank in area
Anderson	71,330	15	337.5	65	Coffee	48,014	28	428.9	54
Bedford	37,586	38	473.7	44	Crockett	14,532	77	265.3	83
Benton	16,537	74	394.8	59	Cumberland	46,802	29	681.6	4
Bledsoe	12,367	81	406.3	57	Davidson	569,891	2	502.3	37
Blount	105,823	11	558.6	23	Decatur	11,731	82	333.9	66
Bradley	87,965	14	328.8	67	De Kalb	17,423	71	304.6	73
Campbell	39,854	33	480.1	42	Dickson	43,156	31	489.9	40
Cannon	12,826	79	265.7	82	Dyer	37,279	39	510.6	35
Carroll	29,475	47	599.1	14	Fayette	28,806	49	704.5	3
Carter	56,742	21	341.1	64	Fentress	16,625	73	498.7	39
Cheatham	35,912	40	302.7	74	Franklin	39,270	34	553.1	25
Chester	15,540	76	288.5	76	Gibson	48,152	27	602.7	13
Claiborne	29,862	46	434.3	50	Giles	29,447	48	611.0	12
Clay	7,976	88	236.1	84	Grainger	20,659	61	280.4	78
Cocke	33,565	42	434.4	49	Greene	62,909	18	621.8	7

County	2000 pop.	Rank in pop.	Sq. miles	Rank in area
Grundy	14,332	78	360.6	63
Hamblen	58,128	20	161.0	93
Hamilton	307,896	4	542.5	27
Hancock	6,786	92	222.3	87
Hardeman	28,105	51	667.6	5
Hardin	25,578	55	577.9	18
Hawkins	53,563	23	486.7	41
Haywood	19,797	64	533.2	29
Henderson	25,522	56	520.1	34
Henry	31,115	45	561.8	21
Hickman	22,295	59	612.7	11
Houston	8,088	87	200.2	88
Humphreys	17,929	66	532.2	30
Jackson	10,984	86	308.9	71
Jefferson	44,294	30	273.8	79
Johnson	17,499	70	298.5	75
Knox	382,032	3	508.5	36
Lake	7,954	89	163.4	91
Lauderdale	27,101	53	470.5	45
Lawrence	39,926	32	617.2	9
Lewis	11,367	84	282.1	77
Lincoln	31,340	44	570.3	20
Loudon	39,086	35	228.6	85
McMinn	49,015	26	430.3	53
McNairy	24,653	57	560.1	22
Macon	20,386	62	307.1	72
Madison	91,837	12	557.1	24
Marion	27,776	52	499.8	38
Marshall	26,767	54	375.4	61
Maury	69,498	17	612.9	10
Meigs	11,086	85	194.9	89
Monroe	38,961	36	635.2	6
Montgomery	134,768	7	539.2	28
Moore	5,740	93	129.2	94

County	2000 pop.	Rank in pop.	Sq. miles	Rank in area
Morgan	19,757	65	522.1	33
Obion	32,450	43	544.9	26
Overton	20,118	63	433.4	51
Perry	7,631	90	414.9	55
Pickett	4,945	95	162.9	92
Polk	16,050	75	435.1	48
Putnam	62,315	19	401.0	58
Rhea	28,400	50	315.9	69
Roane	51,910	24	361.0	62
Robertson	54,433	22	476.5	43
Rutherford	182,023	5	619.0	8
Scott	21,127	60	532.1	31
Sequatchie	11,370	83	265.9	81
Sevier	71,170	16	592.3	15
Shelby	897,472	1	754.9	1
Smith	17,712	68	314.4	70
Stewart	12,370	80	457.7	47
Sullivan	153,048	6	413.0	56
Sumner	130,449	8	529.4	32
Tipton	51,271	25	459.4	46
Trousdale	7,259	91	114.2	95
Unicoi	17,667	69	186.1	90
Union	17,808	67	223.6	86
Van Buren	5,508	94	273.5	80
Warren	38,276	37	432.7	52
Washington	107,198	10	326.2	68
Wayne	16,842	72	734.0	2
Weakley	34,895	41	580.3	17
White	23,102	58	376.7	60
Williamson	126,638	9	582.7	16
Wilson	88,809	13	570.6	19

Source: U.S. Census Bureau; National Association of Counties.

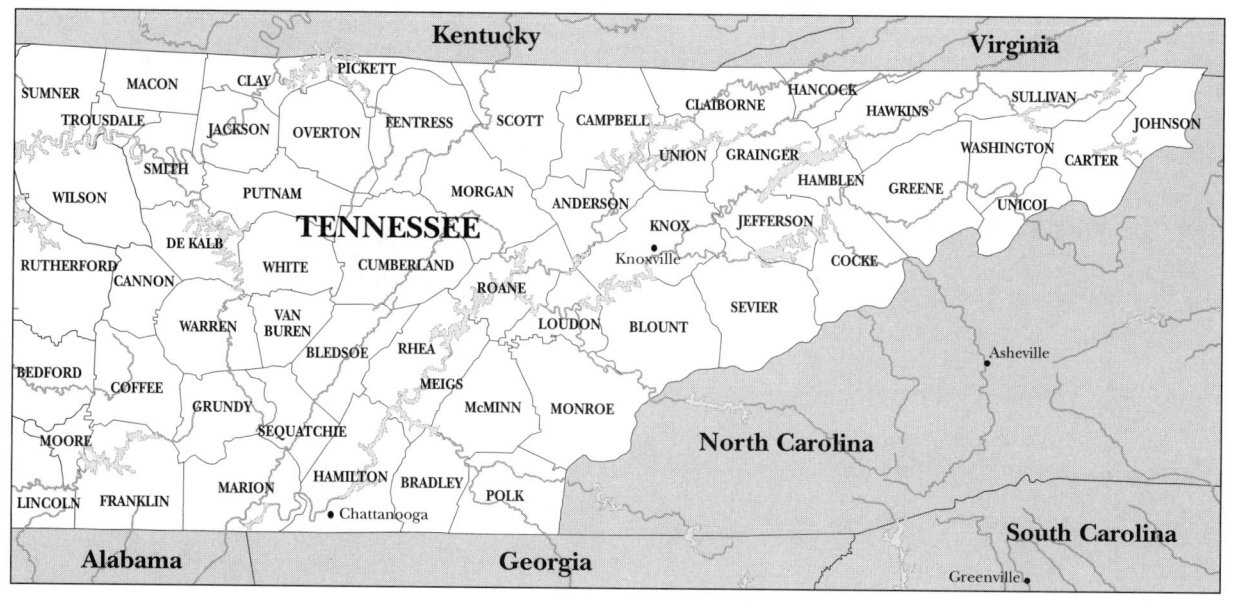

Cities

With 10,000 or more residents

Rank	City	Population	Rank	City	Population
1	Memphis	650,100	28	Tullahoma	17,994
2	Nashville-Davidson (capital)	545,524	29	Farragut	17,720
3	Knoxville	173,890	30	Dyersburg	17,452
4	Chattanooga	155,554	31	Shelbyville	16,105
5	Clarksville	103,455	32	Greeneville	15,198
6	Murfreesboro	68,816	33	Springfield	14,329
7	Jackson	59,643	34	East Brainerd	14,132
8	Johnson City	55,469	35	Goodlettsville	13,780
9	Kingsport	44,905	36	Elizabethton	13,372
10	Franklin	41,842	37	Athens	13,220
11	Hendersonville	40,620	38	McMinnville	12,749
12	Bartlett	40,543	39	Red Bank	12,418
13	Germantown	37,348	40	Mount Juliet	12,366
14	Cleveland	37,192	41	Dickson	12,244
15	Columbia	33,055	42	Middle Valley	11,854
16	Collierville	31,872	43	Sevierville	11,757
17	Oak Ridge	27,387	44	Soddy-Daisy	11,530
18	Smyrna	25,569	45	Union City	10,876
19	Morristown	24,965	46	Lawrenceburg	10,796
20	Bristol	24,821	47	Brownsville	10,748
21	Cookeville	23,923	48	Martin	10,515
22	Brentwood	23,445	49	Millington	10,433
23	Gallatin	23,230	50	Lewisburg	10,413
24	Maryville	23,120	51	Bloomingdale	10,350
25	East Ridge	20,640			
26	Lebanon	20,235			
27	La Vergne	18,687			

Population figures are from 2000 census.

Source: U.S. Bureau of the Census.

Index to Tables

DEMOGRAPHICS

Resident state and national populations, 1970-2004

Population figures given in thousands

	State pop.	U.S. pop.	Share	Rank
1970	3,926	203,302	1.9%	17
1980	4,591	226,546	2.0%	17
1985	4,715	237,924	2.0%	17
1990	4,877	248,765	2.0%	17
1995	5,327	262,761	2.0%	17
2000	5,689	281,425	2.0%	16
2004	5,901	293,655	2.0%	16

Source: U.S. Census Bureau, Current Population Reports, 2006.

Resident population by age, 2004

Age Group	Total persons
Under 5 years	385,000
5 to 17 years	1,007,000
18 to 24 years	576,000
25 to 34 years	828,000
35 to 44 years	887,000
45 to 54 years	852,000
55 to 64 years	629,000
65 to 74 years	407,000
75 to 84 years	248,000
85 years and older	84,000
All age groups	5,901,000
Portion of residents 65 and older	12.5%
National rank in portion of oldest residents	27
National average	12.4%

Population figures are rounded to nearest thousand persons;
figures include armed forces personnel stationed in the state.
Source: U.S. Bureau of the Census, 2006.

Resident population by race, Hispanic origin, 2004

Category	State pop.	Share	U.S.
All residents	5,901	100.00%	100.00%
Non-Hispanic white	4,611	78.14%	67.37%
Hispanic white	152	2.58%	13.01%
Other Hispanic	15	0.25%	1.06%
African American	991	16.79%	12.77%
Native American	17	0.29%	0.96%
Asian, Pacific Islander	74	1.25%	4.37%
Two or more categories	56	0.95%	1.51%

Population figures are in thousands. Persons counted as "Hispanic" (Latino) may be of any race. Because of overlapping categories, categories may not add up to 100%. Shares in column 3 are percentages of each category within the state; these figures may be compared to the national percentages in column 4.
Source: U.S. Bureau of the Census, 2006.

Projected state population, 2000-2030

Year	Population
2000	5,689,000
2005	5,965,000
2010	6,231,000
2015	6,502,000
2020	6,781,000
2025	7,073,000
2030	7,381,000
Population increase, 2000-2030	1,692,000
Percentage increase, 2000-2030	29.7

Projections are based on data from the 2000 census.
Source: U.S. Census Bureau.

VITAL STATISTICS

Infant mortality rates, 1980-2002

	1980	1990	2000	2002
All state residents	13.5	10.3	9.1	9.4
All U.S. residents	12.6	9.2	9.4	9.1
All state white residents	11.9	7.3	6.8	7.0
All U.S. white residents	10.6	7.6	5.7	5.8
All state black residents	19.3	17.9	18.0	18.3
All U.S. black residents	22.2	18.0	14.1	14.4

Figures represent deaths per 1,000 live births of resident infants under 1 year old, exclusive of fetal deaths. Figures for all residents include members of other racial categories not listed separately.
Source: U.S. Census Bureau, *Statistical Abstract of the United States,* 2006.

Abortion rates, 1990 and 2000

	1990	2000
Total abortions	19,000	19,000
Rate per 1,000 women	16.1	15.2
U.S. rate	25.7	21.3
Rank	30	24

Numbers of abortions are rounded to nearest thousand; ranks are based on rates.
Source: U.S. Census Bureau.

Marriages and divorces, 2004

Total marriages	67,500
Rate per 1,000 population	11.4
National rate per 1,000 population	7.4
Rank among all states	4
Total divorces	29,800
Rate per 1,000 population	5.0
National rate per 1,000 population	3.7
Rank among all states	5

Figures are for all marriages and divorces performed within the state, including those of nonresidents; totals are rounded to the nearest hundred. Ranks are for highest to lowest figures; note that divorce data are not available for five states.
Source: U.S. National Center for Health Statistics, *Vital Statistics of the United States,* 2006.

Death rates by leading causes, 2002
Deaths per 100,000 resident population

Cause	State	U.S.
Heart disease	279.9	241.7
Cancer	215.9	193.2
Cerebrovascular diseases	68.7	56.4
Accidents other than motor vehicle	47.3	37.0
Motor vehicle accidents	21.6	15.7
Chronic lower respiratory diseases	51.9	43.3
Diabetes mellitus	30.2	25.4
HIV	6.0	4.9
Suicide	13.4	11.0
Homicide	8.1	6.1
All causes	976.4	847.3
Rank in overall death rate among states		11

Figures exclude nonresidents who died in the state. Causes of death follow International Classification of Diseases. Rank is from highest to lowest death rate in the United States.
Source: U.S. National Center for Health Statistics, *National Vital Statistics Report,* 2006.

ECONOMY

Gross state product, 1990-2004
In current dollars

Year	State product	Nat'l product	State share
1990	$94.6 billion	$5.67 trillion	1.67%
2000	$174.3 billion	$9.75 trillion	1.79%
2002	$191.4 billion	$10.41 trillion	1.84%
2003	$203.1 billion	$10.92 trillion	1.86%
2004	$216.9 billion	$11.65 trillion	1.86%

Source: U.S. Bureau of Economic Analysis, *Survey of Current Business,* July, 2005.

Gross state product by industry, 2003
In billions of dollars

Construction	$6.7
Manufacturing	35.1
Wholesale trade	13.2
Retail trade	18.1
Finance & insurance	11.8
Information	6.3
Professional services	9.0
Health care & social assistance	14.8
Government	22.1
Total state product	$191.2
Total U.S. product	$10,289.2
State share of U.S. total	1.86%
Rank among all states	18

Total figures include industries not listed separately. Amounts are in chained 2000 dollars.
Source: U.S. Bureau of Economic Analysis, *Survey of Current Business,* July, 2005.

Personal income per capita, 1990-2004
In current dollars

	1990	2000	2004
Per capita income	$16,692	$26,097	$30,005
U.S. average	$19,477	$29,845	$32,937
Rank among states	36	34	35

Source: U.S. Bureau of Economic Analysis, *Survey of Current Business,* April, 2005.

Energy consumption, 2001
In trillions of British thermal units (BTU), except as noted

Total energy consumption

Total state energy consumption	2,195
Total U.S. energy consumption	96,275
State share of U.S. total	2.28%
Rank among states	15

Per capita consumption (In millions of BTU)

Total state per capita consumption	382
Total U.S. per capita consumption	338
Rank among states	16

End-use sectors

Residential	500
Commercial	369
Industrial	746
Transportation	581

Sources of energy

Petroleum	708
Natural gas	265
Coal	688
Hydroelectric power	63
Nuclear electric power	299

Figures for totals include categories not listed separately.
Source: U.S. Energy Information Administration, *State Energy Data Report,* 2001.

Nonfarm employment by sectors, 2004

Total persons	2,701,000
Construction	118,000
Manufacturing	412,000
Trade, transportation, utilities	587,000
Information	50,000
Finance, insurance, real estate	142,000
Professional & business services	301,000
Education & health services	320,000
Leisure, hospitality, arts, organizations	253,000
Other services, including repair & maintenance	102,000
Government	414,000

Figures are rounded to nearest thousand persons. "Total" includes mining and natural resources, not listed separately.
Source: U.S. Bureau of Labor Statistics, 2006.

Foreign exports, 1990-2004
In millions of dollars

Year	State	U.S.	State share
1990	3,746	394,045	0.95%
1996	8,094	624,767	1.30%
1997	9,233	688,896	1.34%
2000	11,592	712,055	1.48%
2003	12,612	724,006	1.87%
2004	16,123	769,332	2.10%

Rank among all states in 2004 16

U.S. total does not include U.S. dependencies.
Source: U.S. Census Bureau, *U.S. Merchandise Trade,* series FT 900,
2000; U.S. Census Bureau, *U.S. International Trade in Goods and
Services,* Series FT 900, 2005.

LAND USE

Federally owned land, 2003
Areas in acres

	State	U.S.	State share
Total area	26,728,000	2,271,343,000	1.18%
Nonfederal land	24,712,000	1,599,584,000	1.54%
Federal land	2,016,000	671,759,000	0.30%
Federal share	7.5%	29.6%	—

Areas are rounded to nearest thousand acres. Figures for federally
owned land do not include trust properties.
Source: U.S. General Services Administration, *Federal Real Property
Profile,* 2006.

Land use, 1997
In acres, rounded to nearest thousand

Total surface area 26,974,000
Total nonfederal rural land. 22,597,000
Percentage rural land 83.8%
Cropland 4,644,000
Conservation Reserve Program (CRP*) land. . . . 374,000
Pastureland 4,990,000
Rangeland . . . . (nil)
Forestland 12,042,000
Other rural land 547,000

*CRP is a federal program begun in 1985 to assist private
landowners to convert highly erodible cropland to vegetative
cover for ten years. Note that some categories of land overlap.
Source: U.S. Department of Agriculture, Natural Resources and
Conservation Service, and Iowa State University, Statistical
Laboratory, *Summary Report, 1997 National Resources Inventory,*
revised December, 2000.

Farms and crop acreage, 2004

	State	U.S.	Share	Rank
Farms	85,000	2,113,000	4.02%	4
Acres (millions)	12	937	1.28%	24
Acres per farm	136	443	—	44

Source: U.S. Department of Agriculture, National Agricultural
Statistics Service. Numbers of farms are rounded to nearest
thousand units; acreage figures are rounded to nearest million.
Rankings, including ties, are based on rounded figures.

GOVERNMENT AND FINANCE

Units of local government, 2002

	State	Total U.S.	Rank
All local governments	930	87,525	31
Counties	92	3,034	11
Municipalities	349	19,429	23
Townships	0	16,504	—
School districts	14	13,506	44
Special districts	475	35,052	27

Only 48 states have county governments, 20 states have township
governments ("towns" in New England, Minnesota, New York,
and Wisconsin), and 46 states have school districts. Special
districts encompass such functions as natural resources, fire
protection, and housing and community development.
Source: U.S. Census Bureau, *Census of Governments.*

State government revenue, 2002

Total revenue . . . . $17,952 mill.
General revenue . . . . $17,620 mill.
Per capita revenue $3,042
U.S. per capita average $3,689
Rank among states 47

Intergovernment revenue
Total . . . . $7,316 mill.
From federal government . . . . $7,078 mill.

Charges and miscellaneous
Total . . . . $2,506 mill.
Current charges . . . . $1,713 mill.
Misc. general income . . . . $792 mill.
Insurance trust revenue . . . . $332 mill.

Taxes
Total . . . . $7,798 mill.
Per capita taxes $1,347
Rank among states 48
Property taxes . . . . (nil)
Sales taxes . . . . $6,046 mill.
License taxes . . . . $836 mill.
Individual income taxes . . . . $146 mill.
Corporate income taxes . . . . $503 mill.
Other taxes . . . . $267 mill.

Total revenue figures include items not listed separately here.
Source: U.S. Bureau of the Census.

State government expenditures, 2002

General expenditures
Total state expenditures	$20,029 mill.
Intergovernmental	$4,478 mill.

Per capita expenditures
State	$3,193
Average of all states	$3,859
Rank among states	45

Selected direct expenditures
Education	$3,315 mill.
Public welfare	$6,319 mill.
Health, hospital	$1,237 mill.
Highways	$1,206 mill.
Police protection	$125 mill.
Corrections	$390 mill.
Natural resources	$227 mill.
Parks and recreation	$103 mill.
Government administration	$433 mill.
Interest on debt	$198 mill.
Total direct expenditures	$14,011 mill.

Totals include items not listed separately.
Source: U.S. Census Bureau.

POLITICS

Governors since statehood

D = Democrat; R = Republican; O = other;
(r) resigned; (d) died in office; (i) removed from office

John Sevier (O)	1796-1801
Archibald Roane (O)	1801-1803
John Sevier (O)	1803-1809
Willie Blount (O)	1809-1815
Joseph McMinn (O)	1815-1821
William Carroll (O)	1821-1827
Sam Houston (O)	(r) 1827-1829
William Hall (O)	1829
William Carroll (D)	1829-1835
Newton Cannon (O)	1835-1839
James K. Polk (D)	1839-1841
James C. Jones (O)	1841-1845
Aaron V. Brown (D)	1845-1847
Neill S. Brown (O)	1847-1849
William Trousdale (D)	1849-1851
William B. Campbell (O)	1851-1853
Andrew Johnson (D)	1853-1857
Isham G. Harris* (D)	(i) 1857-1865
Andrew Johnson**	(r) 1862-1865
Edward H. East	1865
William G. Brownlow (R)	(r) 1865-1869
DeWitt C. Senter (R)	1869-1871
John C. Brown (D)	1871-1875
James D. Porter (D)	1875-1879
Albert S. Marks (D)	1879-1881
Alvin Hawkins (R)	1881-1883
William B. Bate (D)	1883-1887

Robert L. Taylor (D)	1887-1891
John P. Buchanan (D)	1891-1893
Peter Turney (D)	1893-1897
Robert L. Taylor (D)	1897-1899
Benton McMillin (D)	1899-1903
James B. Frazier (D)	(r) 1903-1905
John I. Cox (D)	1905-1907
Malcolm R. Patterson (D)	1907-1911
Benjamin W. Hooper (R)	1911-1915
Thomas C. Rye (D)	1915-1919
Albert H. Roberts (D)	1919-1921
Alfred A. Taylor (R)	1921-1923
Austin L. Peay (D)	(d) 1923-1927
Henry H. Horton (D)	1927-1933
Hill McAlister (D)	1933-1937
Gordon W. Browning (D)	1937-1939
Prentice Cooper (D)	1939-1945
James M. McCord (D)	1945-1949
Gordon W. Browning (D)	1949-1953
Frank G. Clement (D)	1953-1959
Buford Ellington (D)	1959-1963
Frank G. Clement (D)	1963-1967
Buford Ellington (D)	1967-1971
Winfield C. Dunn (R)	1971-1975
Leonard Ray Blanton (D)	1975-1979
Lamar Alexander (R)	1979-1987
Ned Ray McWherter (D)	1987-1995
Don Sundquist (R)	1995-2003
Phil Bredesen (D)	2003-

*Confederate governor
**Union governor

Composition of congressional delegations, 1989-2007

	Dem	Rep	Total
House of Representatives			
101st Congress, 1989			
State delegates	6	3	9
Total U.S.	259	174	433
102d Congress, 1991			
State delegates	6	3	9
Total U.S.	267	167	434
103d Congress, 1993			
State delegates	6	3	9
Total U.S.	258	176	434
104th Congress, 1995			
State delegates	4	5	9
Total U.S.	197	236	433
105th Congress, 1997			
State delegates	4	5	9
Total U.S.	206	228	434
106th Congress, 1999			
State delegates	4	5	9
Total U.S.	211	222	433

(continued)

	Dem	Rep	Total
107th Congress, 2001			
State delegates	4	5	9
Total U.S.	211	221	432
108th Congress, 2003			
State delegates	5	4	9
Total U.S.	205	229	434
109th Congress, 2005			
State delegates	5	4	9
Total U.S.	202	231	433
110th Congress, 2007			
State delegates	5	4	9
Total U.S.	233	202	435
Senate			
101st Congress, 1989			
State delegates	2	0	2
Total U.S.	55	45	100
102d Congress, 1991			
State delegates	2	0	2
Total U.S.	56	44	100
103d Congress, 1993			
State delegates	2	0	2
Total U.S.	57	43	100
104th Congress, 1995			
State delegates	0	2	2
Total U.S.	46	53	99
105th Congress, 1997			
State delegates	0	2	2
Total U.S.	45	55	100
106th Congress, 1999			
State delegates	0	2	2
Total U.S.	45	54	99
107th Congress, 2001			
State delegates	0	2	2
Total U.S.	50	50	100
108th Congress, 2003			
State delegates	0	2	2
Total U.S.	48	51	99
109th Congress, 2005			
State delegates	0	2	2
Total U.S.	44	55	99
110th Congress, 2007			
State delegates	0	2	2
Total U.S.	49	49	98

Figures are for starts of first sessions. Totals are for Democrat (Dem.) and Republican (Rep.) members only. House membership totals under 435 and Senate totals under 100 reflect vacancies and seats held by independent party members. When the 110th Congress opened, the Senate's two independent members caucused with the Democrats, giving the Democrats control of the Senate.

Source: U.S. Congress, *Congressional Directory.*

Composition of state legislature, 1990-2006

	Democrats	Republicans
State House (99 seats)		
1990	57	42
1992	63	36
1994	59	40
1996	61	38
1998	59	40
2000	59	40
2002	54	45
2004	53	46
2006	53	46
State Senate (33 seats)		
1990	20	13
1992	19	14
1994	18	15
1996	18	15
1998	18	15
2000	18	15
2002	18	15
2004	16	17
2006	16	17

Figures for total seats may include independents and minor party members. Numbers reflect results of elections in listed years; elected members usually take their seats in the years that follow.
Source: Council of State Governments; *State Elective Officials and the Legislatures.*

Voter participation in presidential elections, 2000 and 2004

	2000	2004
Voting age population		
State	4,305,000	4,510,000
Total United States	209,831,000	220,377,000
State share of U.S. total	2.05	2.05
Rank among states	16	16
Portion of voting age population casting votes		
State	48.2%	54.0%
United States	50.3%	55.5%
Rank among states	36	36

Population figures are rounded to nearest thousand and include all residents, regardless of eligibility to vote.
Source: U.S. Census Bureau.

HEALTH AND MEDICAL CARE

Medical professionals
Physicians in 2003 and nurses in 2001

	U.S.	State
Physicians in 2003		
Total	774,849	15,178
Share of U.S. total		1.95%
Rate	266	260
Rank		19
Nurses in 2001		
Total	2,262,020	48,880
Share of U.S. total		2.16%
Rate	793	850
Rank		22

Rates are numbers of physicians and nurses per 100,000 resident population; ranks are based on rates.

Source: American Medical Association, *Physician Characteristics and Distribution in the U.S.*; U.S. Department of Health and Human Services, Health Resources and Services Administration.

Health insurance coverage, 2003

	State	U.S.
Total persons covered	5,131,000	243,320,000
Total persons not covered	778,000	44,961,000
Portion not covered	13.2%	15.6%
Rank among states	29	—
Children not covered	150,000	8,373,000
Portion not covered	10.8%	11.4%
Rank among states	19	—

Totals are rounded to nearest thousand. Ranks are from the highest to the lowest percentages of persons *not* insured.

Source: U.S. Census Bureau, Current Population Reports.

AIDS, syphilis, and tuberculosis cases, 2003

Disease	U.S. cases	State cases	Rank
AIDS	44,232	835	12
Syphilis	34,270	876	11
Tuberculosis	14,874	285	12

Source: U.S. Centers for Disease Control and Prevention.

Cigarette smoking, 2003
Residents over age 18 who smoke

	U.S.	State	Rank
All smokers	22.1%	25.7%	8
Male smokers	24.8%	27.3%	16
Female smokers	20.3%	24.2%	3

Cigarette smokers are defined as persons who reported having smoked at least 100 cigarettes during their lifetimes and who currently smoked at least occasionally.

Source: U.S. Centers for Disease Control and Prevention, *Morbidity and Mortality Weekly Report*, 53, no. 44 (November 12, 2004).

HOUSING

Home ownership rates, 1985-2004

	1985	1990	1995	2000	2004
State	67.6%	68.3%	67.0%	70.9%	71.6%
Total U.S.	63.9%	63.9%	64.7%	67.4%	69.0%
Rank among states	27	20	30	23	27

Net change in state home ownership rate, 1985-2004 . . . . +4.0%
Net change in U.S. home ownership rate, 1985-2004 . . . . +5.1%

Percentages represent the proportion of owner households to total occupied households.

Source: U.S. Census Bureau, 2006.

Home sales, 2000-2004
In thousands of units

Existing home sales	2000	2002	2003	2004
State sales	100.4	112.0	128.8	156.1
Total U.S. sales	5,171	5,631	6,183	6,784
State share of U.S. total	1.94%	1.99%	2.08%	2.30%
Sales rank among states	20	20	16	14

Units include single-family homes, condos, and co-ops.

Source: National Association of Realtors, Washington, D.C., *Real Estate Outlook: Market Trends & Insights*.

Values of owner-occupied homes, 2003

	State	U.S.
Total units	1,281,000	58,809,000
Value of units		
Under $100,000	43.8%	29.6%
$100,000-199,999	40.4%	36.9%
$200,000 or more	15.8%	33.5%
Median value	$110,000	$142,275
Rank among all states		35

Units are owner-occupied one-family houses whose numbers are rounded to nearest thousand. Data are extrapolated from survey samples.
Source: U.S. Census Bureau, American Community Survey.

EDUCATION

Public school enrollment, 2002

Prekindergarten through grade 8
State enrollment 674,000
Total U.S. enrollment. 34,135,000
State share of U.S. total 1.97%

Grades 9 through 12
State enrollment 254,000
Total U.S. enrollment. 14,067,000
State share of U.S. total 1.81%

Enrollment rates
State public school enrollment rate. 91.4%
Overall U.S. rate 90.4%
Rank among states in 2002. 17
Rank among states in 1995. 14

Enrollment figures (which include unclassified students) are rounded to nearest thousand pupils during fall school term. Enrollment rates are based on enumerated resident population estimate for July 1, 2002.
Source: U.S. National Center for Education Statistics.

Public college finances, 2003-2004

FTE enrollment in public institutions of higher education
Students in state institutions. 169,400
Students in all U.S. public institutions 9,916,600
State share of U.S. total 1.71
Rank among states 20

State and local government appropriations for higher education
State appropriation per FTE $5,053
National average. $5,716
Rank among states 33
State & local tax revenue going to higher education 8.9%

FTE = full-time equivalent in public postsecondary programs, including summer sessions; student numbers are rounded to nearest hundred. Funding figures for 2003-2004 academic year include financial aid to students in state public institutions and exclude money for research, agriculture experiment stations, teaching hospitals, and medical schools; figures are rounded to nearest thousand dollars.
Source: Higher Education Executive Officers, Denver, Colorado.

TRANSPORTATION AND TRAVEL

Highway mileage, 2003

Interstate highways	1,073
Other freeways and expressways	146
Arterial roads	8,935
Collector roads.	17,905
Local roads.	60,459
Urban roads	20,418
Rural roads.	68,100
Total state mileage.	88,518
U.S. total	3,974,107
State share	2.23%
Rank among states	21

Note that combined urban and rural road mileage matches the total of the other categories.
Source: U.S. Federal Highway Administration.

Motor vehicle registrations and driver licenses, 2003

Vehicle registrations	State	U.S.	Share	Rank
Autos, trucks, buses	4,796,000	231,390,000	2.07%	16
Autos only	2,782,000	135,670	2.05%	16
Motorcycles	94,000	5,328,000	1.76%	19
Driver licenses	4,204,000	196,166,000	2.14%	16

Figures, which do not include vehicles owned by military services, are rounded to the nearest thousand. Figures for automobiles include taxis.
Source: U.S. Federal Highway Administration.

Domestic travel expenditures, 2003

Spending by U.S. residents on overnight trips and day trips of at least 50 miles from home

Total expenditures within state	$10.58 bill.
Total expenditures within U.S.	$490.87 bill.
State share of U.S. total	2.2%
Rank among states	14

Source: Travel Industry Association of America.

Retail gasoline prices, 2003-2007

Average price per gallon at the pump

Year	U.S.	State
2003	$1.267	$1.192
2004	$1.316	$1.244
2005	$1.644	$1.612
2007	$2.298	$2.139

Excise tax per gallon in 2004	21.0¢
Rank among all states in 2007 prices	46

Prices are averages of all grades of gasoline sold at the pump during March months in 2003-2005 and during February, 2007. Averages for 2006, during which prices rose higher, are not available.
Source: U.S. Energy Information Agency, *Petroleum Marketing Monthly* (2003-2005 data); American Automobile Association (2007 data).

CRIME AND LAW ENFORCEMENT

State and local police officers, 2000-2004

	2000	2002	2004
Total officers			
U.S.	654,601	665,555	675,734
State	13,700	15,174	15,585*
*Net change, 2000-2004			+13.76%
Officers per 1,000 residents			
U.S.	2.33	2.31	2.30
State	2.41	2.62	2.64
State rank	11	7	7

Totals include state and local police and sheriffs.
Source: Carsey Institute, University of New Hampshire.

Crime rates, 2003

Incidents per 100,000 residents

Crimes	State	U.S.
Violent crimes		
Total incidents	688	475
Murder	7	6
Forcible rape	36	32
Robbery	160	142
Aggravated assault	485	295
Property crimes		
Total incidents	4,379	3,588
Burglary	1,082	741
Larceny/theft	2,845	2,415
Motor vehicle theft	452	433
All crimes	5,067	4,063

Source: U.S. Federal Bureau of Investigation, *Crime in the United States,* annual.

State prison populations, 1980-2003

	State	U.S.	State share
1980	7,022	305,458	2.30%
1990	10,388	708,393	1.47%
1996	15,626	1,025,624	1.52%
2000	22,166	1,391,261	1.59%
2003	25,403	1,470,045	1.73%

State figures exclude prisoners in federal penitentiaries.
Source: U.S. Bureau of Justice Statistics, *Prisoners in 2003.*

Texas

Location: South

Area and rank: 261,914 square miles (678,358 square kilometers); 268,601 square miles (695,677 square kilometers) including water; second largest state in area

Coastline: 367 miles (591 kilometers) on the Gulf of Mexico

Shoreline: 3,359 miles (5,406 kilometers)

Population and rank: 22,490,000 (2004); second largest state in population

Capital city: Austin (656,562 people in 2000 census)

Largest city: Houston (1,953,631 people in 2000 census)

In keeping with Texas's reputation for great size, its capitol building in Austin is the largest capitol building in the United States, except for the national Capitol Building in Washington, D.C., which is not as tall. (©Mike Norton/Dreamstime.com)

Became an independent republic: March 2, 1836

Entered Union and rank: December 29, 1845; twenty-eighth state

Present constitution adopted: 1876

Counties: 254

State name: "Texas" comes from an Indian word meaning "friends"

State nickname: Lone Star State

Motto: Friendship

State flag: One-third (vertical) is blue with white star, other two-thirds (horizontal) red and white

Highest point: Guadalupe Peak—8,749 feet (2,667 meters)

Lowest point: Gulf of Mexico—sea level

Highest recorded temperature: 120 degrees Fahrenheit (49 degrees Celsius)—Seymour, 1936

Lowest recorded temperature: –23 degrees Fahrenheit (–31 degrees Celsius)—Seminole, 1933

State song: "Texas, Our Texas"

State tree: Pecan

State flower: Bluebonnet

State bird: Mockingbird

State fish: Guadalupe bass

National parks: Big Bend, Guadalupe Mountains

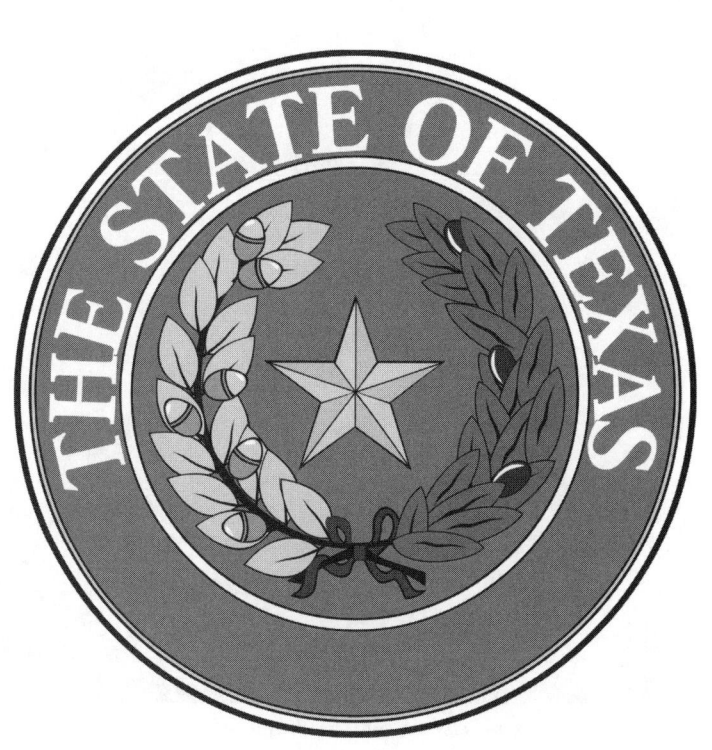

Texas History

Until Alaska was admitted as the forty-ninth state in 1959, Texas was the largest of the United States and still is the largest of the contiguous forty-eight states, occupying one-twelfth of the entire American land mass. With a total area of more than a quarter of a million square miles, it stretches almost eight hundred miles from its eastern boundary in Arkansas and Louisiana to its western extremes at Mexico and New Mexico. On the south it is bordered by the Gulf of Mexico and Mexico. Its northern boundary, Oklahoma, lies 730 miles from its southern extreme.

Texas is the only state in the Union ruled under six flags: those of Spain, France, Mexico, the Republic of Texas, the Confederate States of America, and the United States. Early explorers found this vast area intimidating, but modern transportation and a wealth of natural resources, particularly oil and natural gas, helped Texas achieve the second largest population of the United States.

Early History. The earliest settlers in Texas were American Indians who dwelt there before 12,000 B.C.E. By 5000 B.C.E., the early residents were farming and hunting with bows and arrows. In far western Texas, remnants of Pueblo dwellings similar to those found in New Mexico have been unearthed. Indian mounds like those found in the western parts of Illinois, Tennessee, Louisiana, and Mississippi were discovered in east Texas.

Exploration and Settlement. The earliest explorations of Texas were made by Spaniards. In 1519, Alonso de Piñeda sailed along the Gulf of Mexico coastline from Florida to Mexico, establishing Spain's claim to the land that lay along it. By 1528 Alvar Núñez Cabeza de Vaca explored the interior. During the 1540's, Francisco Vásquez de Coronado and Hernando de Soto both led expeditions into Texas, but their reports made the territory sound so forbidding that explorers avoided the area for the next half century.

It was not until 1682, after René-Robert Cavelier, Sieur de La Salle, declared Texas a possession of France, that the Spaniards took a renewed interest in the area. The French were driven out by Native Americans, but in 1690 the Spanish renewed their claim by establishing two missions among the American Indians in east Texas. By 1716 they had established five missions in east Texas.

Late nineteenth century drawing of the Mexican siege of the Alamo in 1836. (Library of Congress)

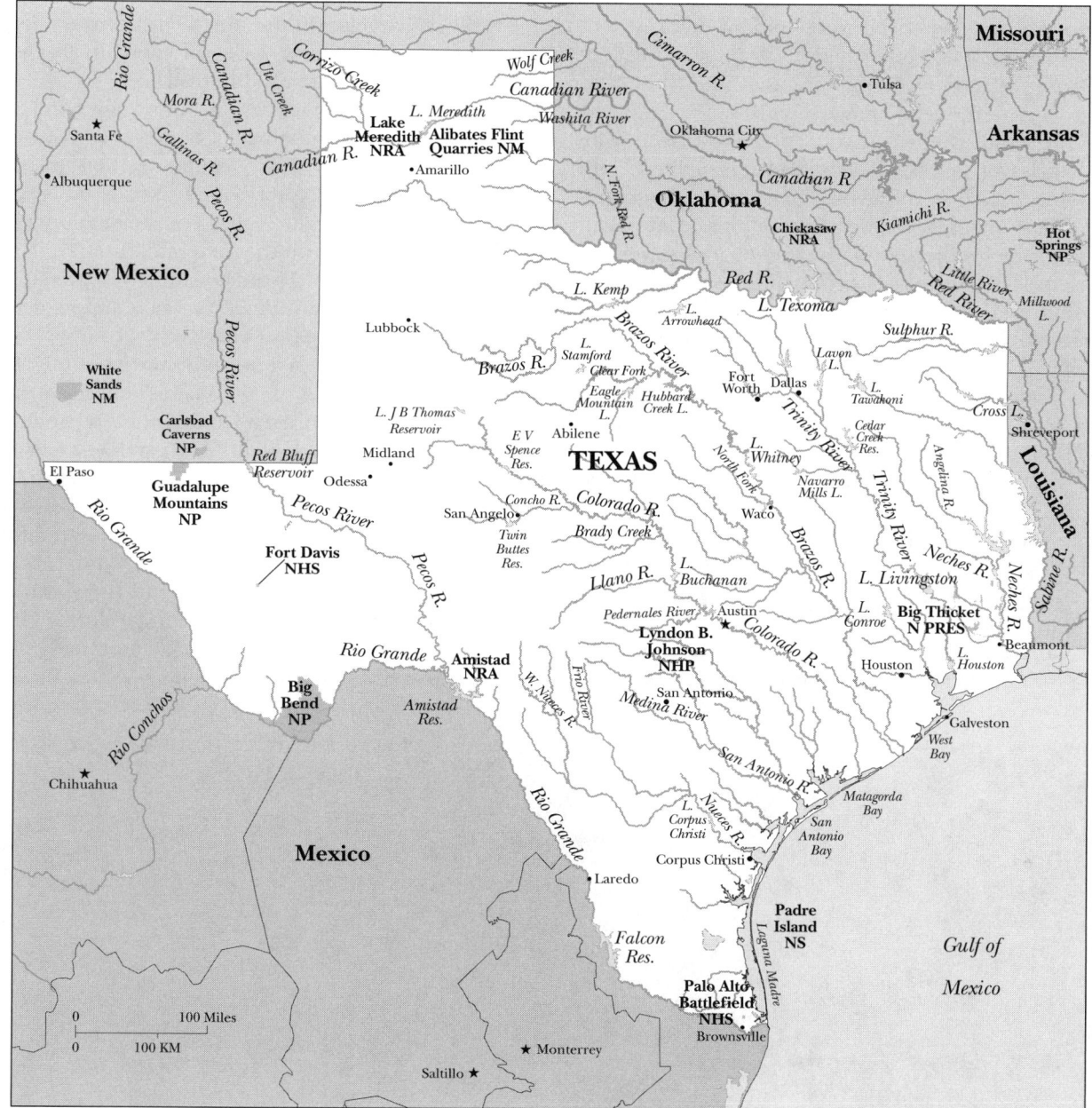

The Native American population of the state ranged from Cherokees in the east, who had been displaced from their lands in other areas, to the Tonkawa, nomadic plains Indians in the central part of the area, to the Coahuitecan and Karankawa tribes, the most primitive of the Native American dwellers, along the Gulf coast. The Lipan Apache, the Comanche, the Kiowa, and the Kiowa Apache inhabited the west.

The U.S. Claim to Texas. Louisiana was ceded to Spain in 1762. By 1800 Texas had established three permanent Spanish settlements: San Antonio, Goliad, and Nacogdoches. In 1800, France took the title to Louisiana, which was sold to the United States in 1803. The boundary between the Spanish and French claims in this area had never been established, so the United States now held a tenuous claim to Texas.

When Texas became part of the new nation of Mexico in 1821, colonization was encouraged. Moses Austin came from Missouri with three hundred families who were given land. Austin's son Stephen brought in more settlers after his father died. Land was plentiful, and land grants were generous and easily obtained.

By 1835 about twenty thousand settlers had arrived in east Texas, bringing with them more than four thousand slaves to work in the cotton fields, thereby establishing Texas as a slave state. In the same year, Mexican general Antonio López de Santa Anna waged war against the Texans during the Texas Revolution, taking about 350 prisoners, who were summarily executed. The following year, he stormed the Alamo, taking control from the few Texans remaining inside.

As Anglo-American immigrants flooded into the area, the United States sought to purchase Texas. The Mexican government, which held claims to the region, tried unsuccessfully to discourage American immigration. Tensions arose between the United States and Mexico, which objected to the presence of slavery in Texas. In 1836, Texas declared its independence as the Republic of Texas, a status it held until it was annexed as the twenty-eighth state of the United States in 1845.

Cotton, an important crop in eastern Texas during its early settlement, made slave labor attractive to those who raised cotton. With slavery as a part of Texan economy, Texas joined the Confederate States of America in 1861, sixteen years after it had gained admission to the Union.

The Early Texas Economy. Agriculture became a major element in the early economy of Texas, some 85 percent of whose land consists of farms and ranches. Cattle and poultry production are significant in the state. Citrus fruit was grown early in the southern areas along the Gulf of Mexico and the Rio Grande. Industry

was slow to develop in the nineteenth century, largely because Texas did not have sufficient hydroelectric power to drive mechanized industry.

Texas came into its own economically after 1901 when the great Spindletop oil field was discovered in southeastern Texas near Beaumont. This discovery triggered a rush to explore other parts of the state for oil, and it was soon found that Texas rested on a huge subterranean sea of oil that extended beyond its land mass into the Gulf of Mexico. Natural gas was also discovered in such quantities that Texas supplied more than a third of the nation's supply.

The oil rush brought enormous revenues into Texas and created hundreds of millionaires almost overnight. The state's population grew from about three million in 1900 to almost four million in 1910, partly because of oil. By 1990, Texas had almost seventeen million residents, making it the third most populous of the United States. By 2004, it was home to more than twenty-two million.

The sale of oil and natural gas was important to the Texas economy. The discovery of these two fuels spurred the growth of manufacturing industries in the state, which now had the reasonable and ready supply of energy it had previously lacked.

Oil rig by the Gulf of Mexico, where the discovery of massive oil fields in 1901 triggered the transformation of Texas's economy. (PhotoDisc)

Ultramodern skyline of Dallas, which overtook San Antonio to become Texas's second-largest city in the 2000 census. (Photo-Disc)

The Move to Manufacturing. Contemporary Texas is one of the ten most productive manufacturing states in the Union. Oil refining and petrochemical companies are among the largest manufacturing industries in the state, most of them centered around the Houston-Beaumont-Port Arthur area in the southeastern portion. In 1961, Houston was chosen as the location of the Manned Spacecraft Center, at which astronauts are trained. It is the control center for the U.S. government's manned space ventures. The establishment of this center brought into Texas considerable other industry that focuses on the manufacture of transportation equipment, including aircraft, automobile assembly plants, and mobile-home manufacturing.

Giant food processing plants grew up to process the livestock, poultry, and vegetables the state produces in abundance. Texas is also preeminent in the manufacturing of machinery, including the complex equipment used in oil exploration and drilling. A thriving mining industry exists, along with extensive textile, clothing, and timber operations.

Transportation. Because of its enormous size, Texas early developed a comprehensive transportation system that, during the early days, involved boat transportation along the Gulf of Mexico and on it rivers, as well as rail transportation served by fourteen thousand miles of track. As the highway system grew to the point that it was the largest in the United States, with sixty-five thousand miles of paved roads, Texans relied more on automobiles than on trains for transportation, so passenger service waned.

During the late twentieth century, Texas had splendid air transportation. The climate is good for flying, and the great distance between major cities make flying the most reasonable means of rapid transport. In 1974, the opening of the Dallas-Fort Worth International Airport, the third largest airport in the world, established Texas as an important hub for many national and international airlines. This airport has the second greatest passenger volume in the United States.

Modern Population. Texas has always had a mix of cultures. In the southern areas along the Rio Grande live many people of Mexican descent, some of whose families have lived there for two hundred years. These people are technically American citizens, but their ties to Mexico remain strong. The Anglo-American population includes not only people of British extraction but also large numbers of Germans, in San Antonio, New Braunfels, Seguin, and other towns in central Texas. Eastern and southern Europeans are well represented in the state's population, as are people from the Middle Eastern countries, especially the major oil-producing ones.

During the late twentieth century, about one-third of all Texans were of African American or Hispanic lineage. Spanish is a second language throughout much of Texas and is used along with English in most of its restaurants, hotels, and stores.

Politics. Texas represents an interesting mix of political conservatism and populism. Texans are staunch individualists, yet the state was essentially a one-party state until the election of George W. Bush as its Republican governor in 1994.

Realizing that Texas is a politically important state, with thirty-two electoral votes, national politicians have flocked to it looking for support. Among these was President John F. Kennedy, who went to Texas in November, 1963, to support Democrats running for public office and to help assure his own victory there when he ran for reelection in 1964. Kennedy was assassinated in Dallas, Texas, by Lee Harvey Oswald. He was succeeded by his vice president, Texan Lyndon Baines Johnson, who remained in office until 1969.

The last year of the twentieth century was notable for Texas, as its governor—George W. Bush, son of former U.S. president and fellow Texan George H. W. Bush—decided to run for the presidency of the United States. He was subsequently elected to the position and resigned as governor in December, 2000. Republican lieutenant governor Rick Perry assumed the office. In the 2004 presidential election, Bush handily won his home state's electoral votes over Democrat John Kerry.

The 2002 midterm elections in Texas saw Perry elected governor in his own right. He won the election by a 58-40 percent margin against Democrat Tony Sanchez, who spent more than $59 million of his own money in the campaign. The same year, Texas Republicans began a plan to place more Republicans in the U.S. Congress through redistricting. The plan became highly controversial; at one point, Democratic state legislators fled the state for Oklahoma to ensure the lack of a legislative quorum for adoption of the plan. It was challenged in court but eventually (in mid-2006) was upheld by the U.S. Supreme Court, except for one congressional district.

In the 2004 presidential election, President Bush had no difficulty again gaining the state's electoral votes, winning by a 61-38 percent margin. The following year, a Texas star Republican politician and House majority leader in Washington, Tom DeLay, was indicted for campaign finance law violations and subsequently resigned his seat.

Wildfires. Around the turn of the twenty-first century, Texas—particularly west Texas—in common with other western states, endured numerous wildfires. In September, 2000, news organizations reported that the state had taken the lead in the number of wildfires, with thirty-five large ones under way, destroying homes, threatening towns, and forcing evacuations. Continuing dry conditions in west Texas brought little respite in future years. In 2006, a week of wildfires in March alone killed thousands of cattle on ranches of the Panhandle region. These fires killed an estimated ten thousand animals. In all, nearly five million acres burned between Christmas, 2005, and late March, 2006.

Prisoners and Executions. Texas was also notable for its large prison population and number of death sentences and executions. The state's prison population of 163,000 was the largest in the nation. Some 45 percent of its death sentences were overturned on appeal; but the number of executions in its history was eight times higher than the next closest state. Although in 2000 the total number executed in the nation dropped 14 percent, the number executed in Texas (forty) was the highest number ever executed by a state in a single year.

Enron. An event that seared the nation's consciousness, especially in Texas, was the Enron debacle. Before its bankruptcy, Houston-based Enron was one of the world's leading energy companies, with more than twenty thousand employees and 2000 revenues of $101 billion, or so it claimed. However, on November 30, 2001, it filed for bankruptcy. Thousands of Texans and others lost their jobs and their life savings. The company was found to have fraudulent business practices; a number of executives pleaded guilty to a variety of crimes and went to jail. One committed suicide. In 2006, two top company officials, CEO Kenneth Lay and his successor as CEO, Jeffrey Skilling, were tried and found guilty of a number of crimes. Both were headed for long jail terms after an October, 2006, sentencing date, but Lay died of a heart attack before sentencing.

R. Baird Shuman
Updated by the Editor

Texas Time Line

1519	Texas is claimed for Spain by Spanish explorer Alonso de Piñeda.
Nov. 6, 1528	Alvar Núñez Cabeza de Vaca explores interior Texas.
1541	Francisco Vásquez de Coronado explores west Texas.
1541	Hernando de Soto explores central Texas.
1682	René-Robert Cavelier, Sieur de La Salle, claims Texas for France; Spaniards establish permanent settlement in Ysleta in west Texas.

1685	La Salle builds fort near Matagora Bay on the Gulf coast.
1690	Spanish establish missions in east Texas.
1691	Texas officially becomes a Spanish province.
1716	Spanish revitalize their mission settlements to thwart the French.
May 1, 1718	Alamo mission is established in what later becomes San Antonio.
1821	Texas becomes part of the new nation of Mexico.
1835	Twenty thousand southerners arrive in east Texas with four thousand slaves.
Oct. 2, 1835	Texas Revolution begins.
Mar. 2, 1836	Republic of Texas, independent of Mexico, is formed.
Mar. 6, 1836	Mexican general Santa Anna's troops capture the Alamo.
1837	United States recognizes Republic of Texas.
1839	Texas State Library is established in Austin.
1839	Education Act of 1839 promises a university system.
Dec. 29, 1845	Texas enters the Union as twenty-eighth state.
Feb. 1, 1861	Texas secedes from the Union, joining the Confederacy.
1865	Texas frees its slaves following the Civil War.
Mar. 30, 1870	Texas is readmitted to the United States.
1876	State constitution is adopted.
1883	University of Texas opens in Austin.
Sept. 8, 1900	Galveston is devastated by hurricane that kills six thousand.
1901	Spindletop oil field is discovered.
1915	Compulsory school attendance law passed.
1931	Discovery of the rich east Texas oil field.
1944	U.S. Supreme Court outlaws state's whites-only primary voting law.
1950	Supreme Court bans racial segregation at University of Texas Law School.
1953	Texas recovers offshore tidal oil fields from U.S. government.
1961	Houston is chosen for Manned Spacecraft Center.
Nov. 22, 1963	President John F. Kennedy is assassinated in Dallas; Texan Lyndon Baines Johnson becomes president of the United States.
1965	Reapportionment of state legislature assures concept of one person, one vote.
1966	Federal courts ban payment of poll tax as a condition of voting.
1968	HemisFair '68 is held to mark San Antonio's 250th anniversary.
1969	Amistad Dam is completed on Rio Grande to serve United States and Mexico.
1970	Hurricane devastates Corpus Christi.
1974	Dallas-Fort Worth International Airport opens.
1988	Drought disaster is declared in Texas.
1988	Waxahachie is chosen as the site of the Superconductor Super Collider.
1990	Two barges and oil tanker collide near Galveston Bay, spilling 500,000 gallons of oil.
1994	Texas has 394 prisoners on death row, the most in the nation.
1994	George W. Bush is elected first Republican governor.
1999	Amoco announces billion-barrel oil discovery in Gulf of Mexico off Texas coast.
Sept., 2000	Thirty-five wildfires are reported burning in west Texas.
Nov. 7, 2000	Texas favorite son and former governor George W. Bush wins the state's presidential electoral votes, with 59 percent of the vote.
Nov. 30, 2001	Thousands of Texans lose their jobs as Houston-based Enron Corporation files for bankruptcy.
Nov. 2, 2004	Bush wins state's presidential balloting by a margin of 61-38 percent.
Sept. 28, 2005	Texas grand jury indicts House Majority Leader Tom DeLay for conspiring to violate state election laws. DeLay later resigns from Congress.
Dec., 2005- Mar., 2006	Wildfires burn five million acres and kill ten thousand cattle in the Panhandle region.

Notes for Further Study

Published Sources. One of the best overviews of Texas is found in James L. Haley's *Texas: From Spindletop Through World War II* (1993), which, in a series of short essays, captures a great deal of Texas history. Haley also brings readers a sweeping overview of the state's past in *Passionate Nation: The Epic History of Texas* (2006). E. G. Littlejohn's *Texas History Stories* (2005) relates for young adult readers the stories of thirteen heroes or events in Texas history, including Cabeza de Vaca, Sam Houston, and the Alamo.

Pete A. Y. Gunter and Max Oelschlager explore some of the nefarious land dealings in Texas in their somewhat specialized *Texas Land Ethics* (1997). The question of capital punishment in Texas is well addressed in Ken Light's *Texas Death Row* (1997), which contains haunting illustrations and sometimes frightening commentary about the Texas justice system. W. Dirk Raat considers the clash of contrasting cultures in *Mexico and the United States: Ambivalent Cultures* (1996), which is nicely supplemented by the essays edited by Oscar J.

Martinez titled *U.S.-Mexican Borderlands: Historical and Contemporary Perspective* (1996). A guidebook that does double duty as a history text is *Exploring Texas History: Weekend Adventures* (2005) by Elaine E. Galit and Vikk Simmons. Likewise, T. Lindsay Baker's *Building the Lone Star State: An Illustrated Guide to Historic Sites* (1986) will prove useful to those planning to travel in the state.

Because Texas is a vast entity with distinct cultural and historical regions, a student of the state's history will appreciate several titles that explore particular locales. Jerry Thompson's *A Wild and Vivid Land: An Illustrated History of the Texas Border* (1997) offers excellent pictures and interesting commentary about south Texas. The story of the multitudes who struggled to make the Lower Rio Grande Valley their home can be found in James A. McAllen and Margaret H. McAllen's *I Would Rather Sleep in Texas: A History of the Lower Rio Grande Valley and the People of the Santa Anita Land Grant* (2003). *Deep Time and the Texas High Plains: History and Geology* (2005) by

Texas is the only state with three cities with populations of more than one million people; Houston, pictured here, is the largest. (PhotoDisc)

Paul H. Carson examines the human and natural history in the Texas High Plains and upper Brazos River region. *Frontier Texas: History of a Borderland to 1880* (2004) by Robert F. Pace and Donald S. Frazier details the history of western Texas. Edited by Françoise Lagarde, *French in Texas: History, Migration, Culture* (2003) explores the French presence and influence on Texas history, arts, education, religion, and business.

William Curry Holden's *Alkalai Trails: Or, Social and Economic Movements of the Texas Frontier, 1846-1900* (1998) offers a detailed and lucid presentation of the economic growth of Texas from the time of the Mexican War to the beginning of the twentieth century. Among the issues dealt with during this period was the question of immigration, particularly from Mexico, which Kenneth L. Stewart and Arnold De Leon address fully in *Not Room Enough: Mexicans, Anglos, and Socioeconomic Change in Texas, 1850-1900* (1993). Focusing on later times in the economic history of the state, the contributors to *The Depression in the Southwest* (1980), edited by Donald W. Whisenhunt, write about the effects on Texas of the great droughts of the 1930's and the economic upheaval throughout the United States. *Oil in Texas: The Gusher Age, 1895-1945* (2002) by Diana Davids Olien and Roger M. Olien details the discovery of oil and the profound effects it had on the state's economy. Two standard college textbooks offer good insight into the history and practice of state politics: *Practicing Texas Politics* (12th ed., 2003) by Lyle C. Brown, et al. and *Texas Politics Today* (12th ed., 2005).

Web Resources. A very useful Web site for research on the state is Texas Online (www.state.tx.us/), which presents information categorized by Business, Living, Learning, Visiting, Working, and Government. Texas Travel (www.traveltex .com/) is an attractive site that details tourist activities in the state. Another Web site (www.texas.com) provides links to the major cities in the state, as well as national parks in the state and the major universities, among other features.

Those interested in library sources and general information regarding the state should consult the Texas State Library and Archives Commission (www.tsl.state.tx.us/), whose Areas of General Interest section provides extensive information for the general user. This site also offers complete texts of books, Library of Congress access, and a means of asking questions by electronic mail. The Handbook of Texas Online (www.tsha.utexas.edu/handbook/online/) is an excellent resource, offering a multidisciplinary encyclopedia of Texas history, geography, and culture. The state constitution can be accessed and questions asked about it on a Web site (www .capitol.state.tx.us/txconst/toc.html) that focuses on the interpretation of the constitution.

Counties

County	2000 pop.	Rank in pop.	Sq. miles	Rank in area
Anderson	55,109	53	1,070.9	55
Andrews	13,004	151	1,500.7	21
Angelina	80,130	41	801.6	195
Aransas	22,497	106	252.0	250
Archer	8,854	174	909.8	127
Armstrong	2,148	237	913.7	122
Atascosa	38,628	71	1,232.2	38
Austin	23,590	100	652.6	224
Bailey	6,594	191	826.7	193
Bandera	17,645	127	791.8	100
Bastrop	57,733	52	888.5	167
Baylor	4,093	211	870.8	179
Bee	32,359	84	880.2	173
Bell	237,974	19	1,059.0	59
Bexar	1,392,931	4	1,246.9	36
Blanco	8,418	176	711.3	212
Borden	729	251	898.9	156
Bosque	17,204	128	989.3	79
Bowie	89,306	36	887.9	168
Brazoria	241,767	18	1,386.9	27
Brazos	152,415	23	585.8	232
Brewster	8,866	173	6,193.0	1
Briscoe	1,790	240	900.3	151
Brooks	7,976	181	943.3	88
Brown	37,674	73	944.0	87
Burleson	16,470	131	665.6	222
Burnet	34,147	79	995.3	74

County	2000 pop.	Rank in pop.	Sq. miles	Rank in area
Caldwell	32,194	86	545.8	235
Calhoun	20,647	113	512.4	238
Callahan	12,905	153	898.7	158
Cameron	335,227	11	905.6	133
Camp	11,549	158	197.5	252
Carson	6,516	193	923.2	107
Cass	30,438	90	937.5	92
Castro	8,285	178	898.4	159
Chambers	26,031	94	599.4	229
Cherokee	46,659	61	1,052.3	62
Childress	7,688	184	710.4	214
Clay	11,006	160	1,097.9	50
Cochran	3,730	219	775.2	205
Coke	3,864	215	898.9	155
Coleman	9,235	169	1,272.9	34
Collin	491,675	8	847.7	186
Collingsworth	3,206	226	918.8	112
Colorado	20,390	114	963.0	82
Comal	78,021	42	561.5	234
Comanche	14,026	146	937.8	90
Concho	3,966	214	991.5	76
Cooke	36,363	76	873.8	177
Coryell	74,978	44	1,051.9	63
Cottle	1,904	238	901.2	146
Crane	3,996	213	785.6	203
Crockett	4,099	210	2,807.6	8
Crosby	7,072	188	899.6	154

(continued)

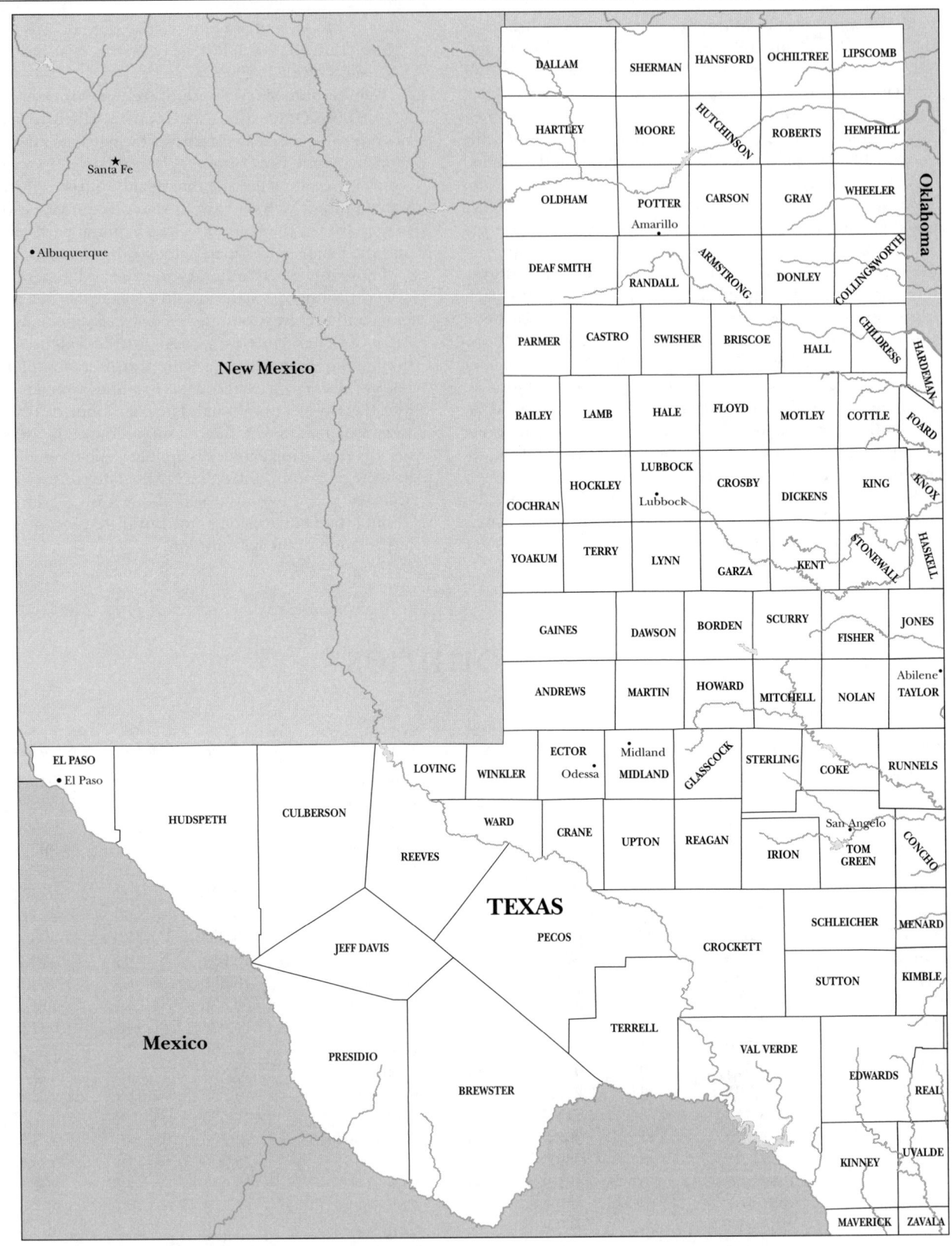

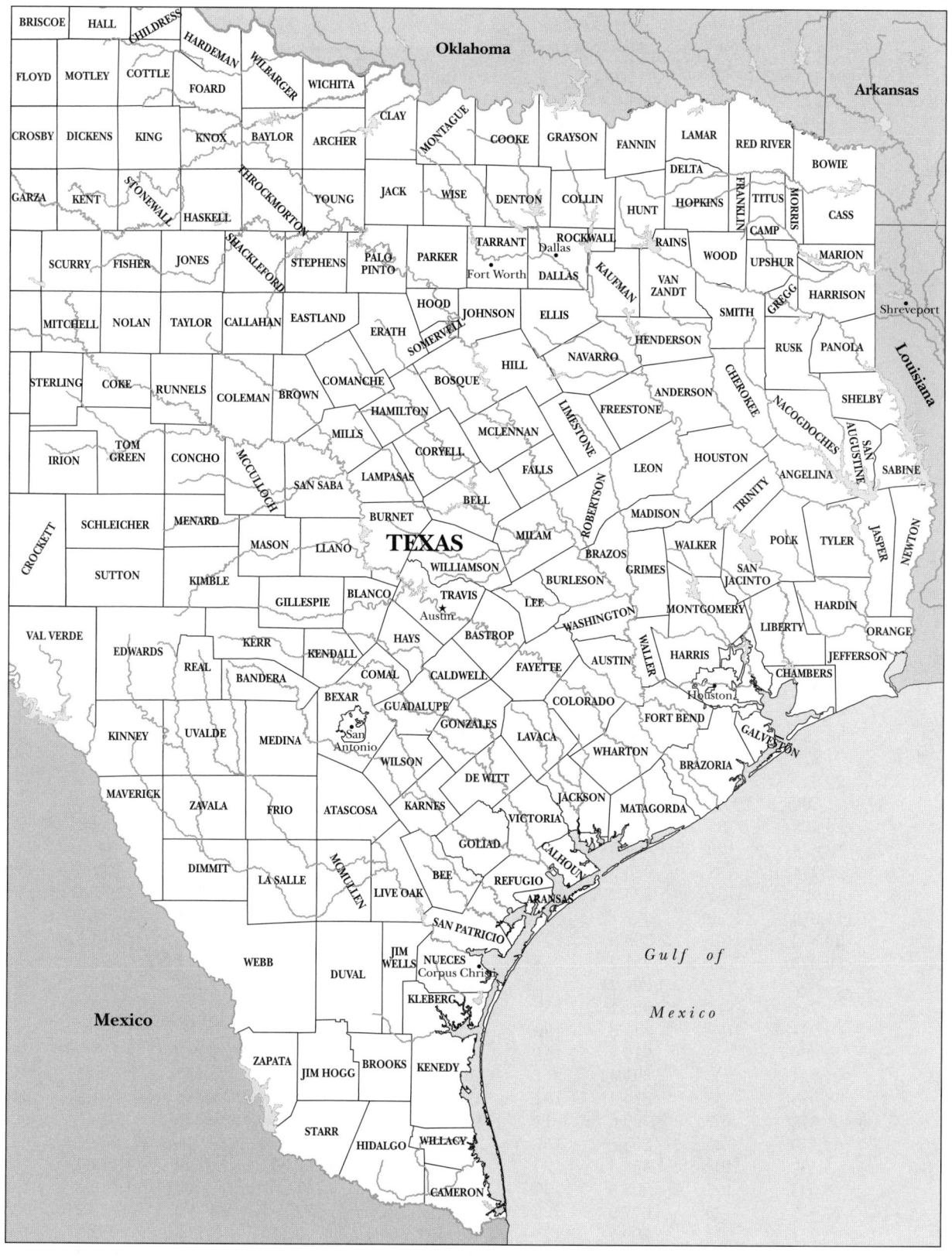

County	2000 pop.	Rank in pop.	Sq. miles	Rank in area	County	2000 pop.	Rank in pop.	Sq. miles	Rank in area
Culberson	2,975	230	3,812.7	5	Houston	23,185	102	1,231.0	39
Dallam	6,222	194	1,504.8	18	Howard	33,627	80	902.9	140
Dallas	2,218,899	2	879.9	174	Hudspeth	3,344	223	4,571.3	3
Dawson	14,985	140	902.1	143	Hunt	76,596	43	841.2	187
Deaf Smith	18,561	122	1,497.4	22	Hutchinson	23,857	98	887.4	169
Delta	5,327	200	277.2	247	Irion	1,771	241	1,051.6	64
Denton	432,976	9	888.5	166	Jack	8,763	175	917.4	115
DeWitt	20,013	117	909.3	130	Jackson	14,391	144	829.5	192
Dickens	2,762	232	904.3	135	Jasper	35,604	77	937.5	91
Dimmit	10,248	164	1,331.0	29	Jeff Davis	2,207	234	2,264.6	11
Donley	3,828	216	929.8	100	Jefferson	252,051	14	903.6	137
Duval	13,120	149	1,792.9	13	Jim Hogg	5,281	202	1,136.2	43
Eastland	18,297	123	926.1	103	Jim Wells	39,326	69	864.7	180
Ector	121,123	27	901.1	147	Johnson	126,811	25	729.4	210
Edwards	2,162	236	2,119.9	12	Jones	20,785	112	931.1	98
El Paso	111,360	31	1,013.1	71	Karnes	15,446	137	750.4	208
Ellis	679,622	6	940.0	89	Kaufman	71,313	46	786.1	202
Erath	33,001	81	1,086.4	52	Kendall	23,743	99	662.5	223
Falls	18,576	121	769.1	207	Kenedy	414	252	1,456.9	25
Fannin	31,242	89	891.6	164	Kent	859	249	902.4	142
Fayette	21,804	109	950.1	85	Kerr	43,653	64	1,106.3	49
Fisher	4,344	208	901.2	145	Kimble	4,468	207	1,250.8	35
Floyd	7,771	183	992.3	75	King	356	253	912.3	124
Foard	1,622	243	706.7	215	Kinney	3,379	221	1,363.5	28
Fort Bend	354,452	10	875.0	175	Kleberg	31,549	88	871.1	178
Franklin	9,458	168	285.7	246	Knox	4,253	209	854.2	183
Freestone	17,867	125	885.3	170	Lamar	48,499	56	917.1	116
Frio	16,252	133	1,133.1	45	Lamb	14,709	141	1,016.3	70
Gaines	14,467	143	1,502.4	19	Lampasas	17,762	126	712.1	211
Galveston	250,158	15	398.7	243	LaSalle	5,866	197	1,489.0	23
Garza	4,872	204	895.6	160	Lavaca	19,210	118	970.0	81
Gillespie	20,814	111	1,061.2	58	Lee	15,657	136	628.6	226
Glasscock	1,406	245	900.8	148	Leon	15,335	138	1,072.1	53
Goliad	6,928	189	853.6	184	Liberty	70,154	47	1,159.8	42
Gonzales	18,628	120	1,067.9	57	Limestone	22,051	108	908.9	131
Gray	22,744	104	928.3	102	Lipscomb	3,057	228	932.2	96
Grayson	110,595	32	933.7	94	Live Oak	12,309	155	1,036.4	68
Gregg	111,379	30	274.1	248	Llano	17,044	129	934.9	93
Grimes	23,552	101	793.8	199	Loving	67	254	673.1	221
Guadalupe	89,023	37	711.2	213	Lubbock	242,628	17	899.6	153
Hale	36,602	75	1,004.7	72	Lynn	6,550	192	891.9	163
Hall	3,782	217	903.1	138	McCulloch	8,205	180	1,069.4	56
Hamilton	8,229	179	835.8	190	McLennan	213,517	20	1,041.9	67
Hansford	5,369	199	919.9	111	McMullen	851	250	1,113.1	48
Hardeman	4,724	206	695.4	217	Madison	12,940	152	469.7	240
Hardin	48,073	58	894.4	162	Marion	10,941	161	381.2	244
Harris	3,400,578	1	1,729.0	14	Martin	4,746	205	914.9	118
Harrison	62,110	49	898.8	157	Mason	3,738	218	932.1	97
Hartley	5,537	198	1,462.4	24	Matagorda	37,957	72	1,114.5	47
Haskell	6,093	196	903.0	139	Maverick	47,297	60	1,280.2	33
Hays	97,589	35	677.9	220	Medina	39,304	70	1,327.9	30
Hemphill	3,351	222	909.7	128	Menard	2,360	233	902.0	144
Henderson	73,277	45	874.4	176	Midland	116,009	28	900.3	150
Hidalgo	569,463	7	1,569.1	15	Milam	24,238	97	1,016.8	69
Hill	32,321	85	962.4	83	Mills	5,151	203	748.2	209
Hockley	22,716	105	908.3	132	Mitchell	9,698	166	910.1	126
Hood	41,100	68	421.6	241	Montague	19,117	119	930.7	99
Hopkins	31,960	87	784.8	204	Montgomery	293,768	13	1,044.3	66

County	2000 pop.	Rank in pop.	Sq. miles	Rank in area	County	2000 pop.	Rank in pop.	Sq. miles	Rank in area
Moore	20,121	115	899.7	152	Starr	53,597	54	1,223.1	40
Morris	13,048	150	254.5	249	Stephens	9,674	167	894.7	161
Motley	1,426	244	989.4	78	Sterling	1,393	246	923.4	106
Nacogdoches	59,203	51	946.8	86	Stonewall	1,693	242	918.7	113
Navarro	45,124	62	1,071.2	54	Sutton	4,077	212	1,453.9	26
Newton	15,072	139	932.8	95	Swisher	8,378	177	900.5	149
Nolan	15,802	135	912.1	125	Tarrant	1,446,219	3	863.5	181
Nueces	313,645	12	835.9	189	Taylor	126,555	26	915.7	117
Ochiltree	9,006	171	917.6	114	Terrell	1,081	247	2,357.9	10
Oldham	2,185	235	1,500.7	20	Terry	12,761	154	889.9	165
Orange	84,966	39	356.4	245	Throckmorton	1,850	239	912.4	123
Palo Pinto	27,026	93	953.0	84	Titus	28,118	92	410.6	242
Panola	22,756	103	801.0	196	Tom Green	104,010	34	1,522.2	17
Parker	88,495	38	903.6	136	Travis	812,280	5	989.4	77
Parmer	10,016	165	881.7	172	Trinity	13,779	147	692.9	218
Pecos	16,809	130	4,764.0	2	Tyler	20,871	110	923.0	109
Polk	41,133	67	1,057.4	60	Upshur	35,291	78	587.7	231
Potter	113,546	29	909.4	129	Upton	3,404	220	1,241.8	37
Presidio	7,304	186	3,855.8	4	Uvalde	25,926	95	1,556.6	16
Rains	9,139	170	232.1	251	Val Verde	44,856	63	3,170.7	7
Randall	104,312	33	914.5	119	Van Zandt	48,140	57	848.8	185
Reagan	3,326	224	1,175.4	41	Victoria	84,088	40	882.6	171
Real	3,047	229	700.0	216	Walker	61,758	50	787.5	201
Red River	14,314	145	1,050.2	65	Waller	32,663	82	513.6	237
Reeves	13,137	148	2,636.1	9	Ward	10,909	162	835.6	191
Refugio	7,828	182	770.3	206	Washington	30,373	91	609.3	228
Roberts	887	248	924.1	104	Webb	193,117	21	3,357.0	6
Robertson	16,000	134	854.6	182	Wharton	41,188	66	1,090.2	51
Rockwall	43,080	65	128.8	254	Wheeler	5,284	201	914.3	120
Runnels	11,495	159	1,054.5	61	Wichita	131,664	24	627.7	227
Rusk	47,372	59	923.6	105	Wilbarger	14,676	142	971.1	80
Sabine	10,469	163	490.3	239	Willacy	20,082	116	596.7	230
San Augustine	8,946	172	527.9	236	Williamson	249,967	16	1,124.4	46
San Jacinto	22,246	107	570.7	233	Wilson	32,408	83	807.2	194
San Patricio	67,138	48	691.8	219	Winkler	7,173	187	841.1	188
San Saba	6,186	195	1,134.5	44	Wise	48,793	55	904.7	134
Schleicher	2,935	231	1,310.7	31	Wood	36,752	74	650.3	225
Scurry	16,361	132	902.6	141	Yoakum	7,322	185	799.8	197
Shackelford	3,302	225	914.0	121	Young	17,943	124	922.4	110
Shelby	25,224	96	794.2	198	Zapata	12,182	156	996.8	73
Sherman	3,186	227	923.1	108	Zavala	11,600	157	1,298.6	32
Smith	174,706	22	928.5	101					
Somervell	6,809	190	187.2	253					

Source: U.S. Census Bureau; National Association of Counties.

Cities
With 10,000 or more residents

Rank	City	Population	Rank	City	Population
1	Houston	1,953,631	8	Corpus Christi	277,454
2	Dallas	1,188,580	9	Plano	222,030
3	San Antonio	1,144,646	10	Garland	215,768
4	Austin (capital)	656,562	11	Lubbock	199,564
5	El Paso	563,662	12	Irving	191,615
6	Fort Worth	534,694	13	Laredo	176,576
7	Arlington	332,969	14	Amarillo	173,627

(continued)

Rank	City	Population
15	Pasadena	141,674
16	Brownsville	139,722
17	Grand Prairie	127,427
18	Mesquite	124,523
19	Abilene	115,930
20	Beaumont	113,866
21	Waco	113,726
22	Carrollton	109,576
23	McAllen	106,414
24	Wichita Falls	104,197
25	Midland	94,996
26	Richardson	91,802
27	Odessa	90,943
28	San Angelo	88,439
29	Killeen	86,911
30	Tyler	83,650
31	Denton	80,537
32	Lewisville	77,737
33	Longview	73,344
34	College Station	67,890
35	Baytown	66,430
36	Bryan	65,660
37	Sugar Land	63,328
38	Round Rock	61,136
39	Victoria	60,603
40	Port Arthur	57,755

Rank	City	Population	Rank	City	Population
41	Harlingen	57,564	100	Corsicana	24,485
42	Galveston	57,247	101	Rosenberg	24,043
43	The Woodlands	55,649	102	Greenville	23,960
44	North Richland Hills	55,635	103	Marshall	23,935
45	Temple	54,514	104	Cloverleaf	23,508
46	McKinney	54,369	105	San Benito	23,444
47	Missouri City	52,913	106	University Park	23,324
48	Flower Mound	50,702	107	Denison	22,773
49	Edinburg	48,465	108	Eagle Pass	22,413
50	Bedford	47,152	109	Plainview	22,336
51	Pharr	46,660	110	Seguin	22,011
52	Euless	46,005	111	Watauga	21,908
53	League City	45,444	112	Southlake	21,519
54	Mission	45,408	113	Waxahachie	21,426
55	Rowlett	44,503	114	Alvin	21,413
56	Allen	43,554	115	Burleson	20,976
57	Grapevine	42,059	116	Kerrville	20,425
58	Texas City	41,521	117	Benbrook	20,208
59	Haltom City	39,018	118	Colleyville	19,636
60	DeSoto	37,646	119	Balch Springs	19,375
61	Pearland	37,640	120	Alice	19,010
62	Conroe	36,811	121	Weatherford	19,000
63	New Braunfels	36,494	122	Brownwood	18,813
64	Spring	36,385	123	Schertz	18,694
65	Hurst	36,273	124	Bay City	18,667
66	Duncanville	36,081	125	Orange	18,643
67	Coppell	35,958	126	Angleton	18,130
68	Atascocita	35,757	127	Rockwall	17,976
69	Sherman	35,082	128	Pampa	17,887
70	Huntsville	35,078	129	West Odessa	17,799
71	Texarkana	34,782	130	Palestine	17,598
72	San Marcos	34,733	131	Nederland	17,422
73	Del Rio	33,867	132	Harker Heights	17,308
74	Frisco	33,714	133	Dickinson	17,093
75	Fort Hood	33,711	134	Mineral Wells	16,946
76	Lufkin	32,709	135	Canyon Lake	16,870
77	Cedar Hill	32,093	136	Pflugerville	16,335
78	La Porte	31,880	137	Ennis	16,045
79	Mission Bend	30,831	138	South Houston	15,833
80	Nacogdoches	29,914	139	Jollyville	15,813
81	Channelview	29,685	140	Groves	15,733
82	Copperas Cove	29,592	141	Stafford	15,681
83	Friendswood	29,037	142	Bellaire	15,642
84	Deer Park	28,520	143	Gatesville	15,591
85	Georgetown	28,339	144	Gainesville	15,538
86	Mansfield	28,031	145	Brushy Creek	15,371
87	Farmers Branch	27,508	146	Wylie	15,132
88	Keller	27,345	147	Uvalde	14,929
89	Socorro	27,152	148	Stephenville	14,921
90	Weslaco	26,935	149	Universal City	14,849
91	The Colony	26,531	150	White Settlement	14,831
92	Lake Jackson	26,386	151	Portland	14,827
93	San Juan	26,229	152	Donna	14,768
94	Cedar Park	26,049	153	Alamo	14,760
95	Cleburne	26,005	154	Belton	14,623
96	Paris	25,898	155	Hereford	14,597
97	Lancaster	25,894	156	Humble	14,579
98	Kingsville	25,575	157	Sulphur Springs	14,551
99	Big Spring	25,233	158	Borger	14,302

(continued)

Rank	City	Population
159	West University Place	14,211
160	Addison	14,166
161	Aldine	13,979
162	Mount Pleasant	13,935
163	Jacksonville	13,868
164	New Territory	13,861
165	Dumas	13,747
166	La Marque	13,682
167	Mercedes	13,649
168	Terrell	13,606
169	Port Neches	13,601
170	Taylor	13,575
171	Pecan Grove	13,551
172	Brenham	13,507
173	Beeville	13,129
174	Forest Hill	12,949
175	Canyon	12,875
176	Levelland	12,866
177	Robstown	12,727
178	Freeport	12,708
179	Saginaw	12,374
180	Highland Village	12,173
181	Port Lavaca	12,035
182	Rio Grande City	11,923
183	Katy	11,775

Rank	City	Population
184	Vernon	11,660
185	Lockhart	11,615
186	Converse	11,508
187	Vidor	11,440
188	Sweetwater	11,415
189	Corinth	11,325
190	Kilgore	11,301
191	Athens	11,297
192	Henderson	11,273
193	Wells Branch	11,271
194	Cinco Ranch	11,196
195	Hewitt	11,085
196	Richmond	11,081
197	San Elizario	11,046
198	El Campo	10,945
199	Burkburnett	10,927
200	Seagoville	10,823
201	Snyder	10,783
202	Galena Park	10,592
203	La Homa	10,433
204	Clute	10,424
205	Jacinto City	10,302

Population figures are from 2000 census.
Source: U.S. Bureau of the Census.

Index to Tables

DEMOGRAPHICS

Resident state and national populations, 1970-2004

Population figures given in thousands

	State pop.	U.S. pop.	Share	Rank
1970	11,199	203,302	5.5%	4
1980	14,229	226,546	6.3%	3
1985	16,273	237,924	6.8%	3
1990	16,986	248,765	6.8%	3
1995	18,959	262,761	7.1%	2
2000	20,852	281,425	7.4%	2
2004	22,490	293,655	7.7%	2

Source: U.S. Census Bureau, Current Population Reports, 2006.

Resident population by age, 2004

Age Group	Total persons
Under 5 years	1,843,000
5 to 17 years	4,424,000
18 to 24 years	2,400,000
25 to 34 years	3,336,000
35 to 44 years	3,338,000
45 to 54 years	2,981,000
55 to 64 years	1,952,000
65 to 74 years	1,214,000
75 to 84 years	756,000
85 years and older	246,000
All age groups	22,490,000

Portion of residents 65 and older	9.9%
National rank in portion of oldest residents	46
National average	12.4%

Population figures are rounded to nearest thousand persons; figures include armed forces personnel stationed in the state.
Source: U.S. Bureau of the Census, 2006.

Resident population by race, Hispanic origin, 2004

Category	State pop.	Share	U.S.
All residents	22,490	100.00%	100.00%
Non-Hispanic white	11,190	49.76%	67.37%
Hispanic white	7,536	33.51%	13.01%
Other Hispanic	245	1.09%	1.06%
African American	2,633	11.71%	12.77%
Native American	153	0.68%	0.96%
Asian, Pacific Islander	742	3.30%	4.37%
Two or more categories	235	1.04%	1.51%

Population figures are in thousands. Persons counted as "Hispanic" (Latino) may be of any race. Because of overlapping categories, categories may not add up to 100%. Shares in column 3 are percentages of each category within the state; these figures may be compared to the national percentages in column 4.
Source: U.S. Bureau of the Census, 2006.

Projected state population, 2000-2030

Year	Population
2000	20,852,000
2005	22,775,000
2010	24,649,000
2015	26,586,000
2020	28,635,000
2025	30,865,000
2030	33,318,000
Population increase, 2000-2030	12,466,000
Percentage increase, 2000-2030	59.8

Projections are based on data from the 2000 census.
Source: U.S. Census Bureau.

VITAL STATISTICS

Infant mortality rates, 1980-2002

	1980	1990	2000	2002
All state residents	12.2	8.1	5.7	6.4
All U.S. residents	12.6	9.2	9.4	9.1
All state white residents	11.2	6.7	5.1	5.6
All U.S. white residents	10.6	7.6	5.7	5.8
All state black residents	18.8	14.7	11.4	13.5
All U.S. black residents	22.2	18.0	14.1	14.4

Figures represent deaths per 1,000 live births of resident infants under 1 year old, exclusive of fetal deaths. Figures for all residents include members of other racial categories not listed separately.
Source: U.S. Census Bureau, Statistical Abstract of the United States, 2006.

Abortion rates, 1990 and 2000

	1990	2000
Total abortions	97,000	89,000
Rate per 1,000 women	23.1	18.8
U.S. rate	25.7	21.3
Rank	19	18

Numbers of abortions are rounded to nearest thousand; ranks are based on rates.
Source: U.S. Census Bureau.

Marriages and divorces, 2004

Total marriages	176,300
Rate per 1,000 population	7.8
National rate per 1,000 population	7.4
Rank among all states	17
Total divorces	81,900
Rate per 1,000 population	3.6
National rate per 1,000 population	3.7
Rank among all states	26

Figures are for all marriages and divorces performed within the state, including those of nonresidents; totals are rounded to the nearest hundred. Ranks are for highest to lowest figures; note that divorce data are not available for five states.
Source: U.S. National Center for Health Statistics, Vital Statistics of the United States, 2006.

Death rates by leading causes, 2002
Deaths per 100,000 resident population

Cause	State	U.S.
Heart disease	199.5	241.7
Cancer	156.9	193.2
Cerebrovascular diseases	48.4	56.4
Accidents other than motor vehicle	37.8	37.0
Motor vehicle accidents	18.5	15.7
Chronic lower respiratory diseases	35.4	43.3
Diabetes mellitus	26.0	25.4
HIV	4.9	4.9
Suicide	10.6	11.0
Homicide	6.5	6.1
All causes	714.1	847.3
Rank in overall death rate among states		45

Figures exclude nonresidents who died in the state. Causes of death follow International Classification of Diseases. Rank is from highest to lowest death rate in the United States.
Source: U.S. National Center for Health Statistics, National Vital Statistics Report, 2006.

ECONOMY

Gross state product, 1990-2004
In current dollars

Year	State product	Nat'l product	State share
1990	$384.1 billion	$5.67 trillion	6.77%
2000	$722.8 billion	$9.75 trillion	7.41%
2002	$775.5 billion	$10.41 trillion	7.45%
2003	$821.9 billion	$10.92 trillion	7.52%
2004	$880.9 billion	$11.65 trillion	7.56%

Source: U.S. Bureau of Economic Analysis, *Survey of Current Business*, July, 2005.

Gross state product by industry, 2003
In billions of dollars

Construction	$32.1
Manufacturing	101.3
Wholesale trade	54.3
Retail trade	61.3
Finance & insurance	50.6
Information	38.5
Professional services	49.4
Health care & social assistance	44.7
Government	86.1
Total state product	$769.4
Total U.S. product	$10,289.2
State share of U.S. total	7.48%
Rank among all states	3

Total figures include industries not listed separately. Amounts are in chained 2000 dollars.
Source: U.S. Bureau of Economic Analysis, *Survey of Current Business*, July, 2005.

Personal income per capita, 1990-2004
In current dollars

	1990	2000	2004
Per capita income	$17,421	$28,313	$30,222
U.S. average	$19,477	$29,845	$32,937
Rank among states	31	23	32

Source: U.S. Bureau of Economic Analysis, *Survey of Current Business*, April, 2005.

Energy consumption, 2001
In trillions of British thermal units (BTU), except as noted

Total energy consumption
Total state energy consumption	12,029
Total U.S. energy consumption	96,275
State share of U.S. total	12.49%
Rank among states	1

Per capita consumption (In millions of BTU)
Total state per capita consumption	564
Total U.S. per capita consumption	338
Rank among states	5

End-use sectors
Residential	1,570
Commercial	1,356
Industrial	6,426
Transportation	2,677

Sources of energy
Petroleum	5,521
Natural gas	4,435
Coal	1,493
Hydroelectric power	12
Nuclear electric power	399

Figures for totals include categories not listed separately.
Source: U.S. Energy Information Administration, *State Energy Data Report*, 2001.

Nonfarm employment by sectors, 2004

Total persons	9,478,000
Construction	543,000
Manufacturing	890,000
Trade, transportation, utilities	1,943,000
Information	226,000
Finance, insurance, real estate	595,000
Professional & business services	1,088,000
Education & health services	1,145,000
Leisure, hospitality, arts, organizations	883,000
Other services, including repair & maintenance	359,000
Government	1,656,000

Figures are rounded to nearest thousand persons. "Total" includes mining and natural resources, not listed separately.
Source: U.S. Bureau of Labor Statistics, 2006.

Foreign exports, 1990-2004
In millions of dollars

Year	State	U.S.	State share
1990	32,931	394,045	8.36%
1996	66,862	624,767	10.70%
1997	76,184	688,896	11.06%
2000	103,866	712,055	13.27%
2003	98,846	724,006	14.63%
2004	117,245	769,332	15.24%

Rank among all states in 2004. 1

U.S. total does not include U.S. dependencies.

Source: U.S. Census Bureau, *U.S. Merchandise Trade*, series FT 900, 2000; U.S. Census Bureau, *U.S. International Trade in Goods and Services*, Series FT 900, 2005.

LAND USE

Federally owned land, 2003
Areas in acres

	State	U.S.	State share
Total area	168,218,000	2,271,343,000	7.41%
Nonfederal land	165,046,000	1,599,584,000	10.32%
Federal land	3,172,000	671,759,000	0.47%
Federal share	1.9%	29.6%	—

Areas are rounded to nearest thousand acres. Figures for federally owned land do not include trust properties.

Source: U.S. General Services Administration, *Federal Real Property Profile*, 2006.

Land use, 1997
In acres, rounded to nearest thousand

Total surface area	171,052,000
Total nonfederal rural land	155,530,000
Percentage rural land	90.9%
Cropland.	26,938,000
Conservation Reserve Program (CRP*) land . . .	3,906,000
Pastureland	15,914,000
Rangeland	95,745,000
Forestland	10,816,000
Other rural land	2,211,000

*CRP is a federal program begun in 1985 to assist private landowners to convert highly erodible cropland to vegetative cover for ten years. Note that some categories of land overlap.

Source: U.S. Department of Agriculture, Natural Resources and Conservation Service, and Iowa State University, Statistical Laboratory, *Summary Report, 1997 National Resources Inventory*, revised December, 2000.

Farms and crop acreage, 2004

	State	U.S.	Share	Rank
Farms	229,000	2,113,000	10.84%	1
Acres (millions)	130	937	13.87%	1
Acres per farm	568	443	—	13

Source: U.S. Department of Agriculture, National Agricultural Statistics Service. Numbers of farms are rounded to nearest thousand units; acreage figures are rounded to nearest million. Rankings, including ties, are based on rounded figures.

GOVERNMENT AND FINANCE

Units of local government, 2002

	State	Total U.S.	Rank
All local governments	4,784	87,525	3
Counties	254	3,034	1
Municipalities	1,196	19,429	2
Townships	0	16,504	—
School districts	1,089	13,506	1
Special districts	2,245	35,052	3

Only 48 states have county governments, 20 states have township governments ("towns" in New England, Minnesota, New York, and Wisconsin), and 46 states have school districts. Special districts encompass such functions as natural resources, fire protection, and housing and community development.

Source: U.S. Census Bureau, *Census of Governments.*

State government revenue, 2002

Total revenue	$60,588 mill.
General revenue	$62,181 mill.
Per capita revenue	$2,862
U.S. per capita average	$3,689
Rank among states	48

Intergovernment revenue	
Total	$21,385 mill.
From federal government	$20,672 mill.

Charges and miscellaneous	
Total	$12,134 mill.
Current charges	$6,115 mill.
Misc. general income	$6,019 mill.
Insurance trust revenue	−$1,593 mill.

Taxes	
Total	$28,662 mill.
Per capita taxes	$1,319
Rank among states	49
Property taxes	(nil)
Sales taxes	$23,577 mill.
License taxes	$3,778 mill.
Individual income taxes	(nil)
Corporate income taxes	(nil)
Other taxes	$1,307 mill.

Total revenue figures include items not listed separately here.

Source: U.S. Bureau of the Census.

State government expenditures, 2002

General expenditures

Total state expenditures	$70,274 mill.
Intergovernmental	$16,681 mill.

Per capita expenditures

State	$2,842
Average of all states	$3,859
Rank among states	49

Selected direct expenditures

Education	$11,558 mill.
Public welfare	$14,607 mill.
Health, hospital	$4,385 mill.
Highways	$5,111 mill.
Police protection	$389 mill.
Corrections	$3,036 mill.
Natural resources	$621 mill.
Parks and recreation	$86 mill.
Government administration	$1,310 mill.
Interest on debt	$950 mill.
Total direct expenditures	$45,090 mill.

Totals include items not listed separately.
Source: U.S. Census Bureau.

POLITICS

Governors since statehood

D = Democrat; R = Republican; O = other;
(r) resigned; (d) died in office; (i) removed from office

James Pinckney Henderson (D)	1846-1847
George T. Wood (D)	1847-1849
Peter H. Bell (D)	(r) 1849-1853
James W. Henderson (D)	1853
Elisha M. Pease (D)	1853-1857
Hardin R. Runnels (D)	1857-1859
Sam Houston (D)	(r) 1859-1861
Edward Clark (D)	1861
Francis R. Lubbock (D)	1861-1863
Pendleton Murrah (D)	(r) 1863-1865
Fletcher S. Stockdale (D)	(i) 1865
Andrew J. Hamilton	1865-1866
James W. Throckmorton (D)	(i) 1866-1867
Elisha M. Pease	(r) 1867-1869
Edmund J. Davis (R)	1870-1874
Richard Coke (D)	(r) 1874-1876
Richard B. Hubbard (D)	1876-1879
Oran M. Roberts (D)	1879-1883
John Ireland (D)	1883-1887
Lawrence ("Sul") Ross (D)	1887-1891
James S. Hogg (D)	1891-1895
Charles A. Culberson (D)	1895-1899
Joseph D. Sayers (D)	1899-1903
Samuel W. T. Lanham (D)	1903-1907
Thomas M. Campbell (D)	1907-1911
Oscar B. Colquitt (D)	1911-1915
James E. Ferguson (D)	(i) 1915-1917

William P. Hobby (D)	1917-1921
Patrick M. Neff (D)	1921-1925
Miriam A. Ferguson (D)	1925-1927
Daniel Moody (D)	1927-1931
Ross S. Sterling (D)	1931-1933
Miriam A. Ferguson (D)	1933-1935
James V. Allred (D)	1935-1939
Wilbert Lee O'Daniel (D)	(r) 1939-1941
Coke R. Stevenson (D)	1941-1947
Beauford H. Jester (D)	(d) 1947-1949
Allan Shivers (D)	1949-1957
Price Daniel (D)	1957-1963
John B. Connally, Jr. (D)	1963-1969
Preston E. Smith (D)	1969-1973
Dolph Briscoe (D)	1973-1979
William P. Clements, Jr. (R)	1979-1983
Mark White (D)	1983-1987
William P. Clements, Jr. (R)	1987-1991
Ann Richards (D)	1991-1995
George W. Bush (R)	1995-2000
J. Richard Perry (R)	2000-

Composition of congressional delegations, 1989-2007

	Dem	Rep	Total
House of Representatives			
101st Congress, 1989			
State delegates	19	8	27
Total U.S.	259	174	433
102d Congress, 1991			
State delegates	19	8	27
Total U.S.	267	167	434
103d Congress, 1993			
State delegates	21	9	30
Total U.S.	258	176	434
104th Congress, 1995			
State delegates	17	13	30
Total U.S.	197	236	433
105th Congress, 1997			
State delegates	16	14	30
Total U.S.	206	228	434
106th Congress, 1999			
State delegates	17	13	30
Total U.S.	211	222	433
107th Congress, 2001			
State delegates	17	13	30
Total U.S.	211	221	432
108th Congress, 2003			
State delegates	17	15	32
Total U.S.	205	229	434
109th Congress, 2005			
State delegates	11	21	32
Total U.S.	202	231	433

(continued)

	Dem	Rep	Total
110th Congress, 2007			
State delegates	13	19	32
Total U.S.	233	202	435

Senate			
101st Congress, 1989			
State delegates	1	1	2
Total U.S.	55	45	100
102d Congress, 1991			
State delegates	1	1	2
Total U.S.	56	44	100
103d Congress, 1993			
State delegates	1	1	2
Total U.S.	57	43	100
104th Congress, 1995			
State delegates	0	2	2
Total U.S.	46	53	99
105th Congress, 1997			
State delegates	0	2	2
Total U.S.	45	55	100
106th Congress, 1999			
State delegates	0	2	2
Total U.S.	45	54	99
107th Congress, 2001			
State delegates	0	2	2
Total U.S.	50	50	100
108th Congress, 2003			
State delegates	0	2	2
Total U.S.	48	51	99
109th Congress, 2005			
State delegates	0	2	2
Total U.S.	44	55	99
110th Congress, 2007			
State delegates	0	2	2
Total U.S.	49	49	98

Figures are for starts of first sessions. Totals are for Democrat (Dem.) and Republican (Rep.) members only. House membership totals under 435 and Senate totals under 100 reflect vacancies and seats held by independent party members. When the 110th Congress opened, the Senate's two independent members caucused with the Democrats, giving the Democrats control of the Senate.

Source: U.S. Congress, *Congressional Directory.*

Composition of state legislature, 1990-2006

	Democrats	Republicans
State House (150 seats)		
1990	93	57
1992	91	58
1994	89	61
1996	82	68
1998	78	72
2000	78	72
2002	62	88
2004	63	87
2006	69	81
State Senate (31 seats)		
1990	22	9
1992	18	13
1994	17	14
1996	14	16
1998	15	16
2000	15	16
2002	12	19
2004	12	19
2006	11	20

Figures for total seats may include independents and minor party members. Numbers reflect results of elections in listed years; elected members usually take their seats in the years that follow.

Source: Council of State Governments; *State Elective Officials and the Legislatures.*

Voter participation in presidential elections, 2000 and 2004

	2000	2004
Voting age population		
State	15,040,000	16,223,000
Total United States	209,831,000	220,377,000
State share of U.S. total	7.17	7.36
Rank among states	2	2
Portion of voting age population casting votes		
State	42.6%	45.7%
United States	50.3%	55.5%
Rank among states	47	49

Population figures are rounded to nearest thousand and include all residents, regardless of eligibility to vote.

Source: U.S. Census Bureau.

HEALTH AND MEDICAL CARE

Medical professionals
Physicians in 2003 and nurses in 2001

	U.S.	State
Physicians in 2003		
Total	774,849	46,802
Share of U.S. total		6.01%
Rate	266	212
Rank		40
Nurses in 2001		
Total	2,262,020	129,710
Share of U.S. total		5.73%
Rate	793	607
Rank		47

Rates are numbers of physicians and nurses per 100,000 resident population; ranks are based on rates.

Source: American Medical Association, *Physician Characteristics and Distribution in the U.S.*; U.S. Department of Health and Human Services, Health Resources and Services Administration.

Health insurance coverage, 2003

	State	U.S.
Total persons covered	16,484,000	243,320,000
Total persons not covered	5,374,000	44,961,000
Portion not covered	24.6%	15.6%
Rank among states	1	—
Children not covered	1,264,000	8,373,000
Portion not covered	20.0%	11.4%
Rank among states	1	—

Totals are rounded to nearest thousand. Ranks are from the highest to the lowest percentages of persons *not* insured.

Source: U.S. Census Bureau, Current Population Reports.

AIDS, syphilis, and tuberculosis cases, 2003

Disease	U.S. cases	State cases	Rank
AIDS	44,232	3,413	4
Syphilis	34,270	3,996	2
Tuberculosis	14,874	1,594	2

Source: U.S. Centers for Disease Control and Prevention.

Cigarette smoking, 2003
Residents over age 18 who smoke

	U.S.	State	Rank
All smokers	22.1%	22.1%	25
Male smokers	24.8%	26.7%	19
Female smokers	20.3%	17.6%	46

Cigarette smokers are defined as persons who reported having smoked at least 100 cigarettes during their lifetimes and who currently smoked at least occasionally.

Source: U.S. Centers for Disease Control and Prevention, *Morbidity and Mortality Weekly Report*, 53, no. 44 (November 12, 2004).

HOUSING

Home ownership rates, 1985-2004

	1985	1990	1995	2000	2004
State	60.5%	59.7%	61.4%	63.8%	65.6%
Total U.S.	63.9%	63.9%	64.7%	67.4%	69.0%
Rank among states	45	42	43	44	45

Net change in state home ownership rate, 1985-2004	+5.1%
Net change in U.S. home ownership rate, 1985-2004	+5.1%

Percentages represent the proportion of owner households to total occupied households.

Source: U.S. Census Bureau, 2006.

Home sales, 2000-2004
In thousands of units

Existing home sales	2000	2002	2003	2004
State sales	381.8	412.4	425.4	485.5
Total U.S. sales	5,171	5,631	6,183	6,784
State share of U.S. total	7.38%	7.32%	6.88%	7.16%
Sales rank among states	3	3	3	3

Units include single-family homes, condos, and co-ops.

Source: National Association of Realtors, Washington, D.C., *Real Estate Outlook: Market Trends & Insights*.

Values of owner-occupied homes, 2003

	State	U.S.
Total units	4,179,000	58,809,000
Value of units		
Under $100,000	50.6%	29.6%
$100,000-199,999	34.8%	36.9%
$200,000 or more	14.6%	33.5%
Median value	$99,139	$142,275
Rank among all states		42

Units are owner-occupied one-family houses whose numbers are rounded to nearest thousand. Data are extrapolated from survey samples.
Source: U.S. Census Bureau, American Community Survey.

EDUCATION

Public school enrollment, 2002

Prekindergarten through grade 8
State enrollment 3,080,000
Total U.S. enrollment. 34,135,000
State share of U.S. total 9.02%

Grades 9 through 12
State enrollment 1,180,000
Total U.S. enrollment. 14,067,000
State share of U.S. total 8.39%

Enrollment rates
State public school enrollment rate. 97.0%
Overall U.S. rate 90.4%
Rank among states in 2002 2
Rank among states in 1995 1

Enrollment figures (which include unclassified students) are rounded to nearest thousand pupils during fall school term. Enrollment rates are based on enumerated resident population estimate for July 1, 2002.
Source: U.S. National Center for Education Statistics.

Public college finances, 2003-2004

FTE enrollment in public institutions of higher education
Students in state institutions. 812,900
Students in all U.S. public institutions 9,916,600
State share of U.S. total 8.20
Rank among states. 2

State and local government appropriations for higher education
State appropriation per FTE $5,282
National average. $5,716
Rank among states 28
State & local tax revenue going to higher
education 9.5%

FTE = full-time equivalent in public postsecondary programs, including summer sessions; student numbers are rounded to nearest hundred. Funding figures for 2003-2004 academic year include financial aid to students in state public institutions and exclude money for research, agriculture experiment stations, teaching hospitals, and medical schools; figures are rounded to nearest thousand dollars.
Source: Higher Education Executive Officers, Denver, Colorado.

TRANSPORTATION AND TRAVEL

Highway mileage, 2003

Interstate highways 3,233
Other freeways and expressways 1,170
Arterial roads. 28,537
Collector roads. 63,508
Local roads 205,539
Urban roads 83,287
Rural roads 218,700
Total state mileage 301,987
U.S. total 3,974,107
State share 7.60%
Rank among states. 1

Note that combined urban and rural road mileage matches the total of the other categories.
Source: U.S. Federal Highway Administration.

Motor vehicle registrations and driver licenses, 2003

Vehicle registrations	State	U.S.	Share	Rank
Autos, trucks, buses	14,889,000	231,390,000	6.43%	2
Autos only	7,842,000	135,670	5.78%	4
Motorcycles	258,000	5,328,000	4.84%	6
Driver licenses	13,498,000	196,166,000	6.88%	2

Figures, which do not include vehicles owned by military services, are rounded to the nearest thousand. Figures for automobiles include taxis.
Source: U.S. Federal Highway Administration.

Domestic travel expenditures, 2003

Spending by U.S. residents on overnight trips and day trips of at least 50 miles from home

Total expenditures within state	$31.47 bill.
Total expenditures within U.S.	$490.87 bill.
State share of U.S. total	6.4%
Rank among states	3

Source: Travel Industry Association of America.

Retail gasoline prices, 2003-2007

Average price per gallon at the pump

Year	U.S.	State
2003	$1.267	$1.184
2004	$1.316	$1.200
2005	$1.644	$1.572
2007	$2.298	$2.156

Excise tax per gallon in 2004	20.0¢
Rank among all states in 2007 prices	42

Prices are averages of all grades of gasoline sold at the pump during March months in 2003-2005 and during February, 2007. Averages for 2006, during which prices rose higher, are not available.

Source: U.S. Energy Information Agency, *Petroleum Marketing Monthly* (2003-2005 data); American Automobile Association (2007 data).

CRIME AND LAW ENFORCEMENT

State and local police officers, 2000-2004

	2000	2002	2004
Total officers			
U.S.	654,601	665,555	675,734
State	46,050	47,710	49,119*
*Net change, 2000-2004			+6.66%
Officers per 1,000 residents			
U.S.	2.33	2.31	2.30
State	2.21	2.19	2.18
State rank	22	21	21

Totals include state and local police and sheriffs.
Source: Carsey Institute, University of New Hampshire.

Crime rates, 2003

Incidents per 100,000 residents

Crimes	State	U.S.
Violent crimes		
Total incidents	553	475
Murder	6	6
Forcible rape	36	32
Robbery	167	142
Aggravated assault	343	295
Property crimes		
Total incidents	4,595	3,588
Burglary	994	741
Larceny/theft	3,158	2,415
Motor vehicle theft	444	433
All crimes	5,148	4,063

Source: U.S. Federal Bureau of Investigation, *Crime in the United States*, annual.

State prison populations, 1980-2003

	State	U.S.	State share
1980	29,892	305,458	9.79%
1990	50,042	708,393	7.06%
1996	132,383	1,025,624	12.91%
2000	166,719	1,391,261	11.98%
2003	166,911	1,470,045	11.35%

State figures exclude prisoners in federal penitentiaries.
Source: U.S. Bureau of Justice Statistics, *Prisoners in 2003*.

Utah

Location: Rocky Mountains

Area and rank: 82,168 square miles (212,816 square kilometers); 84,904 square miles (219,901 square kilometers) including water; twelfth largest state in area

Coastline: none

Population and rank: 2,389,000 (2004); thirty-fourth largest state in population

Capital and largest city: Salt Lake City (181,743 people in 2000 census)

Became territory: September 9, 1850

Entered Union and rank: January 4, 1896; forty-fifth state

Present constitution adopted: 1896

Counties: 29

Utah's capital and largest city, Salt Lake City, looking south, with the domed state capitol building visible at the left. (Corbis)

State name: "Utah" is derived from a Ute word meaning "people of the mountains"

State nickname: Beehive State

Motto: Industry

State flag: Blue field with variant of the state seal

Highest point: Kings Peak—13,528 feet (4,123 meters)

Lowest point: Beaverdam Wash—2,000 feet (610 meters)

Highest recorded temperature: 117 degrees Fahrenheit (47 degrees Celsius)—St. George, 1985

Lowest recorded temperature: –69 degrees Fahrenheit (–56 degrees Celsius)—Peter's Sink, 1985

State song: "Utah, This is the Place" (replaces "Utah, We Love Thee")

State tree: Blue spruce

State flower: Sego lily

State bird: California gull

State fish: Bonneville cutthroat trout

State animal: Rocky Mountain elk

National parks: Arches, Bryce Canyon, Canyonlands, Capitol Reef, Zion

Utah History

As is attested by archaeological evidence, Utah's territory has been continuously inhabited through the past eleven thousand years. The earliest indigenous peoples hunted with spears, used baskets to gather wild foods, and made stone tools. Later peoples, besides hunting and gathering, grew maize. Utes and Paiutes arrived about six hundred years ago, followed later by Navajos. When Anglo-Americans began settling the Utah region, these American Indians, together with the Shoshones and Bannocks, were most numerous.

The first non-Native Americans to enter the region were Spaniards and Mexicans. Juan Maria Rivera made two expeditions to the area in 1765. In 1776, two priests of the Franciscan Order, Fathers Francisco Atanasio Domínguez and Francisco Silvestre Vélez de Escalante, led an expedition from Santa Fe, now in New Mexico, seeking passage to Monterey, California. No further expeditions were recorded until the early nineteenth century, when trade between Santa Fe and Indians of the Utah region became common. From then until the 1840's, numerous fur traders and other mountain men visited the area for varying lengths of time, and many pioneers and adventurers on their way to California traveled across it, but no permanent settlements were established. In 1824, the famous scout Jim Bridger came upon the Great Salt Lake and, tasting its briny water, believed it an ocean.

In its formative period, Utah's inhospitable terrain and geographically remote location far from both the populous east and the growing Pacific region were principal factors in its destiny. On one hand, its arid and mountainous landscape dissuaded early travelers from settling, but on the other, its remoteness attracted the people whose predominance most influenced its character from first settlement to the present day. Those were the Mormons, hearty, closely knit, deeply religious, hard-working folk, who adapted well to Utah's harsh topography.

Arrival of the Mormons. Numbering about three million today, Mormons are formally members of the Church of Jesus Christ of Latter-day Saints. They take their name from the title the Book of Mormon, an important holy book along with the Bible. A principal belief is that Jesus appeared in the New World after His crucifixion. After their church was founded in 1830 by Joseph Smith in Fayette, New York, Mormons were persecuted wherever they settled. Non-Mormons feared their aloofness from society and what appeared as strange ways, such as their communal economy and theocratic organizational structure, in which religious and civic affairs were intertwined. What antagonized others most, however, was the Mormon belief in polygamy, families with several wives, a church doctrine that emerged during the 1850's. Leaving New York in 1831, Smith and his followers moved to Ohio, but trouble there led to expulsion in 1838-1839. Settling in the Illinois town of Nauvoo, by 1842 they had aroused deep resentment in that state. Arrested in 1844,

Utah's "This Is the Place" Monument marks the spot where Brigham Young arrived with the first Mormon settlers in the Salt Lake Valley in 1847. (Utah Travel Council/Frank Jensen)

Smith and his brother were murdered by a mob. Two years later, led by Brigham Young, a man of exceptional leadership qualities, the Mormons fled Illinois, venturing west into unsettled territory in search of secure autonomy. Young, traveling with an advance party, upon sighting the Great Salt Lake Valley in 1847, is said to have declared, "This is the place."

Since their beginnings the Mormons had sent missionaries to other states and western European countries to gain adherents. Now in their new desert home, they called their followers to join them, and Mormons began arriving in the thousands, especially from northern Europe. By 1850 a number of towns had been founded; within Brigham Young's lifetime, some 350 settlements were established. By 1900 the number had grown to 500 settlements in Utah and surrounding states, the result of the Mormon policy of colonization. The towns, based on communal ownership, were planned communities of farmers and tradesmen.

Becoming a Territory. Meanwhile, after the Mexican War of 1846, the Mormon territory became part of the United States, and the community's autonomy was once more put in jeopardy. Mormons had participated in the war on the American side, sending a volunteer battalion on a famous march from Kansas to San Diego. In 1849-1850, Brigham Young declared the Mormon settlement a new state of Deseret, after the word for honeybee in the Book of Mormon. With Young as governor, church leaders filled all offices. Deseret encompassed an immense area extending to San Diego in Southern California, giving access to a port for Mormon immigration and trade. Congress, however, suspicious of the proposed state's huge size and theocratic polity, rejected it, setting up instead the smaller, but still large, territory of Utah, including Nevada, Wyoming, and parts of Colorado. Utah Territory's size was progressively pared, until 1868, when the future state's present borders were drawn. Brigham Young was the first territorial governor.

The Mormon Church did its utmost to populate its territory, issuing a call for members to gather there. In 1849, the church set up a Perpetual Emigrating Fund, used to bring poor members from distant places. Mormons soon began arriving in the thousands from northern Europe, including many from the British Isles. In the end, the fund raised hundreds of thousands of dollars for Mormon emigration.

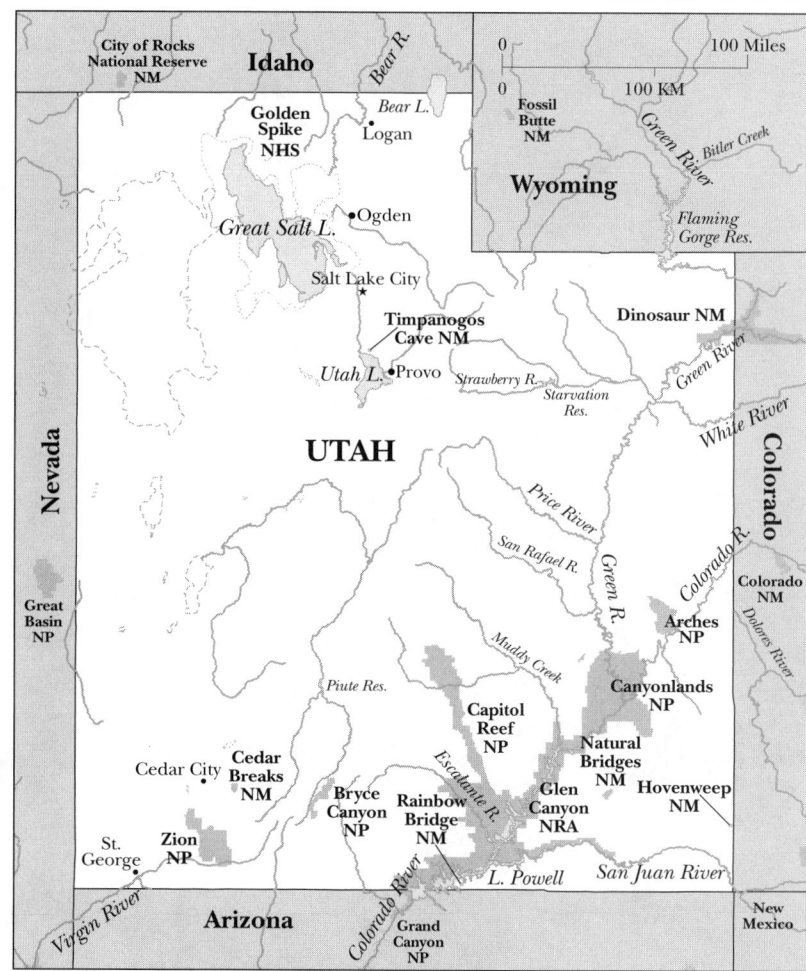

Conflicts with non-Mormons. Relations between Mormons and non-Mormons were tense, and conflicts frequent. Outsiders were excluded from positions of power and influence, and mutual suspicion abounded. Mormons recalled persecution; non-Mormons questioned Mormon loyalty to American democracy. In 1857, rumors of Mormon rebellion against the United States led the administration of President James Buchanan to send some 2,500 troops to occupy Salt Lake City and its environs—events known as the Utah War. Mormon attacks on the troops' supply trains did little to relieve federal anxieties.

Later, the Mormon Church's official neutrality in the Civil War had a similar effect. Young was stripped of his office, and a non-Mormon was installed as governor by the U.S. government. Then, in the darkest chapter of Utah's history, Mormons slaughtered more than one hundred non-Mormon civilian men, women, and children traveling through southern Utah from Missouri and Arkansas. However, after some negotiation, peace was achieved in 1858, though further incidents recurred during the 1860's, when federal soldiers returned.

With some of the most visually striking geological formations in the world, southeastern Utah's Monument Valley has provided settings for more Western films than any other place in the United States. (Jon Sullivan/PD Photo.org)

Besides trouble with non-Mormons and with Washington, D.C., the new territory also experienced conflicts with American Indians. At first Brigham Young's Indian policy was successful in securing peace. American Indian resentment over settler occupation of their lands soon led to hostilities, however. In 1853, the Walker War, named for a Ute chief, broke out, but it ended the next year when Young persuaded the Utes to lay down their arms. Bannock and Shoshone raids continued in northern Utah until 1863, when U.S. Army troops defeated them. Peace was restored in 1867, but raids continued until late 1872. More conflicts occurred in the twentieth century, but by the mid-1920's American Indian aggression had receded. By century's end, however, Native Americans used the legal system to further their interests.

While these events were taking place, others occurred that would have far-reaching effects on Mormon-dominated Utah. Non-Mormons were arriving in significant numbers to work mines, after silver and lead were discovered in Bingham Canyon, near Salt Lake City. Mormons had previously made such discoveries, but were discouraged from exploiting them for fear of attracting outsiders and losing labor needed to produce necessities. Other non-Mormons opened stores or other businesses.

At this time, the nation's communications were progressing. For a scant nineteen months in 1860-1861, the Pony Express road across Utah carried mail from St. Joseph, Missouri, to Sacramento, California. The arrival of the telegraph linking the nation from coast to coast and the completion of a transcontinental railroad in 1869 opened Utah's products to national markets, and a boom began in railroad feeder lines to transport them.

From Territory to State. As the territory progressed economically, it sought entrance to the Union as a state. This proved a formidable task, since distrust of Mormons was prevalent. In 1852, Brigham Young had publicly acknowledged Mormon polygamy. During the

1870's and 1880's, Congress passed acts prohibiting this practice. Utah petitioned for statehood seven times before it was successful. Opposition to statehood receded only after 1890, when Mormon leader Wilford Woodruff issued a manifesto renouncing polygamy. In 1895, a constitution was drafted outlawing this practice and separating church and state; the following year Utah became the nation's forty-fifth state.

Utah's new constitution called for several elected officials in the executive branch, some of whom cannot be reelected. In keeping with a tradition of strong leadership authority, governors have more power than those of nearby states. Most judges are elected, however, and the legislature is bicameral.

Into the American Mainstream. The old ways of the original Mormon settlers died hard. When the last survivor of the 1847 trek from Illinois died in Idaho during the 1920's, thousands of Mormons trooped north to pay their final respects. By then, Utah had begun decisive change that would transform it into a modern society. By World War I Utah was entering the American mainstream. The social landscape was increasingly urbanized, and the economy was developing. New ores, especially copper, were mined, and smelting became a large industry. Labor unions emerged, and with them labor conflict appeared. The Depression hit the state particularly hard, and severe droughts in 1931 and 1934 did not help matters. However, as elsewhere in the nation, the coming of World War II eased economic hardship, as federal defense dollars combined with conscription to lessen unemployment.

Postwar Developments. After World War II, Utah passed from being an agricultural and mining state to an industrial state. A Geneva steel plant opened in 1943, and federal investment in defense industries during the decades that followed spurred industrialization. Utah became a principal site of missile development, and other defense industries took root.

By the 1980's and 1990's a number of high-tech industries that were growing in importance were located in Utah. The state was becoming more politically and culturally sophisticated. Environmental politics entered the scene, and figures such as Utah senator Orrin Hatch became important in Washington politics. As the end of the century approached, Utah had moved from a predominantly industrial to a service economy, as tourism and other service industries expanded. While the position of the Mormon Church remained strong, barely more than a

century of statehood had seen Utah move squarely into the modern world.

Wildfires. Like other Western states, Utah approached the turn of the twenty-first century by experiencing a series of devastating wildfires each summer. By August of 2000, for example, more than sixty extensive wildfires existed in ten Western states, including Utah. Fire danger was the result of drought, with at least two-thirds of the state suffering from severe or extreme long-term drought conditions and nearly the whole of the state suffering from such conditions in the short term. In August, 2001, federal aid was given to fight an out-of-control fire near Provo. Satellite images in June, 2002, showed large fires burning in the state. In 2004, the American Red Cross responded with aid to victims of four wildfires. In June, 2005, wildfires in southwestern Utah restricted travel and caused town evacuations.

The Kennecott Copper Mine was one of several new mining ventures that transformed Utah's economy during the early twentieth century. (Utah Travel Council/Frank Jensen)

In July, 2006, two large wildfires burned nearly four square miles of land.

Polygamy. Also early in the twenty-first century, the most controversial aspect of Utah's Mormon past came to public notice when a polygamy case was tried for the first time in fifty years. In May 2001, polygamist Tom Green, a fifty-two-year-old man who had five wives and twenty-nine children, was tried, convicted, and sentenced to five years imprisonment for bigamy and nonsupport. The following year, Green was convicted of child rape, since his fifth wife was thirteen years old. It was reported, however, that such cases are just the tip of the iceberg and that it is an open secret that some thirty thousand Mormons maintain polygamist families in Utah and other Western states.

Politics. In 2000, while most of the nation was narrowly divided between the two main presidential contenders, Utah was not. Republican George W. Bush took the state with 67 percent of the vote, with just 26 percent for Al Gore. Veteran senator Orrin Hatch won a similar victory, with two-thirds of the vote. Two of the state's congressional districts went to Republicans. The contest for governor also went to a republican, Mike Leavitt, who was reelected to his third term, only the second governor in Utah history to have been elected three times. In 2002, the state's sole Democratic seat in Congress nearly went to a Republican, with both candidates taking 49 percent of the vote; incumbent James David Matheson narrowly won in a 2,014-vote victory, after claiming 56 percent of the vote in 2000. In August 2003, Leavitt was nominated by President Bush to head the U.S. Environmental Protection Agency. Upon confirmation in October, he resigned as governor and was succeeded by the state's first female governor, Olene S. Walker. The state's Republican Party, however, declined to place her on the 2004 primary ballot, despite substantial public support. As a result, Republican Jon Huntsman, Jr., was elected governor in the November election.

Charles F. Bahmueller

Utah Time Line

1776	Fathers Francisco Silvestre Vélez de Escalante and Francisco Atanasio Domínguez seek a new route from New Mexico to California and explore Utah.
1821	Utah's territory becomes part of Mexico.
1824	Trappers arrive in northern Utah; Jim Bridger discovers Great Salt Lake.
1825	Jedediah Smith passes through Utah in the first overland expedition to California.
1841	First wagon train of settlers crosses Utah en route to California.
1842	John C. Frémont and Kit Carson explore the Great Basin.
1843	Fort Buenaventura is established.
July 24, 1847	First party of Mormon pioneers arrive in the Salt Lake Valley.
1848	Utah is ceded to the United States after Mexican War.
Mar. 12, 1849	Constitutional convention declares the state of Deseret, which encompasses the entire Great Basin.
1850	Utah Territory is organized.
1852	Mormon Church publicly acknowledges doctrine of plural marriage; begins the construction of Salt Lake Temple.
1853	Walker War with Ute Indians begins over slavery among the Indians.
1853	Grasshopper plagues endanger crops.
1857-1858	Federal government forcibly removes Governor Brigham Young from office as Utah War begins.
1862	Silver and lead are discovered in Bingham Canyon.
1865-1868	Black Hawk War with Utes is last major American Indian conflict in state.
May 10, 1869	Union Pacific and Central Pacific railroads meet at Promontory.
1869	First non-Mormon church building in Utah is constructed.
1869	John Wesley Powell explores the Colorado River.
1874	Poland Act passed in Congress, making it legal to prosecute Mormons for practicing polygamy.
1875	Holy Cross Sisters open Holy Cross Hospital, their first in the United States.
1879	First telephone service is established in Ogden.
1887	Edmunds Act is passed by Congress, outlawing cohabitation.
1890	Mormon Church president Wilford Woodruff issues a manifesto ending church-sanctioned polygamy.
1891	B'Nai Israel Temple is dedicated in Salt Lake City.

Jan. 4, 1896	Utah becomes the forty-fifth state.
1906	Open-pit copper mining begins in Bingham Canyon.
1911	Strawberry Reservoir is completed.
1914	Auto racing begins on the Bonneville Salt Flats near Great Salt Lake.
1919	Zion National Park is established.
1928	Bryce Canyon National Park is established.
1942-1945	Topaz, Japanese American Relocation Camp, operates near Delta during World War II.
1943	Geneva steel plant begins operation in Utah County.
1952	Six-mile Duchesne Tunnel carrying irrigation water is completed.
1956	Congress creates Colorado River Storage Project.
1964	Flaming Gorge Dam on the Green River is dedicated.
1964	Glen Canyon Dam in Arizona creates Lake Powell, nation's second largest artificial lake.
1965	Canyonlands National Park is opened.
1985	Utah's Jake Garn becomes first U.S. senator to fly in space.
1995	Salt Lake City is announced as the site for the 2002 Winter Olympics.
Nov. 7, 2000	In the presidential election, George W. Bush wins Utah's five electoral votes with 67 percent of the vote.
May, 2001	In the first such case tried in fifty years, polygamist Tom Green is convicted of bigamy and non-support.
Oct. 28, 2003	Governor Mike Leavitt is confirmed by the U.S. Senate as tenth administrator of the U.S. Environmental Protection Agency.
Nov. 2, 2004	George W. Bush wins 71 percent of presidential vote. After the incumbent was not renominated, Republican Jon Huntsman, Jr., wins the governor's race.
June, 2005	Wildfires in southwestern Utah restrict travel and cause town evacuations.

Eastern Utah's Arches National Park is one of the state's five national parks. (PhotoDisc)

Notes for Further Study

Published Sources. For an overview of the state's history, see Thomas G. Alexander's *Utah, the Right Place: The Official Centennial History* (1995), Charles S. Peterson's *Utah: A Bicentennial History* (1984), and Dean L. May's *Utah: A People's History* (1987). Edward Leo Lyman wrote *Political Deliverance: The Mormon Quest for Utah Statehood* (1986) about the struggle to be recognized as a state. For an account of Utah's founding father, readers should see *Brigham Young and the Expanding American Frontier* (1995) by Newell G. Bringhurst. Edited by Jeffery E. Sells, the essays in *God and Country: Politics in Utah* (2005) detail the enormous impact that religion has played in state politics historically and in the modern era. Richard Abanes's *One Nation Under Gods: A History of the Mormon Church* (2002) offers a balanced view of the history of the most important religion in the state's development. *Being Different: Stories of Utah's Minorities* (2001), edited by Stanford J. Layton, offers fourteen essays which detail the history of ethnic groups in the state, including Jewish, Scandinavian, and Japanese American settlers.

For information on Utah's indigenous peoples, *Discover Native America: Arizona, Colorado, New Mexico, and Utah* (1995) by Tish Minear and Janet Limon explores Indians of the state; *Cowboys and Cave Dwellers: Basketmaker Archaeology in Utah's Grand Gulch* (1997) by Fred M. Blackburn and Ray A. Williamson examines ancient Indian artifacts; and *Sacred Images: A Vision of Native American Art* (1996) by Leslie G. Kelen et al. looks at early Utah art. A state of great rugged beauty, Utah lends itself to numerous books that detail its natural history and attractions. On the state's geography and geology, see David L. Petersen's *Zion National Park* (1993), F. A. Barnes's *Utah Canyon Country* (1994), and *Geology Underfoot in Southern Utah* (2006) by Richard L. Orndorff, Robert W. Wieder, and David

G. Futey. *Compass American Guides: Utah* (6th ed., 2005) by Tom Wharton and Gayen Wharton and *Utah's National Parks* (2d ed., 2001) by Rod Adkison are excellent guides to the area's vacation areas. With this rich and varied landscape, however, comes varied struggles over ideas about its use, as detailed in *Contested Landscape: The Politics of Wilderness in Utah and the West* (1999), edited by Doug Goodman and Daniel McCool.

Web Resources. For Web sites on Utah state government, one might begin with the state of Utah site (www.utah.gov/). This site has links to state agencies, services, education, travel, and other topics. Utah's governor maintains a site (governor .state.ut.us), which has links to numerous topics and documents such as education, transportation, and technology. The Utah Historical Society (history.utah.gov/) maintains an extensive page that gives a summary of Utah's history and has sections on state archaeology and historic preservation, as well as a link to the Utah History Research Center, in which people can search on ancestors, maps, and newspaper clippings, among many more features. A remarkable compendium of Utah history found online is the Utah History Encyclopedia (www.media.utah.edu/UHE/UHEindex.html).

An enormous amount of detailed, often fascinating historical narrative is found in the History of the Church of Jesus Christ of Latter-day Saints (www.familysearch.org/). Another good site for researching genealogy is Stevenson's Genealogy Center (www.sgenealogy.com/). Utah's indigenous peoples are discussed at Online Utah (www.onlineutah.com/indian history.shtml). To view interesting demographic data on the state, visit the U.S. Census Bureau's QuickFacts page on Utah (quickfacts.census.gov/qfd/states/49000.html).

Counties

County	2000 pop.	Rank in pop.	Sq. miles	Rank in area	County	2000 pop.	Rank in pop.	Sq. miles	Rank in area
Beaver	6,005	24	2,590.1	13	Rich	1,961	27	1,028.6	23
Box Elder	42,745	7	5,723.7	4	Salt Lake	898,387	1	737.4	25
Cache	91,391	5	1,164.6	22	San Juan	14,413	16	7,820.7	1
Carbon	20,422	13	1,478.6	20	Sanpete	22,763	12	1,588.2	19
Daggett	921	29	698.4	26	Sevier	18,842	14	1,910.4	17
Davis	238,994	3	304.5	29	Summit	29,736	10	1,871.2	18
Duchesne	14,371	17	3,238.4	12	Tooele	40,735	8	6,945.9	2
Emery	10,860	19	4,452.1	7	Uintah	25,224	11	4,477.3	6
Garfield	4,735	25	5,174.5	5	Utah	368,536	2	1,998.4	16
Grand	8,485	20	3,681.8	9	Wasatch	15,215	15	1,180.9	21
Iron	33,779	9	3,298.5	11	Washington	90,354	6	2,427.2	15
Juab	8,238	21	3,391.9	10	Wayne	2,509	26	2,460.5	14
Kane	6,046	23	3,992.2	8	Weber	196,533	4	575.6	28
Millard	12,405	18	6,589.6	3					
Morgan	7,129	22	609.1	27					
Piute	1,435	28	757.9	24					

Source: U.S. Census Bureau; National Association of Counties.

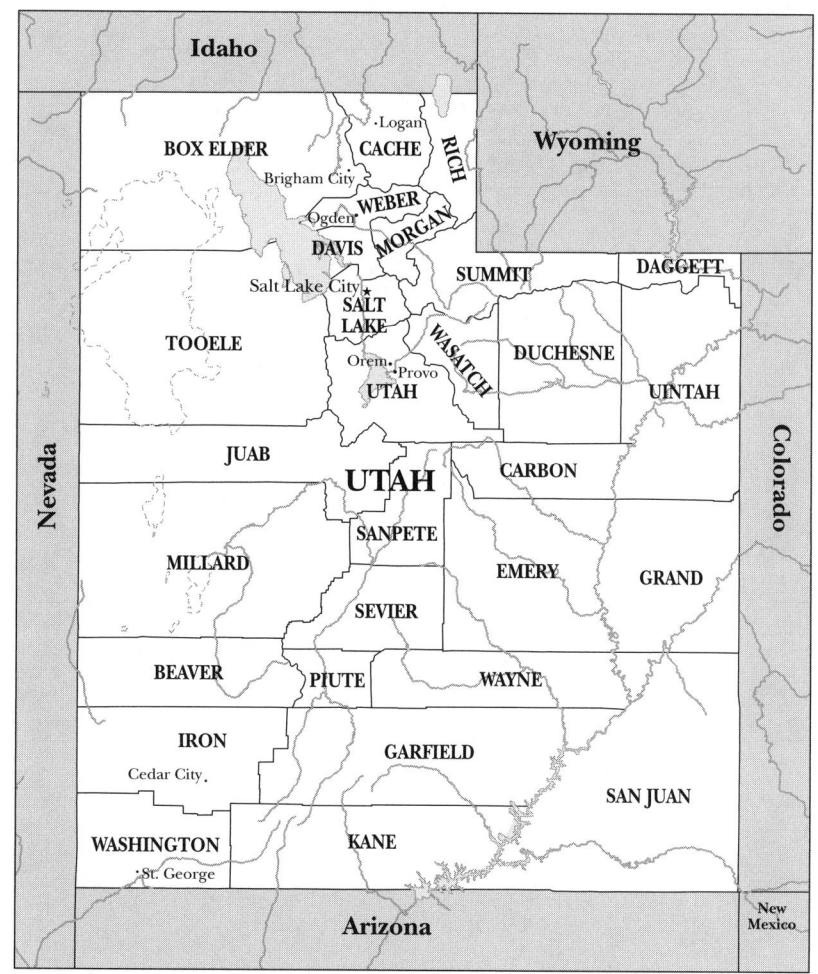

Cities

With 10,000 or more residents

Rank	City	Population	Rank	City	Population
1	Salt Lake City (capital)	181,743	18	Cottonwood Heights	27,569
2	West Valley City	108,896	19	Midvale	27,029
3	Provo	105,166	20	Clearfield	25,974
4	Sandy	88,418	21	Draper	25,220
5	Orem	84,324	22	Riverton	25,011
6	Ogden	77,226	23	Pleasant Grove	23,468
7	West Jordan	68,336	24	Magna	22,770
8	Layton	58,474	25	Tooele	22,502
9	Taylorsville	57,439	26	South Salt Lake	22,038
10	St. George	49,663	27	American Fork	21,941
11	Logan	42,670	28	East Millcreek	21,385
12	Bountiful	41,301	29	Cedar City	20,527
13	Murray	34,024	30	Springville	20,424
14	Kearns	33,659	31	Kaysville	20,351
15	Roy	32,885	32	Spanish Fork	20,246
16	Millcreek	30,377	33	Lehi	19,028
17	South Jordan	29,437	34	Cottonwood West	18,727

(continued)

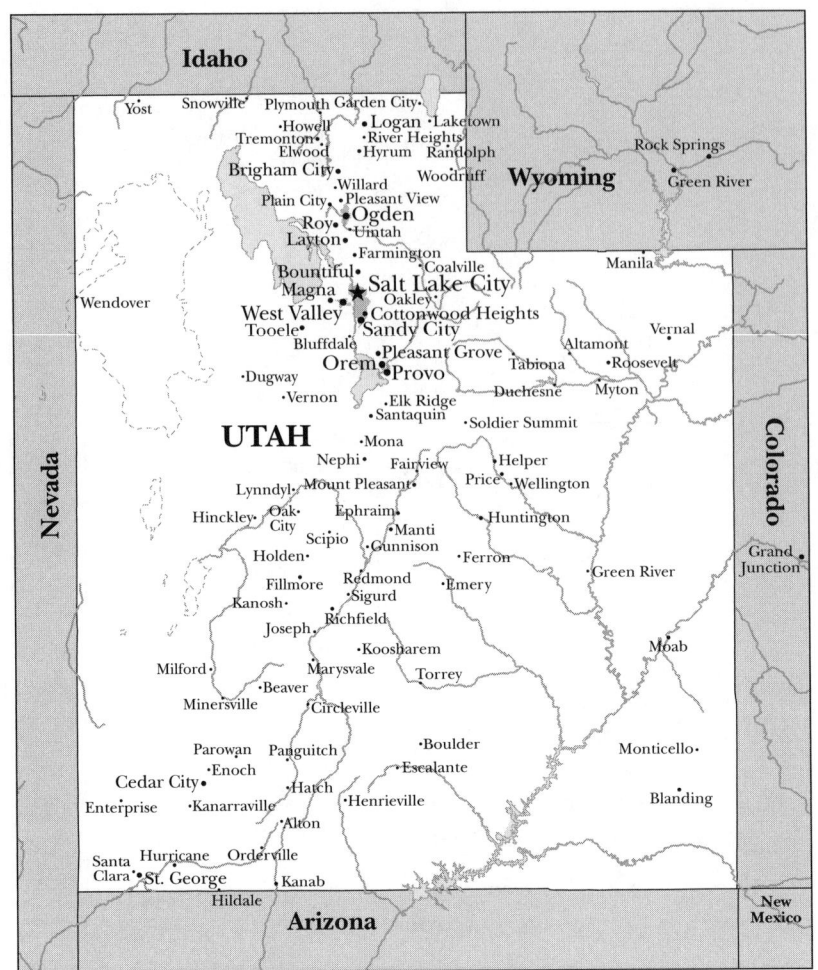

Rank	City	Population
35	Brigham City	17,411
36	North Ogden	15,026
37	Centerville	14,585
38	Holladay	14,561
39	South Ogden	14,377
40	Payson	12,716
41	Clinton	12,585

Rank	City	Population
42	Farmington	12,081
43	Canyon Rim	10,428
44	Oquirrh	10,390

Population figures are from 2000 census.

Source: U.S. Bureau of the Census.

Index to Tables

DEMOGRAPHICS

Resident state and national populations, 1970-2004

Population figures given in thousands

	State pop.	U.S. pop.	Share	Rank
1970	1,059	203,302	0.5%	36
1980	1,461	226,546	0.6%	36
1985	1,643	237,924	0.7%	35
1990	1,723	248,765	0.7%	35
1995	2,014	262,761	0.8%	34
2000	2,233	281,425	0.8%	34
2004	2,389	293,655	0.8%	34

Source: U.S. Census Bureau, Current Population Reports, 2006.

Resident population by age, 2004

Age Group	Total persons
Under 5 years	233,000
5 to 17 years	507,000
18 to 24 years	313,000
25 to 34 years	399,000
35 to 44 years	291,000
45 to 54 years	268,000
55 to 64 years	170,000
65 to 74 years	111,000
75 to 84 years	71,000
85 years and older	26,000
All age groups	2,389,000

Portion of residents 65 and older	8.7%
National rank in portion of oldest residents	49
National average	12.4%

Population figures are rounded to nearest thousand persons;
figures include armed forces personnel stationed in the state.
Source: U.S. Bureau of the Census, 2006.

Resident population by race, Hispanic origin, 2004

Category	State pop.	Share	U.S.
All residents	2,389	100.00%	100.00%
Non-Hispanic white	2,003	83.84%	67.37%
Hispanic white	238	9.96%	13.01%
Other Hispanic	15	0.63%	1.06%
African American	23	0.96%	12.77%
Native American	32	1.34%	0.96%
Asian, Pacific Islander	62	2.60%	4.37%
Two or more categories	31	1.30%	1.51%

Population figures are in thousands. Persons counted as "Hispanic" (Latino) may be of any race. Because of overlapping categories, categories may not add up to 100%. Shares in column 3 are percentages of each category within the state; these figures may be compared to the national percentages in column 4.
Source: U.S. Bureau of the Census, 2006.

Projected state population, 2000-2030

Year	Population
2000	2,233,000
2005	2,418,000
2010	2,595,000
2015	2,783,000
2020	2,990,000
2025	3,226,000
2030	3,485,000
Population increase, 2000-2030	1,252,000
Percentage increase, 2000-2030	56.1

Projections are based on data from the 2000 census.
Source: U.S. Census Bureau.

VITAL STATISTICS

Infant mortality rates, 1980-2002

	1980	1990	2000	2002
All state residents	10.4	7.5	5.2	5.6
All U.S. residents	12.6	9.2	9.4	9.1
All state white residents	10.5	6.0	5.1	5.5
All U.S. white residents	10.6	7.6	5.7	5.8
All state black residents	27.3	—	—	—
All U.S. black residents	22.2	18.0	14.1	14.4

Figures represent deaths per 1,000 live births of resident infants under 1 year old, exclusive of fetal deaths. Figures for all residents include members of other racial categories not listed separately. The Census Bureau considers the post-1980 figures for black residents to be too small to be statistically meaningful.
Source: U.S. Census Bureau, *Statistical Abstract of the United States,* 2006.

Abortion rates, 1990 and 2000

	1990	2000
Total abortions	4,000	4,000
Rate per 1,000 women	9.2	6.6
U.S. rate	25.7	21.3
Rank	45	45

Numbers of abortions are rounded to nearest thousand; ranks are based on rates.
Source: U.S. Census Bureau.

Marriages and divorces, 2004

Total marriages	13,200
Rate per 1,000 population	5.5
National rate per 1,000 population	7.4
Rank among all states	47
Total divorces	9,300
Rate per 1,000 population	3.9
National rate per 1,000 population	3.7
Rank among all states	19

Figures are for all marriages and divorces performed within the state, including those of nonresidents; totals are rounded to the nearest hundred. Ranks are for highest to lowest figures; note that divorce data are not available for five states.
Source: U.S. National Center for Health Statistics, *Vital Statistics of the United States,* 2006.

Death rates by leading causes, 2002
Deaths per 100,000 resident population

Cause	State	U.S.
Heart disease	128.5	241.7
Cancer	102.6	193.2
Cerebrovascular diseases	39.0	56.4
Accidents other than motor vehicle	30.8	37.0
Motor vehicle accidents	14.2	15.7
Chronic lower respiratory diseases	26.0	43.3
Diabetes mellitus	22.2	25.4
HIV	n/a	4.9
Suicide	14.7	11.0
Homicide	2.3	6.1
All causes	566.3	847.3
Rank in overall death rate among states		49

Figures exclude nonresidents who died in the state. Causes of death follow International Classification of Diseases. Rank is from highest to lowest death rate in the United States.
Source: U.S. National Center for Health Statistics, *National Vital Statistics Report,* 2006.

ECONOMY

Gross state product, 1990-2004
In current dollars

Year	State product	Nat'l product	State share
1990	$31.4 billion	$5.67 trillion	0.55%
2000	$67.9 billion	$9.75 trillion	0.70%
2002	$73.6 billion	$10.41 trillion	0.71%
2003	$76.7 billion	$10.92 trillion	0.70%
2004	$82.4 billion	$11.65 trillion	0.71%

Source: U.S. Bureau of Economic Analysis, *Survey of Current Business,* July, 2005.

Gross state product by industry, 2003
In billions of dollars

Construction	$3.6
Manufacturing	8.0
Wholesale trade	3.9
Retail trade	6.3
Finance & insurance	6.6
Information	2.9
Professional services	4.4
Health care & social assistance	3.8
Government	9.9
Total state product	$71.6
Total U.S. product	$10,289.2
State share of U.S. total	0.70%
Rank among all states	33

Total figures include industries not listed separately. Amounts are in chained 2000 dollars.
Source: U.S. Bureau of Economic Analysis, *Survey of Current Business,* July, 2005.

Personal income per capita, 1990-2004
In current dollars

	1990	2000	2004
Per capita income	$14,913	$23,878	$26,606
U.S. average	$19,477	$29,845	$32,937
Rank among states	47	43	46

Source: U.S. Bureau of Economic Analysis, *Survey of Current Business,* April, 2005.

Energy consumption, 2001
In trillions of British thermal units (BTU), except as noted

Total energy consumption

Total state energy consumption	725
Total U.S. energy consumption	96,275
State share of U.S. total	0.75%
Rank among states	36

Per capita consumption (In millions of BTU)

Total state per capita consumption	318
Total U.S. per capita consumption	338
Rank among states	32

End-use sectors

Residential	140
Commercial	140
Industrial	233
Transportation	213

Sources of energy

Petroleum	261
Natural gas	168
Coal	390
Hydroelectric power	5
Nuclear electric power	0

Figures for totals include categories not listed separately.
Source: U.S. Energy Information Administration, *State Energy Data Report,* 2001.

Nonfarm employment by sectors, 2004

Total persons	1,103,000
Construction	73,000
Manufacturing	115,000
Trade, transportation, utilities	219,000
Information	30,000
Finance, insurance, real estate	65,000
Professional & business services	138,000
Education & health services	123,000
Leisure, hospitality, arts, organizations	102,000
Other services, including repair & maintenance . . .	33,000
Government	199,000

Figures are rounded to nearest thousand persons. "Total" includes mining and natural resources, not listed separately.
Source: U.S. Bureau of Labor Statistics, 2006.

Foreign exports, 1990-2004
In millions of dollars

Year	State	U.S.	State share
1990	1,596	394,045	0.41%
1996	3,296	624,767	0.53%
1997	3,239	688,896	0.47%
2000	3,221	712,055	0.41%
2003	4,115	724,006	0.61%
2004	4,718	769,332	0.61%

Rank among all states in 2004 31

U.S. total does not include U.S. dependencies.
Source: U.S. Census Bureau, *U.S. Merchandise Trade,* series FT 900, 2000; U.S. Census Bureau, *U.S. International Trade in Goods and Services,* Series FT 900, 2005.

LAND USE

Federally owned land, 2003
Areas in acres

	State	U.S.	State share
Total area	52,697,000	2,271,343,000	2.32%
Nonfederal land	17,672,000	1,599,584,000	1.10%
Federal land	35,025,000	671,759,000	5.21%
Federal share	66.5%	29.6%	—

Areas are rounded to nearest thousand acres. Figures for federally owned land do not include trust properties.
Source: U.S. General Services Administration, *Federal Real Property Profile,* 2006.

Land use, 1997
In acres, rounded to nearest thousand

Total surface area 54,339,000
Total nonfederal rural land. 17,599,000
Percentage rural land 32.4%
Cropland 1,679,000
Conservation Reserve Program (CRP*) land. . . . 216,000
Pastureland 695,000
Rangeland 10,733,000
Forestland. 1,883,000
Other rural land 2,392,000

*CRP is a federal program begun in 1985 to assist private landowners to convert highly erodible cropland to vegetative cover for ten years. Note that some categories of land overlap.
Source: U.S. Department of Agriculture, Natural Resources and Conservation Service, and Iowa State University, Statistical Laboratory, S*ummary Report, 1997 National Resources Inventory,* revised December, 2000.

Farms and crop acreage, 2004

	State	U.S.	Share	Rank
Farms	15,000	2,113,000	0.71%	36
Acres (millions)	12	937	1.28%	24
Acres per farm	758	443	—	11

Source: U.S. Department of Agriculture, National Agricultural Statistics Service. Numbers of farms are rounded to nearest thousand units; acreage figures are rounded to nearest million. Rankings, including ties, are based on rounded figures.

GOVERNMENT AND FINANCE

Units of local government, 2002

	State	Total U.S.	Rank
All local governments	605	87,525	40
Counties	29	3,034	36
Municipalities	236	19,429	32
Townships	0	16,504	—
School districts	40	13,506	40
Special districts	300	35,052	38

Only 48 states have county governments, 20 states have township governments ("towns" in New England, Minnesota, New York, and Wisconsin), and 46 states have school districts. Special districts encompass such functions as natural resources, fire protection, and housing and community development.
Source: U.S. Census Bureau, *Census of Governments.*

State government revenue, 2002

Total revenue. . . . . $8,468 mill.
General revenue . . . . $8,623 mill.
Per capita revenue $3,717
U.S. per capita average $3,689
Rank among states 26

Intergovernment revenue
Total . . . . $2,279 mill.
From federal government . . . . $2,267 mill.

Charges and miscellaneous
Total . . . . $2,419 mill.
Current charges . . . . $1,675 mill.
Misc. general income . . . . $744 mill.
Insurance trust revenue . . . . −$288 mill.

Taxes
Total . . . . $3,925 mill.
Per capita taxes $1,693
Rank among states 33
Property taxes . . . . (nil)
Sales taxes . . . . $2,023 mill.
License taxes . . . . $148 mill.
Individual income taxes . . . . $1,605 mill.
Corporate income taxes . . . . $111 mill.
Other taxes . . . . $38 mill.

Total revenue figures include items not listed separately here.
Source: U.S. Bureau of the Census.

State government expenditures, 2002

General expenditures

Total state expenditures	$10,107 mill.
Intergovernmental	$2,171 mill.

Per capita expenditures

State	$3,942
Average of all states	$3,859
Rank among states	24

Selected direct expenditures

Education	$2,351 mill.
Public welfare	$1,573 mill.
Health, hospital	$685 mill.
Highways	$728 mill.
Police protection	$104 mill.
Corrections	$268 mill.
Natural resources	$179 mill.
Parks and recreation	$60 mill.
Government administration	$462 mill.
Interest on debt	$188 mill.
Total direct expenditures	$6,972 mill.

Totals include items not listed separately.
Source: U.S. Census Bureau.

POLITICS

Governors since statehood
D = Democrat; R = Republican; O = other;
(r) resigned; (d) died in office; (i) removed from office

Heber M. Wells (R)	1896-1905
John C. Cutler (R)	1905-1909
William Spry (R)	1909-1917
Simon Bamberger (D)	1917-1921
Charles R. Mabey (R)	1921-1925
George H. Dern (D)	1925-1933
Henry H. Blood (D)	1933-1941
Herbert B. Maw (D)	1941-1949
Joseph Bracken Lee (D)	1949-1957
George D. Clyde (R)	1957-1965
Calvin L. Rampton (D)	1965-1977
Scott M. Matheson (R)	1977-1985
Norman H. Bangerter (R)	1985-1993
Mike Leavitt (R)	1993-2003
Olene Smith Walker (R)	2003-2005
Jon Meade Huntsman, Jr. (R)	2005-

Composition of congressional delegations, 1989-2007

	Dem	Rep	Total
House of Representatives			
101st Congress, 1989			
State delegates	1	2	3
Total U.S.	259	174	433
102d Congress, 1991			
State delegates	2	1	3
Total U.S.	267	167	434
103d Congress, 1993			
State delegates	2	1	3
Total U.S.	258	176	434
104th Congress, 1995			
State delegates	0	3	3
Total U.S.	197	236	433
105th Congress, 1997			
State delegates	0	3	3
Total U.S.	206	228	434
106th Congress, 1999			
State delegates	0	3	3
Total U.S.	211	222	433
107th Congress, 2001			
State delegates	1	2	3
Total U.S.	211	221	432
108th Congress, 2003			
State delegates	1	2	3
Total U.S.	205	229	434
109th Congress, 2005			
State delegates	1	2	3
Total U.S.	202	231	433
110th Congress, 2007			
State delegates	1	2	3
Total U.S.	233	202	435
Senate			
101st Congress, 1989			
State delegates	0	2	2
Total U.S.	55	45	100
102d Congress, 1991			
State delegates	0	2	2
Total U.S.	56	44	100
103d Congress, 1993			
State delegates	0	2	2
Total U.S.	57	43	100
104th Congress, 1995			
State delegates	0	2	2
Total U.S.	46	53	99
105th Congress, 1997			
State delegates	0	2	2
Total U.S.	45	55	100

(continued)

	Dem	Rep	Total
106th Congress, 1999			
State delegates	0	2	2
Total U.S.	45	54	99
107th Congress, 2001			
State delegates	0	2	2
Total U.S.	50	50	100
108th Congress, 2003			
State delegates	0	2	2
Total U.S.	48	51	99
109th Congress, 2005			
State delegates	0	2	2
Total U.S.	44	55	99
110th Congress, 2007			
State delegates	0	2	2
Total U.S.	49	49	98

Figures are for starts of first sessions. Totals are for Democrat (Dem.) and Republican (Rep.) members only. House membership totals under 435 and Senate totals under 100 reflect vacancies and seats held by independent party members. When the 110th Congress opened, the Senate's two independent members caucused with the Democrats, giving the Democrats control of the Senate.
Source: U.S. Congress, *Congressional Directory.*

Composition of state legislature, 1990-2006

	Democrats	Republicans
State House (75 seats)		
1990	31	44
1992	26	49
1994	20	55
1996	20	55
1998	21	54
2000	21	54
2002	19	56
2004	19	56
2006	20	55
State Senate (29 seats)		
1990	10	19
1992	11	18
1994	10	19
1996	9	20
1998	11	18
2000	11	18
2002	7	22
2004	8	21
2006	8	21

Figures for total seats may include independents and minor party members. Numbers reflect results of elections in listed years; elected members usually take their seats in the years that follow.
Source: Council of State Governments; *State Elective Officials and the Legislatures.*

Voter participation in presidential elections, 2000 and 2004

	2000	2004
Voting age population		
State	1,522,000	1,649,000
Total United States	209,831,000	220,377,000
State share of U.S. total	0.73	0.75
Rank among states	34	35
Portion of voting age population casting votes		
State	50.6%	56.3%
United States	50.3%	55.5%
Rank among states	30	30

Population figures are rounded to nearest thousand and include all residents, regardless of eligibility to vote.
Source: U.S. Census Bureau.

HEALTH AND MEDICAL CARE

Medical professionals
Physicians in 2003 and nurses in 2001

	U.S.	State
Physicians in 2003		
Total	774,849	4,987
Share of U.S. total		0.64%
Rate	266	212
Rank		40
Nurses in 2001		
Total	2,262,020	13,830
Share of U.S. total		0.61%
Rate	793	607
Rank		47

Rates are numbers of physicians and nurses per 100,000 resident population; ranks are based on rates.
Source: American Medical Association, *Physician Characteristics and Distribution in the U.S.*; U.S. Department of Health and Human Services, Health Resources and Services Administration.

Health insurance coverage, 2003

	State	U.S.
Total persons covered	2,055,000	243,320,000
Total persons not covered	298,000	44,961,000
Portion not covered	12.7%	15.6%
Rank among states	31	—
Children not covered	69,000	8,373,000
Portion not covered	9.0%	11.4%
Rank among states	24	—

Totals are rounded to nearest thousand. Ranks are from the highest to the lowest percentages of persons *not* insured.
Source: U.S. Census Bureau, Current Population Reports.

AIDS, syphilis, and tuberculosis cases, 2003

Disease	U.S. cases	State cases	Rank
AIDS	44,232	75	39
Syphilis	34,270	72	36
Tuberculosis	14,874	39	39

Source: U.S. Centers for Disease Control and Prevention.

Cigarette smoking, 2003
Residents over age 18 who smoke

	U.S.	State	Rank
All smokers	22.1%	12.0%	50
Male smokers	24.8%	14.0%	50
Female smokers	20.3%	9.9%	50

Cigarette smokers are defined as persons who reported having
  smoked at least 100 cigarettes during their lifetimes and who
  currently smoked at least occasionally.
Source: U.S. Centers for Disease Control and Prevention, *Morbidity
  and Mortality Weekly Report,* 53, no. 44 (November 12, 2004).

HOUSING

Home ownership rates, 1985-2004

	1985	1990	1995	2000	2004
State	71.5%	70.1%	71.5%	72.7%	74.9%
Total U.S.	63.9%	63.9%	64.7%	67.4%	69.0%
Rank among states	6	9	7	15	8

Net change in state home ownership rate, 1985-2004	+3.4%
Net change in U.S. home ownership rate, 1985-2004	+5.1%

Percentages represent the proportion of owner households to total
  occupied households.
Source: U.S. Census Bureau, 2006.

Home sales, 2000-2004
In thousands of units

Existing home sales	2000	2002	2003	2004
State sales	35.5	40.9	43.9	43.6
Total U.S. sales	5,171	5,631	6,183	6,784
State share of U.S. total	0.69%	0.73%	0.71%	0.64%
Sales rank among states	35	35	35	36

Units include single-family homes, condos, and co-ops.
Source: National Association of Realtors, Washington, D.C., *Real
  Estate Outlook: Market Trends & Insights.*

Values of owner-occupied homes, 2003

	State	U.S.
Total units	488,000	58,809,000
Value of units		
Under $100,000	11.2%	29.6%
$100,000-199,999	60.8%	36.9%
$200,000 or more	28.0%	33.5%
Median value	$156,657	$142,275
Rank among all states		19

Units are owner-occupied one-family houses whose numbers are
  rounded to nearest thousand. Data are extrapolated from
  survey samples.
Source: U.S. Census Bureau, American Community Survey.

EDUCATION

Public school enrollment, 2002

Prekindergarten through grade 8

State enrollment	343,000
Total U.S. enrollment.	34,135,000
State share of U.S. total	1.00%

Grades 9 through 12

State enrollment	147,000
Total U.S. enrollment.	14,067,000
State share of U.S. total	1.04%

Enrollment rates

State public school enrollment rate.	95.5%
Overall U.S. rate	90.4%
Rank among states in 2002	4
Rank among states in 1995	2

Enrollment figures (which include unclassified students) are
  rounded to nearest thousand pupils during fall school term.
  Enrollment rates are based on enumerated resident population
  estimate for July 1, 2002.
Source: U.S. National Center for Education Statistics.

Public college finances, 2003-2004

FTE enrollment in public institutions of higher education

Students in state institutions 108,600
Students in all U.S. public institutions 9,916,600
State share of U.S. total 1.10
Rank among states 32

State and local government appropriations for higher education

State appropriation per FTE $5,048
National average $5,716
Rank among states 35
State & local tax revenue going to higher
    education 10.2%

FTE = full-time equivalent in public postsecondary programs,
    including summer sessions; student numbers are rounded to
    nearest hundred. Funding figures for 2003-2004 academic year
    include financial aid to students in state public institutions and
    exclude money for research, agriculture experiment stations,
    teaching hospitals, and medical schools; figures are rounded to
    nearest thousand dollars.
Source: Higher Education Executive Officers, Denver, Colorado.

TRANSPORTATION AND TRAVEL

Highway mileage, 2003

Interstate highways 940
Other freeways and expressways 7
Arterial roads 3,360
Collector roads 7,838
Local roads 30,571
Urban roads 8,189
Rural roads 34,527
Total state mileage 42,716
U.S. total 3,974,107
State share 1.07%
Rank among states 36

Note that combined urban and rural road mileage matches the
    total of the other categories.
Source: U.S. Federal Highway Administration.

Motor vehicle registrations and driver licenses, 2003

Vehicle registrations	State	U.S.	Share	Rank
Autos, trucks, buses	2,006,000	231,390,000	0.87%	32
Autos only	1,014,000	135,670	0.75%	31
Motorcycles	38,000	5,328,000	0.71%	35
Driver licenses	1,548,000	196,166,000	0.79%	34

Figures, which do not include vehicles owned by military services,
    are rounded to the nearest thousand. Figures for automobiles
    include taxis.
Source: U.S. Federal Highway Administration.

Domestic travel expenditures, 2003
Spending by U.S. residents on overnight trips and
day trips of at least 50 miles from home

Total expenditures within state . . . . $3.73 bill.
Total expenditures within U.S. . . . . $490.87 bill.
State share of U.S. total 0.8%
Rank among states 37

Source: Travel Industry Association of America.

Retail gasoline prices, 2003-2007
Average price per gallon at the pump

Year	U.S.	State
2003	$1.267	$1.247
2004	$1.316	$1.362
2005	$1.644	$1.580
2007	$2.298	$2.295

Excise tax per gallon in 2004 . . . . 24.5¢
Rank among all states in 2007 prices 23

Prices are averages of all grades of gasoline sold at the pump
    during March months in 2003-2005 and during February, 2007.
    Averages for 2006, during which prices rose higher, are not
    available.
Source: U.S. Energy Information Agency, *Petroleum Marketing
    Monthly* (2003-2005 data); American Automobile Association
    (2007 data).

CRIME AND LAW ENFORCEMENT

State and local police officers, 2000-2004

	2000	2002	2004
Total officers			
U.S.	654,601	665,555	675,734
State	4,641	4,636	4,525*
*Net change, 2000-2004			−2.50%
Officers per 1,000 residents			
U.S.	2.33	2.31	2.30
State	2.08	2.00	1.89
State rank	26	31	33

Totals include state and local police and sheriffs.
Source: Carsey Institute, University of New Hampshire.

Crime rates, 2003
Incidents per 100,000 residents

Crimes	State	U.S.
Violent crimes		
Total incidents	249	475
Murder	3	6
Forcible rape	38	32
Robbery	53	142
Aggravated assault	155	295
Property crimes		
Total incidents	4,226	3,588
Burglary	713	741
Larceny/theft	3,182	2,415
Motor vehicle theft	330	433
All crimes	4,475	4,063

Source: U.S. Federal Bureau of Investigation, *Crime in the United States*, annual.

State prison populations, 1980-2003

	State	U.S.	State share
1980	932	305,458	0.31%
1990	2,496	708,393	0.35%
1996	3,972	1,025,624	0.39%
2000	5,637	1,391,261	0.41%
2003	5,763	1,470,045	0.39%

State figures exclude prisoners in federal penitentiaries.
Source: U.S. Bureau of Justice Statistics, *Prisoners in 2003.*

Vermont

Location: New England

Area and rank: 9,249 square miles (23,956 square kilometers); 9,615 square miles (24,903 square kilometers) including water; forty-third largest state in area

Coastline: none

Population and rank: 621,000 (2004); forty-ninth largest state in population

Capital city: Montpelier (8,035 people in 2000 census)

Largest city: Burlington (38,889 people in 2000 census)

Entered Union and rank: March 4, 1791; fourteenth state

Present constitution adopted: 1793

The statehouse in Montpelier, decorated for Vermont's bicentennial celebration in 1991. (©ThomasWalters/Dreamstime.com)

Counties: 14

State name: "Vermont" is taken from the French "*vert mont,*" for "green mountain"

State nickname: Green Mountain State

Motto: Vermont, Freedom and Unity

State flag: Blue field with state coat of arms

Highest point: Mount Mansfield—4,393 feet (1,339 meters)

Lowest point: Lake Champlain—95 feet (29 meters)

Highest recorded temperature: 105 degrees Fahrenheit (41 degrees Celsius)—1911

Lowest recorded temperature: –50 degrees Fahrenheit (–46 degrees Celsius)—Bloomfield, 1933

State song: "These Green Mountains" (replaces "Hail, Vermont!")

State tree: Sugar maple

State flower: Red clover

State bird: Hermit thrush

State animal: Morgan horse

Vermont History

ermont is the seventh smallest state. The only New England state not bordered by the Atlantic Ocean, Vermont is bordered by New Hampshire in the east, New York on the west, Massachusetts in the south, and Quebec, Canada, in the north. Vermont owns more than half of Lake Champlain, which makes up half of the state's western border.

Vermont's terrain has a little of everything, from the Taconic Mountains, with good granite quarries, to the Champlain Valley, with the flattest land and best soil in the state, to the Green Mountains, which run through the middle of the state. There are about 430 lakes and ponds in Vermont, 420 named peaks, and forests on about 80 percent of the land. The waterways in the state provide trade routes to Canada and New York, and the forests produce hardwood, paper, and the nation's largest supply of maple syrup.

Native American Lands. Until the sixteenth century, Vermont land was inhabited by Abenaki, Mahican, and Pennacook Indians, all members of the Algonquian tribe. Then the land was overtaken by tribes of the powerful Iroquois Confederacy. When French settlers arrived during the seventeenth century, they allied themselves with the Algonquians, because they wanted to trade furs with them. The first permanent white settlement in Vermont was Fort Dummer in the southeast, built by the English to protect Massachusetts residents from French and American Indian raids. There were never any major battles between Native Americans and Europeans over land, as there were in the rest of New England. Still, American Indians were made unwelcome in the state, and they made up less than 2 percent of Vermont's population during the late twentieth century.

At Vermont's Battle of Bennington in 1777, the Continental army defeated a major British force. (Library of Congress)

Settlement of Vermont. After French explorer Samuel de Champlain settled Quebec and Montreal, he traveled south on the Richelieu River into the lake named for him. In 1609, he claimed the Vermont area for France, naming the mountains *Vert Mont* (green mountains). The French built a few military posts to protect their land and established a fur trade with the Algonquians, but Vermont, unlike the other New England states and New York, was not settled for a long time.

In 1724, Dutch newcomers moved into the southwest of the state, and in 1750 Vermont began to attract settlers. Benning Wentworth, the royal governor of New Hampshire, sold pieces of land west of the Connecticut River to pay off his debts, though he had no claims to the region. Between 1750 and 1764, 138 towns on 3 million acres were established, and the area was called the New Hampshire Grants.

From 1754 to 1763, the French and Indian War raged because of land disputes between the French and British. Fighting in the Lake Champlain area ended with the British, with Iroquois allies, defeating the French and Algonquians. The 1763 Treaty of Paris, ending the war, gave control of Vermont to Great Britain.

The governor of New York, George Clinton, had also been making claims on the New Hampshire Grants. After he decreed that settlers in the Grants should pay New York for their land, the landowners in the Grants went to King George III of England with their cause. The king sided with the Grants residents, ordering Clinton not to bother them or to issue any land grants for land that was not his. However, in 1769-1770 Clinton gave titles to 600,000 acres in the Grants and tried to evict those who lived there. Some Vermonters, called the Bennington Nine, fought New York's claims to the area and formed a regiment, the Green Mountain Boys, led by Ethan Allen. The group drove the New York settlers out of the region.

The American Revolution. The Green Mountain Boys were active in the American Revolution (1775-1783), capturing Fort Ticonderoga, a British military post, and a British ship in 1775. Even though they logically should have sided with the British for supporting their claims to the Vermont land, they were more interested in liberty for the United States. American Indians fought on the British side, hoping to be able to keep some of their rightful land, in vain. The only Revolutionary battle fought for Vermont took place in August of 1777 at the Battle of Bennington. Although the battle took place on New York land, the fight remains significant to Vermonters because Vermont won, leading to the defeat of the British at Saratoga, a turning point in the war.

Independence. In 1777, the residents of the New Hampshire Grants declared their independence from England and New York and called their state New Connecticut. Five months later, they changed the name to Vermont. In 1777, they drafted a constitution; the Bill of Rights from that year would be used for more than two hundred years. In 1778, Vermont declared itself independent of the Continental Congress, because the region believed the Congress was a danger to Vermont's liberty; the area made a separate peace treaty with Britain.

Although the Congress wanted to invade Vermont, General George Washington warned against it, but he advised Vermont governor Thomas Chittenden to relinquish his claims to thirty-five New Hampshire and fourteen New York towns. In 1790, Vermont paid New York thirty thousand dollars for disputed land. In 1791, it became the fourteenth state, but its people never forgot its tradition of independence and the fact that it was, unlike the rest of New England, never an English colony.

Like its neighbor New Hampshire, Vermont is rich in granite quarries. (Vermont Department of Tourism & Marketing)

Industry. Vermont's early industry depended on water and timber, of which the state had plenty. Gristmills, sawmills, and paper mills were built on the state's fast streams. In 1805, Brattleboro became a printing center, and cities such as Brandon became iron-mining hubs. The first canal built in the United States was at Bellows Falls in the Connecticut River in 1802, and steamboats began operating on Lake Champlain in 1808, carrying goods to and from Canada. The Embargo Act of 1807 mandated against trade between the United States and foreign countries, so Vermonters had to smuggle food and lumber into Canada in order to maintain their livelihoods.

A special breed of horse, the Justin Morgan, was bred to plow hilly farms in the state, and Spanish merino sheep were imported for the manufacture of wool, leading to the opening of tanneries, carding mills, and finally textile factories. During the 1870's-1880's industries and cities grew, but Vermont never became fully industrialized, like the rest of New England, with huge cities and numerous factories. The state stayed mostly rural. In fact, the Great Depression of the 1930's did not really affect Vermont because the state was so rural.

Economy. During the War of 1812 the economy boomed, because the production of wool was essential for troops fighting Britain. However, after the war, in 1814, trade with Britain resumed, lowering wool prices. By 1820 the economy was doing poorly, and thousands of people left the state. The construction of the Champlain-Hudson Canal in 1823 and the Erie Canal in 1825 helped trade, but by the 1840's Vermonters were leaving again because of cheaper land in the West and depleted resources and topsoil in the state. The residents who stayed behind turned to dairy farming, which would be Vermont's main industry for more than one hundred years.

Although during the 1820's-1850's the population was declining, more so-called summer people were visiting the state for the refreshing air and spring waters. Tourism became a big business, and Vermont was the first state to open a state publicity service to encourage tourism, in 1891. After the Civil War (1861-1865) agriculture stayed in decline, and more Vermonters took the federal government's offer of cheap land in the West. However, immigrants began flocking to the state, from Ireland, Scotland, Italy, Spain, and Sweden. During the late twentieth century most immigrants, about 9 percent, were from Quebec.

World War II. The Vermont General Assembly declared war on Germany in September of 1941, three months before Pearl Harbor was attacked. Because Vermont men in training for the war returned fire under attack at sea, they declared war. The state sent fifty thousand soldiers to the war. Vermont experienced a huge population growth after the 1940's, with people looking to return to a quieter, simpler way of life. The state was still two-thirds rural, with the highest proportion of rural residents in the country.

Independent Thinkers. Vermont never followed the religious movements of the rest of New England, such as the Puritan or Congregationalist faiths. For this they were deemed atheistic sinners by the surrounding communities.

Vermont was very antislavery, providing numerous stops on the Underground Railroad, the escape route for slaves out of the South. Vermonters were so antislavery that more than 75 percent voted for Abraham Lincoln in 1860 than for opponent Stephen Douglas,

who was a native Vermonter. Vermont contributed more than $9 million and thirty-five thousand men to the Civil War effort on the Union side.

After the Civil War the state became notoriously Republican-minded, and it remained that way until 1958. During the 1950's and 1960's, it became more liberal, electing a Democrat, William H. Meyer, to the House of Representatives for the first time in more than one hundred years. In 1974, Patrick Leahy became the first Democratic senator from Vermont since the inception of the Republican Party in 1854.

Environment and Industry. Soon after World War II, Vermont became a huge ski attraction, due to the invention of the mechanized rope tow to pull skiers up a mountain. The downside of this technology and influx of people is that the environment suffered. In 1970, the Environmental Control Law was passed to cut down on pollution and development. It stated that developers would have to prove their projects would have no adverse effects on the surrounding environment.

By the 1990's, the service industry was the largest in the state, accounting for 67 percent of the workforce

Vermont is the nation's leading producer of maple syrup, which is made from a sugar extracted from maple trees. (Vermont Department of Tourism & Marketing/Andre Jenny)

and 62 percent of the gross state product (GSP), mostly in the tourism and leisure fields. Manufacturing accounted for 21 percent of the workers and 26 percent of the GSP, and agriculture only applied to 6 percent of the workers and 1 percent of the GSP. However, 40 percent of the dairy in New England comes from Vermont, and it is the leading producer of maple syrup in the United States.

Civil Unions. Vermont began the new millennium with a public controversy. In *Baker v. Vermont* (1999), the Vermont Supreme Court ruled that the state must provide same-sex couples the same rights and privileges as heterosexual couples. This ruling provoked lively public debate between those who favored same-sex marriage and those who opposed it. As a compromise, the legislature decided upon "civil unions" legislation. Such unions would give nearly identical rights to same-sex couples as accorded to traditional opposite-sex marriages in state (not federal) law. The state House of Representatives passed the bill 79-68, and the Senate passed it 19-11, after which it was signed into law by Governor Howard Dean.

Electoral Politics. The presidential election in 2000 was won by a substantial margin by Al Gore over George W. Bush. Gore received 51 percent to the Texas gover- nor's 41 percent of the vote, gaining Gore the state's three electoral votes. In other races, voters returned former Burlington mayor Bernie Sanders to Congress. Sanders had first been elected when he scored a tremendous upset of a sitting member in 1990. He then became the first independent member of Congress since 1950. Having been reelected four times, in 2000 he scored a fifth reelection, taking 70 percent of the vote. In 2002, Sanders won 65 percent of the vote and in 2004, 69 percent. His politics were consistently left of center, including a 2002 vote against authorizing the use of force in Iraq. In 2006, Sanders announced that he would run for the seat in the U.S. Senate being vacated by his friend Jim Jeffords, formerly a Republican, who switched to Independent and subsequently announced his retirement. The state's other U.S. senator, Democrat Patrick Leahy, was easily reelected in 2004, receiving nearly 71 percent of the vote. It was noteworthy that Leahy was one of two senators targeted in the anthrax terrorist attacks of October, 2001. The letter addressed to him was misdirected, however, and never arrived in his offices. Discovered on November 16, the letter was laced with far more potent anthrax than the initial anthrax letters first sent during the week of September 18.

Church Street in Vermont's largest city, Burlington. (Vermont Department of Tourism & Marketing)

By 2002, both Vermont's public life and the nation's politics were affected by the political decisions of Governor Howard Dean. Dean, a medical doctor, abandoned medicine for politics in 1982, when he was elected to the state legislature. Assuming the office of governor in 1991 when the governor died, he was re-elected to five two-year terms of office, winning in 2000 by 50.4 percent to his opponent's 37 percent of the vote. In 2002, however, Dean decided against reelection, allowing Republican state treasurer Jim Douglas, by a narrow 3 percent margin, to succeed him. Dean then announced his candidacy for president. While not successful, his candidacy was credited with energizing the Democrats' political base. Dean went on to become chairperson of the Democratic National Committee, a consequential position from which by 2006 he was exercising considerable influence. In the 2004 presidential poll, Democrat John Kerry, from neighboring Massachusetts, scored a substantial 59-39 percent victory over the sitting president.

Lauren M. Mitchell
Updated by the Editor

Vermont Time Line

1500's	Algonquian tribes are overtaken by Iroquois tribes.
1609	Samuel de Champlain claims Vermont for France.
1666	First French settlement, Forte Sainte Anne, is built on Isle La Motte.
1690	First English trading post, Chimney Point Fort, is constructed.
1724	British found first permanent settlement, Fort Dummer, in southeast.
1752	First maple syrup is made by Europeans.
1754-1763	French and Indian War is fought in Lake Champlain region.
1763	Control of Vermont passes to Britain; New Hampshire and New York lay claims to the land.
1770	Green Mountain Boys regiment forms to protect Vermont from New York control.
1775	Green Mountain Boys capture Fort Ticonderoga during the Revolution.
Jan. 15, 1777	Vermont declares its independence from Britain and establishes republic.
July, 1777	State constitution is written; Vermont becomes first state to abolish slavery.
1785	First marble quarry in United States opens in Vermont.
1790	New York sells its land claims in Vermont for thirty thousand dollars.
1790	First U.S. patent is given to Samuel Hopkins of Pittsford for making potash out of wood ashes.
Mar. 4, 1791	Vermont becomes fourteenth state.
1791	University of Vermont is founded.
1793	First American copper mine opens at Strafford.
1800	Middlebury College is chartered.
1802	Bellows Falls canal is first in the country.
1805	Montpelier becomes state capital.
1814	First school of higher education for women opens at Middlebury.
1823	Champlain-Hudson canal opens.
1848	First railroad opens.
1861	Vermont is first state to offer troops to Union during Civil War.
Oct., 1864	Confederate soldiers raid Saint Albans, in northernmost Civil War confrontation.
1896	Vermont is first state to implement an absentee voting law.
Aug. 3, 1923	Calvin Coolidge is sworn in as U.S. president in Plymouth Notch, Vermont.
1931	First state income tax is instituted.
1933	First ski tow in the country opens at Woodstock, Vermont.
1938	Hurricane kills five, causes $12 million in damage.
Sept. 11, 1941	Vermont declares war on Germany.
1954	Vermont's Consuelo N. Bailey is first woman in country elected a lieutenant governor.
1958	William Meyer is first Vermont Democrat elected to Congress since 1854.
1964	Vermont votes Democratic in a presidential race for the first time in its history.
1970	Environmental Conservation Agency is established.
1974	Patrick Leahy is first Democratic senator elected in Vermont since 1854.
Jan. 26, 1976	Vermont Nuclear Power Corporation closes as a safety precaution.

(continued)

1976	Abenaki Indians are given official status to qualify for federal benefits; the next year the status is revoked by Governor Richard Snelling.
1985	Madeline Kunin becomes first elected female governor of Vermont.
Mar. 11, 1992	Ice floes dam Winooski River, flooding Montpelier.
June 17, 1992	Vermont supreme court denies a claim by Abenaki Indians to 150 square miles of land.
2000	Governor Howard Dean signs into law a civil unions bill for same-sex couples.
Nov. 7, 2000	Al Gore gains Vermont's three electoral votes in presidential balloting; Governor Dean reelected to fifth term.
Oct., 2001	Senator Patrick Leahy targeted in anthrax terrorist attacks.
Nov. 5, 2002	Republican Jim Douglas elected to succeed five-term governor Howard Dean.
Nov. 2, 2004	Independent congress member Bernie Sanders is reelected for the sixth time.

Notes for Further Study

Published Sources. *Vermont: A History* (1993) by Charles T. Morrissey is a good place to learn the background of the state. Other good general history books include *The Story of Vermont* (1999) by Christopher McGrory Klyza and Stephen C. Trombulak and *Tales of Vermont Ways and People* (1989) by Bertha Sanford Dodge. *Hands on the Land: A History of the Vermont Landscape* (2000) by Jan Albers offers a look into the natural, environmental, social, and human history of the state, and *Freedom and Unity: A History of Vermont* (2004) by Michael Sherman et al. gives the reader a comprehensive narrative of the state's history, from prehistoric times to the present day. Excellent books for the traveler to Vermont are *The Beauty of Vermont* (1998) by Tom Slayton and Elizabeth Bassett's *Nature Walks in Northern Vermont and the Champlain Valley* (1998). For more specialized studies, readers should see *The Abenaki* (1996) by Elaine Landau, *Vermont Native Americans* (2004) by Carole Marsh, and *The Original Vermonters: Native Inhabitants, Past and Present* (1994) by William A. Haviland and Marjory W. Power. *The Vermont Encyclopedia* (2003) by John J. Duffy et al. offers seven overview essays on several topics, including the state's culture, politics, and demographics, which are then followed by more than one thousand entries. *Vermont Off the Beaten Path* (6th ed., 2004) by Barbara Radcliffe Rogers and Stillman Rogers offers a good tourist guide to the state's attractions.

A good overview of early America is found in *Voyages and Explorations of Samuel de Champlain, Sixteen Four to Sixteen Sixteen* (1973), Champlain's own writings edited by Edward Gaylord Bourne. *The Great Warpath: British Military Sites from Albany to Crown Point* (1999) by David R. Starbuck is an excellent report from an archaeologist detailing the lives of soldiers during the Revolution, including accounts from Fort Ticonderoga. Stewart H. Holbrook's *Ethan Allen* (1992) and

Michael T. Hahn's *Ethan Allen: A Life of Adventure* (1994) chronicle the life of the Revolutionary soldier. Civil War history is recounted in *Full Duty: Vermonters in the Civil War* (1995) by Howard Coffin and *A War of the People: Vermont Civil War Letters* (1999) edited by Jeffrey D. Marshall. The latter contains correspondence written by Vermont soldiers in the 1860's.

Web Resources. The best place to start for Vermont information and links to other Web sites is the official state site (vermont.gov/). Vermont Judiciary (www.state.vt.us/courts) has calendars and court schedules, Vermont Legislative Home Page (www.leg.state.vt.us) has fiscal facts, schedules, reports, and documents, and Vermont Democratic Party (www.vt democrats.org/) contains information on that party, with links to party members. For tourist and travel information, Link Vermont (www.linkvermont.com) offers a calendar of events, rental listings, and more, from the Board of Tourism. Vermont.com (www.vermont.com) also offers lodging and entertainment updates.

Virtual Vermont (www.virtualvermont.com/index.php ?loc=www.virtualvermont.com/history/index.html) provides articles on historical topics and links for further historical research. Another good Web site related to the state's history is Samuel de Champlain (www.samueldechamplain .com/, which gives background about the explorer and his findings. About the Ethan Allen Homestead (www.uvm.edu/ ~vhnet/hertour/eallen/eahome.html) has good information about the Green Mountain Boys. The French and Indian War site (www.militaryheritage.com/7yrswar.htm) has much information and many links to other resources. The Abenaki Home Page (millennianet.com/slmiller/abenaki) contains maps, history of the Native American tribe, and links. Also good is the Traditional Abenaki Web site (www.bmuschool .org/webquests/webquest1/Traditional.html).

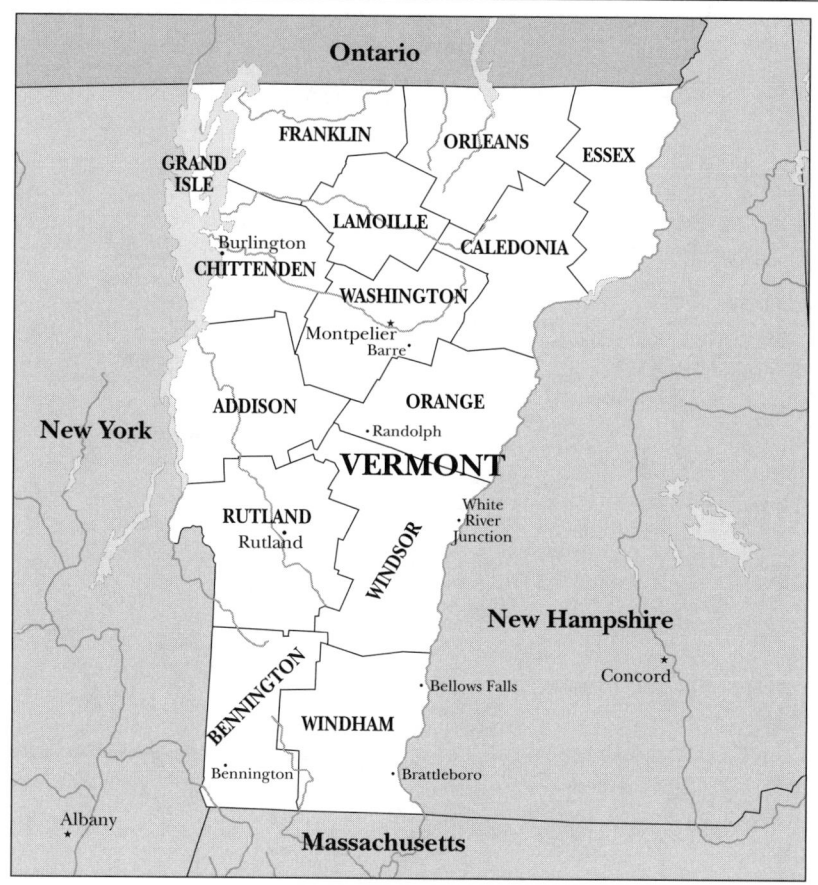

Counties

County	2000 pop.	Rank in pop.	Sq. miles	Rank in area
Addison	35,974	8	770.0	4
Bennington	36,994	7	676.3	8
Caledonia	29,702	9	651.0	10
Chittenden	146,571	1	539.0	12
Essex	6,459	14	665.3	9
Franklin	45,417	5	637.1	11
Grand Isle	6,901	13	82.6	14
Lamoille	23,233	12	460.6	13

County	2000 pop.	Rank in pop.	Sq. miles	Rank in area
Orange	28,226	10	688.7	7
Orleans	26,277	11	696.9	5
Rutland	63,400	2	932.2	2
Washington	58,039	3	689.6	6
Windham	44,216	6	788.8	3
Windsor	57,418	4	971.3	1

Source: U.S. Census Bureau; National Association of Counties.

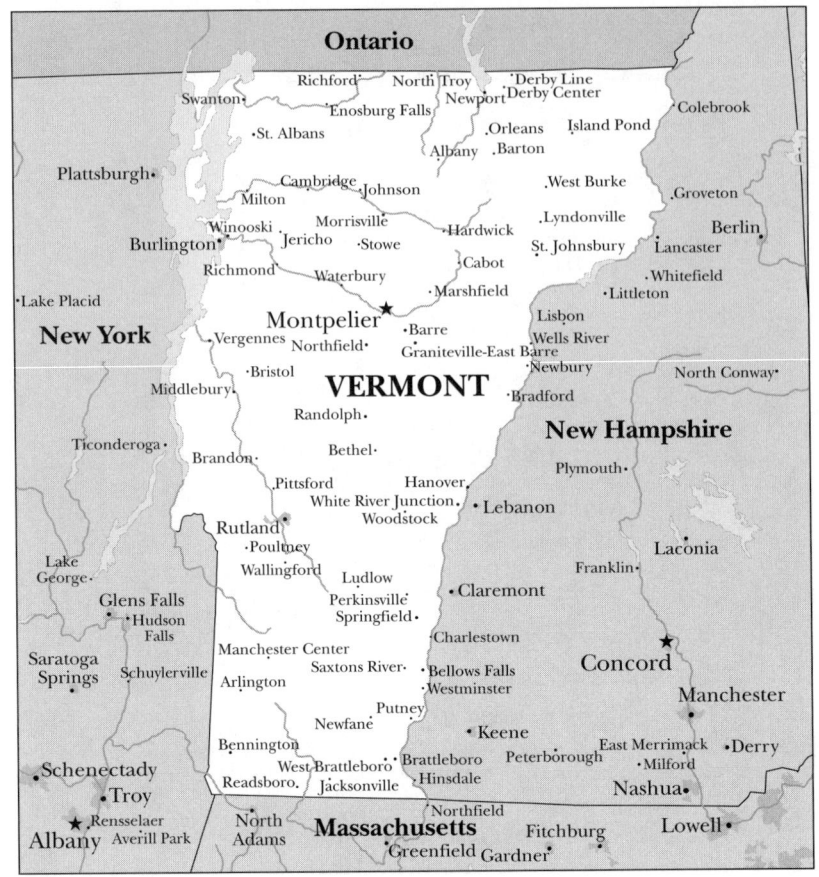

Cities

With 6,000 or more residents

Rank	City	Population	Rank	City	Population
1	Burlington	38,889	13	Brattleboro	8,289
2	Essex	18,626	14	Middlebury	8,183
3	Rutland	17,292	15	Montpelier (capital)	8,035
4	Colchester	16,986	16	Williston	7,650
5	South Burlington	15,814	17	St. Albans	7,650
6	Bennington	15,737	18	St. Johnsbury	7,571
7	Brattleboro	12,005	19	Shelburne	6,944
8	Hartford	10,367	20	Winooski	6,561
9	Milton	9,479	21	Swanton	6,203
10	Barre	9,291			
11	Springfield	9,078			
12	Essex Junction	8,591			

Population figures are from 2000 census.
Source: U.S. Bureau of the Census.

Index to Tables

DEMOGRAPHICS

Resident state and national populations, 1970-2004

Population figures given in thousands

	State pop.	U.S. pop.	Share	Rank
1970	445	203,302	0.2%	48
1980	511	226,546	0.2%	48
1985	530	237,924	0.2%	49
1990	563	248,765	0.2%	48
1995	589	262,761	0.2%	49
2000	609	281,425	0.2%	48
2004	621	293,655	0.2%	49

Source: U.S. Census Bureau, Current Population Reports, 2006.

Resident population by age, 2004

Age Group	Total persons
Under 5 years	31,000
5 to 17 years	104,000
18 to 24 years	62,000
25 to 34 years	70,000
35 to 44 years	95,000
45 to 54 years	105,000
55 to 64 years	74,000
65 to 74 years	41,000
75 to 84 years	28,000
85 years and older	11,000
All age groups	621,000

Portion of residents 65 and older	13.0%
National rank in portion of oldest residents	20
National average	12.4%

Population figures are rounded to nearest thousand persons;
figures include armed forces personnel stationed in the state.
Source: U.S. Bureau of the Census, 2006.

Resident population by race, Hispanic origin, 2004

Category	State pop.	Share	U.S.
All residents	621	100.00%	100.00%
Non-Hispanic white	597	96.14%	67.37%
Hispanic white	5	0.81%	13.01%
Other Hispanic	1	0.16%	1.06%
African American	4	0.64%	12.77%
Native American	2	0.32%	0.96%
Asian, Pacific Islander	6	0.97%	4.37%
Two or more categories	7	1.13%	1.51%

Population figures are in thousands. Persons counted as "Hispanic" (Latino) may be of any race. Because of overlapping categories, categories may not add up to 100%. Shares in column 3 are percentages of each category within the state; these figures may be compared to the national percentages in column 4.
Source: U.S. Bureau of the Census, 2006.

Projected state population, 2000-2030

Year	Population
2000	609,000
2005	631,000
2010	653,000
2015	673,000
2020	691,000
2025	703,000
2030	712,000
Population increase, 2000-2030	103,000
Percentage increase, 2000-2030	16.9

Projections are based on data from the 2000 census.
Source: U.S. Census Bureau.

VITAL STATISTICS

Infant mortality rates, 1980-2002

	1980	1990	2000	2002
All state residents	10.7	6.4	6.0	4.4
All U.S. residents	12.6	9.2	9.4	9.1
All state white residents	10.7	5.9	6.1	4.5
All U.S. white residents	10.6	7.6	5.7	5.8

Figures represent deaths per 1,000 live births of resident infants under 1 year old, exclusive of fetal deaths. Figures for all residents include members of other racial categories not listed separately. The Census Bureau considers the figures for black residents to be too small to be statistically meaningful.
Source: U.S. Census Bureau, *Statistical Abstract of the United States,* 2006.

Abortion rates, 1990 and 2000

	1990	2000
Total abortions	3,000	2,000
Rate per 1,000 women	21.5	12.7
U.S. rate	25.7	21.3
Rank	23	31

Numbers of abortions are rounded to nearest thousand; ranks are based on rates.
Source: U.S. Census Bureau.

Marriages and divorces, 2004

Total marriages	6,000
Rate per 1,000 population	9.6
National rate per 1,000 population	7.4
Rank among all states	6
Total divorces	2,400
Rate per 1,000 population	3.9
National rate per 1,000 population	3.7
Rank among all states	19

Figures are for all marriages and divorces performed within the state, including those of nonresidents; totals are rounded to the nearest hundred. Ranks are for highest to lowest figures; note that divorce data are not available for five states.
Source: U.S. National Center for Health Statistics, *Vital Statistics of the United States,* 2006.

Death rates by leading causes, 2002
Deaths per 100,000 resident population

Cause	State	U.S.
Heart disease	222.2	241.7
Cancer	198.5	193.2
Cerebrovascular diseases	54.3	56.4
Accidents other than motor vehicle	38.9	37.0
Motor vehicle accidents	12.7	15.7
Chronic lower respiratory diseases	44.8	43.3
Diabetes mellitus	28.2	25.4
HIV	n/a	4.9
Suicide	14.9	11.0
Homicide	n/a	6.1
All causes	823.1	847.3
Rank in overall death rate among states		34

Figures exclude nonresidents who died in the state. Causes of death follow International Classification of Diseases. Rank is from highest to lowest death rate in the United States.
Source: U.S. National Center for Health Statistics, *National Vital Statistics Report,* 2006.

ECONOMY

Gross state product, 1990-2004
In current dollars

Year	State product	Nat'l product	State share
1990	$11.7 billion	$5.67 trillion	0.21%
2000	$17.7 billion	$9.75 trillion	0.18%
2002	$19.4 billion	$10.41 trillion	0.19%
2003	$20.5 billion	$10.92 trillion	0.19%
2004	$22.1 billion	$11.65 trillion	0.19%

Source: U.S. Bureau of Economic Analysis, *Survey of Current Business,* July, 2005.

Gross state product by industry, 2003
In billions of dollars

Construction	$0.8
Manufacturing	3.2
Wholesale trade	1.1
Retail trade	1.8
Finance & insurance	1.2
Information	0.8
Professional services	1.0
Health care & social assistance	1.7
Government	2.4
Total state product	$19.6
Total U.S. product	$10,289.2
State share of U.S. total	0.19%
Rank among all states	50

Total figures include industries not listed separately. Amounts are in chained 2000 dollars.

Source: U.S. Bureau of Economic Analysis, *Survey of Current Business,* July, 2005.

Personal income per capita, 1990-2004
In current dollars

	1990	2000	2004
Per capita income	$17,876	$27,680	$32,770
U.S. average	$19,477	$29,845	$32,937
Rank among states	27	28	19

Source: U.S. Bureau of Economic Analysis, *Survey of Current Business,* April, 2005.

Energy consumption, 2001
In trillions of British thermal units (BTU), except as noted

Total energy consumption

Total state energy consumption	164
Total U.S. energy consumption	96,275
State share of U.S. total	0.17%
Rank among states	50

Per capita consumption (In millions of BTU)

Total state per capita consumption	267
Total U.S. per capita consumption	338
Rank among states	40

End-use sectors

Residential	48
Commercial	33
Industrial	31
Transportation	52

Sources of energy

Petroleum	89
Natural gas	8
Coal	(z)
Hydroelectric power	9
Nuclear electric power	44

Figures for totals include categories not listed separately.
(z) Indicates less than 0.5 trillion BTU.

Source: U.S. Energy Information Administration, *State Energy Data Report,* 2001.

Nonfarm employment by sectors, 2004

Total persons	303,000
Construction	17,000
Manufacturing	37,000
Trade, transportation, utilities	59,000
Information	6,000
Finance, insurance, real estate	13,000
Professional & business services	21,000
Education & health services	53,000
Leisure, hospitality, arts, organizations	33,000
Other services, including repair & maintenance . . .	10,000
Government	52,000

Figures are rounded to nearest thousand persons. "Total" includes mining and natural resources, not listed separately.

Source: U.S. Bureau of Labor Statistics, 2006.

Foreign exports, 1990-2004
In millions of dollars

Year	State	U.S.	State share
1990	1,154	394,045	0.29%
1996	3,302	624,767	0.53%
1997	3,811	688,896	0.55%
2000	4,097	712,055	0.52%
2003	2,627	724,006	0.39%
2004	3,283	769,332	0.43%

Rank among all states in 2004 33

U.S. total does not include U.S. dependencies.
Source: U.S. Census Bureau, *U.S. Merchandise Trade*, series FT 900, 2000; U.S. Census Bureau, *U.S. International Trade in Goods and Services*, Series FT 900, 2005.

LAND USE

Federally owned land, 2003
Areas in acres

	State	U.S.	State share
Total area	5,937,000	2,271,343,000	0.26%
Nonfederal land	5,487,000	1,599,584,000	0.34%
Federal land	450,000	671,759,000	0.07%
Federal share	7.6%	29.6%	—

Areas are rounded to nearest thousand acres. Figures for federally owned land do not include trust properties.
Source: U.S. General Services Administration, *Federal Real Property Profile*, 2006.

Land use, 1997
In acres, rounded to nearest thousand

Total surface area.	6,154,000
Total nonfederal rural land	5,183,000
Percentage rural land	84.2%
Cropland	607,000
Conservation Reserve Program (CRP*) land	(nil)
Pastureland	338,000
Rangeland	(nil)
Forestland.	4,150,000
Other rural land	88,000

*CRP is a federal program begun in 1985 to assist private landowners to convert highly erodible cropland to vegetative cover for ten years. Note that some categories of land overlap.
Source: U.S. Department of Agriculture, Natural Resources and Conservation Service, and Iowa State University, Statistical Laboratory, *Summary Report, 1997 National Resources Inventory*, revised December, 2000.

Farms and crop acreage, 2004

	State	U.S.	Share	Rank
Farms	6,000	2,113,000	0.28%	42
Acres (millions)	1	937	0.11%	41
Acres per farm	195	443	—	35

Source: U.S. Department of Agriculture, National Agricultural Statistics Service. Numbers of farms are rounded to nearest thousand units; acreage figures are rounded to nearest million. Rankings, including ties, are based on rounded figures.

GOVERNMENT AND FINANCE

Units of local government, 2002

	State	Total U.S.	Rank
All local governments	733	87,525	35
Counties	14	3,034	43
Municipalities	47	19,429	43
Towns (townships)	237	16,504	17
School districts	283	13,506	20
Special districts	152	35,052	44

Only 48 states have county governments, 20 states have township governments ("towns" in New England, Minnesota, New York, and Wisconsin), and 46 states have school districts. Special districts encompass such functions as natural resources, fire protection, and housing and community development.
Source: U.S. Census Bureau, *Census of Governments.*

State government revenue, 2002

Total revenue.	$3,260 mill.
General revenue	$3,229 mill.
Per capita revenue	$5,238
U.S. per capita average	$3,689
Rank among states.	5
Intergovernment revenue	
Total	$1,087 mill.
From federal government	$1,041 mill.
Charges and miscellaneous	
Total	$624 mill.
Current charges	$324 mill.
Misc. general income	$300 mill.
Insurance trust revenue.	–$3 mill.
Taxes	
Total	$1,518 mill.
Per capita taxes	$2,465
Rank among states.	5
Property taxes	$391 mill.
Sales taxes	$570 mill.
License taxes.	$74 mill.
Individual income taxes	$408 mill.
Corporate income taxes.	$37 mill.
Other taxes	$39 mill.

Total revenue figures include items not listed separately here.
Source: U.S. Bureau of the Census.

State government expenditures, 2002

General expenditures

Total state expenditures . . . . $3,512 mill.
Intergovernmental . . . . $919 mill.

Per capita expenditures

State $5,343
Average of all states $3,859
Rank among states 3

Selected direct expenditures

Education . . . . $524 mill.
Public welfare . . . . $756 mill.
Health, hospital . . . . $82 mill.
Highways . . . . $239 mill.
Police protection . . . . $48 mill.
Corrections . . . . $80 mill.
Natural resources . . . . $65 mill.
Parks and recreation . . . . $15 mill.
Government administration . . . . $192 mill.
Interest on debt . . . . $134 mill.
Total direct expenditures . . . . $2,372 mill.

Totals include items not listed separately.
Source: U.S. Census Bureau.

POLITICS

Governors since statehood

D = Democrat; R = Republican; O = other;
(r) resigned; (d) died in office; (i) removed from office

Thomas Chittenden . . . . (d) 1791-1797
Paul Brigham 1797
Isaac Tichenor (O) 1797-1807
Israel Smith (O) 1807-1808
Isaac Tichenor (O) 1808-1809
Jonas Galusha (O) 1809-1813
Martin Chittenden (O) 1813-1815
Jonas Galusha (O) 1815-1820
Richard Skinner (O) 1820-1823
Cornelius P. Van Ness (O) 1823-1826
Ezra Butler (O) 1826-1828
Samuel C. Crafts (O) 1828-1831
William A. Palmer (O) 1831-1835
Silas H. Jenison (O) 1835-1841
Charles Paine (O) 1841-1843
John Mattocks (O) 1843-1844
William Slade (O) 1844-1846
Horace Eaton (O) 1846-1848
Carlos Coolidge (O) 1848-1850
Charles K. Williams (O) 1850-1852
Erastus Fairbanks (O) 1852-1853
John S. Robinson (D) 1853-1854
Stephen Royce (O) 1854-1856
Ryland Fletcher (R) 1856-1858
Hiland Hall (R) 1858-1860

Erastus Fairbanks (R) 1860-1861
Frederick Holbrook (R) 1861-1863
John G. Smith (R) 1863-1865
Paul Dillingham (R) 1865-1867
John B. Page (R) 1867-1869
Peter T. Washburn (R) . . . . (d) 1869-1870
George W. Hendee (R) 1870
John W. Stewart (R) 1870-1872
Julius Converse (R) 1872-1874
Asahel Peck (R) 1874-1876
Horace Fairbanks (R) 1876-1878
Redfield Proctor (R) 1878-1880
Roswell Farnham (R) 1880-1882
John L. Barstow (R) 1882-1884
Samuel E. Pingree (R) 1884-1886
Ebenezer J. Ormsbee (R) 1886-1888
William P. Dillingbam (R) 1888-1890
Carroll S. Page (R) 1890-1892
Levi K. Fuller (R) 1892-1894
Urban A. Woodbury (R) 1894-1896
Josiah Grout (R) 1896-1898
Edward C. Smith (R) 1898-1900
William W. Stickney (R) 1900-1902
John G. McCullough (R) 1902-1904
Charles J. Bell (R) 1904-1906
Fletcher D. Proctor (R) 1906-1908
George H. Prouty (R) 1908-1910
John A. Mead (R) 1910-1912
Allen M. Fletcher (R) 1912-1915
Charles W. Gates (R) 1915-1917
Horace F. Graham (R) 1917-1919
Percival W. Clement (R) 1919-1921
James Hartness (R) 1921-1923
Redfield Proctor, Jr. (R) 1923-1925
Franklin S. Billings (R) 1925-1927
John E. Weeks (R) 1927-1931
Stanley C. Wilson (R) 1931-1935
Charles M. Smith (R) 1935-1937
George D. Aiken (R) 1937-1941
William H. Wills (R) 1941-1945
Mortimer R. Proctor (R) 1945-1947
Ernest W. Gibson, Jr. (R) . . . . (r) 1947-1950
Harold J. Arthur (R) 1950-1951
Lee E. Emerson (R) 1951-1955
Joseph B. Johnson (R) 1955-1959
Robert T. Stafford (R) 1959-1961
Frank Ray Keyser, Jr. (R) 1961-1963
Phillip H. Hoff (D) 1963-1969
Deane C. Davis (R) 1969-1973
Thomas P. Salmon (D) 1973-1977
Richard A. Snelling (R) 1977-1985
Madeleine Kunin (D) 1985-1991
Richard A. Snelling (R) . . . . (d) 1991
Howard Dean (D) 1991-2003
Jim Douglas (R) 2003-

Composition of congressional delegations, 1989-2007

	Dem	Rep	Total
House of Representatives			
101st Congress, 1989			
State delegates	0	1	1
Total U.S.	259	174	433
102d Congress, 1991			
State delegates	0	0	0
Total U.S.	267	167	434
103d Congress, 1993			
State delegates	0	0	0
Total U.S.	258	176	434
104th Congress, 1995			
State delegates	0	0	0
Total U.S.	197	236	433
105th Congress, 1997			
State delegates	0	0	0
Total U.S.	206	228	434
106th Congress, 1999			
State delegates	0	0	0
Total U.S.	211	222	433
107th Congress, 2001			
State delegates	0	0	0
Total U.S.	211	221	432
108th Congress, 2003			
State delegates	0	0	0
Total U.S.	205	229	434
109th Congress, 2005			
State delegates	0	0	0
Total U.S.	202	231	433
110th Congress, 2007			
State delegates	1	0	1
Total U.S.	233	202	435
Senate			
101st Congress, 1989			
State delegates	1	1	2
Total U.S.	55	45	100
102d Congress, 1991			
State delegates	1	1	2
Total U.S.	56	44	100
103d Congress, 1993			
State delegates	1	1	2
Total U.S.	57	43	100
104th Congress, 1995			
State delegates	1	1	2
Total U.S.	46	53	99
105th Congress, 1997			
State delegates	1	1	2
Total U.S.	45	55	100

	Dem	Rep	Total
106th Congress, 1999			
State delegates	1	1	2
Total U.S.	45	54	99
107th Congress, 2001			
State delegates	1	1	2
Total U.S.	50	50	100
108th Congress, 2003			
State delegates	1	0	2
Total U.S.	48	51	99
109th Congress, 2005			
State delegates	1	0	2
Total U.S.	44	55	99
110th Congress, 2007			
State delegates	1	0	2
Total U.S.	49	49	98

Figures are for starts of first sessions. Totals are for Democrat (Dem.) and Republican (Rep.) members only. House membership totals under 435 and Senate totals under 100 reflect vacancies and seats held by independent party members. Vermont had one Independent-Socialist representative during the sessions in which no Democrats or Republicans are listed and an independent senator in the 108th, 109th, and 110th Congresses. When the 110th Congress opened, the Senate's two independent members caucused with the Democrats, giving the Democrats control of the Senate.

Source: U.S. Congress, *Congressional Directory.*

Composition of state legislature, 1990-2006

	Democrats	Republicans
State House (148 seats)		
1990	73	75
1992	87	57
1994	86	61
1996	89	57
1998	79	67
2000	77	67
2002	69	74
2004	83	60
2006	93	49
State Senate (30 seats)		
1990	15	15
1992	14	16
1994	12	18
1996	17	13
1998	17	13
2000	17	13
2002	19	11
2004	21	9
2006	23	7

Figures for total seats may include independents and minor party members. Numbers reflect results of elections in listed years; elected members usually take their seats in the years that follow.

Source: Council of State Governments; *State Elective Officials and the Legislatures.*

Voter participation in presidential elections, 2000 and 2004

	2000	2004
Voting age population		
State	464,000	487,000
Total United States	209,831,000	220,377,000
State share of U.S. total	0.22	0.22
Rank among states	48	47
Portion of voting age population casting votes		
State	63.5%	64.2%
United States	50.3%	55.5%
Rank among states	5	10

Population figures are rounded to nearest thousand and include all residents, regardless of eligibility to vote.
Source: U.S. Census Bureau.

HEALTH AND MEDICAL CARE

Medical professionals
Physicians in 2003 and nurses in 2001

	U.S.	State
Physicians in 2003		
Total	774,849	2,250
Share of U.S. total		0.29%
Rate	266	363
Rank		4
Nurses in 2001		
Total	2,262,020	5,820
Share of U.S. total		0.26%
Rate	793	949
Rank		9

Rates are numbers of physicians and nurses per 100,000 resident population; ranks are based on rates.
Source: American Medical Association, *Physician Characteristics and Distribution in the U.S.*; U.S. Department of Health and Human Services, Health Resources and Services Administration.

Health insurance coverage, 2003

	State	U.S.
Total persons covered	553,000	243,320,000
Total persons not covered	58,000	44,961,000
Portion not covered	9.5%	15.6%
Rank among states	49	—
Children not covered	5,000	8,373,000
Portion not covered	3.9%	11.4%
Rank among states	50	—

Totals are rounded to nearest thousand. Ranks are from the highest to the lowest percentages of persons *not* insured.
Source: U.S. Census Bureau, Current Population Reports.

AIDS, syphilis, and tuberculosis cases, 2003

Disease	U.S. cases	State cases	Rank
AIDS	44,232	16	46
Syphilis	34,270	1	49
Tuberculosis	14,874	9	47

Source: U.S. Centers for Disease Control and Prevention.

Cigarette smoking, 2003
Residents over age 18 who smoke

	U.S.	State	Rank
All smokers	22.1%	19.6%	41
Male smokers	24.8%	19.8%	45
Female smokers	20.3%	19.4%	32

Cigarette smokers are defined as persons who reported having smoked at least 100 cigarettes during their lifetimes and who currently smoked at least occasionally.
Source: U.S. Centers for Disease Control and Prevention, *Morbidity and Mortality Weekly Report*, 53, no. 44 (November 12, 2004).

HOUSING

Home ownership rates, 1985-2004

	1985	1990	1995	2000	2004
State	69.5%	72.6%	70.4%	68.7%	72.0%
Total U.S.	63.9%	63.9%	64.7%	67.4%	69.0%
Rank among states	17	3	14	34	25

Net change in state home ownership rate, 1985-2004 . . . . . +2.5%
Net change in U.S. home ownership rate, 1985-2004 . . . . . +5.1%

Percentages represent the proportion of owner households to total occupied households.
Source: U.S. Census Bureau, 2006.

Home sales, 2000-2004
In thousands of units

Existing home sales	2000	2002	2003	2004
State sales	12.1	13.0	14.5	14.2
Total U.S. sales	5,171	5,631	6,183	6,784
State share of U.S. total	0.23%	0.23%	0.23%	0.21%
Sales rank among states	48	48	48	49

Units include single-family homes, condos, and co-ops.
Source: National Association of Realtors, Washington, D.C., *Real Estate Outlook: Market Trends & Insights*.

Values of owner-occupied homes, 2003

	State	*U.S.*
Total units	111,000	58,809,000
Value of units		
Under $100,000	27.3%	29.6%
$100,000-199,999	49.3%	36.9%
$200,000 or more	23.4%	33.5%
Median value	$138,457	$142,275
Rank among all states		24

Units are owner-occupied one-family houses whose numbers are rounded to nearest thousand. Data are extrapolated from survey samples.
Source: U.S. Census Bureau, American Community Survey.

EDUCATION

Public school enrollment, 2002

Prekindergarten through grade 8
State enrollment. 68,000
Total U.S. enrollment. 34,135,000
State share of U.S. total 0.20%

Grades 9 through 12
State enrollment. 32,000
Total U.S. enrollment. 14,067,000
State share of U.S. total 0.23%

Enrollment rates
State public school enrollment rate. 92.5%
Overall U.S. rate 90.4%
Rank among states in 2002. 12
Rank among states in 1995 5

Enrollment figures (which include unclassified students) are rounded to nearest thousand pupils during fall school term. Enrollment rates are based on enumerated resident population estimate for July 1, 2002.
Source: U.S. National Center for Education Statistics.

Public college finances, 2003-2004

FTE enrollment in public institutions of higher education
Students in state institutions 17,800
Students in all U.S. public institutions 9,916,600
State share of U.S. total 0.18
Rank among states 50

State and local government appropriations for higher education
State appropriation per FTE $2,575
National average $5,716
Rank among states 50
State & local tax revenue going to higher
education 3.0%

FTE = full-time equivalent in public postsecondary programs, including summer sessions; student numbers are rounded to nearest hundred. Funding figures for 2003-2004 academic year include financial aid to students in state public institutions and exclude money for research, agriculture experiment stations, teaching hospitals, and medical schools; figures are rounded to nearest thousand dollars.
Source: Higher Education Executive Officers, Denver, Colorado.

TRANSPORTATION AND TRAVEL

Highway mileage, 2003

Interstate highways	320
Other freeways and expressways	19
Arterial roads	1,299
Collector roads	3,129
Local roads	9,592
Urban roads	1,382
Rural roads.	12,977
Total state mileage.	14,359
U.S. total	3,974,107
State share	0.36%
Rank among states	46

Note that combined urban and rural road mileage matches the total of the other categories.
Source: U.S. Federal Highway Administration.

Motor vehicle registrations and driver licenses, 2003

Vehicle registrations	*State*	*U.S.*	*Share*	*Rank*
Autos, trucks, buses	516,000	231,390,000	0.22%	50
Autos only	272,000	135,670	0.20%	48
Motorcycles	26,000	5,328,000	0.49%	43
Driver licenses	543,000	196,166,000	0.28%	47

Figures, which do not include vehicles owned by military services, are rounded to the nearest thousand. Figures for automobiles include taxis.
Source: U.S. Federal Highway Administration.

Domestic travel expenditures, 2003
Spending by U.S. residents on overnight trips and
day trips of at least 50 miles from home

Total expenditures within state	$1.37 bill.
Total expenditures within U.S.	$490.87 bill.
State share of U.S. total	0.3%
Rank among states	48

Source: Travel Industry Association of America.

Retail gasoline prices, 2003-2007
Average price per gallon at the pump

Year	U.S.	State
2003	$1.267	$1.284
2004	$1.316	$1.365
2005	$1.644	$1.675
2007	$2.298	$2.407

Excise tax per gallon in 2004	20.0¢
Rank among all states in 2007 prices	9

Prices are averages of all grades of gasoline sold at the pump
during March months in 2003-2005 and during February, 2007.
Averages for 2006, during which prices rose higher, are not
available.

Source: U.S. Energy Information Agency, *Petroleum Marketing
Monthly* (2003-2005 data); American Automobile Association
(2007 data).

CRIME AND LAW ENFORCEMENT

State and local police officers, 2000-2004

	2000	2002	2004
Total officers			
U.S.	654,601	665,555	675,734
State	893	956	1,065*
*Net change, 2000-2004			+19.26%
Officers per 1,000 residents			
U.S.	2.33	2.31	2.30
State	1.47	1.55	1.71
State rank	50	49	43

Totals include state and local police and sheriffs.
Source: Carsey Institute, University of New Hampshire.

Crime rates, 2003
Incidents per 100,000 residents

Crimes	State	U.S.
Violent crimes		
Total incidents	110	475
Murder	2	6
Forcible rape	20	32
Robbery	10	142
Aggravated assault	79	295
Property crimes		
Total incidents	2,200	3,588
Burglary	478	741
Larceny/theft	1,618	2,415
Motor vehicle theft	104	433
All crimes	2,310	4,063

Source: U.S. Federal Bureau of Investigation, *Crime in the United
States*, annual.

State prison populations, 1980-2003

	State	U.S.	State share
1980	480	305,458	0.16%
1990	1,049	708,393	0.15%
1996	1,119	1,025,624	0.11%
2000	1,697	1,391,261	0.12%
2003	1,944	1,470,045	0.13%

State figures include jail inmates but exclude prisoners in federal
penitentiaries.
Source: U.S. Bureau of Justice Statistics, *Prisoners in 2003*.

Virginia

Location: Atlantic coast

Area and rank: 39,598 square miles (102,558 square kilometers); 42,769 square miles (110,772 square kilometers) including water; thirty-seventh largest state in area

Coastline: 112 miles (180 kilometers) on the Atlantic Ocean

Shoreline: 3,315 miles (5,335 kilometers)

Population and rank: 7,460,000 (2004); twelfth largest state in population

Capital city: Richmond (197,790 people in 2000 census)

Largest city: Virginia Beach (425,257 people in 2000 census)

Entered Union and rank: June 25, 1788; tenth state

Present constitution adopted: 1970

The neoclassical design of Virginia's state capitol building in Richmond was inspired by the architectural designs of Thomas Jefferson. (Virginia Tourism Corporation)

Counties: 95, as well as 39 independent cities

State name: Virginia was named after England's Queen Elizabeth I, who was known as the Virgin Queen

State nickname: The Old Dominion; Mother of Presidents; Cavalier State

Motto: *Sic semper tyrannis* (Thus always to tyrants)

State flag: Dark blue field with state coat of arms in white border

Highest point: Mount Rogers—5,729 feet (1,746 meters)

Lowest point: Atlantic Ocean—sea level

Highest recorded temperature: 110 degrees Fahrenheit (43 degrees Celsius)—Balcony Falls, 1954

Lowest recorded temperature: –30 degrees Fahrenheit (–34 degrees Celsius)—Mountain Lake Biological Station, 1985

State song: (No official song; "Carry Me Back to Old Virginia" is former state song; "Shenandoah" is the interim state song)

State tree: American dogwood

State flower: American dogwood

State bird: Cardinal

National park: Shenandoah

Virginia History

One of the most historic of all the American states, Virginia played pivotal roles during the colonial period, the American Revolution and the Civil War. Following the adoption of the Constitution, Virginians had a major influence in shaping the direction and destiny of the early nation, and four of the first five American Presidents, from George Washington through James Monroe, were from Virginia. In fact, a Virginian held the presidency for 24 out of the first 28 years of the United States.

Early Inhabitants and European Settlement. Compared to other portions of the east coast, Native Americans seem to have arrived fairly late in the Virginia area, settling there after 8,000 B.C.E. In the Piedmont area to the west, the tribes of the Sioux language family included Manahoac, Monacan, and Tutelo. In the southwestern portion were the Cherokee while the Nottoway were found in the southeast; both of these were part of the Iroquoian language community. To the north, along the upper portions of Chesapeake Bay, the Susquehanna had migrated into the region from the area which is now Pennsylvania. These were also Iroquoian speakers. Along the lower portions of the Chesapeake Bay coast itself, including the area where the first English settlers arrived, the dominant Native Americans were the Algonquian-speaking members of the group known as the "Powhatan Confederacy," named after its powerful chieftain.

In addition to hunting and fishing, especially along the bountiful coastal waters of the Chesapeake Bay, the tribes turned to agriculture, which flourished in the excellent soil and long, warm growing season of the area. One of their major innovations was the growth and cultivation of tobacco, which the Native Americans passed on to English settlers shortly after their arrival in 1607.

The English colony of Jamestown, founded on a peninsula jutting into the Chesapeake Bay, was part of a grandiose land grant from the English king James I which stretched from what is now southern Maine to California and included both the island of Bermuda and the modern Canadian province of Ontario. However, despite the imperial designs, during its early days Jamestown was hard pressed to simply survive and barely weathered internal division, attacks by the Native Americans, disease, and near starvation. Under the leadership of Captain John Smith, the new colony endured and by the 1620's was exporting tobacco to England as a cash crop. The cultivation of tobacco and other crops was transformed in 1619 when the first Africans arrived in the colony as indentured servants; by the 1630's slavery had been introduced and in 1661 it was legalized. Slavery was to remain an essential part of Virginia's plantation economy until the end of the American Civil War.

A Rich Colony Leads a Revolution. The first legislative assembly in the English colonies gathered in Jamestown in 1619. Even though Virginia became a royal colony in 1624 the House of Burgesses, as the assembly was known, remained a potent force in colonial affairs, including encouraging growth and development, including expansion beyond the Blue Ridge Mountains to the west. In eastern Virginia, especially

Mount Vernon, the plantation home of George Washington, the first president of the United States. (Virginia Tourism Corporation)

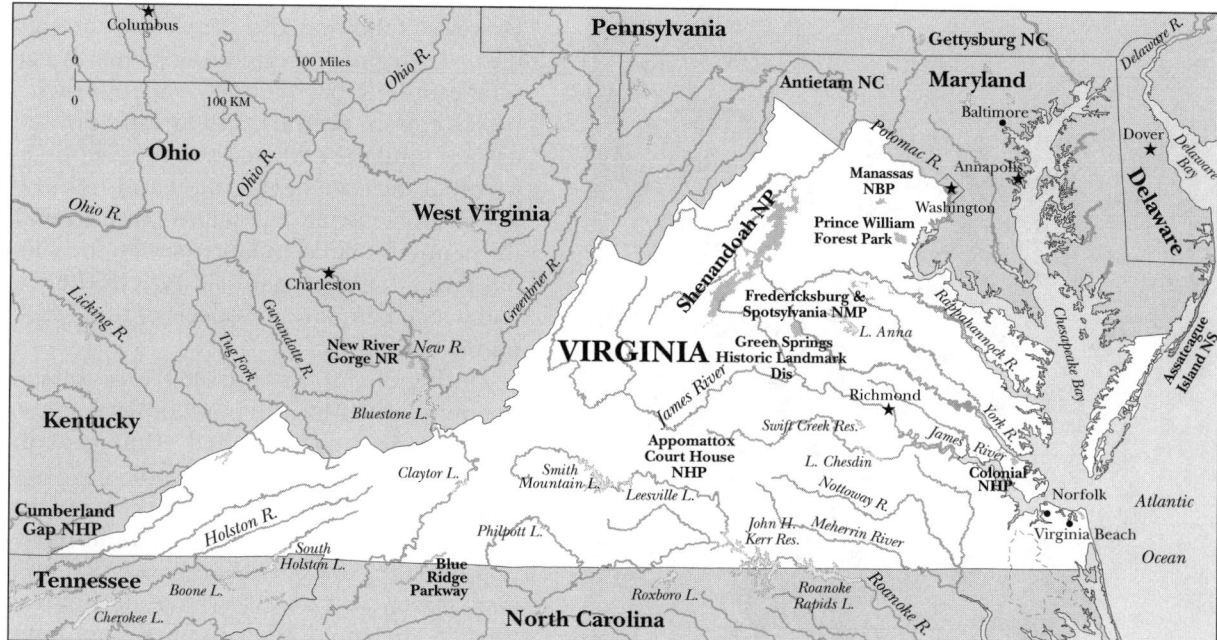

along the rich lands of the tidewater, tobacco farming brought enormous wealth to planters, merchants, and traders. By the middle of the eighteenth century, Virginia was among the richest of the American colonies.

It was also among the most independently minded. In 1676, Virginian Nathaniel Bacon led a popular revolt against despotic colonial governor Sir William Berkeley. As early as 1765 the Virginia House of Burgesses had officially opposed the Stamp Act and in 1769 Virginia launched a boycott of all British goods to protest additional taxes which the colonists regarded as unfair and illegal. It was at the Virginia Convention of 1775 that Patrick Henry delivered the speech which included his famous words, "Give me liberty, or give me death." Henry's sentiment was given more practical form in June, 1776, when Virginia officially declared itself independent from Great Britain. On July 4, 1776, the Declaration of Independence, largely written by Virginian Thomas Jefferson, extended this freedom to all thirteen colonies.

Virginia provided both leaders and a battleground for the American Revolution. George Washington was named commander of the Continental army, while other military leaders included George Rogers Clark, Daniel Morgan and "Light-Horse Harry" Lee, father of Robert E. Lee. The founder of the American Navy, John Paul Jones, was a Virginian, although born in Scotland. The climactic battle of the Revolution came with the combined American and French defeat of British forces under Lord Cornwallis at the siege of Yorktown. This victory ensured final victory for the American cause.

A New Nation and Civil War. Virginians were active in the creation and growth of the new United States.

The Constitution, which replaced the ineffective Articles of Confederation, was largely drafted by James Madison, who later became the fourth president of the United States. He shared that office with a number of others from his state, including George Washington, our first president; Thomas Jefferson, the third; and James Monroe, the fifth. In all, Virginians held the position of chief executive for 24 of the first 28 years of the new nation. In addition, the most influential chief justice of the United States, John Marshall, was a Virginian. He served from 1801 through 1835 and established the independent judiciary as an essential branch of the American federal government.

Although a southern, slave-holding state, Virginia had not taken the radical position held by others such as South Carolina during the intense national debate over slavery. The seizure of the federal arsenal at Harpers Ferry in 1859 by abolitionist John Brown, who hoped to spark a slave revolt, was put down by Colonel Robert E. Lee of the U.S. Army. When the first seven states seceded from the Union after the election of Abraham Lincoln in 1860, Virginia refrained from action. It did not leave the Union until April, 1861, after Lincoln had called up volunteers to suppress the rebellion. When Richmond, less than a hundred miles from Washington, D.C., was named capital of the Confederacy, it ensured that the major battles of the Civil War would be fought in Virginia.

Over the next four years, Robert E. Lee and the Confederate Army of Northern Virginia repulsed repeated attacks by federal forces. Aided by generals such as "Jeb" Stuart and "Stonewall" Jackson, Lee defeated Union forces that greatly outnumbered his own. In his classic 1863 victory at Chancellorsville, however, Lee

Natural arch in Virginia's Blue Ridge Mountains. (PhotoDisc)

lost his best lieutenant when Stonewall Jackson was killed by his own troops, and later that summer Lee and his army were defeated at Gettysburg. During the bloody campaigns of 1864 Union general Ulysses S. Grant wore down Lee's troops and brought about the Confederate surrender at Appomattox Courthouse in April, 1865, effectively ending the Civil War.

A Modern State. During the Civil War Virginia had lost the western part of its territory when counties beyond the mountains loyal to the Union formed a new state, West Virginia, which entered the Union in 1863. Following the Civil War, Virginia went through the harsh period of Reconstruction imposed on the other states of the defeated Confederacy. During this time, Robert E. Lee lost his U.S. citizenship and Jefferson Davis was imprisoned at Fort Monroe on Chesapeake Bay. Virginia was readmitted to the Union on January 26, 1870.

Prior to the war, Virginia had been an industrial and manufacturing leader in the South. Its Tredegar Ironworks in Richmond, for example, was the Confederacy's most important supplier of metal and weapons.

However, following the devastation brought by the war, Virginia reverted to a primarily agricultural economy, based largely on crops such as tobacco, cotton, peanuts, and forestry products. It was not until the early years of the twentieth century that the state began to recover its industrial and manufacturing capabilities. By the middle of the century, thanks in large part to the stimulus of production during World War II, these again had become important aspects of the state's economic base.

During the 1970's and 1980's, Virginia, in cooperation with Maryland and other neighboring states, made a concentrated effort to clean up and restore Chesapeake Bay, whose environment had been severely damaged by decades of neglect and pollution. More than one hundred rivers flow into the bay, some of them originating as far away as New York and West Virginia, but many of them rising in Virginia itself. Excess nutrients from agricultural fertilizer and organic chemicals have been two of the major elements damaging conditions in the bay. However, by 1992 efforts at environmental stewardship had reached the point where more than three-quarters of the bay (78 percent) was reported as being in "excellent" condition. This was good news for Virginia's seafood industry, in particular for the fishers who harvest world-famous Virginia oysters and blue crabs.

Fishing is indeed important to the state, but the modern Virginia economy is a diverse one. Agriculture, much of it located in the fertile Shenandoah Valley and in the southwestern portion of the state, remains a mainstay, with tobacco, corn, and other grains as significant crops. Shipbuilding and ship repair remain important along the coast, especially in the Hampton-Norfolk-Portsmouth area which also is the site of a major U.S. Naval base. Manufacturing, including electronic equipment and other technologically sophisticated products, is important; Virginia is one of the nation's major producers of synthetic fibers. In northern Virginia many residents are employed by the federal government. Because of its great natural beauty and multitude of historical sites, Virginia's tourism industry is a key part of its economy. This economic diversity means that the state retains a position it has long held in its history—that of being one of the leading states in the nation.

Social Progress. The year 2000 greeted Virginia with auspicious news. First, federal studies showed that in 1999, the state's poverty level had dropped to the lowest point in twenty years. The new rates were lower not only absolutely but also in statistical significance. Second, drug use in the state had declined among youth. Among twelve- to seventeen-year-olds, Virginia had the lowest rate of drug use in the nation, 4.7 percent.

Terrorist Attacks. Virginia was directly involved with the September 11, 2001, terrorist attacks since the site of one attack was located in northern Virginia, near the city of Arlington. At 9:37 A.M., American Airlines Flight 77, a Boeing 757, crashed into the Pentagon. All on board the plane, 59 people, died in the crash; 125 people in the Pentagon were killed. Numerous eyewitnesses saw the plane crash, and conspiracy theories that a missile and not a jetliner hit the building have been shown to be without foundation. A memorial to the tragedy was scheduled to open at the site in 2008.

Shortly after the September 11 attacks, Virginia struggled again with terrorist acts. During the anthrax attacks between September and November, 2001, a State Department mail room worker in Sterling, Virginia, contracted inhalation anthrax. In an unrelated case, a Salvadoran immigrant living in the state was accused of having facilitated the acquisition of fraudulent driver licenses by five of the 9/11 hijackers. During the same year, federal agents raided sixteen Muslim homes, businesses, and schools in Virginia that were suspected as fronts for terrorists. Many of those sought were housed in a single house in Herndon, near Washington, D.C. In 2002, the American accused of fighting with the Taliban in Afghanistan, John Walker Lindh, was tried and convicted in Alexandria.

Beltway Snipers. In October, 2002, another tragedy unfolded in Virginia, as well as in Washington, D.C., and Maryland. A killing rampage that terrorized the region began with a series of random shootings. The spree lasted from October 2 until October 24, during which ten persons were killed and three others were critically wounded. Five shootings, from October 9 until October 19, took place in Virginia. Two persons were later found guilty of the murders, John Allen Muhammad and Lee Boyd Malvo. The two were said to be motivated in part by an attempt to extort $10 million from the U.S. government. Initial trials were held in Virginia, and Muhammad received the death sentence.

Politics. Virginia politics were characterized by a variety of twists and turns. George W. Bush won the state's thirteen electoral votes in 2000 with a 52-45 percent victory over Democrat Al Gore. Bush repeated the win in 2004, this time by 55 to 45 percent. In a much-watched race for U.S. Senate, Democrat Chuck Robb was defeated by former governor George Allen, dashing Democrats' hopes of keeping control of the Senate. In 2001, campaigning as a moderate for governor, Democrat Mark Warner won the statehouse and went on to become the most popular Virginia governor in modern memory, with approval ratings of up to a remarkable 75 percent. The state's senior U.S. senator, John Warner, was easily reelected in 2002. Wrongdoing, however, sullied Virginia's public life. In 2003, the head of the Republican Party in the state pleaded guilty to illegal wiretapping in order to eavesdrop on Democrats' planning sessions.

Hurricanes. While Virginia is not often considered a state badly affected by hurricanes, during the early years of the twenty-first century, hurricanes were responsible for serious damage and a number of deaths, as they had done in the 1990's. In 2001, Tropical Storm Allison killed one person and spawned a hurricane; and 2004 hurricanes Charley, Gaston, Ivan, and Jeanne brought death and damage to the state. Worst of all, however, was 2003, when, on September 18, Hurricane Isabel—although downgraded to a tropical storm by the time it hit Virginia—was directly responsible for killing ten persons, causing $1.85 billion in damage in the state, and spawning a tornado over Norfolk.

Michael Witkoski
Updated by the Editor

The headquarters of the U.S. Department of Defense, the Pentagon Building is so closely associated with the national capital that the fact that it is actually in Arlington, Virginia, is often overlooked. This April, 2002, satellite photo shows the reconstruction work done on the building's west side after a hijacked jetliner was flown into the building on September 11, 2001. (U.S. Geological Survey)

Virginia Time Line

1500's	Iroquois Indians flourish in south and Algonquians in the north.
1606	King James I of England charters company to colonize Virginia.
May 13, 1607	Jamestown is founded; John Smith becomes leader of colony.
1612	John Rolfe begins cultivation of tobacco.
1619	Virginia creates House of Burgesses, the first representative assembly in New World.
1619	First black indentured servants arrive.
1622	War with Native Americans results in death of many colonists.
1624	Virginia Company's charter is revoked.
1635	First free school is established in Virginia.
1661	Virginia legalizes slavery.
1693	College of William and Mary is chartered at Williamsburg.
1699	Williamsburg becomes capital, replacing Jamestown.
1716	First theater in United States is built at Williamsburg.
1776	Virginia declares its independence from Great Britain.
1779	Richmond is named state capital.
Oct. 19, 1781	Lord Cornwallis surrenders to George Washington at Yorktown, effectively ending the American Revolution.
1784	Virginia cedes its northwestern lands to United States.
June 26, 1788	Virginia ratifies U.S. Constitution, becoming tenth state to enter the Union.
Apr. 30, 1789	Virginia native George Washington becomes first president of United States.
1801	Thomas Jefferson becomes president of the United States; John Marshall becomes chief justice of the United States.
1819	Thomas Jefferson founds University of Virginia in Charlottesville.
1831	Nat Turner's slave rebellion suppressed.

Colonial-era carriage rolling through Williamsburg, which was rebuilt to appear as it did in colonial times, when it was the capital of Virginia. (Virginia Tourism Corporation)

Oct. 16, 1859	John Brown seizes arsenal at Harpers Ferry; later is captured, tried, and hanged for treason.
Apr. 17, 1861	Virginia secedes from Union.
July 21, 1861	Union army is routed at Bull Run (Manassas) in first major battle of the Civil War.
June 20, 1863	West Virginia becomes separate state.
Apr. 9, 1865	General Robert E. Lee surrenders to General Ulysses S. Grant at Appomattox Courthouse, ending Civil War.
Jan. 26, 1870	Virginia is readmitted to the Union.
1908	Staunton becomes first city in United States with a city-manager form of government.
1926	John D. Rockefeller, Jr., oil tycoon, restores colonial Williamsburg.
1964	Chesapeake Bay Bridge-Tunnel is completed.
1966	U.S. Supreme Court rules Virginia's poll tax unconstitutional, outlawing the tax in all states.
1970	New state constitution is adopted.
1985	Hurricane Juan brings devastating floods.
1990	Virginia's Douglas Wilder becomes first African American governor elected in the United States.
1992	78 percent of Chesapeake Bay is in excellent environmental condition.
1999	Poverty in Virginia drops to the lowest level in twenty years.
Sept. 11, 2001	Hijacked airliner is flown into the Pentagon Building in Arlington.
Oct. 2-24, 2002	Virginia is terrorized by the "Beltway snipers," who shoot five persons within the state.
Sept. 18, 2003	Hurricane Isabel kills ten persons.

Notes for Further Study

Published Sources. Good history books on Virginia include Chiles Larson's *Virginia's Past Today* (1998), which examines the legacy and meaning of Virginia's historic past; Lovis Rubin's *Virginia: A History* (1984), a solid history with excellent discussions of the colonial period, the Civil War and Reconstruction, and economic and cultural developments following 1900; and *The Edge of the South: Life in Nineteenth-Century Virginia* (1991), edited by Edward Ayers and John C. Willis, which provides a fascinating glimpse of Virginia during the period from the Revolution to the Civil War. The period between Reconstruction and the Civil Rights era is discussed in Parke Rouse's *We Happy WASPS: Virginia in the Days of Jim Crow and Harry Byrd* (1996). *The Planting of New Virginia: Settlement and Landscape in the Shenandoah Valley* (2004) by Warren Hofstra studies the eighteenth century cultural history and landscape of town and country in western Virginia. David Hackett Fischer and James C. Kelly's *Bound Away: Virginia and the Westward Movement* (2000) studies three stages of historical migration to, from, and within the state. For younger readers, *Virginia* (2004) by Sandra Pobst and *Virginia* (2004) by Roberta Wiener and James R. Arnold offer accessible, well-illustrated accounts of the state's history, geography, and culture.

For readers interested in the Civil War experience in the state, *Virginia's Civil War* (2005), edited by Peter Wallenstein and Bertram Wyatt-Brown, presents a collection of twenty symposium papers which provide a comprehensive survey of the war period. *Contested Borderland: The Civil War in Appalachian Kentucky and Virginia* (2006) by Brian D. McKnight focuses specifically on the military tactics and civilian involvement situated on the border separating eastern Kentucky and southwestern Virginia.

Virginia is a state defined by the famous men and women who lived there. Lyon G. Tyler's *Encyclopedia of Virginia Biography* (1998) is an excellent source of information about that subject. *Virginia History and Government: 1850 to the Present* (1986) by Daniel Fleming Paul Slayton, and Edgar Toppin is a valuable survey of Virginia during some of its most turbulent and decisive periods.

Web Resources. Because of its many resources for history, tourism, industry, and agriculture, Virginia has a constantly expanding presence on the Internet. An excellent place to begin is the official site, Virginia! Welcome to the Commonwealth (www.state.va.us), which offers a wealth of information and provides links to many other sites. Those interested in Virginia's history, including its rich heritage of colonial and Civil War materials, should consult the Sons of Confederate Veterans site (www.scv.org) or the State Historical Society (www.vahistorical.org/). Another site worth visiting for students who wish to learn about practically any aspect of Virginia life, history, and culture is the Library of Virginia (www.lva.lib.va.us/); its Virginia History and Culture Resources page (www.lva.lib.va.us/whatwedo/k12/vhr/index.htm) is especially helpful. Virginia has long been recognized as one of the most naturally beautiful and varied of the southeastern states, and this aspect of the state is well presented on the home page of the Virginia Natural Heritage Program (www.state.va.us/dcr/dnh/).

The U.S. Census Bureau's QuickFacts (quickfacts.census.gov/qfd/states/51000.html) is a good place to view demographic data about the state and its inhabitants.

Virginia Indians (falcon.jmu.edu/~ramseyil/vaindians.htm) offers detailed information about the state's indigenous cultures.

Counties

County	2000 pop.	Rank in pop.	Sq. miles	Rank in area	County	2000 pop.	Rank in pop.	Sq. miles	Rank in area
Accomack	38,305	27	454.6	35	Halifax	37,355	28	813.8	4
Albemarle	79,236	12	722.8	6	Hanover	86,320	9	472.8	32
Alleghany	12,926	74	445.9	37	Henrico	262,300	3	238.1	78
Amelia	11,400	82	356.8	53	Henry	57,930	18	382.4	48
Amherst	31,894	36	475.3	29	Highland	2,536	95	415.9	42
Appomattox	13,705	69	333.7	57	Isle of Wight	29,728	40	315.9	63
Arlington	189,453	5	25.9	95	James City	48,102	23	142.9	90
Augusta	65,615	14	971.7	1	King and Queen	6,630	92	316.3	62
Bath	5,048	94	531.9	18	King George	16,803	60	180.0	87
Bedford	60,371	16	754.8	5	King William	13,146	72	275.4	71
Bland	6,871	90	358.7	51	Lancaster	11,567	80	133.2	91
Botetourt	30,496	38	542.7	15	Lee	23,589	47	437.2	39
Brunswick	18,419	56	566.2	13	Loudoun	169,599	6	519.9	19
Buchanan	26,978	43	503.9	23	Louisa	25,627	45	497.5	25
Buckingham	15,623	65	580.9	12	Lunenburg	13,146	71	431.8	40
Campbell	51,078	22	504.5	22	Madison	12,520	76	321.5	60
Caroline	22,121	51	532.6	17	Mathews	9,207	85	85.7	94
Carroll	29,245	41	476.5	28	Mecklenburg	32,380	35	624.0	9
Charles City	6,926	89	182.5	86	Middlesex	9,932	84	130.3	92
Charlotte	12,472	78	475.0	30	Montgomery	83,629	11	388.2	47
Chesterfield	259,903	4	425.7	41	Nelson	14,445	67	472.4	33
Clarke	12,652	75	176.6	88	New Kent	13,462	70	209.8	82
Craig	5,091	93	330.1	59	Northampton	13,093	73	207.4	83
Culpeper	34,262	32	381.2	50	Northumberland	12,259	79	192.3	84
Cumberland	9,017	86	298.5	66	Nottoway	15,725	64	314.7	64
Dickenson	16,395	63	332.7	58	Orange	25,881	44	341.7	55
Dinwiddie	24,533	46	503.8	24	Page	23,177	49	311.1	65
Essex	9,989	83	257.8	76	Patrick	19,407	55	483.2	27
Fairfax	969,749	1	395.6	46	Pittsylvania	61,745	15	970.9	2
Fauquier	55,139	20	650.3	8	Powhatan	22,377	50	261.3	75
Floyd	13,874	68	381.5	49	Prince Edward	19,720	54	352.8	54
Fluvanna	20,047	53	287.4	68	Prince George	33,047	34	265.6	74
Franklin	47,286	24	692.1	7	Prince William	280,813	2	338.4	56
Frederick	59,209	17	414.6	43	Pulaski	35,127	29	320.6	61
Giles	16,657	62	357.9	52	Rappahannock	6,983	88	266.6	73
Gloucester	34,780	31	216.6	80	Richmond	8,809	87	191.5	85
Goochland	16,863	59	284.5	69	Roanoke	85,778	10	250.7	77
Grayson	17,917	57	442.7	38	Rockbridge	20,808	52	599.7	11
Greene	15,244	66	156.6	89	Rockingham	67,725	13	851.2	3
Greensville	11,560	81	295.5	67	Russell	30,308	39	474.7	31

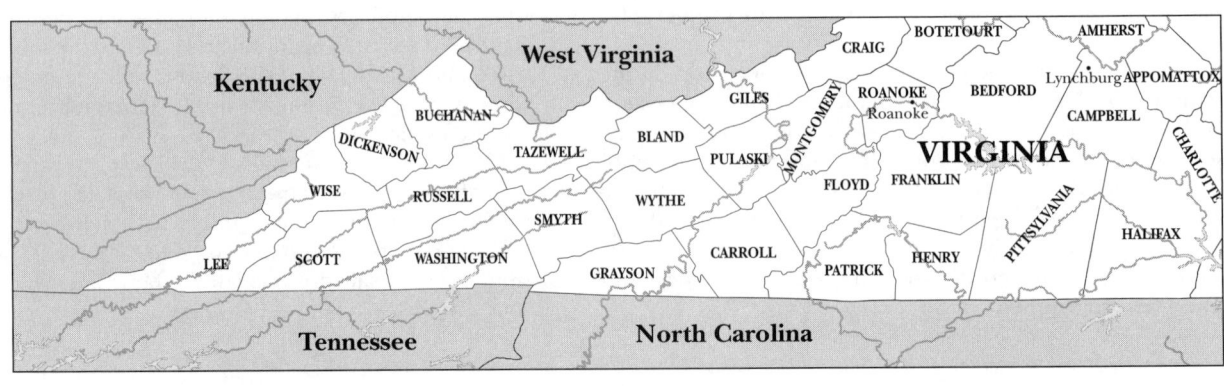

County	2000 pop.	Rank in pop.	Sq. miles	Rank in area
Scott	23,403	48	536.6	16
Shenandoah	35,075	30	512.2	21
Smyth	33,081	33	452.1	36
Southampton	17,482	58	600.3	10
Spotsylvania	90,395	8	400.9	45
Stafford	92,446	7	270.0	72
Surry	6,829	91	279.1	70
Sussex	12,504	77	490.8	26
Tazewell	44,598	25	519.8	20
Warren	31,584	37	213.7	81
Washington	51,103	21	564.2	14
Westmoreland	16,718	61	229.2	79
Wise	40,123	26	403.4	44

County	2000 pop.	Rank in pop.	Sq. miles	Rank in area
Wythe	27,599	42	463.3	34
York	56,297	19	105.6	93

Virginia has 39 independent cities: Alexandria, Bristol, Buena Vista, Charlottesville, Chesapeake, Clifton Forge, Colonial Heights, Covington, Danville, Emporia, Fairfax, Falls Church, Franklin, Fredericksburg, Galax, Hampton, Harrisonburg, Hopewell, Lexington, Lynchburg, Manassas, Manassas Park, Martinsville, Newport News, Norfolk, Norton, Petersburg, Poquoson, Portsmouth, Radford, Richmond, Roanoke, Salem, South Boston, Staunton, Suffolk, Virginia Beach, Waynesboro, and Williamsburg.

Source: U.S. Census Bureau; National Association of Counties.

Cities
With 10,000 or more residents

Rank	City	Population	Rank	City	Population
1	Virginia Beach	425,257	7	Hampton	146,437
2	Norfolk	234,403	8	Alexandria	128,283
3	Chesapeake	199,184	9	Portsmouth	100,565
4	Richmond (capital)	197,790	10	Roanoke	94,911
5	Arlington	189,453	11	Lynchburg	65,269
6	Newport News	180,150	12	Suffolk	63,677

(continued)

Rank	City	Population
13	Burke	57,737
14	Reston	56,407
15	Dale City	55,971
16	Annandale	54,994
17	Centreville	48,661
18	Danville	48,411
19	Charlottesville	45,049
20	Tuckahoe	43,242
21	Chantilly	41,041
22	Harrisonburg	40,468
23	Blacksburg	39,573
24	McLean	38,929
25	Manassas	35,135
26	Petersburg	33,740
27	Woodbridge	31,941
28	Franconia	31,907
29	Mechanicsville	30,464
30	Springfield	30,417
31	Lake Ridge	30,404
32	Oakton	29,348
33	Mount Vernon	28,582
34	West Springfield	28,378
35	Leesburg	28,311
36	Jefferson	27,422
37	Cave Spring	24,941
38	Salem	24,747
39	Staunton	23,853
40	Winchester	23,585
41	Bailey's Crossroads	23,166
42	Hopewell	22,354
43	Herndon	21,655
44	Fairfax	21,498
45	Groveton	21,296
46	Newington	19,784
47	Waynesboro	19,520
48	Fredericksburg	19,279

Rank	City	Population
49	Tysons Corner	18,540
50	Chester	17,890
51	Lorton	17,786
52	Bristol	17,367
53	Christiansburg	16,947
54	Colonial Heights	16,897
55	Hybla Valley	16,721
56	Bon Air	16,213
57	Idylwood	16,005
58	Radford	15,859
59	Lincolnia	15,788
60	Montclair	15,728
61	Martinsville	15,416
62	Highland Springs	15,137
63	Rose Hill	15,058
64	Laurel	14,875
65	Vienna	14,453
66	Hollins	14,309
67	Wolf Trap	14,001
68	Front Royal	13,589
69	Fort Hunt	12,923
70	Glen Allen	12,562
71	East Highland Park	12,488
72	Williamsburg	11,998
73	Madison Heights	11,584
74	Poquoson	11,566
75	Bull Run	11,337
76	Merrifield	11,170
77	Lakeside	11,157
78	Timberlake	10,683
79	Falls Church	10,377
80	Manassas Park	10,290

Population figures are from 2000 census.
Source: U.S. Bureau of the Census.

Index to Tables

DEMOGRAPHICS

Resident state and national populations, 1970-2004
Population figures given in thousands

	State pop.	U.S. pop.	Share	Rank
1970	4,651	203,302	2.3%	14
1980	5,347	226,546	2.4%	14
1985	5,715	237,924	2.4%	13
1990	6,189	248,765	2.5%	12
1995	6,671	262,761	2.5%	12
2000	7,079	281,425	2.5%	12
2004	7,460	293,655	2.5%	12

Source: U.S. Census Bureau, Current Population Reports, 2006.

Resident population by age, 2004

Age Group	Total persons
Under 5 years	498,000
5 to 17 years	1,307,000
18 to 24 years	748,000
25 to 34 years	1,015,000
35 to 44 years	1,173,000
45 to 54 years	1,093,000
55 to 64 years	778,000
65 to 74 years	453,000
75 to 84 years	291,000
85 years and older	103,000
All age groups	7,460,000

Portion of residents 65 and older	11.4%
National rank in portion of oldest residents	40
National average	12.4%

Population figures are rounded to nearest thousand persons; figures include armed forces personnel stationed in the state.
Source: U.S. Bureau of the Census, 2006.

Resident population by race, Hispanic origin, 2004

Category	State pop.	Share	U.S.
All residents	7,460	100.00%	100.00%
Non-Hispanic white	5,122	68.66%	67.37%
Hispanic white	380	5.09%	13.01%
Other Hispanic	46	0.62%	1.06%
African American	1,483	19.88%	12.77%
Native American	24	0.32%	0.96%
Asian, Pacific Islander	335	4.49%	4.37%
Two or more categories	115	1.54%	1.51%

Population figures are in thousands. Persons counted as "Hispanic" (Latino) may be of any race. Because of overlapping categories, categories may not add up to 100%. Shares in column 3 are percentages of each category within the state; these figures may be compared to the national percentages in column 4.
Source: U.S. Bureau of the Census, 2006.

Projected state population, 2000-2030

Year	Population
2000	7,079,000
2005	7,553,000
2010	8,010,000
2015	8,467,000
2020	8,917,000
2025	9,364,000
2030	9,825,000
Population increase, 2000-2030	2,746,000
Percentage increase, 2000-2030	38.8

Projections are based on data from the 2000 census.
Source: U.S. Census Bureau.

VITAL STATISTICS

Infant mortality rates, 1980-2002

	1980	1990	2000	2002
All state residents	13.6	10.2	6.9	7.4
All U.S. residents	12.6	9.2	9.4	9.1
All state white residents	11.9	7.4	5.4	5.5
All U.S. white residents	10.6	7.6	5.7	5.8
All state black residents	19.8	19.5	12.4	14.6
All U.S. black residents	22.2	18.0	14.1	14.4

Figures represent deaths per 1,000 live births of resident infants under 1 year old, exclusive of fetal deaths. Figures for all residents include members of other racial categories not listed separately.
Source: U.S. Census Bureau, *Statistical Abstract of the United States,* 2006.

Abortion rates, 1990 and 2000

	1990	2000
Total abortions	35,000	29,000
Rate per 1,000 women	22.6	18.1
U.S. rate	25.7	21.3
Rank	20	19

Numbers of abortions are rounded to nearest thousand; ranks are based on rates.
Source: U.S. Census Bureau.

Marriages and divorces, 2004

Total marriages	62,500
Rate per 1,000 population	8.4
National rate per 1,000 population	7.4
Rank among all states	11
Total divorces	30,100
Rate per 1,000 population	4.0
National rate per 1,000 population	3.7
Rank among all states	18

Figures are for all marriages and divorces performed within the state, including those of nonresidents; totals are rounded to the nearest hundred. Ranks are for highest to lowest figures; note that divorce data are not available for five states.
Source: U.S. National Center for Health Statistics, *Vital Statistics of the United States,* 2006.

Death rates by leading causes, 2002

Deaths per 100,000 resident population

Cause	State	U.S.
Heart disease	205.0	241.7
Cancer	186.5	193.2
Cerebrovascular diseases	54.3	56.4
Accidents other than motor vehicle	34.0	37.0
Motor vehicle accidents	13.2	15.7
Chronic lower respiratory diseases	37.7	43.3
Diabetes mellitus	21.4	25.4
HIV	3.6	4.9
Suicide	11.0	11.0
Homicide	5.4	6.1
All causes	784.2	847.3
Rank in overall death rate among states		37

Figures exclude nonresidents who died in the state. Causes of death follow International Classification of Diseases. Rank is from highest to lowest death rate in the United States.
Source: U.S. National Center for Health Statistics, *National Vital Statistics Report,* 2006.

ECONOMY

Gross state product, 1990-2004
In current dollars

Year	State product	Nat'l product	State share
1990	$147.0 billion	$5.67 trillion	2.59%
2000	$260.3 billion	$9.75 trillion	2.67%
2002	$288.8 billion	$10.41 trillion	2.77%
2003	$304.1 billion	$10.92 trillion	2.78%
2004	$326.6 billion	$11.65 trillion	2.80%

Source: U.S. Bureau of Economic Analysis, *Survey of Current Business,* July, 2005.

Gross state product by industry, 2003
In billions of dollars

Construction	$12.0
Manufacturing	36.4
Wholesale trade	12.8
Retail trade	19.8
Finance & insurance	18.9
Information	16.6
Professional services	29.3
Health care & social assistance	14.1
Government	45.9
Total state product	$283.9
Total U.S. product	$10,289.2
State share of U.S. total	2.76%
Rank among all states	13

Total figures include industries not listed separately. Amounts are in chained 2000 dollars.
Source: U.S. Bureau of Economic Analysis, *Survey of Current Business,* July, 2005.

Personal income per capita, 1990-2004
In current dollars

	1990	2000	2004
Per capita income	$20,449	$31,087	$35,477
U.S. average	$19,477	$29,845	$32,937
Rank among states	12	12	10

Source: U.S. Bureau of Economic Analysis, *Survey of Current Business,* April, 2005.

Energy consumption, 2001
In trillions of British thermal units (BTU), except as noted

Total energy consumption

Total state energy consumption	2,315
Total U.S. energy consumption	96,275
State share of U.S. total	2.40%
Rank among states	14

Per capita consumption (In millions of BTU)

Total state per capita consumption	322
Total U.S. per capita consumption	338
Rank among states	29

End-use sectors

Residential	549
Commercial	534
Industrial	547
Transportation	685

Sources of energy

Petroleum	911
Natural gas	247
Coal	482
Hydroelectric power	−13
Nuclear electric power	269

Figures for totals include categories not listed separately. The negative figure for hydroelectric power resulted from pumped storage for which more electricity was expended than created during peak demand periods.
Source: U.S. Energy Information Administration, *State Energy Data Report,* 2001.

Nonfarm employment by sectors, 2004

Total persons	3,584,000
Construction	231,000
Manufacturing	299,000
Trade, transportation, utilities	647,000
Information	100,000
Finance, insurance, real estate	189,000
Professional & business services	577,000
Education & health services	380,000
Leisure, hospitality, arts, organizations	320,000
Other services, including repair & maintenance	180,000
Government	652,000

Figures are rounded to nearest thousand persons. "Total" includes mining and natural resources, not listed separately.
Source: U.S. Bureau of Labor Statistics, 2006.

Foreign exports, 1990-2004
In millions of dollars

Year	State	U.S.	State share
1990	9,333	394,045	2.37%
1996	12,215	624,767	1.96%
1997	12,755	688,896	1.85%
2000	11,698	712,055	1.50%
2003	10,853	724,006	1.61%
2004	11,631	769,332	1.51%

Rank among all states in 2004 22

U.S. total does not include U.S. dependencies.
Source: U.S. Census Bureau, *U.S. Merchandise Trade,* series FT 900, 2000; U.S. Census Bureau, *U.S. International Trade in Goods and Services,* Series FT 900, 2005.

LAND USE

Federally owned land, 2003
Areas in acres

	State	U.S.	State share
Total area	25,496,000	2,271,343,000	1.12%
Nonfederal land	22,879,000	1,599,584,000	1.43%
Federal land	2,617,000	671,759,000	0.39%
Federal share	10.3%	29.6%	—

Areas are rounded to nearest thousand acres. Figures for federally owned land do not include trust properties.
Source: U.S. General Services Administration, *Federal Real Property Profile,* 2006.

Land use, 1997
In acres, rounded to nearest thousand

Total surface area	27,087,000
Total nonfederal rural land.	19,886,000
Percentage rural land	73.4%
Cropland	2,918,000
Conservation Reserve Program (CRP*) land	71,000
Pastureland	2,995,000
Rangeland	(nil)
Forestland	13,316,000
Other rural land	587,000

*CRP is a federal program begun in 1985 to assist private landowners to convert highly erodible cropland to vegetative cover for ten years. Note that some categories of land overlap.
Source: U.S. Department of Agriculture, Natural Resources and Conservation Service, and Iowa State University, Statistical Laboratory, *Summary Report, 1997 National Resources Inventory,* revised December, 2000.

Farms and crop acreage, 2004

	State	U.S.	Share	Rank
Farms	48,000	2,113,000	2.27%	18
Acres (millions)	9	937	0.96%	31
Acres per farm	181	443	—	39

Source: U.S. Department of Agriculture, National Agricultural Statistics Service. Numbers of farms are rounded to nearest thousand units; acreage figures are rounded to nearest million. Rankings, including ties, are based on rounded figures.

GOVERNMENT AND FINANCE

Units of local government, 2002

	State	Total U.S.	Rank
All local governments	521	87,525	43
Counties	95	3,034	9
Municipalities	229	19,429	34
Townships	0	16,504	—
School districts	1	13,506	46
Special districts	196	35,052	42

Only 48 states have county governments, 20 states have township governments ("towns" in New England, Minnesota, New York, and Wisconsin), and 46 states have school districts. Special districts encompass such functions as natural resources, fire protection, and housing and community development.
Source: U.S. Census Bureau, *Census of Governments.*

State government revenue, 2002

Total revenue	$23,577 mill.
General revenue	$24,843 mill.
Per capita revenue	$3,416
U.S. per capita average	$3,689
Rank among states	34

Intergovernment revenue
Total	$5,531 mill.
From federal government	$5,377 mill.

Charges and miscellaneous
Total	$6,530 mill.
Current charges	$3,703 mill.
Misc. general income	$2,827 mill.
Insurance trust revenue	−$1,604 mill.

Taxes
Total	$12,781 mill.
Per capita taxes	$1,754
Rank among states	28
Property taxes	$21 mill.
Sales taxes	$4,782 mill.
License taxes	$543 mill.
Individual income taxes	$6,711 mill.
Corporate income taxes	$309 mill.
Other taxes	$416 mill.

Total revenue figures include items not listed separately here.
Source: U.S. Bureau of the Census.

State government expenditures, 2002

General expenditures

Total state expenditures . . . . $28,044 mill.
Intergovernmental . . . . $8,369 mill.

Per capita expenditures

State $3,505
Average of all states $3,859
Rank among states 37

Selected direct expenditures

Education . . . . $4,657 mill.
Public welfare . . . . $3,622 mill.
Health, hospital . . . . $2,186 mill.
Highways . . . . $2,587 mill.
Police protection . . . . $232 mill.
Corrections . . . . $959 mill.
Natural resources . . . . $183 mill.
Parks and recreation . . . . $74 mill.
Government administration . . . . $923 mill.
Interest on debt . . . . $721 mill.
Total direct expenditures . . . . $17,177 mill.

Totals include items not listed separately.
Source: U.S. Census Bureau.

POLITICS

Governors since statehood

D = Democrat; R = Republican; O = other;
(r) resigned; (d) died in office; (i) removed from office

Patrick Henry 1776-1779
Thomas Jefferson 1779-1781
William Fleming 1781
Thomas Nelson 1781
Benjamin Harrison III 1781-1784
Patrick Henry 1784-1786
Edmund J. Randolph 1786-1788
Beverly Randolph 1788-1791
Henry Lee 1791-1794
Robert Brooke 1794-1796
James Wood (O) 1796-1799
James Monroe (O) 1799-1802
John Page (O) 1802-1805
William H. Cabell (O) 1805-1808
John Tyler III (O) . . . . (r) 1808-1811
James Monroe (O) . . . . (r) 1811
George W. Smith (O) . . . . (d) 1811
Peyton Randolph (O) 1811-1812
James Barbour (O) 1812-1814
Wilson C. Nicholas (O) 1814-1816
James P. Preston (O) 1816-1819
Thomas Mann Randolph (O) 1819-1822
James Pleasants, Jr. (O) 1822-1825
John Tyler IV (O) . . . . (r) 1825-1827
William B. Giles (D) 1827-1830
John Floyd (D) 1830-1834

Littleton W. Tazewell (D) . . . . (r) 1834-1836
Wyndham Robertson (D) 1836-1837
David Campbell (D) 1837-1840
Thomas W. Gilmer (O) . . . . (r) 1840-1841
James M. Patton (O) 1841
John Rutherford (O) 1841-1842
John M. Gregory (O) 1842-1843
James McDowell (O) 1843-1846
William Smith (D) 1846-1849
John B. Floyd (D) 1849-1852
Joseph Johnson (D) 1852-1856
Henry A. Wise (D) 1856-1860
John Letcher (D) 1860-1864
William Smith (D) . . . . (i) 1864-1865
Francis H. Pierpoint (D) . . . . (i) 1865-1868
Henry H. Wells . . . . (i) 1868-1869
Gilbert C. Walker 1869-1874
James L. Kemper (D) 1874-1878
Frederick W. M. Holliday (D) 1878-1882
William E. Cameron (O) 1882-1886
Fitzhugh Lee (D) 1886-1890
Philip W. McKinney (D) 1890-1894
Charles T. O'Ferrall (D) 1894-1898
James Hoge Tyler (D) 1898-1902
Andrew J. Montague (D) 1902-1906
Claude A. Swanson (D) 1906-1910
William H. Mann (D) 1910-1914
Henry C. Stuart (D) 1914-1918
Westmoreland Davis (D) 1918-1922
Elbert Lee Trinkle (D) 1922-1926
Harry F. Byrd (D) 1926-1930
John G. Pollard (D) 1930-1934
George C. Perry (D) 1934-1938
James H. Price (D) 1938-1942
Colgate W. Darden, Jr. (D) 1942-1946
William M. Tuck (D) 1946-1950
John S. Battle (D) 1950-1954
Thomas B. Stanley (D) 1954-1958
James Lindsay Almond, Jr. (D) 1958-1962
Albertis S. Harrison, Jr. (D) 1962-1966
Mills E. Godwin, Jr. (D) 1966-1970
Abner Linwood Holton, Jr. (R) 1970-1974
Mills E. Godwin, Jr. (R) 1974-1978
John N. Dalton (R) 1978-1982
Charles S. Robb (D) 1982-1986
Gerald L. Baliles (D) 1986-1990
L. Douglas Wilder (D) 1990-1994
George F. Allen (R) 1994-1998
James S. Gilmore III (R) 1998-2002
Mark Warner (D) 2002-2006
Tim Kaine (D) 2006-

Composition of congressional delegations, 1989-2007

	Dem	Rep	Total
House of Representatives			
101st Congress, 1989			
State delegates	5	5	10
Total U.S.	259	174	433
102d Congress, 1991			
State delegates	6	4	10
Total U.S.	267	167	434
103d Congress, 1993			
State delegates	7	4	11
Total U.S.	258	176	434
104th Congress, 1995			
State delegates	6	5	11
Total U.S.	197	236	433
105th Congress, 1997			
State delegates	6	5	11
Total U.S.	206	228	434
106th Congress, 1999			
State delegates	6	5	11
Total U.S.	211	222	433
107th Congress, 2001			
State delegates	4	6	10
Total U.S.	211	221	432
108th Congress, 2003			
State delegates	3	8	11
Total U.S.	205	229	434
109th Congress, 2005			
State delegates	3	8	11
Total U.S.	202	231	433
110th Congress, 2007			
State delegates	3	8	11
Total U.S.	233	202	435
Senate			
101st Congress, 1989			
State delegates	1	1	2
Total U.S.	55	45	100
102d Congress, 1991			
State delegates	1	1	2
Total U.S.	56	44	100
103d Congress, 1993			
State delegates	1	1	2
Total U.S.	57	43	100
104th Congress, 1995			
State delegates	1	1	2
Total U.S.	46	53	99
105th Congress, 1997			
State delegates	1	1	2
Total U.S.	45	55	100

	Dem	Rep	Total
106th Congress, 1999			
State delegates	1	1	2
Total U.S.	45	54	99
107th Congress, 2001			
State delegates	0	2	2
Total U.S.	50	50	100
108th Congress, 2003			
State delegates	0	2	2
Total U.S.	48	51	99
109th Congress, 2005			
State delegates	0	2	2
Total U.S.	44	55	99
110th Congress, 2007			
State delegates	1	1	2
Total U.S.	49	49	98

Figures are for starts of first sessions. Totals are for Democrat (Dem.) and Republican (Rep.) members only. House membership totals under 435 and Senate totals under 100 reflect vacancies and seats held by independent party members. When the 110th Congress opened, the Senate's two independent members caucused with the Democrats, giving the Democrats control of the Senate.

Source: U.S. Congress, *Congressional Directory.*

Composition of state legislature, 1990-2006

	Democrats	Republicans
State House (100 seats)		
1990	58	41
1992	52	47
1994	52	47
1996	53	46
1998	50	49
2000	47	52
2002	37	61
2004	38	60
2006	40	57
State Senate (40 seats)		
1990	22	18
1992	22	18
1994	22	18
1996	20	20
1998	19	21
2000	18	21
2002	16	24
2004	16	24
2006	17	23

Figures for total seats may include independents and minor party members. Numbers reflect results of elections in listed years; elected members usually take their seats in the years that follow.

Source: Council of State Governments; *State Elective Officials and the Legislatures.*

Voter participation in presidential elections, 2000 and 2004

	2000	2004
Voting age population		
State	5,361,000	5,655,000
Total United States	209,831,000	220,377,000
State share of U.S. total	2.55	2.57
Rank among states	12	12
Portion of voting age population casting votes		
State	51.1%	56.5%
United States	50.3%	55.5%
Rank among states	28	29

Population figures are rounded to nearest thousand and include all residents, regardless of eligibility to vote.
Source: U.S. Census Bureau.

HEALTH AND MEDICAL CARE

Medical professionals
Physicians in 2003 and nurses in 2001

	U.S.	State
Physicians in 2003		
Total	774,849	20,220
Share of U.S. total		2.60%
Rate	266	274
Rank		11
Nurses in 2001		
Total	2,262,020	55,440
Share of U.S. total		2.45%
Rate	793	770
Rank		34

Rates are numbers of physicians and nurses per 100,000 resident population; ranks are based on rates.
Source: American Medical Association, *Physician Characteristics and Distribution in the U.S.*; U.S. Department of Health and Human Services, Health Resources and Services Administration.

Health insurance coverage, 2003

	State	U.S.
Total persons covered	6,424,000	243,320,000
Total persons not covered	962,000	44,961,000
Portion not covered	13.0%	15.6%
Rank among states	30	—
Children not covered	162,000	8,373,000
Portion not covered	8.9%	11.4%
Rank among states	26	—

Totals are rounded to nearest thousand. Ranks are from the highest to the lowest percentages of persons *not* insured.
Source: U.S. Census Bureau, Current Population Reports.

AIDS, syphilis, and tuberculosis cases, 2003

Disease	U.S. cases	State cases	Rank
AIDS	44,232	786	13
Syphilis	34,270	552	17
Tuberculosis	14,874	332	10

Source: U.S. Centers for Disease Control and Prevention.

Cigarette smoking, 2003
Residents over age 18 who smoke

	U.S.	State	Rank
All smokers	22.1%	22.1%	25
Male smokers	24.8%	26.4%	20
Female smokers	20.3%	18.0%	42

Cigarette smokers are defined as persons who reported having smoked at least 100 cigarettes during their lifetimes and who currently smoked at least occasionally.
Source: U.S. Centers for Disease Control and Prevention, *Morbidity and Mortality Weekly Report*, 53, no. 44 (November 12, 2004).

HOUSING

Home ownership rates, 1985-2004

	1985	1990	1995	2000	2004
State	68.5%	69.8%	68.1%	73.9%	73.4%
Total U.S.	63.9%	63.9%	64.7%	67.4%	69.0%
Rank among states	22	10	22	11	14

Net change in state home ownership rate,
1985-2004 . . . . +4.9%
Net change in U.S. home ownership rate,
1985-2004 . . . . +5.1%

Percentages represent the proportion of owner households to total occupied households.
Source: U.S. Census Bureau, 2006.

Home sales, 2000-2004
In thousands of units

Existing home sales	2000	2002	2003	2004
State sales	130.0	150.1	158.3	186.0
Total U.S. sales	5,171	5,631	6,183	6,784
State share of U.S. total	2.51%	2.67%	2.56%	2.74%
Sales rank among states	12	11	11	13

Units include single-family homes, condos, and co-ops.
Source: National Association of Realtors, Washington, D.C., *Real Estate Outlook: Market Trends & Insights*.

Values of owner-occupied homes, 2003

	State	U.S.
Total units	1,632,000	58,809,000
Value of units		
Under $100,000	25.2%	29.6%
$100,000-199,999	35.2%	36.9%
$200,000 or more	39.6%	33.5%
Median value	$162,080	$142,275
Rank among all states 17		

Units are owner-occupied one-family houses whose numbers are rounded to nearest thousand. Data are extrapolated from survey samples.
Source: U.S. Census Bureau, American Community Survey.

EDUCATION

Public school enrollment, 2002

Prekindergarten through grade 8
State enrollment 832,000
Total U.S. enrollment. 34,135,000
State share of U.S. total 2.44%

Grades 9 through 12
State enrollment 346,000
Total U.S. enrollment. 14,067,000
State share of U.S. total 2.46%

Enrollment rates
State public school enrollment rate. 90.6%
Overall U.S. rate 90.4%
Rank among states in 2002. 24
Rank among states in 1995. 19

Enrollment figures (which include unclassified students) are rounded to nearest thousand pupils during fall school term. Enrollment rates are based on enumerated resident population estimate for July 1, 2002.
Source: U.S. National Center for Education Statistics.

Public college finances, 2003-2004

FTE enrollment in public institutions of higher education
Students in state institutions 257,700
Students in all U.S. public institutions 9,916,600
State share of U.S. total 2.60
Rank among states 10

State and local government appropriations for higher education
State appropriation per FTE $4,571
National average. $5,716
Rank among states 41
State & local tax revenue going to higher education 6.5%

FTE = full-time equivalent in public postsecondary programs, including summer sessions; student numbers are rounded to nearest hundred. Funding figures for 2003-2004 academic year include financial aid to students in state public institutions and exclude money for research, agriculture experiment stations, teaching hospitals, and medical schools; figures are rounded to nearest thousand dollars.
Source: Higher Education Executive Officers, Denver, Colorado.

TRANSPORTATION AND TRAVEL

Highway mileage, 2003

Interstate highways	1,118
Other freeways and expressways	224
Arterial roads	8,250
Collector roads.	14,081
Local roads.	47,569
Urban roads	21,011
Rural roads.	50,231
Total state mileage.	71,242
U.S. total	3,974,107
State share	1.79%
Rank among states	28

Note that combined urban and rural road mileage matches the total of the other categories.
Source: U.S. Federal Highway Administration.

Motor vehicle registrations and driver licenses, 2003

Vehicle registrations	State	U.S.	Share	Rank
Autos, trucks, buses	6,346,000	231,390,000	2.74%	11
Autos only	4,044,000	135,670	2.98%	11
Motorcycles	73,000	5,328,000	1.37%	22
Driver licenses	5,046,000	196,166,000	2.57%	12

Figures, which do not include vehicles owned by military services, are rounded to the nearest thousand. Figures for automobiles include taxis.
Source: U.S. Federal Highway Administration.

Domestic travel expenditures, 2003

Spending by U.S. residents on overnight trips and
day trips of at least 50 miles from home

Total expenditures within state	$13.89 bill.
Total expenditures within U.S.	$490.87 bill.
State share of U.S. total	2.8%
Rank among states	10

Source: Travel Industry Association of America.

Retail gasoline prices, 2003-2007

Average price per gallon at the pump

Year	U.S.	State
2003	$1.267	$1.225
2004	$1.316	$1.279
2005	$1.644	$1.596
2007	$2.298	$2.138

Excise tax per gallon in 2004	17.5¢
Rank among all states in 2007 prices	47

Prices are averages of all grades of gasoline sold at the pump
during March months in 2003-2005 and during February, 2007.
Averages for 2006, during which prices rose higher, are not
available.
Source: U.S. Energy Information Agency, *Petroleum Marketing
Monthly* (2003-2005 data); American Automobile Association
(2007 data).

CRIME AND LAW ENFORCEMENT

State and local police officers, 2000-2004

	2000	2002	2004
Total officers			
U.S.	654,601	665,555	675,734
State	16,036	16,552	17,011*
*Net change, 2000-2004			+6.08%
Officers per 1,000 residents			
U.S.	2.33	2.31	2.30
State	2.27	2.27	2.28
State rank	21	16	19

Totals include state and local police and sheriffs.
Source: Carsey Institute, University of New Hampshire.

Crime rates, 2003

Incidents per 100,000 residents

Crimes	State	U.S.
Violent crimes		
Total incidents	276	475
Murder	6	6
Forcible rape	24	32
Robbery	90	142
Aggravated assault	156	295
Property crimes		
Total incidents	2,704	3,588
Burglary	392	741
Larceny/theft	2,070	2,415
Motor vehicle theft	243	433
All crimes	2,980	4,063

Source: U.S. Federal Bureau of Investigation, *Crime in the United
States,* annual.

State prison populations, 1980-2003

	State	U.S.	State share
1980	8,920	305,458	2.92%
1990	17,593	708,393	2.48%
1996	27,655	1,025,624	2.70%
2000	30,168	1,391,261	2.17%
2003	35,067	1,470,045	2.39%

State figures exclude prisoners in federal penitentiaries.
Source: U.S. Bureau of Justice Statistics, *Prisoners in 2003.*

Washington

Location: Northwest Pacific coast

Area and rank: 66,582 square miles (172,447 square kilometers); 71,303 square miles (184,675 square kilometers) including water; twentieth largest state in area

Coastline: 157 miles (253 kilometers) on the Pacific Ocean

Shoreline: 3,026 miles (4,870 kilometers)

Population and rank: 6,204,000 (2004); fifteenth largest state in population

Capital city: Olympia (42,514 people in 2000 census)

Largest city: Seattle (563,374 people in 2000 census)

Became territory: March 2, 1853

State capitol building in Olympia. (State of Washington Tourism Development)

Entered Union and rank: November 11, 1889; forty-second state

Present constitution adopted: 1889

Counties: 39

State name: Washington was named for President George Washington

State nicknames: Evergreen State; Chinook State

Motto: *Al-ki* (American Indian word meaning "by and by")

State flag: Dark green background with state seal

Highest point: Mount Rainier—14,410 feet (4,392 meters)

Lowest point: Pacific Ocean—sea level

Highest recorded temperature: 118 degrees Fahrenheit (48 degrees Celsius)—Ice Harbor Dam, 1961

Lowest recorded temperature: –48 degrees Fahrenheit (–44 degrees Celsius)—Mazama and Winthrop, 1968

State song: "Washington, My Home"

State tree: Western hemlock

State flower: Coast rhododendron

State bird: Willow goldfinch

State fish: Steelhead trout

National parks: Mount Rainier; North Cascades; Olympic

Washington History

Like its southern neighbor Oregon, Washington is divided into two distinct geographical parts, a wet, forested western portion, and a semi-arid east. Washington's forests made it one of the nation's great timber producers, while its dry eastern portion requires extensive irrigation for agricultural productivity. While it shares geographical features with Oregon and Idaho, making up the Pacific Northwest region, Washington's social and political complexion has its own unique qualities. One reason is that unlike Oregon, Washington was not first settled by farmers.

After the earliest period, in which its white inhabitants were predominantly trappers, Washington's early history was dominated by extraction industries, such as gold mining and logging. Later, toward the end of the nineteenth century, large industry brought with it conflict between big business and big labor, which affected the state's social character. Later still, after the middle of the twentieth century, industries that prospered in the state on account of the Cold War left their own indelible imprint on the state's economy, society, and politics.

Early History. The early history of the area that became Washington was dominated by the struggle for control of the region by Great Britain, Russia, and Spain, followed by the United States. By 1775 Spain was sending expeditions up the Pacific coast, mainly to secure a buffer zone between Russian and British claims and its Mexican territory. Russia asserted claims far distant from Alaska, sending landing parties as far south as California. While Spain and Russia dropped out of the competition by the end of the eighteenth century, Britain opposed its former colonies, now a scrappy young republic. The Americans, for their part, strengthened their claims to the region when, after the 1803 Louisiana Purchase, the expedition of Meriwether Lewis and William Clark arrived and wintered by the Pacific at Fort Clatsop.

In 1792, the Americans sent Captain Robert Gray to the northwest, where he discovered the Columbia River and named it after his ship. In the same year, Britain sent an expedition led by George Vancouver to the region. Members of the expedition of British captain James Cook had already discovered the value of sea otter pelts bought from American Indians and sold profitably in China. By 1818 the two nations agreed to share the region. The Pacific North West Company dominated the fur trade until 1821, when it merged with Hudson's Bay Company, which remained the most influential non-Indian power in the area until 1846.

Native American peoples occupied a key position in the fur trade, especially in the beginning, before white trappers appeared in any numbers and before native populations became depleted. Native Americans provided sea otter pelts and other furs to white traders in exchange for manufactured goods, especially those made of metal, unknown in American Indian cultures. These included tools that added to the Native Ameri-

In the twenty-first century, ferryboats remain an important mode of transportation connecting the mainland with the peninsulas and islands of Puget Sound. Washington has one of the largest fleets of auto and passenger ferries in the world.

cans' ability to produce goods for themselves. Indians benefited from material goods, but their contact with whites proved catastrophic, since they contracted small pox and other diseases that decimated their numbers. It has been estimated that the population of Native American peoples on the northwest coast declined during the century following 1774 from about 200,000 to about 40,000, or some 80 percent. Moreover, by the 1820's sea otters were nearly extinct.

By 1810 a second phase of the fur trade began, increasingly dominated by Europeans and centered on beaver and similar mammals. This trade was focused on inland areas and required European trading companies to establish forts and interior avenues of transportation. News of the area finally took hold of the American imagination in the East and Midwest after the success of fur-trading companies illustrated the possibilities of internal development. The stage was set for the arrival of immigrants in large numbers.

The Anglo-American condominium begun in 1818 lasted into the 1840's. By then, however, the U.S. westward expansion, with its drive to possess the continent as its manifest destiny, brought hundreds, then thousands of American settlers to the region. During the early 1840's, Hudson's Bay Company, which was interested in commerce, not settlement, moved its base of operations northward, focusing on the area that became British Columbia. Although American nationalists sought lands north of the fifty-fourth parallel, the

United States, negotiating in 1846 with far-stronger Britain, settled for the forty-eighth parallel as a boundary. Two years later Oregon Territory, including what became Washington, was established.

From Territory to State. After the establishment of Oregon Territory in 1848, the population north of the Columbia River grew rapidly. Accordingly, in 1853 the Territory of Washington was formed. A decade later, gold strikes in the eastern portion led to its breaking off to become separately organized as Idaho Territory. Except for adjustments in Puget Sound's San Juan Islands, Washington's boundaries were now fixed. Sentiment for statehood strengthened during the Civil War, and in 1867 the territorial legislature urged Congress to admit a new state. Not until 1889, however, did Congress pass the required legislation for statehood, admitting Washington into the Union.

As it was growing toward statehood, Washington experienced an ugly social and moral pathology, in the form of anti-Chinese racism. When economic downturns arrived, labor unions made scapegoats of Chinese laborers, who arrived after 1840. Chinese were reviled for driving down wages, and serious incidents occurred, especially during the mid-1880's in Seattle, Tacoma, and other cities, when Chinese were driven out. As a result, the Chinese population in the Pacific Northwest dropped sharply.

If few Chinese could resist ill treatment, the same was not always true of the state's Native American peo-

Seattle, looking south toward Mount Rainier. The prominent Space Needle, at the left, was built for Seattle's 1962 world's fair.
(State of Washington Tourism Development)

ples. Prophetic religious visions encouraging American Indians to live by their old customs were one form of resistance. Suing in the courts was another. Such attempts at peaceful resolution of disputes followed the armed conflicts that occurred, for example, between 1855 and 1859, when the influx of miners after gold strikes alarmed the native peoples. Relations between settlers and Native Americans were complicated by the fact that there were different points of view not only among the federal government, the settlers, and the Indians, but within each group as well. Tribes or subtribal bands sometimes fought among themselves over policy toward white society.

Policy toward the American Indians reflected both idealism and self-interest, resulting in the reservation system. Reservations were designed both to separate tribal societies from the settlers and to "civilize" them, that is, to adapt them to the European ways, "detribalizing" and assimilating them to American society. Native American children were taken to boarding schools for this purpose. The treaty system that reflected this policy was unreliable, however, partly because the U.S. Senate frequently rejected treaties. Moreover, not all tribal members agreed with the treaties as negotiated, and discontent and confusion sometimes followed their signing. Treaties signed in 1854 and 1855 failed to prevent the conflicts of 1855-1858. Both wars and considerable crime broke out among American Indians and settlers between 1850 and 1880. Efforts were made to reform the reservation system and assimilation policy, to little effect. After the 1930's, however, the goal of assimilation was reconsidered. By the 1970's, Native Americans were having considerable success defending tribal rights in the courts.

1880's to 1945. Washington inaugurated its statehood with a government that reflected its past as a frontier society. As the frontier distrusted political power, especially executive power, so did the state. Accordingly, Washington's constitution called for a plural executive, with a number of elected offices, rather than a single, all-powerful governor. These included, besides governor and lieutenant governor, a secretary of state (chief elections officer), attorney general, treasurer, auditor, and others.

The state's politics in the next decades followed national trends as well as home-grown movements. Populism and radical parties and sects arose between 1880 and 1920, making a lasting impact. Reformers were influential because the state saw itself in a formative, malleable stage of collective life. The state's constitution showed strong Populist influence, distrusting big business by banning gifts or loans of public money and credit to private enterprise. The constitution's bill of rights protected individual rights even more than the federal Bill of Rights. Not surprisingly, the People's Party candidate for president received 22 percent of the vote in 1892.

The Progressive movement also deeply affected Washington, as it did its southern neighbor. Around the turn of the century, like Oregon, Washington voters gained the powers of initiative, referendum, and, later, recall elections. Municipal ownership of utilities and urban planning became public policy, and nature conservation, a recurring feature of the state's politics, appeared. In addition, radicalism and utopianism had some influence; the International Workers of the World (IWW), a Marxist party founded in Chicago in 1905, was active on the political fringes prior to and just after World War I.

By the Depression years of the 1930's, radicalism was a spent force, and, as elsewhere in the nation, federal policies attempted to come to the state's rescue. In building dams and in other projects, federal spending became an essential element in the state's economy, prefiguring what was to come. The most important single project was the Grand Coulee dam, but other dams were constructed. In addition, the Civilian Conservation Corps (CCC) was active in parks and forests; and there existed public housing and irrigation projects, among other federal programs.

Power generated from the Columbia River Basin was essential for the defense industries that sprang up during the war years. Among them were atomic development works at Hanford, where the plutonium for the nation's first atomic weapons was produced. Later it was discovered that the Hanford nuclear reactor also produced much radioactive waste that endangered both people and the natural world.

Postwar Economy and Politics. After World War II, many thought the state's economy would suffer badly from the nation's military stand-down, but they were mistaken. The advent of the Cold War brought further defense spending to Washington, including additional development of the Hanford atomic facility. By the 1950's the Boeing Company near Seattle was receiving large contracts from the Pentagon. Federal spending also helped the state with the continuing development of hyroelectric power and crop-irrigation facilities through dam construction. Thanks to voter loyalty, the state was gaining influence in Washington, D.C., through the reelection of its senators Warren Magnuson and Henry "Scoop" Jackson, sometimes called "the senator from Boeing." Later, Representative Tom Foley became Speaker of the U.S. House of Representatives.

To celebrate the success of the state and its principal city, a world's fair was held in Seattle in 1962. Its futuristic free-standing tower, known as a space needle, became an icon of forward-thrusting technological prowess and self-confidence and was widely imitated around the world. As might be expected, the influence of the Boeing Company on the exposition was widely noticeable.

Later decades, however, saw a different side of Washington's success, as environmentally conscious activists sought to counterbalance the influence of timber and other industries. This was especially evident as the state's nuclear-power board defaulted on bonds used to build nuclear reactors, all but one of which were never completed. This was also evident as early as 1974, when Spokane opened Expo '74, the world's first environmental world's fair. By the end of the century, Washington was economically thriving on a balance of "high-tech" industries such as Boeing and Microsoft, tourism, and agriculture. Although anti-Asian sentiment was long outdated, civil rights issues for African Americans remained. Environmental problems, such as the decline of salmon, a state icon, also remained, and there was marked resistance to further economic development that would endanger the state's natural environment.

Terrorism Investigations. Around the dawn of the new millennium, Washington was a focus of Islamic terrorism investigations. The state was jittery after a suspicious customs official at the border crossing in the small town of Port Angeles in late 1999 arrested a Middle Eastern man with explosives in his car. In 2002, a federal grand jury probed whether two defunct Seattle mosques had ties with the terrorist organization al-Qaeda. In July of the same year, federal agents had arrested two men said to have documents in their possession describing methods of poisoning water supplies. One of those arrested had close relations with one of the closed Seattle mosques. There were a series of other raids, indictments, and accusations of terror connections. Thus, U.S. Customs raided a Seattle-area money transfer office run by Somalis, who were also said to be linked with al-Qaeda.

Moreover, in May, 2003, Seattle held a biological and radiological terrorism drill. The terrorist threat that affected the entire West Coast of the nation erupted again in August, 2006, when part of the port of Seattle was closed after bomb-sniffing dogs reacted to shipping containers from Pakistan, though no explosives were found. The state was also subject to homegrown terrorism. In June, 2001, a bomb went off at a Tacoma clinic where abortions were sometimes performed, but no one was hurt.

During this period, officials also grew concerned over Washington's border and its penetration by illegal immigrants. The Seattle-Vancouver, Canada, area functioned as a major port of entry for human smugglers. In 2000, the U.S. and Canada signed a border security pact. However, in the same year, continued smuggling of aliens led to the deaths of several Chinese immigrants found in Seattle shipping containers.

Boeing. Among economic problems in the state, the Boeing Company, one of the state's principal employers, was cited by Federal Aviation Administration inspectors as having more than one hundred specific problems said to be "deeply rooted" and "systemic." The following year, Boeing announced it was relocating corporate headquarters from Seattle, its base since 1916, to Chicago.

Politics. A controversy over the official recognition of an Indian tribe, making it eligible to open gambling facilities, erupted in 2001. In January, the outgoing Clinton administration recognized the Duwamish tribe, but the incoming Bush administration voided the decision, citing procedural errors. Privately, it was suggested that the tribe received recognition as a payoff after it contributed to the Democratic Party. The tribe traces its lineage to renowned Chief Seattle.

In electoral politics, Gary Locke, the nation's first Chinese American governor, was reelected in 2000. In that election, Democrat Al Gore took the state's presidential electoral votes. After confirmation by a recount, Republican U.S. senator Slade Gorton was defeated by Democrat Maria Cantwell, who spent $10 million of her own money, by just 2,229 votes, or .09 percent. Nationally, the state went to Al Gore, who received the state's eleven electoral votes by a 50-45 percent margin.

In the 2004 governor's race, when term limits stopped incumbent Locke from running, an exceptionally close contest put Democrat Christine Gregoire in the statehouse. Several disputed recounts found her the winner over former state senator Dino Rossi by just 129 votes. In the presidential balloting, the Democrats, headed by John Kerry, again won the state's electoral votes, defeating George W. Bush by 53 to 46 percent.

R. Baird Shuman
Updated by the Editor

Washington Time Line

1500's	Spanish and English explorers sail off Washington coast.
1775	Spanish explorers Bruno Hecta and Juan Bidega y Quadra are first Europeans on Washington soil.
1778	English explorer Captain James Cook sights Washington coast.
1788-1794	Great Britain sends twenty-five fur-trading ships to Washington, compared to fifteen sent by the United States.
1790	Spain and Britain sign Nootka Sound Convention, resolving claims to Northwest in British favor.
1792-1795	Explorer George Vancouver surveys Puget Sound and Georgia Gulf region.
1795-1814	U.S. sends ninety fur-trading ships to region, compared to twelve sent by Britain.
1805	Meriwether Lewis and William Clark lead their expedition down Columbia River to the Pacific Ocean.
1807-1811	Canadian explorer and geographer David Thompson travels down Columbia River to the Pacific Ocean.
1818	United States and Britain sign treaty allowing joint occupation of Oregon Country, including Washington.
1825	John McLoughlin of Britain's Hudson's Bay Company completes Fort Vancouver on Columbia River.
1840's	Americans trekking over the Oregon Trail settle in modern Washington.
1844	Election slogan Fifty-Four Forty or Fight adopted during presidential campaign of James K. Polk.
1846	United States and Britain sign treaty fixing northwest U.S. boundary at the forty-ninth parallel.
1848	Congress passes bill creating Oregon Territory, including Washington; General Joseph Lane is appointed territorial governor.
1852	Seattle is settled.
1853	Bill creating Washington Territory is signed into law; Isaac Ingalls Stevens is appointed first governor.
1855	Governor Stevens's efforts to move American Indians to reservations lead to Indian wars.
1858-1859	Indian wars end, and treaties with the tribes are ratified.
1860	Gold strikes in nearby regions lead to increased migration to Washington.
1863	Washington receives present boundaries when neighboring lands become Idaho Territory.
1872	San Juan Islands in Puget Sound awarded to United States, ending dispute with Britain.

Crater of Mount Saint Helens, viewed from the north, several years after the volcano's 1980 eruption. (PhotoDisc)

1883	Completion of transcontinental railroad leads to increased migration from the East.
Nov. 11, 1889	Washington becomes nation's forty-second state.
1897	Klondike gold rush brings boom as merchants provide supplies to miners.
1900	Irrigation of arid eastern Washington lands creates fertile farmland.
1909	Alaska-Yukon-Pacific Exposition held in Seattle to celebrate port's growth.
1917	U.S. entrance into World War I proves a boon to Washington economy.
1919	Nation's first general strike is held in Washington.
1930's	Great Depression brings economic hardship to state.
1930's	Construction on Bonneville and Grand Coulee Dams helps ease economic ills.
1942-1945	World War II provides great stimulus to state's economy.
1942	Federal government establishes Hanford nuclear energy facility, which helps build first atomic bombs.
1950's-1960's	Postwar economy develops industrial, manufacturing sectors.
1960's	Hanford nuclear energy facility begins producing electricity.
1960's	Growth of Boeing Aircraft Company provides important economic expansion in the state.
1962	Seattle's World Fair is signal success and stimulates tourist industry.
1964	United States and Canada approve plan for cooperative development of hydroelectric power.
1970's-1980's	State project to build five nuclear power plants incurs large cost overruns; four are never completed.
1980	Mount Saint Helens, long-dormant volcano, erupts, causing billions of dollars in damage.
1980-1990's	Led by Microsoft and Boeing Corporations, high-tech firms provide significant economic strength to the state.
1983	State nuclear power agency defaults on $2.25 billion of municipal bonds; construction on the power plants ceases.
1999	One hundredth anniversary of Mount Rainier National Park.
Nov. 7, 2000	Al Gore defeats George W. Bush in presidential poll; Democrat Maria Cantwell wins U.S. Senate seat by .09 percent of the vote.
2001	Boeing Company announces relocation of its corporate headquarters from Seattle to Chicago.

(continued)

May 12, 2003	Seattle holds an antiterrorism drill, simulating biological and radiological attacks.
Nov. 2, 2004	Democrat John Kerry wins the state's eleven electoral votes, while Democrat Christine Gregoire wins governorship by 129 votes.
Aug. 16, 2006	Part of the port of Seattle is closed after bomb-sniffing dogs indicate shipping containers might contain explosives.

Notes for Further Study

Published Sources. Several older but still useful titles are a good option for readers interested in Washington's history: Robert Ficken and C. P. LeWarne's *Washington: A Centennial History* (1988), Mary W. Avery's *Washington: A History of the Evergreen State* (1965), and Norman Clark's *Washington: A Bicentennial History* (1976). *Washington: A State of Contrasts* (2001) by Dale A. Lambert examines the complex past and present history of Washington and its unique geographic regions. *Washington's History: The People, Land, and Events of the Far Northwest* (2003) by Harry Ritter explores the events and people who helped in the development of Washington State.

A brief introduction to the study of local history is *Discovering Washington: A Guide to State and Local History* (1989) by Keith Petersen and Mary Reed. Resources on recreation include Ira Spring and Harvey Manning's *One Hundred Classic Hikes in Washington* (1998) and Archie Satterfield and Dale Swensson's *Natural Wonders of Washington: A Guide to Parks, Preserves, and Wild Places* (1996). For those touring the state or a locality, an excellent work is *A Traveler's History of Washington* (1996) by Bill Gulick or *Exploring Washington's Backroads: Highways and Hometowns of the Evergreen State* (2005) by John J. Deviny. The state's geography is discussed in James Scott and R. L. Delorme's *Historical Atlas of Washington* (1988). Native Seattleite Fred Moody, in his fascinating *Seattle and the Demons of Ambition* (2003), details the city's boom-bust economic cycles in the last three decades of the twentieth century and their influence on social and political factors within the city, the state, and across the country.

Web Resources. For government and public resources on the Web, the state of Washington home page is a good starting point (access.wa.gov/). The Washington State Legislature site (www1.leg.wa.gov/legislature/) is extensive, offering links to elected officials, laws and agency rules, and history sites. The Washington State History Museum (www.wshs.org/) is an excellent resource for information on the state's past, as is History Link (www.historylink.org/this_week/index.cfm), an extensive online encyclopedia.

Information on state parks may be found at Washington State Parks (www.parks.wa.gov). For resources on the history of Native Americans, including Washington's tribes, on the Internet, users should consult the Northwest Indian Country site (www.tribaltourism.com/) or (www.kstrom.net/isk/maps/wa/wamap.html). The city of Seattle is important to the state for economic, cultural, and tourist reasons. A good site at which to learn more about the city is the official city page (www.seattle.gov/) or the city's Convention and Visitor's Bureau (www.seeseattle.org/).

Counties

County	2000 pop.	Rank in pop.	Sq. miles	Rank in area
Adams	16,428	31	1,925.0	14
Asotin	20,551	29	635.9	34
Benton	142,475	10	1,703.1	22
Chelan	66,616	17	2,921.6	3
Clallam	64,525	18	1,745.2	20
Clark	345,238	5	627.9	35
Columbia	4,064	37	868.8	31
Cowlitz	92,948	12	1,138.7	28
Douglas	32,603	26	1,820.6	17
Ferry	7,260	36	2,204.0	9
Franklin	49,347	21	1,242.2	27
Garfield	2,397	39	710.5	33
Grant	74,698	13	2,676.4	4
Grays Harbor	67,194	16	1,917.3	15
Island	71,558	14	208.6	38
Jefferson	25,953	27	1,808.8	18
King	1,737,034	1	2,126.1	11
Kitsap	231,969	6	396.0	36
Kittitas	33,362	25	2,296.7	8
Klickitat	19,161	30	1,872.5	16
Lewis	68,600	15	2,407.8	6
Lincoln	10,184	34	2,311.2	7
Mason	49,405	20	961.1	30
Okanogan	39,564	24	5,268.3	1
Pacific	20,984	28	974.6	29
Pend Oreille	11,732	33	1,400.5	25
Pierce	700,820	2	1,675.5	23
San Juan	14,077	32	174.9	39
Skagit	102,979	11	1,735.3	21
Skamania	9,872	35	1,656.5	24
Snohomish	606,024	3	2,090.2	13
Spokane	417,939	4	1,763.8	19
Stevens	40,066	23	2,478.3	5
Thurston	207,355	8	727.1	32
Wahkiakum	3,824	38	264.3	37
Walla Walla	55,180	19	1,270.5	26
Whatcom	166,814	9	2,120.1	12
Whitman	40,740	22	2,159.4	10
Yakima	222,581	7	4,296.1	2

Source: U.S. Census Bureau; National Association of Counties.

Cities

With 10,000 or more residents

Rank	City	Population
1	Seattle	563,374
2	Spokane	195,629
3	Tacoma	193,556
4	Vancouver	143,560
5	Bellevue	109,569
6	Everett	91,488
7	Federal Way	83,259
8	Kent	79,524
9	Yakima	71,845
10	Bellingham	67,171
11	Lakewood	58,211
12	Kennewick	54,693
13	Shoreline	53,025
14	Renton	50,052
15	Redmond	45,256
16	Kirkland	45,054
17	Olympia (capital)	42,514
18	Auburn	40,314
19	Edmonds	39,515
20	Richland	38,708
21	Bremerton	37,259
22	Seattle Hill-Silver Firs	35,311
23	Longview	34,660
24	Cascade-Fairwood	34,580
25	Sammamish	34,104
26	Lynnwood	33,847
27	Puyallup	33,011
28	Pasco	32,066
29	Burien	31,881
30	South Hill	31,623
31	Lacey	31,226
32	Bothell	30,150
33	University Place	29,933
34	Walla Walla	29,686
35	East Hill-Meridian	29,308
36	Des Moines	29,267
37	Wenatchee	27,856
38	Mount Vernon	26,232
39	North Creek	25,742
40	SeaTac	25,496
41	Marysville	25,315
42	Opportunity	25,065
43	Pullman	24,675
44	Paine Field-Lake Stickney	24,383
45	Cottage Lake	24,330
46	Parkland	24,053
47	Picnic Point-North Lynnwood	22,953
48	Inglewood-Finn Hill	22,661

(continued)

Rank	City	Population
49	Mercer Island	22,036
50	Spanaway	21,588
51	North Marysville	21,161
52	White Center	20,975
53	Mountlake Terrace	20,362
54	Bainbridge Island	20,308
55	Oak Harbor	19,795
56	Fort Lewis	19,089
57	Kenmore	18,678
58	Port Angeles	18,397
59	West Lake Stevens	18,071
60	Mukilteo	18,019
61	Orchards	17,852
62	Tukwila	17,181
63	Salmon Creek	16,767
64	Aberdeen	16,461
65	Silverdale	15,816
66	Elk Plain	15,697
67	Ellensburg	15,414
68	Alderwood Manor	15,329
69	Lakeland North	15,085
70	Moses Lake	14,953
71	Centralia	14,742
72	Anacortes	14,557
73	Maple Valley	14,209
74	Bryn Mawr-Skyway	13,977
75	Sunnyside	13,905

Rank	City	Population
76	Monroe	13,795
77	Covington	13,783
78	East Wenatchee Bench	13,658
79	Camano	13,347
80	East Renton Highlands	13,264
81	Lake Forest Park	13,142
82	Tumwater	12,698
83	Martha Lake	12,633
84	Camas	12,534
85	Kingsgate	12,222
86	Five Corners	12,207
87	Kelso	11,895
88	Arlington	11,713
89	Prairie Ridge	11,688
90	Mill Creek	11,525
91	Lakeland South	11,436
92	Union Hill-Novelty Hill	11,265
93	Issaquah	11,212
94	Riverton-Boulevard Park	11,188
95	Enumclaw	11,116
96	Lea Hill	10,871
97	West Valley	10,433
98	Vashon	10,123
99	Dishman	10,031

Population figures are from 2000 census.
Source: U.S. Bureau of the Census.

Index to Tables

DEMOGRAPHICS

Resident state and national populations, 1970-2004

Population figures given in thousands

	State pop.	U.S. pop.	Share	Rank
1970	3,413	203,302	1.7%	22
1980	4,132	226,546	1.8%	20
1985	4,400	237,924	1.9%	20
1990	4,867	248,765	2.0%	18
1995	5,481	262,761	2.1%	15
2000	5,894	281,425	2.1%	15
2004	6,204	293,655	2.1%	15

Source: U.S. Census Bureau, Current Population Reports, 2006.

Resident population by age, 2004

Age Group	Total persons
Under 5 years	387,000
5 to 17 years	1,099,000
18 to 24 years	635,000
25 to 34 years	859,000
35 to 44 years	956,000
45 to 54 years	933,000
55 to 64 years	631,000
65 to 74 years	357,000
75 to 84 years	243,000
85 years and older	103,000
All age groups	6,204,000
Portion of residents 65 and older	11.3%
National rank in portion of oldest residents	43
National average	12.4%

Population figures are rounded to nearest thousand persons;
figures include armed forces personnel stationed in the state.
Source: U.S. Bureau of the Census, 2006.

Resident population by race, Hispanic origin, 2004

Category	State pop.	Share	U.S.
All residents	6,204	100.00%	100.00%
Non-Hispanic white	4,809	77.51%	67.37%
Hispanic white	481	7.75%	13.01%
Other Hispanic	46	0.74%	1.06%
African American	216	3.48%	12.77%
Native American	101	1.63%	0.96%
Asian, Pacific Islander	416	6.71%	4.37%
Two or more categories	180	2.90%	1.51%

Population figures are in thousands. Persons counted as "Hispanic" (Latino) may be of any race. Because of overlapping categories, categories may not add up to 100%. Shares in column 3 are percentages of each category within the state; these figures may be compared to the national percentages in column 4.
Source: U.S. Bureau of the Census, 2006.

Projected state population, 2000-2030

Year	Population
2000	5,894,000
2005	6,205,000
2010	6,542,000
2015	6,951,000
2020	7,432,000
2025	7,996,000
2030	8,625,000
Population increase, 2000-2030	2,731,000
Percentage increase, 2000-2030	46.3

Projections are based on data from the 2000 census.
Source: U.S. Census Bureau.

VITAL STATISTICS

Infant mortality rates, 1980-2002

	1980	1990	2000	2002
All state residents	11.8	7.8	5.2	5.8
All U.S. residents	12.6	9.2	9.4	9.1
All state white residents	11.5	7.3	4.9	5.5
All U.S. white residents	10.6	7.6	5.7	5.8
All state black residents	16.4	20.6	9.4	12.7
All U.S. black residents	22.2	18.0	14.1	14.4

Figures represent deaths per 1,000 live births of resident infants under 1 year old, exclusive of fetal deaths. Figures for all residents include members of other racial categories not listed separately.
Source: U.S. Census Bureau, *Statistical Abstract of the United States,* 2006.

Abortion rates, 1990 and 2000

	1990	2000
Total abortions	33,000	26,000
Rate per 1,000 women	27.7	20.3
U.S. rate	25.7	21.3
Rank	10	17

Numbers of abortions are rounded to nearest thousand; ranks are based on rates.
Source: U.S. Census Bureau.

Marriages and divorces, 2004

Total marriages	40,100
Rate per 1,000 population	6.5
National rate per 1,000 population	7.4
Rank among all states	32
Total divorces	25,200
Rate per 1,000 population	4.1
National rate per 1,000 population	3.7
Rank among all states	16

Figures are for all marriages and divorces performed within the state, including those of nonresidents; totals are rounded to the nearest hundred. Ranks are for highest to lowest figures; note that divorce data are not available for five states.
Source: U.S. National Center for Health Statistics, *Vital Statistics of the United States,* 2006.

Death rates by leading causes, 2002
Deaths per 100,000 resident population

Cause	State	U.S.
Heart disease	183.6	241.7
Cancer	178.9	193.2
Cerebrovascular diseases	61.8	56.4
Accidents other than motor vehicle	36.3	37.0
Motor vehicle accidents	12.5	15.7
Chronic lower respiratory diseases	44.8	43.3
Diabetes mellitus	24.6	25.4
HIV	2.0	4.9
Suicide	13.4	11.0
Homicide	3.5	6.1
All causes	747.0	847.3
Rank in overall death rate among states		43

Figures exclude nonresidents who died in the state. Causes of death follow International Classification of Diseases. Rank is from highest to lowest death rate in the United States.
Source: U.S. National Center for Health Statistics, *National Vital Statistics Report,* 2006.

ECONOMY

Gross state product, 1990-2004
In current dollars

Year	State product	Nat'l product	State share
1990	$115.7 billion	$5.67 trillion	2.04%
2000	$221.3 billion	$9.75 trillion	2.27%
2002	$234.0 billion	$10.41 trillion	2.25%
2003	$245.1 billion	$10.92 trillion	2.24%
2004	$259.8 billion	$11.65 trillion	2.23%

Source: U.S. Bureau of Economic Analysis, *Survey of Current Business,* July, 2005.

Gross state product by industry, 2003
In billions of dollars

Construction	$9.7
Manufacturing	21.0
Wholesale trade	14.1
Retail trade	18.5
Finance & insurance	13.8
Information	21.4
Professional services	15.4
Health care & social assistance	14.3
Government	31.2
Total state product	$229.7
Total U.S. product	$10,289.2
State share of U.S. total	2.23%
Rank among all states	14

Total figures include industries not listed separately. Amounts are in chained 2000 dollars.
Source: U.S. Bureau of Economic Analysis, *Survey of Current Business,* July, 2005.

Personal income per capita, 1990-2004
In current dollars

	1990	2000	2004
Per capita income	$19,865	$31,779	$35,299
U.S. average	$19,477	$29,845	$32,937
Rank among states	16	11	11

Source: U.S. Bureau of Economic Analysis, *Survey of Current Business,* April, 2005.

Energy consumption, 2001
In trillions of British thermal units (BTU), except as noted

Total energy consumption

Total state energy consumption	2,034
Total U.S. energy consumption	96,275
State share of U.S. total	2.11%
Rank among states	16

Per capita consumption (In millions of BTU)

Total state per capita consumption	339
Total U.S. per capita consumption	338
Rank among states	27

End-use sectors

Residential	471
Commercial	377
Industrial	586
Transportation	600

Sources of energy

Petroleum	843
Natural gas	323
Coal	100
Hydroelectric power	557
Nuclear electric power	86

Figures for totals include categories not listed separately.
Source: U.S. Energy Information Administration, *State Energy Data Report,* 2001.

Nonfarm employment by sectors, 2004

Total persons	2,698,000
Construction	164,000
Manufacturing	264,000
Trade, transportation, utilities	519,000
Information	92,000
Finance, insurance, real estate	152,000
Professional & business services	302,000
Education & health services	319,000
Leisure, hospitality, arts, organizations	255,000
Other services, including repair & maintenance	100,000
Government	523,000

Figures are rounded to nearest thousand persons. "Total" includes mining and natural resources, not listed separately.
Source: U.S. Bureau of Labor Statistics, 2006.

Foreign exports, 1990-2004
In millions of dollars

Year	State	U.S.	State share
1990	24,432	394,045	6.20%
1996	26,482	624,767	4.24%
1997	32,752	688,896	4.75%
2000	32,215	712,055	4.12%
2003	34,173	724,006	5.06%
2004	33,793	769,332	4.39%

Rank among all states in 2004. 5

U.S. total does not include U.S. dependencies.
Source: U.S. Census Bureau, *U.S. Merchandise Trade*, series FT 900, 2000; U.S. Census Bureau, *U.S. International Trade in Goods and Services*, Series FT 900, 2005.

LAND USE

Federally owned land, 2003
Areas in acres

	State	U.S.	State share
Total area	42,694,000	2,271,343,000	1.88%
Nonfederal land	29,447,000	1,599,584,000	1.84%
Federal land	13,247,000	671,759,000	1.97%
Federal share	31.0%	29.6%	—

Areas are rounded to nearest thousand acres. Figures for federally owned land do not include trust properties.
Source: U.S. General Services Administration, *Federal Real Property Profile*, 2006.

Land use, 1997
In acres, rounded to nearest thousand

Total surface area	44,035,000
Total nonfederal rural land.	28,508,000
Percentage rural land	64.7%
Cropland	6,656,000
Conservation Reserve Program (CRP*) land . . .	1,017,000
Pastureland	1,193,000
Rangeland	5,857,000
Forestland	12,835,000
Other rural land	951,000

*CRP is a federal program begun in 1985 to assist private landowners to convert highly erodible cropland to vegetative cover for ten years. Note that some categories of land overlap.
Source: U.S. Department of Agriculture, Natural Resources and Conservation Service, and Iowa State University, Statistical Laboratory, *Summary Report, 1997 National Resources Inventory*, revised December, 2000.

Farms and crop acreage, 2004

	State	U.S.	Share	Rank
Farms	35,000	2,113,000	1.66%	26
Acres (millions)	15	937	1.60%	19
Acres per farm	434	443	—	15

Source: U.S. Department of Agriculture, National Agricultural Statistics Service. Numbers of farms are rounded to nearest thousand units; acreage figures are rounded to nearest million. Rankings, including ties, are based on rounded figures.

GOVERNMENT AND FINANCE

Units of local government, 2002

	State	Total U.S.	Rank
All local governments	1,787	87,525	19
Counties	39	3,034	33
Municipalities	279	19,429	28
Townships	0	16,504	—
School districts	296	13,506	18
Special districts	1,173	35,052	8

Only 48 states have county governments, 20 states have township governments ("towns" in New England, Minnesota, New York, and Wisconsin), and 46 states have school districts. Special districts encompass such functions as natural resources, fire protection, and housing and community development.
Source: U.S. Census Bureau, *Census of Governments.*

State government revenue, 2002

Total revenue	$23,813 mill.
General revenue	$22,775 mill.
Per capita revenue	$3,754
U.S. per capita average	$3,689
Rank among states	21
Intergovernment revenue	
Total	$6,348 mill.
From federal government	$6,216 mill.
Charges and miscellaneous	
Total	$3,798 mill.
Current charges	$2,353 mill.
Misc. general income	$1,445 mill.
Insurance trust revenue	$673 mill.
Taxes	
Total	$12,629 mill.
Per capita taxes	$2,082
Rank among states	13
Property taxes	$1,457 mill.
Sales taxes	$9,950 mill.
License taxes	$631 mill.
Individual income taxes	(nil)
Corporate income taxes	(nil)
Other taxes	$590 mill.

Total revenue figures include items not listed separately here.
Source: U.S. Bureau of the Census.

State government expenditures, 2002

General expenditures

Total state expenditures . . . . $30,378 mill.
Intergovernmental. . . . . $6,806 mill.

Per capita expenditures

State $4,147
Average of all states $3,859
Rank among states 21

Selected direct expenditures

Education. $4,825 mill.
Public welfare . . . . $6,151 mill.
Health, hospital . . . . $2,088 mill.
Highways . . . . $1,254 mill.
Police protection. . . . . $175 mill.
Corrections. . . . . $735 mill.
Natural resources . . . . $553 mill.
Parks and recreation . . . . $201 mill.
Government administration. . . . . $539 mill.
Interest on debt . . . . $674 mill.
Total direct expenditures. . . . . $18,354 mill.

Totals include items not listed separately.
Source: U.S. Census Bureau.

POLITICS

Governors since statehood

D = Democrat; R = Republican; O = other;
(r) resigned; (d) died in office; (i) removed from office

Elisha P. Ferry (R) 1889-1893
John H. McGraw (R). 1893-1897
John R. Rogers (D) . . . . (d) 1897-1901
Henry McBride (R) 1901-1905
Albert E. Mead (R) 1905-1909
Samuel G. Cosgrove (R) . . . . (d) 1909
Marion E. Hay (R). 1909-1913
Ernest Lister (D) . . . . (d) 1913-1919
Louis F. Hart (R). 1919-1925
Roland H. Hartley (R). 1925-1933
Clarence D. Martin (D) 1933-1941
Arthur B. Langlie (R) 1941-1945
Monrad C. Wallgren (D) 1945-1949
Arthur B. Langlie (R) 1949-1957
Albert D. Rosellini (D) 1957-1965
Daniel J. Evans (R). 1965-1977
Dixie Lee Ray (D) 1977-1981
John Spellman (R). 1981-1985
Booth Gardner (D) 1985-1993
Mike Lowry (D) 1993-1997
Gary Locke (D) 1997-2005
Christine Gregoire (D) 2005-

Composition of congressional delegations, 1989-2007

	Dem	Rep	Total
House of Representatives			
101st Congress, 1989			
State delegates	5	3	8
Total U.S.	259	174	433
102d Congress, 1991			
State delegates	5	3	8
Total U.S.	267	167	434
103d Congress, 1993			
State delegates	8	1	9
Total U.S.	258	176	434
104th Congress, 1995			
State delegates	3	6	9
Total U.S.	197	236	433
105th Congress, 1997			
State delegates	5	4	9
Total U.S.	206	228	434
106th Congress, 1999			
State delegates	5	4	9
Total U.S.	211	222	433
107th Congress, 2001			
State delegates	6	3	9
Total U.S.	211	221	432
108th Congress, 2003			
State delegates	6	3	9
Total U.S.	205	229	434
109th Congress, 2005			
State delegates	6	3	9
Total U.S.	202	231	433
110th Congress, 2007			
State delegates	6	3	9
Total U.S.	233	202	435
Senate			
101st Congress, 1989			
State delegates	1	1	2
Total U.S.	55	45	100
102d Congress, 1991			
State delegates	1	1	2
Total U.S.	56	44	100
103d Congress, 1993			
State delegates	1	1	2
Total U.S.	57	43	100
104th Congress, 1995			
State delegates	1	1	2
Total U.S.	46	53	99
105th Congress, 1997			
State delegates	1	1	2
Total U.S.	45	55	100

(continued)

	Dem	Rep	Total
106th Congress, 1999			
State delegates	1	1	2
Total U.S.	45	54	99
107th Congress, 2001			
State delegates	2	0	2
Total U.S.	50	50	100
108th Congress, 2003			
State delegates	2	0	2
Total U.S.	48	51	99
109th Congress, 2005			
State delegates	2	0	2
Total U.S.	44	55	99
110th Congress, 2007			
State delegates	2	0	2
Total U.S.	49	49	98

Figures are for starts of first sessions. Totals are for Democrat (Dem.) and Republican (Rep.) members only. House membership totals under 435 and Senate totals under 100 reflect vacancies and seats held by independent party members. When the 110th Congress opened, the Senate's two independent members caucused with the Democrats, giving the Democrats control of the Senate.
Source: U.S. Congress, Congressional Directory.

Composition of state legislature, 1990-2006

	Democrats	Republicans
State House (98 seats)		
1990	58	40
1992	65	33
1994	38	60
1996	45	53
1998	49	49
2000	49	49
2002	52	46
2004	55	43
2006	63	35
State Senate (49 seats)		
1990	24	25
1992	28	21
1994	25	24
1996	23	26
1998	27	22
2000	27	22
2002	24	25
2004	26	23
2006	32	17

Figures for total seats may include independents and minor party members. Numbers reflect results of elections in listed years; elected members usually take their seats in the years that follow.
Source: Council of State Governments; State Elective Officials and the Legislatures.

Voter participation in presidential elections, 2000 and 2004

	2000	2004
Voting age population		
State	4,398,000	4,718,000
Total United States	209,831,000	220,377,000
State share of U.S. total	2.10	2.14
Rank among states	15	14
Portion of voting age population casting votes		
State	56.6%	60.6%
United States	50.3%	55.5%
Rank among states	15	17

Population figures are rounded to nearest thousand and include all residents, regardless of eligibility to vote.
Source: U.S. Census Bureau.

HEALTH AND MEDICAL CARE

Medical professionals
Physicians in 2003 and nurses in 2001

	U.S.	State
Physicians in 2003		
Total	774,849	16,347
Share of U.S. total		2.10%
Rate	266	267
Rank		13
Nurses in 2001		
Total	2,262,020	45,170
Share of U.S. total		2.00%
Rate	793	754
Rank		37

Rates are numbers of physicians and nurses per 100,000 resident population; ranks are based on rates.
Source: American Medical Association, Physician Characteristics and Distribution in the U.S.; U.S. Department of Health and Human Services, Health Resources and Services Administration.

Health insurance coverage, 2003

	State	U.S.
Total persons covered	5,147,000	243,320,000
Total persons not covered	944,000	44,961,000
Portion not covered	15.5%	15.6%
Rank among states	20	—
Children not covered	125,000	8,373,000
Portion not covered	8.4%	11.4%
Rank among states	31	—

Totals are rounded to nearest thousand. Ranks are from the highest to the lowest percentages of persons not insured.
Source: U.S. Census Bureau, Current Population Reports.

AIDS, syphilis, and tuberculosis cases, 2003

Disease	U.S. cases	State cases	Rank
AIDS	44,232	527	20
Syphilis	34,270	239	24
Tuberculosis	14,874	250	18

Source: U.S. Centers for Disease Control and Prevention.

Cigarette smoking, 2003
Residents over age 18 who smoke

	U.S.	State	Rank
All smokers	22.1%	19.5%	42
Male smokers	24.8%	20.9%	41
Female smokers	20.3%	18.2%	39

Cigarette smokers are defined as persons who reported having smoked at least 100 cigarettes during their lifetimes and who currently smoked at least occasionally.

Source: U.S. Centers for Disease Control and Prevention, *Morbidity and Mortality Weekly Report,* 53, no. 44 (November 12, 2004).

HOUSING

Home ownership rates, 1985-2004

	1985	1990	1995	2000	2004
State	66.8%	61.8%	61.6%	63.6%	66.0%
Total U.S.	63.9%	63.9%	64.7%	67.4%	69.0%
Rank among states	31	41	42	45	43

Net change in state home ownership rate,
  1985-2004 . . . . −0.8%
Net change in U.S. home ownership rate,
  1985-2004 . . . . +5.1%

Percentages represent the proportion of owner households to total occupied households.

Source: U.S. Census Bureau, 2006.

Home sales, 2000-2004
In thousands of units

Existing home sales	2000	2002	2003	2004
State sales	112.4	116.3	132.3	147.6
Total U.S. sales	5,171	5,631	6,183	6,784
State share of U.S. total	2.17%	2.07%	2.14%	2.18%
Sales rank among states	13	17	14	15

Units include single-family homes, condos, and co-ops.

Source: National Association of Realtors, Washington, D.C., *Real Estate Outlook: Market Trends & Insights.*

Values of owner-occupied homes, 2003

	State	U.S.
Total units	1,254,000	58,809,000
Value of units		
Under $100,000	9.1%	29.6%
$100,000-199,999	40.8%	36.9%
$200,000 or more	50.1%	33.5%
Median value	$200,235	$142,275
Rank among all states 9		

Units are owner-occupied one-family houses whose numbers are rounded to nearest thousand. Data are extrapolated from survey samples.

Source: U.S. Census Bureau, American Community Survey.

EDUCATION

Public school enrollment, 2002

Prekindergarten through grade 8
State enrollment 697,000
Total U.S. enrollment 34,135,000
State share of U.S. total 2.04%

Grades 9 through 12
State enrollment 318,000
Total U.S. enrollment 14,067,000
State share of U.S. total 2.26%

Enrollment rates
State public school enrollment rate 91.1%
Overall U.S. rate 90.4%
Rank among states in 2002 20
Rank among states in 1995 23

Enrollment figures (which include unclassified students) are rounded to nearest thousand pupils during fall school term. Enrollment rates are based on enumerated resident population estimate for July 1, 2002.

Source: U.S. National Center for Education Statistics.

Public college finances, 2003-2004

FTE enrollment in public institutions of higher education

Students in state institutions. 220,000
Students in all U.S. public institutions 9,916,600
State share of U.S. total 2.22
Rank among states 11

State and local government appropriations for higher education

State appropriation per FTE $5,509
National average. $5,716
Rank among states 24
State & local tax revenue going to higher
 education 7.0%

FTE = full-time equivalent in public postsecondary programs,
 including summer sessions; student numbers are rounded to
 nearest hundred. Funding figures for 2003-2004 academic year
 include financial aid to students in state public institutions and
 exclude money for research, agriculture experiment stations,
 teaching hospitals, and medical schools; figures are rounded to
 nearest thousand dollars.
Source: Higher Education Executive Officers, Denver, Colorado.

TRANSPORTATION AND TRAVEL

Highway mileage, 2003

Interstate highways 764
Other freeways and expressways 290
Arterial roads 7,324
Collector roads. 16,807
Local roads 57,079
Urban roads 19,458
Rural roads 62,806
Total state mileage 82,264
U.S. total 3,974,107
State share 2.07%
Rank among states 25

Note that combined urban and rural road mileage matches the
 total of the other categories.
Source: U.S. Federal Highway Administration.

Motor vehicle registrations and driver licenses, 2003

Vehicle registrations	State	U.S.	Share	Rank
Autos, trucks, buses	5,379,000	231,390,000	2.32%	15
Autos only	2,969,000	135,670	2.19%	15
Motorcycles	141,000	5,328,000	2.65%	13
Driver licenses	4,407,000	196,166,000	2.25%	15

Figures, which do not include vehicles owned by military services,
 are rounded to the nearest thousand. Figures for automobiles
 include taxis.
Source: U.S. Federal Highway Administration.

Domestic travel expenditures, 2003
Spending by U.S. residents on overnight trips and
day trips of at least 50 miles from home

Total expenditures within state . . . . $8.04 bill.
Total expenditures within U.S. . . . . $490.87 bill.
State share of U.S. total 1.6%
Rank among states 21

Source: Travel Industry Association of America.

Retail gasoline prices, 2003-2007
Average price per gallon at the pump

Year	U.S.	State
2003	$1.267	$1.421
2004	$1.316	$1.351
2005	$1.644	$1.697
2007	$2.298	$2.567

Excise tax per gallon in 2004 . . . . 28.0¢
Rank among all states in 2007 prices 4

Prices are averages of all grades of gasoline sold at the pump
 during March months in 2003-2005 and during February, 2007.
 Averages for 2006, during which prices rose higher, are not
 available.
Source: U.S. Energy Information Agency, *Petroleum Marketing
 Monthly* (2003-2005 data); American Automobile Association
 (2007 data).

CRIME AND LAW ENFORCEMENT

State and local police officers, 2000-2004

	2000	2002	2004
Total officers			
U.S.	654,601	665,555	675,734
State	9,580	9,868	9,825*
*Net change, 2000-2004			+2.56%
Officers per 1,000 residents			
U.S.	2.33	2.31	2.30
State	1.63	1.63	1.58
State rank	44	46	48

Totals include state and local police and sheriffs.
Source: Carsey Institute, University of New Hampshire.

Crime rates, 2003
Incidents per 100,000 residents

Crimes	State	U.S.
Violent crimes		
Total incidents	347	475
Murder	3	6
Forcible rape	47	32
Robbery	93	142
Aggravated assault	204	295
Property crimes		
Total incidents	4,755	3,588
Burglary	950	741
Larceny/theft	3,142	2,415
Motor vehicle theft	663	433
All crimes	5,102	4,063

Source: U.S. Federal Bureau of Investigation, *Crime in the United States*, annual.

State prison populations, 1980-2003

	State	U.S.	State share
1980	4,399	305,458	1.44%
1990	7,995	708,393	1.13%
1996	12,527	1,025,624	1.22%
2000	14,915	1,391,261	1.07%
2003	16,148	1,470,045	1.10%

State figures exclude prisoners in federal penitentiaries.
Source: U.S. Bureau of Justice Statistics, *Prisoners in 2003*.

West Virginia

Location: East

Area and rank: 24,087 square miles (62,384 square kilometers); 24,231 square miles (62,758 square kilometers) including water; forty-first largest state in area

Coastline: none

Population and rank: 1,815,000 (2004); thirty-seventh largest state in population

Capital and largest city: Charleston (53,421 people in 2000 census)

Entered Union and rank: June 20, 1863; thirty-fifth state

Present constitution adopted: 1872

Counties: 55

State capitol building in Charleston.

State name: West Virginia takes its name from Virginia, from which it seceded during the Civil War

State nickname: Mountain State

Motto: *Montani semper liberi* (Mountaineers are always free)

State flag: White field bordered in dark blue with the state coat of arms

Highest point: Spruce Knob—4,861 feet (1,482 meters)

Lowest point: Potomac River—240 feet (73 meters)

Highest recorded temperature: 112 degrees Fahrenheit (44 degrees Celsius)—Martinsburg, 1936

Lowest recorded temperature: –37 degrees Fahrenheit (–38 degrees Celsius)—Lewisburg, 1917

State songs: "West Virginia, My Home"; "The West Virginia Hills"; "This Is My West Virginia" ("Take Me Home, Country Roads" is unofficial)

State tree: Sugar maple

State flower: Rhododendron

State bird: Cardinal

State fish: Brook trout

State animal: Black bear

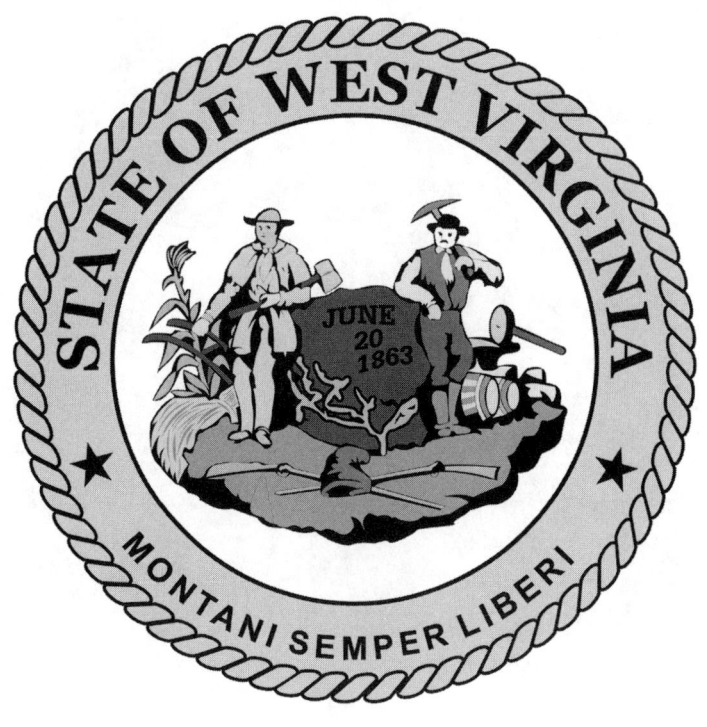

West Virginia History

More than most states, West Virginia has been shaped in its development and its history by its geography. Although part of Virginia for almost a century, it was separated from the coastal and central portions of Virginia by the Allegheny Mountains and was thus removed from the sources of political and economic power and influence. Lying completely within the Appalachian Highlands, the state is mountainous and rugged, and although it is blessed with abundant mineral resources such as coal and natural gas, it has little land available for large-scale agriculture. Travel and transportation have often been extremely difficult and even hazardous, fostering a sense of isolation in the state, which in turn fostered a high degree of independence expressed in the state's official motto, *Montani semper liberi* (mountaineers are always free).

Early Times. Native Americans entered the West Virginia area as early as fifteen thousand years ago; most of them regarded the territory as unfit for permanent settlement and good only as hunting and battle grounds. Later, when the Cherokee, Iroquois, and Shawnee arrived to establish villages, they located them near the major rivers; instead of developing agriculture, they relied on hunting. The tradition of tribal warfare continued, including fights over the springs found throughout the area that were a source of valuable salt, used in food preservation and for trading.

Colonization. The original grant of Virginia by King James I of England included what is now West Virginia. The colonists first explored the western portion of their territory in 1669, when an expedition under John Lederer reached the Blue Ridge Mountains. Thomas Batts and Robert Fallam followed in 1671, striking along the New River and claiming the Ohio Valley for England, a claim that was disputed both by France and by Native Americans. Morgan Morgan, a Welshman, is traditionally considered the first European settler in the West Virginia area, having established Bunker Hill in 1726. Morgan was followed by other colonists, including Germans from Pennsylvania and Scotch Irish from northern Ireland. Although King George III prohibited American colonists from crossing the Allegheny Mountains, this ban was largely ignored, and during the period from 1722 through 1740, the Iroquois and Cherokee ceded their lands to advancing settlers.

The distance and physical barriers between the western settlements and the rest of Virginia began to cause difficulties. In addition, the planters and traders along the Virginia tidewater and eastern rivers exerted a monopoly on the state's political and economic life. Settlers beyond the

West Virginia takes its nickname, the "Mountain State," from its rugged terrain. (PhotoDisc)

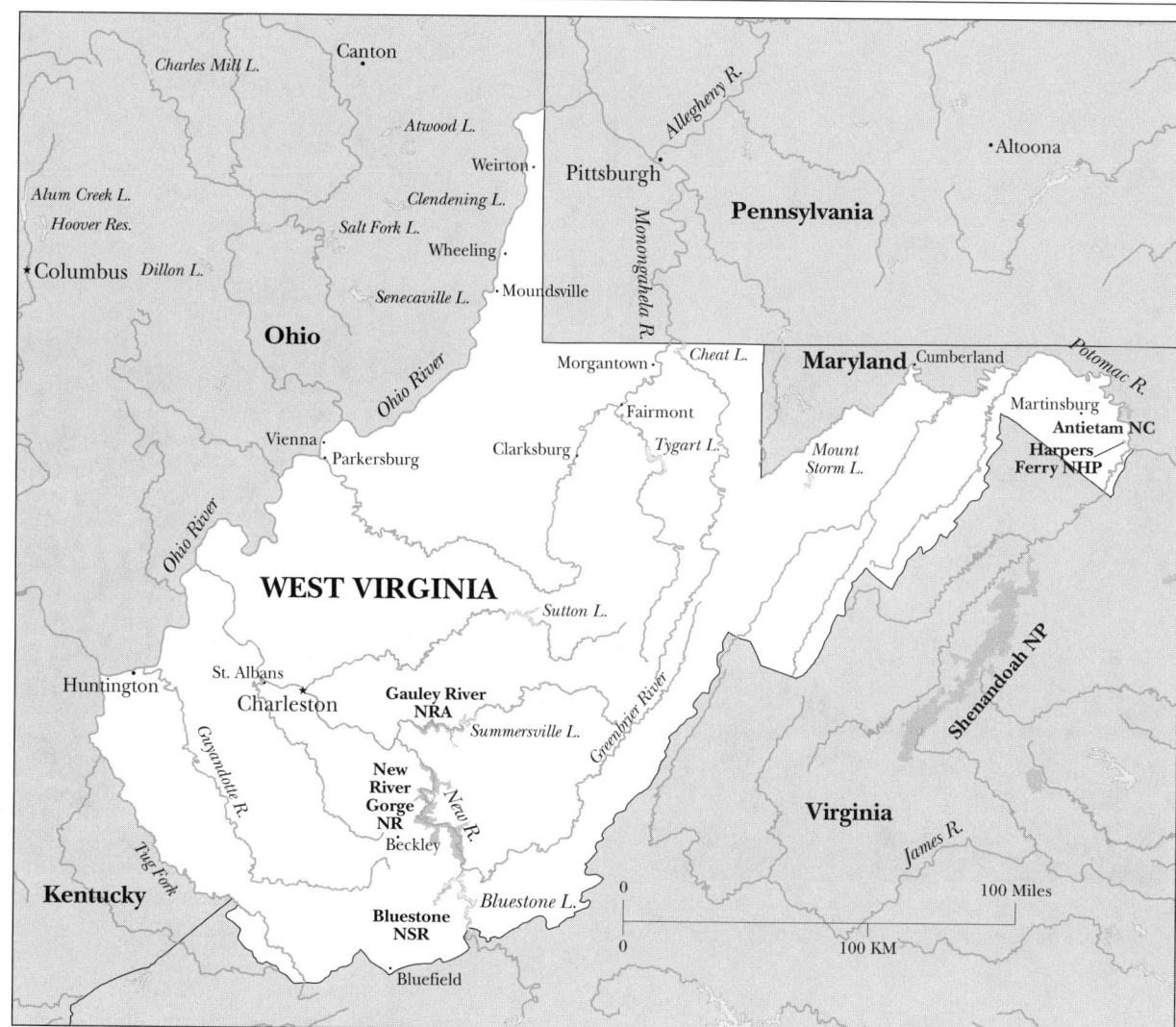

Alleghenies grew restive, and by 1776, when the American colonies were ready to break with Great Britain, western Virginia was asking the Continental Congress for independence from Virginia. The necessities of the ensuing American Revolution put this request on hold, however. As part of Virginia, it joined the Union in 1788.

Independence and Civil War. Following American independence, political and economic power in Virginia shifted more than ever toward the tidewater and eastern section, where slaveholders were dominant. The west was unsuccessful in its requests for fairness during the revision of the state constitution in 1829, and it continued to suffer from neglect by the Richmond state government. Poor roads, inadequate schools, higher taxes, neglected economic development, and lack of representation in the state legislature were among the west's major complaints. Some, but not all, were addressed in a new state constitution adopted in 1851, but the movement toward separate statehood continued.

In 1859, John Brown, a militant abolitionist from Kansas, seized the federal armory at Harpers Ferry as the first step in a revolt. He was soon captured, tried, and hanged for treason. Soon the nation was in the throes of the Civil War, and Virginia joined other southern states in seceding from the Union. The largely non-slave-holding and pro-Union western counties summoned a convention in Wheeling in August, 1861, and formed a government for a new state to be known as Kanawha. In November of that year a second convention at Wheeling adopted the name of West Virginia and began drafting a constitution. In December, 1862, President Abraham Lincoln approved an act admitting the new state, which entered the Union the following June.

In the aftermath of the Civil War arose one of the most famous feuds in American history, that of the Hatfields and the McCoys. Both families lived along both banks of the Tug River, which forms the border between Kentucky and West Virginia. The precise cause of the feud is unknown. Some have suggested the theft of

Suspension bridge at Wheeling, the town in which West Virginia delegates voted to secede from Virginia in 1861. Wheeling later briefly served as the new state's capital. (West Virginia Division of Tourism & Parks/Steve Shaluta, Jr.)

a McCoy hog by a Hatfield; others, a forbidden romance between a McCoy girl and a Hatfield boy. Whatever the underlying reasons, the feud began in earnest during 1882, when a West Virginia Hatfield was killed by Kentucky McCoys. As the feud escalated, West Virginia authorities sought to suppress it by legal action, even taking their case to the U.S. Supreme Court. When the feud finally came to an end during the late 1880's, more than a dozen people had been killed.

Coal Mining and Coal Strikes. Following the Civil War, West Virginia advanced in exploitation of its major resources, primarily timber, coal, and natural gas. Coal had been discovered as early as 1742, but the deposits were not effectively mined until after the Civil War, primarily because of transportation difficulties. When these difficulties were solved by the spread of the railroads, West Virginia became the leading producer of bituminous, or soft, coal in North America. In addition to its abundance and relative ease of mining, the state's coal proved to be remarkably free from sulfur and other impurities, making it even more valuable.

Although coal was the chief source of West Virginia's revenues, it was also a major cause of internal problems. Coal mining was hard and dangerous work, and

mine owners insisted on long hours and low pay for their workers. Deaths in mine disasters were frequent, and the toll was often high: in 1907, 537 persons died in mining accidents, 362 of them in one mine alone, the worst single mining disaster in U.S. history. Efforts to organize and unionize the miners to fight for better pay and working conditions were met with bitter hostility by mine owners, other businesses, and even the state and federal governments. Time and again, West Virginia governors declared martial law and called up the National Guard to put down strikes and other union-organizing efforts. The struggles reached a peak of violence in the years between the end of World War I and the Great Depression. In 1920, the Matewan Massacre led to the deaths of more than ten people during a confrontation between miners and their supporters in the community and mine owners and their forces. As a result, the United Mine Workers of America saw an increase in its membership, but its work toward better conditions was smothered when federal troops were ordered into the area. The strikes and conflicts continued until New Deal programs and the need for increased coal supplies for defense production in World War II brought better conditions to the mines.

Into the Future. The market for coal was often uncertain, and prices for the product could fall to low levels. Because of this, its isolation, poor economic base, and inadequate schools, West Virginia suffered from a high degree of poverty, which reached its depth during the Great Depression. As part of Appalachia, the mountainous region stretching from Pennsylvania to upper Alabama, West Virginia was among the prime targets for massive federal assistance, especially during the Great Society's War on Poverty during the administration of President Lyndon Johnson. Funding was made available for roads, schools, retraining for workers, forest restoration, and the fight against rural poverty. Entire communities, especially in the more remote areas of the state, were aided by these efforts. In addition, the state's private sector began to revive.

Following World War II, coal production proved uncertain, largely because it was linked to the availability of other energy sources, such as oil, and to environmental concerns about matters such as strip mining. The timber industry, which had been a source of income for the area since the mid-eighteenth century, expanded greatly after steam power replaced hydroelectric power during the late nineteenth century. Natural gas, which had been discovered in 1815, was also plentiful in the state. However, manufacturing became the major source of income for the state, ahead of mining and timbering combined. Chief products were first steel and later chemicals and allied products.

In 1960, West Virginia played a major role in U.S. presidential politics when its Democratic presidential primary pitted candidate John F. Kennedy against Hubert H. Humphrey. Kennedy's landslide victory over Humphrey (almost 61 percent of the vote) caused Humphrey to withdraw from the race and, more important, demonstrated that a Catholic such as Kennedy could have a chance at victory. In the November presidential election Kennedy won the presidency. Political analysts regarded the West Virginia primary as a turning point in Kennedy's campaign and its results among the most important in American politics.

As the twentieth century ended, West Virginia continued to diversify its economic base, adding to mining, forestry, and manufacturing and drawing increasingly on recreation and tourism. The completion of major interstate highways through the state made travel easier and faster and encouraged development of the southern portion of the state, where vast areas of largely untouched natural beauty lured visitors, campers, and nature enthusiasts. Once an isolated and difficult-to-reach territory, West Virginia was rapidly becoming a destination for a variety of travelers.

General Elections. A West Virginia tradition was observed in the 2000 general election when the state again chose Democrat Robert Byrd for the U.S. Senate, this time by a remarkable 78-20 percent margin. By 2006, Byrd, first elected in 1958, had served forty-eight years, longer than any other senator in American history, eclipsing the record of Senator Strom Thurmond of South Carolina. In other contests, Democrats tended to dominate the balloting in this long-time Democratic state. Thus, Democrat Bob Wise narrowly unseated Governor Cecil H. Underwood by a 50-48 percent margin. Two notable exceptions to the state's left-leaning bent were Republican Shelley Capito, a first-term member of Congress, who defeated a determined challenge by a wealthy opponent who spent $5 million of his own money. The other notable exception was the 52-46 percent victory by George W. Bush over Democrat Al Gore. It was only the fourth time since 1932 that a Republican has been able to win the state's electoral votes.

In 2004, predictions that the president would pay dearly for removing steel tariffs were proved wrong. Bush took the state with an enhanced majority, 56-43 percent. Despite the Republican president's wider victory, Democrat Joe Manchin III eliminated the opposition for the governor's mansion with a significantly greater margin, 63-34 percent. The incumbent, Bob Wise, decided not to present himself for reelection after admitting an affair with a state employee.

Economic Difficulties. As the new century approached, West Virginia faced difficult economic and demographic problems. The state found itself rapidly losing population. In fact, it had fewer residents in 2000 than it had had in 1940, and the sharpest national declines in state populations were found in West Virginia and one other state. The state's economy was performing poorly, with welfare caseloads rising rapidly. Welfare caseloads rose in thirty-three states, but West Virginia was one of three states in which caseloads increased the most.

When the state's steel industry—along with those of states such as nearby Pennsylvania and Ohio—experienced a price squeeze from foreign producers, President Bush stepped in to support a probe on steel prices. Later he placed tariffs on steel that aided the employment situation in affected states. The fact that President Bill Clinton was widely believed to have lost the state for Al Gore by refusing to act on the difficulties facing the steel industry was not lost on the new administration. In 2003, however, Bush lifted the steel tariffs to avert a trade war, despite the widespread expectation that he would pay a political price in the next presidential election. Economic difficulties of a different kind were apparent when West Virginia doctors protested the growing costs of malpractice insurance.

Jessica Lynch. Also in 2003, the state found itself at the center of national attention when West Virginia soldier Pfc. Jessica Lynch returned home following service in Iraq. Lynch had been captured while on a mission and was dramatically rescued from a hospital after a tip from an Iraqi, who was later granted asylum in the United States. Stories followed that she was a hero, that she fought off the Iraqis as long as she could, and that she had been ill-treated while captive. When she returned to West Virginia, she was joyously received. Lynch herself, however, denied she was a heroine, saying that her gun had jammed, and she never fired a shot; she also said she had no recollection of mistreatment in captivity. After receiving an honorable medical discharge from the service, in 2005, she entered college in West Virginia and successfully returned to private life.

Michael Witkoski
Updated by the Editor

West Virginia Time Line

1500's	Cherokee, Iroquois, and Shawnee tribes inhabit West Virginia area.
1609	English king James I grants area to Virginia colony.
1669	Explorer John Lederer becomes first European to see West Virginia.
1671	Thomas Batts and Robert Fallam explore New River valley and claim land for England.
1725	Fur traders enter area west of Appalachians.
1726	Morgan Morgan establishes first permanent English settlement in West Virginia near Bunker Hill.
1742	Peter Salley discovers coal on Coal River at Racine.

Antislavery leader John Brown leading his raid on Harpers Ferry, in an imaginative mural painted in the late 1930's by John Steuart Curry. (National Archives)

1749	Jacob Marlin and Stephen Sewell establish first recorded settlement west of Allegheny Mountains.
1768	Iroquois cede lands to British in Treaty of Fort Stanwix.
1774	Colonists defeat alliance of Native Americans at battle of Point Pleasant, in what is considered the first battle of the Revolution.
June 26, 1788	Virginia ratifies Constitution, becoming tenth state to enter the Union.
1790	First iron-ore furnace west of Allegheny Mountains opens on Kings Creek.
1794	"Mad Anthony" Wayne defeats Native Americans at Fallen Timbers.
1815	First gas well in United States is drilled near Charleston.
1818	Cumberland Road opens to Wheeling.
1819	State constitutional crisis grows over division between eastern and western portions of state.
1851	Virginia adopts new constitution with concessions to western portion of the state.
1853	Baltimore and Ohio Railroad reaches Wheeling.
Oct. 16, 1859	John Brown raids federal armory at Harpers Ferry; is later tried, convicted, and hanged for treason at Charles Town.
1861	Convention at Wheeling nullifies Virginia ordinance of secession and establishes loyal Union government.
June 20, 1863	West Virginia enters Union as thirty-fifth state.
1867	State university is chartered at Morgantown.
1870	State capital is moved to Charleston.
1872	West Virginia adopts new state constitution.
1875	State capital is moved to Wheeling.
1885	State capital is moved back to Charleston.
1896	State begins first rural free mail delivery in United States.
1907	Five mine disasters kill 537 people.
1920	Ten people are killed in Matewan Massacre during bitter coal strike.
1921	National Guard and U.S. Army troops put down coal strike.
1938	Tygart Dam on Tygart River is completed.
1954	West Virginia Turnpike is completed.
1962	Green Bank movable radio telescope, world's largest, begins operations.
1965	Major gas field is found near Charleston.
1966	Summersville Dam on Gauley River is dedicated.
1967	Some forty people die in collapse of suspension bridge over Ohio River at Point Pleasant.
1972	Failure of dam on Buffalo Creek produces flash flood that kills more than one hundred people.
1977	Workers complete New River Gorge Bridge, world's longest single-arch steel span.
1988	Major oil spill pollutes Monongahela and Ohio rivers, endangering water supplies.
1996	Charlotte Pritt becomes first woman nominated for governor by a major political party in West Virginia.
1996	West Virginia coal industry sets production record at 174 million tons.
1998	Marie Redd becomes first female African American elected to West Virginia state senate.
Nov. 7, 2000	George W. Bush wins the state's five electoral votes by a 54-46 percent margin.
Apr. 12, 2003	Having been rescued in Iraq, Private Jessica Lynch is flown to the U.S. for medical treatment.
Nov. 2, 2004	President Bush enhances his majority, winning the state by 56-43 percent, while Joe Manchin is elected governor by 63-34 percent.
June 10, 2006	Robert Byrd becomes the longest serving member ever of the U.S. Senate, having served forty-eight years.

Notes for Further Study

Published Sources. Three good general studies of West Virginia are Otis K. Rice's *West Virginia: A History* (1985), an academic but well-written survey of the state's development that is objective; John Alexander Williams's *West Virginia: A History* (Rev. ed., 2001), a very good overview of West Virginia from early days to more modern times; and Anna Smucker's *History of West Virginia* (2004). *The Americanization of West Virginia: Creating a Modern Industrial State, 1916-1925* (1998) by John C. Hennen is an excellent study of what is probably the major transition in West Virginia's history, which brought it into the modern world at a price that was sometimes terrible to individuals and communities. One of the states hardest hit by the Great Depression, West Virginia was in many ways a test case for President Franklin Roosevelt's New Deal. Jerry Bruce Thomas's *An Appalachian New Deal: West Virginia in the Great Depression* (1998) examines the plans, attempts, and consequences that resulted from the New Deal's implementation. In *To Save the Land and People: A History of Opposition to Surface Coal Mining in Appalachia* (2003), Chad Montrie traces the roots and effects of the twentieth-century movement to outlaw surface mining in Appalachia.

Drawing from archival letters and records of military orders and dispatches, Tim McKinney's *The Civil War in West Virginia* (2005) presents a good overview of the state's experiences with the Civil War. Written by Charles J. Rawling and originally published in 1887, *History of the First Regiment West Virginia Infantry* remains the only history of the First West Virginia Infantry ever published. A reprint, published in 2002 and edited by McKinney, enhances Rawling's original work with an index, photographs, biographical data, and statistical analysis of the regiment's service.

The West Virginia Encyclopedia (2006), edited by Ken Sullivan, brings together more than two thousand articles on the state's history, geography, historic individuals, and culture. *The 55 West Virginias: A Guide to the State's Counties* (1998) by E. Lee North is an excellent introduction to the varieties of history,

geography, and culture in the state. The diverse state receives its due in this study of the Mountain State's individual counties. *West Virginia Off the Beaten Path* (5th ed., 2004) by Su Clauson-Wicker serves as an excellent guidebook for travelers.

Web Resources. An excellent starting point for material on history and current events is the state of West Virginia Main Page (www.state.wv.us). This has links to the many government agencies and departments that have statistics and connections to additional resources. The West Virginia State Archives (www.wvculture.org/history/wvsamenu.html) provides access to a wide range of historical information about West Virginia and its development. The Famous West Virginians Page (members.aol.com/jeff560/wv-fam.html) documents historically important individuals from the state, while West Virginia in the Civil War (www.wvcivilwar.com/) is a thorough site detailing war operations in the state. West Virginia History and Genealogy (www.usgennet.org/usa/wv/state1/) is a good destination for those interested in family ancestry.

A good source for introductory and general information, as well as good links to other sites, is West Virginia Online (www.wvonline.com). Those planning a trip to the state should consult either West Virginia Wild and Wonderful (www.wvtourism.com/) or the West Virginia Division of Natural Resources (www.wvdnr.gov/), which offers information about outdoor activities and park recreation.

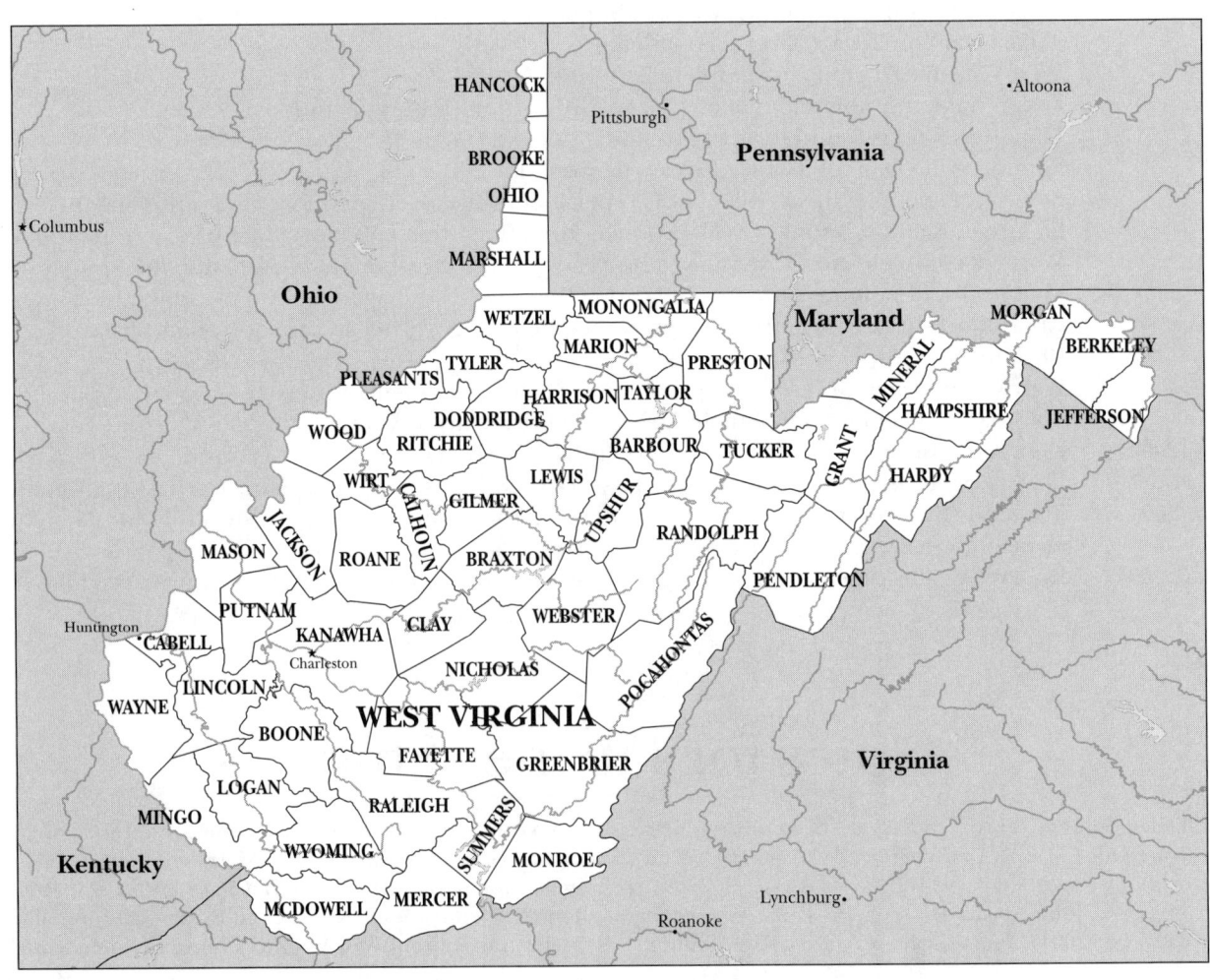

Winery in West Virginia's Summers County. (West Virginia Division of Tourism & Parks/David E. Fattaleh)

Counties

County	2000 pop.	Rank in pop.	Sq. miles	Rank in area
Barbour	15,557	36	340.8	38
Berkeley	75,905	6	321.2	41
Boone	25,535	28	503.0	16
Braxton	14,702	39	513.5	14
Brooke	25,447	29	88.9	54
Cabell	96,784	2	281.6	45
Calhoun	7,582	50	280.6	46
Clay	10,330	45	342.4	37
Doddridge	7,403	52	320.5	42
Fayette	47,579	11	664.0	6
Gilmer	7,160	54	340.1	39
Grant	11,299	43	477.2	19
Greenbrier	34,453	17	1,021.3	2
Hampshire	20,203	32	641.8	9
Hancock	32,667	18	83.0	55
Hardy	12,669	42	583.4	11
Harrison	68,652	7	416.1	29
Jackson	28,000	22	465.8	21
Jefferson	42,190	14	209.6	50
Kanawha	200,073	1	903.2	4
Lewis	16,919	34	388.8	30
Lincoln	22,108	31	437.5	24
Logan	37,710	15	454.2	22
McDowell	27,329	23	534.8	13
Marion	56,598	9	309.7	43
Marshall	35,519	16	307.0	44
Mason	25,957	26	431.9	25
Mercer	62,980	8	420.5	27
Mineral	27,078	24	327.8	40
Mingo	28,253	21	422.6	26
Monongalia	81,866	4	361.2	33
Monroe	14,583	40	473.4	20
Morgan	14,943	38	229.0	49
Nicholas	26,562	25	648.7	7
Ohio	47,427	12	106.2	53
Pendleton	8,196	49	698.0	5
Pleasants	7,514	51	130.7	52
Pocahontas	9,131	48	940.3	3
Preston	29,334	19	648.4	8
Putnam	51,589	10	346.3	36
Raleigh	79,220	5	607.0	10
Randolph	28,262	20	1,039.8	1
Ritchie	10,343	44	453.5	23
Roane	15,446	37	483.6	18
Summers	12,999	41	361.2	32
Taylor	16,089	35	172.8	51
Tucker	7,321	53	418.9	28
Tyler	9,592	47	257.6	47
Upshur	23,404	30	354.8	35
Wayne	42,903	13	505.8	15
Webster	9,719	46	556.1	12
Wetzel	17,693	33	359.2	34
Wirt	5,873	55	233.0	48
Wood	87,986	3	367.4	31
Wyoming	25,708	27	500.9	17

Source: U.S. Census Bureau; National Association of Counties.

Cities

With 10,000 or more residents

Rank	City	Population
1	Charleston (capital)	53,421
2	Huntington	51,475
3	Parkersburg	33,099
4	Wheeling	31,419
5	Morgantown	26,809
6	Weirton	20,411
7	Fairmont	19,097
8	Beckley	17,254
9	Clarksburg	16,743
10	Martinsburg	14,972

Rank	City	Population
11	South Charleston	13,390
12	Teays Valley	12,704
13	St. Albans	11,567
14	Bluefield	11,451
15	Vienna	10,861
16	Cross Lanes	10,353

Population figures are from 2000 census.
Source: U.S. Bureau of the Census.

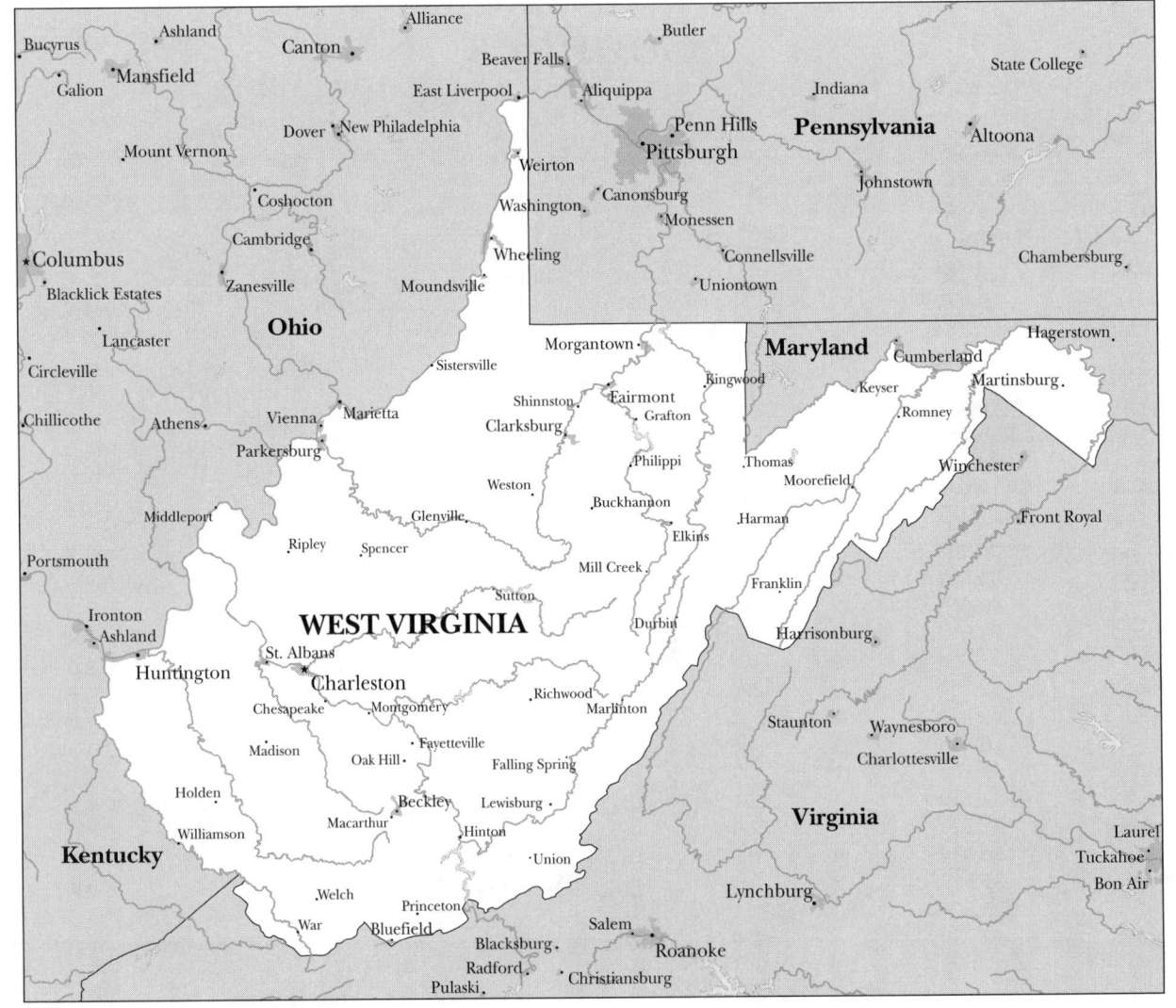

Index to Tables

DEMOGRAPHICS

Resident state and national populations, 1970-2004

Population figures given in thousands

	State pop.	U.S. pop.	Share	Rank
1970	1,744	203,302	0.9%	34
1980	1,950	226,546	0.9%	34
1985	1,907	237,924	0.8%	34
1990	1,793	248,765	0.7%	34
1995	1,824	262,761	0.7%	35
2000	1,808	281,425	0.6%	37
2004	1,815	293,655	0.6%	37

Source: U.S. Census Bureau, Current Population Reports, 2006.

Resident population by age, 2004

Age Group	Total persons
Under 5 years	101,000
5 to 17 years	284,000
18 to 24 years	173,000
25 to 34 years	227,000
35 to 44 years	252,000
45 to 54 years	284,000
55 to 64 years	217,000
65 to 74 years	144,000
75 to 84 years	102,000
85 years and older	33,000
All age groups	1,815,000

Portion of residents 65 and older	15.3%
National rank in portion of oldest residents	2
National average	12.4%

Population figures are rounded to nearest thousand persons;
figures include armed forces personnel stationed in the state.
Source: U.S. Bureau of the Census, 2006.

Resident population by race, Hispanic origin, 2004

Category	State pop.	Share	U.S.
All residents	1,815	100.00%	100.00%
Non-Hispanic white	1,714	94.44%	67.37%
Hispanic white	14	0.77%	13.01%
Other Hispanic	1	0.06%	1.06%
African American	58	3.20%	12.77%
Native American	4	0.22%	0.96%
Asian, Pacific Islander	10	0.55%	4.37%
Two or more categories	15	0.83%	1.51%

Population figures are in thousands. Persons counted as "Hispanic" (Latino) may be of any race. Because of overlapping categories, categories may not add up to 100%. Shares in column 3 are percentages of each category within the state; these figures may be compared to the national percentages in column 4.
Source: U.S. Bureau of the Census, 2006.

Projected state population, 2000-2030

Year	Population
2000	1,808,000
2005	1,819,000
2010	1,829,000
2015	1,823,000
2020	1,801,000
2025	1,766,000
2030	1,720,000
Population decrease, 2000-2030	−88,000
Percentage decrease, 2000-2030	−4.9

Projections are based on data from the 2000 census.
Source: U.S. Census Bureau.

VITAL STATISTICS

Infant mortality rates, 1980-2002

	1980	1990	2000	2002
All state residents	11.8	9.9	7.6	9.1
All U.S. residents	12.6	9.2	9.4	9.1
All state white residents	11.4	8.1	7.4	8.5
All U.S. white residents	10.6	7.6	5.7	5.8
All state black residents	21.5	—	—	—
All U.S. black residents	22.2	18.0	14.1	14.4

Figures represent deaths per 1,000 live births of resident infants under 1 year old, exclusive of fetal deaths. Figures for all residents include members of other racial categories not listed separately. The Census Bureau considers the post-1980 figures for black residents to be too small to be statistically meaningful.
Source: U.S. Census Bureau, Statistical Abstract of the United States, 2006.

Abortion rates, 1990 and 2000

	1990	2000
Total abortions	3,000	3,000
Rate per 1,000 women	7.8	6.8
U.S. rate	25.7	21.3
Rank	47	44

Numbers of abortions are rounded to nearest thousand; ranks are based on rates.
Source: U.S. Census Bureau.

Marriages and divorces, 2004

Total marriages	13,200
Rate per 1,000 population	7.3
National rate per 1,000 population	7.4
Rank among all states	26
Total divorces	8,600
Rate per 1,000 population	4.7
National rate per 1,000 population	3.7
Rank among all states	9

Figures are for all marriages and divorces performed within the state, including those of nonresidents; totals are rounded to the nearest hundred. Ranks are for highest to lowest figures; note that divorce data are not available for five states.
Source: U.S. National Center for Health Statistics, Vital Statistics of the United States, 2006.

Death rates by leading causes, 2002
Deaths per 100,000 resident population

Cause	State	U.S.
Heart disease	343.5	241.7
Cancer	258.2	193.2
Cerebrovascular diseases	69.9	56.4
Accidents other than motor vehicle	53.1	37.0
Motor vehicle accidents	23.0	15.7
Chronic lower respiratory diseases	68.2	43.3
Diabetes mellitus	47.0	25.4
HIV	1.1	4.9
Suicide	15.3	11.0
Homicide	5.3	6.1
All causes	1,166.3	847.3
Rank in overall death rate among states		1

Figures exclude nonresidents who died in the state. Causes of death follow International Classification of Diseases. Rank is from highest to lowest death rate in the United States.
Source: U.S. National Center for Health Statistics, National Vital Statistics Report, 2006.

ECONOMY

Gross state product, 1990-2004
In current dollars

Year	State product	Nat'l product	State share
1990	$28.3 billion	$5.67 trillion	0.50%
2000	$41.7 billion	$9.75 trillion	0.43%
2002	$45.3 billion	$10.41 trillion	0.44%
2003	$46.7 billion	$10.92 trillion	0.43%
2004	$49.8 billion	$11.65 trillion	0.43%

Source: U.S. Bureau of Economic Analysis, *Survey of Current Business,* July, 2005.

Gross state product by industry, 2003
In billions of dollars

Construction	$1.6
Manufacturing	5.1
Wholesale trade	2.1
Retail trade	4.0
Finance & insurance	1.7
Information	1.4
Professional services	1.7
Health care & social assistance	4.0
Government	7.1
Total state product	$43.2
Total U.S. product	$10,289.2
State share of U.S. total	0.42%
Rank among all states	40

Total figures include industries not listed separately. Amounts are in chained 2000 dollars.
Source: U.S. Bureau of Economic Analysis, *Survey of Current Business,* July, 2005.

Personal income per capita, 1990-2004
In current dollars

	1990	2000	2004
Per capita income	$14,493	$21,900	$25,872
U.S. average	$19,477	$29,845	$32,937
Rank among states	48	49	48

Source: U.S. Bureau of Economic Analysis, *Survey of Current Business,* April, 2005.

Energy consumption, 2001
In trillions of British thermal units (BTU), except as noted

Total energy consumption

Total state energy consumption	762
Total U.S. energy consumption	96,275
State share of U.S. total	0.79%
Rank among states	34

Per capita consumption (In millions of BTU)

Total state per capita consumption	423
Total U.S. per capita consumption	338
Rank among states	10

End-use sectors

Residential	157
Commercial	111
Industrial	311
Transportation	183

Sources of energy

Petroleum	215
Natural gas	152
Coal	872
Hydroelectric power	10
Nuclear electric power	0

Figures for totals include categories not listed separately.
Source: U.S. Energy Information Administration, *State Energy Data Report,* 2001.

Nonfarm employment by sectors, 2004

Total persons	736,000
Construction	35,000
Manufacturing	63,000
Trade, transportation, utilities	137,000
Information	12,000
Finance, insurance, real estate	31,000
Professional & business services	58,000
Education & health services	111,000
Leisure, hospitality, arts, organizations	68,000
Other services, including repair & maintenance	55,000
Government	143,000

Figures are rounded to nearest thousand persons. "Total" includes mining and natural resources, not listed separately.
Source: U.S. Bureau of Labor Statistics, 2006.

Foreign exports, 1990-2004
In millions of dollars

Year	State	U.S.	State share
1990	1,550	394,045	0.39%
1996	2,169	624,767	0.35%
1997	2,276	688,896	0.33%
2000	2,219	712,055	0.28%
2003	2,380	724,006	0.35%
2004	3,262	769,332	0.42%

Rank among all states in 2004 34

U.S. total does not include U.S. dependencies.
Source: U.S. Census Bureau, *U.S. Merchandise Trade*, series FT 900, 2000; U.S. Census Bureau, *U.S. International Trade in Goods and Services*, Series FT 900, 2005.

LAND USE

Federally owned land, 2003
Areas in acres

	State	U.S.	State share
Total area	15,411,000	2,271,343,000	0.68%
Nonfederal land	14,144,000	1,599,584,000	0.88%
Federal land	1,266,000	671,759,000	0.19%
Federal share	8.2%	29.6%	—

Areas are rounded to nearest thousand acres. Figures for federally owned land do not include trust properties.
Source: U.S. General Services Administration, *Federal Real Property Profile*, 2006.

Land use, 1997
In acres, rounded to nearest thousand

Total surface area	15,508,000
Total nonfederal rural land.	13,252,000
Percentage rural land	85.5%
Cropland	864,000
Conservation Reserve Program (CRP*) land	(nil)
Pastureland	1,527,000
Rangeland	(nil)
Forestland	10,582,000
Other rural land	279,000

*CRP is a federal program begun in 1985 to assist private landowners to convert highly erodible cropland to vegetative cover for ten years. Note that some categories of land overlap.
Source: U.S. Department of Agriculture, Natural Resources and Conservation Service, and Iowa State University, Statistical Laboratory, S*ummary Report, 1997 National Resources Inventory*, revised December, 2000.

Farms and crop acreage, 2004

	State	U.S.	Share	Rank
Farms	21,000	2,113,000	0.99%	34
Acres (millions)	4	937	0.43%	39
Acres per farm	173	443	—	40

Source: U.S. Department of Agriculture, National Agricultural Statistics Service. Numbers of farms are rounded to nearest thousand units; acreage figures are rounded to nearest million. Rankings, including ties, are based on rounded figures.

GOVERNMENT AND FINANCE

Units of local government, 2002

	State	Total U.S.	Rank
All local governments	686	87,525	38
Counties	55	3,034	28
Municipalities	234	19,429	33
Townships	0	16,504	—
School districts	55	13,506	39
Special districts	342	35,052	34

Only 48 states have county governments, 20 states have township governments ("towns" in New England, Minnesota, New York, and Wisconsin), and 46 states have school districts. Special districts encompass such functions as natural resources, fire protection, and housing and community development.
Source: U.S. Census Bureau, *Census of Governments*.

State government revenue, 2002

Total revenue.	$9,130 mill.
General revenue	$8,053 mill.
Per capita revenue	$4,461
U.S. per capita average	$3,689
Rank among states	17

Intergovernment revenue	
Total	$2,899 mill.
From federal government	$2,847 mill.

Charges and miscellaneous	
Total	$1,602 mill.
Current charges	$772 mill.
Misc. general income	$830 mill.
Insurance trust revenue	$1,025 mill.

Taxes	
Total	$3,552 mill.
Per capita taxes	$1,968
Rank among states	17
Property taxes.	$4 mill.
Sales taxes	$1,921 mill.
License taxes	$175 mill.
Individual income taxes	$1,035 mill.
Corporate income taxes	$220 mill.
Other taxes	$198 mill.

Total revenue figures include items not listed separately here.
Source: U.S. Bureau of the Census.

State government expenditures, 2002

General expenditures

Total state expenditures	$9,409 mill.
Intergovernmental	$1,454 mill.

Per capita expenditures

State	$4,189
Average of all states	$3,859
Rank among states	18

Selected direct expenditures

Education	$1,181 mill.
Public welfare	$2,136 mill.
Health, hospital	$299 mill.
Highways	$986 mill.
Police protection	$48 mill.
Corrections	$170 mill.
Natural resources	$174 mill.
Parks and recreation	$68 mill.
Government administration	$426 mill.
Interest on debt	$238 mill.
Total direct expenditures	$6,107 mill.

Totals include items not listed separately.
Source: U.S. Census Bureau.

POLITICS

Governors since statehood

D = Democrat; R = Republican; O = other;
(r) resigned; (d) died in office; (i) removed from office

Arthur I. Boreman (O)	(r) 1863-1869
Daniel D. T. Farnsworth (R)	1869
William E. Stevenson (R)	1869-1871
John J. Jacob (D)	1871-1877
Henry M. Mathews (D)	1877-1881
Jacob B. Jackson (D)	1881-1885
Emanuel Willis Wilson (D)	1885-1890
Aretas B. Fleming (D)	1890-1893
William A. MacCorkle (D)	1893-1897
George W. Atkinson (R)	1897-1901
Albert B. White (R)	1901-1905
William M. O. Dawson (R)	1905-1909
William E. Glasscock (R)	1909-1913
Henry D. Hatfield (R)	1913-1917
John J. Cornwell (D)	1917-1921
Ephriam F. Morgan (R)	1921-1925
Howard M. Gore (R)	1925-1929
William G. Conley (R)	1929-1933
Herman G. Kump (D)	1933-1937
Homer A. Holt (D)	1937-1941
Matthew M. Neely (D)	1941-1945
Clarence W. Meadows (D)	1945-1949
Okey L. Patteson (D)	1949-1953
William C. Marland (D)	1953-1957
Cecil H. Underwood (D)	1957-1961
William W. Barron (D)	1961-1965

Hulett C. Smith (D)	1965-1969
Arch A. Moore, Jr. (R)	1969-1977
John D. Rockefeller IV (D)	1977-1985
Arch A. Moore, Jr. (R)	1985-1989
Gaston Caperton (D)	1989-1997
Cecil H. Underwood (R)	1997-2001
Bob Wise (D)	2001-2005
Joe Manchin (D)	2005-

Composition of congressional delegations, 1989-2007

	Dem	Rep	Total
House of Representatives			
101st Congress, 1989			
State delegates	4	0	4
Total U.S.	259	174	433
102d Congress, 1991			
State delegates	4	0	4
Total U.S.	267	167	434
103d Congress, 1993			
State delegates	3	0	3
Total U.S.	258	176	434
104th Congress, 1995			
State delegates	3	0	3
Total U.S.	197	236	433
105th Congress, 1997			
State delegates	3	0	3
Total U.S.	206	228	434
106th Congress, 1999			
State delegates	3	0	3
Total U.S.	211	222	433
107th Congress, 2001			
State delegates	2	1	3
Total U.S.	211	221	432
108th Congress, 2003			
State delegates	2	1	3
Total U.S.	205	229	434
109th Congress, 2005			
State delegates	2	1	3
Total U.S.	202	231	433
110th Congress, 2007			
State delegates	2	1	3
Total U.S.	233	202	435
Senate			
101st Congress, 1989			
State delegates	2	0	2
Total U.S.	55	45	100
102d Congress, 1991			
State delegates	2	0	2
Total U.S.	56	44	100

(continued)

	Dem	Rep	Total
103d Congress, 1993			
State delegates	2	0	2
Total U.S.	57	43	100
104th Congress, 1995			
State delegates	2	0	2
Total U.S.	46	53	99
105th Congress, 1997			
State delegates	2	0	2
Total U.S.	45	55	100
106th Congress, 1999			
State delegates	2	0	2
Total U.S.	45	54	99
107th Congress, 2001			
State delegates	2	0	2
Total U.S.	50	50	100
108th Congress, 2003			
State delegates	2	0	2
Total U.S.	48	51	99
109th Congress, 2005			
State delegates	2	0	2
Total U.S.	44	55	99
110th Congress, 2007			
State delegates	2	0	2
Total U.S.	49	49	98

Figures are for starts of first sessions. Totals are for Democrat (Dem.) and Republican (Rep.) members only. House membership totals under 435 and Senate totals under 100 reflect vacancies and seats held by independent party members. When the 110th Congress opened, the Senate's two independent members caucused with the Democrats, giving the Democrats control of the Senate.

Source: U.S. Congress, *Congressional Directory.*

Composition of state legislature, 1990-2006

	Democrats	Republicans
State House (100 seats)		
1990	74	26
1992	79	21
1994	69	30
1996	74	25
1998	75	25
2000	75	25
2002	68	32
2004	68	32
2006	72	28
State Senate (34 seats)		
1990	33	1
1992	32	2
1994	26	8
1996	25	9
1998	29	5
2000	29	5
2002	24	10
2004	21	13
2006	23	11

Figures for total seats may include independents and minor party members. Numbers reflect results of elections in listed years; elected members usually take their seats in the years that follow.

Source: Council of State Governments; *State Elective Officials and the Legislatures.*

Voter participation in presidential elections, 2000 and 2004

	2000	2004
Voting age population		
State	1,407,000	1,431,000
Total United States	209,831,000	220,377,000
State share of U.S. total	0.67	0.65
Rank among states	36	36
Portion of voting age population casting votes		
State	46.1%	52.8%
United States	50.3%	55.5%
Rank among states	41	40

Population figures are rounded to nearest thousand and include all residents, regardless of eligibility to vote.

Source: U.S. Census Bureau.

HEALTH AND MEDICAL CARE

Medical professionals
Physicians in 2003 and nurses in 2001

	U.S.	State
Physicians in 2003		
Total	774,849	4,168
Share of U.S. total		0.54%
Rate	266	230
Rank		31
Nurses in 2001		
Total	2,262,020	15,850
Share of U.S. total		0.70%
Rate	793	880
Rank		18

Rates are numbers of physicians and nurses per 100,000 resident population; ranks are based on rates.

Source: American Medical Association, *Physician Characteristics and Distribution in the U.S.*; U.S. Department of Health and Human Services, Health Resources and Services Administration.

Health insurance coverage, 2003

	State	U.S.
Total persons covered	1,491,000	243,320,000
Total persons not covered	296,000	44,961,000
Portion not covered	16.6%	15.6%
Rank among states	17	—
Children not covered	34,000	8,373,000
Portion not covered	8.4%	11.4%
Rank among states	31	—

Totals are rounded to nearest thousand. Ranks are from the highest to the lowest percentages of persons *not* insured.

Source: U.S. Census Bureau, Current Population Reports.

AIDS, syphilis, and tuberculosis cases, 2003

Disease	U.S. cases	State cases	Rank
AIDS	44,232	95	38
Syphilis	34,270	11	44
Tuberculosis	14,874	21	43

Source: U.S. Centers for Disease Control and Prevention.

Cigarette smoking, 2003
Residents over age 18 who smoke

	U.S.	State	Rank
All smokers	22.1%	27.4%	2
Male smokers	24.8%	27.6%	14
Female smokers	20.3%	27.2%	2

Cigarette smokers are defined as persons who reported having smoked at least 100 cigarettes during their lifetimes and who currently smoked at least occasionally.

Source: U.S. Centers for Disease Control and Prevention, *Morbidity and Mortality Weekly Report*, 53, no. 44 (November 12, 2004).

HOUSING

Home ownership rates, 1985-2004

	1985	1990	1995	2000	2004
State	75.9%	72.0%	73.1%	75.9%	80.3%
Total U.S.	63.9%	63.9%	64.7%	67.4%	69.0%
Rank among states	1	5	3	5	1

Net change in state home ownership rate,
1985-2004 . . . . +4.4%

Net change in U.S. home ownership rate,
1985-2004 . . . . +5.1%

Percentages represent the proportion of owner households to total occupied households.

Source: U.S. Census Bureau, 2006.

Home sales, 2000-2004
In thousands of units

Existing home sales	2000	2002	2003	2004
State sales	22.9	28.1	28.9	36.0
Total U.S. sales	5,171	5,631	6,183	6,784
State share of U.S. total	0.44%	0.50%	0.47%	0.53%
Sales rank among states	41	39	40	38

Units include single-family homes, condos, and co-ops.

Source: National Association of Realtors, Washington, D.C., *Real Estate Outlook: Market Trends & Insights*.

Values of owner-occupied homes, 2003

	State	U.S.
Total units	387,000	58,809,000
Value of units		
Under $100,000	62.0%	29.6%
$100,000-199,999	30.4%	36.9%
$200,000 or more	7.6%	33.5%
Median value	$85,709	$142,275
Rank among all states		46

Units are owner-occupied one-family houses whose numbers are
  rounded to nearest thousand. Data are extrapolated from
  survey samples.
Source: U.S. Census Bureau, American Community Survey.

EDUCATION

Public school enrollment, 2002

Prekindergarten through grade 8
State enrollment 200,000
Total U.S. enrollment. 34,135,000
State share of U.S. total 0.59%

Grades 9 through 12
State enrollment. 82,000
Total U.S. enrollment. 14,067,000
State share of U.S. total 0.58%

Enrollment rates
State public school enrollment rate. 96.5%
Overall U.S. rate 90.4%
Rank among states in 2002 3
Rank among states in 1995 4

Enrollment figures (which include unclassified students) are
  rounded to nearest thousand pupils during fall school term.
  Enrollment rates are based on enumerated resident population
  estimate for July 1, 2002.
Source: U.S. National Center for Education Statistics.

Public college finances, 2003-2004

FTE enrollment in public institutions of higher education
Students in state institutions 69,500
Students in all U.S. public institutions 9,916,600
State share of U.S. total 0.70
Rank among states 37

**State and local government appropriations for higher
education**
State appropriation per FTE $4,135
National average $5,716
Rank among states 45
State & local tax revenue going to higher
  education 9.3%

FTE = full-time equivalent in public postsecondary programs,
  including summer sessions; student numbers are rounded to
  nearest hundred. Funding figures for 2003-2004 academic year
  include financial aid to students in state public institutions and
  exclude money for research, agriculture experiment stations,
  teaching hospitals, and medical schools; figures are rounded to
  nearest thousand dollars.
Source: Higher Education Executive Officers, Denver, Colorado.

TRANSPORTATION AND TRAVEL

Highway mileage, 2003

Interstate highways 549
Other freeways and expressways 9
Arterial roads 3,170
Collector roads 8,777
Local roads. 24,488
Urban roads 3,190
Rural roads 33,803
Total state mileage. 36,993
U.S. total 3,974,107
State share 0.93%
Rank among states 38

Note that combined urban and rural road mileage matches the
  total of the other categories.
Source: U.S. Federal Highway Administration.

Motor vehicle registrations and driver licenses, 2003

Vehicle registrations	State	U.S.	Share	Rank
Autos, trucks, buses	1,409,000	231,390,000	0.61%	37
Autos only	756,000	135,670	0.56%	36
Motorcycles	19,000	5,328,000	0.36%	47
Driver licenses	1,272,000	196,166,000	0.65%	37

Figures, which do not include vehicles owned by military services,
  are rounded to the nearest thousand. Figures for automobiles
  include taxis.
Source: U.S. Federal Highway Administration.

Domestic travel expenditures, 2003
Spending by U.S. residents on overnight trips and
day trips of at least 50 miles from home

Total expenditures within state . . . . $1.80 bill.
Total expenditures within U.S. . . . . $490.87 bill.
State share of U.S. total 0.4%
Rank among states 43

Source: Travel Industry Association of America.

Retail gasoline prices, 2003-2007
Average price per gallon at the pump

Year	U.S.	State
2003	$1.267	$1.256
2004	$1.316	$1.298
2005	$1.644	$1.647
2007	$2.298	$2.358

Excise tax per gallon in 2004 . . . . 27.0¢
Rank among all states in 2007 prices 10

Prices are averages of all grades of gasoline sold at the pump
during March months in 2003-2005 and during February, 2007.
Averages for 2006, during which prices rose higher, are not
available.
Source: U.S. Energy Information Agency, *Petroleum Marketing
Monthly* (2003-2005 data); American Automobile Association
(2007 data).

CRIME AND LAW ENFORCEMENT

State and local police officers, 2000-2004

	2000	2002	2004
Total officers			
U.S.	654,601	665,555	675,734
State	3,128	3,028	3,177*
*Net change, 2000-2004			+1.57%
Officers per 1,000 residents			
U.S.	2.33	2.31	2.30
State	1.73	1.68	1.75
State rank	39	44	40

Totals include state and local police and sheriffs.
Source: Carsey Institute, University of New Hampshire.

Crime rates, 2003
Incidents per 100,000 residents

Crimes	State	U.S.
Violent crimes		
Total incidents	258	475
Murder	4	6
Forcible rape	16	32
Robbery	40	142
Aggravated assault	197	295
Property crimes		
Total incidents	2,359	3,588
Burglary	562	741
Larceny/theft	1,603	2,415
Motor vehicle theft	195	433
All crimes	2,617	4,063

Source: U.S. Federal Bureau of Investigation, *Crime in the United
States,* annual.

State prison populations, 1980-2003

	State	U.S.	State share
1980	1,257	305,458	0.41%
1990	1,565	708,393	0.22%
1996	2,749	1,025,624	0.27%
2000	3,856	1,391,261	0.28%
2003	4,758	1,470,045	0.32%

State figures exclude prisoners in federal penitentiaries.
Source: U.S. Bureau of Justice Statistics, *Prisoners in 2003.*

Wisconsin

Location: Upper Midwest

Area and rank: 54,314 square miles (140,673 square kilometers); 65,503 square miles (169,653 square kilometers) including water; twenty-fifth largest state in area

Coastline: none

Population and rank: 5,509,000 (2004); twentieth largest state in population

Capital city: Madison (208,054 people in 2000 census)

Largest city: Milwaukee (596,974 people in 2000 census)

Became territory: July 4, 1836

Entered Union and rank: May 29, 1848; thirtieth state

Present constitution adopted: 1848

Counties: 72

State name: "Wisconsin" comes from a Chippewa word meaning "grassy place"

State nickname: Badger State

Motto: Forward

State flag: Field of royal blue with state coat of arms, state name in white above, "1848" below

State capitol building in Madison. (Wisconsin Department of Tourism/Bob Queen)

Highest point: Timms Hill—1,951 feet (595 meters)

Lowest point: Lake Michigan—579 feet (176 meters)

Highest recorded temperature: 114 degrees Fahrenheit (46 degrees Celsius)—Wisconsin Dells, 1936

Lowest recorded temperature: –54 degrees Fahrenheit (–48 degrees Celsius)—Danbury, 1922

State song: "On, Wisconsin"

State tree: Sugar maple

State flower: Wood violet

State bird: Robin

State fish: Musky (Muskellunge)

State animal: Badger

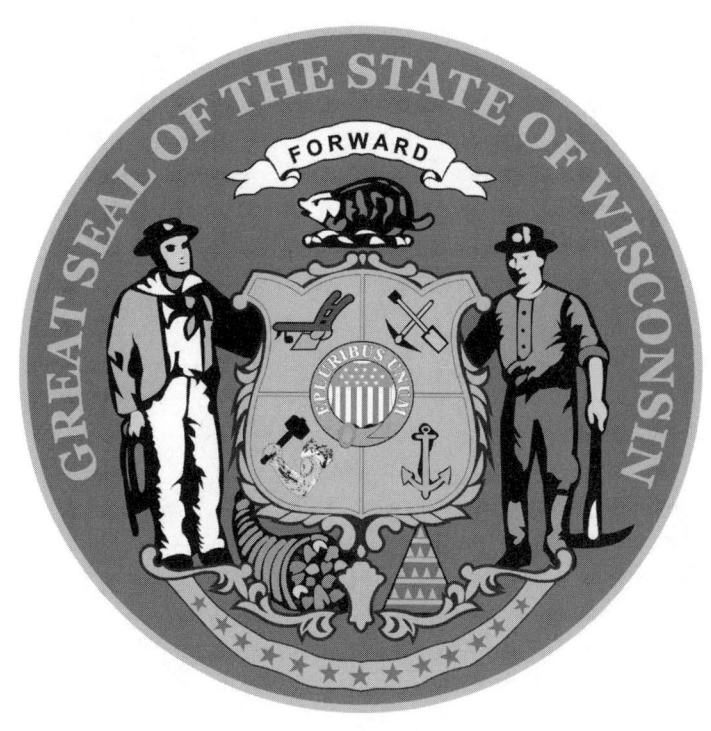

Wisconsin History

Influenced by a landscape shaped by ancient glaciers, Wisconsin developed into a state with three distinct regions. The southeast corner of Wisconsin, along the shore of Lake Michigan, is an urban, industrial area, dominated by Milwaukee, the state's largest city. The northern third of the state is a sparsely populated area of forests and lakes, primarily used for tourism and recreation. Between these two regions, the southern, western, and central areas of the state are productive agricultural lands, particularly in dairy farming.

Early History. During the last two million years, glaciers advanced and retreated over much of North America. The last major advance began about twenty-five thousand years ago and reached its greatest extent around fifteen thousand years ago. At this time, it covered nearly two-thirds of Wisconsin. A smaller advance, about ten thousand years ago, covered only the northern part of the state. As a result of this glacial activity, this area now contains numerous streams and marshes,

Lookout tower atop Timms Hill, whose altitude of 1,951 feet makes it the highest elevation in Wisconsin. (Jon Sullivan/ PD Photo.org)

as well as more than fourteen thousand lakes. The areas of older glacial activity, which have been subjected to erosion, now contain flat plains and rolling hills. The southwest part of the state, which was not covered by glaciers, is an area of ridges and valleys carved by rivers.

The first humans to inhabit the area arrived about twelve thousand years ago, when much of northern Wisconsin was still covered with glaciers. These people, known as the Paleo-Indian culture, hunted bison and other large animals. About ten thousand years ago, as the climate warmed, the people of the Archaic culture hunted large and small animals and gathered wild plants for food. About three thousand years ago, the people of the Woodland culture used bows and arrows to hunt, made pottery, and built large mounds. About one thousand years ago, the people of the Mississippian culture lived in large, permanent villages and grew corn, beans, and squash.

During the early seventeenth century, just before Europeans arrived in the area, the major Native American peoples living in Wisconsin included the Santee Dakota in the northwest, the Menominee in the northeast, the Iowa in the southwest, and the Winnebago in the southeast. In addition to crops associated with the Mississippian culture, the peoples of northern Wisconsin also subsisted on wild rice growing in wetlands.

During the 1640's, the Iroquois, a powerful confederation of Native Americans living in the New York area, launched a series of wars against Native Americans living to the west. The Iroquois were enemies of the French, while the peoples living in the Great Lakes region were generally allied with the French and participated in the French fur trade. The wars drove many Native American peoples westward into Wisconsin, including the Potawatomi, the Ojibwa, the Sauk, the Fox, the Ottawa, the Huron, the Miami, the Mascouten, and the Kickapoo. Many of these peoples later moved farther west, but the Ojibwa, the Menominee, the Winnebago, and the Potawatomi remained in the state. Other Native American peoples moved westward into Wisconsin during the 1820's, including the Oneida, the Stockbridge, the Munsee, and the Brotherton. Most Native Americans in Wisconsin now live on reservations in the northern part of the state or in Milwaukee.

Exploration and Settlement. The first European known to reach Wisconsin was the French explorer Jean Nicolet. In 1634, Nicolet journeyed from Lake Huron through the strait between the Upper and Lower Peninsulas of Michigan, becoming the first European to reach Lake Michigan. He then sailed into Green Bay,

a narrow inlet of Lake Michigan, and reached Wisconsin. Here he negotiated a peace treaty with the Winnebago. In 1671, the French missionary Claude-Jean Allouez founded a mission at Green Bay. A fort was built on the site in 1717, and Green Bay served as the center of the fur trade in the area for one hundred years.

At the end of the French and Indian War, a struggle between France and Great Britain for control of North America, the area was acquired by the British. At the end of the American Revolution, twenty years later, the area was acquired by the United States. Wisconsin was part of the Northwest Territory from 1787 to 1800, part of the Indiana Territory from 1800 to 1809, part of the Illinois Territory from 1809 to 1818, and part of the Michigan Territory from 1818 to 1836. The Wisconsin Territory was created in 1836.

American settlement of the area began slowly. Although the future site of Milwaukee was settled as early as 1800, it did not develop into a town for thirty years. The United States built Fort Howard at Green Bay in 1816 and began building the town of Green Bay in 1829. The opening of the Erie Canal in 1825, linking the Hudson River with Lake Erie, made travel between the heavily populated eastern states and the sparsely populated Great Lakes region much easier. The discovery of lead ores in southwestern Wisconsin during the 1820's also encouraged settlers. Mineral Point, established in the area of the lead mines in 1827, quickly became the most important settlement in the area and served as the first territorial capital.

Statehood and Economic Growth. At first, the Wisconsin Territory was settled mostly by Americans from eastern states. The lead mines brought immigrants from Cornwall, a region of southwestern England fa-

Wisconsin's dairy farms have made the state one of the nation's leading producers of milk products. (PhotoDisc)

mous for mines, during the 1830's. These were soon followed by immigrants from Germany, Ireland, and Italy moving into southwestern Wisconsin. German immigrants also settled in Milwaukee during the 1840's. After losing a large part of its western lands to the newly created Iowa Territory in 1838, the Wisconsin Territory became the thirtieth state ten years later.

After statehood, settlers entered Wisconsin from eastern and southern states, Germany, Poland, Scandinavia, and the British Isles. As lead mining played a less important role in the state, dairy farming and other forms of agriculture came to dominate the economy. Several institutes of higher learning were founded during the late 1840's, and the nation's first kindergarten was opened in Watertown in 1856.

The national crisis over slavery led to the creation of the Republican Party of Wisconsin in Ripon in 1854. During the Civil War, Wisconsin was firmly on the side of the Union. The Republican Party continued to dominate state politics for a century. The war brought industrial development to Milwaukee, and the city went on to be an important center of labor-union activity.

During the 1870's, zinc ores were discovered in southwestern Wisconsin. Zinc mining remained an important industry in the state for more than one hundred years. The 1870's also saw the rise of the production of lumber in the northern part of the state. Lumber resources were nearly depleted by the 1920's,

so the forestry industry turned from lumber to the production of woodpulp for papermaking. This would remain an important part of the economy. Iron mining developed in northern Wisconsin during the 1880's and continued into the 1960's.

The Twentieth Century. Wisconsin played an important role in the Progressive movement of the early twentieth century, as political reformers fought corruption and the influence of the railroads and other powerful business interests. A national leader in the Progressive movement, Wisconsin native Robert Marion La Follette, Sr., served as governor of the state from 1900 to 1906, and as a U.S. senator from 1906 until his death in 1925. The Progressive movement remained a faction within the Republican Party until 1934, when the Wisconsin Progressive Party was created. The party rejoined the Republicans in 1946, but many of its members joined the Democratic Party instead.

Influenced by the Progressive movement and labor unions, Milwaukee elected Socialist mayors in 1910, 1916, and 1948. Despite the state's reputation for reformist and radical politics, it also produced numerous conservative politicians. One of the most controversial was Wisconsin native Joseph Raymond McCarthy, who served as a U.S. senator from 1946 until his death in 1957. McCarthy drew national attention with accusations that a large number of Communists had infiltrated the government of the United States.

During the Great Depression of the 1930's, Wisconsin's economy, balanced between manufacturing and agriculture, suffered less than that of most states. Agriculture in particular remained remarkably stable, with Wisconsin leading the nation in dairy farming after 1920. Despite this stability, Wisconsin, like the rest of the nation, saw a shift in its population from farmlands to cities. During the 1920's, about half of the state's residents lived in rural areas; by the 1980's, about two-thirds of the population lived in urban areas.

The need for military equipment during World War II greatly increased industrial production in the southeastern part of Wisconsin and made it one of the leading manufacturing states in the nation. The rise in the tourism industry in the second half of the twentieth century also greatly benefited the economy. Wisconsin's economy was slowed by a nationwide recession during the late 1980's, but to a lesser extent than most other states. During the 1990's, Wisconsin maintained a reputation for economic stability, an honest, efficient state government, and innovative, if controversial, public policies.

Politics. As in much of the nation, the 2000 presidential contest in Wisconsin was closely fought. In the end, the Democratic Party ticket of Al Gore and John Edwards defeated George W. Bush and Dick Cheney by just 5,396 votes out of 2.275 million votes cast. By attracting some 95,000 votes, the third party candidacy of maverick reformer Ralph Nader made the race closer than it might have been without him.

In the 2002 midterm elections, the state had one fewer seat in Congress, which was lost to the 2000 census. When the election was over, the state's eight seats in Congress were evenly divided between Republicans and Democrats. Most interest, however, centered on the governor's race between newcomer Democrat Jim Doyle and the incumbent governor, Scott McCallum. The contest was characterized as exceptionally hostile, and the candidates resorted to name-calling. A major issue was the state's ballooning budget deficit, slated to reach $2.8 billion following two years. In the end, Doyle won by 45 to 41 percent, with a libertarian candidate taking 11 percent. In the 2004 presidential poll, Democrat John Kerry narrowly defeated Bush, winning the state by about 11,500 votes out of nearly 3 million votes cast.

Commerce and Headlines. Globalization touched Wisconsin's famed brewing industry, founded by German immigrants in the nineteenth century. South African Breweries bought the Miller Brewing Company of Milwaukee from its New York-based owners. Tariff rules also affected the state when in 2003, after threats of retaliatory action by Europe and elsewhere, President Bush lifted the tariffs on steel that he had imposed the previous year. Many steel users in Wisconsin and nearby states were negatively affected by the action.

An international issue closer to home involved the state's northern neighbor. Canada sold prescription drugs to U.S. customers at substantial discounts to local prices. Because drug prices were a hardship for lower-

With ports on Lake Superior, Lake Michigan, and the Mississippi River, Wisconsin has excellent access to world shipping. (Wisconsin Department of Tourism)

income people, in 2004 the state of Wisconsin, like neighboring Minnesota, opened a state Web site to assist its residents in purchasing drugs more cheaply.

A tragic occurrence took place in 2004, when an immigrant from Laos, claiming that he was attacked first and racially taunted, killed six Wisconsin hunters. How-ever, after some of the dead were found to have been shot in the back and survivors gave a different account of the incident, he was found guilty of murder.

Rose Secrest
Updated by the Editor

Wisconsin Time Line

1600's	Native Americans farm Wisconsin land.
1634	French explorer Jean Nicolet sails into Green Bay and becomes the first European to reach Wisconsin.
1640's	Iroquois begin a series of wars against other Native Americans, driving them west into Wisconsin.
1671	French missionary Claude-Jean Allouez founds a mission at Green Bay.
1717	French build a fort at Green Bay.
1763	End of the French and Indian War brings the area under British control.
1783	End of the American Revolution brings the area under the control of the United States.
1787	Wisconsin becomes part of the Northwest Territory.
1800	Future site of Milwaukee is settled.
1800	Wisconsin becomes part of the Indiana Territory.
1809	Wisconsin becomes part of the Illinois Territory.
1816	Americans build a fort at Green Bay.
Dec. 3, 1818	Wisconsin becomes part of the Michigan Territory.
1820's	Lead mining begins in Wisconsin.
1825	Opening of the Erie Canal improves transportation from eastern states to Wisconsin and other Great Lake states.
1827	Mineral Point is founded.
1830's	Cornish miners become the first major group of European immigrants to settle in the area.
1836	Wisconsin Territory is created, with the territorial capital at Mineral Point.
1837	Territorial capital is moved to Burlington.
1838	Newly formed settlement of Madison becomes the territorial capital.
1840's	Large numbers of German immigrants arrive.
1846	Beloit College in Beloit and Carroll College in Waukesha are founded.
1847	Carthage College in Kenosha and Lawrence University in Appleton are founded.
May 29, 1848	Wisconsin is admitted to the Union.
1849	University of Wisconsin is founded at Madison.
1854	Republican Party of Wisconsin is created at Ripon.
1856	Nation's first kindergarten is established at Watertown.
1857	Marquette University is founded in Milwaukee.
1863	Ripon College is founded in Ripon.
1870's	Zinc mining and lumber production begin in Wisconsin.
1875	Free high schools are established by state law.
1880's	Iron mining begins in the state.
1890's	Large numbers of Polish and Italian immigrants arrive.
1898	Saint Norbert College is founded in De Pere.
1900	Robert Marion La Follette, Sr., is elected governor.
1906	La Follette is elected a U.S. senator.
1910	First Socialist mayor of Milwaukee is elected.
1920	For the first time, Wisconsin leads the nation in dairy farming.
1920's	Lumber production declines.
1936	University of Wisconsin hires painter John Steuart Curry as the nation's first artist-in-residence.
1946	Wisconsin's Joseph Raymond McCarthy is elected a U.S. senator.

1960's	Iron mining declines.
1970's	Zinc mining declines.
1971	University of Wisconsin merges with the Wisconsin State University system, creating one of the largest university systems in the nation.
1982	Community Options Program is created, allowing the elderly to be cared for in homelike settings.
1983	Laws are passed allowing health maintenance organizations (HMOs) to exist in the state, greatly changing health care.
1990	Population reaches 4.9 million.
1997	Population reaches 5.2 million.
1999	BadgerCare, a state program designed to provide medical insurance for low-income families, is created.
Nov. 7, 2000	Republican presidential candidate Al Gore wins Wisconsin's electoral votes by 5,396 votes out of 2.275 million votes cast.
Nov. 2, 2002	Democratic challenger Jim Doyle defeats Republican incumbent Scot McCallum in a bitterly fought race for governor.
Nov. 21, 2004	Claiming he was racially taunted, a Laotian immigrant kills six Wisconsin hunters.

Notes for Further Study

Published Sources. For the student new to the subject, a good starting place is *Wisconsin* (1998) by Jean F. Blashfield, which discusses the state's geography, history, natural resources, economy, culture, and people. Originally printed in 1941, the *WPA Guide to Wisconsin: The Federal Writers' Project Guide to 1930's Wisconsin* was reprinted by the Wisconsin State Historical Society in 2006 because of its comprehensive information on state history, people, resources, art, architecture, folklore, and traditions. The new edition has an authoritative introduction by Wisconsin historian Norman K. Risjord. Joan M. Jensen's *Calling This Place Home: Women on the Wisconsin Frontier, 1850-1925* (2006) provides readers with an understanding of how women shaped the state's history and how broader developments shaped their lives.

In order to understand the political process in Wisconsin, a useful resource is Jack Stark's *The Wisconsin State Constitution: A Reference Guide* (1997). An excellent, often dramatic account of how laws are made in the state is found in *The Art of Legislative Politics* (1994) by Tom Loftus, which uses examples of political battles in Wisconsin over controversial topics such as abortion, gun control, and education. *Power to the People: An American State at Work* (1996) by former Wisconsin governor Tommy G. Thompson presents an interesting look at state politics from an insider's viewpoint. The economic changes in Wisconsin during the 1990's are discussed in *The End of the Line: Lost Jobs, New Lives in Postindustrial America* (1994) by Kathryn Marie Dudley, which deals with the closing of an automobile manufacturing plant in Racine and its aftereffects.

A visual guide to the state's history is provided in *Wisconsin's Past and Present: A Historical Atlas* (1998) by members of the Wisconsin Cartographer's Guild. Frank L. Klement's *Wisconsin in the Civil War: The Home Front and the Battle Front, 1861-1865* (1997) provides a detailed account of a period often overlooked in Wisconsin history. *Indian Nations of Wisconsin: Histories of Endurance and Renewal* (2001) by Patty Loew presents a collection of brief histories of twelve indigenous groups who have maintained their presence in Wisconsin

from the point of European contact to the present. *Wisconsin Indians* (2d ed., 2002) by Nancy Oestreich Lurie offers another good discussion of this topic. *Roadside Geology of Wisconsin* (2004) by Robert H. Dott, Jr., and John W. Attig offers thirty-five interpretive road guides to the geologic history of the state's landscapes, as well as maps, photographs, and a glossary.

Web Resources. Several Web sites offer useful guides to the enormous variety of information about the state available on the Internet. A portal site offering access to a host of other sites is the state of Wisconsin's official site (www.wisconsin .gov/). Another source of general information is Wisconline (www.wisconline.com), which lists upcoming events in the state, provides detailed information on current weather conditions, and supplies an unusual star map displaying the constellations visible from Wisconsin at particular times. An excellent discussion of law and the lawmaking process is found at the Wisconsin Legislature (www.legis.state.wi.us/). Statistical data from the U.S. Census Bureau's QuickFacts (quickfacts.census.gov/qfd/states/55000.html) are a good way to discern local and regional demographic trends.

Travel in Wisconsin is the subject of Wisconsin Department of Tourism (www.travelwisconsin.com), which also provides maps of the state. Outstanding Web sites dedicated to the major cities in the state include Madison.com (www.madison.com), which also provides links to the city's newspapers, and Milwaukee Online (www.onmilwaukee.com/), which also provides information for tourists. Official Web sites for the city governments can be found at City of Madison (www.ci .madison.wi.us) and City of Milwaukee (www.ci.mil.wi.us/display/router.asp). Of the many sites dedicated to the state's history, a good place to start is the Wisconsin Historical Society (www.wisconsinhistory.org/), which provides links to archives and historical libraries. Excellent information on many of the Native American peoples living in Wisconsin is provided by Great Lakes Intertribal Council Native Wisconsin Home Page (www.glitc.org/).

Counties

County	2000 pop.	Rank in pop.	Sq. miles	Rank in area
Adams	18,643	55	647.8	43
Ashland	16,866	58	1,043.9	11
Barron	44,963	29	862.9	25
Bayfield	15,013	66	1,476.4	2
Brown	226,778	4	528.7	56
Buffalo	13,804	67	684.5	42
Burnett	15,674	64	821.5	28
Calumet	40,631	35	319.9	68
Chippewa	55,195	25	1,010.5	13
Clark	33,557	41	1,215.7	7
Columbia	52,468	26	773.9	33
Crawford	17,243	57	572.8	52
Dane	426,526	2	1,202.2	8
Dodge	85,897	17	882.4	22
Door	27,961	44	482.7	59
Douglas	43,287	31	1,309.3	4
Dunn	39,858	36	852.1	26
Eau Claire	93,142	16	637.7	45
Florence	5,088	71	488.1	58
Fond du Lac	97,296	14	723.0	39
Forest	10,024	68	1,014.1	12
Grant	49,597	28	1,147.9	9
Green	33,647	40	584.0	50
Green Lake	19,105	53	354.3	65
Iowa	22,780	48	762.7	35
Iron	6,861	70	757.3	36
Jackson	19,100	54	987.3	15
Jefferson	74,021	21	557.1	53

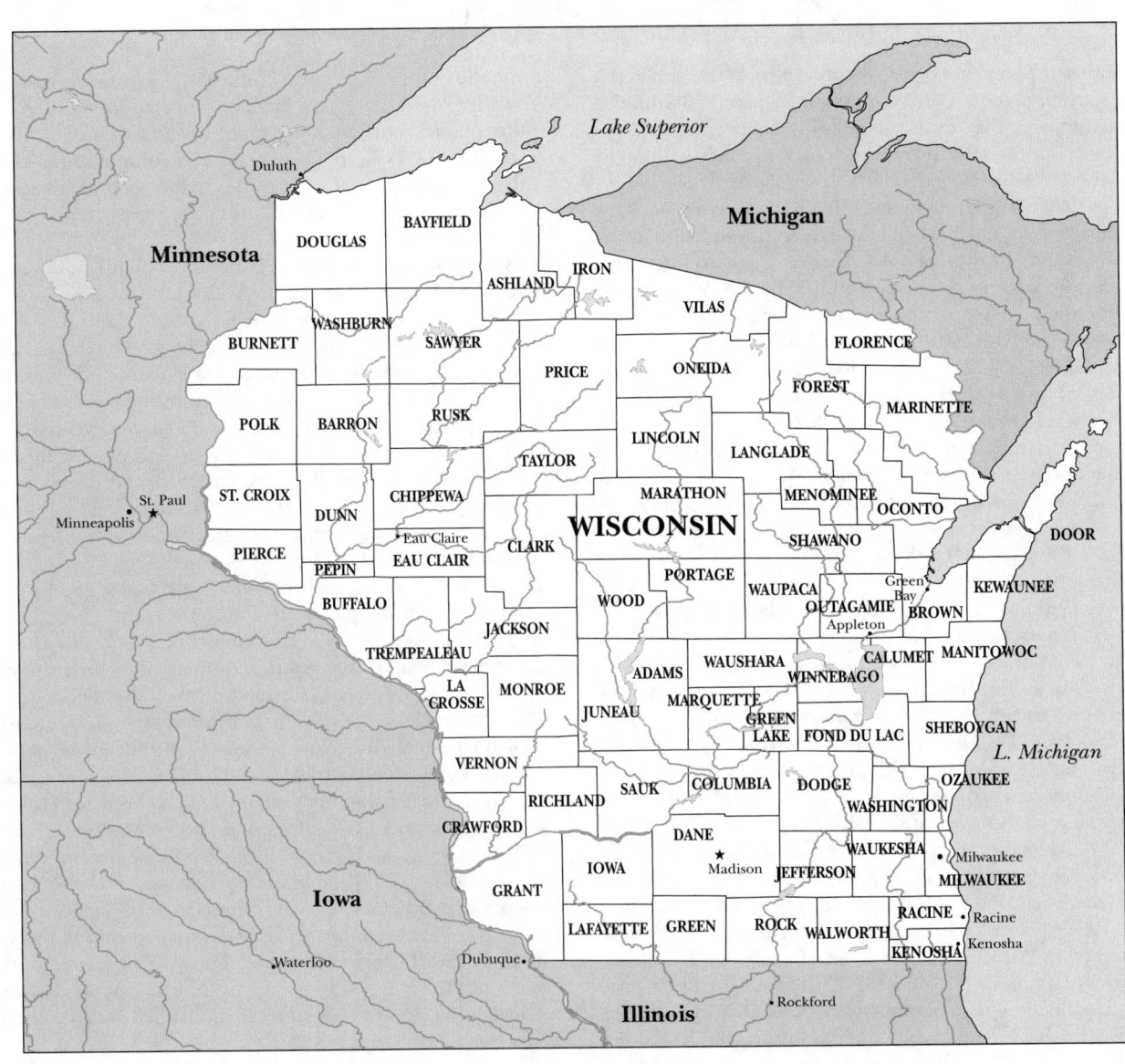

County	2000 pop.	Rank in pop.	Sq. miles	Rank in area
Juneau	24,316	46	767.7	34
Kenosha	149,577	9	272.8	69
Kewaunee	20,187	51	342.7	66
La Crosse	107,120	13	452.8	61
Lafayette	16,137	60	633.6	46
Langlade	20,740	50	872.7	24
Lincoln	29,641	42	883.0	21
Manitowoc	82,887	18	591.6	48
Marathon	125,834	10	1,545.1	1
Marinette	43,384	30	1,402.0	3
Marquette	15,832	62	455.5	60
Menominee	4,562	72	358.0	64
Milwaukee	940,164	1	241.6	70
Monroe	40,899	33	900.9	19
Oconto	35,634	39	998.1	14
Oneida	36,776	38	1,124.7	10
Outagamie	160,971	6	640.4	44
Ozaukee	82,317	19	232.0	72
Pepin	7,213	69	232.3	71
Pierce	36,804	37	576.5	51
Polk	41,319	32	917.3	17
Portage	67,182	22	806.4	30
Price	15,822	63	1,252.7	6

County	2000 pop.	Rank in pop.	Sq. miles	Rank in area
Racine	188,831	5	333.1	67
Richland	17,924	56	586.3	49
Rock	152,307	8	720.5	41
Rusk	15,347	65	913.2	18
St. Croix	63,155	23	722.0	40
Sauk	55,225	24	837.7	27
Sawyer	16,196	59	1,256.5	5
Shawano	40,664	34	892.6	20
Sheboygan	112,646	12	513.7	57
Taylor	19,680	52	975.0	16
Trempealeau	27,010	45	734.1	38
Vernon	28,056	43	795.0	31
Vilas	21,033	49	872.8	23
Walworth	93,759	15	555.4	55
Washburn	16,036	61	809.7	29
Washington	117,493	11	430.8	63
Waukesha	360,767	3	555.6	54
Waupaca	51,731	27	751.1	37
Waushara	23,154	47	626.1	47
Winnebago	156,763	7	438.6	62
Wood	75,555	20	792.9	32

Source: U.S. Census Bureau; National Association of Counties.

Cities
With 10,000 or more residents

Rank	City	Population
1	Milwaukee	596,974
2	Madison (capital)	208,054
3	Green Bay	102,313
4	Kenosha	90,352
5	Racine	81,855
6	Appleton	70,087
7	Waukesha	64,825
8	Oshkosh	62,916
9	Eau Claire	61,704
10	West Allis	61,254
11	Janesville	59,498
12	La Crosse	51,818
13	Sheboygan	50,792
14	Wauwatosa	47,271
15	Fond du Lac	42,203
16	Brookfield	38,649
17	Wausau	38,426
18	New Berlin	38,220
19	Beloit	35,775
20	Greenfield	35,476
21	Manitowoc	34,053
22	Menomonee Falls	32,647
23	Franklin	29,494
24	Oak Creek	28,456
25	West Bend	28,152

Rank	City	Population
26	Superior	27,368
27	Stevens Point	24,551
28	Neenah	24,507
29	Caledonia	23,614
30	Mount Pleasant	23,142
31	Mequon	21,823
32	Watertown	21,598
33	Muskego	21,397
34	South Milwaukee	21,256
35	De Pere	20,559
36	Fitchburg	20,501
37	Sun Prairie	20,369
38	Marshfield	18,800
39	Wisconsin Rapids	18,435
40	Cudahy	18,429
41	Grand Chute	18,392
42	Germantown	18,260
43	Ashwaubenon	17,634
44	Menasha	16,331
45	Pleasant Prairie	16,136
46	Middleton	15,770
47	Allouez	15,443
48	Beaver Dam	15,169
49	Menomonie	14,937
50	Onalaska	14,839

(continued)

Rank	City	Population
51	Greendale	14,405
52	Whitefish Bay	14,163
53	Shorewood	13,763
54	Howard	13,546
55	Whitewater	13,437
56	Glendale	13,367
57	Kaukauna	12,983
58	Chippewa Falls	12,925
59	Two Rivers	12,639
60	River Falls	12,560
61	Oconomowoc	12,382
62	Stoughton	12,354
63	Brown Deer	12,170
64	Weston	12,079
65	Bellevue Town	11,828
66	Bellevue	11,828
67	Pewaukee	11,783

Rank	City	Population
68	Marinette	11,749
69	Fort Atkinson	11,621
70	Cedarburg	10,908
71	Hartford	10,905
72	Monroe	10,843
73	Waupun	10,718
74	Baraboo	10,711
75	Plover	10,520
76	Little Chute	10,476
77	Port Washington	10,467
78	Richfield	10,373
79	Grafton	10,312
80	Merrill	10,146

Population figures are from 2000 census.
Source: U.S. Bureau of the Census.

Index to Tables

DEMOGRAPHICS

Resident state and national populations, 1970-2004

Population figures given in thousands

	State pop.	U.S. pop.	Share	Rank
1970	4,418	203,302	2.2%	16
1980	4,706	226,546	2.1%	16
1985	4,748	237,924	2.0%	16
1990	4,892	248,765	2.0%	16
1995	5,185	262,761	1.9%	18
2000	5,364	281,425	1.9%	18
2004	5,509	293,655	1.9%	20

Source: U.S. Census Bureau, Current Population Reports, 2006.

Resident population by age, 2004

Age Group	Total persons
Under 5 years	338,000
5 to 17 years	970,000
18 to 24 years	575,000
25 to 34 years	696,000
35 to 44 years	840,000
45 to 54 years	826,000
55 to 64 years	550,000
65 to 74 years	349,000
75 to 84 years	256,000
85 years and older	111,000
All age groups	5,509,000
Portion of residents 65 and older	13.0%
National rank in portion of oldest residents	20
National average	12.4%

Population figures are rounded to nearest thousand persons;
figures include armed forces personnel stationed in the state.
Source: U.S. Bureau of the Census, 2006.

Resident population by race, Hispanic origin, 2004

Category	State pop.	Share	U.S.
All residents	5,509	100.00%	100.00%
Non-Hispanic white	4,749	86.20%	67.37%
Hispanic white	218	3.96%	13.01%
Other Hispanic	19	0.34%	1.06%
African American	328	5.95%	12.77%
Native American	51	0.93%	0.96%
Asian, Pacific Islander	108	1.96%	4.37%
Two or more categories	56	1.02%	1.51%

Population figures are in thousands. Persons counted as "Hispanic" (Latino) may be of any race. Because of overlapping categories, categories may not add up to 100%. Shares in column 3 are percentages of each category within the state; these figures may be compared to the national percentages in column 4.
Source: U.S. Bureau of the Census, 2006.

Projected state population, 2000-2030

Year	Population
2000	5,364,000
2005	5,554,000
2010	5,727,000
2015	5,883,000
2020	6,005,000
2025	6,088,000
2030	6,151,000
Population increase, 2000-2030	787,000
Percentage increase, 2000-2030	14.7

Projections are based on data from the 2000 census.
Source: U.S. Census Bureau.

VITAL STATISTICS

Infant mortality rates, 1980-2002

	1980	1990	2000	2002
All state residents	10.3	8.2	6.6	6.9
All U.S. residents	12.6	9.2	9.4	9.1
All state white residents	9.7	7.7	5.5	5.6
All U.S. white residents	10.6	7.6	5.7	5.8
All state black residents	18.5	19.0	17.2	18.9
All U.S. black residents	22.2	18.0	14.1	14.4

Figures represent deaths per 1,000 live births of resident infants under 1 year old, exclusive of fetal deaths. Figures for all residents include members of other racial categories not listed separately.
Source: U.S. Census Bureau, *Statistical Abstract of the United States,* 2006.

Abortion rates, 1990 and 2000

	1990	2000
Total abortions	15,000	11,000
Rate per 1,000 women	13.5	9.6
U.S. rate	25.7	21.3
Rank	36	40

Numbers of abortions are rounded to nearest thousand; ranks are based on rates.
Source: U.S. Census Bureau.

Marriages and divorces, 2004

Total marriages	34,100
Rate per 1,000 population	6.2
National rate per 1,000 population	7.4
Rank among all states	40
Total divorces	17,000
Rate per 1,000 population	3.1
National rate per 1,000 population	3.7
Rank among all states	33

Figures are for all marriages and divorces performed within the state, including those of nonresidents; totals are rounded to the nearest hundred. Ranks are for highest to lowest figures; note that divorce data are not available for five states.
Source: U.S. National Center for Health Statistics, *Vital Statistics of the United States,* 2006.

Death rates by leading causes, 2002
Deaths per 100,000 resident population

Cause	State	U.S.
Heart disease	237.5	241.7
Cancer	199.0	193.2
Cerebrovascular diseases	63.9	56.4
Accidents other than motor vehicle	41.8	37.0
Motor vehicle accidents	16.0	15.7
Chronic lower respiratory diseases	42.9	43.3
Diabetes mellitus	24.9	25.4
HIV	1.4	4.9
Suicide	11.5	11.0
Homicide	3.5	6.1
All causes	863.4	847.3
Rank in overall death rate among states		28

Figures exclude nonresidents who died in the state. Causes of death follow International Classification of Diseases. Rank is from highest to lowest death rate in the United States.
Source: U.S. National Center for Health Statistics, *National Vital Statistics Report,* 2006.

ECONOMY

Gross state product, 1990-2004
In current dollars

Year	State product	Nat'l product	State share
1990	$100.3 billion	$5.67 trillion	1.77%
2000	$176.2 billion	$9.75 trillion	1.81%
2002	$189.5 billion	$10.41 trillion	1.82%
2003	$198.1 billion	$10.92 trillion	1.81%
2004	$211.7 billion	$11.65 trillion	1.82%

Source: U.S. Bureau of Economic Analysis, *Survey of Current Business,* July, 2005.

Gross state product by industry, 2003
In billions of dollars

Construction $7.5
Manufacturing 43.6
Wholesale trade. 10.6
Retail trade 13.9
Finance & insurance 13.6
Information 6.0
Professional services. 7.7
Health care & social assistance. 14.1
Government 19.5

Total state product. $186.4
Total U.S. product $10,289.2
State share of U.S. total 1.81%
Rank among all states 19

Total figures include industries not listed separately. Amounts are in chained 2000 dollars.
Source: U.S. Bureau of Economic Analysis, *Survey of Current Business,* July, 2005.

Personal income per capita, 1990-2004
In current dollars

	1990	2000	2004
Per capita income	$18,072	$28,570	$32,157
U.S. average	$19,477	$29,845	$32,937
Rank among states	23	19	21

Source: U.S. Bureau of Economic Analysis, *Survey of Current Business,* April, 2005.

Energy consumption, 2001
In trillions of British thermal units (BTU), except as noted

Total energy consumption
Total state energy consumption 1,863
Total U.S. energy consumption 96,275
State share of U.S. total 1.94%
Rank among states 19

Per capita consumption (In millions of BTU)
Total state per capita consumption 345
Total U.S. per capita consumption. 338
Rank among states 25

End-use sectors
Residential. 401
Commercial 313
Industrial 729
Transportation 422

Sources of energy
Petroleum 668
Natural gas. 363
Coal 495
Hydroelectric power 21
Nuclear electric power 120

Figures for totals include categories not listed separately.
Source: U.S. Energy Information Administration, *State Energy Data Report,* 2001.

Nonfarm employment by sectors, 2004

Total persons 2,803,000
Construction 126,000
Manufacturing 502,000
Trade, transportation, utilities. 540,000
Information 50,000
Finance, insurance, real estate. 158,000
Professional & business services 251,000
Education & health services 376,000
Leisure, hospitality, arts, organizations 250,000
Other services, including repair & maintenance 135,000
Government 412,000

Figures are rounded to nearest thousand persons. "Total" includes mining and natural resources, not listed separately.
Source: U.S. Bureau of Labor Statistics, 2006.

Foreign exports, 1990-2004
In millions of dollars

Year	State	U.S.	State share
1990	5,158	394,045	1.31%
1996	9,504	624,767	1.52%
1997	10,125	688,896	1.47%
2000	10,508	712,055	1.34%
2003	11,510	724,006	1.70%
2004	12,706	769,332	1.65%

Rank among all states in 2004 20

U.S. total does not include U.S. dependencies.

Source: U.S. Census Bureau, *U.S. Merchandise Trade*, series FT 900, 2000; U.S. Census Bureau, *U.S. International Trade in Goods and Services*, Series FT 900, 2005.

LAND USE

Federally owned land, 2003
Areas in acres

	State	U.S.	State share
Total area	35,011,000	2,271,343,000	1.54%
Nonfederal land	33,029,000	1,599,584,000	2.06%
Federal land	1,982,000	671,759,000	0.30%
Federal share	5.7%	29.6%	—

Areas are rounded to nearest thousand acres. Figures for federally owned land do not include trust properties.

Source: U.S. General Services Administration, *Federal Real Property Profile*, 2006.

Land use, 1997
In acres, rounded to nearest thousand

Total surface area	35,920,000
Total nonfederal rural land.	30,374,000
Percentage rural land	84.6%
Cropland.	10,613,000
Conservation Reserve Program (CRP*) land	661,000
Pastureland	2,994,000
Rangeland	(nil)
Forestland	14,448,000
Other rural land	1,658,000

*CRP is a federal program begun in 1985 to assist private landowners to convert highly erodible cropland to vegetative cover for ten years. Note that some categories of land overlap.

Source: U.S. Department of Agriculture, Natural Resources and Conservation Service, and Iowa State University, Statistical Laboratory, *Summary Report, 1997 National Resources Inventory,* revised December, 2000.

Farms and crop acreage, 2004

	State	U.S.	Share	Rank
Farms	77,000	2,113,000	3.64%	8
Acres (millions)	16	937	1.71%	18
Acres per farm	203	443	—	32

Source: U.S. Department of Agriculture, National Agricultural Statistics Service. Numbers of farms are rounded to nearest thousand units; acreage figures are rounded to nearest million. Rankings, including ties, are based on rounded figures.

GOVERNMENT AND FINANCE

Units of local government, 2002

	State	Total U.S.	Rank
All local governments	3,048	87,525	11
Counties	72	3,034	19
Municipalities	585	19,429	11
Towns (townships)	1,265	16,504	7
School districts	442	13,506	12
Special districts	684	35,052	17

Only 48 states have county governments, 20 states have township governments ("towns" in New England, Minnesota, New York, and Wisconsin), and 46 states have school districts. Special districts encompass such functions as natural resources, fire protection, and housing and community development.

Source: U.S. Census Bureau, *Census of Governments.*

State government revenue, 2002

Total revenue	$20,874 mill.
General revenue	$22,874 mill.
Per capita revenue	$4,205
U.S. per capita average	$3,689
Rank among states	15
Intergovernment revenue	
Total	$7,031 mill.
From federal government	$5,913 mill.
Charges and miscellaneous	
Total	$4,029 mill.
Current charges	$2,374 mill.
Misc. general income	$1,655 mill.
Insurance trust revenue	–$2,000 mill.
Taxes	
Total	$11,814 mill.
Per capita taxes	$2,172
Rank among states	11
Property taxes	$92 mill.
Sales taxes	$5,428 mill.
License taxes	$728 mill.
Individual income taxes	$4,974 mill.
Corporate income taxes	$445 mill.
Other taxes	$148 mill.

Total revenue figures include items not listed separately here.

Source: U.S. Bureau of the Census.

State government expenditures, 2002

General expenditures
Total state expenditures . . . . $26,749 mill.
Intergovernmental . . . . $9,523 mill.

Per capita expenditures
State $4,250
Average of all states $3,859
Rank among states 16

Selected direct expenditures
Education. $3,197 mill.
Public welfare . . . . $4,136 mill.
Health, hospital . . . . $968 mill.
Highways . . . . $1,272 mill.
Police protection . . . . $97 mill.
Corrections. $873 mill.
Natural resources . . . . $378 mill.
Parks and recreation . . . . $54 mill.
Government administration. . . . . $603 mill.
Interest on debt . . . . $737 mill.
Total direct expenditures. . . . . $13,596 mill.

Totals include items not listed separately.
Source: U.S. Census Bureau.

POLITICS

Governors since statehood
D = Democrat; R = Republican; O = other;
(r) resigned; (d) died in office; (i) removed from office

Nelson Dewey (D) 1848-1852
Leonard J. Farwell (O) 1852-1854
William A. Barstow (D) . . . . (r) 1854-1856
Arthur MacArthur (D) 1856
Coles Bashford (R) 1856-1858
Alexander W. Randall (R). 1858-1862
Louis P. Harve(r)y (R) 1862
Edward Saloman (R) 1862-1864
James T. Lewis (R) 1864-1866
Lucius Fairchild (R) 1866-1872
Cadwallader C. Washburn (R) 1872-1874
William R. Taylor (D) 1874-1876
Harrison Ludington (D) 1876-1878
William E. Smith (D) 1878-1882
Jeremiah M. Rusk (D) 1882-1889
William D. Hoard (R) 1889-1891
George W. Peck (D) 1891-1895
William H. Upham (R) 1895-1897
Edward Scofield (R) 1897-1901
Robert M. LaFollette (R) . . . . (r) 1901-1906
James O. Davidson (R) 1906-1911
Francis E. McGovern (R) 1911-1915
Emanuel L. Philipp (R) 1915-1921
John J. Blaine (R) 1921-1927
Fred R. Zimmerman (R) 1927-1929
Walter J. Kohler (R) 1929-1931
Philip F. LaFollette (R) 1931-1933

Albert G. Schmedeman (D) 1933-1935
Philip F. LaFollette (O) 1935-1939
Julius P. Heil (R) 1939-1943
Walter S. Goodland (R) . . . . (d) 1943-1947
Oscar Rennebohm (R) 1947-1951
Walter J. Kohler, Jr. (R) 1951-1957
Vernon W. Thomson (R) 1957-1959
Gaylord A. Nelson (D). 1959-1963
John W. Reynolds, Jr. (D) 1963-1965
Warren P. Knowles (R) 1965-1971
Patrick J. Lucey (D) . . . . (r) 1971-1977
Martin Schreiber (D) 1977-1979
Lee S. Dreyfus (R) 1979-1983
Anthony S. Earl (D) 1983-1987
Tommy G. Thompson (R). 1987-2001
Scott McCallum (R) . . . . (r) 2001-2003
Jim Doyle (D) 2003-

Composition of congressional delegations, 1989-2007

	Dem	Rep	Total
House of Representatives			
101st Congress, 1989			
State delegates	5	4	9
Total U.S.	259	174	433
102d Congress, 1991			
State delegates	4	5	9
Total U.S.	267	167	434
103d Congress, 1993			
State delegates	4	5	9
Total U.S.	258	176	434
104th Congress, 1995			
State delegates	5	4	9
Total U.S.	197	236	433
105th Congress, 1997			
State delegates	5	4	9
Total U.S.	206	228	434
106th Congress, 1999			
State delegates	5	4	9
Total U.S.	211	222	433
107th Congress, 2001			
State delegates	5	4	9
Total U.S.	211	221	432
108th Congress, 2003			
State delegates	4	4	8
Total U.S.	205	229	434
109th Congress, 2005			
State delegates	4	4	8
Total U.S.	202	231	433
110th Congress, 2007			
State delegates	5	3	8
Total U.S.	233	202	435

(continued)

	Dem	Rep	Total
Senate			
101st Congress, 1989			
State delegates	1	1	2
Total U.S.	55	45	100
102d Congress, 1991			
State delegates	1	1	2
Total U.S.	56	44	100
103d Congress, 1993			
State delegates	2	0	2
Total U.S.	57	43	100
104th Congress, 1995			
State delegates	2	0	2
Total U.S.	46	53	99
105th Congress, 1997			
State delegates	2	0	2
Total U.S.	45	55	100
106th Congress, 1999			
State delegates	2	0	2
Total U.S.	45	54	99
107th Congress, 2001			
State delegates	2	0	2
Total U.S.	50	50	100
108th Congress, 2003			
State delegates	2	0	2
Total U.S.	48	51	99
109th Congress, 2005			
State delegates	2	0	2
Total U.S.	44	55	99
110th Congress, 2007			
State delegates	2	0	2
Total U.S.	49	49	98

Figures are for starts of first sessions. Totals are for Democrat (Dem.) and Republican (Rep.) members only. House membership totals under 435 and Senate totals under 100 reflect vacancies and seats held by independent party members. When the 110th Congress opened, the Senate's two independent members caucused with the Democrats, giving the Democrats control of the Senate.

Source: U.S. Congress, *Congressional Directory.*

Composition of state legislature, 1990-2006

	Democrats	Republicans
State Assembly (99 seats)		
1990	58	41
1992	51	47
1994	48	51
1996	47	52
1998	45	54
2000	44	55
2002	40	59
2004	39	60
2006	47	52
State Senate (33 seats)		
1990	19	14
1992	16	17
1994	16	17
1996	17	16
1998	17	16
2000	17	16
2002	15	18
2004	14	19
2006	18	15

Figures for total seats may include independents and minor party members. Numbers reflect results of elections in listed years; elected members usually take their seats in the years that follow.

Source: Council of State Governments; *State Elective Officials and the Legislatures.*

Voter participation in presidential elections, 2000 and 2004

	2000	2004
Voting age population		
State	4,010,000	4,201,000
Total United States	209,831,000	220,377,000
State share of U.S. total	1.91	1.91
Rank among states	18	18
Portion of voting age population casting votes		
State	64.8%	71.3%
United States	50.3%	55.5%
Rank among states	4	3

Population figures are rounded to nearest thousand and include all residents, regardless of eligibility to vote.

Source: U.S. Census Bureau.

HEALTH AND MEDICAL CARE

Medical professionals
Physicians in 2003 and nurses in 2001

	U.S.	State
Physicians in 2003		
Total	774,849	13,769
Share of U.S. total		1.77%
Rate	266	252
Rank		24
Nurses in 2001		
Total	2,262,020	49,610
Share of U.S. total		2.19%
Rate	793	918
Rank		13

Rates are numbers of physicians and nurses per 100,000 resident population; ranks are based on rates.

Source: American Medical Association, *Physician Characteristics and Distribution in the U.S.*; U.S. Department of Health and Human Services, Health Resources and Services Administration.

Health insurance coverage, 2003

	State	U.S.
Total persons covered	4,836,000	243,320,000
Total persons not covered	593,000	44,961,000
Portion not covered	10.9%	15.6%
Rank among states	40	—
Children not covered	104,000	8,373,000
Portion not covered	7.7%	11.4%
Rank among states	39	—

Totals are rounded to nearest thousand. Ranks are from the highest to the lowest percentages of persons *not* insured.

Source: U.S. Census Bureau, Current Population Reports.

AIDS, syphilis, and tuberculosis cases, 2003

Disease	U.S. cases	State cases	Rank
AIDS	44,232	184	32
Syphilis	34,270	111	33
Tuberculosis	14,874	66	34

Source: U.S. Centers for Disease Control and Prevention.

Cigarette smoking, 2003
Residents over age 18 who smoke

	U.S.	State	Rank
All smokers	22.1%	22.1%	25
Male smokers	24.8%	24.0%	27
Female smokers	20.3%	20.3%	26

Cigarette smokers are defined as persons who reported having smoked at least 100 cigarettes during their lifetimes and who currently smoked at least occasionally.

Source: U.S. Centers for Disease Control and Prevention, *Morbidity and Mortality Weekly Report*, 53, no. 44 (November 12, 2004).

HOUSING

Home ownership rates, 1985-2004

	1985	1990	1995	2000	2004
State	63.8%	68.3%	67.5%	71.8%	73.3%
Total U.S.	63.9%	63.9%	64.7%	67.4%	69.0%
Rank among states	37	20	24	18	15

Net change in state home ownership rate, 1985-2004 . . . . +9.5%

Net change in U.S. home ownership rate, 1985-2004 . . . . +5.1%

Percentages represent the proportion of owner households to total occupied households.

Source: U.S. Census Bureau, 2006.

Home sales, 2000-2004
In thousands of units

Existing home sales	2000	2002	2003	2004
State sales	91.6	105.5	105.9	116.8
Total U.S. sales	5,171	5,631	6,183	6,784
State share of U.S. total	1.77%	1.87%	1.71%	1.72%
Sales rank among states	22	22	22	22

Units include single-family homes, condos, and co-ops.

Source: National Association of Realtors, Washington, D.C., *Real Estate Outlook: Market Trends & Insights.*

Values of owner-occupied homes, 2003

	State	U.S.
Total units	1,193,000	58,809,000
Value of units		
Under $100,000	29.9%	29.6%
$100,000-199,999	49.7%	36.9%
$200,000 or more	20.4%	33.5%
Median value	$131,908	$142,275
Rank among all states 26		

Units are owner-occupied one-family houses whose numbers are rounded to nearest thousand. Data are extrapolated from survey samples.
Source: U.S. Census Bureau, American Community Survey.

EDUCATION

Public school enrollment, 2002

Prekindergarten through grade 8
State enrollment 592,000
Total U.S. enrollment. 34,135,000
State share of U.S. total 1.73%

Grades 9 through 12
State enrollment 290,000
Total U.S. enrollment. 14,067,000
State share of U.S. total 2.06%

Enrollment rates
State public school enrollment rate. 87.9%
Overall U.S. rate 90.4%
Rank among states in 2002. 38
Rank among states in 1995. 47

Enrollment figures (which include unclassified students) are rounded to nearest thousand pupils during fall school term. Enrollment rates are based on enumerated resident population estimate for July 1, 2002.
Source: U.S. National Center for Education Statistics.

Public college finances, 2003-2004

FTE enrollment in public institutions of higher education
Students in state institutions 218,900
Students in all U.S. public institutions 9,916,600
State share of U.S. total 2.21
Rank among states 12

State and local government appropriations for higher education
State appropriation per FTE $5,941
National average $5,716
Rank among states 18
State & local tax revenue going to higher
education 8.2%

FTE = full-time equivalent in public postsecondary programs, including summer sessions; student numbers are rounded to nearest hundred. Funding figures for 2003-2004 academic year include financial aid to students in state public institutions and exclude money for research, agriculture experiment stations, teaching hospitals, and medical schools; figures are rounded to nearest thousand dollars.
Source: Higher Education Executive Officers, Denver, Colorado.

TRANSPORTATION AND TRAVEL

Highway mileage, 2003

Interstate highways 745
Other freeways and expressways 238
Arterial roads. 11,870
Collector roads. 21,408
Local roads. 79,009
Urban roads 20,293
Rural roads 92,977
Total state mileage 113,270
U.S. total 3,974,107
State share 2.85%
Rank among states 13

Note that combined urban and rural road mileage matches the total of the other categories.
Source: U.S. Federal Highway Administration.

Motor vehicle registrations and driver licenses, 2003

Vehicle registrations	State	U.S.	Share	Rank
Autos, trucks, buses	4,647,000	231,390,000	2.01%	17
Autos only	2,578,000	135,670	1.90%	18
Motorcycles	240,000	5,328,000	4.50%	7
Driver licenses	3,766,000	196,166,000	1.92%	19

Figures, which do not include vehicles owned by military services, are rounded to the nearest thousand. Figures for automobiles include taxis.
Source: U.S. Federal Highway Administration.

Domestic travel expenditures, 2003

Spending by U.S. residents on overnight trips and
day trips of at least 50 miles from home

Total expenditures within state	$7.16 bill.
Total expenditures within U.S.	$490.87 bill.
State share of U.S. total	1.5%
Rank among states	25

Source: Travel Industry Association of America.

Retail gasoline prices, 2003-2007

Average price per gallon at the pump

Year	U.S.	State
2003	$1.267	$1.241
2004	$1.316	$1.291
2005	$1.644	$1.654
2007	$2.298	$2.315

Excise tax per gallon in 2004	29.1¢
Rank among all states in 2007 prices	20

Prices are averages of all grades of gasoline sold at the pump
during March months in 2003-2005 and during February, 2007.
Averages for 2006, during which prices rose higher, are not
available.

Source: U.S. Energy Information Agency, *Petroleum Marketing
Monthly* (2003-2005 data); American Automobile Association
(2007 data).

CRIME AND LAW ENFORCEMENT

State and local police officers, 2000-2004

	2000	2002	2004
Total officers			
U.S.	654,601	665,555	675,734
State	12,323	11,347	12,839*
*Net change, 2000-2004			+4.19%
Officers per 1,000 residents			
U.S.	2.33	2.31	2.30
State	2.30	2.09	2.33
State rank	18	25	16

Totals include state and local police and sheriffs.
Source: Carsey Institute, University of New Hampshire.

Crime rates, 2003

Incidents per 100,000 residents

Crimes	State	U.S.
Violent crimes		
Total incidents	221	475
Murder	3	6
Forcible rape	22	32
Robbery	80	142
Aggravated assault	116	295
Property crimes		
Total incidents	2,883	3,588
Burglary	485	741
Larceny/theft	2,172	2,415
Motor vehicle theft	225	433
All crimes	3,104	4,063

Source: U.S. Federal Bureau of Investigation, *Crime in the United
States,* annual.

State prison populations, 1980-2003

	State	U.S.	State share
1980	3,980	305,458	1.30%
1990	7,465	708,393	1.05%
1996	12,991	1,025,624	1.27%
2000	20,754	1,391,261	1.49%
2003	22,614	1,470,045	1.54%

State figures exclude prisoners in federal penitentiaries.
Source: U.S. Bureau of Justice Statistics, *Prisoners in 2003.*

Wyoming

Location: Rocky Mountains

Area and rank: 97,105 square miles (251,501 square kilometers); 97,818 square miles (253,349 square kilometers) including water; ninth largest state in area

Coastline: none

Population and rank: 507,000 (2004); fiftieth largest state in population

Capital and largest city: Cheyenne (53,011 people in 2000 census)

Became territory: May 19, 1869

Entered Union and rank: July 10, 1890; forty-fourth state

State capitol building in Cheyenne. (©James Blank/Weststock)

Present constitution adopted: 1890

Counties: 23, as well as Yellowstone National Park

State name: "Wyoming" is derived from the Delaware Indian word meaning "mountains and valleys alternating"

State nickname: Equality State

Motto: Equal rights

State flag: Blue field with border of white and red with white silhouette of buffalo bearing the state seal in blue

Highest point: Gannett Peak—13,804 feet (4,207 meters)

Lowest point: Belle Fourche River—3,099 feet (945 meters)

Highest recorded temperature: 114 degrees Fahrenheit (46 degrees Celsius)—Basin, 1900

Lowest recorded temperature: –63 degrees Fahrenheit (–53 degrees Celsius)—Moran, 1933

State song: "Wyoming"

State tree: Cottonwood

State flower: Indian paintbrush

State bird: Meadowlark

National parks: Grand Teton, Yellowstone

Wyoming History

Wyoming is an expansive, arid land of high sweeping plains punctuated by series of mountain ranges. Its average elevation is some 6,700 feet above sea level. Travelers have frequently remarked on the state's austere beauty: "Nature has collected all of her beauties together," explorer John C. Frémont wrote of the region in 1842, "in one chosen place." Passing through the state's southern tier at night, travelers are mesmerized by multiple, simultaneous lightning storms illuminating vast plains, jagged mountains silhouetted in the background.

For all its magnificence, however, for much of its history Wyoming has been only the path to somewhere else. Today, Wyoming's immense emptiness supports fewer than half a million people, a diminishing portion of whom are destined to lead rugged lives employed in mining, livestock grazing, and agriculture. Memory of the state's colorful past is kept alive by frequent rodeos, roundups, and frontier celebrations. Each summer tourists flock to its spectacular scenery—to Jackson Hole, the Grand Tetons, and incomparable Yellowstone, the world's first national park.

Early History. According to archaeological evidence, the earliest immigrants to Wyoming arrived about eleven thousand years ago, leaving various traces. In 1965, two dwellings testifying to the habitation of the earliest peoples were discovered near Guernsey, on the North Platte River, southeast of Casper. For many years immense herds of buffalo roamed the midwestern plains. They attracted many migrating peoples from Asia who traversed the Bering Straits, many of them inhabiting the Wyoming region—tribes such as the Arap-

Rising to 13,770 feet, Grand Teton (center) is the tallest mountain in western Wyoming's Teton Range. In 1929, the region surrounding the mountain was made into Grand Teton National Park. (Jon Sullivan/PD Photo.org)

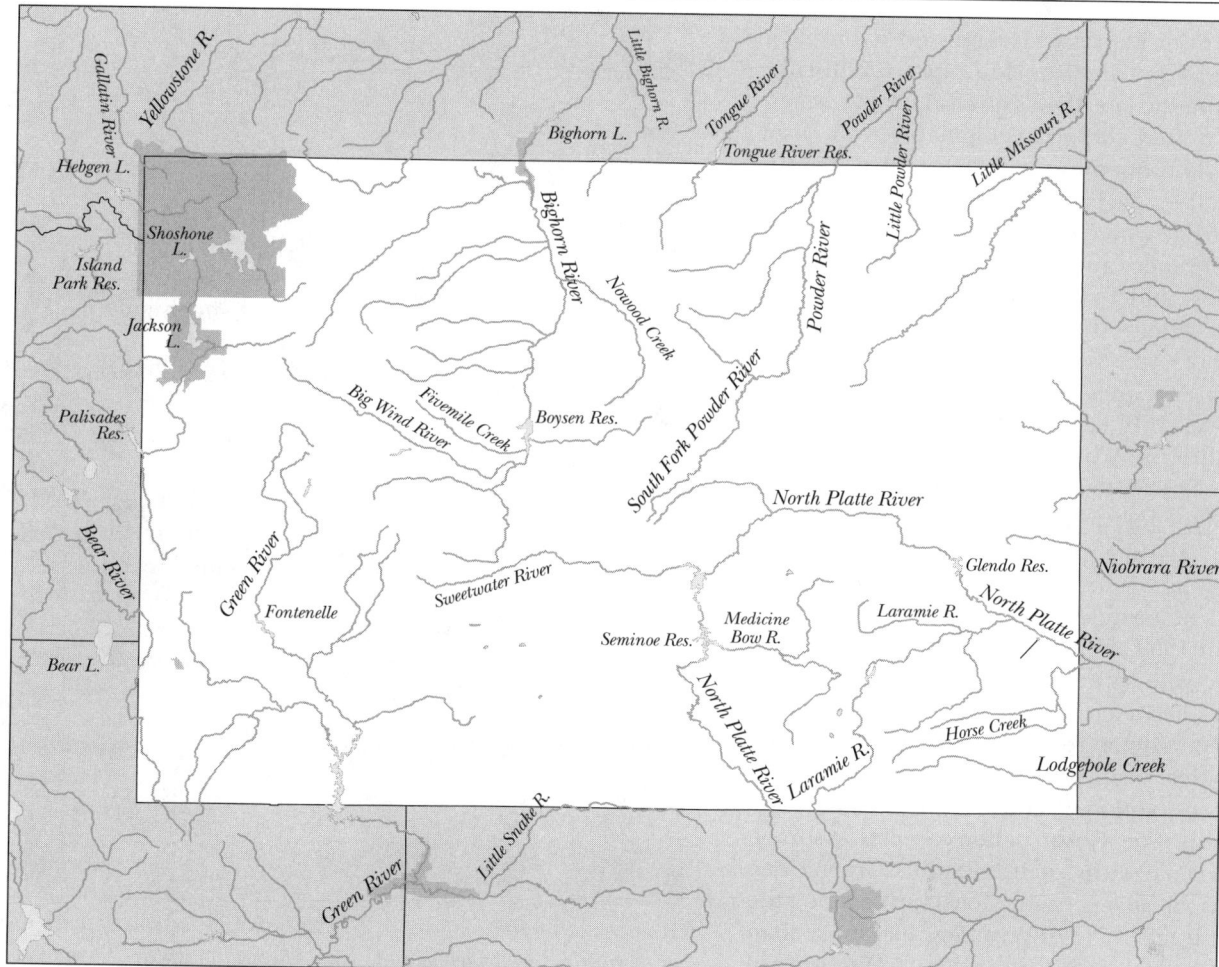

aho, Bannock, Crow, Cheyenne, Sioux, and Shoshone.

Earliest contact between these peoples and whites may have occurred during the mid-eighteenth century, when French trappers entered the area. Extensive exploration did not begin until the following century, however, after the United States concluded the Louisiana Purchase in 1803 and President Thomas Jefferson sent Meriwether Lewis and William Clark to chart what the nation had bought. By then, parts of Wyoming had been claimed by Spain, France, and Great Britain. It required several more acquisitions for Wyoming's modern territory to be completed. The 1819 treaty with Spain, the partition of Texas after the Lone Star Republic joined the Union in 1845, the agreement with Britain over the Columbia River country in 1846, and the Treaty of Guadalupe Hidalgo in 1848 all included land within the state's modern borders.

Exploration. Fur trading was the initial stimulus to exploring Wyoming. The first American to do so was a former member of the Lewis and Clark expedition, John Colter. In 1807, Colter traveled across the Yellowstone area, where he sighted its geothermal activity. Other fur traders crossed Wyoming going to and from Astoria, Oregon. During the 1820's, more fur trappers

and traders made their way west, many of them to Wyoming. In 1825, an annual gathering of these men, who included Indians, was inaugurated that lasted for fifteen years. In 1834, traders founded Fort William, later renamed Fort Laramie, which became the area's first permanent trading post. In 1843, famous scout Jim Bridger founded a second trading post near the western end of the state, east of Evanston.

At about the same time, John C. Frémont led a party through the region guided by scout Kit Carson. Frémont's reports to Congress on his explorations spurred provision for protection of migrants on the Oregon Trail, and in 1849, the government purchased Fort William, which by then was known as Fort John. Wyoming had become a pathway for tens of thousands of migrants and adventurers using several trails leading west, including the Oregon, California, and Mormon Trails. These trails traversed the South Pass through the Rocky Mountains, continued to Fort Bridger, then divided. The first Mormon party passed through in 1847. A Mormon colony established near the Utah border perished in a blizzard in 1856. A succession of outposts was established during the 1860's, including telegraph stations and stage coach and freight line stops. In 1860-

1861, Pony Express riders crossed Wyoming in their epic journey from Missouri to California.

From the late 1840's onward, Native Americans viewed these developments with suspicion. The opening of the Bozeman Trail in 1863 after gold was discovered in Montana particularly alarmed them, as settlers streamed in. Native Americans and settlers made and broke treaties, and fighting continued throughout the decade. Settlers began to arrive in greater numbers when gold was discovered in the South Pass area in 1867 and later when coal was found. To keep the Bozeman Trail operating, the U.S. Army opened Fort Phil Kearny in 1866. The Sioux, led by Chief Red Cloud, detested the fort and determined to raze it. More than 150 white men were killed in its defense, including 81, led by Captain W. J. Fetterman, killed in a single battle. The army closed the fort in 1868 after concluding a treaty with the Sioux, who agreed not to oppose the building of a railroad in the south.

Becoming a Territory. The greatest influx of settlers occurred with railroads, beginning with the Union Pacific, which crossed Wyoming in 1868. Construction camps that sprang up became towns, such as Rawlins, Green River, and Rock Springs; more towns arose along the great trails. By 1870 Wyoming had more than nine thousand white inhabitants. Discovery of gold in the Black Hills of the Dakotas led to fierce Indian resistance, when thousands of settlers ignored treaty provisions and moved into territory the Sioux considered sacred. Bloody battles were fought with the U.S. Army. Peace was finally restored in 1876, when the last of the Indian fighters fled or surrendered and settled on reservations.

By then Wyoming had undergone development as a separate society. The coming of the railroad led to the formation of Wyoming Territory in 1868. Population jumped to more than twenty thousand in 1880 and to some sixty-two thousand in 1890. Mining was supplemented by cattle grazing and shipments of longhorns from Texas on their way to market. Sheep also made their appearance, setting the stage for protracted struggle between sheep- and cattlemen later immortalized in Hollywood films. Oil had been known to exist in the region since the 1830's, when it was used to grease wagon wheels. In 1883, the first well was drilled in the Dallas Field, in the Wind River region.

Politically, Wyoming Territory was growing up quickly. In 1869, it became the first territorial legislature to allow women to vote, serve on juries, and hold office. In 1924, it was first to elect a woman governor. However, in certain respects it remained primitive. The Wyoming Stock Growers Association, formed as a local

Women voting in Cheyenne in 1888. Wyoming was one of the first states or territories to give women the vote—largely to induce them to come to the predominantly male territory. (Library of Congress)

association in 1873, grew powerful enough to enforce its own vigilante law in defense of its interests. During the 1890's, matters deteriorated with the decline of the cattle industry and ruinous cattle rustling, by groups such as the notorious Hole-in-the-Wall Gang. Homesteaders, who fenced off the open range, arrived. In 1892, the association decided to act, embarking on the Johnson County cattle war. Texas gunmen, hired to murder a list of enemies, killed two men before the law stepped in. Later during the 1890's more violence occurred with the influx of sheepherders, blamed for the inability of cattle to find sufficient food.

Statehood. These events aside, by the turn of the century Wyoming was fast becoming part of the nation. In 1889, without waiting for passage of a congressional enabling act, a proposed state constitution was drawn up. The following year Wyoming became the nation's forty-fourth state. It arrived into the Union with a progressive constitution that included a provision for women's suffrage. The constitution also included fulsome support for popular sovereignty and freedom of religion. Judges would be elected, not appointed, on a nonpartisan basis. The constitution was made difficult to amend.

The state's politics have been marked by both conservative and maverick tendencies. During the 1980's, one of its senators, Dick Cheney, was selected secretary of defense, and another, Alan Simpson, was widely admired by political opponents for his candor and civility. Wyoming has also been noted for its patriotism. Despite its small size, it contributed to the Spanish-American War of 1898, surpassing its quota of volunteers. It also sent twelve thousand to World War I.

Economically, Wyoming was able to increase its agriculture after the turn of the century through irrigation, as homesteaders continued to arrive. In addition, tourism became more economically significant for the state, as better roads and railroad service made it easier for people to reach scenic areas such as Yellowstone. The Depression, however, hit the state hard, though an increase in oil production and New Deal projects helped hard-pressed wage earners.

World War II and Postwar Developments. World War II found Wyoming's patriotic spirit intact, as tens of thousands of men and hundreds of women went off to war. At home the economy bustled with government's demands for food and mineral deposits for the war effort. After the war, the state continued to prosper, when the Cold War brought more federal government spending. Atomic weapons production brought lucrative mining ventures when uranium was discovered in

the state, and military spending increased when Wyoming was chosen as a primary site for testing of intercontinental missiles.

The state's population continued to grow, from 92,000 at the turn of the century to 290,000 in 1950 and 40,000 more a decade later. After that time, however, growth was uneven, advancing only 2,000 from 1960 to 1970 and actually losing ground from 1980 to 1990. By then, although it had grown to more than 450,000, comparatively little manufacturing in the state and the difficulty of agriculture still placed it at the bottom of the list of state populations. Economically, although services provide some 60 percent of the state's income, it is heavily dependent on the land, through mining, grazing, and construction. By the 1990's, the state was attempting to broaden its economic base, especially by developing tourism. Politically, the state was divided between those who favored economic development and those who looked to the conservation of the state's natural resources.

Wildfires. Around the turn of the twenty-first century, Wyoming began annual battles against the destructive forces of nature in the form of wildfires. Such fires were nothing new to the state; in 1988, 36 percent of Yellowstone National Park was ravaged by wildfires that continuously burned throughout the summer. Only the first snows of the year, in September, extin-

Yellowstone National Park's Old Faithful geyser may be Wyoming's most famous landmark. (PhotoDisc)

guished them. In August, 2000, hundreds of homes were threatened by fire in the Casper area. By 2002, four years of extensive and severe drought enhanced the fire menace. In June, 2002, fires near the South Dakota border were easily visible on satellite images. That year, over 270 wildfires burned more than 100,000 acres in the state. In late August of the following year, some 18,300 acres on the east side of Yellowstone Park had burned and many more fires were under way. In August, 2006, hundreds of elite federal firefighters were sent to the Casper area to battle wildfires threatening hundreds of homes.

Politics. The general election of 2000 saw a nearly complete Republican sweep of electoral office races. George W. Bush and his Wyoming-bred running mate Dick Cheney, who represented the state as congress member from 1979 to 1989, took 69 percent of the vote to Al Gore's 28 percent. Craig Thomas, newly elected to the U.S. Senate, outdistanced the presidential ticket with his 74 percent of the vote. Incumbent congresswoman Barbara Cubin won 67 percent of the ballots. More remarkable, however, was that the Republican electoral sweep extended to many minor officials. Observers believed that the Republican victory was the result of Cheney's reputation in the state.

The 2002 election, without the Bush-Cheney coattails, still went to the Republicans in the Congress, both House and Senate, as Mike Enzi easily outdistanced his Republican opponent by a margin of 73 to 27 percent,

and Barbara Cubin won by the diminished margin of 61 to 36 percent. In an upset, however, the governor's race was won by Democrat Dave Freudenthal by 50-48 percent. The sitting governor, Republican Jim Geringer, was barred from running by term limit laws. In 2004, Bush-Cheney again claimed the state, again with 69 percent of the balloting.

Environmental Issues. As would be expected of a large Western state, environmental politics touched Wyoming's public landscape during the early twenty-first century. In 2001, a proposed methane exploration in the Powder River region was canceled because no appropriate environmental studies had been undertaken. Thereafter, the issue continued to divide those of competing interests without a resolution. A dispute also simmered, at times coming to a boil, between environmentalists and snowmobilers over the vehicles' use in Yellowstone and Grand Teton national parks. A Clinton administration ban on the use of snowmobiles in the parks by 2003 was lifted by the Bush administration in 2001; the administration stipulated that use would be limited, and noise and air pollution must be abated. In December, 2003, a Washington, D.C., federal court struck down the decision to lift the ban. A few months later, however, a Wyoming federal judge reversed this decision. Afterward, snowmobiles and snowcoaches continued to be allowed.

Charles F. Bahmueller

Wyoming Time Line

1742-1743	François de La Vérendrye enters Wyoming.
1807	John Colter is first white American to enter Wyoming.
1812	Returning party from Astoria builds first known cabin in Wyoming, on North Platte River near Bessemer Bend.
1825	Fur trade begins.
1832	First wagons travel through South Pass; Fort Bonneville, near modern Daniel, is established.
1834	Fort Laramie, first permanent trading post in Wyoming, is established as Fort William.
1842	John C. Frémont enters Wyoming.
1843	Fort Bridger, second permanent settlement, is established by Jim Bridger and Louis Vasquez.
1849	U.S. government purchases Fort Laramie.
1852	First school opens, at Fort Laramie.
1852	Fort Supply, the first agricultural settlement, is established by Mormons near Fort Bridger; later deserted and burned.
1860	Pony Express mail service begins.
1862	Fort Halleck is established on Overland Trail.
1863	Bozeman Trail is opened.
1863	First newspaper in Wyoming, the *Daily Telegraph*, is established at Fort Bridger.
1863	Fort Reno is established.
1866	Fort Phil Kearny is established on Bozeman Trail.
1866	Cheyenne is founded; Union Pacific Railroad enters Wyoming.

In 1906, Wyoming's Devil's Tower became the first site in the United States to receive federal protection as a "national monument." (PhotoDisc)

July 25, 1868	Wyoming Territory is created.
1869	Wind River Reservation for Shoshone Indians is created.
May 19, 1869	Wyoming Territory is formally organized.
1873	Yellowstone Park, world's first national park, is created.
1876	Cheyenne-Black Hills stage line is launched.
1877	Agreement is made with Shoshone Indians to allow Arapahoes to move to Wind River Reservation.
1880	Electric lights are introduced in Cheyenne.
1885	Chinese Massacre takes place at Rock Springs.
1886	Northwestern Railroad reaches eastern boundary.
1887	University of Wyoming opens.
1889	Wyoming constitutional convention takes place.
July 10, 1890	Wyoming is admitted to Union as forty-fourth state.
1892	Johnson County Invasion occurs.
1893	Cort F. Meyer is elected state superintendent of public instruction, becoming the first woman in the country elected to a state office.
1906	Devil's Tower National Monument opens, the first "national monument" in the United States.
1918	Uranium is discovered near Lusk.

(continued)

1922	Salt Creek Oil Field opens.
1925	Nellie Tayloe Ross becomes the first woman governor in the country.
1925	Teapot Dome scandal transpires.
1935	State sales tax is adopted.
1939	Trona, marketed as baking soda, is discovered in Sweetwater County.
1949	Severe blizzard paralyzes state.
1978	World's largest radio telescope is built on Jelm Mountain.
1990	Voters approve term limitation initiative.
1995	Wolves are reintroduced to Yellowstone National Park.
Jul.-Sept. 1998	More than 240 wildfires consume nearly 800,000 acres of Yellowstone National Park; fires are not completely out until November.
June-Sept., 2002	Hundreds of wildfires burn more than 100,000 acres across Wyoming.
Nov. 5, 2002	Republican Mike Enzi wins U.S. Senate seat; Democrat Dave Freudenthal wins election upset by 3,800 votes to become governor.
Feb. 10, 2004	Wyoming federal court overturns previous decision banning snowmobiles in Yellowstone National Park.
Aug., 2006	Four hundred elite federal firefighters sent to battle wildfires in Casper area.

Notes for Further Study

Published Sources. Books on Wyoming government include Robert B. Keiter and Tim Newcomb's *The Wyoming Constitution* (1993), Oliver Walter's *Equality State: Government and Politics in Wyoming* (1988), and Lewis L. Gould's *Wyoming from Territory to Statehood* (1989). Historical accounts of the state include Taft A. Larson, *History of Wyoming* (1990); *Frontier Spirit: The Story of Wyoming* (1996) by Craig Sodaro and Randy Adams; and *Readings in Wyoming History* (1996) by Phil Roberts. Not to be overlooked is the New Deal's Federal Writers Project's American Guide series publication *Wyoming: A Guide to Its History, Highways, and People*, originally published in 1941 but reprinted in 1981 because of its still-useful information. Barbara Fifer's *Wyoming's Historic Forts* (2001) uses full-color and historical black-and-white photographs, as well as brief historical text, in its coverage of the places and people on America's western frontier. *Ancient Visions: Petroglyphs and Pictographs of the Wind River and Bighorn Country, Wyoming and Montana* (2004) by Julie Francis and Lawrence Loendorf is pertinent for its academic discussion of prehistoric sites.

For Wyoming's Indian tribes, see Speaks Lightning's *Indians of Idaho, Montana, and Wyoming: A Winter Count* (1999); Joel C. Janetski's *The Indians of Yellowstone Park* (1987); and Bert Webber's *Indians Along the Oregon Trail: The Tribes of Nebraska, Wyoming, Idaho, Oregon, and Washington Identified* (1992). For an account of Indian wars, see *The Indian Wars of the West and Frontier Army Life, 1862-1898* (1998), edited by Robert Lester. An aspect of Native American artifacts is presented in Mary Helen Hendry's *Indian Rock Art in Wyoming* (1983). For the Chinese Massacre at Rock Springs, see Craig Storti, *Incident at Bitter Creek: The Story of the Rock Creek Chinese Massacre* (1991). Yellowstone Park is examined from varying perspectives in *Yellowstone Ecology: A Road Guide* (1992) by Sharon Eversman et al. The state's geology is discussed more generally in Darwin R. Spearing and David R. Lageson, *Roadside Geology of Wyoming* (1988).

A comprehensive guide to Wyoming can be found in the *Ultimate Wyoming Atlas and Travel Encyclopedia* (2003) by Michael Dougherty, which offers more than 130 maps and information about every town and city in the state. *Compass Guides Wyoming* (4th ed., 2004) by local writer Nathaniel Burt provides an insider view to the history and attractions of his state.

Web Resources. For information on Wyoming government, see the state's home page (wyoming.gov/), which has numerous links, including to some county and city sites. The governor's home page at this site has a calendar of events of the state for each month. At the judicial branch site (courts.state.wy.us), Wyoming supreme court opinions, as well as other information on the judiciary, are given.

The state's history can be accessed at the Wyoming History Home page (home pages.rootsweb.com/~sabthomp/wyo ming/wyoming.htm), Wyoming Tales and Trails (www.wyomingtalesandtrails.com/), and the Wyoming State Historical Society (wyshs.org/index.htm). For information about the state's Native Americans, see, for example, Access Genealogy's page on the state (www.accessgenealogy.com/native/wyoming/), the Northern Arapaho site (www.northernarapaho.com/), or the Montana-Wyoming Tribal Leaders Council (www.mtwytlc.com/).

Yellowstone National Park can be accessed at the Total Yellowstone Page (www.yellowstone-natl-park.com/) or at the National Park Service's page on the park (www.nps.gov/yell/). Jackson Hole, the gateway to the Grand Tetons, has an attractive and informative site (www.jacksonhole.com/). The Wyoming State Library (www-wsl.state.wy.us/) offers links for research purposes of all kinds when one follows the Wyomingites and Site Visitors link on the home page. The Wyoming News site (www.wyomingnews.com/news/index.asp), sponsored by the *Wyoming Tribune Eagle*, provides visitors current news stories about the state and its regions.

Counties

County	2000 pop.	Rank in pop.	Sq. miles	Rank in area
Albany	32,014	6	4,273.8	8
Big Horn	11,461	15	3,137.1	13
Campbell	33,698	5	4,796.9	7
Carbon	15,639	11	7,896.6	3
Converse	12,052	14	4,254.9	9
Crook	5,887	21	2,858.7	14
Fremont	35,804	4	9,182.7	2
Goshen	12,538	13	2,225.5	20
Hot Springs	4,882	22	2,004.0	23
Johnson	7,075	18	4,166.4	10
Laramie	81,607	1	2,686.2	15
Lincoln	14,573	12	4,069.3	11
Natrona	66,533	2	5,340.1	5

County	2000 pop.	Rank in pop.	Sq. miles	Rank in area
Niobrara	2,407	23	2,625.9	16
Park	25,786	8	6,942.7	4
Platte	8,807	16	2,085.0	21
Sheridan	26,560	7	2,523.4	17
Sublette	5,920	20	4,881.6	6
Sweetwater	37,613	3	10,425.9	1
Teton	18,251	10	4,007.9	12
Uinta	19,742	9	2,081.8	22
Washakie	8,289	17	2,240.2	19
Weston	6,644	19	2,397.9	18

Source: U.S. Census Bureau; National Association of Counties.

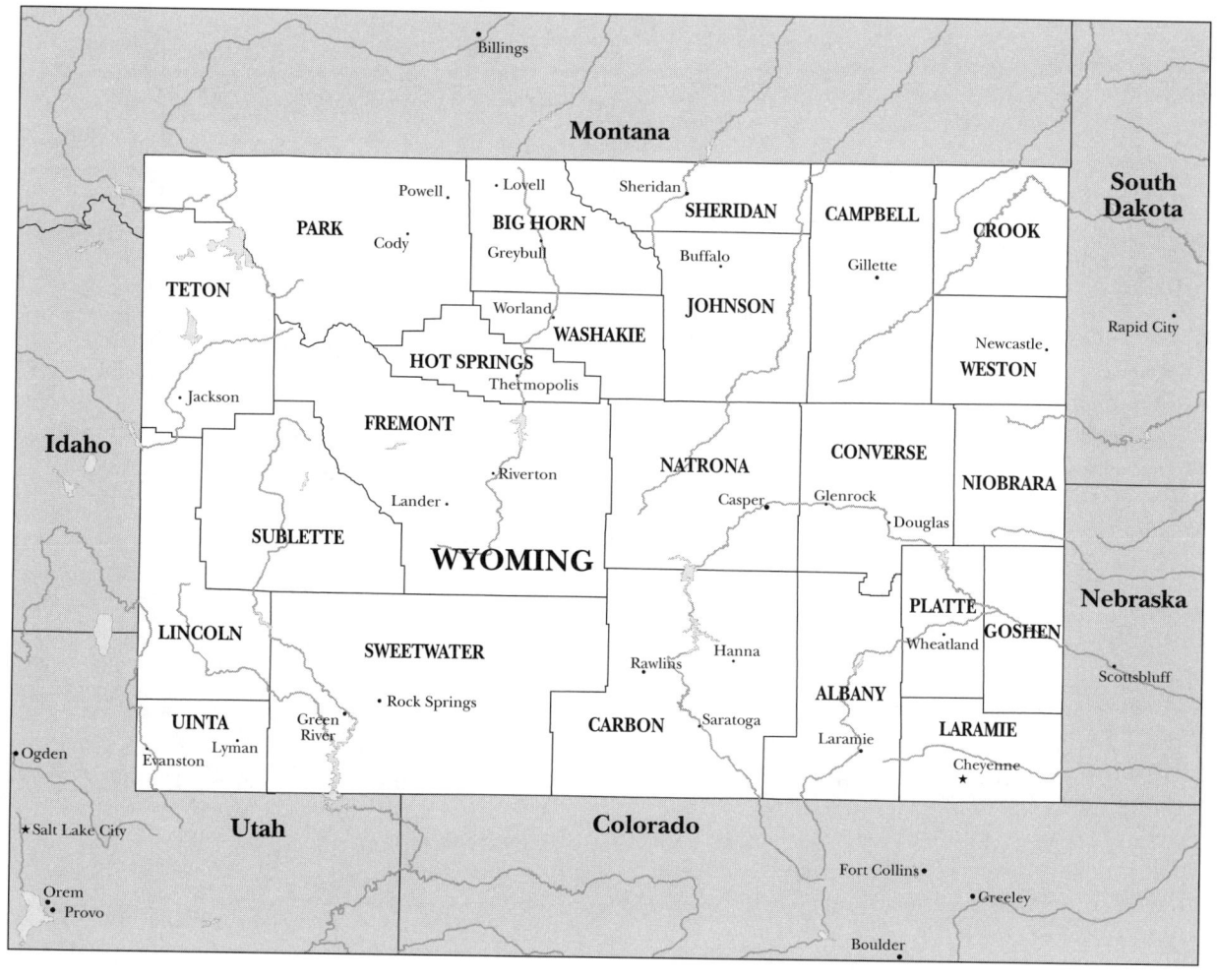

Cities

With 6,000 or more residents

Rank	City	Population
1	Cheyenne (capital)	53,011
2	Casper	49,644
3	Laramie	27,204
4	Gillette	19,646
5	Rock Springs	18,708
6	Sheridan	15,804
7	Green River	11,808
8	Evanston	11,507

Rank	City	Population
9	Riverton	9,310
10	Cody	8,835
11	Jackson	8,647
12	Rawlins	8,538
13	Lander	6,867

Population figures are from 2000 census.
Source: U.S. Bureau of the Census.

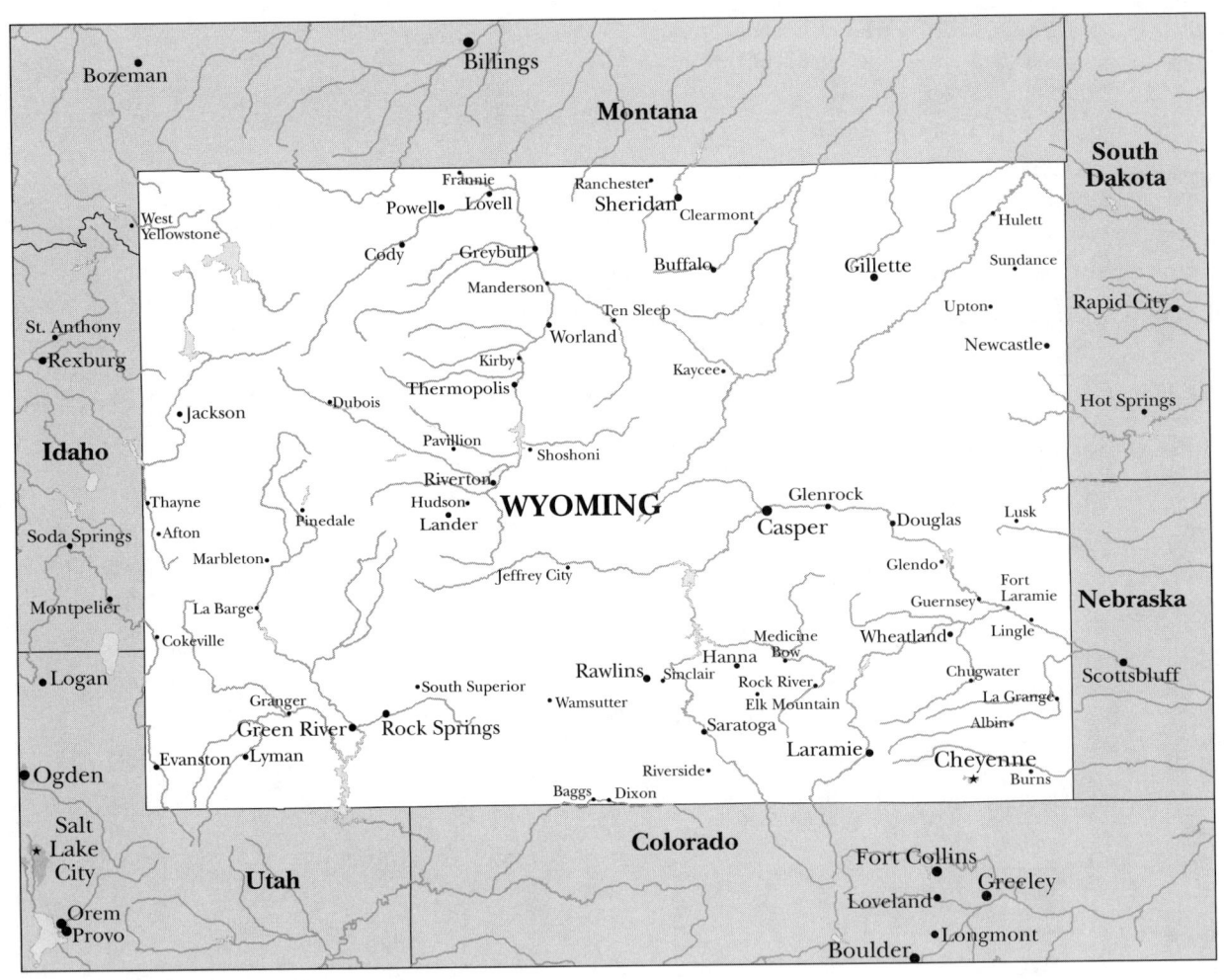

Index to Tables

DEMOGRAPHICS

Resident state and national populations, 1970-2004

Population figures given in thousands

	State pop.	U.S. pop.	Share	Rank
1970	332	203,302	0.2%	49
1980	470	226,546	0.2%	49
1985	500	237,924	0.2%	50
1990	454	248,765	0.2%	50
1995	485	262,761	0.2%	50
2000	494	281,425	0.2%	50
2004	507	293,655	0.2%	50

Source: U.S. Census Bureau, Current Population Reports, 2006.

Resident population by age, 2004

Age Group	Total persons
Under 5 years	31,000
5 to 17 years	86,000
18 to 24 years	57,000
25 to 34 years	61,000
35 to 44 years	69,000
45 to 54 years	84,000
55 to 64 years	57,000
65 to 74 years	33,000
75 to 84 years	21,000
85 years and older	7,000
All age groups	507,000

Portion of residents 65 and older	12.1%
National rank in portion of oldest residents	33
National average	12.4%

Population figures are rounded to nearest thousand persons;
figures include armed forces personnel stationed in the state.
Source: U.S. Bureau of the Census, 2006.

Resident population by race, Hispanic origin, 2004

Category	State pop.	Share	U.S.
All residents	507	100.00%	100.00%
Non-Hispanic white	449	88.56%	67.37%
Hispanic white	31	6.11%	13.01%
Other Hispanic	3	0.59%	1.06%
African American	4	0.79%	12.77%
Native American	12	2.37%	0.96%
Asian, Pacific Islander	3	0.59%	4.37%
Two or more categories	6	1.18%	1.51%

Population figures are in thousands. Persons counted as "Hispanic" (Latino) may be of any race. Because of overlapping categories, categories may not add up to 100%. Shares in column 3 are percentages of each category within the state; these figures may be compared to the national percentages in column 4.
Source: U.S. Bureau of the Census, 2006.

Projected state population, 2000-2030

Year	Population
2000	494,000
2005	507,000
2010	520,000
2015	528,000
2020	531,000
2025	529,000
2030	523,000
Population increase, 2000-2030	29,000
Percentage increase, 2000-2030	5.9

Projections are based on data from the 2000 census.
Source: U.S. Census Bureau.

VITAL STATISTICS

Infant mortality rates, 1980-2002

	1980	1990	2000	2002
All state residents	9.8	8.6	6.7	6.7
All U.S. residents	12.6	9.2	9.4	9.1
All state white residents	9.3	7.5	6.5	6.8
All U.S. white residents	10.6	7.6	5.7	5.8
All state black residents	25.9	—	—	—
All U.S. black residents	22.2	18.0	14.1	14.4

Figures represent deaths per 1,000 live births of resident infants under 1 year old, exclusive of fetal deaths. Figures for all residents include members of other racial categories not listed separately. The Census Bureau considers the post-1980 figures for black residents to be too small to be statistically meaningful.
Source: U.S. Census Bureau, *Statistical Abstract of the United States,* 2006.

Abortion rates, 1990 and 2000

	1990	2000
Total abortions	<1,000	<1,000
Rate per 1,000 women	4.4	0.9
U.S. rate	25.7	21.3
Rank	50	50

Numbers of abortions are rounded to nearest thousand; ranks are based on rates.
Source: U.S. Census Bureau.

Marriages and divorces, 2004

Total marriages	4,800
Rate per 1,000 population	9.4
National rate per 1,000 population	7.4
Rank among all states	7
Total divorces	2,700
Rate per 1,000 population	5.3
National rate per 1,000 population	3.7
Rank among all states	3

Figures are for all marriages and divorces performed within the state, including those of nonresidents; totals are rounded to the nearest hundred. Ranks are for highest to lowest figures; note that divorce data are not available for five states.
Source: U.S. National Center for Health Statistics, *Vital Statistics of the United States,* 2006.

Death rates by leading causes, 2002

Deaths per 100,000 resident population

Cause	State	U.S.
Heart disease	201.5	241.7
Cancer	172.2	193.2
Cerebrovascular diseases	48.7	56.4
Accidents other than motor vehicle	58.0	37.0
Motor vehicle accidents	31.5	15.7
Chronic lower respiratory diseases	65.0	43.3
Diabetes mellitus	29.1	25.4
HIV	n/a	4.9
Suicide	21.1	11.0
Homicide	4.6	6.1
All causes	837.0	847.3
Rank in overall death rate among states		32

Figures exclude nonresidents who died in the state. Causes of death follow International Classification of Diseases. Rank is from highest to lowest death rate in the United States.
Source: U.S. National Center for Health Statistics, *National Vital Statistics Report,* 2006.

ECONOMY

Gross state product, 1990-2004
In current dollars

Year	State product	Nat'l product	State share
1990	$13.2 billion	$5.67 trillion	0.23%
2000	$17.4 billion	$9.75 trillion	0.18%
2002	$20.3 billion	$10.41 trillion	0.19%
2003	$22.3 billion	$10.92 trillion	0.20%
2004	$24.3 billion	$11.65 trillion	0.21%

Source: U.S. Bureau of Economic Analysis, *Survey of Current Business,* July, 2005.

Gross state product by industry, 2003
In billions of dollars

Construction	$1.0
Manufacturing	1.3
Wholesale trade	0.8
Retail trade	1.4
Finance & insurance	0.6
Information	0.4
Professional services	0.6
Health care & social assistance	0.9
Government	2.8
Total state product	$19.9
Total U.S. product	$10,289.2
State share of U.S. total	0.19%
Rank among all states	48

Total figures include industries not listed separately. Amounts are in chained 2000 dollars.
Source: U.S. Bureau of Economic Analysis, *Survey of Current Business,* July, 2005.

Personal income per capita, 1990-2004
In current dollars

	1990	2000	2004
Per capita income	$18,002	$28,460	$34,306
U.S. average	$19,477	$29,845	$32,937
Rank among states	25	21	15

Source: U.S. Bureau of Economic Analysis, *Survey of Current Business,* April, 2005.

Energy consumption, 2001
In trillions of British thermal units (BTU), except as noted

Total energy consumption

Total state energy consumption	439
Total U.S. energy consumption	96,275
State share of U.S. total	0.46%
Rank among states	42

Per capita consumption (In millions of BTU)

Total state per capita consumption	890
Total U.S. per capita consumption	338
Rank among states	2

End-use sectors

Residential	39
Commercial	51
Industrial	238
Transportation	111

Sources of energy

Petroleum	157
Natural gas	104
Coal	500
Hydroelectric power	9
Nuclear electric power	0

Figures for totals include categories not listed separately.
Source: U.S. Energy Information Administration, *State Energy Data Report,* 2001.

Nonfarm employment by sectors, 2004

Total persons	255,000
Construction	19,000
Manufacturing	10,000
Trade, transportation, utilities	49,000
Information	4,000
Finance, insurance, real estate	11,000
Professional & business services	15,000
Education & health services	22,000
Leisure, hospitality, arts, organizations	31,000
Other services, including repair & maintenance . . .	10,000
Government	65,000

Figures are rounded to nearest thousand persons. "Total" includes mining and natural resources, not listed separately.
Source: U.S. Bureau of Labor Statistics, 2006.

Foreign exports, 1990-2004
In millions of dollars

Year	State	U.S.	State share
1990	264	394,045	0.07%
1996	481	624,767	0.08%
1997	560	688,896	0.08%
2000	503	712,055	0.06%
2003	582	724,006	0.09%
2004	680	769,332	0.09%

Rank among all states in 2004 48

U.S. total does not include U.S. dependencies.
Source: U.S. Census Bureau, *U.S. Merchandise Trade*, series FT 900, 2000; U.S. Census Bureau, *U.S. International Trade in Goods and Services*, Series FT 900, 2005.

LAND USE

Federally owned land, 2003
Areas in acres

	State	U.S.	State share
Total area	62,343,000	2,271,343,000	2.74%
Nonfederal land	30,812,000	1,599,584,000	1.93%
Federal land	31,532,000	671,759,000	4.69%
Federal share	50.6%	29.6%	—

Areas are rounded to nearest thousand acres. Figures for federally owned land do not include trust properties.
Source: U.S. General Services Administration, *Federal Real Property Profile*, 2006.

Land use, 1997
In acres, rounded to nearest thousand

Total surface area 62,603,000
Total nonfederal rural land. 32,773,000
Percentage rural land 52.4%
Cropland 2,174,000
Conservation Reserve Program (CRP*) land 247,000
Pastureland 1,146,000
Rangeland 27,302,000
Forestland 1,004,000
Other rural land 900,000

*CRP is a federal program begun in 1985 to assist private landowners to convert highly erodible cropland to vegetative cover for ten years. Note that some categories of land overlap.
Source: U.S. Department of Agriculture, Natural Resources and Conservation Service, and Iowa State University, Statistical Laboratory, *Summary Report, 1997 National Resources Inventory*, revised December, 2000.

Farms and crop acreage, 2004

	State	U.S.	Share	Rank
Farms	9,000	2,113,000	0.43%	40
Acres (millions)	34	937	3.63%	8
Acres per farm	3,743	443	—	1

Source: U.S. Department of Agriculture, National Agricultural Statistics Service. Numbers of farms are rounded to nearest thousand units; acreage figures are rounded to nearest million. Rankings, including ties, are based on rounded figures.

GOVERNMENT AND FINANCE

Units of local government, 2002

	State	Total U.S.	Rank
All local governments	722	87,525	36
Counties	23	3,034	37
Municipalities	98	19,429	40
Townships	0	16,504	—
School districts	55	13,506	38
Special districts	546	35,052	24

Only 48 states have county governments, 20 states have township governments ("towns" in New England, Minnesota, New York, and Wisconsin), and 46 states have school districts. Special districts encompass such functions as natural resources, fire protection, and housing and community development.
Source: U.S. Census Bureau, *Census of Governments.*

State government revenue, 2002

Total revenue . . . . $2,770 mill.
General revenue . . . . $2,768 mill.
Per capita revenue $5,546
U.S. per capita average $3,689
Rank among states 4

Intergovernment revenue
Total . . . . $1,169 mill.
From federal government . . . . $1,113 mill.

Charges and miscellaneous
Total . . . . $505 mill.
Current charges . . . . $112 mill.
Misc. general income . . . . $393 mill.
Insurance trust revenue . . . . −$48 mill.

Taxes
Total . . . . $1,094 mill.
Per capita taxes $2,193
Rank among states 9
Property taxes . . . . $144 mill.
Sales taxes . . . . $544 mill.
License taxes . . . . $95 mill.
Individual income taxes . . . . (nil)
Corporate income taxes . . . . (nil)
Other taxes . . . . $311 mill.

Total revenue figures include items not listed separately here.
Source: U.S. Bureau of the Census.

State government expenditures, 2002

General expenditures
Total state expenditures . . . . $2,948 mill.
Intergovernmental . . . . $975 mill.

Per capita expenditures
State $5,228
Average of all states $3,859
Rank among states 5

Selected direct expenditures
Education . . . . $287 mill.
Public welfare . . . . $372 mill.
Health, hospital . . . . $104 mill.
Highways . . . . $354 mill.
Police protection . . . . $25 mill.
Corrections . . . . $83 mill.
Natural resources . . . . $125 mill.
Parks and recreation . . . . $22 mill.
Government administration . . . . $93 mill.
Interest on debt . . . . $72 mill.
Total direct expenditures . . . . $1,634 mill.

Totals include items not listed separately.
Source: U.S. Census Bureau.

POLITICS

Governors since statehood
D = Democrat; R = Republican; O = other;
(r) resigned; (d) died in office; (i) removed from office

Francis E. Warren (R) . . . . (r) 1890
Amos W. Barber (R) 1890-1893
John E. Osborne (D) 1893-1895
William A. Richards (R) 1895-1899
DeForest Richards (R) . . . . (d) 1899-1903
Fennimore Chatterton (R) 1903-1905
Bryant B. Brooks (R) 1905-1911
Joseph M. Carey (D) 1911-1915
John B. Kendrick (D) . . . . (r) 1915-1917
Frank L. Houx (D) 1917-1919
Robert D. Carey (R) 1919-1923
William B. Ross (D) . . . . (d) 1923-1924
Frank E. Lucas (R) 1924-1925
Nellie T. Ross (D) 1925-1927
Frank C. Emerson (R) . . . . (d) 1927-1931
Alonzo M. Clark (R) 1931-1933
Leslie A. Miller (D) 1933-1939
Nels H. Smith (R) 1939-1943
Lester C. Hunt (D) . . . . (r) 1943-1949
Arthur G. Crane (R) 1949-1951
Frank A. Barrett (R) . . . . (r) 1951-1953
Clifford J. Rogers (R) 1953-1955
Milward L. Simpson (R) 1955-1959
John J. Hickey (D) . . . . (r) 1959-1961
John R. Gage (D) 1961-1963
Clifford P. Hansen (R) 1963-1967

Stanley K. Hathaway (R) 1967-1975
Edgar J. Herschler (D) 1975-1987
Mike Sullivan (D) 1987-1995
Jim Geringer (R) 1995-2003
Dave Freudenthal (D) 2003-

Composition of congressional delegations, 1989-2007

	Dem	Rep	Total
House of Representatives			
101st Congress, 1989			
State delegates	0	1	1
Total U.S.	259	174	433
102d Congress, 1991			
State delegates	0	1	1
Total U.S.	267	167	434
103d Congress, 1993			
State delegates	0	1	1
Total U.S.	258	176	434
104th Congress, 1995			
State delegates	0	1	1
Total U.S.	197	236	433
105th Congress, 1997			
State delegates	0	1	1
Total U.S.	206	228	434
106th Congress, 1999			
State delegates	0	1	1
Total U.S.	211	222	433
107th Congress, 2001			
State delegates	0	1	1
Total U.S.	211	221	432
108th Congress, 2003			
State delegates	0	1	1
Total U.S.	205	229	434
109th Congress, 2005			
State delegates	0	1	1
Total U.S.	202	231	433
110th Congress, 2007			
State delegates	0	1	1
Total U.S.	233	202	435
Senate			
101st Congress, 1989			
State delegates	0	2	2
Total U.S.	55	45	100
102d Congress, 1991			
State delegates	0	2	2
Total U.S.	56	44	100
103d Congress, 1993			
State delegates	0	2	2
Total U.S.	57	43	100

(continued)

	Dem	Rep	Total
104th Congress, 1995			
State delegates	0	2	2
Total U.S.	46	53	99
105th Congress, 1997			
State delegates	0	2	2
Total U.S.	45	55	100
106th Congress, 1999			
State delegates	0	2	2
Total U.S.	45	54	99
107th Congress, 2001			
State delegates	0	2	2
Total U.S.	50	50	100
108th Congress, 2003			
State delegates	0	2	2
Total U.S.	48	51	99
109th Congress, 2005			
State delegates	0	2	2
Total U.S.	44	55	99
110th Congress, 2007			
State delegates	0	2	2
Total U.S.	49	49	98

Figures are for starts of first sessions. Totals are for Democrat (Dem.) and Republican (Rep.) members only. House membership totals under 435 and Senate totals under 100 reflect vacancies and seats held by independent party members. When the 110th Congress opened, the Senate's two independent members caucused with the Democrats, giving the Democrats control of the Senate.

Source: U.S. Congress, *Congressional Directory.*

Composition of state legislature, 1990-2006

	Democrats	Republicans
State House (64 seats in 1990; 60 seats thereafter)		
1990	22	42
1992	19	41
1994	13	47
1996	17	43
1998	17	43
2000	17	43
2002	15	45
2004	14	46
2006	17	43
State Senate (30 seats)		
1990	10	20
1992	10	20
1994	10	20
1996	9	21
1998	10	20
2000	10	20
2002	10	20
2004	7	23
2006	7	23

Figures for total seats may include independents and minor party members. Numbers reflect results of elections in listed years; elected members usually take their seats in the years that follow.

Source: Council of State Governments; *State Elective Officials and the Legislatures.*

Voter participation in presidential elections, 2000 and 2004

	2000	2004
Voting age population		
State	366,000	390,000
Total United States	209,831,000	220,377,000
State share of U.S. total	0.17	0.18
Rank among states	50	50
Portion of voting age population casting votes		
State	58.3%	62.6%
United States	50.3%	55.5%
Rank among states	11	14

Population figures are rounded to nearest thousand and include all residents, regardless of eligibility to vote.

Source: U.S. Census Bureau.

HEALTH AND MEDICAL CARE

Medical professionals
Physicians in 2003 and nurses in 2001

	U.S.	State
Physicians in 2003		
Total	774,849	963
Share of U.S. total		0.12%
Rate	266	192
Rank		45
Nurses in 2001		
Total	2,262,020	3,780
Share of U.S. total		0.17%
Rate	793	765
Rank		35

Rates are numbers of physicians and nurses per 100,000 resident population; ranks are based on rates.
Source: American Medical Association, *Physician Characteristics and Distribution in the U.S.*; U.S. Department of Health and Human Services, Health Resources and Services Administration.

Health insurance coverage, 2003

	State	U.S.
Total persons covered	411,000	243,320,000
Total persons not covered	78,000	44,961,000
Portion not covered	15.9%	15.6%
Rank among states	19	—
Children not covered	15,000	8,373,000
Portion not covered	12.5%	11.4%
Rank among states	13	—

Totals are rounded to nearest thousand. Ranks are from the highest to the lowest percentages of persons *not* insured.
Source: U.S. Census Bureau, Current Population Reports.

AIDS, syphilis, and tuberculosis cases, 2003

Disease	U.S. cases	State cases	Rank
AIDS	44,232	8	48
Syphilis	34,270	4	47
Tuberculosis	14,874	4	50

Source: U.S. Centers for Disease Control and Prevention.

Cigarette smoking, 2003
Residents over age 18 who smoke

	U.S.	State	Rank
All smokers	22.1%	24.6%	18
Male smokers	24.8%	25.2%	24
Female smokers	20.3%	24.1%	4

Cigarette smokers are defined as persons who reported having smoked at least 100 cigarettes during their lifetimes and who currently smoked at least occasionally.
Source: U.S. Centers for Disease Control and Prevention, *Morbidity and Mortality Weekly Report*, 53, no. 44 (November 12, 2004).

HOUSING

Home ownership rates, 1985-2004

	1985	1990	1995	2000	2004
State	73.2%	68.9%	69.0%	71.0%	72.8%
Total U.S.	63.9%	63.9%	64.7%	67.4%	69.0%
Rank among states	3	16	19	22	19

Net change in state home ownership rate,
  1985-2004 . . . . −0.4%
Net change in U.S. home ownership rate,
  1985-2004 . . . . +5.1%

Percentages represent the proportion of owner households to total occupied households.
Source: U.S. Census Bureau, 2006.

Home sales, 2000-2004
In thousands of units

Existing home sales	2000	2002	2003	2004
State sales	9.6	10.6	11.4	13.2
Total U.S. sales	5,171	5,631	6,183	6,784
State share of U.S. total	0.19%	0.19%	0.18%	0.19%
Sales rank among states	50	50	50	50

Units include single-family homes, condos, and co-ops.
Source: National Association of Realtors, Washington, D.C., *Real Estate Outlook: Market Trends & Insights*.

Values of owner-occupied homes, 2003

	State	U.S.
Total units	105,000	58,809,000
Value of units		
Under $100,000	38.5%	29.6%
$100,000-199,999	44.7%	36.9%
$200,000 or more	16.8%	33.5%
Median value	$116,360	$142,275
Rank among all states 33		

Units are owner-occupied one-family houses whose numbers are rounded to nearest thousand. Data are extrapolated from survey samples.
Source: U.S. Census Bureau, American Community Survey.

EDUCATION

Public school enrollment, 2002

Prekindergarten through grade 8
State enrollment. 60,000
Total U.S. enrollment. 34,135,000
State share of U.S. total 0.18%

Grades 9 through 12
State enrollment. 28,000
Total U.S. enrollment. 14,067,000
State share of U.S. total 0.20%

Enrollment rates
State public school enrollment rate. 95.4%
Overall U.S. rate 90.4%
Rank among states in 2002 5
Rank among states in 1995 3

Enrollment figures (which include unclassified students) are rounded to nearest thousand pupils during fall school term. Enrollment rates are based on enumerated resident population estimate for July 1, 2002.
Source: U.S. National Center for Education Statistics.

Public college finances, 2003-2004

FTE enrollment in public institutions of higher education
Students in state institutions 22,200
Students in all U.S. public institutions 9,916,600
State share of U.S. total 0.22
Rank among states 49

State and local government appropriations for higher education
State appropriation per FTE. $11,358
National average. $5,716
Rank among states. 1
State & local tax revenue going to higher education 14.7%

FTE = full-time equivalent in public postsecondary programs, including summer sessions; student numbers are rounded to nearest hundred. Funding figures for 2003-2004 academic year include financial aid to students in state public institutions and exclude money for research, agriculture experiment stations, teaching hospitals, and medical schools; figures are rounded to nearest thousand dollars.
Source: Higher Education Executive Officers, Denver, Colorado.

TRANSPORTATION AND TRAVEL

Highway mileage, 2003

Interstate highways	913
Other freeways and expressways	5
Arterial roads	3,673
Collector roads.	10,884
Local roads.	12,007
Urban roads	2,504
Rural roads.	24,978
Total state mileage.	27,482
U.S. total	3,974,107
State share	0.69%
Rank among states	42

Note that combined urban and rural road mileage matches the total of the other categories.
Source: U.S. Federal Highway Administration.

Motor vehicle registrations and driver licenses, 2003

Vehicle registrations	State	U.S.	Share	Rank
Autos, trucks, buses	620,000	231,390,000	0.27%	49
Autos only	232,000	135,670	0.17%	50
Motorcycles	28,000	5,328,000	0.53%	40
Driver licenses	378,000	196,166,000	0.19%	50

Figures, which do not include vehicles owned by military services, are rounded to the nearest thousand. Figures for automobiles include taxis.
Source: U.S. Federal Highway Administration.

Domestic travel expenditures, 2003

Spending by U.S. residents on overnight trips and
day trips of at least 50 miles from home

Total expenditures within state	$1.71 bill.
Total expenditures within U.S.	$490.87 bill.
State share of U.S. total	0.3%
Rank among states	44

Source: Travel Industry Association of America.

Retail gasoline prices, 2003-2007

Average price per gallon at the pump

Year	U.S.	State
2003	$1.267	$1.311
2004	$1.316	$1.306
2005	$1.644	$1.649
2007	$2.298	$2.186

Excise tax per gallon in 2004	14.0¢
Rank among all states in 2007 prices	35

Prices are averages of all grades of gasoline sold at the pump
during March months in 2003-2005 and during February, 2007.
Averages for 2006, during which prices rose higher, are not
available.

Source: U.S. Energy Information Agency, *Petroleum Marketing
Monthly* (2003-2005 data); American Automobile Association
(2007 data).

CRIME AND LAW ENFORCEMENT

State and local police officers, 2000-2004

	2000	2002	2004
Total officers			
U.S.	654,601	665,555	675,734
State	1,192	1,239	1,279*
*Net change, 2000-2004			+7.30%
Officers per 1,000 residents			
U.S.	2.33	2.31	2.30
State	2.41	2.48	2.53
State rank	11	11	9

Totals include state and local police and sheriffs.
Source: Carsey Institute, University of New Hampshire.

Crime rates, 2003

Incidents per 100,000 residents

Crimes	State	U.S.
Violent crimes		
Total incidents	262	475
Murder	3	6
Forcible rape	27	32
Robbery	17	142
Aggravated assault	216	295
Property crimes		
Total incidents	3,321	3,588
Burglary	521	741
Larceny/theft	2,641	2,415
Motor vehicle theft	159	433
All crimes	3,583	4,063

Source: U.S. Federal Bureau of Investigation, *Crime in the United
States*, annual.

State prison populations, 1980-2003

	State	U.S.	State share
1980	534	305,458	0.17%
1990	1,110	708,393	0.16%
1996	1,499	1,025,624	0.15%
2000	1,680	1,391,261	0.12%
2003	1,872	1,470,045	0.13%

State figures exclude prisoners in federal penitentiaries.
Source: U.S. Bureau of Justice Statistics, *Prisoners in 2003*.

District of Columbia

Location: Atlantic coast

Area and rank: 61.4 square miles (159 square kilometers); 683 square miles (177 square kilometers) including water; if it were a state, it would rank fifty-first largest in area

Coastline: none

Population and rank: 554,000 (2004); if it were a state, it would be fiftieth largest in population, ahead of Wyoming

Became municipal corporation: February 21, 1871

Present form of government adopted: 1975

The National Capitol Building from the west, the side facing the Washington Monument and Lincoln Memorial. (PhotoDisc)

District name: "Columbia" is the Latin form of Christopher Columbus's surname; the city of Washington was named after former president George Washington the year after he died

District nicknames: Capital City; The District

Motto: *Justitia omnibus* (Justice to all)

District flag: Three red stars above two horizontal red stripes on a white field

Highest point: Tenleytown—410 feet (125 meters)

Lowest point: Potomac and Anacostia River shores—sea level

Highest recorded temperature: 106 degrees Fahrenheit (41 degrees Celsius), 1918 and 1930

Lowest recorded temperature: −15 degrees Fahrenheit (−26 degrees Celsius), 1899

District song: "The Star-Spangled Banner"

District tree: Scarlet oak

District flower: American beauty rose

District bird: Wood thrush

District of Columbia History

Situated on the east bank of the Potomac River and bordering the states of Virginia and Maryland, the District of Columbia is coextensive with the modern city of Washington, the federal capital of the United States. The district came into existence through the provision in the U.S. Constitution (1787) of a site where the nation's capital would be located. Article I, section 8 of the document gave the U.S. Congress exclusive power to govern a district, not larger than one hundred square miles, "to become the seat of government of the United States."

Origins and Early Development. After 1776, the capital of the newly independent nation resided in either Philadelphia or New York. Just where the site of the new capital would be—farther to the south or to the north—was a matter of some dispute among northern and southern states during the early years under the new Constitution. The dispute was put to rest through the diplomatic skill of Thomas Jefferson. Being a southerner, Jefferson wanted the new capital to be in his part of the country. At a private dinner in New York in 1790, he prevailed upon Secretary of the Treasury Alexander Hamilton to consent to a southern location in exchange for support for Hamilton's proposal for federal assumption of state debts.

The district was established following congressional acts of 1790 and 1791. President George Washington selected the site's exact location, just seven miles north

Home to one of the premier collections of historical artifacts in the world, Washington's Smithsonian Institution got its start during the early nineteenth century with the bequest of James Smithson (1765-1829), a British subject who never visited the United States. (PhotoDisc)

of his ancestral home, Mount Vernon. Land for the diamond-shaped district straddling the Potomac River was ceded by both Virginia and Maryland. No sooner had the district been born, however, than the people of Virginia had second thoughts and began clamoring for their state's land to be returned. In 1846, when Congress ordered the return of the ceded territory, which included the city and county of Alexandria, Virginia finally got its wish. As a consequence, the modern map of the district has the appearance of a diamond with its lower left facet broken off.

Construction of Federal City, as the district was originally known, began during the early 1790's. Among the early projects was construction of an official residence for the president. Work on the presidential mansion, later called the White House, began in 1792, and construction of the Capitol Building, which was to house the Congress, began a year later. For the city's overall design, the plan of Pierre Charles L'Enfant was chosen. However, L'Enfant, who had emigrated from his native France at the time of the American Revolution, was soon found to be so obnoxious in pursuing execution of his design that Washington fired him. L'Enfant was to spend the rest of his life unsuccessfully seeking the compensation that he believed he deserved for his work.

On December 1, 1800, the new capital city, now known as Washington (George Washington had died the previous year), was ready to receive the federal government, which was relocated from Philadelphia. On February 27, 1801, the district was officially made subject to the authority of Congress. A census revealed that it had some 14,103 residents, of whom 10,066 were white, 793 were "free negroes," and 3,244 were slaves.

Peaceful operation of the new capital, however, was short lived. In 1812, war with Great Britain broke out, and two years later British troops entered the city, looting and burning its public buildings. Members of the government, including President James Madison and First Lady Dolley Madison, were forced to flee for their lives. The presidential mansion was among the troops' victims, though not before the soldiers helped themselves to a presidential feast abandoned by its hastily departing residents.

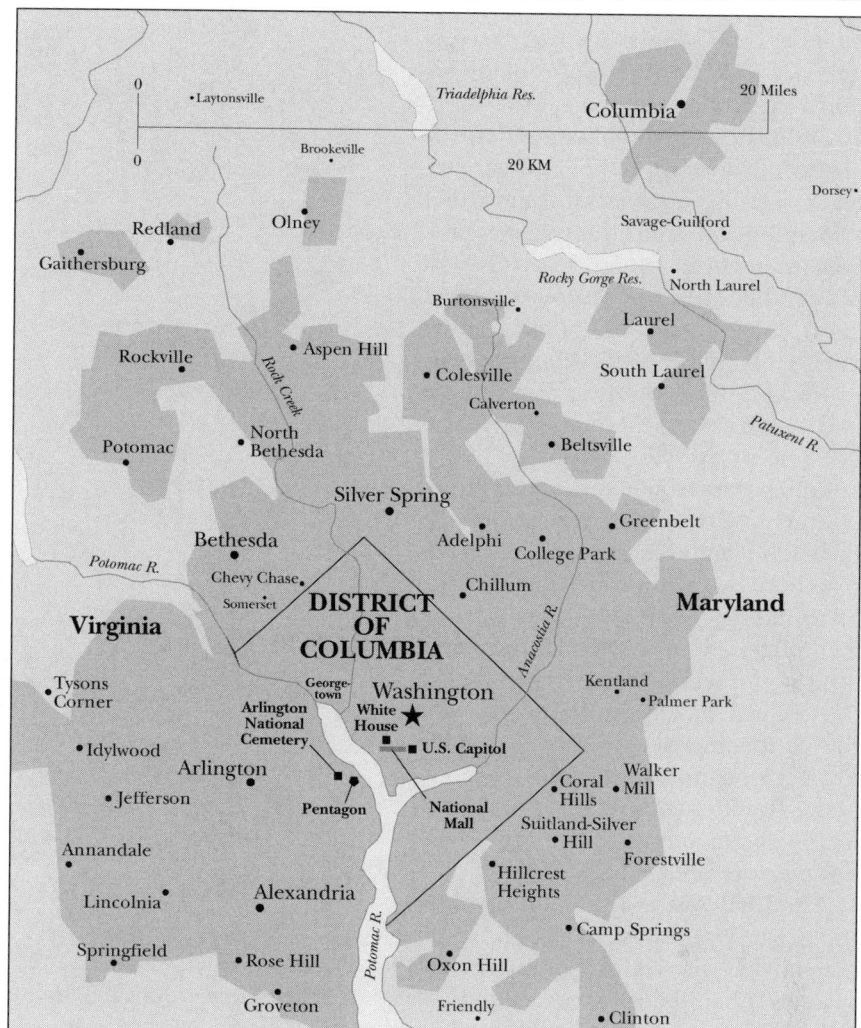

Whitewashed to hide its war scars, the mansion was afterward known as the White House. Its first inhabitants were President John Adams and his wife Abigail, who found their new official home a cold and drafty place in which few comforts were to be found. The mansion's colorful history includes being thoroughly trashed in a celebration of Andrew Jackson's election in 1828. A century later, during the administration of President Calvin Coolidge, its condition had deteriorated so badly that a piano fell partly through one its rotten floors. In 1950, after president Harry S. Truman was sternly warned of the building's dangerous condition, the White House was completely gutted and reconstructed. The president's family moved to the Blair House across the street during the process.

During its opening decades, the city of Washington in the District of Columbia was hardly the grand and bustling metropolis of the modern era. The new capital was a rural town of frequently muddy dirt roads and fetid marshes that bred disease-bearing mosquitoes. Stifling summer heat drove many residents out of the city. Washington was also a town of boarding houses for members of Congress, who arrived first by coach and later by train from the nation's expanding four corners.

Besides the city of Washington, the district included the city of Georgetown, many of whose habitations and other structures date from the early years of the nineteenth century. Development of Washington's suburbs, on the other hand, did not begin until shortly before the Civil War. Prior to 1846, the district comprised two counties, Washington and Alexandria.

Some of the city's imposing public buildings date from the various periods of the nineteenth century. After the British burned the city in 1814, reconstruction was begun. Work on the Capitol Building—including a new, more magnificent dome to replace the somewhat petite version that existed before the Civil War and expanded quarters for the House and Senate—was a notable project consuming decades to complete. President Abraham Lincoln demanded that work on the dome continue throughout the Civil War.

The Civil War Era. The outbreak of the Civil War in April, 1861, often placed the District of Columbia, still sparsely inhabited with a population of only a few thousand, in imminent danger of attack by the nearby Confederacy. To defend the capital, President Lincoln created the Army of the Potomac, raising the district's population by some thousands. The growth of the federal government made necessary by the war also contributed to the expansion of the town's population.

In 1862, slavery was abolished in the district, preceding both the Emancipation Proclamation—which was issued the following year—and the Thirteenth Amendment to the U.S. Constitution, which permanently ended slavery in the nation. Moreover, in 1867, Congress granted black men the right to vote in local elections. Meanwhile, shortly after the close of the Civil War, Washington's history was stained by President Lincoln's martyrdom at the hands of John Wilkes Booth. On April 14, 1865, at Ford's Theatre, during a performance of the play *Our American Cousin*, Booth shot Lincoln. The president died early the following morning.

Library of Congress and Public Monuments. After the close of the Civil War, the district set about continuing the construction of federal buildings. One of these was the Library of Congress, which had begun with Thomas Jefferson's library as its founding collection.

The Washington Monument around 1860, during the long hiatus when construction was stopped. The monument was finally completed in 1884. (Library of Congress)

Following that time, the library's size grew to more than ten million volumes. By law, a copy of every book published within the United States must be deposited in the library. The library also collects large numbers of foreign publications.

During the 1880's, the lovely and ornate Thomas Jefferson Building was constructed on Capitol Hill. By the early twenty-first century, this branch of the library was drawing thousands of visitors each year. The more utilitarian James Madison Building, a product of post-World War II America, stands nearby and houses much of the collection, as well as electronic equipment open to the public to search the library's holdings.

Among the most significant public monuments completed during the post-Civil War era is the Washington Monument, which required some forty years to complete. The monument was built in two stages. About one-quarter of it was completed between 1848 and 1856, the rest between 1876 and 1884. The long period during which construction was halted made Washington the subject of considerable public derision. The stages of the monument's construction are clearly visible in the structure itself, as the stones for the bottom quarter and top three-quarters differ noticeably in coloration. When it finally opened in 1888, the 555-foot-high monument was the tallest building in the world. The following year, however, France's new Eiffel Tower in Paris eclipsed it.

When the district was given a territorial government in 1871, its second governor, Alexander Shepard, set about creating the amenities worthy of a national capital. He ordered paved streets, sidewalks, and street lamps. These additions bankrupted local government, however, leading Congress to abolish territorial government and rule the district itself over the following century. As the twentieth century approached, plans were made to develop more public monuments. Dozens of imposing new buildings were erected, as the capital of a rising nation began to take shape.

The District During the Twentieth Century. The twentieth century saw the completion of the modern city that Washington, D.C., has become. The Lincoln and Jefferson Memorials and other parts of the National Mall were conceived and constructed. A law to build a memorial to Lincoln was passed in 1911; the memorial opened in 1922. Twelve years later, Congress passed a resolution to build a memorial to Jefferson, and in 1943 the Jefferson Memorial was dedicated. In addition, vast edifices housing the federal bureaucracy, many of them dating from the New Deal era (1933-1945) under President Franklin D. Roosevelt, and others of later vintage, such as the Federal Bureau of Investigation (FBI) and Ronald Reagan buildings, were constructed.

The National Archives Building on Pennsylvania Avenue opened its doors in 1935 to exhibit the Declaration of Independence, the U.S. Constitution, and the Bill of Rights. These priceless relics of the nation's founding descend deep into the earth each night for their protection and are raised each morning just before the archive opens its doors to the public.

Among other improvements was the opening of Union Station, near Capitol Hill, in 1907. The terminal remained a focal point of transit activity until the 1950's, when it fell into decline. It was reconstructed in opulent splendor during the mid-1980's. During the early years of the twenty-first century, twenty million people a year passed through it. Earlier, the 1907 opening of the station prompted the Pennsylvania Railroad to remove its tracks and terminal from the National Mall. A nineteenth century transportation canal on the mall was also filled in, and this central promenade and gathering place gradually assumed its current form.

Washington has not always been the scene of positive events, however. In 1932, a "Bonus Army" of more than ten thousand impoverished men seeking immediate payment of funds promised to World War I veterans was violently expelled from the city by a U.S. Army force commanded by Douglas MacArthur. During World War II and afterward during the Cold War (1946-1991), spies—some of them trusted Americans—plied their trade in the city, often in the service of the Soviet Union. Moreover, significant areas of the city, especially Northeast Washington, became impoverished and crime-ridden.

Post-World War II Years. From the 1960's to the 1980's and beyond, Washington was the scene of the "K Street" phenomenon: The headquarters of hundreds of well-financed lobbying organizations became located on this renowned—or notorious—avenue. The corridors of power frequented by well-heeled lobbyists came to be known as "Gucci Gulch." Watering holes known as "power bars," such as the Round Robin Bar at the Willard Hotel on Pennsylvania Avenue, appeared, and the institution of the "power lunch" took shape, as the effects of the intrusion of a large influx of money into American politics became visible.

During the 1960's and 1970's, the District of Columbia was also the scene of numerous demonstrations protesting the Vietnam War, as well as numerous Civil Rights movement marches. The most memorable of these was the March on Washington in August, 1963, climaxed by the Reverend Martin Luther King, Jr.'s, famed "I Have a Dream" speech at the Lincoln Memorial. After King was assassinated in early 1968, Washington was wracked with rioting, as African American residents expressed their outrage.

Meanwhile, new buildings added to the capital city included such public landmarks as the Kennedy Center on the banks of the Potomac and private ones, such as the nearby Watergate Hotel and office complex, where, in 1972, a burglary of Democratic Party Headquarters eventuated in the nation's worst political scandal and the eventual resignation of President Richard M. Nixon.

Government of the District. When the District of Columbia became the center of American national government in 1800, it was not yet coextensive with the city of Washington, situated within it. At that time it also contained the separate city of Georgetown and the county of Washington. After creating a succession of local government institutions, in 1871 Congress combined the governments of Georgetown and Washington and the county of Washington into a single territorial District of Columbia government.

In 1874, territorial government was temporarily replaced by a government of three commissioners. In 1878, Congress replaced this government with a municipal corporation, headed by three commissioners appointed by the president, to govern the district as a whole. This form of government continued until 1967. In 1968, voters gained the right to elect a board of education. Finally, in 1973, in response to voter demands,

Congress passed the District of Columbia Home Rule Act, allowing for a locally elected mayor and city council government, an arrangement that continued into the twenty-first century.

The Twenty-third Amendment of the U.S. Constitution, ratified in 1961, granted District of Columbia residents the right to determine three electoral college votes at presidential elections. Voters also elect a non-voting delegate to the U.S. House of Representatives. Efforts to elevate the district to the status of a state, however, have repeatedly failed, leaving the district's tax-paying residents without voting members in either house of Congress.

In 1978, Congress passed the District of Columbia Voting Rights Amendment, which would have given the district the same congressional representation as states. However, when the time allowed for the amendment's ratification elapsed in 1985, only sixteen states had ratified it. In 1980, voters approved creation of a constitution for a state of New Columbia. However, despite ratification by the district's voters of a constitution in 1982, statehood remained elusive, leading the district to place the motto "Taxation Without Representation" on its license plates, recalling the colonial American grievances against Britain during the eighteenth century.

The Modern Era. The most significant event for Washington, D.C., during the early years of the twenty-first century was the September 11, 2001, attack on the headquarters of the Department of Defense, the Pentagon Building in nearby Virginia. Terrorists crashed a commercial passenger jet plane laden with fuel into the building. Later, it was learned that the Capitol Building itself had been targeted by a hijacked plane, which was brought down in Pennsylvania by its passengers. Afterward, Washington became the site of intense security measures against terrorist attack. Streets previously accessible by automobile, notably the section of Pennsylvania Avenue in front of the White House, were closed to traffic. Shortly after the September 11 attacks, an anthrax-laced letter arrived at the offices of a member of the U.S. Senate—a similar letter to a second senator was not delivered—affecting an entire office building and further terrorizing the city. This event served only to intensify Washington's sense of being under siege. Physical barriers and other security measures became common features of daily life in the city.

A further blight on civil life in the district occurred in 2002, when snipers killed ten persons and critically injured three others in Washington and surrounding areas in Maryland and Virginia during three weeks in October. The killings finally ended on October 24, when suspects, who were later convicted, were taken into custody.

Despite war and tragedy, the District of Columbia continued to be the epicenter of government and the sometimes-raucous national politics of the United States. Marches and demonstrations still frequently mark the nation's open and democratic government, and the gracious expanses of the National Mall and other sites of public monuments, museums, and governmental and private institutions continue to attract millions of visitors annually from throughout the nation and across the globe.

Charles F. Bahmueller

District of Columbia Time Line

1787	Provision is made in the new U.S. Constitution for a "District (not exceeding ten Miles square) to become the seat of the government of the United States."
1790	Residency Act of 1790 gives President George Washington the power to choose a site on the East Bank of the Potomac River for a new capital city.
Jan. 22, 1791	President Washington appoints commissioners for surveying district of the new capital city.
Jan. 24, 1791	Washington selects a site seven miles from his home Mount Vernon for the new federal district, which includes land from Maryland and Virginia.
Dec. 1, 1800	Federal capital moves from Philadelphia to new federal district, later known as Washington, D.C.
1802	Congress grants the first municipal charter to the new national capital.
1814	During the War of 1812, President James Madison and his administration flee Washington ahead of advancing British troops.
1814	British troops maraud through the District of Columbia, burning and looting public buildings, including the Presidential Mansion, and killing inhabitants.
1846	Congress passes a law returning the portion of the district's land donated by Virginia, including the city of Alexandria.
Apr. 16, 1862	Congress abolishes slavery in the District of Columbia.

Apr. 14, 1865	President Abraham Lincoln is shot in Ford's Theatre while watching a play; he dies the next morning.
1867	Congress grants the right to vote to black residents of the District of Columbia.
Feb. 21, 1871	Congress replaces the government of the district with a territorial government under a municipal corporation.
1874	Territorial government of the District of Columbia is abolished and a temporary government is installed.
June 11, 1878	Organic Act of 1878 makes the district into a municipal corporation governed by three presidentially appointed commissioners.
1907	Union Station opens; serves as the district's transportation hub for nearly five decades.
May 30, 1922	Lincoln Memorial is dedicated.
July 28, 1932	Federal troops under General Douglas MacArthur evict thousands of Depression-impoverished veterans from "Bonus Army" camps in Washington.
Apr. 13, 1943	Jefferson Memorial is dedicated.
Nov. 1, 1950	Two members of a Puerto Rican nationalist group attempt to shoot their way into Blair House, the temporary residence of the president, as part of an attempted assassination of the president.
Mar. 1, 1954	Four Puerto Rican nationalists, using automatic pistols, fire thirty rounds into the House of Representatives from the visitors' gallery, injuring four members, one seriously.
1961	Twenty-third Amendment of the U.S. Constitution gives district voters the right to three electoral votes in presidential elections.
August, 1963	City is the site of a massive Civil Rights movement march, which is capped by Martin Luther King, Jr.'s, "I Have a Dream" speech.
June 17, 1972	Burglary at the Democratic Party's offices in the Watergate complex sets off chain of events and revelations known as the Watergate scandal.
1973	Congress approves the District of Columbia Self Government Act, under which the district is governed by an elected mayor and a thirteen-member city council.
1975	Home rule begins with Walter Washington as the first elected mayor.
Mar. 29, 1978	First segment of the Washington Metro, the district's subway, opens.

(continued)

Begun in 1976, Washington's modern subway system has grown to five lines, which serve the District of Columbia and surrounding communities in Maryland and Virginia. (PhotoDisc)

1982	Voters approve a draft constitution for the proposed new state of New Columbia.
1992	U.S. House of Representatives approves statehood for the District of Columbia, but the Senate votes it down.
Sept. 11, 2001	Terrorists crash hijacked passenger jetliner into the Pentagon in nearby northern Virginia.
Oct. 2001	Letters mailed from New Jersey to two U.S. senators contain deadly anthrax spores and terrorize the capital; two district postal workers die in the attacks.
Oct. 2002	Snipers kill ten and wound three critically in attacks in and around Washington. John Allen Muhammad and Lee Boyd Malvo are apprehended and later convicted for the crimes.

Notes for Further Study

Published Sources. Useful books for a variety of research interests include *Washington Through Two Centuries: A History in Maps and Images* by Joseph R. Passonneau (2004), which presents a comprehensive history of the city of Washington and the District of Columbia; *On This Spot: Pinpointing the Past in Washington, D.C.* by Douglas E. Evelyn (1992), which locates significant events, building sites, and the like in the district; and *Old Washington, D.C. in Early Photographs, 1846-1932* (1980) by Robert Reed, which presents a wealth of early photographic materials. Other good sources include *Washington Seen: A Photographic History, 1875-1965* by Fredric M. Miller, Jr., and Howard Gillette; and *Capital Losses: A Cultural History of Washington's Destroyed Buildings* (1979) by James M. Goode.

Washington, D.C. Past and Present, by author-photographer Peter R. Penczer (1998) provides a well-illustrated, plainspoken and entertaining look at the city's history. The book includes 127 pairs of then-and-now photographs, many of them vintage in character, of Washington, D.C., and its Virginia and Maryland suburbs. For fascinating accounts of several dimensions of the Capitol Hill building where Congress meets, see William C. Allen's *A History of the United States Capitol: A Chronicle of Design, Construction, and Politics* (2005) and *The United States Capitol: Its Architecture and Decoration*, by Henry Hope Reed and photographer Anne Day (2005). For a more sweeping look at art in the history of Washington, see Bruce R. Smith's *Art and History of Washington D.C.* (2006).

Web Resources. A good place to begin one's online search for information related to the District of Columbia is the city's official tourism Web site (www.washington.org/index .cfm?blnNavView=True&idContentType=36&idCurrentPage =7). It provides area maps, community links, and information on upcoming events, among many other features. The city's official government site (www.dc.gov/) is also a valuable Internet stop. It provides information about getting around the city, the district's history, living and working in the area, and the "mayor's corner," a section that gives links to the mayor's blog, contact information, and the mayor's schedule and newsletter. D.C. Pages (dcpages.com/cgi-bin/jump.cgi? ID= 11576) provides a helpful interactive map of the city; clicking on any of the points-of-interest icons produces a pop-up window that, for example, gives information on the history of a monument, its operating hours and price of admission, photographs, and tips of other sites nearby. Both the Smithsonian Institution (www.si.edu/) and the National Gallery of Art (www.nga.gov/) have excellent Web sites, as does the Architect of the Capitol (www.aoc.gov/), which provides detailed information about the Capitol complex, including its history, visiting information, and preservation efforts. The U.S. House of Representatives (www.house.gov/house/tour_dc .shtml) gives numerous links to organizations and historic sites in the vicinity as well as its legislative schedule and links to individual congress members; the U.S. Senate (www .senate.gov/) has a similar site. For information about doing business in the city, visit the D.C. Chamber of Commerce (www.dcchamber.org/).

Index to Tables

DEMOGRAPHICS

Resident district and national populations, 1980-2004

Population figures given in thousands

	District pop.	U.S. pop.	Share
1980	638	226,546	0.3%
1990	607	248,791	0.2%
1995	581	266,278	0.2%
2000	572	281,425	0.2%
2004	554	293,655	0.2%

Source: U.S. Census Bureau, Current Population Reports, 2006.

Resident population by age, 2004

Age Group	Total persons
Under 5 years	35,000
5 to 17 years	75,000
18 to 24 years	58,000
25 to 34 years	108,000
35 to 44 years	82,000
45 to 54 years	72,000
55 to 64 years	56,000
65 to 74 years	34,000
75 to 84 years	24,000
85 years and older	9,000
All age groups	554,000
Portion of residents 65 and older	12.1%
National rank in portion of oldest residents, if D.C. were a state	33
National average	12.4%

Population figures are rounded to nearest thousand persons; figures include armed forces personnel stationed in the state.
Source: U.S. Bureau of the Census, 2006.

Resident population by race, Hispanic origin, 2004

Category	Dist. pop.	Share	U.S.
All residents	554	100.00%	100.00%
Non-Hispanic white	168	30.32%	67.37%
Hispanic white	39	7.04%	13.01%
Other Hispanic	8	1.44%	1.06%
African American	319	57.58%	12.77%
Native American	2	0.36%	0.96%
Asian, Pacific Islander	17	3.07%	4.37%
Two or more categories	8	1.44%	1.51%

Population figures are in thousands. Persons counted as "Hispanic" (Latino) may be of any race. Because of overlapping categories, categories may not add up to 100%. Shares in column 3 are percentages of each category within the district; these figures may be compared to the national percentages in column 4.
Source: U.S. Bureau of the Census, 2006.

Projected district population, 2000-2030

Year	Population
2000	572,000
2005	551,000
2010	530,000
2015	506,000
2020	481,000
2025	455,000
2030	433,000
Population decrease, 2000-2030	−139,000
Percentage decrease, 2000-2030	−24.2

Projections are based on data from the 2000 census.
Source: U.S. Census Bureau.

VITAL STATISTICS

Infant mortality rates, 1980-2002

	1980	1990	2000	2002
All district residents	25.0	20.7	12.0	11.3
All U.S. residents	12.6	9.2	9.4	9.1
All district white residents	17.8	—	17.8	—
All U.S. white residents	10.6	7.6	5.7	5.8
All district black residents	26.7	24.6	16.1	14.5
All U.S. black residents	22.2	18.0	14.1	14.4

Figures represent deaths per 1,000 live births of resident infants under 1 year old, exclusive of fetal deaths. Figures for all residents include members of other racial categories not listed separately. The Census Bureau considers the 1990 and 2002 figures for white residents to be too small to be statistically meaningful.
Source: U.S. Census Bureau, Statistical Abstract of the United States, 2006.

Abortion rates, 1990 and 2000

	1990	2000
Total abortions	21,000	10,000
Rate per 1,000 women	133.1	68.1
U.S. rate	25.7	21.3
Rank if district were a state	1	1

Numbers of abortions are rounded to nearest thousand; ranks are based on rates.
Source: U.S. Census Bureau.

Marriages and divorces, 2004

Total marriages 2,900
Rate per 1,000 population. 5.3
National rate per 1,000 population 7.4
Rank if the district were a state 48

Total divorces 900
Rate per 1,000 population. 1.7
National rate per 1,000 population 3.7
Rank if the district were a state 45

Figures are for all marriages and divorces performed within the district, including those of nonresidents; totals are rounded to the nearest hundred. Ranks are for highest to lowest figures; note that divorce data are not available for five states.
Source: U.S. National Center for Health Statistics, Vital Statistics of the United States, 2006.

Death rates by leading causes, 2002

Deaths per 100,000 resident population

Cause	District	U.S.
Heart disease	291.8	241.7
Cancer	227.4	193.2
Cerebrovascular diseases	48.9	56.4
Accidents other than motor vehicle	35.0	37.0
Motor vehicle accidents	10.2	15.7
Chronic lower respiratory diseases	23.3	43.3
Diabetes mellitus	33.5	25.4
HIV	40.8	4.9
Suicide	5.4	11.0
Homicide	40.1	6.1
All causes	1,024.9	847.3
Rank in overall death rate if the district were a state		5

Figures exclude nonresidents who died in the district. Causes of death follow International Classification of Diseases. Rank is from highest to lowest death rate in the United States.
Source: U.S. National Center for Health Statistics, National Vital Statistics Report, 2006.

ECONOMY

Gross district product, 1990-2004
In current dollars

Year	District product	Nat'l product	District share
1990	$40.1 billion	$5.67 trillion	0.71%
2000	$58.4 billion	$9.75 trillion	0.60%
2002	$67.2 billion	$10.41 trillion	0.65%
2003	$70.7 billion	$10.92 trillion	0.65%
2004	$75.3 billion	$11.65 trillion	0.65%

Source: U.S. Bureau of Economic Analysis, *Survey of Current Business,* July, 2005.

District product by industry, 2003
In billions of dollars

Construction	$0.7
Manufacturing	0.2
Wholesale trade	0.7
Retail trade	1.0
Finance & insurance	3.6
Information	4.7
Professional services	12.7
Health care & social assistance	2.9
Government	22.1
Total district product	$64.1
Total U.S. product	$10,289.2
District share of U.S. total	0.62%
Rank if district were a state	36

Total figures include industries not listed separately. Amounts are in chained 2000 dollars.
Source: U.S. Bureau of Economic Analysis, *Survey of Current Business,* July, 2005.

Personal income per capita, 1990-2004
In current dollars

	1990	2000	2004
Per capita income	$26,473	$40,456	$51,803
U.S. average	$19,477	$29,845	$32,937
Rank if district were a state	1	2	1

Source: U.S. Bureau of Economic Analysis, *Survey of Current Business,* April, 2005.

Energy consumption, 2001
In trillions of British thermal units (BTU), except as noted

Total energy consumption

Total district energy consumption	168
Total U.S. energy consumption	96,275
District share of U.S. total	0.17%
Rank if the district were a state	50

Per capita consumption (In millions of BTU)

Total district per capita consumption	294
Total U.S. per capita consumption	338
Rank if the district were a state	38

End-use sectors

Residential	34
Commercial	104
Industrial	4
Transportation	26

Sources of energy

Petroleum	34
Natural gas	31
Coal	1
Hydroelectric power	0
Nuclear electric power	0

Figures for totals include categories not listed separately.
Source: U.S. Energy Information Administration, *State Energy Data Report,* 2001.

Nonfarm employment by sectors, 2004

Total persons	672,000
Construction	12,000
Manufacturing	3,000
Trade, transportation, utilities	28,000
Information	24,000
Finance, insurance, real estate	31,000
Professional & business services	143,000
Education & health services	92,000
Leisure, hospitality, arts, organizations	51,000
Other services, including repair & maintenance	59,000
Government	231,000

Figures are rounded to nearest thousand persons. "Total" includes mining and natural resources, not listed separately.
Source: U.S. Bureau of Labor Statistics, 2006.

Foreign exports, 2000-2005
In millions of dollars

Year	District	U.S.	District share
2000	1,003	712,055	0.13%
2001	1,034	678,560	0.15%
2002	1,066	648,800	0.16%
2003	809	724,006	0.12%
2004	1,164	769,332	0.15%
2005	825	853,765	0.10%

Rank among states in 2004, if district were a state 46

U.S. total does not include U.S. dependencies.
Source: Northeast-Midwest Institute; U.S. Census Bureau, *U.S. Merchandise Trade,* series FT 900, 2000; U.S. Census Bureau, *U.S. International Trade in Goods and Services,* Series FT 900, 2005.

LAND USE

Federally owned land, 2003
Areas in acres

	District	U.S.	District share
Total area	39,000	2,271,343,000	(s)
Nonfederal land	29,000	1,599,584,000	(s)
Federal land	10,000	671,759,000	(s)
Federal share	26.3%	29.6%	—

Areas are rounded to nearest thousand acres. Figures for federally owned land do not include trust properties. (s) District shares of national land are less than one-one hundredth of 1 percent.
Source: U.S. General Services Administration, *Federal Real Property Profile,* 2006.

GOVERNMENT AND FINANCE

Units of local government, 2002

	District	Total U.S.	Rank
All local governments	2	87,525	51
Counties	0	3,034	—
Municipalities	1	19,429	50
Townships	0	16,504	—
School districts	0	13,506	—
Special districts	1	35,052	51

Only 48 states have county governments, 20 states have township governments ("towns" in New England, Minnesota, New York, and Wisconsin), and 46 states have school districts. Special districts encompass such functions as natural resources, fire protection, and housing and community development. Rank numbers reflect what the district's positions would be if it were a state.
Source: U.S. Census Bureau, *Census of Governments.*

POLITICS

Mayors since home rule

The administration of the District of Columbia has gone through several reorganizations since the district was created. From 1790 until 1871, the city of Georgetown had its own mayors, as did the separate city of Washington, from 1802 to 1871. From 1871 to 1874 the district was administered under appointed governors, and from 1874 until 1975 it was under the Board of Commissioners, which was appointed by the president of the United States. The chair of the board, who was designated "president," was de facto mayor, or mayor-commissioner. When the district was placed under home rule in 1975, the last appointed mayor, Walter Washington, became the first elected mayor.

Walter Washington (D)	1975-1979
Marion S. Barry (D)	1979-1991
Sharon Pratt Kelly* (D)	1991-1995
Marion S. Barry (D)	1995-1999
Anthony A. Williams (D)	1999-2007
Adrian M. Fenty (D)	2007-

*Kelly began her term as Sharon Pratt Dixon.

Voter participation in presidential elections, 2000 and 2004

	2000	2004
Voting age population		
District	456,000	444,000
Total United States	209,831,000	220,377,000
District share of U.S. total	0.22	0.20
Rank if district were a state	48	50
Portion of voting age population casting votes		
District	44.2%	51.3%
United States	50.3%	55.5%
Rank if district were a state	46	42

Population figures are rounded to nearest thousand and include all residents, regardless of eligibility to vote.
Source: U.S. Census Bureau.

HEALTH AND MEDICAL CARE

Medical professionals
Physicians in 2003 and nurses in 2001

	U.S.	District
Physicians in 2003		
Total	774,849	4,329
Share of U.S. total		0.56%
Rate	266	768
Rank if district were a state		1
Nurses in 2001		
Total	2,262,020	8,600
Share of U.S. total		0.38%
Rate	793	1,498
Rank if district were a state		1

Rates are numbers of physicians and nurses per 100,000 resident population; ranks are based on rates.
Source: American Medical Association, *Physician Characteristics and Distribution in the U.S.*; U.S. Department of Health and Human Services, Health Resources and Services Administration.

Health insurance coverage, 2003

	District	U.S.
Total persons covered	475,000	243,320,000
Total persons not covered	79,000	44,961,000
Portion not covered	14.3%	15.6%
Rank if district were a state	24	—
Children not covered	12,000	8,373,000
Portion not covered	11.4%	11.4%
Rank if district were a state	18	—

Totals are rounded to nearest thousand. Ranks are from the highest to the lowest percentages of persons *not* insured.
Source: U.S. Census Bureau, Current Population Reports.

AIDS, syphilis, and tuberculosis cases, 2003

Disease	U.S. cases	District cases	Rank
AIDS	44,232	961	(12)
Syphilis	34,270	330	(23)
Tuberculosis	14,874	79	(33)

Rank numbers reflect the district's position if it were a state.
Source: U.S. Centers for Disease Control and Prevention.

Cigarette smoking, 2003
Residents over age 18 who smoke

	U.S.	District	Rank
All smokers	22.1%	22.3%	25
Male smokers	24.8%	26.2%	23
Female smokers	20.3%	19.0%	33

Cigarette smokers are defined as persons who reported having smoked at least 100 cigarettes during their lifetimes and who currently smoked at least occasionally. Rank numbers reflect what the district's position would be if it were a state.
Source: U.S. Centers for Disease Control and Prevention, *Morbidity and Mortality Weekly Report*, 53, no. 44 (November 12, 2004).

HOUSING

Home ownership rates, 1985-2004

	1985	1990	1995	2000	2004
District	37.4%	36.4%	39.2%	41.9%	45.6%
Total U.S.	63.9%	63.9%	64.7%	67.4%	69.0%
Rank if district were a state	51	51	51	51	51

Net change in district home ownership rate, 1985-2004 . . . . +8.2%
Net change in U.S. home ownership rate, 1985-2004 . . . . +5.1%

Percentages represent the proportion of owner households to total occupied households.
Source: U.S. Census Bureau, 2006.

Home sales, 2000-2004
In thousands of units

Existing home sales	2000	2002	2003	2004
District sales	10.6	11.2	12.1	13.4
Total U.S. sales	5,171	5,631	6,183	6,784
District share of U.S. total	0.20%	0.20%	0.20%	0.20%
Sales rank if district were a state	50	50	50	50

Units include single-family homes, condos, and co-ops.
Source: National Association of Realtors, Washington, D.C., *Real Estate Outlook: Market Trends & Insights.*

Values of owner-occupied homes, 2003

	District	U.S.
Total units	76,000	58,809,000
Value of units		
Under $100,000	9.1%	29.6%
$100,000-199,999	31.5%	36.9%
$200,000 or more	59.5%	33.5%
Median value	$248,171	$142,275
Rank if district were a state 4		

Units are owner-occupied one-family houses whose numbers are rounded to nearest thousand. Data are extrapolated from survey samples.
Source: U.S. Census Bureau, American Community Survey.

EDUCATION

Public school enrollment, 2002

Prekindergarten through grade 8
District enrollment. 59,000
Total U.S. enrollment. 34,135,000
District share of U.S. total 0.17%

Grades 9 through 12
District enrollment. 17,000
Total U.S. enrollment. 14,067,000
District share of U.S. total 0.12%

Enrollment rates
District public school enrollment rate 99.2%
Overall U.S. rate 90.4%
Rank if the district were a state in 2002. 1

Enrollment figures (which include unclassified students) are rounded to nearest thousand pupils during fall school term. Enrollment rates are based on enumerated resident population estimate for July 1, 2002.
Source: U.S. National Center for Education Statistics.

TRANSPORTATION AND TRAVEL

Highway mileage, 2003

Interstate highways 13
Other freeways and expressways 22
Arterial roads 264
Collector roads 152
Local roads 1,085

Total district mileage 1,536
U.S. total 3,974,107
District share 0.04%
Rank if the district were a state 51

Note that all district roads are regarded as urban.
Source: U.S. Federal Highway Administration.

Motor vehicle registrations and driver licenses, 2003

Vehicle registrations	District	U.S.	Share	Rank
Autos, trucks, buses	228,000	231,390,000	0.01%	51
Autos only	184,000	135,670	0.14%	51
Motorcycles	1,000	5,328,000	0.02%	51
Driver licenses	313,000	196,166,000	0.16%	51

Figures, which do not include vehicles owned by military services, are rounded to the nearest thousand. Figures for automobiles include taxis. Rank figures indicate where the district would rank if it were a state.
Source: U.S. Federal Highway Administration.

Domestic travel expenditures, 2003
Spending by U.S. residents on overnight trips and day trips of at least 50 miles from home

Total expenditures within district . . . . $4.28 bill.
Total expenditures within U.S. . . . . $490.87 bill.
State share of U.S. total 0.9%
Rank if the district were a state 33

Source: Travel Industry Association of America.

CRIME AND LAW ENFORCEMENT

Crime rates, 2003
Incidents per 100,000 residents

Crimes	District	U.S.
Violent crimes		
Total incidents	1,608	475
Murder	44	6
Forcible rape	49	32
Robbery	700	142
Aggravated assault	816	295
Property crimes		
Total incidents	5,800	3,588
Burglary	829	741
Larceny/theft	3,213	2,415
Motor vehicle theft	1,758	433
All crimes	7,408	4,063

Source: U.S. Federal Bureau of Investigation, *Crime in the United States*, annual.

District prison populations, 1990-2003

	District	U.S.	District share
1990	9,947	773,919	1.28%
2000	7,456	1,391,261	0.54%
2003	n/a	1,470,045	n/a

District figures include jail inmates but exclude prisoners in federal penitentiaries.
Source: U.S. Bureau of Justice Statistics, *Prisoners in 2003*.

Appendixes

Index to Appendixes

General Bibliography

This bibliography lists books containing material about a wide variety of topics pertaining to the states collectively. Additional sources on individual states can be found in the Notes for Further Study at the end of each chapter.

General References

Brockenhauer, Mark H., and Stephen F. Cunha. *National Geographic: Our Fifty States.* Washington, D.C.: National Geographic Society, 2004. This vibrant book designed for young adults takes readers on a state-by-state tour of America and covers such topics as each state's history, economic strengths, and other noteworthy facts.

Cheney, Lynne. *Our Fifty States: A Family Adventure Across America.* New York: Simon & Schuster, 2006. Illustrated guide to the states that discusses each state and the important people, ideas, and events that have shaped its history.

Davis, Kenneth C. *Don't Know Much About the Fifty States.* New York: HarperCollins Children's Books, 2004. Colorful and engaging book for young readers that is organized in question-and-answer format. Each state entry contains trivia, a map, a chart with basic facts, and photographs.

Fifer, Barbara. *Everyday Geography of the United States: The Essential Guide to the Fifty States.* New York: Black Dog and Leventhal, 2003. Colorful reference book packed with maps, quizzes, statistics, and trivia about each of the fifty states.

Forte, Imogene. *One Nation, Fifty States.* Rev. ed. Nashville, Tenn.: Incentive, 2002. Designed with teachers in mind, this book offers tips for content-based lessons, enrichment activities, and evaluation activities, all related to the fifty states.

Gutman, Bill. *The Look-It-Up Book of the Fifty States.* New York: Random House, 2002. Brings together historical, geographical, and miscellaneous information about each of the fifty states.

Howe, Randy. *Flags of the Fifty States and Their Incredible Histories: The Complete Guide to America's Most Powerful Symbols.* Guilford, Conn.: Lyons Press, 2002. Pictorial presentation of the state flags and the forces that came to bear on what was ultimately chosen to become each territory's emblem—politics, geography, economics, and conflicts of an era.

Nault, Jennifer. *Guide to American States: Fact Book.* New York: Weigl, 2002. Accessible book about the fifty states designed for a young-adult audience.

Ross, Wilma S. *Fabulous Facts About the Fifty States.* 4th rev. ed. New York: Scholastic, 1997. Written for a young-adult audience, this book includes maps and good basic information about each state.

Nation Building and Statehood

Conle, Patrick T., and John P. Kaminski, eds. *Bill of Rights and the States: The Colonial and Revolutionary Origins of American Liberties.* Madison, Wis.: Madison House, 1992. Fourteen individual state essays, three introductory essays, maps, and five dozen illustrations elucidate the early and complex struggles for statehood of the nation's first states. Also covers the local and regional interests that shaped the debate over individual rights and the eventual adoption of the Bill of Rights.

Edling, Max M. *A Revolution in Favor of Government: Origins of the U.S. Constitution and the Making of the American State.* New York: Oxford University Press, 2003. Fine study of the origins of nationhood and the roles that the newly formed states played in the process.

Isenberg, Alison. *Downtown America: A History of the Place and the People Who Made It.* Chicago: University of Chicago Press, 2004. Uses conference reports, maps, real estate appraisals, marketing studies, and federal guidelines to detail the rise and fall of American urban centers in several states and the efforts to reshape these areas in the late twentieth century. A good comparative study of American cities and state and local governments.

Laney, Garrine P. *Statehood Process of the Fifty States.* New York: Novinka Books, 2002. Traces the history of the statehood process and looks at how each of the fifty states came to join as one nation.

Perl, Lila. *It Happened in America: True Stories from the Fifty States.* New York: Henry Holt, 1996. Uses engaging historical anecdotes to instruct younger readers about states' pasts.

Shearer, Benjamin F. *Uniting States: The Story of Statehood for the Fifty United States.* Westport, Conn.: Greenwood Press, 2004. Fifty-one essays and more than ninety maps tell the story of how each of the fifty states in the Union became part of, and remained, one nation.

Whitehead, John S. *Completing the Union: Alaska, Hawaii, and the Battle for Statehood.* Albuquerque: University of New Mexico Press, 2004. Chronicles the thirteen-year process to admit Alaska and Hawaii to the union of states and argues that this lengthy struggle was caused by many of the events surrounding the Cold War.

Government and Politics

Dresang, Dennis L., and James J. Goslinghow. *Politics and Policy in American States and Communities.* 4th ed. New York: Pearson Longman, 2004. Examines how citizens of individual states are affected by decisions of governmental officials and, in turn, how they can influence public policy via partisan politics within state governments.

Gray, Virginia. *American States and Cities.* 2d ed. New York: Longman, 1997. Study of the role that modern-day state governments play in shaping the political life of the nation.

Gray, Virginia, Herbert Jacob, and Russell L. Hanson. *Politics in the American States: A Comparative Analysis.* 8th ed. Washington, D.C.: CQ Press, 2004. Introduces state politics in the United States, discusses the impact of initiatives and referenda on state politics, and analyzes parties and elections, utilizing results from the 2002 elections.

Harrison, Robert. *Congress, Progressive Reform, and the New American State.* New York: Cambridge University Press, 2004. Harrison uses case studies of reform legislation enacted by Congress during the early twentieth century to explore the nature of progressivism and the processes of political change that resulted in the establishment of the modern American states.

Hird, John A. *Power, Knowledge, and Politics: Policy Analysis in the States.* Washington, D.C.: Georgetown University Press, 2005. Examines the development and limitations of policy analysis within the states.

Jewell, Malcolm, and Sarah McCally-Morehouse. *Political Parties and Elections in American States.* 4th ed. Washington, D.C.: CQ Press, 2001. Provides cross-state data and case studies that place state political systems in a national context, an approach that allows readers to understand how and why parties differ across the country.

Kearney, Richard C., and Ann Bowman. *State and Local Government: The Essentials.* Boston: Houghton Mifflin, 2000. Discusses interrelationships between state and local governments, including the roles of state constitutions, citizen participation and elections, and political parties, interest groups, and campaigns.

Keefe, William J., and Morris S. Ogul. *American Legislative Process: Congress and the States.* 10th ed. Upper Saddle River, N.J.: Prentice Hall, 2001. Fourteen chapters provide excellent analysis of the legislative process at both the federal and state levels, discussing, for example, legislatures and legislators in the political system, the legislative structure for decision making, and state interaction with the executive and the courts.

Kemp, Roger L., ed. *How American Governments Work: A Handbook of City, County, Regional, State, and Federal Operations.* Jefferson, N.C.: McFarland, 2002. Divided into two parts, this book first examines the status of American cities in the twenty-first century and their relationships with county governments. The second part examines connections among regional, state, and federal governments.

Krane, Dale, Platon N. Rigos, and Melvin Hill. *Home Rule in America: A Fifty State Handbook.* Washington, D.C.: CQ Press, 2000. In this volume, an expert from each state describes how the concept of home rule manifests there, considering what actions local governments can and cannot pursue; the degree to which power is centralized at the state capital; how home rule varies according to government function; and the impact on such issues as taxes, land annexation, and citizen access.

Mladenka, Kenneth R., and Kim Quaile Hill. *Democratic Governance in American States and Cities.* 2d ed. Belmont, Calif.: Wadsworth, 1996. Examines the interplay between local and state governments.

Shefter, Martin. *Political Parties and the State: The American Historical Experience.* Princeton, N.J.: Princeton University Press, 1994. Collection of articles by Shefter examines the emergence of strong political parties and the changing balance among parties and bureaucracies within states across America.

Smith, Kevin B., et al. *Governing States and Localities.* Washington, D.C.: CQ Press, 2005. Discusses a wide array of topics regarding state governments, including the way in which federalism operates, state constitutions, political culture and participation, the court system, and education, health, and safety agencies in individual states.

Teaford, Jon C. *Rise of the States: Evolution of American State Government.* Baltimore: Johns Hopkins University Press, 2002. A noted urban historian, Teaford studies the development of state government in the United States from the end of the nineteenth century to the end of the twentieth century. He argues that states continually adapted and expanded throughout the past century and actively assumed new responsibilities, developed new sources of revenue, and created new institutions.

Wilkinson, Herbert A. *The American Doctrine of State Succession.* 1934. Reprint. Westport, Conn.: Greenwood Press, 1975. Classic study that evaluates state succession as it affects public law and government, private law and private rights, nationality, public debts and financial obligations, and treaties.

Contemporary Issues

Cleary, Edward L., and Allen D. Hertzke, eds. *Representing God at the Statehouse: Religion and Politics in the American States.* Lanham, Md.: Rowman & Littlefield, 2006. Nine essays offer a comparative view of religion and politics at the state government level.

Fisher, Peter S., and Alan H. Peters. *Industrial Incentives: Competition Among American Cities and States.* Kalamazoo, Mich.: W. E. Upjohn Institute for Employment Research, 1998. Carefully researched book that explores how economic development incentives vary across different types of firms and across states.

Hansen, Susan B. *Globalization and the Politics of Pay: Policy Choices in the American States.* Washington, D.C.: Georgetown University Press, 2006. Explores how the states have responded to the increasing pressure to cut labor costs in an integrated global economy.

Heller, Donald E., ed. *The States and Public Higher Education Policy: Affordability, Access, and Accountability.* Baltimore: Johns Hopkins University Press, 2001. Good comparative analyses that address the access, affordability, and accountability in higher education across the states.

Segers, Mary C., and Timothy A. Byrnes, eds. *Abortion Politics in American States.* Armonk, N.Y.: M. E. Sharpe, 1995. One dozen case studies examine the abortion issue at the state government level, describing how the political, religious, and institutional conditions shape how the debate is conducted in specific states and its results through the mid-1990's.

Smith, Jonathan E., and John A. Agnew, eds. *American Space/American Place: Geographies of the Contemporary United States.* New York: Routledge, 2002. Unique study that compares the American ideal of liberty, equality, individual opportunity, and social improvement with the contemporary conditions of the regions, states, and localities. The authors examine factors within states such as education, health, welfare, economic and industrial development, and race, gender, and class relations.

Vale, Thomas. *The American Wilderness: Reflections on Nature Protection in the United States.* Charlottesville: University of Virginia Press, 2005. Analyzes efforts across the nation's states to protect nature, focusing on varying meanings of wilderness and nature, the national park system, outdoor recreation, and conservation organizations, among other topics.

Regional and Travel Studies

Allen, Barbara, and Thomas J. Schlereth, eds. *Sense of Place: American Regional Cultures.* Lexington: University Press of Kentucky, 1990. One dozen essays by folklorists explore legends, anecdotes, songs, food, architecture, and crafts from a wide range of locales within the American states.

America's Historic Sites. 3 vols. Pasadena, Calif.: Salem Press, 2000. Well-illustrated state-by-state survey of important historic sites that provides a wealth of detailed information on each place. Coverage encompasses the District of Columbia.

Biggers, Shirley Hoover. *American Author Houses, Museums, Memorials, and Libraries: A State-by-State Guide.* Jefferson, N.C.: McFarland, 2000. Thorough travel guide that provides information on the sites throughout the country at which authors are commemorated—museums, library collections, grave sites, memorial walks, and monuments.

Cayton, Andrew R., and Susan E. Gray, eds. *American Midwest: Essays in Regional History.* Bloomington: Indiana University Press, 2001. Experts on various aspects of midwestern history consider the question of regional identity as a useful way of thinking about the history of the American Midwest.

Colombo, Marcella. *American Southwest: Places and History.* New York: Stewart, Tabori & Chang, 1998. Stunning photographs and engaging text characterize this region's history and cultural attractions.

Dregni, Eric. *Midwest Marvels: Roadside Attractions Across Iowa, Minnesota, the Dakotas, and Wisconsin.* Minneapolis: University of Minnesota Press, 2006. Engaging travel guide that emphasizes the region's quirky and distinct roadside sculptures, monuments, and replicas, allowing readers to gain a unique sense of the area's history.

Evans, Sterling, ed. *The Borderlands of the American and Canadian Wests: Essays on Regional History of the Forty-Ninth Parallel.* Lincoln: University of Nebraska Press, 2006. Examines the social conditions, history, group identity, and formation of regionalism along the northern borders of the United States.

Feintuch, Burt, and David H. Watters, eds. *The Encyclopedia of New England: The Culture and History of an American Region.* New Haven, Conn.: Yale University Press, 2005. Collection of essays discussing the history and culture of New England.

Ferris, William, ed. *The Greenwood Encyclopedia of American Regional Cultures.* 8 vols. Westport, Conn.: Greenwood Press, 2004. This multivolume set examines the social life and customs, history, and civilization of the major regions of the country, including the Great Plains, the Pacific Northwest, the Mid-Atlantic, and the Rocky Mountains.

Gelbert, Doug. *American Revolutionary War Sites, Memorials, Museums, and Library Collections: A State-by-State Guidebook to Places Open to the Public.* Jefferson, N.C.: McFarland, 1998. Thorough guide to the places that shaped the outcome of the Civil War throughout several American states.

Hauck, Eldon. *American Capitols: An Encyclopedia of the State, National, and Territorial Capital Edifices of the United States.* Jefferson, N.C.: McFarland, 2004. Provides detailed historical profiles of the capitol buildings of every state, the federal government in Washington, D.C., and those of American Samoa, Guam, the Northern Mariana Islands, Puerto Rico, and the Virgin Islands. State entries average four to six pages each, are arranged alphabetically, and include a wealth of fascinating historical trivia.

Jensen, Jamie. *Road Trip USA: Cross-Country Adventures on America's Two-Lane Highways.* 3d ed. New York: Avalon Travel, 2006. Unique travel guide that emphasizes alternative routes through the American states, providing mile-by-mile highlights about obscure towns, roadside curiosities, and local lore.

Jordan-Bychkov, Terry G. *The Upland South: The Making of an American Folk Region and Landscape.* Santa Fe, N.Mex.: Center for American Places, 2003. Describes the region that runs from Virginia and North Carolina west through Kentucky, Tennessee, Arkansas, Oklahoma, Texas, and their bordering states. A geographer, Jordan-Bychkov explores the region's character through an analysis of its traditional cultural landscape.

Kaiser, Harvey H. *An Architectural Guidebook to the National Parks: The Southwest—Arizona, New Mexico, Texas.* Layton, Utah: Gibbs Smith, 2003. Tours historic structures of America's national parks, focusing on the historical significance, natural beauty, and important events related to each building.

Monmonier, Mark. *From Squaw Tit to Whorehouse Meadow: How Maps Name, Claim, and Inflame.* Chicago: University of Chicago Press, 2006. Examination of cartographic history from the early twentieth century, when mapmakers created salacious, bawdy, and even derogatory place names. Monmonier discusses efforts of modern cartographers to reconcile these names with cultural sensitivity, providing readers with fascinating insight into the history of place names across the American states.

Pomeroy, Earl. *The Pacific Slope: A History of California, Oregon, Washington, Idaho, Utah, and Nevada.* Reno: University of Nevada Press, 2003. Synthesizes the history of six western states by examining the historical forces that created them.

Schwantes, Carlos Arnaldo. *Pacific Northwest: An Interpretive History.* Rev. ed. Lincoln: University of Nebraska Press, 1996. Comprehensive view of the Pacific Northwest's collective history; the revised edition has new sections on early mining in the Pacific Northwest, sea routes to Oregon in the early discovery and contact period, the environment of the region, and politics since 1945.

Williams, John Alexander. *Appalachia: A History.* Chapel Hill: University of North Carolina Press, 2002. Brings together a discussion of the region's social, political, environmental, economic, and popular history over the span of four and one-half centuries.

Statistics

Farley, Reynolds, and John Haaga, eds. *The American People: Census 2000.* New York: Russell Sage Foundation, 2005. Presents and evaluates numerous socioeconomic trends derived from the 2000 U.S. Census.

Health United States 2005: Chartbook on Trends in the Health of Americans. Hyattsville, Md.: Department of Health and Human Services, Centers for Disease Control and Prevention, National Center for Health Statistics, 2006. Provides a range of health status indicators for all fifty states.

Morgan, Kathleen O'Leary, and Scott Morgan, eds. *Crime State Rankings 2006: Crime in the Fifty United States.* 13th ed. Lawrence, Kans.: Morgan Quitno Press, 2006. Comparative look at the ways in which state residents are impacted by crime and how local and state governments deal with it.

_____. *Education State Rankings 2002-2003: Pre K-12 Education in the United States.* Lawrence, Kans.: Morgan Quitno Press, 2002. Evaluates public education across the states using statistical and comparative data.

_____. *Health Care State Rankings 2005: Health Care in the Fifty United States.* Lawrence, Kans: Morgan Quitno Press, 2002. Five hundred tables compare health care statistics from state to state alphabetically and by order in rank, covering a wide range of topics such as births and reproductive health, deaths by various causes, rates of incidence of disease, and issues of physical fitness.

_____. *State Trends: Measuring Change in the Fifty United States.* Lawrence, Kans.: Morgan Quitno Press, 2005. Uses statistical data to compare sectors related to economic conditions, medical care, public welfare, and higher education, among others, across the states.

New Strategist Publications, eds. *Access to Poverty in the United States.* Ithaca, N.Y.: New Strategist, 2003. Provides comparative, state-by-state information derived from the 2002 Current Population Survey on the Poverty Status, Health Insurance Coverage, and Pension Plan Participation of Americans.

_____. *Americans and Their Homes: Demographics of Homeownership.* Ithaca, N.Y.: New Strategist, 2005. Brings together state-by-state data published in the U.S. Census Bureau's 2003 American Housing Survey and puts it in the context of trends since 1990, including regional variations, household income, and buying behavior.

Slater, Courtenay, and Martha G. Davis. *State Profiles: The Population and Economy of Each U.S. State.* 3d ed. Lanham, Md.: Bernan Press, 2006. Each state is covered by a succinct, standardized chapter that allows for easy data comparisons between states and with national and regional averages.

Sperling, Bert, and Peter Sander. *Cities Ranked and Rated: More than Four Hundred Metropolitan Areas Evaluated in the U.S. and Canada.* Hoboken, N.J.: Wiley, 2004. Considers individual cities' rankings in measures such as population, economy and jobs, cost of living, climate, education, and crime. The discussion allows readers to gain a better understanding of state, regional, and local governments' priorities, strengths, and weaknesses and provides insight into local and state government policy making.

Strawser, Cornelia J., ed. *Business Statistics of the United States: Patterns of Economic Change.* 10th ed. Lanham, Md.: Bernan Press, 2005. Good overall view of the economic conditions within America, both nationally and by state. The book is arranged in four parts covering the U.S. economy, industry profiles, historical data, and regional and state data.

U.S. Census Bureau. *Statistical Abstract of the United States*. Washington, D.C.: U.S. Department of Commerce, Economics, and Statistics Administration, U.S. Census Bureau, 2005. The standard statistical source for a range of data about the population of the United States. Most of this data is also available on the Census Bureau's Web site.

Sarah Hilbert

Guide to Web Resources

Finding information about the states online is straightforward and facile, thanks to the ease of using search engines such as google.com, yahoo.com, altavista.com, excite.com, and ask.com. Search engines are huge indexes that attempt to include every word from every page of the entire World Wide Web in their databases. Basic facts about the fifty states are readily available; one may simply type the name of any given state into a search engine to begin. Often, the state's official government and tourist sites will be among the first "hits" search engines will find. Following links from such pages will launch a fruitful search process. However, because there is so much information available on the Web, search results using names of states or general terms may amount to literally thousands of hits, making it necessary to develop strategies to separate the wheat from the chaff. The various online search engines organize their databases in subtly distinct ways, so it is important that users consult several different search engines when attempting to find information.

At the end of each state history essay in *The 50 States*, readers will find several general Web URLs listed for that particular state. This appendix is centered on ways in which Internet users can find worthwhile Web sites that speak in some way to the states as a whole, while also offering them the choice to "drill down" and find information on individual states.

Search Techniques

Those looking for more in-depth and meaningful information on the states need to refine their search strategies. Users generally can find solid information by searching on refined and very narrow search terms or by searching on phrases, using reputable, well-organized sites that are "deep" in their content. Well-honed search terms provide Internet users with specific, targeted content. For example, instead of searching on "Colorado" or "Colorado history," one might search on "Colorado gold rush," "Colorado pioneers," or "Colorado Chicano civil rights."

The narrower the search phrase, the more targeted the results. If one wants a search engine to find hits based exactly on both the terms and the word order of terms used, it is necessary to place quotation marks around the search terms. Users can also consider regions of the United States, such as the Pacific Northwest, Great Plains, or the Mid-Atlantic states; typing these terms paired with words such as "agriculture," "economic growth," or "cultural history" to produce relevant hits.

For those with a bit more time, perhaps one of the most interesting ways to search the Internet is to start with a reputable, well-organized site and allow some time for "wandering" within the site, following internal links to deeper content housed therein. Moreover, these kinds of sites often provide well-considered and researched external links that will take users to other, equally valuable Web sites. The process of good Web searching is an exploratory one that can produce exponential results if approached correctly.

Reputable Web destinations and those that change least frequently are typically hosted by government and academic institutions. Many commercial and personal sites are also suitable resources for research. The URL can tell users about the nature of the Web site. Personal pages often contain the names of Web sites' hosts, and domain names usually indicate the sites' origins. The URLs of U.S. government sites contain *.gov*, *.mil*, or *.us*. URLs of educational sites contain *.edu*; nonprofits carry the *.org* domain. For more information about searching the Web and evaluating Web sites, consult Tilburg University's very informative online tutorial (www.tilburguniversity.nl/services/library/instruction/www/onlinecourse/).

Exploring Online Content

The following discussions of three content-rich sites will demonstrate the potential of doing online research on the states.

Library of Congress (www.loc.gov/index.html) is an excellent, well-organized Internet destination, that, given competent navigation of the site, will present users with links to the library's vast and thoroughly interesting collections, many of which speak directly to American states' culture, statehood, and history. On the site's home page, users should head first for the Kids and Families section; there, one will find the library's American Memory collection (memory.loc.gov/ammem/index.html), which is organized by topics, many of which are directly related to the fifty states, including Cities and Towns, African American History, Women's History, Architecture and Landscape, and Immigration and American Expansion. Upon selecting one of these topics, users will find a substantial listing of various photographs, multimedia resources, personal narratives, and historic ephemera that one can peruse online.

The Library of Congress also presents its America's Story from America's Library section (www.americaslibrary.gov/cgi-bin/page.cgi), designed for children and young adults. Users can choose the Explore the States section and use games, trivia, and articles to learn all about any state's history, culture, government, and modern life. Finally, The Local Legacies section (www.loc.gov/folklife/roots/ac-home.html) is a great place to learn more about the country's diverse culture state by state. Users can choose any state from the U.S. map and gain access to lists of links for state fairs, cultural institutions, local museums, and leisure activities.

The National Archives or **NARA** (www.archives.gov/) preserves a portion of all documents and materials created in the course of business conducted by the United States federal government. These records prove important for Internet users who are conducting a search on any topic relating to state or national government or history and want to find letters, reports, notes, memos, photographs, and other primary sources. Be aware that the full breadth of the archives' collection is accessible only by making a visit to local NARA agencies (see www.archives.gov/locations/). However, the Web site does maintain a well-organized Archives Research Catalog (www.archives.gov/research/arc/), which allows users to find many historical documents and photographs pertaining to the states. Visiting the Search Hints page (www.archives.gov/research/arc/topics/) will present one with a list of topics on what research can be conducted online.

Cable television's **History Channel** (www.historychannel.com/) has a wide range of information about historical events and figures from around the world, but users can quickly narrow down their search for historical information on American states by using the site's search function, which is found on every page of the site in the upper-left-hand corner. A simple search on "California," for example, will yield a lengthy page that includes a table of the state's basic factual information and short essays about its land and resources, climate information, population, education, cultural life, economy, and history. One will also see a television listing of programs on the History Channel that pertain to that particular state. Users can also type the name of an American region into the search box. A search on "American Southwest," for example, yielded links to pages about American Indian Languages, Art, and Architecture, as well as sections that explore the region's historic ties to Latin America.

The site also has a comprehensive map section on North America (www.historychannel.com/maps/category.jsp?cat=14585826), in which users can select a state (organized by letter breaks) and be presented with a number of links that detail many facets of the states' histories. The site's Speeches and Videos section (www.historychannel.com/broadband/home/) offers, by selecting North America as a search parameter, a comprehensive collection of audiovisual clips on American states' history.

Web Resources

The following sites are worthwhile, content-rich sites on which users will be able to spend some time finding information about the states.

- **The U.S. Census Bureau** provides the QuickFacts section (quickfacts.census.gov/qfd/), which allows users to select any state and find a range of statistical information about the state's demographics. On each state page, users can use drop-down menus to select any county in the state, or any city or town with more than twenty-five thousand people, and see comparable statistics for these particular locales. The bureau's FactFinder page (factfinder.census.gov/home/saff/main.html?_lang=en) is also helpful.

- **FirstGov.gov** (www.firstgov.gov/) serves as the U.S. government's official Web portal for information pertaining to national and state government. On the home page, users can select from the categories listed across the top; most will likely find the greatest amount of useful information on the category titled For Citizens. Users can also select from the left-hand navigational column information on federal, state, local, and tribal governments; an A-Z government agency index; data and statistics; and contact information for national, state, and local government offices.

- **World Atlas.com** has a section of its colorful, engaging Web site devoted to the United States (worldatlas.com/webimage/countrys/namerica/us.htm). Users can select any one of links for the fifty states; this leads to an individual state page, which gives a brief overview of the state's history and provides links for Famous Natives, Fast Facts, Flag and Symbols, Landforms, Land Statistics, Maps, Time Line of History, Weather, and Further Links.

- **State and Local Government on the Net** (www.statelocalgov.net/) serves as a portal site for the Web sites of thousands of state agencies and city and county governments. Drop-down menus on the home page's left-hand side allow users to select by state, topic, or local government.

- **Fed Stats** (www.fedstats.gov/) serves as a gateway to statistics about the fifty states from more than one hundred federal agencies. Users have two options to search the site via drop-down menus: by state or by agencies by subject. The site also has topics lists, map statistics, and a listing of kids' pages on government agencies Web sites.

- **Kaiser Family Foundation State Health Facts.org** (www.statehealthfacts.kff.org/cgi-bin/healthfacts.cgi) is a thorough and often-updated site which provides both cross-state comparisons of data on various health-related topics and individual state profiles from its home page.

- **GeoData.gov** (gos2.geodata.gov/wps/portal/gos) is a fascinating Web site that allows users to use maps and geographic data for state research. Fire mapping, the journey of Meriwether Lewis and William Clark, and state recreational sites are some of the special interest maps available from the home page; choosing from Data Categories such as agriculture, biology and ecology, and transportation networks will yield users statistical state data and maps related to the category. State and city maps are also available.

- **State Capitals Newsletters** (statecapitals.com/) allows users to track upcoming legislation in states across the country. Each of these weekly newsletters focuses on one legislative or regulatory topic in order to give a national perspective on state lawmaking. Topics include Lottery and Casino Regulation, Public Health, Response to Terrorism, and Gay Rights, among countless others. The Subject Index statecapitals.com/subjectindex.html) is perhaps the best place to start one's search.

- **HelloMetro.com** (www.hellometro.com/) allows users to access local city guides for large U.S. cities. The city sites provide information on local businesses, movie show times, local music bands and artists, and classifieds. Each city page also has a brief article on the city's history and its facts and places.

- **Public Broadcasting System American Experience** (www.pbs.org/wgbh/amex/) is the companion Web site to the network's acclaimed television series that focuses on American history and culture; programs are often about individual states, cities, or regions. The site offers users the means to do additional research on televised programs. By visiting the Archives section (www.pbs.org/wgbh/amex/archives .html), users will find a list of topics organized by theme, alphabet, and chronology. The Special Features section provides links to maps, quizzes, and photographic galleries.

- **Access Genealogy Native American Indian Genealogy** (www.accessgenealogy.com/native/) allows users to select a state and then follow the link to a page that describes the state's tribes—organized by linguistics and geography—and their histories and current populations.

- **American Local History Network** (www.alhn.org/) is a nonprofit organization that operates as a portal site for a number of independent historical and genealogical Web sites, all of which are organized by state or by topic. This is an excellent starting place for online researchers on state history and historical state residents.

Sarah Hilbert

Order in Which the States Entered the Union

Rank	State	Entered Union
1	Delaware	December 7, 1787
2	Pennsylvania	December 12, 1787
3	New Jersey	December 18, 1787
4	Georgia	January 2, 1788
5	Connecticut	January 9, 1788
6	Massachusetts	February 6, 1788
7	Maryland	April 28, 1788
8	South Carolina	May 23, 1788
9	New Hampshire	June 21, 1788
10	Virginia	June 25, 1788
11	New York	July 26, 1788
12	North Carolina	November 21, 1789
13	Rhode Island	May 29, 1790
14	Vermont	March 4, 1791
15	Kentucky	June 1, 1792
16	Tennessee	June 1, 1796
17	Ohio	March 1, 1803
18	Louisiana	April 30, 1812
19	Indiana	December 11, 1816
20	Mississippi	December 10, 1817
21	Illinois	December 3, 1818
22	Alabama	December 14, 1819
23	Maine	March 15, 1820
24	Missouri	August 10, 1821
25	Arkansas	June 15, 1836
26	Michigan	January 26, 1837
27	Florida	March 3, 1845
28	Texas	December 29, 1845
29	Iowa	December 28, 1846
30	Wisconsin	May 29, 1848
31	California	September 9, 1850
32	Minnesota	May 11, 1858
33	Oregon	February 14, 1859
34	Kansas	January 29, 1861
35	West Virginia	June 20, 1863
36	Nevada	October 31, 1864
37	Nebraska	March 1, 1867
38	Colorado	August 1, 1876
39	North Dakota	November 2, 1889
40	South Dakota	November 2, 1889
41	Montana	November 8, 1889
42	Washington	November 11, 1889
43	Idaho	July 3, 1890
44	Wyoming	July 10, 1890
45	Utah	January 4, 1896
46	Oklahoma	November 16, 1907
47	New Mexico	January 6, 1912
48	Arizona	February 14, 1912
49	Alaska	January 3, 1959
50	Hawaii	August 21, 1959

States Ranked by Area
In square miles

Rank	State	Land area	Including water	Rank	State	Land area	Including water
1	Alaska	570,374	656,424	29	New Carolina	48,718	53,821
2	Texas	261,914	268,601	30	New York	47,224	54,475
3	California	155,973	163,707	31	Mississippi	46,914	48,434
4	Montana	145,556	147,046	32	Pennsylvania	44,820	46,058
5	New Mexico	121,365	121,598	33	Louisiana	43,566	51,843
6	Arizona	114,000	114,006	34	Tennessee	41,220	42,146
7	Nevada	109,806	110,567	35	Ohio	40,953	44,828
8	Colorado	103,730	104,100	36	Kentucky	39,732	40,411
9	Wyoming	97,105	97,818	37	Virginia	39,598	42,769
10	Oregon	96,003	98,386	38	Indiana	35,870	36,420
11	Idaho	82,751	83,574	39	Maine	30,865	35,387
12	Utah	82,168	84,904	40	South Carolina	30,111	32,007
13	Kansas	81,823	82,282	41	West Virginia	24,087	24,231
14	Minnesota	79,617	86,943	42	Maryland	9,775	12,407
15	Nebraska	76,644	77,358	43	Vermont	9,249	9,615
16	South Dakota	75,898	77,121	44	New Hampshire	8,969	9,351
17	North Dakota	68,994	70,704	45	Massachusetts	7,838	10,555
18	Missouri	68,898	69,709	46	New Jersey	7,419	8,722
19	Oklahoma	68,679	69,903	47	Hawaii	6,423	10,932
20	Washington	66,582	71,303	48	Connecticut	4,845	5,544
21	Michigan	58,110	96,810	49	Delaware	1,982	2,489
22	Georgia	57,919	59,441	50	Rhode Island	1,045	1,545
23	Iowa	55,875	56,276	(51)	District of Columbia	61.4	68.3
24	Illinois	55,593	57,918				
25	Wisconsin	54,314	65,503				
26	Florida	53,997	65,758				
27	Arkansas	52,075	53,182				
28	Alabama	50,750	52,423				

States are ranked by their land surfaces; ranking number for the District of Columbia shows what its position would be if it were a state.

Source: U.S. Bureau of the Census.

100 Largest U.S. Cities in the 2000 Census

Rank	City	State	Population	Rank	City	State	Population
1	New York	New York	8,008,278	52	Santa Ana	California	337,977
2	Los Angeles	California	3,694,820	53	Pittsburgh	Pennsylvania	334,563
3	Chicago	Illinois	2,896,016	54	Arlington	Texas	332,969
4	Houston	Texas	1,953,631	55	Cincinnati	Ohio	331,285
5	Philadelphia	Pennsylvania	1,517,550	56	Anaheim	California	328,014
6	Phoenix	Arizona	1,321,045	57	Islip	New York	322,612
7	San Diego	California	1,223,400	58	Toledo	Ohio	313,619
8	Dallas	Texas	1,188,580	59	Tampa	Florida	303,447
9	San Antonio	Texas	1,144,646	60	Oyster Bay	New York	293,925
10	Detroit	Michigan	951,270	61	Buffalo	New York	292,648
11	San Jose	California	894,943	62	St. Paul	Minnesota	287,151
12	Indianapolis	Indiana	781,870	63	Corpus Christi	Texas	277,454
13	San Francisco	California	776,733	64	Aurora	Colorado	276,393
14	Hempstead	New York	755,924	65	Raleigh	North Carolina	276,093
15	Jacksonville	Florida	735,617	66	Newark	New Jersey	273,546
16	Columbus	Ohio	711,470	67	Lexington-Fayette	Kentucky	260,512
17	Austin	Texas	656,562	68	Anchorage	Alaska	260,283
18	Baltimore	Maryland	651,154	69	Louisville	Kentucky	256,231
19	Memphis	Tennessee	650,100	70	Riverside	California	255,166
20	Milwaukee	Wisconsin	596,974	71	St. Petersburg	Florida	248,232
21	Boston	Massachusetts	589,141	72	Bakersfield	California	247,057
22	El Paso	Texas	563,662	73	Stockton	California	243,771
23	Seattle	Washington	563,374	74	Birmingham	Alabama	242,820
24	Denver	Colorado	554,636	75	Jersey City	New Jersey	240,055
25	Nashville-Davidson	Tennessee	545,524	76	Norfolk	Virginia	234,403
26	Charlotte	North Carolina	540,828	77	Baton Rouge	Louisiana	227,818
27	Fort Worth	Texas	534,694	78	Hialeah	Florida	226,419
28	Portland	Oregon	529,121	79	Lincoln	Nebraska	225,581
29	Oklahoma City	Oklahoma	506,132	80	Greensboro	North Carolina	223,891
30	Tucson	Arizona	486,699	81	North Hempstead	New York	222,611
31	New Orleans	Louisiana	484,674	82	Plano	Texas	222,030
32	Las Vegas	Nevada	478,434	83	Rochester	New York	219,773
33	Cleveland	Ohio	478,403	84	Glendale	Arizona	218,812
34	Long Beach	California	461,522	85	Akron	Ohio	217,074
35	Albuquerque	New Mexico	448,607	86	Garland	Texas	215,768
36	Brookhaven	New York	448,248	87	Babylon	New York	211,792
37	Kansas City	Missouri	441,545	88	Madison	Wisconsin	208,054
38	Fresno	California	427,652	89	Fort Wayne	Indiana	205,727
39	Virginia Beach	Virginia	425,257	90	Fremont	California	203,413
40	Atlanta	Georgia	416,474	91	Scottsdale	Arizona	202,705
41	Sacramento	California	407,018	92	Montgomery	Alabama	201,568
42	Oakland	California	399,484	93	Shreveport	Louisiana	200,145
43	Mesa	Arizona	396,375	94	Lubbock	Texas	199,564
44	Tulsa	Oklahoma	393,049	95	Chesapeake	Virginia	199,184
45	Omaha	Nebraska	390,007	96	Mobile	Alabama	198,915
46	Minneapolis	Minnesota	382,618	97	Des Moines	Iowa	198,682
47	Honolulu	Hawaii	371,657	98	Grand Rapids	Michigan	197,800
48	Miami	Florida	362,470	99	Richmond	Virginia	197,790
49	Colorado Springs	Colorado	360,890	100	Yonkers	New York	196,086
50	St. Louis	Missouri	348,189				
51	Wichita	Kansas	344,284				

Source: U.S. Census Bureau.

100 Largest U.S. Counties by Area

Rank	County	State	Sq. miles	Rank	County	State	Sq. miles
1	Yukon-Koyukuk (c)	Alaska	157,121	53	Kodiak Island (b)	Alaska	6,463
2	North Slope (b)	Alaska	87,861	54	Washoe	Nevada	6,343
3	Bethel (c)	Alaska	40,633	55	Siskiyou	California	6,287
4	Valdez-Cordova (c)	Alaska	36,945	56	St. Louis	Minnesota	6,226
5	Northwest Arctic (b)	Alaska	35,863	57	Brewster	Texas	6,193
6	Kings	New York	26,796	58	Cochise	Arizona	6,170
7	Southeast Fairbanks (c)	Alaska	25,994	59	Chaves	New Mexico	6,071
8	Matanuska-Susitna (b)	Alaska	24,694	60	Pershing	Nevada	6,009
9	Lake and Peninsula (b)	Alaska	23,632	61	Fresno	California	5,963
10	Nome (c)	Alaska	23,001	62	Cherry	Nebraska	5,961
11	San Bernardino	California	20,062	63	Klamath	Oregon	5,945
12	Dillingham (c)	Alaska	18,675	64	Rio Arriba	New Mexico	5,858
13	Coconino	Arizona	18,619	65	Wrangell-Petersburg (c)	Alaska	5,808
14	Nye	Nevada	18,147	66	Box Elder	Utah	5,724
15	Elko	Nevada	17,182	67	Beaverhead	Montana	5,543
16	Wade Hampton (c)	Alaska	17,124	68	San Juan	New Mexico	5,514
17	Kenai Peninsula (b)	Alaska	16,079		Yuma	Arizona	5,514
18	Mohave	Arizona	13,312	70	Lander	Nevada	5,494
19	Skagway-Hoonah-Angoon (c)	Alaska	12,881	71	McKinley	New Mexico	5,449
20	Denali (b)	Alaska	12,750	72	Pinal	Arizona	5,370
21	Apache	Arizona	11,206	73	Natrona	Wyoming	5,340
22	Lincoln	Nevada	10,635	74	Okanogan	Washington	5,268
23	Sweetwater	Wyoming	10,426	75	Garfield	Utah	5,175
24	Inyo	California	10,192	76	Phillips	Montana	5,140
25	Harney	Oregon	10,135	77	Flathead	Montana	5,099
26	Navajo	Arizona	9,954	78	Douglas	Oregon	5,037
27	Malheur	Oregon	9,888	79	Rosebud	Montana	5,012
28	Humboldt	Nevada	9,648	80	Big Horn	Montana	4,995
29	Maricopa	Arizona	9,204	81	Churchill	Nevada	4,929
30	Pima	Arizona	9,187	82	Custer	Idaho	4,926
31	Fremont	Wyoming	9,183	83	Valley	Montana	4,921
32	White Pine	Nevada	8,877	84	Sublette	Wyoming	4,882
33	Idaho	Idaho	8,485	85	Lincoln	New Mexico	4,831
34	Kern	California	8,142	86	Tulare	California	4,824
35	Lake	Oregon	8,136	87	Campbell	Wyoming	4,797
36	Yavapai	Arizona	8,124	88	Las Animas	Colorado	4,773
37	Clark	Nevada	7,911	89	Gila	Arizona	4,768
38	Carbon	Wyoming	7,897	90	Pecos	Texas	4,764
39	San Juan	Utah	7,821	91	Moffat	Colorado	4,743
40	Owyhee	Idaho	7,678	92	San Miguel	New Mexico	4,717
41	Yakutat City (b)	Alaska	7,650	93	Garfield	Montana	4,668
42	Fairbanks North Star (b)	Alaska	7,362	94	Graham	Arizona	4,630
43	Prince of Wales-Outer Ketchikan (c)	Alaska	7,324	95	Hudspeth	Texas	4,571
				96	Lemhi	Idaho	4,564
44	Riverside	California	7,208	97	Lassen	California	4,558
45	Aleutians East (b)	Alaska	6,985	98	Lane	Oregon	4,554
46	Tooele	Utah	6,946	99	Cibola	New Mexico	4,540
47	Park	Wyoming	6,943	100	Grant	Oregon	4,529
48	Catron	New Mexico	6,928				
49	Aroostook	Maine	6,672				
50	Socorro	New Mexico	6,647				
51	Otero	New Mexico	6,627				
52	Millard	Utah	6,590				

(b) = Alaska borough county; (c) = census area county. Figures for areas are rounded to nearest square mile.

Source: U.S. Census Bureau; National Association of Counties.

State Population Ranks, 1980-2004

State	Rank				Percent change in population		
	1980	1990	2000	2004	1980-1990	1990-2000	2000-2004
Alabama	22	22	23	23	3.8	10.1	1.9
Alaska	50	49	48	47	36.9	14.0	4.5
Arizona	29	24	20	18	34.8	40.0	12.0
Arkansas	33	33	33	32	2.8	13.7	3.0
California	1	1	1	1	26.0	13.6	6.0
Colorado	28	26	24	22	14.0	30.6	7.0
Connecticut	25	27	29	29	5.8	3.6	2.9
Delaware	47	46	45	45	12.1	17.6	6.0
Florida	7	4	4	4	32.7	23.5	8.8
Georgia	13	11	10	9	18.6	26.4	7.8
Hawaii	39	41	42	42	14.9	9.3	4.2
Idaho	41	42	39	39	6.7	28.5	7.7
Illinois	5	6	5	5	*	8.7	2.4
Indiana	12	14	14	14	1.0	9.7	2.6
Iowa	27	30	30	30	4.7	5.4	1.0
Kansas	32	32	32	33	4.8	8.5	1.7
Kentucky	23	23	25	26	0.7	9.6	2.6
Louisiana	19	21	22	24	0.4	5.9	1.0
Maine	38	38	40	40	9.2	3.8	3.3
Maryland	18	19	19	19	13.4	10.8	4.9
Massachusetts	11	13	13	13	4.9	5.5	1.1
Michigan	8	8	8	8	0.4	6.9	1.8
Minnesota	21	20	21	21	7.4	12.4	3.7
Mississippi	31	31	31	31	2.2	10.5	2.0
Missouri	15	15	17	17	4.1	9.4	2.8
Montana	44	44	44	44	1.6	12.9	2.7
Nebraska	35	36	38	38	0.5	8.4	2.1
Nevada	43	39	35	35	50.1	66.3	16.8
New Hampshire	42	40	41	41	20.5	11.4	5.2
New Jersey	9	9	9	10	5.2	8.6	3.4
New Mexico	37	37	36	36	16.3	20.1	4.6
New York	2	2	3	3	2.5	5.5	1.3
North Carolina	10	10	11	11	12.8	21.3	6.1
North Dakota	46	47	47	48	-2.1	0.5	-1.2
Ohio	6	7	7	7	0.5	4.7	0.9
Oklahoma	26	28	27	28	4.0	9.7	2.1
Oregon	30	29	28	27	7.9	20.4	5.1
Pennsylvania	4	5	6	6	0.2	3.4	1.0
Rhode Island	40	43	43	43	5.9	4.5	3.1
South Carolina	24	25	26	25	11.7	15.1	4.6
South Dakota	45	45	46	46	0.8	8.5	2.1
Tennessee	17	17	16	16	6.2	16.7	3.7
Texas	3	3	2	2	19.4	22.8	7.9
Utah	36	35	34	34	17.9	29.6	7.0
Vermont	48	48	49	49	10.0	8.2	2.1
Virginia	14	12	12	12	15.8	14.4	5.4
Washington	20	18	15	15	17.8	21.1	5.3
West Virginia	34	34	37	37	-8.0	0.8	0.4
Wisconsin	16	16	18	20	4.0	9.6	2.7
Wyoming	49	50	50	50	-3.4	8.9	2.6
District of Columbia	—	—	—	—	-4.9	5.7	3.2
United States	—	—	—	—	9.8	13.1	4.3

*Change is less than 0.05 percent.
Source: U.S. Census Bureau, Current Population Reports, 2006.

States Ranked by Infant Mortality Rates, 2002

Rank	State	Rate
1	Maine	4.4
	Vermont	4.4
3	Massachusetts	4.9
4	New Hampshire	5.0
5	Iowa	5.3
6	Minnesota	5.4
7	California	5.5
	Alaska	5.5
9	Utah	5.6
10	New Jersey	5.7
11	Oregon	5.8
	Washington	5.8
13	Nevada	6.0
	New York	6.0
15	Idaho	6.1
	Colorado	6.1
17	North Dakota	6.3
	New Mexico	6.3
19	Texas	6.4
	Arizona	6.4
21	South Dakota	6.5

Rank	State	Rate
	Connecticut	6.5
23	Wyoming	6.7
24	Wisconsin	6.9
25	Nebraska	7.0
	Rhode Island	7.0
27	Kansas	7.1
28	Kentucky	7.2
29	Hawaii	7.3
30	Illinois	7.4
	Virginia	7.4
32	Florida	7.5
	Montana	7.5
	Maryland	7.5
35	Pennsylvania	7.6
36	Indiana	7.7
37	Ohio	7.9
38	Michigan	8.1
	Oklahoma	8.1
40	North Carolina	8.2
41	Arkansas	8.3
42	Missouri	8.5

Rank	State	Rate
43	Delaware	8.7
44	Georgia	8.9
45	Alabama	9.1
	West Virginia	9.1
47	South Carolina	9.3
48	Tennessee	9.4
49	Mississippi	10.3
	Louisiana	10.3
(51)	District of Columbia	11.3
—	United States	7.0

Figures represent deaths per 1,000 live births of resident infants under 1 year old, exclusive of fetal deaths; ranking number for the District of Columbia shows what its position would be if it were a state.

Source: U.S. Census Bureau, *Statistical Abstract of the United States,* 2006.

States Ranked by Abortion Rates, 2000

	State	Abortions	Rate
1	New York	165,000	39.1
2	New Jersey	66,000	36.3
3	Nevada	14,000	32.2
4	Florida	103,000	31.9
5	Delaware	5,000	31.3
6	California	236,000	31.2
7	Maryland	35,000	29.0
8	Rhode Island	6,000	24.1
9	Oregon	17,000	23.5
10	Illinois	64,000	23.2
11	Hawaii	6,000	22.1
12	Michigan	46,000	21.6
13	Kansas	12,000	21.4
	Massachusetts	30,000	21.4
15	Connecticut	15,000	21.1
16	North Carolina	38,000	21.0
17	Washington	26,000	20.3
18	Texas	89,000	18.8
19	Virginia	29,000	18.1
20	Georgia	32,000	16.9
21	Ohio	40,000	16.5
	Arizona	18,000	16.5
23	Colorado	16,000	15.9
24	Tennessee	19,000	15.2
25	New Mexico	6,000	14.7
26	Pennsylvania	37,000	14.3
	Alabama	14,000	14.3
28	Minnesota	15,000	13.5
	Montana	3,000	13.5
30	Louisiana	13,000	13.0

	State	Abortions	Rate
31	Vermont	2,000	12.7
32	Alaska	2,000	11.7
33	Nebraska	4,000	11.6
34	New Hampshire	3,000	11.2
35	Oklahoma	7,000	10.1
36	North Dakota	1,000	9.9
	Maine	3,000	9.9
38	Iowa	6,000	9.8
	Arkansas	6,000	9.8
40	Wisconsin	11,000	9.6
41	Indiana	12,000	9.4
42	South Carolina	8,000	9.3
43	Idaho	2,000	7.0
44	West Virginia	3,000	6.8
45	Missouri	8,000	6.6
	Utah	4,000	6.6
47	Mississippi	4,000	5.9
48	South Dakota	1,000	5.5
49	Kentucky	5,000	5.3
50	Wyoming	<1,000	0.9
(1)	District of Columbia	10,000	68.1
—	United States	1,313,000	21.3

States are ranked by abortion rates per 1,000 women; abortion numbers are rounded to nearest thousand; ranking number for the District of Columbia shows what its position would be if it were a state.

Source: U.S. Census Bureau, *Statistical Abstract of the United States,* 2006.

States Ranked by Gross State Product, 2004
In billions of dollars

	State	Gross product	Share of national product		State	Gross product	Share of national product
1	California	$1,543.8	13.25%	30	Oklahoma	$107.2	0.92%
2	New York	$899.7	7.72%	31	Nevada	$99.4	0.85%
3	Texas	$880.9	7.56%	32	Kansas	$99.1	0.85%
4	Florida	$594.5	5.10%	33	Utah	$82.4	0.71%
5	Illinois	$528.9	4.54%	34	Arkansas	$80.1	0.69%
6	Pennsylvania	$468.8	4.02%	35	Mississippi	$76.2	0.65%
7	Ohio	$418.3	3.59%	36	Nebraska	$67.9	0.58%
8	New Jersey	$415.9	3.57%	37	New Mexico	$60.9	0.52%
9	Michigan	$372.8	3.20%	38	Delaware	$54.5	0.47%
10	Georgia	$340.7	2.92%	39	New Hampshire	$52.1	0.45%
11	North Carolina	$335.4	2.88%	40	Hawaii	$50.1	0.43%
12	Virginia	$326.6	2.80%	41	West Virginia	$49.8	0.43%
13	Massachusetts	$317.7	2.73%	42	Idaho	$43.4	0.37%
14	Washington	$259.8	2.23%	43	Maine	$43.3	0.37%
15	Indiana	$227.3	1.95%	44	Rhode Island	$41.9	0.36%
16	Maryland	$226.5	1.94%	45	Alaska	$33.9	0.29%
17	Minnesota	$225.6	1.94%	46	South Dakota	$29.4	0.25%
18	Tennessee	$216.9	1.86%	47	Montana	$27.7	0.24%
19	Wisconsin	$211.7	1.82%	48	Wyoming	$24.3	0.21%
20	Missouri	$203.2	1.74%	49	North Dakota	$23.6	0.20%
21	Colorado	$200.0	1.72%	50	Vermont	$22.1	0.19%
22	Arizona	$199.7	1.71%	(36)	District of Columbia	$75.3	0.65%
23	Connecticut	$187.1	1.61%	—	United States	$11.65 trillion	100%
24	Louisiana	$152.0	1.30%				
25	Alabama	$138.5	1.19%				
26	Kentucky	$135.4	1.16%				
27	South Carolina	$135.3	1.16%				
28	Oregon	$128.1	1.10%				
29	Iowa	$114.3	0.98%				

Ranking number for the District of Columbia shows what its position would be if it were a state.

Source: U.S. Bureau of Economic Analysis, *Survey of Current Business*, July 2005.

States Ranked by Per Capita Income, 2004

Rank	State	2004	Rank	State	2004
1	Connecticut	$45,398	30	Maine	$30,566
2	Massachusetts	$41,801	31	Iowa	$30,560
3	New Jersey	$41,332	32	Texas	$30,222
4	Maryland	$39,247	33	Indiana	$30,094
5	New York	$38,228	34	Georgia	$30,051
6	New Hampshire	$37,040	35	Tennessee	$30,005
7	Colorado	$36,063	36	Oregon	$29,971
8	Minnesota	$35,861	37	North Carolina	$29,246
	Delaware	$35,861	38	Arizona	$28,442
10	Virginia	$35,477	39	Oklahoma	$28,089
11	Washington	$35,299	40	Alabama	$27,795
12	California	$35,019	41	Kentucky	$27,709
13	Alaska	$34,454	42	Louisiana	$27,581
14	Illinois	$34,351	43	South Carolina	$27,172
15	Wyoming	$34,306	44	Idaho	$27,098
16	Rhode Island	$33,733	45	Montana	$26,857
17	Nevada	$33,405	46	Utah	$26,606
18	Pennsylvania	$33,348	47	New Mexico	$26,191
19	Vermont	$32,770	48	West Virginia	$25,872
20	Hawaii	$32,160	49	Arkansas	$25,725
21	Wisconsin	$32,157	50	Mississippi	$24,650
22	Michigan	$31,954	(1)	District of Columbia	$51,803
23	Florida	$31,455	—	United States	$32,937
24	North Dakota	$31,398			
25	Nebraska	$31,339			
26	Ohio	$31,322			
27	South Dakota	$30,856			
28	Kansas	$30,811			
29	Missouri	$30,608			

Ranking numbers for the District of Columbia show what its
position would be if it were a state.

Source: U.S. Bureau of Economic Analysis, *Survey of Current Business,*
April, 2005.

States Ranked by Total Energy Consumption, 2001

Rank	State	Total BTUs	Per capita BTUs	Per capita Rank
1	Texas	12,029 trill.	564 mill.	5
2	California	7,853 trill.	227 mill.	48
3	Florida	4,135 trill.	253 mill.	44
	New York	4,135 trill.	217 mill.	49
5	Ohio	3,982 trill.	350 mill.	23
6	Pennsylvania	3,923 trill.	319 mill.	31
7	Illinois	3,870 trill.	309 mill.	35
8	Louisiana	3,500 trill.	784 mill.	3
9	Michigan	3,120 trill.	312 mill.	34
10	Georgia	2,881 trill.	343 mill.	26
11	Indiana	2,802 trill.	457 mill.	7
12	North Carolina	2,591 trill.	316 mill.	33
13	New Jersey	2,500 trill.	294 mill.	38
14	Virginia	2,315 trill.	322 mill.	29
15	Tennessee	2,195 trill.	382 mill.	16
16	Washington	2,034 trill.	339 mill.	27
17	Alabama	1,943 trill.	435 mill.	9
18	Kentucky	1,880 trill.	462 mill.	6
19	Wisconsin	1,863 trill.	345 mill.	25
20	Missouri	1,815 trill.	322 mill.	29
21	Minnesota	1,745 trill.	350 mill.	23
22	South Carolina	1,549 trill.	382 mill.	16
	Massachusetts	1,549 trill.	242 mill.	46
24	Oklahoma	1,540 trill.	444 mill.	8
25	Maryland	1,420 trill.	264 mill.	41
26	Arizona	1,353 trill.	255 mill.	43
27	Colorado	1,270 trill.	287 mill.	39
28	Mississippi	1,173 trill.	410 mill.	12
29	Iowa	1,151 trill.	392 mill.	14
30	Arkansas	1,106 trill.	411 mill.	11
31	Oregon	1,064 trill.	307 mill.	36
32	Kansas	1,044 trill.	387 mill.	15
33	Connecticut	853 trill.	249 mill.	45
34	West Virginia	762 trill.	423 mill.	10
35	Alaska	737 trill.	1,164 mill.	1
36	Utah	725 trill.	318 mill.	32
37	New Mexico	679 trill.	371 mill.	20
38	Nevada	629 trill.	301 mill.	37
39	Nebraska	627 trill.	365 mill.	22
40	Idaho	501 trill.	379 mill.	19
41	Maine	491 trill.	382 mill.	16
42	Wyoming	439 trill.	890 mill.	2
43	North Dakota	407 trill.	640 mill.	4
44	Montana	366 trill.	404 mill.	13
45	New Hampshire	322 trill.	256 mill.	42
46	Delaware	293 trill.	368 mill.	21
47	Hawaii	282 trill.	230 mill.	47
48	South Dakota	248 trill.	327 mill.	28
49	Rhode Island	227 trill.	215 mill.	50
50	Vermont	164 trill.	267 mill.	40
(50)	District of Columbia	168 trill.	294 mill.	(38)
—	United States	96,275 trill.	338 mill.	—

Ranking numbers for the District of Columbia show what its position would be if it were a state.

Source: U.S. Energy Information Administration, *State Energy Data Report*, 2001.

States Ranked by Value of Foreign Exports, 2004
In billions of dollars

	State	Total	Share		State	Total	Share
1	Texas	$117.245	15.24%	30	Kansas	$4.931	0.64%
2	California	$109.968	14.29%	31	Utah	$4.718	0.61%
3	New York	$44.401	5.77%	32	Arkansas	$3.493	0.45%
4	Michigan	$35.625	4.63%	33	Vermont	$3.283	0.43%
5	Washington	$33.793	4.39%	34	West Virginia	$3.262	0.42%
6	Ohio	$31.208	4.06%	35	Mississippi	$3.179	0.41%
7	Illinois	$30.214	3.93%	36	Oklahoma	$3.178	0.41%
8	Florida	$28.982	3.77%	37	Alaska	$3.157	0.41%
9	Massachusetts	$21.837	2.84%	38	Idaho	$2.915	0.38%
10	Louisiana	$19.922	2.59%	39	Nevada	$2.907	0.38%
11	Georgia	$19.633	2.55%	40	Maine	$2.432	0.32%
12	New Jersey	$19.192	2.49%	41	Nebraska	$2.316	0.30%
13	Indiana	$19.109	2.48%	42	New Hampshire	$2.286	0.30%
14	Pennsylvania	$18.487	2.40%	43	Delaware	$2.053	0.27%
15	North Carolina	$18.115	2.35%	44	New Mexico	$2.046	0.27%
16	Tennessee	$16.123	2.10%	45	Rhode Island	$1.286	0.17%
17	Arizona	$13.423	1.74%	46	North Dakota	$1.008	0.13%
18	South Carolina	$13.376	1.74%	47	South Dakota	$826	0.11%
19	Kentucky	$12.992	1.69%	48	Wyoming	$680	0.09%
20	Wisconsin	$12.706	1.65%	49	Montana	$565	0.07%
21	Minnesota	$12.678	1.65%	50	Hawaii	$405	0.05%
22	Virginia	$11.631	1.51%				
23	Oregon	$11.172	1.45%	(46)	District of Columbia	$1.164	0.15%
24	Alabama	$9.037	1.17%	—	United States	$769.332	100%
25	Missouri	$8.997	1.17%				
26	Connecticut	$8.559	1.11%				
27	Colorado	$6.651	0.86%				
28	Iowa	$6.394	0.83%				
29	Maryland	$5.746	0.75%				

Ranking number for the District of Columbia shows what its position would be if it were a state.

Source: U.S. Census Bureau, *U.S. International Trade in Goods and Services*, Series FT 900, 2005.

States Ranked by Amount of Federally Owned Land, 2003

Areas in acres

	State	Federally owned area	Total area	Federal share of state		State	Federally owned area	Total area	Federal share of state
1	Alaska	243,847,000	365,482,000	66.7%	31	West Virginia	1,266,000	15,411,000	8.2%
2	Nevada	64,589,000	70,264,000	91.9%	32	South Carolina	1,236,000	19,374,000	6.4%
3	California	46,980,000	100,207,000	46.9%	33	Alabama	1,202,000	32,678,000	3.7%
4	Arizona	36,495,000	72,688,000	50.2%	34	New Hampshire	830,000	5,769,000	14.4%
5	Idaho	35,136,000	52,933,000	66.4%	35	Pennsylvania	724,000	28,804,000	2.5%
6	Utah	35,025,000	52,697,000	66.5%	36	Hawaii	672,000	4,106,000	16.4%
7	Wyoming	31,532,000	62,343,000	50.6%	37	Illinois	651,000	35,795,000	1.8%
8	Oregon	30,639,000	61,599,000	49.7%	38	Kansas	642,000	52,511,000	1.2%
9	Montana	29,239,000	93,271,000	31.3%	39	Indiana	534,000	23,158,000	2.3%
10	New Mexico	26,518,000	77,766,000	34.1%	40	Ohio	458,000	26,222,000	1.7%
11	Colorado	23,175,000	66,486,000	34.9%	41	Vermont	450,000	5,937,000	7.6%
12	Washington	13,247,000	42,694,000	31.0%	42	Iowa	302,000	35,860,000	0.8%
13	Florida	4,606,000	34,721,000	13.3%	43	New York	242,000	30,681,000	0.8%
14	Arkansas	3,956,000	33,599,000	11.8%	44	Maryland	192,000	6,319,000	3.0%
15	Michigan	3,638,000	36,492,000	10.0%	45	New Jersey	180,000	4,813,000	3.7%
16	North Carolina	3,602,000	31,403,000	11.5%	46	Maine	164,000	19,848,000	0.8%
17	Minnesota	3,535,000	51,206,000	6.9%	47	Massachusetts	106,000	5,035,000	2.1%
18	Texas	3,172,000	168,218,000	1.9%	48	Delaware	30,000	1,266,000	2.3%
19	Virginia	2,617,000	25,496,000	10.3%	49	Connecticut	15,000	3,135,000	0.5%
20	South Dakota	2,314,000	48,882,000	4.7%	50	Rhode Island	5,000	677,000	0.8%
21	Georgia	2,314,000	37,295,000	6.2%	(50)	District of Columbia	10,000	39,000	26.3%
22	Missouri	2,238,000	44,248,000	5.1%	—	United States	671,759,000	2,271,343,000	29.6%
23	Mississippi	2,101,000	30,223,000	7.0%					
24	Tennessee	2,016,000	26,728,000	7.5%					
25	Wisconsin	1,982,000	35,011,000	5.7%					
26	Kentucky	1,706,000	25,512,000	6.7%					
27	Louisiana	1,502,000	28,868,000	5.2%					
28	Nebraska	1,459,000	49,032,000	3.0%					
29	North Dakota	1,333,000	44,452,000	3.0%					
30	Oklahoma	1,332,000	44,088,000	3.0%					

Areas are rounded to nearest thousand acres; ranking number for the District of Columbia shows what its position would be if it were a state.

Source: U.S. General Services Administration, *Federal Real Property Profile,* 2006.

States Ranked by Farm Acreage, 2004

Rank	State	Acres	Share	Rank	State	Acres	Share
1	Texas	130,000,000	13.87%	29	Florida	10,000,000	1.07%
2	Montana	60,000,000	6.40%		Michigan	10,000,000	1.07%
3	Kansas	47,000,000	5.02%	31	Alabama	9,000,000	0.96%
4	Nebraska	46,000,000	4.91%		North Carolina	9,000,000	0.96%
5	New Mexico	45,000,000	4.80%		Virginia	9,000,000	0.96%
6	South Dakota	44,000,000	4.70%	34	Louisiana	8,000,000	0.85%
7	North Dakota	39,000,000	4.16%		Pennsylvania	8,000,000	0.85%
8	Oklahoma	34,000,000	3.63%		New York	8,000,000	0.85%
	Wyoming	34,000,000	3.63%	37	Nevada	6,000,000	0.64%
10	Iowa	32,000,000	3.42%	38	South Carolina	5,000,000	0.53%
11	Colorado	31,000,000	3.31%	39	West Virginia	4,000,000	0.43%
12	Missouri	30,000,000	3.20%	40	Maryland	2,000,000	0.21%
13	Illinois	28,000,000	2.99%	41	Alaska	1,000,000	0.11%
	Minnesota	28,000,000	2.99%		Delaware	1,000,000	0.11%
15	California	27,000,000	2.88%		Hawaii	1,000,000	0.11%
16	Arizona	26,000,000	2.77%		Maine	1,000,000	0.11%
17	Oregon	17,000,000	1.81%		Massachusetts	1,000,000	0.11%
18	Wisconsin	16,000,000	1.71%		New Jersey	1,000,000	0.11%
19	Indiana	15,000,000	1.60%		Vermont	1,000,000	0.11%
	Ohio	15,000,000	1.60%	48	Connecticut	(under 500,000)	—
	Washington	15,000,000	1.60%		New Hampshire	(under 500,000)	—
22	Arkansas	14,000,000	1.49%		Rhode Island	(under 500,000)	—
	Kentucky	14,000,000	1.49%	—	All states	937,000,000	100%
24	Idaho	12,000,000	1.28%				
	Tennessee	12,000,000	1.28%				
	Utah	12,000,000	1.28%				
27	Georgia	11,000,000	1.17%				
	Mississippi	11,000,000	1.17%				

Figures are rounded to nearest million acres; District of Columbia has no statistically significant farm acreage.

Source: U.S. Department of Agriculture, National Agricultural Statistics Service.

Local Government Units, 2002

	All units		Counties		Municipalities		Townships	
	Number	Rank	Number	Rank	Number	Rank	Number	Rank
Alabama	1,171	26	67	20	451	19	0	—
Alaska	175	48	12	44	149	37	0	—
Arizona	638	39	15	42	87	41	0	—
Arkansas	1,588	20	75	18	499	17	0	—
California	4,409	4	57	26	475	18	0	—
Colorado	1,928	16	62	24	270	29	0	—
Connecticut	580	41	0	—	30	45	149	19
Delaware	339	45	3	47	57	42	0	—
Florida	1,191	25	66	21	404	21	0	—
Georgia	1,448	21	156	2	531	16	0	—
Hawaii	19	50	3	47	1	50	0	—
Idaho	1,158	27	44	32	200	35	0	—
Illinois	6,903	1	102	6	1,291	1	1,431	3
Indiana	3,085	10	91	12	567	12	1,008	9
Iowa	1,975	15	99	8	948	4	0	—
Kansas	3,887	5	104	5	627	8	1,299	6
Kentucky	1,439	22	119	3	424	20	0	—
Louisiana	473	44	60	25	302	26	0	—
Maine	826	34	16	40	22	46	467	12
Maryland	265	46	23	37	157	36	0	—
Massachusetts	841	33	5	46	45	44	306	15
Michigan	2,804	12	83	15	533	14	1,242	8
Minnesota	3,482	7	87	14	854	7	1,793	1
Mississippi	1,000	29	82	16	296	27	0	—
Missouri	3,422	8	114	4	946	5	312	14
Montana	1,127	28	54	29	129	38	0	—
Nebraska	2,791	13	93	10	531	15	446	13
Nevada	210	47	16	40	19	47	0	—
New Hampshire	559	42	10	45	13	48	221	18
New Jersey	1,412	24	21	39	324	24	242	16
New Mexico	858	32	33	35	101	39	0	—
New York	3,420	9	57	26	616	9	929	11
North Carolina	960	30	100	7	541	13	0	—
North Dakota	2,735	14	53	30	360	22	1,332	4
Ohio	3,636	6	88	13	942	6	1,308	5
Oklahoma	1,798	18	77	17	590	10	0	—
Oregon	1,439	22	36	34	240	31	0	—
Pennsylvania	5,031	2	66	21	1,018	3	1,546	2
Rhode Island	118	49	0	—	8	49	31	20
South Carolina	701	37	46	31	269	30	0	—
South Dakota	1,866	17	66	21	308	25	940	10
Tennessee	930	31	92	11	349	23	0	—
Texas	4,784	3	254	1	1,196	2	0	—
Utah	605	40	29	36	236	32	0	—
Vermont	733	35	14	43	47	43	237	17
Virginia	521	43	95	9	229	34	0	—
Washington	1,787	19	39	33	279	28	0	—
West Virginia	686	38	55	28	234	33	0	—
Wisconsin	3,048	11	72	19	585	11	1,265	7
Wyoming	722	36	23	37	98	40	0	—
District of Columbia	2	(51)	0	—	1	(50)	0	—
United States	87,525		3,034		19,429		16,504	

Townships are designated "towns" in New England, Minnesota, New York, and Wisconsin), and 46 states have school districts. Special districts encompass such functions as natural resources, fire protection, and housing and community development. Ranking numbers for the District of Columbia shows what its positions would be if it were a state.

Source: U.S. Census Bureau, *Census of Governments.*

States Ranked by General Revenue, 2002

Rank	State	Total revenue (billions)	Per capita revenue	Per capita rank	Rank	State	Total revenue (billions)	Per capita revenue	Per capita rank
1	California	$141.48	$4,044	18	28	Colorado	$13.88	$3,085	40
2	New York	$92.90	$4,851	7	29	Oklahoma	$12.76	$3,658	42
3	Texas	$62.18	$2,862	48	30	Mississippi	$11.04	$3,851	27
4	Florida	$47.00	$2,817	49	31	Iowa	$11.03	$3,757	29
5	Pennsylvania	$46.54	$3,775	28	32	Arkansas	$10.53	$3,890	24
6	Michigan	$40.89	$4,071	14	33	Kansas	$9.18	$3,384	43
7	Illinois	$40.34	$3,205	39	34	Utah	$8.62	$3,717	26
8	Ohio	$40.23	$3,526	38	35	New Mexico	$8.48	$4,570	9
9	New Jersey	$33.90	$3,952	16	36	West Virginia	$8.05	$4,461	17
10	North Carolina	$29.97	$3,606	25	37	Nevada	$6.17	$2,844	44
11	Massachusetts	$26.48	$4,129	8	38	Hawaii	$6.04	$4,894	3
12	Georgia	$26.11	$3,058	45	39	Nebraska	$5.99	$3,468	33
13	Virginia	$24.84	$3,416	34	40	Maine	$5.60	$4,315	13
14	Wisconsin	$22.87	$4,205	15	41	Alaska	$5.42	$8,462	1
15	Washington	$22.78	$3,754	21	42	Rhode Island	$4.84	$4,524	10
16	Minnesota	$21.91	$4,360	12	43	Delaware	$4.63	$5,748	2
17	Indiana	$20.01	$3,249	36	44	New Hampshire	$4.39	$3,442	50
18	Maryland	$19.91	$3,659	31	45	Idaho	$4.38	$3,257	32
19	Missouri	$18.65	$3,284	41	46	Montana	$3.72	$4,086	20
20	Louisiana	$17.66	$3,944	23	47	Vermont	$3.23	$5,238	5
21	Tennessee	$17.62	$3,042	47	48	North Dakota	$2.87	$4,526	11
22	Alabama	$15.99	$3,567	35	49	Wyoming	$2.77	$5,546	4
23	Arizona	$15.86	$2,916	46	50	South Dakota	$2.60	$3,424	37
24	Kentucky	$15.81	$3,866	22	—	All states	$1,062.31	$3,689	—
25	Connecticut	$15.38	$4,447	6					
26	South Carolina	$14.48	$3,526	30					
27	Oregon	$14.31	$4,060	19					

Source: U.S. Census Bureau.

States Ranked by Government Expenditures, 2002

Rank	State	Total expenditure (billions)	Per capita	Per capita rank	Rank	State	Total expenditure (billions)	Per capita	Per capita rank
1	California	$184.93	$4,521	11	28	Colorado	16.82	3,257	44
2	New York	119.20	5,045	7	29	Oklahoma	14.73	3,697	31
3	Texas	70.27	2,842	49	30	Mississippi	12.74	3,998	23
4	Pennsylvania	55.17	3,824	28	31	Iowa	12.72	3,895	26
5	Ohio	52.59	3,713	30	32	Arkansas	11.52	3,930	25
6	Florida	51.83	2,833	50	33	Kansas	10.59	3,546	36
7	Michigan	49.18	4,364	15	34	Utah	10.11	3,942	24
8	Illinois	49.13	3,391	39	35	New Mexico	10.08	4,975	8
9	New Jersey	41.99	3,841	27	36	West Virginia	9.41	4,189	18
10	North Carolina	33.12	3,556	35	37	Hawaii	7.45	5,386	2
11	Massachusetts	32.85	4,433	13	38	Alaska	7.40	10,456	1
12	Washington	30.38	4,147	21	39	Nevada	7.35	2,881	48
13	Georgia	30.05	3,180	46	40	Nebraska	6.54	3,599	34
14	Virginia	28.04	3,505	37	41	Maine	6.27	4,378	14
15	Wisconsin	26.74	4,250	16	42	Rhode Island	5.77	4,534	10
16	Minnesota	26.69	4,672	9	43	Idaho	5.23	3,444	38
17	Maryland	23.32	3,798	29	44	New Hampshire	4.82	3,278	43
18	Indiana	22.21	3,343	41	45	Delaware	4.65	5,252	4
19	Missouri	20.84	3,299	42	46	Montana	4.27	4,159	19
20	Connecticut	20.12	5,070	6	47	Vermont	3.51	5,343	3
21	Tennessee	20.03	3,193	45	48	North Dakota	3.02	4,436	12
22	South Carolina	20.01	4,154	20	49	Wyoming	2.95	5,228	5
23	Kentucky	18.41	4,004	22	50	South Dakota	2.77	3,361	40
24	Louisiana	18.32	3,611	32	—	All states	1,280.29	3,859	—
25	Arizona	18.12	2,986	47					
26	Oregon	18.03	4,228	17					
27	Alabama	18.00	3,608	33					

Per capita figures are based on total general expenditures.

Source: U.S. Census Bureau.

Apportionment of Seats in the House of Representatives, 1900-2000

State	2000	1990	1980	1970	1960	1950	1940	1930	1910-1920	1900	net change, 1900-2000	Rank in 2000
Alabama	7	7	7	7	8	9	9	9	10	9	−2	22
Alaska	1	1	1	1	1	1	—	—	—	—	+1	44
Arizona	8	6	5	4	3	2	2	1	1	—	+8	18
Arkansas	4	4	4	4	4	6	7	7	7	7	−3	31
California	53	52	45	43	38	30	23	20	11	8	+45	1
Colorado	7	6	6	5	4	4	4	4	4	3	+4	22
Connecticut	5	6	6	6	6	6	6	6	5	5	+0	27
Delaware	1	1	1	1	1	1	1	1	1	1	+0	44
Florida	25	23	19	15	12	8	6	5	4	3	+22	4
Georgia	13	11	10	10	10	10	10	10	12	11	+2	9
Hawaii	2	2	2	2	2	1	—	—	—	—	+2	39
Idaho	2	2	2	2	2	2	2	2	2	1	+1	39
Illinois	19	20	22	24	24	25	26	27	27	25	−6	5
Indiana	9	10	10	11	11	11	11	12	13	13	−4	14
Iowa	5	5	6	6	7	8	8	9	11	11	−6	27
Kansas	4	4	5	5	5	6	6	7	8	8	−4	31
Kentucky	6	6	7	7	7	8	9	9	11	11	−5	25
Louisiana	7	7	8	8	8	8	8	8	8	7	+0	22
Maine	2	2	2	2	2	3	3	3	4	4	−2	39
Maryland	8	8	8	8	8	7	6	6	6	6	+2	18
Massachusetts	10	10	11	12	12	14	14	15	16	14	−4	13
Michigan	15	16	18	19	19	18	17	17	13	12	+3	8
Minnesota	8	8	8	8	8	9	9	9	10	9	−1	18
Mississippi	4	5	5	5	5	6	7	7	8	8	−4	31
Missouri	9	9	9	10	10	11	13	13	16	16	−7	14
Montana	1	1	2	2	2	2	2	2	2	1	+0	44
Nebraska	3	3	3	3	3	4	4	5	6	6	−3	34
Nevada	3	2	2	1	1	1	1	1	1	1	+2	34
New Hampshire	2	2	2	2	2	2	2	2	2	2	+0	39
New Jersey	13	13	14	15	15	14	14	14	12	10	+3	9
New Mexico	3	3	3	2	2	2	2	1	1	—	+3	34
New York	29	31	34	39	41	43	45	45	43	37	−8	3
North Carolina	13	12	11	11	11	12	12	11	10	10	+3	9
North Dakota	1	1	1	1	2	2	2	2	3	2	−1	44
Ohio	18	19	21	23	24	23	23	24	22	21	−3	7
Oklahoma	5	6	6	6	6	6	8	9	8	5	+0	27
Oregon	5	5	5	4	4	4	4	3	3	2	+3	27
Pennsylvania	19	21	23	25	27	30	33	34	36	32	−13	5
Rhode Island	2	2	2	2	2	2	2	2	3	2	+0	39
South Carolina	6	6	6	6	6	6	6	6	7	7	−1	25
South Dakota	1	1	1	2	2	2	2	2	3	2	−1	44
Tennessee	9	9	9	8	9	9	10	9	10	10	−1	14
Texas	32	30	27	24	23	22	21	21	18	16	+16	2
Utah	3	3	3	2	2	2	2	2	2	1	+2	34
Vermont	1	1	1	1	1	1	1	1	2	2	−1	44
Virginia	11	11	10	10	10	10	9	9	10	10	+1	12
Washington	9	9	8	7	7	7	6	6	5	3	+6	14
West Virginia	3	3	4	4	5	6	6	6	6	5	−2	34
Wisconsin	8	9	9	9	10	10	10	10	11	11	−3	18
Wyoming	1	1	1	1	1	1	1	1	1	1	+0	44
Totals	435	435	435	435	435	437	435	435	435	391	+44	—

Alaska (admitted, 1959), Arizona (1912), Hawaii (1959), New Mexico (1912), and Oklahoma (1907) were given representatives by the censuses that preceded their formal admissions to the union. Note that there was no reapportionment after the 1920 census.
Source: U.S. Census Bureau.

States Ranked by Numbers of Seats in Their Legislatures, 2006

Rank	State	Total	Lower house	Upper house
1	New Hampshire	424	400	24
2	Pennsylvania	253	203	50
3	Georgia	236	180	56
4	New York	212	150	62
5	Minnesota	201	134	67
6	Massachusetts	200	160	40
7	Missouri	197	163	34
8	Maryland	188	141	47
9	Connecticut	187	151	36
10	Maine	186	151	35
11	Texas	181	150	31
12	Vermont	180	150	30
13	Illinois	177	118	59
14	Mississippi	174	122	52
15	North Carolina	170	120	50
	South Carolina	170	124	46
17	Kansas	165	125	40
18	Florida	160	120	40
19	Iowa	150	100	50
	Indiana	150	100	50
	Montana	150	100	50
22	Oklahoma	149	101	48
23	Michigan	148	110	38
24	Washington	147	98	49
25	Louisiana	144	105	39
26	North Dakota	141	94	47
27	Virginia	140	100	40

Rank	State	Total	Lower house	Upper house
	Alabama	140	105	35
29	Kentucky	138	100	38
30	Arkansas	135	100	35
31	West Virginia	134	100	34
32	Wisconsin	132	99	33
	Tennessee	132	99	33
	Ohio	132	99	33
35	California	120	80	40
	New Jersey	120	80	40
37	Rhode Island	113	75	38
38	New Mexico	112	70	42
39	South Dakota	105	70	35
	Idaho	105	70	35
41	Utah	104	75	29
42	Colorado	100	65	35
43	Arizona	90	60	30
	Oregon	90	60	30
	Wyoming	90	60	30
46	Hawaii	76	51	25
47	Nevada	63	42	21
48	Delaware	62	41	21
49	Alaska	60	40	20
50	Nebraska*	49	—	—
—	All states	7,382	5,411	1,971

*Nebraska's legislature is unicameral.

Source: National Conference of State Legislatures.

States Ranked by Voting Participation in 2004 Presidential Election

Rank	State	Voting age population	Percent voting	Rank	State	Voting age population	Percent voting
1	Minnesota	3,861,000	73.3	30	Utah	1,649,000	56.3
2	Maine	1,035,000	71.6	31	Illinois	9,475,000	55.7
3	Wisconsin	4,201,000	71.3	32	New Jersey	6,543,000	55.2
4	New Hampshire	995,000	68.2	33	Oklahoma	2,664,000	55.0
5	Oregon	2,742,000	67.0	34	Alabama	3,436,000	54.8
6	Alaska	467,000	66.9	35	North Carolina	6,423,000	54.5
	South Dakota	580,000	66.9	36	Tennessee	4,510,000	54.0
8	Iowa	2,274,000	66.3	37	New Mexico	1,411,000	53.6
9	Ohio	8,680,000	64.8	38	Indiana	4,637,000	53.2
10	Vermont	487,000	64.2	39	Mississippi	2,153,000	52.9
11	Michigan	7,579,000	63.8	40	West Virginia	1,431,000	52.8
12	North Dakota	495,000	63.1	41	Rhode Island	837,000	52.2
13	Montana	719,000	62.7	42	South Carolina	3,173,000	51.0
14	Wyoming	390,000	62.6	43	Georgia	6,497,000	50.8
15	Missouri	4,370,000	62.5		New York	14,655,000	50.8
16	Colorado	3,423,000	62.2		Arkansas	2,076,000	50.8
17	Washington	4,718,000	60.6	46	Arizona	4,197,000	48.0
18	Pennsylvania	9,569,000	60.3	47	Nevada	1,731,000	47.9
19	Nebraska	1,313,000	59.3	48	California	26,297,000	47.2
20	Connecticut	2,665,000	59.2	49	Texas	16,223,000	45.7
21	Massachusetts	4,952,000	59.1	50	Hawaii	964,000	44.5
22	Delaware	637,000	58.9	(42)	District of Columbia	444,000	51.3
23	Idaho	1,021,000	58.6	—	United States	220,377,000	55.5
24	Louisiana	3,351,000	58.0				
25	Kansas	2,052,000	57.9				
26	Maryland	4,163,000	57.3				
27	Florida	13,394,000	56.8				
28	Kentucky	3,166,000	56.7				
29	Virginia	5,655,000	56.5				

Population figures are rounded to nearest thousand and include all residents of voting age, regardless of eligibility to vote. Ranking number for the District of Columbia shows what its position would be if it were a state.

Source: U.S. Census Bureau.

States Ranked by Numbers of Physicians, 2003
Based on rate per 100,000 residents

Rank	State	Rate	Total	Rank	State	Rate	Total
1	Massachusetts	443	28,474	30	Michigan	238	24,004
2	Maryland	414	22,819	31	South Carolina	230	9,521
3	New York	391	75,048		West Virginia	230	4,168
4	Vermont	363	2,250	33	Kentucky	227	9,348
5	Connecticut	362	12,603		Montana	227	2,079
6	Rhode Island	350	3,770	35	Alaska	222	1,439
7	Hawaii	310	3,901	36	Georgia	221	19,222
	New Jersey	310	26,804	37	Kansas	218	5,947
9	Pennsylvania	295	36,421	38	Indiana	215	13,346
10	Minnesota	278	14,088		South Dakota	215	1,640
11	Virginia	274	20,220	40	Alabama	212	9,547
12	Illinois	272	34,461		Texas	212	46,802
13	Maine	267	3,485		Utah	212	4,987
	Washington	267	16,347	43	Arizona	209	11,679
15	Louisiana	265	11,904	44	Arkansas	202	5,516
16	New Hampshire	263	3,392	45	Wyoming	192	963
17	Oregon	262	9,342	46	Iowa	188	5,544
18	California	261	92,470	47	Nevada	185	4,152
19	Tennessee	260	15,178	48	Mississippi	182	5,240
20	Colorado	255	11,600	49	Oklahoma	172	6,034
	Ohio	255	29,153	50	Idaho	170	2,324
22	Delaware	253	2,069	(1)	District of Columbia	768	4,329
	North Carolina	253	21,287	—	United States	266	774,849
24	Wisconsin	252	13,769				
25	Florida	248	42,213				
26	Nebraska	242	4,216				
27	Missouri	241	13,732				
	North Dakota	241	1,529				
29	New Mexico	239	4,473				

Ranking number for the District of Columbia shows what its
    position would be if it were a state.
Source: American Medical Association, *Physician Characteristics and
    Distribution in the U.S.*; U.S. Department of Health and Human
    Services, Health Resources and Services Administration.

States Ranked by Percentage of Persons Covered by Health Insurance, 2003

Rank	State	Persons covered	Persons not covered	Portion covered
1	Minnesota	4,633,000	444,000	91.3%
2	Vermont	553,000	58,000	90.5%
3	Hawaii	1,126,000	127,000	89.9%
4	Rhode Island	946,000	108,000	89.8%
5	New Hampshire	1,133,000	131,000	89.7%
6	Maine	1,150,000	133,000	89.6%
	Connecticut	3,065,000	357,000	89.6%
8	Massachusetts	5,685,000	682,000	89.3%
9	North Dakota	563,000	69,000	89.1%
	Wisconsin	4,836,000	593,000	89.1%
	Michigan	8,838,000	1,080,000	89.1%
12	Missouri	5,004,000	620,000	89.0%
	Kansas	2,389,000	294,000	89.0%
14	Delaware	729,000	91,000	88.9%
15	Nebraska	1,532,000	195,000	88.7%
	Iowa	2,593,000	329,000	88.7%
17	Pennsylvania	10,771,000	1,384,000	88.6%
18	Ohio	9,885,000	1,362,000	87.9%
19	South Dakota	659,000	91,000	87.8%
20	Utah	2,055,000	298,000	87.3%
21	Virginia	6,424,000	962,000	87.0%
22	Tennessee	5,131,000	778,000	86.8%
23	Indiana	5,296,000	853,000	86.1%
	Maryland	4,731,000	762,000	86.1%
25	Kentucky	3,537,000	574,000	86.0%
	New Jersey	7,378,000	1,201,000	86.0%
27	Alabama	3,798,000	629,000	85.8%
28	South Carolina	3,481,000	584,000	85.6%
	Illinois	10,810,000	1,818,000	85.6%
30	New York	16,104,000	2,866,000	84.9%
31	Washington	5,147,000	944,000	84.5%
32	Wyoming	411,000	78,000	84.1%
33	Georgia	7,162,000	1,409,000	83.6%
34	West Virginia	1,491,000	296,000	83.4%
35	Arizona	4,626,000	951,000	83.0%
36	Colorado	3,708,000	772,000	82.8%
	Oregon	2,957,000	613,000	82.8%
38	North Carolina	6,829,000	1,424,000	82.7%
39	Arkansas	2,206,000	465,000	82.6%
40	Mississippi	2,343,000	511,000	82.1%
41	Florida	13,849,000	3,071,000	81.8%
42	California	28,895,000	6,499,000	81.6%
43	Idaho	1,107,000	253,000	81.4%
44	Alaska	523,000	122,000	81.1%
	Nevada	1,824,000	426,000	81.1%
46	Montana	739,000	177,000	80.6%
47	Oklahoma	2,737,000	701,000	79.6%
48	Louisiana	3,517,000	912,000	79.4%
49	New Mexico	1,457,000	414,000	77.9%
50	Texas	16,484,000	5,374,000	75.4%
(28)	District of Columbia	475,000	79,000	85.7%
—	United States	243,320,000	44,961,000	84.4%

Ranking number for the District of Columbia shows what its position would be if it were a state.

Source: U.S. Census Bureau, Current Population Reports.

States Ranked by Numbers of AIDS cases, 2003

Rank	State	Cases	Rank	State	Cases	Rank	State	Cases
1	California	5,967	21	Mississippi	509	41	Nebraska	60
2	New York	5,133	22	Indiana	506	42	Maine	52
3	Florida	4,774	23	Alabama	471	43	New Hampshire	37
4	Texas	3,413	24	Missouri	404	44	Idaho	25
5	Georgia	1,907	25	Colorado	368	45	Alaska	17
6	Pennsylvania	1,906	26	Nevada	279	46	Vermont	16
7	Illinois	1,734	27	Oregon	242	47	South Dakota	13
8	Maryland	1,572	28	Kentucky	220	48	Wyoming	8
9	New Jersey	1,514	29	Delaware	216	49	Montana	7
10	North Carolina	1,102	30	Oklahoma	214	50	North Dakota	2
11	Louisiana	1,048	31	Arkansas	189	(12)	District of Columbia	961
12	Tennessee	835	32	Wisconsin	184	—	United States	44,232
13	Virginia	786	33	Minnesota	179			
14	South Carolina	778	34	Kansas	111			
15	Ohio	775		New Mexico	111			
16	Massachusetts	757	36	Hawaii	110			
17	Connecticut	733	37	Rhode Island	102			
18	Michigan	676	38	West Virginia	95			
19	Arizona	628	39	Iowa	75			
20	Washington	527		Utah	75			

Ranking number for the District of Columbia shows what its position would be if it were a state.

Source: U.S. Centers for Disease Control and Prevention.

States Ranked by Percentage of Residents Who Smoke, 2003

Rank	State	All smokers	Male	Female	Rank	State	All smokers	Male	Female
1	Kentucky	30.8	33.8	28.1	31	New York	21.6	24.8	18.8
2	West Virginia	27.4	27.6	27.2	32	Nebraska	21.3	23.6	19.0
3	Missouri	27.3	31.2	23.8	33	New Hampshire	21.2	22.4	20.2
4	Louisiana	26.6	30.3	23.2	34	Minnesota	21.1	22.4	19.9
5	Alaska	26.3	30.3	21.9	35	Arizona	21.0	23.8	18.2
6	Michigan	26.2	30.2	22.3		Oregon	21.0	23.1	18.9
7	Indiana	26.1	28.6	23.8	37	North Dakota	20.5	22.0	19.0
8	Tennessee	25.7	27.3	24.2	38	Kansas	20.4	21.0	19.7
9	Mississippi	25.6	31.1	20.7	39	Maryland	20.2	23.0	17.7
10	South Carolina	25.5	28.5	22.8	40	Montana	19.9	19.5	20.3
	Pennsylvania	25.5	27.1	24.1	41	Vermont	19.6	19.8	19.4
12	Ohio	25.4	26.9	24.0	42	New Jersey	19.5	21.2	17.9
13	Alabama	25.3	28.5	22.4		Washington	19.5	20.9	18.2
14	Nevada	25.2	29.0	21.3	44	Massachusetts	19.2	20.0	18.4
	Oklahoma	25.2	27.8	22.7	45	Idaho	19.0	19.5	18.5
16	Arkansas	24.8	27.6	22.3	46	Connecticut	18.7	19.7	17.9
	North Carolina	24.8	28.0	21.9	47	Colorado	18.5	19.6	17.5
18	Wyoming	24.6	25.2	24.1	48	Hawaii	17.3	20.1	14.4
19	Illinois	24.3	28.3	20.5	49	California	16.8	20.5	13.2
20	Florida	23.9	26.0	22.1	50	Utah	12.0	14.0	9.9
21	Maine	23.6	23.1	24.0	(25)	District of Columbia	22.3	26.2	19.0
22	Georgia	22.8	25.8	20.0	—	United States	22.1	24.8	20.3
23	South Dakota	22.7	24.7	20.7					
24	Rhode Island	22.4	23.8	21.1					
25	Texas	22.1	26.7	17.6					
	Wisconsin	22.1	24.0	20.3					
	Virginia	22.1	26.4	18.0					
28	New Mexico	22.0	23.6	20.5					
29	Delaware	21.9	26.0	18.2					
30	Iowa	21.7	22.8	20.7					

Smokers are persons who reported having smoked at least 100 cigarettes during their lifetimes and who currently smoked at least occasionally. Ranking number for the District of Columbia shows what its position would be if it were a state.

U.S. Centers for Disease Control and Prevention, *Morbidity and Mortality Weekly Report* 53, no. 44 (November 12, 2004).

States Ranked by Percentage of Home Ownership, 2004

Rank	State	Percentage	Rank	State	Percentage	Rank	State	Percentage
1	West Virginia	80.3%	21	Missouri	72.4%	41	South Dakota	68.5%
2	Alabama	78.0%		Montana	72.4%	42	Alaska	67.2%
3	Delaware	77.3%	23	Florida	72.2%	43	Washington	66.0%
4	Michigan	77.1%	24	Maryland	72.1%	44	Nevada	65.7%
5	Minnesota	76.4%	25	Vermont	72.0%	45	Texas	65.6%
6	South Carolina	76.2%	26	Connecticut	71.7%	46	Massachusetts	63.8%
7	Indiana	75.8%	27	Tennessee	71.6%	47	Rhode Island	61.5%
8	Pennsylvania	74.9%	28	New Mexico	71.5%	48	Hawaii	60.9%
	Utah	74.9%	29	Nebraska	71.2%	49	California	59.7%
10	Maine	74.7%	30	Oklahoma	71.1%	50	New York	54.8%
11	Kentucky	74.3%		Colorado	71.1%	(51)	District of Columbia	45.6%
12	Mississippi	74.0%	32	Georgia	70.9%	—	United States	69.0%
13	Idaho	73.7%	33	Louisiana	70.6%			
14	Virginia	73.4%	34	North Dakota	70.0%			
15	New Hampshire	73.3%	35	Kansas	69.9%			
	Wisconsin	73.3%	36	North Carolina	69.8%			
17	Iowa	73.2%	37	Arkansas	69.1%			
18	Ohio	73.1%	38	Oregon	69.0%			
19	Wyoming	72.8%	39	New Jersey	68.8%			
20	Illinois	72.7%	40	Arizona	68.7%			

Percentages represent the proportion of owner households to total occupied households. Ranking number for the District of Columbia shows what its position would be if it were a state.

Source: U.S. Census Bureau, 2006.

States Ranked by Volume of Home Sales, 2004

Rank	State	Units	Share	Rank	State	Units	Share
1	California	610,100	8.99%	31	Connecticut	72,500	1.07%
2	Florida	526,500	7.76%	32	Iowa	71,100	1.05%
3	Texas	485,500	7.16%	33	Arkansas	60,900	0.90%
4	Illinois	307,500	4.53%	34	Mississippi	58,100	0.86%
	New York	307,500	4.53%	35	New Mexico	50,600	0.75%
6	Ohio	275,700	4.06%	36	Utah	43,600	0.64%
7	Pennsylvania	244,600	3.61%	37	Nebraska	39,800	0.59%
8	Georgia	215,800	3.18%	38	West Virginia	36,000	0.53%
9	Michigan	213,400	3.15%	39	Hawaii	35,500	0.52%
10	North Carolina	192,600	2.84%	40	Maine	33,600	0.50%
11	New Jersey	188,700	2.78%	41	Idaho	32,000	0.47%
12	Arizona	186,800	2.75%	42	New Hampshire	27,200	0.40%
13	Virginia	186,000	2.74%	43	Montana	24,200	0.36%
14	Tennessee	156,100	2.30%	44	Alaska	23,000	0.34%
15	Washington	147,600	2.18%	45	Rhode Island	19,200	0.28%
16	Missouri	141,800	2.09%	46	Delaware	18,900	0.28%
17	Massachusetts	141,700	2.09%	47	South Dakota	17,300	0.26%
18	Maryland	140,600	2.07%	48	North Dakota	14,500	0.21%
19	Minnesota	137,400	2.03%	49	Vermont	14,200	0.21%
20	Indiana	130,500	1.92%	50	Wyoming	13,200	0.19%
21	Colorado	126,000	1.86%	(50)	District of Columbia	13,400	0.20%
22	Wisconsin	116,800	1.72%	—	United States	6,740,000	100%
23	Alabama	112,000	1.65%				
24	Nevada	99,800	1.47%				
25	South Carolina	99,300	1.46%				
26	Oklahoma	93,600	1.38%				
27	Oregon	90,700	1.34%				
28	Kentucky	89,300	1.32%				
29	Louisiana	79,600	1.17%				
30	Kansas	73,400	1.08%				

Figures for units, which are rounded to nearest hundred, include single-family houses, condos, and co-ops. Ranking number for the District of Columbia shows what its position would be if it were a state.

Source: National Association of Realtors, Washington, D.C., *Real Estate Outlook: Market Trends & Insights.*

States Ranked by Values of Owner-Occupied Houses, 2003

	State	Total	Median		State	Total	Median
1	California	5,921,000	$334,426	30	Montana	173,000	$118,887
2	Hawaii	185,000	$324,661	31	New Mexico	363,000	$118,764
3	Massachusetts	1,259,000	$309,736	32	Idaho	284,000	$118,174
4	New Jersey	1,795,000	$245,573	33	Wyoming	105,000	$116,360
5	Connecticut	765,000	$226,202	34	Pennsylvania	3,002,000	$110,020
6	Colorado	1,062,000	$210,398	35	Tennessee	1,281,000	$110,000
7	New Hampshire	280,000	$208,403	36	Missouri	1,256,000	$108,625
8	Rhode Island	212,000	$205,244	37	Indiana	1,419,000	$106,840
9	Washington	1,254,000	$200,235	38	Kentucky	812,000	$104,103
10	New York	2,804,000	$198,883	39	Nebraska	389,000	$100,539
11	Maryland	1,255,000	$186,139	40	Kansas	611,000	$100,257
12	Alaska	112,000	$174,146	41	Louisiana	892,000	$99,215
13	Oregon	709,000	$171,039	42	Texas	4,179,000	$99,139
14	Nevada	433,000	$170,333	43	South Dakota	146,000	$96,977
15	Minnesota	1,259,000	$169,778	44	Alabama	947,000	$96,106
16	Delaware	185,000	$165,739	45	Iowa	688,000	$91,427
17	Virginia	1,632,000	$162,080	46	West Virginia	387,000	$85,709
18	Illinois	2,563,000	$160,551	47	Oklahoma	749,000	$85,502
19	Utah	488,000	$156,657	48	Mississippi	560,000	$85,142
20	Arizona	1,165,000	$146,124	49	Arkansas	556,000	$83,699
21	Florida	3,508,000	$144,507	50	North Dakota	129,000	$81,796
22	Michigan	2,417,000	$141,413	(4)	District of Columbia	76,000	$248,171
23	Georgia	1,745,000	$140,734	—	United States	58,809,000	$147,275
24	Vermont	111,000	$138,457				
25	Maine	267,000	$134,846				
26	Wisconsin	1,193,000	$131,908				
27	North Carolina	1,678,000	$125,428				
28	South Carolina	818,000	$121,290				
29	Ohio	2,727,000	$118,956				

Units are owner-occupied one-family houses; numbers are rounded to nearest thousand. Data are extrapolated from survey samples. Ranking number for the District of Columbia shows what its position would be if it were a state.

Source: U.S. Census Bureau, American Community Survey.

States Ranked by Total Public School Enrollment, 2002

Rank	State	Total enrollment	Prekindergarten-grade 8	Grades 9-12	Enrollment rate Percent	Enrollment rate Rank
1	California	6,357,000	4,529,000	1,828,000	92.6	10
2	Texas	4,260,000	3,080,000	1,180,000	97.0	2
3	New York	2,888,000	2,017,000	871,000	85.8	46
4	Florida	2,540,000	1,809,000	731,000	89.7	30
5	Illinois	2,085,000	1,488,000	597,000	88.5	35
6	Ohio	1,838,000	1,284,000	554,000	87.8	40
7	Pennsylvania	1,817,000	1,242,000	575,000	84.6	48
8	Michigan	1,785,000	1,254,000	531,000	93.7	7
9	Georgia	1,496,000	1,089,000	407,000	92.1	14
10	New Jersey	1,368,000	979,000	389,000	87.9	38
11	North Carolina	1,336,000	964,000	372,000	90.3	28
12	Virginia	1,178,000	832,000	346,000	90.6	24
13	Washington	1,015,000	697,000	318,000	91.1	20
14	Indiana	1,004,000	714,000	290,000	85.9	45
15	Massachusetts	983,000	701,000	282,000	90.2	29
16	Arizona	937,000	660,000	277,000	88.6	34
17	Tennessee	928,000	674,000	254,000	91.4	17
18	Missouri	925,000	653,000	272,000	88.9	31
19	Wisconsin	882,000	592,000	290,000	87.9	38
20	Maryland	866,000	610,000	256,000	85.6	47
21	Minnesota	847,000	568,000	279,000	90.6	24
22	Colorado	751,000	534,000	217,000	91.0	21
23	Alabama	740,000	534,000	206,000	90.8	22
24	Louisiana	731,000	537,000	194,000	84.2	49
25	South Carolina	695,000	501,000	194,000	93.2	8
26	Kentucky	661,000	477,000	184,000	91.4	18
27	Oklahoma	625,000	449,000	176,000	97.8	1
28	Connecticut	570,000	406,000	164,000	91.3	19
29	Oregon	554,000	382,000	172,000	88.2	36
30	Mississippi	492,000	360,000	132,000	88.9	31
31	Utah	490,000	343,000	147,000	95.5	4
32	Iowa	482,000	326,000	156,000	92.6	10
33	Kansas	471,000	322,000	149,000	92.2	13
34	Arkansas	451,000	319,000	132,000	90.6	24
35	Nevada	370,000	271,000	99,000	90.8	22
36	New Mexico	320,000	224,000	96,000	86.5	43
37	Nebraska	285,000	195,000	90,000	88.1	37
38	West Virginia	282,000	200,000	82,000	96.5	3
39	Idaho	248,000	173,000	75,000	91.5	16
40	New Hampshire	208,000	144,000	64,000	88.7	33
41	Maine	205,000	142,000	63,000	91.6	15
42	Hawaii	184,000	131,000	53,000	86.3	44
43	Rhode Island	160,000	113,000	47,000	87.2	42
44	Montana	150,000	101,000	49,000	90.6	24
45	Alaska	134,000	94,000	40,000	94.9	6
46	South Dakota	128,000	87,000	41,000	87.7	41
47	Delaware	116,000	82,000	34,000	81.6	50
48	North Dakota	104,000	69,000	35,000	92.9	9
49	Vermont	100,000	68,000	32,000	92.5	12
50	Wyoming	88,000	60,000	28,000	95.4	5
(51)	District of Columbia	76,000	59,000	17,000	99.2	(1)
—	United States	48,202,000	34,135,000	14,067,000	90.4	—

Enrollment figures (which include unclassified students) are rounded to nearest thousand pupils during fall school term. Enrollment rates are based on enumerated resident population estimate for July 1, 2002. Ranking number for the District of Columbia shows what its position would be if it were a state.

Source: U.S. National Center for Education Statistics.

States Ranked by Total College Enrollments, 2002

Rank	State	Institutions	Enrollments			
			Total students	Public institutions	Private institutions	Full-time students
1	California	400	2,474,000	2,121,000	353,000	1,186,000
2	Texas	200	1,152,000	1,007,000	146,000	643,000
3	New York	310	1,107,000	611,000	497,000	763,000
4	Florida	161	792,000	618,000	174,000	426,000
5	Illinois	175	777,000	554,000	223,000	427,000
6	Pennsylvania	257	655,000	370,000	284,000	466,000
7	Michigan	109	606,000	496,000	110,000	340,000
8	Ohio	179	588,000	442,000	146,000	387,000
9	North Carolina	126	447,000	368,000	79,000	284,000
10	Massachusetts	119	431,000	188,000	243,000	287,000
11	Virginia	100	405,000	337,000	68,000	238,000
12	Arizona	71	402,000	307,000	94,000	215,000
13	Georgia	124	398,000	317,000	80,000	258,000
14	New Jersey	57	362,000	289,000	72,000	213,000
15	Missouri	119	348,000	214,000	134,000	207,000
16	Indiana	99	342,000	259,000	83,000	232,000
17	Washington	78	339,000	293,000	46,000	210,000
18	Wisconsin	68	329,000	268,000	61,000	207,000
19	Minnesota	113	324,000	236,000	88,000	206,000
20	Maryland	63	300,000	247,000	53,000	157,000
21	Colorado	76	282,000	234,000	49,000	156,000
22	Tennessee	89	262,000	194,000	68,000	186,000
23	Alabama	75	246,000	218,000	29,000	165,000
24	Louisiana	87	232,000	198,000	35,000	169,000
25	Kentucky	79	225,000	189,000	37,000	141,000
26	Oregon	57	205,000	174,000	31,000	118,000
27	Iowa	62	203,000	146,000	57,000	142,000
28	South Carolina	63	202,000	168,000	34,000	134,000
29	Oklahoma	53	198,000	171,000	27,000	128,000
30	Kansas	60	188,000	168,000	20,000	110,000
31	Utah	25	179,000	136,000	43,000	114,000
32	Connecticut	45	171,000	109,000	62,000	102,000
33	Mississippi	41	147,000	134,000	13,000	111,000
34	Arkansas	46	127,000	114,000	14,000	85,000
35	New Mexico	43	121,000	112,000	9,000	64,000
36	Nebraska	38	117,000	92,000	25,000	76,000
37	Nevada	14	96,000	90,000	6,000	42,000
38	West Virginia	37	94,000	80,000	14,000	69,000
39	Rhode Island	13	77,000	39,000	39,000	53,000
40	Idaho	14	72,000	58,000	14,000	49,000
41	New Hampshire	25	69,000	41,000	28,000	45,000
42	Hawaii	20	65,000	48,000	17,000	40,000
43	Maine	32	63,000	45,000	18,000	37,000
44	Delaware	10	49,000	37,000	12,000	31,000
45	South Dakota	27	48,000	38,000	10,000	32,000
46	North Dakota	22	46,000	41,000	5,000	36,000
47	Montana	22	45,000	41,000	4,000	34,000
48	Vermont	27	37,000	21,000	15,000	26,000
49	Wyoming	9	33,000	31,000	2,000	18,000
50	Alaska	8	30,000	28,000	1,000	12,000
(39)	District of Columbia	16	91,000	6,000	85,000	58,000
—	U.S. military (service schools)	5	14,000	14,000	NA	14,000
—	United States	4,168	16,612,000	12,752,000	3,860,000	9,946,000

Enrollment numbers are rounded to nearest thousand students and exclude students taking courses by mail, radio, or television. Data are for all degree-granting institutions at the opening of the 2002-2003 academic year. Ranking number for the District of Columbia shows what its position would be if it were a state.

Source: U.S. National Center for Education Statistics, *Digest of Education Statistics.*

States Ranked by Total Highway Mileage, 2003

Rank	State	Total	Interstate highways	Other roads
1	Texas	301,987	3,233	298,754
2	California	169,549	2,458	167,091
3	Illinois	138,526	2,170	136,356
4	Kansas	135,012	874	134,138
5	Minnesota	131,893	912	130,981
6	Missouri	124,685	1,181	123,504
7	Ohio	123,522	1,574	121,948
8	Michigan	122,222	1,243	120,979
9	Pennsylvania	120,423	1,758	118,665
10	Florida	120,375	1,471	118,904
11	Georgia	116,534	1,245	115,289
12	Iowa	113,516	782	112,734
13	Wisconsin	113,270	745	112,525
14	New York	113,124	1,674	111,450
15	Oklahoma	112,578	930	111,648
16	North Carolina	102,160	1,019	101,141
17	Arkansas	98,541	656	97,885
18	Indiana	94,597	1,169	93,428
19	Alabama	94,434	905	93,529
20	Nebraska	93,198	482	92,716
21	Tennessee	88,518	1,073	87,445
22	Colorado	86,821	956	85,865
23	North Dakota	86,782	572	86,210
24	South Dakota	83,688	679	83,009
25	Washington	82,264	764	81,500
26	Kentucky	77,011	763	76,248
27	Mississippi	74,105	685	73,420
28	Virginia	71,242	1,118	70,124
29	Montana	69,450	1,192	68,258
30	South Carolina	66,230	842	65,388
31	Oregon	65,951	728	65,223
32	New Mexico	63,953	1,000	62,953
33	Louisiana	60,937	904	60,033
34	Arizona	57,529	1,167	56,362
35	Idaho	46,927	611	46,316
36	Utah	42,716	940	41,776
37	New Jersey	38,952	431	38,521
38	West Virginia	36,993	549	36,444
39	Massachusetts	35,590	569	35,021
40	Nevada	33,977	560	33,417
41	Maryland	30,688	481	30,207
42	Wyoming	27,482	913	26,569
43	Maine	22,693	367	22,326
44	Connecticut	21,089	346	20,743
45	New Hampshire	15,630	235	15,395
46	Vermont	14,359	320	14,039
47	Alaska	14,230	1,082	13,148
48	Rhode Island	6,415	71	6,344
49	Delaware	5,894	41	5,853
50	Hawaii	4,309	55	4,254
(51)	District of Columbia	1,536	13	1,523
—	United States	3,974,107	46,508	3,927,599

Ranking number for the District of Columbia shows what its position would be if it were a state.

Source: U.S. Federal Highway Administration.

States Ranked by Total Registered Vehicles, 2003

Rank	State	Total vehicles	Automobiles	Licensed drivers
1	California	30,248,000	18,699,000	22,657,000
2	Texas	14,889,000	7,842,000	13,498,000
3	Florida	14,526,000	8,564,000	12,906,000
4	New York	10,802,000	8,313,000	11,357,000
5	Ohio	10,536,000	6,519,000	7,656,000
6	Pennsylvania	9,724,000	6,121,000	8,370,000
7	Illinois	9,250,000	5,769,000	8,054,000
8	Michigan	8,540,000	4,805,000	7,065,000
9	Georgia	7,730,000	4,192,000	5,758,000
10	New Jersey	6,712,000	4,449,000	5,729,000
11	Virginia	6,346,000	4,044,000	5,046,000
12	North Carolina	6,119,000	3,654,000	6,015,000
13	Indiana	5,739,000	3,252,000	4,536,000
14	Massachusetts	5,479,000	3,615,000	4,646,000
15	Washington	5,379,000	2,969,000	4,407,000
16	Tennessee	4,796,000	2,782,000	4,204,000
17	Wisconsin	4,647,000	2,578,000	3,766,000
18	Minnesota	4,525,000	2,502,000	3,036,000
19	Missouri	4,460,000	2,600,000	3,966,000
20	Alabama	4,329,000	1,771,000	3,598,000
21	Maryland	3,877,000	2,479,000	3,552,000
22	Louisiana	3,714,000	1,997,000	3,120,000
23	Arizona	3,574,000	1,992,000	3,819,000
24	Kentucky	3,389,000	1,959,000	2,800,000
25	Iowa	3,369,000	1,883,000	1,978,000
26	South Carolina	3,162,000	1,915,000	2,919,000
27	Oklahoma	3,074,000	1,623,000	2,348,000
28	Oregon	3,061,000	1,545,000	2,590,000
29	Connecticut	2,964,000	2,041,000	2,660,000
30	Kansas	2,314,000	834,000	1,987,000
31	Colorado	2,027,000	888,000	2,975,000
32	Utah	2,006,000	1,014,000	1,548,000
33	Mississippi	1,951,000	1,139,000	1,886,000
34	Arkansas	1,889,000	955,000	1,998,000
35	Nebraska	1,677,000	855,000	1,311,000
36	New Mexico	1,509,000	694,000	1,236,000
37	West Virginia	1,409,000	756,000	1,272,000
38	Idaho	1,301,000	554,000	921,000
39	Nevada	1,222,000	624,000	1,488,000
40	New Hampshire	1,145,000	656,000	968,000
41	Maine	1,052,000	619,000	932,000
42	Montana	1,010,000	437,000	705,000
43	Hawaii	903,000	525,000	834,000
44	South Dakota	827,000	388,000	555,000
45	Rhode Island	806,000	549,000	731,000
46	North Dakota	694,000	346,000	460,000
47	Delaware	687,000	419,000	585,000
48	Alaska	637,000	261,000	481,000
49	Wyoming	620,000	232,000	378,000
50	Vermont	516,000	272,000	543,000
(51)	District of Columbia	228,000	184,000	313,000
—	United States	231,390,000	135,670,000	196,166,000

Figures, which do not include vehicles owned by military services, are rounded to the nearest thousand. Figures for automobiles include taxis. Ranking number for the District of Columbia shows what its position would be if it were a state.

Source: U.S. Federal Highway Administration.

States Ranked by Total Domestic Travel Expenditures, 2003

In billions of dollars

Rank	State	Total	Share	Rank	State	Total	Share
1	California	$61.08	12.4%	29	Alabama	$5.55	1.1%
2	Florida	$42.89	8.7%	30	Kentucky	$5.43	1.1%
3	Texas	$31.47	6.4%		Mississippi	$5.43	1.1%
4	New York	$27.73	5.6%	32	Iowa	$4.63	0.9%
5	Illinois	$21.60	4.4%	33	Oklahoma	$4.21	0.9%
6	Nevada	$19.32	3.9%	34	New Mexico	$4.08	0.8%
7	Pennsylvania	$15.24	3.1%	35	Arkansas	$3.97	0.8%
8	New Jersey	$14.73	3.0%	36	Kansas	$3.85	0.8%
9	Georgia	$14.52	3.0%	37	Utah	$3.73	0.8%
10	Virginia	$13.89	2.8%	38	Nebraska	$2.77	0.6%
11	North Carolina	$12.63	2.6%	39	New Hampshire	$2.69	0.5%
12	Ohio	$12.43	2.5%	40	Idaho	$2.21	0.4%
13	Michigan	$11.99	2.4%	41	Montana	$2.06	0.4%
14	Tennessee	$10.58	2.2%	42	Maine	$1.99	0.4%
15	Massachusetts	$9.95	2.0%	43	West Virginia	$1.80	0.4%
16	Colorado	$9.19	1.9%	44	Wyoming	$1.71	0.3%
17	Missouri	$9.18	1.9%	45	South Dakota	$1.52	0.3%
18	Arizona	$9.15	1.9%	46	Rhode Island	$1.43	0.3%
19	Louisiana	$9.06	1.8%	47	Alaska	$1.38	0.3%
20	Maryland	$9.01	1.8%	48	Vermont	$1.37	0.3%
21	Washington	$8.04	1.6%	49	North Dakota	$1.24	0.3%
22	Minnesota	$7.95	1.6%	50	Delaware	$1.14	0.2%
23	Hawaii	$7.49	1.5%	(33)	District of Columbia	$4.28	0.9%
24	South Carolina	$7.22	1.5%	—	United States	$490.87	100%
25	Wisconsin	$7.16	1.5%				
26	Connecticut	$6.71	1.4%				
27	Indiana	$6.69	1.4%				
28	Oregon	$5.56	1.1%				

Ranking number for the District of Columbia shows what its
  position would be if it were a state.

Source: Travel Industry Association of America.

States Ranked by Gas Prices, 2007
Average prices per gallon at the pump

Rank	State	Price	Rank	State	Price	Rank	State	Price
1	Hawaii	$3.003	20	Wisconsin	$2.315	39	Alabama	$2.172
2	California	$2.693	21	Rhode Island	$2.302	40	Arkansas	$2.164
3	Nevada	$2.581	22	Massachusetts	$2.299	41	Montana	$2.157
4	Washington	$2.567	23	Utah	$2.295	42	Texas	$2.156
5	Oregon	$2.525	24	New Hampshire	$2.292	43	Minnesota	$2.149
6	New York	$2.499	25	New Mexico	$2.265	44	New Jersey	$2.148
7	Connecticut	$2.464	26	Maryland	$2.258		Mississippi	$2.148
8	Alaska	$2.441	27	Nebraska	$2.256	46	Tennessee	$2.139
9	Vermont	$2.407	28	Colorado	$2.246	47	Virginia	$2.138
10	West Virginia	$2.358	29	North Carolina	$2.238	48	South Carolina	$2.110
11	Illinois	$2.357	30	South Dakota	$2.237	49	Oklahoma	$2.086
12	Ohio	$2.355	31	Kentucky	$2.226	50	Missouri	$2.084
13	Indiana	$2.353		Delaware	$2.226			
14	Arizona	$2.341	33	Iowa	$2.212	(10)	District of Columbia	$2.373
15	Michigan	$2.337	34	North Dakota	$2.201			
16	Florida	$2.333	35	Wyoming	$2.186	—	United States	$2.298
17	Pennsylvania	$2.329	36	Louisiana	$2.181			
18	Maine	$2.327	37	Georgia	$2.174			
19	Idaho	$2.320	38	Kansas	$2.173			

Prices are averages of all grades sold at the pump during early February, 2007.

Source: American Automobile Association.

States Ranked by Crime Rates, 2003

Incidents per 100,000 residents

Rank	State	All crimes	Violent crimes	Property crimes	Rank	State	All crimes	Violent crimes	Property crimes
1	Arizona	6,145	513	5,632	30	Indiana	3,711	353	3,358
2	Hawaii	5,508	270	5,238	31	Wyoming	3,583	262	3,321
3	South Carolina	5,271	794	4,477	32	Montana	3,463	365	3,098
4	Florida	5,182	730	4,452	33	Minnesota	3,380	263	3,117
5	Texas	5,148	553	4,595	34	Rhode Island	3,281	286	2,995
6	Washington	5,102	347	4,755	35	Iowa	3,233	272	2,961
7	Oregon	5,078	296	4,782	36	Idaho	3,152	243	2,909
8	Tennessee	5,067	688	4,379	37	Wisconsin	3,104	221	2,883
9	Louisiana	4,996	646	4,350	38	Massachusetts	3,019	469	2,550
10	Nevada	4,902	614	4,288	39	Virginia	2,980	276	2,704
11	Oklahoma	4,812	506	4,306	40	Kentucky	2,944	262	2,682
12	New Mexico	4,789	665	4,124	41	Connecticut	2,915	308	2,607
13	North Carolina	4,733	455	4,278	42	New Jersey	2,910	366	2,544
14	Georgia	4,709	454	4,255	43	Pennsylvania	2,829	398	2,431
15	Maryland	4,505	704	3,801	44	New York	2,713	465	2,248
16	Missouri	4,488	473	4,015	45	West Virginia	2,617	258	2,359
17	Alabama	4,479	430	4,049	46	Maine	2,566	109	2,457
18	Utah	4,475	249	4,226	47	Vermont	2,310	110	2,200
19	Kansas	4,390	396	3,994	48	New Hampshire	2,203	149	2,054
20	Alaska	4,335	593	3,742	49	South Dakota	2,175	173	2,002
21	Colorado	4,286	345	3,941	50	North Dakota	2,174	78	2,096
22	Arkansas	4,077	456	3,621	(1)	District of Columbia	7,408	1,608	5,800
23	Mississippi	4,046	326	3,720	—	United States	4,063	475	3,588
24	Delaware	4,042	658	3,384					
25	California	4,003	579	3,424					
26	Nebraska	4,000	289	3,711					
27	Ohio	3,974	333	3,641					
28	Illinois	3,841	557	3,284					
29	Michigan	3,788	511	3,277					

Ranking number for the District of Columbia shows what its position would be if it were a state.

Source: U.S. Federal Bureau of Investigation, *Crime in the United States,* annual.

States Ranked by Prison Inmate Populations, 2003

Rank	State	Total prisoners	Portion of U.S. total	Rank	State	Total prisoners	Portion of U.S. total
1	Texas	166,911	11.35%	30	Nevada	10,543	0.72%
2	California	164,487	11.19%	31	Massachusetts	10,232	0.70%
3	Florida	79,594	5.41%	32	Kansas	9,132	0.62%
4	New York	65,198	4.44%	33	Iowa	8,546	0.58%
5	Michigan	49,358	3.36%	34	Minnesota	7,865	0.54%
6	Georgia	47,208	3.21%	35	Delaware	6,794	0.46%
7	Ohio	44,778	3.05%	36	New Mexico	6,223	0.42%
8	Illinois	43,418	2.95%	37	Idaho	5,887	0.40%
9	Pennsylvania	40,890	2.78%	38	Hawaii	5,828	0.40%
10	Louisiana	36,047	2.45%	39	Utah	5,763	0.39%
11	Virginia	35,067	2.39%	40	West Virginia	4,758	0.32%
12	North Carolina	33,560	2.28%	41	Alaska	4,527	0.31%
13	Arizona	31,170	2.12%	42	Nebraska	4,040	0.27%
14	Missouri	30,303	2.06%	43	Montana	3,620	0.25%
15	Alabama	29,253	1.99%	44	Rhode Island	3,527	0.24%
16	New Jersey	27,246	1.85%	45	South Dakota	3,026	0.21%
17	Tennessee	25,403	1.73%	46	New Hampshire	2,434	0.17%
18	Maryland	23,791	1.62%	47	Maine	2,013	0.14%
19	South Carolina	23,719	1.61%	48	Vermont	1,944	0.13%
20	Mississippi	23,182	1.58%	49	Wyoming	1,872	0.13%
21	Indiana	23,069	1.57%	50	North Dakota	1,239	0.08%
22	Oklahoma	22,821	1.55%	—	*All states*	1,470,045	100%
23	Wisconsin	22,614	1.54%				
24	Connecticut	19,846	1.35%				
25	Colorado	19,671	1.34%				
26	Kentucky	16,622	1.13%				
27	Washington	16,148	1.10%				
28	Arkansas	13,084	0.89%				
29	Oregon	12,715	0.86%				

State figures exclude prisoners in federal penitentiaries; some state figures include jail inmates. U.S. total includes both state and federal prison inmates. No 2003 data are available for the District of Columbia.

Source: U.S. Bureau of Justice Statistics, *Prisoners in 2003*.

Index

INDEX

Economy. *See* **Employment, nonfarm; Exports, foreign; Gross state product; Income, personal**

Education. *See* **Government expenditures; Public college finances; School enrollment**

Elections. *See* **Congressional delegations, composition of; Legislatures, state; Presidential elections**

Employment, nonfarm

Energy consumption

Exports, foreign

Farms. *See also* **Industries;
Land use**

Federally owned land. *See* **Land,
federally owned**

Finance. *See* **Industries**

Foreign exports. *See* **Exports,
foreign**

Forest land. *See* **Land use**

Gasoline prices

Government. *See* **Industries;
Local government units**

Government administration. *See*
Government expenditures

Government employment. *See*
Employment, nonfarm

Health. *See* **Death rates; Government expenditures; Health insurance; Infant mortality**

Health insurance

Heart disease. *See* **Death rates**

Higher education. *See* **Public college finances**

Highway mileage

Highways. *See* **Government expenditures**

Hispanics. *See* **Population, by race and Hispanic origin**

HIV. *See* **Death rates**